There's more to this program than meets the page.

Get course tools and resources any time you need with the **Sag mal** Supersite.

Why Supersite means better learning:

- Engages and focuses students
- Improves student performance
- Saves you time with auto-grading, quick setup, and reporting tools
- Provides flexibility to personalize your course
- Offers cost-saving digital options

Visit vistahigherlearning.com/new-supersite to learn more.

2nd EDITION

SAG MAL

AN INTRODUCTION TO GERMAN LANGUAGE AND CULTURE

Christine Anton

Tobias Barske

Megan McKinstry

VISTA®
HIGHER LEARNING

Boston, Massachusetts

Publisher: José A. Blanco

Editorial Development: Judith Bach, Aliza B. Krefetz

Project Management: Kayli Brownstein, Cécile Engeln, Sharon Inglis, Tiffany Kayes

Rights Management: Ashley Dos Santos, Jorgensen Fernandez, Caitlin O'Brien

Technology Production: Egle Gutiérrez, Paola Ríos Schaaf

Design: Gabriel Noreña, Andrés Vanegas

Production: Manuela Arango, Oscar Díez, Erik Restrepo

Student Text ISBN: 978-1-68004-334-1
Instructor's Annotated Edition ISBN: 978-1-68004-336-5
Library of Congress Control Number: 2015948688

1 2 3 4 5 6 7 8 9 WC 20 19 18 17 16 15

INSTRUCTOR'S ANNOTATED EDITION

TABLE OF CONTENTS

The Vista Higher Learning Story

Your Specialized Foreign Language Publisher

Independent, specialized, and privately owned, Vista Higher Learning was founded in 2000 with one mission: to raise the teaching and learning of world languages to a higher level. This mission is based on the following beliefs:

- It is essential to prepare students for a world in which learning another language is a necessity, not a luxury.
- Language learning should be fun and rewarding, and all students should have the tools they need to achieve success.
- Students who experience success learning a language will be more likely to continue their language studies both inside and outside the classroom.

With this in mind, we decided to take a fresh look at all aspects of language instructional materials. Because we are specialized, we dedicate 100 percent of our resources to this goal and base every decision on how well it supports language learning.

That is where you come in. Since our founding, we have relied on the invaluable feedback of language instructors and students nationwide. This partnership has proved to be the cornerstone of our success, allowing us to constantly improve our programs to meet your instructional needs.

The result? Programs that make language learning exciting, relevant, and effective through:

- unprecedented access to resources
- a wide variety of contemporary, authentic materials
- the integration of text, technology, and media
- a bold and engaging textbook design

By focusing on our singular passion, we let you focus on yours.

The Vista Higher Learning Team

VISTA®
HIGHER LEARNING

500 Boylston Street, Suite 620, Boston, MA 02116-3736 TOLL-FREE: 800-618-7375
TELEPHONE: 617-426-4910 FAX: 617-426-5209 www.vistahigherlearning.com

GETTING TO KNOW SAG MAL SECOND EDITION

Vibrant and original, **SAG MAL**, Second Edition, takes a fresh, student-friendly approach to introductory German, aimed at making students' learning and instructors' teaching easier, more enjoyable, and more successful. **SAG MAL** develops students' speaking, listening, reading, and writing skills so that they will be able to express their own ideas and interact with others meaningfully and in real-life contexts.

NEW to the Second Edition

- Enhanced Supersite—groundbreaking technology with powerful course management tools and a simplified user experience, now with iPad®-friendly* features and vText

- Enhanced Virtual Chat activities that simulate real conversation

- Online administration of oral testing, using the Virtual Chat format

- Additional Instructor Resources, including Task-based activities—for use in class or for assessment, and illustration bank for use with instructor-created activities

- Vocabulary Tools, including customizable study lists for vocabulary words

- Three new authentic **Zapping** TV-clips

- New Kurzfilm, *Bienenstich ist aus*, in Unit 12

- New **Lesen** reading, *Der Panther*, by Rainer Maria Rilke, in Unit 12

- Revised textbook content—with increased scaffolding, more recycling of lesson-specific vocabulary, and adjustments to the grammar sequence

Plus, the original hallmark features of SAG MAL

- A unique, easy-to-navigate design with color-coded lesson sections and visually engaging textbook pages featuring content designed for instructional impact and visual appeal

- Distinctive and cohesive integration of video—from a specially shot **Fotoroman** dramatic series to authentic TV clips and short films in the **Zapping** feature in every unit

- A unique vocabulary practice sequence that alternates between recognition and production practice at every level of discourse: words, phrases or sentences, and dialogues, including listening comprehension activities in each lesson

- A unique four-part practice sequence for every grammar point, moving from form focused **Jetzt sind Sie dran!** activities to directed **Anwendung** activities, to communicative, interactive **Kommunikation** activities, and finallly, to open-ended activities in **Wiederholung** that recycle previously learned material

- **Tipp** and **Achtung** boxes with linguistic and cultural notes, **Ressourcen** boxes with correlations to student supplements and **Querverweis** boxes with grammar cross-references

- Systematic development of reading and writing skills, incorporating learning strategies and a process approach

- A rich, contemporary cultural presentation of the everyday lives of German speakers

- Groundbreaking technology designed to expand learning and teaching options, including online textbook and web-only activities, with Partner Chats and Virtual Chats for pair activities

- vText—the interactive, online text—perfect for hybrid courses

*Students must use a computer for audio recording and select presentations and tools that require Flash or Shockwave.

Table of Contents

			Kontext	Fotoroman

Kultur	**Strukturen**	**Weiter geht's**

Kontext   Fotoroman

Kontext

Fotoroman

		Kontext	**Fotoroman**

Kultur

Strukturen

Weiter geht's

THE *SAG MAL* SUPERSITE

The **SAG MAL** Supersite is a learning environment designed especially for world language instruction, based on feedback from language educators. Its simplified interface, innovative new tools, and seamless textbook-technology integration will help you reach students and build their love of language.

For students:

- engaging media
- motivating user experience
- improved performance
- helpful resources

For educators:

- freedom to teach
- powerful course management
- time-saving tools
- enhanced support

Partner Chat

RESOURCES

Specialized resources ensure successful implementation.

- Online assessments and Testing Program files in editable formats
- Audio- and videoscripts with English translations
- Grammar presentation slides
- Digital Image & Illustration Bank

- Info Gap Activities
- Sample syllabus
- Sample lesson plan
- Digital Image Bank
- Answer keys

CONTENT

Meaningful, integrated content means less prep time and a more powerful student experience. (See page IAE-16 for details.)

EDUCATOR TOOLS

Enhanced online tools facilitate instruction and save time.

Easy course management

A powerful setup wizard lets you customize your course settings, copy previous courses to save time, and create your all-in-one gradebook. Grades for teacher-created assignments (pop quizzes, class participation, etc.) can be incorporated for a true, up-to-date cumulative grade.

Customized content

Tailor the Supersite to fit your needs. Create your own open-ended or video Partner Chat activities, add video or outside resources, and modify existing content with your own personalized notes.

Grading tools

Grade efficiently via spot-checking, student-by-student, and question-by-question options. Use in-line editing tools to give targeted feedback and voice comments—it's the perfect tool for busy language educators!

Assessment solutions

Administer online quizzes and tests from the Testing Program or develop your own—such as open-ended writing prompts or chat activities for an oral assessment portfolio. Plus, new tools allow for time limits and password protection.

Plus!

- Single sign-on for easy integration with your school's LMS
- Live Chat for video chat, audio chat, and instant messaging with students
- A communication center for announcements, notifications, and help requests
- An option for hiding content from a course
- Voiceboards for oral assignments, group discussions, homework, and more
- Reporting tools for summarizing student data

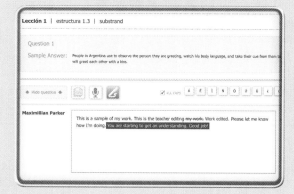

In-line editing

Each section of your textbook comes with activities on the **SAG MAL** Supersite, many of which are auto-graded with immediate feedback. Plus, the Supersite is iPad®-friendly*, so it can be accessed on the go! Visit **vhlcentral.com** to explore the wealth of exciting resources.

KONTEXT
- Image-based vocabulary activity with audio
- Additional activities for extra practice
- **Aussprache und Rechtschreibung** presentation followed by record-compare activities

- Textbook activities, including audio activities
- Chat activities for conversational skill-building and oral practice

FOTOROMAN
- Streaming video for all 24 episodes of the **Fotoroman** with instructor-controlled options for subtitles
- Textbook activities

- **Zusammenfassung** section where key vocabulary and grammar from the episode are called-out
- Additional activities for extra practice

KULTUR
- Culture reading
- Internet search activity

- Textbook activities
- Additional activities for extra practice

STRUKTUREN
- Grammar presentations
- Chat activities for conversational skill-building and oral practice
- **Zapping** streaming video of TV clip or short film

- Textbook activities
- Additional activities for extra practice

WEITER GEHT'S

Panorama
- Interactive map with statistics and cultural notes
- Additional activity for extra practice

Im Internet
- Internet search activity
- Textbook activity with auto-grading

Lesen
- Audio-sync reading
- Additional online-only practice activities
- Textbook activities

Hören
- Textbook activities
- Additional activities for extra practice

Schreiben
- Submit your writing assignment online

WORTSCHATZ
- Audio recordings of all vocabulary items
- Vocabulary tools

Plus! Also found on the Supersite:

- All textbook and lab audio MP3 files
- Communication center for instructor notifications and feedback
- A single gradebook for all Supersite activities

- WebSAM online Workbook/Video Manual and Lab Manual
- **v̂Text** online, interactive student edition with access to Supersite activities, audio, and video

*Students must use a computer for audio-recording.

VIRTUAL INTERACTIVE TEXT

v̂Text

This interactive text includes the complete Student Edition and integrated Supersite resources that can be accessed from any computer.

- Access all textbook activities with a mouse icon, audio, and video right from the vText—now you have a single platform for completing assignments and accessing resources

- Submit work online and have it flow directly into your instructor's gradebook

- Take notes or highlight important information right on the vText page

- Quickly search table of contents or browse by page number

- Print vocabulary and grammar pages for use as study guides

- Access on the go—now iPad® friendly*

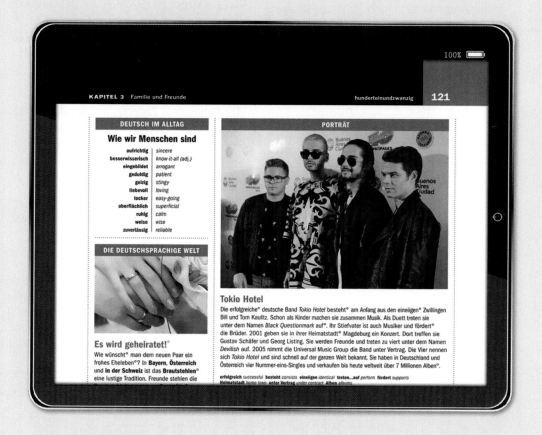

PROGRAM COMPONENTS

Students

Print

- **Student Edition**
  Available in hardcover or loose-leaf format

- **Student Activities Manual
  (Workbook/Video Manual/
  Lab Manual) (SAM)**
  The Workbook contains the workbook
  activities for each textbook lesson.

  The Video Manual contains activities for the
  Fotoroman Video. The Lab Manual contains
  lab activities for each textbook lesson for use
  with the Lab Audio Program.

Online

- **Supersite**
  Student access to the Supersite
  (**vhlcentral.com**) is provided with the purchase
  of a new student edition. See page IAE-16 for
  all Supersite resources available to students.

- **vText**
  This virtual, interactive student edition
  provides students with a digital text, plus
  interactive links to all Supersite activities
  and media.

- **WebSAM**
  Online version of the Student Activities Manual
  (Workbook/Video Manual/Lab Manual)

Instructors

Print

- **Instructor's Annotated Edition (IAE)**
  This IAE contains a wealth of teaching
  information. The expanded trim size and
  enhanced design make the annotations
  easy to reference.

Online

- **Instructor Supersite**
  The password-protected Instructor Supersite
  offers the resources, tools, and content
  necessary to facilitate language instruction,
  and allows instructors to assign activities
  and track student progress through its course
  management system. See pages IAE-14 and
  IAE-15 for details.

- **Video Program**
  The **Fotoroman**, **Zapping**, and **Kurzfilm** video
  programs are available on the Supersite.
  *For a physical **Fotoroman** DVD (from the
  Sag Mal 1e program), contact your Modern
  Language Specialist.*

- **Testing Program**
  The Testing Program is provided in RTF format.

  - Vocabulary and grammar quiz
    for each lesson

  - Unit tests

  - 2 cumulative exams
    (1 for units 1–6; 1 for units 7–12)

ICONS AND *RESSOURCEN* BOXES

Icons

These icons in the Second Edition of **SAG MAL** alert you to the type of activity or section involved.

Icons legend			
🎧	Listening activity/section	Ⓢ	Content found on the Supersite: audio, video, and presentations
	Activity on the Supersite		Information Gap activity
👥	Pair activity	▦	Worksheet activity
👨‍👨‍👦	Group activity	♻	Recycling activity

- The Information Gap activities and Worksheet activities require handouts that your instructor will give you.
- The listening icon indicates that audio is available. You will see it in the **Kontext**, **Aussprache und Rechtschreibung**, **Hören**, and **Wortschatz** sections.
- The Supersite icon appears on pages for which there is online content, such as audio, video, or presentations.
- The recycling icon tells you that you will need to use vocabulary and/or grammar learned in previous lessons.

Ressourcen Boxes

Ressourcen boxes let you know exactly which print and technology ancillaries you can use to reinforce and expand on every section of each lesson in your textbook. They include page numbers, when applicable.

Ressourcen boxes legend			
SAM WB: pp. 29–30	Workbook	SAM VM: pp. 219–220	Video Manual
SAM LM: p. 17	Lab Manual	Ⓢ	SAG MAL Supersite vhlcentral.com

SAG MAL at-a-glance

UNIT OPENERS

outline the content and features of each unit.

Familie und Freunde

KAPITEL
3

LEKTION 3A	LEKTION 3B	WEITER GEHT'S
Kontext Seite 96–99 • Johanna Schmidts Familie • Final consonants	**Kontext** Seite 114–117 • Wie sind sie? • Consonant clusters	Seite 134–140 **Panorama: Die Vereinigten Staaten und Kanada** **Lesen:** Read an article about pets. **Hören:** Listen to a conversation between two friends. **Schreiben:** Write a letter to a friend. **Kapitel 3 Wortschatz**
Fotoroman Seite 100–101 • Ein Abend mit der Familie	**Fotoroman** Seite 118–119 • Unsere Mitbewohner	
Kultur Seite 102–103 • Eine deutsche Familie	**Kultur** Seite 120–121 • Auf unsere Freunde!	
Strukturen Seite 104–113 • 3A.1 Possessive adjectives • 3A.2 Descriptive adjectives and adjective agreement • Wiederholung • Zapping	**Strukturen** Seite 122–133 • 3B.1 Modals • 3B.2 Prepositions with the accusative • 3B.3 The imperative • Wiederholung	

Unit opener photos highlight scenes from the **Fotoroman** that illustrate the unit theme. They are snapshots of the characters that students will come to know throughout the program.

Content lists break down each unit into its two lessons and one **Weiter Geht's** section, giving you an at-a-glance summary of the vocabulary, grammar, cultural topics, and language skills covered in the unit.

Ⓢupersite

Supersite resources are available for every section of each unit at **vhlcentral.com.** Icons show you which textbook activities are also available online, and where additional practice activities are available. The description next to the Ⓢ icon indicates what additional resources are available for each section: videos, audio recordings, readings, presentations, and more!

Supersite features vary by access level. Visit **vistahigherlearning.com** to explore which Supersite level is right for you.

KONTEXT

presents and practices vocabulary in meaningful contexts.

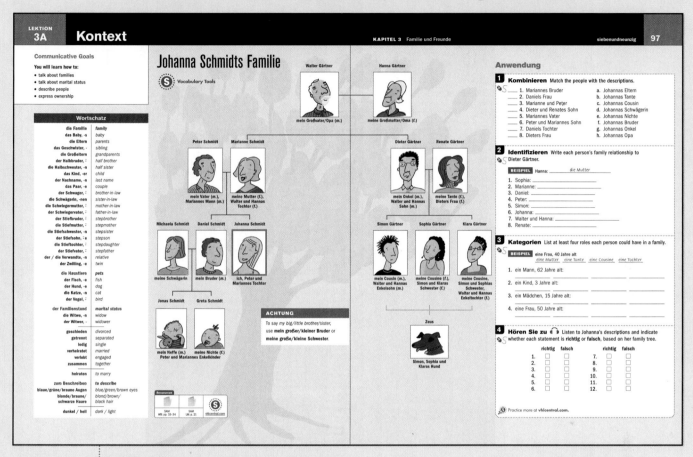

Communicative goals highlight the real-life tasks you will be able to carry out in German by the end of each lesson.

Illustrations introduce high-frequency vocabulary through expansive, full-color images.

Wortschatz sidebars call out important theme-related vocabulary in easy-to-reference German-English lists.

Ressourcen boxes let you know what print and technology ancillaries reinforce and expand on every section of every lesson.

Achtung boxes give you additional information about how and when to use certain vocabulary words or grammar structures.

Kontext always contains an audio activity that accompanies either the **Anwendung** or the **Kommunikation** practice activities. Anwendung follows a pedagogical sequence that starts with simpler, shorter, discrete recognition activities and builds toward longer, more complex production activities.

Ⓢupersite

- Audio recordings of all vocabulary items
- Audio for **Kontext** listening activity
- Image-based vocabulary activity with audio
- Textbook activities
- Additional online-only practice activities

Supersite features vary by access level. Visit **vistahigherlearning.com** to explore which Supersite level is right for you.

KONTEXT

practices vocabulary using communication activities.

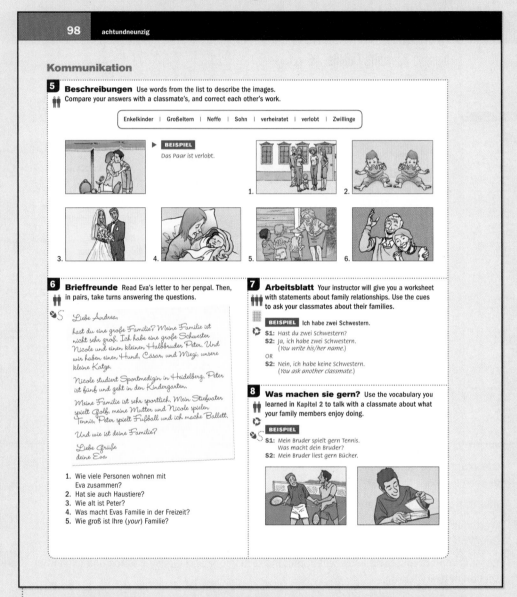

Kommunikation activities make use of discourse-level prompts, allowing you to use the vocabulary creatively in interactions with a partner, a small group, or the entire class.

Icons provide on-the-spot visual cues for pair, small group, language recycling, listening-based, and worksheet-based or information gap activities.

Supersite

- Chat activities for conversational skill-building and oral practice

Supersite features vary by access level. Visit **vistahigherlearning.com** to explore which Supersite level is right for you.

AUSSPRACHE UND RECHTSCHREIBUNG
presents the rules of German pronunciation and spelling.

Explanations of German pronunciation and spelling are presented clearly, with abundant model words and phrases. The red highlighting feature focuses your attention on the target structure.

Practice pronunciation and spelling at the word- and sentence-levels. The final activity features illustrated sayings and proverbs that present the target structures in an entertaining cultural context.

The headset icon at the top of the page indicates that the explanation and activities are recorded for convenient use in or outside of class.

Ⓢupersite

- Audio recording of the **Aussprache und Rechtschreibung** presentation
- Record-and-compare activities

Supersite features vary by access level. Visit **vistahigherlearning.com** to explore which Supersite level is right for you.

FOTOROMAN

tells the story of a group of students living in Berlin.

Fotoroman is a versatile episodic video that can be assigned as homework, presented in class, or used as review.

Conversations reinforce vocabulary from **Kontext**. They also preview structures from the upcoming **Strukturen** section in context.

Personen features the cast of recurring **Fotoroman** characters, including four college students: George, Sabite, Meline, and Hans.

Nützliche Ausdrücke calls out the most important words and expressions from the **Fotoroman** episode that have not been formally presented. This vocabulary is not tested. The blue numbers refer to the grammar structures presented in the lesson.

Übungen activities include comprehension questions, a communicative task, and a research-based task.

Supersite

- Streaming video for all 24 episodes of the **Fotoroman**
- End-of-video **Zusammenfassung** section where key vocabulary and grammar from the episode are called out
- Textbook activities

Supersite features vary by access level. Visit **vistahigherlearning.com** to explore which Supersite level is right for you.

KULTUR

explores cultural themes introduced in **KONTEXT.**

LEKTION 3B **Kultur**

KAPITEL 3 Familie und Freunde — hunderteinundzwanzig 121

IM FOKUS

Auf unsere Freunde!°

Reading

TIPP

In German, many adjectives can be transformed into nouns.

bekannt → **der / die Bekannte**
known — *acquaintance*

besonders → **(etwas) Besonderes**
special — *something special*

gleich → **das Gleiche**
same — *the same one/the same thing*

In dieser° Facebook-Zeit haben wir alle viele „Freunde". Was ist also ein Kumpel°, mit dem Sie hin und wieder auf Partys gehen, und was ist ein echter° Freund? Deutsche sagen nicht so schnell „Freund" wie Amerikaner. In Deutschland ist es etwas Besonderes° ein „Freund" zu sein.

Wirklich gute Freunde hat man in Deutschland wahrscheinlich höchstens° vier oder fünf. Ein echter Freund zu sein bedeutet, dass° man sich sehr gut und vielleicht auch schon sehr lange kennt°. Die meisten Leute in Deutschland sagen, dass sie ihre Freunde schon aus der Schule oder aus der Kinderzeit kennen. Nur weil° man einmal zusammen Kaffee getrunken hat°, ist man noch lange kein Freund.

In der Gruppe kennen sich alle mehr oder weniger gut. Trotzdem° nennen sich die Leute in einer Gruppe „Kumpel", nicht „Freunde". Die anderen Leute, die man kennt, nennt man meistens „Bekannte".

Es gibt also drei Gruppen von Menschen um eine Person: Die meisten Menschen sind Bekannte. Die größere Gruppe sind die Kumpel. Und nur eine sehr kleine Gruppe sind richtige Freunde. Aber mit diesen Freunden kann man alles teilen°. Also: Auf Freunde!

Auf unsere Freunde! *Here's to our friends!* **dieser** *this* **Kumpel** *buddy* **echter** *real* **etwas Besonderes** *something special* **wahrscheinlich höchstens** *probably at most* **bedeutet, dass** *means that* **sich... kennt** *know each other* **Nur weil** *Just because* **getrunken hat** *has drunk* **Trotzdem** *Nevertheless* **teilen** *share*

DEUTSCH IM ALLTAG

Wie wir Menschen sind

aufrichtig	*sincere*
besserwisserisch	*know-it-all (adj.)*
eingebildet	*arrogant*
geduldig	*patient*
geizig	*stingy*
liebevoll	*loving*
locker	*easy-going*
oberflächlich	*superficial*
ruhig	*calm*
weise	*wise*
zuverlässig	*reliable*

DIE DEUTSCHSPRACHIGE WELT

Es wird geheiratet!°

Wie wünscht° man dem neuen Paar ein frohes Eheleben°? In **Bayern**, **Österreich** und **in der Schweiz** ist das **Brautstehlen°** eine lustige Tradition. Freunde stehlen die Braut und bringen sie von Gaststätte° zu Gaststätte. Der Bräutigam° muss sie finden... und alle Getränke bezahlen°! Die **Deutschen** und die **Österreicher** tragen den Ring meistens an der rechten° Hand. Aber **in der Schweiz** trägt man ihn an der linken° Hand. Die ist dem Herzen näher°.

Es wird geheiratet! *Someone's getting married!* **wünscht** *wishes* **Eheleben** *married life* **Brautstehlen** *stealing of the bride* **Gaststätte** *restaurant* **Bräutigam** *groom* **Getränke bezahlen** *pay for the drinks* **rechten** *right* **linken** *left* **dem Herzen näher** *closer to the heart*

PORTRÄT

Tokio Hotel

Die erfolgreiche° deutsche Band *Tokio Hotel* besteht° am Anfang aus den eineiigen° Zwillingen Bill und Tom Kaulitz. Schon als Kinder machen sie zusammen Musik. Als Duett treten sie unter dem Namen *Black Questionmark* auf°. Ihr Stiefvater ist auch Musiker und fördert° die Brüder. 2001 geben sie in ihrer Heimatstadt° Magdeburg ein Konzert. Dort treffen sie Gustav Schäfer und Georg Listing. Sie werden Freunde und treten zu viert unter dem Namen *Devilish* auf. 2005 nimmt die Universal Music Group die Band unter Vertrag°. Die Vier nennen sich *Tokio Hotel* und sind schnell auf der ganzen Welt bekannt. Sie haben in Deutschland und Österreich vier Nummer-eins-Singles und verkaufen bis heute weltweit über 7 Millionen Alben°.

erfolgreich *successful* **besteht** *consists* **eineiigen** *identical* **treten...auf** *perform* **fördert** *supports* **Heimatstadt** *home town* **unter Vertrag** *under contract* **Alben** *albums*

IM INTERNET

Sind die Hochzeitsbräuche (*wedding traditions*) anders (*different*) in Deutschland als in den USA?

Find out more at **vhlcentral.com**.

ÜBUNGEN

1 Was fehlt? Complete the statements.

1. In Deutschland sagt man nicht so schnell _______ zu einer neuen Person.
2. Viele Deutsche kennen ihre Freunde aus der _______ und aus der Kinderzeit.
3. Gute _______ nennt man in Deutschland nur vier oder fünf Personen.
4. Für _______ und für Deutsche hat das Wort „Freund" nicht die gleiche Bedeutung.
5. In _______ ist ein Freund jemand, den (*whom*) man sehr gut kennt.
6. Einen echten Freund kennt man sehr gut und oft auch sehr _______.
7. Es gibt _______ Gruppen von Menschen um eine Person.
8. In einer _______ sind alle gute Kumpel.
9. Die meisten Menschen, die man kennt, nennt man _______.
10. Die Gruppe der Freunde ist eine sehr _______ Gruppe.

Practice more at **vhlcentral.com.**

2 Richtig oder falsch? Indicate whether each statement is **richtig** or **falsch**. Correct the false statements.

1. In Österreich ist es Tradition, den Bräutigam zu stehlen.
2. In Deutschland trägt man den Ehering an der rechten Hand.
3. Prinz Ernst August ist der Sohn von Kaiser Wilhelm II.
4. Prinz Ernst August mag (*likes*) die Paparazzi.
5. Alexandra ist die Tochter von Prinzessin Caroline von Monaco und Prinz Ernst August von Hannover.

3 Wie sind sie? In pairs, describe each person in the photo on p. 120. How old do you think they are? What do you think their personalities are like? Are they friends or just classmates?

Ressourcen vhlcentral.com

Im Fokus presents an in-depth reading about the lesson's cultural theme. Full-color photos bring to life important aspects of the topic, while charts support the main text with statistics and additional information.

Tipp boxes provide helpful tips for reading and understanding German.

Porträt spotlights notable people, places, events, and products from the German-speaking world. This article is thematically linked to the lesson.

Deutsch im Alltag presents additional vocabulary related to the lesson theme, showcasing words and phrases used in everyday spoken German. This vocabulary is not tested.

Die deutschsprachige Welt focuses on the people, places, dialects, and traditions in regions where German is spoken. This short article is thematically linked to the lesson.

Im Internet boxes, with provocative questions and photos, direct you to the **SAG MAL** Supersite where you can continue to learn about the topics in **Kultur**.

Supersite

- **Kultur** reading
- **Im Internet** research activity expands on the lesson theme
- Textbook activities
- Additional online-only practice activities

Supersite features vary by access level. Visit **vistahigherlearning.com** to explore which Supersite level is right for you.

STRUKTUREN

presents German grammar in a graphic-intensive format.

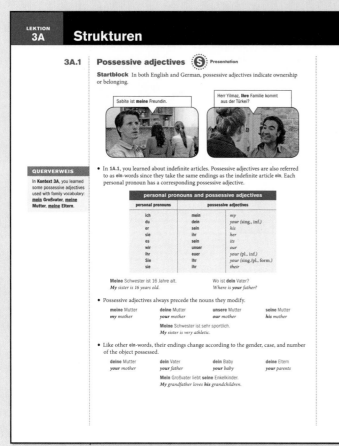

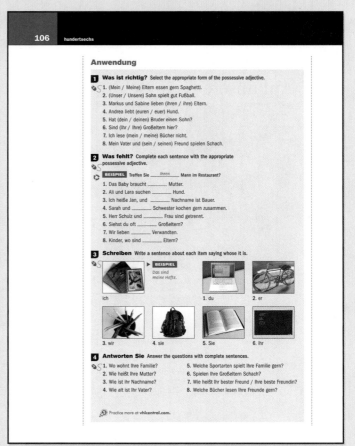

Format includes one to two pages of explanation for each grammar point, followed by one to two pages of activities. Two to three grammar points are featured in each lesson.

Startblock eases you into each grammar explanation, with definitions of grammatical terms and reminders about grammar concepts with which you are already familiar.

Photos from the **Fotoroman** consistently integrate the lesson's video episode with the grammar explanations.

Querverweis boxes call out information covered in earlier lessons or provide cross-references to related topics you will see in future units.

Achtung boxes clarify potential sources of confusion and provide supplementary information.

Jetzt sind Sie dran! is your first opportunity to practice the new grammar point.

Anwendung offers a wide range of guided activities that combine lesson vocabulary and previously learned material with the new grammar point.

Kommunikation activities provide opportunities for self-expression using the lesson grammar and vocabulary. These activities feature interaction with a partner, in small groups, or with the whole class.

(S)upersite

- Grammar presentations
- Textbook activities
- Additional online-only practice activities
- Chat activities for conversational skill-building and oral practice

WIEDERHOLUNG
pulls the lesson together.

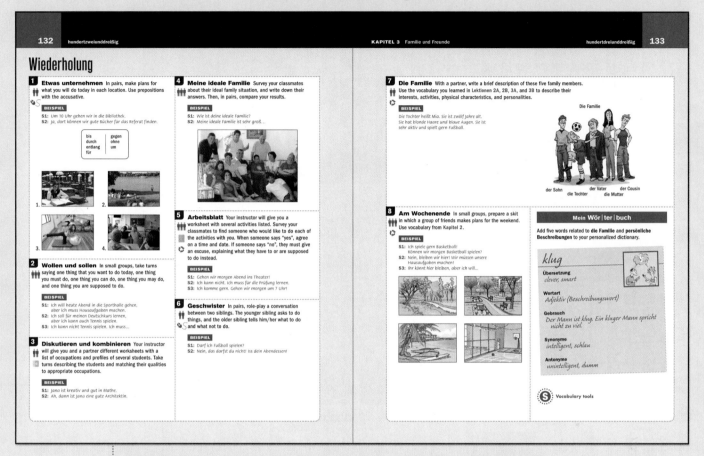

Wiederholung activities integrate the lesson's grammar points and vocabulary with previously learned vocabulary and structures, providing consistent, built-in review as you progress through the text.

Pair and group icons indicate communicative activities such as role play, games, personal questions, interviews, and surveys.

Information gap activities, identified by interlocking puzzle pieces, engage you and a partner in problem-solving situations.

Recycling icons call out the activities in which you will practice the lesson's grammar and vocabulary along with previously learned material.

Mein Wörterbuch in the B lesson of each unit offers the opportunity to increase your vocabulary and contextualize new words.

Supersite

- Chat activities for conversational skill-building and oral practice

Supersite features vary by access level. Visit **vistahigherlearning.com** to explore which Supersite level is right for you.

ZAPPING AND KURZFILM

feature TV clips and short-subject films.

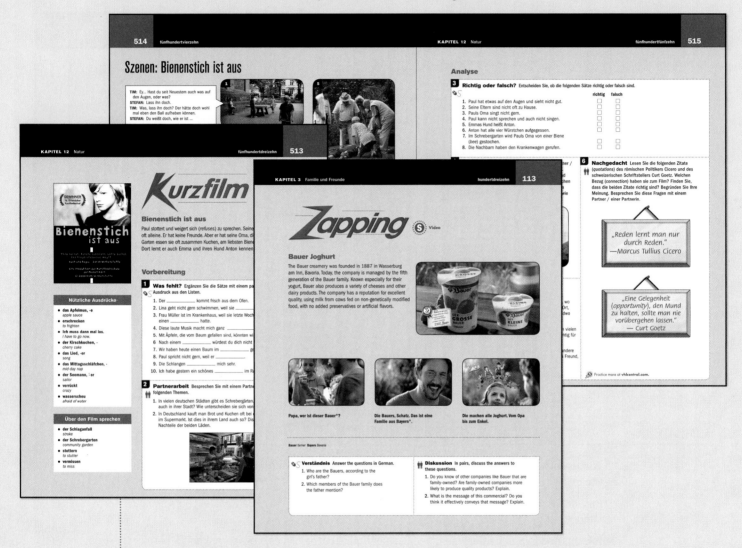

Zapping presents TV commercials and public service announcements from the German-speaking world in Units 1 through 9. Post-viewing activities check comprehension.

Kurzfilm in Units 10, 11, and 12 features short films from contemporary German-speaking filmmakers.

Summary provides context for each film.

Vorbereitung pre-viewing activities set the stage for the short films and provide key information to facilitate comprehension.

Analysen post-viewing activities encourage you to explore the broader themes presented in each film.

Ⓢupersite

- Streaming video of the TV clip or short film with instructor-controlled subtitle options
- Textbook activities

Supersite features vary by access level. Visit **vistahigherlearning.com** to explore which Supersite level is right for you.

WEITER GEHT'S

Panorama presents geographical, historical, and cultural information about the German-speaking world.

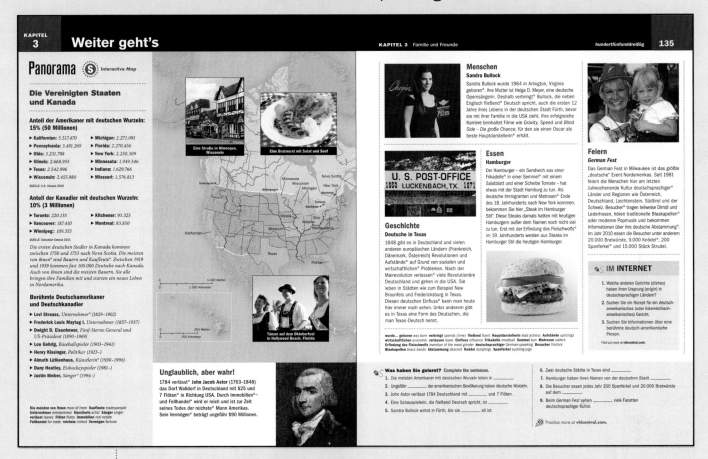

Panorama offers interesting facts about the featured city, region, or country.

Maps point out major geographical features and situate the featured region in the context of its immediate surroundings.

Readings explore different aspects of the featured region's culture, such as history, landmarks, fine art, literature, and insight into everyday life.

Unglaublich aber wahr! highlights an intriguing fact about the featured region.

Comprehension questions check your understanding of key ideas.

Supersite

- Interactive map with statistics and cultural notes
- **Im Internet** research activity
- Textbook activities
- Additional online-only practice activity

Supersite features vary by access level. Visit **vistahigherlearning.com** to explore which Supersite level is right for you.

WEITER GEHT'S

Lesen provides practice for reading skills in the context of the unit's theme.

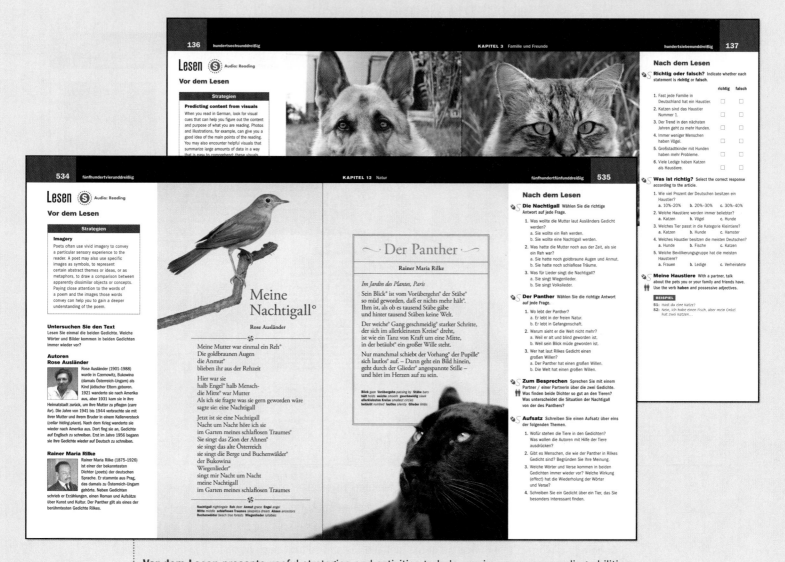

Vor dem Lesen presents useful strategies and activities to help you improve your reading abilities.

Readings are tied to the lesson theme and recycle vocabulary and grammar you have learned. The selections in Units 1 through 9 are cultural texts. The selections in Units 10 through 12 are authentic literary texts.

Nach dem Lesen consists of post-reading activities that check your comprehension.

ⓢupersite

- Audio-sync reading that highlights text as it is being read
- Textbook activities

Supersite features vary by access level. Visit **vistahigherlearning.com** to explore which Supersite level is right for you.

WEITER GEHT'S

Hören and **Schreiben** develop listening and writing skills in the context of the unit's theme.

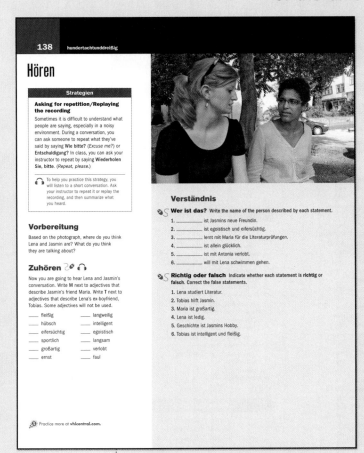

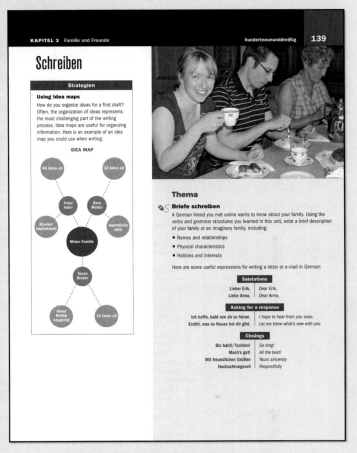

Hören uses a recorded conversation or narration to develop your listening skills in German. **Strategien** and **Vorbereitung** prepare you to listen to the audio recording.

Zuhören guides you through the recorded segment, and **Verständnis** checks your understanding of what you heard.

In the **Schreiben** section, **Strategien** provides useful preparation for the writing task presented in **Thema**.

Thema presents a writing topic and includes suggestions for approaching it. It also provides words and phrases that may be useful in writing about the topic.

Ⓢupersite

- Audio for **Hören** activities
- Textbook activities
- Additional online-only practice activity
- Composition engine writing activity for **Schreiben**

Supersite features vary by access level. Visit **vistahigherlearning.com** to explore which Supersite level is right for you.

WORTSCHATZ
summarizes the unit's active vocabulary.

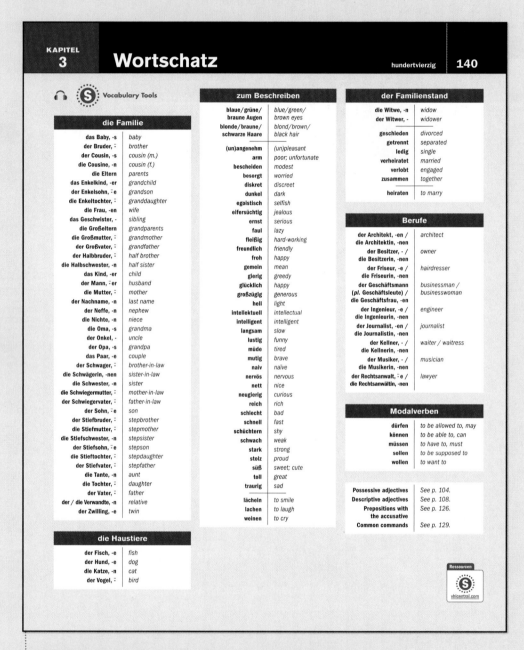

Wortschatz presents the unit's active vocabulary in logical groupings, including notation of plural forms.

Ⓢupersite

- Audio recordings of all vocabulary items
- Vocabulary tools

Supersite features vary by access level. Visit **vistahigherlearning.com** to explore which Supersite level is right for you.

THE *FOTOROMAN* EPISODES

Fully integrated with your textbook, the **SAG MAL Fotoroman** contains 24 dramatic episodes—one for each lesson of the text. The episodes relate the adventures of four college students who are studying in Berlin.

The **Fotoroman** dialogues in the printed textbook lesson are an abbreviated version of the dramatic episode featured in the video. Therefore, each **Fotoroman** section can be used as preparation before you view the corresponding video episode, as post-viewing reinforcement, or as a stand-alone section.

As you watch the video, you will see the characters interact using the vocabulary and grammar you are studying. Their conversations incorporate new vocabulary and grammar with previously taught language. At the conclusion of each episode, the **Zusammenfassung** segment summarizes the key language functions and grammar points used in the episode.

THE CAST

Learn more about each of the characters you'll meet in **SAG MAL Fotoroman:**

George
is from Milwaukee, Wisconsin. He is studying Architecture.

Hans
is from Straubing, in Bavaria. He studies Political Science and History.

Meline
is from Vienna. She is studying Business.

Sabite
is from Berlin. She studies Art.

SAG MAL AND THE *STANDARDS FOR FOREIGN LANGUAGE LEARNING*

Since 1982, when the ACTFL Proficiency Guidelines were first published, that seminal document and its subsequent revisions have influenced the teaching of modern languages in the United States. **SAG MAL**, Second Edition, was written with the concerns and philosophy of the ACTFL Proficiency Guidelines in mind, incorporating a proficiency-oriented approach from its planning stages.

SAG MAL's pedagogy was also informed from its inception by the Standards for Foreign Language Learning in the 21st Century. First published in 1996 under the auspices of the National Standards in Foreign Language Education Project, the Standards are organized into five goal areas, often called the Five Cs: Communication, Cultures, Connections, Comparisons, and Communities.

Since **SAG MAL**, Second Edition, takes a communicative approach to the teaching and learning of German, the Communication goal is central to the student text. For example, the diverse formats used in the **Kommunikation** and **Wiederholung** activities in each lesson—pair work, small group work, class circulation, information gap, task-based, and so forth—engage students in communicative exchanges, providing and obtaining information, and expressing feelings, emotions, and ideas. The **Schreiben** section focuses on developing students' communication skills in writing. The Cultures goal is most overtly evident in the **Fotoroman** and **Kultur** sections, as well as in the **Panorama** feature in the **Weiter geht's** section at the end of each unit. Students can also acquire information and recognize distinctive cultural viewpoints in the literary texts of the Lesen sections. **SAG MAL**, Second Edition, also weaves culture into virtually every page, exposing students to the multiple facets of practices, products, and perspectives of the German-speaking world. In keeping with the Connections goal, students can connect with other disciplines such as communications, business, geography, history, fine arts, science, and math in the **Zapping** and **Panorama** features. Moreover, Im Internet boxes in **Kultur** and **Panorama** support the Connections and Communities goals as students work through those sections and complete the related activities on the **SAG MAL**, Second Edition, Supersite. Asfor the Comparisons goal, it is reflected in **Aussprache** und **Rechtschreibung** and the **Strukturen** sections.

Special Standards icons appear on the student text pages of your Instructor's Annotated Edition to call out sections that have a particularly strong relationship with the Standards. These are a few examples of how **SAG MAL**, Second Edition, was written with the Standards firmly in mind, but you will find many more as you work with the student textbook and its ancillaries.

Communication Understand and be understood: read and listen to understand German speakers, converse with others, and share your thoughts clearly through speaking and writing.

Cultures Experience German, Austrian, and Swiss culture through the viewpoints, places, objects, behaviors, and beliefs important to the national identity of these countries.

Connections Apply what you learn in your German course to your other studies; apply what you know from other courses to your German studies.

Comparisons Discover in which ways the language and culture of the German-speaking world are like your own—and how they differ.

Communities Engage with German-speaking communities locally, nationally, and internationally both in your courses and beyond—for life.

LEARNING TO USE YOUR INSTRUCTOR'S ANNOTATED EDITION

SAG MAL, Second Edition, offers you a comprehensive, thoroughly developed Instructor's Annotated Edition (IAE). It features student text pages overprinted with answers to all activities with discrete responses. Each page also contains annotations for a few selected activities that were written to complement and support varied teaching styles, to extend the already rich contents of the student textbook, and to save you time in class preparation and course management.

Because the **SAG MAL**, Second Edition, IAE is different from instructor's editions available with other German programs, this section is designed as a quick orientation to the principal types of instructor annotations it contains. As you familiarize yourself with them, it is important to know that the annotations are suggestions only. The questions, sentences, models, or simulated instructor-student exchanges presented are not meant to be prescriptive or limiting. You are encouraged to view these suggested "scripts" as flexible points of departure that will help you achieve your instructional goals.

For the Unit Opening Page

- **Suggestion** A discussion topic idea, based on the Unit Opener photo

For the Lessons

- **Suggestion** Teaching suggestions for working with on-page materials, carrying out specific activities, and presenting new vocabulary or grammar

- **Expansion** Expansions and variations on activities

- **Vorbereitung** Suggestions for talking about the **Fotoroman** pages before students have watched the video or studied the pages

- **Nützliche Ausdrücke** A list of expressions taken from the **Fotoroman** that students may need to study before watching the episode

Please check the **SAG MAL**, Second Edition, Supersite at **vhlcentral.com**
for additional teaching support.

COURSE PLANNING

The entire **SAG MAL**, Second Edition, program was developed with an eye to flexibility and ease of use in a wide variety of course configurations. **SAG MAL**, Second Edition, can be used in courses taught on semester or quarter systems, and in courses that complete the book in two or three semesters. Here are some sample course plans that illustrate how **SAG MAL**, Second Edition, can be used in different academic situations. You should, of course, feel free to organize your courses in the way that best suits your students' needs and your instructional objectives.

Two-Semester System

The following chart illustrates how **SAG MAL**, Second Edition, can be completed in a two-semester course.

Semester 1	Semester 2
Units 1–6	Units 7–12

Three-Semester or Quarter System

This chart shows how **SAG MAL**, Second Edition, can be used in a three-semester or quarter course. The units are divided over each semester/quarter, allowing students to absorb the material at a steady pace.

Semester/Quarter 1	Semester/Quarter 2	Semester/Quarter 3
Units 1–4	Units 5–8	Units 9–12

Four-Semester System

This chart shows how **SAG MAL**, Second Edition, can be used in a four-semester course.

Semester 1	Semester 2	Semester 3	Semester 1
Units 1–3	Units 4–6	Units 7–9	Units 10–12

Sample Lesson Plan and Syllabus

The sample two-semester syllabus and **Kapitel 3** lesson plan for **SAG MAL**, Second Edition, are available on the instructor's section of the **SAG MAL**, Second Edition, Supersite at **vhlcentral.com**. You will find general suggestions, as well as plans for the two lessons in each unit and end-of-unit **Weiter geht's** section. The sample syllabus and lesson plan are not intended to be prescriptive. You should feel free to present lesson materials as you see fit, tailoring them to your own teaching preferences and to your students' learning styles. It is our hope that you will find the **SAG MAL**, Second Edition, program very flexible: simply pick and choose from its arrayof instructional resources, and sequence the material in the way that makes the most sense for your course.

GENERAL TEACHING CONSIDERATIONS

Orienting Students to the Student Textbook

Because **SAG MAL**, Second Edition, treats interior and graphic design as an integral part of students' language-learning experience, you may want to take a few minutes to orient students to the student textbook. Have them flip through one unit, and point out that the units are all organized exactly the same way, with two short lessons and a concluding **Weiter geht's** section. Also point out that the major sections of each lesson are color-coded for easy navigation: green for **Kontext**; orange for **Fotoroman**; red for **Kultur**; blue for **Strukturen**, **Zapping**, and **Wiederholung**; and purple for **Weiter geht's** and **Wortschatz**. Because of these design elements, students can be confident that they will always know "where they are" in their textbook.

Emphasize that sections are self-contained, occupying either a full page or a spread of two facing pages, thereby eliminating "bad breaks." Finally, call students' attention to the use of color to highlight key information in elements such as charts, diagrams, word lists, activity models, titles, and help boxes such as **Achtung!**, **Tipp**, and **Querverweis**.

Flexible Lesson Organization

SAG MAL, Second Edition, uses a flexible lesson organization designed to meet the needs of diverse teaching styles, instructional goals, and institutional requirements. For example, you can begin with the unit opening page and progress sequentially through a unit. If you do not want to devote class time to grammar, you can assign the Strukturen explanations for outside study, freeing up class time for other purposes, such as developing oral communication skills; building listening, reading, and writing skills; learning more about the German-speaking world; or working with the video program. You might decide to work with the **Weiter geht's** section in order to focus on students' reading skills and their knowledge of German-speaking regions. On the other hand, you might prefer to skip these sections entirely, or to draw from them selectively, depending on your classroom needs and the interests of your students. If you plan on using the **SAG MAL**, Second Edition, Testing Program, however, be aware that its tests and exams check students' command of language presented in **Kontext** and vocabulary called out in text and charts on the **Strukturen** pages. The language presented in the **Nützliche Ausdrücke** boxes of the **Fotoroman** and the Deutsch im **Alltag** boxes on **Kultur** pages is not tested.

Identifying Active Vocabulary

All words and expressions taught in the **Kontext** illustrations and lists are considered active, testable vocabulary. Likewise, new vocabulary called out in **Strukturen**, including tables, charts, and boxes, is considered active and testable. At the end of each unit, **Wortschatz** provides a convenient one-page summary of the items that students should know and that may appear on quizzes, tests, or exams. The phrases and expressions in **Fotoroman** are not part of the active vocabulary load. You will want to point this out to students.

TAKING INTO ACCOUNT THE AFFECTIVE DIMENSION

While many factors contribute to the quality and success rate of learning experiences, two factors are particularly germane to language learning. One is students' beliefs about how language is learned; the other is language-learning anxiety.

As studies show and experienced instructors know, students often come to modern language courses either with a lack of knowledge about how to approach language learning or with mistaken notions about how to do so. For example, many students believe that making mistakes when speaking the target language must be avoided because doing so will lead to permanent errors. Others are convinced that learning another language is like learning any other academic subject. In other words, they believe that success is guaranteed, provided they attend class regularly, learn the assigned vocabulary words and grammar rules, and study for exams. In fact, in a study of college-level beginning language learners in the United States, over one third of the participants thought that they could become fluent if they studied the language for only one hour a day for two years or less. Mistaken and unrealistic beliefs such as these can cause frustration and ultimately demotivation, thereby significantly undermining students' ability to achieve a successful language-learning experience.

Another factor that can negatively impact students' language-learning experiences is language-learning anxiety. As Professor Elaine K. Horwitz of The University of Texas at Austin and Senior Consulting Editor of **VISTAS**, First Edition, wrote, "Surveys indicate that up to one-third of American foreign language students feel moderately to highly anxious about studying another language. Physical symptoms of foreign language anxiety can include heart-pounding or palpitations, sweating, trembling, fast breathing, and general feelings of unease." The late Dr. Philip Redwine Donley, **VISTAS** co-author and author of articles on language-learning anxiety, spoke with many students who reported feeling nervous or apprehensive in their classes. They mentioned freezing when called on by their instructors or going inexplicably blank when taking tests. Some so dreaded their classes that they skipped them or dropped the course.

Based on what Vista Higher Learning learned from instructors and students using our highly successful introductory Spanish and French programs, **SAG MAL**, Second Edition, contains several features aimed at reducing students' language anxiety and supporting their successful language learning. First of all, the highly structured, visually dramatic interior design of the **SAG MAL**, Second Edition, student text was conceived as a learning tool to make students feel comfortable with the content and confident about navigating the lessons. In addition, the student text provides marginal boxes that assist students by making relevant connections with new information or reminding them of previously learned concepts.

GENERAL SUGGESTIONS FOR USING THE SAG MAL *FOTOROMAN* VIDEO EPISODES

The **Fotoroman** section in each lesson and the **Fotoroman** video were created as interlocking pieces. All photos in **Fotoroman** are actual video stills from the corresponding video episode, while the printed conversations are abbreviated versions of the dramatic segment. Both the **Fotoroman** conversations and their expanded video versions represent comprehensible input at the discourse level; they were purposely written to use language from the corresponding lesson's **Kontext** and **Strukturen** sections. Thus, as of **Episode 2** in **Lektion 1B**, they recycle known language, preview grammar points students will study later in the lesson, and, in keeping with **Krashen's** concept of "i + 1," contain some amount of unknown language.

Because the **Fotoroman** textbook sections and the dramatic episodes of the **Fotoroman** video are so closely connected, you may use them in many different ways. For instance, you can use **Fotoroman** as a preview, presenting it before showing the video episode. You can also show the video episode first and follow up with **Fotoroman**. You can even use **Fotoroman** as a stand-alone, video-independent section.

Depending on your teaching preferences and campus facilities, you might decide to show all video episodes in class or to assign them solely for viewing outside the classroom. You could begin by showing the first one or two episodes in class to familiarize yourself and students with the characters, storyline, style, and **Zusammenfassung** sections. After that, you could work in class only with **Fotoroman** and have students view the remaining video episodes outside of class. No matter which approach you choose, students have ample materials to support viewing the video independently and processing it in a meaningful way. For each video episode, there are activities in the **Fotoroman** section of the corresponding textbook lesson, as well as additional activities in the **SAG MAL**, Second Edition, Video Manual section of the *Student Activities Manual*.

You might also want to use the **Fotoroman** video in class when working with the **Strukturen** sections. You could play the parts of the dramatic episode that correspond to the video stills in the grammar explanations or show selected scenes and ask students to identify certain grammar points.

You could also focus on the **Zusammenfassung** sections that appear at the end of each episode to summarize the key language functions and grammar points used. In class, you could play the parts of the **Zusammenfassung** section that exemplify individual grammar points as you progress through each **Strukturen** section. You could also wait until you complete a **Strukturen** section and review it and the lesson's **Kontext** section by showing the corresponding **Zusammenfassung** section in its entirety.

On the **SAG MAL**, Second Edition, Supersite, instructors can control what, if any, subtitles students can see. They are available in German or in English, and in transcript format.

When showing the **Fotoroman** video segments in your classes, you might want to implement a process approach. You could start with an activity that prepares students for the video segment, implementing the vocabulary they learned in the **Kontext** section. This could be followed by an activity that students do while you play parts of, or the entire, video segment. The final activity, done in the same class period or in the next one as warm-up, could recap what students saw and heard and move beyond the video segment's topic. The following suggestions for using the **Fotoroman** video segments in class are in addition to those on the individual pages of the Instructor's Annotated Edition, and they can be carried out as described or expanded upon in any number of ways.

Before viewing

- Ask students to guess what the segment might be about based on what they've learned in Kontext or by asking them to look at the video stills.

- Have pairs make a list of the lesson vocabulary they expect to hear in the video.

- Read a list of true-false or multiple-choice questions about the video to the class, and have students use what they know about the characters to guess the answers. Have them confirm their guesses after watching the segment.

While viewing

- Show the video segment with the audio turned off and ask students to use lesson vocabulary and previously learned structures to describe what they see. Have them confirm their guesses by showing the segment again with the audio on.

- Have students refer to the list of words they brainstormed before viewing the video and put a check in front of any words they actually hear or see in the segment.

- First, have students simply watch the video. Then, show it again and ask students to take notes on what they see and hear. Finally, have them compare their notes in pairs or groups for confirmation.

- Print the episode's videoscript from the Supersite and white out words and expressions related to the lesson theme. Distribute the scripts for pairs or groups to complete as cloze paragraphs.

- Show the video segment before moving on to Kontext to jump-start the lesson's vocabulary, grammar, and cultural focus. Have students tell you what vocabulary and grammar they recognize from previous lessons.

After viewing

- Have students say what aspects of the information presented in the corresponding textbook lesson are included in the video segment.

- Ask groups to write a brief summary of the content of the video segment. Have them exchange papers with another group for peer review.

- Have students pick one new aspect of the corresponding textbook lesson's cultural theme that they learned about from watching the video segment. Then ask them to research more about that topic and write a list or paragraph to expand on it.

Zapping

ABOUT *ZAPPING* TV CLIPS AND SHORT FILMS

A TV clip or a short film from the German-speaking world appears in the first **Lektion** of each **Kapitel**. The purpose of this feature is to expose students to the language and culture contained in authentic media pieces. The following list of the television commercials and short films is organized by **Kapitel** and **Lektion** for your convenience.

SAG MAL, Second Edition, **Zapping** clips

Kapitel 1
Deutsche Bahn
(29 seconds)

Kapitel 4
Yello Strom
(39 seconds)

Kapitel 7
Urlaub im grünen Binnenland
(3 minutes, 41 seconds)

Kapitel 2
TU Berlin
(1 minute, 15 seconds)

Kapitel 5
Real
(26 seconds)

Kapitel 8
Mercedes Benz
(35 seconds)

Kapitel 3
Bauer Joghurt
(33 seconds)

Kapitel 6
Hausarbeit
(1 minute, 13 seconds)

Kapitel 9
Central Krankenversicherung
(25 seconds)

SAG MAL, Second Edition, short films

Kapitel 10
Fanny
(13 minutes, 45 seconds)

Kapitel 11
Die Berliner Mauer
(15 minutes)

Kapitel 12
Bienenstich ist aus
(15 minutes)

ABOUT STRATEGIES IN *LESEN*, *HÖREN*, AND *SCHREIBEN*

SAG MAL, Second Edition, takes a process approach to the development of reading, listening, and writing skills. These are lists of the different strategies taught in each unit so that you may refer to them in one convenient place.

Lesen

Kapitel 1	Recognizing cognates	**Kapitel 7**	Predicting content from the title
Kapitel 2	Predicting content through formats	**Kapitel 8**	Guessing meaning from context
Kapitel 3	Predicting content from visuals	**Kapitel 9**	Reading for the main idea
Kapitel 4	Scanning	**Kapitel 10**	Analyzing repetition
Kapitel 5	Skimming	**Kapitel 11**	Identifying perspective
Kapitel 6	Recognizing word families	**Kapitel 12**	Analyzing imagery

Hören

Kapitel 1	Listening for words you know	**Kapitel 8**	Recognizing the genre of spoken discourse
Kapitel 2	Listening for cognates		
Kapitel 3	Asking for repetition	**Kapitel 9**	Using background information
Kapitel 4	Listening for the gist	**Kapitel 10**	Guessing the meaning of words from context
Kapitel 5	Listening for key words	**Kapitel 11**	Listening for linguistic clues
Kapitel 6	Using background knowledge	**Kapitel 12**	Taking notes
Kapitel 7	Using visual cues		

Schreiben

Kapitel 1	Writing in German	**Kapitel 8**	Expressing and supporting opinions
Kapitel 2	Brainstorming	**Kapitel 9**	Using linking words
Kapitel 3	Using idea maps	**Kapitel 10**	Using note cards
Kapitel 4	Adding details	**Kapitel 11**	Writing strong introductions and conclusions
Kapitel 5	Using a dictionary		
Kapitel 6	Reporting on an interview	**Kapitel 12**	Considering audience and purpose
Kapitel 7	Making an outline		

ACKNOWLEDGMENTS

On behalf of its authors and editors, Vista Higher Learning expresses its sincere appreciation to the instructors nationwide who reviewed materials from **SAG MAL**. Their input and suggestions were vitally helpful in forming and shaping the Second Edition in its final, published form.

We also extend a special thank you to the contributing writers of **SAG MAL**, Second Edition, whose hard work was central to the publication.

REVIEWERS

Tim Altanero
Austin Community College, TX

Jennifer Aykens
Northern Virginia Community College, VA

Kim Bowen
Spring Arbor University, MI

Annette Budzinski-Luftig
Northeastern State University, OK

Lisa Coffield
Idaho State University, ID

Sandra Dillon
Idaho State University, ID

Elizabeth Kay Dyer
Quincy University, IL

Christine Eaton
University of South Alabama, AL

Sonja Fritzsche
Illinois Wesleyan University, IL

Stephen Grollman
Concordia College, MN

Rachel J. Halverson
Washington State University, WA

Eleanor ter Horst
University of South Alabama, AL

Connie Hubbard
Black Hills State University, SD

Nan Hussey
Bethel College, IN

Kristopher Imbrigotta
University of Puget Sound, WA

Jennifer Kelley
University of Cincinnati, OH

Thomas Kiddie
West Virginia State University, WV

Randall Kloko
University of Central Florida, FL

REVIEWERS

Irene Lee
SUNY Plattsburgh, NY

Christiane Pyle
Southern Oregon University, OR

Erich Lichtscheidl
Montgomery County Community College, PA

Eckhard Rolz
South Dakota State University, SD

Connie Manwaring
Utah Valley University, UT

Ulrike Schellhammer
University of Dayton, OH

Richard March
Northern Virginia Community College, VA

Gabriele Steiner
Modesto Jr College, CA

Laura McLary
University of Portland, OR

Susanne Taylor
Hanover College, IN

Helen Morris-Keitel
Bucknell Univerisity, PA

Pamela Thuswaldner
Gordon College, MA

David E. Nagle
Towson University, MD

Matthias Vogel
University of Oregon, OR

Marion Pasricha
Daytona State College, FL

2nd EDITION

SAG MAL

AN INTRODUCTION TO
GERMAN LANGUAGE AND CULTURE

Hallo! Wie geht's?

Suggestion Ask students what the people in the photo are doing and what they might be saying to each other. Ask if students know any German greetings.

Communicative Goals

You will learn how to:

- greet people and say good-bye
- make introductions
- use polite expressions

Active vocabulary Point out that all expressions used in the illustration are glossed in the **Wortschatz** on p.46. Tell students that they are responsible for learning all terms listed in the **Wortschatz**, as well as vocabulary introduced on the **Strukturen** pages. This is the content they will be expected to know for tests and quizzes.

Wortschatz

Begrüßung und Abschied	hellos and good-byes
Guten Morgen.	Good morning.
Guten Abend.	Good evening.
Gute Nacht.	Good night.
Bis dann.	See you later.
Bis gleich.	See you soon.
Bis morgen.	See you tomorrow.
Auf Wiedersehen.	Good-bye.
Schönen Tag noch!	Have a nice day!
Prima.	Great.
Es geht.	So-so.
(Nicht) schlecht.	(Not) bad.
Mir geht's nicht (so) gut.	I'm not (so) well.
Höflichkeiten	polite expressions
Gern geschehen.	My pleasure.
Entschuldigung.	Excuse me.
Entschuldigen Sie.	Excuse me. (form.)
Es tut mir leid.	I'm sorry.
ja	yes
nein	no
sich vorstellen	introducing oneself
Wie heißen Sie?	What is your name? (form.)
Schön dich/Sie kennen zu lernen.	Nice to meet you. (inf./form.)
Personen	people
die Frau	woman
der Freund / die Freundin	friend (m./f.)
der Junge	boy
das Mädchen	girl
der Mann	man
Herr	Mr.
Frau	Mrs.; Ms.
wo?	where?
hier	here
da/dort	there

Suggestion Point out that **Morgen** with a capital *M* means *morning*, as in **Guten Morgen**, while **morgen** with a lowercase *m* means *tomorrow*, as in **bis morgen**.

Suggestion Point out that the informal question **Wie heißt du?** is used in the dialogue between Markus and Anna on p.3.

Suggestion Point out that **Frau** is used to address a woman regardless of her marital status.

Suggestion Explain that German speakers often end a phone conversation with **Auf Wiederhören** (*Until we hear each other again*) instead of **Auf Wiedersehen** (*Until we see each other again*).

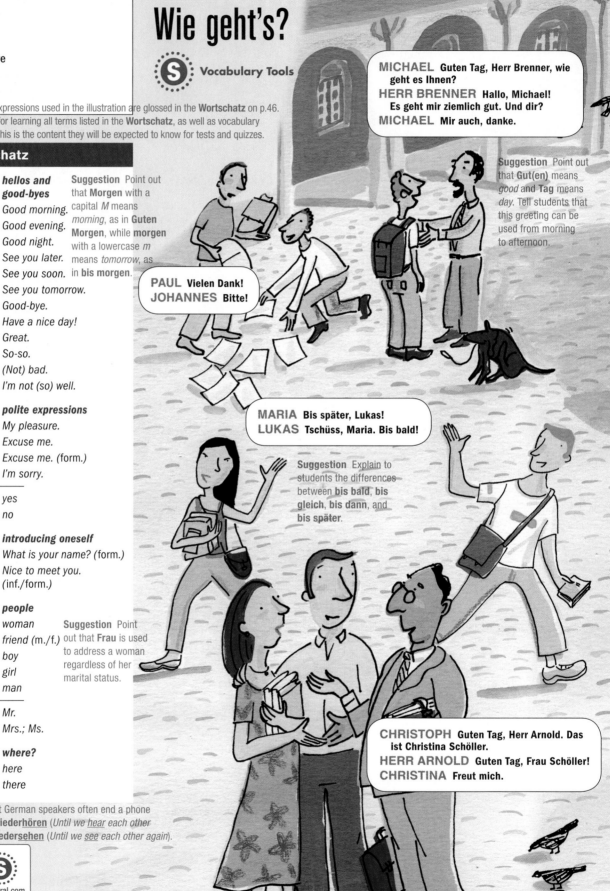

Wie geht's?

Vocabulary Tools

MICHAEL Guten Tag, Herr Brenner, wie geht es Ihnen?
HERR BRENNER Hallo, Michael! Es geht mir ziemlich gut. Und dir?
MICHAEL Mir auch, danke.

PAUL Vielen Dank!
JOHANNES Bitte!

MARIA Bis später, Lukas!
LUKAS Tschüss, Maria. Bis bald!

CHRISTOPH Guten Tag, Herr Arnold. Das ist Christina Schöller.
HERR ARNOLD Guten Tag, Frau Schöller!
CHRISTINA Freut mich.

Suggestion Point out that **Gut(en)** means *good* and **Tag** means *day*. Tell students that this greeting can be used from morning to afternoon.

Suggestion Explain to students the differences between **bis bald**, **bis gleich**, **bis dann**, and **bis später**.

ACHTUNG

There are formal and informal ways of saying *you* in German. Use **du** and its plural, **ihr**, in informal address; use **Sie** in formal situations.

MARKUS **Guten Tag, ich heiße Markus. Und du? Wie heißt du?**
ANNA **Ich heiße Anna.**
MARKUS **Angenehm, Anna.**

Suggestion Have students take turns greeting each other and introducing themselves using vocabulary from this section.

SOFIA **Guten Tag, Katrin!**
KATRIN **Hallo, Sofia!**
SOFIA **Wie geht's?**
KATRIN **Mir geht's gut, danke! Und wie geht es dir? Alles klar?**
SOFIA **Sehr gut, danke!**

Anwendung

1 Was passt? Put these expressions into the correct categories.

Bitte!	die Frau	der Mann
Danke.	der Freund	Tschüss!
Entschuldigung.	Guten Tag.	Wie geht's?

1 Suggestion Ask students to suggest additional items from this section that could be listed in each category.

Polite expressions	People	Hellos and good-byes
Danke.	die Frau	Wie geht's?
Entschuldigung.	der Mann	Guten Tag.
Bitte!	der Freund	Tschüss!

2 Was fehlt? Complete each conversation with the appropriate word.

1. —_____Vielen_____ Dank!
   —_____Gern_____ geschehen!
2. —Guten Morgen. Ich _____heiße_____ Daniel.
   —Guten _____Morgen_____, Daniel.
3. —Hallo, Lina! _____Wie_____ geht's?
   —_____Ziemlich/Sehr_____ gut.
4. —Auf _____Wiedersehen_____, Frau Stein. Schönen Tag noch!
   —_____Danke/Vielen Dank_____.
5. —Hallo, David. Das _____ist_____ Lara.
   —Hallo, Lara. Schön, dich _____kennen_____ zu lernen.
6. —Guten Abend, Herr Klein. Wie geht es _____Ihnen_____?
   —Hallo, Tom. Es geht _____mir_____ gut, danke. Und dir?

2 Expansion Have students write two more lines of dialogue for each conversation. Remind them to pay careful attention to the use of **du** and **Sie**.

3 Kurze Gespräche 🎧 Listen to the conversations and decide whether each conversation is **höflich** (*formal*) or **vertraulich** (*informal*).

	höflich	vertraulich
1.	☐	☑
2.	☑	☐
3.	☐	☑
4.	☐	☑
5.	☑	☐
6.	☐	☑

3 Suggestion Before playing the audio recording, ask students to brainstorm ways of indicating formal and informal speech, such as the use of titles and last names versus first names.

4 Antworten Sie 🎧 Provide an appropriate response to each question or statement you hear.

1. Ich heiße [name].
2. Gut, danke.
3. Freut mich.
4. Gern geschehen.
5. Tschüss.
6. Danke.

4 Suggestion Have students listen to the recording and respond out loud to each prompt. Then, have them listen again and write down their answers.

🖱 Practice more at **vhlcentral.com**.

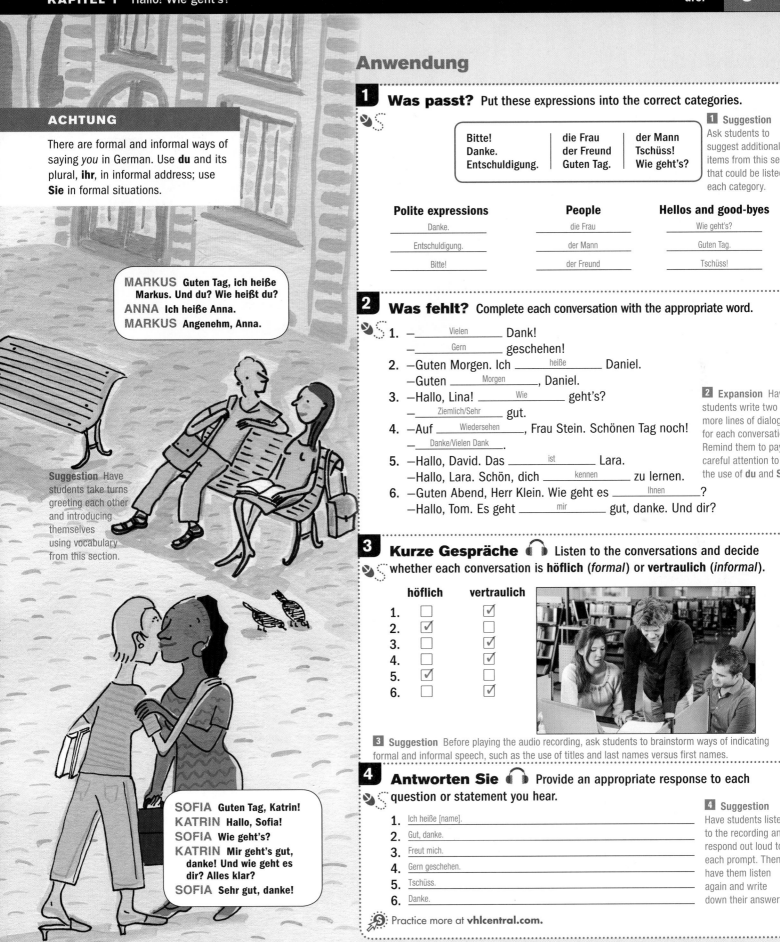

Kommunikation

5 Minidialoge
With a partner, select the response that best completes each conversation, then role-play the mini-dialogues.

5 Suggestion Before playing the audio recording, ask students to brainstorm ways of indicating formal and informal speech, such as the use of titles and last names versus first names.

1. —Guten Tag, Frau Meier!
   a.—Hallo, Frau Schneider!   **b.** —Nicht schlecht.
2. —Danke, Sabine.
   a.—Bitte.   **b.** —Bis bald!
3. —Auf Wiedersehen!
   a. —Prima.   **b.**—Tschüss!
4. —Wie heißen Sie?
   a.—Ich heiße Paul.   **b.** —Vielen Dank.
5. —Wie geht es Ihnen, Herr Huber?
   a. —Bis dann.   **b.**—Danke, gut.
6. —Ich heiße Anka.
   a.—Freut mich.   **b.** —Entschuldigung.
7. —Gute Nacht, Lara. Bis morgen.
   a.—Ja, bis dann.   **b.** —Freut mich.
8. —Guten Tag, Herr Melchior. Das ist mein Freund.
   a. —Gern geschehen.   **b.**—Angenehm.

6 Begrüßungen
In small groups, look at the illustrations, then act out a short dialogue in which the people greet each other, ask each other's names, and ask each other how they are. Pay attention to the use of **du** and **Sie**. Answers will vary.

1. Professor Fink

2. Frau Sperber

3. Anja

4. Franz

6 Suggestion Have students act out their conversations in front of the class.

7 Diskutieren und kombinieren
Your instructor will give you and a partner worksheets with descriptions of five people. Use the information from your worksheet to introduce yourself and talk about how you are. Role-play each of the five people on your worksheet. Answers will vary.

BEISPIEL

S1: Hallo, ich heiße Martin. Und du?
S2: Hallo, ich heiße Sandra. Wie geht's?
S1: Ziemlich gut. Und dir?

8 Kennen lernen
In groups of three, introduce yourself and ask your partners how they are. Then introduce your partners to the members of another group. Answers will vary.

BEISPIEL

S1: Hallo, ich heiße Sina. Und wie heißt du?
S2: Ich heiße Katja. Hallo, Sina.
S1: Und wie geht's dir?
S2: Prima, danke. Und wie geht's dir?
S1: Ziemlich gut. Katja, das hier ist Thomas.
S3: Hallo, Katja. Schön dich kennen zu lernen.

Aussprache und Rechtschreibung Audio

 ## The German alphabet

The German alphabet is made up of the same 26 letters as the English alphabet. Although the alphabet is the same, many of the letters (**Buchstaben**) are pronounced differently.

Suggestion Pronounce the words **Buchstabe** and **Beispiel** for students and ask them what they think these words mean.

Buchstabe		Beispiel	Buchstabe		Beispiel	Buchstabe		Beispiel
a	(ah)	**A**bend	i	(ih)	**I**dee	r	(err)	**R**egen
b	(beh)	**B**utter	j	(yot)	**j**a	s	(ess)	**s**ingen
c	(tseh)	**C**elsius, **C**afé	k	(kah)	**K**atze	t	(teh)	**t**anzen
			l	(ell)	**l**esen	u	(ooh)	**U**niversität
d	(deh)	**d**anke	m	(emm)	**M**utter	v	(fau)	**V**ogel, **V**ase
e	(eh)	**E**lefant	n	(enn)	**N**ase	w	(veh)	**W**asser
f	(eff)	**f**inden	o	(oh)	**O**per	x	(iks)	**X**ylophon
g	(geh)	**g**ut	p	(peh)	**P**apier	y	(üpsilon)	**Y**acht, **T**yp
h	(hah)	**h**allo	q	(koo)	**Q**uatsch	z	(tset)	**Z**elt

Suggestion Tell students that, except in words or names of foreign origin, the letter **c** is only used in the letter combinations **ch** and **sch**.

Suggestion Tell students that the letter **v** is pronounced like an English *v* in words of foreign origin. Ex.: **Vanille, Viktor, Vatikan, Venedig**.

The symbol **ß** (**Eszett** or **scharfes s**) is used instead of a double **s** in certain words. **Eszett** is never used at the beginning of a word. It is capitalized as **SS**.

ß (Eszett, scharfes S)   **Stra**ß**e** (*street*)

Suggestion Tell students that ß is not used at all in Switzerland. In Swiss German, **Straße** is written as **Strasse**.

An **Umlaut** (¨) can be added to the vowels **a**, **o**, and **u**, changing their pronunciation.

a	**Apfel**	ä	(a-Umlaut)	**Äpfel**
o	**Ofen**	ö	(o-Umlaut)	**Öfen**
u	**Mutter**	ü	(u-Umlaut)	**Mütter**

Suggestion Explain that the words with umlauts in these examples are the plural forms of the words to their left. Also point out that when used as a vowel, the letter **y** is pronounced like **ü**. Ex.: **Typ, typisch**.

In German, all nouns are capitalized, no matter where they appear in a sentence. When spelling aloud, say **großes a** for *capital a*, or **kleines a** for *lowercase a*. To ask how a word is spelled, say: **Wie schreibt man das?** (lit. *How does one write this?*)

 1 **Aussprechen** Practice saying the German alphabet and sample words aloud.

 2 **Buchstabieren** Spell these words aloud in German.

1. hallo
2. Morgen
3. studieren
4. Explosion
5. typisch
6. Universität
7. Bäcker
8. Straße
9. Juwelen
10. Frühling
11. tanzen
12. Querflöte

2 **Expansion** Ask students to identify cognates. Tell students the meanings of any unfamiliar words.

 3 **Sprichwörter** Practice reading these sayings aloud.

Wer A sagt, muss auch B sagen.[1]

Übung macht den Meister.[2]

[1] You have to finish what you've started. (lit. *Whoever says A must also say B.*)
[2] Practice makes perfect.

Ressourcen

SAM: LM: p. 2   vhlcentral.com

Willkommen in Berlin! Ⓢ Video

Meline und George kommen nach Berlin. Hier treffen sie Sabite und Hans.
Ist es eine freundliche Begrüßung (*friendly welcome*)?

Vorbereitung Before showing the video, have students preview the images and text on the page and guess what this episode will be about. Encourage them to focus on overall comprehension of the video, and not to worry if they don't understand every word.

MELINE (*am Telefon*) Lukas... ah, Kreuzberg, okay. Lukas...

SABITE Hallo?
GEORGE Hallo. Ich bin George. Wie heißt du?
SABITE Ich heiße Sabite. Nett dich kennen zu lernen.
GEORGE Nett dich kennen zu lernen, Sabite.

SABITE Alles in Ordnung?
GEORGE Hier sind die Schlüssel. Danke, vielen Dank.
SABITE Gern geschehen. Keine Ursache. Bis später.

GEORGE *Talk to you later.* Auf Wiederhören.

HANS Entschuldigung. Was für ein Chaos! Hier ist die Bürste... und der Lippenstift. Und hier ist das Handy.
MELINE (*am Telefon*) Tschüss, Lukas.

HANS Ich heiße Hans. Schönen Tag!

1 **Richtig oder falsch?** Choose whether each statement is **richtig** (*true*) or **falsch** (*false*).

1. Sabite hilft (*helps*) Hans. Falsch.
2. Meline ist am Flughafen (*airport*). Falsch.
3. George hat (*has*) die Schlüssel. Richtig.
4. Meline telefoniert mit (*calls*) Lukas. Richtig.
5. George trifft (*meets*) Sabite. Richtig.

6. Hans geht es ganz okay. Falsch.
7. Meline geht nach (*is going to*) Kreuzberg. Richtig.
8. Meline hat eine Bürste, einen Lippenstift und ein Handy. Richtig.
9. Sabite geht es gut. Richtig.
10. Hans sagt: „Willkommen in München." Falsch.

PERSONEN

George

Hans

Meline

Sabite

MELINE Ich bin's, Meline.
SABITE Meline, hallo. Nett dich kennen zu lernen.
MELINE Freut mich. Wie geht es dir?
SABITE Mir geht es gut.

SABITE Oh, das ist George. Hallo, George. Das ist Meline. Meline, George.
GEORGE Hallo.
MELINE Nett dich kennen zu lernen.
GEORGE Freut mich.

HANS George?
GEORGE Ja!
HANS Hallo! Ich bin Hans. Willkommen in Deutschland. Nett dich kennen zu lernen. Wie geht's?
GEORGE Ganz okay.

GEORGE Das ist Sabite.
SABITE Hallo.
HANS Hi.

Nützliche Ausdrücke

- **Wie heißt du?**
  What's your name?
- **Nett dich kennen zu lernen.**
  Nice to meet you.
- **Ist jemand da?**
  Anyone there?
- **Keine Ursache.**
  Don't mention it.
- **Auf Wiederhören.**
  Talk to you later.
- **Was für ein Chaos!**
  What a mess!
- **der Lippenstift**
  lipstick
- **das Handy**
  cell phone
- **Freut mich.**
  It's a pleasure.
- **Willkommen in Deutschland.**
  Welcome to Germany.

  1A.1
- **Hier ist die Bürste.**
  Here's the brush.

  1A.2
- **Hier sind die Schlüssel.**
  Here are the keys.

  1A.3
- **Ich bin George.**
  I'm George.

Suggestion Tell students that they will learn more about the grammar structures previewed in each episode in the lesson's **Strukturen** section.

2 **Zum Besprechen** Imagine that you and your partner are exchange students meeting for the first time. Greet each other, give your names, and be sure to include an appropriate goodbye. Be prepared to present your conversation to the class. Answers will vary.

2 **Suggestion** This activity can also be done with groups of three or more.

3 **Vertiefung** Germany's tallest structure is the television tower (**Fernsehturm**) in Berlin. Use the Internet to find its nicknames in German. Answers include: Telespargel, St. Walter

Ressourcen

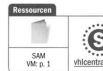

SAM
VM: p. 1

vhlcentral.com

Hallo, Deutschland!  Reading

SAYING "HELLO" CAN BE A COMPLEX social interaction. Should you shake hands? Kiss cheeks? Keep your distance? The answers depend on where you are, who you are, and who you're talking to.

In general, Germans shake hands more than Americans do, and eye contact is an important feature of this gesture. If you've just been introduced to someone, shake hands, look them in the eye, and say **Freut mich**. In a business setting, a handshake is more or less obligatory, but friends may or may not shake hands when greeting. As in North America, friends in Germany, Austria, and Switzerland can often be seen greeting each other with a hug or a kiss on the cheek.

Greetings vary depending on time of day, level of formality, and region. In formal situations, you can say **Guten Morgen** in the morning, **Guten Tag** from morning to late afternoon, and **Guten Abend** in the evening. In Bavaria or Austria, you are likely to hear **Grüß Gott°** at any time of day. **Hallo**, **Tag**, and **Grüß dich°** are all common informal greetings. In Bavaria, use **Servus°** to say hello or goodbye to friends.

Deciding between informal and polite forms of address requires some judgment. In general, use the familiar forms **du** and **ihr** with children, teenagers, family members, and fellow

students. Use the polite form **Sie** with anyone else until they invite you to call them **du**. Always use **Sie** with people with whom you are not on a first-name basis. Address men as **Herr** and women as **Frau**, regardless of their marital status.

Grüß Gott *Hello. (lit. Greet God)* **Grüß dich** *Hello. (lit. Greet you (inf.))* **Servus** *Hello; Good-bye (inf.)*

1 **Richtig oder falsch?** Indicate whether each statement is **richtig** (*true*) or **falsch** (*false*). Correct any false statements.

1. **Hallo** is an appropriate greeting to use with friends. Richtig.

2. When meeting someone new, shake hands and say **Freut mich**. Richtig.

3. You should always use **Sie** with other students.
   Falsch. You should use **du** with other students.

4. You should shake hands to greet business partners. Richtig.

5. German friends often greet each other with a hug. Richtig.

6. **Guten Abend** is an appropriate way to greet your boss in the morning.
   Falsch. **Guten Morgen** is an appropriate greeting in the morning.

7. You are more likely to hear **Grüß Gott** in Austria than in Berlin. Richtig.

8. **Du** is used to address adults you don't know.
   Falsch. **Du** is used with friends and family, not with strangers.

9. It is appropriate to address children with **du**. Richtig.

10. When you are not sure whether to use **Sie** or **du**, you should follow the lead of the other person. Richtig.

 Practice more at **vhlcentral.com**.

Deutsch im Alltag Have students take turns practicing the greetings from the list. Remind them that these items are not active vocabulary.

DEUTSCH IM ALLTAG

Wie geht's?

Geht's dir gut?	*Are you all right? (inf.)*
Und dir?	*And you? (inf.)*
Geht es Ihnen gut?	*Are you all right? (form.)*
Und Ihnen?	*And you? (form.)*
So weit, so gut.	*So far, so good.*
Spitze!	*Great!*
Schön dich zu sehen.	*Nice to see you. (inf.)*
Schön Sie zu sehen.	*Nice to see you. (form.)*
Herzlich willkommen.	*Welcome.*
Was geht?	*What's up?*

DIE DEUTSCHSPRACHIGE WELT

Auf Wiedersehen, Goodbye

One characteristic feature of the German language is its wealth of regional differences. Many dialects have their own greetings, from **Moin Moin** along the North Sea Coast to Switzerland's **Grüezi mitenand**. But how do German speakers say good-bye?

- **Auf Wiedersehen** and **tschüss** are the most standard good-byes.
- The formal Swiss counterpart is **Uf Widerluege.**
- The informal **Mach's gut** is similar in meaning to *Take care.*
- In Baden-Württemberg and the Saarland, **Ade** is common.
- In Austria, **Pfiati** is often used among friends.

Die deutschsprachige Welt Have students locate the countries and regions mentioned here in the map on p. 40 of their textbooks.

PORTRÄT

Das Brandenburger Tor°

On December 22, 1989, thousands cheered as West German Chancellor Helmut Kohl walked through the Brandenburg Gate to shake hands with East German Prime Minister Hans Modrow. It was the first time since the construction of the **Berliner Mauer°** in 1961 that East and West Germans had been permitted to pass through the gate.

Built in 1791, the **Brandenburger Tor** was one of fourteen toll gates that encircled the city. Over the next two centuries, the **Tor** withstood an invasion by Napoleon's soldiers, falling bombs in World War II, and the Cold War partition of East and West Germany. Today, the **Tor** is one of Berlin's most popular attractions, a symbol of German unity, and a monument to Berlin's tumultuous past.

Suggestion Tell students the origin and meaning of some regional greetings: **Moin Moin** derives from a Dutch word meaning *good* or *beautiful*. **Grüezi mitenand** means *Hello everyone* and is used to greet multiple people. **Pfiati** is derived from **Pfüat di**, meaning *(May God) protect you*. **Tschüss** is derived from *ciao*, and **Ade** from *adieu*.

Tor *Gate* **Berliner Mauer** *Berlin Wall*

⚡ IM INTERNET

Fashionably late isn't always fashionable. How do German and American manners differ when it comes to punctuality, greetings, and formality?

Find out more at **vhlcentral.com**.

Expansion Show students pictures of various people (an elderly person, a child, a teacher, etc.) and ask how they would greet each person.

2 **Was haben Sie gelernt?** Answer the questions. Answers may vary.

1. How would you say good-bye to a friend or fellow student in a German-speaking country? List three options.
   Tschüss, Ade, Pfiati, Mach's gut.
2. What did Germans celebrate at the Brandenburg Gate in 1989?
   They celebrated the opening of the border crossing and the fall of the Berlin Wall.
3. Name some historical events that occurred near the Brandenburg Gate.
   The invasion of Berlin by Napoleon, WWII, the building of the Wall, the fall of the Wall.
4. What does the Brandenburg Gate now symbolize?
   It symbolizes German unity.

3 **Sie sind dran** In pairs, practice meeting and greeting people in these situations. Answers will vary.

1. It's 10 a.m. and you run into your German professor at the grocery store. What do you say?
2. Now you're purchasing your groceries. How do you say "hello" and "good-bye" to the cashier?
3. Just as you're leaving the store, you run into an old friend. Say "hi" and ask how your friend is doing.

Ressourcen

vhlcentral.com

Strukturen

1A.1

Gender, articles, and nouns  Presentation

Startblock Like English nouns, German nouns can be either singular or plural and may be preceded by a definite or indefinite article. Unlike English nouns, all German nouns have a gender. German nouns are always capitalized, regardless of where they appear in a sentence.

Was für **ein Chaos**!

Hier ist **die Bürste**. Hier ist **das Handy**.

Gender

- All German nouns have a gender: masculine, feminine, or neuter. While most nouns referring to males are masculine and most nouns referring to females are feminine, the genders of nouns representing objects and ideas need to be memorized.

MASCULINE	FEMININE	NEUTER
der **Mann**	die **Frau**	das **Buch**
*the **man***	*the **woman***	*the **book***
der **Junge**	die **Blume**	das **Mädchen**
*the **boy***	*the **flower***	*the **girl***

- Nouns ending with -**in** that refer to people are always feminine.

die Freund**in**	die Student**in**	die Professor**in**
*the (**female**) friend*	*the (**female**) student*	*the (**female**) professor*

- Other feminine noun endings include -**ei**, -**heit**, -**schaft**, -**ung**, and -**tät**.

die **Bäckerei**	die **Freundschaft**	die **Universität**
*the **bakery***	*the **friendship***	*the **university***

Definite and indefinite articles

- The definite article, equivalent to *the* in English, precedes a noun and indicates its gender. The masculine article is **der**, the feminine article is **die**, and the neuter article is **das**.

MASCULINE	FEMININE	NEUTER
der **Tisch**	die **Tür**	das **Fenster**
the table	*the door*	*the window*

- The definite article **die** is used with all plural nouns, regardless of gender.

	SINGULAR	PLURAL	
MASCULINE	**der** Tisch	**die** Tische	*the tables*
FEMININE	**die** Tür	**die** Türen	*the doors*
NEUTER	**das** Fenster	**die** Fenster	*the windows*

- The indefinite article **ein(e)** corresponds to *a* or *an* in English. It precedes the noun and matches its gender. Note that both masculine and neuter nouns take the form **ein**, while feminine nouns take **eine**.

MASCULINE	FEMININE	NEUTER
ein Tisch	**eine** Tür	**ein** Fenster
a table	*a door*	*a window*
ein Mann	**eine** Frau	**ein** Mädchen
a man	*a woman*	*a girl*

- There is no plural form of the indefinite article.

Er ist **ein Mann**.   Sie sind **Männer**.
*He is **a man**.*   *They are **men**.*

Compound nouns

- Compound words are very common in German. As in English, two or more simple nouns can be combined to form a compound noun.

die Nacht   +   das Hemd   =   **das Nachthemd**
night   *shirt*   *nightshirt*

Hier ist **der Lippenstift**.

- The gender and number of a compound noun is determined by the last noun in the compound.

das Haus   +   **die** Aufgabe   =   **die Hausaufgabe**
house   *assignment*   *homework*

die Nacht   +   **der** Tisch   =   **der Nachttisch**
night   *table*   *night table*

Jetzt sind Sie dran! Tell students that all the nouns listed are singular.

Expansion Give students additional examples of nouns that can combine to form compounds. Have them figure out the appropriate articles for the compound forms. Ex.: **das Land** (*the country*) **+ die Karte** (*the map*) **= die Landkarte** (*the (country) map*); **der Arm** (*the arm*) **+ das Band** (*the strap*) **+ die Uhr** (*the clock*) **= die Armbanduhr** (*the watch*).

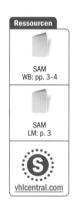

Ressourcen

SAM
WB: pp. 3–4

SAM
LM: p. 3

Ⓢ
vhlcentral.com

Jetzt sind Sie dran!   Indicate the gender of each noun: **Maskulinum, Femininum,** or **Neutrum.**

	Maskulinum	Femininum	Neutrum
1. der Mann	☑	☐	☐
2. die Freundin	☐	☑	☐
3. der Junge	☑	☐	☐
4. das Hemd	☐	☐	☑
5. die Aufgabe	☐	☑	☐
6. ein Freund	☑	☐	☐

	Maskulinum	Femininum	Neutrum
7. eine Frau	☐	☑	☐
8. ein Mädchen	☐	☐	☑
9. ein Tisch	☑	☐	☐
10. eine Nacht	☐	☑	☐
11. die Universität	☐	☑	☐
12. ein Buch	☐	☐	☑

Anwendung

1 **Was fehlt?** Write the appropriate article.

der, die, das	ein, eine
1. ___das___ Fenster	5. ___eine___ Frau
2. ___der___ Tisch	6. ___eine___ Tür
3. ___der___ Student	7. ___ein___ Mann
4. ___die___ Freundschaft	8. ___ein___ Mädchen

2 **Ergänzen Sie** Write each noun in the appropriate column. Include the definite and indefinite article.

> Bäckerei | Haus
> Buch | Hemd
> Freund | Junge
> Freundin | Studentin

Maskulinum	Femininum	Neutrum
der Mann; ein Mann	die Bäckerei; eine Bäckerei	das Buch; ein Buch
der Freund; ein Freund	die Freundin; eine Freundin	das Haus; ein Haus
der Junge; ein Junge	die Studentin; eine Studentin	das Hemd; ein Hemd

3 **Sätze** Complete each sentence with the appropriate definite or indefinite article.

1. ___Der___ Junge heißt Paul.
2. Wie heißt ___die___ Professorin?
3. Jasmin ist ___ein___ Mädchen.
4. ___Das___ Buch ist prima!
5. ___Die___ Türen sind hier.
6. Lara ist ___eine___ gute Studentin.

4 **Bilden Sie Wörter** Write the compound word with the appropriate definite article.

> ▶ **BEISPIEL**
> das Haus + die Aufgabe =
> *die Hausaufgabe*

1. die Kinder + der Garten
= ___der Kindergarten___

2. der Schlaf (*sleep*) +
das Zimmer (*room*) =
das Schlafzimmer

3. das Telefon +
die Nummer =
die Telefonnummer

4. der Computer +
das Spiel (*game*) =
das Computerspiel

 Practice more at **vhlcentral.com.**

Kommunikation

5 **Was ist das?** In pairs, take turns identifying each person or object. Provide both the definite and indefinite articles.

▶ **BEISPIEL**
S1: *der Junge*
S2: *ein Junge*

1. das Buch, ein Buch

2. die Frau, eine Frau

3. der Mann, ein Mann

4. die Tür, eine Tür

5. das Fenster, ein Fenster

6. das Mädchen, ein Mädchen

6 **Was passt zusammen?** In pairs, take turns creating compound nouns using words from the list. Write down each compound noun with the appropriate article. Sample answers are provided.

der Schlüssel

der Ring

▶ **BEISPIEL**
S1: *der Schlüssel / der Ring*
S2: *der Schlüsselring*

der Handschuh, die Hauskatze, der Nachtbus, der Eisbär

die Hand

der Schuh

die Nacht

der Bus

das Haus

die Katze

das Eis

der Bär

6 Suggestion Tell students the compounds they come up with don't have to be real words in German. Have them read out loud the compound words they created. Then, share with them the actual compounds (provided as sample answers) that can be made from combining the words listed, and have students guess their meanings.

7 **Was zeichne ich?** In small groups, take turns drawing pictures of nouns you've learned so far, for your partners to guess. The person who guesses correctly is the next to draw. Don't forget the article! Answers will vary.

8 **Gedächtnisspiel** Play a memory game. The first player says a noun with the appropriate definite or indefinite article, and the next player repeats the previous noun and says his or her own. Go around the class until someone forgets an item or uses the wrong article. That player starts the next round.

1A.2 **Plurals** **Presentation**

Startblock Plurals in German follow several patterns. These patterns can help you remember the plural form of each noun you learn.

- In German dictionaries and vocabulary lists, singular nouns are listed along with a notation that indicates how to form the plural. There are five main patterns for forming plural nouns.

ACHTUNG

The best way to be sure of a noun's plural form is to memorize it when you learn the singular form. Being familiar with the patterns of plural formation can make this process easier.

Suggestion Point out that irregular plural forms exist in English as well as German. Ask students to brainstorm examples. Ex.: *child, children; mouse, mice; woman, women; deer, deer.*

ACHTUNG

Two plurals that do not follow the standard pattern for feminine nouns are **die Mütter**, plural of **Mutter**, and **die Töchter** (*daughters*), plural of **Tochter**.

Ressourcen

SAM
WB: pp. 5–6

SAM
LM: p. 4

vhlcentral.com

notation	singular	plural
- ..	das Fenster ⟶ die Fenster die Mutter (*mother*) ⟶ die Mütter	
-e ..e	der Freund ⟶ die Freunde der Stuhl (*chair*) ⟶ die Stühle	
-er ..er	das Kind (*child*) ⟶ die Kinder der Mann ⟶ die Männer	
-n -en -nen	der Junge ⟶ die Jungen die Frau ⟶ die Frauen die Freundin ⟶ die Freundinnen	
-s	der Park ⟶ die Parks	

- Most masculine and neuter nouns form the plural by adding -**e** or -**er**. Plurals with the -**er** ending always add an **Umlaut** when the vowel in the singular form is **a**, **o**, or **u**.

  der Tag (*day*) ⟶ die Tage   das Buch ⟶ die Bücher

- If the singular form of a noun ends in -**el**, -**en**, or -**er**, there is no additional plural ending, but an **Umlaut** is added to the stem vowel **a**, **o**, or **u**.

  der Apfel (*apple*) ⟶ die Äpfel   das Zimmer (*room*) ⟶ die Zimmer

- For feminine nouns ending with -**in**, add -**nen** to form the plural.

  die Freundin ⟶ die Freundinnen   die Studentin ⟶ die Studentinnen

- For most other feminine nouns, add -**n** if the singular form ends in -**e**, -**el**, or -**er**. Add -**en** if it does not. Note that feminine plurals with these endings never add an **Umlaut**.

  die Blume (*flower*) ⟶ die Blumen   die Frau ⟶ die Frauen

- The -**s** ending is added to most words borrowed from other languages and to most nouns ending with vowels other than **e**.

  das Sofa ⟶ die Sofas   das Auto ⟶ die Autos

Jetzt sind Sie dran! Write the plural form of each singular noun and vice versa.

Singular

1. das Café _____die Cafés_____
2. die Studentin _____die Studentinnen_____
3. der Stuhl _____die Stühle_____
4. die Tochter _____die Töchter_____

Plural

5. die Zimmer _____das Zimmer_____
6. die Universitäten _____die Universität_____
7. die Äpfel _____der Apfel_____
8. die Studenten _____der Student_____

Anwendung und Kommunikation

1 Schreiben Write the plural form.

1. das Buch ___die Bücher___
2. der Mann ___die Männer___
3. der Tag ___die Tage___
4. die Blume ___die Blumen___
5. die Mutter ___die Mütter___

6. das Auto ___die Autos___
7. der Junge ___die Jungen___
8. die Tür ___die Türen___
9. das Kind ___die Kinder___
10. der Park ___die Parks___

2 Plural Complete each sentence with the plural form of the appropriate word.

BEISPIEL Holiday Inn und Marriott sind ___Hotels___.

Apfel	Buch	Freundin
Auto	Computer	Hotel
Blume	Freund	Tag

1. BMW und Volkswagen sind ___Autos___.
2. Rosen und Tulpen (*tulips*) sind ___Blumen___.
3. Dell, HP und Acer sind ___Computer___.
4. Granny Smith und Macintosh sind ___Äpfel___.
5. Eine Woche (*week*) hat sieben (*seven*) ___Tage___.
6. Anna, Monika und Emma sind ___Freundinnen___.
7. *Harry Potter* und *Sag mal* sind ___Bücher___.
8. Lukas und Felix sind ___Freunde___.

2 **Suggestion** Remind students that they learned in **1A.1** that there is no plural form of the indefinite article.

3 Was ist das? In pairs, take turns identifying each object, place, or person. Give both singular and plural forms. Sample answers are provided.

▶ **BEISPIEL**
S1: *die Blume*
S2: *die Blumen*

1. das Mädchen, die Mädchen/ das Kind, die Kinder

2. der Park, die Parks

3. der Junge, die Jungen/ das Kind, die Kinder

4. das Auto, die Autos

5. das Fenster, die Fenster

6. die Tür, die Türen

7. der Stuhl, die Stühle

3 **Expansion** Write nouns from this lesson's vocabulary on the back of note cards and distribute them to students. Have each student make a drawing of their noun on the opposite side of the card. Then have them take turns identifying each other's drawings and giving the plural form of each noun.

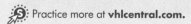 Practice more at **vhlcentral.com.**

1A.3

Subject pronouns, *sein*, and the nominative case

 **Presentation**

Lukas, **du bist**...

Ich bin George.

Subject pronouns

QUERVERWEIS

German speakers often use the third-person singular pronoun **man** where English speakers would say *one* or *you*.

You will learn more about the use of **man** in **7B.3**.

Suggestion Tell students that **ich** is capitalized only when it begins a sentence, unlike the pronoun *I* in English. Remind them that the formal **Sie** is always capitalized.

- In German, as in English, any noun can be replaced with an equivalent pronoun. A subject pronoun replaces a noun that functions as the subject of a sentence.

Maria ist nett.   **Sie** ist nett.   **Der Junge** ist groß.   **Er** ist groß.
Maria is nice.   *She is nice.*   *The boy is tall.*   *He is tall.*

subject pronouns		
	singular	**plural**
1ˢᵗ person	**ich** *I*	**wir** *we*
2ⁿᵈ person	**du** *you* (inf.) **Sie** *you* (form.)	**ihr** *you* (inf.) **Sie** *you* (form.)
3ʳᵈ person	**er** *he/it* **sie** *she/it* **es** *it*	**sie** *they*

- The gender of a noun determines the gender of the pronoun that replaces it. German uses **er** for all masculine nouns, **sie** for all feminine nouns, and **es** for all neuter nouns.

Der Tisch ist klein. ▶ **Er** ist klein.   **Das Buch** ist neu. ▶ **Es** ist neu.
The table is small.   *It's small.*   *The book is new.*   *It's new.*

Suggestion Give students additional examples using **sie** and **Sie** and have them figure out which meaning is intended, based on context.

- The pronoun **Sie/sie** can mean *you*, *she*, *it*, or *they*, depending on context. Write **Sie** with a capital **S** to mean *you* in a formal context, and **sie** with a lowercase **s** to mean *she*, *it*, or *they*.

Das ist Frau Hansen.
   Sie ist Professorin.
That's Mrs. Hansen. **She** *is a professor.*

Das sind Lara und Jonas.
   Sie sind Studenten.
That's Lara and Jonas. **They're** *students.*

Woher kommen **Sie**?
Where are **you** *from?*

The verb *sein*

- **Sein** (*To be*) is an irregular verb: its conjugation does not follow a predictable pattern.

Suggestion
Explain to students that the conjugation of a verb is the set of verb forms corresponding to the different possible subjects.

sein (*to be*)			
singular		**plural**	
ich **bin**	*I am*	wir **sind**	*we are*
du **bist**	*you are* (inf.)	ihr **seid**	*you are* (inf.)
Sie **sind**	*you are* (form.)	Sie **sind**	*you are* (form.)
er/sie/es **ist**	*he/she/it is*	sie **sind**	*they are*

Ich bin Amerikaner.   **Sie ist** Deutsche.   **Wir sind** Freunde.
I'm American.   *She's German.*   *We are friends.*

Suggestion Point out that the conjugated form of **sein** is the same for **wir**, **Sie**, and **sie** (*pl.*). Tell students that all verbs have the same conjugated form for these three subjects.

Suggestion Point out that **Amerikaner** and **Deutsche** are nouns, even though they are translated as adjectives in this context. Tell students that the feminine form of **Amerikaner** is **Amerikanerin**, and the masculine form of **Deutsche** is **Deutscher**.

The nominative case

- German has four *cases* that indicate the function of each noun in a sentence. The case of a noun determines the form of the definite or indefinite article that precedes the noun, the form of any adjectives that modify the noun, and the form of the pronoun that can replace the noun.

QUERVERWEIS

You will learn more about cases in **1B.1**, **3B.2**, **4B.1**, **4B.2**, and **8B.1**.

German cases		
Nominativ	**Der** Professor ist alt.	*The professor is old.*
Akkusativ	Ich verstehe **den** Professor.	*I understand the professor.*
Dativ	Der Assistent zeigt **dem** Professor den neuen Computer.	*The assistant is showing the professor the new computer.*
Genitiv	Das ist der Assistent **des** Professor**s**.	*This is the professor's assistant.*

Suggestions

- Tell students that dictionaries and vocabulary lists always give nouns in their nominative form.
- Tell students that the set of forms that change depending on the number, case, and gender of a word are called declensions (**die Deklination**, -en).

- The grammatical subject of a sentence is always in the nominative case (**der Nominativ**). Subject pronouns are, by definition, nominative pronouns. The nominative case is also used for nouns that follow a form of **sein**, **werden** (*to become*), or **bleiben** (*to stay, to remain*).

    Das ist **eine gute Idee**.   Wir bleiben **Freunde**.
    *That's **a good idea**.*   *We're still **friends**.*

- The definite and indefinite articles you learned in **1A.1** are the forms used with nouns in the nominative case.

nominative articles				
	masculine	**feminine**	**neuter**	**plural**
definite	der Junge	die Frau	das Mädchen	die Jungen
indefinite	ein Junge	eine Frau	ein Mädchen	– Jungen

Ressourcen

SAM
WB: pp. 7–8

SAM
LM: p. 5

S

vhlcentral.com

 Jetzt sind Sie dran!   For each noun, write the correct subject pronoun. For each pronoun, write the appropriate form of **sein**.

1. der Apfel _____ *er* _____
2. das Haus _____ *es* _____
3. die Jungen _____ *sie* _____
4. die Hausaufgabe _____ *sie* _____
5. Brigitte und ich _____ *wir* _____
6. die Studentin und du _____ *ihr* _____
7. wir _____ *sind* _____
8. ihr _____ *seid* _____
9. du _____ *bist* _____
10. Sie _____ *sind* _____
11. ich _____ *bin* _____
12. er _____ *ist* _____

Anwendung

1 Was ist richtig? Select the appropriate subject pronoun.

1. (**Ihr** / Wir) seid in Deutschland.
2. (**Er** / Ich) ist Katjas Freund.
3. (Du / **Sie**) sind nett!
4. (**Ihr** / Ich) seid Amerikaner.
5. (**Wir** / Ich) sind Deutsche.
6. (**Ich** / Du) bin Studentin.
7. (Es / **Du**) bist prima!
8. (Ihr / **Sie**) ist intelligent.

2 Expansion Have students transform the subjects of items 1, 4, 6, and 8 into subject pronouns.

2 Was fehlt? Write the correct form of sein.

1. Herr und Frau Schlüter ___sind___ dort.
2. Lena und ich ___sind___ hier.
3. Ich ___bin___ Anna.
4. Du ___bist___ Student.
5. Herr Professor, Sie ___sind___ Experte.
6. Das Buch ___ist___ sehr interessant.
7. Ihr ___seid___ Kinder.
8. Das Fenster und die Tür ___sind___ offen (open).

3 Sätze ergänzen Write the pronoun and the appropriate form of sein.

▶ **BEISPIEL**

___Sie sind___ im (at the) Restaurant.

1. ___Sie sind___ Freundinnen.

2. ___Er ist___ Deutschprofessor.

3. Mia, Tim und ich, ___wir sind___ Studenten.

4. Sara, ___du bist___ allein (alone).

5. ___Sie ist___ müde (tired).

6. Jan und du, ___ihr seid___ Freunde.

4 Bilden Sie Sätze Write complete sentences using sein. Then, replace the subjects with subject pronouns, where possible.

BEISPIEL Samuel / Professor
Samuel ist Professor. Er ist Professor.

1. Lukas und ich / Studenten
   Lukas und ich sind Studenten. Wir sind Studenten.
2. du / nett
   Du bist nett.
3. es / ein gutes (good) Buch
   Es ist ein gutes Buch.
4. Michael und du / in Deutschland
   Michael und du seid in Deutschland. Ihr seid in Deutschland.
5. Danielle und Johanna / Deutsche
   Danielle und Donna sind Deutsche. Sie sind Deutsche.
6. ich / Amerikaner
   Ich bin Amerikaner.
7. Sie / unfair, Frau Henke
   Sie sind unfair, Frau Henke.
8. das Haus / gigantisch
   Das Haus ist gigantisch. Es ist gigantisch.

 Practice more at **vhlcentral.com**.

Kommunikation

5 **Was sehen Sie?** These pictures have been mislabeled. In pairs, take turns reading and correcting the labels. Answers will vary.

▶ **BEISPIEL** Kinder

S1: *Das sind Kinder.*
S2: *Nein, das sind Studentinnen.*

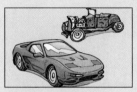

1. Stühle

2. ein Tisch

3. ein Professor

4. Autos

5. Männer

6. ein Fenster

6 **Beschreibungen** Tell your partner that you are like each of the people listed. Answers will vary.

BEISPIEL Paul / in Amerika (du)
　　　　　　Jan und Sara / tolerant (ihr)

S1: *Paul ist in Amerika, und du?*
S2: *Ich bin auch in Amerika. Jan und Sara sind tolerant, und ihr?*
S1: *Wir sind auch tolerant.*

1. die Professorin / intelligent (du)
2. Klara und Tim / Freunde (ihr)

3. Felix / romantisch (du)
4. Max und Lisa / Studenten (ihr)

6 **Suggestion** Model pronunciation of the cognates used in this activity.

7 **Freut mich!** In groups of three, role-play these situations. Each person should say something about him-/herself using a form of **sein**.

BEISPIEL

S1: *Hallo, ich bin Max.*
S2: *Hallo, Max. Schön dich kennen zu lernen.*
　　　Ich bin Sara und das ist Julia. Wir sind Studentinnen.

7 **Expansion** Have group members introduce themselves to the rest of the class.

1. You are meeting your classmates for the first time. Introduce yourself and ask how each person is doing.

2. You and your friend are invited to a birthday party. Exchange greetings and introduce yourselves to other guests.

Wiederholung

NATIONAL STANDARDS communication

4 Expansions

- Repeat this activity using the cards students created for **Memory-Spiel**.
- Divide the class into teams and play Pictionary using the lesson vocabulary.

1 Memory-Spiel
With a partner, create a set of cards to play Memory, featuring ten nouns you learned in this lesson. For each noun you draw, create a matching card showing the word with the definite article. Shuffle the cards and place them face down. Take turns matching pictures and words. Answers will vary.

2 Freut mich!
In pairs, practice introducing yourselves in formal and informal situations. Answers will vary.

3 Schatzsuche
With a partner, find one word or phrase from this lesson that corresponds to each description. Compete against other pairs to see which team can complete their list first. Remember: all words must be spelled correctly, nouns must be preceded by the appropriate definite article, and no word or phrase can be used more than once. Answers will vary.

1. a feminine plural noun
2. a formal greeting
3. an informal way to say goodbye
4. a neuter noun that refers to a person
5. a response to the question "**Wie geht's**?"
6. a plural noun ending in -**s**
7. a sentence using a subject pronoun with **sein**
8. a noun that has identical singular and plural forms

4 Was ist das?
In pairs, take turns identifying the objects and people.

▶ **BEISPIEL**
S1: Was ist das?
S2: Das ist ein Auto.

1. Das ist ein Buch.

2. Das ist eine Blume./Das sind Blumen.

3. Das ist ein Fenster.

4. Das ist ein Sofa.

5. Das ist ein Park.

6. Das sind Kinder.

5 Diskutieren und kombinieren
Your instructor will give you and a partner two worksheets with different images and labels. Work together to form the compound words.

6 Arbeitsblatt
Your instructor will give you a worksheet (**das Arbeitsblatt**). Ask your classmates to say their names and spell them for you. Don't forget to greet them, ask how they are, and say thank you! Answers will vary.

BEISPIEL
S1: Guten Morgen!
S2: Hallo!
S1: Wie geht's?
S2: Es geht mir gut.
S1: Wie heißt du?
S2: Ich heiße Nadia.
S1: Wie schreibt man das?
S2: N-A-D-I-A.
S1: Wie ist dein Nachname (*last name*)?
S2: Mueller. M-U-E-L-L-E-R.
S1: Danke!

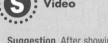 Video

Suggestion After showing students the video, ask questions to facilitate comprehension. Ex: In the first scene, why do some of the people in the child's drawing have blank faces? In the second scene, why are the children happier?

Familien fahren° besser mit der Bahn

Deutsche Bahn (**DB**) is the German railway company, based in Berlin. The **Deutsche Bahn** offers a **Sparpreis** (*discount price*) for families. Children under age 15 ride free when accompanied by an adult and pay half-price fares when traveling alone. This advertisement presents the **Deutsche Bahn** as a convenient and comfortable transportation option for families, allowing parents and children to interact and enjoy themselves on the way to their destination.

Die Bahn macht mobil: www.bahn.de

Sag mal°, weißt du noch, wie die Beiden von vorne aussehen?°

Warum fragst du mich?° Du kennst die länger als ich.°

Jetzt mit Gratiseis° für Kinder.

fahren *ride* **Sag mal** *Say...* **weißt du..., wie die Beiden von vorne aussehen?** *do you know what those two look like from the front?* **Warum fragst du mich?** *Why are you asking me?* **Du kennst die länger als ich.** *You've known them longer than me.* **Gratiseis** *free popsicle*

 Verständnis Circle the correct answers.

1. How much does the **DB** family package cost?
   a. 49 euro   b. 60 euro   c. 39 euro   d. 55 euro
2. What do children riding the train receive?
   a. Bücher   b. Äpfel   c. Eis   d. Blumen

 Diskussion Discuss the following questions with a partner. Answers will vary.

1. What is train service like in your country? How do you think it compares with the services offered by the **Deutsche Bahn**?
2. Does this commercial make you want to travel by train in Germany? Why or why not?

Communicative Goals

You will learn how to:
- talk about classes
- talk about schedules

Suggestion Point out that many of these vocabulary items are compound nouns. Ask students to identify the compound nouns, then help them to figure out the meaning of the component words.

Wortschatz

im Unterricht	*in class*
der Computer, -	*computer*
das Ergebnis, -se	*result; score*
das Foto, -s	*photo*
die Frage, -n	*question*
die Hausaufgabe, -n	*homework*
der Kalender, -	*calendar*
die Klasse, -n	*class*
der Kuli, -s	*ball-point pen*
das Lehrbuch, ̈er	*(university) textbook*
die Note, -n	*grade (on an assignment)*
die Notiz, -en	*note*
das Problem, -e	*problem*
die Prüfung, -en	*test; exam*
der Radiergummi, -s	*eraser*
die Sache, -n	*thing*
das Schulbuch, ̈er	*(K–12) textbook*
die Stunde, -n	*lesson*
der Taschenrechner, -	*calculator*
der Tisch, -e	*table; desk*
die Tür, -en	*door*
das Zeugnis, -se	*report card; grade report*
Da ist/sind...	*There is/are...*
Ist/Sind hier...?	*Is/Are there... here?*
Hier ist/sind...	*Here is/are...*
Was ist das?	*What is that?*
Orte	*places*
das Klassenzimmer, -	*classroom*
die Schule, -n	*school*
die Universität, -en	*university, college*
die Bibliothek, -en	*library*
die Mensa, Mensen	*(university) cafeteria*
Personen	*people*
Wer ist das?	*Who is it?*
der Klassenkamerad, -en / die Klassenkameradin, -nen	*(K-12) classmate*
der Kommilitone, -n / die Kommilitonin, -nen	*(university) classmate*
der Professor, -en / die Professorin, -nen	*professor*
der Student, -en / die Studentin, -nen	*(university) student*

In der Schule Ⓢ Vocabulary Tools

die Uhr, -en

der Rucksack, ̈e

der Bleistift, -e

das Fenster, -

Suggestion Tell students that **Schüler(in)** refers to a student in elementary school through high school, while **Student(in)** refers to a college or university student.

der Schüler, -

das Buch, ̈er

die Schülerin, -nen

das Heft, -e

das Wörterbuch, ̈er

der Stift, -e

der Papierkorb, ̈e

ACHTUNG

Don't confuse **Da ist...** (*There is...*) with **Das ist...** (*This is...*).

das Blatt Papier, (*pl.* Blätter Papier)

Ressourcen

SAM WB: pp. 9–10

SAM LM: p. 6

Ⓢ vhlcentral.com

die Tafel, -n

DEUTSCHLAND

LIECHTENSTEIN

DIE SCHWEIZ ÖSTERREICH

die Karte, -n

der Lehrer, -
(die Lehrerin, -nen *f.*)

der Schreibtisch, -e

der Stuhl, ⸚e

Anwendung

1 Expansion Ask students what other words from the lesson vocabulary could be included in each group.

1 Was passt nicht? Select the word that doesn't belong.

1. der Professor / das Problem / die Universität / die Studentin
2. das Fenster / das Schulbuch / die Notizen / das Heft
3. der Stift / der Bleistift / der Papierkorb / der Kuli
4. die Tafel / der Schreibtisch / der Stuhl / die Prüfung
5. die Tür / das Ergebnis / der Tisch / die Uhr
6. das Problem / der Radiergummi / die Frage / das Ergebnis

2 Ergänzen Sie Select the words that best complete each sentence.

1. Annika ist...
   a. der Stuhl.   b. die Schülerin.   c. die Stunde.
2. Wer ist das? Das ist...
   a. der Bleistift.   b. der Taschenrechner.   c. der Professor.
3. Wo sind die Bücher? Sie sind...
   a. in der Bibliothek.   b. im Ergebnis.   c. im Papierkorb.
4. Frau Meier ist...
   a. die Lehrerin.   b. die Schülerin.   c. die Schule.
5. Im Klassenzimmer sind...
   a. Tische.   b. Noten.   c. Universitäten.
6. Das Quiz und der Test sind...
   a. Hausaufgaben.   b. Prüfungen.   c. Ergebnisse.

3 Was ist das? Label each item.

3 Suggestion Have students identify items in your own classroom. Ask students: **Ist hier eine Uhr? Wo ist die Tür?**, etc.

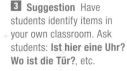

▶ **BEISPIEL** *der Bleistift*

1. ___der Stift/ der Kuli___   2. ___das Buch/das Schulbuch/das Lehrbuch/das Wörterbuch___   3. ___der Stuhl___

4. ___der Rucksack___   5. ___die Uhr___   6. ___die Tür___

4 Zuordnungen 🎧 Write each word you hear in the correct category.

Orte	Personen
1. die Schule	5. die Freundin
2. die Mensa	6. der Lehrer
3. das Klassenzimmer	7. die Professorin
4. die Universität	8. der Schüler

🖎 Practice more at **vhlcentral.com.**

4 Expansion Have students give the plural form of each word.

Kommunikation

5 Was ist das? In pairs, take turns pointing at items and people in your classroom and asking each other to identify them. Answers will vary.

BEISPIEL

S1: Was ist das?
S2: Das ist ein Bleistift. Wer ist das?
S1: Das ist der Professor.

5 Expansion Repeat the activity as a class, having students ask and answer questions about items in the classroom.

6 Im Rucksack List six items that are in your backpack. Then, work with a partner and compare lists.
Answers will vary.

In meinem (*my*) Rucksack ist/sind...

1. _____
2. _____
3. _____
4. _____
5. _____
6. _____

In _____s Rucksack ist/sind...

1. _____
2. _____
3. _____
4. _____
5. _____
6. _____

WERKZEUG

To say that something belongs to someone, add an **-s** to the person's name (**Marias Heft**; **Julians Buch**). Add an apostrophe if the name already ends in **-s** (**Niklas' Heft**; **Tobias' Buch**).

6 Expansion Bring in a bag filled with items such as pens, a calendar, a calculator, and so on. Pull them out one by one and ask students: **Ist das ein Bleistift oder ein Kuli? Ist das eine Uhr oder ein Taschenrechner? Ein Schulbuch oder ein Wörterbuch?** etc.

7 Ist da...? In pairs, take turns asking each other questions about what you see in the illustration. Answers will vary.

BEISPIEL

S1: Ist da ein Papierkorb?
S2: Nein. Da ist ein Bleistift. Ist da...?

8 Ratespiel Play Pictionary as a class. Answers will vary.

- Take turns going to the board and drawing images representing words from the lesson vocabulary.
- The person drawing may not write any letters or numbers.
- The person who correctly identifies the drawing in German gets to go next.

Aussprache und Rechtschreibung Audio

🎧 The vowels *a, e, i, o,* and *u*

Each German vowel may be pronounced with either a long or a short sound. A vowel followed by **h** is always long. A double **oo**, **aa**, or **ee** also indicates a long vowel sound. In some words, long **i** is spelled **ie**.

| Fahne | wen | ihn | doof | Mut | diese |

A vowel followed by two or more consonant sounds is usually short.

| Pfanne | wenn | in | Sonne | Mutter | singst |

When the German letter **e** appears in the unstressed syllable at the end of a word, it is pronounced like the *e* in the English word *the*.

| danke | Schule | Frage | Klasse | Dinge | Vase |

In certain words, an **Umlaut** (¨) is added to the vowel **a**, **o**, or **u**, changing the pronunciation of the vowel.

| Bank | Bänke | schon | schön | Bruder | Brüder |

Suggestion To produce the **ü** sound, tell students to round their lips as if to pronounce the letter **u**, but then make the long **i** sound.

---

1 **Aussprechen** Practice saying these words aloud.

1. Kahn / kann
2. beten / Betten
3. Robe / Robbe
4. Buch / Butter
5. den / denn
6. Saat / satt
7. Rogen / Roggen
8. Sack / Säcke
9. Wort / Wörter
10. Stuhl / Stühle
11. Hefte
12. Tage

1 **Expansion** Tell students the meanings of any unfamiliar words.

2 **Nachsprechen** Practice saying these sentences aloud.

1. Der Mann kam ohne Kamm.
2. Wir essen Bienenstich und trinken Kaffee.
3. Am Sonntag und am Montag scheint die Sonne.
4. Das U-Boot ist unter Wasser.
5. Ich habe viele Freunde in der Schule.
6. Der Mantel mit den fünf Knöpfen ist schöner als die Mäntel mit einem Knopf.

3 **Sprichwörter** Practice reading these sayings aloud.

¹ Tell me who your friends are, and I will tell you who you are.
² The early bird catches the worm.

Ressourcen

SAM LM: p. 7

vhlcentral.com

Oh, George! 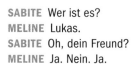 Video

George und Hans treffen (*meet*) Meline und Sabite im Biergarten.
Melines Handy klingelt...

Vorbereitung Have students review the **Nützliche Ausdrücke** before watching the video, in order to preview the episode content.

1

SABITE Wer ist es?
MELINE Lukas.
SABITE Oh, dein Freund?
MELINE Ja. Nein. Ja.

2

MELINE Wir haben Probleme.

3

MELINE Hast du einen Freund?
SABITE Ja. Torsten. Er ist Student.
MELINE Hast du ein Bild?

4

GEORGE Sabite? Sabite, hallo.
SABITE Hallo.
HANS Hallo.
SABITE Was ist da drin?
GEORGE Lehrbücher! Wörterbuch... Hefte...
Stifte... Kalender.
HANS Hast du auch einen Computer?

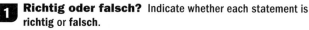

5

KELLNERIN Bitte schön?
HANS Ein Wasser, bitte.
GEORGE Einen Kaffee und ein
Stück Strudel.

MELINE Ich habe keinen Freund mehr.
SABITE Wie geht's dir?
MELINE Mir geht es sehr gut.

6

1 **Richtig oder falsch?** Indicate whether each statement is richtig or falsch.

1. George hat ein Wörterbuch. Richtig.
2. Sabite hat ein Bild von (*of*) Torsten. Richtig.
3. George will (*wants*) das Brandenburger Tor sehen (*to see*). Richtig.
4. Im Bauhaus-Museum gibt es viele Bücher. Falsch.
5. Meline telefoniert mit Lukas. Richtig.

6. Die Kellnerin hat einen Freund. Richtig.
7. Torsten ist Student. Richtig.
8. Hans hat einen Stadtplan. Richtig.
9. Die Kellnerin heißt Laura. Falsch.
10. George bestellt (*orders*) Kaffee und Steak. Falsch.

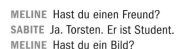

PERSONEN

George   Hans   Meline   Sabite   Kellnerin

GEORGE Ich habe eine Idee. Hast du einen Stadtplan?
HANS Ja!
GEORGE Was muss ich in Berlin sehen? Das Brandenburger Tor!
HANS Checkpoint Charlie!

SABITE Potsdamer Platz!
GEORGE Marlene-Dietrich-Platz!
KELLNERIN Das Bode-Museum. Und das Jüdische Museum!

HANS Wie viele Kurse hast du belegt?
SABITE Ah, vier.
MELINE Bauhaus-Museum.
HANS Ja!
MELINE Im Bauhaus-Museum gibt es viele...
SABITE Stühle! Viele Stühle. Und Tische.

GEORGE Wie heißt sie?
SABITE Ähm, Leyna? Oh, George.
HANS Sie hat einen Freund?
GEORGE Ja.

Nützliche Ausdrücke

- **Prost!**
  Cheers!
- **Wer ist es?**
  Who is it?
- **Hast du ein Bild?**
  Do you have a picture?
- **Was ist da drin?**
  What's in there?
- **Hast du auch einen Computer?**
  Do you have a computer, too?
- **die Kellnerin**
  waitress
- **Bitte schön?**
  May I take your order?; May I help you?
- **das Wasser**
  water
- **der Kaffee**
  coffee
- **das Stück Strudel**
  a piece of strudel
- **Ich habe keinen Freund mehr.**
  I don't have a boyfriend anymore.
- **die Idee**
  idea
- **der Stadtplan**
  city map
- **Was muss ich in Berlin sehen?**
  What do I have to see in Berlin?
- **Ist alles in Ordnung?**
  Is everything alright?
- **Wie heißt sie?**
  What's her name?

1B.1
- **Wir haben Probleme.**
  We have problems.

1B.2
- **Hast du einen Stadtplan?**
  Do you have a city map?

1B.3
- **—Wie viele Kurse hast du?**
  —How many classes are you taking?
- **—Vier.**
  —Four.

---

2 Zum Besprechen With a partner, role-play a scene where one of you plays the waiter (**Kellner**) or waitress at a **Biergarten** and the other plays a customer ordering food. Here are some common items to order. Answers will vary.

eine Cola	ein Stück Strudel
einen Kaffee	einen Tee
einen Saft (*juice*)	ein Wasser

2 Suggestion This activity can also be done with groups of three or more. Have students take turns playing the roles of server and customers.

3 Vertiefung The characters mention several important sites and museums in Berlin. Research these and other monuments and plan a day of sightseeing in Berlin to present to the class. Mention at least three sites that interest you and include their names in German. Answers will vary.

3 Suggestion Preview the expression **es gibt** and encourage students to list some of the things they can see at each site.

Die Schulzeit  Reading

Suggestion Explain that the **Abitur** is awarded based on a points system. For each course and each exam they take, students can earn a maximum of 15 points. At the completion of all courses and exams, the points are tallied, and students are awarded a final grade from 1 to 6. The minimum qualifying score for the **Abitur** is 280 points (out of 840).

ALTHOUGH THE WORD AND THE concept were invented by **Friedrich Fröbel**, a teacher in 19th-century Germany, **Kindergarten** is not a part of today's German public school system. There are many privately-run **Kindergärten**, but attendance is not universal.

Public school for German children starts at age six, with **Grundschule°**. For the first four years, all **Grundschüler** attend school together. But after age ten, students are streamed into three different kinds of schools, usually as recommended by their teacher.

The most academically rigorous option is **Gymnasium**. **Gymnasium** lasts eight years, and graduates need to pass difficult exit exams to earn their **Abitur°**. The "Abi" gives students access to competitive internships and a university education.

A more vocationally-oriented option is **Hauptschule**. Students typically finish **Hauptschule** at age 15 or 16. They may then attend **Berufsfachschule°**, where they can train for a variety of professions, from mechanics to physical therapy.

The third option is **Realschule**, which has stricter academic requirements than **Hauptschule**. After graduation, students may seek further schooling that will lead them into careers like banking, IT, or social work.

This three-track system has been in use for decades, but in recent years it has come under serious criticism. The **Abitur** is associated with higher social status, and more and more families push to have their children admitted into **Gymnasium**. **Realschule** still generally leads to solid employment opportunities, but there is now a stigma attached to **Hauptschule**, which makes the job search more difficult for its graduates.

In some states, there is a fourth option for secondary school students: the **Gesamtschule°**. These comprehensive schools have no entrance requirements. They offer college preparatory classes for students who perform well, general education classes for students with average performance, and remedial courses for those who need additional support. **Gesamtschulen** were introduced in 1969 with the hope of eliminating inequalities associated with the three-track system, but they have been slow to take root.

Grundschule *elementary school* **Abitur** *high school diploma* **Berufsfachschule** *vocational school* **Gesamtschule** *comprehensive school*

Suggestion Tell students that the Austrian and Swiss version of the **Abitur** is called **die Matura**.

ÜBUNGEN

1 **Was fehlt?** Complete the statements.

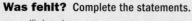

1. ___Kindergarten___ is not part of the German public school system.
2. ___Friedrich Fröbel___ invented the word **Kindergarten**.
3. German elementary school is called ___Grundschule___.
4. Children normally begin school at age ___six___.
5. **Grundschule** lasts ___four___ years.

6. After age ten, students are streamed into three kinds of schools: **Gymnasium**, **Hauptschule**, and ___Realschule___.
7. **Gymnasium** graduates receive a diploma called the ___Abitur___.
8. Students who have earned their **Abitur** can attend ___university___.
9. After finishing ___Hauptschule___, students may attend **Berufsfachschule**.
10. The ___Gesamtschule___ offers an alternative to the three-track system.

 Practice more at **vhlcentral.com**.

DEUTSCH IM ALLTAG

Die Schule

die Abschlussfeier, -n	*graduation*
die Pause, -n	*recess*
der Schulleiter, -	*(male) principal*
die Schulleiterin, -nen	*(female) principal*
bestehen	*to pass a test*
durchfallen	*to flunk; to fail*
schwänzen	*to cut class*
langweilig	*boring*

DIE DEUTSCHSPRACHIGE WELT

Ein süßer° Beginn

In German-speaking countries, the first day of school is a festive occasion. Excited **Erstklässler°** are presented with **Schultüten** by their parents on the morning of their first day of school. The **Schultüte** is a decorated paper cone, filled with candies, chocolates, school supplies, and other treats. With their unopened **Tüten** in hand, the **Erstklässler** set off for **Grundschule. Alles Gute für den ersten Schultag!°**

süßer *sweet* **Erstklässler** *first-graders* **Alles Gute für den ersten Schultag!** *Best wishes on your first day of school!*

Noten in Deutschland

Deutsche Noten:	1	2	3	4	5/6
US-Äquivalente:	A/A+	A-/B+	B/B-	C/D	D-/F

PORTRÄT

Der Schultag

The school day in Germany typically lasts from 7:30 or 8:00 in the morning until 1:00 in the afternoon, with a 15-20 minute mid-morning break, called the **Große Pause**. Many schools do not have cafeterias, since students go home at lunch time. They then have the afternoon to do homework and participate in extracurricular activities. Students have only 6 weeks of summer vacation, but they get longer breaks during the school year, with 2 weeks off in the fall, 2 weeks for Christmas, and 2 weeks in the spring.

Die Deutschsprachige Welt Tell students that children often craft their own **Schultüten** in **Kindergarten**. Their parents then fill the **Tüten** before the first day of **Grundschule**.

TIPP

The German word for *one* is **eins**. A straight-A student is called **ein(e) Einserschüler(in)**.

⚬⚬ IM INTERNET

Subjects: What subjects do students study at **Gymnasium**? What are **Pflichtfächer**? What are **Wahlfächer**?

Find out more at **vhlcentral.com**.

---

2 **Richtig oder falsch?** Indicate whether each statement is **richtig** or **falsch**. Correct the false statements.

1. Most German students eat lunch in their school cafeterias.
   Falsch. Many schools do not have cafeterias, since students go home at lunch time.
2. Students get a midmorning break called the **Große Pause**. **Richtig.**
3. Students get 12 weeks of vacation every summer.
   Falsch. Students have only 6 weeks of summer vacation.
4. Children in their first year of school are called **Kindergärtner**.
   Falsch. They are called **Erstklässler**.
5. The **Schultüte** is a test that elementary school students take on the first day. **Falsch.** The **Schultüte** is a cone full of treats.

3 **Die Schule: anders in Deutschland** In pairs, discuss the similarities and differences between school life in Germany or other German-speaking countries and in your country. What do you like best about each system? Why?

Suggestion Tell students that many changes to the German educational system have been proposed and/or implemented over the last decade. **Gymnasium** originally lasted nine years, but was shortened to eight, and the government is considering extending the number of years spent in elementary school and lengthening the school day.

1B.1

Haben and the accusative case

Startblock To describe what someone or something has, use the irregular verb **haben** with the accusative case.

Haben

haben (*to have*)			
ich habe	*I have*	**wir haben**	*we have*
du hast	*you have* (inf.)	**ihr habt**	*you have* (inf.)
Sie haben	*you have* (form.)	**Sie haben**	*you have* (form.)
er/sie/es hat	*he/she/it has*	**sie haben**	*they have*

Ich **habe** ein Buch.
*I **have** a book.*

Greta **hat** eine Karte.
*Greta **has** a map.*

Wir **haben** eine Frage.
*We **have** a question.*

The accusative case

- In **1A.3**, you learned that the function of a noun in a sentence determines its case, as well as the case of any article or adjective that modifies it. A noun that functions as a direct object is in the accusative case (**der Akkusativ**).

definite articles				
	masculine	**feminine**	**neuter**	**plural**
nominative	**der** Stuhl	**die** Tür	**das** Fenster	**die** Notizen
accusative	**den** Stuhl	**die** Tür	**das** Fenster	**die** Notizen

indefinite articles				
	masculine	**feminine**	**neuter**	**plural**
nominative	**ein** Stuhl	**eine** Tür	**ein** Fenster	**–** Notizen
accusative	**einen** Stuhl	**eine** Tür	**ein** Fenster	**–** Notizen

Der Lehrer hat **den Stift**.
*The teacher has **the pen**.*

Sie öffnet **die Tür**.
*She's opening **the door**.*

Ich kaufe **einen Schreibtisch**.
*I'm buying **a desk**.*

Wir haben hier **ein Problem**.
*We have **a problem** here.*

Suggestion Give students additional examples to illustrate the use of the accusative with direct objects and the nominative with predicate nouns. Ex.: **Markus ist ein guter Freund. Sabine hat einen guten Freund.**

Jetzt sind Sie dran! | In the first column, complete the sentences using **haben**. In the second column, indicate whether each underlined phrase is in the **Nominativ (N)** or **Akkusativ (A)** case.

1. Wir ___haben___ die Bücher.
2. Ich ___habe___ Fotos.
3. Herr Müller ___hat___ ein Haus.
4. Ihr ___habt___ morgen Schule.
5. Max und Julia ___haben___ viele Hausaufgaben.
6. Lena ___hat___ eine Theorie.

N 7. Sie ist <u>eine gute Schülerin</u>.
A 8. David hat <u>eine Frage</u>.
A 9. Ich habe <u>ein Problem</u>.
A 10. Du hast <u>einen Stuhl</u>.
N 11. Ihr seid <u>Studenten</u>.
A 12. Herr Meier trinkt <u>ein Glas Wasser</u>.

Anwendung und Kommunikation

1 **Bilden Sie Sätze** Write complete sentences.

 BEISPIEL ich / haben / ein Radiergummi

Ich habe einen Radiergummi.

1. du / haben / ein Computer   Du hast einen Computer.
2. ihr / haben / ein Taschenrechner   Ihr habt einen Taschenrechner.
3. der Lehrer / haben / ein Buch   Der Lehrer hat ein Buch.
4. wir / haben / ein Problem   Wir haben ein Problem.
5. ich / haben / eine Frage   Ich habe eine Frage.
6. das Mädchen / haben / ein Freund   Das Mädchen hat einen Freund.

2 **Was haben wir?** Rewrite each sentence using **haben** with the subject provided.

 BEISPIEL Das ist ein Computer. (Inge)

Inge hat einen Computer.

1. Das ist ein Rucksack. (Peter)   Peter hat einen Rucksack.
2. Das ist ein Kuli. (ich)   Ich habe einen Kuli.
3. Das ist ein Schulbuch. (ihr)   Ihr habt ein Schulbuch.
4. Das sind Fotos. (du)   Du hast Fotos.
5. Das ist ein Wörterbuch. (Erik und Nina)   Erik und Nina haben ein Wörterbuch.
6. Das ist eine Karte. (wir)   Wir haben eine Karte.

3 **Was haben sie?** With a partner, take turns saying what each person has.

▶ **BEISPIEL**

Patrick hat Fotos.

Patrick

1. du

Du hast Bücher.

2. die Kommilitonen

Die Kommilitonen/Sie haben Hefte.

3. Bettina

Bettina/Sie hat eine Uhr.

4. ich

Ich habe einen Taschenrechner.

5. du und Abdel

Du und Abdel/Ihr habt einen Rucksack.

6. wir

Wir haben einen Computer.

4 **Im Klassenzimmer** In groups, take turns discussing what items are in your classroom and what each of you has brought to class.   Answers will vary.

BEISPIEL

S1: *Was haben wir hier?*
S2: *Wir haben Stühle und Bänke.*

S1: *Was hast du?*
S2: *Ich habe ein Heft.*

4 **Expansion** Call on individual students and have them describe what they and their group members have brought to class. Ex.: **Er hat ein Heft und einen Bleistift. Ich habe auch ein Heft und sie hat einen Kuli.**

 Practice more at **vhlcentral.com.**

1B.2

Suggestion Explain that German uses case to indicate the function of a noun, whereas English relies more heavily on word order. Thus, in German, subject and object can switch positions without changing function. Ex.: **Der Junge hat einen Computer. Einen Computer hat der Junge.**

Expansion For additional practice, ask students yes-or-no questions and have them answer with affirmative statements. Ex.: **Hast du einen Rucksack? Ja, ich habe einen Rucksack.**

QUERVERWEIS

You will learn more about word order and conjunctions in **6A.3** and **10A.1**.

You will learn how to form negative statements in **2B.3**.

Ressourcen

SAM
WB: pp. 13–14

SAM
LM: p. 9

vhlcentral.com

Word order Presentation

Startblock By changing the order of words in a sentence, you can shift emphasis or turn a statement into a yes-or-no question.

Statements

- In German, the verb is always the second element in a statement. The first element is often the subject, but it can also be a time expression or a prepositional phrase.

1ST	2ND	3RD
Ich	**habe**	heute Abend viele Hausaufgaben.

*I **have** a lot of homework tonight.*

Heute Abend	**habe**	ich viele Hausaufgaben.

*Tonight I **have** a lot of homework.*

- A direct or indirect object may be placed in first position, but this is a less common phrasing, used to place emphasis on the object. When the subject is not the first element in the sentence, it immediately follows the verb.

1ST	2ND	3RD
Viele Hausaufgaben	**habe**	ich heute Abend.

*I **have** a lot of homework tonight.*

- You can use the conjunctions **und** (*and*), **aber** (*but*), and **oder** (*or*) to combine two statements into one sentence, without affecting the word order of either statement.

Heute Abend haben wir viele
Hausaufgaben **und** morgen haben wir Unterricht.
*Tonight we have a lot of homework **and** tomorrow we have class.*

Yes-or-no questions

- To turn a statement into a yes-or-no question, move the verb to the first position. Move the subject to the second position, since it must immediately follow the verb. Use **ja** or **nein** to respond to this type of question.

STATEMENT	QUESTION
Die Professorin ist nett.	▶ **Ist die Professorin** nett?
The professor is nice.	*Is the professor nice?*
Jetzt habt ihr einen Computer.	▶ **Habt ihr jetzt** einen Computer?
Now you have a computer.	*Do you have a computer now?*

You may want to preview negation by modeling a few simple statements using **nicht**. (Ex. **Der Apfel ist nicht gut. Das Buch ist nicht schlecht. Die Professorin ist nicht nett.**) Remind students that they learned the word **nicht** lexically in **1A Kontext**, in the expression **nicht schlecht**. However, emphasize that **nicht** should not be used to negate a noun, and that students will learn more about negation in the next unit.

Jetzt sind Sie dran! **Turn each statement into a yes-or-no question.**

1. Ich habe ein Buch.
   Habe ich ein Buch?/Hast du ein Buch? /Haben Sie ein Buch?

2. Ich bin Studentin.
   Bin ich Studentin?/Bist du Studentin?/Sind Sie Studentin?

3. Das sind Kommilitonen.
   Sind das Kommilitonen?

4. Der Apfel ist gut.
   Ist der Apfel gut?

5. Wir haben viele Fotos.
   Haben wir viele Fotos?/Habt ihr viele Fotos?/Haben Sie viele Fotos?

6. Tobias und Jasmin haben Rucksäcke.
   Haben Tobias und Jasmin Rucksäcke?

7. Lukas hat einen Taschenrechner.
   Hat Lukas einen Taschenrechner?

8. Ich habe ein Problem.
   Habe ich ein Problem?/Hast du ein Problem? /Haben Sie ein Problem?

Anwendung und Kommunikation

1 **Sätze** Combine each pair of sentences using **oder**, **aber**, or **und**, as indicated.

BEISPIEL Ben hat gute Noten. David hat schlechte Noten. (aber)

Ben hat gute Noten, aber David hat schlechte Noten.

1. Du hast ein Blatt Papier. Ich habe einen Bleistift. (und) Du hast ein Blatt Papier und ich habe einen Bleistift.
2. Ist das Buch gut? Ist es schlecht? (oder) Ist das Buch gut oder ist es schlecht?
3. Es geht mir ziemlich gut. Ich habe ein Problem. (aber) Es geht mir ziemlich gut, aber ich habe ein Problem.
4. Ist Ela da? Ist sie im Unterricht? (oder) Ist Ela da oder ist sie im Unterricht?
5. Wir haben heute viele Hausaufgaben. Morgen haben wir eine Prüfung. (und)
   Wir haben heute viele Hausaufgaben und morgen haben wir eine Prüfung
6. Ich heiße Sophia. Das ist Mia. (und) Ich heiße Sophia und das ist Mia.

2 **Noch einmal** Rewrite each sentence twice, changing the order of the underlined elements.

BEISPIEL <u>Ich</u> habe <u>heute</u> (*today*) <u>eine Prüfung</u>.

Heute habe ich eine Prüfung.
Eine Prüfung habe ich heute.

1. <u>Tim</u> hat <u>heute Abend</u> <u>Deutschhausaufgaben</u>. Heute Abend hat Tim Deutschhausaufgaben. Deutschhausaufgaben hat Tim heute Abend.
2. <u>Max und Lisa</u> haben <u>ein Haus</u> <u>in Berlin</u>. Ein Haus haben Max und Lisa in Berlin. In Berlin haben Max und Lisa ein Haus. Max und Lisa haben in Berlin ein Haus.
3. <u>Wir</u> sind <u>jetzt</u> <u>im Unterricht.</u> Jetzt sind wir im Unterricht. Im Unterricht sind wir jetzt.
4. <u>Ich</u> bin <u>jetzt</u> <u>in Berlin</u>. Jetzt bin ich in Berlin. In Berlin bin ich jetzt.

3 **Wer hat was?** In pairs, take turns asking and answering questions.

BEISPIEL Professor / Problem (nein / Frage)

S1: *Hat der Professor ein Problem?*
S2: *Nein, er hat eine Frage.*

1. Frau / Blatt Papier (nein / Foto) Hat die Frau ein Blatt Papier? Nein, sie hat ein Foto.
2. Emil und ich / Bleistifte (ja) Haben Emil und ich Bleistifte? Ja, ihr habt Bleistifte.
3. Lehrerin / Kalender (ja) Hat die Lehrerin (einen) Kalender? Ja, sie hat (einen) Kalender.
4. Schüler / Buch (nein / Heft) Hat der Schüler/Haben die Schüler ein Buch? Nein, er hat/sie haben ein Heft.

4 **Was ist los?** In groups, take turns asking and answering yes-or-no questions about the image. Answers will vary.

BEISPIEL

S1: *Haben die Schüler Bücher?*
S2: *Ja, sie haben Bücher.*

 Practice more at **vhlcentral.com.**

1B.3

Numbers Presentation

Startblock As in English, numbers in German follow patterns. Memorizing the numbers from **1** to **20** will help you learn numbers **21** and above.

Sabite hat **vier** Kurse.

George ist **21** Jahre alt.

- Every number up to one million is written as a single word. Numbers from **13** to **19** follow a pattern similar to English, adding the ending **-zehn** to each single-digit number. Numbers from **21** to **99** repeat this pattern, adding **und** plus the number in the tens place to each single-digit number: [ones] + **und** + [tens].

25 = **fünf** + **und** + **zwanzig** ▶ **fünfundzwanzig**

numbers 0–99			
0 null	10 zehn	20 zwanzig	30 dreißig
1 eins	11 elf	21 einundzwanzig	31 einunddreißig
2 zwei	12 zwölf	22 zweiundzwanzig	40 vierzig
3 drei	13 dreizehn	23 dreiundzwanzig	45 fünfundvierzig
4 vier	14 vierzehn	24 vierundzwanzig	50 fünfzig
5 fünf	15 fünfzehn	25 fünfundzwanzig	60 sechzig
6 sechs	16 sechzehn	26 sechsundzwanzig	70 siebzig
7 sieben	17 siebzehn	27 siebenundzwanzig	80 achtzig
8 acht	18 achtzehn	28 achtundzwanzig	90 neunzig
9 neun	19 neunzehn	29 neunundzwanzig	99 neunundneunzig

- Note that the **s** in **eins** is dropped at the beginning of a compound word.

41 = eins + vierzig ▶ **ein**undvierzig   **81** = eins + achtzig ▶ **ein**undachtzig

- Likewise, **sechs** and **sieben** are shortened when they precede the letter **z**.

16 = **sech**zehn   **66** = sechsund**sech**zig
17 = **sieb**zehn   **77** = siebenund**sieb**zig

- In German, decimals are indicated by a comma (**Komma**), not a period (**Punkt**). When giving a unit of measurement (length, currency, etc.), say the unit instead of **Komma**. Note that units of currency are usually written after the number.

25,4 = fünfundzwanzig **Komma** vier   **0,5** = null **Komma** fünf
4,99 € = vier **Euro** neunundneunzig   **10,18 m** = zehn **Meter** achtzehn

- Use **Wie viel?** to ask *How much?* and **Wie viele?** to ask *How many?*

Wie viel kostet das Buch?   **Wie viele** Blätter Papier habt ihr?
How much does the book cost?   *How many pieces of paper do you have?*

numbers 100 and higher			
100	(ein)hundert	1.000	(ein)tausend
101	hunderteins	1.300	tausenddreihundert
128	hundertachtundzwanzig	5.000	fünftausend
200	zweihundert	10.000	zehntausend
300	dreihundert	50.000	fünfzigtausend
400	vierhundert	100.000	hunderttausend
500	fünfhundert	460.000	vierhundertsechzigtausend
600	sechshundert	1.000.000	eine Million
700	siebenhundert	1.050.000	eine Million fünfzigtausend
800	achthundert	7.000.000	sieben Millionen
900	neunhundert	1.000.000.000	eine Milliarde

- Note that German uses a period where English typically uses a comma to separate thousands, millions, etc.

2.320.000	1.999,99 €	5.225,00 $
2,320,000	*€1,999.99*	*$5,225.00*

- Numbers in the millions and higher are written as separate words.

2.016.000
zwei Millionen sechzehntausend

1.000.050.000
eine Milliarde fünfzigtausend

Mathematical expressions

- Use these expressions to talk about math.

mathematical expressions					
+	plus	×	mal	=	ist (gleich)
–	minus	÷	geteilt durch	%	Prozent

6 + 7 = 13
Sechs plus sieben ist dreizehn.
Six plus seven is thirteen.

8 – 2 = 6
Acht minus zwei ist gleich sechs.
Eight minus two equals six.

3 · 3 = 9
Drei mal drei ist gleich neun.
Three times three equals nine.

20 : 5 = 4
Zwanzig geteilt durch fünf ist vier.
Twenty divided by five is four.

Suggestion Have students practice reading these numbers aloud.

ACHTUNG

Note that German speakers typically use the symbol · to indicate multiplication and the symbol : to indicate division.

Ressourcen

SAM
WB: pp. 15–16

SAM
LM: p. 10

vhlcentral.com

Jetzt sind Sie dran! Write each number or equation in words.

1. 37
   siebenunddreißig

2. 212
   zweihundertzwölf

3. 49
   neunundvierzig

4. 368
   dreihundertachtundsechzig

5. 24
   vierundzwanzig

6. 75
   fünfundsiebzig

7. 1991
   eintausendneunhunderteinundneunzig

8. 587
   fünfhundertsiebenundachtzig

9. 16 + 15 = 31
   Sechzehn plus fünfzehn ist (gleich) einunddreißig.

10. 97 – 17 = 80
    Siebenundneunzig minus siebzehn ist achtzig.

11. 18 : 9 = 2
    Achtzehn geteilt durch neun ist zwei.

12. 12 · 3 = 36
    Zwölf mal drei ist sechsunddreißig.

Anwendung

1 **Eins, zwei, drei...** Fill in the missing number, then write the number in words.

BEISPIEL 0, 5, 10, __15__ , 20; ___fünfzehn___

1. 2, 4, __6__, 8, 10; ___sechs___
2. 0, 10, 20, __30__, 40; ___dreißig___
3. 670, 671, 672, 673, __674__; ___sechshundertvierundsiebzig___
4. 3.456, 3.457, 3.458, __3.459__, 3.460; ___dreitausendvierhundertneunundfünfzig___
5. 35, 40, 45, 50, __55__; ___fünfundfünfzig___
6. 1.899.996, 1.899.997, 1.899.998, 1.899.999, __1.900.000__; ___eine Million neunhunderttausend___

2 **Wie alt bist du?** With a partner, take turns asking and saying how old each person is.

BEISPIEL Anna: 16

S1: Wie alt ist Anna?
S2: Sie ist sechzehn Jahre alt.

1. Tim: 19 Er ist neunzehn Jahre alt.
2. Sara: 11 Sie ist elf Jahre alt.
3. Herr Wolf: 73 Er ist dreiundsiebzig Jahre alt.
4. Frau Öztürk: 101 Sie ist hunderteins Jahre alt.

5. Niklas: 5 Er ist fünf Jahre alt.
6. Herr Braun: 42 Er ist zweiundvierzig Jahre alt.
7. Jasmin: 21 Sie ist einundzwanzig Jahre alt.
8. Frau Schröder: 67 Sie ist siebenundsechzig Jahre alt.

3 **Was sehen Sie?** Write how many there are of each item.

BEISPIEL

(860) Student
Da sind achthundertsechzig Studenten.

(5.937) Buch
1. ___Da sind fünftausendneunhundertsiebenunddreißig Bücher.___

(16) Mädchen
2. Da sind sechzehn Mädchen.

(217) Tisch
3. Da sind zweihundertsiebzehn Tische.

(54) Auto
4. Da sind vierundfünfzig Autos.

(12) Stuhl
5. Da sind zwölf Stühle.

(4) Studentin
6. Da sind vier Studentinnen.

4 **Matheprofi** In pairs, take turns reading the equations out loud.

1. $67 + 4 = 71$
2. $16 + 28 = 44$
3. $91 - 6 = 85$
4. $45 - 7 = 38$

5. $24 : 4 = 6$
6. $989 : 43 = 23$
7. $58 \cdot 2 = 116$
8. $213 \cdot 3 = 639$

1. Siebenundsechzig plus vier ist (gleich) einundsiebzig.
2. Sechzehn plus achtundzwanzig ist (gleich) vierundvierzig.
3. Einundneunzig minus sechs ist (gleich) fünfundachtzig.
4. Fünfundvierzig minus sieben ist (gleich) achtunddreißig.
5. Vierundzwanzig geteilt durch vier ist (gleich) sechs.
6. Neunhundertneunundachtzig geteilt durch dreiundvierzig ist (gleich) dreiundzwanzig.
7. Achtfünfzig mal zwei ist (gleich) (ein) hundertsechzehn.
8. Zweihundertdreizehn mal drei ist (gleich) sechshundertneunundreißig.

 Practice more at **vhlcentral.com.**

Kommunikation

5 **Wie viele Einwohner hat...?** In pairs, discuss the population of each city.

> **BEISPIEL** München: 1.330.440
>
> **S1:** Wie viele Einwohner (*inhabitants*) hat München?
> **S2:** München hat eine Million dreihundertdreißigtausendvierhundertvierzig Einwohner.

1. Berlin: 3.450.889   Berlin hat drei Millionen vierhundertfünfzigtausendachthundertneunundachtzig Einwohner.
2. Gelsenkirchen: 259.744   Gelsenkirchen hat zweihundertneunundfünfzigtausendsiebenhundertvierundvierzig Einwohner.
3. Hamburg: 1.783.975   Hamburg hat eine Million siebenhundertdreiundachtzigtausendneunhundertfünfundsiebzig Einwohner.
4. Dresden: 532.058   Dresden hat fünfhundertzweiunddreißigtausendachtundfünfzig Einwohner.
5. Stuttgart: 601.646   Stuttgart hat sechshunderteintausendsechshundertsechsundvierzig Einwohner.

6 **Wie viel kostet...?** In pairs, take turns asking about and saying the cost of each item. Answers will vary.

> **BEISPIEL**
>
> **S1:** Wie viel kostet ein Computer?
> **S2:** Er kostet eintausenddreihundertvierundzwanzig Euro siebzehn.

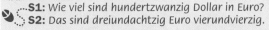

Auto	Apfel
Haus	Blume
Tisch	Heft
Computer	Stuhl

7 **Wie viel sind...?** In pairs, discuss these exchange rates.

> **BEISPIEL** $120 = 83,44 €
>
> **S1:** Wie viel sind hundertzwanzig Dollar in Euro?
> **S2:** Das sind dreiundachtzig Euro vierundvierzig.

1. $450 = 312,70 €
2. $573 = 452,08 CHF (Schweizer Franken)
3. 781,45 € = 86.074,17 ¥ (Yen)
4. $1.628,50 = £985,88 (Pfund Sterling)
5. 3.816 € = £3.321,67
6. 6.487,15 CHF = $8.222,89
7. $14.005,90 = 9.733,30 €
8. £251.029 = $414.884,04

8 **Ich habe mehr!** In small groups, take turns exaggerating the number of items you have at home.

> **BEISPIEL**
>
> **S1:** Ich habe sieben Kulis.
> **S2:** Ich habe dreihundertfünfundneunzig Taschenrechner!
> **S3:** Und ich habe neuntausendvierundzwanzig Stifte!

1.253.687

6 **Suggestion** Bring in price listings from German-language web sites and have students read the prices aloud.

7 **Answers**
1. vierhundertfünfzig Dollar/ dreihundertzwölf Euro siebzig.
2. fünfhundertdreiundsiebzig Dollar/ vierhundertzweiundfünfzig Schweizer Franken acht.
3. siebenhunderteinundachtzig Euro fünfundvierzig/sechsundacht-zigtausendvierundsiebzig Yen siebzehn.
4. eintausendsechshundertachtund-zwanzig Dollar fünfzig/neunhun-dertfünfundachtzig Pfund Sterling achtundachtzig.
5. dreitausendachthundertsechzehn Euro/dreitausenddreihundertein-undzwanzig Pfund Sterling sieben-undsechzig.
6. sechstausendvierhundertsieben-undachtzig Schweizer Franken fünfzehn/achttausendzweihun-dertzweiundzwanzig Dollar neun-undachtzig.
7. vierzehntausendfünf Dollar neun-zig/neuntausendsiebenhundert-dreiunddreißig Euro dreißig.
8. zweihunderteinundfünfzigtau-sendneunundzwanzig Pfund Sterling/vierhundertvierzehntau-sendachthundertvierundachtzig Dollar vier.

8 **Expansion** Ask each student to make a list of items and quantities before beginning this activity. (Ex: **7 Kulis, 86 Rucksäcke, 98 Taschenrechner**....) As they do the activity, have students write down the numbers they hear and then compare with what their partner actually said.

Wiederholung

1 Fragespiel

In pairs, play a question game (Fragespiel) using the lesson vocabulary. Choose a person or object in the classroom. Your partner will ask yes-or-no questions to figure out the word you've chosen. Answers will vary.

BEISPIEL

S1: *Bist du eine Sache?*
S2: *Nein.*
S1: *Bist du eine Person?*
S2: *Ja.*
S1: *Hast du einen Schreibtisch?*
S2: *Ja.*
S1: *Bist du ein Lehrer?*
S2: *Genau (Exactly)!*

1 Suggestion Help students to select vocabulary that they can ask questions about. Circulate around the room to ensure that everyone is forming appropriate questions.

2 Mathe

Write two numbers between 1 and 100 on separate index cards. Then, in small groups, make a pile of everyone's cards, shuffle, and take turns drawing two cards from the pile. The person who draws must create a math problem using the numbers. The first person to answer the math problem correctly draws next. Answers will vary.

BEISPIEL

S1: *(draws 55 and 5)* *Fünfundfünfzig geteilt durch fünf.*
S2: *Fünfundfünfzig geteilt durch fünf ist elf.*

2 Expansion Have the whole class play this game, as a group or in teams.

3 Ratespiel

In small groups, collect the items listed. One student leaves the group while the others distribute the items among themselves. The student then returns and tries to guess who has each item. Answers will vary.

BEISPIEL

S1: *Hast du den Radiergummi?*
S2: *Nein.*
S1: *Hat Megan den Radiergummi?*
S2: *Nein, Simon hat den Radiergummi.*

3 Suggestion Remind students to pay attention to articles when using nouns in the accusative case.

der Bleistift	der Radiergummi
das Buch	der Rucksack
das Heft	der Taschenrechner
der Kuli	die Uhr

4 Im Schreibwarenladen

In groups of three, make a shopping list of school supplies. Then, role-play a trip to the store to buy the items you need. Present your scene to the class. Answers will vary.

BEISPIEL

S1: *Guten Tag.*
S2: *Guten Tag. Haben Sie hier Hefte und Bleistifte?*
S1: *Ja, wir haben hier Hefte und Bleistifte.*
S3: *Wie viel kosten die Hefte?*
S1: *Sie kosten fünf Euro neunzig.*

5 Diskutieren und kombinieren

Your instructor will give you and your partner worksheets with different pictures of a classroom. Do not look at each other's pictures. Ask and answer questions to identify seven differences (**Unterschiede**) between the two pictures. Answers will vary.

BEISPIEL

S1: *Ich habe zwei Türen. Hast du auch zwei Türen?*
S2: *Nein. Ich habe eine Tür. Hast du einen Lehrer?*
S1: *Ja, ich habe auch einen Lehrer. Hast du...?*

6 Arbeitsblatt

Your instructor will give you a game board. Play the game with your partners. Count the spaces aloud in German as you play.

7 **Interview** Interview as many classmates as possible to find out if these statements (**Behauptungen**) apply to them. Write down their names.

BEISPIEL

S1: Hallo! Hast du einen Bleistift?
S2: Ja, ich habe einen Bleistift./
Nein, aber ich habe einen Kuli.

Behauptung	Name
1. Ich habe einen Bleistift.	Alexia
2. Ich bin 21 Jahre alt.	Markus
3. Ich habe ein Wörterbuch.	
4. Es geht mir gut.	
5. Ich bin Amerikaner(in).	
6. Ich bin Student(in).	
7. Ich habe ein Heft.	
8. Ich habe viele Hausaufgaben.	

8 **Galgenmännchen** In small groups, play Hangman using the vocabulary you learned in **Lektion 1A** and **Lektion 1B**. For nouns, include the definite article. Give your partners a hint about each word. Answers will vary.

BEISPIEL

S1: Es ist eine Person/eine Sache / ein Ort /
ein Ausdruck (*expression*).
S2: Hat das Wort ein S?
S1: Nein. / Ja, das Wort hat zwei S.

8 Suggestion Tell students that letters of the alphabet are neuter.

Mein Wör|ter|buch

Throughout this book, you will be encouraged to keep a personalized dictionary. By associating words with images, examples of usage (**Gebrauch**), synonyms, and antonyms, you will create entries that are relevant to you, and you will be better able to retain these new words.

Add five words to your personalized dictionary related to the themes **Begrüßung und Abschied** and **In der Schule**.

Sehr erfreut.

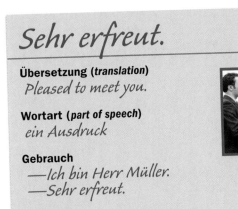

Übersetzung (translation)
Pleased to meet you.

Wortart (part of speech)
ein Ausdruck

Gebrauch
—Ich bin Herr Müller.
—Sehr erfreut.

Synonyme
Freut mich. / Angenehm. / Schön dich/Sie kennen zu lernen.

Antonyme
—

 **Vocabulary tools**

Panorama (S) Interactive Map

Die deutschsprachige Welt°

Länder° mit Deutsch als Amtssprache°

▶ Belgien
▶ Deutschland
▶ Italien (Region: Südtirol)
▶ Liechtenstein
▶ Luxemburg
▶ Österreich
▶ die Schweiz

Bevölkerung°

▶ **Belgien:** *10,4 Millionen Einwohner° (77.000 deutsche Muttersprachler°)*
▶ **Deutschland:** *81,1 Millionen Einwohner*
▶ **Italien:** *61,7 Millionen Einwohner (336.000 deutsche Muttersprachler)*
▶ **Liechtenstein:** *37.313 Einwohner*
▶ **Luxemburg:** *520.672 Einwohner (474.000 deutsche Muttersprachler)*
▶ **Österreich:** *8,2 Millionen Einwohner*
▶ **die Schweiz:** *8,1 Millionen Einwohner (4,8 Millionen deutsche Muttersprachler)*

QUELLE: das Haus der deutschen Sprache

Hauptstädte°

▶ **Belgien:** *Brüssel*
▶ **Deutschland:** *Berlin*
▶ **Liechtenstein:** *Vaduz*
▶ **Luxemburg:** *Luxemburg*
▶ **Österreich:** *Wien*
▶ **die Schweiz:** *Bern*

Wien, Österreichs Hauptstadt

Bern, Hauptstadt der Schweiz

Landesgrenzen
● **Stadt**
◉ **Landeshauptstadt**
✪ **Hauptstadt**

Unglaublich, aber wahr!

Belgien hat drei offizielle Sprachen°: Französisch, Niederländisch und Deutsch. Die deutschsprachige Region ist im Osten Belgiens. Circa° 76.000 Menschen leben° hier. Viele Belgier sprechen mindestens° zwei Sprachen.

deutschsprachige Welt *German-speaking world* **Länder** *countries*
Amtssprache *official language* **Bevölkerung** *population*
Einwohner *inhabitants* **Muttersprachler** *native speakers*
Hauptstädte *capitals* **Sprachen** *languages* **Circa** *Approximately*
leben *live* **mindestens** *at least*

Österreich

Die Alpen

Die Alpen sind das höchste Gebirge° in Europa. Es ist circa 1.200 Kilometer lang, und 29% sind in Österreich. Deshalb heißt Österreich auch die „Alpenrepublik". In Österreich leben circa 4 Millionen Menschen° in den Alpen. Das sind 50% aller Österreicher. Der höchste Berg° in Österreich ist der Großglockner. Er ist 3.798 Meter hoch.

Die Schweiz

Schokolade

Die Schweiz ist bekannt für Banken, Uhren, Messer° und natürlich° Schokolade. Die bekanntesten Schokoladenfirmen sind Lindt, Tobler, Sprüngli und Suchard. Suchard produziert Milka Schokolade. Vor allem die Schweizer essen Schokolade gern°. Pro Jahr isst° jeder Schweizer 11,7 Kilogramm Schokolade. Niemand° auf der Welt isst mehr Schokolade als° die Schweizer. In Deutschland isst man 11,4 Kilogramm Schokolade pro Person, in Österreich 7,9, und in den USA nur 5,2 Kilogramm.

Die Hanse Point out that the Hanse was the precursor to the European Union and one of the first international trade unions.

Geschichte

Die Hanse

Die Deutsche Hanse ist eine Union von Kaufleuten°. Sie existiert zwischen Mitte des 12. Jahrhunderts° und Mitte des 17. Jahrhunderts. Bis zu 200 Städte im nördlichen Europa sind in der Union, wie zum Beispiel Zuidersee (heutiges° Holland), Hamburg, Bremen und Lübeck (heutiges Deutschland), Stockholm (heutiges Schweden), Danzig (heutiges Polen) und Riga (heutiges Lettland°). Diese Städte liegen° vor allem an der Nordsee und der Ostsee°.

Die Berliner Mauer
Tell students that *3,40 Meter* is read out loud as **drei Meter vierzig**.

Deutschland

Die Berliner Mauer°

Vom 13. August 1961 bis 9. November 1989 ist die Berliner Mauer eine Grenze° zwischen° Ost- und Westberlin. Die Mauer umgibt° ganz Westberlin und kreiert eine Insel°. Sie ist das Symbol des Kalten Krieges°. Die Mauer ist 156,4 Kilometer lang. Sie ist zwischen 3,40 Meter und 4,20 Meter hoch. Rund um Westberlin stehen 302 Beobachtungstürme°.

höchste Gebirge *highest mountain range* **Menschen** *people* **Berg** *mountain* **Mauer** *Wall* **Grenze** *border* **zwischen** *between* **umgibt** *surrounds* **kreiert eine Insel** *creates an island* **des Kalten Krieges** *of the Cold War* **Beobachtungstürme** *watchtowers* **Messer** *knives* **natürlich** *of course* **essen... gern** *like to eat* **isst** *eats* **Niemand** *Nobody* **mehr... als** *more... than* **von Kaufleuten** *of merchants* **des 12. Jahrhunderts** *of the 12ᵗʰ century* **heutiges** *present-day* **Lettland** *Latvia* **liegen** *are located* **Ostsee** *Baltic Sea*
Die Berliner Mauer Tell students that the dates **13. August** and **9. November** are read out loud as **der dreizehnte August** and **der neunte November**. Explain that students will learn more about reading and writing dates in 2A.3.

IM INTERNET

1. Machen Sie eine Liste mit den wichtigsten (*most important*) Städten in Deutschland, Österreich und der Schweiz.

2. Der 9. November 1989 ist das Ende der Berliner Mauer. Suchen Sie (*Look for*) Informationen über diesen Tag.

Find out more at **vhlcentral.com**.

Was haben Sie gelernt? Complete the statements.

1. Belgien hat __drei__ offizielle Sprachen.

2. Die deutschsprachige Region ist im __Osten__ Belgiens.

3. Ein anderer (*other*) Name für Österreich ist die __Alpenrepublik__.

4. Der __Großglockner__ ist der höchste Berg in Österreich.

5. Die Berliner Mauer existiert von 1961 bis __1989__.

6. Die Berliner Mauer ist 156,4 __Kilometer__ lang.

7. Die Schweizer Firma Suchard produziert __Milka__ Schokolade.

8. Jeder __Schweizer__ isst 11,7 Kilogramm Schokolade pro Jahr.

9. Die Hanse existiert im __nördlichen__ Europa.

10. Bis zu __200__ Städte sind in der Hanse.

Lesen  Audio: Reading

Vor dem Lesen

Strategien

Recognizing cognates

Cognates are words in two or more languages that are similar in meaning and in spelling. Look for cognates to increase your comprehension when you read in German. However, watch out for false cognates. For example, you've already learned that in German, **Note** means *grade*, not *note*. Likewise, **bald** means *soon*, not *bald*, and **fast** means *almost*, not *fast*. Can you guess the meaning of these German words?

das Café	das Programm
der Doktor	das Restaurant
das Hotel	der Sommer
der Juli	das Telefon
das Museum	das Theater

Untersuchen Sie den Text

Look at this text. What kind of information does it present? Where do you usually find such information? Can you guess what this is?

Suchen Sie verwandte Wörter

Read the list of cognates in **Strategien** again. How many of them can you find in the reading? Do you see any additional cognates? Can you guess their English equivalents?

Raten Sie die Bedeutung

Besides using cognates and words you already know, you can also use context to guess the meaning of unfamiliar words. Find the following words in the reading and try to figure out what they mean. Compare your answers with a classmate's.

ägyptisch	Platz
Abakus	Straße

Adressbuch

Ägyptisches Museum

✉ **Residenzstraße 1**   📱 (089) 29 85 46
80333 München

Christian Hunner

✉ **Pfarrstraße 16**   📱 (089) 2 10 28 84
80667 München

Sparda-Bank

✉ **Arnulfstraße 15**   📱 (089) 5 51 42 – 4 00
80335 München

Heideck Apotheke°

✉ **Heideckstraße 31**   📱 (089) 1 57 52 52
80637 München

Il Galeone Ristorante Pizzeria

✉ **Hornsteinstraße 18**   📱 (089) 94 46 47 03
81679 München

Andreas Spitzauer

✉ **Appenzeller Straße 95**   📱 (089) 75 67 19
81475 München

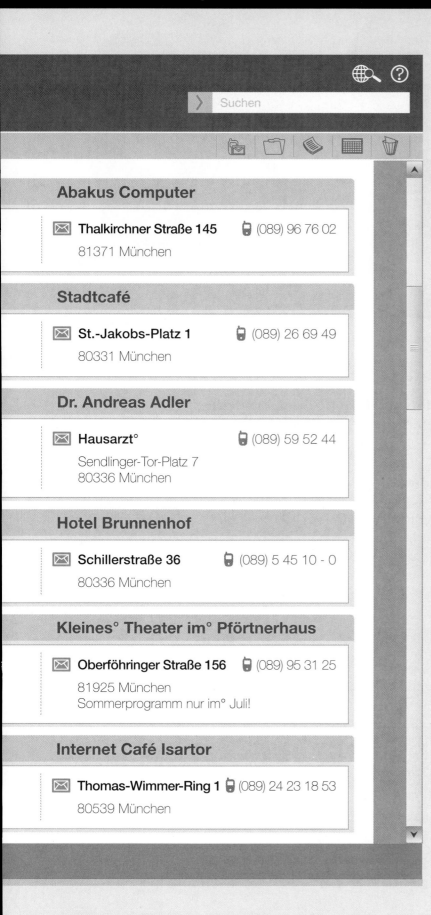

Abakus Computer

 Thalkirchner Straße 145 📱 (089) 96 76 02
81371 München

Stadtcafé

✉ **St.-Jakobs-Platz 1** 📱 (089) 26 69 49
80331 München

Dr. Andreas Adler

✉ **Hausarzt°** 📱 (089) 59 52 44
Sendlinger-Tor-Platz 7
80336 München

Hotel Brunnenhof

✉ **Schillerstraße 36** 📱 (089) 5 45 10 - 0
80336 München

Kleines° Theater im° Pförtnerhaus

✉ **Oberföhringer Straße 156** 📱 (089) 95 31 25
81925 München
Sommerprogramm nur im° Juli!

Internet Café Isartor

✉ **Thomas-Wimmer-Ring 1** 📱 (089) 24 23 18 53
80539 München

Apotheke pharmacy **Hausarzt** family physician **Kleines** Small **im** in (the) **nur im** only in (the)

Nach dem Lesen

Wohin gehen sie? Say where each of these people should go, based on the clues.

BEISPIEL Lena loves to eat pasta but hates to cook.
Il Galeone Ristorante Pizzeria

1. Frau Scholz needs to reserve some hotel rooms.
   Hotel Brunnenhof

2. Christiane's computer is broken.
   Abakus Computer

3. Herr Meier thinks he has the flu.
   Dr. Adler/Heideck Apotheke/Hausarzt

4. Nina would like to see some ancient Egyptian art.
   Ägyptisches Museum

5. Herr and Frau Hansel want to go somewhere for coffee or tea.
   Stadtcafé/Internet Café Isartor

6. Andrea is meeting some friends for Italian food.
   Il Galeone Ristorante Pizzeria

7. Frau Müller needs to buy some aspirin for her daughter.
   Heideck Apotheke

8. Thomas wants to take his girlfriend to a play.
   Kleines Theater im Pförtnerhaus

9. Herr Trüb needs to deposit his paycheck.
   Sparda-Bank

10. Sebastian's computer is broken, but he needs to send an e-mail.
    Internet Café Isartor/Abakus Computer

Unsere Einträge Select three listings from the reading and use them as models to create similar listings in German that advertise places or services in your area.

BEISPIEL

Stonydale Bank
Hunter Straße 206
50555 Stonydale
Tel. (555) 337-0665

Suggestion You may want to have students complete this activity in pairs.

Hören

Strategien

Listening for words you know

You can get the gist of a conversation by listening for words and phrases you already know.

 To help you practice this strategy, listen to these statements and make a list of the words you have already learned.

_____   _____

_____   _____

Vorbereitung

Where are the people in the photograph? What are they doing? Do you think they know each other? Why or why not? What do you think they are talking about?

Zuhören

As you listen, check the words you associate with Tanja and those you associate with Rainer.

Tanja

☑ der Taschenrechner

__ der Computer

☑ das Blatt Papier

☑ zwei Bleistifte

__ die Prüfung

Rainer

__ der Radiergummi

☑ die Hausaufgaben

__ das Heft

☑ das Problem

__ die Karte

Verständnis

 Richtig oder falsch? Based on the conversation you heard, indicate whether each statement is **richtig** or **falsch**.

1. Rainer ist Deutschprofessor.
   Falsch. _____

2. Tanja geht es gut.
   Richtig. _____

3. Rainer braucht (*needs*) einen Taschenrechner.
   Richtig. _____

4. Tanja hat ein Problem mit den Hausaufgaben.
   Falsch. _____

5. Rainer hat einen Bleistift für Tanja.
   Falsch. _____

6. Tanja hat ein Blatt Papier für Rainer.
   Richtig. _____

7. Tanja hat zwei Bleistifte.
   Richtig. _____

8. Rainer hilft (*helps*) Tanja bei den Hausaufgaben.
   Falsch. _____

 Stellen Sie sich vor! Introduce yourself in German to a classmate you do not know well.

- Greet your partner.
- Ask his or her name.
- Ask how he or she is doing.
- Introduce your partner to another student.
- Say good-bye.

Suggestion Students often gravitate towards other students they already know. Make sure to direct students to new partners.

Schreiben

Strategien

Writing in German

Writing can take many forms and serve many functions. You might write an e-mail to get in touch with someone, a blog entry to share your feelings or opinions, or an essay to persuade others to accept a point of view. Good writing requires time, thought, effort, and a lot of practice. Here are some tips to help you write more effectively in German.

DO

- Try to write your ideas in German.
- Decide what the purpose of your writing will be.
- Make an outline of your ideas.
- Use the grammar and vocabulary that you know.
- Use your textbook for examples of punctuation, style conventions, and expressions in German.
- Use your imagination and creativity to make your writing interesting.
- Put yourself in your reader's place to determine if your writing is interesting.

DON'T

- Don't translate your ideas from English to German.
- Don't simply repeat what is in the textbook or on a Web page.
- Don't use an online translator.
- Don't use a bilingual dictionary until you have learned how to use it effectively.

Strategien Emphasize the importance of outlining ideas in German, instead of translating from English. Encourage students to use the vocabulary and grammar they already know to complete this **Thema**.

Thema

 Machen Sie eine Liste

A group of German-speaking students will be spending a year at your school. Put together a list of people and places that might be useful or interesting to them. Your list should include:

- Your name, address, phone number(s), and e-mail address
- The names of two or three other students in your German class, their addresses, phone numbers, and e-mail addresses
- Your German instructor's name, office phone number, and e-mail address
- The names, addresses, and phone numbers of three places near your school where students like to go (a bookstore, a café or restaurant, a movie theater, etc.)

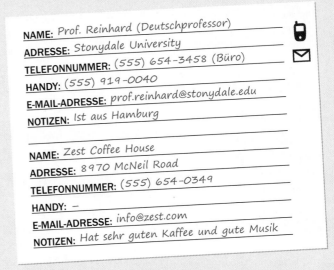

NAME: Prof. Reinhard (Deutschprofessor)
ADRESSE: Stonydale University
TELEFONNUMMER: (555) 654-3458 (Büro)
HANDY: (555) 919-0040
E-MAIL-ADRESSE: prof.reinhard@stonydale.edu
NOTIZEN: Ist aus Hamburg

NAME: Zest Coffee House
ADRESSE: 8970 McNeil Road
TELEFONNUMMER: (555) 654-0349
HANDY: –
E-MAIL-ADRESSE: info@zest.com
NOTIZEN: Hat sehr guten Kaffee und gute Musik

 Vocabulary Tools

Begrüßung und Abschied

Hallo./Guten Tag.	Hello.
Guten Morgen.	Good morning.
Guten Abend.	Good evening.
Gute Nacht.	Good night.
Bis bald./Bis gleich.	See you soon.
Bis dann./ Bis später.	See you later.
Bis morgen.	See you tomorrow.
Auf Wiedersehen.	Good-bye.
Schönen Tag noch!	Have a nice day!
Tschüss.	Bye.
Alles klar?	Is everything OK?
Wie geht's (dir)?	How are you? (inf.)
Wie geht es Ihnen?	How are you? (form.)
Prima.	Great.
Sehr gut.	Very well.
Ziemlich gut.	Fine.
Und dir/Ihnen?	And you?
Mir auch.	Me, too.
Es geht.	So-so.
(Nicht) schlecht.	(Not) bad.
Mir geht's (sehr) gut.	I'm (very) well.
Mir geht's nicht (so) gut.	I'm not (so) well.

sich vorstellen

Wie heißt du?	What is your name? (inf.)
Wie heißen Sie?	What is your name? (form.)
Und du/Sie?	And you? (inf./form.)
Das ist.../ Das sind...	This is.../ These are...
Ich heiße...	My name is...
Freut mich./ Angenehm.	Pleased to meet you.
Schön dich/Sie kennen zu lernen.	Nice to meet you. (inf./form.)

im Unterricht

das Blatt Papier, (pl. Blätter Papier)	sheet of paper
der Bleistift, -e	pencil
das Buch, ¨er	book
der Computer, -	computer
das Ergebnis, -se	result; score
das Fenster, -	window
das Foto, -s	photo
die Frage, -n	question
die Hausaufgabe, -n	homework
das Heft, -e	notebook
der Kalender, -	calendar
die Karte, -n	map
die Klasse, -n	class
das Klassenzimmer, -	classroom
der Kuli, -s	ball-point pen
das Lehrbuch, ¨er	(university) textbook
die Note, -n	grade (on an assignment)
die Notiz, -en	note
der Papierkorb, ¨e	wastebasket
das Problem, -e	problem
die Prüfung, -en	test; exam
der Radiergummi, -s	eraser
der Rucksack, ¨e	backpack
der Schreibtisch, -e	desk
die Sache, -n	thing
das Schulbuch, ¨er	(K–12) textbook
der Stift, -e	pen
der Stuhl, ¨e	chair
die Stunde, -n	lesson
die Tafel, -n	(black/white) board
der Taschenrechner, -	calculator
der Tisch, -e	table; desk
die Tür, -en	door
die Uhr, -en	clock
das Wörterbuch, ¨er	dictionary
das Zeugnis, -se	report card; grade report
Da ist/sind...	There is/are...
Ist/Sind...hier?	Is/Are there... here?
Hier ist/sind...	Here is/are...
Was ist das?	What is that?

Orte

die Schule, -n	school
die Universität, -en	university, college
die Bibliothek, -en	library
die Mensa, Mensen	(university) cafeteria
wo?	where?
hier	here
da / dort	there

Höflichkeiten

Danke.	Thank you.
Vielen Dank.	Thank you very much.
Bitte.	Please./ You're welcome.
Gern geschehen.	My pleasure.
Entschuldigung.	Excuse me.
Entschuldigen Sie.	Excuse me. (form.)
Es tut mir leid.	I'm sorry.
ja	yes
nein	no

Personen

die Frau, -en	woman
der Freund, -e / die Freundin, -nen	friend
der Junge, -n	boy
der Klassenkamerad, -en / die Klassenkameradin, -nen	(K-12) classmate
der Kommilitone, -n /die Kommilitonin, -nen	(university) classmate
der Lehrer, - / die Lehrerin, -nen	teacher
das Mädchen, -	girl
der Mann, ¨er	man
der Professor, -en / die Professorin, -nen	professor
der Schüler, - / die Schülerin, -nen	(K–12) student
der Student, -en / die Studentin, -nen	(university) student
Herr	Mr.
Frau	Mrs.; Ms.
Wer ist das?	Who is it?

Nouns and articles	See pp. 10-11.
Compound nouns	See p. 11.
Plurals	See p. 14.
Subject pronouns	See p. 16.
sein	See p. 17.
Nominative articles	See p. 17.
haben	See p. 30.
Accusative articles	See p. 30.
Yes-or-no questions	See p. 32.
Numbers and math expressions	See pp. 34–35.

Schule und Studium

Suggestion Ask students who the people in the
photo are, where they are, and what they are doing.

Kontext

Communicative Goals

You will learn how to:

- talk about classes
- ask questions
- tell time

Tell students that **an der Universität** means *at the university*. Point out that **der** is a feminine article in the dative case, and that the dative is used in certain phrases describing locations, including the expressions **in der Schule** (*at school*) and **im Unterricht** (*in class*) from **1B Kontext**. They will learn more about the dative case in **Lektion 4B**.

An der Universität

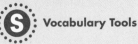
Vocabulary Tools

Suggestion Explain to students that the **Abschlusszeugnis** is a document similar to a transcript, itemizing the course credits required to obtain a degree, including grades and GPA.

Wortschatz

das Studium	*studies*	**Suggestion** Explain that a **Diplom** is one of the degrees awarded by universities, in addition to others such as the **Magister** and the **Staatsexamen**.
der Abschluss, ⁼e/ das Diplom, -e	*degree*	
das Abschlusszeugnis, -se/ das Diplom, -e	*diploma*	
der Dozent, -en / die Dozentin, -nen	*college/university instructor*	
das Fach, ⁼er	*subject*	
das Seminar, -e	*seminar*	
das Stipendium, -en	*scholarship*	
die Veranstaltung, -en	*class; course*	
die Vorlesung, -en	*lecture*	

belegen	*to take (a class)*
gehen	*to go*
lernen	*to study; to learn*
studieren	*to study; to major in*

Orte	*places*
das Café, -s	*café*
der Hörsaal, Hörsäle	*lecture hall*
der Seminarraum, -räume	*college classroom*
die Sporthalle, -n	*gym*

zum Beschreiben	*to describe*
einfach	*easy*
interessant	*interesting*
langweilig	*boring*
nützlich / nutzlos	*useful / useless*
schwierig	*difficult*

der Stundenplan	*schedule*
der Montag, -e	*Monday*
der Dienstag, -e	*Tuesday*
der Mittwoch, -e	*Wednesday*
der Donnerstag, -e	*Thursday*
der Freitag, -e	*Friday*
der Samstag, -e	*Saturday*
der Sonntag, -e	*Sunday*
die Stunde, -n	*hour*
die Woche, -n	*week*
das Wochenende, -n	*weekend*
die Zeit, -en	*time*

montags/dienstags/ mittwochs	*on Mondays/Tuesdays/ Wednesdays*
morgens	*in the morning*
nachmittags	*in the afternoon*
abends	*in the evening*

MEDIZIN

(die) Biologie

(die) Architektur

Ich studiere Physik (f.) und Chemie (f.).

Was studierst du?

(die) Kunst

(die) Mathematik

$E = MC^2$

$x = 2 + 2$ $3(x + 2)$ $(a - b)$

C++

(die) Informatik

Ressourcen

SAM WB: pp. 17–18

SAM LM: p. 11

vhlcentral.com

ACHTUNG

Don't use an article when talking about a school subject or sport, or identifying someone's profession.

Julian studiert Psychologie.
Julian is studying psychology.

Anna spielt Basketball.
Anna plays basketball.

Herr Fischer ist Dozent.
Mr. Fischer is a university teacher.

(die) Psychologie

(die) Fremdsprachen (f., pl.)

(die) Wirtschaft

(die) Geschichte

(die) Naturwissenschaften (f., pl.)

Suggestion Emphasize that **studieren** means *to study* in the sense of examining something or pursuing an academic subject, while **lernen** is used in the context of learning information or studying for a test.

Anwendung

Suggestion Explain that the term **Veranstaltungen** can refer to **Vorlesungen**, **Seminare**, or other scheduled events.

1 **Was passt zusammen?** Match related words in the two columns.

_f_ 1. der Computer	a. die Fremdsprache
_c_ 2. die Vorlesung	b. die Sporthalle
_d_ 3. die Biologie	c. der Hörsaal
_e_ 4. das Diplom	d. die Naturwissenschaft
_h_ 5. Montag, Dienstag, Mittwoch...	e. der Abschluss
_a_ 6. Deutsch	f. die Informatik
_g_ 7. Sigmund Freud	g. die Psychologie
_b_ 8. der Basketball	h. die Woche

2 **Das Unileben** Listen to the conversation between Hannah and Mehmet and indicate which classes each of them is taking this semester.

Veranstaltungen	Mehmet	Hannah
Mathematik	X	
Physik	X	
Chemie		
Geschichte	X	X
Literatur	X	X
Kunst	X	
Psychologie		X
Medizin		X
Informatik		

3 **Was fehlt?** Complete the sentences. Use each word once.

abends	Naturwissenschaften
Dozentin	Seminarraum
Fremdsprachen	Stipendium
Hörsaal	Wirtschaft

1. Die Vorlesung von Professor Huber ist im ___Hörsaal___ C.
2. Chemie, Physik und Biologie sind ___Naturwissenschaften___.
3. Frau Klein ist ___Dozentin___ an der Uni.
4. Für ein Studium in ___Wirtschaft/Naturwissenschaften___ ist Mathematik nützlich.
5. Spanisch, Italienisch und Chinesisch sind ___Fremdsprachen___.
6. Wir haben eine Veranstaltung in diesem (*this*) ___Seminarraum___.
7. Eva hat ein ___Stipendium___ und studiert in England.
8. Morgens und nachmittags gehen die Studenten in Seminare und Vorlesungen, und ___abends___ gehen sie in die Bibliothek.

 Practice more at **vhlcentral.com**.

Kommunikation

4 Auf dem Campus

Write a caption for each picture. Complete the sentences to say what each person is studying and add one sentence giving your opinion of each course. In pairs, take turns reading your sentences out of order. Your partner must decide which picture each sentence refers to. Sample answers are provided.

4 Suggestion Before students do this activity, you may want to have them preview the conjugation of **studieren**, taught in **2A.1**. Call on individual students and ask: **Was studierst du?**

▶ **BEISPIEL**

Max studiert __Informatik__.
__Informatik ist schwierig.__

1. Daniela studiert __Spanisch__.
Spanisch ist nützlich.

2. Björn studiert __Psychologie__.
Psychologie ist einfach.

3. Anna studiert __Chemie__.
Chemie ist nutzlos.

4. Mia und ich studieren __Architektur__.
Architektur ist interessant.

5 Ihr Studium

Indicate whether each statement is **richtig** or **falsch**, in your opinion. Then, compare your answers with a classmate's. Answers will vary.

BEISPIEL

S1: Chemie ist nützlich. Richtig oder falsch?
S2: Falsch. Chemie ist nutzlos.

	richtig	falsch
1. Mathematik ist schwierig.	☐	☐
2. Fremdsprachen sind nützlich.	☐	☐
3. Literatur ist interessant.	☐	☐
4. Ein Abschluss in Psychologie ist nutzlos.	☐	☐
5. Prüfungen in Geschichte sind einfach.	☐	☐
6. Ein Wirtschaftstudium ist langweilig.	☐	☐

6 Arbeitsblatt

Your instructor will give you a worksheet. Keep a record of your classmates' answers to share with the class.

BEISPIEL

S1: Ist Mathematik einfach oder schwierig?
S2: Mathematik ist schwierig, aber nützlich.

7 Diskutieren und kombinieren

Your instructor will give you and a partner different worksheets. Each worksheet includes part of Sarah's weekly schedule. In pairs, take turns asking each other questions to fill in the missing information and complete the schedule.

BEISPIEL

S1: Hat Sarah montags Chemie?
S2: Nein, sie hat mittwochs Chemie.
S1: Hat sie montags Geschichte?
S2: Ja, sie hat montagnachmittags Geschichte.
S1: Hat sie...?

5 Expansion Read the statements out loud and have students vote on whether each is **richtig** or **falsch**. Then have a class discussion about the results of the poll.

Aussprache und Rechtschreibung Audio

🎧 Consonant sounds

Although most German consonants sound very similar to their English counterparts, there are five letters that represent different sounds than they do in English: **g**, **j**, **v**, **w**, and initial **c**, which will be discussed in **Lektion 6B**.

The German letter **g** has three different pronunciations. At the end of a syllable or before a **t**, it is pronounced like the *k* in the English word *keep*. In the suffix **-ig**, the **g** is pronounced like the German **ch**. Otherwise, **g** is pronounced like the *g* in the English word *garden*.

Ta**g**	bele**g**t	schwieri**g**	**g**ehen	fra**g**en

The German letter **j** is pronounced very similarly to the letter *y* in the English word *young*. However, in a small number of loanwords from other languages, **j** may be pronounced like the *j* in *job* or the *g* in *mirage*.

jung	**J**anuar	**j**a	**j**obben	**J**ournal

The German letter **v** is pronounced like the *f* in the English word *fable*. In a few loanwords from other languages, **v** is pronounced like the *v* in the English word *vase*.

vier	**V**orlesung	**V**ase	Uni**v**ersität	**V**olleyball

The German letter **w** is pronounced like the *v* in the English word *vote*.

wissen	Mitt**w**och	**W**irtschaft	**W**ort	Sch**w**ester

Suggestion Tell students that the pronunciation of the final **-ig** sound has several regional variations.

Suggestion Have students look at the sample words and sentences on this page to identify cognates and words they already know. Tell students the meanings of any unfamiliar words or phrases.

1 **Aussprechen** Practice saying these words aloud.

1. Garten
2. Essig
3. Weg
4. Jahr
5. Journalist
6. joggen
7. Vater
8. verstehen
9. Violine
10. Wasser
11. zwischen
12. weil

2 **Nachsprechen** Practice saying these sentences aloud.

1. Wir wollen wissen, wie wir das wissen sollen.
2. In vier Wochen wird Veronikas Vater wieder in seiner Villa wohnen.
3. Gestern war Gregors zwanzigster Geburtstag.
4. Jeden Tag soll ich Gemüse und Grünzeug wie Salat essen.
5. Meine Schwester studiert Jura an der Universität Jena.
6. Viele Studenten jobben, um das Studium zu finanzieren.

3 **Sprichwörter** Practice reading these sayings aloud.

Es ist nicht alles Gold, was glänzt.[1]

Was ich nicht weiß, macht mich nicht heiß.[2]

[1] All that glitters is not gold.

[2] Ignorance is bliss. (lit. *What I don't know, doesn't bother me.*)

Ressourcen

SAM
LM: p. 12

vhlcentral.com

Fotoroman

Checkpoint Charlie Video

George und Hans reden über (*talk about*) das Studium und über Meline und Sabite. Ist Hans in Sabite verliebt (*in love*)?

Vorbereitung Have students look at scene 7 and try to guess what Hans is reacting to. After they have watched the video, have them review their predictions.

1

GEORGE Woher kommst du?
HANS Ich komme aus Straubing. Das ist in Bayern.
GEORGE Wie viele Menschen leben dort?
HANS Hmm... etwa 100.000.

2

HANS Woher kommst du?
GEORGE Milwaukee, Wisconsin.
HANS Wie viel Uhr ist es dort?
GEORGE Wie viel Uhr ist es hier?
HANS Es ist Viertel vor zwei.
GEORGE Der Zeitunterschied ist sieben Stunden. Also Viertel vor sieben morgens.

3

HANS Alles in Ordnung?
GEORGE Ich studiere Architektur, belege Kurse in Städtebau, Physik, Mathematik und Philosophie!

4

HANS Und du belegst einen Deutschkurs, nicht wahr? Studieren ist nicht leicht. George, du bist ein Mitbewohner und Freund. Ich helfe dir.
GEORGE Wann?
HANS Morgens. Um 5.00 Uhr!

5

GEORGE Hey! Wir sind da!
HANS Check...
GEORGE ...point Charlie.

GEORGE Sabite kommt aus Prenzlauer Berg. Und Meline?
HANS Was ist mit Meline?
GEORGE Woher kommt sie?
HANS Wien.

6

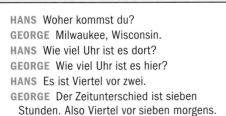

---

1 **Wer ist das?** Which character does each statement describe: George, Meline, Sabite, or Hans?

1. __George__ hält ein Referat über Architektur und Kunst.
2. __Meline__ kommt aus Wien.
3. __George__ belegt einen Deutschkurs.
4. __Hans__ kommt aus Straubing.
5. __George__ studiert Architektur.

6. __George__ ist Hans' Mitbewohner und Freund.
7. __Sabite__ liest Bücher über Kunst und Mode.
8. __Sabite__ kommt aus Prenzlauer Berg.
9. __George__ kommt aus Milwaukee.
10. __Hans__ hilft (*helps*) George morgens um 5.00 Uhr.

PERSONEN

George   Hans

HANS Sabite ist ganz anders. Sie liest Bücher über Kunst und Mode.

GEORGE Mode ist nutzlos. Ich halte am 20. Oktober ein Referat über Architektur und Kunst in Berlin. Sabite hilft mir.

HANS Was?

GEORGE Sabite studiert Kunst. Ich halte bald das Referat. Sie hilft mir.

GEORGE Alles in Ordnung, Hans?

HANS Ja, alles klar. Lernst du Philosophie mit Meline?

GEORGE Wo liegt das Problem?

HANS Was?

GEORGE Hans, findest du Sabite...

HANS Sabite ist nur eine Freundin.

GEORGE Okay.

HANS Also, ähm... hat Sabite einen Freund? Nein?

GEORGE Ich glaube nicht, dass sie einen hat.

HANS Du und Sabite, ihr seid nicht...?

GEORGE Nein!

HANS Okay.

GEORGE Okay.

Nützliche Ausdrücke

- **etwa**
  about
- **Wie viel Uhr ist es dort?**
  What time is it there?
- **der Zeitunterschied**
  time difference
- **Und du belegst einen Deutschkurs, nicht wahr?**
  And you're taking a German class, aren't you?
- **Ich helfe dir.**
  I'll help you.
- **Was ist mit Meline?**
  What's with Meline?
- **ein Referat halten**
  to give a presentation
- **Alles klar!**
  All right!
- **Wo liegt das Problem?**
  Where's the problem?
- **Sabite ist nur eine Freundin.**
  Sabite's just a friend.
- **Ich glaube nicht, dass sie einen hat.**
  I don't think she has one.

  2A.1
- **Sabite studiert Kunst.**
  Sabite is studying art.

  2A.2
- **Woher kommst du?**
  Where are you from?

  2A.3
- **Es ist Viertel vor zwei.**
  It's a quarter to two.

---

2 **Zum Besprechen** In this episode, the characters talk about their classes. With a partner, discuss your schedule and course load. Mention what you are studying, how many courses you are taking, and which courses you have in the morning, afternoon, or evenings.
Answers will vary.

S1: *Was studierst du?*
S2: *Ich studiere Fremdsprachen und Geschichte. Und du?*

3 **Vertiefung** George and Hans visit Checkpoint Charlie on their walk in Berlin. Find out more about this well-known landmark. What is its significance? What streets are nearby? What does "Charlie" refer to?
Sample answers: It was the main crossing point of the Berlin Wall; it is located at the junction of Friedrichstraße, Zimmerstraße, and Mauerstraße; "Charlie" comes from the letter C in the NATO phonetic alphabet.

Ressourcen

SAM
VM: p. 3   vhlcentral.com

Uni-Zeit, Büffel-Zeit°  Reading

HISTORICALLY, UNIVERSITY EDUCATION in Germany has been government-funded and free for all students. In the past few decades, some states introduced modest tuition fees—usually 500 Euros per semester. However, the fees proved so unpopular that they have since been abolished. As of October 2014, all public universities are again tuition-free, even for foreign students.

Apart from cost, there are other significant differences between German and American university life. German universities typically offer only a limited amount of dormitory housing. Most students live off campus, either commuting from home or renting an apartment shared with other students. Unlike in most American Universities, students must decide on a major before they begin their studies, and there is little flexibility in the choice of courses.

In the past few decades, there has been an initiative to standardize degree requirements between countries. Part of this restructuring has included a push to transition from 4- to 6-year **Diplom** and **Magister**° degrees to 3-year **Bachelor** degrees. This change has met with resistance from students, including complaints that it simply compresses the original curriculum into a shorter time frame. Many students also object to the shift toward a heavier workload with more frequent testing.

The percentage of students studying at private universities remains very small, but it is gradually increasing. Whereas public universities have had problems with over-crowding, private institutions can offer smaller class sizes, giving students more contact with professors.

Statistische Informationen zum Thema Studium	
Neue Studenten pro Jahr°	ca. 1.000.000
Studenten, die nach dem° Bachelor weiter studieren°	78%
Bachelor-Studenten, die zum Studieren ins Ausland gehen°	15%
Bachelor-Absolventen°, die 1,5 Jahre nach dem Abschluss Arbeit° haben	ca. 97%

QUELLE: Der Tagesspiegel

Büffel-Zeit *cramming time* **Diplom, Magister** *degrees available before the education reform* **pro Jahr** *per year* **die nach dem** *who after the* **weiter studieren** *continue their studies* **ins Ausland gehen** *go abroad* **Absolventen** *graduates* **Arbeit** *work*

1 **Richtig oder falsch?** Indicate whether each statement is **richtig** or **falsch**. Correct the false statements.

1. The majority of universities in Germany are public. Richtig.

2. German universities have always charged tuition fees.
   Falsch. Historically, German universities have not charged tuition fees.

3. Students in Germany have accepted reforms in education wholeheartedly.
   Falsch. There has been resistance from some students.

4. It takes more time to earn a **Bachelor**'s degree than it did to earn the **Magister** or the **Diplom**. Falsch. It takes less time.

5. Students now have a lighter workload with fewer tests.
   Falsch. There has been a shift toward a heavier workload with more frequent tests.

6. A small percentage of students study at private universities. Richtig.

7. Private and public universities charge the same tuition fees.
   Falsch. Private universities charge tuition, but public universities are free.

8. The majority of German students leave school after completing their Bachelor degree. Falsch. The majority of students continue their studies.

9. Most German students study abroad. Falsch. 15% go abroad.

10. In Germany, most students live in dormitories. Falsch. Most students live off campus.

 Practice more at **vhlcentral.com.**

DEUTSCH IM ALLTAG

Die Uni

der Besserwisser, -	know-it-all
der Mitbewohner, - / die Mitbewohnerin, -nen	roommate
das Referat, -e	presentation
das Schwarze Brett	bulletin board
das Studentenwohnheim, -e	dormitory
die Studiengebühr, -en	tuition fee
büffeln	to cram (for a test)

DIE DEUTSCHSPRACHIGE WELT

Der Bologna-Prozess

Die Bildungsminister° der Europäischen Union treffen sich erstmals° 1999 in Bologna in Italien. Das Ziel°: international einheitliche° Universitäts-Abschlüsse in ganz Europa und hohe° Mobilität für Studenten. In Europa müssen° Universitäten die Hochschulbildung° standardisieren. Bis zum° Jahre 2010 will man einen gemeinsamen° europäischen Hochschulraum° entwickeln°. Er wird im März 2010 in Budapest und Wien offiziell eröffnet°. 47 Mitgliedsländer° nehmen daran teil°.

Bildungsminister *secretaries of education* **treffen... erstmals** *meet for the first time* **Ziel** *goal* **einheitliche** *standardized* **hohe** *high* **müssen** *must* **Hochschulbildung** *higher education* **Bis zum** *Until* **gemeinsam** *common* **Hochschulraum** *Higher Education Area* **entwickeln** *develop* **eröffnet** *opened* **Mitgliedsländer** *member countries* **nehmen... teil** *participate*

PORTRÄT

Suggestion Tell students that Paracelsus is famous for his statement: "**Alle Ding' sind Gift, und nichts ohn' Gift; allein die Dosis macht, daß ein Ding kein Gift ist.**" This is often paraphrased in English as "The dose makes the poison", a central principle of toxicology.

Uni Basel

Universität Basel (gegründet° 1460): Viele brillante Wissenschaftler° belegen hier Vorlesungen und machen ihren° Abschluss in Medizin, Philosophie oder Psychologie. Der exzentrische Paracelsus (1493-1541) ist hier Professor für Medizin. Auch Holbein (1497-1543), Jung (1875-1961) und Hesse (1877-1962) leben° in Basel. Aber der berühmteste° Professor hier ist der Philosoph Friedrich Nietzsche (1844-1900).

Heute ist die Universität in Basel voller Leben° und sehr modern. Mehr als 13.000 Studenten sind hier. Viele studieren Biowissenschaften°. Andere° lernen Literatur, Wirtschaft oder Mathematik – für 850 Schweizer Franken im Semester.

gegründet *founded* **Wissenschaftler** *scientists* **machen ihren** *make their* **leben** *live* **berühmteste** *most famous* **voller Leben** *full of life* **Biowissenschaften** *life sciences* **Andere** *Others*

☁ IM INTERNET

Österreichische Universitäten. Wie ist das Studium in Österreich? Ist es mit dem (*with the*) deutschem System vergleichbar (*comparable*)?

Find out more at **vhlcentral.com**.

Expansion Have students search online for more information about the people mentioned in this article, as well as other famous intellectuals from Basel. Have them share their findings with the class.

2 **Was fehlt?** Complete the sentences.

1. Nach der Bologna-Erklärung müssen viele Länder in Europa die Hochschulbildung _standardisieren_.

2. Der Bologna-Prozess hat als Ziel international einheitliche _(Universitäts-)Abschlüsse_.

3. Heute lernen Studenten in Basel _Biowissenschaften_, Literatur, Wirtschaft oder Mathematik.

4. Der berühmteste Professor der Universität Basel ist _(Friedrich) Nietzsche_.

3 **Studentenleben** In pairs, discuss the similarities and differences between student life in German-speaking countries and in the United States. Would you like to study in a German-speaking country? Which system do you think is best? Give reasons for your answers.
Answers will vary.

3 **Suggestion** Ask students what they like and dislike about their college experience. Is tuition too high? Is the workload too heavy? Can they imagine studying the same amount of material in three years?

Ressourcen

vhlcentral.com

2A.1 Regular verbs  Presentation

Startblock Most German verbs follow predictable conjugation patterns in which a set of endings is added to the verb stem.

Ich **studiere** Architektur.

Lernst du Philosophie mit Meline?

QUERVERWEIS

In **Kapitel 1**, you learned the irregular verbs **sein** and **haben**. You will learn more about irregular verbs in **2B.1**.

ACHTUNG

Depending on the context, **sie studiert** can be translated as *she studies, she is studying,* or *she does study.*

- To form the present tense of a regular verb, drop the **-en** or **-n** ending from the infinitive and add **-e, -st, -t,** or **-en/-n** to the stem.

	studieren (to study)		wandern (to hike)	
ich	studiere	*I study*	wandere	*I hike*
du	studierst	*you study*	wanderst	*you hike*
Sie	studieren	*you study*	wandern	*you hike*
er/sie/es	studiert	*he/she studies*	wandert	*he/she hikes*
wir	studieren	*we study*	wandern	*we hike*
ihr	studiert	*you study*	wandert	*you hike*
Sie	studieren	*you study*	wandern	*you hike*
sie	studieren	*they study*	wandern	*they hike*

Studierst du Physik?
Are you studying physics?

Sie wandern im Sommer.
They go hiking in the summer.

- Regular verbs whose stems end in **-d** or **-t** add an **e** before the endings **-st** or **-t** for ease of pronunciation.

arbeiten (to work)			
ich arbeite	*I work*	wir arbeiten	*we work*
du arbeitest	*you work*	ihr arbeitet	*you work*
Sie arbeiten	*you work*	Sie arbeiten	*you work*
er/sie/es arbeitet	*he/she/it works*	sie arbeiten	*they work*

Suggestion Tell students that infinitives consist of a stem and an ending. Reinforce this idea by writing infinitives on the board and modeling the conjugation patterns. Ask students to identify the stem of each verb.

Lena **arbeitet** in München.
Lena works in Munich.

Findest du Mathematik interessant?
Do you find math interesting?

QUERVERWEIS

As in English, the simple present can sometimes be used to talk about a future action. You will learn more about this usage in **2B.2**.

Wartet ihr auf eure Freunde?
Are you waiting for your friends?

Die Hefte **kosten** zu viel.
The notebooks cost too much.

- Verbs whose stems end in **-gn** or **-fn** also add an **-e** before the endings **-st** and **-t**.

  Es regnet morgen.
  It's going to rain tomorrow.

  Öffnest du das Fenster?
  Are you opening the window?

- If a verb stem ends in **-s**, **-ß**, **-x**, or **-z**, the **-s** is dropped from the second person singular ending.

ACHTUNG

Note that the **du**, **er/sie/es**, and **ihr** forms of **heißen** are identical.

heißen (*to be named*)			
ich heiße	*I am named*	wir heißen	*we are named*
du heißt	*you are named*	ihr heißt	*you are named*
Sie heißen	*you are named*	Sie heißen	*you are named*
er/sie/es heißt	*he/she/it is named*	sie heißen	*they are named*

Du heißt Jonas, nicht wahr?
Your name is Jonas, right?

Mein Hund **heißt** Fritz.
My dog's name is Fritz.

Martin **reist** oft in die Schweiz.
Martin often travels to Switzerland.

Ihr **grüßt** den Professor nicht?
You're not going to greet the professor?

Suggestion Remind students that new verbs are also vocabulary items. Tell students that they should be able to recognize these verbs in all of their present-tense forms, but they will learn more about how to use them in later units.

QUERVERWEIS

Some verbs, including **bringen**, **finden**, **gehen**, and **schreiben** are regular in the present tense and irregular in the past tense.

You will learn more about past tense forms in **5A.1**, **5B.1**, and **6A.1**.

common regular verbs (present tense)			
antworten	*to answer*	leben	*to live*
bauen	*to build*	lernen	*to learn; to study*
bedeuten	*to mean*	lieben	*to love*
begrüßen	*to greet*	machen	*to do; to make*
belegen	*to take (a class)*	öffnen	*to open*
brauchen	*to need*	regnen	*to rain*
bringen	*to bring*	reisen	*to travel*
finden	*to find*	sagen	*to say*
fragen	*to ask*	schreiben	*to write*
gehen	*to go*	spielen	*to play*
hören	*to hear; to listen to*	suchen	*to look for*
kaufen	*to buy*	verstehen	*to understand*
kommen	*to come*	warten	*to wait*
korrigieren	*to correct*	wiederholen	*to repeat*
kosten	*to cost*	wohnen	*to live (somewhere)*

Kaufst du Kaffee im Supermarkt?
Do you buy coffee at the supermarket?

Was **bedeutet** das auf Englisch?
What does that mean in English?

Ich **lerne** Deutsch.
I'm learning German.

Wir **belegen** Biologie.
We're taking Biology.

Ressourcen

SAM
WB: pp. 19-20

SAM
LM: p. 13

(S)

vhlcentral.com

Jetzt sind Sie dran! **Write the appropriate form of the verb.**

1. Wir ___lernen___ (lernen) Deutsch.

2. Der Student ___wiederholt___ (wiederholen) den Satz (*sentence*).

3. Ich ___warte___ (warten) auf den Bus.

4. Die Lehrerin ___korrigiert___ (korrigieren) die Prüfungen.

5. Du ___belegst___ (belegen) fünf Veranstaltungen.

6. Das Universitätsstudium ___kostet___ (kosten) sehr viel.

7. Ihr ___versteht___ (verstehen) Mathematik.

8. Wir ___brauchen___ (brauchen) viel Papier und viele Bleistifte für den Unterricht.

9. Anja und Thomas ___begrüßen___ (begrüßen) den Dozenten.

10. Ich ___kaufe___ (kaufen) eine Tasse Kaffee in der Mensa.

11. Wir ___machen___ (machen) nachmittags Hausaufgaben.

12. Du ___öffnest___ (öffnen) die Tür.

Anwendung

1 **Was ist richtig?** Select the verb that best completes each sentence.

1. Astrid und Jonas (wohnen / bedeuten) in Berlin.
2. Michaela (sucht / korrigiert) den Seminarraum.
3. Ich (baue / studiere) Informatik und Mathematik.
4. Wir (belegen / grüßen) sehr viele Vorlesungen.
5. (Belegst / Lebst) du in Deutschland oder in Österreich?
6. Ihr (macht / kauft) nachmittags Hausaufgaben.
7. (Warten / Kosten) Sie auf (*for*) den Bus, Professor Meier?
8. Du (sagst / reist) im Sommer nach (*to*) Spanien und Italien.

2 Expansion Have students write their own dialogues about the courses they are taking.

2 **Was fehlt?** Maria and Tim are meeting for lunch. Complete their conversation with the correct verb forms.

MARIA Hallo, Tim! Wie (1) __geht__ (gehen) es dir? Wie ist das Deutschseminar?

TIM Ach, es geht mir ziemlich gut. Im Seminar (2) __schreibt__ (schreiben) der Dozent viel an die Tafel, aber ich (3) __verstehe__ (verstehen) es gut. Und du? Wie (4) __findest__ (finden) du das Informatikseminar?

MARIA Ich (5) __liebe__ (lieben) Informatik! Wir (6) __bauen__ (bauen) heute einen Computer.

TIM Vielleicht (*Maybe*) (7) __belege__ (belegen) ich nächstes Semester auch Informatik. (8) __Machst__ (Machen) du viele Hausaufgaben?

MARIA Ja! Samstags und sonntags (9) __lerne__ (lernen) ich immer (*always*).

TIM Oje. Samstags und sonntags (10) __spielen__ (spielen) Max und ich Computer.

3 **Schreiben** Write complete sentences using the cues.

1. ich / kaufen / einen Apfel   Ich kaufe einen Apfel.
2. David / brauchen / das Wörterbuch   David braucht das Wörterbuch.
3. du / arbeiten / freitags und samstags   Du arbeitest freitags und samstags.
4. Lara / suchen / das Deutschbuch   Lara sucht das Deutschbuch.
5. Josef und ich / spielen / Basketball   Josef und ich spielen Basketball.
6. lernen / ihr / Spanisch / ?   Lernt ihr Spanisch?
7. der Dozent / wiederholen / das Experiment   Der Dozent wiederholt das Experiment.
8. Hans und Jana / leben / in Irland   Hans und Jana leben in Irland.
9. regnen / es / ?   Regnet es?
10. öffnen / du / das Fenster / ?   Öffnest du das Fenster?

*Practice more at **vhlcentral.com**.*

Kommunikation

4 **Was fehlt?** Complete the sentences, and then, with a partner, take turns asking and explaining what each person is doing.

▶ **BEISPIEL**

Du ___hörst___ Musik.
S1: *Was mache ich?*
S2: *Du hörst Musik.*

1. Herr Becker ___arbeitet___.

2. Wir ___spielen___ Tennis.

3. Ihr ___lernt___ viel.

4. Ich ___kaufe___ ein neues Fahrrad.

5. Heinrich ___begrüßt___ den Mann.

6. Hans ___liebt___ Emma.

5 **Bilden Sie Sätze** In pairs, use items from each column to create six sentences. You may use some items more than once. Answers will vary.

BEISPIEL *Ich höre Musik.*

A	B	C
ich	hören	Deutsch
du	lernen	Hausaufgaben
Alena	lieben	Kunst
Anna und ich	machen	Musik
ihr	spielen	Naturwissenschaft
die Studenten	verstehen	Tennis

6 **Persönliche Fragen** In pairs, take turns asking and answering the questions. Answers will vary.

1. Wie viele Kurse belegst du?
2. Lernst du Fremdsprachen?
3. Gehst du oft in die Sporthalle?

4. Was machst du morgens?
5. Was machst du nachmittags?
6. Was machst du abends?

6 Expansion Have students write a paragraph about themselves, including their name, age, major, and class schedule.

7 **Gespräch** In pairs, fill in Student 2's half of the dialogue, then continue the conversation with your partner using at least four more regular verbs. Answers will vary.

S1: Hallo! Studierst du hier an der Uni?
S2: …
S1: Ich auch! Was studierst du?
S2: …
S1: Ist Wirtschaft schwierig?
S2: …
S1: Montags und mittwochs habe ich Geschichte. Und du?
S2: …

2A.2 | **Interrogative words**  Presentation

Startblock Use interrogative words to ask for information.

Wie viele Menschen leben dort?

Was ist mit Meline?

Suggestion Ask students additional questions using interrogatives from the list, and have students answer. Ex.: **Was ist das? Wer ist sie?**, etc.

interrogatives			
wann?	*when?*	**wie?**	*how?*
warum?	*why?*	**wie viel(e)?**	*how much/many?*
was?	*what?*	**wo?**	*where?*
welcher/welche/welches?	*which?*	**woher?**	*where (from)?*
wer/wen?	*who/whom?*	**wohin?**	*where (to)?*

- To ask an information question (one that cannot be answered with **ja** or **nein**), begin the question with an interrogative word.

Wann beginnen wir?	**Warum** machst du das?	**Wo** ist Frau Schultz?
When do we start?	*Why are you doing that?*	*Where is Mrs. Schultz?*

- Use **wer** when the person you're asking about is the grammatical subject of the verb and **wen** when the person is the direct object of the verb.

Wer begrüßt den Professor?	**Wen** begrüßt der Professor?
Who is greeting the professor?	*Who(m) is the professor greeting?*

- The form of **welcher** depends on the gender and number of the noun it modifies. Its three forms (**welcher/welche/welches**) have the same endings as the masculine, feminine/plural, and neuter forms of the definite article (**der/die/das**).

Welche Professorin lehrt Mathematik?	**Welcher Student** belegt Mathematik?
Which professor teaches mathematics?	*Which student is taking math?*

- Use **woher** to ask people where they are from and **wohin** to ask where they are going.

—**Woher** kommen Sie?	—**Wohin** geht ihr?
—Ich komme **aus Wien**.	—Wir gehen **in die Bibliothek**.
—*Where are you **from**?*	—*Where are you going?*
—*I'm **from Vienna**.*	—*We're going **to the library**.*

Jetzt sind Sie dran! | Select the appropriate interrogative for each question. | **Expansion** Have students take turns asking each other the questions and giving logical answers, where possible.

1. (Woher / Wer) kommst du?
2. (Wohin / Wann) haben wir Deutsch?
3. (Was / Wohin) reisen wir?
4. (Wer / Wo) braucht ein Blatt Papier?
5. (Welche / Woher) Seminare sind einfach?
6. (Wer / Wen) liebst du?

Anwendung und Kommunikation

 1 Was fehlt? Complete each sentence with an appropriate interrogative word.

1. _____Wann/Wo_____ spielen wir Tennis?
2. _____Wann/Woher_____ kommt die Dozentin?
3. _____Was_____ kaufst du für das Studium?
4. _____Warum/Wann_____ brauchst du einen Computer?
5. ___Wo/Wann/Wie viel/Was___ lernst du?
6. _____Wie_____ alt bist du?
7. ___Welche/Wie viele___ Kurse belegst du?
8. _____Wie viel_____ Zeit haben wir abends?

 2 Schreiben Write questions using the cues. Pay attention to word order.

BEISPIEL Marie und Alex / woher / kommen
Woher kommen Marie und Alex?

1. der Hörsaal / wo / ist Wo ist der Hörsaal?
2. wie / die Deutschvorlesung / ist Wie ist die Deutschvorlesung?
3. gehen / wann / wir / in die Bibliothek Wann gehen wir in die Bibliothek?
4. einen Kuli / wer / braucht Wer braucht einen Kuli?
5. machst / was / du / samstags Was machst du samstags?
6. wohin / gehen / nachmittags / die Studenten Wohin gehen die Studenten nachmittags?
7. welches / belegt / Seminar / ihr Welches Seminar belegt ihr?
8. lernt / warum / Paul / so viel Warum lernt Paul so viel?

3 Fragen In pairs, write a question for each response. Sample answers are provided.

BEISPIEL Ich komme aus Wien.
Woher kommst du?

 1. Karl hat montags, mittwochs und freitags Vorlesungen. Wann hat Karl Vorlesungen?
 2. Die Universitätsbibliothek hat 3.726 Bücher. Wie viele Bücher hat die Universitätsbibliothek?
3. Das Seminar ist langweilig. Was ist langweilig?/Welches Seminar ist langweilig?
4. Das Heft kostet 3,50 €. Wie viel kostet das Heft?
5. Ich brauche das Buch *Siddhartha* für die Literaturvorlesung. Welches Buch brauchst du für die Literaturvorlesung?
6. Ich wohne in Berlin. Wo wohnst du?
7. Der Dozent wiederholt die Frage. Wer wiederholt die Frage?
8. Anna liebt Paul. Wen liebt Anna?

4 Interview Prepare six questions about college life using interrogative words. Then, survey your classmates. Answers will vary.

4 Expansion Have each group of students make a set of flashcards with interrogative pronouns. One student chooses a card and asks a question with the selected word to someone in the group. That person must answer the question and select the next card.

Practice more at **vhlcentral.com.**

2A.3

Talking about time and dates Presentation

Startblock Like English, German uses cardinal numbers (*one*, *two*, *three*) to tell time and ordinal numbers (*first*, *second*, *third*) to give dates.

Telling time

- To ask *What time is it?*, say **Wie spät ist es?** or **Wie viel Uhr ist es?**. To answer, say **Es ist** + [*hour*] + **Uhr** + [*minutes*].

Es ist ein Uhr./
Es ist eins.

Es ist zwei Uhr./
Es ist zwei.

Es ist zwölf Uhr./
Es ist Mittag/Mitternacht.

- Use **vor** and **nach** to indicate minutes before and after the hour. Use **Viertel vor** for *quarter to* and **Viertel nach** for *quarter past*. In these constructions, omit the word **Uhr**.

Es ist **Viertel vor** elf./
Es ist zehn Uhr fünfundvierzig.

Es ist **zwanzig nach** vier./
Es ist vier Uhr zwanzig.

- Use **halb** to mean *half an hour before*. Note that it is not equivalent to the English phrase *half past*.

Es ist **halb zehn**.
Es ist neun Uhr dreißig.

Es ist **halb sieben**.
Es ist sechs Uhr dreißig.

- Use the 24-hour clock when talking about train schedules, movie listings, and official timetables. Do not use the expressions **Viertel vor**, **Viertel nach**, or **halb** with the 24-hour clock.

  20.30 Uhr = zwanzig Uhr dreißig
  8:30 p.m.

  18.45 Uhr = achtzehn Uhr fünfundvierzig
  6:45 p.m.

- To specify the time at which an event or activity will take place, use **um** + [*time*].

  —**Um wie viel Uhr** beginnt der Film?
  —*What time* does the movie start?

  —**Um** sechzehn Uhr zehn.
  —*At four-ten p.m.*

Ordinal numbers

- The ordinal numbers (**die Ordinalzahlen**) from 1st to 19th are formed, with a few exceptions, by adding **-te** to the corresponding cardinal numbers. To form all other ordinals, add **-ste** to the cardinal forms. Use a period to indicate the abbreviated form of an ordinal number.

ordinal numbers

1.	erste	first	7.	siebte	seventh	19.	neunzehnte	nineteenth
2.	zweite	second	8.	achte	eighth	20.	zwanzigste	twentieth
3.	dritte	third	9.	neunte	ninth	31.	einunddreißigste	thirty-first
4.	vierte	fourth	10.	zehnte	tenth	55.	fünfundfünfzigste	fifty-fifth
5.	fünfte	fifth	11.	elfte	eleventh	100.	hundertste	hundredth
6.	sechste	sixth	12.	zwölfte	twelfth	1000.	tausendste	thousandth

der **erste** Dozent
the **first** instructor

die **zweite** Vorlesung
the **second** lecture

das **dritte** Fach
the **third** subject

Dates

die Monate (*months*)			
Januar	April	Juli	Oktober
Februar	Mai	August	November
März	Juni	September	Dezember

Januar ist der erste Monat.
January is the first month.

Dezember ist der zwölfte Monat.
December is the twelfth month.

- Answer the question **Der Wievielte ist heute?** (*What is the date today?*) with **Heute ist der** + [*ordinal number* (+ *month*)].

  Heute ist **der erste Mai**.
  *Today is **May first.***

  Heute ist **der einunddreißigste**.
  *Today is **the thirty-first**.*

  23. März 2010 ⟶ **23.3.2010**
  March 23rd, 2010 ⟶ *3/23/2010*

  7. Oktober 2014 ⟶ **7.10.2014**
  October 7th, 2014 ⟶ *10/7/2014*

- To specify the day on which an event or activity takes place, use **am** before the date, and add **-n** to the ordinal number. Use the question **Wann hast du Geburtstag?** to ask someone when their birthday is.

  Ich habe **am 7. (siebten) Juli** Geburtstag.
  *My birthday is **on July 7th**.*

  Am 1. (ersten) Januar beginnt das neue Jahr.
  *The new year begins **on January 1st**.*

- The pattern **am** + [*time expression*] is also used with days of the week.

  am Montag
  on Monday

  am Dienstag
  on Tuesday

  am Wochenende
  on the weekend

- Like English, German uses cardinal numbers to refer to a particular year.

  1895 = achtzehnhundertfünfundneunzig

  2016 = zweitausendsechzehn

QUERVERWEIS

To form the accusative of ordinal numbers, add **-n** before masculine nouns. The feminine and neuter forms do not change.

Du trinkst deinen zweiten Kaffee.
You're having your second coffee.

Ich antworte auf die dritte Frage.
I'm answering the third question.

You will learn more about nominative and accusative adjective endings in **3A.2**

ACHTUNG

In writing, the day also comes before the month. Remember that an ordinal number is indicated by putting a period after the number.

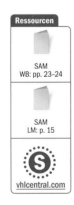

Ressourcen

SAM
WB: pp. 23–24

SAM
LM: p. 15

(S)
vhlcentral.com

Jetzt sind Sie dran!

Expansion Write some additional times and dates on the board and have students read them aloud.

Suggestion Show students this alternative question/answer pattern for recognition purposes only: **Den Wievielten haben wir heute? Heute haben wir den zweiundzwanzigsten Juni.** Point out the use of the accusative article and the **-n** added to the ordinal number.

A. Select the correct time.

1. **7:15 a.m.** Es ist (Viertel nach / Viertel vor) sieben.
2. **2:00 p.m.** Es ist zwei Uhr (morgens / nachmittags).
3. **10:30 a.m.** Es ist (halb zehn / halb elf) vormittags.
4. **12:00 p.m.** Es ist (Mittag / Mitternacht).
5. **7:55 a.m.** Es ist (acht / sieben) Uhr fünfundfünfzig.
6. **8:37 p.m.** Es ist (zwanzig Uhr / achtzehn Uhr) siebenunddreißig.

B. Write the correct date.

7. **14. Februar** Heute ist der ___vierzehnte___ Februar.
8. **28. Dezember** Heute ist der ___achtundzwanzigste___ Dezember.
9. **3. Juli** Heute ist der ___dritte___ Juli.
10. **30. Mai** Heute ist der ___dreißigste___ Mai.
11. **11. Oktober** Heute ist der ___elfte___ Oktober.
12. **7. August** Heute ist der ___siebte___ August.

Anwendung

1 Was ist richtig? Select the sentence that refers to the time shown.

1. **Es ist zwei Uhr.**/ Es ist drei Uhr.

2. **Es ist Viertel vor eins.**/ Es ist zwölf Uhr vierzig.

3. Es ist fünf Uhr zwanzig. / **Es ist zehn vor drei.**

4. **Es ist zwei Uhr fünfundvierzig.**/ Es ist Viertel vor zwei.

2 Wie spät ist es? Write a sentence indicating the time shown on each clock or watch.

▶ **BEISPIEL**
Es ist Viertel nach vier.

p.m.

1. Es ist halb eins. / Es ist zwölf Uhr dreißig.

2. Es ist ein Uhr. / Es ist eins.

p.m.

3. Es ist Viertel nach fünf. / Es ist siebzehn Uhr fünfzehn.

p.m.

4. Es ist zehn nach acht. / Es ist zwanzig Uhr zehn.

a.m.

5. Es ist halb sechs. / Es ist fünf Uhr dreißig.

a.m.

6. Es ist Viertel vor elf. / Es ist zehn Uhr fünfundvierzig.

7. Es ist zwölf nach zwei. / Es ist vierzehn Uhr zwölf.

a.m.

8. Es ist fünf nach sieben. / Es ist sieben Uhr fünf.

p.m.

9. Es ist fünf vor vier. / Es ist drei Uhr fünfundfünfzig.

10. Es ist fünfundzwanzig vor Mittag. / Es ist fünfundzwanzig vor zwölf. / Es ist elf Uhr fünfunddreißig.

3 Suggestion Reinforce the difference between **am elften Oktober** and **der elfte Oktober**. Ex.: **Am elften Oktober haben Sie eine Prüfung. Der elfte Oktober ist ein Samstag.**

3 Wer hat Geburtstag? Write out the date indicated to say when each person's birthday is.

BEISPIEL Angela Merkel hat am (17.) _siebzehnten_ Juli Geburtstag.

1. Arnold Schwarzenegger hat am (30.) ___dreißigsten___ Juli Geburtstag.

2. Heidi Klum hat am (1.) ___ersten___ Juni Geburtstag.

3. Karl Lagerfeld hat am (10.) ___zehnten___ September Geburtstag.

4. Michael Fassbender hat am (2.) ___zweiten___ April Geburtstag.

5. Die Tennisspielerin Steffi Graf hat am (14.) ___vierzehnten___ Juni Geburtstag.

6. Der Fußballspieler Mesut Özil hat am (15.) ___fünfzehnten___ Oktober Geburtstag.

7. Die Musikerin Nena hat am (24.) ___vierundzwanzigsten___ März Geburtstag.

8. Der Musiker Herbert Grönemeyer hat am (12.) ___zwölften___ April Geburtstag.

9. Der Schauspieler (actor) Christoph Waltz hat am (4.) ___vierten___ Oktober Geburtstag.

10. Die Schauspielerin Sibel Kekilli hat am (16.) ___sechzehnten___ Juni Geburtstag.

 Practice more at **vhlcentral.com**.

Kommunikation

4 **Um wie viel Uhr...?** In pairs, look at the class schedule. Take turns asking and answering questions about the start times of classes. Answers will vary.

BEISPIEL

S1: Wann und um wie viel Uhr ist Literatur?
S2: Literatur ist dienstags und donnerstags um halb neun.

	Montag	Dienstag	Mittwoch	Donnerstag	Freitag
8.30		Literatur		Literatur	Chemie
9.25	Biologie	Biologie	Biologie		Chemie
10.20		Kunst		Kunst	
11.15	Informatik		Informatik		Informatik
12.10	Mathematik	Deutsch	Deutsch	Deutsch	Mathematik

4 Expansion Ask students to describe their own schedules. In pairs, have them take turns asking and answering questions about their own classes and activities.

5 **Der Wievielte ist heute?** In pairs, take turns pointing at different dates on the calendar and having your partner tell you the date. Answers will vary.

BEISPIEL

S1: Der Wievielte ist heute?
S2: Heute ist der dritte Oktober.

Oktober						
Montag	Dienstag	Mittwoch	Donnerstag	Freitag	Samstag	Sonntag
		1	2	3	4	5
6	7	8	9	10	11	12
13	14	15	16	17	18	19
20	21	22	23	24	25	26
27	28	29	30	31		

5 Expansion Bring an example of movie listings, TV schedules, or course schedules from a German university. In pairs, have students ask and answer questions about the schedules.

5 Suggestion Point out that on German calendars and schedules, **Montag** is listed as the first day of the week and **Sonntag** as the last.

6 **Geburtstage** Ask your classmates when their birthdays are. Find out whose birthday is closest to yours. Answers will vary.

BEISPIEL

S1: Wann hast du Geburtstag?
S2: Ich habe am siebten Dezember Geburtstag. Und wann hast du Geburtstag?
S1: Ich habe am neunten Oktober Geburtstag.

7 **Interview** In pairs, take turns asking and answering the questions. Answers will vary.

BEISPIEL

S1: Wann hast du Deutschvorlesung?
S2: Montags, mittwochs und freitags um Viertel nach elf. Und du?

1. Welcher Tag ist heute?
2. Wann hast du Geburtstag?
3. Wann gehst du in die Sporthalle?
4. Wie spät ist es?
5. Um wie viel Uhr gehst du in die Mensa?
6. Wann hast du Unterricht?

Wiederholung

4 Expansion Show a time zone map and ask what time it is in a given place. Ex.: **Wie viel Uhr ist es in Bangkok?**

1 Graffiti In small groups, take turns drawing items from the lesson vocabulary and guessing what they are.
Answers will vary.

BEISPIEL

S1: Ist das ein Diplom?
S2: Nein!
S3: Ist das ein Stipendium?
S2: Ja, richtig!

2 Verabredungen Take turns asking and answering questions using the cues and the images. Answers will vary.

▶ **BEISPIEL**

S1: Wohin reist du im Sommer?
S2: Ich reise nach Spanien.

reisen

1. gehen 2. lernen 3. kosten

4. kaufen 5. hören 6. begrüßen

3 Feste Ask your classmates on what day these holidays fall. Add three additional holidays. Answers will vary.

BEISPIEL Weihnachten (*Christmas*)

S1: Wann ist Weihnachten?
S2: Weihnachten ist am 25. Dezember.

3 Suggestion Provide students with a calendar to consult for this activity.

- Silvester (*New Year's Eve*)
- Neujahrstag (*New Year's Day*)
- Columbus-Tag
- Halloween
- Veteranentag
- Heiligabend (*Christmas Eve*)

3 Suggestion Tell students about the German celebrations of **Aprilscherz, der Tag der Arbeit, and Erntedankfest** and explain how they differ from their American equivalents.

4 Zeitzonen In pairs, take turns telling your partner what time it is in each North American city and asking what time it is in a German-speaking country. Answers will vary.

BEISPIEL

S1: In Pittsburgh ist es fünfzehn Uhr zwölf. Wie viel Uhr ist es in Österreich?
S2: In Österreich ist es einundzwanzig Uhr zwölf. In Calgary ist es halb vier. Wie viel Uhr ist es in Deutschland?

Uhrzeit in...	Uhrzeit in Deutschland / in Österreich / in der Schweiz
Pittsburgh, PA: 15.12	+ 6 Stunden
Calgary, AB: 3.30	+ 8 Stunden
Fairbanks, AK: 22.54	+ 11 Stunden
Ft. Stockton, TX: 11.45	+ 7 Stunden
Hope, BC: 15.28	+ 9 Stunden
London, ON: 3.09	+ 6 Stunden
Needles, CA: 12.30	+ 9 Stunden
Tifton, FL: 21.36	+ 6 Stunden
Winnipeg, MB: 20.15	+ 7 Stunden

5 Arbeitsblatt Your instructor will give you a worksheet. Talk with your classmates to figure out the starting lineup of a race.

5 Suggestion Make sure students understand that **der Wievielte** is the masculine form and **die Wievielte** is the feminine form.

BEISPIEL

S1: Der Wievielte bist du?
S2: Ich bin der vierzehnte. Die wievielte bist du?
S1: Ich bin die achte.
S1 schreibt: Ben ist der vierzehnte.
S2 schreibt: Sarah ist die achte.

6 Diskutieren und kombinieren You and your partner each have two schedules. One shows your activities. The other shows a partial list of your partner's activities, with one activity missing each day. Ask and answer questions to complete both schedules.

BEISPIEL

S1: Was machst du am Sonntag um neun Uhr morgens?
S2: Ich mache Hausaufgaben. Und was machst du am Freitag um vier Uhr nachmittags?
S1: Ich habe Yoga.

Zapping

S Video

TU Berlin

The **Technische Universität Berlin**, or **TU Berlin**, is a modern-looking institution with a long and impressive history. Founded in 1879, the **TU** is one of the biggest technical universities in Germany, and the only one in Berlin to offer an engineering degree (**Ingenieur-Abschluss**). The TU also has a larger percentage of international students (**Studenten aus dem Ausland**) than any other German university.

Suggestion After showing students the video, ask questions to facilitate comprehension. Ex.: What types of subjects do students study at the TU? What degrees are offered at the TU?

Vier Unis hat die Stadt zu bieten°. Die TU ist die zweitälteste°.

Nach vorn° präsentiert sie sich modern und sachlich°.

„Wir haben die Ideen° für die Zukunft°" heißt der Leitspruch°.

zu bieten *to offer* **zweitälteste** *second oldest* **Nach vorn** *From the front* **sachlich** *functional* **Ideen** *ideas* **Zukunft** *future* **Leitspruch** *motto*

 Verständnis Circle the correct answers.

1. What percentage of **TU** students come from abroad?
   a. 5   b. 10   c. 20   d. 30

2. Which of the following is *not* one of the key subjects (**Schwerpunkte**) offered by the **TU**?
   a. Mathematik   b. Architektur   c. Physik   d. Chemie

 Diskussion Discuss the following questions with a partner. Answers will vary.

1. In what ways is the **TU Berlin** similar to your school? How is it different?

2. Would you like to study at the **TU Berlin**? Why or why not?

Communicative Goals

You will learn how to:

- talk about sports
- talk about leisure activities

Remind students to omit the article when talking about a sport: **Stefan spielt Basketball.** Point out that **der Basketball** refers to the actual ball: **Julia kauft einen Basketball.**

Sport und Freizeit 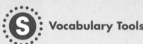 Vocabulary Tools

Wortschatz

Sportarten	*sports*
(der) (American) Football	football
(das) Golf	golf
(das) Hockey	hockey
(der) Volleyball	volleyball
das Schwimmbad, ̈er	swimming pool
das Spiel, -e	game
der Sport	sports
das Stadion, Stadien	stadium
Fahrrad fahren (fährt)	to ride a bicycle
Ski fahren	to ski
schwimmen	to swim
trainieren	to practice
Freizeitaktivitäten	*leisure activities*
der Berg, -e	mountain
das Fahrrad, ̈er	bicycle
die Freizeit	free time
das Hobby, -s	hobby
der Park, -s	park
der Strand, ̈e	beach
der Wald, ̈er	forest
angeln gehen	to go fishing
campen gehen	to go camping
essen gehen	to eat out
spazieren gehen	to go for a walk
klettern	to (rock) climb
kochen	to cook
(ein Pferd) reiten	to ride (a horse)
schreiben	to write
Spaß haben/machen	to have fun / to be fun
singen	to sing
tanzen	to dance
wandern	to hike

Suggestion Have students preview the conjugation of **fahren**, which will be covered in 2B.1. Explain that **fahren** is listed with its third-person singular form because it has a stem change in the present tense.

ACHTUNG

Infinitives can be used as nouns in German. **Freitags habe ich Schwimmen. Samstags habe ich Reiten.** Infinitives used as nouns are neuter.

die Spielerinnen (*sing.* die Spielerin)

Sie spielen Tennis (*n.*).

das Spielfeld, -er/ der Platz, ̈e

der Ball, ̈e

die Mannschaft, -en

der Spieler, -

Er spielt Fußball. (spielen)

Sie verliert nicht gern. (verlieren)

die Karten (*sing.* die Karte)

Er gewinnt. (gewinnen)

ACHTUNG

Use **gern** or **nicht gern** after a verb to say that you *like* or *don't like* doing something.

Lisa singt gern.
Lisa likes to sing.

Ich spiele nicht gern Tennis.
I don't like playing tennis.

You will learn more about the uses of **gern** in **Lektion 4A**.

Basketball (*m.*)

der Basketball

Sie spielen gern Schach (*n.*).

Baseball (*m.*)

Leichtathletik (*f.*)

Anwendung

1 Expansion Have students list additional words that could belong to each grouping.

1 Was passt nicht? Indicate the word that doesn't belong.

1. a. Basketball
   b. Schach
   c. Golf
   d. Tennis

2. **a. der Strand**
   b. der Spieler
   c. das Stadion
   d. der Platz

3. a. reiten
   b. schwimmen
   c. singen
   d. klettern

4. a. der Rucksack
   b. das Camping
   c. der Berg
   d. das Spielfeld

5. a. spazieren gehen
   b. kochen
   c. wandern
   d. reiten

6. a. die Freizeit
   b. die Schule
   c. die Aktivität
   d. das Hobby

2 Was fehlt? Complete the sentences with words from the list.

| Fußball | Schwimmbad | Spaß | spazieren | Tennisspielerinnen |

1. Serena und Venus Williams sind ___Tennisspielerinnen___.
2. Ski fahren macht im Winter viel ___Spaß___.
3. Wir schwimmen im ___Schwimmbad___.
4. Auf dem Spielfeld spielen wir ___Fußball___.
5. Im Park gehen wir ___spazieren___.

3 Zuordnen Write the activity that describes each picture.

Sample answers are provided.

▶ **BEISPIEL**

Leichtathletik trainieren

3 Expansion Ask students what they do in their free time. Ex.: **Spielen Sie Baseball oder Basketball? Fahren Sie Ski? Gehen Sie im Park spazieren?**

1. Ski fahren

2. campen gehen

3. Fahrrad fahren

4. Basketball spielen

4 Das Wochenende 🎧 Listen to the conversation between Lukas, Max, and Michaela, and indicate who will be doing each activity.

	Lukas	Max	Michaela
1. Tennis spielen		✓	
2. kochen			✓
3. lernen		✓	✓
4. tanzen		✓	✓
5. klettern	✓		
6. Videospiele spielen	✓		

Practice more at **vhlcentral.com**.

Kommunikation

---

5 **Berühmte Sportler** In pairs, match the athletes with the descriptions.

BEISPIEL

S1: Er spielt Fußball und kommt aus England.
S2: Es ist David Beckham.

  c   **1.** Er kommt aus der Schweiz und spielt Tennis.

  f   **2.** Er spielt Basketball.

  b   **3.** Sie ist eine Tennisspielerin aus Deutschland.

  d   **4.** Er schwimmt und hat viele olympische Medaillen (*medals*).

  a   **5.** Sie ist eine Skifahrerin aus Amerika.

  e   **6.** Er kommt aus Kalifornien und spielt Golf.

a. Lindsay Vonn
b. Steffi Graf
c. Roger Federer
d. Michael Phelps
e. Tiger Woods
f. LeBron James

5 Expansion Have students come up with their own prompts, real or fictitious. Ex.: **Sie ist groß und blond und sie spielt Gitarre und singt.** (Taylor Swift) **Er ist Hogwarts-Schüler.** (Harry Potter) **Sein Alter ego heißt „Slim Shady".** (Eminem)

---

6 **Machst du das gern?** In pairs, take turns telling each other whether you like or dislike each activity. Sample answers are provided.

BEISPIEL

S1: Ich schwimme gern. Und du?
S2: Ich schwimme auch gern. / Ich schwimme nicht gern.

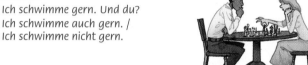

1. Ich spiele (nicht) gern Schach.

2. Ich tanze (nicht) gern.

3. Ich spiele (nicht) gern Fußball.

4. Ich reite (nicht) gern.

---

7 **Arbeitsblatt** Your instructor will give you a worksheet with information about activities. Ask your classmates what they like to do in their free time.

BEISPIEL Volleyball spielen

S1: Spielst du gern Volleyball?
S2: Ja. Ich spiele gern Volleyball./Nein. Ich spiele nicht gern Volleyball.

7 Suggestion Tell students to find at least one person for each activity.

angeln gehen	reiten	Fußball spielen
campen gehen	schwimmen	Schach spielen
kochen	singen	tanzen
spazieren gehen	Baseball spielen	Tennis trainieren
klettern	Basketball spielen	wandern

8 **Pantomime** Play charades in groups of four. Take turns acting out activities from the lesson vocabulary. The person who guesses the activity goes next. Answers will vary.

BEISPIEL

S1: Ist es Baseball?
S2: Nein.
S3: Ist es Tennis?
S2: Ja, es ist Tennis!

Aussprache und Rechtschreibung Audio

 Diphthongs: *au, ei/ai, eu/äu*

When one vowel sound glides into another vowel sound in the same syllable, the complex sound produced is called a diphthong. In German, this complex sound is said quickly and is not drawn out as it is in English. There are three diphthongs in German: **au**, **ei/ai**, and **eu/äu**.

faul	**aus**	**Leine**	**Mais**	**neun**	**täuschen**

The German diphthong written **au** begins with the vowel sound of the *o* in the English word *pod* and ends with a sound similar to the *oo* in the English word *loose*.

auf	**Frau**	**Bauch**	**Haus**	**auch**

The German diphthong written as **ei** or **ai** is pronounced very similarly to the *i* in the English word *time*. Remember that the German **ie** is not a diphthong, but simply a way of writing the long **i** sound, as in the word **sieben**.

Freitag	**Zeit**	**Mai**	**Eis**	**schreiben**

The German diphthong written as **eu** or **äu** is pronounced very similarly to the *oi* in the English word *coin*.

Zeugnis	**Freund**	**Häuser**	**Europa**	**Deutsch**

 1 **Aussprechen** Practice saying these words aloud.

1. laufen
2. Kaufhaus
3. Rauch
4. Maus
5. mein
6. Wein
7. Mainz
8. reiten
9. treu
10. freuen
11. Leute
12. läuft

 2 **Nachsprechen** Practice saying these sentences aloud.

1. Die Mäuse laufen einfach im Zimmer herum.
2. Tausende Leute gehen an uns vorbei.
3. Am Freitag habe ich leider keine Zeit.
4. Paul macht eine Europareise mit Freunden.
5. Meine Frau kauft ein neues Haus außerhalb von Mainz.
6. Für den Sauerbraten brauchen wir Rotweinessig.

3 **Sprichwörter** Practice reading these sayings aloud.

Einem geschenkten Gaul schaut man nicht ins Maul.[2]

Schuster, bleib bei deinen Leisten.[1]

[1] Stick with what you know. (lit. Cobbler, stick with your shoe stretchers.)

[2] Don't look a gift horse in the mouth.

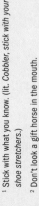

Ressourcen

SAM
LM: p. 17

vhlcentral.com

Ein Picknick im Park Video

George und Meline treffen Sabite und Torsten im Park. Sie sprechen über
Sport und ihre Hobbys. Kommt Meline Torsten zu nahe (*too close*)?

Vorbereitung Have students preview the images and
write down three questions they want to have answered
when they watch the video.

NATIONAL
communication
cultures
STANDARDS

TORSTEN Das Fußballspiel beginnt um
halb acht.
SABITE Es ist Viertel nach sechs. Niemand ist
hier. George kommt von der Uni.

TORSTEN Spielt er Fußball?
SABITE Er spielt Baseball in der Freizeit. Er ist
in einer Uni-Mannschaft.
TORSTEN Hat Meline Hobbys?
SABITE Sie fährt Ski und spielt Tennis. Sie
gewinnt alles.

GEORGE Oh, vielen Dank! Wo sind Hans
und Meline?
SABITE Meline kommt aus der Bibliothek. Hans
hat eine Vorlesung.
GEORGE Studierst du auch, Torsten?
TORSTEN Ja. Ich studiere Chemie und Biologie.

MELINE Ich bringe Dessert!
GEORGE Sabite, ich glaube, Hans...
MELINE Hans. Hallo, Torsten, nett dich kennen
zu lernen.
TORSTEN Gleichfalls, Meline.

MELINE Du studierst Medizin?
TORSTEN Biologie.
MELINE Fährst du Ski?
TORSTEN Nee, meine Familie fährt nicht
Ski. Aber ich wandere und klettere.

MELINE Ich komme aus Wien. Alle fahren
Ski in den österreichischen Alpen. Wir
haben viele Sportarten: Skifahren,
Klettern, Fahrradfahren, Golf und Tennis.
Spielst du auch Tennis?
SABITE Äh, Meline?
MELINE Hmmm?
SABITE Gehen wir spazieren.

1 **Was ist richtig?** Choose the words that best complete the sentences.

1. Torsten und Sabite sind (im Park / im Café).
2. George kommt (aus dem Stadion / von der Uni).
3. Meline fährt Ski und spielt (Golf / Tennis).
4. Torsten studiert Chemie und (Biologie / Physik).
5. Meline bringt (Kaffee / Dessert).

6. Alle fahren (Ski / Bob) in den österreichischen Alpen.
7. Sabite ist eifersüchtig auf (*jealous of*) (Meline / Torsten).
8. Meline trennt keine (Klassenkameraden / Paare).
9. (Frau Yilmaz / Herr Yilmaz) macht morgen Sauerbraten.
10. Hans weiß nicht, dass Sabite einen (Mitbewohner / Freund) hat.

Expansion Have students write simple sentences
with the words that were not chosen.

PERSONEN

Torsten

Sabite

George

Meline

SABITE Meline. Wir sind Mitbewohnerinnen. Freundinnen.
MELINE Und?
SABITE „Spielst du auch Tennis?"

MELINE Sabite. Keine Sorge. Ich trenne keine Paare.
SABITE Es ist okay, ich verstehe.

SABITE George, Meline, meine Mutter macht morgen Sauerbraten. Kommt ihr zum Abendessen?
MELINE Oh, danke, Sabite. Wir kommen.
TORSTEN Frau Yilmaz ist eine gute Köchin.
GEORGE Wow, vielen Dank. Und Hans?
SABITE Ich frage ihn.

MELINE Hans weiß nicht, dass Sabite einen Freund hat, oder?
GEORGE Er hat keine Ahnung.

Nützliche Ausdrücke

- **Niemand ist hier.**
  Nobody's here.

- **die Uni-Mannschaft**
  varsity team

- **Sie gewinnt alles.**
  She wins at everything.

- **glauben**
  to believe

- **aber**
  but

- **Alle fahren Ski in den österreichischen Alpen.**
  Everyone in the Austrian Alps skis.

- **Gehen wir spazieren.**
  Let's go for a walk.

- **Keine Sorge.**
  Don't worry.

- **das Abendessen**
  dinner

- **der Koch / die Köchin**
  cook

- **Hans weiß nicht, dass Sabite einen Freund hat, oder?**
  Hans doesn't know Sabite has a boyfriend, does he?

- **Er hat keine Ahnung.**
  He doesn't have a clue.

2B.1
- **Meine Familie fährt nicht Ski.**
  My family doesn't ski.

2B.2
- **Meine Mutter macht morgen Sauerbraten.**
  My mother is making sauerbraten tomorrow.

2B.3
- **Ich trenne keine Paare.**
  I wouldn't break up a couple.

---

2 **Zum Besprechen** In this episode, the characters talk about their favorite sports and pastimes. Interview your classmates to find out who shares your interests. Who likes the same sports? Who has the same hobbies? Answers will vary.

2 **Suggestion** Refer students to the script for scenes 3, 5, and 6 for model questions they can use to interview their classmates.

3 **Suggestion** Point out that the United States national soccer team has a German coach, Jürgen Klinsmann. Ask if any students saw the 2014 World Cup games, including the championship match between Germany and Argentina.

3 **Vertiefung** Fußball is one of the most popular sports in Germany. What is the name of the German national soccer league? Find the names of four prominent German soccer teams. Which team won last year's championship? (Fußball-)Bundesliga; Sample answers: FC Bayern München, VfL Wolfsburg, Bayer Leverkusen, Borussia Mönchengladbach; Answers will vary.

3 **Expansion** Have students research popular soccer players from Germany, Austria, and Switzerland and share their names with the class.

Ressourcen

SAM
VM: pp. 4

vhlcentral.com

IM FOKUS

Skifahren im Blut°  Reading

IN ALPINE VILLAGES, LEARNING TO SKI is like learning to walk. Almost everyone does it, starting at a very young age. The beginner slopes are full of preschool-aged children taking their first lessons. Skiing courses were required in Austrian schools until 1995, and many schools in Bavaria and Austria still offer **Skiwoche°**, a chaperoned week-long ski trip, as part of their curriculum.

Many of the world's best skiers come from German-speaking countries. Carina Vogt is a German **Skisprung-Weltmeisterin°** and **Olympiasiegerin°**.

Vogt won the first gold medal ever awarded for women's ski jumping at the 2014 Sochi Winter Olympic games, and in 2015 she won two World Cup gold medals for ski jumping, coming in third overall in women's events. In honor of her achievements, there is now a street named after her in her home town of Degenfeld in Baden-Württemberg.

Austrian Marcel Hirscher specializes in slalom and giant slalom. The son of two ski instructors, Hirscher has been skiing since age 2. In 2015, at the age of 26, he became the first **Weltmeister** ever to win the overall World Cup title for men's ski events four times in a row.

While the Alpine skiing tradition remains strong, environmental and economic sustainability have become major concerns. Ski tourism has had a serious impact on the ecology of the Alpine regions. With rising temperatures due to climate change, lack of snow is also becoming an issue. Snowmaking is expensive and uses vast amounts of water. And, while large ski resorts continue to draw visitors from all over the world, skiing is becoming less affordable for locals, with some smaller ski areas struggling to remain in business.

Blut *blood* **Skiwoche** *ski week* **Skisprung-Weltmeisterin** *ski jump world champion* **Olympiasiegerin** *Olympic gold medalist* **Jährliche Anzahl an** *Annual number of* **mehr als** *more than* **Einnahmen** *revenue* **Arbeitsplätze** *jobs* **Pistenfläche** *skiable area*

Österreich: Ski-Paradies	
Jährliche Anzahl an° Skitouristen	mehr als° 15,4 Millionen
Jährliche Einnahmen° durch Skifahren	mehr als 11 Milliarden Euro
Arbeitsplätze° im Skitourismus	312.625
Pistenfläche°	25.400 Hektar (254 km²)
Alpine Skiweltmeisterschaft 2015: Medaillen für Österreich	9 (5 Gold, 3 Silber, 1 Bronze)

QUELLE: Trend Wirtschaftsmagazin

ÜBUNGEN

1 Was fehlt? Complete the statements.

1. Austrian schools had mandatory ski classes until ___1995___.
2. In Bavaria and Austria, many school classes travel to the mountains for ___Skiwoche___.
3. ___Carina Vogt___ won the first ever Olympic gold medal for women's ski jumping.
4. Vogt won two ___World Cup___ gold medals in 2015.

5. There is a street named after Vogt in the town of ___Degenfeld___.
6. ___Marcel Hirscher___ started skiing at age 2.
7. Hirscher was the first ever four-time ___Weltmeister___ in men's ski events.
8. ___Snowmaking___ uses excessive quantities of water.
9. Ski tourism accounts for ___312,625___ jobs in Austria.
10. Austria won ___9___ medals in the 2015 Alpine Skiing World Championships.

Practice more at **vhlcentral.com.**

DEUTSCH IM ALLTAG

Mehr Freizeit

der Fan, -s	*fan*
die Meisterschaft, -en	*championship*
der Spielstand, ⁻e	*score*
das Tor, -e	*goal (in soccer, etc.)*
faulenzen	*to relax; to be lazy*
joggen	*to jog*
fit	*in good shape*
sportlich	*athletic*
Los!	*Start!; Go!*

DIE DEUTSCHSPRACHIGE WELT

Die Deutschen und das Fahrrad

In Deutschland hat man im Schnitt° 6 Stunden und 34 Minuten Freizeit am Tag. Populäre Hobbys der Deutschen sind Videospiele, Lesen und natürlich° Sport. Die Deutschen sind leidenschaftliche° Fahrradfahrer. Kilometerlange Radwege° durchkreuzen° das Land, wie etwa° die Romantische Straße° in Bayern: sie führt an Schlössern° und vielseitigen Landschaften° vorbei°.

im Schnitt *on average* **natürlich** *of course*
leidenschaftliche *passionate* **Radwege** *bike trails*
durchkreuzen *cross* **wie etwa** *such as* **Straße** *road*
Schlössern *castles* **vielseitigen Landschaften** *varied*
landscapes **führt an... vorbei** *leads past*
Suggestion Tell students that **die Romantische Straße** is
a road with an adjacent bike path that runs 350 km from Würzburg to Füssen.

PORTRÄT

Tooooooor!

Der talentierte und populäre Fußballer **Mesut Özil** spielt international für Deutschland. 2014 ist die deutsche Fußballnationalmannschaft in Brasilien bei der Weltmeisterschaft°. In allen sieben Spielen steht Mesut Özil in der Startelf°. Er erzielt° drei Tore und wird° mit der deutschen Nationalmannschaft Weltmeister. Özil ist Deutscher mit türkischer Abstammung° und kommt aus Gelsenkirchen. Er ist Moslem und betet vor jedem° Spiel. Man sagt, die Familie Özil ist ein gutes Beispiel für erfolgreiche° Integration von Ausländern° in Deutschland. Aber Özil spielt nicht nur° für deutsche Mannschaften. Seit° 2013 spielt er in England, für *Arsenal London*.

Weltmeisterschaft *World Cup* **Startelf** *starting line-up*
erzielt *scores* **wird** *becomes* **mit türkischer Abstammung**
of Turkish descent **betet vor jedem** *prays before every*
erfolgreiche *successful* **Ausländern** *foreigners*
nicht nur *not only* **Seit** *Since*

⟳ IM INTERNET

Wandern: Was sind beliebte Wanderwege° in der Schweiz?

beliebte Wanderwege *popular hiking trails*

Find out more at **vhlcentral.com**.

---

2 **Richtig oder falsch?** In pairs, correct the false statements.

	richtig	falsch
1. On average, Germans have more than six hours of leisure time per day.	☑	☐
2. Biking is a popular sport in Germany.	☑	☐
3. Mesut Özil played in six games in the 2014 World Cup. Özil played in seven games.	☐	☑
4. Mesut Özil grew up in Turkey. He grew up in the German town of Gelsenkirchen.	☐	☑

3 **Bekannte Sportler** In pairs, take turns role-playing famous athletes who play each of the sports listed. Your partner must guess who you are.

Answers will vary.

BEISPIEL

S1: *Ich spiele Fußball und komme aus Deutschland.*
S2: *Bist du Mesut Özil?*

1. Golf	4. Tennis
2. Baseball	5. Basketball
3. Schwimmen	6. Fußball

2B.1

Stem-changing verbs  Presentation

QUERVERWEIS

See **2A.1** to review the present-tense conjugations of regular verbs.

Startblock Certain irregular verbs follow predictable patterns of spelling changes in their present-tense conjugations. These verbs use the regular endings, but have changes to their stem vowels in the **du** and **er/sie/es** forms. Most stem-changing verbs follow one of four patterns in the present tense.

ACHTUNG

The formal **Sie** forms are the same as the plural **sie** forms for all verbs. Starting in this lesson, **Sie** and **sie** (*pl.*) forms will be listed together in verb tables.

- a ⟶ ä

schlafen (*to sleep*)			
ich schlafe	*I sleep*	wir schlafen	*we sleep*
du schläfst	*you sleep*	ihr schlaft	*you sleep*
er/sie/es schläft	*he/she/it sleeps*	Sie/sie schlafen	*you/they sleep*

Schläfst du jede Nacht acht Stunden?
***Do* you *sleep* eight hours every night?**

Sie **schlafen** im Studentenwohnheim.
*They **sleep** in the dormitory.*

- au ⟶ äu

laufen (*to run*)			
ich laufe	*I run*	wir laufen	*we run*
du läufst	*you run*	ihr lauft	*you run*
er/sie/es läuft	*he/she/it runs*	Sie/sie laufen	*you/they run*

Mehmet **läuft** am Strand.
*Mehmet **runs** on the beach.*

Sie **laufen** über das Spielfeld.
*They're **running** across the field.*

- e ⟶ i

	essen (*to eat*)		sprechen (*to speak*)	
ich	esse	*I eat*	spreche	*I speak*
du	isst	*you eat*	sprichst	*you speak*
er/sie/es	isst	*he/she/it eats*	spricht	*he/she/it speaks*
wir	essen	*we eat*	sprechen	*we speak*
ihr	esst	*you eat*	sprecht	*you speak*
Sie/sie	essen	*you/they eat*	sprechen	*you/they speak*

Wir **essen** in der Mensa.
*We're **eating** in the cafeteria.*

Sprichst du Englisch?
***Do* you *speak* English?**

- Besides an **e ⟶ i** vowel change, **nehmen** (*to take*) and **werden** (*to become*) have additional changes in the **du** and **er/sie/es** forms.

ACHTUNG

Remember: when the verb stem ends in **-s**, drop the **-s** from the second-person singular ending.

	nehmen (*to take*)		werden (*to become*)	
ich	nehme	*I take*	werde	*I become*
du	nimmst	*you take*	wirst	*you become*
er/sie/es	nimmt	*he/she/it takes*	wird	*he/she/it becomes*
wir	nehmen	*we take*	werden	*we become*
ihr	nehmt	*you take*	werdet	*you become*
Sie/sie	nehmen	*you/they take*	werden	*you/they become*

Du **nimmst** jeden Tag den Bus.
*You **take** the bus every day.*

Ein Anfänger **wird** mit der Zeit Experte.
*A beginner **becomes** an expert over time.*

- e ⟶ ie

lesen (*to read*)			sehen (*to see*)	
ich	lese	*I read*	sehe	*I see*
du	liest	*you read*	siehst	*you see*
er/sie/es	liest	*he/she/it reads*	sieht	*he/she/it sees*
wir	lesen	*we read*	sehen	*we see*
ihr	lest	*you read*	seht	*you see*
Sie/sie	lesen	*you/they read*	sehen	*you/they see*

Du **liest** viele Bücher.
*You **read** a lot of books.*

Seht ihr die Spieler?
*Do you **see** the players?*

- This table summarizes some common verbs with stem changes in the present tense. When a verb with a present-tense stem change is presented in this text, it will be listed with its third-person singular form: **lesen (liest)**.

common stem-changing verbs (present tense)			
a ⟶ ä		**e ⟶ i**	
braten	*to fry*	brechen	*to break*
fahren	*to go*	essen	*to eat*
fallen	*to fall*	geben	*to give*
fangen	*to catch*	helfen	*to help*
lassen	*to let, to allow*	nehmen	*to take*
schlafen	*to sleep*	sprechen	*to speak*
tragen	*to carry; to wear*	treffen	*to hit; to meet*
waschen	*to wash*	vergessen	*to forget*
		werden	*to become*
		werfen	*to throw*
au ⟶ äu		**e ⟶ ie**	
laufen	*to run*	empfehlen	*to recommend*
		lesen	*to read*
		sehen	*to see*
		stehlen	*to steal*

Fährst du nach Berlin?
*Are you **going** to Berlin?*

Es **gibt** dort ein sehr gutes Café.
*There **is** a very good café there.*

Suggestion Remind students that new verbs are also vocabulary items. Tell students that they should be able to recognize these verbs in all of their present-tense forms, but they will learn more about how to use them in later units.

ACHTUNG

The verb **geben** is used in certain idiomatic expressions, such as **Es gibt** (*There is/There are*). Idiomatic expressions do not translate literally to English.

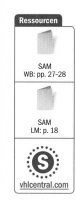

Ressourcen

SAM
WB: pp. 27–28

SAM
LM: p. 18

vhlcentral.com

Jetzt sind Sie dran! Write the appropriate form of the verb.

1. Ich ___esse___ (essen) viele Äpfel.
2. Du ___hilfst___ (helfen) Sophie.
3. Ich ___gebe___ (geben) Tobias ein Buch.
4. Peter ___nimmt___ (nehmen) ein Taxi.
5. Ihr ___fahrt___ (fahren) gern Fahrrad.
6. Wir ___tragen___ (tragen) Rucksäcke.

7. Anna ___wird___ (werden) Informatikprofessorin.
8. Du ___liest___ (lesen) viele Bücher.
9. Er ___schläft___ (schlafen) bis 8 Uhr morgens.
10. Ihr ___sprecht___ (sprechen) Deutsch.
11. Die Schüler ___sehen___ (sehen) einen Film.
12. Du ___vergisst___ (vergessen) die Hausaufgaben.

Anwendung

1 **Was ist richtig?** Select the verb that best completes each sentence.

 1. Hannah (schläft / ~~isst~~) viele Äpfel.

2. Ich (lese / ~~brate~~) ein Schnitzel.

3. Du (~~fährst~~ / triffst) einen Porsche.

4. Wir (helfen / ~~waschen~~) den Hund.

5. Alena und Daniel (treffen / ~~sprechen~~) Deutsch, Englisch und Polnisch.

6. Ihr (~~läuft~~ / fangt) 8 Kilometer.

7. Du (~~liest~~ / wird) viele Bücher.

8. Du (gibst / ~~triffst~~) Jasmin im Café.

2 **Schreiben** Write complete sentences using the cues.

 1. Herr Schmidt / empfehlen / das Schnitzel
Herr Schmidt empfiehlt das Schnitzel.

2. ich / wissen / die Antwort
Ich weiß die Antwort.

3. du / fahren / das Auto
Du fährst das Auto.

4. wir / treffen / Katrina und Paul
Wir treffen Katrina und Paul.

5. Angela / lesen / gern
Angela liest gern.

6. du / sprechen / Deutsch
Du sprichst Deutsch.

7. ich / werden / Architekt
Ich werde Architekt.

8. Peter / stehlen / einen Apfel
Peter stiehlt einen Apfel.

3 **Was sehen Sie?** Complete the sentences. Sample answers are provided.

▶ **BEISPIEL**

Peter __läuft__ gern im Park.

1. Sie __schlafen__ in der Hängematte.

2. Tobi __wäscht__ das Auto.

3. Der Footballspieler __fängt__ den Ball.

4. Hans __liest__ das Buch.

5. Er __isst__ eine Bratwurst.

6. Ingrid __trifft__ Rolf im Museum.

 Practice more at **vhlcentral.com.**

Kommunikation

4 **Bilden Sie Sätze** In pairs, create six logical sentences with items from each column. Some items may be used more than once. Answers will vary.

BEISPIEL *Du empfiehlst die Torte.*

A	B	C
ich	empfehlen	Fußball im Stadion
du	lesen	Goethes *Faust*
Nina	sehen	die Torte
Elsa und ich	spielen	23 Jahre alt
Bianca und du	sprechen	viele Fremdsprachen
Olivia und Markus	werden	einen Film

5 **Wie bitte?** Adele is talking to her mother on the phone. You hear only Adele's side of the conversation. In pairs, reconstruct her mother's questions. Sample answers are provided.

BEISPIEL Ich fahre am Wochenende nach Hause (*home*).
Wann fährst du nach Hause?

1. Ja, ich schlafe gut.
   Schläfst du gut?
2. Ich esse um 7 Uhr abends.
   Wann isst du?
3. Ja, ich lese viel.
   Liest du viel?
4. Ich sehe Matthias im Unterricht.
   Wo siehst du Matthias? / Wen siehst du im Unterricht?
5. Ja, wir sprechen im Unterricht Deutsch.
   Sprecht ihr im Unterricht Deutsch?
6. Ja, Matthias und ich nehmen zusammen (*together*) den Bus.
   Nehmt ihr zusammen den Bus?
7. Ich treffe Matthias nachmittags im Café.
   Wo/Wann triffst du Matthias?
8. Ja, ich fahre oft Fahrrad.
   Fährst du oft Fahrrad?

6 **Wer macht was?** Use the cues to ask your classmates whether they participate in these activities. Answers will vary.

BEISPIEL
S1: *Spielst du Fußball im Stadion?*
S2: *Nein, aber ich laufe im Park. Läufst du auch im Park?*

Fahrrad fahren	im Park laufen	im Stadion Fußball spielen
Ski fahren	im Schwimmbad schwimmen	Bälle werfen und fangen
viele Bücher lesen	den Bus nehmen	Freunde im Café treffen

6 Expansion Have students take notes on their classmates' answers and report their findings to the class. Ex.: **Michael spielt Baseball im Stadion. Anna fährt Fahrrad im Park.**

7 **Im Park** In pairs, write a paragraph that describes the activities of the people shown. Use each of the verbs from the list at least once. Answers will vary.

BEISPIEL
S1: *Die Frauen gehen im Park spazieren.*
S2: *Die Kinder reiten im Park.*

fahren	sehen
laufen	gehen
reiten	spielen
schlafen	treffen

2B.2

Present tense used as future  Presentation

Startblock In German, as in English, you can use the present tense with certain time expressions to talk about the future.

Heute Abend spielen wir Fußball.

Morgen macht meine Mutter Sauerbraten.

- The adverbs **heute** (*today*), **morgen** (*tomorrow*), and **übermorgen** (*the day after tomorrow*) are commonly used with the present tense to express future ideas. Use them with these time expressions to specify the time of day at which a future action will occur.

common time expressions			
Morgen	*morning*	Nachmittag	*afternoon*
Vormittag	*midmorning*	Abend	*evening*
Mittag	*noon*	Nacht	*night*

Morgen gehen wir einkaufen.
Tomorrow we're going shopping.

Heute Nachmittag gehe ich schwimmen.
This afternoon I'm going swimming.

- In **2A.3**, you learned to use **am** before dates and days of the week. Also use **am** with **Morgen, Vormittag, Mittag, Nachmittag, Abend,** or **Wochenende** to specify when something will occur. When both the day of the week and the time of day are specified, they form a compound noun: **Dienstagmittag, Mittwochabend.**

Am Wochenende gehen wir angeln.
*We're going fishing **this weekend**.*

Am Freitagnachmittag gehe ich zum Arzt.
*I'm going to the doctor's **Friday afternoon**.*

- Use **im** with months and seasons (**Frühling, Sommer, Herbst, Winter**).

Im Februar fahre ich Ski.
*I'm going skiing **in February**.*

Im Frühling gehe ich wandern.
*I'm going hiking **this spring**.*

- The adjective **nächste** (*next*) can be used with time-related nouns such as days of the week, seasons, and months. In this usage, it takes accusative endings.

nächsten Sommer
next summer

nächste Woche
next week

nächstes Jahr
next year

Jetzt sind Sie dran! Select the appropriate word or phrase.

1. Wir fahren (nächstes / nächste) Woche nach Polen.
2. (Am / Im) Montagvormittag gehe ich spazieren.
3. (Heute Abend / Abend) spielt ihr Karten.
4. Ursula fährt (am / im) Februar Ski.
5. Wir wandern (nächsten / nächstes) Freitag im Wald.
6. (Morgen Nachmittag / Nachmittag) fahre ich Fahrrad.
7. Wir gehen (Nacht / übermorgen) klettern.
8. (Nächsten / Nächstes) Wochenende spielst du Tennis.

Anwendung und Kommunikation

1 Was passt? Select the appropriate time expression.

1. Die nächste Prüfung ist (Nachmittag / (übermorgen)).
2. Ich fahre ((im)/ am) März in Urlaub.
3. Spielst du ((am)/ im) Abend Hockey?
4. Peter und Bettina fahren ((nächstes)/ nächste) Wochenende in die Berge.
5. Gehst du (Nachmittag / (heute Nachmittag)) klettern?
6. (Nächstes / (Nächsten)) Sommer fahren wir an den Strand.

2 Bilden Sie Sätze Write sentences using the cues.

1. ich / gehen / heute Nachmittag / angeln   Ich gehe heute Nachmittag angeln.
2. übermorgen / spielen / Roland / Baseball   Übermorgen spielt Roland Baseball.
3. nächstes Jahr / fahren / Anja / an den Strand   Nächstes Jahr fährt Anja an den Strand.
4. Patrick / treffen / Bianca / am Abend   Patrick trifft Bianca am Abend.
5. am Sonntagabend / kochen / wir   Am Sonntagabend kochen wir.
6. du / fahren / im Winter / Ski   Du fährst im Winter Ski.

3 Sätze In pairs, use items from each column to make up sentences describing what each person is going to do. Answers will vary.

BEISPIEL

Wir sehen heute Abend einen Film.

A	B	C	D
ich	Fahrrad fahren	am Freitag	für einen Marathonlauf
du	gehen	heute Nacht	im Park
Angelika	spazieren gehen	im Dezember	nach Österreich
wir	reisen	im Frühling	Freunde im Restaurant
ihr	trainieren	morgen Nachmittag	in die Disko
Otto und Gabi	treffen	nächstes Jahr	in den Bergen

3 Expansion Have students ask each other about their own plans for each of the times listed in column C. Ex.: **Was machst du am Freitag?**

4 Fernsehen In pairs, decide which TV programs you want to watch, and take turns asking each other when they will be on. Answers will vary.

BEISPIEL

S1: *Wann kommt TV total?*
S2: *TV total kommt morgen Abend / Mittwochabend.*

	Dienstag (heute)	Mittwoch	Donnerstag
10.00 Uhr	Reisen für Genießer	Lindenstraße	Türkisch für Anfänger
15.00 Uhr	Sport Aktuell	Das Supertalent	Die Sendung mit der Maus
19.00 Uhr	Formel 1	Hallo Deutschland	Deutschland sucht den Superstar
23.00 Uhr	Bauer sucht Frau	TV total	Familien im Brennpunkt

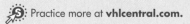 Practice more at **vhlcentral.com.**

2B.3 | **Negation**  Presentation

Startblock In 1B.2, you learned to make affirmative statements and ask yes-or-no questions. To negate a statement or ask a negative question, use **nicht** or **kein**.

Nein, meine Familie fährt **nicht** Ski.

Ich trenne **keine** Paare.

Nicht

QUERVERWEIS

You have already learned to use **nicht** in the expressions **nicht schlecht** and **nicht (so) gut** (in **1A Kontext**) and **nicht gern** (in **2B Kontext**)

ACHTUNG

Ich spiele kein Tennis means *I don't play tennis (at all).* **Ich spiele nicht Tennis** means *I'm not playing tennis (at the moment).*

- In negative statements or questions, place **nicht** after the subject, conjugated verb, direct object, and definite time expressions, but before other sentence elements.

Ich gehe heute in die Sporthalle.
I'm going to the gym today.
▶ Ich gehe heute **nicht** in die Sporthalle.
I'm not going to the gym today.

Brauchst du den Fußball?
Do you need the soccer ball?
▶ Brauchst du den Fußball **nicht**?
Don't you need the soccer ball?

Die Spieler sind hier.
The players are here.
▶ Die Spieler sind **nicht** hier.
The players are not here.

Mathematik ist einfach.
Math is easy.
▶ Mathematik ist **nicht** einfach.
Math is not easy.

- In some cases, the placement of **nicht** depends on which element of a statement the speaker wants to emphasize.

Ich spiele **nicht** Golf mit Tobias.
Ich spiele mit Tobias Tennis.
I'm not playing golf with Tobias.
I'm playing tennis with Tobias.

Ich spiele **nicht** mit Tobias Golf.
Ich spiele mit Moritz Golf.
I'm not playing golf with Tobias.
I'm playing golf with Moritz.

Wir sehen den Film heute **nicht**.
We're not seeing the film today.

Wir sehen den Film morgen, **nicht** heute.
We're seeing the film tomorrow, not today.

Die Studenten essen **nicht** in der Mensa.
The students aren't eating in the dining hall.

Die Studenten essen in der Mensa **nicht** gern.
The students don't like to eat in the dining hall.

Hans weiß es **nicht**?

Er hat **keine** Ahnung.

Kein

- **Kein** is the negative form of the indefinite article **ein**. Use **kein** to negate a noun preceded by an indefinite article or by no article.

—Spielen Sie Tennis?
—*Do you play tennis?*

▶ —Nein, wir spielen **kein** Tennis.
—*No, we don't play tennis.*

—Hat er ein Hobby?
—*Does he have a hobby?*

▶ —Nein, er hat **keine** Hobbys.
—*No, he has no hobbies.*

QUERVERWEIS

Words that have the same endings as **ein** are often called **ein**-words. You will learn about other **ein**-words in **3A.1**.

- **Kein** follows the same patterns of gender and case endings as **ein**. Note that, unlike **ein**, **kein** has a plural form.

kein				
	masculine	**feminine**	**neuter**	**plural**
nominative **accusative**	kein Ball keinen Ball	keine Freizeit keine Freizeit	kein Spiel kein Spiel	keine Karten keine Karten

—Hast du **einen** Fußball?
—*Do you have a soccer ball?*

▶ —Nein, ich habe **keinen** Fußball.
—*No, I don't have a soccer ball.*

—Ist das **ein** Stadion?
—*Is that a stadium?*

▶ —Nein, das ist **kein** Stadion.
—*No, that's not a stadium.*

—Sind das Basketballspieler?
—*Are those guys basketball players?*

▶ —Nein, das sind **keine** Basketballspieler.
—*No, those aren't basketball players.*

Suggestion Point out that the responses **Ja**, **Nein**, and **Doch** at the beginning of a sentence do not affect subject-verb word order.

Doch

- The word **doch** has no exact equivalent in English. Use it to contradict a negative question or statement.

—Ich habe **keine** Freunde.
—*I don't have any friends.*

▶ —**Doch**, du hast viele Freunde!
—*No, you have lots of friends!*

—Gehst du **nicht** zum Strand?
—*Aren't you going to the beach?*

▶ —**Doch**, ich gehe zum Strand.
—*Yes, I'm going to the beach.*

Ressourcen

SAM
WB: pp. 31–32

SAM
LM: p. 20

Ⓢ
vhlcentral.com

Jetzt sind Sie dran! Complete the sentences with the appropriate form of **nicht** or **kein**.

1. Der Volleyballspieler ist __*nicht*__ so fit.
2. Stefan hat __keinen__ Fußball.
3. Wir machen die Hausaufgaben __nicht__.
4. Übermorgen habe ich __keine__ Vorlesung.
5. Uwe trainiert __nicht__ und verliert das Spiel.
6. Ich habe __kein__ Foto.

7. Bernhard spielt viel Fußball, aber er gewinnt __keine__ Spiele.
8. Du schwimmst __nicht__ im Schwimmbad.
9. Wir sehen den Film __nicht__.
10. Ihr habt __keine__ Freizeit.
11. Am Donnerstag fahren wir __nicht__ in die Berge.
12. Es gibt hier __kein__ Stadion.

Anwendung

1 **Verneinen Sie** Negate the sentences using **nicht**.

1. Wir haben die Karten.
   Wir haben die Karten nicht.
2. Ich vergesse die Hausaufgaben.
   Ich vergesse die Hausaufgaben nicht.
3. Wir reiten am Wochenende.
   Wir reiten am Wochenende nicht.
4. Simon und Katrina sind hier.
   Simon und Katrina sind nicht hier.
5. Du gehst in die Bibliothek.
   Du gehst nicht in die Bibliothek.

6. Ihr verliert das Volleyballspiel.
   Ihr verliert das Volleyballspiel nicht.
7. Thomas und Brigitte schwimmen am Nachmittag.
   Thomas und Brigitte schwimmen am Nachmittag nicht.
8. Am Sonntag gehen wir angeln.
   Am Sonntag gehen wir nicht angeln.

2 **Antworten Sie** Answer the questions using **kein**.

BEISPIEL

S1: *Hast du Hobbys?*
S2: *Nein, ich habe keine Hobbys.*

1. Hat Peter ein Fahrrad?
   Nein, Peter hat kein Fahrrad.
2. Habt ihr Freizeit?
   Nein, wir haben keine Freizeit.
3. Sind das Spielerinnen?
   Nein, das sind keine Spielerinnen.
4. Ist Berlin ein Land (*country*)?
   Nein, Berlin ist kein Land.
5. Ist Alexandra eine Hockeyspielerin?
   Nein, Alexandra ist keine Hockeyspielerin.

6. Hast du einen Basketball?
   Nein, ich habe keinen Basketball.
7. Gibt es dort ein Stadion?
   Nein, es gibt dort kein Stadion.
8. Spielst du Volleyball?
   Nein, ich spiele keinen Volleyball.
9. Ist Salzburg ein Berg?
   Nein, Salzburg ist kein Berg.
10. Haben Sie Karten?
    Nein, ich habe keine Karten.

3 **Was fehlt?** Complete the conversation with **nicht**, **kein**, or **doch**.

KARIN Hallo, Alina! Geht's dir gut? Kommst du (1) ___nicht___ heute Abend zum Training?

ALINA Heute Abend? (2) ___Doch___! Aber morgen komme ich (3) ___nicht___.

KARIN Warum (4) ___nicht___?

ALINA Ich habe (5) ___keine___ Zeit! Wir haben sehr viele Biologiehausaufgaben und übermorgen habe ich auch eine Chemieprüfung!

KARIN Belegst du nicht vier Veranstaltungen?

ALINA (6) ___Doch___, ich belege Biologie, Chemie, Physik und auch Mathematik.

Practice more at **vhlcentral.com**.

Kommunikation

4 **Expansion** Have students create their own questions to ask their partners.

4 **Partnerinterview** In pairs, take turns asking each other questions. Contradict your partner's questions using **nicht, kein,** or **doch.** Sample answers are provided.

BEISPIEL

S1: Hast du einen Basketball?
S2: Nein, ich habe keinen Basketball.
S1: Tanzt du nicht am Wochenende?
S2: Doch, ich tanze am Wochenende.

1. Spielst du Hockey?
   Nein, ich spiele kein Hockey.
2. Wanderst du im Wald?
   Nein, ich wandere nicht im Wald.
3. Fährst du im Dezember Fahrrad?
   Nein, im Dezember fahre ich nicht Fahrrad.
4. Hast du keine Hobbys?
   Doch, ich habe viele Hobbys.

5. Trainierst du für einen Marathonlauf?
   Nein, ich trainiere für keinen Marathonlauf.
6. Hast du nicht viele Hausaufgaben?
   Doch, ich habe viele Hausaufgaben.
7. Schwimmst du im Schwimmbad?
   Nein, ich schwimme nicht im Schwimmbad.
8. Bist du Tennisspieler(in)?
   Nein, ich bin kein Tennisspieler / keine Tennisspielerin.

5 **Das stimmt nicht!** In pairs, take turns making false statements about the photos. Correct your partner's false statements by negating them, then supply the correct answer. Answers will vary.

▶ **BEISPIEL**

S1: Die Frau fährt Auto.
S2: Nein, sie fährt nicht Auto. Sie fährt Fahrrad.

1.

2.

3.

4.

5.

6.

6 **Ich habe es schlecht** In pairs, take turns coming up with exaggerations using **nicht** and **kein.** Contradict your partner's exaggerations using **doch.** Answers will vary.

BEISPIEL

S1: Wir haben keine Freizeit!
S2: Doch, wir haben viel Freizeit!

7 **Trauriger Jörn** In small groups, explain why Jörn is sad, using negative statements. Answers will vary.

BEISPIEL

S1: Jörn hat keine Freunde.
S2: Er lernt nicht und hat keine guten Noten.

Wiederholung

1 **Expansion** Have students add their partner's name to the list and ask questions in order to fill out their partner's row in the chart.

1 Gute Freunde
In pairs, look at the information provided about each person. Decide which of them are friends, based on their interests. Answers will vary.

BEISPIEL Heidi fährt Ski und Florian fährt auch Ski. Heidi und Florian sind Freunde.

	Tennis spielen	Musik hören	Bücher lesen	Ski fahren	Fahrrad fahren	Fremdsprachen sprechen
Heidi	✓	✓		✓	✓	✓
Daniela		✓			✓	✓
Magda	✓		✓	✓		✓
Klaus		✓			✓	✓
Florian	✓		✓	✓		✓
Oliver		✓		✓		✓

2 Begriffe raten
In small groups, take turns drawing pictures based on words or phrases you learned in **Lektionen 2A** and **2B**. The first person to guess the word or phrase draws next. Answers will vary.

BEISPIEL

S1: Spielt er Schach?
S2: Nein. Er spielt nicht Schach.
S3: Spielt er Karten?
S2: Ja, richtig!

3 Viele Fragen
Start a conversation with a classmate using the questions as prompts. Ask follow-up questions using time expressions. Answers will vary.

BEISPIEL

S1: Machst du viele Hausaufgaben?
S2: Ja, ich mache viele Hausaufgaben.
S1: Hast du heute Hausaufgaben in Geschichte?
S2: Nein, ich habe heute keine Hausaufgaben in Geschichte.

1. Liest du viele Bücher?
2. Reist du im Winter nach Kanada?
3. Sprichst du Deutsch?
4. Verstehst du Mathematik?
5. Machst du viel Sport?
6. Spielst du Schach?
7. Isst du viel Pizza?
8. Fährst du viel Fahrrad?

4 Diskutieren und kombinieren
Your instructor will give you and your partner different worksheets showing two schedules. Take turns asking and answering questions to find out the missing information from your partner's schedule.

BEISPIEL

S1: Wann gehst du ins Stadion?
S2: Nächsten Montag um halb fünf nachmittags.

5 Vermischtes
Use the cues to form questions. Then, in pairs, take turns asking and answering the questions. Answers will vary.

BEISPIEL

S1: Hast du heute Abend Freizeit?
S2: Nein, ich habe heute Abend keine Freizeit.

1. angeln gehen / du / am Sonntag
2. Tennis spielen / du / samstags
3. gehen / du / oft / in die Sporthalle
4. Tennisschuhe / haben / keine / du
5. du / reiten / am Wochenende
6. du / schlafen / viel / sonntags
7. für die Prüfung / lernen / nicht / du
8. du / nicht / aus Berlin / kommen

6 Arbeitsblatt
Your instructor will give you and your partner each a worksheet. Take turns asking questions to find each other's battleships.

BEISPIEL

S1: Liest Otto ein Buch?
S2: Treffer (*Hit*)! Er liest ein Buch./ Nein, kein Treffer. Er liest nicht.

	lesen	arbeiten
Otto		
Lukas und Maria		🚢

7 Marias Leben In pairs, take turns asking and answering questions about

Maria's activities. Sample answers are provided.

▶ **BEISPIEL**

Dienstag, 9.15

S1: Was macht Maria am Dienstag um Viertel nach neun morgens?

S2: Am Dienstag um Viertel nach neun morgens macht Maria Hausaufgaben.

1. morgen, 10.30
Was macht Maria vormittags um halb elf? Vormittags um halb elf lernt Maria Deutsch.

2. heute, 12.00
Was macht Maria heute Mittag? Heute Mittag spielt Maria Tennis.

3. Samstag, 14.00
Was macht Maria am Samstag um zwei Uhr nachmittags? Am Samstag um zwei Uhr nachmittags liest Maria ein Buch.

4. heute Nachmittag, 14.25
Was macht Maria heute Nachmittag um fünf vor halb drei? Heute Nachmittag um fünf vor halb drei trinkt Maria einen Kaffee.

5. nächsten Montag, 17.45
Was macht Maria nächsten Montag um Viertel vor sechs nachmittags? Nächsten Montag um Viertel vor sechs nachmittags trifft Maria eine Freundin.

6. Freitag, 23.15
Was macht Maria am Freitag um Viertel nach elf abends? Am Freitag um Viertel nach elf abends schläft Maria.

8 Minigeschichte In small groups, make up a story about the people in the picture. Be as detailed as possible. You may want to give the people names.
Answers will vary.

BEISPIEL

S1: Es ist Samstag und viele Studenten trainieren im Stadion.

S2: Niklas und David sind Basketballspieler, aber sie trainieren nicht...

fangen	trainieren
gewinnen	treffen
laufen	verlieren
spielen	werfen

Mein Wör|ter|buch

Add five words related to the themes **an der Universität** and **Sport und Freizeit** to your personalized dictionary.

die Klausur, -en

Übersetzung
exam

Wortart
das Substantiv

Gebrauch
Ich lerne viel für die Klausur.

Synonyme
die Prüfung, das Examen, der Test

Antonyme
—

S Vocabulary tools

Panorama 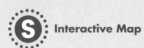 Interactive Map

Berlin

Die Stadt in Zahlen

▶ **Fläche:** *892 km² (Quadratkilometer)*

▶ **Einwohner° der Stadt Berlin:** *3.443.570*

▶ **Ausländer° in Berlin:** *503.945 (aus 186 Ländern)*

▶ **Touristen (2013):** *11.324.947*

▶ **Fastfood:** *Döner Kebap, erfunden° 1971 von Mehmet Aygün in Berlin; etwa 1.600 Verkaufsstellen° Currywurst (70 Millionen pro Jahr), erfunden 1949 von Herta Heuwer in Berlin; etwa 200 Verkaufsstellen*

▶ **Touristenattraktionen:** *das Brandenburger Tor, der Reichstag, die Gedächtniskirche, der Gendarmenmarkt, der Alexanderplatz, das Holocaust-Mahnmal, die Museumsinsel, der Potsdamer Platz, das Nikolaiviertel.*

QUELLE: Berlin - offizielles Hauptstadtportal

Berühmte Berliner

▶ **Friedrich II. (Friedrich der Große),** *König von Preußen° (1712–1786)*

▶ **Alexander von Humboldt,** *Naturforscher° (1769–1859)*

▶ **Gustav Langenscheidt,** *Deutschlehrer und Verlagsbuchhändler° (1832–1895)*

▶ **Berthold Brecht,** *Dramatiker° (1898–1956)*

▶ **Marlene Dietrich,** *Schauspielerin° und Sängerin° (1901–1992)*

▶ **Thomas „Icke" Häßler,** *Fußballspieler (1966–)*

▶ **Franziska van Almsick,** *Schwimmerin (1978–)*

Einwohner *inhabitants* **Ausländer** *foreigners* **erfunden** *invented* **Verkaufsstellen** *points of sale* **König von Preußen** *King of Prussia* **Naturforscher** *naturalist* **Verlagsbuchhändler** *publisher* **Dramatiker** *playwright* **Schauspielerin** *actress* **Sängerin** *singer* **Weltkrieg** *World War* **in Trümmern** *in ruins* **Gebäude zerstört** *buildings destroyed* **Wohnungen** *apartments* **Krankenhäuser** *hospitals* **beschädigt** *damaged*

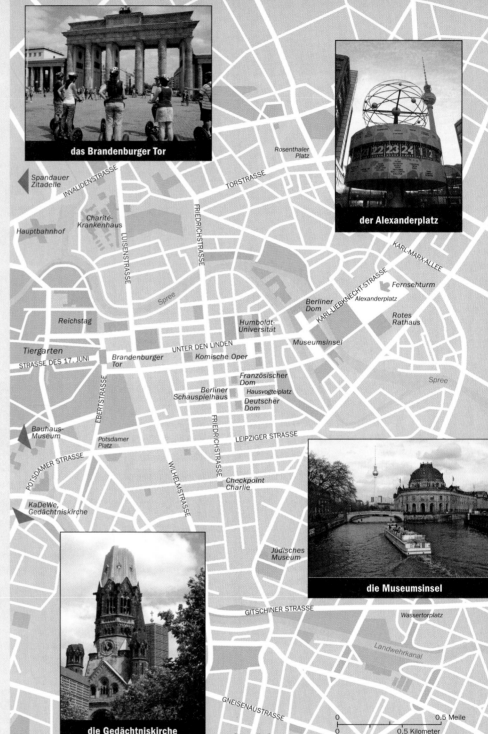

das Brandenburger Tor

der Alexanderplatz

die Museumsinsel

die Gedächtniskirche

Unglaublich aber wahr!

Am 2. Mai 1945 endet der 2. Weltkrieg° in Berlin. 28.5 km² der Stadt liegen in Trümmern°. Im Zentrum sind etwa 50% der Gebäude zerstört°. Etwa 600.000 Wohnungen° sind komplett zerstört. Die Infrastruktur der Stadt, Straßen, Schulen und Krankenhäuser° sind schwer beschädigt°. In Berlin leben noch 2,8 Millionen Menschen, vor dem Krieg sind es 4,3 Millionen.

Geschichte

Das DDR Museum

Seit 1989 sind Berlin und ganz Deutschland nicht mehr geteilt°. Das DDR Museum beleuchtet° das Leben in der ehemaligen° DDR: die Mauer, die Stasi° und den Alltag°. Die Ausstellung ist interaktiv. Man kann sich in einen echten° Trabant° oder ein authentisches DDR-Wohnzimmer° setzen. Geschichte zum Anfassen°!

Sport

Olympische Spiele 1936

Die Olympischen Sommerspiele 1936 finden vom 1. bis 16. August 1936 in Berlin statt°. 3.961 Athleten aus 49 Nationen nehmen an den Spielen teil° – ein neuer Rekord. Der bekannteste° Sportler dieser Spiele ist der amerikanische Leichtathlet Jesse Owens. Er gewinnt vier Goldmedaillen. Der erfolgreichste° deutsche Athlet ist der Kunstturner° Konrad Frey mit drei Goldmedaillen, einer Silbermedaille und zwei Bronzemedaillen. Die Nationalsozialisten missbrauchen° die Spiele als Propaganda.

Architektur

Der Reichstag°

Zwischen 1884 und 1894 errichtet der Architekt Paul Wallot den Reichstag. Er ist das wichtigste° Gebäude der deutschen Politik: bis 1918 trifft sich hier der Reichstag des Deutschen Kaiserreichs°, danach das Parlament der Weimarer Republik, und seit 1999 der Deutsche Bundestag. 1933 ist der legendäre Reichstagsbrand°. Heute besuchen Touristen oft die Glaskuppel. Sie ist 23,5 Meter hoch°, 40 Meter breit° und 800 Tonnen schwer°. Im Sommer 1995 verhüllen° die Künstler Christo und Jeanne-Claude den Reichstag komplett. 5 Millionen Besucher° kommen nach Berlin, um den Reichstag zu sehen.

Kultur

Karneval der Kulturen

Berlin ist eine internationale Stadt mit mehr als 500.000 Menschen aus 186 Ländern. Seit 1996 gibt es jedes Jahr ein Fest, um die Internationalität und Kulturenvielfalt° Berlins zu feiern: den Karneval der Kulturen. Es gibt einen großen Umzug° mit etwa 5.000 Teilnehmern und ein viertägiges Straßenfest mit mehr als 800 Künstlern – Musik, Tanz, Performance – aus über 70 Ländern. 2011 besuchen fast 1,5 Millionen Menschen das Event in Berlin-Kreuzberg. 750.000 sehen den Umzug. An den vier Tagen kann man viele kulinarische und handwerkliche° Sachen genießen°.

IM INTERNET

1. Suchen Sie Informationen über Marlene Dietrich. Wann beginnt ihre (*her*) Karriere? Suchen Sie die drei bekanntesten Filme.

2. Was ist die Museumsinsel? Suchen Sie Informationen über mindestens (*at least*) drei Museen der Museumsinsel.

3. Suchen Sie Beispiele für „Ostalgie" (*nostalgia for the East*).

Find out more at **vhlcentral.com**.

---

geteilt *divided* **beleuchtet** *illuminates* **ehemaligen** *former* **Stasi** *secret police* **Alltag** *everyday* **echten** *real* **Trabant** *car produced in East Germany* **Wohnzimmer** *living room* **zum Anfassen** *to touch* **finden... statt** *take place* **nehmen... teil** *participate* **bekannteste** *most well-known* **erfolgreichste** *most successful* **Kunstturner** *gymnast* **missbrauchen** *misuse* **Reichstag** *parliament building* **wichtigste** *most important* **des Deutschen Kaiserreichs** *of the German empire* **Reichstagsbrand** *Reichstag fire* **hoch** *high* **breit** *wide* **schwer** *heavy* **verhüllen** *cover with fabric* **Besucher** *visitors* **Kulturenvielfalt** *cultural diversity* **Umzug** *parade* **handwerkliche** *crafts* **genießen** *enjoy*

 Was haben Sie gelernt? Complete the sentences.

1. Die Fläche Berlins ist _____892_____ Quadratkilometer.

2. Nach dem 2. Weltkrieg sind __(etwa) 600.000__ Wohnungen in Berlin zerstört.

3. Seit _____1989_____ ist Berlin nicht mehr geteilt.

4. Im __DDR Museum__ kann man ein DDR-Wohnzimmer sehen.

5. Der erfolgreichste deutsche Athlet bei den Olympischen Spielen 1936 ist __Konrad Frey__.

6. An den Olympischen Spielen 1936 nehmen 3.961 __Athleten__ teil.

7. Paul Wallot errichtet den Reichstag zwischen _____1884_____ und 1894.

8. Im Sommer 1995 kommen 5 Millionen __Besucher__ nach Berlin, um den Reichstag zu sehen.

9. Der Karneval der Kulturen dauert (*lasts*) ____vier____ Tage.

10. Besucher sehen Künstler – Musiker, Tänzer etc. – aus über ____70____ Ländern beim Karneval der Kulturen.

 Practice more at **vhlcentral.com**.

Lesen Audio: Reading

Vor dem Lesen

Strategien

Predicting content through formats

Recognizing the format of a text can help you to predict its content. For example, invitations, greeting cards, and classified ads follow easily identifiable formats, which usually give you a general idea of the information they contain. Look at the text below and identify it based on its format.

Uhrzeit	Montag	Dienstag	Mittwoch	Donnerstag	Freitag
7.55	Deutsch	Französisch	Biologie	Religion	Mathe
8.40	Englisch	Musik	Geschichte	Physik	Mathe
9.40	Sport	Geschichte	Mathe	Französisch	Englisch
10.25	Sport	Mathe	Englisch	Französisch	Chemie
11.25	Religion	Physik	Erdkunde	Erdkunde	Musik
12.10	Sozialkunde	Chemie	Deutsch	Deutsch	Bio

If you guessed that this is a page from a student's weekly planner, you are correct. You can now infer that it contains information about a student's weekly schedule, including days, times, classes, and activities.

Texte verstehen

Briefly look at the document. What is its format? What kind of information is given? How is it organized? What are the visual components? What types of documents usually contain these elements?

Verwandte Wörter

You have already learned that you can use cognates, as well as format, to help you predict the content of a document. With a classmate, make a list of all the cognates you find in the reading selection. Based on these cognates and the format of the document, can you guess what this document is and what it is for?

Karlswald-Universität
Studienkolleg Mittelhessen

4 Stunden pro Tag (Montag–Freitag)
2 Tutorien pro Woche

Kurse
- Grundstufe: Anfänger°
- Stufe 1: Einführung° I
- Stufe 2: Einführung II
- Stufe 3: fortgeschritten° I
- Stufe 4: fortgeschritten II
- Stufe 5/6: Vorbereitung° auf die DSH-Prüfung

Kosten
- Einstufungstest: 50 Euro
- Stufe 1, 2, 3 und 4: 410 Euro pro Kurs
- Stufe 5/6: 620 Euro

Unterbringung°
- In Studentenwohnheimen
- In Privatwohnungen

Studienkolleg Mittelhessen
Friedrichstraße 3 | D-35032 Marburg

ausländische *foreign* **die... wollen** *who want* **Anfänger** *beginner* **Einführung** *introduction*
fortgeschritten *advanced* **Vorbereitung** *preparation* **Unterbringung** *accommodations*

Die Deutschkurse an der Karlswald-Universität:
Deutschtraining für ausländische° Studenten, die
in Karlswald studieren wollen°.

Stufe 1–4 vom 3. Januar bis 14. Februar
Stufe 5/6 vom 3. Januar bis 22. März

Große Auswahl° zusätzlicher Aktivitäten:

- Tagesausflüge° zu Städten der Region
  (Frankfurt, Eisenach, Heidelberg)
- Besuche von Sehenswürdigkeiten°
  (Elisabethkirche, Marburger Schloss)
- Besuche von Kulturveranstaltungen°
  (Theaterproduktionen, Konzerte)
- Sport und andere Aktivitäten

Suggestion Encourage
students to record
unfamiliar words and
phrases that they
learn from this reading
in their personalized
dictionaries.

Intensives Training in Hörverständnis°, Leseverständnis und Textproduktion.

Tel.: (06421) 28 23 651 - Fax.: (06421) 28 23 652
www.uni-karlswald.de/studienkolleg

Auswahl *selection* **Tagesausflüge** *day trips* **Sehenswürdigkeiten** *places of interest*
Kulturveranstaltungen *cultural events* **Hörverständnis** *listening comprehension*

Nach dem Lesen

 Antworten Sie Select the option that best
completes the statement.

1. Das ist eine Broschüre für...
   a. ein deutsches Gymnasium.
   b. ein Institut für Deutschkurse.
   c. Studenten, die Englisch lernen wollen.

2. Studenten, die kein Deutsch sprechen, nehmen
   den Kurs...
   a. Grundstufe.   b. Stufe 3.   c. Stufe 5/6.

3. Jeden (*Every*) Tag haben Studenten in
   einem Kurs...
   a. 4 Stunden Deutschunterricht.
   b. 4 Stunden Tutorien.
   c. 2 Stunden Deutschunterricht.

4. Der Test am Ende der Stufe 5/6...
   a. ist intensives Training.
   b. hat kein Hörverständnis.
   c. heißt DSH-Prüfung.

5. Studenten wohnen...
   a. bei deutschen Familien.
   b. im Studentenwohnheim.
   c. in Frankfurt.

6. An Wochenenden besuchen Studenten...
   a. Studentenheime und Privatwohnungen.
   b. Frankfurt und andere Städte.
   c. die Universität.

Suggestion Go over
the answers with the
whole class or have
students check their
answers in pairs.

7. Kurse kosten...
   a. 50 Euro.
   b. 1.030 Euro.
   c. 410 oder 620 Euro.

8. Die Kurse der Stufe 1, 2, 3 und 4 dauern...
   a. 4 Wochen.   **b.** 6 Wochen.   c. 11 Wochen.

 Richtig oder falsch? Mark the appropriate box.

	richtig	falsch
1. Das Studienkolleg Mittelhessen ist für deutsche Studenten.	☐	☑
2. Die Deutschkurse sind 5 Stunden jeden Tag.	☐	☑
3. Es gibt Tagesausflüge nach Frankfurt, Eisenach und Heidelberg.	☑	☐
4. Das Studienkolleg ist in der Friedrichstraße 3, D-35032 Marburg.	☑	☐

Hören

Strategien

Listening for cognates

You already know that cognates are words that have similar spellings and meanings in two or more languages, like *telephone* and **Telefon** or *activity* and **Aktivität**. Listen for cognates to improve your comprehension of spoken German.

 To help you practice this strategy, listen to these statements. Write down all the cognates you hear.

Vorbereitung

Based on the photograph, who do you think Julian and Anni are? Where are they? Do they know each other well? Where are they going this morning? What are they talking about?

Zuhören

Listen to the conversation and list any cognates you hear. Listen again and complete the highlighted portions of Julian's schedule.

4. April   Montag

9.30	*Kaffee mit Jasmin in der Cafeteria*	14.30	
10.00	*Seminar zur eng-lischen Literatur*	15.00	lernen mit David
10.30		15.30	
11.00		16.00	
11.30		16.30	
12.00	*Mittagessen mit Karl in der Mensa*	17.00	Fußball spielen
12.30		17.30	
13.00		18.00	
13.30		18.30	
14.00	Englischvorlesung	19.00	*Konzert im Kulturladen*

 Practice more at **vhlcentral.com**.

Verständnis

 Richtig oder falsch? Indicate whether each sentence is **richtig** or **falsch**. Correct any false statements.

1. Anni lernt morgens in der Bibliothek.
   Richtig.

2. Julian und Anni studieren Architektur.
   Falsch. Julian studiert englische Literatur und Anni studiert Architektur.

3. Um 9.30 Uhr trinkt Julian mit Jasmin Kaffee.
   Richtig.

4. Anni hat um 2 Uhr eine Vorlesung.
   Falsch. Julian hat um 2 Uhr eine Vorlesung.

5. Anni findet Architektur interessant.
   Richtig.

6. Anni und Julian haben langweilige Professoren.
   Richtig.

7. Julian und Anni gehen am Nachmittag Fußball spielen.
   Falsch. Julian geht am Nachmittag Fußball spielen.

8. Julian geht am Abend in ein Konzert.
   Richtig.

 Pläne In pairs, discuss your plans for this weekend, including where and when you will do each activity.

Suggestion To check answers for **Zuhören**, have students work in pairs and ask each other questions about Julian's schedule.

Schreiben

Strategien

Brainstorming

Brainstorming can help you generate ideas on a specific topic. Before you begin writing, you should spend 10–15 minutes brainstorming, jotting down any ideas about the topic that occur to you. Whenever possible, try to write down your ideas in German. Express your ideas in single words or phrases, and jot them down in any order. While brainstorming, do not worry about whether your ideas are good or bad. Selecting and organizing ideas should be the second stage of your writing. The more ideas you write down while you are brainstorming, the more options you will have to choose from later on, when you start to organize your ideas.

Hobbys...
laufen
campen gehen
Tennis spielen
kochen
tanzen
schreiben
schwimmen
Fahrrad fahren

Thema

 Eine persönliche Beschreibung

Write a description of yourself to post on a Web site in order to find a German-speaking e-pal. Your description should include:

- your name and where you are from.
- your birthday.
- the name of your university and where it is located.
- the courses you are currently taking and your opinion of each one.
- your hobbies and pastimes.
- any other information you would like to include.

Hallo!

Ich heiße Erik Schneider und ich komme aus Köln. Ich studiere Physik an der Technischen Universität in Berlin. Ich fahre Ski, spiele Tennis und fahre Fahrrad...

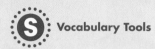 **Vocabulary Tools**

das Studium

der Abschluss, ¨e/ das Diplom, -e	degree
das Abschlusszeugnis, -se/ das Diplom, -e	diploma
der Dozent, -en / die Dozentin, -nen	college/university instructor
das Fach, ¨er	subject
das Seminar, -e	seminar
das Stipendium, -en	scholarship
die Veranstaltung, -en	class; course
die Vorlesung, -en	lecture
(die) Architektur	architecture
(die) Biologie	biology
(die) Chemie	chemistry
(die) Fremdsprache, -n	foreign language
(die) Geschichte	history
(die) Informatik	computer science
(die) Kunst, ¨e	art
(die) Literatur	literature
(die) Mathematik	math
(die) Medizin	medicine
(die) Naturwissenschaft, -en	science
(die) Physik	physics
(die) Psychologie	psychology
(die) Wirtschaft	business
belegen	to take (a class)
gehen	to go
lernen	to study; to learn
studieren	to study; to major in

Orte

das Café, -s	café
der Hörsaal, Hörsäle	lecture hall
der Seminarraum, -räume	(college/university) classroom
die Sporthalle, -n	gym

zum Beschreiben

einfach	easy
interessant	interesting
langweilig	boring
nützlich	useful
nutzlos	useless
schwierig	difficult

der Stundenplan

der Montag, -e	Monday
der Dienstag, -e	Tuesday
der Mittwoch, -e	Wednesday
der Donnerstag, -e	Thursday
der Freitag, -e	Friday
der Samstag, -e	Saturday
der Sonntag, -e	Sunday
die Stunde, -n	hour
die Woche, -n	week
das Wochenende, -n	weekend
die Zeit, -en	time
morgens	in the morning
nachmittags	in the afternoon
abends	in the evening
montags	on Mondays
dienstags	on Tuesdays
mittwochs	on Wednesdays
donnerstags	on Thursdays
freitags	on Fridays
samstags	on Saturdays
sonntags	on Sundays

Sportarten

(der) Baseball	baseball
(der) Basketball	basketball
(der) (American) Football	football
(der) Fußball	soccer
(das) Golf	golf
(das) Hockey	hockey
(die) Leichtathletik	track and field
(das) Tennis	tennis
(der) Volleyball	volleyball
der Ball, ¨e	ball
die Mannschaft, -en	team
das Schwimmbad, ¨er	swimming pool
das Spiel, -e	game
der Spieler, - / die Spielerin, -nen	player
das Spielfeld, -er/ der Platz, ¨e	field, court
der Sport	sports
das Stadion, Stadien	stadium
Fahrrad fahren	to ride a bicycle
Ski fahren	to ski
gewinnen	to win
schwimmen	to swim
spielen	to play
trainieren	to practice
verlieren	to lose

Freizeit

der Berg, -e	mountain
das Fahrrad, ¨er	bicycle
die Freizeit	free time
die Freizeitaktivität, -en	leisure activity
das Hobby, -s	hobby
die Karte, -n	card
der Park, -s	park
das Schach	chess
der Strand, ¨e	beach
der Wald, ¨er	forest
angeln gehen	to go fishing
campen gehen	to go camping
essen gehen	to eat out
spazieren gehen	to go for a walk
klettern	to (rock) climb
kochen	to cook
(ein Pferd) reiten	to ride (a horse)
schreiben	to write
Spaß haben/machen	to have fun / to be fun
singen	to sing
tanzen	to dance
wandern	to hike

Ausdrücke

Sie spielen gern Schach.	They like to play chess.
Sie verliert nicht gern.	She doesn't like to lose.

Regular verbs	See pp. 56–57.
Interrogative words	See p. 60.
Telling time	See p. 62.
Ordinal numbers and dates	See p. 63.
gern/nicht gern	See p. 69.
Stem-changing verbs	See pp. 76–77.
Common time expressions	See p. 80.
Negative words	See pp. 82–83.

Familie und Freunde

Suggestion Ask students: Who are the people in the photo and what are they doing?

Kontext

Communicative Goals

You will learn how to:

- talk about families
- talk about marital status
- describe people
- express ownership

Suggestion Point out to students that **die Eltern** has no singular form. Mention that nouns like **Eltern** and **Leute**, which exist only in the plural, have no grammatical gender in German.

Johanna Schmidts Familie

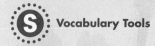 **Vocabulary Tools**

Wortschatz

die Familie	*family*
das Baby, -s	*baby*
die Eltern	*parents*
das Geschwister, -	*sibling*
die Großeltern	*grandparents*
der Halbbruder, ⁇	*half brother*
die Halbschwester, -n	*half sister*
das Kind, -er	*child*
der Nachname, -n	*last name*
das Paar, -e	*couple*
der Schwager, ⁇	*brother-in-law*
die Schwägerin, -nen	*sister-in-law*
die Schwiegermutter, ⁇	*mother-in-law*
der Schwiegervater, ⁇	*father-in-law*
der Stiefbruder, ⁇	*stepbrother*
die Stiefmutter, ⁇	*stepmother*
die Stiefschwester, -n	*stepsister*
der Stiefsohn, ⁇e	*stepson*
die Stieftochter, ⁇	*stepdaughter*
der Stiefvater, ⁇	*stepfather*
der / die Verwandte, -n	*relative*
der Zwilling, -e	*twin*
die Haustiere	*pets*
der Fisch, -e	*fish*
der Hund, -e	*dog*
die Katze, -n	*cat*
der Vogel, ⁇	*bird*
der Familienstand	*marital status*
die Witwe, -n	*widow*
der Witwer, -	*widower*
geschieden	*divorced*
getrennt	*separated*
ledig	*single*
verheiratet	*married*
verlobt	*engaged*
zusammen	*together*
heiraten	*to marry*
zum Beschreiben	*to describe*
blaue/grüne/braune Augen	*blue/green/brown eyes*
blonde/braune/ schwarze Haare	*blond/brown/ black hair*
dunkel / hell	*dark / light*

Suggestion Point out to students that **Geschwister** is primarily used in the plural. Model this usage by asking individual students whether they have any siblings. Ex.: **Hast du noch Geschwister? Ja, ich habe eine Schwester und zwei Brüder.**

Point out that whereas *hair* in English is a collective singular noun, **die Haare** is a plural noun. Explain that **das Haar** refers to a single hair, or to hair in general.

Walter Gärtner

mein Großvater/Opa (*m.*)

Peter Schmidt   **Marianne Schmidt**

mein Vater (*m.*), Mariannes Mann (*m.*)

meine Mutter (*f.*), Walter und Hannas Tochter (*f.*)

Michaela Schmidt   **Daniel Schmidt**   **Johanna Schmidt**

meine Schwägerin   **mein Bruder (*m.*)**   **ich, Peter und Mariannes Tochter**

Jonas Schmidt   **Greta Schmidt**

mein Neffe (*m.*)   **meine Nichte (*f.*)**
Peter und Mariannes Enkelkinder

ACHTUNG

To say *my big/little brother/sister,* use **mein großer/kleiner Bruder** or **meine große/kleine Schwester**.

Hanna Gärtner

meine Großmutter/Oma (f.)

Dieter Gärtner   **Renate Gärtner**

mein Onkel (m.),   meine Tante (f.),
Walter und Hannas   Dieters Frau (f.)
Sohn (m.)

Simon Gärtner   **Sophia Gärtner**   **Klara Gärtner**

mein Cousin (m.),   meine Cousine (f.),   meine Cousine,
Walter und Hannas   Simon und Klaras   Simon und Sophias
Enkelsohn (m.)   Schwester (f.)   Schwester,
Walter und Hannas
Enkeltochter (f.)

Zeus

Simon, Sophia und
Klaras Hund

Anwendung

1 **Expansion** Get students started by asking them questions about their own families. Ex.: **Haben Sie Geschwister?**

1 **Kombinieren** Match the people with the descriptions.

_g_ 1. Mariannes Bruder
_d_ 2. Daniels Frau
_a_ 3. Marianne und Peter
_c_ 4. Dieter und Renates Sohn
_h_ 5. Mariannes Vater
_f_ 6. Peter und Mariannes Sohn
_e_ 7. Daniels Tochter
_b_ 8. Dieters Frau

a. Johannas Eltern
b. Johannas Tante
c. Johannas Cousin
d. Johannas Schwägerin
e. Johannas Nichte
f. Johannas Bruder
g. Johannas Onkel
h. Johannas Opa

2 **Identifizieren** Write each person's family relationship to Dieter Gärtner.

BEISPIEL Hanna: _die Mutter_

1. Sophia: _die Tochter_
2. Marianne: _die Schwester_
3. Daniel: _der Neffe_
4. Peter: _der Schwager_
5. Simon: _der Sohn_
6. Johanna: _die Nichte_
7. Walter und Hanna: _die Eltern_
8. Renate: _die Frau_

3 **Kategorien** List at least four roles each person could have in a family.
Sample answers are provided.

BEISPIEL eine Frau, 40 Jahre alt
eine Mutter   eine Tante   eine Cousine   eine Tochter

1. ein Mann, 62 Jahre alt:
   ein Schwager   ein Großvater   ein Schwiegervater   ein Vater
2. ein Kind, 3 Jahre alt:
   ein Sohn   ein Neffe   ein Enkelsohn   ein Bruder
3. ein Mädchen, 15 Jahre alt:
   eine Cousine   eine Schwester   eine Tochter   eine Enkeltochter
4. eine Frau, 50 Jahre alt:
   eine Oma   eine Tante   eine Schwägerin   eine Mutter

4 **Hören Sie zu** Listen to Johanna's descriptions and indicate whether each statement is **richtig** or **falsch**, based on her family tree.

	richtig	falsch		richtig	falsch
1.	✓	☐	7.	☐	✓
2.	☐	✓	8.	☐	✓
3.	✓	☐	9.	✓	☐
4.	✓	☐	10.	☐	✓
5.	☐	✓	11.	☐	✓
6.	✓	☐	12.	✓	☐

 Practice more at **vhlcentral.com**.

Kommunikation

5 Beschreibungen
Use words from the list to describe the images.

Compare your answers with a classmate's, and correct each other's work. Sample answers are provided.

> Enkelkinder | Großeltern | Neffe | Sohn | verheiratet | verlobt | Zwillinge

▶ **BEISPIEL**

Das Paar ist verlobt.

5 Suggestion Give students cues to help them complete this activity. Ask them questions about the pictures. Ex.: **Wer sind die Leute? Wie alt ist das Kind?**

1. Das Kind ist der Neffe.

2. Die Babys sind Zwillinge.

3. Der Mann und die Frau sind verheiratet.

4. Die Mutter hat einen Sohn.

5. Die Großmutter hat drei Enkelkinder.

6. Die Großeltern begrüßen die Familie.

6 Brieffreunde
Read Eva's letter to her penpal. Then, in pairs, take turns answering the questions.
Sample answers are provided.

Liebe Andrea,

hast du eine große Familie? Meine Familie ist nicht sehr groß. Ich habe eine große Schwester Nicole und einen kleinen Halbbruder Peter. Und wir haben einen Hund, Cäsar, und Miezi, unsere kleine Katze.

Nicole studiert Sportmedizin in Heidelberg. Peter ist fünf und geht in den Kindergarten.

Meine Familie ist sehr sportlich. Mein Stiefvater spielt Golf, meine Mutter und Nicole spielen Tennis, Peter spielt Fußball und ich mache Ballett.

Und wie ist deine Familie?

Liebe Grüße deine Eva

6 Expansion Have students write their own responses to Eva's letter. You might provide them with real postcards which they have to "mail" back to you. Encourage volunteers to read their letters aloud to the class.

1. Wie viele Personen wohnen mit Eva zusammen? Drei Personen wohnen mit Eva zusammen: der Stiefvater, die Mutter, der Halbbruder.
2. Hat sie auch Haustiere? Ja, sie hat zwei Haustiere: einen Hund und eine Katze.
3. Wie alt ist Peter? Er ist fünf (Jahre alt).
4. Was macht Evas Familie in der Freizeit? Der Stiefvater spielt Golf, die Mutter und die Schwester spielen Tennis, der Halbbruder spielt Fußball und Eva macht Ballett.
5. Wie groß ist Ihre (*your*) Familie? Answers will vary.

7 Arbeitsblatt
Your instructor will give you a worksheet with statements about family relationships. Use the cues to ask your classmates about their families.

BEISPIEL Ich habe zwei Schwestern.

S1: Hast du zwei Schwestern?
S2: Ja, ich habe zwei Schwestern. (*You write his/her name.*)
OR
S2: Nein, ich habe keine Schwestern. (*You ask another classmate.*)

7 Suggestion Ask volunteers to share their results with the class.

8 Was machen sie gern?
Use the vocabulary you learned in **Kapitel 2** to talk with a classmate about what your family members enjoy doing.

BEISPIEL

S1: Mein Bruder spielt gern Tennis. Was macht dein Bruder?
S2: Mein Bruder liest gern Bücher.

Aussprache und Rechtschreibung Audio

🎧 Final consonants

The German consonants **b**, **d**, and **g** generally sound quite similar to their English counterparts.

Ball	**Bruder**	**Dezember**	**bringen**	**Golf**

However, when **b** appears at the end of a word or syllable, or before a **t**, it is pronounced like a **p**.

ab	**habt**	**gelb**	**Staub**	**liebt**

When **d** appears at the end of a word or syllable, it is pronounced like a **t**. The **-dt** letter combination is also pronounced **t**.

Geld	**Hund**	**Stadt**	**sind**	**Fahrrad**

As you learned in **2A**, when **g** appears at the end of a word or before a **t**, it is pronounced like a **k**. In standard German, **-ig** at the end of a word is pronounced like the German **ch**. For more about the **ch** sound, see **Lektion 6A**.

klug	**bringt**	**Tag**	**sagt**	**zwanzig**

Suggestion Remind students that the pronunciation of the final **-ig** sound has several regional variations.

1 Aussprechen Practice saying these words aloud.

1. Bank
2. sieben
3. Laub
4. lobt
5. danken
6. Boden
7. Abend
8. gehen
9. Junge
10. Berg
11. fragt
12. schwierig

2 Nachsprechen Practice saying these sentences aloud.

1. Der Dieb klaut ein Fahrrad.
2. Der Besucher fragt Manfred ruhig um Rat.
3. Bernds Geschwister sind freundlich und großzügig.
4. Viele Diebe klauen viele Fahrräder.
5. Ingrids böser Bruder ist gierig und gemein.
6. Jörg sitzt im Zug und singt ein Lied.

Suggestion Have students look at the sample words and sentences on this page to identify cognates and words they already know. Tell students the meanings of any unfamiliar words or phrases.

3 Sprichwörter Practice reading these sayings aloud.

Kindermund tut Wahrheit kund.[1]

Geld regiert die Welt.[2]

[1] Out of the mouths of babes. (lit. The mouths of children make known the truth.)
[2] Money rules the world.

Ressourcen

SAM
LM: p. 22

vhlcentral.com

Ein Abend mit der Familie Video

Die Freunde essen bei Familie Yilmaz. Alle wissen (*know*), Torsten ist Sabites Freund. Alle, nur einer nicht.

Vorbereitung Have students scan the images on the pages before they watch the video and try to guess what this episode will be about.

ANKE Hallo! Willkommen, ich bin Sabites Mutter.
GEORGE Freut mich sehr, Sie kennen zu lernen, Frau Yilmaz. Ich bin George Bachman.

SABITE George, das ist meine jüngere Schwester, Zeynep.
GEORGE Hallo, Zeynep, nett dich kennen zu lernen.
SABITE Und das ist unser Vater.
GEORGE Herr Yilmaz, freut mich.

ANKE Das sind die Patatesli Sigara Böregi von Faiks Großmutter.
MELINE Herr Yilmaz, Ihre Familie kommt aus der Türkei?
FAIK Ja. Ich komme aus Ankara. Ich habe dort Cousins und einen Onkel. Haben Sie Geschwister?
MELINE Ich habe drei ältere Schwestern. Eine ist verheiratet, eine ist getrennt, eine ist verlobt. Ich habe auch eine Nichte, sie heißt Ava und ist 12.

GEORGE Meine Eltern sind geschieden. Meine Urgroßeltern kommen aus Heidelberg.
TORSTEN Mein Onkel lebt in Heidelberg. Er ist Professor. Es ist eine schöne Stadt.

SABITE Hallo, Hans.
HANS Tut mir leid, dass ich zu spät komme.

HANS Hallo!
SABITE Hans, das sind meine Eltern, Anke und Faik.
HANS Guten Abend, Herr Yilmaz. Guten Abend, Frau Yilmaz. Für Sie.
ANKE Danke.
HANS Sehr erfreut.

---

1 **Richtig oder falsch?** Indicate whether each statement is **richtig** or **falsch**.

1. Sabite hat einen jüngeren Bruder. Falsch.
2. Meline hat zwei ältere Schwestern. Falsch.
3. Melines Nichte heißt Ava. Richtig.
4. Faik kommt aus Ankara. Richtig.
5. Es gibt Sauerbraten bei Familie Yilmaz. Richtig.

6. Georges Eltern sind verheiratet. Falsch.
7. Torstens Onkel lebt in München. Falsch.
8. Georges Urgroßeltern kommen aus Berlin. Falsch.
9. Hans' Familie kommt aus Bayern. Richtig.
10. Max ist 18 und spielt Basketball. Falsch.

PERSONEN

 Anke
 Faik
 George
 Hans
 Meline
 Sabite
 Torsten
Zeynep

HANS Bist du ihr Bruder?
TORSTEN Nein, Sabite ist meine Freundin. Ich bin Torsten. Nett dich kennen zu lernen.
HANS Freut mich.
MELINE Börek?
HANS Nein danke.

MELINE Frau Yilmaz, Ihr Sauerbraten ist köstlich.
ANKE Danke, Meline. Hans? Alles in Ordnung? Du isst nichts.
HANS Hmm? Ja, danke.

FAIK Hans, Ihre Familie kommt aus Bayern?
HANS Ja.
TORSTEN Ich habe eine Tante in München. Hast du Geschwister, Hans?
HANS Mein Bruder, Max, ist 18. Er ist sportlich und spielt gern Fußball.
MELINE Hat er eine Freundin?

SABITE Hans, alles in Ordnung?
MELINE Sabite!
SABITE Was?
MELINE Hans.
SABITE Was ist mit Hans? Oh. Ooooh.
ANKE Wir haben Strudel!

Nützliche Ausdrücke

- **Freut mich sehr, Sie kennen zu lernen.**
  Pleased to meet you.
- **Das ist meine jüngere Schwester.**
  This is my younger sister.
- **die Türkei**
  Turkey
- **Haben Sie Geschwister?**
  Do you have any siblings?
- **die Urgroßeltern**
  great-grandparents
- **Tut mir leid, dass ich zu spät komme.**
  Sorry for being late.
- **der Sauerbraten**
  marinated beef
- **Ihr Sauerbraten ist köstlich.**
  Your sauerbraten is delicious.
- **Er ist sportlich und spielt gern Fußball.**
  He's athletic and likes to play soccer.
- **Alles in Ordnung?**
  Everything OK?
- **einladen**
  to invite
- **das Abendessen**
  dinner

  3A.1
- **Das ist unser Vater.**
  This is our father.

  3A.2
- **Es ist eine schöne Stadt.**
  It's a beautiful city.

---

2 Zum Besprechen Draw your family tree. Include your parents, siblings, aunts, uncles, and grandparents. Then "introduce" your family to a classmate. Answers will vary.

BEISPIEL

S1: *Das ist meine Tante Sie heißt Paula. Sie wohnt in New Jersey.*
S2: *Das ist mein Onkel. Er heißt...*

2 Expansion Have students present their partners' families to another pair.

3 Erweiterung Boreks are a popular Turkish snack with many varieties. In pairs, research another popular Turkish dish, and share your findings with the class. Answers will vary.

Ressourcen

 SAM VM: p. 5

 vhlcentral.com

Eine deutsche Familie  Reading

TANJA UND JENS SIND EIN deutsches Ehepaar mit zwei Kindern. Sie haben zwei Söhne, Finn und Lukas. Finn ist 11 Jahre alt und in die 5. Klasse. Lukas ist zwei Jahre älter als Finn und geht schon° in die 7. Klasse. Die Familie hat eine große Wohnung° und einen schönen Garten vor dem Haus. Jens arbeitet den ganzen Tag in einem Büro°. Tanja arbeitet als Krankenschwester°, aber sie ist nachmittags immer zu Hause, wenn Finn und Lukas um eins von der Schule nach Hause kommen. Abends spielen sie zusammen Fußball im Park oder fahren Fahrrad am Rhein.

In der Familie macht auch Jens Hausarbeit°, aber Tanja kocht und putzt° trotzdem mehr. Die Familie fährt einmal im Jahr zusammen in den Urlaub°.

Sind Jens und Tanja also eine „typisch" deutsche Familie? Das Leben in Deutschland ist vielfältiger geworden°. In der Wohnung links neben Jens und Tanja lebt eine Einwandererfamilie°, rechts von ihnen lebt ein allein erziehender° Vater mit seiner Tochter. Was ist also „typisch" für die deutsche Familie von heute? Vielleicht einfach Zusammenhalt° und Liebe.

Mit wem° die Deutschen leben (%)

	Eltern	allein	Partner	allein mit Kind	sonstige°
18–24	63,5	15,9	15,8	1,4	3,4
25–29	19,8	25,2	48,6	3,1	3,3
30–34	6,8	20,1	66,9	4,5	1,7
35–44	3,3	14,9	74,1	6,3	1,4
45–54	1,3	13,6	78,8	5,0	1,4
55–64	0,3	16,9	79,4	2,2	1,3
65–74	0,1	25,0	70,8	2,1	2,1
75–79	0	41,8	52,0	2,2	3,9
80+	0	58,7	30,1	2,5	3,4

QUELLE: Bundesministerium

schon *already* **Wohnung** *apartment* **Büro** *office* **Krankenschwester** *nurse* **Hausarbeit** *housework* **putzt** *cleans* **Urlaub** *vacation* **ist vielfältiger geworden** *has become more diverse* **Einwandererfamilie** *family of immigrants* **allein erziehender** *single parent* **Zusammenhalt** *sticking together* **Mit wem** *With whom* **sonstige** *miscellaneous*

Expansion Have students read the data in the chart aloud to practice saying numbers.

Was fehlt? Complete the statements.

1. Jens' Frau heißt ___Tanja___.
2. Jens' ___Söhne___ heißen Finn und Lukas.
3. Am Tag arbeitet ___Jens___ im Büro.
4. Tanja ___arbeitet___ als Krankenschwester.
5. Am Vormittag sind Finn und Lukas in der ___Schule___.
6. Am Abend spielen Jens, Finn, Lukas und Tanja Fußball oder ___fahren Fahrrad___ am Rhein.

7. Jens macht in der Familie auch ___Hausarbeit___.
8. Die Familie fährt gemeinsam in den ___Urlaub___.
9. In Deutschland leben die meisten (*most*) 18- bis 24-Jährigen mit ihren (*their*) ___Eltern___.
10. Die meisten Deutschen, die älter als (*older than*) 80 Jahre sind, leben ___allein___.

DEUTSCH IM ALLTAG

Die Familie

die Ehe	marriage
die Einzelkind	only child
das Einzelkind	only child
die Hochzeit	wedding
die Mama	mom
der erste/zweite Mann	first/second husband
der Papa	dad
die Urgroßmutter	great-grandmother
der Urgroßvater	great-grandfather
der / die Verlobte	fiancé(e)
adoptieren	to adopt

DIE DEUTSCHSPRACHIGE WELT

Die Liebe

Ein Kuss° ist nicht nur° ein Kuss. In den meisten Teilen° Deutschlands sagt man „Kuss". Aber es gibt andere Möglichkeiten°, „Kuss" in der deutschsprachigen Welt zu sagen. **In der Schweiz** und **in Liechtenstein** sagt man „Müntschi". **In Österreich** und **in Bayern** ist ein Kuss ein „Bussi" oder ein „Busserl". **Auf Kölsch** (der Dialekt von Köln) ist das ein „Bütz".

Und wie sagt man „Ich liebe dich"? Ein paar° Varianten: **In Bayern** und **in Österreich** sagt man „I mog di". **In der Schweiz** geht das so: „I liäbä di". Und **die Berliner** sagen „Ick liebe Dir".

Kuss kiss **nur** only **meisten Teilen** most parts **Möglichkeiten** possibilities **Ein paar** A couple of

PORTRÄT

Angela Merkel

Seit November 2005 hat Deutschland eine Bundeskanzlerin°: **Angela Merkel**. Viele Deutsche finden Merkel pragmatisch und solide, und im Magazin Forbes steht, sie ist eine der mächtigsten° Frauen der Welt. Die CDU°-Politikerin hat keine Kinder, aber sie hat einen wichtigen Unterstützer°, ihren Mann, Joachim Sauer. Sauer ist Professor für Chemie an der Humboldt-Universität in Berlin. Er hält sich am liebsten von den Medien fern°, aber wenn die mächtigsten Politiker der Welt zusammen essen, ist Sauer oft dabei. Und wer wäscht im Hause Sauer-Merkel die Wäsche°? Beide!

Bundeskanzlerin female chancellor **eine der mächtigsten** one of the most powerful **CDU** Christian Democratic Union **Unterstützer** supporter **hält sich am liebsten von den Medien fern** prefers to stay away from the media **wäscht… die Wäsche** does the laundry

⚲S IM INTERNET

Scheidung (*Divorce*): Eine Epidemie in den deutschsprachigen Ländern?

Find out more at **vhlcentral.com.**

---

2 **Richtig oder falsch?** Indicate whether each statement is **richtig** or **falsch**. Correct the false statements.

⚲S 1. Der Dialekt, den man in Köln spricht, heißt „Bayerisch".
   Falsch. Der Dialekt heißt Kölsch.
2. „I liäbä di" ist die schweizerische Art (*Swiss way*), „Ich liebe dich" zu sagen. Richtig.
3. Angela Merkel hat zwei Kinder.
   Falsch. Angela Merkel hat keine Kinder.
4. Joachim Sauer ist mit Angela Merkel verheiratet. Richtig.
5. Joachim Sauer ist der deutsche Bundespräsident.
   Falsch. Joachim Sauer ist Professor für Chemie.

3 **Sie sind dran** Use vocabulary from **Deutsch im Alltag** to write six sentences describing a famous American family. Then share the description with your classmates. Answers will vary.

3A.1 **Possessive adjectives** Ⓢ Presentation

Startblock In both English and German, possessive adjectives indicate ownership or belonging.

> Sabite ist **meine** Freundin.

> Herr Yilmaz, **Ihre** Familie kommt aus der Türkei?

QUERVERWEIS

In **Kontext 3A**, you learned some possessive adjectives used with family vocabulary: <u>**mein**</u> **Großvater**, <u>**meine**</u> **Mutter**, <u>**meine**</u> **Eltern**.

- In **1A.1**, you learned about indefinite articles. Possessive adjectives are also referred to as **ein**-words since they take the same endings as the indefinite article **ein**. Each personal pronoun has a corresponding possessive adjective.

personal pronouns and possessive adjectives		
personal pronouns	**possessive adjectives**	
ich	mein	*my*
du	dein	*your* (sing., inf.)
er	sein	*his*
sie	ihr	*her*
es	sein	*its*
wir	unser	*our*
ihr	euer	*your* (pl., inf.)
Sie	Ihr	*your* (sing./pl., form.)
sie	ihr	*their*

Meine Schwester ist 16 Jahre alt.
My sister is 16 years old.

Wo ist **dein** Vater?
Where is your father?

- Possessive adjectives always precede the nouns they modify.

meine Mutter	**deine** Mutter	**unsere** Mutter	**seine** Mutter
my mother	*your mother*	*our mother*	*his mother*

Meine Schwester ist sehr sportlich.
My sister is very athletic.

- Like other **ein**-words, their endings change according to the gender, case, and number of the object possessed.

deine Mutter	**dein** Vater	**dein** Baby	**deine** Eltern
your mother	*your father*	*your baby*	*your parents*

Mein Großvater liebt **seine** Enkelkinder.
My grandfather loves his grandchildren.

- Like other **ein**-words, possessive adjectives have no added endings before singular masculine or neuter nouns in the nominative, or before singular neuter nouns in the accusative.

nominative and accusative of *ein*-words				
	masculine	**feminine**	**neuter**	**plural**
nominative	ein Vater unser Vater	eine Mutter unsere Mutter	ein Kind unser Kind	keine Brüder unsere Brüder
accusative	einen Vater unseren Vater	eine Mutter unsere Mutter	ein Kind unser Kind	keine Brüder unsere Brüder

Ihr Kind ist 3 Jahre alt.
Her child is 3 years old.

Tobias liebt **seinen** Bruder.
*Tobias loves **his** brother.*

- The formal possessive adjective **Ihr** corresponds to the formal personal pronoun **Sie**. The possessive adjective **ihr** can mean either *her* or *their*, depending on context.

Wo sind **Ihre** Eltern?
*Where are **your** parents?*

Rolf und Heike kochen für **ihre** Kinder.
*Rolf and Heike cook for **their** children.*

Christa kocht für **ihre** Enkelkinder.
*Christa cooks for **her** grandchildren.*

- The possessive adjective **euer** drops the second **e** when an ending is added. The possessive adjective **unser** may drop the **e** in the stem when an ending is added, but this form is rare.

euer Enkelsohn	**eure** Familie	**unser** Sohn	**uns(e)re** Tochter
your grandson	*your family*	*our son*	*our daughter*

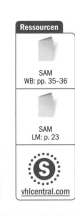

Ressourcen

SAM
WB: pp. 35–36

SAM
LM: p. 23

vhlcentral.com

Jetzt sind Sie dran!   Write the correct forms of the possessive adjectives.

Nominativ

mein

1. __meine__ Idee

dein

2. __deine__ Eltern

sein

3. __sein__ Wörterbuch

ihr

4. __ihr__ Familienstand

Akkusativ

mein

5. __meinen__ Bruder

dein

6. __deine__ Frage

sein

7. __seine__ Familie

ihr

8. __ihr__ Kind

Nominativ

unser

9. __unser__ Fahrrad

euer

10. __eure__ Mannschaft

Ihr

11. __Ihr__ Nachname

ihr

12. __ihre__ Hausaufgaben

Akkusativ

unser

13. __uns(e)re__ Verwandten

euer

14. __euren__ Sohn

Ihr

15. __Ihre__ Hunde

ihr

16. __ihr__ Problem

Anwendung

1 **Was ist richtig?** Select the appropriate form of the possessive adjective.

1. (Mein / ⟨Meine⟩) Eltern essen gern Spaghetti.
2. (⟨Unser⟩ / Unsere) Sohn spielt gut Fußball.
3. Markus und Sabine lieben (ihren / ⟨ihre⟩) Eltern.
4. Andrea liebt (⟨euren⟩ / euer) Hund.
5. Hat (⟨dein⟩ / deinen) Bruder einen Sohn?
6. Sind (Ihr / ⟨Ihre⟩) Großeltern hier?
7. Ich lese (mein / ⟨meine⟩) Bücher nicht.
8. Mein Vater und (⟨sein⟩ / seinen) Freund spielen Schach.

2 **Was fehlt?** Complete each sentence with the appropriate possessive adjective.

> **BEISPIEL** Treffen Sie _____*Ihren*_____ Mann im Restaurant?

1. Das Baby braucht ___*seine*___ Mutter.
2. Ali und Lara suchen ___*ihren*___ Hund.
3. Ich heiße Jan, und ___*mein*___ Nachname ist Bauer.
4. Sarah und ___*ihre*___ Schwester kochen gern zusammen.
5. Herr Schulz und ___*seine*___ Frau sind getrennt.
6. Siehst du oft ___*deine*___ Großeltern?
7. Wir lieben ___*unsere*___ Verwandten.
8. Kinder, wo sind ___*eure*___ Eltern?

3 Expansion Model using possessive adjectives with students' belongings. Ex.: **Ist das sein Kuli? Nein, das ist ihr Kuli.**

3 **Schreiben** Write a sentence about each item saying whose it is.

> **BEISPIEL**
> *Das sind meine Hefte.*

ich

1. du Das ist dein Computer. **2. er** Das ist sein Fahrrad.

3. wir Das sind unsere Bleistifte. **4. sie** Das ist ihr Rucksack. **5. Sie** Das ist Ihr Buch. **6. ihr** Das ist eure Tafel.

4 **Antworten Sie** Answer the questions with complete sentences. Answers will vary.

1. Wo wohnt Ihre Familie?
2. Wie heißt Ihre Mutter?
3. Wie ist ihr Nachname?
4. Wie alt ist Ihr Vater?
5. Welche Sportarten spielt Ihre Familie gern?
6. Spielen Ihre Großeltern Schach?
7. Wie heißt Ihr bester Freund / Ihre beste Freundin?
8. Welche Bücher lesen Ihre Freunde gern?

Practice more at **vhlcentral.com.**

Kommunikation

5 **Familie und Freunde** With your partner, take turns asking and answering these questions. Answers will vary.

BEISPIEL

S1: Hat deine Mutter Haustiere?
S2: Ja, meine Mutter hat zwei Haustiere. Ihre Katze heißt Muffin und ihr Hund heißt Sam. Wie ist dein Vater?
S1: Mein Vater ist Lehrer. Er ist vierzig Jahre alt und hat zwei Brüder.

1. Hat deine Mutter Haustiere?
2. Wie ist dein Vater?
3. Wieviele Kinder haben deine Eltern?
4. Wo wohnt deine Familie?
5. Was machen deine Freunde am Samstag?
6. Was studiert dein bester Freund oder deine beste Freundin?

6 **Meine Familie** Use the cues to form questions. Then interview your classmates about their family members. Sample answers are provided.

BEISPIEL

S1: Spricht deine Mutter Deutsch?
S2: Ja, meine Mutter spricht Deutsch.
S3: Nein, meine Mutter spricht kein Deutsch.

1. Bruder / spielen / Fußball Spielt dein Bruder Fußball?
2. Vater / haben / ein Hund Hat dein Vater einen Hund?
3. Eltern / lesen / Bücher Lesen deine Eltern Bücher?
4. Großmutter / spielen / Tennis Spielt deine Großmutter Tennis?
5. Schwester / haben / grüne Augen Hat deine Schwester grüne Augen?
6. Onkel und Tante / fahren / Ski Fahren dein Onkel und deine Tante Ski?
7. Verwandte / schreiben / E-Mails Schreiben deine Verwandten E-Mails?
8. Familie / sein / groß Ist deine Familie groß?

7 **Ich sehe etwas** Tell the class about something of yours that you can see in the classroom. Then, repeat what the people before you said they saw. Answers will vary.

BEISPIEL

S1: Ich sehe meinen Fußball.
S2: Ich sehe mein Buch und Stefan sieht seinen Fußball.
S3: Ich sehe meine Fotos, Maria sieht ihr Buch und Stefan sieht seinen Fußball.

8 **Familienporträt** In small groups, take turns describing your family. Use possessive pronouns in the nominative and accusative case. After everyone has spoken, take turns describing your partners' families to the rest of the class. Answers will vary.

BEISPIEL

S1: Das ist Inga. Ihre Mutter hat grüne Augen und braune Haare.
S2: Das ist Michael. Seine Mutter ist Lehrerin.

5 **Expansion** After pairs have shared their answers, ask them to repeat what has been said, using the appropriate possessive adjective.
Ex.: **S1: Meine Mutter hat braune Augen. S2: Seine/Ihre Mutter hat braune Augen.**

6 **Expansion** If students answer a question negatively, encourage them to mention a different family member for whom the statement is true.
Ex.: **Spricht deine Mutter Deutsch? Nein, meine Mutter spricht kein Deutsch. Aber mein Vater spricht Deutsch.**

QUERVERWEIS

In **2A Kontext**, you learned a few adjectives to describe school subjects. In **3A Kontext**, you learned some additional adjectives to describe eye color, hair color, and marital status.

3A.2

Descriptive adjectives and adjective agreement

 **Presentation**

Startblock Adjectives can describe people, places, or things. Here are some adjectives commonly used to describe people and their physical attributes.

physical description			
alt	*old*	hübsch	*pretty*
blond	*blond*	jung	*young*
braunhaarig	*brown-haired*	klein	*small; short (stature)*
dick	*fat; thick*	kurz	*short (hair)*
dunkelhaarig	*dark-haired*	lang	*long (hair)*
dünn	*thin*	lockig	*curly*
glatt	*straight (hair)*	rothaarig	*red-headed*
groß	*big; tall*	schlank	*slim*
großartig	*terrific*	schön	*pretty; beautiful*
gut aussehend	*handsome*	schwarzhaarig	*black-haired*
hässlich	*ugly*	sportlich	*athletic*

- Use an adjective with no added endings after the verbs **sein**, **werden**, and **bleiben** (*to remain*).

  Mein Bruder ist **klein**.
  *My brother is **short**.*

  Seine Mutter bleibt **sportlich**.
  *His mother stays **in shape**.*

  Deine Schwester wird **groß**.
  *Your sister is getting **tall**.*

- When you use an adjective before a noun, you need to include an adjective ending.

  Meine **großen** Schwestern spielen Fußball.
  *My **big** sisters play soccer.*

  Das ist eine **hübsche** Katze.
  *That's a **pretty** cat.*

Suggestion Tell students that **der**-words include the definite articles, **dieser** (*this*), **mancher** (*some*), **jeder** (*each*), and **solcher** (*such*), while **ein**-words include the indefinite articles, **kein**, and possessive adjectives.

- Adjective endings depend on the case, number, and gender of the noun they modify, and whether they are preceded by a **der**-word, an **ein**-word, or neither.

  Sie lieben ihren **jungen** Sohn.
  *They love their **young** son.*

  Das **kleine** Baby hat **blaue** Augen.
  *The **little** baby has **blue** eyes.*

QUERVERWEIS

For more about **der**-words, see **8B.2**.

- Adjectives after a **der**-word have these endings.

after *der*-words				
	masculine	**feminine**	**neuter**	**plural**
nominative	der **groß**e Bruder	die **blond**e Schwester	das **jung**e Kind	die **alt**en Großeltern
accusative	den **groß**en Bruder	die **blond**e Schwester	das **jung**e Kind	die **alt**en Großeltern

Der **alte** Mann dort ist mein Opa.
*The **old** man over there is my grandpa.*

Ich liebe die **hübschen** Häuser in dieser Straße.
*I love the **pretty** houses on this street.*

Die **große** Frau ist meine Tante.
*The **tall** woman is my aunt.*

Irene sucht ihren **kleinen** Cousin.
*Irene is looking for her **little** cousin.*

- Adjectives preceded by an **ein**-word have these endings.

after *ein*-words				
	masculine	**feminine**	**neuter**	**plural**
nominative	ein groß**er** Bruder	eine blond**e** Schwester	ein jung**es** Kind	meine alt**en** Großeltern
accusative	einen groß**en** Bruder	eine blond**e** Schwester	ein jung**es** Kind	meine alt**en** Großeltern

Mein **großer** Bruder ist ein **guter** Golfspieler.
*My **big** brother is a **good** golf player.*

Herr Wirth hat eine **sportliche** Tochter.
*Mr. Wirth has an **athletic** daughter.*

Ist deine **kleine** Schwester hier?
*Is your **little** sister here?*

Seine Großmutter hat einen **schönen** Vogel.
*His grandmother has a **beautiful** bird.*

- Unpreceded adjectives have these endings.

unpreceded				
	masculine	**feminine**	**neuter**	**plural**
nominative	rot**er** Wein	dick**e** Milch	alt**es** Brot	groß**e** Fische
accusative	rot**en** Wein	dick**e** Milch	alt**es** Brot	groß**e** Fische

Kleine Kinder brauchen **gute** Eltern.
***Small** children need **good** parents.*

Mein Vater hat **braune** Augen.
*My father has **brown** eyes.*

Altes Brot schmeckt nicht so gut.
***Old** bread doesn't taste so good.*

Unsere Geschwister haben **lockige** Haare.
*Our siblings have **curly** hair.*

- If multiple adjectives precede the same noun, they all take the same ending.

Ist das **kleine**, **rothaarige** Mädchen deine Schwester?
*Is the **little**, **red-headed** girl your sister?*

Sie hat einen **großen**, **gut aussehenden** Bruder.
*She has a **tall**, **good-looking** brother.*

- Use **sehr** before an adjective to mean *very*. The adverb **sehr** does not take any additional endings.

Ihre Haare sind **sehr** lang.
*Her hair is **very** long.*

Ich lese ein **sehr** gutes Buch.
*I'm reading a **very** good book.*

ACHTUNG

Some adjectives ending in -**el**, such as **dunkel**, drop the **e** in the stem when an ending is added.
Das ist ein dunkles Foto.
That's a dark photo.

Suggestion Point out that most endings for preceded adjectives are either -**e** or -**en**, and that the only other possible endings are -**er**, -**es**, and -**em**.

QUERVERWEIS

You learned the adverb **sehr** in **1A Kontext**, in the expression **sehr gut**. You will learn more about adverbs in **4A.1**.

Ressourcen

SAM
WB: pp. 37–38

SAM
LM: p. 24

vhlcentral.com

Jetzt sind Sie dran! Write the nominative or accusative form of the adjectives.

Nominativ

1. der ___schlanke___ (schlank) Vater
2. ein ___verheirateter___ (verheiratet) Mann
3. die ___große___ (groß) Familie
4. eine ___alte___ (alt) Schwägerin
5. das ___verlobte___ (verlobt) Paar
6. die ___sportlichen___ (sportlich) Enkelkinder

Akkusativ

7. einen ___jungen___ (jung) Vater
8. die ___ledigen___ (ledig) Verwandten
9. einen ___dünnen___ (dünn) Hund
10. ein ___hübsches___ (hübsch) Mädchen
11. den ___kleinen___ (klein) Sohn
12. das ___blonde___ (blond) Kind

Anwendung

1 **Kombinieren** Match each adjective with its opposite.

_d_ 1. hässlich   a. jung
_f_ 2. kurz   b. dick
_e_ 3. blond   c. klein
_a_ 4. alt   d. schön
_c_ 5. groß   e. schwarzhaarig
_b_ 6. dünn   f. lang
_g_ 7. lockig   g. glatt

2 **Was fehlt?** Complete the sentences.

1. Ich habe einen ____großen____ (groß) Bruder.
2. Mein ____großer____ (groß) Bruder spielt Fußball.
3. Er hat einen ____kleinen____ (klein) Hund.
4. Der ____kleine____ (klein) Hund hat sehr ____kurze____ Haare.
5. Seine ____kurzen____ (kurz) Haare sind auch sehr ____dünn____ (dünn).
6. Hast du auch so einen ____kleinen____ (klein), ____schönen____ (schön) Hund?

3 **Was ist richtig?** Select the adjective that best completes each sentence.

BEISPIEL Martin ist sehr nett und freundlich.
Er ist ein ____großartiger____ (hässlicher, sportlicher, großartiger) Junge.

1. Sein Vater fährt viel Fahrrad und Ski. Er ist ein sehr ____sportlicher____ (sportlicher, alter, blonder) Mann.
2. Deine Schwester hat schöne Haare. Sie ist ein ____hübsches____ (großes, hässliches, hübsches) Mädchen.
3. Meine Mutter hat keine lockigen Haare. Sie hat ____glatte____ (kleine, lange, glatte) Haare.
4. Meine Eltern sind nicht mehr zusammen. Ich habe ____geschiedene____ (verheiratete, kurze, geschiedene) Eltern.
5. Ihre Enkeltochter ist 2 Jahre alt. Sie ist ein ____junges____ (junges, hässliches, dickes) Kind.
6. Die Großeltern sind 80 Jahre alt. Die ____alten____ (hübschen, alten, kleinen) Großeltern spielen Schach am Wochenende.

4 **Schreiben** Replace the underlined words with the words in parentheses and make any necessary changes.

BEISPIEL Das kleine Mädchen ist sehr sportlich. (die)
Die kleinen Mädchen sind sehr sportlich.

1. Der rothaarige Sohn spielt Fußball. (mein) Mein rothaariger Sohn spielt Fußball.
2. Ihr Großvater liest das lange Buch. (ein) Ihr Großvater liest ein langes Buch.
3. Ich belege einen schwierigen Kurs. (den) Ich belege den schwierigen Kurs.
4. Der kurze, dünne Junge ist nicht sehr sportlich. (die) Die kurzen, dünnen Jungen sind nicht sehr sportlich.
5. Siehst du die kleinen Kinder? (das) Siehst du das kleine Kind?

Practice more at **vhlcentral.com**.

Kommunikation

5 **Die Familie Müller** In pairs, take turns describing the members of the Müller family. Answers will vary.

BEISPIEL
Moritz ist alt und klein.

Michael   Petra   Inez

Rex

Moritz

Alexander

6 **Ein guter Freund** Interview a classmate to learn about one of his/her friends. Use the questions below and add three more of your own. Answers will vary.

BEISPIEL
S1: *Hat deine beste Freundin lange Haare?*
S2: *Nein, sie hat kurze Haare.*

- Wie heißt er/sie?
- Wie alt ist er/sie?
- Ist er/sie groß oder klein?
- Hat er/sie blaue Augen?
- Ist er/sie dunkelhaarig?
- Ist er/sie sportlich?
- Ist er ein guter Student? / Ist sie eine gute Studentin?

6 **Expansions**
- Have students bring in photos of their family or friends. Ask students to describe the people in the photos to classmates.
  Ex.: **Das ist mein sportlicher Vater und hier ist meine hübsche Mutter.**
- Have students describe their partners' friends to the class.

7 **Raten Sie** Choose a famous person. In small groups, take turns asking yes-or-no questions to determine the identity of each person. Answers will vary.

BEISPIEL
S1: *Ist sie eine Frau?*
S2: *Ja.*
S3: *Hat sie blaue Augen?*
S2: *Nein.*

8 **Beschreiben** Pick one of your family members and describe him or her to your partner. Take notes on your partner's description, and be prepared to describe his or her family member to the class. Answers will vary.

BEISPIEL
Mein Onkel ist ein großer Mann. Er hat kurze schwarze Haare...

- Wie alt ist er/sie?
- Wie ist sein/ihr Familienstand?
- Hat er/sie Kinder?

- Macht er/sie Sport?
- Hat er/sie Haustiere?
- Woher kommt er/sie?

8 **Suggestion** Tell students they can describe an actual family member or invent a fictional person.

Wiederholung

1 Wer ist wer?
In pairs, take turns choosing a person from the list and giving clues to help your partner guess which person you've chosen. Answers will vary.

BEISPIEL

S1: Mein Vater ist ihr Mann. Meine Schwester ist ihre Tochter. Wer ist sie?
S2: Sie ist deine Mutter.

Bruder	Schwester
Cousin	Schwiegermutter
Enkeltochter	Sohn
Großvater	Tante
Schwager	Vater

2 Saras Familie
In pairs, say what each person in Sara's family is like and what he or she likes to do. Use vocabulary from **Kontext 2B.** Answers will vary.

BEISPIEL

S1: Wie ist Saras Bruder?
S2: Ihr Bruder ist groß. Er spielt gern Tennis.

Bruder

1. Cousin 2. Neffe 3. Tante

4. Onkel 5. Großvater 6. Schwägerin

3 Arbeitsblatt
Your instructor will give you a worksheet with instructions to play Family Bingo. Get a different name for each square of the grid, then share your findings with the class. Answers will vary.

BEISPIEL

S1: Paula, hast du einen großen Bruder?
S2: Ja, mein Bruder Stefan ist sehr groß.
S1: Paula hat einen großen Bruder.

4 Verschiedene Menschen
In small groups, take turns picking someone in the illustration and describing him/her. The next person repeats the description and adds to it. Keep going around the group, trying to add as many details as possible. Answers will vary.

BEISPIEL

S1: Die Frau heißt Fatima. Sie ist hübsch.
S2: Die Frau heißt Fatima. Sie ist hübsch und liest gern.
S3: Die Frau heißt Fatima. Sie ist hübsch und liest gern. Morgen geht sie spazieren.

Daniel Fatima Annika

Mert und Lara

Yusuf und Tobias

Jana und Alexander

Emil und Eva

5 Diskutieren und kombinieren
Your instructor will give you and your partner each a picture of a family. Ask questions to find the six differences between the two pictures. Answers will vary.

BEISPIEL

S1: Ist Renate blond?
S2: Nein. Renate ist nicht blond. Sie ist dunkelhaarig.

6 Stammbaum
Create an illustrated family tree, and share it with a classmate. Tell your partner about each of your family members, including their names, how they are related to you, what they are like, and what they like or don't like to do. Answers will vary.

BEISPIEL

S1: Das ist meine Schwester. Sie heißt Steffi. Sie ist sehr sportlich.
S2: Fährt Steffi gern Fahrrad?

S Video

Bauer Joghurt

The Bauer creamery was founded in 1887 in Wasserburg am Inn, Bavaria. Today, the company is managed by the fifth generation of the Bauer family. Known especially for their yogurt, Bauer also produces a variety of cheeses and other dairy products. The company has a reputation for excellent quality, using milk from cows fed on non-genetically modified food, with no added preservatives or artificial flavors.

Papa, wer ist dieser Bauer°?

Die Bauers, Schatz. Das ist eine Familie aus Bayern°.

Die machen alle Joghurt. Vom Opa bis zum Enkel.

Bauer *farmer* **Bayern** *Bavaria*

 Verständnis Answer the questions in German.

1. Who are the Bauers, according to the girl's father? eine Familie aus Bayern

2. Which members of the Bauer family does the father mention? den Opa, den Enkel / das Enkelkind

 Diskussion In pairs, discuss the answers to these questions. Answers will vary.

1. Do you know of other companies like Bauer that are family-owned? Are family-owned companies more likely to produce quality products? Explain.

2. What is the message of this commercial? Do you think it effectively conveys that message? Explain.

Communicative Goals

You will learn how to:
- describe people
- express an attitude about an action
- give instructions

Wie sind sie?  Vocabulary Tools

Wortschatz

persönliche Beschreibungen	*personal descriptions*
(un)angenehm	*(un)pleasant*
arm	*poor; unfortunate*
bescheiden	*modest*
egoistisch	*selfish*
ernst	*serious*
freundlich	*friendly*
gemein	*mean*
gierig	*greedy*
großzügig	*generous*
intellektuell	*intellectual*
intelligent	*intelligent*
langsam	*slow*
mutig	*brave*
naiv	*naïve*
nervös	*nervous*
nett	*nice*
neugierig	*curious*
reich	*rich*
schlecht	*bad*
schüchtern	*shy*
schwach	*weak*
stolz	*proud*
toll	*great*
lächeln	*to smile*
lachen	*to laugh*
weinen	*to cry*
Berufe	*professions*
der Architekt, -en / die Architektin, -nen	*architect*
der Geschäftsmann (*pl.* Geschäftsleute) / die Geschäftsfrau, -en	*businessman / businesswoman*
der Ingenieur, -e / die Ingenieurin, -nen	*engineer*
der Journalist, -en / die Journalistin, -nen	*journalist*
der Rechtsanwalt, ¨e / die Rechtsanwältin, -nen	*lawyer*

Er ist stark.

der Kellner, - (die Kellnerin, -nen)

Er ist schnell.

Er ist fleißig.

Sie sind faul.

der Besitzer, - (die Besitzerin, -nen)

diskret

müde

eifersüchtig

Sie ist besorgt.

Er ist traurig.

 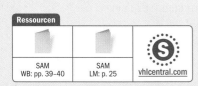
ACHTUNG

Note that the plural of **der Geschäftsmann** is **die Geschäftsleute**; **die Leute** means *people*.

Anwendung

1 Expansion Bring in pictures of famous people with different professions and ask students: **Wie heißt diese Person? Was ist ihr/sein Beruf?**

1 **Kombinieren** Match these famous people with their professions.

_d_ 1. Sheryl Sandberg		a. Architekt
_f_ 2. Ferdinand Porsche		b. Rechtsanwältin
_a_ 3. Walter Gropius		c. Musiker
_e_ 4. Diane Sawyer		d. Geschäftsfrau
_c_ 5. Ludwig van Beethoven		e. Journalistin
_b_ 6. Sonia Sotomayor		f. Ingenieur

2 **Gegenteile** Complete each sentence with the opposite adjective.

1. Der Geschäftsmann ist nicht <u>arm</u>, er ist ___reich___.
2. Die Musiker sind nicht <u>traurig</u>, sie sind ___glücklich/froh___.
3. Die Besitzerin ist nicht <u>gierig</u>, sie ist ___großzügig___.
4. Die Kellnerin ist nicht <u>langsam</u>, sie ist ___schnell___.
5. Die Tennisspieler sind nicht <u>schwach</u>, sie sind ___stark___.
6. Der Rechtsanwalt ist nicht <u>fleißig</u>, er ist ___faul___.
7. Die Architektin ist nicht <u>stolz</u>, sie ist ___bescheiden___.
8. Unser Hund ist nicht <u>gemein</u>, er ist ___freundlich/nett___.

2 Expansion Introduce adjectives with visuals: **Ist diese Person schnell oder langsam? Sportlich oder unsportlich? Freundlich oder gemein?** etc.

3 **Was fehlt?** Select the word that best describes each person.

bescheiden	gierig	müde	stark
faul	glücklich	nervös	süß
fleißig	intelligent	neugierig	traurig

1. Klara arbeitet viel und schnell. Sie ist ___fleißig___.
2. Ben hat sehr gute Noten. Er ist ___intelligent___.
3. Philip hat viel Stress. Er ist ___nervös___.
4. Emma lacht und lächelt viel. Sie ist ___glücklich___.
5. Maria macht keine Hausaufgaben. Sie ist ___faul___.
6. Tom schläft nicht viel. Er ist ___müde___.
7. Erik weint. Er ist ___traurig___.
8. Greta hat viele Fragen. Sie ist ___neugierig___.

4 **Hören Sie zu** 🎧 You will hear descriptions of three people. Listen carefully and indicate whether the statements are **richtig** or **falsch**.

	richtig	falsch
1. Florian ist Journalist.	☐	☑
2. Stefanie hat zwei Kinder.	☑	☐
3. Franz' Hund heißt Argus.	☐	☑
4. Stefanies Mann findet seinen Beruf langweilig.	☐	☑
5. Florian ist ein angenehmer Boss.	☑	☐
6. Stefanie und Klaus sind reich.	☐	☑
7. Florians Auto ist sehr alt.	☐	☑
8. Franz ist ein stolzer Opa.	☑	☐

4 Expansion Play the audio again and have students correct the false statements.

Practice more at **vhlcentral.com.**

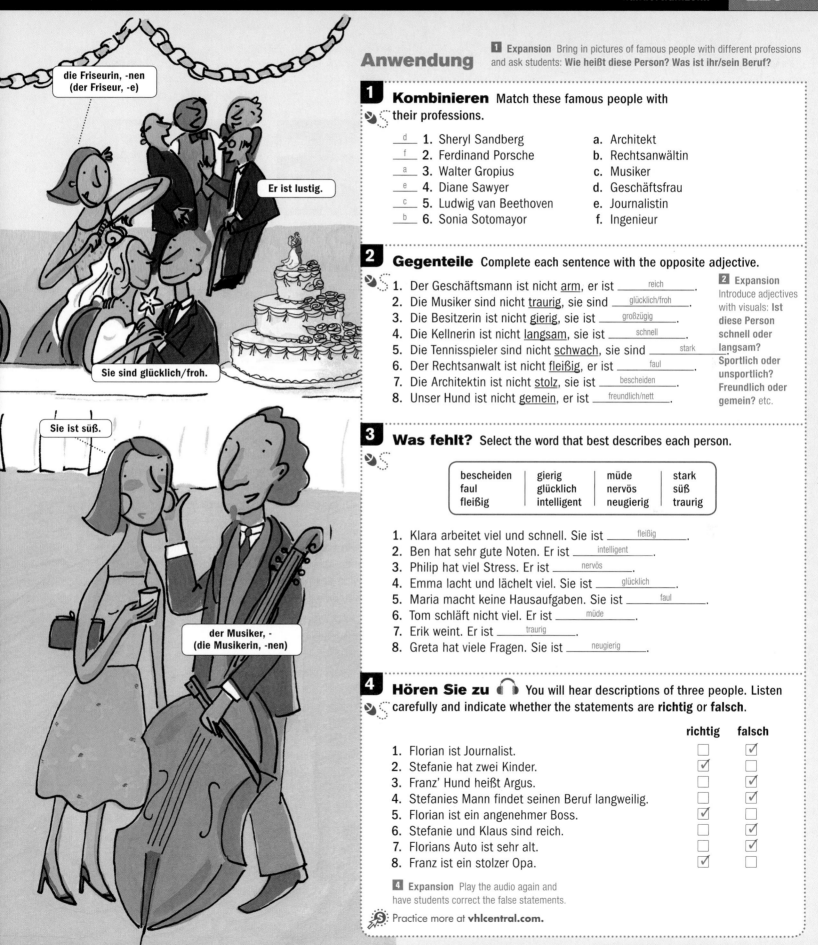

die Friseurin, -nen (der Friseur, -e)

Er ist lustig.

Sie sind glücklich/froh.

Sie ist süß.

der Musiker, - (die Musikerin, -nen)

Kommunikation

7 Suggestion Have students brainstorm a list of adjectives to describe themselves and their ideal partner before they start composing their ads.

5 Berufe In pairs, take turns replying to the questions based on the images.

▶ **BEISPIEL**

S1: Ist Karl Musiker?
S2: Nein, er ist Kellner.

1. Ist Helga Ingenieurin?
Nein, sie ist Geschäftsfrau/Rechtsanwältin.

2. Ist Ulrich Architekt?
Nein, er ist Friseur.

3. Sind Markus, Jan und Tobias Rechtsanwälte?
Nein, sie sind Musiker.

4. Ist Birgit Kellnerin?
Nein, sie ist Journalistin.

5. Ist Stefan Friseur?
Nein, er ist Geschäftsmann.

6. Ist Claudia Musikerin?
Nein, sie ist Ingenieurin/Architektin.

6 Partnersuche Read Georg's personal ad and discuss with a partner whether Maria or Jessica would be a better match for him. Be ready to defend your opinion to the class. Answers will vary.

Georg, 32 Jahre

Hallo! Ich heiße Georg, ich bin 32 Jahre alt, 182 cm groß, schlank, dunkelhaarig und habe braune Augen. Ich bin ein netter Mann, optimistisch und intelligent. Ich habe viele Hobbys, spiele Fußball, Tennis und Handball, sehe gern Filme und koche auch gern und gut. Ich bin geschieden und habe eine kleine Tochter. Meine ideale Partnerin ist zwischen 26 und 32 Jahre alt, nicht zu klein (ca. 168 cm), blond, schlank, aktiv und sportlich. Sie muss gern essen und sie muss Kinder gern haben! Wenn du das bist, dann schicke mir eine E-Mail an nettergeorg@gvz.de.

6 Expansion Ask students to explain their choice of the ideal partner for Georg. Encourage them to use opposite adjectives. Ex.: **Jessica ist nicht groß, sie ist klein**.

Maria
23 Jahre
groß (182 cm)
lustig
schüchtern
aktiv

Jessica
28 Jahre
klein (165 cm)
sportlich
intellektuell
schlank

8 Suggestion As a class, brainstorm some of the questions partners will need to ask for this activity. Ex.: **Wo wohnst du? Was ist dein Beruf? Bist du verheiratet? Wie viele Kinder hast du?** Have pairs act out their conversations for the class.

7 Wunschpartner Now it's your turn to write a personal ad. Using Georg's ad as a model, describe yourself and your ideal girlfriend or boyfriend. Include details such as profession, age, physical characteristics, and personality. In groups, take turns reading the ads and guessing who wrote them.

8 Klassentreffen Imagine you are at the 10th reunion for your high-school class. With a partner, role-play a conversation between two old friends who haven't seen each other since graduation.

- Find out where your friend now lives and what his or her profession is.
- Ask about your friend's marital status, whether he or she has children, and, if so, what they are like.
- Ask your friend to describe his or her significant other.

9 Klatsch und Tratsch Heike is catching up with her cousin Lisa, who is a real **Klatschbase** (gossip). With a partner, write a conversation between Heike and Lisa in which Lisa gives her opinion of the guests at a recent family wedding. Answers will vary.

9 Expansion Hand out pictures of famous people to pairs or groups of students and ask them to write some gossip about each person.

BEISPIEL

S1: Wie ist Peters Frau?
S2: Sie ist hübsch und sehr schlank, aber eine unangenehme Person und ein bisschen gemein. Sie ist Journalistin, also der intellektuelle Typ.

Aussprache und Rechtschreibung Audio

🎧 Consonant clusters

Some German consonant combinations are not common in English. In the clusters **gn**, **kn**, **pf**, and **ps**, both consonants are pronounced. Do not add a vowel sound between these consonants when you pronounce them.

Gnom	**Kn**ödel	**Pf**erd	Na**pf**	**ps**ychisch

The German **ng** is always pronounced like the English *ng* in *singer*, never like the consonant combination in *finger*, regardless of where it appears in a word.

Ri**ng**	fa**ng**en	ju**ng**	Prüfu**ng**en	entla**ng**

Some German letters represent the sound of a consonant cluster. The letter **x** is pronounced like the consonant combination **ks**. The letter **z** and the consonant combinations **tz** and **ts** are pronounced like the *ts* in the English word *hats*. The letter combination **qu** is pronounced *kv*.

e**x**tra	**Z**ahn	**Qu**alität	si**tz**t	**Äqu**ator

1 **Aussprechen** Practice saying these words aloud.

1. Gnade
2. knicken
3. Pfeil
4. Topf
5. Pseudonym
6. lang
7. bringen
8. Examen
9. Zoo
10. Mozart
11. Quatsch
12. Aquarell

Suggestion Have students look at the sample words and sentences on this page to identify cognates and words they already know. Tell students the meanings of any unfamiliar words or phrases.

2 **Nachsprechen** Practice saying these sentences aloud.

1. Die Katze streckt sich und legt den Kopf in den Nacken.
2. Felix fängt eine Qualle aus dem Ozean.
3. Der Zoowärter zähmt ein quergestreiftes Zebra.
4. Herr Quast brät Knödel in der Pfanne.
5. Der Gefangene bittet Xerxes um Gnade.
6. Das Taxi fährt kreuz und quer durch die Schweiz.

3 **Sprichwörter** Practice reading these sayings aloud.

Pferde lassen sich zum Wasser bringen, aber nicht zum Trinken zwingen.[1]

Nachts sind alle Katzen grau.[2]

[1] You can lead a horse to water, but you can't make it drink.
[2] At night, all cats are grey.

Unsere Mitbewohner Video

George trifft Meline im Museum und Hans trifft Sabite am Brandenburger Tor.
Sie reden über ihre Mitbewohner. Oder über mehr?

Vorbereitung Before showing the video, ask students to brainstorm what adjectives they would use to describe each of the characters. Write these words on the board.

NATIONAL STANDARDS communication cultures

1

GEORGE Hallo, Meline. Wer ist das?
MELINE Fritz Sommer. Langweilig. George, du sollst nicht immer alles so ernst nehmen.
GEORGE Du bist lustig.
MELINE Und du bist süß, mein kleiner amerikanischer Freund.

2

HANS Hallo, Sabite!
SABITE Hallo, Hans! Wie geht's? Oh, sei nicht traurig. Du bist nett und großzügig. Können wir Freunde sein?

3

MELINE Oh, armer Hans!
GEORGE Sei nicht gemein, Meline.
MELINE Bin ich nicht. Sabite ist künstlerisch, lebhaft und verrückt.

4

MELINE Hans ist intellektuell, aber naiv.
GEORGE Ihn als Mitbewohner zu haben, ist langweilig. Er liest und sieht fern bis um zwei Uhr früh. Ich habe morgens Uni.
MELINE Kann er nicht ohne Fernsehen lernen?
GEORGE Nein, das kann er nicht.

5

GEORGE Ist Sabite eine gute Mitbewohnerin?
MELINE Sabite ist eine liebenswürdige und bescheidene Person. Ihre Kunst ist hässlich und schlecht!

SABITE Ich bin so stolz auf dich, Hans. Du bist ein echter Freund. Danke, dass du mir hilfst.
HANS Keine Ursache.
SABITE Meline ist gemein.
HANS Meline ist unangenehm.

6

1 **Wer ist das?** Which character does each statement describe: George, Meline, Sabite, or Hans?

1. _____George_____ ist besorgt um seine Noten.
2. _____Meline_____ hat schöne Augen.
3. _____Sabite_____ macht hässliche und schlechte Kunst.
4. Jungen finden _____Meline_____ geheimnisvoll und faszinierend.
5. _____Hans_____ ist nett und großzügig.

6. _____Hans_____ ist ein echter Freund.
7. _____George_____ ist ein netter Typ.
8. _____Sabite_____ ist künstlerisch, lebhaft und verrückt.
9. _____George_____ ist süß.
10. _____Hans_____ ist intellektuell, aber naiv.

PERSONEN   George   Hans   Meline   Sabite

7

SABITE Ich möchte, dass sie einen neuen Freund hat.
HANS Bist du eifersüchtig?
SABITE Was?
HANS Sie ist lebhaft und hübsch. Sie hat sehr schöne Augen. Jungen finden sie geheimnisvoll und faszinierend.

8

SABITE Ist George ein guter Mitbewohner?
HANS Er ist ein netter Typ. Er ist besorgt um seine Noten. Ich sehe nachts fern und lese und er lernt bis zwei Uhr morgens.

9

SABITE Findest du sie hübsch?
HANS Wen?
SABITE Meline.
HANS Ich weiß nicht.

10

GEORGE Meline, Sabite meint es ernst mit Torsten. Du darfst nicht...
MELINE Ich finde nicht, dass sie gut zusammenpassen. Aber mach dir keine Sorgen. Ich kann sie nicht auseinanderbringen. Sie machen bald Schluss, auch ohne meine Hilfe.

Nützliche Ausdrücke

- **etwas ernst nehmen**
  to take something seriously

- **Du bist lustig.**
  You should talk. (lit. You're funny.)

- **Ihn als Mitbewohner zu haben, ist langweilig.**
  Having him as a roommate is boring.

- **Sei nicht traurig.**
  Don't be sad.

- **Danke, dass du mir hilfst.**
  Thanks for helping me.

- **Keine Ursache.**
  You're welcome.

- **Ich möchte, dass sie einen neuen Freund hat.**
  I want her to get a new boyfriend.

- **Jungen finden sie geheimnisvoll und faszinierend.**
  Boys find her mysterious and fascinating.

- **besorgt sein um**
  to be worried about

- **Du darfst nicht...**
  You mustn't...

- **Ich finde nicht, dass sie gut zusammenpassen.**
  I don't think they're a good match.

- **Schluss machen**
  to break up

  3B.1

- **Ich kann sie nicht auseinanderbringen.**
  I can't break them up.

  3B.2

- **Er ist besorgt um seine Noten.**
  He's worried about his grades.

  3B.3

- **Mach dir keine Sorgen.**
  Don't worry.

2 **Schreiben** Write a brief description of a well-known person in your school or community, using as many descriptive adjectives as you can. Do not mention his/her name. Be prepared to read your description to the class, who will guess this person's identity. Answers will vary.

freundlich	intellektuell	schüchtern
glücklich	lustig	traurig
großzügig	mutig	...

3 **Vertiefung** Research a famous German person and present him/her to the class. Use adjectives to describe his/her physical appearance and personality. Be prepared to share your description with your classmates. Answers will vary.

3 **Suggestion** You may wish to assign individuals for students to research, such as Diane Kruger, Hermann Hesse, Wilhelm Röntgen, Hugo Boss, etc.

Ressourcen

SAM VM: p. 6

 vhlcentral.com

Suggestion Point out to students that, as they have seen in the **Fotoroman**, German speakers also use **Freund/Freundin** to refer to a boyfriend or girlfriend. Encourage students to think about misunderstandings that might arise from the different ways that Americans and Germans use the word "friend."

IM FOKUS

Auf unsere Freunde!  Reading

TIPP

In German, many adjectives can be transformed into nouns.

bekannt → **der / die Bekannte**
known   *acquaintance*

besonders → **(etwas) Besonderes**
special   *something special*

gleich → **das Gleiche**
same   *the same one/the same thing*

IN DIESER° FACEBOOK-ZEIT HABEN wir alle viele „Freunde". Was ist also ein Kumpel°, mit dem Sie hin und wieder auf Partys gehen, und was ist ein echter° Freund? Deutsche sagen nicht so schnell „Freund" wie Amerikaner. In Deutschland ist es etwas Besonderes° ein „Freund" zu sein.

Wirklich gute Freunde hat man in Deutschland wahrscheinlich höchstens° vier oder fünf. Ein echter Freund zu sein bedeutet, dass° man sich sehr gut und vielleicht auch schon sehr lange kennt°. Die meisten Leute in Deutschland sagen, dass sie ihre Freunde schon aus der Schule oder aus der Kinderzeit kennen. Nur

weil° man einmal zusammen Kaffee getrunken hat°, ist man noch lange kein Freund.

In der Gruppe kennen sich alle mehr oder weniger gut. Trotzdem° nennen sich die Leute in einer Gruppe „Kumpel", nicht „Freunde". Die anderen Leute, die man kennt, nennt man meistens „Bekannte".

Es gibt also drei Gruppen von Menschen um eine Person: Die meisten Menschen sind Bekannte. Die größere Gruppe sind die Kumpel. Und nur eine sehr kleine Gruppe sind richtige Freunde. Aber mit diesen Freunden kann man alles teilen°. Also: Auf Freunde!

Auf unsere Freunde! *Here's to our friends!* **dieser** *this* **Kumpel** *buddy* **echter** *real* **etwas Besonderes** *something special* **wahrscheinlich höchstens** *probably at most* **bedeutet, dass** *means that* **sich... kennt** *know each other* **Nur weil** *Just because* **getrunken hat** *has drunk* **Trotzdem** *Nevertheless* **teilen** *share*

ÜBUNGEN

1 **Was fehlt?** Complete the statements.

1. In Deutschland sagt man nicht so schnell <u>Freund</u> zu einer neuen Person.

2. Viele Deutsche kennen ihre Freunde aus der <u>Schule</u> und aus der Kinderzeit.

3. Gute <u>Freunde</u> nennt man in Deutschland nur vier oder fünf Personen.

4. Für <u>Amerikaner</u> und für Deutsche hat das Wort „Freund" nicht die gleiche Bedeutung.

5. In <u>Deutschland</u> ist ein Freund jemand, den (*whom*) man sehr gut kennt.

6. Einen echten Freund kennt man sehr gut und oft auch sehr <u>lange</u>.

7. Es gibt <u>drei</u> Gruppen von Menschen um eine Person.

8. In einer <u>Gruppe</u> sind alle gute Kumpel.

9. Die meisten Menschen, die man kennt, nennt man <u>Bekannte</u>.

10. Die Gruppe der Freunde ist eine sehr <u>kleine</u> Gruppe.

Practice more at **vhlcentral.com.**

DEUTSCH IM ALLTAG

Wie wir Menschen sind

aufrichtig	*sincere*
besserwisserisch	*know-it-all (adj.)*
eingebildet	*arrogant*
geduldig	*patient*
geizig	*stingy*
liebevoll	*loving*
locker	*easy-going*
oberflächlich	*superficial*
ruhig	*calm*
weise	*wise*
zuverlässig	*reliable*

DIE DEUTSCHSPRACHIGE WELT

Es wird geheiratet!°

Wie wünscht° man dem neuen Paar ein
frohes Eheleben°? In **Bayern**, **Österreich**
und **in der Schweiz** ist das **Brautstehlen**°
eine lustige Tradition. Freunde stehlen die
Braut und bringen sie von Gaststätte°
zu Gaststätte. Der Bräutigam° muss sie
finden... und alle Getränke bezahlen°!
Die **Deutschen** und die **Österreicher** tragen
den Ring meistens an der rechten° Hand.
Aber **in der Schweiz** trägt man ihn an der
linken° Hand. Die ist dem Herzen näher°.

Es wird geheiratet! *Someone's getting married!*
wünscht *wishes* **Eheleben** *married life* **Brautstehlen**
stealing of the bride **Gaststätte** *restaurant* **Bräutigam**
groom **Getränke bezahlen** *pay for the drinks* **rechten**
right **linken** *left* **dem Herzen näher** *closer to the heart*

PORTRÄT

Tokio Hotel

Die erfolgreiche° deutsche Band *Tokio Hotel* besteht° am Anfang aus den eineiigen° Zwillingen
Bill und Tom Kaulitz. Schon als Kinder machen sie zusammen Musik. Als Duett treten sie
unter dem Namen *Black Questionmark* auf°. Ihr Stiefvater ist auch Musiker und fördert°
die Brüder. 2001 geben sie in ihrer Heimatstadt° Magdeburg ein Konzert. Dort treffen sie
Gustav Schäfer und Georg Listing. Sie werden Freunde und treten zu viert unter dem Namen
Devilish auf. 2005 nimmt die Universal Music Group die Band unter Vertrag°. Die Vier nennen
sich *Tokio Hotel* und sind schnell auf der ganzen Welt bekannt. Sie haben in Deutschland und
Österreich vier Nummer-eins-Singles und verkaufen bis heute weltweit über 7 Millionen Alben°.

erfolgreich *successful* **besteht** *consists* **eineiigen** *identical* **treten...auf** *perform* **fördert** *supports*
Heimatstadt *home town* **unter Vertrag** *under contract* **Alben** *albums*

⟳ IM INTERNET

Sind die Hochzeitsbräuche (*wedding traditions*)
anders (*different*) in Deutschland als in den USA?

Find out more at **vhlcentral.com**.

3 **Suggestion** You may want to teach students the expression **ich glaube**.

---

2 **Richtig oder falsch?** Indicate whether each statement is **richtig**
or **falsch**. Correct the false statements.

1. In Österreich ist es Tradition, den Bräutigam zu stehlen.
   Falsch. Es ist Tradition, die Braut zu stehlen.
2. In Deutschland trägt man den Ehering an der rechten Hand. Richtig.
3. *Tokio Hotel* ist eine erfolgreiche Band aus Österreich.
   Falsch. Die Band kommt aus Deutschland.
4. Bill und Tom Kaulitz sind Cousins. Falsch. Sie sind Brüder.
5. *Tokio Hotel* verkauft bis heute über 7 Millionen Alben. Richtig.

3 **Wie sind sie?** In pairs, describe each person in the photo on p. 120.
How old do you think they are? What do you think their personalities are
like? Are they friends or just classmates? Answers will vary.

Die deutschsprachige Welt Tell students that weddings in
Germany typically have two parts: the legal ceremony (which
is required) at the **Standesamt**, and the church wedding. After
the legal ceremony, friends and family may gather in front of
the bride's home to break pottery, because "**Scherben bringen**
Glück" (*shards bring happiness*).

Ressourcen

vhlcentral.com

Strukturen

3B.1

Modals Ⓢ Presentation

Startblock In both English and German, modal verbs modify the meaning of another verb.

Können wir Freunde sein?

Oh, George, du **darfst** nicht so ernst sein.

- Modals express an attitude towards an action, such as permission, obligation, ability, desire, or necessity. *May*, *can*, and *must* are examples of English modals.

Suggestion Explain to students that there are six modals in total. The modal **mögen** will be presented in **4A.2**.

modals	
dürfen	*to be allowed to, may*
können	*to be able to, can*
müssen	*to have to, must*
sollen	*to be supposed to*
wollen	*to want to*

- Except for **sollen**, all of the German modals are irregular in their present tense singular forms.

modals in the present tense					
	dürfen	**können**	**müssen**	**sollen**	**wollen**
ich	darf	kann	muss	soll	will
du	darfst	kannst	musst	sollst	willst
er/sie/es	darf	kann	muss	soll	will
wir	dürfen	können	müssen	sollen	wollen
ihr	dürft	könnt	müsst	sollt	wollt
Sie/sie	dürfen	können	müssen	sollen	wollen

Expansion Give students example sentences in English, with and without modals, to illustrate their use. Ex.: *He does his homework. He should do his homework. He must do his homework. He can do his homework. He wants to do his homework. He is allowed to do his homework.* Point out how each modal changes the meaning of the sentence.

- When you use a modal to modify the meaning of another verb, put the conjugated form of the modal in second position. Put the infinitive of the other verb at the end of the sentence.

Ich **muss** Französisch **lernen**.
*I **have to study** French.*

Ich **will** Französisch **lernen**.
*I **want to learn** French.*

- To form a yes-or-no question, move the modal verb to the beginning of the sentence, while the verb it modifies remains at the end.

> **Willst** du Wasser **trinken**?
> *Do you **want to drink** water?*

> **Könnt** ihr eurer Mutter **helfen**?
> *Can you **help** your mother?*

- **Dürfen** expresses permission.

> Mama, **darf** ich heute Nachmittag schwimmen gehen?
> *Mom, **may** I go swimming this afternoon?*

> Nein, Lina, du **darfst** heute nicht schwimmen gehen.
> *No, Lina, you **may** not go swimming today.*

- **Können** expresses ability.

> Peter **kann** Ski fahren.
> *Peter **can** ski.*

> **Kannst** du Fahrrad fahren?
> *Can you ride a bicycle?*

- **Müssen** expresses obligation.

> Jasmin und Moritz **müssen** viel lernen.
> *Jasmin and Moritz **have to** study a lot.*

> **Muss** Maria Spanisch lernen?
> *Does Maria **have to** learn Spanish?*

- **Sollen** conveys the expectation that a task be completed (*to be supposed to*). Note that, unlike the English *should* or *ought*, **sollen** implies an expectation that comes from someone other than the subject.

> Du **sollst** das Buch lesen.
> *You **are supposed to** read the book.*

> **Soll** ich nach Hause gehen?
> ***Should** I go home?*

- **Wollen** expresses desire.

> Sie **wollen** Musikerinnen werden.
> *They **want to** become musicians.*

> **Willst** du eine Katze haben?
> *Do you **want to** get a cat?*

Ressourcen

SAM
WB: pp. 41–42

SAM
LM: p. 27

Ⓢ
vhlcentral.com

Jetzt sind Sie dran!   **Complete the sentences.**

1. Die Lehrerin __soll__ (sollen) langsam sprechen.
2. Ihr __sollt__ (sollen) eure Hausaufgaben nicht vergessen.
3. Was __sollen__ (sollen) wir heute machen?
4. Der Musiker __kann__ (können) Gitarre spielen.
5. Ich __kann__ (können) meinen Rucksack nicht finden.
6. __Kannst__ (Können) du nach Deutschland reisen?
7. Du __musst__ (müssen) ein Wörterbuch kaufen.
8. Ein Geschäftsmann __muss__ (müssen) sehr fleißig sein.

9. Wir __müssen__ (müssen) das Matheproblem an die Tafel schreiben.
10. Das Paar __darf__ (dürfen) heiraten.
11. Die Kinder __dürfen__ (dürfen) hier Fußball spielen.
12. Du __darfst__ (dürfen) nicht in das Klassenzimmer gehen.
13. Ich __will__ (wollen) Architektin werden.
14. Die Kinder __wollen__ (wollen) Fremdsprachen studieren.
15. __Wollt__ (Wollen) ihr die Fotos sehen?

Anwendung

1 **Entscheiden Sie** Select the correct form of the modal.

1. Ich (sollen / soll) Gitarre spielen.
2. Wir (dürfen / darf) keine Schokolade essen.
3. (Willst / Wollt) du in die Bibliothek gehen?
4. Ihr (musst / müsst) eure Großeltern begrüßen.
5. Annika (kann / können) ihre Cousine nicht finden.
6. Max und Nils (kann / können) samstags lange schlafen.

2 **Was fehlt?** Complete the sentences.

1. Die Kellner _____sollen_____ (sollen) das Essen bringen.
2. Du _____kannst_____ (können) Deutsch lernen.
3. Wir _____müssen_____ (müssen) einen Beruf finden.
4. Ihr _____dürft_____ (dürfen) einen Film sehen.
5. Ich _____will_____ (wollen) Journalist werden.

3 **Schreiben** Rewrite the sentences using the cues.

BEISPIEL Antonia ist Musikerin. (wollen)
Antonia will Musikerin sein.

1. Die Ingenieure bauen eine neue Maschine. (müssen) Die Ingenieure müssen eine neue Maschine bauen.
2. Der Journalist reist nach Deutschland. (dürfen) Der Journalist darf nach Deutschland reisen.
3. Die Geschäftsfrau und der Geschäftsmann sind nicht gierig. (sollen)
Die Geschäftsfrau und der Geschäftsmann sollen nicht gierig sein.
4. Meine Tante und ich tanzen Tango. (können) Meine Tante und ich können Tango tanzen.
5. Ich werde Friseurin. (wollen) Ich will Friseurin werden.

4 **Expansion** Have students use these questions as the basis for a partner interview. Instead of using the subjects given, have them pose the questions to one another.
Ex.: **Darfst du schwimmen gehen? Ja, ich darf schwimmen gehen.**

4 **Fragen** Use the cues to form questions about the images.

BEISPIEL
ich / schwimmen
gehen / dürfen

Darf ich schwimmen gehen?

1. du / Ski fahren / können
Kannst du Ski fahren?

2. ich / jetzt lernen / sollen
Soll ich jetzt lernen?

3. Erika / Fußball spielen / wollen
Will Erika Fußball spielen?

4. wir / Musik hören / dürfen
Dürfen wir Musik hören?

5. Thomas / Musiker werden / wollen
Will Thomas Musiker werden?

6. ihr / viele Bücher lesen / müssen
Müsst ihr viele Bücher lesen?

 Practice more at **vhlcentral.com.**

Kommunikation

5 Expansion Have students say what they want to do and let other students give them advice. Ex.: **Ich will gute Noten bekommen. Du musst viel lernen.**

5 **Viele Wünsche** In pairs, take turns saying what each person wants to do. Then, imagine what they must or should do to achieve that goal.

Sample answers are provided.

> **BEISPIEL** mein Bruder / nach Deutschland fahren
>
> **S1:** *Mein Bruder will nach Deutschland fahren.*
> **S2:** *Er soll Deutsch lernen.*

1. meine Freundin / Architektin werden   Meine Freundin will Architektin werden.
2. ich / das Fußballspiel gewinnen   Ich will das Fußballspiel gewinnen.
3. wir / einen Hund haben   Wir wollen einen Hund haben.
4. mein Vater / ein neues Auto kaufen   Mein Vater will ein neues Auto kaufen.
5. meine Schwester / gute Noten haben   Meine Schwester will gute Noten haben.
6. mein Onkel / kurze Haare haben   Mein Onkel will kurze Haare haben.

6 **Berufe** With a partner, offer advice to help these people get the jobs they want. Answers will vary.

> **BEISPIEL** Mira und Maria / Ingenieurinnen
>
> **S1:** *Mira und Maria wollen Ingenieurinnen werden.*
> **S2:** *Sie sollen viel lernen.*

1. Emil und Hasan / Rechtsanwälte
2. David und Hanna / Musiker
3. Julia / Journalistin
4. Greta und Dilara / Geschäftsfrauen

7 **Einladungen** In small groups, take turns inviting each other to take part in these activities. If you turn down an invitation, explain what you want to do, should do, or must do instead, and suggest a different activity. Answers will vary.

> **BEISPIEL**
>
> **S1:** *Willst du Tennis spielen?*
> **S2:** *Ich kann nicht. Ich muss Hausaufgaben machen. Aber wir können morgen spazieren gehen.*

1.

2.

3.

4.

5.

6.

3B.2 Prepositions with the accusative  Presentation

Startblock In **1B.1**, you learned the accusative endings for definite and indefinite articles. You also learned that the direct object in German always takes the accusative case. In addition, the objects of certain prepositions are always in the accusative case.

Das Trinkgeld ist **für den Kellner**.
The tip is for the waiter.

Der Hund läuft **durch die Wälder**.
The dog is running through the woods.

- Prepositions and prepositional phrases describe time, manner, and place, and answer the questions *when*, *how*, and *where*.

um 8 Uhr
at 8 o'clock

ohne meinen Bruder
without my brother

gegen die Wand
against the wall

- Here are some common accusative prepositions.

prepositions with the accusative							
bis	*until, to*	entlang	*along*	gegen	*against*	pro	*per*
durch	*through*	für	*for*	ohne	*without*	um	*around; at (time)*

Der Besitzer kommt **durch die Tür**.
The owner is coming through the door.

Was hast du **gegen meinen Freund**?
What do you have against my boyfriend?

- The prepositions **durch**, **für**, and **um**, when followed by the neuter definite article **das**, may be contracted to **durchs**, **fürs**, and **ums**. These contractions are frequently used in speech and are acceptable in writing.

Das Spielzeug ist **fürs** Baby.
The toy is for the baby.

Die Kinder laufen **ums** Haus.
The kids are running around the house.

- The accusative preposition **bis** is frequently used with time expressions. When **bis** comes before a proper noun, such as **Samstag** or **März**, no article is necessary.

Ich bin **bis April** in Deutschland.
I'm in Germany until April.

Wir bleiben **bis nächsten Monat** in Köln.
We are staying in Cologne until next month.

- **Pro** is also an accusative preposition. The object it precedes takes no article.

Der Kellner verdient 300 Euro **pro Woche**.
The waiter earns 300 euros per week.

Das Auto fährt 230 Kilometer **pro Stunde**.
The car goes 230 kilometers per hour.

- The accusative is also used with objects that precede **entlang**.

Wir gehen **den Fluss entlang**.
We are going down the river.

Ich fahre **die Straße entlang**.
I'm driving along the road.

Ressourcen

SAM
WB: pp. 43–44

SAM
LM: p. 28

vhlcentral.com

 **Jetzt sind Sie dran!** **Select the preposition that best completes each sentence.**

1. Die Frau geht (ohne / pro) ihren Mann einkaufen.
2. Der Hund läuft (durch / gegen) den Park.
3. Die Mutter braucht ein Spielzeug (um / für) ihre Tochter.
4. Was haben die Besitzer (gegen / bis) die Musik?
5. Die Kellnerin geht (durch / um) den Tisch.

6. Die Taxifahrt kostet 2 € (für / pro) Kilometer.
7. Ich gehe den Fluss (entlang / bis).
8. Die Journalisten arbeiten (gegen / bis) Mitternacht.

Anwendung und Kommunikation

1 **Was ist richtig?** Select the preposition that best completes each sentence.

> bis | entlang | für | gegen | ohne | um

1. ____Um____ 8 Uhr muss ich arbeiten.
2. Der kleine Junge wirft den Ball ____gegen____ die Wand.
3. ____Ohne____ meine Schwester gehe ich nicht campen.
4. Das Auto fährt die Straße ____entlang____.
5. Sara kauft einen Kaffee ____für____ ihre Mutter.
6. Mein Onkel spielt ____bis____ 6 Uhr Fußball.

2 **Bilden Sie Sätze** Write eight sentences using items from each column. Pay attention to word order and accusative endings. Use each preposition once.

BEISPIEL Herr und Frau Becker / heute Abend eine Party geben / um / 8 Uhr
Heute Abend um 8 Uhr geben Herr und Frau Becker eine Party.

der Besitzer	angeln gehen	bis	Haustiere
du	beginnen	durch	Woche
ich	in Berlin bleiben	entlang	der Park
die Journalistin	50 Stunden arbeiten	für	19 Uhr
das Konzert	fahren	gegen	Samstag
Herr Bauer	laufen	ohne	die Straße
meine Schwester	lernen	pro	mein Bruder
wir	sein	um	die Prüfung

3 **Umfrage** In pairs, take turns asking and answering the questions. Answers will vary.

BEISPIEL

S1: *Um wie viel Uhr fährst du zur Uni?*
S2: *Ich fahre um 8 Uhr zur Uni.*

1. Um wie viel Uhr beginnt dein Unterricht?
2. Wie viele Stunden schläfst du pro Nacht?
3. Für wen kaufst du gern Blumen?
4. Ohne was kannst du nicht leben?
5. Gegen welche Mannschaften spielst du gern?

4 **Die Geburtstagsfeier** In small groups, write four sentences describing the illustration. Use at least four prepositions with the accusative.

Possible answers: Der Hund läuft durch das Spielfeld. Die Äpfel sind für die Kinder. Die Jungen spielen ohne ihre Schwester. Die Eltern wollen um 12 Uhr essen.

 Practice more at **vhlcentral.com**.

3B.3

The imperative Presentation

Startblock Imperatives are used to express commands, requests, suggestions, directions, and instructions.

Sei nicht traurig.

Mach dir keine Sorgen!

- The imperative forms are based on the present-tense conjugation patterns of **du**, **wir**, **ihr**, and **Sie**.

the *Imperativ* conjugation	
Indikativ	**Imperativ**
du kaufst	kauf(e)
ihr kauft	kauft
Sie kaufen	kaufen Sie
wir kaufen	kaufen wir

Mach deine Hausaufgaben!
Do your homework!

Backen wir einen Kuchen!
Let's bake a cake!

- To form an informal singular command, drop the **-st** from the present-tense **du** form of the verb. As in English, omit the subject pronoun with the second-person imperative.

Antworte auf die Frage!
Answer the question!

Schreib deinen Eltern eine E-Mail.
Write your parents an email.

- Verbs with an **a** to **ä** vowel change do not retain this change in the imperative. However, **e** to **ie** and **e** to **i** changes are retained in the imperative for **du**.

Fahr langsam!
Drive slowly!

Lies das Buch.
Read the book.

Nimm den Bleistift.
Take the pencil.

- The informal plural **ihr** command is identical to the present-tense form, without the pronoun.

Esst die Äpfel, Kinder!
Eat the apples, kids!

Lernt für die Prüfung.
Study for the exam.

- For formal commands, keep the subject **Sie** and invert the subject/verb word order of the present tense. Remember that the singular and plural forms are identical.

Probieren Sie den Kuchen!
Try the cake!

Warten Sie bitte hier.
Please wait here.

- The first person plural command is equivalent to the English *Let's....* As with **Sie**, invert the subject/verb order of the present tense for **wir**.

Essen wir den Kuchen.
Let's eat the cake.

Gehen wir spazieren.
Let's go for a walk.

ACHTUNG

Verbs that contain a double **s** in the infinitive do not drop an **s** in the informal singular imperative.

Iss das Gemüse, Tanja!
Eat your vegetables, Tanja!

- In a negative command, **nicht** or **kein** follows the imperative form.

Fahren Sie nicht so schnell!
Don't drive so fast!

Hör keine laute Musik!
Don't listen to loud music!

Arbeite nicht so langsam!
Don't work so slowly!

Macht kein Theater!
Don't make a fuss!

- Use **bitte** to soften a command and make it polite. **Bitte** can be placed almost anywhere in a sentence, as long as it doesn't separate the verb from the subject pronoun **wir** or **Sie**.

Öffnen Sie **bitte** Ihren Rucksack.
*Open your backpack, **please**.*

Schlaft **bitte** nicht im Unterricht!
***Please** don't sleep in class!*

Geh nach Hause, **bitte**.
*Go home, **please**.*

Bitte nehmen Sie Platz.
***Please** take a seat.*

- The modals **können** and **wollen** are often used instead of the imperative for polite requests.

Können Sie mir helfen?
***Can** you help me?*

Wollen wir gehen?
***Shall** we go?*

- The verb **sein** has irregular imperative forms.

Sei lieb!
***Be** good! (sing., inf.)*

Seid diskret!
***Be** discreet! (pl., inf.)*

Seien Sie mutig!
***Be** brave! (form.)*

Seien wir realistisch.
***Let's be** realistic.*

- On signs or labels, and in recipes or printed instructions, infinitives are often used instead of imperatives. Here are some common commands and instructions found in everyday situations. Notice that in some cases, a command is conveyed by using an infinitive or the word **verboten** (*forbidden*), rather than the imperative.

common commands	
Drücken.	*Push.*
Ziehen.	*Pull.*
Bring mir...	*Bring me...*
Langsam fahren.	*Slow down.*
Warte.	*Wait.*
Sprechen Sie bitte langsamer.	*Please speak more slowly.*
Türen schließen.	*Keep doors closed.*
Rauchen verboten.	*No smoking.*
Betreten des Rasens verboten.	*Keep off the grass.*
Keine Zufahrt.	*Do not enter.*
Parkverbot.	*No parking.*

QUERVERWEIS

See **2B.3** to review the use of **nicht** and **kein**.

Ressourcen

SAM
WB: pp. 45–46

SAM
LM: p. 29

vhlcentral.com

Jetzt sind Sie dran! Select the correct imperative form to complete each sentence.

1. Herr Professor Braun, (sprecht / sprechen Sie) bitte langsamer.
2. Schüler, (öffnen Sie / öffnet) eure Bücher auf Seite 34.
3. Philip, (vergiss / vergessen wir) deine Hausaufgaben nicht!
4. Kinder, (seid / sei) freundlich und nett!
5. Wir haben morgen eine Prüfung. (Lernen wir / Lernt) zusammen.
6. Nina, (fahrt / fahr) nicht so schnell!
7. Herr und Frau Schmidt, (warte / warten Sie) bitte einen Moment.
8. Wir haben Hunger. (Essen wir / Iss) den Strudel.

Anwendung

1 **Was fehlt?** Complete the sentences using the imperative.

BEISPIEL Sebastian, _____Komm_____ (kommen)!

1. Herr Schneider, ___wiederholen Sie___ (wiederholen) bitte.
2. Marie und Lukas, _____esst_____ (essen) langsamer!
3. Felix, _____sei_____ (sein) nicht gemein!
4. Frau Fischer und Herr Wagner, ___nehmen Sie___ (nehmen) bitte eine Karte.
5. Paul und Else, _____macht_____ (machen) bitte kein Theater!
6. _____Sprechen_____ (sprechen) wir Deutsch!

2 **Bilden Sie Sätze** Write imperative commands for each person using the cues.

BEISPIEL Herr Braun: nicht so schnell fahren
Herr Braun, fahren Sie nicht so schnell!

1. Klara: Tennis mit Jan spielen Klara, spiel Tennis mit Jan!
2. Wir: durch den Park gehen Gehen wir durch den Park!
3. Max und Lara: den Text auf Seite 27 lesen Max und Lara, lest/lesen Sie den Text auf Seite 27!
4. Herr Gärtner: heute bis 8 Uhr bleiben Herr Gärtner, beiben Sie heute bis 8 Uhr!
5. Frau Weber: nicht nervös sein Frau Weber, seien Sie nicht nervös!
6. Niklas: um 6 Uhr nach Hause kommen Niklas, komm um 6 Uhr nach Hause!

3 **Schreiben** Tell these people not to do what they are doing. Sample answers are provided.

BEISPIEL Lara ist eifersüchtig.
Sei nicht eifersüchtig, Lara!

3 **Expansion** Have students give additional affirmative commands for this activity. Ex.: **1. Seien Sie nicht gierig, Herr Becker! Seien Sie großzügig und nett!**

1. Herr Becker ist gierig.
   Seien Sie nicht gierig, Herr Becker!
2. Tom und Jonas weinen.
   Weint nicht, Tom und Jonas!
3. Lukas spielt schlechte Musik.
   Spiel keine schlechte Musik, Lukas!
4. Frau Weber kauft hässliche Sachen.
   Kaufen Sie keine hässlichen Sachen, Frau Weber!
5. Max und Lukas schreiben an die Wand.
   Schreibt nicht an die Wand, Max und Lukas!
6. Wir bleiben hier.
   Bleiben wir nicht hier!
7. Hanna telefoniert 4 Stunden pro Tag.
   Hanna, telefonier nicht 4 Stunden pro Tag!
8. Otto und Emma essen den Kuchen.
   Esst den Kuchen nicht, Otto und Emma!

4 **Konjugieren** Write a command for each image using the cues. Sample answers are provided.

1. wir Tanzen wir.

2. Nils Nils, wirf den Ball!

3. Kinder / eure Bücher
   Kinder, öffnet eure Bücher.

4. Frau Schulze / ein Glas Wasser
   Frau Schulze, trinken Sie ein Glas Wasser.

5. wir Gehen wir spazieren.

6. Greta / ein Bonbon
   Greta, nimm ein Bonbon.

Practice more at **vhlcentral.com.**

Kommunikation

5 **Befehle** In small groups, write eight sentences using **sollen**. Then, trade lists with another group and convert their sentences into commands. Answers will vary.

BEISPIEL

S1: *Du sollst deine Hausaufgaben machen.*
S2: *Mach deine Hausaufgaben.*

6 **Guter Rat** In pairs, use the imperative to give advice to each person or group. Answers will vary.

BEISPIEL deine Professorin
Sprechen Sie bitte langsamer!

1. deine Kommilitonen
2. deine beste Freundin oder dein bester Freund
3. deine Eltern oder deine Großeltern
4. dein Bruder oder deine Schwester
5. dein Dozent oder deine Dozentin
6. deine Katze oder dein Hund

7 **Ein paar Ratschläge** In pairs, list ten pieces of advice that you would give to a new German exchange student at your school. Use the affirmative and negative forms of the imperative. Answers will vary.

BEISPIEL

S1: *Sei fleißig, aber nicht zu ernst!*
S2: *Vergiss nicht deine Hausaufgaben!*

8 **Simon sagt** In groups of five, play Simon Says. One student gives commands using the **du**, **Sie**, **ihr**, and **wir** forms. The group members must perform or mime the activity, but only if the speaker says **"Simon sagt"**. The first person to make a mistake becomes the new leader. Answers will vary.

BEISPIEL

S1: *Simon sagt: „Tanzen wir!"*
OR
S1: *Laura und Michael, lauft um den Tisch!*

essen	laufen	schreiben
fahren	nehmen	sprechen
hören	öffnen	tanzen
fangen	sagen	weinen
lachen	schlafen	wiederholen

8 **Suggestion** If nobody makes a mistake, tell students to change leaders after three commands.

8 **Expansion** You may want to introduce students to the traditional German game **Kommando Pimperle**, similar to Simon Says.

Wiederholung

1 Etwas unternehmen

In pairs, make plans for what you will do today in each location. Use prepositions with the accusative. Answers will vary.

BEISPIEL

S1: Um 10 Uhr gehen wir in die Bibliothek.
S2: Ja, dort können wir gute Bücher für das Referat finden.

bis	gegen
durch	ohne
entlang	um
für	

1.

2.

3.

4.

2 Wollen und sollen

In small groups, take turns saying one thing that you want to do today, one thing you must do, one thing you can do, one thing you may do, and one thing you are supposed to do. Answers will vary.

BEISPIEL

S1: Ich will heute Abend in die Sporthalle gehen, aber ich muss Hausaufgaben machen.
S2: Ich soll für meinen Deutschkurs lernen, aber ich kann auch Tennis spielen.
S3: Ich kann nicht Tennis spielen. Ich muss...

3 Diskutieren und kombinieren

Your instructor will give you and a partner different worksheets with a list of occupations and profiles of several students. Take turns describing the students and matching their qualities to appropriate occupations. Answers will vary.

BEISPIEL

S1: Jana ist kreativ und gut in Mathe.
S2: Ah, dann ist Jana eine gute Architektin.

3 Expansion After partners have matched each student to the profession indicated, have them brainstorm alternative professions that would be compatible with the qualities listed.

4 Meine ideale Familie

Survey your classmates about their ideal family situation, and write down their answers. Then, in pairs, compare your results. Answers will vary.

BEISPIEL

S1: Wie ist deine ideale Familie?
S2: Meine ideale Familie ist sehr groß...

5 Arbeitsblatt

Your instructor will give you a worksheet with several activities listed. Survey your classmates to find someone who would like to do each of the activities with you. When someone says "yes", agree on a time and date. If someone says "no", they must give an excuse, explaining what they have to or are supposed to do instead. Answers will vary.

BEISPIEL

S1: Gehen wir morgen Abend ins Theater!
S2: Ich kann nicht. Ich muss für die Prüfung lernen.
S3: Ich komme gern. Gehen wir morgen um 7 Uhr!

6 Geschwister

In pairs, role-play a conversation between two siblings. The younger sibling asks to do things, and the older sibling tells him/her what to do and what not to do. Answers will vary.

BEISPIEL

S1: Darf ich Fußball spielen?
S2: Nein, das darfst du nicht! Iss dein Abendessen!

7 **Die Familie** With a partner, write a brief description of these five family members. Use the vocabulary you learned in **Lektionen 2A**, **2B**, **3A**, and **3B** to describe their interests, activities, physical characteristics, and personalities. Answers will vary.

BEISPIEL

Die Tochter heißt Mia. Sie ist zwölf Jahre alt. Sie hat blonde Haare und blaue Augen. Sie ist sehr aktiv und spielt gern Fußball.

7 **Suggestion** Encourage students to be creative in their descriptions, and to include information about how the characters are related to one another.

Die Familie

der Sohn   der Vater   der Cousin
    die Tochter   die Mutter

8 **Am Wochenende** In small groups, prepare a skit in which a group of friends makes plans for the weekend. Use vocabulary from **Kapitel 2.** Answers will vary.

BEISPIEL

S1: *Ich spiele gern Basketball! Können wir morgen Basketball spielen?*
S2: *Nein, bleiben wir hier! Wir müssen unsere Hausaufgaben machen!*
S3: *Ihr könnt hier bleiben, aber ich will...*

8 **Suggestion** Before dividing students into groups, have the class brainstorm a list of possible activities that could take place in the locations pictured.

Mein Wör|ter|buch

Add five words related to **die Familie** and **persönliche Beschreibungen** to your personalized dictionary.

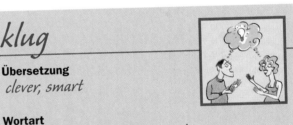

klug

Übersetzung
clever, smart

Wortart
Adjektiv (Beschreibungswort)

Gebrauch
Der Mann ist klug. Ein kluger Mann spricht nicht zu viel.

Synonyme
intelligent, schlau

Antonyme
unintelligent, dumm

 **Vocabulary tools**

Panorama Ⓢ Interactive Map

Die Vereinigten Staaten und Kanada

NATIONAL
connections
cultures
STANDARDS

Anteil der Amerikaner mit deutschen Wurzeln: 15% (50 Millionen)

- ▶ **Kalifornien:** *5.517.470*
- ▶ **Pennsylvania:** *3.491.269*
- ▶ **Ohio:** *3.231.788*
- ▶ **Illinois:** *2.668.955*
- ▶ **Texas:** *2.542.996*
- ▶ **Wisconsin:** *2.455.980*

- ▶ **Michigan:** *2.271.091*
- ▶ **Florida:** *2.270.456*
- ▶ **New York:** *2.250.309*
- ▶ **Minnesota:** *1.949.346*
- ▶ **Indiana:** *1.629.766*
- ▶ **Missouri:** *1.576.813*

QUELLE: U.S. Census 2010

Anteil der Kanadier mit deutschen Wurzeln: 10% (3 Millionen)

- ▶ **Toronto:** *220.135*
- ▶ **Vancouver:** *187.410*
- ▶ **Winnipeg::** *109.355*

- ▶ **Kitchener:** *93.325*
- ▶ **Montreal:** *83.850*

QUELLE: Canadian Census 2011

Die ersten deutschen Siedler in Kanada kommen zwischen 1750 und 1753 nach Nova Scotia. Die meisten von ihnen° sind Bauern und Kaufleute°. Zwischen 1919 und 1939 kommen fast 100.000 Deutsche nach Kanada. Auch von ihnen sind die meisten Bauern. Sie alle bringen ihre Familien mit und starten ein neues Leben in Nordamerika.

Berühmte Deutschamerikaner und Deutschkanadier

- ▶ **Levi Strauss,** *Unternehmer° (1829–1902)*
- ▶ **Frederick Louis Maytag I,** *Unternehmer (1857–1937)*
- ▶ **Dwight D. Eisenhower,** *Fünf-Sterne General und US-Präsident (1890–1969)*
- ▶ **Lou Gehrig,** *Baseballspieler (1903–1941)*
- ▶ **Henry Kissinger,** *Politiker (1923–)*
- ▶ **Almuth Lütkenhaus,** *Künstlerin° (1930–1996)*
- ▶ **Dany Heatley,** *Eishockeyspieler (1981–)*
- ▶ **Justin Bieber,** *Sänger° (1994–)*

Die meisten von ihnen *most of them* **Kaufleute** *tradespeople*
Unternehmer *entrepreneur* **Künstlerin** *artist* **Sänger** *singer*
verlässt *leaves* **Flöten** *flutes* **Immobilien** *real estate*
Fellhandel *fur trade* **reichste** *richest* **Vermögen** *fortune*

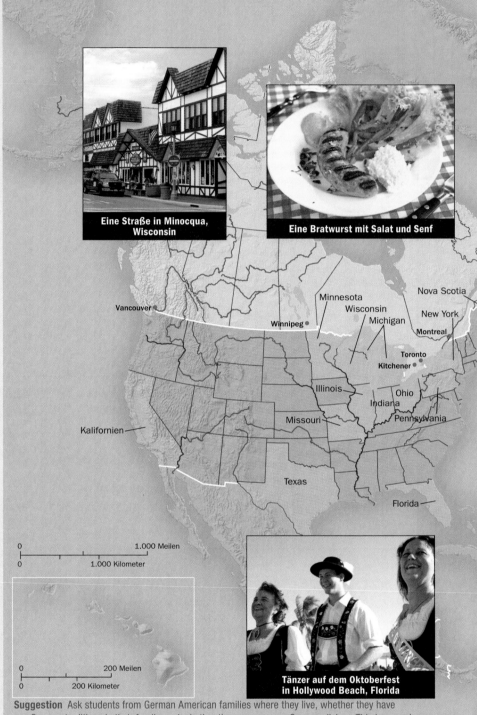

Eine Straße in Minocqua, Wisconsin

Eine Bratwurst mit Salat und Senf

Nova Scotia
Minnesota
Wisconsin
New York
Vancouver
Winnipeg
Michigan
Montreal
Toronto
Kitchener
Illinois
Ohio
Indiana
Missouri
Pennsylvania
Kalifornien
Texas
Florida

0 — 1.000 Meilen
0 — 1.000 Kilometer

0 — 200 Meilen
0 — 200 Kilometer

Tänzer auf dem Oktoberfest in Hollywood Beach, Florida

Suggestion Ask students from German American families where they live, whether they have any German traditions in their family, and whether they prepare any German dishes. This is a good opportunity to explore the richness of German American culture in the United States, and also to point out how some German customs have evolved.

Unglaublich, aber wahr!

1784 verlässt° **John Jacob Astor** (1763–1848) das Dorf Walldorf in Deutschland mit $25 und 7 Flöten° in Richtung USA. Durch Immobilien°- und Fellhandel° wird er reich und ist zur Zeit seines Todes der reichste° Mann Amerikas. Sein Vermögen° beträgt ungefähr $90 Millionen.

Menschen

Sandra Bullock

Sandra Bullock wurde 1964 in Arlington, Virginia geboren°. Ihre Mutter ist Helga D. Meyer, eine deutsche Opernsängerin. Deshalb verbringt° Bullock, die neben Englisch fließend° Deutsch spricht, auch die ersten 12 Jahre ihres Lebens in der deutschen Stadt Fürth, bevor sie mit ihrer Familie in die USA zieht. Ihre erfolgreiche Karriere beinhaltet Filme wie *Gravity, Speed* und *Blind Side – Die große Chance*, für den sie einen Oscar als beste Hauptdarstellerin° erhält.

Geschichte

Deutsche in Texas

1848 gibt es in Deutschland und vielen anderen europäischen Ländern (Frankreich, Dänemark, Österreich) Revolutionen und Aufstände° auf Grund von sozialen und wirtschaftlichen° Problemen. Nach der Mairevolution verlassen° viele Revolutionäre Deutschland und gehen in die USA. Sie leben in Städten wie zum Beispiel New Braunfels und Fredericksburg in Texas. Diesen deutschen Einfluss° kann man heute hier immer noch sehen. Unter anderem gibt es in Texas eine Form des Deutschen, die man Texas-Deutsch nennt.

Essen

Hamburger

Der Hamburger – ein Sandwich aus einer Frikadelle° in einer Semmel° mit einem Salatblatt und einer Scheibe Tomate – hat etwas mit der Stadt Hamburg zu tun. Als deutsche Immigranten und Matrosen° Ende des 18. Jahrhunderts nach New York kommen, bekommen Sie hier „Steak im Hamburger Stil". Diese Steaks damals hatten mit heutigen Hamburgern außer dem Namen noch nicht viel zu tun. Erst mit der Erfindung des Fleischwolfs° im 19. Jahrhunderts werden aus Steaks im Hamburger Stil die heutigen Hamburger.

Feiern

German Fest

Das German Fest in Milwaukee ist das größte „deutsche" Event Nordamerikas. Seit 1981 feiern die Menschen hier am letzten Juliwochenende Kultur deutschsprachiger° Länder und Regionen wie Österreich, Deutschland, Liechtenstein, Südtirol und der Schweiz. Besucher° tragen teilweise Dirndl und Lederhosen, hören traditionelle Blaskapellen° oder moderne Popmusik und bekommen Informationen über ihre deutsche Abstammung°. Im Jahr 2010 essen die Besucher unter anderem 20.000 Bratwürste, 9.000 Knödel°, 200 Spanferkel° und 15.000 Stück Strudel.

 IM INTERNET

1. Welche anderen Gerichte (*dishes*) haben ihren Ursprung (*origin*) in deutschsprachigen Ländern?

2. Suchen Sie ein Rezept für ein deutsch-amerikanisches (oder österreichisch-amerikanisches) Gericht.

3. Suchen Sie Informationen über eine berühmte deutsch-amerikanische Person.

Find out more at **vhlcentral.com**.

---

wurde... geboren *was born* **verbringt** *spends (time)* **fließend** *fluent* **Hauptdarstellerin** *lead actress* **Aufstände** *uprisings* **wirtschaftlichen** *economic* **verlassen** *leave* **Einfluss** *influence* **Frikadelle** *meatball* **Semmel** *bun* **Matrosen** *sailors* **Erfindung des Fleischwolfs** *invention of the meat grinder* **deutschsprachiger** *German-speaking* **Besucher** *Visitors* **Blaskapellen** *brass bands* **Abstammung** *descent* **Knödel** *dumplings* **Spanferkel** *suckling pigs*

 Was haben Sie gelernt? Complete the sentences.

1. Die meisten Amerikaner mit deutschen Wurzeln leben in _Kalifornien_.

2. Ungefähr _15 %_ der amerikanischen Bevölkerung haben deutsche Wurzeln.

3. John Astor verlässt 1784 Deutschland mit _$25_ und 7 Flöten.

4. Eine Schauspielerin, die fließend Deutsch spricht, ist _Sandra Bullock_.

5. Sandra Bullock wohnt in Fürth, bis sie _12 Jahre_ alt ist.

6. Zwei deutsche Städte in Texas sind _New Braunfels_ und Fredericksburg

7. Hamburger haben ihren Namen von der deutschen Stadt _Hamburg_.

8. Die Besucher essen jedes Jahr 200 Spanferkel und 20.000 Bratwürste auf dem _German Fest_.

9. Beim *German Fest* sehen _Besucher_ viele Facetten deutschsprachiger Kultur.

 Practice more at **vhlcentral.com**.

Lesen

 Audio: Reading

Vor dem Lesen

Strategien

Predicting content from visuals

When you read in German, look for visual cues that can help you figure out the content and purpose of what you are reading. Photos and illustrations, for example, can give you a good idea of the main points of the reading. You may also encounter helpful visuals that summarize large amounts of data in a way that is easy to comprehend; these visuals include bar graphs, pie charts, flow charts, lists of percentages, and other diagrams.

Die beliebtesten° Haustiere

In Deutschland gibt es Haustiere in mehr als° 12 Millionen Haushalten.

Katzen	**16,5%** der Haushalte
Hunde	**13,8%** der Haushalte
Kleintiere	**5,9%** der Haushalte
Vögel	**5,7%** der Haushalte
Aquarien°	**5,7%** der Haushalte

Auch in Österreich und der Schweiz sind Katzen und Hunde die beliebtesten Haustiere.

beliebtesten *most popular* **mehr als** *more than* **Aquarien** *fish tanks*

Texte verstehen 👥👥 Take a quick look at the visual elements of the article in order to generate a list of ideas about its content. Then compare your list with a classmate's. What elements did you both notice? What aspects did your partner notice that didn't catch your eye? Discuss and consolidate your ideas to produce a final list to share with the class.

Hunde und Katzen

Für viele Deutsche, Österreicher und Schweizer sind Haustiere sehr wichtig. Allerdings gibt es in diesen Ländern weit weniger vierbeinige° Freunde als in anderen europäischen Ländern. Zum Beispiel hat in Deutschland nur etwa jeder Vierte ein Haustier.

Welche Tiere findet man bei Deutschen, Österreichern und Schweizern am häufigsten°? Oft hört man, der Hund ist des Deutschen bester Freund. Statistiken zeigen° allerdings, dass nicht Hunde, sondern Katzen das Haustier Nummer 1 im deutschsprachigen Raum sind. Hunde stehen nur an Nummer 2.

vierbeinige *four-legged* **am häufigsten** *most frequently* **zeigen** *show*

Außerdem geht der allgemeine° Trend hin zu mehr° Katzen und weniger° Hunden. Andere beliebte Tiere sind Kleintiere wie Kaninchen° und Hamster. Vögel singen immer weniger in deutschsprachigen Haushalten°.

Haustiere sind oft ein wichtiger Teil° der Familie. Kinder lernen durch sie, soziale Kontakte zu pflegen°. Großstadtkinder, die mit einem Hund leben, haben später° oft weniger Probleme mit Kriminalität. Vor allem bei Singles sind Katzen beliebt, da sie alleine sein können, aber auch eine Art Partnerersatz sind.

Wer hat welches Haustier?

Status	Katzen	Hunde	Fische	Vögel
Ledig	23%	18%	7%	5%
Verheiratet	18%	18%	6%	5%
Frauen	17%	18%	7%	5%
Männer	17%	18%	6%	5%

allgemeine *general* **mehr** *more* **weniger** *fewer* **Kaninchen** *bunnies* **Haushalten** *households*
ein wichtiger Teil *an important part* **pflegen** *to cultivate* **später** *later*

Nach dem Lesen

Richtig oder falsch? Indicate whether each statement is **richtig** or **falsch**.
Expansion Have students correct the false statements.

	richtig	falsch
1. Fast jede Familie in Deutschland hat ein Haustier. <small>Jeder Vierte in Deutschland hat ein Haustier.</small>	☐	☑
2. Katzen sind das Haustier Nummer 1.	☑	☐
3. Der Trend in den nächsten Jahren geht zu mehr Hunden. <small>Der Trend in den nächsten Jahren geht zu mehr Katzen.</small>	☐	☑
4. Immer weniger Menschen haben Vögel.	☑	☐
5. Großstadtkinder mit Hunden haben mehr Probleme. <small>Großstadtkinder mit Hunden haben weniger Probleme.</small>	☐	☑
6. Viele Ledige haben Katzen als Haustiere.	☑	☐

Was ist richtig? Select the correct response according to the article.

1. Wie viel Prozent der Deutschen besitzen ein Haustier?
   a. 10%–20% b. 20%–30% c. 30%–40%

2. Welche Haustiere werden immer beliebter?
   a. Katzen b. Vögel c. Hunde

3. Welches Tier passt in die Kategorie Kleintiere?
   a. Katzen b. Hunde c. Hamster

4. Welches Haustier besitzen die meisten Deutschen?
   a. Hunde b. Fische c. Katzen

5. Welche Bevölkerungsgruppe hat die meisten Haustiere?
   a. Frauen b. Ledige c. Verheiratete

Meine Haustiere With a partner, talk about the pets you or your family and friends have. Use the verb **haben** and possessive adjectives.

BEISPIEL

S1: *Hast du eine Katze?*
S2: *Nein, ich habe einen Fisch, aber mein Onkel hat zwei Katzen...*

Hören

Strategien

Asking for repetition/Replaying the recording

Sometimes it is difficult to understand what people are saying, especially in a noisy environment. During a conversation, you can ask someone to repeat what they've said by saying **Wie bitte?** (*Excuse me?*) or **Entschuldigung?** In class, you can ask your instructor to repeat by saying **Wiederholen Sie, bitte.** (*Repeat, please.*)

 To help you practice this strategy, you will listen to a short conversation. Ask your instructor to repeat it or replay the recording, and then summarize what you heard.

Vorbereitung

Based on the photograph, where do you think Lena and Jasmin are? What do you think they are talking about?

Zuhören

Now you are going to hear Lena and Jasmin's conversation. Write **M** next to adjectives that describe Jasmin's friend Maria. Write **T** next to adjectives that describe Lena's ex-boyfriend, Tobias. Some adjectives will not be used.

__M__ fleißig	____ langweilig
____ hübsch	__M__ intelligent
__T__ eifersüchtig	__T__ egoistisch
____ sportlich	____ langsam
__M__ großartig	__T__ verlobt
____ ernst	____ faul

Vor dem Hören Ask students questions about the two women in the picture to help them guess what they might be talking about. Brainstorm possible topics for the women's conversation and write them on the board. Ex.: **Über was sprechen Lena und Jasmin? Über die Arbeit? Über Familie? Über die Liebe?**

Verständnis

Wer ist das? Write the name of the person described by each statement.

1. ___Maria___ ist Jasmins neue Freundin.
2. ___Tobias___ ist egoistisch und eifersüchtig.
3. ___Jasmin___ lernt mit Maria für die Literaturprüfungen.
4. ___Lena___ ist allein glücklich.
5. ___Tobias___ ist mit Antonia verlobt.
6. ___Jasmin___ will mit Lena schwimmen gehen.

Richtig oder falsch Indicate whether each statement is **richtig** or **falsch**. Correct the false statements.

1. Lena studiert Literatur. Falsch. Jasmin studiert Literatur.
2. Tobias hilft Jasmin. Falsch. Maria hilft Jasmin.
3. Maria ist großartig. Richtig.
4. Lena ist ledig. Richtig.
5. Geschichte ist Jasmins Hobby. Richtig.
6. Tobias ist intelligent und fleißig. Falsch. Tobias ist egoistisch und eifersüchtig.

Schreiben

NATIONAL
communication
cultures
STANDARDS

Using idea maps

How do you organize ideas for a first draft? Often, the organization of ideas represents the most challenging part of the writing process. Idea maps are useful for organizing information. Here is an example of an idea map you could use when writing.

IDEA MAP

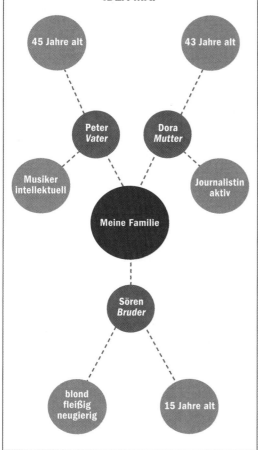

Successful Language Learning Remind students to write their notes in German. Emphasize that they should not translate directly from English. Encourage them to use words and phrases they are familiar with and not rely too heavily on the dictionary.

Thema

 Briefe schreiben

A German friend you met online wants to know about your family. Using the verbs and grammar structures you learned in this unit, write a brief description of your family or an imaginary family, including:

- Names and relationships
- Physical characteristics
- Hobbies and interests

Suggestion Tell students that it may be helpful to write their idea maps on note cards, so that they can easily rearrange the ideas if necessary.

Here are some useful expressions for writing a letter or e-mail in German:

Salutations	
Lieber Erik,	*Dear Erik,*
Liebe Anna,	*Dear Anna,*

Asking for a response	
Ich hoffe, bald von dir zu hören.	*I hope to hear from you soon.*
Erzähl, was es Neues bei dir gibt.	*Let me know what's new with you.*

Closings	
Bis bald!/Tschüss!	*So long!*
Mach's gut!	*All the best!*
Mit freundlichen Grüßen	*Yours sincerely*
Hochachtungsvoll	*Respectfully*

Suggestion Tell students that when the salutation ends with a comma, it is considered part of the first sentence of the letter, and the word that follows is not capitalized (unless it's a noun). Point out that an exclamation mark can be used instead of a comma, in which case the text that follows does start with a capitalized word.

Suggestion Point out the differences in formality in the closing expressions. For example, **Tschüss!** and **Mach's gut!** should only be used with friends and family, whereas **Mit freundlichen Grüßen** or **Hochachtungsvoll** are more formal.

 **Vocabulary Tools**

die Familie

das Baby, -s	baby
der Bruder, ⸚	brother
der Cousin, -s	cousin (m.)
die Cousine, -n	cousin (f.)
die Eltern	parents
das Enkelkind, -er	grandchild
der Enkelsohn, ⸚e	grandson
die Enkeltochter, ⸚	granddaughter
die Frau, -en	wife
das Geschwister, -	sibling
die Großeltern	grandparents
die Großmutter, ⸚	grandmother
der Großvater, ⸚	grandfather
der Halbbruder, ⸚	half brother
die Halbschwester, -n	half sister
das Kind, -er	child
der Mann, ⸚er	husband
die Mutter, ⸚	mother
der Nachname, -n	last name
der Neffe, -n	nephew
die Nichte, -n	niece
die Oma, -s	grandma
der Onkel, -	uncle
der Opa, -s	grandpa
das Paar, -e	couple
der Schwager, ⸚	brother-in-law
die Schwägerin, -nen	sister-in-law
die Schwester, -n	sister
die Schwiegermutter, ⸚	mother-in-law
der Schwiegervater, ⸚	father-in-law
der Sohn, ⸚e	son
der Stiefbruder, ⸚	stepbrother
die Stiefmutter, ⸚	stepmother
die Stiefschwester, -n	stepsister
der Stiefsohn, ⸚e	stepson
die Stieftochter, ⸚	stepdaughter
der Stiefvater, ⸚	stepfather
die Tante, -n	aunt
die Tochter, ⸚	daughter
der Vater, ⸚	father
der / die Verwandte, -n	relative
der Zwilling, -e	twin

die Haustiere

der Fisch, -e	fish
der Hund, -e	dog
die Katze, -n	cat
der Vogel, ⸚	bird

zum Beschreiben

blaue/grüne/braune Augen	blue/green/brown eyes
blonde/braune/schwarze Haare	blond/brown/black hair
(un)angenehm	(un)pleasant
arm	poor; unfortunate
bescheiden	modest
besorgt	worried
diskret	discreet
dunkel	dark
egoistisch	selfish
eifersüchtig	jealous
ernst	serious
faul	lazy
fleißig	hard-working
freundlich	friendly
froh	happy
gemein	mean
gierig	greedy
glücklich	happy
großzügig	generous
hell	light
intellektuell	intellectual
intelligent	intelligent
langsam	slow
lustig	funny
müde	tired
mutig	brave
naiv	naïve
nervös	nervous
nett	nice
neugierig	curious
reich	rich
schlecht	bad
schnell	fast
schüchtern	shy
schwach	weak
stark	strong
stolz	proud
süß	sweet; cute
toll	great
traurig	sad
lächeln	to smile
lachen	to laugh
weinen	to cry

der Familienstand

die Witwe, -n	widow
der Witwer, -	widower
geschieden	divorced
getrennt	separated
ledig	single
verheiratet	married
verlobt	engaged
zusammen	together
heiraten	to marry

Berufe

der Architekt, -en / die Architektin, -nen	architect
der Besitzer, - / die Besitzerin, -nen	owner
der Friseur, -e / die Friseurin, -nen	hairdresser
der Geschäftsmann (pl. Geschäftsleute) / die Geschäftsfrau, -en	businessman / businesswoman
der Ingenieur, -e / die Ingenieurin, -nen	engineer
der Journalist, -en / die Journalistin, -nen	journalist
der Kellner, - / die Kellnerin, -nen	waiter / waitress
der Musiker, - / die Musikerin, -nen	musician
der Rechtsanwalt, ⸚e / die Rechtsanwältin, -nen	lawyer

Modalverben

dürfen	to be allowed to, may
können	to be able to, can
müssen	to have to, must
sollen	to be supposed to
wollen	to want to

Possessive adjectives	See p. 104.
Descriptive adjectives	See p. 108.
Prepositions with the accusative	See p. 126.
Common commands	See p. 129.

Essen

Suggestion Have students look at the photo and identify the people and items they see. Ask them what they think this unit will be about.

Communicative Goals

You will learn how to:

- talk about food
- talk about grocery shopping

Lebensmittel

 **Vocabulary Tools**

Suggestion Tell students that Germans typically buy fresh bread from a bakery, rather than the supermarket.

Wortschatz

Geschäfte	*stores*
die Bäckerei, -en	*bakery*
die Eisdiele, -n	*ice cream shop*
das Feinkostgeschäft, -e	*delicatessen*
das Fischgeschäft, -e	*fish store*
die Konditorei, -en	*pastry shop*
das Lebensmittelgeschäft, -e	*grocery store*
der Markt, ⸚e	*market*
die Metzgerei, -en	*butcher shop*
der Supermarkt, ⸚e	*supermarket*
einkaufen gehen	*to go shopping*
verkaufen	*to sell*
Essen	*food*
das Brot, -e	*bread*
das Brötchen, -	*roll*
die Butter	*butter*
der Joghurt, -s	*yogurt*
der Käse, -	*cheese*
das Öl, -e	*oil*
das Olivenöl, -e	*olive oil*
die Pasta	*pasta*
der Reis	*rice*
das Rezept, -e	*recipe*
die Zutat, -en	*ingredient*

Suggestion Tell students that many German speakers treat **Paprika** as a masculine noun and that some also treat **Joghurt** as a feminine or neuter noun, especially in Austria and Switzerland.

Fleisch und Fisch	*meat and fish*
die Garnele, -n	*shrimp*
das Hähnchen, -	*chicken*
die Meeresfrüchte (*pl.*)	*seafood*
das Rindfleisch	*beef*
der Schinken, -	*ham*
das Schweinefleisch	*pork*
der Thunfisch	*tuna*
das Würstchen, -	*sausage*

Obst und Gemüse	*fruits and vegetables*
die Ananas, -	*pineapple*
die Artischocke, -n	*artichoke*
die Himbeere, -n	*raspberry*
die Melone, -n	*melon*
die Traube, -n	*grape*

die Orange, -n

die Birne, -n

die Erdbeere, -n

der Pfirsich, -e

Obst

die Banane, -n

der Apfel, ⸚

die Kartoffel, -n

Gemüse

die Zwiebel, -n

die rote Paprika (*pl.* die roten Paprika)

die Karotte, -n

die Aubergine, -n

die grüne Bohne (*pl.* die grünen Bohnen)

der Knoblauch

der Pilz, -e

die Tomate, -n

Suggestion Tell students that some words have more than one accepted plural form. Ex.: **die Ananas/die Ananasse; die Paprika/die Paprikas.**

Anwendung

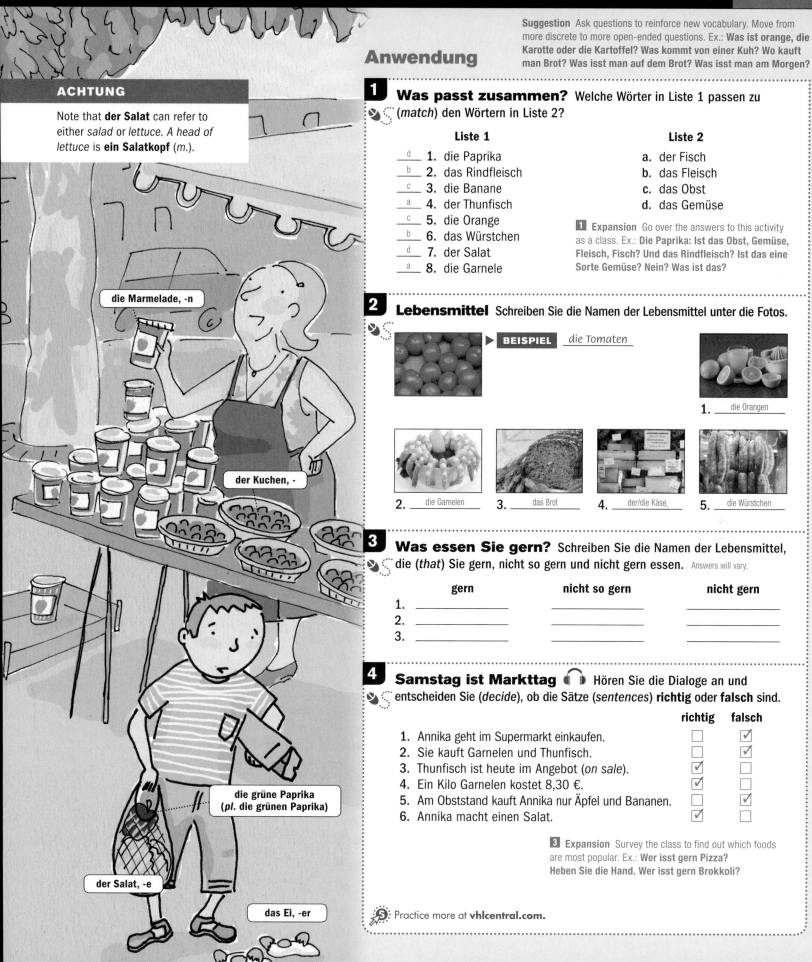

ACHTUNG

Note that **der Salat** can refer to either *salad* or *lettuce*. A head of lettuce is **ein Salatkopf** (*m.*).

die Marmelade, -n

der Kuchen, -

die grüne Paprika
(*pl.* die grünen Paprika)

der Salat, -e

das Ei, -er

1 **Was passt zusammen?** Welche Wörter in Liste 1 passen zu (*match*) den Wörtern in Liste 2?

Liste 1	Liste 2
_d_ **1.** die Paprika	**a.** der Fisch
_b_ **2.** das Rindfleisch	**b.** das Fleisch
_c_ **3.** die Banane	**c.** das Obst
_a_ **4.** der Thunfisch	**d.** das Gemüse
_c_ **5.** die Orange	
_b_ **6.** das Würstchen	
_d_ **7.** der Salat	
_a_ **8.** die Garnele	

1 Expansion Go over the answers to this activity as a class. Ex.: **Die Paprika: Ist das Obst, Gemüse, Fleisch, Fisch? Und das Rindfleisch? Ist das eine Sorte Gemüse? Nein? Was ist das?**

2 **Lebensmittel** Schreiben Sie die Namen der Lebensmittel unter die Fotos.

▶ **BEISPIEL** *die Tomaten*

1. die Orangen

2. die Garnelen **3.** das Brot **4.** der/die Käse **5.** die Würstchen

3 **Was essen Sie gern?** Schreiben Sie die Namen der Lebensmittel, die (*that*) Sie gern, nicht so gern und nicht gern essen. Answers will vary.

	gern	nicht so gern	nicht gern
1.			
2.			
3.			

4 **Samstag ist Markttag** 🎧 Hören Sie die Dialoge an und entscheiden Sie (*decide*), ob die Sätze (*sentences*) **richtig** oder **falsch** sind.

	richtig	falsch
1. Annika geht im Supermarkt einkaufen.	☐	☑
2. Sie kauft Garnelen und Thunfisch.	☐	☑
3. Thunfisch ist heute im Angebot (*on sale*).	☑	☐
4. Ein Kilo Garnelen kostet 8,30 €.	☑	☐
5. Am Obststand kauft Annika nur Äpfel und Bananen.	☐	☑
6. Annika macht einen Salat.	☑	☐

3 Expansion Survey the class to find out which foods are most popular. Ex.: **Wer isst gern Pizza? Heben Sie die Hand. Wer isst gern Brokkoli?**

Practice more at **vhlcentral.com**.

Kommunikation

5 Was kann man hier kaufen? Welche drei Lebensmittel können
Sie in den Geschäften kaufen? Vergleichen Sie (*Compare*) die Antworten mit einem
Partner / einer Partnerin. Answers will vary.

▶ **BEISPIEL**

in der Eisdiele
das Eis
der Kaffee
die Cola

5 Expansion Check students' answers by asking:
**Was kauft man beim Bäcker? Was kauft man in
der Metzgerei? Was kauft man auf dem Markt?**

1. beim Bäcker

_____
_____
_____

TIPP

Auf Deutsch sagt man:

Ich kaufe Brot **beim** Bäcker.

Ich kaufe Fleisch **in
der** Metzgerei.

Ich kaufe Fisch
im Fischgeschäft/
im Supermarkt.

Ich kaufe Obst und
Gemüse **auf dem** Markt.

2. in der Metzgerei

_____
_____
_____

3. auf dem Markt

_____
_____
_____

4. im Supermarkt

_____
_____
_____

5. im Fischgeschäft

_____
_____
_____

6 Kochen mit Freunden Sie und Ihre Freunde
wollen am Abend zusammen kochen. Diskutieren Sie,
was Sie alles brauchen und wer was kaufen soll
(*who should buy what*). Answers will vary.

BEISPIEL

S1: *Wer bringt Obst und Gemüse?*
S2: *Ich bringe Salat. Thomas, bringst du das Obst?*
S3: *Ja, ich kann Trauben und Birnen bringen.*

7 Arbeitsblatt Sie sind Geschäftsbesitzer und Ihre
Mitstudenten müssen erraten (*guess*), was man bei
Ihnen kaufen kann und welches Geschäft Sie haben.

BEISPIEL

S1: *Verkaufen Sie Bananen?*
S2: *Nein.*
S3: *Verkaufen Sie Wurst?*
S2: *Ja.*
S1: *Haben Sie eine Metzgerei?*

8 Essen und trinken Fragen Sie Ihre Mitstudenten,
was sie gern oder nicht gern essen und trinken. Finden
Sie mindestens (*at least*) eine Person, die denselben
Geschmack (*the same taste*) hat wie Sie. Answers will vary.

BEISPIEL

S1: *Ich esse gern Brot und Nutella am Morgen. Isst du
auch Nutella?*
S2: *Nein, ich esse nicht gern Nutella.*
S3: *Ich esse gern Brot und Nutella. Und ich trinke morgens
Kaffee. Du auch?*

Aussprache und Rechtschreibung Audio

🎧 The German s, z, and c

The s sound in German is represented by **s**, **ss**, or **ß**. At the end of a word, **s**, **ss**, and **ß** are pronounced like the s in the English word *yes*. Before a vowel, **s** is pronounced like the s in the English word *please*.

Reis	**Professor**	**weiß**	**Supermarkt**	**Käse**

The German **z** is pronounced like the *ts* in the English word *bats*, whether it appears at the beginning, middle, or end of a word. The combination **tz** is also pronounced *ts*. The ending -**tion** is always pronounced *-tsion*.

Pilze	**Zwiebel**	**Platz**	**Besitzer**	**Kaution**

Only in loan words does the letter **c** appear directly before a vowel. Before **e** or **i**, the letter **c** is usually pronounced *ts*. Before other vowels, it is usually pronounced like the c in *cat*. The letter combination **ck** is pronounced like the *ck* in the English word *packer*.

Cent	**Celsius**	**Computer**	**backen**	**Bäckerei**

1 **Aussprechen** Wiederholen Sie die Wörter, die Sie hören.

1. lassen
2. lasen
3. weißer
4. weiser
5. sinnlos
6. seitens
7. selbst
8. Zeile
9. Katzen
10. letztes
11. Campingplatz
12. Fleck

2 **Nachsprechen** Wiederholen Sie die Sätze, die Sie hören.

1. Der Musiker geht am Samstag zum Friseur.
2. Es geht uns sehr gut.
3. Die Zwillinge essen eine Pizza mit Pilzen, Zwiebeln und Tomaten.
4. Jetzt ist es Zeit in den Zoo zu gehen.
5. Der Clown sitzt im Café und spielt Computerspiele.
6. Ich esse nur eine Portion Eis.

3 **Sprichwörter** Wiederholen Sie die Sprichwörter, die Sie hören.

Suggestion Tell students that people in Southern Germany, Austria, and Switzerland typically pronounce **s** like the s in *yes*, even before vowels.

2 **Suggestion** Tell students that tuna, eggs, shrimp, and corn are all common pizza toppings in Germany.

> Aus den Augen, aus dem Sinn.[1]

> Gegensätze ziehen sich an.[2]

[1] Out of sight, out of mind.
[2] Opposites attract.

Ressourcen

SAM
LM: p. 31

vhlcentral.com

Börek für alle Video

George und Hans treffen Meline und Sabite im Supermarkt. George hat eine
Idee: Er macht Börek für seine Freunde. Aber kann George kochen?

Vorbereitung Have students scan the images and
try to guess what the characters will buy. Have them
create a grocery shopping list for the boys and another
one for the girls.

1

GEORGE Was möchtest du heute essen?
HANS Hmmm. Ich esse gerne Fleisch.
  Rindfleisch, Schweinefleisch und Wurst...
GEORGE Los! Auf zur Fleischtheke!
HANS Ja!

2

SABITE Ich esse gern Tofu mit Pilzen
  und Erdbeeren.
HANS Erdbeeren und was?
SABITE Pilze. Mit Tofu.

3

GEORGE Sabite, welche Zutaten kommen
  in die Börek von deiner Mutter? Wir können
  sie kochen.
SABITE Hmm. Lass mich überlegen. Kartoffeln,
  Blätterteig, Zwiebeln. Kartoffeln kochen,
  Zwiebeln braten, Teig aufrollen. Backen.

4

GEORGE Ich mache heute Abend Börek!
SABITE Wir bringen Käse und Brot mit. Wann
  sollen wir kommen?
GEORGE Kommt um halb sieben vorbei.
SABITE Perfekt.
MELINE Was ist perfekt?

5

MELINE Müssen wir mit Hans und
  George essen?
SABITE Ach, Meline, sei nett.

HANS Muss Meline mit uns essen? Sie ist
  extrem unangenehm. Ich finde, das ist
  eine ausgesprochen schlechte Idee.
GEORGE Meline ist lustig. Du magst
  sie bestimmt.
HANS Das glaube ich kaum.
GEORGE Sie mag dich bestimmt.

6

ÜBUNGEN

1 **Was fehlt?** Ergänzen Sie die Sätze mit den richtigen Informationen.

1. Hans isst gern Schweinefleisch und (Rindfleisch / Tofu).
2. Sabite isst gern Tofu mit Pilzen und (Wurst / Erdbeeren).
3. In die Börek von Frau Yilmaz kommen (Pilze / Zwiebeln).
4. Man muss die Zwiebeln (waschen / braten).
5. Meline und Sabite sollen um (zehn nach sieben / halb sieben)
   bei Hans und George sein.

6. Sie bringen (Käse und Brot / Käse und Wurst) mit.
7. Hans findet die Idee ausgesprochen (schlecht / gut).
8. In Georges Börek ist kein (Blätterteig / Schafskäse).
9. Sabite ruft morgen (ihre Mutter / ihre Oma) an.
10. Hans und George haben noch (Milch und Äpfel / Joghurt
    und Bananen).

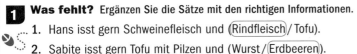

PERSONEN George Hans Meline Sabite

GEORGE Tada! Prost!
HANS Prost!

SABITE George! Was...
GEORGE Ich weiß es nicht!

SABITE Wo ist der Schafskäse? Er gibt ihnen erst noch den Geschmack.
GEORGE Schafskäse? Wieso...
SABITE Oh, nein. Oh, George, es tut mir leid! Ich rufe morgen meine Mutter an und schreibe es dann auf.

GEORGE Es ist schon okay. Der Butterkäse und das Brot liegen dort.
MELINE Ich brate Eier und Kartoffeln.
HANS Gute Idee. Wir haben hier oben noch Joghurt und Bananen.
SABITE Hier stehen noch Butter und Marmelade für das Brot!

Nützliche Ausdrücke

- **die Wurst**
  cold cuts
- **Los! Auf zur Fleischtheke!**
  Let's go! To the butcher's counter!
- **der Blätterteig**
  phyllo dough
- **aufrollen**
  roll up
- **Kommt um halb sieben vorbei!**
  Come over at half past six!
- **Brauchen wir noch etwas?**
  Do we need anything else?
- **Ich finde, das ist eine ausgesprochen schlechte Idee.**
  I think it's an extremely bad idea.
- **Das glaube ich kaum.**
  I hardly think so.
- **Ich weiß es nicht!**
  I don't know!
- **der Schafskäse**
  Feta cheese

4A.1
- **Ich mache heute Abend Börek!**
  I'm making boreks tonight!

4A.2
- **Du magst sie bestimmt.**
  You really will like her.

4A.3
- **Ich rufe morgen meine Mutter an und schreibe es dann auf.**
  I'll call my mother tomorrow, and I'll write it down.

Suggestion Explain to students that **Wurst** can refer to either sausage or cold cuts.

2 **Zum Besprechen** Sie und ein Freund möchten heute Abend eine Party geben. Spielen Sie mit einem Partner einen Dialog. Welches Essen wollen Sie servieren? Welche Zutaten brauchen Sie? Müssen Sie einkaufen gehen? Wie kochen Sie das Essen? Answers will vary.

2 **Expansion** Have students work in groups to talk about German food. Have they ever tried German food? What dishes have they heard of? Are there any German stores or restaurants in your area? Invite students from German-American families to share family recipes with the class.

3 **Vertiefung** Suchen Sie bekannte Lebensmittelhersteller (*food brands*) in Deutschland, wie Knorr, Maggi oder Haribo. Finden Sie drei bekannte Produkte. Präsentieren Sie der Klasse Ihre Resultate. Answers will vary.

Ressourcen

SAM VM: p. 7

 vhlcentral.com

Suggestion Before reading, ask students about their own shopping habits: **Wo kaufen Sie Ihr Essen? Hat Ihre Stadt einen „Farmer's Market"? Was kann man da kaufen?**

Der Wiener Naschmarkt  Reading

IN DEUTSCHLAND, ÖSTERREICH und der Schweiz hat fast jede Stadt° einen Marktplatz°. Er ist normalerweise im Zentrum der Stadt.

Stände am Naschmarkt	
Lebensmittel	31
Gastronomie°	27
Obst und Gemüse	20
Fleischwaren	9
Backwaren°	8
Fisch	5
Blumen	2
Milchprodukte	2
Wein	1
Bier	1
Sonstiges°	1

QUELLE: Edition moKKa

Große Städte haben oft mehr als einen Marktplatz. Berühmte° Marktplätze sind der Viktualienmarkt in München, der Alexanderplatz in Berlin, der Helvetiaplatz in Zürich und der Naschmarkt in Wien.

Der Naschmarkt ist einer der 26 Märkte in Wien. Er existiert seit über° 80 Jahren und liegt° sehr zentral. Viele Stände° auf dem Naschmarkt sind von Montag bis Samstag zwischen° 9 und 21 Uhr offen. Vor allem° samstagmorgens bei gutem Wetter° findet man alte und junge Menschen an den Ständen. Die Atmosphäre ist lebendig°: Menschen unterhalten sich° und Kunden handeln mit den Verkäufern°.

Märkte wie der Wiener Naschmarkt haben auch viele verschiedene° Waren: Es gibt Käse, Fleisch, Wurst, Obst und Gemüse. Natürlich gibt es auch Milchprodukte wie Käse und Joghurt. Außerdem° kann man Blumen oder Seife° kaufen. Der Markt ist auch sehr international mit italienischen, griechischen, türkischen und asiatischen Ständen.

fast jede Stadt *almost every city* **Marktplatz** *market square* **Berühmte** *Famous* **existiert seit über** *has existed for more than* **liegt** *is located* **Stände** *stands* **zwischen** *between* **Vor allem** *Especially* **bei gutem Wetter** *when the weather is nice* **lebendig** *lively* **unterhalten sich** *chat* **Kunden handeln mit den Verkäufern** *buyers negotiate with the vendors* **verschiedene** *different* **Außerdem** *In addition* **Seife** *soap* **Gastronomie** *prepared foods* **Backwaren** *baked goods* **Sonstiges** *Other*

ÜBUNGEN

1 **Der Wiener Naschmarkt** Ergänzen Sie die Sätze.

1. Jede Stadt in Deutschland, <u>Österreich</u> und der Schweiz hat einen Marktplatz.
2. Der Marktplatz ist normalerweise im <u>Zentrum</u> der Stadt.
3. Ein berühmter Marktplatz in Berlin heißt <u>Alexanderplatz</u>.
4. In Wien gibt es <u>26</u> Märkte.
5. Der Naschmarkt existiert seit über <u>80</u> Jahren.
6. Viele Stände sind zwischen 9 und <u>21</u> Uhr offen.
7. Die Atmosphäre auf dem Naschmarkt ist <u>lebendig</u>.
8. Der Naschmarkt ist sehr international mit italienischen, griechischen, <u>türkischen</u> und asiatischen Waren.
9. An fünf Ständen kann man <u>Fisch</u> kaufen.
10. Auf dem Naschmarkt gibt es <u>20</u> Obst- und Gemüsestände.

: Practice more at **vhlcentral.com**.

DEUTSCH IM ALLTAG

Auf dem Markt

Ich hätte gern...	*I would like...*
ein Dutzend Eier	*a dozen eggs*
ein Pfund Kartoffeln	*a pound of potatoes*
100 Gramm Käse	*100 grams of cheese*
Das macht 3,80 €.	*That's € 3.80.*
Sonst noch etwas?	*Anything else?*
Was wünschen Sie?	*What would you like?*
Wie viel kostet das?	*How much is that?*

DIE DEUTSCHSPRACHIGE WELT

Das ist eine Tomate, oder?

Deutsche und Österreicher sprechen Deutsch, aber es gibt verschiedene Vokabeln. Deutsche sagen „Tomate". Was sagen Österreicher? Hier ist eine kurze Liste mit Essensvokabeln:

In Deutschland	In Österreich
die Aprikose°	die Marille
grüne Bohnen	Fisolen
das Brötchen	die Semmel
das Hackfleisch°	das Faschierte
die Kartoffel	der Erdapfel
der Meerrettich°	der Kren
der Quark°	der Topfen
die Sahne°	der Obers
die Tomate	der Paradeiser

Aprikose *apricot* **Hackfleisch** *ground meat* **Meerrettich** *horseradish* **Quark** *curd cheese* **Sahne** *cream*

PORTRÄT

Wolfgang Puck

Wolfgang Puck ist ein österreichischer Koch°. Er lebt und arbeitet in den USA, hat aber auch Restaurants in Toronto, Dubai, London, Singapur und Tokio. Er ist sehr erfolgreich°: Der Umsatz° seiner Firmen ist mehr als 300 Millionen Dollar pro Jahr. In den USA hat er mehr als 70 Restaurants: Bistros, Cafés und Gourmetrestaurants. Ein sehr berühmtes und sehr teures° Restaurant ist das Spago in Beverly Hills. Das Essen in seinen Restaurants ist nicht nur amerikanisch. In fast jedem Restaurant kann man neben amerikanischen Burgern auch Wiener Schnitzel° und Kärntner Kasnudeln° bestellen.

Koch *chef* **erfolgreich** *successful* **Umsatz** *total revenue* **teures** *expensive*
Wiener Schnitzel *Viennese schnitzel* **Kärntner Kasnudeln** *South Austrian cheese noodles*

IM INTERNET

Wie viele Christkindlmärkte gibt es in Österreich? Wo sind sie? Welche Christkindlmärkte sind sehr berühmt?

Find out more at **vhlcentral.com**.

---

2 **Richtig oder falsch?** Korrigieren Sie die falschen Aussagen.

1. Das Brötchen heißt Semmel in Österreich. Richtig.
2. Eine Tomate heißt Marille in Österreich. Falsch. Sie heißt ein Paradeiser.
3. Wolfgang Puck ist ein deutscher Koch. Falsch. Er ist ein österreicher Koch.
4. Wolfgang Puck hat Restaurants nur in den USA.
   Falsch. Er hat Restaurants auch in Toronto, Dubai, London, Singapur und Tokio.
5. In fast jedem Restaurant von Wolfgang Puck kann man Wiener Schnitzel bestellen. Richtig.

3 **Auf dem Naschmarkt** Spielen Sie ein Gespräch zwischen einem Kunden (*customer*) und einem Verkäufer auf dem Naschmarkt. Integrieren Sie die folgenden Informationen: Grüße, zwei Produkte, Preise, Bezahlung (*payment*), Abschiede. Answers will vary.

BEISPIEL
3 Suggestion Encourage students to use phrases from the **Deutsch im Alltag** box in their role-plays.

S1: *Guten Tag.*
S2: *Grüß Gott. Kann ich Ihnen helfen?*
S1: *Ja. Ich hätte gerne...*

Ressourcen

vhlcentral.com

4A.1

Suggestion Teach students the mnemonic device "TMP" to help them remember that adverbs of Time come before adverbs of Manner, which come before adverbs of Place.

Suggestion On the board, write the sentence: **Ein Student fährt heute Nachmittag zu schnell zum Supermarkt.** Have students underline the adverbial phrases and identify which one describes time, which describes manner, and which describes place.

QUERVERWEIS

In **2B**, you learned to use the adverb **gern(e)** (*lit.* gladly) with a verb to say that you enjoy an activity.

See **1B.2** to review basic word order in German.

See **2A.3** to review other adverbs related to time and date.

Adverbs Presentation

Startblock In German, as in English, adverbs are words or phrases that modify a verb, an adjective, or another adverb. Adverbs describe *when*, *how*, or *where* an action takes place.

Ich gehe **wirklich gern** einkaufen.

Ich mache **heute Abend** Börek!

- An adverb usually comes immediately before the adjective or adverb it modifies. Adverbs that frequently modify adjectives or other adverbs include **fast** (*almost*), **noch** (*yet; still; in addition*), **nur** (*only*), **schon** (*already*), **sehr, so** (*so*), **wirklich** (*really*), **ziemlich** (*quite*), and **zu** (*too*).

  Der Kuchen ist **fast** fertig.
  *The cake is **almost** ready.*

  Du isst **viel zu** schnell.
  *You eat **much too** quickly.*

- When an adverb modifies a verb, it generally comes immediately after the verb it modifies. Adverbs of time or place can also come directly before the verb.

  Ich esse **täglich** Gemüse.
  *I eat vegetables **every day**.*

  Morgens trinken wir **immer** Kaffee.
  *We **always** drink coffee **in the morning**.*

- Here are some common adverbs of time, manner, and place.

adverbs					
Wann?		**Wie?**		**Wo?**	
immer	*always*	allein	*alone*	da/dort	*there*
jetzt	*now*	bestimmt	*definitely*	drüben	*over there*
nie	*never*	leider	*unfortunately*	hier	*here*
oft	*often*	vielleicht	*maybe*	überall	*everywhere*
selten	*rarely*	zusammen	*together*	woanders	*somewhere else*
täglich	*daily*				

- Adverbs of time indicate *when* or *how frequently* an event occurs and answer the questions **wann?** and **wie oft?** (*how often?*).

  Wir gehen **morgen** einkaufen.
  *We're going shopping **tomorrow**.*

  Ich esse **selten** Kuchen.
  *I **rarely** eat cake.*

- If there is more than one time expression in a sentence, general time references are placed before adverbs of specific time.

  Die Bäckerei öffnet **am Sonntag um 9 Uhr**.
  *The bakery opens at **9 o'clock on Sunday**.*

  Samstag morgens um 11 Uhr frühstücke ich mit meinem Vater.
  *I have breakfast with my father **every Saturday morning at 11 o'clock**.*

ACHTUNG

In English, you can turn an adjective into an adverb by adding the ending *-ly*.

In German, you can turn an adjective into an adverb by placing it after the verb you want to modify:

Peter ist ein gesunder Junge.
Peter is a healthy boy.

Peter isst sehr gesund.
Peter eats very healthily.

- Adverbs of manner indicate *how* an action is done. They answer the question **wie?**

  Ich mache das **allein**.
  I'm doing this by myself.

  Du spielst **wirklich gut** Tennis.
  You play tennis really well.

- Adverbs of place describe locations or directions and answer the questions **wo?**, **wohin?**, and **woher?**

  Woher kommst du?
  Where are you from?

  Ich komme **aus Deutschland**.
  I'm from Germany.

  Wohin geht ihr?
  Where are you going?

  Wir gehen **in die Eisdiele**.
  We're going to the ice cream shop.

- When there is more than one adverbial expression in a sentence, adverbs of time come first, followed by adverbs of manner, then adverbs of place.

  Papa kauft **heute in der Konditorei** eine Geburtstagstorte.
  Dad is getting a birthday cake today at the pastry shop.

  Wir fahren **zusammen zum Supermarkt**.
  We're going to the supermarket together.

  Heute Abend esse ich **vielleicht im Restaurant**.
  Maybe I'll eat at a restaurant tonight.

  Sie essen **morgen Abend bestimmt woanders**.
  They are definitely eating somewhere else tomorrow night.

- In **2B.3** you learned how to negate sentences with **nicht**. In sentences with adverbial expressions, **nicht** usually *precedes* general expressions of time, manner, and place, but *follows* adverbs of specific time.

  Wir kaufen **nicht oft** Fleisch im Supermarkt.
  We don't often buy meat at the supermarket.

  Ich will **am Montag nicht** in die Schule gehen.
  I don't want to go to school on Monday.

  Die Gäste sind **noch nicht hier**.
  The guests aren't here yet.

  Wir können **nicht mehr hier** warten.
  We can't wait here anymore.

Suggestion Point out to students that adverbs can make their speech and writing more informative and expressive. Give them a sample sentence, such as **Anna geht spazieren**. Ask them to make it more vivid by adding adverbs that describe where, how, and when the action takes place.

Ressourcen

SAM
WB: pp. 49–50

SAM
LM: p. 32

S
vhlcentral.com

Jetzt sind Sie dran! | Geben Sie an (*Indicate*), ob die Adverbien die Zeit, die Art und Weise (*manner*) oder den Ort beschreiben.

1. Wir kochen heute Abend <u>zusammen</u>. _Art und Weise_
2. Marina ist <u>immer</u> besorgt. _Zeit_
3. Die Eltern trinken <u>gern</u> Rotwein. _Art und Weise_
4. Das Lebensmittelgeschäft ist <u>dort drüben</u>. _Ort_
5. Meine Schwester isst <u>nie</u> Obst und Gemüse. _Zeit_
6. Ihr trinkt <u>selten</u> Kaffee. _Zeit_
7. Du machst deine Hausaufgaben <u>allein</u>. _Art und Weise_
8. Ich fahre <u>schnell</u> zur Universität. _Art und Weise_
9. Petra hat <u>jetzt</u> keine Zeit. _Zeit_
10. Ich esse <u>oft</u> Käse und Brot. _Zeit_
11. Kann man Auberginen <u>überall</u> kaufen? _Ort_
12. Wir bleiben <u>hier</u> in Berlin. _Ort_

Anwendung

1 **Was ist richtig?** Wählen Sie (*Choose*) das adverbiale Element, das am besten passt.

 Ich gehe (die ganze Nacht / im Restaurant / morgens) in den Unterricht.

1. Yusuf macht (in der Bibliothek / im Fitnessstudio / in der Bäckerei) Hausaufgaben.
2. Wir möchten später (selten / beim Bäcker / im Park) ein Picknick machen.
3. Efe geht (im Hörsaal / im Supermarkt / im Café) einkaufen.
4. Das Restaurant ist (oft / überall / zusammen) voll (*crowded*).
5. Das Rezept ist (jetzt / fast / wirklich) einfach.
6. Thomas isst (dort / selten / allein) Fleisch.
7. Der Kuchen ist (abends / am Wochenende / sehr) gut.
8. Zum Mittagessen gehen wir (leider / in die Mensa / überall).

2 **Auf dem Campus** Setzen Sie das Adverb an die richtige Stelle.

BEISPIEL Wir essen um 6 Uhr. (immer)
Wir essen immer um 6 Uhr.

1. David vergisst immer seine Hausaufgaben. (fast)
David vergisst fast immer seine Hausaufgaben.

2. Ich gehe im Supermarkt einkaufen. (oft)
Ich gehe oft im Supermarkt einkaufen.

3. Paula geht nachmittags spazieren. (auf dem Campus)
Paula geht nachmittags auf dem Campus spazieren.

4. Die Studenten essen in der Mensa. (nicht gern)
Die Studenten essen nicht gern in der Mensa.

5. Ihr lernt in der Bibliothek. (abends)
Ihr lernt abends in der Bibliothek.

6. Du gehst freitags tanzen. (im Club)
Du gehst freitags im Club tanzen.

7. Die Professorin korrigiert die Prüfungen. (am Sonntag)
Die Professorin korrigiert am Sonntag die Prüfungen./Die Professorin korrigiert die Prüfungen am Sonntag.

8. Julius fährt nach Berlin. (am Wochenende)
Julius fährt am Wochenende nach Berlin.

3 Suggestion Remind students that they do not need to use words from each column in every sentence. Create one sentence together as a class, before having students work in groups.

3 **Was machen diese Leute?** Bilden Sie Sätze mit zwei Adverbien. Setzen Sie die Wörter in die richtige Reihenfolge (*order*). Answers will vary.

Subjekt	Objekt	Verb	Adverbien	
ich	das Auto	backen	gern	selten
du	die Hausaufgaben	fahren	jetzt	im Sommer
mein Vater	den Hund	kaufen	nächstes Jahr	überall
wir	einen Kuchen	machen	nie	um 9 Uhr
du und Dieter	einen Obstsalat	wandern	oft	am Wochenende
meine Freunde	einen Snack	waschen	schnell	zusammen

Practice more at **vhlcentral.com**.

Kommunikation

4 **Wie und warum?** Was machen die Personen, wie machen Sie das und warum? Erfinden Sie (*Make up*) ein kurzes Szenario. Benutzen Sie (*Use*) jedes der folgenden Adverbien nur einmal (*once*): allein, langsam, oft, selten, vielleicht, zusammen. Sample answers are provided.

▶ **BEISPIEL**

S1: Wie geht er?
S2: Er geht schnell. Wohin geht er?
S3: Er geht vielleicht in den Park.

1. Sie lernen zusammen.

2. Er liest allein.

3. Er kocht vielleicht Reis.

4. Sie fährt langsam.

5. Sie fährt oft Fahrrad.

5 **Partnergespräch** Stellen Sie Ihrem Partner / Ihrer Partnerin Fragen. Answers will vary.

 BEISPIEL

S1: Wie oft kochst du?
S2: Ich koche sehr oft. / Ich koche selten.

 1. Wann lernst du?

2. Wann sind deine Kurse?

3. Wie oft gehst du in die Mensa?

4. Wann machst du deine Mittagspause?

5. Wie oft gehst du tanzen?

6. Wie oft fährst du zu den Großeltern?

6 **Meine Mitstudenten** Finden Sie für jede Aktivität eine Person aus Ihrer Klasse.

 BEISPIEL

S1: Isst du oft Fisch?
S2: Nein, ich esse nicht oft Fisch.
S3: Und du?

oft / Fisch essen
gut / Gitarre spielen
täglich / in der Sporthalle trainieren
selten / Gemüse essen
gern / am Wochenende tanzen gehen
oft / Schokomilch trinken
nie / samstags im Haus bleiben
immer / Eier zum Frühstück essen
gut / kochen können

6 Suggestion Before students begin the activity, make sure they know how to form the questions properly. Emphasize that they must answer using complete sentences. During the activity, circulate around the room and interact with students, asking them questions and keeping them on task.

4A.2 The modal *mögen*  Presentation

Startblock In 2B Kontext, you learned to express likes and dislikes using **gern** and **nicht gern**. Another way of expressing liking is with the modal **mögen**.

ACHTUNG

While **gern** is always used with a verb, **mögen** is typically used with a noun:
Wir <u>mögen</u> **Erdbeeren.**
But: **Wir** <u>essen gern</u> **Erdbeeren.**

Ich <u>mag keinen</u> **Tee.**
But: **Ich** <u>trinke nicht gern</u> **Tee.**

Since **gern** is an adverb, it can also be used in combination with **mögen**, for emphasis:

Was <u>magst</u> **du** <u>gern</u>**?**
Das <u>mag</u> **ich** <u>nicht so gern</u>**.**

Hey! Ich **mag** das! Danke.

Meline ist lustig. Du **magst** sie bestimmt.

- Like all the modal verbs, **mögen** is irregular in the singular.

QUERVERWEIS

See **3B.1** to review the other modal verbs: **dürfen**, **können**, **müssen**, **sollen**, and **wollen**.

See **2B.3** to review negation.

You will learn more about subjunctive forms in **9B.1**.

Suggestion Point out that, as with other modals, the **er/sie/es** form of **mögen** is identical to its **ich** form.

mögen (*to like*)			
ich mag	*I like*	wir mögen	*we like*
du magst	*you like*	ihr mögt	*you like*
er/sie/es mag	*he/she/it likes*	Sie/sie mögen	*you/they like*

- While most modals modify another verb, **mögen** almost always modifies a noun.

Mögt ihr diesen Joghurt?
*Do you **like** this yogurt?*

Nein, diesen Joghurt **mögen** wir **nicht**.
*No, we **don't like** that yogurt.*

- Depending on context, you can use either **nicht** or **kein** to negate a statement with **mögen**.

Ich **mag keine** grünen Paprika.
*I **don't like** green peppers.*

Magst du rote Paprika?
*Do you **like** red peppers?*

Nein, rote Paprika **mag** ich auch **nicht**.
*No, I **don't like** red peppers either.*

- **Möchten** is the subjunctive form of **mögen**. Use **möchten** for polite requests and to say what you *would like* to have or do. **Möchten** may be followed by either a verb or a noun.

möchten			
ich möchte	*I would like*	wir möchten	*we would like*
du möchtest	*you would like*	ihr möchtet	*you would like*
er/sie/es möchte	*he/she/it would like*	Sie/sie möchten	*you/they would like*

Wir **möchten** Fußball spielen.
*We **would like** to play soccer.*

Möchten Sie Kaffee oder Tee?
***Would** you **like** coffee or tea?*

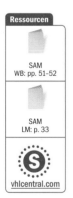
Suggestion Explain to students that "**Ich mag keine grünen Paprika.**", "**Grüne Paprika mag ich nicht.**", and "**Ich mag grüne Paprika nicht gern.**" all convey the same idea, but with slightly different emphasis.

Jetzt sind Sie dran!

Ergänzen Sie die Lücken mit den richtigen Formen der Modalverben **mögen** oder **möchten**.

1. Die Kinder _mögen_ (mögen) Schokolade.
2. Ich _mag_ (mögen) keinen Fußball.
3. Julia _möchte_ (möchten) in die Konditorei gehen.
4. _Möchtest_ (Möchten) du Pasta oder Reis?
5. Anne _mag_ (mögen) russische Literatur.
6. _Möchten_ (Möchten) Sie einen Tisch am Fenster?
7. Ihr _möchtet_ (möchten) zur Bäckerei gehen.
8. _Magst_ (Mögen) du Meeresfrüchte nicht?
9. Ich _möchte_ (möchten) kein Fleisch essen.
10. Unsere Katzen _mögen_ (mögen) unseren Hund nicht.
11. _Mögt_ (Mögen) ihr Garnelen?
12. Wir _möchten_ (möchten) Pasta.

Anwendung und Kommunikation

1 **Wer mag was?** Schreiben Sie die Sätze um. Benutzen Sie **mögen** anstatt **essen** oder **trinken gern.** Some answers may vary.

> **BEISPIEL** Ich esse nicht gern Garnelen.
> *Ich mag keine Garnelen. / Ich mag Garnelen nicht.*

1. Meine Schwester isst gern Schokolade. Meine Schwester mag Schokolade.
2. Meine Eltern essen gern Bananen zum Frühstück. Meine Eltern mögen Bananen zum Frühstück.
3. Ich esse nicht gern Auberginen. Ich mag Auberginen nicht./Ich mag keine Auberginen.
4. Mein Mann und ich essen gern Pizza. Mein Mann und ich mögen Pizza.
5. Esst ihr gern Würstchen? Mögt ihr Würstchen?
6. Trinkst du nicht gern Kaffee? Magst du keine Kaffee?/Magst du Kaffee nicht?

2 **Pläne** Ergänzen Sie die Sätze mit der richtigen Form von **möchten** und mit Wörtern aus der Liste.

> am Wochenende Fußball spielen | schlafen
> im Biergarten essen | tanzen
> heiraten | Tennis spielen

> ▶ **BEISPIEL**
> **Ben und Simon**
> *möchten am Wochenende Fußball spielen.*

1. Elias und Emma
möchten heiraten

2. Paula, du
möchtest schlafen

3. Professor Klein
möchte Tennis spielen

4. Alex und du, ihr
möchtet tanzen

5. Marie und ich, wir
möchten im Biergarten essen

3 **Was magst du?** Fragen Sie Ihren Partner / Ihre Partnerin, was er/sie (nicht) mag. Fragen Sie auch nach den anderen Personen in seiner/ihrer Familie. Answers will vary.

> **BEISPIEL**
> **S1:** *Magst du Thunfisch?*
> **S2:** *Nein, aber ich mag Käse.*
> **S1:** *Und dein Bruder? Mag er Thunfisch?*
> **S2:** *Nein, aber er mag Würstchen.*

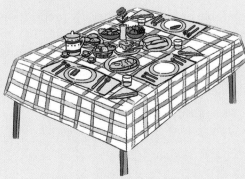

3 **Suggestion** You may want to teach students the words **igitt** and **lecker** for use in this activity.

2 **Expansion** Have students write 5 sentences about what *they* would like to do this weekend, using **möchten**.

 Practice more at **vhlcentral.com.**

4A.3 Separable and inseparable prefix verbs  Presentation

Startblock In German, many verbs have a prefix in their infinitive form.

Ich gehe wirklich gern **einkaufen**.

Lass mich **überlegen**.

Suggestion Tell students that separable prefix verbs are the "drama queens" of the grammar world. They like to "break up" and "get back together". They break off from the main verb and move to the end of the clause in the indicative and the imperative, but get back together when used with modals.

- A verb with a prefix has the same conjugations as its base form, but the added prefix changes the meaning.

  Sucht ihr eure Eltern?
  *Are you **looking for** your parents?*

  Besucht ihr eure Verwandten?
  *Do you **visit** your relatives?*

- Some prefixes are always attached to the verb and others can be separated from it.

  Jakob **verkauft** sein Fahrrad.
  *Jakob **is selling** his bike.*

  Ich **kaufe** im Supermarkt **ein**.
  *I **shop** at the supermarket.*

QUERVERWEIS

See **2B.1** to review the present tense of irregular verbs like **fangen** and **schlafen**.

The verb **vorstellen** is often used reflexively. You will learn more about reflexive verbs in **9A.1** and **9A.2**.

Suggestion Give students the name of a celebrity and ask them to write sentences about what this celebrity does on a typical Saturday, using 5-6 separable or inseparable prefix verbs. Create the first sentence as a class.

- Here are some of the most common separable and inseparable prefix verbs.

verbs with separable prefixes	
anfangen	*to begin*
ankommen	*to arrive*
anrufen	*to call*
aufstehen	*to get up*
ausgehen	*to go out*
einkaufen	*to shop*
einschlafen	*to fall asleep*
mitbringen	*to bring along*
mitkommen	*to come along*
vorbereiten	*to prepare*
vorstellen	*to introduce*
zuschauen	*to watch*
zurückkommen	*to come back*

verbs with inseparable prefixes	
beantworten	*to answer*
besprechen	*to discuss*
bestellen	*to order*
besuchen	*to visit*
bezahlen	*to pay (for)*
erklären	*to explain*
verkaufen	*to sell*
verbringen	*to spend (time)*
überlegen	*to think over*
wiederholen	*to repeat*

ACHTUNG

When speaking, place the stress on the prefix of a separable prefix verb: **anrufen**, **einschlafen**. The prefix of an inseparable prefix verb is never stressed: **verkaufen**, **wiederholen**.

- Separable prefixes are generally prepositions (**an**, **aus**, **mit**) or other parts of speech that carry meaning and can stand alone. In contrast, most inseparable prefixes (**be-**, **er-**, **ver-**) have no independent meaning and never stand alone.

  Heute Abend **gehen** wir zusammen **aus**.
  *Tonight we**'re going out** together.*

  Stefan **steht** jeden Morgen um 6 Uhr **auf**.
  *Stefan **gets up** at 6 o'clock every morning.*

  Ich **bestelle** die Pasta mit Garnelen.
  *I**'m ordering** the pasta with shrimp.*

  Ihr **verkauft** euer Auto?
  *You**'re selling** your car?*

- When using a separable prefix verb in the present tense or the imperative, move the prefix to the end of the sentence or clause.

Wir **kaufen** auf dem Markt **ein**.
We're shopping at the market.

Kommst du **zurück**?
Are you coming back?

Bitte **stellen** Sie die Frau **vor**.
Please introduce the woman.

Ruf deine Eltern **an**!
Call your parents!

Wir **bringen** Käse und Brot **mit**.

Wir **laden** Meline und Sabite zu uns zu Börek **ein**?

- To make the sentence negative, add **nicht** immediately before the separable prefix.

Ich komme **nicht** zurück.
I'm not coming back.

Ruf deine Eltern **nicht** an!
Don't call your parents!

- When using a modal with a separable prefix verb, move the infinitive of the separable prefix verb to the end of the sentence.

Die Mädchen **möchten** morgen Abend **ausgehen**.
The girls want to go out tomorrow night.

Ich **muss** mit meinen Hausaufgaben **anfangen**.
I need to start my homework.

- The prefix of an inseparable prefix verb always remains attached to the beginning of the verb.

Ich **bezahle** die Lebensmittel.
I'll pay for the groceries.

Wiederholen Sie den Satz.
Repeat the sentence.

ACHTUNG

In this book, separable prefix verbs will be presented with their third person present-tense form in parentheses: **einkaufen (kauft... ein)**

Expansion Before they begin the **Jetzt sind Sie dran!** activity, have students identify which verbs have separable prefixes and which do not.

Ressourcen

SAM
WB: pp. 53–54

SAM
LM: p. 34

S

vhlcentral.com

Jetzt sind Sie dran!   **Schreiben Sie die richtige Form des Verbs in Klammern.**

1. Ich ___wiederhole___ den Satz. (wiederholen)
2. Wir ___rufen___ unsere Freunde ___an___. (anrufen)
3. Erwin und Marta ___verkaufen___ ihr Haus. (verkaufen)
4. Du musst heute Abend noch ___einkaufen___. (einkaufen)
5. Der Student ___stellt___ seine Eltern ___vor___. (vorstellen)

6. ___Gehen___ wir am Wochenende ___aus___? (ausgehen)
7. Papa ___bestellt___ gern Meeresfrüchte. (bestellen)
8. Ich ___verbringe___ eine Woche in Zürich. (verbringen)
9. Kannst du Brot ___mitbringen___? (mitbringen)
10. Wir ___besuchen___ unsere Verwandten in Salzburg. (besuchen)

Anwendung

1 Expansion Have students work in pairs to create mini-dialogues using two or three commands from this activity. Ex.: **Frau Meinedienerin, wir haben nichts zu essen. Kaufen Sie ein! Jawohl, Herr Herrschigern!** Have pairs perform their dialogues for the class.

1 Befehle Geben Sie Befehle (*commands*) in der **Sie**-Form.

BEISPIEL

aufstehen
Stehen Sie auf.

1. anrufen   Rufen Sie an.
2. einkaufen   Kaufen Sie ein.
3. bezahlen   Bezahlen Sie.
4. zuschauen   Schauen Sie zu.
5. nicht mitkommen   Kommen Sie nicht mit.

6. überlegen   Überlegen Sie.
7. anfangen   Fangen Sie an.
8. nicht einschlafen   Schlafen Sie nicht ein.
9. zurückkommen   Kommen Sie zurück.
10. nicht ausgehen   Gehen Sie nicht aus.

2 Fragen Formulieren Sie die Fragen um und benutzen Sie (*use*) dabei die angegebenen (*indicated*) Modalverben.

BEISPIEL

Kommst du mit? (können)
Kannst du mitkommen?

1. Gehst du aus? (wollen)   Willst du ausgehen?
2. Kaufen wir ein? (sollen)   Sollen wir einkaufen?
3. Kommt Lisa mit? (müssen)   Muss Lisa mitkommen?

4. Fangt ihr an? (möchten)   Möchtet ihr anfangen?
5. Schläfst du ein? (dürfen)   Darfst du einschlafen?
6. Schaut Nils zu? (können)   Kann Nils zuschauen?

3 Was machen sie? Schreiben Sie zu jedem (*each*) Foto einen Satz und benutzen Sie Präfixverben.

> Freunde anrufen
> heute Abend ausgehen
> die Bücher bezahlen
> einkaufen
>
> einschlafen
> die Grammatik erklären
> euren Hund mitbringen

▶ **BEISPIEL**
Herr Schröder
Herr Schröder erklärt die Grammatik.

ich
1. Ich schlafe ein.

Jana und Lina
2. Jana und Lina rufen Freunde an.

Emma und ihre Freunde
3. Emma und ihre Freunde gehen heute Abend aus.

Stefanie
4. Stefanie bezahlt die Bücher.

Frau Neumann und ihre Tochter
5. Frau Neumann und ihre Tochter kaufen ein.

ihr
6. Ihr bringt euren Hund mit.

 Practice more at **vhlcentral.com**.

Kommunikation

 4 Mein Tag Füllen Sie einen Terminkalender mit Ihren Informationen aus und diskutieren Sie dann mit Ihrem Partner / Ihrer Partnerin, was Sie täglich so machen. Answers will vary.

BEISPIEL

S1: Ich stehe um 8 Uhr auf. Und du?
S2: Ich stehe um 8.30 Uhr auf. Meine erste Vorlesung fängt um 10 Uhr an. Und deine?

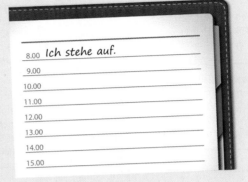

8.00 *Ich stehe auf.*
9.00
10.00
11.00
12.00
13.00
14.00
15.00

5 Wer ist das? Wählen Sie eine Person und schreiben Sie zwei Dinge auf, die diese (*this*) Person macht. Ihre Mitstudenten müssen raten (*guess*), wer es ist. Answers will vary.

BEISPIEL

S1: Sie kommt um 8 Uhr zur Uni.
Sie erklärt die Hausaufgaben und beantwortet unsere Fragen.
S2: Ist es die Professorin?

anfangen	ausgehen	besuchen	erklären	verbringen
ankommen	beantworten	bezahlen	mitbringen	vorbereiten
anrufen	besprechen	einkaufen	mitkommen	zurückkommen

6 Ein Picknick machen Sie und Ihre Freunde planen ein Picknick. Diskutieren Sie, wer was kauft, wer was mitbringt und was Sie alles machen müssen. Answers will vary.

BEISPIEL

S1: Sollen wir viele Freunde anrufen?
S2: Ja, und wir müssen auch viel Essen mitbringen.
S3: Ich bringe Wurst und Käse mit!

Wiederholung

1 Was magst du? Fragen Sie einen Partner / eine Partnerin, was er/sie mag oder nicht mag. Answers will vary.

BEISPIEL

S1: Magst du Hähnchen mit Reis?
S2: Ja, ich mag Hähnchen mit Reis. Und du?
S1: Nein, ich mag Hähnchen mit Reis nicht. Magst du...?

Würstchen mit Brot	Schweinefleisch mit Kartoffeln
Thunfisch mit Zwiebeln	Auberginen mit Tomaten
Pasta mit Pilzen	Schinken mit Brot
Hähnchen mit Reis	Pasta mit Käse
Garnelen mit Tomaten	Rindfleisch mit Salat

2 Das Wochenende Sagen Sie, was die Personen am Wochenende machen möchten. Wechseln Sie sich (*Take turns*) mit einem Partner / einer Partnerin ab. Answers will vary.

BEISPIEL

S1: Was möchte Klara am Wochenende machen?
S2: Klara möchte am Wochenende gern lesen.

Klara

1. Petra und Klaus

2. Paul, Manfred, Andrea und Monika

3. Inge

4. Robert

3 Arbeitsblatt Fragen Sie Ihre Mitstudenten, wie oft, wie und wo sie diese Lebensmittel essen. Answers will vary.

BEISPIEL

S1: Wie oft isst du Eier in der Mensa?
S2: Ich esse selten Eier in der Mensa.

4 Was machen sie? Ein Student / Eine Studentin spielt eine Situation. Die anderen Studenten raten (*guess*) die Situation. Benutzen Sie vollständige (*complete*) Sätze. Answers will vary.

BEISPIEL

S1: Fährst du Fahrrad?
S2: Nein.
S1: Reitest du ein Pferd?
S2: Ja.

aufstehen	im Restaurant	einschlafen
ausgehen	bestellen	Fahrrad fahren
einen Kuchen	einen Freund	ein Pferd reiten
backen	besuchen	Volleyball spielen

5 Diskutieren und kombinieren Sie bekommen eine Tabelle von Ihrem Professor / Ihrer Professorin. Fragen Sie einen Partner / eine Partnerin, wann die Personen die Aktivitäten machen.

BEISPIEL

S1: Wann geht Alex Lebensmittel einkaufen?
S2: Alex geht am Samstag Lebensmittel einkaufen.

6 Der Wochenplan Entscheiden Sie (*Decide*), was Sie diese Woche machen wollen. Suchen Sie andere Studenten in der Gruppe, die das Gleiche planen und finden Sie eine gemeinsame Zeit, wann sie das machen können. Answers will vary.

BEISPIEL

S1: Willst du diese Woche einkaufen gehen?
S2: Ja, ich will diese Woche einkaufen gehen.
S1: Können wir zusammen einkaufen gehen?
S2: Ja, gern.
S1: Hast du am Mittwoch Zeit?
S2: Nein, am Mittwoch habe ich keine Zeit. Hast du am Donnerstag Zeit?
S1: Ja, am Donnerstag habe ich Zeit. Um wie viel Uhr...

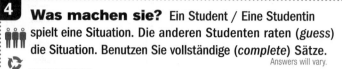

Zapping

Ⓢ Video

Yello Strom

Die Firma Yello Strom ist eine deutsche Stromfirma°. In Deutschland können Kunden° zwischen verschiedenen° Stromfirmen wählen. Kundenservice° ist deshalb aber auch ein wichtiger Aspekt, um neue Kunden zu gewinnen. Yello Strom ist eine kreative Firma mit neuen Ideen. Kundenservice ist sehr wichtig für diese Firma. In diesem Werbeclip zeigt° die Firma, dass Kunden bei Yello Strom nur mit echten Menschen reden!

Auf dem Wochenmarkt°

„Sie haben drei gelbe° Bananen gewählt°."

„Guter Service geht anders°."

Stromfirma *electric company* **Kunden** *customers* **verschiedenen** *different* **Kundenservice** *customer service* **zeigt** *shows* **Wochenmarkt** *farmer's market* **gelbe** *yellow* **gewählt** *selected* **anders** *differently*

 Verständnis Beantworten Sie die Fragen mit den Informationen aus dem Video.

1. Was möchte die Frau auf dem Markt?
   Sie möchte drei ____Äpfel____.

2. Was versteht der Verkäufer?
   Er versteht drei ___(gelbe) Bananen___.

 Diskussion Diskutieren Sie die folgenden Fragen mit einem Partner / einer Partnerin. Answers will vary.

1. Wie finden Sie Telefonmenüs? Funktionieren sie gut? Sind sie praktisch oder frustrierend?

2. Wie findest du die Werbung (*commercial*)? Ist die Situation lustig oder nicht so lustig?

Kontext

Communicative Goals

You will learn how to:

- talk about food and meals
- describe flavors

Im Restaurant

S Vocabulary Tools

Wortschatz

im Restaurant	*at the restaurant*
die Beilage, -n	side dish
das Besteck	silverware
die Flasche, -n	bottle
der erste/zweite Gang	first/second course
das Gericht, -e	dish
die Hauptspeise, -n	main course
der Nachtisch, -e	dessert
die Rechnung, -en	check
die Tasse, -n	cup
das Trinkgeld	tip
die Vorspeise, -n	appetizer
Mahlzeiten	*meals*
das Abendessen	dinner
das Frühstück	breakfast
das Mittagessen	lunch
der Snack, -s	snack
Getränke	*drinks*
das Bier	beer
der Kaffee	coffee
die Milch	milk
das Mineralwasser	sparkling water
der Saft, ¨e	juice
der Tee	tea
das stille Wasser	still water
der Wein	wine
Essen beschreiben	*talking about food*
der Geschmack, ¨e	flavor; taste
fade	bland
lecker	delicious
leicht	light
salzig	salty
scharf	spicy
schwer	rich, heavy
süß	sweet
Ausdrücke	*expressions*
Ich hätte gern(e)...	I would like...
auf Diät sein	to be on a diet
hausgemacht	homemade

Explain that **ein Gericht** refers to a particular food item whereas **ein Teller** is the plate on which it is served.

Suggestion Point out the compound words **Hauptspeise**, **Vorspeise**, and **Speisekarte**. Ask students for a synonym for **Speise**.

Suggestion Point out that the word **Snack** has come into German from English. Tell students that Germans also use the word **die Zwischenmahlzeit**, while Austrians often say **die Jause**.

Suggestion Point out that the noun **Geschmack** comes from the verb **schmecken**.

Ressourcen

SAM
WB: pp. 55–56

SAM
LM: p. 35

S vhlcentral.com

der Koch, ¨e
(die Köchin, -nen *f.*)

Die Suppe schmeckt gut.
(schmecken)

der Kellner, -
(die Kellnerin, -nen *f.*)

die Gabel, -n

die Speisekarte, -n

die Serviette, -n

der Teller, -

das Messer, -

die Tischdecke, -n

ACHTUNG

Use the prefix **Lieblings-** to indicate that something is your favorite.

Pizza ist mein Lieblingsgericht.

Sie bestellen.
(bestellen)

das Salz

das Glas, ¨er

der Pfeffer

der Esslöffel, -

der Teelöffel, -

Speisekarte

Speisekarte

Speisekarte

Suggestion Tell students that a soup spoon may also be referred to as **der Suppenlöffel**.

Anwendung

1 Expansion Have each pair come up with their own set of four words, and have the class guess which is the "odd word out".

1 **Was passt nicht?** Welches Wort passt nicht zu den anderen?

1. a. die Gabel
   b. das Messer
   c. die Serviette
   d. der Löffel

2. a. die Milch
   b. der Saft
   c. der Kaffee
   d. das Salz

3. a. die Speisekarte
   b. die Flasche
   c. die Tasse
   d. das Glas

4. a. salzig
   b. stolz
   c. scharf
   d. süß

5. a. die Kellnerin
   b. die Köchin
   c. der Saft
   d. der Koch

6. a. das Mittagessen
   b. die Beilage
   c. das Abendessen
   d. das Frühstück

2 **Wie schmeckt's?** Beschreiben Sie (*Describe*) den Geschmack der Lebensmittel. Sample answers are provided.

 BEISPIEL Die Bratwurst ist
scharf.

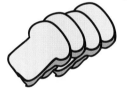

1. Der Saft ist
   süß.

2. Die Suppe ist
   schwer.

3. Der Salat ist
   leicht.

4. Der Käse ist
   salzig.

5. Das Brot ist
   fade.

6. Der Kuchen ist
   lecker.

3 **Was bestellen wir?** Hören Sie den Dialog an und markieren Sie, was Tom, Klara und Murat bestellen.

3 Expansion Ask students questions to check their answers. Encourage them to respond with complete sentences. Ex.: **Wer bestellt das Steak? Was trinkt Murat? Wer möchte den Meeresfrüchtesalat?**

Essen	Tom	Klara	Murat
1. Steak	☑	☐	☐
2. Cola	☐	☐	☑
3. Meeresfrüchtesalat	☐	☑	☐
4. stilles Wasser	☑	☐	☐
5. gemischter Salat	☑	☐	☐
6. Brot	☐	☑	☐
7. Mineralwasser	☐	☑	☐
8. Rindfleisch	☐	☐	☑

 Practice more at **vhlcentral.com**.

Kommunikation

4 Verschiedene Mahlzeiten

Fragen Sie Ihren Partner / Ihre Partnerin, welche Mahlzeiten auf den Fotos zu sehen sind. Wechseln Sie sich ab (*Take turns*). Sample answers are provided.

▶ **BEISPIEL**

das Frühstück

S1: Ist das das Frühstück?
S2: Nein, das ist das Abendessen.

1. die Vorspeise
Ist das die Vorspeise?
Nein, das ist der Nachtisch.

2. die Hauptspeise
Ist das die Hauptspeise?
Nein, das ist ein Getränk.

3. der Nachtisch
Ist das der Nachtisch?
Nein, das ist das Mittagessen.

4. das Abendessen
Ist das das Abendessen?
Nein, das ist das Frühstück.

5. ein Snack
Ist das ein Snack?
Nein, das ist das Abendessen.

6. das Mittagessen
Ist das das Mittagessen?
Nein, das ist ein Snack.

5 Wo möchten wir heute Abend essen?

Sie möchten heute Abend ins Restaurant essen gehen. Lesen Sie die Speisekarte und überlegen Sie, was Sie zu jedem (*for each*) Gang bestellen wollen. Answers will vary.

Suggestion Explain to students that **Nachspeise** and **Dessert** are synonyms for **Nachtisch** commonly used on restaurant menus.

BEISPIEL

S1: Ich möchte gern den Tomatensalat mit Mozzarella als ersten Gang.
S2: Ich auch! Und als zweiten Gang bestelle ich das Hähnchen mit Reis.
S3: Wollt ihr auch Getränke bestellen?

7 Expansion Have students work in groups to create a commercial for their "ideal restaurant" and present it to the class. You may want to provide prompts. Ex.: **Unser Restaurant ist/hat... Das Essen ist... Wir servieren... In unserem Restaurant kann man... Die Atmosphäre ist... Die Kellner sind...**

Speisekarte

Vorspeisen
Tagessuppe
Chef-Salat mit Schinken, Käse und Ei
Bauern-Salat mit Schafskäse, Zwiebeln
    und Oliven
Tomatensalat mit Mozzarella

Beilagen
Kartoffelsalat
Karottensalat
Grüner Salat
Kartoffelpuffer
Sauerkraut

Nachspeisen
Apfelkuchen
Bananen mit Schokolade
hausgemachter Joghurt mit
    Himbeermarmalade
Obstsalat

Hauptspeisen
Würstchen mit Brötchen
Thunfisch mit Salat
Hähnchen mit Reis
Rindfleisch mit Pommes frites
Schweinefleisch mit Kartoffeln
Pasta mit Garnelen
Pasta mit Käse

Getränke
stilles Wasser   Milch
Mineralwasser   Kaffee
Orangensaft   Tee

6 Stress im Restaurant!

Sie sind im Restaurant und der Kellner bringt Ihr Essen. Aber auf dem Tisch gibt es kein Besteck, kein Brot, keine Getränke, kein Salz und so weiter. Sagen Sie dem Kellner, was er noch alles bringen soll. Answers will vary.

BEISPIEL

S1: Kann ich bitte auch Gabel und Messer haben?
S2: Und bitte zwei Glas Wasser!
S3: Natürlich. Möchten sie noch etwas (*anything else*)?

7 Diskutieren und kombinieren

Wie sind die Restaurants „Zum Grünen Baum" und „Zur Stadtmauer"? Fragen Sie Ihren Partner / Ihre Partnerin, und ergänzen Sie die fehlenden (*missing*) Informationen.

BEISPIEL

S1: Was für ein Restaurant ist „Zur Stadtmauer"?
S2: Es ist ein vegetarisches Bistro. Und was für ein Restaurant ist „Zum Grünen Baum"?
S1: Dort gibt es traditionelle deutsche Gerichte. Welche Vorspeisen gibt es im Bistro?

Aussprache und Rechtschreibung Audio

🎧 The German *s* in combination with other letters

The letter combination **sch** is pronounced like the *sh* in the English word *fish*.

| Fisch | Schinken | Geschäft | Fleisch | Schule |

When an **s** appears at the beginning of a word in front of the letter **p** or **t**, it is also pronounced like the *sh* in *fish*. A prefix added to the word will not change the pronunciation of the **s**. However, if the **sp** or **st** letter combination occurs in the middle or at the end of a word, the **s** is pronounced like the *s* in the English word *restore*.

| Speise | stoppen | versprechen | Aspirin | Fenster |

In a few words borrowed from other languages, **sh** and **ch** are also pronounced like the *sh* in *fish*.

| Chauffeur | Cashewnuss | Shampoo | Champignon | charmant |

At the beginning of a word, the letter combination **tsch** is pronounced like the *ch* in *chat*. In the middle or at the end of a word, **tsch** is pronounced like the *tch* in *catch*.

| tschüss | Tschad | Tschechien | Rutsch | Klatschbase |

---

1 Aussprechen Wiederholen Sie die Wörter, die Sie hören.

1. Schaft
2. waschen
3. Sport
4. Strudel
5. aufstehen
6. Kasten
7. Aspekt
8. Putsch
9. platschen
10. Kutscher

2 Nachsprechen Wiederholen Sie die Sätze, die Sie hören.

1. Im Lebensmittelgeschäft kaufst du Schinken und Fisch.
2. In der Schule schwimmen alle Schüler im Schwimmbad.
3. Studenten spielen gern Videospiele.
4. Auf der Speisekarte steht Käsespätzle.
5. Der Tscheche sagt nicht mal tschüss.
6. Ich wünsche dir einen guten Rutsch ins neue Jahr!

3 Sprichwörter Wiederholen Sie die Sprichwörter, die Sie hören.

2 Suggestion Point out that **Einen guten Rutsch ins neue Jahr!** is a common New Year's greeting in German.

2 Expansion Item 2 is a tongue twister. Have students take turns trying to say it as quickly as possible. You may also want to teach students the tongue twister **Fischers Fritz fischt frische Fische.**

Besser spät als nie.[1]

Reden ist Silber; Schweigen ist Gold.[2]

Ressourcen

SAM
LM: p. 36

vhlcentral.com

Die Rechnung, bitte!  Ⓢ Video

Vorbereitung Have students scan the script to find words and expressions related to food.

Torsten und Sabite sind bei einem romantischen Abendessen in einem schönen Restaurant. Aber es bleibt nicht so romantisch...

KELLNER Wir bieten eine leckere hausgemachte Pilzsuppe an. Nicht zu schwer.
SABITE Davon nehme ich einen Teller, bitte. Und als zweiten Gang nehme ich die Rindsrouladen.
KELLNER Sehr gerne. Und für Sie, mein Herr?
TORSTEN Als Vorspeise nehme ich den Salat und als Hauptspeise das Wiener Schnitzel, mit Salzkartoffeln, bitte.
KELLNER Ausgezeichnet.

SABITE Sie haben sehr gutes Essen in diesem Restaurant.
TORSTEN Ja. Meine ältere Schwester empfiehlt es guten Freunden wärmstens.

KELLNER Möchten Sie gerne noch einen Nachtisch?
MELINE Ach, ich muss auf meine Figur achten!
KELLNER Oh, nein, Sie sind doch extrem...
LORENZO Wir nehmen ein Stück Schwarzwälder Kirschtorte. Zwei Gabeln.
MELINE Und zwei Kaffee bitte.

SABITE Hallo!
MELINE Sabite! Hallo! Sabite, das ist Lorenzo. Lorenzo, das ist meine Mitbewohnerin, Sabite.
LORENZO Ciao.

LORENZO Ich komme aus Milano.
MELINE Lorenzo ist geschäftlich in Berlin. Er arbeitet im Bereich internationale Finanzen.
LORENZO Bist du auch Studentin?
SABITE Ja, ich studiere Kunst.

SABITE Ich liebe die Kunst von Kandinsky und Klee. Aber Italien hat die Meister... Michelangelo... Da Vinci...
LORENZO Ja. Du musst sie mal aus der Nähe sehen.
SABITE Ich hoffe, sie eines Tages sehen zu können. Mein Vater kommt aus der Türkei. Ich möchte dort gern ein Semester lang studieren.

communication cultures NATIONAL STANDARDS

1 Richtig oder falsch? Entscheiden Sie, ob die folgenden Sätze **richtig** oder **falsch** sind.

1. Sabite nimmt die Pilzsuppe und die Roulade. Richtig.
2. Torsten bestellt ein Schnitzel mit Salzkartoffeln. Richtig.
3. Torstens Schwester empfiehlt ihren Freunden das Restaurant. Richtig.
4. Meline und Lorenzo bestellen zwei Stück Schwarzwälder Kirschtorte. Falsch.
5. Lorenzo kommt aus Italien. Richtig.

6. Er studiert Kunst. Falsch.
7. Sabite mag die Kunst von Klee und Picasso. Falsch.
8. Sie möchte ein Jahr in der Türkei studieren. Falsch.
9. Sie möchte Istanbul kennen lernen. Richtig.
10. Sabite findet Torsten egoistisch. Richtig.

1 Expansion Have students correct the false sentences.

PERSONEN

 Torsten   **Sabite**   **Meline**   **Lorenzo**   **Kellner**

SABITE Torsten, ist alles in Ordnung?
TORSTEN Türkei? Du möchtest in der Türkei studieren?
SABITE Ich möchte Istanbul kennen lernen.

SABITE Hör auf. Noch studiert niemand in der Türkei. Entschuldige bitte.
TORSTEN Sabite!

SABITE Torsten ist... ist... ist so egoistisch!

TORSTEN Frauen. Und du bist also nicht Lukas?
LORENZO Die Rechnung, bitte!

Nützliche Ausdrücke

- **anbieten**
  to offer
- **Davon nehme ich einen Teller, bitte.**
  I would like a bowl of that, please.
- **die Rindsroulade**
  beef roulade
- **die Salzkartoffeln**
  boiled potatoes
- **Ich muss auf meine Figur achten.**
  I have to watch my weight.
- **die Schwarzwälder Kirschtorte**
  Black Forest cake
- **Er ist geschäftlich in Berlin.**
  He's in Berlin on business.
- **Er arbeitet im Bereich internationale Finanzen.**
  He works in international finance.
- **Ich hoffe, sie eines Tages sehen zu können.**
  I hope to see them someday.
- **ein Semester lang**
  for one semester
- **Hör auf!**
  Cut it out!
- **Noch studiert niemand in der Türkei.**
  No one's studying in Turkey just yet.

4B.1
- **Meine ältere Schwester empfiehlt es guten Freunden wärmstens.**
  My older sister highly recommends it to her close friends.

4B.2
- **Du musst sie mal aus der Nähe sehen.**
  You should see them up close.

2 **Zum Besprechen** Wählen Sie zu dritt ein Gericht aus Deutschland, Österreich oder der Schweiz und machen Sie eine Liste mit Zutaten. Präsentieren Sie der Klasse dann die Liste. Ihre Kommilitonen müssen das Gericht erraten (*guess*).   Answers will vary.

2 **Expansion** Name some well-known German, Austrian or Swiss dishes (**Kaiserschmarrn, Sauerbraten, Knödel,** etc.), and ask students to find the main ingredients. Write any new words on the board.

3 **Vertiefung** In den USA ist Wiener Schnitzel vielleicht das berühmteste (*most famous*) Gericht aus den deutschsprachigen Ländern. Wissen Sie, woher es kommt? Kennen Sie andere Gerichte, die den Namen von Städten haben?   Sample answers: Wiener Schnitzel: Wien (*Vienna*); Frankfurter (Würstchen), Hamburger, Nürnberger (Bratwürstchen), Berliner (*jelly doughnut*), Kassler (*smoked pork chop*)

Ressourcen

SAM
VM: p. 8

vhlcentral.com

Suggestion Before having students read the article, ask whether they like to spend time in cafés or coffee houses. Do they like to study in cafés? What are their favorite cafés in town? How much do they spend on coffee every week?

IM FOKUS

Wiener Kaffeehäuser Ⓢ Reading

Typische Cafépreise	
Kleiner Schwarzer	2,80 €
Kleiner Brauner	2,90 €
Melange	3,90 €
Großer Schwarzer	4,20 €
Großer Brauner	4,30 €
Einspänner	4,90 €
Kapuziner	4,90 €
Pharisäer	6,60 €

QUELLE: Café Korb in Wien

KAFFEEHÄUSER IN ÖSTERREICH HABEN eine lange Tradition. Kaffeehäuser gibt es seit dem 18. Jahrhundert. In Wien findet man heute mindestens° 1.100 Kaffeehäuser. Typischerweise serviert ein Kellner einen Kaffee auf einem silbernen Tablett° mit einem Löffel, einem Glas Wasser und einem Keks. In den Kaffeehäusern trinkt man aber auch andere Getränke wie Kakao, Wasser und Wein. Zum Kaffee isst man oft Apfelstrudel, Gugelhupf° oder Sachertorte°. Oft besuchen Gäste° ein Kaffeehaus, bestellen einen Kaffee und bleiben viele Stunden. Hier diskutieren Gäste auch über Politik, Sport und andere Themen.

Wiener Kaffeehäuser haben spezielle Vokabeln: Sahne° heißt Obers. Ein kleiner oder großer Brauner ist ein Kaffee serviert mit Obers in einer kleinen Schale°. Eine Melange ist halb° Kaffee und halb geschäumte° Milch. Ein Kapuziner ist ein kleiner Mokka (ein Schwarzer oder Espresso pur) mit wenig Milch.

Es gibt auch andere Cafés in Wien. In einer Espresso-Bar trinkt man vor allem° Espresso und Cappuccino wie in Italien. In Stehcafés trinken Gäste Kaffee sehr schnell oder nehmen den Kaffee mit. Café-Konditoreien sind nicht nur Cafés. In der Konditorei kaufen Kunden hausgemachte Kuchen und Süßigkeiten°. Die neueste Version eines Cafés ist der amerikanische Import Starbucks. Hier findet man vor allem jüngere Österreicher.

mindestens *at least* **Tablett** *tray* **Gugelhupf** *Bundt cake* **Sachertorte** *chocolate torte* **Gäste** *guests* **Sahne** *cream* **Schale** *dish* **halb** *half* **geschäumte** *foamed* **vor allem** *above all* **Süßigkeiten** *sweets*

Suggestion Have students compare Viennese coffee prices to what they normally pay, keeping the exchange rate in mind. Ask: **Wie viel kostet der Kapuziner? Ist das teuer? Wie viel bezahlen Sie für Ihr Lieblingskaffeegetränk?**

ÜBUNGEN

1 **Wiener Kaffeehäuser** Ergänzen Sie die Sätze.

1. Wiener Kaffeehäuser haben eine ___lange___ Tradition.

2. In Wien findet man mehr als ___1.100___ Kaffeehäuser.

3. Auf einem Tablett serviert der Kellner den Kaffee, einen Löffel, ein ___Glas Wasser___ und einen Keks.

4. Gäste bleiben oft ___viele___ Stunden.

5. Neben Kaffee kann man auch ___Kakao___, Wasser oder Wein trinken.

6. Typisches Essen in Kaffeehäusern sind ___Apfelstrudel___, Gugelhupf und Sachertorte.

7. Ein Melange ist halb Kaffee und halb ___(geschäumte) Milch___.

8. In Wien gibt es auch Espresso-Bars, ___Stehcafés___ und Café-Konditoreien.

9. In einer Espresso-Bar trinken Gäste Kaffee wie in ___Italien___.

10. Ein Kapuziner im Café Korb kostet ___4,90 €___.

Ⓟ Practice more at **vhlcentral.com**.

Am Tisch

Die Rechnung, bitte!	*Check, please!*
Die Speisekarte, bitte!	*The menu, please!*
Guten Appetit!	*Enjoy your meal!*
Noch einen Wunsch?	*Anything else?*
Herr Ober!	*Waiter!*
Prost!	*Cheers!*
Zum Wohl!	*Cheers!*

Ausländische Spezialitäten

In Deutschland besteht die Bevölkerung°
ungefähr zu 8% aus° Ausländern°, in der
Schweiz sind es fast 23%. Die Ausländer
kommen aus vielen Ländern wie Italien,
Griechenland°, der Türkei, Nordafrika und
dem ehemaligen° Jugoslawien. Deshalb°
ist die Restaurantszene in Deutschland,
Österreich und der Schweiz auch sehr
international. In jeder° Stadt gibt es
Restaurants mit italienischen, griechischen
und verschiedenen° asiatischen Speisen.
Vor allem in Großstädten ist die Auswahl°
sehr groß. Die populärsten Restaurants sind
definitiv italienisch, aber man findet auch
sehr viele asiatische Restaurants.

Bevölkerung *population* **besteht... aus** *consists of*
Ausländern *foreigners* **Griechenland** *Greece*
ehemaligen *former* **Deshalb** *Therefore* **jeder** *every*
verschiedenen *various* **Auswahl** *selection*

Figlmüller

Das Figlmüller ist ein sehr altes Restaurant in Wien. Es ist „die Heimat° des Schnitzels", ein
Paradies für Schnitzelfans. Man findet das Restaurant in der Wollzeile im Zentrum Wiens.
Das Restaurant existiert seit über 100 Jahren und ist berühmt° für seine Schnitzel, ein
Stück Schweinefleisch mit Semmelbröselhülle°. Die Schnitzel sind ziemlich groß, dünn
und sehr knusprig°. Dazu gibt es österreichische Weine. Bier und Kaffee gibt es hier nicht.
Auch Süßspeisen finden Gäste nicht auf der Speisekarte. Aber Schnitzel sind hier sehr
wichtig. Alle Ober servieren die Schnitzel in einem schwarzen Smoking°!

Heimat *home* **berühmt** *famous* **Semmelbröselhülle** *bread crumb crust* **knusprig** *crisp* **Smoking** *tuxedo*

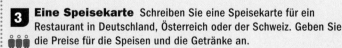

✎S IM INTERNET

Suchen Sie Informationen über die Mensa an der
Universität Wien. Was können Studenten essen?
Was können Studenten trinken? Wie viel kostet
das Essen?

Find out more at **vhlcentral.com**.

3 **Expansion** After each group creates a menu, have them act out a short restaurant role-play using phrases
from the **Deutsch im Alltag** box. Have students request the menu, order their food, and finally pay for it.

---

2 **Richtig oder falsch?** Korrigieren Sie die falschen Aussagen.

1. In deutschsprachigen Ländern gibt es viele internationale Restaurants.
   Richtig.
2. Die beliebtesten internationalen Restaurants sind italienisch. Richtig.
3. Das Restaurant Figlmüller ist ein sehr altes Restaurant in Wien. Richtig.
4. Das Restaurant Figlmüller hat eine Spezialität: Apfelstrudel.
   Falsch. Die Spezialität ist Schnitzel.
5. Fast 23% der Bevölkerung in Deutschland sind Ausländer.
   Falsch. Fast 23% der Bevölkerung in der Schweiz sind Ausländer.

3 **Eine Speisekarte** Schreiben Sie eine Speisekarte für ein
Restaurant in Deutschland, Österreich oder der Schweiz. Geben Sie
die Preise für die Speisen und die Getränke an.

BEISPIEL *Restaurant „Zur Post"*

Hauptspeisen		Nachtische	
Schweinebraten	6,90 €	*Obstsalat*	3,10 €
Pizza Marinara	5,50 €	*Tiramisu*	3,50 €

Ressourcen

vhlcentral.com

4B.1

Suggestion Remind students that the subject is "who does it", the direct object is "what gets `verbed", and the indirect object is "for whom or to whom".

QUERVERWEIS

See **1A.3** and **1B.1** to review the use of the nominative and accusative case.

You will learn more about verbs that take dative objects in **5A.3**

Suggestion To help students memorize the definite articles, teach them the nonsense words "rese, nese, mrmn". These words are derived from the last letter of each article, moving from left to right across the table.

Suggestion To help students memorize the indefinite articles, teach them the nonsense phrase "blank-e blank-e, en-e, blank-e, mrmn (Blankie, blankie, any blankie, Merman?)", also derived from the endings placed on the article, moving from left to right across the table.

QUERVERWEIS

See **3A.1** to review the use of possessive adjectives.

The dative  Presentation

Suggestion Provide the class with sentences in both German and English, and have students identify the subject, direct object, and indirect object. Point out the semantic difference between sentences such as: **Ich bringe den Kindern die Schokolade,** and **Ich bringe der Schokolade die Kinder,** or **Der Hund beißt den Mann,** and **Den Hund beißt der Mann.**

Startblock In **1B.1**, you learned that the direct object of a verb is always in the accusative case. When a verb has an indirect object, it is always in the dative case.

- An object in the dative case indicates *to whom* or *for whom* an action is performed.

  Ich bringe **dem Lehrer** einen Apfel.
  *I'm bringing **the teacher** an apple.*

  Zeig **der Professorin** deine Arbeit.
  *Show your work **to the professor**.*

- Verbs that are frequently used with a dative object include **zeigen** (*to show*), **geben**, **bringen**, **empfehlen**, and **gehören** (*to belong to*). Note that the verbs **helfen** and **danken** also take a dative object, even though their English equivalents normally take a direct object.

  Wir helfen **den Kindern**.
  *We're helping (giving help to) **the kids**.*

  Sie dankt **dem Kellner**.
  *She's thanking (giving thanks to) **the waiter**.*

- The forms of the definite and indefinite articles that accompany dative nouns differ from the forms in the nominative or accusative case.

definite articles	masculine	feminine	neuter	plural
nominative	der Kellner	die Kellnerin	das Kind	die Kinder
accusative	den Kellner	die Kellnerin	das Kind	die Kinder
dative	dem Kellner	der Kellnerin	dem Kind	den Kindern

indefinite articles	masculine	feminine	neuter	plural
nominative	ein Kellner	eine Kellnerin	ein Kind	keine Kinder
accusative	einen Kellner	eine Kellnerin	ein Kind	keine Kinder
dative	einem Kellner	einer Kellnerin	einem Kind	keinen Kindern

  Der Kellner bringt **der Frau** einen Salat.
  *The waiter is bringing **the woman** a salad.*

  Ich empfehle **einem Freund** das Restaurant.
  *I'm recommending the restaurant **to a friend**.*

- The endings for possessive adjectives are the same as the endings for the indefinite articles.

possessive adjectives	masculine	feminine	neuter	plural
nominative	mein Koch	meine Köchin	mein Kind	meine Kinder
accusative	meinen Koch	meine Köchin	mein Kind	meine Kinder
dative	meinem Koch	meiner Köchin	meinem Kind	meinen Kindern

  Der Kellner bringt **meiner Frau** einen Salat.
  *The waiter is bringing **my wife** a salad.*

  Wir empfehlen unseren **Freunden** das Restaurant.
  *We recommend the restaurant **to our friends**.*

- When using plural nouns in the dative case, add **-n** to any noun whose plural form does not already end in **-n** or **-s**.

nominative plural	dative plural
die Teller	den Tellern
die Esslöffel	den Esslöffeln
die Kaffees	den Kaffees
die Rechnungen	den Rechnungen

- A small number of singular masculine nouns also add the ending **-n** or **-en** in the accusative and dative cases. The **n**-nouns you have learned so far are: **der Architekt, der Dozent, der Journalist, der Junge, der Neffe,** and **der Student**.

Nils backt **seinem Neffen** einen Apfelkuchen.
*Nils is baking an apple pie **for his nephew**.*

Ich schreibe **dem Dozenten** eine E-Mail.
*I'm writing an e-mail **to the instructor**.*

- In the dative case, an adjective preceded by an **ein**-word or a **der**-word always ends in **-en**.

Anna kauft **dem kleinen** Jungen ein Eis.
*Anna is buying an ice cream for **the little** boy.*

Ich gebe **meiner kleinen** Schwester eine Banane.
*I'm giving **my little** sister a banana.*

- Adjectives in the dative that are not preceded by an article have endings similar to the definite article endings.

	masculine	feminine	neuter	plural
unpreceded adjective endings				
nominative	süß**er** Kuchen	süß**e** Melone	süß**es** Getränk	süß**e** Äpfel
accusative	süß**en** Kuchen	süß**e** Melone	süß**es** Getränk	süß**e** Äpfel
dative	süß**em** Kuchen	süß**er** Melone	süß**em** Getränk	süß**en** Äpfeln

Ich biete **guten** Freunden immer gutes Essen an.
*I always serve good food to **good** friends.*

Die Lehrerin hilft **neuen** Studenten gern.
*The teacher likes to help **new** students.*

- Use the dative question word **wem** to ask *to whom?*

nominative	accusative	dative
wer?	**wen?**	**wem?**

Wem gibst du das Geschenk?
***To whom** are you giving the present?*

Ich gebe **meiner Mutter** das Geschenk.
*I'm giving the present **to my mother**.*

Wem gehört diese Tasse?
*Who does this cup belong **to**?*

Sie gehört **meinem Opa**.
*It belongs **to my grandpa**.*

QUERVERWEIS

You will learn more about **n**-nouns in **8B.1**.

See **3A.2** to review adjective agreement in the nominative and accusative case.

See **2A.2** to review question words.

ACHTUNG

In sentences with both direct and indirect objects, the dative object comes before the accusative object.

Suggestion Students often forget to add **-n** in the dative plural. Write sentences on the board in which the **n** is missing, and ask students to find the mistakes. Ex.: **Der Koch kocht den** Kinder **eine leckere Suppe. Die Kinder bringen ihren** Freunde **viele Geschenke.**

Suggestion Point out to students that these endings are similar to the endings of the definite articles, and also follow the "rese, nese, mrmn" pattern.

Ressourcen

SAM
WB: pp. 57–58

SAM
LM: p. 37

vhlcentral.com

Jetzt sind Sie dran! **Wählen Sie den richtigen Artikel.**

1. Mama dankt (der / dem) Kellner.
2. Ich gebe (dem / der) Professorin die Hausaufgaben.
3. Moritz gibt (seiner / seinem) Mutter ein Parfüm.
4. Die Professorin hilft (ihren / ihrem) Studenten mit der Grammatik.
5. Die Großmutter backt (ihrem / ihrer) Enkelkind einen Kuchen.
6. Ich schreibe (dem / der) Besitzer eine E-Mail.

Anwendung

1 **Was fehlt?** Ergänzen Sie die Sätze mit den richtigen Substantivformen im Dativ.

BEISPIEL deine Freundin: Kaufst du _deiner Freundin_ einen MP3-Player?

1. meine Partnerin: Ich zeige ___meiner Partnerin___ die Hausaufgaben.
2. ihr Mann: Sie gibt ___ihrem Mann___ einen Kuss.
3. die Freunde: Er macht ___den Freunden___ ein leckeres Essen.
4. unser Opa: Ich schreibe ___unserem Opa___ eine lange E-Mail.
5. die alte Frau: Er bringt ___der alten Frau___ ein Mineralwasser.
6. die Kellnerin: Der Koch gibt ___der Kellnerin___ eine Tasse Tee.

2 **Pluralformen** Geben Sie die richtigen Pluralformen im Dativ an.

1. dem alten Hund: ___den alten Hunden___
2. seiner lieben Tante: ___seinen lieben Tanten___
3. der netten Katze: ___den netten Katzen___
4. einem neugierigen Journalisten: ___neugierigen Journalisten___
5. dem kleinen Mädchen: ___den kleinen Mädchen___
6. keiner stolzen Frau: ___keinen stolzen Frauen___
7. dem mutigen Kind: ___den mutigen Kindern___
8. ihrem großen Neffen: ___ihren großen Neffen___
9. meinem faulen Bruder: ___meinen faulen Brüdern___

3 **Dativobjekte** Ergänzen Sie die Sätze mit der richtigen Form im Dativ.

1. Die Kellnerin empfiehlt ___meinen Brüdern___ (meine Brüder) die Vorspeise.
2. ___Wem___ (Wer) bringst du die Flasche Wein?
3. Ich gebe ___der Kellnerin___ (die Kellnerin) ein Trinkgeld.
4. Der gute Student hilft ___schlechten Studenten___ (schlechte Studenten) oft.
5. Du gibst ___einem schönen Mädchen___ (ein schönes Mädchen) rote Rosen.
6. ___Wem___ (Wer) soll ich das Besteck geben?
7. Kannst du ___meiner Mutter___ (meine Mutter) einen Nachtisch empfehlen?
8. Ich zeige ___meinem Freund___ (mein Freund) die Rechnung.
9. Die Kinder helfen ___ihren Eltern___ (ihre Eltern) gern.
10. Der Junge gibt ___den alten Hunden___ (die alten Hunde) Würstchen.

4 **Nettigkeiten** Bilden Sie Sätze. Sample answers are provided.

BEISPIEL sie / der Kellner / ein Trinkgeld / geben
Sie geben dem Kellner ein Trinkgeld.

1. die Frau / ihre Mutter / ein Kuchen / geben   Die Frau gibt ihrer Mutter einen Kuchen.
2. ich / der Hund / sein Essen / vorbereiten   Ich bereite dem Hund sein Essen vor.
3. der Schüler / die Lehrerin / eine Postkarte / schreiben   Der Schüler schreibt der Lehrerin eine Postkarte.
4. er / seine Tochter / eine Vorspeise / bestellen   Er bestellt seiner Tochter eine Vorspeise.
5. die Köchin / das Kind / ein Brötchen / geben   Die Köchin gibt dem Kind ein Brötchen.
6. meine Frau / die Oma / eine Beilage / mitbringen   Meine Frau bringt der Oma eine Beilage mit.

Practice more at **vhlcentral.com.**

Kommunikation

5 **Was für ein Chaos!** Ihr Haus ist ein totales Chaos. Fragen Sie Ihren Partner / Ihre Partnerin, wem die Sachen gehören, die im Haus herumliegen. Answers will vary.

▶ **BEISPIEL**

S1: Wem gehört der Pullover?
S2: Er gehört meiner Schwester.

meine Eltern	die Köchin
eine Freundin	meine Schwester
der Kellner	ein Student

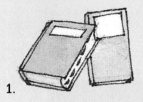

1.   2.   3.

4.   5.   6.

6 **Geschenke** Sehen Sie die Speisekarte auf Seite 164 an und erzählen Sie Ihrem Partner / Ihrer Partnerin, welche Gerichte Sie Ihrer Familie und Ihren Freunden empfehlen. Answers will vary.

BEISPIEL meine Tante

S1: Ich empfehle meiner Tante den Chef-Salat. Was empfiehlst du deiner Oma?
S2: Ich empfehle meiner Oma einen kleinen Tomatensalat mit Mozzarella!

1. Mutter/Vater
2. Großeltern
3. Lehrer/Lehrerin
4. Cousin/Cousine

5. Onkel/Tante
6. bester Freund/beste Freundin
7. Bruder/Schwester
8. Kommilitonen

7 **Wem tust du einen Gefallen?** Beantworten Sie die Fragen von Ihrem Partner / Ihrer Partnerin. Answers will vary.

BEISPIEL

S1: Wem zeigst du dein Zeugnis?
S2: Ich zeige meinen Eltern mein Zeugnis. Und du?

1. Wem schreibst du Postkarten im Sommer?
2. Wem kochst du ein Essen?
3. Wem kaufst du ein Buch?

4. Wem hilfst du bei den Hausaufgaben?
5. Wem stellst du deine Eltern vor?
6. Wem backst du einen Kuchen?

6 **Suggestions**
• Even if students have been working well with the accusative and dative in isolation, they often have difficulty when they must use both cases in the same sentence. It may be helpful to have charts on the board, and to emphasize that the person who receives the recommendation will be in the dative, while the recommended dish will be in the accusative.
• Give students a few minutes to look at the menu on p. 164 and decide on their recommendations before they begin working with partners. Emphasize that they will be working with *both* the accusative and the dative. Ask a student volunteer to put an example on the board.

4B.2

Prepositions with the dative  Presentation

Suggestion Teach students the mnemonic device of singing the dative prepositions in alphabetical order to the tune of Strauss's *Donauwalzer* ("Blue Danube").

QUERVERWEIS

See **3B.2** to review prepositions that take an object in the accusative case.

ACHTUNG

The prepositions **nach** and **zu** are also used in the set expressions **nach Hause** (*home*) and **zu Hause** (*at home*). **Ich gehe jetzt nach Hause. Er bleibt immer zu Hause.**

Suggestion Emphasize that the phrases **zu Hause** and **nach Hause** are idiomatic and should be memorized as "sound bites".

Startblock Certain prepositions are always followed by an object in the dative case.

Mein Vater kommt **aus der Türkei**.

Ich glaube, es ist alles okay **mit den beiden**.

- Most dative prepositional phrases provide information about time and location.

prepositions with the dative			
aus	*from*	nach	*after; to*
außer	*except for*	seit	*since; for*
bei	*at; near; with*	von	*from*
mit	*with*	zu	*to; for; at*

Willst du **bei meinen Eltern** essen?
*Do you want to eat **at my parents' house**?*

Zum Geburtstag bekomme ich Geschenke.
*I get presents **on my birthday**.*

- Use **nach** before the names of countries or cities. Use **zu** with people, businesses, or other locations.

Wir fliegen morgen **nach Berlin**.
*We're flying **to Berlin** tomorrow.*

Gehst du **zur Bäckerei**?
*Are you going **to the bakery**?*

- The preposition **seit** is used with time expressions to indicate *since when* or *for how long* something has been taking place.

Seit wann wohnst du in Berlin?
***Since when** have you been living in Berlin?*

Ich wohne **seit einem Jahr** in Berlin.
*I've been living in Berlin **for one year**.*

- The prepositions **bei**, **von**, and **zu** can combine with the definite article **dem** to form contractions. The preposition **zu** also forms a contraction with the definite article **der**.

bei + dem = **beim**   zu + dem = **zum**
von + dem = **vom**   zu + der = **zur**

Wir kaufen oft **beim** Supermarkt ein.
*We often shop **at the** supermarket.*

Ich esse immer Eier **zum** Frühstück.
*I always have eggs **for** breakfast.*

Ressourcen

SAM
WB: pp. 59–60

SAM
LM: p. 38

vhlcentral.com

Jetzt sind Sie dran!   **Wählen Sie die passenden Präpositionen.**

1. Der beste Tisch ist (aus dem /(beim)) Fenster.
2. Wann fährst du ((zum)/ mit dem) Supermarkt?
3. ((Vom)/ Außer dem) Supermarkt gibt es hier keine Geschäfte.
4. Deine Familie kommt (mit /(aus)) den USA.
5. ((Seit)/ Außer) zwei Jahren lerne ich Spanisch.
6. Ninas Freund fährt (nach der /(zur)) Universität.
7. Ich wohne (zu /(bei)) meinen Eltern.
8. Wir essen Pizza ((mit)/ bei) Besteck.

Anwendung und Kommunikation

1 **Was ist richtig?** Wählen Sie die passenden Präpositionen.

BEISPIEL Wir wohnen (seit / um) fünf Jahren hier.

1. Daniel kommt (mit / aus) Hamburg.
2. Er studiert (bei / seit) sechs Semestern an der Uni Heidelberg.
3. Er wohnt (mit / von) drei Freunden zusammen.
4. Alle drei Monate fährt er (nach / zu) Hause zu seinen Eltern.
5. Seine Mutter ist immer extrem glücklich, wenn ihr Sohn (nach / zu) Hause ist.
6. Am Wochenende spielt er (aus / mit) seinem Vater Tennis.
7. (Außer / Aus) seinen Eltern besucht er auch seine Großeltern.
8. Daniel hat nächste Woche Geburtstag und er bekommt (nach / von) seinem Opa ein neues Auto.

2 **Wer ist das?** Setzen Sie die fehlenden Dativpräpositionen ein.

Christoph Waltz kommt (1) ___aus___ Österreich. Seine Großmutter arbeitet als junge Frau als Schauspielerin (*actress*) (2) ___bei___ einem Theater und (3) ___von___ dieser Großmutter hat er sein Talent. Waltz ist (4) ___seit___ vielen Jahren als ein großartiger Schauspieler berühmt. Für seine Rollen in den Filmen *Inglourious Basterds* und *Django Unchained* gewinnt er zwei Oscars. Beide Filme sind (5) ___von___ Quentin Tarantino. Waltz wohnt (6) ___mit___ seiner Frau in Hollywood, London und Berlin.

3 **Seit wann?** Seit wann macht Ihr Partner / Ihre Partnerin die folgenden Aktivitäten? Answers will vary.

BEISPIEL heute Vorlesungen haben

S1: *Seit wann hast du heute Vorlesungen?*
S2: *Ich habe seit 10 Uhr Vorlesung. Und du?*

1. hier studieren
2. Deutsch lernen
3. Kaffee trinken
4. einen Computer haben
5. ein Handy haben
6. Auto fahren

4 **Fotoalbum** Sehen Sie die Fotos an und beantworten Sie die Fragen von Ihrem Partner / Ihrer Partnerin. Answers will vary.

▶ **BEISPIEL**

S1: *Woher kommt Eriks Opa?*
S2: *Er kommt aus der Schweiz.*

1. Mit wem spricht Anna?
2. Wohin reisen Lena und Jasmin?
3. Wohin geht Annika?
4. Seit wann arbeitet Felix im Restaurant?

3 **Suggestion** Native speakers of English often try to use the present perfect with **seit**. Remind students to use the present tense in this exercise.

4 **Suggestion** Have students take turns asking and answering the questions. Make sure they understand that they should base their answers on the pictures, but that there is no single correct answer for each question, and they are welcome to respond imaginatively.

Wiederholung

1 Ankes Familie
Ankes Familie ist in einem Restaurant. Was bringt der Kellner den Familienmitgliedern (*family members*) zu trinken? Answers will vary.

> **BEISPIEL** die Schwester
>
> **S1:** *Was bringt der Kellner Ankes Schwester?*
> **S2:** *Er bringt ihrer Schwester ein Glas Milch.*

der Kaffee die Milch	das Mineralwasser der Orangensaft	das stille Wasser der Tee

1. der Onkel
2. die Eltern
3. der Bruder
4. die Oma
5. die Tante
6. der Opa

2 Der Koch
Fragen Sie den Koch, was er den Personen zum Essen macht. Wechseln Sie sich ab. Sample answers are provided.

> **BEISPIEL**
>
> **S1:** *Herr Müller, was machen Sie dem Musiker zum Frühstück?*
> **S2:** *Ich mache dem Musiker ein Schinkenbrot.*

der Musiker / das Frühstück

1. die Journalistin / das Abendessen
Herr Müller, was machen Sie der Journalistin zum Abendessen? Ich mache der Journalistin eine Suppe.

2. die Architektin / das Mittagessen
Herr Müller, was machen Sie der Architektin zum Mittagessen? Ich mache der Architektin Rindfleisch.

3. die Friseurin / das Mittagessen
Herr Müller, was machen Sie der Friseurin zum Mittagessen? Ich mache der Friseurin einen kleinen Salat.

4. der Geschäftsmann / das Abendessen
Herr Müller, was machen Sie dem Geschäftsmann zum Abendessen? Ich mache dem Geschäftsmann Fisch mit Garnelen.

5. die Dozentin / das Abendessen
Herr Müller, was machen Sie der Dozentin zum Abendessen? Ich mache der Dozentin Hähnchen mit Kartoffeln.

6. der Ingenieur / das Mittagessen
Herr Müller, was machen Sie dem Ingenieur zum Mittagessen? Ich mache dem Ingenieur Pasta.

3 Wie schmeckt's?
Sagen Sie einem Partner / einer Partnerin, was die Personen essen und wie sie es finden. Answers will vary.

> **BEISPIEL**
>
> **S1:** *Wie findet die Frau die Erdbeeren?*
> **S2:** *Sie sind der Frau zu süß.*

fade	lecker	leicht	salzig	scharf	süß

1. der Mann
2. die Frau
3. das Mädchen

4. die Studenten
5. der Junge
6. die Kinder

4 Diskutieren und kombinieren
Sie sind Kellner / Kellnerin im Restaurant. Was sollen Sie den Gästen bringen? Fragen Sie Ihren Partner / Ihre Partnerin. Answers will vary.

> **BEISPIEL**
>
> **S1:** *Was braucht der junge Mann?*
> **S2:** *Bring dem jungen Mann eine Serviette.*
> **S1:** *Was braucht die alte Frau?*
> **S2:** *Bring der alten Frau eine Gabel.*

4 Suggestion Briefly review vocabulary, to make sure students recall the names and genders of all the items pictured before beginning this activity.

5 Arbeitsblatt
Sie bekommen von Ihrem Professor / Ihrer Professorin eine Liste mit diversen Aktivitäten. Suchen Sie Kommilitonen, die diese Aktivitäten machen. Answers will vary.

> **BEISPIEL**
>
> **S1:** *Isst du täglich Eier zum Frühstück?*
> **S2:** *Ja, ich esse täglich Eier zum Frühstück.*
> OR
> **S1:** *Wohnst du bei deinen Eltern?*
> **S2:** *Nein, ich wohne nicht bei meinen Eltern.*

6 Wie lange?

6 **Wie lange?** Finden Sie vier Dinge heraus, die Ihr Partner / Ihre Partnerin gern macht. Fragen Sie ihn/sie, seit wann er/sie das schon macht.

BEISPIEL

S1: *Was spielst du gern?*
S2: *Ich spiele gern Tennis.*
S1: *Seit wann spielst du Tennis?*
S2: *Seit drei Jahren.*

7 **Interview** Führen Sie ein Interview mit einem Partner / einer Partnerin. Wenn eine Person fertig ist, tauschen Sie (*exchange*) Rollen. Answers will vary.

BEISPIEL

S1: *Bei wem wohnst du im Sommer?*
S2: *Ich wohne bei meinem Bruder.*

1. Woher kommst du?
2. Seit wann studierst du an der Uni?
3. Gehst du gern zum Supermarkt einkaufen?
4. Mit wem telefonierst du gern?
5. Bei wem wohnst du im Sommer?
6. Wohin möchtest du reisen?

8 **Poetische Präpositionen** Schreiben Sie mit einem Partner / einer Partnerin ein Gedicht aus fünf Sätzen. Außer der letzten Zeile (*line*) soll jede Zeile mit einer Dativ- oder Akkusativpräposition beginnen.

BEISPIEL

Mit dem Ball spiele ich.
Bei dem Metzger kaufen wir ein.
Durch die Stadt läuft die Mutter.
Außer Anton isst die Familie.
Der Hund schläft ein.

Mein Wör | ter | buch

Schreiben Sie noch fünf weitere Wörter in Ihr persönliches Wörterbuch zu den Themen **Lebensmittel** und **im Restaurant**.

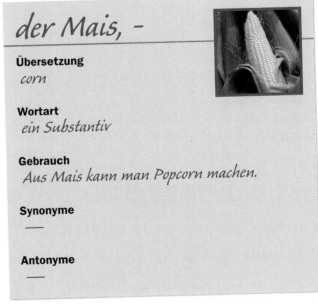

der Mais, -

Übersetzung
corn

Wortart
ein Substantiv

Gebrauch
Aus Mais kann man Popcorn machen.

Synonyme
—

Antonyme
—

 Vocabulary tools

Weiter geht's

Panorama Interactive Map

Österreich

Österreich in Zahlen

▶ **Fläche°:** *83.855 km² (Quadratkilometer) (60% der Fläche sind gebirgig°)*

▶ **Bevölkerung:** *8,2 Millionen Menschen*

▶ **9 Bundesländer°:** *Burgenland, Kärnten, Niederösterreich, Oberösterreich, Salzburg, Steiermark, Tirol, Vorarlberg, Wien*

▶ **Städte:** *Wien (1,7 Mio. Einwohner), Graz (264.000), Linz (190.000), Salzburg (148.000) und Innsbruck (121.000)*

▶ **Berge:** *der Großglockner (3.797 m), die Wildspitze (3.774 m)*

▶ **Flüsse°:** *die Donau, der Inn*

▶ **Währung°:** *der Euro (€) (seit 2002)*

▶ **Wichtige Industriezweige°:** *Banken, Tourismus*

▶ **Touristenattraktionen:** *Bergsport, Salzburger Festspiele°, Spanische Hofreitschule°, Wintertourismus*

Touristen können in Städten wie Wien und Salzburg viel Kultur genießen° oder in den Alpen Berg- und Wintersport betreiben. Für Firmen ist Österreich interessant, weil die Unternehmenssteuer° sehr niedrig° ist.

QUELLE: Österreichische Botschaft, Washington

Berühmte Österreicher

▶ **Maria Theresia,** *Kaiserin° (1717–1780)*

▶ **Wolfgang Amadeus Mozart,** *Komponist (1756–1791)*

▶ **Sigmund Freud,** *Neurologe (1856–1939)*

▶ **Gustav Klimt,** *Künstler° (1862–1918)*

▶ **Lise Meitner,** *Physikerin (1878–1968)*

▶ **Friedensreich Hundertwasser,** *Architekt (1928–2000)*

▶ **Elfriede Jelinek,** *Autorin (1946–)*

▶ **Falco,** *Musiker (1957–1998)*

Fläche *surface area* **gebirgig** *mountainous* **Bundesländer** *states* **Flüsse** *rivers* **Währung** *currency* **Wichtige Industriezweige** *Important industries* **Festspiele** *festivals* **Hofreitschule** *Riding School* **genießen** *enjoy* **Unternehmenssteuer** *business tax* **niedrig** *low* **Kaiserin** *empress* **Künstler** *artist* **Pfefferminzbonbons** *peppermint candies* **Geschmacksrichtung** *flavor* **jedem** *every* **Lakritz** *licorice* **Köpfe** *heads* **Spendern** *dispensers*

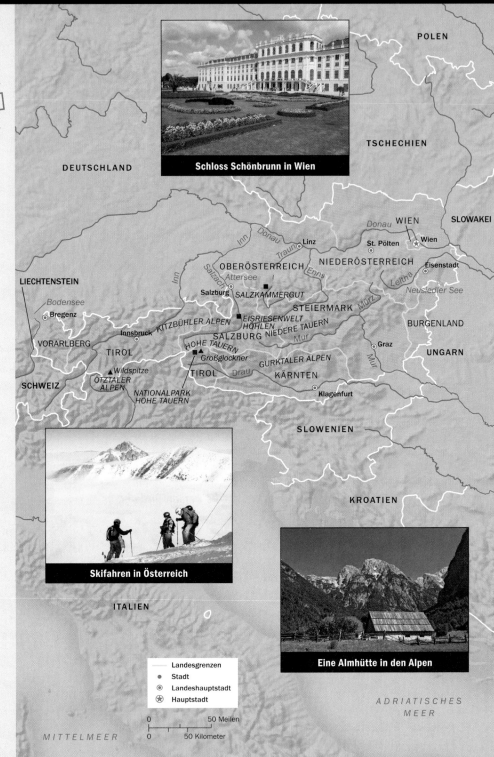

Schloss Schönbrunn in Wien

Skifahren in Österreich

Eine Almhütte in den Alpen

Landesgrenzen
● Stadt
◉ Landeshauptstadt
✹ Hauptstadt

0   50 Meilen
0   50 Kilometer

Unglaublich, aber wahr!

Der Österreicher Eduard Haas III. fängt 1927 an, Pfefferminzbonbons° mit dem Namen PEZ zu verkaufen. Der Name PEZ kommt von der ersten Geschmacksrichtung°, PfeffErminZ. PEZ gibt es heute mit jedem° Geschmack, sogar Chlorophyll und Lakritz°! Seit 1952 gibt es lustige Köpfe° auf den Spendern° wie Mickey Mouse und Donald Duck.

Politik

Internationale Institutionen in Wien

Politisch ist Österreich ein neutrales Land. Es ist Mitglied° in der Europäischen Union, aber nicht in der NATO. Seit 1980 ist Wien einer von vier Hauptsitzen° der Vereinten Nationen°. Die anderen Hauptsitze sind New York, Genf und Nairobi. Andere internationale Organisationen in Wien sind die IAEA (Internationale Organisation für Atomenergie) und die OPEC.

Sport

Olympische Spiele

Olympische Spiele und Österreich bedeuten vor allem° Olympische Winterspiele und alpiner Skisport. 1964 und 1976 treffen sich° Sportler aus aller Welt zu den Olympischen Winterspielen in Innsbruck. Erfolgreiche° österreichische Olympioniken° sind Felix Gottwald (nordischer Kombinierer°) mit drei Gold-, einer Silber- und drei Bronzemedaillen. Der Skispringer° Thomas Morgenstern und der Skifahrer Toni Sailer gewinnen jeweils° drei Goldmedaillen. In alpinen Skidisziplinen gewinnen Österreicher mehr Medaillen als jedes andere Land der Welt (34 Gold-, 39 Silber- und 41 Bronzemedaillen).

Musik

Familie von Trapp in Amerika

Viele kennen° die Familie von Trapp aus dem Film *The Sound of Music*. Aber was passiert° mit der Familie nach der Emigration? 1939 emigriert die Familie mit nur vier Dollar in der Tasche° nach Amerika. Die von Trapps machen als „Trapp Family Singers" Karriere und kaufen 1942 eine Farm in Stowe, Vermont. Auch heute kann man die Farm als Gasthaus° besuchen — und man kann mit den von Trapps Weihnachten° feiern.

Architektur

Friedensreich Hundertwasser

Hundertwasser ist ein kontroverser österreichischer Architekt und Künstler. Er beginnt in den 50er Jahren in Österreich als Künstler mit revolutionären Ideen. Die Beziehung° zwischen Mensch und Natur ist ein zentrales Thema in seiner Kunst. Heute kann man seine Häuser in der ganzen Welt finden: in Magdeburg und Essen (Deutschland), in Napa Valley (USA), in Tel Aviv (Israel) und in Kawakawa (Neuseeland). Das Hundertwasserhaus in Wien ist ein Touristenmagnet und auch die Fassade der Müllverbrennungsanlage° Spittelau ist sehr berühmt.

⊘S IM INTERNET

1. Wer sind die besten österreichischen Frauen bei Olympischen Spielen?

2. Was bedeuten dem Architekten Hundertwasser die Ideen Fensterrecht, Baummieter und Spiralhaus?

Find out more at **vhlcentral.com**.

Mitglied *member* **Hauptsitzen** *head offices* **Vereinten Nationen** *United Nations* **vor allem** *especially* **treffen sich** *meet* **Erfolgreiche** *Successful* **Olympioniken** *Olympic champions* **nordischer Kombinierer** *Nordic combined skier* **Skispringer** *ski jumper* **jeweils** *each* **kennen** *know* **passiert** *happens* **Tasche** *pocket* **Gasthaus** *inn* **Weihnachten** *Christmas* **Beziehung** *relationship* **Müllverbrennungsanlage** *waste incineration plant*

 Was haben Sie gelernt? Ergänzen Sie die Sätze.

1. Der Name __PEZ__ kommt von Pfefferminz.

2. Seit __1952__ gibt es lustige Köpfe auf den PEZ-Spendern.

3. Offiziell ist Österreich ein __neutrales__ Land.

4. Wien ist seit __1980__ einer von vier Hauptsitzen der Vereinten Nationen.

5. 1939 emigriert die Familie __von Trapp__ nach Amerika.

6. Die Familie von Trapp kauft 1942 eine Farm in __Stowe__ in Vermont.

7. 1964 und __1976__ sind die Olympischen Winterspiele in Innsbruck.

8. In alpinen Skidisziplinen gewinnen die Österreicher __mehr__ Medaillen als jedes andere Land.

9. Hundertwasser ist ein kontroverser österreichischer __Architekt__ und Künstler.

10. Hundertwassers Häuser kann man in Österreich, Deutschland, den USA, Israel und __Neuseeland__ finden.

 Practice more at **vhlcentral.com**.

Lesen Audio: Reading

Vor dem Lesen

Strategien

Scanning

Scanning involves glancing over a document in search of specific information. For example, you can scan a document to identify its format, to find cognates, to locate visual clues about the document's content, or to find specific facts. Scanning allows you to learn a great deal about a text without having to read it word for word.

Textart Was für ein Text ist das? Erklären Sie Ihre Antwort einem Partner / einer Partnerin.

eine E-Mail	**(ein Blog)**
eine Broschüre	ein Memo
eine Einkaufsliste	ein Artikel

Auf einen Blick Sehen Sie sich mit einem Partner / einer Partnerin den Text an.

A. Schreiben Sie drei Aktivitäten auf, die Sie im Text finden. *Sample answers are provided.*

schlafen
Inlineskates fahren
klettern

B. Welche Lehnwörter (*loan words*) und Kognate können Sie im Text finden? Diskutieren Sie Ihre Antworten. *Sample answers are provided.*

Sofas	Musik
Konzerthalle	Brunch
Jamsession	Inlineskates

---

   http://www.die-ersten-monate-in-graz.com

Die ersten Monate in Graz

über mich	Hauptseite	Fotos	Kontakt

Besuch!   12. Oktober

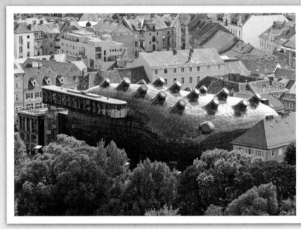

Das Kunsthaus

Am Freitag besuchen mich meine Freunde Lukas, Jan und Paul für ein Wochenende in Graz. Super! Vier Jahre lang haben wir zusammen in Wien studiert. Jetzt sehen wir uns nur selten. Jan wohnt in Linz, Lukas arbeitet in Wien und Paul studiert immer noch. Alle können bei mir übernachten. Ich habe ein Gästezimmer° und zwei Sofas im Wohnzimmer°. Das funktioniert prima! Schlafen werden wir an diesem Wochenende ohnehin° nicht! Am Freitag geht's erstmal in die Hopfenlaube, eine tolle Konzerthalle, für eine Jamsession. Da ist die Musik immer toll und wir können über die guten alten Zeiten reden. Am Samstag geht's dann ins Café Schwalbennest frühstücken. Nach der langen Nacht ist ein guter Brunch extrem wichtig°. Das Café ist ganz in der Nähe° meiner Wohnung°. Anschließend° gehen wir bei schönem Wetter° eine Runde im Volksgarten Inlineskates fahren. Der Volksgarten ist total

Gästezimmer *guest bedroom* **Wohnzimmer** *living room* **ohnehin** *anyhow*
wichtig *important* **in der Nähe** *near to* **Wohnung** *apartment*
Anschließend *Afterwards* **bei schönem Wetter** *in nice weather*

☆▼ · Suche 🔍

schön und sehr zentral gelegen°. Später können wir auch noch die Treppen° zum Grazer Schlossberg hochklettern°. Vom Uhrturm kann man die ganze Stadt super sehen inklusive der wunderschönen Innenstadt. Und was machen wir bei Regen°? Dann können wir das Kunsthaus Graz besuchen. Dort gibt es immer moderne Ausstellungen°. Ich freue mich schon auf° das Wochenende und auf meine alten Freunde.

Archiv

▶ Prüfungsstress ☹
▶ Glücklich!
▶ Die Uni
▶ Es ist schon wieder° Montag…
▶ September
▶ August
▶ Juli
▶ Juni
▶ Mai
▶ April
▶ März

Der Uhrturm

zentral gelegen *centrally located* **Treppen** *stairs* **hochklettern** *to climb up*
Regen *rain* **Ausstellungen** *exhibits* **freue mich…auf** *look forward to*
schon wieder *once again*

Nach dem Lesen

 Das richtige Wort Ergänzen Sie die Aussagen mit den richtigen Informationen.

1. Am Freitag besuchen drei Freunde die Stadt ___Graz___ für ein Wochenende.

2. Am ___Freitag___ gehen die Freunde in die Hopfenlaube.

3. Am Samstag essen die Freunde ___Frühstück/Brunch___ im Café Schwalbennest.

4. Anschließend gehen sie Inlineskates fahren im ___Volksgarten___.

5. Später können sie die ___Treppen___ zum Grazer Schlossberg hochklettern.

6. Bei Regen besuchen sie ___das Kunsthaus Graz___.

 Informationen Schreiben Sie die richtigen Antworten. Schreiben Sie ganze Sätze.
Sample answers are provided.

BEISPIEL Wo wohnt Lukas?
Lukas wohnt in Wien.

1. Wer besucht Graz am Wochenende?
   Lukas, Jan und Paul besuchen Graz.

2. Warum wollen die Freunde in die Hopfenlaube gehen?
   Die Musik da ist toll.

3. Wann frühstücken die Freunde im Café Schwalbennest?
   Sie frühstücken dort am Samstag.

4. Was machen die Freunde im Volksgarten?
   Die Freunde fahren im Volksgarten Inlineskates.

5. Was kann man vom Uhrturm sehen?
   Man kann die ganze Stadt super sehen.

6. Was kann man im Kunsthaus Graz sehen?
   Im Kunsthaus Graz kann man moderne Ausstellungen sehen.

 Ihre Heimatstadt Stellen Sie einem Partner / einer Partnerin Fragen: Was kann oder soll man in Ihrer Heimatstadt (*hometown*) machen?

BEISPIEL

S1: *Was muss man in deiner Heimatstadt sehen?*
S2: *In meiner Heimatstadt muss man das Kunstmuseum sehen.*
S1: *Wo kann man gut essen?*

Suggestion Give students a minute to prepare their lists of sights, and provide them with vocabulary as needed.

Hören

Strategien

Listening for the gist

When you listen to a conversation in German, try to figure out the main ideas that are being expressed, rather than trying to catch every word. Listening for the gist can help you follow what someone is saying, even if you can't hear or understand some of the words.

 To help you practice this strategy, you will listen to three sentences. Jot down a brief summary of what you hear.

Vorbereitung

Schauen Sie sich das Foto an. Wer ist auf dem Foto? Wo sind sie? Was machen sie?

Zuhören

Hören Sie sich den Podcast mit Andrea und der Reporterin an. Lesen Sie dann die Liste. Hören Sie sich den Podcast ein zweites Mal an und markieren Sie die Zutaten, die Sie hören.

Pilze	Nudeln
Kartoffel	Zwiebeln
Butter	Salz
Milch	Pfirsiche
Tomaten	Paprika
Schinken	Pfeffer
Knoblauch	Eier

Verständnis

Eine Zusammenfassung Ergänzen Sie die Zusammenfassung (*summary*) von dem Podcast mit Wörtern von der Liste.

den Schinken	die Nudeln	eine Reporterin
findet	frische Pilze	salzig
lecker	einen Podcast	schmeckt
Pfeffer	probieren	Zwiebeln

1. Wir hören ___einen Podcast___ mit der Köchin Andrea.
2. In der Küche sind Andrea und ___eine Reporterin___.
3. Im Moment kann man auf dem Markt ___frische Pilze___ kaufen.
4. Heute kocht Andrea Nudeln mit Pfifferlingen (*chanterelles*). Sie sind sehr ___lecker___.
5. Die Pfifferlinge passen gut zum Schinken – er ist ziemlich ___salzig___.
6. Man braucht auch Vollmilch, Butter und ___Zwiebeln___.
7. Erst kocht Andrea ___die Nudeln___.
8. Dann brät sie ___den Schinken___ mit Butter.
9. Am Ende kommen noch Salz und ___Pfeffer___ dazu.
10. Die Reporterin ___findet___ das Gericht lecker!

 Und Sie? Bereiten Sie mit einem Partner / einer Partnerin ein Rezept für eine Pizza vor. Welche Zutaten sollen auf die Pizza?

BEISPIEL

S1: *Was soll alles auf die Pizza?*
S2: *Pilze, Zwiebeln, Tomaten…*

Schreiben

Strategien

Adding details

How can you make your writing more informative or more interesting? You can add details by answering the "W" questions: Who? What? When? Where? Why? The answers to these questions will provide useful information that can be incorporated into your writing. Here are some useful question words that you have already learned.

Wer?	Wo?
Was?	Warum?
Wann?	Wie?

Compare these two statements.

„Ich muss einkaufen gehen."

„Nach der Schule muss ich Eier kaufen. Mit den Eiern kann ich eine leckere Omelette kochen."

While both statements give the same basic information (the writer needs to go shopping), the details provided in the second statement are much more informative.

Thema

 ### Grüße nach Salzburg

Sie entschließen sich (*decide*), ein Jahr in Österreich zu verbringen und bei einer Familie zu leben. Schreiben Sie eine Karte an Ihre Gastfamilie (*host family*). Sagen Sie der Familie, was Sie gern sehen wollen und was Sie machen wollen. Schreiben Sie fünf Sätze. Nennen Sie (*Give*) Details. Beantworten Sie dabei Fragen mit **wer?**, **was?**, **wo?**, **wie?** und **wann?**

Liebe Gastfamilie, bald komme ich nach Salzburg. Dann können wir zusammen den Uhrturm besuchen...

 **Vocabulary Tools**

Geschäfte

die Bäckerei, -en	bakery
die Eisdiele, -n	ice cream shop
das Feinkostgeschäft, -e	delicatessen
das Fischgeschäft, -e	fish store
die Konditorei, -en	pastry shop
das Lebensmittelgeschäft, -e	grocery store
der Markt, ⸚e	market
die Metzgerei, -en	butcher shop
der Supermarkt, ⸚e	supermarket
einkaufen gehen	to go shopping
verkaufen	to sell

Essen

das Brot, -e	bread
das Brötchen, -	roll
die Butter	butter
das Ei, -er	egg
der Joghurt, -s	yogurt
der Käse, -	cheese
der Kuchen, -	cake; pie
die Marmelade, -n	jam
das Öl, -e	oil
das Olivenöl, -e	olive oil
die Pasta	pasta
der Reis	rice
das Rezept, -e	recipe
die Zutat, -en	ingredient

Fleisch und Fisch

die Garnele, -n	shrimp
das Hähnchen, -	chicken
die Meeresfrüchte (pl.)	seafood
das Rindfleisch	beef
der Schinken, -	ham
das Schweinefleisch	pork
der Thunfisch	tuna
das Würstchen, -	sausage

Mahlzeiten

das Abendessen	dinner
das Frühstück	breakfast
das Mittagessen	lunch
der Snack, -s	snack

Obst und Gemüse

die Ananas, -	pineapple
der Apfel, ⸚	apple
die Artischocke, -n	artichoke
die Aubergine, -n	eggplant
die Banane, -n	banana
die Birne, -n	pear
die grüne Bohne (pl. die grünen Bohnen)	green bean
die Erdbeere, -n	strawberry
die Himbeere, -n	raspberry
die Karotte, -n	carrot
die Kartoffel, -n	potato
der Knoblauch	garlic
die Melone, -n	melon
die Orange, -n	orange
die grüne Paprika (pl. die grünen Paprika)	green pepper
die rote Paprika (pl. die roten Paprika)	red pepper
der Pfirsich, -e	peach
der Pilz, -e	mushroom
der Salat, -e	lettuce; salad
die Tomate, -n	tomato
die Traube, -n	grape
die Zwiebel, -n	onion

Getränke

das Bier	beer
der Kaffee	coffee
die Milch	milk
das Mineralwasser	sparkling water
der Saft, ⸚e	juice
der Tee	tea
das stille Wasser	still water
der Wein	wine

Essen beschreiben

der Geschmack, ⸚e	flavor; taste
fade	bland
lecker	delicious
leicht	light
salzig	salty
scharf	spicy
schwer	rich, heavy
süß	sweet

im Restaurant

die Beilage, -n	side dish
das Besteck	silverware
der Esslöffel, -	soup spoon
die Flasche, -n	bottle
die Gabel, -n	fork
der erste/zweite Gang, ⸚	first/second course
das Glas, ⸚er	glass
das Gericht, -e	dish
die Hauptspeise, -n	main course
der Kellner, - / die Kellnerin, -nen	waiter / waitress
der Koch, ⸚e / die Köchin, -nen	cook
das Messer, -	knife
der Nachtisch, -e	dessert
der Pfeffer	pepper
die Rechnung, -en	check
das Salz	salt
die Serviette, -n	napkin
die Speisekarte, -n	menu
die Suppe, -n	soup
die Tasse, -n	cup
der Teelöffel, -	teaspoon
der Teller, -	plate
die Tischdecke, -n	tablecloth
das Trinkgeld	tip
die Vorspeise, -n	appetizer
bestellen	to order
schmecken	to taste

Ausdrücke

Ich hätte gern(e)... / Ich möchte	I would like...
auf Diät sein	to be on a diet
hausgemacht	homemade
mögen	to like

Adverbs	See p. 150.
Separable and inseparable prefix verbs	See p. 156.
Dative articles and possessive adjectives	See pp. 170–171.
Dative prepositions	See p. 174.

Feiern

5

Suggestion Have students guess the meaning of the unit title **Feiern** based on the image shown. Ask: **Was feiern Meline, Hans und Sabite?**

Communicative Goals

You will learn how to:

- talk about celebrations
- talk about life events

Feste feiern  **S** Vocabulary Tools

Suggestion Tell students that because of the influence of English, one often sees the plural form **Parties** on blogs and in advertising. Remind them that the correct plural form is still **Partys**.

Wortschatz

Feste	*celebrations*
der Feiertag, -e	*holiday*
die Karte, -n	*card*
die Party, -s	*party*
das Zimmer, -	*room*
anstoßen (stößt... an)	*to toast*
bekommen	*to receive*
einladen (lädt... ein)	*to invite*
feiern	*to celebrate*
eine Party geben	*to throw a party*
(keinen) Spaß haben	*(not) to have fun*
schenken	*to give (a gift)*
überraschen	*to surprise*
Herzlichen Glückwunsch!	*Congratulations!*
besondere Anlässe	*special occasions*
die Ehe, -n	*marriage*
der/die Frischvermählte, -n	*newlywed*
die Geburt, -en	*birth*
der Geburtstag, -e	*birthday*
die Hochzeit, -en	*wedding*
der Jahrestag, -e	*anniversary*
(das) Silvester	*New Year's Eve*
(das) Weihnachten	*Christmas*
in Rente gehen	*to retire*
einen Abschluss machen	*to graduate*
Ausdrücke	*expressions*
die Freundschaft, -en	*friendship*
das Glück	*happiness*
der Kuss, ¨e	*kiss*
die Liebe	*love*

Suggestion Point out to students that **Anlässe** is the plural form of **der Anlass**.

Suggestion Tell students that many German speakers also treat **Silvester** as a masculine noun.

Suggestion Tell students that the phrase **Ich lade dich ein** can also mean *It's my treat.*

Suggestion Teach students the verb form **küssen.**

der Gast, ¨e

der Gastgeber, -

die Gastgeberin, -nen

die Torte, -n

das Eis

der Keks, -e

die Süßigkeiten (*pl.*)

der Sekt

das Gebäck

der Eiswürfel, -

Suggestion Tell students that Germans don't typically use ice cubes in their drinks.

Expansion Ask students to cut out pictures from magazines that depict words on the vocabulary list and bring them to class. Have students work in groups, taking turns asking about and identifying the pictures.

Herzlichen Glückwunsch zum Geburtstag, Hans!

der Ballon, -s

die Überraschung, -en

Suggestion Tell students that the plural form **die Ballone** is also used, especially in Southern Germany, Austria, and Switzerland.

das Geschenk, -e

Anwendung

1 Suggestion Go over the first few items together, as a class.

1 Was passt zusammen? Welche Wörter in der linken Spalte (*column*) passen am besten zu den Wörtern in der rechten Spalte?

a/b	1. der Geburtstag	a. der Kuchen
d	2. der Gast	b. die Karte
f/e	3. die Ehe	c. das Silvester
a	4. die Torte	d. die Gastgeberin
c	5. das Weihnachten	e. die Liebe
e/f	6. der Kuss	f. die Frischvermählten

2 Feste und Feiertage Ergänzen Sie die Sätze.

1. An nationalen __Feiertagen__ muss man nicht arbeiten.
2. An Halloween kommen Kinder an die Haustür und man gibt ihnen __Süßigkeiten__.
3. Zum Geburtstag bekommt man __Geschenke/Karten__.
4. An Silvester stößt man um Mitternacht mit __Sekt__ an.
5. Nach 50 Ehejahren feiert man die goldene __Hochzeit__.
6. In Deutschland geht man normalerweise mit 67 Jahren in __Rente__.

3 Eine Party für Max 🎧 Hören Sie sich den Dialog an und markieren Sie dann die richtigen Aussagen.

3 Expansion Have students write a second dialogue that takes place at Max's surprise party, then act it out for the class.

	richtig	falsch
1. Max hat nächsten Monat Geburtstag.	☐	☑
2. Max braucht ein bisschen Spaß.	☑	☐
3. Max plant seine Geburtstagsparty selbst.	☐	☑
4. Max spielt in der Basketballmannschaft.	☑	☐
5. Zum Geburtstag kommen zehn Personen.	☐	☑
6. Die Party ist bei Emil.	☑	☐
7. Die Freunde kaufen das Geschenk zusammen.	☑	☐
8. Zum Geburtstag bekommt Max einen Baseball.	☐	☑

4 Satzsalat Bilden Sie Sätze mit den diversen Elementen.

Answers will vary. Sample answers are provided.

BEISPIEL *Die Eltern bereiten eine Geburtstagsparty vor.*

die Eltern	anstoßen	die Kinder
die Gäste	bekommen	eine Geburtstagsparty
der Gastgeber	einladen	eine Geburtstagstorte
das Geburtstagskind	mitbringen	ein Geschenk
die Verwandten	vorbereiten	mit einem Getränk

1. Die Verwandten bringen ein Geschenk mit.
2. Das Geburtstagskind bekommt eine Geburtstagstorte.
3. Die Gastgeber laden die Kinder ein.
4. Die Gäste stoßen mit einem Getränk an.

4 Suggestion Have students identify the separable prefix verbs before they complete this activity.

 Practice more at **vhlcentral.com.**

ACHTUNG

Use the preposition **zu** to say *on Christmas* or *on New Year's Eve:*
Zu Silvester feiern wir bei meinem Bruder.

Expansion Bring in a box with one or more objects inside and tell students it is an **Überraschung**. Have them ask yes-or-no questions to figure out what the object is.

Kommunikation

7 Suggestion Write the following useful phrases on the board: **Auf meinem Bild sind …, Mein Bild hat …,** and **Hast du das auch auf deinem Bild?** Make sure students understand that they should not show each other their pictures. Model this by protectively holding your sheet of paper and saying: **Mein Partner darf mein Bild nicht sehen.**

5 Besondere Anlässe Was feiern die Personen auf den Bildern? Bilden Sie mit Ihrem Partner / Ihrer Partnerin zusammen einen Satz zu jedem Bild. Answers will vary. Sample answers are provided.

▶ **BEISPIEL**

Matthias hat heute Geburtstag.

5 Suggestion Encourage students to be inventive and detailed in their descriptions.

Matthias

1. Lena
Lena macht ihren Abschluss.

2. Kerstin und Simon
Kerstin und Simon feiern ihre Hochzeit.

3. die Familie Hartmann
Die Familie Hartmann feiert Weihnachten.

4. Andreas und seine Freunde Andreas gibt eine Silvesterparty für seine Freunde.

5. Herr Aydin
Herr Aydin ist jetzt in Rente.

6. Martin
Martin gibt seiner Freundin einen Kuss.

6 Eine Einladung Lesen Sie Kiaras Einladung an ihre Verwandten und beantworten Sie mit Ihrem Partner / Ihrer Partnerin die Fragen zum Text.
Answers will vary. Sample answers are provided.

Von:	Kiara Gökda
An:	Familie Özer; Familie Celik; Murat Gökda; Familie Gökda; Ela Cengiz; Kenan Cengiz; Alik Aymaz; Familie Yilmaz
Betreff:	Feier für meine Eltern

Hallo an alle,

im Mai feiern unsere Eltern ihre silberne Hochzeit. 25 Jahre – unglaublich! Mein Bruder Murat und ich planen eine Feier für sie am Samstag, dem 5. Mai, im Restaurant „Zum Alten Markt" hier in München. Unsere Idee ist, dass wir alle, wir beide und ihr, ihnen eine Reise nach Marokko schenken. Die Reise ist für eine Woche und kostet 520 Euro pro Person.

Wir hoffen, ihr könnt kommen und macht bei dem Geschenk mit.

Kiara

1. Warum schreibt Kiara die E-Mail? Sie plant eine Feier für ihre Eltern.
2. Wie lange sind die Eltern verheiratet? Sie sind 25 Jahre verheiratet.
3. Was wollen sie den Eltern schenken? Sie wollen den Eltern eine Reise nach Marokko schenken.
4. Von wem ist das Geschenk? Das Geschenk ist von Kiara und Murat und den Verwandten.
5. Wie viel Geld braucht Kiara für das Geschenk? Sie braucht 1.040 Euro für das Geschenk.
6. Wann und wo ist die Feier?
Sie ist am 5. Mai im Restaurant „Zum Alten Markt" in München.

7 Diskutieren und kombinieren Finden Sie die sieben kleinen Unterschiede auf den Bildern, die Sie von Ihrem Professor / Ihrer Professorin bekommen. Answers will vary.

BEISPIEL

S1: *Auf meinem Bild sind fünf Personen. Wie viele Personen sind auf deinem Bild?*
S2: *Auf meinem Bild sind sechs Personen.*

8 Feiern wir! Sie planen eine Party für nächstes Wochenende. Beraten Sie (*Discuss*), wo Sie die Party machen wollen, wen Sie einladen, was Sie alles brauchen, wer Essen macht, wer die Getränke kauft, welche Musik Sie hören möchten und so weiter. Answers will vary.

BEISPIEL

S1: *Bei wem wollen wir die Party machen?*
S2: *Bei Hanna? Sie wohnt bei ihren Eltern, und ihr Haus ist ziemlich groß. Und wen wollen wir einladen?*
S3: *Wir können unsere Freunde vom Basketball einladen.*

8 Expansion Have students plan an actual party as the culmination of this unit. Make sure students use German to discuss the plans.

Aussprache und Rechtschreibung  Audio

🎧 The consonantal *r*

To pronounce the German consonant **r**, start by placing the tip of your tongue against your lower front teeth. Then, raise the back of your tongue toward the roof of your mouth. Let air flow from the back of your throat over your tongue creating a soft vibrating sound from the roof of your mouth.

Rock	rot	Brille	Freund	Jahrestag

Note that the consonant **r** sound always precedes a vowel.

Orange	frisch	fahren	Rucksack	Paprika

When the German **r** comes at the end of a word or a syllable, it sounds more like a vowel than a consonant. This *vocalic* **r** sound will be discussed in **Lektion 9A**.

Suggestion Tell students that in some parts of Bavaria and Austria, the **r** sound is produced with the tongue at the front of the mouth, and sounds similar to the Spanish r.

1 **Aussprechen** Wiederholen Sie die Wörter, die Sie hören.

1. Rente
2. rosa
3. reden
4. Schrank
5. schreiben
6. sprechen
7. Sprudel
8. Straße
9. gestreift
10. frisch
11. Bruder
12. tragen
13. grau
14. Haare
15. Amerika
16. studieren

2 **Nachsprechen** Wiederholen Sie die Sätze, die Sie hören.

1. Veronika trägt einen roten Rock.
2. Mein Bruder schreibt einen Brief.
3. Rolf reist mit Rucksack nach Rosenheim.
4. Regensburg und Bayreuth liegen in Bayern.
5. Warum fahren Sie nicht am Freitag?
6. Marie und Robert sprechen Russisch.
7. Drei Krokodile fressen frische Frösche.
8. Im Restaurant bestellt die Frau Roggenbrot mit Radieschen.

3 **Sprichwörter** Wiederholen Sie die Sprichwörter, die Sie hören.

Rede, so lernst du reden.[1]

Der Krug geht so lange zum Brunnen, bis er bricht.[2]

[1] You learn how to do something by doing it. (lit. Speak, if you want to learn how to speak.)

[2] If you overdo it, you'll wear yourself out. (lit. The pitcher goes to the well until it breaks.)

Ressourcen

SAM
LM: p. 40

 vhlcentral.com

Fotoroman

Frohes neues Jahr! Video

Vorbereitung Have students preview the scenes and write down one adjective to describe each scene.

Meline und Sabite wollen Silvester feiern, aber Torsten und Lorenzo haben andere Pläne. Da klingelt es plötzlich an der Tür...

1

SABITE Torsten! Es ist Silvester! Aber es sind Weihnachtsferien! Die Uni fängt erst wieder in zwei Wochen an. Warte mal.

2

MELINE Niemand lernt an Silvester. Man geht auf Partys und hat Spaß. Du hast eine wunderschöne Freundin, Torsten. Verlange nicht von ihr, das neue Jahr ohne dich zu beginnen. Bist du ihr immer noch böse?

3

SABITE Torsten? Dir auch ein frohes neues Jahr!

4

MELINE Lorenzo ist in der Stadt. Wir gehen später am Abend essen und danach gehen wir zu einer Party am Brandenburger Tor.
SABITE Schön, dass du Silvester mit ihm feierst.
MELINE Wir haben Spaß zusammen. Wieso kommst du nicht mit uns mit? Es sind bestimmt eine Million Leute da.
SABITE Ich mag keine Menschenmassen. Danke für die Einladung.

5

MELINE Sind Hans und George schon aus Bayern zurück? Wo ist Lorenzo?
SABITE Er ist nicht da! Es wird langsam spät.
MELINE Voicemail.
SABITE Nur die Ruhe, Meline.
MELINE Lorenzo!

GEORGE UND HANS Frohes neues Jahr!!!!
GEORGE Wir haben die Party einfach zu euch gebracht!
HANS George hat das Licht in eurer Wohnung gesehen.
GEORGE Hans hat Meline schreien gehört.
MELINE Ich habe nicht geschrien.
HANS Wo ist Lorenzo?
MELINE Ha, ha, ha, Hans. Wo ist denn deine neue Freundin?

6

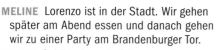

1 **Richtig oder falsch?** Entscheiden Sie, ob die folgenden Sätze richtig oder falsch sind.

1. Torsten will Silvester lernen. Richtig.
2. Lorenzo ist in der Stadt. Richtig.
3. Meline und Lorenzo wollen ins Kino gehen. Falsch.
4. Es sind eine Million Leute am Fernsehturm. Falsch.
5. George und Hans haben Licht in der Wohnung gesehen. Richtig.

6. Hans hat Meline singen gehört. Falsch.
7. George und Hans sind auf einer Party in Kreuzberg gewesen. Richtig.
8. Meline möchte, dass Hans und George zurück zur Party gehen. Falsch.
9. Hans hat Kekse gebacken. Falsch.
10. George möchte mit seinen Freunden anstoßen. Richtig.

PERSONEN

 George   Hans   Meline   Sabite

7

HANS Gut, dann gehen wir eben zurück zur Party in Kreuzberg.
SABITE Ah, ah! Geht nicht. Ich bin so froh, dass ihr hier seid. Frohes neues Jahr, Hans, George.
MELINE Bitte geht nicht. Ich habe Sekt.

8

HANS Ich habe einen Stollen für uns gebacken.
SABITE Oh, sieht lecker aus. Bitte schön.
HANS Danke. Hier, reich mal rüber.
MELINE Oh, Hans, er schmeckt genau wie der von meiner Mutter!

9

MELINE Es ist Mitternacht! Frohes neues Jahr!

10

GEORGE Ich möchte gern mit euch anstoßen, meine neuen Freunde. *Happy New Year!*
SABITE *Mutlu yillar.*

Nützliche Ausdrücke

- **Silvester**
  New Year's Eve
- **die Weihnachtsferien**
  winter break
- **Die Uni fängt erst wieder in zwei Wochen an.**
  Classes don't begin for two weeks.
- **wunderschön**
  gorgeous
- **Bist du ihr immer noch böse?**
  Are you still mad at her?
- **Frohes neues Jahr!**
  Happy New Year!
- **die Menschenmassen**
  crowds
- **Nur die Ruhe!**
  Relax!
- **Hans hat Meline schreien gehört.**
  Hans heard Meline yelling.
- **Reich mal rüber!**
  Hand it over!

5A.1
- **Ich habe einen Stollen für uns gebacken.**
  I baked a stollen for us.

5A.2
- **Verlange nicht von ihr, das neue Jahr ohne dich zu beginnen.**
  Don't make her start the new year without you.

5A.3
- **Schön, dass du Silvester mit ihm feierst.**
  It's great that you're celebrating New Year's with him.

2 **Zum Besprechen** Planen Sie zu dritt eine Silvesterparty. Machen Sie eine Einkaufsliste und eine Gästeliste. Soll die Party ein Motto (*theme*) haben? Was müssen die Gäste mitbringen? Answers will vary.

3 **Vertiefung** Finden Sie heraus (*Find out*), warum der letzte Tag im Jahr in der deutschsprachigen Welt **Silvester** heißt. Woher kommt der Name? Seit wann heißt der Tag so? Possible answer: Seit 1582 heißt der letzte Tag des Jahres Silvester, benannt nach dem Todestag von Papst Silvester I. (31. Dezember).

Suggestion Explain to students that Hans speaks in Bavarian at the end of this episode: **Is' scho' recht. A guat's Nei's!** (**Du hast Recht. Ein gutes Neues!**)

Ressourcen

SAM VM: p. 9

 vhlcentral.com

Expansion As a post-reading exercise, show students pictures of the places or things mentioned (ex., **Prinzessin Therese, Bierzelte, ein Karussell, eine Brille**), and ask them to explain what each picture has to do with **Oktoberfest**, as described in the text.

IM FOKUS

Das Oktoberfest Reading

Suggestion Before they read the text, ask students what they know about **Oktoberfest**. Create a mind-map by writing the word **Oktoberfest** on the board and asking students what they associate with the event.

AM 12. OKTOBER 1810 HEIRATET Kronprinz Ludwig (der spätere König Ludwig I. von Bayern) Prinzessin Therese. Vor den Toren Münchens°

Das Oktoberfest	
Erstes Oktoberfest:	1810
Ort:	Theresienwiese
Fläche:	0,42 km² (Quadratkilometer)
Besucher:	mehr als 6 Millionen Gäste
Festzelte:	14 große und 20 kleine
Schweinswürste:	112.772 Paar
Schweinshaxen°:	78.216
Abfall°:	935 Tonnen
Verlorene Gegenstände°:	275 Brillen° und 380 Handys

QUELLE: offizielles Stadtportal für München

feiern Menschen aus ganz Bayern die königliche Hochzeit auf einem Feld. Dieses Feld heißt heute noch Theresienwiese. Viele Menschen nennen es einfach die Wiesn, ein Wort aus der bayerischen Umgangssprache°. 1810 kann man Pferderennen° auf der Theresienwiese sehen und in den nächsten Jahren wiederholt man diese Pferderennen. Das ist der Anfang des Oktoberfests.

Im Jahr 1818 gibt es das erste Karussell° beim Oktoberfest. Heute findet man neben Karussells und Festzelten° auch Willenborgs Riesenrad° und einen Flohzirkus° für Kinder. Aus Wettergründen° beginnt das

Oktoberfest bereits im September. Traditionell ist der erste Tag immer der erste Samstag nach dem 15. September. Der Oberbürgermeister° Münchens zapft° das erste Bierfass° an und sagt dann: „O'zapft is!" Das ist Bayerisch und bedeutet „Es ist angezapft!" Der letzte Tag ist der erste Sonntag im Oktober. In über 200 Jahren findet das Oktoberfest 24-mal wegen° Cholera oder Kriegen° nicht statt°.

den Toren Münchens the gates of Munich **bayerischen Umgangssprache** Bavarian vernacular **Pferderennen** horse races **Karussell** merry-go-round **Festzelten** pavilions **Riesenrad** Ferris wheel **Flohzirkus** flea circus **aus Wettergründen** due to weather concerns **Oberbürgermeister** mayor **zapft... an** taps **Bierfass** beer barrel **wegen** due to **Kriegen** wars **findet... statt** takes place **Schweinshaxen** pork knuckles **Abfall** garbage **Verlorene Gegenstände** Lost items **Brillen** eyeglasses

Suggestion To help students process the information in the statistics box, give them a series of sentence fragments to complete. Ex.: **Das erste Oktoberfest war... Die Besucher essen... Die Besucher verlieren jedes Jahr...**

ÜBUNGEN

1 **Richtig oder falsch?** Sind die Aussagen **richtig** oder **falsch**? Korrigieren Sie die falschen Aussagen.

1. Das erste Oktoberfest findet 1815 statt.
   Falsch. Das erste Oktoberfest findet 1810 statt.
2. Die Menschen feiern die Hochzeit von Kronprinz Ludwig und Prinzessin Therese in Nürnberg.
   Falsch. Die Menschen feiern die Hochzeit in München.
3. In der bayerischen Umgangssprache heißt die Theresienwiese „Wiesn".
   Richtig.
4. Das erste Karussell gibt es 1815. Falsch. Das erste Karussell gibt es 1816.
5. Für Kinder gibt es heute auch einen Flohzirkus. Richtig.

6. Der erste Tag des Oktoberfests ist immer der erste Sonntag nach dem 15. September.
   Falsch. Der erste Tag des Oktoberfests ist der erste Samstag nach dem 15. September.
7. Der Münchener Oberbürgermeister zapft das erste Bierfass an. Richtig.
8. In über 200 Jahren findet das Oktoberfest 20-mal nicht statt.
   Falsch. Es findet 24-mal nicht statt.
9. Mehr als 10 Millionen Gäste besuchen das Oktoberfest jedes Jahr.
   Falsch. Mehr als 6 Millionen Gäste besuchen das Oktoberfest jedes Jahr.
10. Zu den verlorenen Gegenständen gehören 275 Brillen und 380 Handys. Richtig.

Practice more at **vhlcentral.com**.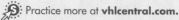

Suggestion Have students highlight key words before reading each paragraph. Ex.: **heiratet, Prinzessin Therese, feiern, Hochzeit, Feld, München, Pferderennen.** Then ask simple comprehension questions built around the key words and have them scan the paragraph to find answers: **Wer heiratet? Wann? Wo ist die Hochzeit?**

Expansion Teach students to sing a German Christmas carol, such as "**O Tannenbaum**". Explain that Christmas is a major holiday in German-speaking countries, but be culturally sensitive toward students who don't celebrate Christmas.

DEUTSCH IM ALLTAG

Herzlichen Glückwunsch

Alles Gute zum Geburtstag!	*Happy birthday!*
Ein gutes neues Jahr!	*Happy New Year!*
Frohe Ostern!	*Happy Easter!*
Frohe Weihnachten!	*Merry Christmas!*
Gute Besserung!	*Get well!*
Hals- und Beinbruch!	*Break a leg!*
Viel Glück!	*Good luck!*

DIE DEUTSCHSPRACHIGE WELT

Weihnachten

Am 6. Dezember besucht Sankt Nikolaus Kinder in vielen Gegenden° Deutschlands, Österreichs und der Schweiz. Brave° Kinder bekommen Schokolade, Nüsse° und andere Süßigkeiten. Manchmal bringt der Sankt Nikolaus einen Partner mit. Diese zweite Person heißt Krampus im Süden und Knecht Ruprecht im Norden. Er soll böse° Kinder erschrecken°.

Die Weihnachtsfeiertage sind der 25. und 26. Dezember. Geschenke bekommen Kinder aber schon am 24. Dezember, dem Heiligen Abend. Das Christkind, ein blonder Engel°, bringt Geschenke, und Familien öffnen sie am gleichen Abend.

in vielen Gegenden *in many areas* **Brave** *Well-behaved* **Nüsse** *nuts* **böse** *naughty* **erschrecken** *scare* **Engel** *angel*

PORTRÄT

Die Sternsinger

Suggestion Ask students what differences they've noticed between Christmas as it is celebrated in their country and Christmas in German-speaking countries.

Vor allem in Bayern und Österreich sind die Sternsinger ein sehr bekanntes Brauchtum°. Drei Kinder oder junge Leute verkleiden sich° als die Heiligen Drei Könige° Caspar, Melchior und Balthasar. Sie gehen zwischen dem 27. Dezember und dem 6. Januar, dem Tag des Dreikönigsfestes, von Haus zu Haus. Sie singen Lieder in den Häusern, sprechen ein Gebet° und sagen ein Gedicht° auf. Dann schreiben sie mit Kreide° einen Segen° über° die Haustür. In Deutschland sammeln° die Sternsinger seit dem 16. Jahrhundert Geld für wohltätige Zwecke°, vor allem für Kinder in Not°. Die Aktion Dreikönigssingen ist weltweit° die größte organisierte Hilfsaktion von Kindern für Kinder. Alleine im Jahr 2013 sammeln die Sternsinger fast 70 Millionen Euro.

Brauchtum *tradition* **verkleiden sich** *dress up* **Könige** *kings* **Gebet** *prayer* **Gedicht** *poem* **Kreide** *chalk* **Segen** *blessing* **über** *over* **sammeln** *collect* **wohltätige Zwecke** *charitable causes* **in Not** *in need* **weltweit** *worldwide*

⚲ IM INTERNET

Welche anderen Feste und Festivals werden in Deutschland, Österreich und der Schweiz gefeiert?

Find out more at **vhlcentral.com**.

Expansion Have students research more details about **Nikolaustag** and **Weihnachten**. Ask them: **Was macht man mit seinen Schuhen am Nikolaustag? Was trägt der Ruprecht mit sich? Wer ist der Weihnachtsmann?**

2 Was fehlt? Ergänzen Sie die Sätze.

1. Sankt Nikolaus besucht Kinder am __6. Dezember__.
2. Brave Kinder bekommen __Schokolade__, Nüsse und andere Süßigkeiten.
3. Weihnachtsgeschenke bringt in Deutschland, Österreich und der Schweiz __das Christkind__.
4. Zwischen dem 27. Dezember und dem __6. Januar__ gehen Sternsinger von Haus zu Haus.

3 Wie feiern Sie zu Hause? Wählen Sie mit einem Partner / einer Partnerin einen Feiertag in Ihrem Land. Was feiert man an diesem Tag, wie feiert man den Tag, wann feiert man und welche regionalen Variationen gibt es? Präsentieren Sie Ihre Beschreibung den Kommilitonen. Die Mitstudenten müssen den Feiertag erraten (guess).

3 Suggestion Give students a model to help them understand how to approach this activity. Ex.: **Ich denke an einen Feiertag. Mein Feiertag ist im Herbst. An diesem Tag muss man nicht arbeiten. Der Tag ehrt den Arbeiter. Das ist ein amerikanischer Feiertag. Die Deutschen haben auch so einen Feiertag, aber dort feiert man ihn am ersten Mai. Welcher Feiertag ist das?** (Labor Day)

Ressourcen

vhlcentral.com

5A.1

The *Perfekt* (Part 1) Presentation

Startblock In English, there are several ways of talking about events in the past: *I ate, I have eaten, I was eating.* In German, all of these meanings can be expressed with the **Perfekt** tense.

QUERVERWEIS

In **6A.1** and **6B.1**, you will learn about the **Präteritum**, a past tense used mainly in writing.

Wir **haben** die Party einfach zu euch **gebracht**.

Ich **habe** einen Stollen für uns **gebacken**.

The *Perfekt* tense

QUERVERWEIS

Most verbs form the **Perfekt** with **haben**. You will learn about forming the **Perfekt** with **sein** in **5B.1**.

- To form the **Perfekt**, use a present tense form of **haben** or **sein** with the *past participle* of the verb that expresses the action.

  Ich **habe** zu viel Kuchen **gegessen**.
  *I **ate** too much cake.*

  Wir **haben** den Kindern Geschenke **gekauft**.
  *We **bought** the kids presents.*

Forming past participles

- German verbs can be grouped into three main categories, based on the way their past participles are formed.

  Ich **habe** eine Torte **gemacht**.
  *I **made** a cake.*

  Wir **haben** Kekse **gegessen**.
  *We **ate** cookies.*

  Er **hat** eine CD **gebrannt**.
  *He **burned** a CD.*

ACHTUNG

The **-et** ending is added to verb stems ending in **-d**, **-t**, or a consonant cluster, to make pronunciation easier: **Es hat geregnet**.

- Most German verbs are *weak*. Form the past participle of a weak verb by adding **ge-** before the verb stem and **-t** or **-et** after the stem.

common weak verbs			
infinitive	**past participle**	**infinitive**	**past participle**
arbeiten	gearbeitet	lernen	gelernt
feiern	gefeiert	öffnen	geöffnet
hören	gehört	sagen	gesagt
kaufen	gekauft	spielen	gespielt
lachen	gelacht	tanzen	getanzt

Haben Sie eine Flasche Sekt **gekauft**?
*Did you **buy** a bottle of champagne?*

Ich **habe** mit den Gästen **geredet**.
*I **chatted** with the guests.*

Suggestion Write on the board: **ge-** + stem + **-t** and have students copy it down in their notes. Give students the infinitives of other weak verbs, and have them figure out the past participles, based on the pattern. Ex.: **kochen, machen**.

- Verbs ending in **-ieren** are almost always weak. Their past participles end in **-t**, but omit the **ge-** prefix.

  Der Lehrer **hat** die Hausaufgaben **korrigiert**.
  *The teacher **corrected** the homework.*

  Wie lange **habt** ihr in Deutschland **studiert**?
  *How long **did** you **study** in Germany?*

  Suggestion Point out that the past participle of **verlieren** is an exception: **Ich habe verloren**.

- To form the past participle of a *strong* verb, add **ge-** before the verb stem and **-en** after. Strong verbs may be regular or irregular in the present, but verbs that have a stem change in the present tense are almost always strong verbs in the **Perfekt**.

Wir **haben** unsere Freunde **gesehen**.
*We **saw** our friends.*

Ich **habe** meinen Eltern **geholfen**.
*I **helped** my parents.*

- Note that many strong verbs have a stem change in the past participle.

common strong verbs			
infinitive	past participle	infinitive	past participle
essen	ge**g**essen	schlafen	geschlafen
finden	gef**u**nden	schreiben	geschr**ie**ben
geben	gegeben	sprechen	gespr**o**chen
heißen	geheißen	tragen	getragen
helfen	geh**o**lfen	treffen	getr**o**ffen
lesen	gelesen	trinken	getr**u**nken
nehmen	gen**o**mmen	waschen	gewaschen

Habt ihr den Bus nach Hause **genommen**?
*Did you **take** the bus home?*

Sie **hat** viele Bücher **geschrieben**.
*She's **written** a lot of books.*

Hast du gut **geschlafen**?
*Did you **sleep** well?*

Was **habt** ihr auf der Party **getragen**?
*What **did** you **wear** to the party?*

- There is a small group of verbs called *mixed* verbs. The past participles of mixed verbs have a **ge-** prefix and end in **-t** like weak verbs, but they have irregular stems like many strong verbs.

common mixed verbs	
infinitive	past participle
brennen (*to burn*)	ge**brann**t
bringen	ge**brach**t
denken (*to think*)	ge**dach**t
nennen (*to name*)	ge**nann**t
rennen (*to run*)	ge**rann**t

Habt ihr an die Hochzeit **gedacht**?
*Were you **thinking** about the wedding?*

Sie **haben** ihr Kind Johanna **genannt**.
*They **named** their child Johanna.*

Suggestion Show students the verb list in **Appendix A**. Give them the infinitive of a strong or mixed verb, and have them check the appendix to find the past participle.

Suggestion Tell students that there are 10 vowel change patterns for the past forms of strong verbs, which will become more apparent when they learn the **Präteritum** in **Kapitel 6**: **ei-e-ie, ei-i-i, i-a-u, i-a-o, ie-o-o, e-a-o, e-a-e, e-o-o, a-u-a, a-ie-a**. Emphasize that while it is useful to be aware of these patterns, they still need to memorize which verbs are strong or mixed and what if any stem changes they have.

ACHTUNG

You cannot tell which category a verb belongs to by looking at the infinitive. You must learn the past participle of a verb along with its present tense forms.

QUERVERWEIS

See **Appendix A** for a complete list of past participles for all strong and mixed verbs taught in this book.

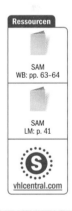

Ressourcen

SAM
WB: pp. 63–64

SAM
LM: p. 41

Ⓢ
vhlcentral.com

Jetzt sind Sie dran! **Ergänzen Sie die Sätze mit den richtigen Formen der Hilfsverben und der Partizipien.**

1. Wir ___haben___ Monikas Geburtstag ___gefeiert___. (feiern)
2. Die Katzen ___haben___ viel Milch ___getrunken___. (trinken)
3. Unsere Freunde ___haben___ viel Spaß ___gehabt___. (haben)
4. Jens ___hat___ mit seinen Geschenken ___gespielt___. (spielen)
5. Ich ___habe___ am Montag ___gearbeitet___. (arbeiten)
6. Peter ___hat___ vier Jahre an der Uni ___studiert___. (studieren)

7. Die Gäste ___haben___ dem Geburtstagskind viele Geschenke ___gegeben___. (geben)
8. ___Habt___ ihr die Bücher ___gelesen___? (lesen)
9. ___Hast___ du an die Pläne ___gedacht___? (denken)
10. Wir ___haben___ sehr viel ___gelacht___. (lachen)
11. ___Habt___ ihr Süßigkeiten ___gegessen___? (essen)
12. Meine Freundin ___hat___ einen Hund ___adoptiert___. (adoptieren)

Anwendung

1 Suggestion Make sure students understand the meaning of these verbs before you begin. Practice pronunciation of **schreiben/geschrieben** and tell students to highlight the "vowel swap" in their books.

1 Expansion Mime *correcting, reading, eating,* and *finding* and ask students **Was habe ich gemacht?** They must produce sentences in the perfect to describe the action you mimed. Ex.: **Sie haben Hausaufgaben korrigiert. Sie haben Ihr Handy gefunden.**

2 Suggestion Ask students to identify the mixed verb (**denken**) before doing this activity. Also, practice pronunciation of **gearbeitet** by having students repeat after you.

3 Suggestion Remind students that when they learn a new verb, there is usually no way to know if it is strong or weak, and that while there are some patterns, they still need to learn participles on a verb-by-verb basis.

1 **Was passt zusammen?** Welche Verben in Spalte 1 entsprechen (*match*) den Partizipien in Spalte 2?

_c_ 1. essen		a. gebracht
_f_ 2. finden		b. geholfen
_b_ 3. helfen		c. gegessen
_e_ 4. schreiben		d. genommen
_a_ 5. bringen		e. geschrieben
_d_ 6. nehmen		f. gefunden

2 **Das Perfekt** Setzen Sie die Verben ins Perfekt.

BEISPIEL tanzen (ich)
ich habe getanzt

1. kaufen (du) du hast gekauft
2. lernen (wir) wir haben gelernt
3. feiern (er) er hat gefeiert
4. arbeiten (Sie) Sie haben gearbeitet
5. hören (ihr) ihr habt gehört
6. regnen (es) es hat geregnet
7. kochen (sie, *sing.*) sie hat gekocht
8. denken (ich) ich habe gedacht

3 **Was haben sie gemacht?** Ergänzen Sie die Sätze mit der richtigen Form von **haben** und dem passenden Partizip.

1. Ich ___habe___ einen neuen Rucksack ___gekauft___. (kaufen)
2. Julius ___hat___ seine Freunde ___getroffen___. (treffen)
3. ___Habt___ ihr das Fußballspiel mit Paul ___diskutiert___? (diskutieren)
4. Der Koch ___hat___ die Zwiebeln ___gewaschen___. (waschen)
5. ___Hast___ du mit deinem Bruder ___gesprochen___? (sprechen)
6. Anna ___hat___ ihre Tochter zum Friseur ___gebracht___. (bringen)
7. Kiara ___hat___ eine Party ___gegeben___. (geben)
8. Professor Schulz, ___haben___ Sie meine Arbeit ___korrigiert___? (korrigieren)

4 **Am Wochenende** Was haben diese Personen am Wochenende gemacht? Schreiben Sie zu jedem Foto einen Satz im Perfekt. Answers will vary. Sample answers are provided.

BEISPIEL
meine Eltern und ich
Meine Eltern und ich haben Karten gespielt.

1. Herr Peters
Herr Peters hat gelesen.

2. Erik und Emil
Erik und Emil haben Tee getrunken.

3. Jessica
Jessica hat geschlafen.

4. Nina
Nina hat getanzt.

5. Hasan
Hasan hat sein Auto gewaschen.

6. Sara und Max
Sara und Max haben im Restaurant gegessen.

 Practice more at **vhlcentral.com**.

Kommunikation

5 **Letzten Sommer** Fragen Sie Ihren Partner / Ihre Partnerin, was er/sie letzten Sommer gemacht hat. Answers will vary.

1. Hast du viel geschlafen?
2. Hast du viel gegessen?
3. Hast du gearbeitet? Wo?
4. Hast du Deutsch gelernt?

5. Hast du Sport gemacht?
6. Hast du oft Freunde getroffen?
7. Hast du etwas gekauft? Was?
8. Hast du viele Filme gesehen? Welche?

6 **Auf Dieters Geburtstagsparty** Sehen Sie mit einem Partner / einer Partnerin das Bild (*picture*) an. Was haben die Personen auf Dieters Geburtstagsparty gemacht?

BEISPIEL

S1: *Jutta hat Karaoke gesungen.*
S2: *Ja, und ihre Freunde haben viel gelacht.*

7 **Im Deutschkurs** Fragen Sie Ihre Kommilitonen, was man heute im Deutschkurs gemacht hat. Vergleichen Sie die Antworten in Ihrer Gruppe.

BEISPIEL

S1: *Habt ihr gelesen?*
S2: *Ja, wir haben gelesen.*
S3: *Wer hat gelacht?*
S1: *Ben hat gelacht!*

antworten	schlafen
diskutieren	schreiben
essen	singen
lachen	spielen
lernen	sprechen
lesen	trinken

7 **Suggestion** Divide students into small groups and ask each group to come up with their own sample question, using verbs from the word bank. Write their suggestions on the board.

8 **Meine Großeltern** Erzählen Sie den Studenten/Studentinnen in Ihrer Gruppe, was Ihre Großeltern gemacht haben, als sie jünger waren (*when they were younger*).

BEISPIEL

S1: *Mein Großvater hat immer viele Geschenke für seine Kinder gekauft.*
S2: *Meine Großmutter hat jeden Tag Kuchen oder Kekse gebacken.*
S3: *Meine Großeltern haben oft Karten gespielt.*

8 **Suggestion** Smaller groups are recommended for this activity. Tell students that if they don't know much about their grandparents, they can be creative and make something up.

QUERVERWEIS

See **Lektion 1A.3** to review the nominative pronouns.

Suggestion Give students a moment to read through the list of accusative pronouns. Then, with their books closed, have them provide the accusative form of each nominative pronoun you give them.

Suggestion Remind students that a noun following the verb **sein** is *not* a direct object and is in the nominative case.

Suggestion The song **"Ich will"** by Rammstein is full of pronouns and features ample repetition. Give students a fill-in-the-blanks worksheet containing the song lyrics, with the pronouns omitted. Have students listen to the song and fill in the missing pronouns.

5A.2 | **Accusative pronouns**

Startblock Just as nouns in the nominative case can be replaced by nominative pronouns, nouns in the accusative case can be replaced by accusative pronouns.

personal pronouns				
	nominative		**accusative**	
singular	ich	*I*	**mich**	*me*
	du	*you* (inf.)	**dich**	*you* (inf.)
	Sie	*you* (form.)	**Sie**	*you* (form.)
	er/sie/es	*he/she/it*	**ihn/sie/es**	*him/her/it*
plural	wir	*we*	**uns**	*us*
	ihr	*you* (inf.)	**euch**	*you* (inf.)
	Sie	*you* (form.)	**Sie**	*you* (form.)
	sie	*they*	**sie**	*them*

Wer hat **die Torte** gebacken?
*Who baked **the cake**?*

Ich habe **sie** gebacken.
*I baked **it**.*

- You learned in **1B.1** that direct objects are always in the accusative case. An accusative pronoun replaces a noun that functions as a direct object.

  Er hat **mich** überrascht.
  *He surprised **me**.*

  Hast du **ihn** geküsst?
  *Did you kiss **him**?*

- In **3B.2**, you learned that certain prepositions are always followed by the accusative. A pronoun that follows an accusative preposition must be in the accusative case.

  Wir haben eine Überraschung **für dich**.
  *We have a surprise **for you**.*

  Ihr fahrt **ohne mich** zur Hochzeit.
  *You're going to the wedding **without me**.*

- In simple sentences, accusative pronouns go directly after the conjugated verb. If the sentence has a modal verb, the accusative pronoun goes after the conjugated modal verb.

  Ich sehe **euch** jeden Tag.
  *I see **you** every day.*

  Ich muss **es** heute machen.
  *I have to do **it** today.*

- In the **Perfekt**, place the accusative pronoun directly after the conjugated helping verb.

  Sie haben **uns** zur Party eingeladen.
  *They invited **us** to the party.*

  Wir haben **sie** mit einer Torte überrascht.
  *We surprised **them** with a cake.*

- In sentences with inverted word order, such as yes-or-no questions, place the accusative pronoun after the subject.

  Siehst du **sie** oft?
  *Do you see **her** often?*

  Morgen rufe ich **dich** an.
  *I'll call **you** tomorrow.*

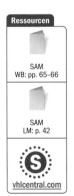

Ressourcen

SAM
WB: pp. 65–66

SAM
LM: p. 42

vhlcentral.com

Jetzt sind Sie dran! **Wählen Sie die richtigen Pronomen.**

1. Das Buch? Du sollst (**es**/ ihn) lesen.
2. Da sind die Ballons. Siehst du (**sie**/ uns) nicht?
3. Ihr müsst ohne (**uns**/ euch) ins Kino gehen.
4. Ich finde Paul süß und habe (uns / **ihn**) geküsst.
5. Jana und dich? Wir finden (**euch**/ sie) nett.
6. Sophia, warte! Ich habe eine Karte für (**dich**/ ihn).
7. Die große Liebe? Gibt es (uns / **sie**)?
8. Nina, liebst du (**mich**/ dich)?

Anwendung und Kommunikation

1 **Bei meinen Eltern** Ersetzen Sie (*Substitute*) die unterstrichenen
Wörter mit Akkusativpronomen.

> **BEISPIEL** Ich sehe <u>Peter</u>.
> *Ich sehe ihn.*

1. Ich rufe <u>meinen Freund</u> an.
   Ich rufe ihn an.
2. Mein Freund besucht <u>mich und</u>
   <u>meine Familie</u>.
   Mein Freund besucht uns.
3. Mein Bruder kocht <u>das Essen</u>
   für uns.
   Mein Bruder kocht es für uns.

4. Mein Vater isst <u>die Suppe</u> gern.
   Mein Vater isst sie gern.
5. Meine Schwester kauft <u>die Erdbeeren</u>
   auf dem Markt.
   Meine Schwester kauft sie auf dem Markt.
6. Mein Freund sagt: „Ich besuche <u>dich</u>
   <u>und deine Eltern</u> gern.“
   Mein Freund sagt: „Ich besuche euch gern.“

2 **Sätze bilden** Bilden Sie logische Sätze mit den angegebenen Wörtern.
Ersetzen Sie die Wörter in Klammern (*parentheses*) mit Akkusativpronomen.
Answers may vary. Sample answers are provided.

> **BEISPIEL** (die Erdbeeren) essen wollen
> *Ich will sie essen.*

1. (das Buch)
   lesen müssen
   Ich muss es lesen.

2. (Lisa) einladen
   wollen
   Ich will sie einladen.

3. (der Film) sehen
   möchten
   Ich möchte ihn sehen.

4. (das Auto)
   kaufen sollen
   Ich soll es kaufen.

5. (Hausaufgaben)
   machen müssen
   Ich muss sie machen.

3 **Die Überraschungsparty** Ihr Partner / Ihre Partnerin fragt Sie über
die Party am Samstag bei Max. Beantworten Sie die Fragen und benutzen
Sie Akkusativpronomen. Answers may vary. Sample answers are provided.

> **BEISPIEL** **S1:** *Ruft ihr Emil und Maria an?*
> **S2:** *Ja, wir rufen sie an.*

1. Ist es eine Party für Max?
   Ja, es ist eine Party für ihn.
2. Lädst du Erik ein?
   Ja, ich lade ihn ein.
3. Kommt Erik ohne seine Freundin?
   Ja, er kommt ohne sie.
4. Hast du das Geschenk
   schon gekauft?
   Ja, ich habe es schon gekauft.

5. Bringst du deine Cousins mit?
   Nein, ich bringe sie nicht mit.
6. Soll ich den Kuchen mitbringen?
   Ja, du sollst ihn mitbringen.
7. Können wir dort laute Musik hören?
   Ja, ihr könnt sie dort hören.
8. Überraschen wir Max?
   Ja, wir überraschen ihn.

3 **Suggestion** Students are
sometimes confused when
answering **wir** questions with
ihr. You may wish to do item 7
together as a class.

4 **Der Computer** Erstellen Sie ein Gespräch mit den angegebenen
Wörtern. Benutzen Sie Akkusativpronomen. Answers will vary.

> **BEISPIEL** der Computer
> **S1:** *Meine Eltern haben ihn für mich gekauft.*
> **S2:** *Ohne ihn kann ich nicht lernen.*
> **S3:** *Ich finde ihn schlecht.*

das Eis	das Geschenk
der Gastgeber	die Karten
der Geburtstag	die Kekse

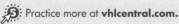

Practice more at **vhlcentral.com**.

5A.3

Dative pronouns  : Presentation

ACHTUNG

Be careful when deciding whether the pronoun you need is a direct or an indirect object.

Ich sehe ihn.
[direct object]

Ich gebe ihm das Buch.
[indirect object]

QUERVERWEIS

In **2B** and **4A.2**, you learned to use **gern** and **mögen** to express liking. Use **gefallen** to say that you like the way something looks or sounds.

Die Musik gefällt mir.
Der Film hat mir gefallen.

ACHTUNG

In **4B.2**, you learned that certain prepositions are always followed by the dative case. If a dative preposition is followed by a pronoun, use a dative pronoun: **mit mir, von ihnen, bei uns**

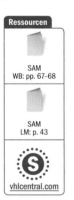

Ressourcen

SAM
WB: pp. 67–68

SAM
LM: p. 43

(S)

vhlcentral.com

Startblock Use dative pronouns in place of dative nouns to indicate *to whom* or *for whom* an action is done.

- You learned in **4B.1** that indirect objects are always in the dative case. When the indirect object is a pronoun rather than a noun, use a dative pronoun.

Suggestion Give students two or three simple sentences that feature pronouns, and have them identify the subjects, the direct objects, the indirect objects, and any objects of prepositions. Use humorous or dramatic sentences to keep students engaged.

personal pronouns			
	nominative	**accusative**	**dative**
singular	ich du Sie er/sie/es	mich dich Sie ihn/sie/es	mir dir Ihnen ihm/ihr/ihm
plural	wir ihr Sie sie	uns euch Sie sie	uns euch Ihnen ihnen

Musst du **ihr** eine E-Mail schreiben?
*Do you have to write **her** an e-mail?*

Wir wollen **euch** die Stadt zeigen.
*We want to show **you** the city.*

- In **4B.1**, you learned that the verbs **helfen, danken,** and **gehören** always take an object in the dative case. Here are some other verbs that always take a dative object.

antworten	*to answer*	**glauben**	*to believe*
folgen	*to follow*	**gratulieren**	*to congratulate*
gefallen (gefällt)	*to please*	**passen**	*to fit*

Das gefällt **mir** sehr gut.
I like that a lot.

Ich glaube **dir** nicht.
*I don't believe **you**.*

Gehört das **euch**?
*Does this belong to **you**?*

Antworte **mir**!
*Answer **me**!*

- When one object is a noun and the other is a pronoun, place the pronoun first.

Gib **mir** einen Kuss!
*Give **me** a kiss!*

Zeig **es** dem Lehrer!
*Show **it** to the teacher!*

- When a sentence has both a direct and an indirect object and both are pronouns, place the dative pronoun after the accusative pronoun.

Ich habe **dem Gastgeber das Geschenk** gegeben.
*I gave **the present** to the host.*

Ich habe **es ihm** gegeben.
*I gave **it** to him.*

Suggestion Point out to students that in item 4, **Backen** is used as a noun. Explain that in this context, **beim Backen** means *with the baking.*

 **Jetzt sind Sie dran!** Wählen Sie den richtigen Fall (*case*) für die unterstrichenen Wörter: Nominativ (N), Akkusativ (A), oder Dativ (D).

___D___ 1. Er hat <u>ihr</u> eine Blume gegeben.

___N___ 2. <u>Wir</u> bringen Wein und Käse zur Party mit.

___A___ 3. Hast du <u>sie</u> zu Weihnachten besucht?

___D___ 4. Kannst du <u>mir</u> beim Backen helfen?

___D___ 5. Ich danke <u>euch</u> für die Fotos von der Hochzeit.

___N___ 6. Vielleicht glaubt <u>seine Mutter</u> ihm nicht.

___A___ 7. Gabi besucht <u>dich</u> am Wochenende, nicht?

___D___ 8. Das Geschenk ist von <u>ihr</u>.

Anwendung und Kommunikation

1 **Meine Tante** Ersetzen Sie die Dativobjekte mit Dativpronomen.

> **BEISPIEL** Meine Tante hat mit <u>meiner Mutter</u> telefoniert.
> *Meine Tante hat mit ihr telefoniert.*

1. Ich habe viel von <u>meiner Tante Marie</u> gelernt. Ich habe viel von ihr gelernt.
2. Ich habe oft bei <u>Tante Marie und Onkel Hans</u> geschlafen. Ich habe oft bei ihnen geschlafen.
3. Sie haben immer mit <u>mir und meinem Bruder</u> gespielt. Sie haben immer mit uns gespielt.
4. Mein Onkel hat <u>meinem Bruder</u> oft geholfen. Mein Onkel hat ihm oft geholfen.
5. „Tante Marie, kann ich bei <u>dir und Onkel Hans</u> wohnen?" „Tante Marie, kann ich bei euch wohnen?"

2 **Was ist richtig?** Wählen Sie in jedem Satz das richtige Pronomen.

1. Wir haben (ihr / sie) das Geschenk gegeben.
2. Gehören (euch / ihn) die Karten?
3. Hast du (ihn / ihm) zum Geburtstag gratuliert?
4. Haben die Gäste mit (sie / ihnen) angestoßen?
5. Wer hat außer (dir / dich) Kuchen gegessen?
6. Und das Baby? Habt ihr (ihm / es) auch gesehen?
7. Wann feiert ihr die Hochzeit? Feiert ihr (sie / ihr) im Sommer?
8. Lädst du (mich / mir) auch ein?

3 **Alles Gute zum Geburtstag!** Erzählen Sie Ihrem Partner / Ihrer Partnerin, was Sie diesen Personen zum Geburtstag schenken. Answers will vary.

> **BEISPIEL**
>
> Ihre Mutter
> **S1:** *Was schenkst du deiner Mutter zum Geburtstag?*
> **S2:** *Ich schenke ihr einen kleinen Hund! Und deiner Mutter?*
> **S1:** *Meine Mutter mag Hunde nicht. Ich schenke ihr einen Computer.*

1. Ihr Bruder
2. Ihre Großeltern
3. Ihre Schwester
4. Ihre Katze
5. Ihr Vater
6. Ihr Professor / Ihre Professorin

4 **Danke schön!** Erfinden Sie mit Ihren Kommilitonen eine Geschichte (*story*) über die Personen auf dem Bild. Answers will vary.

> **BEISPIEL**
>
> **S1:** *Die junge Frau ruft ihre Schwester an.*
> **S2:** *Sie dankt ihr für das Geburtstagsgeschenk.*
> **S3:** *Nein! Sie gratuliert ihr zu ihrem Abschluss...*

anrufen	einladen	gratulieren (zu)
antworten (auf)	gefallen	helfen
danken (für)	gehören	kaufen
einkaufen	glauben	schreiben

 Practice more at **vhlcentral.com**.

4 Suggestion Circulate among groups and provide vocabulary as needed. Allow students to focus on content and comprehensibility rather than on accuracy.

4 Expansion Have students write their stories down, this time paying closer attention to grammatical correctness. Have them read their stories out loud to the class.

Wiederholung

1 Auf der Party
Wer hat dieses Essen gemacht und diese Geschenke gekauft? Answers will vary.

BEISPIEL

S1: Wer hat den Apfelsaft gekauft?
S2: Anja hat ihn gekauft.

backen	kaufen
bringen	machen
gehören	schenken

2 Suggestion Before beginning this activity, have students review the gender of each food item listed, to make sure they apply the appropriate pronouns in the accusative.

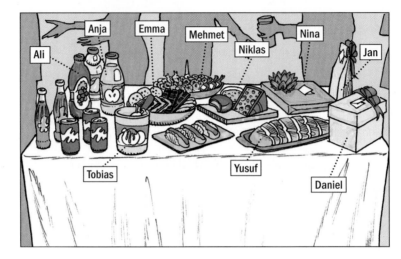

2 Was isst du gern?
Was isst Ihr Partner / Ihre Partnerin gern? Benutzen Sie Wörter aus der Liste in den Fragen und Akkusativpronomen in den Antworten. Answers will vary.

BEISPIEL

S1: Isst du gern Garnelen?
S2: Nein, ich esse sie nicht gern.

2 Expansion Have students jot down which foods their partner likes and report back to the class.

Auberginen	Pilze
Eis	Schinken
Gebäck	Schweinefleisch
Kekse	Süßigkeiten
Knoblauch	Torten
Meeresfrüchte	Trauben
Pfirsiche	Würstchen

3 Arbeitsblatt
Wer hat in Ihrer Klasse diese Aktivitäten gemacht? Schreiben Sie die Namen der Kommilitonen auf. Fragen Sie dann weiter nach mehr Informationen. Answers will vary.

3 Suggestion You may wish to set a time limit for this activity, or encourage students to go as quickly as possible, to help them stay on task.

BEISPIEL

S1: Hast du zu viel gegessen? Wann?
S2: Ich habe an Thanksgiving zu viel gegessen.

4 Geschenke
Was haben Sie und Ihr Partner / Ihre Partnerin Freunden und Familie zum Geburtstag oder zu Weihnachten geschenkt? Answers will vary.

BEISPIEL

S1: Was hast du deiner Mutter zum Geburtstag geschenkt?
S2: Ich habe ihr einen schönen Terminkalender geschenkt.

5 Diskutieren und kombinieren
Sie und Ihr Partner / Ihre Partnerin bekommen unterschiedliche Blätter mit Bildern von einer Party. Beschreiben Sie mit Ihrem Partner / Ihrer Partnerin Laras Aktivitäten. Answers will vary.

BEISPIEL

S1: Um halb acht hat Lara mit einem Freund gesprochen. Was hat sie um acht Uhr gemacht?
S2: Um acht Uhr hat sie gesungen.

6 Und Sie?
Was haben Sie auf der letzten Party gemacht? Was haben die anderen in der Gruppe gemacht? Answers will vary.

BEISPIEL

S1: Auf der Party am Freitagabend habe ich getanzt. Und du? Hast du auf der letzten Party getanzt?
S2: Nein, ich habe nicht getanzt. Aber ich habe auf der Party am Samstagabend Musik gehört. Das mache ich gern.

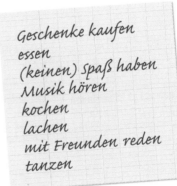

Geschenke kaufen
essen
(keinen) Spaß haben
Musik hören
kochen
lachen
mit Freunden reden
tanzen

4 Suggestion Emphasize correct use of case. Students may need a moment to formulate their questions in writing before they speak with their partners.

S Video

Shopping im Großmarkt

Großmärkte, wo es alles gibt, liegen im Trend. In Deutschland gibt es sie in fast jeder Stadt. Dazu gehören beispielsweise Marktkauf, Kaufland oder Real. Diese Märkte machen es für den Verbraucher° leicht, denn man findet fast alles unter einem Dach°. Allein Real hat in Deutschland etwa 300 Filialen°. Man findet dort neben Lebensmitteln wie Fleisch, Fisch und Brot auch Kosmetik, alles für den Haushalt, Elektroartikel, Fahrrad- und Autozubehör°, Spielwaren, alles fürs Baby, für Tiere, Sportartikel und Bekleidung°. Oft findet man tolle Angebote und Schnäppchen°. Die Märkte haben meistens° eine gute Verkehrsanbindung° und Parken ist kein Problem.

Ich gehe kurz was einkaufen. Braucht jemand° was?

Nö, ach... doch, für unser Wellness-Wochenende, Mädels?

Suggestion Point out that **nö** is an informal variant of **nein**, similar to *nope* in English. Explain that **Praktikant** is an **n**-noun.

Gesichtsmasken°, Biogurken°, Bademäntel°... und einen neuen Praktikanten°.

Verbraucher *customer* **Dach** *roof* **Filialen** *chain stores* **Autozubehör** *car accessories* **Bekleidung** *clothes* **Schnäppchen** *bargains* **meistens** *usually* **Verkehrsanbindung** *access to transportation* **jemand** *anyone* **Gesichtsmasken** *face masks* **Biogurken** *organic cucumbers* **Bademäntel** *bathrobes* **Praktikanten** *intern*

 Verständnis Beantworten Sie die Fragen mit den Informationen aus dem Video.

1. Welches Getränk wollen die Kolleginnen zum Wellness-Wochenende mitbringen?
   a. Karrottensaft   b. grünen Tee   c. stilles Wasser
2. Was möchten die Kolleginnen nicht?
   a. Conditioner und Bodylotion   b. eine Torte und Kekse
   c. einen DVD-Player und Filme

Diskussion Besprechen Sie die folgenden Fragen mit einem Partner/einer Partnerin. Answers will vary.

1. Gehen Sie gern im Großmarkt einkaufen? Warum oder warum nicht?
2. Sie planen ein Wellness-Wochenende mit Freunden. Was müssen Sie alles im Großmarkt finden?

Communicative Goals

You will learn how to:

- describe clothing
- talk about shopping

Kleidung  Vocabulary Tools

Wortschatz

Kleidung	*clothing*
die Bluse, -n	*blouse*
die Brille, -n	*glasses*
der Handschuh, -e	*glove*
die Jeans, -	*jeans*
der Mantel, ⸚	*coat*
der Pullover, -	*sweater*
die Socke, -n	*sock*
der Stiefel, -	*boot*
das Sweatshirt, -s	*sweatshirt*
das Trägerhemd, -en	*tank top*
das T-Shirt, -s	*T-shirt*
die Unterwäsche	*underwear*

Einkaufen	*shopping*
die Baumwolle	*cotton*
die Farbe, -n	*color*
die Kleidergröße, -n	*size*
das Leder	*leather*
der Kunde, -n / die Kundin, -nen	*customer*
die Seide	*silk*
der Verkäufer, - / die Verkäuferin, -nen	*salesperson*
die Wolle	*wool*

im Angebot	*on sale*
einfarbig	*solid colored*
eng	*tight*
gestreift	*striped*
kurzärmlig	*short-sleeved*
langärmlig	*long-sleeved*
weit	*loose; big*

anziehen (zieht... an)	*to put on*

Suggestion Tell students that **Jeans** may be used in the singular (**Ich trage eine Jeans**) or plural (**Meine Jeans sind alt**).

Suggestion Tell students that **Kleider** can also mean clothing, in general. Ex: **Hast du neue Kleider gekauft?**

Suggestion Give students sample sentences using the verb anziehen. Ex.: **Ich ziehe eine Jacke an.**

Ressourcen		
SAM WB: pp. 69–70	SAM LM: p. 44	vhlcentral.com

Labels within illustration: der Hut, ⸚e · der Badeanzug, ⸚e · Er ist teuer. · die Krawatte, -n · der Gürtel, - · das Kleid, -er · das Hemd, -en · die kurze Hose (*pl.* die kurzen Hosen) · die Turnschuhe (*sing.* der Turnschuh) · Er trägt einen Anzug (*pl.* ⸚e). (tragen) · die Handtasche, -n · gelb · grün · lila · rosa · grau · schwarz · orange · blau · braun · weiß · rot

Suggestion Use items in the classroom to practice color, or bring a bag of assorted colorful objects and ask students to name the colors they see. Ask: **Welche Farbe hat der Tisch? Welche Farbe hat die Tafel? Welche Farbe hat Jakes Sweatshirt?**

2 Expansion Ask students additional questions to practice colors. Ex: **Welche Farbe hat die Sonne? Welche Farbe hat ein Ei? Welche Farbe hat Spinat? Welche Farbe hat ein Panther? Welche Farbe haben deine Augen?**

ACHTUNG

Note that the adjectives **lila** and **rosa** are invariable: they do not vary in case, number, or gender to match the noun they modify.
Ich mag den lila Hut.

die Sonnenbrille, -n

die Mütze, -n

die Halskette, -n

der Schal, -s

die Jacke, -n

Es ist günstig.

die Hose, -n

der Rock, -̈e

der Schuh, -e

Suggestion Point out to students that while English uses the plural to talk about *pants*, the German word **Hose** is singular.

Expansion Write the conjugation of **tragen** on the board and practice pronunciation. Describe what you are wearing and ask questions about what students are wearing. Ex.: **Wer trägt ein blaues T-Shirt? Wie viele Studenten tragen heute eine Jeans? Welche Farbe hat Leslies Jacke? Was trägt Molly?**

Anwendung

1 Was passt nicht? Welches Wort passt nicht zu den anderen?

BEISPIEL lila, grün, (hell)

1. (die Unterwäsche), der Mantel, die Jacke
2. teuer, günstig, (langärmlig)
3. das Leder, die Seide, (die Farbe)
4. die Schuhe, (die Halsketten), die Stiefel
5. (die Verkäuferin), die Mütze, der Schal
6. das Kleid, der Rock, (die Krawatte)

2 Farben bezeichnen Nennen Sie die Farben von den Dingen, die Sie auf den Fotos sehen.

1. gelb

2. weiß

3. rot

4. rosa

5. braun

6. schwarz/dunkelgrau

3 Semesterferien Manfred plant eine kurze Reise in die Schweizer Alpen. Hören Sie an, was Manfred sagt, und markieren Sie am Ende die Kleidungsstücke, die er kaufen will.

	ja	nein			ja	nein
1. einen Pullover	☐	☑	5. eine Lederjacke		☐	☑
2. Skistiefel	☑	☐	6. eine Skihose		☑	☐
3. eine Jeans	☑	☐	7. eine Skijacke		☐	☑
4. ein Hemd	☐	☑	8. einen Mantel		☑	☐

4 Passende Kleidungsstücke Welche Kleidungsstücke trägt man in diesen Situationen? Answers will vary. Sample answers are provided.

1. Hasan trägt am Strand seine <u>Sonnenbrille</u>.
2. Zum Wandern in den Alpen soll man <u>gute Schuhe</u> tragen.
3. Im Winter trägt Alexandra ihren <u>Mantel</u> und ihren Pullover.
4. Zum Schwimmen trägt Lena ihren <u>Badeanzug</u>.
5. Für ihren Abschlussball kauft Emma ein schönes <u>Kleid</u>.

3 Suggestion Prepare students for the listening task by asking what kind of clothing one needs in specific situations. Ex: **Es ist ein sehr heißer Tag. Was trage ich am besten? Ich gehe schwimmen. Was brauche ich? Was packe ich für einen Skiurlaub?**

Practice more at **vhlcentral.com**.

Kommunikation

5 Was tragen die Leute? Beschreiben Sie mit Ihrem Partner / Ihrer Partnerin die Kleidungsstücke von den Personen auf den Fotos. Answers will vary. Sample answers are provided.

die Tennisspielerin

> **BEISPIEL**
>
> *Die Tennisspielerin trägt ein weißes Trägerhemd und einen weißen Tennisrock.*

5 Suggestion Give students sample adjective phrases that model correct endings for all genders in the accusative. Ex.: *masculine:* **einen roten Rock;** *feminine:* **eine gelbe Bluse;** *neuter:* **ein weißes Hemd;** *plural:* **grüne Socken.**

1. Thomas Thomas trägt einen grauen Mantel, Jeans und einen schwarzen Pullover.

2. der Geschäftsmann Der Geschäftsmann trägt ein blaues Hemd und eine schwarze Hose.

3. die Studentin Die Studentin trägt einen roten Pullover, eine dunkle Hose und einen braunen Rucksack.

4. die Kinder Die Kinder tragen weiße T-Shirts, grüne kurze Hosen, weiße Socken und Turnschuhe.

5. Frau Walter Frau Walter trägt einen hellbraunen Mantel, einen hellbraunen Schal, und eine schwarze Handtasche.

6. Herr Huber Herr Huber trägt einen hellen Anzug und einen dunklen Hut.

6 Diskutieren und kombinieren Finden Sie die sieben kleinen Unterschiede auf den Bildern, die Sie von Ihrem Professor / Ihrer Professorin bekommen. Answers will vary.

> **BEISPIEL**
>
> **S1:** *Trägt die Person auf deinem Bild (picture) eine Jeans?*
> **S2:** *Nein, sie trägt einen Rock.*

7 Wir gehen auf eine Party! Annika lädt Ihren Deutschkurs zu einer Party ein. Besprechen Sie mit Ihren Kommilitonen, was für eine Party es wird und was Sie für die Fete anziehen wollen. Answers will vary.

> **BEISPIEL**
>
> **S1:** *Annikas Fete ist morgen Abend. Was soll ich anziehen? Vielleicht meine enge, schwarze Jeans und ein schwarzes T-Shirt.*
> **S2:** *Hmm, ganz in schwarz? Ich bringe auch einen Badeanzug mit. Sie hat ein Schwimmbad im Garten.*
> **S3:** *Soll ich dann auch einen Hut und eine Sonnenbrille mitnehmen?*

7 Suggestion Have each group report back to the class about who will be wearing what to the party.

8 Im Kaufhaus Schreiben Sie in kleinen Gruppen einen Dialog im Kaufhaus. Sprechen Sie mit dem Verkäufer / der Verkäuferin über die Kleider, die Sie brauchen, aus welchem Material sie sein sollen, für welchen Anlass Sie einkaufen und so weiter. Answers will vary.

> **BEISPIEL**
>
> **S1:** *Guten Tag. Kann ich Ihnen helfen?*
> **S2:** *Ja, ich brauche für eine Hochzeitsfeier ein passendes Kleid.*
> **S3:** *Und ich brauche einen Anzug. Schwarz oder dunkelgrau.*

ein baumwollenes Nachthemd
ein dunkelblaues Abendkleid
gute Wanderschuhe
einen rot gestreiften Badeanzug
eine flexible Skibrille
traditionelle Lederhosen
warme Stiefel
weiße Tenniskleidung

6 Expansion Draw a **Strichmännchen** wearing assorted items of clothing, but do not show students the picture. Ask them to draw a stick figure and clothe him according to your oral description. Then, reveal your drawing so students can compare it to their own.

Aussprache und Rechtschreibung Audio

The letter combination *ch* (Part 1)

The letter combination **ch** has two distinct pronunciations, which depend on its placement within a word. To pronounce **ch** after the vowels **a**, **o**, **u**, and **au**, start by pressing the tip of your tongue against your lower front teeth and raising the back of the tongue to the roof of the mouth. Then blow out air through the small space between the back of the tongue and the roof of the mouth.

| Nachname | Tochter | Buch | brauchen | acht |

In loanwords, **ch** may appear at the beginning of a word. In these words, the **ch** is sometimes pronounced like the *k* in the English word *king*. It may also be pronounced like the *sh* in the English word *ship*.

| Chaos | Chor | Christ | Chance | Chef |

Expansion Have students come up with a class motto including as many ch-sounds following a back vowel as possible.

 1 **Aussprechen** Wiederholen Sie die Wörter, die Sie hören.

1. lachen
2. nach
3. auch
4. gesprochen
5. geflochten
6. brauchen
7. fluchen
8. Tuch
9. flache

2 **Nachsprechen** Wiederholen Sie die Sätze, die Sie hören.

1. Wir haben schon wieder Krach mit den Nachbarn.
2. Christians Tochter macht die Nachspeise.
3. Die Kinder waren nass bis auf die Knochen.
4. Hast du Bauchweh?
5. Der Schüler sucht ein Buch über Fremdsprachen.
6. Jochen kocht eine Suppe mit Lauch.

Vorgetan und nachgedacht hat manchem großes Leid gebracht.[2]

 3 **Sprichwörter** Wiederholen Sie die Sprichwörter, die Sie hören.

Wo Rauch ist, da ist auch Feuer.[1]

[1] Where there's smoke, there's fire.
[2] Look before you leap.
(*lit.* Doing before thinking has brought great suffering to many.)

Ressourcen

SAM
LM: p. 45

 vhlcentral.com

Sehr attraktiv, George! Video

Meline findet Georges Stil nicht sehr attraktiv. Kann sie ihm helfen, attraktive Kleidung zu finden?

Vorbereitung Ask students to describe what George and Meline are wearing in each scene.

GEORGE Hallo, Meline.
MELINE Hallo, George.
GEORGE Wer ist das gewesen?
MELINE Esteban Aurelio Gómez de la Garza.
Kommt aus Madrid. Langweilig.
GEORGE Hast du seit Silvester mit Lorenzo gesprochen?
MELINE Lorenzo ist unhöflich gewesen.
Ich habe ihn gelöscht.

GEORGE Ich gehe zur Kaiser-Wilhelm-Gedächtnis-Kirche. Möchtest du gern mitkommen?
MELINE Ja.

GEORGE Franz Schwechten hat das Originalbauwerk entworfen.
MELINE Im neuromanischen Baustil.
GEORGE Du weißt viel über Architektur.
MELINE Ich kann lesen. Das steht hier alles. Dort ist eine Tafel!

MELINE George, lass es bleiben. Komm. Ich weiß, wie ich dir helfen kann.
GEORGE Mir mit was helfen?
MELINE George, du bist nicht in den USA. Männer in Europa tragen keine Jeans und Turnschuhe. Schau.

GEORGE Woher hast du gewusst, dass das passiert?
MELINE Du kennst deine Architektur. Und ich kenne die Menschen. Gehen wir.

MELINE Wie sieht's aus da drin, George? George?
GEORGE Okay?
MELINE Komm, lass mich mal sehen!

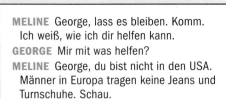

1 **Was fehlt?** Ergänzen Sie die Sätze mit den richtigen Informationen.

1. Esteban Aurelio Gómez de la Garza kommt aus (Madrid / Barcelona).
2. George möchte zur (Berliner Mauer / Kaiser-Wilhelm-Gedächtnis-Kirche) gehen.
3. (Franz Beckenbauer / Franz Schwechten) hat das Originalbauwerk entworfen.
4. George weiß viel über (Kleidung / Architektur).
5. Meline kann George mit seiner (Kleidung / Hausaufgabe) helfen.

6. Männer in Europa tragen keine (Jeans und Turnschuhe / Seidenkrawatten).
7. Meline findet die Kleidung im Geschäft zu (teuer / hässlich).
8. George empfiehlt Meline einen Freund aus einem anderen (Land / Beruf).
9. Mit dem Hut und der (Sonnenbrille / Jacke) sieht George sehr europäisch aus.
10. Meline hat eine schöne (Halskette / Handtasche) gesehen.

PERSONEN George   Meline

7

MELINE Dieser Pullover ist zu eng. Die Hosen sind zu lang. Du musst ein gestreiftes Hemd unter dem Pullover anziehen, kein einfarbiges. Was meinst du?

GEORGE Mir gefallen die Stiefel?

MELINE Das ist alles falsch. Zu teuer, zu teuer. Diese sind ein Schnäppchen. Wo ist der Verkäufer?

GEORGE Warum bin ich in diesen Laden gekommen? Ich sehe lächerlich aus.

8

MELINE Blau? Nein. Schwarz? Nein. Grün? Nein. Okay. Zieh dieses Hemd... und diese Hose an... mit... dieser Seidenkrawatte. Komm schon! Wir haben nicht den ganzen Tag Zeit.

9

GEORGE Wie wäre es du denn mal mit einer Person aus einem anderen Beruf?

MELINE Wie Architektur?

GEORGE Ähmm... nein. Literatur oder Philosophie. Informatik oder Geschichte? Wie Hans.

10

MELINE Sehr attraktiv, George. Setz diese Sonnenbrille auf. Hut. So sieht ein europäischer Mann aus.

GEORGE Hast du gehört, was ich gesagt habe?

MELINE Zieh schnell deine Jeans wieder an. Ich habe eine Handtasche gesehen. Die muss ich unbedingt kaufen. Hans. Also wirklich.

Nützliche Ausdrücke

- **die Kirche**
  church
- **Franz Schwechten hat das Originalbauwerk entworfen.**
  Franz Schwechten designed the original structure.
- **Im neuromanischen Baustil.**
  In the neo-Romanesque style.
- **die Tafel**
  plaque
- **George, lass es bleiben.**
  George, don't even try.
- **Mir mit was helfen?**
  Help me with what?
- **Woher hast du gewusst, dass das passiert?**
  How did you know that was going to happen?
- **Wie sieht's aus da drin, George?**
  How's it going in there, George?
- **lächerlich**
  ridiculous
- **Wir haben nicht den ganzen Tag Zeit.**
  We don't have all day.
- **unbedingt**
  at all costs

  5B.1
- **Wer ist das gewesen?**
  Who was that?

  5B.2
- **Du weißt viel über Architektur.**
  You know a lot about architecture.
- **Und ich kenne die Menschen.**
  And I know people.

  5B.3
- **George, du bist nicht in den USA.**
  George, you're not in the U.S.
- **Warum bin ich in diesen Laden gekommen?**
  Why did I come into this store?

2 **Zum Besprechen** Bilden Sie Gruppen zu dritt und diskutieren Sie: Was denken Sie über Mode? Ist sie Ihnen wichtig? Was ist Ihre Lieblingskleidung? Answers will vary.

3 **Vertiefung** Suchen Sie einen bekannten Designer oder eine bekannte Designerin aus Deutschland, Österreich, der Schweiz oder Liechtenstein und finden Sie Informationen zu ihm/ihr im Internet. Geben Sie vor Ihrer Klasse eine kurze Präsentation. Research possibilities include: Karl Lagerfeld, Wolfgang Joop, Jil Sander, Helmut Lang

3 **Suggestion** Encourage students to bring photos of their chosen designer and his/her fashions to share with the class.

Ressourcen

SAM
VM: p. 10

vhlcentral.com

IM FOKUS

Deutsche Modewelt Ⓢ Reading

> **TIPP**
>
> The symbol **m²** stands for **Quadratmeter** (*square meters*).

FRANKREICH UND ITALIEN SIND klassische Modeländer. Aber in Deutschland entwirft° und produziert man auch viel Mode und Kleidung. Ähnlich wie° in Frankreich und Italien gibt es berühmte Modedesigner:

Karl Lagerfeld, Wolfgang Joop und Jil Sander sind internationale Stars. Deutsche Marken° wie Hugo Boss, Bogner und Escada sind weltweit° bekannt.

Mode spielt in Deutschland eine große Rolle für die Wirtschaft. Deutschland gehört heute zu den führenden° Mode-Exporteuren. Jedes Jahr importieren deutsche Firmen aber auch Kleidung im Wert von 36,2 Milliarden Euro nach Deutschland: Deutschland ist einer der größten internationalen Kleiderimporteure. Im Bereich° der Sportmode sind deutsche Firmen wie Adidas und Puma überall bekannt. Diese beiden Firmen haben ihren Hauptsitz° in Herzogenaurach, einer kleinen Stadt in Bayern. In Berlin findet man das größte Warenhaus° auf dem europäischen Kontinent: das Kaufhaus des Westens (KaDeWe), mit rund 60.000 m² Verkaufsfläche°. Die wichtigsten Modestädte in Deutschland sind Berlin und Düsseldorf. Auch München wird für Mode immer wichtiger.

Deutschland ist ein Magnet für Modeexperten aus der ganzen Welt. In Düsseldorf findet zweimal pro Jahr die CPD (Collections Premieren Düsseldorf) statt°. Das ist die größte Modemesse° weltweit. In München kommen Fachbesucher° aus über 100 Ländern zweimal pro Jahr zur ISPO (Internationale Fachmesse für Sportartikel und Sportmode), wo rund 2.500 Aussteller° neue Sportkleidung und Accessoires präsentieren. Die PREMIUM Internationale Fachmesse für Mode findet in Berlin auch zweimal pro Jahr statt. Hier findet man viele junge Modeschöpfer°.

Kleidergrößen			
Frauenkleider		**Männerhosen**	
Deutschland	USA	Deutschland	USA (Bundweite/Länge in Zoll°)
30	2	44	30/32
32	4	46	32/32
34	6	48	33/32
36	8	50	34/32
38	10	52	36/34
40	12	54	38/34
42	14	56	40/34
44	16		

Modewelt *world of fashion* **entwirft** *designs* **Ähnlich wie** *Similar to* **Marken** *brands* **weltweit** *worldwide* **führenden** *leading* **Bereich** *area* **Hauptsitz** *headquarters* **Warenhaus** *department store* **Verkaufsfläche** *sales floor* **findet... statt** *takes place* **Modemesse** *fashion trade fair* **Fachbesucher** *trade visitors* **Aussteller** *exhibitors* **Modeschöpfer** *fashion designers* **Zoll** *inches*

ÜBUNGEN

1 **Richtig oder falsch?** Sind die Aussagen **richtig** oder **falsch?** Korrigieren Sie die falschen Sätze.

1. Frankreich und Italien sind die klassischen Modeländer. Richtig.
2. Mode spielt in Deutschland keine große Rolle. Falsch. Mode spielt in Deutschland eine große Rolle.
3. Karl Lagerfeld und Jil Sander sind internationale Modestars. Richtig.
4. Deutschland ist ein großer Mode-Exporteur. Richtig.
5. Puma und Adidas sind Sportmodefirmen aus Bayern. Richtig.

6. Das größte Warenhaus auf dem europäischen Kontinent ist in Frankreich. Falsch. Das größte Warenhaus auf dem europäischen Kontinent ist das KaDeWe in Berlin.
7. In Deutschland gibt es viele internationale Modemessen. Richtig.
8. Die Herren-Mode-Woche/Inter-Jeans ISPO kann man zweimal pro Jahr in Berlin besuchen. Falsch. Die ISPO kann man zweimal pro Jahr in München besuchen.
9. Das KaDeWe ist die größte Modemesse der Welt. Falsch. Die CPD ist die größte Modemesse der Welt.
10. Jil Sander und Wolfgang Joop sind bekannte deutsche Designer. Richtig.

Ⓢ Practice more at **vhlcentral.com**.

Suggestion Remind students that when dealing with long sentences, identifying the subject and verb can help them to figure out the gist.

DEUTSCH IM ALLTAG

Modevokabeln

der letzte Schrei	the latest thing
der Stil	style
angesagt	trendy
ausgefallen	offbeat
elegant	elegant
gut gekleidet	well-dressed
modisch	fashionable
schlecht gekleidet	badly dressed

DIE DEUTSCHSPRACHIGE WELT

Die Tracht

Das Wort „Tracht" bezeichnet° oft traditionelle oder historische Kleidung. In der Alpenregion, genauer gesagt° in Bayern und in Österreich, bezieht sich° das Wort heute auf Lederhosen für Männer und Dirndl für Frauen. Männer tragen neben° Lederhosen, Hosenträger°, Haferlschuhe° und Bundhosenstrümpfe°. Frauen in Dirndl tragen eine weiße Bluse mit Puffärmeln° und ein Kropfband°. Ursprünglich° waren Lederhosen und Dirndl Arbeitskleidung, aber heute sieht man sie bei Umzügen° wie dem Oktoberfest.

bezeichnet denotes **genauer gesagt** more precisely
bezieht sich refers to **neben** in addition to
Hosenträger suspenders **Haferlschuhe** brogue shoes
Bundhosenstrümpfe long socks **Puffärmeln** puffed sleeves
Kropfband choker **Ursprünglich** originally **Umzügen** parades

PORTRÄT

Rudolf Moshammer

Rudolf Moshammer war ein bekannter bayerischer Modedesigner. International war er nicht so bekannt wie Karl Lagerfeld oder Jil Sander. Aber namhafte° Kunden wie zum Beispiel Arnold Schwarzenegger, Siegfried und Roy, José Carreras und Carl XVI. Gustaf von Schweden kauften seine Mode. Moshammer verkaufte seine Designs in der Münchner Boutique Carneval de Venise, einem Geschäft an der Maximilianstraße im Herzen Münchens. Neben seiner Mode war Moshammer berühmt für seine Yorkshire-Hündin Daisy, seine aufwendige° schwarze Frisur° mit zwei Locken im Gesicht° und sein soziales Engagement für Obdachlose°. Im Januar 2005 wurde Moshammer in seiner Münchner Villa ermordet°.

Suggestion Tell students that nowadays one rarely sees Germans dressed **in Tracht**, even in Bavaria--except, as mentioned in the article, **bei Festen und Umzügen.**

namhafte famous **aufwendige** lavish **Frisur** hairstyle **Gesicht** face **Obdachlose** homeless people
wurde... ermordet was murdered

⚲ IM INTERNET

Suchen Sie Namen bekannter Designer in Deutschland, Österreich und der Schweiz.

Find out more at **vhlcentral.com.**

---

2 **Mode in Bayern** Ergänzen Sie die Sätze.

1. Eine Tracht ist traditionelle und historische ___Kleidung___.

2. Ursprünglich waren ___Lederhosen___ und Dirndl Arbeitskleidung.

3. Arnold Schwarzenegger und José Carreras waren zwei namhafte ___Kunden___ von Rudolf Moshammer.

4. Rudolf Moshammers Boutique war in ___München___.

5. Moshammers Yorkshire-Hündin heißt ___Daisy___.

3 **Campusmode** Besprechen Sie mit einem Partner / einer Partnerin, was Studenten auf dem Campus tragen: Gibt es eine Campusmode? Tragen Sie diese Kleidung auch gern? Welche Kleidung sollen Studenten tragen?

BEISPIEL

S1: Viele Studenten tragen gern Jeans mit Sweatshirt zum Frühstück. Wie findest du das?

S2: Das gefällt mir. Blaue Jeans und einfarbige Sweatshirts passen gut zusammen.

Ressourcen

vhlcentral.com

5B.1

The *Perfekt* (Part 2)  Presentation

Startblock In 5A.1, you learned that most verbs form the **Perfekt** with **haben**. However, certain types of verbs form the **Perfekt** with **sein**.

> Wer **ist** das **gewesen**?

> Sie **ist** vor sechs Monaten von Köln nach Berlin **gezogen**.

The *Perfekt* with *sein*

QUERVERWEIS

See **1B.1** to review the function of direct objects.

ACHTUNG

Use the adverb **gestern** to say that something happened *yesterday*.

Gestern sind wir zum Park gelaufen. Paul ist gestern Abend auf eine Party gegangen.

Suggestion Remind students that this rule is helpful as a general guideline, but that ultimately, they will need to memorize the correct participles and auxiliaries on a verb-by-verb basis.

Suggestion Point out to students that **bleiben** and **sein** are an exception to the "change of condition or location" rule.

- Only a few verbs form the **Perfekt** with **sein**. They are all verbs that indicate a change of condition or location. These verbs never take a direct object.

  Die Pflanzen **sind** schnell **gewachsen**.
  *The plants **grew** quickly.*

  Peter **ist** krank **gewesen**.
  *Peter **got** sick.*

  Wir **sind** zusammen nach Innsbruck **gefahren**.
  *We **drove** to Innsbruck together.*

  Ich **bin** vom Fahrrad **gefallen**.
  *I **fell** off my bike.*

- To form the **Perfekt** tense of a verb with **sein**, use a conjugated form of **sein** plus the past participle of the verb that expresses the action.

  Amira **ist** schon nach Hause **gegangen**.
  *Amira already **went** home.*

  Mein Opa **ist** gestern nach
    München **gefahren**.
  *My grandpa **went** to Munich yesterday.*

  Sie **sind** gestern Abend **gekommen**.
  *They **came** last night.*

  Letzten Sommer **sind** wir nach
    Italien **gereist**.
  *Last summer we **traveled** to Italy.*

- Both **sein** and **bleiben** are conjugated with **sein** in the **Perfekt**. Note that the past participle of **sein** is **gewesen**.

  Ich **bin** in der Bibliothek **geblieben**.
  *I **stayed** in the library.*

  Vor zwei Jahren **bin** ich in Istanbul **gewesen**.
  *Two years ago I **was** in Istanbul.*

- Here is a list of common verbs that take **sein** in the **Perfekt**. Note that most are strong verbs.

Suggestion Have students identify whether each verb listed describes a "change of location" or a "change of state".

verbs that form the *Perfekt* with *sein*			
infinitive	**past participle**	**infinitive**	**past participle**
bleiben	geblieben	reisen	gereist
fahren	gefahren	sein	gewesen
fallen	gefallen	steigen (*to climb*)	gestiegen
gehen	gegangen	sterben (*to die*)	gestorben
kommen	gekommen	wachsen (*to grow*)	gewachsen
laufen	gelaufen	wandern	gewandert
passieren (*to happen*)	passiert	werden	geworden

Was **ist passiert**?
*What **happened**?*

Ich **bin** gerade zwanzig **geworden**.
*I just **turned** twenty.*

Word order in the *Perfekt*

- In **1B.2**, you learned that the conjugated verb is always in second position in a statement and in first position in a yes-or-no question. In the **Perfekt**, the conjugated form of **haben** or **sein** is always in second position for statements and first in yes-or-no questions.

Hast du seit Silvester mit Lorenzo **gesprochen**?

Lorenzo **ist** unhöflich **gewesen**.

Die roten Schuhe **haben** nicht viel **gekostet**.
*The red shoes **didn't cost** very much.*

Seid ihr im Sommer viel **gereist**?
*Did you **travel** a lot over the summer?*

- In statements and questions, always place the past participle at the end of the sentence or clause.

Ich **habe** gestern ein neues Kleid **gekauft**.
*I **bought** a new dress yesterday.*

Wo **hast** du die tollen Stiefel **gekauft**?
*Where **did** you **buy** those awesome boots?*

QUERVERWEIS

See **1B.2** and **2A.2** to review word order in simple sentences.

Ressourcen

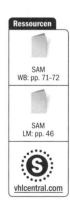

SAM
WB: pp. 71–72

SAM
LM: pp. 46

Ⓢ
vhlcentral.com

Jetzt sind Sie dran! Wählen Sie das passende Hilfsverb.

1. Wir (sind / haben) den ganzen Abend bei unseren Eltern gewesen.
2. Ich (bin / habe) nicht lange auf der Party geblieben.
3. (Ist / Hat) Philip eine teure Sonnenbrille gekauft?
4. Leider (ist / hat) Jasmins Katze letzte Woche gestorben.
5. Wann (seid / habt) ihr nach Italien gereist?
6. Ich (bin / habe) einen schicken Rock aus Seide getragen.
7. (Bist / Hast) du die Kleider gewaschen?
8. Michael (ist / hat) zum Kaufhof gefahren.
9. Meine Eltern (sind / haben) mir Handschuhe geschenkt.
10. Leider (ist / hat) mein Bleistift ins Wasser gefallen.
11. Ihr (seid / habt) nicht viel gelaufen.
12. (Bist / Hast) du ohne Brille ins Theater gegangen?

Anwendung

1 Perfektformen Ergänzen Sie die Sätze mit den richtigen Formen von **sein** und den Partizipien.

1. Ich ___bin___ am Samstag zu Michaela ___gegangen___. (gehen)
2. Meine Mutter ___ist___ fünf Kilometer ___gelaufen___. (laufen)
3. Die Wintermonate ___sind___ sehr warm ___gewesen___. (sein)
4. Wann ___ist___ Sigmund Freud ___gestorben___? (sterben)
5. Jan und Klara, ihr ___seid___ zu spät ___gekommen___. (kommen)
6. Zu Silvester ___sind___ wir zu Hause ___geblieben___. (bleiben)
7. ___Bist___ du letzten Sommer durch Europa ___gereist___? (reisen)
8. Professor Schmidt, wann ___sind___ Sie nach Hause ___gefahren___? (fahren)

2 Expansion Have students play pictionary using sentences in the **Perfekt**. Choose sentences with verbs that are easy to depict in a drawing. Ex.: **Mein Hund ist geschwommen**.

2 Letzten Juli Beschreiben Sie, was diese Personen letzten Juli **gemacht haben.** Answers may vary. Sample answers are provided.

> nach Nürnberg fahren | am Strand laufen
> von einem Stuhl fallen | nach Europa reisen
> nach Hause kommen | schwimmen gehen

▶ **BEISPIEL** Mein Bruder Max
ist am Strand gelaufen.

1. Anja
ist nach Hause gekommen

2. Mein Neffe Emil
ist von einem Stuhl gefallen

3. Professor Aydin
ist nach Europa gereist

4. Frau Weber
ist nach Nürnberg gefahren

5. Meine Cousins
sind schwimmen gegangen

3 In letzter Zeit Bilden Sie Sätze im Perfekt. Benutzen Sie **sein** als Hilfsverb. Answers may vary. Sample answers are provided.

BEISPIEL meine Oma / kommen / zu meiner Abschlussfeier
Meine Oma ist zu meiner Abschlussfeier gekommen.

1. fahren / du / nach Hause
Bist du nach Hause gefahren?
2. meine Eltern und ich / reisen / im Januar / nach Österreich
Meine Eltern und ich sind im Januar nach Österreich gereist.
3. mein Freund / bleiben / bei seinen Eltern / in Berlin
Mein Freund ist bei seinen Eltern in Berlin geblieben.
4. ich / werden / nach der Party / sehr müde
Ich bin nach der Party sehr müde geworden.
5. dein Baby / wachsen / so schnell
Dein Baby ist so schnell gewachsen!
6. gehen / ihr / auf die Hochzeit / von Nils und Julia
Seid ihr auf die Hochzeit von Nils und Julia gegangen?

 Practice more at **vhlcentral.com.**

Kommunikation

4 **Bilden Sie Sätze** Was hat Ihrer Partner / Ihre Partnerin zu Silvester gemacht? Stellen Sie ihm/ihr sechs logische Fragen darüber. Benutzen Sie das Perfekt und verwenden Sie Wörter aus jeder Spalte. Answers will vary.

BEISPIEL

S1: Bist du mit deinen Freunden auf eine Party gegangen?
S2: Ja, wir sind zusammen auf eine Party gegangen!

A	B	C
ich	bleiben	mit dem Auto
du	fahren	nicht
das Wetter	gehen	neue Kleider
der/die Gastgeber(in)	kommen	bei deine Eltern
ihr	passieren	mit deinen Freunden
deine Freunde	sein	warm
was?	tragen	zu spät

5 **Historische Personen** Erraten Sie mit Ihrer Gruppe, was jede von diesen historischen Personen in ihrem Leben gemacht hat. Answers will vary. Sample answers are provided.

BEISPIEL George Washington

Er ist Präsident von Amerika gewesen.

fallen	laufen	sein
gehen	reisen	spielen
helfen	schreiben	werden

1. Julia Child / Kochbücher
   Sie hat Kochbücher geschrieben.
2. Babe Ruth / Baseball
   Er hat Baseball gespielt.
3. Angela Merkel / Kanzlerin von Deutschland
   Sie ist Kanzlerin von Deutschland geworden.
4. Humpty Dumpty / die Mauer
   Er ist von der Mauer gefallen.
5. Mutter Teresa / arme Leute
   Sie hat armen Leuten geholfen.
6. Marco Polo / nach China
   Er ist nach China gereist.

5 **Expansion** For homework, have students research biographical information about a famous person of their choice and write ten simple sentences about that person in the **Perfekt**. In class, students must present their sentences and have classmates guess who the person is.

6 **Semesterferien** Fragen Sie Ihren Partner / Ihre Partnerin, was er/sie in den Semesterferien (*semester break*) gemacht hat. Answers will vary.

BEISPIEL

S1: Bist du in den Semesterferien gereist?
S2: Nein, ich bin hier geblieben. Ich habe in einer Pizzeria gearbeitet. Und du?
S1: Meine Familie und ich sind nach Deutschland gefahren.

arbeiten	spazieren gehen
bleiben	kommen
fahren	reisen
einkaufen gehen	sein
schwimmen gehen	wandern

7 **Als Kind** Machen Sie mit einem Partner / einer Partnerin ein Interview über Ihre Kindheit (*childhood*). Wenn Sie fertig sind, tauschen Sie die Rollen.

BEISPIEL gern zur Schule gehen

S1: Bist du gern zur Schule gegangen?
S2: Ja, ich bin gern zur Schule gegangen. Aber meine Hausaufgaben habe ich nicht immer gern gemacht!

1. ein guter Schüler / eine gute Schülerin sein
2. nach der Schule mit Freunden spielen
3. oft zu spät zur Schule kommen
4. Fahrrad fahren
5. im Sommer mit den Eltern reisen
6. gern ins Schwimmbad gehen
7. am Wochenende zu Hause bleiben
8. einen Hund oder eine Katze haben

7 **Suggestion** If you hear many mistakes in the formation of participles or use of the correct auxiliary, interrupt this activity to form some sample questions together with the class.

5B.2 Wissen and kennen  Presentation

Startblock In German, the verbs **wissen** and **kennen** are used to express different types of knowledge.

Du **weißt** viel über Architektur.

Ich **kenne** die Menschen.

QUERVERWEIS

The verb **wissen** is often used with dependent clauses. You will learn about dependent clauses in **10A.3**.

ACHTUNG

The verb **wissen** is used in many common idiomatic expressions:

Weißt du was?
You know what?

Weißt du das bestimmt?
Are you sure about that?

Woher soll ich das wissen?
How should I know?

QUERVERWEIS

To review the formation of mixed verbs, see **5A.1**.

- Use **wissen** to express the idea of *knowing a fact* or piece of information. **Wissen** is irregular in its present-tense singular forms.

wissen (*to know information*)			
ich weiß	*I know*	wir wissen	*we know*
du weißt	*you know*	ihr wisst	*you know*
er/sie/es weiß	*he/she/it knows*	Sie/sie wissen	*you/they know*

Michael **weiß** die Antwort nicht.
Michael doesn't ***know*** *the answer.*

Weißt du Saras Telefonnummer?
Do you ***know*** *Sara's phone number?*

- Use **kennen** to express the idea of *being familiar with* someone or something. **Kennen** always takes a direct object, usually a person or place. It is regular in the present tense.

kennen (*to know, to be familiar with*)			
ich kenne	*I know*	wir kennen	*we know*
du kennst	*you know*	ihr kennt	*you know*
er/sie/es kennt	*he/she/it knows*	Sie/sie kennen	*you/they know*

Ich **kenne** viele Leute.
I ***know*** *a lot of people.*

Du **kennst** Jana schon seit zwei Jahren.
You've ***known*** *Jana for two years.*

- In the **Perfekt**, both **kennen** and **wissen** are mixed verbs; their past participles end in -**t**, but their stems are irregular.

Jan **hat** den Professor sehr gut **gekannt**.
Jan ***knew*** *the professor very well.*

Mein Opa **hat** viel über Kunst **gewusst**.
My grandpa ***knew*** *a lot about art.*

Das **habe** ich nicht **gewusst**.
I ***didn't know*** *that.*

Hast du deine Urgroßeltern **gekannt**?
Did *you* ***know*** *your great grandparents?*

Ressourcen

SAM
WB: pp. 73-74

SAM
LM: p. 47

vhlcentral.com

Jetzt sind Sie dran! Wählen Sie das richtige Verb.

1. (Wisst / Kennt) ihr was?
2. Wir (wissen / kennen) die Musik von Mozart.
3. (Wisst / Kennt) ihr die neue Studentin?
4. (Weiß / Kennt) er das bestimmt?
5. Woher sollen wir das (wissen / kennen)?
6. Du (weißt / kennst) die Antwort nicht.
7. Ich habe ihn nicht gut (gewusst / gekannt).
8. Ich habe das nicht (gewusst / gekannt).

Anwendung und Kommunikation

1 **Wissen und kennen** Ergänzen Sie die richtigen Formen von **kennen** und **wissen**.

Präsens

1. sie (*sing.*) ____kennt____ (kennen)
2. ihr ____wisst____ (wissen)
3. wir ____kennen____ (kennen)
4. du ____weißt____ (wissen)
5. er ____weiß____ (wissen)
6. ich ____kenne____ (kennen)

Perfekt

7. Sie __haben gewusst__ (wissen)
8. du __hast gekannt__ (kennen)
9. ihr __habt gekannt__ (kennen)
10. er __hat gewusst__ (wissen)
11. ich __habe gekannt__ (kennen)
12. wir __haben gewusst__ (wissen)

2 **Wissen oder kennen?** Wählen Sie das passende Verb und ergänzen Sie die Sätze mit den richtigen Formen von **wissen** oder **kennen**.

1. ____Weißt____ du die Telefonnummer von Marie?
2. Wir ____kennen____ ihren Freund, aber wir ____wissen____ nicht viel über ihn.
3. ____Wisst____ ihr das bestimmt?
4. Meine Freundin ____kennt____ Berlin sehr gut.
5. ____Habt____ ihr euch schon letztes Semester ____gekannt____? (Perfekt)
6. Einstein ____hat____ sehr viel über Physik ____gewusst____! (Perfekt)

3 **Die Stadt und der Campus** Fragen Sie Ihren Partner / Ihre Partnerin nach Ihrer Stadt (*city*) und Ihrem Campus. Wen oder was kennen Sie dort? Was wissen Sie darüber? Answers will vary.

3 **Suggestion** Formulate the first few questions and answers together as a class.

BEISPIEL

S1: *Kennst du ein schönes Café?*
S2: *Ja, ich kenne ein sehr schönes Café!*
S1: *Weißt du auch die Adresse?*
S2: *Natürlich weiß ich die: Schillerstraße 5.*

> unsere Stadt
> die Telefonnummer von dem Professor / der Professorin
> ein gutes und nicht so teures Restaurant
> die E-mail-Adressen von deinen Kommilitonen
> einen guten Friseur

4 **Ihre Kommilitonen** Finden Sie ein paar Informationen über die Personen in Ihrer Gruppe.

BEISPIEL

S1: *Wo wohnst du?*
S2: *Ich wohne in Campbell Hall.*
S1: *Kennst du Professor Schmidt?*
S2: *Nein, ich kenne ihn nicht.*

Name: Caroline	
Ich weiß:	1. ihren Namen. (Caroline)
	2. ihre Adresse. (Campbell Hall, Zimmer 204)
	3. ihre Telefonnummer.
Ich kenne:	4. ihre Freundin Katia.
	5. ihren Freund Jeffrey. (Sie spielen Tennis zusammen.)
	6. ihr Lieblingsrestaurant. (Blue Moon)

 Practice more at **vhlcentral.com**.

5B.3

NATIONAL STANDARDS comparisons

Suggestion Before starting with the **Wechselpräpositionen**, help students solidify their existing knowledge of prepositions. Ask them what prepositions are and have them give some examples in both English and German. Remind them that some prepositions always take the accusative, and some always take the dative. Review these prepositions to ensure that students remember their meaning and usage.

Two-way prepositions Presentation

Startblock In 3B.2 and 4B.2, you learned that certain prepositions are always followed by the accusative case, while others are always followed by the dative case. A small number of prepositions can be followed by either the dative or the accusative, depending on the situation.

Was machst du **in diesem Teil** der Stadt?

Warum bin ich **in diesen Laden** gekommen?

- Prepositions that can be followed by either the dative or the accusative are called *two-way prepositions*.

two-way prepositions			
an	*at, on*	über	*above, over*
auf	*on, on top of*	unter	*under*
hinter	*behind*	vor	*in front of*
in	*in, into*	zwischen	*between*
neben	*next to*		

Ich trage ein T-Shirt **unter dem Pullover**.
*I'm wearing a T-shirt **under my sweater**.*

Stell deine Schuhe nicht **auf den Tisch!**
*Don't put your shoes **on the table!***

- Whether you choose a dative or an accusative object to follow a two-way preposition depends on the meaning of the sentence. If the verb indicates *movement toward* a destination, use an object in the accusative.

Ich **fahre** das Auto **in die Garage**.
*I'm **driving** the car **into the garage**.*

Der Hund **geht in die Küche**.
*The dog **is going into the kitchen**.*

- If the verb does *not* indicate movement toward a destination, use an object in the dative case.

ACHTUNG

Remember that dative prepositions *always* take a dative object, even if the verb in the sentence indicates movement: **Ich fahre mit meinem Onkel**.

Suggestion Teach students the rhyme *Where at? Dat! Where to? Accu!* and the German equivalent **Wo? Dativ! Wohin? Akkusativ!** to help them remember this rule. Emphasize that the deciding factor is not just movement, but movement *towards* a destination.

Expansion Use objects in the classroom to demonstrate two-way prepositions. Ex: **Ich lege mein Buch auf den Tisch. Das Buch liegt auf dem Tisch**. In each sentence, emphasize the distinction between *destination* and *location*.

Warum **bist** du heute **auf dem** Kurfürstendamm?

Das Auto **ist in der Garage**.
*The car **is in the garage**.*

Er **arbeitet im Bereich** internationale Finanzen.

Der Hund **isst in der Küche**.
*The dog **eats in the kitchen**.*

- When you use a two-way preposition with a pronoun, make sure to select a pronoun in the appropriate case.

Ich sitze **neben dem alten Mann**.
*I'm sitting **next to the old man**.*

Ich sitze **neben ihm**.
*I'm sitting **next to him**.*

Er hat den Teller **vor seinen Sohn** gestellt.
*He put the plate **in front of his son**.*

Er hat den Teller **vor ihn** gestellt.
*He put the plate **in front of him**.*

- Here are some common contractions of two-way prepositions and definite articles.

an	+	das	⟶	**ans**
auf	+	das	⟶	**aufs**
in	+	das	⟶	**ins**
an	+	dem	⟶	**am**
in	+	dem	⟶	**im**

- The question **wohin?** (*where to?*) asks about movement. When you answer this question with a two-way preposition, always use an object in the accusative case.

Wohin fahren wir morgen?
Where are we going tomorrow?

Wir fahren morgen **in die Stadt**.
*We're going **to the city** tomorrow.*

Wohin gehen die Leute?
Where are the people going?

Sie gehen **ins Konzert**.
*They're going **to the concert**.*

- The question **wo?** (*where?*) asks about location. When you answer this question with a two-way preposition, always use an object in the dative case.

Wo ist mein Schal?
Where is my scarf?

Dein Schal liegt **auf dem Tisch**.
*Your scarf is lying **on the table**.*

- Use the dative after a two-way preposition with a verb that indicates where something is located. Use the accusative with a verb that indicates where something is being placed.

wo?	
hängen	to hang, to be hanging
liegen	to lie
sitzen	to sit
stehen	to stand

wohin?	
hängen	to hang (something)
legen	to lay (down)
setzen	to set (down)
stellen	to put (down)

Das Bild **hängt an der** Wand.
*The picture **is hanging on the** wall.*

Ich **hänge** das Bild **an die** Wand.
*I'm **hanging** the picture **on the** wall.*

QUERVERWEIS

To review the forms of dative and accusative pronouns, see **5A.2** and **5A.3**.

See **3B.2** to review contractions with accusative prepositions. See **4B.2** to review contractions with dative prepositions.

Suggestion Make sure students understand that the "**wo**" verbs all describe location (place) and the "**wohin**" verbs all describe the process of placing something somewhere (placement).

Ressourcen

SAM
WB: pp. 75-76

SAM
LM: p. 48

S

vhlcentral.com

Jetzt sind Sie dran! **Wählen Sie den richtigen Artikel.** **Suggestion** Remind students that they need to look at the verb in order to make a decision about case. Students may have difficulty with item 7 because of the motion verb **fahren**. Point out that the car is your *location*, not your *destination*. You are *in the car*, not moving *towards the car*.

1. Wir wohnen über (einer / eine) Bäckerei.
2. Ich lege den gestreiften Hut auf (den / dem) Tisch.
3. Aha! Unter (den / dem) Tisch liegt meine Mütze.
4. Die Verkäuferin hängt das kurzärmlige Kleid zwischen (die / den) langärmligen Kleider und die Blusen.
5. Matthias trägt selten ein Sweatshirt über (sein / seinem) T-shirt.

6. Dein Schal hängt neben (die / der) Tür.
7. Ich bin in (meinem / mein) Auto gefahren.
8. Frau Vögele braucht Unterwäsche und geht in (ein / einem) Geschäft.
9. Die Katze sitzt gern auf (meine / meiner) Jacke.
10. Seid ihr am Montag wieder in (ein / einem) Konzert gegangen?

Anwendung

1 Präpositionen Ergänzen Sie die Sätze mit den richtigen bestimmten (*definite*) Artikeln.

> **BEISPIEL** Die neue Bäckerei ist zwischen _der_ Metzgerei und _dem_ Supermarkt.

1. Die warme Jacke hängt an ___der___ Tür.
2. Hast du dein Fahrrad hinter ___das___ Haus gestellt?
3. Der Kellner geht um ___den___ Tisch.
4. Trägst du ein Trägerhemd unter ___dem___ T-Shirt?
5. Ich gehe in ___die___ Bibliothek.
6. Sophia und Hans laufen morgens durch ___den___ Park.
7. Die Katze liegt gern neben ___dem___ Fenster.
8. Der Hund ist hinter ___das___ Auto gelaufen.

2 Wo macht man das? Schreiben Sie zu jedem Foto, wo man diese Aktivitäten machen kann.

| die Berge | ein altes Haus | das Restaurant |
| die Bibliothek | der Park | das Stadion |

▶ **BEISPIEL** lesen
in der Bibliothek

1. Fußball spielen
   im Stadion

2. essen
   im Restaurant

3. Ski fahren
   in den Bergen

4. spazieren gehen
   im Park

5. wohnen
   in einem alten Haus

3 Überraschung beim Abendessen Bilden Sie Sätze. Sample answers are provided.

> **BEISPIEL** das Trinkgeld / liegen / auf / der Tisch
> *Das Trinkgeld liegt auf dem Tisch.*

1. der Pizzaservice / bringen / die Pizza / an / die Haustür
   Der Pizzaservice bringt die Pizza an die Haustür.
2. die Großmutter / stellen / Teller und Gläser / auf / der Tisch
   Die Großmutter stellt Teller und Gläser auf den Tisch.
3. die Kinder / sitzen / zwischen / die Eltern
   Die Kinder sitzen zwischen den Eltern.
4. die kleine Lisa / setzen / ihre neue Barbie / neben / ihr großer Bruder
   Die kleine Lisa setzt ihre neue Barbie neben ihren großen Bruder.
5. die leckere Pizza / sein / schon / auf / der Tisch
   Die leckere Pizza ist schon auf dem Tisch.
6. eine kleine Maus / laufen / über / die Teller
   Eine kleine Maus ist über die Teller gelaufen.
7. der Vater / bringen / schnell / die Katze / in / das Zimmer
   Der Vater hat schnell die Katze ins Zimmer gebracht.
8. was / finden / die Familie / später / unter / der Tisch
   Was hat die Familie später unter dem Tisch gefunden?

 Practice more at **vhlcentral.com.**

Kommunikation

4 **Auf und um den Campus** Beantworten Sie die Fragen von Ihrem Partner / Ihrer Partnerin. Answers will vary.

BEISPIEL

S1: Wohin hast du deinen Rucksack gelegt?
S2: Ich habe ihn unter den Tisch gelegt.

1. Wohin können wir zum Kaffee trinken gehen?
2. Wo lernen die Studenten Fremdsprachen?
3. Wohin gehen die Studenten zum Mittagessen?
4. Wo kann ich ein leckeres Eis kaufen?
5. Wohin sollen die Studenten ihre Autos stellen?
6. Wo wanderst du gern?

4 **Suggestion** Make sure partners take turns asking and answering questions.

5 **Wohin gehst du?** Sie wollen diese Aktivitäten machen. Fragen Sie die Studenten / die Studentinnen in Ihrer Gruppe, wohin Sie gehen müssen. Answers will vary.

BEISPIEL frühstücken

S1: Ich will frühstücken. Wohin muss ich gehen?
S2: Du musst in die Mensa gehen.
S3: Ja, in der Mensa kannst du frühstücken.

1. Deutsch lernen
2. Basketball spielen
3. ein Fußballspiel sehen
4. schwimmen

5. Lebensmittel kaufen
6. Bücher lesen
7. Gebäck kaufen
8. mit Freunden zum Essen ausgehen

6 **Hier auf dem Campus** Sarah ist neu an Ihrer Uni. Erfinden Sie mit Ihrem Partner / Ihrer Partnerin zusammen sechs Ratschläge (*pieces of advice*) für sie. Sie können auch andere Verben benutzen. Answers will vary.

BEISPIEL Die Mensa is nicht sehr gut. (essen)
    Iss nicht in der Mensa. Geh ins Café!

1. Das Café ist leider teuer. (bestellen)
2. Dein Zimmer ist sehr warm. (öffnen)
3. Der Deutschkurs ist nicht einfach. (lernen)

4. Parken ist ein Problem. (stellen)
5. Der Park ist abends sehr dunkel. (laufen)

6 **Suggestion** Briefly review formation of the **du**-imperative for each verb.

7 **Was passiert alles im Restaurant?** Erfinden Sie eine Geschichte (*story*) mit den Studenten / die Studentinnen in Ihrer Gruppe über die Personen auf dem Bild. Benutzen Sie Präpositionen. Answers will vary.

BEISPIEL

S1: Die junge Frau ist mit ihrem Mann ins Restaurant gekommen.
S2: Sie sitzt am Tisch neben ihrem Mann.
S3: Ein Kellner stellt einen Teller auf den Tisch...

7 **Suggestion** Make sure students understand that they need to use a preposition in each sentence. You may wish to set a time limit and have groups compete to create the most correct sentences.

Wiederholung

1 Kleidung zu jedem Anlass
Beschreiben Sie mit einem Partner / einer Partnerin, was Tobias und Anna zu jedem (*each*) Anlass tragen. Answers will vary.

BEISPIEL

S1: Was trägt Tobias zur Geburtstagsfeier im Restaurant?
S2: Zur Geburtstagsfeier im Restaurant trägt er eine grüne Hose und ein oranges T-shirt. Und was trägt Anna?

> im Regen (*rain*)
> im Rockkonzert
> in den Bergen, zum Ski fahren
> ins Schwimmbad
> zur Geburtstagsfeier im Restaurant
> zur Sporthalle

2 Arbeitsblatt
Ihr Professor / Ihre Professorin gibt Ihnen ein Blatt mit einigen Fragen und Fakten. Finden Sie eine Person, die die Antwort weiß.

BEISPIEL

S1: Wie heißt der längste (*longest*) Fluss in Österreich?
S2: Ich weiß es nicht. / Ich weiß es. Das ist die Donau.

3 Diskutieren und kombinieren
Sie und ein Partner / eine Partnerin bekommen zwei verschiedene Blätter. Sehen Sie die Bilder an und antworten Sie auf die Fragen von Ihrem Partner / Ihrer Partnerin.

BEISPIEL

S1: Wohin ist Jasmin gegangen?
S2: Sie ist ins Stadion gegangen.
S1: Was macht sie in dem Stadion?
S2: Sie sieht ein Fußballspiel an.

4 Lenas Großeltern
Erzählen Sie mit einem Partner / einer Partnerin von Lenas Großeltern. Benutzen Sie die angegebenen Daten und erfinden Sie (*invent*) weitere (*additional*) Informationen.

BEISPIEL

S1: Lenas Großeltern sind 1967 auf die Uni gegangen.
S2: Im Deutschseminar hat die Oma den Opa gesehen.
S1: Sie hat gedacht: „Er ist der Mann für mich!"

1967	1973	1975	1976	2012
Die Oma sieht den Opa im Deutschseminar.	Oma und Opa machen den Abschluss.	Oma und Opa heiraten.	Die Frischvermählten reisen nach Indien.	Beide gehen in Rente.

5 Unsere Woche
Schreiben Sie auf, was Sie in der letzten Woche gemacht haben. Fragen Sie Ihren Partner / Ihre Partnerin, was er/sie gemacht hat.

BEISPIEL

S1: Am Montag bin ich in die Bibliothek gegangen. Und du, Monika, was hast du gemacht?
S2: Ich bin auf meinem Zimmer geblieben.

meine Woche	ich	mein Partner / meine Partnerin
Montag	Ich bin in die Bibliothek gegangen.	Monika ist auf ihrem Zimmer geblieben.
Dienstag		
Mittwoch		
Donnerstag		
Freitag		
Samstag		
Sonntag		

6 Kennst du diese Person?
Beschreiben Sie eine bekannte Person. Die Gruppe soll erraten, wer es ist.

BEISPIEL

S1: Er hat 2015 einen Oscar gewonnen. Kennt ihr ihn?
S2: Ja, ich kenne ihn. Das ist Eddie Redmayne.

7 **Im Kleidergeschäft** Spielen Sie mit einem Partner / einer Partnerin die Rollen von Verkäufer / Verkäuferin und Kunden / Kundin im Kleidergeschäft. Der Kunde / Die Kundin sucht Kleider für einen besonderen Anlass. Benutzen Sie Wörter aus der Liste.

BEISPIEL

S1: *Kann ich Ihnen helfen?*
S2: *Ja, bitte. Ich suche ein schönes Hemd für eine Party.*

danken	kaufen
glauben	kennen
helfen	passen

8 **Das Klassenzimmer** Beschreiben Sie, wo die Gegenstände (*objects*) und Personen in Ihrem Klassenzimmer sind.

BEISPIEL

S1: *Vor der Tafel steht der Professor.*
S2: *Unter dem Tisch...*

Mein Wör|ter|buch

Schreiben Sie noch fünf weitere Wörter in Ihr persönliches Wörterbuch zu den Themen **Feste feiern** und **Kleidung**.

das Bekleidungsgeschäft, -e

Übersetzung
clothing store

Wortart
ein Substantiv

Gebrauch
Der Verkäufer im Bekleidungsgeschäft hat mir eine neue Bluse verkauft.

Synonyme
der Klamottenladen

Antonyme
—

 **Vocabulary tools**

Weiter geht's

Panorama Interactive Map

Bayern

connections cultures NATIONAL STANDARDS

Bayern in Zahlen

▶ **Fläche:** *70.549 km² (größtes deutsches Bundesland)*

▶ **Bevölkerung:** *12,4 Millionen Menschen (zweite Stelle°
hinter Nordrhein-Westfalen)*

▶ **Religion:** *römisch-katholisch 67,2 %, evangelisch-
lutherisch 24,1%*

▶ **Städte:** *München (1,3 Mio. Einwohner), Nürnberg
(503.500), Augsburg (263.600), Würzburg (133.100)
und Regensburg (134.600)*

▶ **Berge:** *die Zugspitze (2.962 m) (höchster Berg
Deutschlands), Hochfrottspitze (2.649 m), Großer
Arber (1.456 m)*

▶ **Niedrigster Punkt:** *Kahl am Main (107 m)*

▶ **Flüsse:** *die Donau, der Inn*

▶ **Wichtige Industriezweige:** *Automobil, IT, Medien und
Verlage°, Tourismus*

▶ **Touristenattraktionen:** *Befreiungshalle (Kelheim),
Fuggerei (Augsburg), Marienplatz (München),
Schloss Neuschwanstein (Füssen), Steinerne Brücke
(Regensburg), Walhalla (Donaustauf)
Touristen können in Städten wie München, Augsburg
und Regensburg viel Kultur genießen. In den Alpen
oder dem Bayerischen Wald können sie Berg- und
Wintersport treiben. Wirtschaftlich entwickelt sich°
Bayern in den letzten Jahrzehnten von einem Agrar-
zu einem Technologieland.*

QUELLE: Bayerisches Landesportal

Berühmte Bayern

▶ **Adam Ries,** *Mathematiker (1492/93–1559)*

▶ **Levi Strauss,** *Erfinder° der Jeans (1829–1902)*

▶ **Elizabeth „Sisi",** *Kaiserin° von Österreich und
Ungarn (1837–1898)*

▶ **Ludwig II.,** *König von Bayern (1845–1886)*

▶ **Lena Christ,** *Autorin (1881–1920)*

▶ **Franz Josef Strauß,** *Politiker (1915–1988)*

▶ **Dirk Nowitzki,** *Basketballspieler (1978–)*

▶ **Magdalena Neuner,** *Biathletin (1987–)*

Stelle *position* **Verlage** *publishing companies* **entwickelt
sich** *evolves* **Erfinder** *inventor* **Kaiserin** *empress* **Weltkulturerbe** *World
Heritage Site* **herrscht** *exists* **Dialektpfleger** *dialect conservator*
Ortseingängen *city limit* **Verbotsschilder** *ban signs*

Suggestion Tell students that in many
regions of Germany, only the older generation
still speaks the dialect and many dialects
are dying out. In Bavaria, however, the
dialect is still alive and well, and it is closely
intertwined with the Bavarian identity.

HESSEN

SACHSEN

**Steinerne Brücke in Regensburg,
ein UNESCO-Weltkulturerbe°**

Im Bayerischen Wald

Main

Bayreuth

Würzburg

Nürnberg

BAYERN

NATIONALPARK
BAYERISCHER
WALD

Regensburg

Ingolstadt

Straubing

BAYERISCHER WALD

BADEN-
WÜRTTEMBERG

Donau

Isar

Passau

Augsburg

München

Inn

Ammersee

Starnberger See

Chiemsee

Bodensee

Garmisch-
Partenkirchen

NATIONALPARK
BERCHTESGADEN

Zugspitze ▲

— Landesgrenzen
● Stadt
◉ Landeshauptstadt

0 — 25 Meilen
0 — 25 Kilometer

Das Alte Rathaus, München

Unglaublich, aber wahr!

„Auf Wiedersehen" heißt im bayerischen Dialekt
„Servus". In Norddeutschland kann man „Tschüss"
(oder „Tschüß") sagen. In dem bayerischen Dorf
Gotzing herrscht° ein Tschüss-Verbot oder eine
„Tschüss-freie Zone". Hans Triebel, ein
Dialektpfleger°, installiert deshalb an den
Ortseingängen° „Tschüss"-Verbotsschilder°.

Expansion Ask students if they think the **Verbot** rule will work, and whether or not they agree
with imposing that kind of rule. Teach students a few phrases of the Bavarian dialect, such as:
I mog di (Ich mag dich), a Gaudi (ein Riesenspass), and **Schleich di (Hau ab).**

"Tschüß"
freie
Zone

Suggestion Before they read the **Kunst** article, play students the beginning of **Ritt der Walküren**. Ask them if they like it, if they've heard it before, and who composed it. Have them find Bayreuth on the map.

Kunst

Bayreuther Festspiele

Die Bayreuther Festspiele heißen auch Richard-Wagner-Festspiele. Sie finden jedes Jahr in der Stadt Bayreuth im Festspielhaus auf dem Grünen Hügel statt. Die Werke von Richard Wagner, einem berühmten deutschen Komponisten°, kann man während dieses weltberühmten Events seit 1876 sehen. Bei den ersten Festspielen inszeniert Richard Wagner seine Oper° „Der Ring des Nibelungen". Jedes Jahr besuchen 58.000 Zuschauer eine von dreißig Aufführungen° in Bayreuth. Allerdings versuchen° jedes Jahr 500.000 Menschen Karten zu kaufen. Deshalb dauert es bis zu zehn Jahre, bis man eine Karte bekommt.

Städte

Die sieben Hügel° von Bamberg

Bamberg ist eine Stadt in Franken, einer Region in Bayern. Seit 1993 ist sie ein UNESCO-Weltkulturerbe wegen des größten unversehrt erhaltenen° historischen Stadtzentrums in Deutschland. Genauso wie° Rom ist Bamberg auf sieben Hügeln gebaut. Deshalb trägt es auch den Namen „das Fränkische Rom". Die sieben Hügel Bambergs sind der Altenburger Berg, der Domberg, der Michaelsberg, der Abtsberg, der Jakobsberg, der Kaulberg und der Stephansberg. Auf dem Domberg kann man den mächtigen°, viertürmigen Dom° aus dem 13. Jahrhundert° finden.

Industrie

Audi

Suggestion Ask students which other German car brands they are familiar with.

Die Autofirma Audi hat ihren Hauptsitz° in Ingolstadt, Oberbayern. Neben VW, Porsche, BMW und Opel ist Audi einer der wichtigsten Autoproduzenten Deutschlands. Audi baut besonders sportliche Autos. Die Audi-Quattro-Modelle zum Beispiel gibt es seit 1980. Diese Modelle haben permanenten Vierradantrieb°. Zwischen 2000 und 2014 haben Audis das Autosport Rennen dreizehn Mal° gewonnen. Im Jahr 2013 arbeiten 67.000 Mitarbeiter bei Audi. Im gleichen Jahr macht die Firma 49 Milliarden € Umsatz° und baut 1,5 Millionen Autos.

Suggestion Tell students that because of "Mad King Ludwig's" extravagant building projects, he ended his life deeply in debt.

Architektur

Die Schlösser° von Ludwig II.

Ludwig II. ist der bekannteste König Bayerns. Er ist in erster Linie für seine Schlösser weltberühmt. Neben dem bekanntesten Schloss, Schloss Neuschwanstein, ist er auch für das Königshaus am Schachen und Schloss Linderhof verantwortlich°. Auf der Herreninsel im Chiemsee steht der Anfang von Schloss Herrenchiemsee. Dieses Schloss ist aber nicht fertig gebaut. Ludwigs Schlossbauten sind wegen neuer Technologien wichtig°: Stahlbau° und elektrisches Licht° sind integriert. Die Schlösser sind heute die bedeutendsten touristischen Attraktionen Bayerns.

⬧ IM INTERNET

1. Wie viele Touristen besuchen jedes Jahr die Schlösser Ludwigs II.? Wo sind die Schlösser?

2. Was bedeutet der Name *Audi*? Warum gibt es vier Ringe im Unternehmenslogo (*company logo*) von Audi?

Find out more at **vhlcentral.com**.

Komponisten *composer* **Oper** *opera* **Aufführungen** *performances* **versuchen** *try* **Hügel** *hills* **unversehrt erhaltenen** *preserved undamaged* **Genauso wie** *Just like* **mächtigen** *mighty* **viertürmigen Dom** *cathedral with four towers* **Jahrhundert** *century* **Hauptsitz** *headquarters* **Vierradantrieb** *four-wheel drive* **Mal** *times* **Umsatz** *sales* **Schlösser** *castles* **verantwortlich** *responsible* **wichtig** *important* **Stahlbau** *steel construction* **Licht** *light*

⬧ Was haben Sie gelernt? Ergänzen Sie die Sätze.

1. „Auf Wiedersehen" heißt im bayerischen Dialekt „___Servus___".

2. In Gotzing, einem Dorf in Bayern, darf man nicht ___Tschüss/Tschüß___ sagen.

3. Bei den ersten Bayreuther Festspielen inszeniert ___Richard Wagner___ seine Oper „Der Ring des Nibelungen".

4. Jedes Jahr versuchen ___500.000___ Menschen, Karten für die Bayreuther Festspiele zu kaufen.

5. Seit ___1993___ ist Bamberg ein UNESCO-Weltkulturerbe.

6. Genauso wie Rom ist Bamberg auf ___sieben___ Hügeln gebaut.

7. Der Hauptsitz der Firma Audi ist in ___Ingolstadt___.

8. Audis haben ___dreizehn Mal___ das Rennen „24 Stunden von Le Mans" gewonnen.

9. Das bekannteste Schloss von König Ludwig II. ist ___Schloss Neuschwanstein___.

10. Ludwigs Schlossbauten integrieren neue Technologien wie Stahlbau und ___elektrisches Licht___.

⬧ Practice more at **vhlcentral.com**.

Lesen Audio: Reading

Vor dem Lesen

Strategien
Skimming Skimming involves quickly reading through a document to absorb its general meaning. This allows you to understand the main ideas without having to read word for word. When you skim a text, look at its title and subtitles and read the first sentence of each paragraph.

Untersuchen Sie den Text Lesen Sie den Text schnell. Was ist der Titel des Texts? Wie viele Teile hat der Text? Wie heißen die Teile? Sehen Sie sich jetzt die Fotos an. Was ist das Thema des Texts?

Lehnwörter 👥 Sehen Sie sich mit einem Partner / einer Partnerin den Text an und machen Sie eine Liste mit englischen Lehnwörtern (*loanwords*) und Kognaten. Sample answers are provided.
Trend, Internet, Web, traditionell, Millionen, Accessoires, hier, Alternative, Probleme, Internetpräsenz, coole

Suchen 👥 Sehen Sie sich mit einem Partner / einer Partnerin den Text an. Stehen die Informationen im Text oder nicht? Markieren Sie **ja** oder **nein**.

	ja	nein
1. wo Deutsche Kleider kaufen	☑	☐
2. das Internet	☑	☐
3. Modenschauen	☐	☑
4. Designer	☐	☑
5. Warenhäuser	☑	☐
6. Boutiquen	☐	☑
7. Modeketten	☑	☐
8. Flohmärkte	☑	☐

Deutschland heute

Hauptseite   Politik   Wirtschaft

WO KAUFEN DEUTSCHE HEUTE IHRE KLEIDUNG?

In den letzten Jahren gibt es einen neuen Trend: Deutsche kaufen ihre Kleider immer öfter im Internet. Neben dem Web besuchen Deutsche aber auch weiterhin° traditionelle Geschäfte wie Warenhäuser° und Kleidergeschäfte. Nur noch wenige° Deutsche finden ihre Kleidung auf Flohmärkten°.

INTERNET, DAS GROSSE GESCHÄFT

Im Jahr 2014 sind 51 Millionen Deutsche online shoppen gegangen. Mehr als 65 Prozent dieser Internetkäufer haben Bekleidung und Accessoires im Web gekauft. Vor allem Frauen kaufen hier gerne ein; im Jahr 2013 haben mehr als siebzig Prozent aller Frauen Kleidung oder Sportartikel im Internet gekauft. Bei den Männern sind es fast sechzig Prozent.

WARENHÄUSER WERDEN IMMER WENIGER

Warenhäuser wie Karstadt und Galeria Kaufhof sind immer noch eine Alternative für den Kleiderkauf. In den letzten Jahren haben Warenhäuser aber immer größere wirtschaftliche Probleme und viele Warenhäuser schließen°. Zwischen 2009 und 2015 hat Kaufhof mehr als zehn Warenhäuser in Deutschland geschlossen und dieser Trend geht weiter°.

Kultur   Sport   Gesundheit

MODEKETTEN° HABEN ERFOLG°

Kleidergeschäfte wie H&M,
Zara, Esprit und Orsay kann
man heute in allen großen
deutschen Städten finden.
Diese Ketten sind bei jungen
Menschen besonders beliebt.
H&M ist der Marktführer°
in Deutschland. Alle
Modeketten haben immer
mehr Internetpräsenz.

AUF DEM FLOHMARKT

Es gibt immer noch eine
kleine Gruppe Deutscher,
die am Samstagmorgen früh
aufsteht°, um Flohmärkte zu
besuchen. Hier kann man
unter anderem gebrauchte°
Kleidung günstig kaufen.
Es gibt sie in jeder Stadt
besonders im Sommer. Vor
allem coole Klamotten°
aus den 60er und 70er Jahren
findet man hier für wenig Geld.

weiterhin *still* **Warenhäuser** *department stores* **wenige** *few*
Flohmärkten *flea markets* **schließen** *close* **geht weiter** *continues*
Modeketten *Fashion chains* **Erfolg** *success* **Marktführer** *market leader*
gemeinsam *in common* **aufsteht** *gets up* **gebrauchte** *used*
Klamotten *clothes (colloquial)*

Nach dem Lesen

Was fehlt? Ergänzen Sie die Sätze.

1. Deutsche kaufen Kleider vor allem <u>im Internet</u>, in
   Warenhäusern und in Kleidergeschäften.
2. <u>51 Millionen</u> Deutsche sind 2014 im Internet
   einkaufen gegangen.
3. Mehr <u>Frauen</u> als Männer kaufen Kleider
   im Internet.
4. Kaufhof hat mehr als <u>zehn</u> Warenhäuser
   geschlossen.
5. Der Marktführer der Modeketten in Deutschland
   ist <u>H&M</u>.
6. Flohmärkte gibt es besonders im <u>Sommer</u>.

Richtig oder falsch? Sind die Aussagen
richtig oder **falsch?** Korrigieren Sie die
falschen Sätze. Sample answers are provided.

	richtig	falsch
1. Deutsche kaufen Mode immer öfter im Internet.	☑	☐
2. Fast 60 Prozent aller Frauen haben Kleidung oder Sportartikel im Internet gekauft.	☐	☑

Fast 60 Prozent aller Männer haben Kleidung oder Sportartikel im Internet gekauft.

| 3. Karstadt und Galeria Kaufhof sind deutsche Warenhäuser. | ☑ | ☐ |
| 4. Junge Menschen kaufen nicht gern bei H&M ein. | ☐ | ☑ |

Diese Kette ist bei jungen Menschen beliebt.

| 5. Alle Modeketten verkaufen Kleidung auch im Internet. | ☑ | ☐ |
| 6. Auf dem Flohmarkt ist Kleidung teuer. | ☐ | ☑ |

Auf dem Flohmarkt ist Kleidung günstig.

Was tragen Sie? Besprechen Sie in einer
Gruppe: Was tragen Sie gern zu verschiedenen
Anlässen (in der Schule, bei einer Party, zu Hause)?
Wo kaufen Sie Ihre Kleider?

BEISPIEL

S1: *Zu Hause trage ich gerne Jeans und T-Shirts.*
S2: *Wo kaufst du deine Jeans?*
S1: *Meine Jeans kaufe ich im Internet.*
S3: *Ich trage im Sommer gern Kleider.*

Hören

Strategien

Listening for key words

By listening for key words (**Schlüsselwörter**) or phrases, you can identify the subject and main ideas of a conversation or speech, as well as some of the details.

 To practice this strategy, you will listen to a short radio spot. Jot down the key words that help you identify the subject of the radio spot and its main ideas.

Vorbereitung

Schauen Sie sich das Foto an. Wer ist in dem Foto? Wo sind sie? Was machen sie?

Zuhören

Hören Sie sich an, wie Marion Scholz ihre neue Mode beschreibt. Lesen Sie dann die Liste. Hören Sie sich die Beschreibung ein zweites Mal an. Welche Kleidungsartikel tragen die Models?

1. ___ Mütze	7. ___ Rock
2. ✓ Anzug	8. ✓ Gürtel
3. ✓ Hemd	9. ___ Bluse
4. ✓ Kleid	10. ✓ Hut
5. ___ Stiefel	11. ___ Badeanzug
6. ___ Jacke	12. ✓ Socken

Verständnis

 Was fehlt? Ergänzen Sie die Sätze mit den richtigen Informationen.

braun Handtasche	hellblau kurz	lange orange	Sandalen schwarz	Seide weiten

1. Robert trägt einen ___weiten___ Anzug.
2. Die Farbe des Anzugs ist ___hellblau___.
3. Die Sandalen sind ___schwarz___.
4. Elizabeth trägt ein Kleid aus ___Seide___.
5. Am Arm trägt sie eine ___Handtasche___.
6. Ihre ___Sandalen___ sind braun.
7. Carolas Hose und T-Shirt sind ___kurz___.
8. Ihre Hose und ihr T-Shirt sind ___orange___ und gelb.
9. Thomas trägt ___lange___ Socken zu seiner kurzen Hose.
10. Die Kleidung von Thomas ist ___braun___.

Ein Star, ein Fest Wählen Sie einen Star und einen besonderen Anlass. Was trägt der Star zu diesem Anlass? Beschreiben Sie den Star einem Partner / einer Partnerin.

Expansion Show students pictures of celebrities at a **Preisverleihung** such as the Grammy Awards. Have students describe what the celebrities are wearing and then have them vote on the best and worst outfits.

Schreiben

Strategien

Using a dictionary

The dictionary is a useful tool that can provide valuable information about vocabulary. However, in order to use the dictionary correctly, you must understand the elements of each entry.

If you glance at an English-German dictionary, you will notice that its format is similar to that of an English dictionary. Most words are listed with several different definitions, organized by part of speech. The most frequently used meanings are usually listed first.

To find the best word for your needs, refer to the abbreviations and explanatory notes that appear next to each entry. For example, imagine that you are writing about fashion. You want to write *The man is wearing a suit*, but you don't know the German word for *suit*. In the dictionary, you might find an entry like this one:

> **suit** *n.* 1. der Anzug, Anzüge; (*woman's*) das Kostüm, -e 2. der Prozess, -e (*Jur*); 3. die Farbe, -n (*Cards*)

The abbreviation key at the front of the dictionary says that *n.* corresponds to **Substantiv** (*noun*). The second translation is **der Prozess** followed by the abbreviation *Jur*, indicating that it's a law term, and thus that **der Prozess** is a *law suit*. The third word is **die Farbe**, followed by the word *Cards*, indicating that **die Farbe** is a *suit* in a card game. Since **der Anzug** is listed first, you can assume that this is the main translation of the word. The first definition also specifies the difference between a suit for a man, **der Anzug**, and a suit for a woman, **das Kostüm**. Since the other two meanings do not apply to clothing, these details tell you that **der Anzug** is the best choice for your needs.

Thema

Beschreiben Sie

Sehen Sie sich das Bild an. Beschreiben Sie dann in einem Absatz (*paragraph*) den Mann oder die Frau für einen Artikel in einem Modejournal.

Beschreiben Sie das Aussehen (*look*) im Detail. Aus welchem Material sind die Kleider? Wie sind die Kleider geschnitten (*cut*)? Welche Muster (*patterns*) und Farben haben die Kleider? Wo kann man diese Kleider tragen? Sagen Sie auch etwas über den Designer und wo man die Kleider kaufen kann. Am Ende schreiben Sie Ihre Meinung über die Kleidung. Geben Sie dem Artikel einen Titel.

Bevor Sie den Artikel schreiben, machen Sie sich Notizen. Suchen Sie Vokabeln, die Sie brauchen, in einem Wörterbuch.

- Material
- Schnitt
- Muster
- Farben
- Wo kann man es tragen?
- Wo kann man es kaufen?

Neueste Mode

Lederjacken sind wieder in. Dieser Mann trägt eine schwarze Lederjacke mit einem weißen Trägerhemd. Der Schnitt ist…

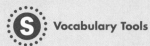 **Vocabulary Tools**

Feste

der Ballon, -s	balloon
der Feiertag, -e	holiday
der Gast, ⸚e	guest
der Gastgeber, - / die Gastgeberin, -nen	host / hostess
das Geschenk, -e	gift
die Karte, -n	card
die Party, -s	party
die Überraschung, -en	surprise
das Zimmer, -	room
anstoßen (stößt... an)	to toast
bekommen	to receive
einladen (lädt... ein)	to invite
feiern	to celebrate
eine Party geben	to throw a party
(keinen) Spaß haben	(not) to have fun
schenken	to give (a gift)
überraschen	to surprise
Herzlichen Glückwunsch!	Congratulations!

Essen und Trinken

das Eis	ice cream
der Eiswürfel, -	ice cube
das Gebäck	pastries; baked goods
der Keks, -e	cookie
der Sekt	champagne
die Süßigkeiten (pl.)	candy
die Torte, -n	cake

besondere Anlässe

die Ehe, -n	marriage
der / die Frischvermählte, -n	newlywed
die Geburt, -en	birth
der Geburtstag, -e	birthday
die Hochzeit, -en	wedding
der Jahrestag, -e	anniversary
(das) Silvester	New Year's Eve
(das) Weihnachten	Christmas
in Rente gehen	to retire
einen Abschluss machen	to graduate

Ausdrücke

die Freundschaft, -en	friendship
das Glück	happiness
der Kuss, ⸚e	kiss
die Liebe	love

Kleidung

der Anzug, ⸚e	suit
der Badeanzug, ⸚e	bathing suit
die Bluse, -n	blouse
die Brille, -n	glasses
der Gürtel, -	belt
die Halskette, -n	necklace
der Handschuh, -e	glove
die Handtasche, -n	purse
das Hemd, -en	shirt
die Hose, -n	pants
die kurze Hose (pl. die kurzen Hosen)	shorts
der Hut, ⸚e	hat
die Jacke, -n	jacket
die Jeans, -	jeans
das Kleid, -er	dress
die Krawatte, -n	tie
der Mantel, ⸚	coat
die Mütze, -n	cap
der Pullover, -	sweater
der Rock, ⸚e	skirt
der Schal, -s	scarf
der Schuh, -e	shoe
die Socke, -n	sock
die Sonnenbrille, -n	sunglasses
der Stiefel, -	boot
das Sweatshirt, -s	sweatshirt
das Trägerhemd, -en	tank top
das T-Shirt, -s	T-shirt
der Turnschuh, -e	sneakers
die Unterwäsche	underwear

Einkaufen

die Baumwolle	cotton
die Farbe, -n	color
die Kleidergröße, -n	size
der Kunde, -n / die Kundin, -nen	customer
das Leder	leather
die Seide	silk
der Verkäufer, - / die Verkäuferin, -nen	salesperson
die Wolle	wool
im Angebot	on sale
günstig	inexpensive
einfarbig	solid colored
eng	tight
gestreift	striped
kurzärmlig	short-sleeved
langärmlig	long-sleeved
teuer	expensive
weit	loose; big
anziehen (zieht... an)	to put on
tragen (trägt)	to wear

Farben

blau	blue
braun	brown
gelb	yellow
grau	gray
grün	green
lila	purple
orange	orange
rosa	pink
rot	red
schwarz	black
weiß	white

Past participles with *haben*	See pp. 194–195.
Accusative pronouns	See p. 198.
Dative pronouns	See p. 200.
Past participles with *sein*	See p. 213.
Wissen and *kennen*	See p. 216.
Two-way prepositions	See p. 218.

Ressourcen

vhlcentral.com

Trautes Heim

Suggestion Ask students: Wo ist George? Was kocht er?

Communicative Goals

You will learn how to:

- describe your home
- talk about living arrangements

Wortschatz

Zimmer	rooms
das Arbeitszimmer, -	home office
der Dachboden, ⸚	attic
das Erdgeschoss, -e	ground floor
das Esszimmer, -	dining room
der Flur, -e	hall
die Küche, -n	kitchen
der erste/zweite Stock	second/third floor
Möbel	*furniture*
das Bild, -er	picture
das Möbelstück, -e	piece of furniture
der Nachttisch, -e	night table
der Schrank, ⸚e	cabinet; closet
die Schublade, -n	drawer
die Treppe, -n	stairway
Orte	*places*
das Haus, ⸚er	house
das Wohnheim, -e	dorm
die Wohnung, -en	apartment
nach rechts/links	to the right/left
Ausdrücke	*expressions*
mieten	to rent
umziehen (zieht... um)	to move
wohnen	to live

ACHTUNG

Note that **mieten** means to rent *from* someone, while **vermieten** means to rent *to* someone. **Ich miete eine kleine Wohnung in der Stadt. Die Familie vermietet ein Zimmer in ihrem Haus.**

Expansion Have students play a memory game to internalize the new vocabulary. The first student starts with **In meiner Wohnung gibt es...** and names an item of furniture. The next student repeats the previous item(s) and adds one. If a student can't repeat the entire sequence, he or she is eliminated. Remind students to use the accusative with **Es gibt.**

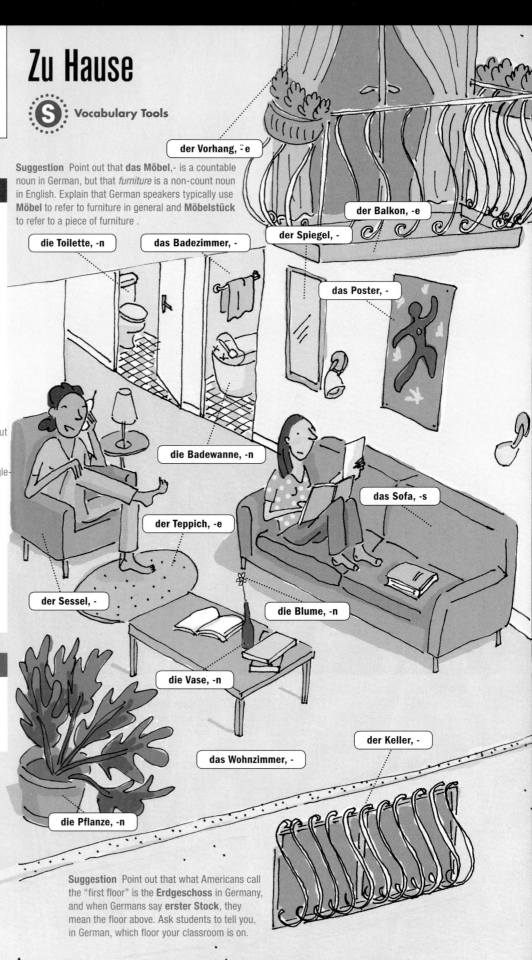

Zu Hause

S Vocabulary Tools

Suggestion Point out that **das Möbel,-** is a countable noun in German, but that *furniture* is a non-count noun in English. Explain that German speakers typically use **Möbel** to refer to furniture in general and **Möbelstück** to refer to a piece of furniture.

der Vorhang, ⸚e

der Balkon, -e

die Toilette, -n

das Badezimmer, -

der Spiegel, -

das Poster, -

Suggestion Point out that many Germans in big cities live in apartments, not single-family homes.

die Badewanne, -n

das Sofa, -s

der Teppich, -e

der Sessel, -

die Blume, -n

die Vase, -n

der Keller, -

das Wohnzimmer, -

die Pflanze, -n

Suggestion Point out that what Americans call the "first floor" is the **Erdgeschoss** in Germany, and when Germans say **erster Stock**, they mean the floor above. Ask students to tell you, in German, which floor your classroom is on.

Suggestion Make sure that students understand the difference between **der Stock** and **der Boden**. Point out that **der Dachboden** is a compound of **das Dach** (*roof*) and **der Boden**.

1 **Expansion** Give students a description of a mixed-up apartment and ask them to tell you where things ought to be. Ex.: **Mein Sofa ist in der Garage. Wo sollte es sein? Mein Bett ist in der Küche. Wo sollte es sein? Meine Bücher sind unter dem Bett. Wo sollten sie sein?**

Anwendung

das Bücherregal, -e

die Wand, ⸚e

die Lampe, -n

das Bett, -en

die Kommode, -n

das Schlafzimmer, -

der Boden, ⸚

die Garage, -n

Suggestion Ask students where they do various activities. Ex.: **Wo schläfst du? Wo isst du? Wo kochst du?**

Expansion Have students create their own **wo**-question using items from the lesson vocabulary. Remind students to use the dative with two-way prepositions since they will be describing location.

1 **Paare finden** Welche Objekte assoziieren Sie mit den Zimmern in einem Haus?

_d_ 1. die Küche		a. das Bücherregal
_b_ 2. das Wohnzimmer		b. das Sofa
_f_ 3. das Esszimmer		c. das Auto
_c_ 4. die Garage		d. die Lebensmittel
_h_ 5. das Badezimmer		e. die Kommode
_e_ 6. das Schlafzimmer		f. der Esstisch
_g_ 7. der Balkon		g. die Blumen
_a_ 8. das Arbeitszimmer		h. die Toilette

2 **Expansion** Have students compile a list of what they have, don't have, or would like to have in their rooms and share it with the class or a partner. Provide a model to demonstrate correct use of the accusative and of **kein**.

2 **Bilder beschriften** Wie heißen die verschiedenen Bereiche (*parts*) in einem Haus?

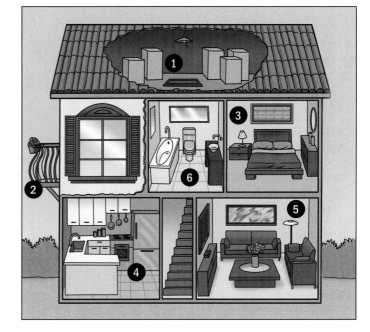

1. ____der Dachboden____   4. ____die Küche____
2. ____der Balkon____   5. ____das Wohnzimmer____
3. ____das Schlafzimmer____   6. ____das Badezimmer____

3 **Was ist richtig?** 🎧 Hören Sie die Definitionen und wählen Sie das Wort, das am besten passt.

1. Flur / (Küche)
2. Wand / (Vorhang)
3. (Badezimmer) / Wohnzimmer
4. (Garage) / Dachboden
5. Rucksack / (Vase)
6. (Bild) / Kommode
7. (Haus) / Esszimmer
8. Bücherregal / (Lampe)

3 **Expansion** Play a guessing game using vocabulary items not mentioned in the recording. Give students clues and have them guess which word you are thinking of. Ex.: **Ich denke an ein Möbelstück. Da schlafe ich. Was ist das? Das steht in meinem Wohnzimmer. Ich sitze darauf. Was ist das?**

 Practice more at **vhlcentral.com**.

Kommunikation

4 Wo ich wohne

Wo ich wohne Arbeiten Sie mit einem Partner / einer Partnerin. Benutzen Sie die Wörter aus den drei Spalten und beschreiben Sie Ihr Zimmer, Ihre Wohnung oder Ihr Haus. Answers will vary.

BEISPIEL

S1: *Meine Wohnung ist ziemlich groß und hat einen kleinen Balkon.*

S2: *Mein Zimmer ist klein. Aber alle meine Möbel sind neu.*

A	B	C
mein Haus mein Zimmer (im Wohnheim) meine Wohnung	ist (nicht) hat (kein)	Badezimmer Balkon Fenster Garage Küche Schlafzimmer Schreibtisch groß/klein alt/neu modern/unmodern

5 Expansion After students have put the dialogue in the correct order, have two volunteers read it aloud.

5 Janas Haus

Janas Haus Klara besucht Jana in ihrem neuen Haus. Bringen Sie den Dialog in eine logische Reihenfolge (*order*). Wenn Sie fertig sind, vergleichen Sie Ihr Haus oder Ihre Wohnung mit Janas Haus.

___4___ **JANA** Sechs Zimmer. Das hier ist das Wohnzimmer und dann hier links die Küche und das Esszimmer.

___1___ **KLARA** Jana, dein neues Haus ist wirklich schön.

___6___ **JANA** Ja, die Küche gefällt meinem Mann sehr gut. Er kocht so gern! So, und hier rechts siehst du den Flur zu den drei Schlafzimmern und den zwei Badezimmern. Es gibt nur den einen Stock.

___3___ **KLARA** Das stimmt. Wie viele Zimmer hat es?

___7___ **KLARA** Ihr braucht ja auch nicht noch mehr Zimmer. Also, ich muss sagen, du hast ein ganz tolles Haus gefunden.

___2___ **JANA** Danke schön. Es ist ziemlich groß. Die alte Wohnung in der Stadt war einfach zu klein.

___5___ **KLARA** Die Küche ist auch super. Da kann dein Mann leckeres Essen kochen.

6 Mein Zimmer

Mein Zimmer Beschreiben Sie zwei Mitstudenten Ihr Zimmer. Answers will vary.

BEISPIEL

S1: *In meinem Zimmer habe ich ein Bett und einen Schreibtisch.*

S2: *Ich habe auch ein Bett, aber ich habe keinen Schreibtisch.*

S3: *Ich habe in meinem Zimmer einen grünen Teppich...*

7 Diskutieren und kombinieren

Diskutieren und kombinieren Arbeiten Sie mit einem Partner / einer Partnerin. Ihr Professor / Ihre Professorin gibt Ihnen zwei verschiedene Blätter mit dem Grundriss (*floor plan*) von Ihrer neuen Wohnung. Sagen Sie Ihrem Partner / Ihrer Partnerin, was Sie alles mitgebracht haben. Er/Sie wird Ihnen sagen, in welche Zimmer Sie die Sachen stellen sollen. Answers will vary.

BEISPIEL

S1: *Ich habe Balkonpflanzen mitgebracht.*

S2: *Stell sie auf den Balkon. Er ist rechts von der Küche. Ich habe...*

7 Suggestion Remind students to use the accusative with two-way prepositions when they tell each other where to place an item.

7 Expansion Review the differences between **stellen**, **legen**, and **hängen**. Place a classroom eraser horizontally on the desk and say: **Ich lege den Schwamm auf den Tisch.** Then stand the eraser on one end and say: **Ich stelle den Schwamm auf den Tisch.** Finally, tape the **Schwamm** to the wall and say: **Ich hänge den Schwamm an die Wand.**

Aussprache und Rechtschreibung Audio

🎧 The letter combination *ch* (Part 2)

To pronounce the soft **ch** after the vowel sounds **i/ie**, **e**, **ä**, **ö**, **ü**, or **ei**, start by placing the tip of your tongue behind your lower teeth. Then pronounce the *h* sound while breathing out forcefully.

Chemie	**rechts**	**Teppich**	**Küche**	**leicht**

Use the same soft **ch** sound when pronouncing the **g** in the suffix **-ig** at the end of a word. However, when there is an adjective ending after the **-ig**, the **g** is pronounced like the hard *g* in the word *garden*. In the combination **-iglich**, the **g** is pronounced like the *k* in the word *kind*. The soft **ch** is also used in the suffix **-lich**, whether or not there is an ending after it.

dreckig	**schmutzig**	**billige**	**königlich**	**freundlichen**

When **ch** appears before an **s**, the letter combination is pronounced like the *x* in the word *fox*. Do not confuse **chs** with the combination **sch**, which is pronounced like the *sh* in the word *shade*.

sechs	**wachsen**	**schlafen**	**waschen**	**Dachs**

When **ch** appears at the beginning of loanwords, its pronunciation varies.

Charakter	**Chip**	**Chef**	**Charterflug**	**Chronik**

1 Aussprechen Wiederholen Sie die Wörter, die Sie hören.

1. Bücher
2. freundlich
3. China
4. zwanzig
5. braunhaarige
6. lediglich
7. höchste
8. Achsel
9. Ochse
10. Chaos
11. checken
12. Charme

2 Nachsprechen Wiederholen Sie die Sätze, die Sie hören.

1. Die königliche Köchin schläft wieder in der Küche.
2. Mein neugieriger Nachbar will täglich mit mir sprechen.
3. Den Rechtsanwalt finden wir freundlich und zuverlässig.
4. Der Chef schickt mich nächstes Jahr nach China.
5. Der Dachs hat einen schlechten Charakter.

2 Suggestion Have students take turns reading the sentences aloud. Explain the meaning of any unfamiliar words.

3 Sprichwörter Wiederholen Sie die Sprichwörter, die Sie hören.

Liebe deinen Nächsten wie dich selbst.[1]

Jedem Tierchen sein Pläsierchen.[2]

[1] Love thy neighbor as thyself.

[2] To each his/her own. (lit. For every creature its own pleasure.)

Fotoroman

Besuch von Max Video

Hans' kleiner Bruder Max kommt ihn in Berlin besuchen. Meline ist
froh, Max kennen zu lernen. Zu froh, in den Augen von Hans.

Vorbereitung Have students read the title
of the episode and discuss in pairs what they
expect to happen in the episode.

NATIONAL communication cultures STANDARDS

1

GEORGE Max!
MAX Hallo, George!
GEORGE Schön, dich wiederzusehen! Wie viele
Nächte schläfst du auf unserem Sofa?
MAX Zwei. Ich bin übers Wochenende in Berlin.
Doch bis Sonntagabend muss ich wieder in
Straubing sein.

2

HANS Warum lernst du eigentlich nicht an
deinem Schreibtisch in deinem Zimmer?
GEORGE Es ist bequemer im Wohnzimmer,
denn die Küche ist gleich nebenan. Und es
ist schön hell hier.
HANS Da ist was dran.
MAX Wir gehen in den Biergarten. Komm
doch mit.

Suggestion Explain to students
that **Servus!** means both *Hello!* and
Goodbye! in Bavaria and Austria.

3

MAX Wir bleiben bestimmt lange dort.
GEORGE Nach dieser Lektion komme
ich herunter.
HANS Alles klar! Okay! Servus!

MAX Das tut mir leid.
MELINE Es ist schon okay. Kein Problem.
HANS Meline, das ist mein kleiner Bruder Max.
MELINE Hallo.
MAX Wir gehen in den Biergarten. Komm doch
mit uns.
MELINE Ich muss nur noch schnell die
Lebensmittel in die Küche bringen.

4

5

MELINE Max, ich kann das Regalbrett
nicht erreichen. Kannst du mir das dort
oben hinstellen?
MAX Deine Wohnung gefällt mir.
MELINE Ja. Die Lampen und Vorhänge
gehören Sabite. Und die ganzen
Gemälde.

MAX Du bist aus Wien?
MELINE Ja. Hast du das an meinem
Akzent erkannt?
MAX Ja. Als Hans zu Weihnachten nach
Hause kam, sprach er übrigens von dir.
MELINE Wirklich? Was hat er gesagt?

6

1 **Wer ist das?** Welche Person(en) beschreiben die folgenden Sätze:
George, Hans, Max, Meline oder Sabite?

1. Er/Sie ist übers Wochenende in Berlin. Max
2. Er/Sie lernt im Wohnzimmer, denn die Küche ist gleich nebenan. George
3. Sie wollen in den Biergarten gehen. Hans und Max
4. Nach einer Lektion kommt er/sie herunter. George

5. Er/Sie muss Lebensmittel in die Küche bringen. Meline
6. Die Wohnung gefällt ihm/ihr. Max
7. Ihm/Ihr gehören die Vorhänge, die Lampen und die Gemälde. Sabite
8. Weihnachten sprach er/sie von Meline. Hans
9. Er/Sie war satt und konnte nicht schlafen. George
10. Er/Sie überlegt, ob (*whether*) Hans und Max wirklich Brüder sind. Meline

PERSONEN

 George   Hans   Meline   Max

7

GEORGE Wir hatten Heiligabend ein riesiges Essen.

HANS Es war drei Uhr früh, am Weihnachtsmorgen.

GEORGE Ich war ja noch total satt und konnte nicht einschlafen.

HANS Es war ja noch total dunkel im Haus.

8

GEORGE Ich ging den Gang hinunter und hörte ein Geräusch.

HANS Max, meine Familie und ich, wir schliefen in unseren Zimmern.

GEORGE Ich ging in die Küche, und am Herd stand ihr Großvater.

HANS Opa Otto bereitete die Weihnachtsgans zu. George überraschte ihn und... „Ja! Wo kommst du denn her?"

9

GEORGE Sie war köstlich! Wo ist Sabite heute Abend?

MELINE Mit Torsten weg.

GEORGE Sind sie immer noch zusammen?

MELINE Ja, aber es ist schwierig seit den Feiertagen.

10

MELINE Ich mag Torsten, aber man sagt an Silvester keine Verabredung ab.

HANS So wie Lorenzo?

MELINE Wer?

HANS Na, Lorenzo. Der Italiener.

MELINE Seid ihr wirklich Brüder?

Nützliche Ausdrücke

- **Doch bis Sonntagabend muss ich wieder in Straubing sein.**
  But by Sunday evening I have to be back in Straubing.

- **Da ist was dran.**
  You have a point there.

- **Servus!**
  So long!

- **Ich kann das Regalbrett nicht erreichen.**
  I can't reach the shelf.

- **Kannst du mir das dort oben hinstellen?**
  Can you put this up there for me?

- **das Gemälde**
  painting

- **Hast du das an meinem Akzent erkannt?**
  Could you tell from my accent?

- **riesig**   • **satt**
  huge   *full (of food)*

- **das Geräusch**   • **der Herd**
  noise   *stove*

- **Opa Otto bereitete die Weihnachtsgans zu.**
  Grandpa Otto was preparing the Christmas goose.

  6A.1
- **Als Hans zu Weihnachten nach Hause kam, sprach er übrigens von dir.**
  When Hans was home for Christmas, he talked about you, by the way.

  6A.2
- **Nach dieser Lektion komme ich herunter.**
  After this lesson, I'll come down.

  6A.3
- **Es ist bequemer im Wohnzimmer, denn die Küche ist gleich nebenan.**
  The living room is more convenient, because it's right next to the kitchen.

2 **Zum Besprechen** George trifft Opa Otto an Heiligabend in der Küche. Bereiten Sie mit einem Partner / einer Partnerin einen kurzen Dialog zwischen George und Opa Otto vor. Präsentieren Sie Ihren Dialog der Klasse. Answers will vary.

Suggestion After each pair has presented their role play, have the class vote on the most interesting, realistic, and convincing performances.

3 **Vertiefung** Suchen Sie im Internet Informationen über die Weihnachtsgans. Woher kommt diese Tradition? In welchen Ländern isst man Weihnachtsgans? Was isst man als Beilage? Schreiben Sie einen kurzen Absatz mit Ihren Ergebnissen. Answers will vary.

Fribourg ⓢ Reading

Suggestion Before students read the article, ask them **Welche Sprachen spricht man in der Schweiz?** Have students locate Fribourg on a map of Switzerland. Have them guess what languages are spoken there, based on its location.

> **TIPP**
>
> The abbreviation **St.** stands for **Sankt**, meaning *Saint*.

Die Architektur Fribourgs bietet° Beispiele vieler historischer Epochen. Die Altstadt im Zentrum ist eines der größten geschlossenen Ortsbilder° des mittelalterlichen° Europa. Die St.-Niklaus-Kathedrale, gebaut zwischen 1283 und 1490, ist das Symbol Fribourgs. Es ist ein Beispiel gotischer Architektur. Die Stadt hat über 200 gotische Gebäude. Den Renaissancestil kann man im Ratzéhof sehen, gebaut zwischen 1581 und 1585. Heute ist dieses Gebäude die Heimat° des Museums für Kunst und Geschichte. Neben den vielen alten Teilen der Stadt kann man auch neue Gebäude finden wie zum Beispiel die Universität (1889) oder die Villenviertel° im Gembachquartier. Viele Villen sind Jugendstil-Bauten°. Bekannt sind in Fribourg auch die alten Brücken° und seine zwölf historischen Brunnen°.

FRIBOURG LIEGT GENAU AN DER Grenze° zwischen deutschsprachiger und französischsprachiger Schweiz. Die Saane fließt° durch die Stadt und trennt sie in zwei Teile°. Im westlichen Teil spricht man Französisch und im östlichen Teil Deutsch. Etwa 63% der Bevölkerung spricht Französisch und 21% spricht Deutsch. Studenten können hier in beiden Sprachen studieren und machen einen großen Teil der über 40.000 Einwohner aus. Die Stadt ist sehr alt und existiert bereits seit 1157. Damals war Fribourg noch deutschsprachig.

Wohnen in der Schweiz
Wohnungen: 4,2 Millionen (2013)
durchschnittliche° Größe: 99 m²
durchschnittlicher Kaufpreis für Wohnungen
• **Bern:** SFr (Schweizer Franken) 750.000
• **Zürich:** SFr 1,4 Millionen
• **durchschnittlicher Mietpreis:** SFr 1.332
• **Mieteranteil°:** 55,8%
QUELLEN: Schweizerisches Bundesamt für Statistik

Expansion Give students numbers and ask them to explain what each number has to do with Fribourg. Ex.: **21%, 1157, 12,** etc.

Grenze *border* **fließt** *flows* **Teile** *parts* **bietet** *offers* **geschlossenen Ortsbilder** *complete townscapes* **mittelalterlichen** *medieval* **Heimat** *home* **Villenviertel** *mansion district* **Jugendstil-Bauten** *Art Nouveau buildings* **Brücken** *bridges* **Brunnen** *wells* **durchschnittliche** *average* **Mieteranteil** *percentage of renters*

Expansion Have students take turns reading aloud from the article. Ask questions to check comprehension and keep the class engaged. Ex.: **Wie heißt der Fluss von Fribourg? Wo spricht man Französisch? Wie viel Prozent der Bevölkerung spricht Französisch?**

ÜBUNGEN

1 Richtig oder falsch? Sind die Aussagen richtig oder falsch? Korrigieren Sie die falschen Aussagen. Answers will vary.

1. Fribourg liegt an der Grenze zwischen der Schweiz und Frankreich.
   Falsch. Fribourg liegt an der Grenze zwischen deutschsprachiger und französischsprachiger Schweiz.
2. Mehr als 60% der Bevölkerung spricht Französisch. Richtig.
3. In Fribourg kann man auf Deutsch oder Französisch studieren. Richtig.
4. Das Symbol Fribourgs ist der Ratzéhof.
   Falsch. Das Symbol Fribourgs ist die St. Niklaus Kathedrale.
5. Der Ratzéhof ist im gotischen Stil gebaut.
   Falsch. Der Ratzéhof ist im Renaissancestil gebaut.
6. Brücken gibt es in Fribourg nicht.
   Falsch. Die alten Brücken in Fribourg sind bekannt.
7. Eine durchschnittliche Wohnung in Zürich kostet SFr 750.000.
   Falsch. Eine durchschnittliche Wohnung in Zürich kostet SFr 1,4 Millionen.
8. Über 50% der Schweizer mieten eine Wohnung. Richtig.

Expansion Have students use an online currency converter to find out how Swiss apartment prices compare to prices in other countries.

Suggestion Remind students that Switzerland is a neutral country, has not joined the EU, and has also kept its own currency, **der Schweizer Franken.**

ⓢ Practice more at **vhlcentral.com.**

DEUTSCH IM ALLTAG

Studentenzimmer

der	
Gemeinschaftsraum	common room
die Kaution	security deposit
die Miete	rent
die Nebenkosten	additional charges
die Wohngemeinschaft (WG)	apartment share
(un)möbliert	(un)furnished
Zimmer frei	vacancy

DIE DEUTSCHSPRACHIGE WELT

Chalets

Chalets sind ein Häusertyp. Es ist ursprünglich ein französisches Wort und bedeutet Sennhütte°. Man kann diese Häuser im Alpenbereich allgemein, insbesondere° aber in der Schweiz finden. Früher haben Hirten° in Chalets gewohnt. Traditionell sind sie aus Holz° gebaut. In den Schweizer Gemeinden° Lenk, Grindelwald, Saanen und Zermatt darf man nur Chalets bauen. Moderne Architektur will man so in den Alpen verhindern°. Heute nennt man oft auch Ferienhäuser° aus Holz Chalets. Sie müssen nicht in einer Bergregion stehen, und man findet sie überall auf der Welt.

Sennhütte herdsman's hut **insbesondere** especially
Hirten shepherds **Holz** wood **Gemeinden** townships
verhindern prevent **Ferienhäuser** vacation homes

PORTRÄT

César Ritz

3 Expansion For homework, have students draw their dream apartments and prepare a written description to present in class.

César Ritz war ein berühmter Schweizer Hotelier. Er wurde am 23. Februar 1850 als dreizehntes Kind einer armen Familie in Niederwald im Goms geboren. Die Schule beendete er nicht. Anfangs arbeitete er als Schuhputzer°, Träger° und Kellner in verschiedenen Hotels. Im Rigi-Kulm-Hotel in der Schweiz wurde er schließlich° Hoteldirektor. 1888 heiratete er die Hoteliersstochter Marie-Louise Beck. Er hatte großen Erfolg als Direktor und eröffnete° 1898 das Grandhotel Le Ritz in Paris, 1906 das Hotel Ritz in London und 1910 das Hotel Ritz in Madrid. Alle Hotels gelten° als absolute Luxushotels. Wegen seines großen Erfolgs nannte König Edward VII. César Ritz den „König der Hoteliers und Hotelier der Könige".

Schuhputzer shoeshine boy **Träger** porter **schließlich** eventually **eröffnete** opened **gelten** count

WOHNUNG ZU VERMIETEN

◉⟲ IM INTERNET

Finden Sie ein Zimmer zum Mieten in einer deutschsprachigen Stadt. Wie groß ist es? Wie viel kostet es? Was ist im Preis inbegriffen (*included*)?

Find out more at **vhlcentral.com**.

3 Suggestion Provide a simple model for this activity describing your own dream apartment. Then ask students about their own preferences. Ex.: **Möchten Sie lieber eine Wohnung mit einem Schwimmbad oder mit einem Atelier? Möchten Sie lieber ein Chalet in den Alpen oder eine Villa am Strand? Möchten Sie lieber ein Schloss in der Schweiz oder eine große Wohnung in Manhattan?**

2 **Was fehlt?** Ergänzen Sie die Sätze.

1. Chalets sind ein Schweizer ___Häusertyp___.
2. In den Schweizer Alpen sind Chalets aus ___Holz___ gebaut.
3. In Lenk und Grindelwald, darf man nur ___Chalets___ bauen.
4. César Ritz ist ein berühmter ___Schweizer___ Hotelier.
5. Er ist das ___dreizehnte___ Kind seiner Eltern.
6. Die Ritz-Hotels in Paris und London sind absolute ___Luxushotels___.

3 **Eine gute Wohnung** Diskutieren Sie mit einem Partner / einer Partnerin über die Wohnung, in der Sie wohnen möchten. Reden Sie über Größe, Preis, und Lage (*location*).

Suggestion Before students read the article on César Ritz, preview the relevant vocabulary and concepts. Show the class a picture of a Swiss **Schule**, a **Schuhputzer**, and a fancy hotel. While showing the pictures say: **Dieser Mann kommt aus einer armen Familie. Er beendet die Schule nicht. Er arbeitet als Schuhputzer. Später eröffnet er ein neues großes Hotel.**, etc.

Ressourcen

vhlcentral.com

6A.1

The *Präteritum*  Presentation

QUERVERWEIS

The **Präteritum** appears most often in writing. You will learn more about the uses of the **Präteritum** in **6B.1**.

ACHTUNG

The **ich** form and the **er/sie/es** form are always identical in the **Präteritum**.

Suggestion Tell students that the **Präteritum** is also frequently called the "simple past". Point out that whereas the perfect tense has two parts --the auxiliary and the participle--, the **Präteritum** only has one.

Suggestion Give students a series of weak verbs and have them guess the simple past forms, based on the pattern shown. Ex: **tanzen, machen, leben, kaufen, mieten, vermieten.**

QUERVERWEIS

See **4A.1** to review the uses of **mögen**.

See **5A.1** to review mixed verbs in the **Perfekt**.

Suggestion Emphasize to students that the past tense forms of mixed and strong verbs must be memorized on a verb-by-verb basis.

Startblock In **5A.1**, you learned to use the **Perfekt** to talk about past events. Another tense, the **Präteritum**, is also used to refer to past events.

- To form the **Präteritum** of weak verbs, add **-te**, **-test**, **-ten**, or **-tet** to the infinitive stem. Add an **-e** before these endings if the stem ends in **-d**, **-t**, or a consonant cluster.

Präteritum of weak verbs			
	sagen	**wohnen**	**arbeiten**
ich	sag**te**	wohn**te**	arbeite**te**
du	sag**test**	wohn**test**	arbeite**test**
er/sie/es	sag**te**	wohn**te**	arbeite**te**
wir	sag**ten**	wohn**ten**	arbeite**ten**
ihr	sag**tet**	wohn**tet**	arbeite**tet**
Sie/sie	sag**ten**	wohn**ten**	arbeite**ten**

Die Kinder **spielten** in ihren Zimmern.
*The children **played** in their rooms.*

Ich **mietete** eine kleine Wohnung.
*I **rented** a small apartment.*

- Modal verbs have the same endings as weak verbs in the **Präteritum**. If the modal stem has an **Umlaut**, the **Umlaut** is dropped.

sollen		**dürfen**	
ich soll**te**	wir soll**ten**	ich durf**te**	wir durf**ten**
du soll**test**	ihr soll**tet**	du durf**test**	ihr durf**tet**
er/sie/es soll**te**	Sie/sie soll**ten**	er/sie/es durf**te**	Sie/sie durf**ten**

Warum **wolltet** ihr einen neuen Teppich kaufen?
*Why **did** you **want** to buy a new rug?*

Bianca **musste** ihre Großeltern besuchen.
*Bianca **had** to visit her grandparents.*

- The modal **mögen** has an additional stem change in the **Präteritum**. Be careful not to confuse the **Präteritum** form **mochte** with the polite form **möchte**.

Anna **möchte** eine neue Lampe für ihr Schlafzimmer.
*Anna **would like** a new lamp for her bedroom.*

Als Junge **mochte** Peter das Zimmer auf dem Dachboden.
*As a boy, Peter **liked** the room in the attic.*

- The **Präteritum** stem of a mixed verb is the same as the stem of its past participle.

Perfekt and *Präteritum* of mixed verbs		
Infinitiv	**Perfekt**	**Präteritum**
bringen	er hat ge**bracht**	er **brachte**
denken	er hat ge**dacht**	er **dachte**
kennen	er hat ge**kannt**	er **kannte**
wissen	er hat ge**wusst**	er **wusste**

Wir **brachten** die Tischlampe ins Arbeitszimmer.
*We **brought** the desk lamp into the office.*

Wusste Daniel Emmas Adresse?
*Did Daniel **know** Emma's address?*

• Strong verbs in the **Präteritum** have irregular stems and add different endings from those of weak verbs.

beginnen	gefallen	liegen
ich begann	ich gefiel	ich lag
du begannst	du gefielst	du lagst
er/sie/es begann	er/sie/es gefiel	er/sie/es lag
wir begannen	wir gefielen	wir lagen
ihr begannt	ihr gefielt	ihr lagt
Sie/sie begannen	Sie/sie gefielen	Sie/sie lagen

irregular verb stems in the *Präteritum*					
bleiben	blieb	helfen	half	sehen	sah
essen	aß	kommen	kam	sprechen	sprach
fahren	fuhr	lesen	las	sterben	starb
finden	fand	nehmen	nahm	tragen	trug
geben	gab	schlafen	schlief	trinken	trank
gehen	ging	schreiben	schrieb	verstehen	verstand

Wir **blieben** gestern zu Hause.
*We **stayed** home yesterday.*

Er **sah** mir in die Augen.
*He **looked** me in the eyes.*

Ich **aß** ein kleines Stück Kuchen.
*I **ate** a little piece of cake.*

Sie **fuhren** nach Frankfurt.
*They **drove** to Frankfurt.*

• The verbs **sein**, **haben**, and **werden** do not follow the pattern of other irregular verbs.

sein	haben	werden
ich war	ich hatte	ich wurde
du warst	du hattest	du wurdest
er/sie/es war	er/sie/es hatte	er/sie/es wurde
wir waren	wir hatten	wir wurden
ihr wart	ihr hattet	ihr wurdet
Sie/sie waren	Sie/sie hatten	Sie/sie wurden

Es **wurde** schnell dunkel.
*It **got** dark quickly.*

Als Kinder **hatten** wir viele Haustiere.
*We **had** a lot of pets when we were kids.*

Suggestion Some students may incorrectly add the **-te** ending to the preterite form of strong verbs, creating nonsense forms such as **begannte** or **gefielte**. Explain that adding -te to a strong verb in its simple past form is like adding the -ed ending to an irregular verb like *sang* or *swam* in English.

ACHTUNG

Note that the **Präteritum** endings for strong verbs follow the same pattern as those of weak and mixed verbs, but without the addition of **-te-** as a past-tense marker.
Also note that the **ich** and **er/sie/es** forms of strong verbs have no added endings in the **Präteritum**.

QUERVERWEIS

See **Appendix A** for a complete list of strong verbs and their **Präteritum** forms.

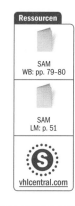

Ressourcen

SAM
WB: pp. 79–80

SAM
LM: p. 51

S

vhlcentral.com

Jetzt sind Sie dran!

Ergänzen Sie die Sätze mit den richtigen Formen der Verben im Präteritum.

1. Wir __*machten*__ (machen) zusammen unsere Hausaufgaben.
2. Die alten Möbel __waren__ (sein) hässlich.
3. Mein Bruder __wollte__ (wollen) ein Motorrad zu Weihnachten.
4. Das Mathebuch __lag__ (liegen) auf dem Schreibtisch.
5. __Hattet__ (Haben) ihr als Kinder einen Hund?
6. Wolfgang __trank__ (trinken) Tee zum Frühstück.
7. In der 8. Klasse __schrieben__ (schreiben) wir jede Woche eine Prüfung.
8. Jan __kaufte__ (kaufen) die Bluse für seine Freundin.
9. __Musstest__ (Müssen) du am Donnerstag lange arbeiten?
10. Unsere Eltern __fuhren__ (fahren) ohne uns in die Türkei.
11. Gestern __gab__ (geben) es Knödel in der Mensa.
12. Ich __fand__ (finden) diese Präsentation interessant.

Anwendung

1 Zeitformen Wählen Sie für jeden Satz die richtige Zeitform (*tense*).

	Präsens	Perfekt	Präteritum
1. Er ist nach Berlin gereist.	☐	☑	☐
2. Sie arbeitete mit seiner Freundin.	☐	☐	☑
3. Mietet ihr ein Haus am Strand?	☑	☐	☐
4. Hast du schon zu Abend gegessen?	☐	☑	☐
5. Sie hatten viel Spaß auf der Party.	☐	☐	☑
6. Wir kaufen die Möbel bei Ikea.	☑	☐	☐
7. Wie fandest du den Film?	☐	☐	☑
8. Ich konnte gestern nicht kommen.	☐	☐	☑

2 Sätze umformen Formen Sie die Sätze vom **Präsens** ins **Präteritum** um.

> **BEISPIEL** Der Fußballspieler geht nach Europa.
> *Der Fußballspieler ging nach Europa.*

1. Die Studentin wohnt bei ihren Eltern.
   Die Studentin wohnte bei ihren Eltern.
2. Seid ihr verheiratet?
   Wart ihr verheiratet?
3. Ich bringe ihnen eine Zimmerpflanze.
   Ich brachte ihnen eine Zimmerpflanze.
4. Die Schüler bauen Legohäuser.
   Die Schüler bauten Legohäuser.

5. Du gibst ihr ein Hochzeitsgeschenk.
   Du gabst ihr ein Hochzeitsgeschenk.
6. Das Haus hat keinen Keller.
   Das Haus hatte keinen Keller.
7. Wir ziehen nach Hamburg um.
   Wir zogen nach Hamburg um.
8. Sie bleiben eine Woche in Paris.
   Sie blieben eine Woche in Paris.

3 Der gestrige Tag Erzählen Sie, was gestern alles passierte. Benutzen Sie das Präteritum.

> **BEISPIEL** ich / wollen / ins Feinkostgeschäft gehen
> *Ich wollte ins Feinkostgeschäft gehen.*

1. die Kinder / dürfen / auf die Geburtstagsfeier gehen Die Kinder durften auf die Geburtstagsfeier gehen.

2. wir / müssen / neue Möbel für das Wohnzimmer kaufen Wir mussten neue Möbel für das Wohnzimmer kaufen.

3. Papa / sollen / seine Hemden in die Schublade legen Papa sollte seine Hemden in die Schublade legen.

4. du / wollen / Blumen für den Balkon kaufen Du wolltest Blumen für den Balkon kaufen.

5. ihr / können / leider nicht lange bei uns bleiben Ihr konntet leider nicht lange bei uns bleiben.

6. Sophia / mögen / die Gemüsesuppe nicht Sophia mochte die Gemüsesuppe nicht.

4 Ein Märchen Ergänzen Sie die Sätze mit den richtigen Präteritumsformen.

Es (1) ___war___ (sein) einmal ein kleines Mädchen. Ihr Name war Aschenputtel. Ihre Mutter (2) ___starb___ (sterben), als sie jung war. Ihr Vater (3) ___fand___ (finden) bald eine neue Frau. Seine neue Frau (4) ___hatte___ (haben) zwei hässliche Töchter. Die Stiefschwestern und die Stiefmutter (5) ___mochten___ (mögen) Aschenputtel nicht. Aschenputtel (6) ___musste___ (müssen) den Boden wischen, die Wäsche waschen und alle Betten machen. Die bösen Stiefschwestern (7) ___trugen___ (tragen) selber schöne Kleider, aber sie (8) ___gaben___ (geben) Aschenputtel nur ein altes, dreckiges Kleid. Eines Tages (*One day*) (9) ___besuchte___ (besuchen) Aschenputtel das Grab (*grave*) ihrer Mutter. Sie (10) ___sprach___ (sprechen) über ihr Unglück (*misfortune*)...

4 Suggestion Ask students if they can guess which famous fairy tale this is. You may want to share the original version of the **Aschenputtel** (*Cinderella*) story with students, and point out how it differs from modern retellings.

4 Expansion For homework, have students write an ending for the story, based on their knowledge of the fairy tale, or from their imaginations.

 Practice more at **vhlcentral.com.**

Kommunikation

5 **Das Leben vor hundert Jahren** Wie war das Leben vor hundert Jahren? Arbeiten Sie mit einem Partner / einer Partnerin und bilden Sie logische Sätze mit Wörtern aus jeder Spalte. Answers will vary.

> **BEISPIEL**
>
> **S1:** Jungen konnten allein in den Wald gehen.
> **S2:** Frauen konnten nicht an einer Universität studieren.

Frauen	dürfen	im Garten schlafen
Hunde	können	nicht so viele Prüfungen korrigieren
Jungen	müssen	an einer Universität studieren
Kinder	sollen	allein in den Wald gehen
Mädchen	wollen	viel arbeiten
Männer		in einem großen Kaufhaus einkaufen
Professoren		Brot backen
Studenten		mit dem Auto fahren

6 **Meine Familie** Erzählen Sie Ihrem Partner / Ihrer Partnerin von Ihrem Familienleben als Kind. Benutzen Sie das Präteritum. Answers will vary.

> **BEISPIEL**
>
> **S1:** Meine Familie wohnte in New York. Mein Vater war Musiker. Er arbeitete auch in einer Bibliothek. Wir gingen oft am Wochenende zu meinen Großeltern...
> **S2:** Ich wohnte zusammen mit meinen Eltern, meinem kleinen Bruder und meiner Oma...

7 **Ein schöner Tag** Erzählen Sie Ihrem Partner / Ihrer Partnerin von einem sehr schönen Tag in Ihrem Leben. Benutzen Sie das Präteritum. Answers will vary.

> **BEISPIEL**
>
> **S1:** Es war ein Samstag. Das Wetter war schön und ich hatte keine Hausaufgaben. Ich ging in die Stadt...
> **S2:** Ein sehr schöner Tag war mein 16. Geburtstag. Meine Eltern hatten ein großes Geschenk für mich und es stand vor der Haustür...

8 **Ein trauriger Tag** Gestern war ein sehr trauriger Tag für Erik. Schreiben Sie mit zwei Mitstudenten zusammen eine Geschichte über Eriks Tag. Benutzen Sie das Präteritum. Answers will vary.

> **BEISPIEL**
>
> Erik ging in die Küche. Er fand ein Blatt Papier. Es war von seiner Freundin...

8 **Expansion** Collect the stories, read them out loud, and have the class guess which group wrote which story. You may want to have students vote for their favorite.

7 **Suggestion** Before having students work with a partner, give them time to take notes and prepare. You might want to give them a list of verbs in the simple past. Ex.: **aß, gab, bekam, ging, fand, trank, machte, sagte, arbeitete, besuchte, spielte, schlief, lag, hatte, war, wohnte, kaufte, verlor.**

6A.2 *Da-, wo-, hin-,* and *her-* compounds  **S** Presentation

Suggestion Write some common **da**-compounds on the board, along with their English equivalents. Ex.: **darüber** (*about that*), **darunter** (*under that*). Give concrete examples for each, such as: **Hier ist mein Rucksack. Darunter ist der Stuhl und darunter ist der Boden.** Have students guess the meanings of other **da**-compounds. Ex.: **dazwischen, danach, daneben, davor, darauf, dahinter**.

QUERVERWEIS

See **3B.2** to review accusative prepositions, **4B.2** to review dative prepositions, and **5B.3** to review two-way prepositions.

Many German verbs are used idiomatically with certain prepositions. You will learn more about these verbs in **7A.2**.

See **4B.1** to review the use of **wen** and **wem**.

Expansion Give students clues using **da**-compounds and have them guess which item in the classroom you're referring to. Ex.: **Damit schreibt man. Darauf sitzen die Studenten. Darunter sind wir alle. Damit lernen wir Deutsch. Max sitzt daneben**. Have students write their own **da**-compound riddles to share with the class.

ACHTUNG

Note that **warten auf** (*to wait for*), **denken an** (*to think about*), and **sprechen über** (*to talk about*) always take accusative objects.

Startblock In German, personal pronouns following a preposition can only refer to people. Special forms are used when the object of the preposition refers to a thing or an idea.

Als Hans zu Weihnachten nach Hause kam, sprach er übrigens **von dir**.

Davon nehme ich einen Teller, bitte.

- In **5A.2** and **5A.3**, you learned to use personal pronouns to refer to the object of a preposition. When the object is a thing or an idea, use a **da**-compound instead.

Kennst du Alex? Wir sind am Samstag **mit ihm** essen gegangen.
*Do you know Alex? We went out to eat **with him** on Saturday.*

Wo ist der Teddybär? Das Baby will **damit** spielen.
*Where's the teddy bear? The baby wants to play **with it**.*

- Form a **da**-compound by adding **da-** to a preposition. If the preposition begins with a vowel, insert an **-r-** after **da-**.

common **da**-compounds	
dafür davon davor	daran darauf darin

Wo ist der Bus? Wir warten seit einer halben Stunde **darauf**.
*Where's the bus? We've been waiting **for it** for half an hour.*

—Hat Max dir ein Geschenk gegeben?
—Ja, und ich habe ihm **dafür** gedankt.
Did Max give you a present?
*—Yes, and I thanked him **for it**.*

- German speakers often drop the **-a-** in **da**-compounds that begin with **dar-**.

Wer ist da **drin**?
*Who's **in there**?*

Denk mal **drüber** nach.
*Think it **over**.*

- Use **wen** or **wem** to ask about the object of a preposition when it refers to a person. When you ask about a thing or idea, use a **wo**-compound.

Mit wem seid ihr ins Restaurant gegangen?
*Who did you go to the restaurant **with**?*

Womit spielt die Katze?
*What is the cat playing **with**?*

- Form a **wo**-compound by combining **wo(r)-** with a preposition.

common **wo**-compounds	
wofür wovon wovor	woran worauf worin

Wofür braucht sie den Spiegel?
*What does she need the mirror **for**?*

Woran denkst du jetzt?
*What are you thinking **about** now?*

Worüber sprecht ihr?
*What are you talking **about**?*

- In **2A.2**, you learned to use **wohin** to ask *where to?* and **woher** to ask *from where?* In conversation, **hin** and **her** can be separated from **wo**, moving to the end of the sentence.

<table>
<tr>
<td>

Wohin soll ich den Spiegel hängen?
Where should I hang the mirror?

Wo gehst du jetzt **hin**?
Where are you going to now?

</td>
<td>

Woher hast du diese Möbel bekommen?
Where did you get this furniture?

Wo kommst du **her**?
Where are you from?

</td>
</tr>
</table>

- Use the adverb **dahin** or **daher** to replace a prepositional phrase expressing motion.

<table>
<tr>
<td>

Reist ihr **in die Schweiz**?
Are you going to Switzerland?

</td>
<td>

Ja, wir reisen **dahin**.
Yes, we're going there.

</td>
</tr>
</table>

- **Hin** or **her** can also be combined with the prefix of a separable prefix verb, to indicate motion. Note that **hin** generally indicates motion *away* from the speaker, while **her** indicates motion *toward* the speaker.

<table>
<tr>
<td>

Birgit **geht** die Treppe **hinauf**.
Birgit is going up the stairs.

Komm **herein** oder geh **hinaus**!
Either come in or go out!

</td>
<td>

Paul **kommt** die Treppe **herunter**.
Paul is coming down the stairs.

Rapunzel, lass dein Haar **herunter**!
Rapunzel, let down your hair!

</td>
</tr>
</table>

Suggestion The **Jetzt sind Sie dran!** activity helps to underscore the fact that **da-** and **wo-**compounds are not used when the pronoun refers to a person. Go over the answers as a class, and emphasize that since items 2, 4, and 7 refer to people, they must use the preposition with a personal pronoun.

- Compound prefixes like **herauf-**, **herein-**, **herunter-**, or **heraus-** are often shortened in spoken German to **rauf-**, **rein-**, **runter-**, **raus-**, and so on.

<table>
<tr>
<td>

Lässt du mich bitte ins Badezimmer **rein**?
Will you please let me into the bathroom?

</td>
<td>

Papa soll die alte Kommode in den Keller **runterbringen**.
Dad is supposed to bring the old dresser down to the basement.

</td>
</tr>
</table>

QUERVERWEIS

See **5B.3** to review the difference between **wo** and **wohin**.

ACHTUNG

The phrase **hin und her** means *back and forth:* **Warum laufen die Kinder hin und her?**

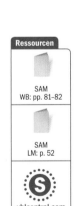

Ressourcen

SAM
WB: pp. 81–82

SAM
LM: p. 52

vhlcentral.com

Jetzt sind Sie dran!   **Wählen Sie die richtigen Formen.**

1. (Woher / Wohin) kommt das Sprichwort „Zeit ist Geld"?
2. (Womit / Mit wem) hast du auf der Party getanzt?
3. (Womit / Mit wem) sollen wir anfangen?
4. Hast du Herrn Schulz gesehen? Ich denke oft (an ihn / daran).
5. (Wohin / Woher) soll ich die Lampe stellen?
6. (Wofür / Für wen) brauchst du so viele Bleistifte?
7. Marie ist wirklich unangenehm. Ich will nicht (damit / mit ihr) sprechen.
8. So eine schöne Vase! Wir danken euch sehr (für sie / dafür).
9. Die neue Wohnung ist wunderschön! Paul und Fabian haben viel (über sie / darüber) geredet.
10. (Woher / Wohin) bekomme ich das Geld für die Miete?

Anwendung

1 **Ersetzungen** Ersetzen Sie die Satzteile mit den entsprechenden **wo-** oder **da-**Komposita.

1. **wo-**: vor dem Kaufhaus ___wovor___
2. **wo-**: unter dem Teppich ___worunter___
3. **da-**: über das Buch ___darüber___
4. **da-**: gegen die Wand ___dagegen___

5. **wo-**: aus Baumwolle ___woraus___
6. **da-**: für das Geschenk ___dafür___
7. **wo-**: mit dem Fahrrad ___womit___
8. **da-**: hinter der Schule ___dahinter___

2 **Suggestion** Before they complete the activity, have students identify which noun is being replaced in each sentence.

2 **Was ist richtig?** Wählen Sie die passenden Präposition + Pronomen-Verbindungen oder die passenden **da-**Komposita.

1. Mias Cousinen wohnen in Wels. Letzten Sommer hat sie (bei ihnen / dabei) gewohnt.
2. Laura gab mir ein Geburtstagsgeschenk und ich dankte ihr (für es / dafür).
3. Frank ist gegen diese Idee und seine Freunde sind auch alle (gegen ihn / dagegen).
4. Meine große Schwester hat mir immer bei den Hausaufgaben geholfen. Ich habe sie täglich (mit ihr / damit) zusammen gemacht.
5. Simon spricht selten über Politik. Seine Freundin diskutiert aber gern (über sie / darüber).

3 **Was fehlt?** Ergänzen Sie die Sätze mit den passenden Wörtern. Bilden Sie Kombinationen mit **hin** oder **her**.

▶ **BEISPIEL**

Jasmin ___geht___ die Treppe ___hinauf___ (hinaufgehen).

1. Der Junge ___klettert___ den Baum ___hinauf___ (hinaufklettern).

2. Der Kellner ___kommt___ mit der Speisekarte ___heraus___ (herauskommen).

3. Herr Scholz ___geht___ in die Metzgerei ___hinein___ (hineingehen).

4. Die Blätter (*leaves*) ___fallen___ von den Bäumen ___herunter___ (herunterfallen).

4 **Fragen bilden** Was sind die Fragen zu den Antworten?

 BEISPIEL Zur Schule fahre ich mit dem Bus.
Womit fährst du zur Schule?

1. Lukas geht mit seiner Schwester ins Theater. Mit wem geht Lukas ins Theater?
2. Sarah ist gegen die Gartentür gefahren. Wogegen ist Sarah gefahren?
3. Das neue Sofa ist aus Leder gemacht. Woraus ist das neue Sofa gemacht?
4. Die Vorlesung war über Neurobiologie. Worüber war die Vorlesung?

 Practice more at **vhlcentral.com.**

Kommunikation

5 Hin oder her? Entscheiden Sie mit Ihrem Partner / Ihrer Partnerin, welches Verb zu jedem Bild passt und beantworten Sie die Fragen. Sample answers are provided.

| herauskommen | hinausgehen | hineingehen | hinfallen | hinstellen |

▶ **BEISPIEL** Was macht der Kellner?
Er stellt das Essen hin.

1. Was ist der Frau passiert?
Sie ist hingefallen.

2. Papa kommt gerade von der Arbeit. Was macht er? Er geht hinein.

3. Was will das Kind machen?
Es will hinausgehen.

4. Herr und Frau Koch waren im Konzert. Was machen sie jetzt?
Sie kommen heraus.

6 So bin ich Stellen Sie Ihrem Partner / Ihrer Partnerin die Fragen. Answers will vary.

BEISPIEL Worüber lachst du oft?
Ich lache oft über meine Katze. Sie ist immer so lustig.

1. Woher kommt deine Familie?
2. Worüber sprichst du gern?
3. Wohin gehst du gern?
4. An wen denkst du oft?

7 Mein bester Freund Wie ist der beste Freund / die beste Freundin von Ihrem Partner / Ihrer Partnerin? Stellen Sie Fragen und benutzen Sie **wo-Komposita** oder Präposition + **wen/wem**. Answers will vary.

BEISPIEL sehr viel wissen / über

S1: *Worüber weiß dein bester Freund sehr viel?*
S2: *Er weiß sehr viel über Rockmusik.*

1. oft denken / an
2. selten Probleme haben / mit
3. gern ausgehen / mit
4. mit dir sprechen / über

8 Mein Zimmer Beschreiben Sie Ihr Zimmer. Benutzen Sie **da-Komposita**. Ihr Partner / Ihre Partnerin versucht dann, ein Bild von Ihrem Zimmer zu zeichnen. Dann tauschen Sie die Rollen. Answers will vary.

BEISPIEL *Da ist mein Bett. Darauf liegt eine Bettdecke von meiner Oma, und darüber hängt ein Poster. Mein Nachttisch steht neben dem Bett. Darauf liegt...*

hängen	links davon	an	über	hinter
liegen	rechts davon	auf	unter	vor
stehen	zwischen	in	neben	

5 Expansion TPR (total physical response) exercises can be useful for demonstrating the difference between **hin** and **her**. Give students a list of commands and have them take turns giving and following the commands Ex.: **Geh zur Tür hin! Komm wieder zu mir her! Geh aus dem Klassenzimmer hinaus! Komm herauf zu mir! Gehen wir beide die Treppe hinunter!**

6 Suggestion Have students ask you the questions, so that they can hear more sample answers. Remind them that they can give creative or humorous responses when answering the questions.

7 Suggestion Introduce the activity by bringing a picture of your own best friend and modeling questions and answers. Ex.: **Das ist ein guter Freund von mir, Todd. Worüber spricht er mit mir? Er spricht gern über sein Hobby, Radfahren. An wen denkt er oft? Er denkt oft an seine Freundin Mary.**

QUERVERWEIS

You learned the conjunctions **und**, **oder**, and **aber** in **1B.2**.

Suggestion Remind students what conjunctions are, and have them give you examples in English. Tell them that German has two kinds —coordinating and subordinating. Explain that coordinating conjunctions have no impact on word order, and are simply inserted between two clauses like a plus sign.

Suggestion Tell students that whenever *but* can be replaced with *rather* in English, the equivalent German conjunction will be **sondern**.

Ressourcen

SAM
WB: pp. 83–84

SAM
LM: p. 53

(S)
vhlcentral.com

6A.3 Coordinating conjunctions (S) Presentation

Startblock Use coordinating conjunctions to combine two related sentences, words, or phrases into a single sentence.

> Ich ging in die Küche, **und** am Herd stand ihr Großvater.

> Es ist bequemer hier, **denn** die Küche ist gleich nebenan.

- The most common coordinating conjunctions are **aber**, **denn** (*for, because*), **oder**, **sondern** (*but rather/instead*), and **und**.

> Ich habe eine Wohnung mit großer Küche gemietet, **denn** ich koche gern.
> *I rented an apartment with a big kitchen, **because** I like to cook.*

> Lina braucht einen Schrank **oder** eine Kommode für ihre Kleider.
> *Lina needs a closet **or** a dresser for her clothes.*

- Both **aber** and **sondern** correspond to the English word *but*. **Sondern** is used after a negated clause and indicates that the two ideas being coordinated are mutually exclusive.

> Erik hat ein großes Sofa, **aber** er sitzt gern auf dem Boden.
> *Erik has a big sofa, **but** he likes to sit on the floor.*

> Meine Wohnung ist nicht im Erdgeschoss, **sondern** im ersten Stock.
> *My apartment is not on the ground floor, **but rather** on the second floor.*

- When two clauses are connected by a coordinating conjunction, both follow normal subject-verb word order. Always use a comma before **aber**, **denn**, and **sondern**.

> Die Katze sitzt auf dem Balkon **und der Hund liegt** auf dem Teppich.
> *The cat is sitting on the balcony **and the dog is lying** on the carpet.*

> Ihr esst immer im Esszimmer, **aber wir essen** gern in der Küche.
> *You always eat in the dining room, **but we** like to **eat** in the kitchen.*

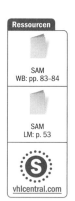

Jetzt sind Sie dran! **Wählen Sie die passende Konjunktion.**

1. Seine Schwester hat einen braunen Sessel (und / sondern) ein blaues Sofa im Wohnzimmer.
2. Im Keller ist es nicht warm, (sondern / aber) kalt.
3. Wir haben ein Haus mit einer großen Garage gekauft, (und / denn) wir haben zwei Autos.
4. Ich liebe Schokolade, (denn / aber) ich bin leider auf Diät.
5. Annika kauft gern Pflanzen für ihr Arbeitszimmer, (aber / denn) sie liebt die Natur.
6. Die Kinder wollen spielen, (sondern / aber) sie müssen ihre Hausaufgaben machen.
7. Wohnst du in einem Haus (oder / sondern) mietest du eine Wohnung?
8. Auf meinem Schreibtisch habe ich eine Lampe (und / denn) ein hübsches Bild von meiner Freundin.
9. Ich parke mein Auto nicht auf der Straße, (sondern / aber) in der Garage.
10. Zieht ihr im Januar (denn / oder) im Februar um?

Anwendung und Kommunikation

1 **Aber oder sondern?** Ergänzen Sie die Sätze mit **aber** oder **sondern**.

1. Nils ist intelligent, ___aber___ ein bisschen schüchtern.

2. Er und seine Frau wohnen in Deutschland, ___aber___ sie kommen aus den USA.

3. Anna studiert nicht mehr an der Universität, ___sondern___ arbeitet jetzt als Architektin.

4. Sie wollten letztes Jahr in ein neues Haus umziehen, ___aber___ es war zu teuer.

5. Ihre Kinder sind nicht in der Schule, ___sondern___ im Kindergarten.

2 **Was und warum** Bilden Sie logische Sätze aus Spalte A und B und verbinden Sie sie mit **aber, oder, denn, und** oder **sondern**. Sample answers are provided.

BEISPIEL

Ich arbeitete gerne mit Antonia, denn sie war sehr fleißig.

A	B
Ich arbeitete immer gerne mit Antonia.	Sie fanden dort einen günstigen Kleiderschrank.
Sie waren beim Möbelhaus Fischer.	Sie war fleißig.
Hannes wollte das gestreifte Hemd kaufen.	Er wollte nicht im Erdgeschoss wohnen.
Sie kauften kein zweites Auto.	Sie kauften ein Fahrrad.
Er wollte ein Zimmer bei einer Familie mieten.	Es war zu eng.
Ich bin heute Abend zu Hause geblieben.	Ich war sehr müde.

3 **Lara und ihre Familie** Erfinden Sie einen passenden Satz zu jedem Bild, und benutzen Sie dabei die angegebenen **Konjunktionen.** Answers will vary.

▶ **BEISPIEL** sondern

Lara hat keinen Hund, sondern eine Katze.

1. oder
2. und

3. und
4. oder

1 **Suggestion** Remind students that **sondern** follows negative statements, so if the first clause contains the word **nicht**, the correct "but" will be probably be **sondern**.

2 Sample answers: Sie waren beim Möbelhaus Fischer und sie fanden dort einen günstigen Kleiderschrank. / Hannes wollte das gestreifte Hemd kaufen, aber es war zu eng. / Sie kauften kein zweites Auto, sondern ein Fahrrad. / Er wollte ein Zimmer bei einer Familie mieten, aber er wollte nicht im Erdgeschoss wohnen. / Ich bin heute Abend zu Hause geblieben, denn ich war sehr müde.

3 **Expansion** Invite students to draw their own simple pictures. Then have them share their pictures in small groups and generate captions together using coordinating conjunctions.

 Practice more at **vhlcentral.com.**

Wiederholung

1 Umzug
Lena reist viel. Sprechen Sie mit einem Partner / einer Partnerin darüber, wo Lena war und was sie machte. Sample answers are provided.

> **BEISPIEL** München / Oktoberfest besuchen
>
> **S1:** In München besuchte Lena das Oktoberfest.
> **S2:** In Berlin...

1. Berlin / das Brandenburger Tor sehen In Berlin sah sie das Brandenburger Tor.
2. Hamburg / ein Konzert hören In Hamburg hörte sie ein Konzert.
3. Düsseldorf / in der Königsallee wohnen In Düsseldorf wohnte sie in der Königsallee.
4. Köln / ein Fahrrad kaufen In Köln kaufte sie ein Fahrrad.
5. Heidelberg / Chemie studieren In Heidelberg studierte sie Chemie.

2 Eine laute Party
Sie sind auf einer Party, aber die Musik ist sehr laut, und Sie können nicht gut hören. Fragen Sie Ihren Partner / Ihre Partnerin, was er/sie gesagt hat. Answers may vary. Sample answers are provided.

> **BEISPIEL** Am Montag / ins Musikgeschäft gehen möchten
>
> **S1:** Am Montag möchte ich ins Musikgeschäft gehen.
> **S2:** Wie bitte? Wohin möchtest du gehen?

1. am Dienstag / in der Mensa essen wollen Wo willst du essen?
2. im Sommer / nach Österreich reisen möchten Wohin möchtest du reisen?
3. am Freitag / im Schwimmbad schwimmen können Wo kannst du schwimmen?
4. am Wochenende / für die Physikprüfung lernen sollen Wofür sollst du lernen?
5. nächste Woche / einen Essay über München schreiben müssen Worüber musst du schreiben?
6. morgen Abend / mit den Eltern im Restaurant essen können Mit wem kannst du essen?/Wo kannst du essen?
7. morgen Nachmittag / lange in der Bibliothek bleiben müssen Wo musst du lange bleiben?
8. im Winter / in den Alpen Ski fahren wollen Wo willst du Ski fahren?

3 Expansion Before beginning the info-gap activity, show students a picture of a room and ask true or false questions about the picture using **da**-compounds. Ex.: **Richtig oder falsch? Das Zimmer hat keine Lampe. Es gibt ein Bett. Daneben ist ein Nachttisch. Darauf liegt ein Buch. Darüber hängt ein Poster.**

3 Diskutieren und kombinieren
Sie und Ihr Partner / Ihre Partnerin bekommen zwei Blätter mit verschiedenen Bildern. Vergleichen Sie die Bilder, und machen Sie eine Liste mit den sieben Unterschieden auf den Bildern. Answers will vary.

> **BEISPIEL**
>
> **S1:** Es gibt nur ein Bett und eine Lampe rechts daneben, vor dem Fenster.
> **S2:** Ich habe auch ein Bett, aber ich habe keine Lampe, ...

4 Im Stadtzentrum
Erzählen Sie Ihrem Partner / Ihrer Partnerin, was Sie am Dienstag im Stadtzentrum machten. Wählen Sie ein Wort aus jeder Spalte und bilden Sie logische Sätze. Answers will vary.

> **BEISPIEL**
>
> **S1:** Am Dienstag lasen wir Bücher in der Bibliothek.
> **S2:** An der Uni sprach ich mit...

A	B	C
Bücher	mit Freunden	essen
Meeresfrüchte	Kaffee	fahren
an der Uni	Kleider	finden
im Café	Steak	kaufen
im Modegeschäft	auf dem Markt	kommen
im Restaurant „Tivoli"	durch die Stadt	lesen
mit dem Fahrrad	in der Bibliothek	spazieren
langsam	in die Stadt	sprechen
spät	nach Hause	trinken

5 Arbeitsblatt
Fragen Sie Ihre Klassenkameraden, ob Sie die Aktivitäten in der Liste gern machen. Finden Sie eine Person für jede Aktivität. Answers will vary.

> **BEISPIEL**
>
> **S1:** Fährst du gern mit dem Fahrrad?
> **S2:** Ja, ich fahre gern damit.

6 Das Wochenende
Erzählen Sie sich gegenseitig, was sie am Wochenende gemacht haben. Nennen Sie mindestens sechs Dinge und auch einen Grund für jede Aktivität. Answers will vary.

> **BEISPIEL**
>
> **S1:** Am Samstagmorgen war ich drei Stunden in der Bibliothek, denn ich musste einen Essay für mein Literaturseminar schreiben.
> **S2:** Am Samstagmorgen war ich nicht in der Bibliothek, sondern ich sollte mit meiner Mannschaft Fußball spielen...

Zapping

(S) Video

Hausarbeit

Das Schweizer Fernsehen° produziert deutschsprachige Fernsehsendungen für das Schweizer Publikum. Die Sendung „Tagesschau" ist das Programm, das täglich die meisten Zuschauer hat. Die folgende TV-Reportage aus der Tagesschau berichtet, wie viel Hausarbeit Schweizer Männer heute machen. Die Reportage basiert auf einer Studie der Schweizer Regierung°. Die Art der Arbeit, die Männer und Frauen zu Hause machen, ist unterschiedlich°.

SF TAGESSCHAU

Hausarbeit
- Frauen: 30 Stunden
- Männer: 18,1 Stunden

Immer mehr Frauen mit Kindern sind berufstätig°.

Väter mit kleinen Kindern helfen mehr im Haushalt.

Dass beide Geschlechter zu Hause gleich viel° arbeiten, davon sind wir noch weit weg°.

Fernsehen television **Regierung** government **unterschiedlich** different **Geschlecht** gender **berufstätig** working **gleich viel** the same amount **weit weg** far away

 Verständnis Beantworten Sie die Fragen mit den Informationen aus dem Video.

1. Laut (according to) des Videos, welche Aktivität machen normalerweise die Männer zu Hause?
   a. Putzen   b. Gartenarbeit   c. Bügeln

2. Welche Aktivität machen Frauen und Männer?
   a. Aufräumen   b. Waschen   c. Kochen

 Diskussion. Besprechen Sie die folgenden Fragen mit einem Partner / einer Partnerin. Answers will vary.

1. Wer macht was in Ihrem Haushalt? Arbeiten die Männer und die Frauen in Ihre Familie gleich viel zu Hause?

2. Schreiben Sie eine kurze Szene über ein berufstätiges Paar. Die beiden Partner diskutieren, wie die Hausarbeit aufgeteilt sein soll.

Communicative Goals

You will learn how to:

- talk about household chores
- talk about appliances

Wortschatz

die Hausarbeit	*housework*
den Tisch decken	*to set the table*
staubsaugen	*to vacuum*
Wäsche waschen	*to do laundry*
Haushaltsartikel	*household items*
die Decke, -n	*blanket*
der Herd, -e	*stove*
die Kaffeemaschine, -n	*coffeemaker*
die Pfanne, -n	*pan*
die Spülmaschine, -n	*dishwasher*
der Staubsauger, -	*vacuum cleaner*
der Toaster, -	*toaster*
der Wäschetrockner, -	*dryer*
die Waschmaschine, -n	*washing machine*
zum Beschreiben	*to describe*
dreckig	*filthy*
ordentlich	*tidy*
sauber	*clean*
schmutzig	*dirty*
Es ist ein Saustall!	*It's a pigsty!*
Verben	*verbs*
aufräumen (räumt... auf)	*to clean up*
putzen	*to clean*
waschen	*to wash*
wischen	*to wipe; to mop*

ACHTUNG

German speakers often shorten a compound when the context is clear:
Anja wirft die Wäsche in den Trockner.
But: **Der Wäschetrockner ist kaputt.**

Suggestion Ask students to describe their house, apartment, or dorm room using three adjectives, including at least one from the **zum Beschreiben** list.

Hausarbeit ⑤ Vocabulary Tools

Expansion Play "vocabulary bingo" with your students. Give students a list of 16 words from **6A** and **6B** and have them fill in a 4 X 4 grid with the words in mixed-up order. Then given an oral definition for each word. Ex: **Das ist grün. Es lebt. Es ist in einem Topf in meinem Wohnzimmer. (Die Pflanze.) Das ist wie ein Besen mit einem Motor. Damit mache ich meine Teppiche sauber. (Der Staubsauger)** As you define a word, students call out the answer and everyone gets to put an 'X' in the corresponding box. The first student to complete a row or column calls out **Ich gewinne**.

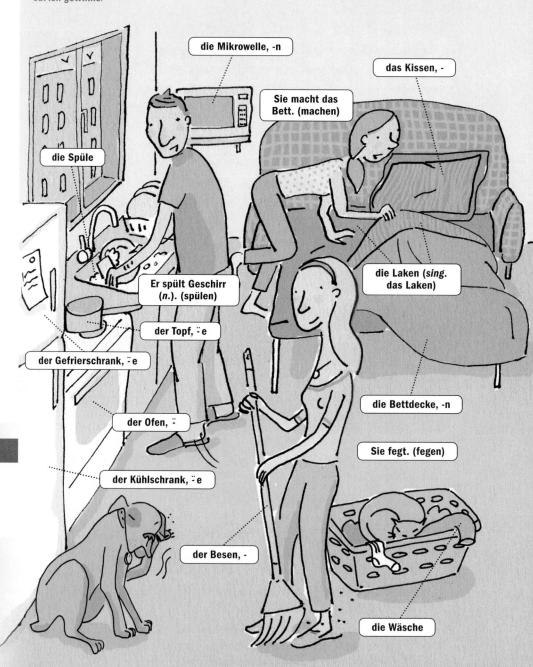

- die Mikrowelle, -n
- das Kissen, -
- Sie macht das Bett. (machen)
- die Spüle
- Er spült Geschirr (*n.*). (spülen)
- die Laken (*sing.* das Laken)
- der Topf, ⸚e
- der Gefrierschrank, ⸚e
- die Bettdecke, -n
- der Ofen, ⸚
- Sie fegt. (fegen)
- der Kühlschrank, ⸚e
- der Besen, -
- die Wäsche

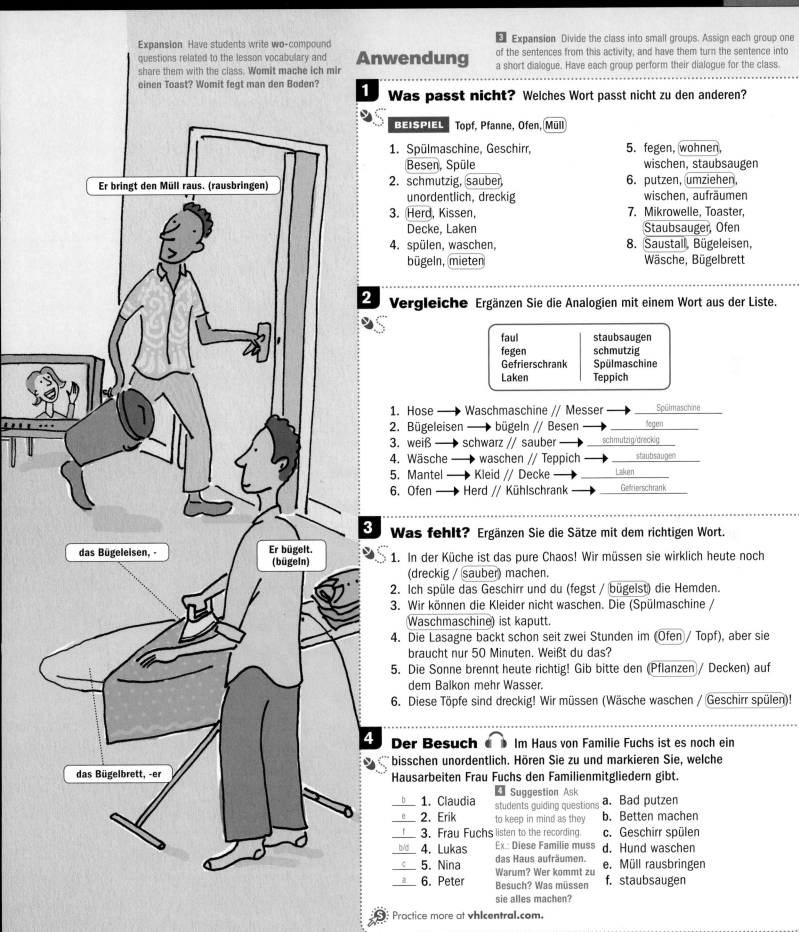

Er bringt den Müll raus. (rausbringen)

das Bügeleisen, -

Er bügelt. (bügeln)

das Bügelbrett, -er

Expansion Have students write **wo**-compound questions related to the lesson vocabulary and share them with the class. **Womit mache ich mir einen Toast? Womit fegt man den Boden?**

Anwendung

3 Expansion Divide the class into small groups. Assign each group one of the sentences from this activity, and have them turn the sentence into a short dialogue. Have each group perform their dialogue for the class.

1 Was passt nicht? Welches Wort passt nicht zu den anderen?

BEISPIEL Topf, Pfanne, Ofen, (Müll)

1. Spülmaschine, Geschirr, (Besen), Spüle
2. schmutzig, (sauber), unordentlich, dreckig
3. (Herd), Kissen, Decke, Laken
4. spülen, waschen, bügeln, (mieten)
5. fegen, (wohnen), wischen, staubsaugen
6. putzen, (umziehen), wischen, aufräumen
7. Mikrowelle, Toaster, (Staubsauger), Ofen
8. (Saustall), Bügeleisen, Wäsche, Bügelbrett

2 Vergleiche Ergänzen Sie die Analogien mit einem Wort aus der Liste.

faul	staubsaugen
fegen	schmutzig
Gefrierschrank	Spülmaschine
Laken	Teppich

1. Hose ⟶ Waschmaschine // Messer ⟶ _Spülmaschine_
2. Bügeleisen ⟶ bügeln // Besen ⟶ _fegen_
3. weiß ⟶ schwarz // sauber ⟶ _schmutzig/dreckig_
4. Wäsche ⟶ waschen // Teppich ⟶ _staubsaugen_
5. Mantel ⟶ Kleid // Decke ⟶ _Laken_
6. Ofen ⟶ Herd // Kühlschrank ⟶ _Gefrierschrank_

3 Was fehlt? Ergänzen Sie die Sätze mit dem richtigen Wort.

1. In der Küche ist das pure Chaos! Wir müssen sie wirklich heute noch (dreckig / (sauber)) machen.
2. Ich spüle das Geschirr und du (fegst / (bügelst)) die Hemden.
3. Wir können die Kleider nicht waschen. Die (Spülmaschine / (Waschmaschine)) ist kaputt.
4. Die Lasagne backt schon seit zwei Stunden im ((Ofen) / Topf), aber sie braucht nur 50 Minuten. Weißt du das?
5. Die Sonne brennt heute richtig! Gib bitte den ((Pflanzen) / Decken) auf dem Balkon mehr Wasser.
6. Diese Töpfe sind dreckig! Wir müssen (Wäsche waschen / (Geschirr spülen))!

4 Der Besuch 🎧 Im Haus von Familie Fuchs ist es noch ein bisschen unordentlich. Hören Sie zu und markieren Sie, welche Hausarbeiten Frau Fuchs den Familienmitgliedern gibt.

_b_ 1. Claudia
_e_ 2. Erik
_f_ 3. Frau Fuchs
_b/d_ 4. Lukas
_c_ 5. Nina
_a_ 6. Peter

4 Suggestion Ask students guiding questions to keep in mind as they listen to the recording. Ex.: **Diese Familie muss das Haus aufräumen. Warum? Wer kommt zu Besuch? Was müssen sie alles machen?**

a. Bad putzen
b. Betten machen
c. Geschirr spülen
d. Hund waschen
e. Müll rausbringen
f. staubsaugen

Practice more at **vhlcentral.com**.

Kommunikation

5 **Räumen wir auf!** Die Wohnung ist mal wieder ein Saustall! Diskutieren Sie mit zwei Mitstudenten, welche Hausarbeiten jeder von Ihnen heute noch macht. Machen Sie dann auch einen Wochenplan, worin steht, wer in der Woche was machen muss, damit (*so that*) die Wohnung sauber bleibt. Answers will vary.

BEISPIEL

S1: *Wer spült das Geschirr?*
S2: *Ich spüle das Geschirr. Und wer…?*

6 **Expansion** After students have completed their partner conversations, ask them whether they think the housework is divided up fairly in their own families.

6 **Hausarbeiten** Besprechen Sie mit Ihrem Partner / Ihrer Partnerin, wer in Ihrer Familie die angegebenen (*indicated*) Hausarbeiten macht. Answers will vary.

BEISPIEL

Betten machen
S1: *Bei uns in der Familie macht meine Mutter die Betten.*
S2: *Ich mache mein Bett jeden Morgen.*

1. Geschirr spülen
2. Kleider bügeln
3. Müll rausbringen
4. Staub wischen
5. Toilette putzen
6. Wäsche waschen

7 **Expansion** Have students write about their own experiences from the day before, using modals in the simple past: What did they have to do yesterday? (**Ich musste…**) What did they want to do? (**Ich wollte…**) What could they or could they not do? (**Ich konnte…**) What did they enjoy doing? (**Ich mochte…**)

7 **Diskutieren und kombinieren** Gestern Abend haben Tim und Lara eine große Party gegeben, aber heute müssen sie alles aufräumen. Ihr Professor / Ihre Professorin gibt Ihnen und Ihrem Partner / Ihrer Partnerin zwei verschiedene Blätter mit Informationen über Tim und Laras Tag. Erzählen Sie einander, was Tim und Lara heute machen. Schreiben Sie dann einen kurzen Absatz über ihren Tag.

BEISPIEL

S1: *Um Viertel nach zehn räumt Lara den Tisch auf. Was macht Tim um Viertel nach zehn?*
S2: *Um Viertel nach zehn macht Tim das Bett.*

8 **Mein Traumhaus** Beschreiben Sie Ihrem Partner / Ihrer Partnerin Ihr Traumhaus: wo ist es, wie groß ist es, wie viele Stockwerke und Zimmer hat es, welche Möbel und Haushaltsartikel haben Sie, und wer macht die diversen Hausarbeiten?

BEISPIEL

S1: *Mein Traumhaus ist am Strand und es hat fünf Schlafzimmer, vier Badezimmer, ein Studierzimmer und auch eine große Garage für drei Autos. Im Garten ist ein Schwimmbad und ein zweites, kleines Haus für meine acht Hunde.*
S2: *Mein Traumhaus ist in der Stadt. Es hat…*

8 **Suggestion** Give students a few minutes to make notes about their dream house before they work with a partner. Encourage them to be creative and to include lots of detail.

Aussprache und Rechtschreibung  (S) Audio

🎧 The German *k* sound

The German **k** is pronounced like the *k* in the English word *kind*. At the end of a syllable, this sound may be written as **ck**.

Kaffee	Laken	Decke	Frack	Kreide

In a few loanwords, the **c** at the beginning of a word is pronounced like a **k**. In other loanwords, the initial **c** may be pronounced similarly to the *ts* in *cats* or the *c* in *cello*.

Computer	Caravan	Couch	Celsius	Cello

When the consonant combination **kn** appears at the beginning of a word, both letters are pronounced. In the combination **nk**, the sound is very similar to the *nk* in the English word *thank*.

Knie	knusprig	Knödel	danken	Schrank

Remember that the **ch** sound and the **k/ck** sound are pronounced differently.

di**ch**	di**ck**	Ba**ch**	Ba**ck**

Suggestion Tell students that a distinctive feature of Swiss German is the pronunciation of the initial k sound, as in the word **Kirche**. It is pronounced as a **k** immediately followed by the back **ch** sound (IPA [*kx*]).

1 **Aussprechen** Wiederholen Sie die Wörter, die Sie hören.

1. Keller
2. Keramik
3. Stock
4. Container
5. Cola
6. Celsius
7. knackig
8. Knallfrosch
9. Bank
10. Hockey
11. lach
12. Lack

2 **Nachsprechen** Wiederholen Sie die Sätze, die Sie hören.

1. In der Küche backt man Kekse.
2. Deine Kleider hängen im Kleiderschrank.
3. In Frankfurt essen glückliche Kinder knackige Bockwürste.
4. Mein Lieblingsmöbelstück ist diese knallrote Couch.
5. Wir kaufen das Cabriolet in Köln.
6. Kann Klaus Knödel kochen?

3 **Sprichwörter** Wiederholen Sie die Sprichwörter, die Sie hören.

Klappern gehört zum Handwerk.[1]

Kommt Zeit, kommt Rat.[2]

[1] Talking it up is part of the trade. (lit. *Rattling is part of the trade.*)
[2] We'll figure it out with time. (lit. *With time comes counsel.*)

Ich putze gern! Video

Vorbereitung In preparation for this episode, have students list in German all the chores they typically do around the house.

Meline und Sabite wollen die Wohnung aufräumen, doch plötzlich hat Meline eine wichtige Verabredung. Muss Sabite jetzt alleine putzen?

communication
cultures

MELINE Super. Ich treffe dich dann dort in einer halben Stunde.
SABITE Wohin gehst du?
MELINE Meine Freundin Beatrice besucht ihre Großmutter in Wilmersdorf und sie haben mich zum Tee zu sich eingeladen.
SABITE Wir haben darüber gesprochen, die Wohnung zu putzen. Sie ist ein Saustall.

MELINE Das können wir doch später machen.
SABITE Meline, seit wir hier eingezogen sind, hast du nicht ein Mal bei der Hausarbeit geholfen. Du hast kein Geschirr gewaschen, den Boden nicht gefegt und auch die Möbel nicht abgestaubt.

MELINE Beatrice und ich sind schon sehr lange Freundinnen und ihre Großmutter ist sehr alt. Man kann doch Staubsaugen nicht mit der Zeit vergleichen, die man mit der Familie verbringt.
SABITE Warte. Nimm den Abfall mit raus.

GEORGE Danke. Geht's dir gut?
SABITE Oh, mir geht es gut! Meline und ich hatten vor, heute die Wohnung aufzuräumen, aber sie hat sich aus dem Staub gemacht.
GEORGE Ich helfe dir.

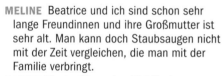

GEORGE Ich wusste nicht, dass Mädchen so...
SABITE Unordentlich sein können?
GEORGE Letzte Woche sah es hier tadellos aus. Was ist passiert?
SABITE Es ist so stressig an der Uni. Wir haben keine Zeit zum Putzen. Und Meline macht keine Hausarbeiten.

SABITE Das kann ich von dir nicht verlangen. Es ist schmutzig hier drin.
GEORGE Ich hatte als Kind ein Zimmer mit meinem Bruder zusammen. Er war superfaul. Ich habe die Betten gemacht und die Wäsche gewaschen.

Suggestion Have students do this activity with their books closed. Divide the class into groups and see how many questions each group can answer correctly.

ÜBUNGEN

1 **Richtig oder falsch?** Entscheiden Sie, ob die folgenden Sätze richtig oder falsch sind.

1. Meline besucht eine Freundin in Wilmersdorf. Richtig.
2. Sabite und Meline wollten die Wohnung putzen. Richtig.
3. Meline hilft oft bei der Hausarbeit. Falsch.
4. Meline muss den Abfall mit rausnehmen. Richtig.
5. Sabite ist glücklich darüber, dass Meline nicht hilft. Falsch.

6. George hatte als Kind ein Zimmer allein. Falsch.
7. Er hat die Betten gemacht und die Wäsche gewaschen. Richtig.
8. Sabite und Meline haben keine Zeit zum Putzen. Richtig.
9. George und Sabite haben Melines Wäsche gefaltet. Falsch.
10. Meline muss ihre Bluse bügeln. Falsch.

PERSONEN

George   Meline   Sabite

Suggestion Explain to students that although there is no official progressive verb form in German, the so-called **am-Progressiv** (or **Rheinische Verlaufsform**) is increasingly common in standard German: **Da du gerade am Bügeln bist...** (*Since you're ironing...*).

SABITE Vielen Dank für deine Hilfe, George.
GEORGE Ich putze gern. Aber sag das bitte nicht Hans.
MELINE Oh, George. Ich dachte, dass du Torsten bist. Beatrices Großmutter hat einen Mandelkuchen gebacken. Das wird euch aufheitern.

Suggestion Tell students that the expression **sich aus dem Staub machen** originally referred to soldiers who, wanting to escape from their compulsory military service, would take advantage of the large amounts of dust kicked up during battles to sneak away without being detected.

SABITE Wir haben die Böden gefegt, das Geschirr gewaschen, den Herd geputzt, Staub gesaugt und abgestaubt.
GEORGE Wir haben die Töpfe und Pfannen weggeräumt und eklige Dinge aus dem Kühlschrank und dem Spülbecken entfernt.

SABITE Deine Wäsche haben wir *nicht* gefaltet.

MELINE Ach, dieses Kleid möchte ich heute Abend anziehen. Jetzt muss ich bügeln.
SABITE Oh, Meline, da du gerade am Bügeln bist... Danke!

Nützliche Ausdrücke

- **Sie haben mich zum Tee zu sich eingeladen.**
  They invited me over for tea.

- **einziehen**
  to move in

- **nicht ein Mal**
  not even once

- **Man kann doch Staubsaugen nicht mit der Zeit vergleichen, die man mit der Familie verbringt.**
  You can't compare vacuuming to spending time with family.

- **Sie hat sich aus dem Staub gemacht.**
  She ran away.

- **tadellos**   • **der Mandelkuchen**
  spotless   *almond cake*

- **aufheitern**   • **eklig**
  to cheer up   *disgusting*

- **Da du gerade am Bügeln bist...**
  Since you're ironing...

6B.1

- **Ich habe die Betten gemacht und die Wäsche gewaschen.**
  I made the beds and did the laundry.

- **Ich hatte als Kind ein Zimmer mit meinem Bruder zusammen.**
  I shared a bedroom with my brother when I was a kid.

6B.2

- **Wir haben die Töpfe und Pfannen weggeräumt und eklige Dinge aus dem Kühlschrank und dem Spülbecken entfernt.**
  We put away all the pots and pans, and got rid of disgusting things from the refrigerator and the kitchen sink.

2 **Zum Besprechen** Stellen Sie sich vor (*Imagine*), Ihre Wohnung ist so ein „Saustall" wie die von Sabite und Meline. Machen Sie zu dritt einen Plan, um die Wohnung aufzuräumen. Wer macht was? Arbeiten Sie zusammen oder alleine? Was machen Sie zuerst? Answers will vary.

3 **Vertiefung** Sabites Professor hat das Gedicht „Kenner und Enthusiast" von Goethe zitiert, um ihr Kunstprojekt zu kommentieren. Suchen Sie das Gedicht im Internet. Finden Sie heraus, wie die Strophe (*stanza*) weitergeht. Um ihn versammelten Männer sich, / Die ihn einen Kenner nannten.

3 **Expansion** In class, discuss the meaning of the Goethe poem "**Kenner und Enthusiast**". For homework, have students find out more about Goethe and prepare a brief report to present to the class.

Ressourcen

SAM
VM: p. 12

vhlcentral.com

Haushaltsgeräte°

 Reading

Suggestion Before they read the text, ask students what appliances they have in their home or dorm and which ones they use the most. Ex.: **Hast du einen Kühlschrank? Eine Mikrowelle? Eine Kaffeemaschine? Welche von diesen Geräten gebrauchst du jeden Tag?**

EINIGE WICHTIGE HAUSHALTSGERÄTE wurden von Technikern deutschsprachiger Länder erfunden°.

Thermoskannen

In einer Thermoskanne bleiben Getränke länger warm. Der Chemnitzer Professor Adolf Ferdinand Weinhold entdeckte° 1881 ein Prinzip, damit Glasgefäße° weniger Wärme verlieren. Reinhold Burger, ein anderer Deutscher, forschte° an einer Nutzung° dieses Prinzips.

1903 registrierte er sein Patent. Die Flaschen hatten eine Silberbeschichtung° und ein schützendes Metallgehäuse°. 1909 verkaufte Burger sein Patent an die Charlottenburger Thermos AG. Deshalb heißen diese Flaschen heute Thermosflaschen. Die erste Serienproduktion fand 1920 statt.

Kaffeefilter

Für das Kaffeekochen braucht man Kaffeefilter. Ein sehr bekannter Name bei Kaffeefiltern ist Melitta. Der

Firmenname geht zurück auf Melitta Bentz aus Dresden. 1908 revolutionierte sie das Kaffeekochen. Sie verwendete° ein Stück Filterpapier und einen durchlöchterten Messingtopf°. Damit filterte sie den bitteren Kaffeesatz°. Aus dieser Idee entstand das Kaffeefiltern mit Kaffeefilter und Filterpapier. Das Patent erhielt Melitta Bentz am 20. Juni 1908 vom Kaiserlichen Patentamt in Berlin.

Nähmaschinen°

Eine Nähmaschine ist eine Maschine für die Kleiderproduktion. Die erste Nähmaschinenfirma, Bernina International AG, wurde von Karl Friedrich Gegauf gegründet°. Gegauf wusste, dass Nähen kompliziert und arbeitsaufwendig° sein kann. 1893 erfand er die erste Hohlsaum°-Nähmaschine der Welt. Damit konnte man 100 Stiche pro Minute nähen. 1885 zerstörte ein Großbrand° die Werkstatt der Gebrüder Gegauf komplett; lediglich der Prototyp der Hohlsaum-Nähmaschine konnte gerettet werden°. Heute ist Bernina eine sehr erfolgreiche Firma in der Schweiz.

Haushaltsgerätehersteller in Deutschland	
Bauknecht: Küchengeräte	1.917 Mitarbeiter in Deutschland
Bosch/Siemens: Haushaltsgeräte	14.642 Mitarbeiter in Deutschland
Liebherr: Kühlschränke und Gefriertruhen°	1.775 Mitarbeiter in Deutschland
Miele: Elektro-Haushaltsgeräte	11.000 Mitarbeiter in Deutschland
Rowenta: Küchen- und Haushaltsgeräte	1.100 Mitarbeiter in Deutschland

QUELLE: Statistisches Bundesamt Deutschland

Haushaltsgeräte appliances **wurden... erfunden** were invented **entdeckte** discovered **Glasgefäße** glass containers **forschte** researched **Nutzung** use **Silberbeschichtung** silver coating **schützendes Metallgehäuse** protective metal casing **verwendete** used **durchlöchterten Messingtopf** perforated brass pot **Kaffeesatz** coffee grounds **Nähmaschinen** sewing machines **wurde... gegründet** was founded **arbeitsaufwendig** labor-intensive **Hohlsaum** hemstitch **seam Großbrand** large fire **gerettet werden** be saved **Gefriertruhen** freezers

Suggestion Remind students that they don't have to understand every word and should focus instead on key words and main themes. Give them targeted pre-reading questions to help them pick out key information. Ex.: **Seit wann gibt es Kühlschränke? Was braucht man für das Kaffeekochen? Wer erfand die erste Hohlsaum-Nähmaschine?**

ÜBUNGEN

1 **Richtig oder falsch?** Sind die Aussagen richtig oder falsch? Korrigieren Sie die falschen Aussagen. Answers will vary.

1. In Thermoskannen bleiben Getränke länger warm. Richtig.

2. Adolf Ferdinand Weinhold registrierte 1903 ein Patent für Thermoskannen. Falsch. Reinhold Burger registrierte das Patent für Thermoskannen.

3. Melitta ist ein bekannter Name bei Kaffeefiltern. Richtig.

4. 1904 revolutionierte Melitta Bentz das Kaffeekochen. Falsch. 1908 revolutionierte Melitta Bentz das Kaffeekochen.

5. Melitta Bentz kommt aus Österreich. Falsch. Melitta Bentz kommt aus Deutschland.

6. Karl Friedrich Gegauf erfand in der Schweiz eine Nähmaschine. Richtig.

7. Seine Nähmaschine nähte 50 Stiche pro Minute. Falsch. Seine Nähmaschine nähte 100 Stiche pro Minute.

8. Der Prototyp der Hohlsaum-Nähmaschine wurde 1885 von einem Großbrand zerstört. Falsch. Der Großbrand zerstörte die Werkstatt der Gebrüder Gegauf, aber nicht den Prototyp der Hohlsaum-Nähmaschine.

9. Miele produziert Elektro-Haushaltsgeräte und hat in Deutschland 11.000 Mitarbeiter. Richtig.

10. Rowenta produziert nur Küchengeräte. Falsch. Rowenta produziert Küchen- und Haushaltsgeräte.

 Practice more at **vhlcentral.com**.

DEUTSCH IM ALLTAG

Materialien

die Fliesen (*pl.*)	*tiles*
der Granit	*granite*
das Holz	*wood*
die Keramik	*ceramic*
der Kunststoff	*plastic*
das Leder	*leather*
der Marmor	*marble*
der Stahl	*steel*

DIE DEUTSCHSPRACHIGE WELT

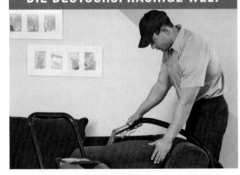

Fachleute Hauswirtschaft°

Ein offizieller Beruf in der Schweiz ist
Fachmann/Fachfrau Hauswirtschaft. Personen
mit diesem Beruf sind Experten für Hausarbeit.
Das Berufsziel°: Menschen fühlen sich in ihrer
Wohnung wohl°. Deshalb putzen sie Zimmer
schnell, gründlich° und umweltschonend°.
Bei Schäden° in Zimmern reparieren sie diese
Schäden. Fachleute Hauswirtschaft arbeiten
in Heimen°, Krankenhäusern°, Hotels und
Restaurants. Die Ausbildung° dauert drei Jahre.
Man muss in einem Betrieb° arbeiten, jede
Woche einen Tag in die Schule gehen und am
Ende Prüfungen machen.

Fachleute Hauswirtschaft *home economics specialists*
Berufsziel *professional aim* **fühlen sich... wohl** *feel
comfortable* **gründlich** *thoroughly* **umweltschonend**
environmentally friendly **Schäden** *damages*
Heimen *(nursing) homes* **Krankenhäusern** *hospitals*
Ausbildung *training* **Betrieb** *firm*

PORTRÄT

Johanna Spyri

Johanna Spyri (1827–1901),
geborene Heusser, war eine sehr
erfolgreiche° Schweizer Autorin.
Sie war das vierte von sechs
Kindern. Bis sie 25 Jahre alt war,
unterrichtete sie ihre jüngeren
Geschwister und half ihrer Mutter
im Haushalt. 1852 heiratete sie den
Rechtsberater Johann Bernhard
Spyri. Ihr Mann war nicht oft zu
Hause und Johanna Spyri mochte
Hausarbeit nicht. Deshalb animierte°
sie ein Freund, der Pastor Cornelius
Rudolph Vietor, zum Schreiben.
1871 veröffentlichte° sie ihre erste
Geschichte „Ein Blatt auf Vronys
Grab". Es war ein großer Erfolg.
Später schrieb sie ihr berühmtestes
Buch „Heidis Lehr- und Wanderjahre"
über das Waisenmädchen° Heidi. Es
ist ein Roman° über die romantische
Idylle der Schweizer Alpen. Dieser
Roman alleine existiert in mehr als
50 Sprachen. Insgesamt schrieb
Spyri 31 Bücher, 27 Erzählbände°
und 48 Erzählungen°.

erfolgreich *successful* **animierte** *encouraged*
veröffentlichte *published* **Waisenmädchen**
orphan girl **Roman** *novel* **Erzählbände**
anthologies **Erzählungen** *stories*

⟳S IM INTERNET

Suchen Sie Stellenangebote als Fachmann/frau
Hauswirtschaft in der Schweiz. Was muss man
machen? Schreiben Sie Beispiele auf.

Find out more at **vhlcentral.com**.

Suggestion Before they read the article on Johanna Spyri, have students
scan the text and underline all the **Präteritum** forms they can find.

---

2 **Was fehlt?** Ergänzen Sie die Sätze.

1. Ein Fachmann / Eine Fachfrau Hauswirtschaft ist ein Experte für Hausarbeit .

2. Fachleute Hauswirtschaft reparieren Schäden in Zimmern.

3. Die Ausbildung für Fachleute Hauswirtschaft dauert 3 Jahre .

4. Johanna Spyri fing mit dem Schreiben an, denn sie mochte Hausarbeit nicht.

5. Das bekannteste Buch Spyris ist über das Waisenmädchen Heidi .

6. Dieses Buch existiert in mehr als 50 Sprachen .

3 **Ihre Traumküche** Diskutieren Sie mit einem Partner / einer Partnerin
Ihre Traumküche. Welche Geräte sind in der Küche? Aus welchen
Materialien ist die Küche? Ist die Traumküche klein, groß, hell, etc.?
Wie sieht die Küche Ihres Partners aus?

3 **Suggestion** Before students work in pairs, have them review the
vocabulary in the **Deutsch im Alltag**, and explain the use of the forms
aus Holz, aus Marmor, aus Plastik, etc. You may want to bring in
pictures of kitchens from home-decorating magazines as a visual aid.

Ressourcen

vhlcentral.com

Strukturen

6B.1

Perfekt versus *Präteritum*  Presentation

Startblock You have learned to use both the **Perfekt** and the **Präteritum** to talk about past events. However, these two tenses are not used interchangeably.

> Ich **habe** es nicht **verstanden**, aber es **hat** mir **gefallen**.

> „Da **warf** ich in ein Eckchen mich, die Eingeweide **brannten**."

- The **Perfekt** tense is most often used in conversation and in informal writing, such as e-mails, blog entries, personal letters, or diaries.

  Habt ihr den Tisch **gedeckt**?
  *Did you **set** the table?*

  Nein, aber wir **haben** den Boden **gewischt**.
  *No, but we **mopped** the floor.*

- The **Präteritum** is generally used in formal or literary writing, such as novels or newspaper articles, or in other formal contexts, such as news reports or speeches. It is sometimes called the *narrative past*, since it is often used to narrate a series of related past events.

  Es **war** einmal eine junge Frau mit dem Namen Aschenputtel.
  *Once upon a time, there **was** a young woman named Cinderella.*

  Jeden Tag **fegte** sie den Boden, **machte** sie die Betten und **spülte** sie das Geschirr.
  *Every day, she **swept** the floors, **made** the beds, and **washed** the dishes.*

- A few specific verbs are commonly used in the **Präteritum**, even in informal contexts. In conversation, German speakers typically use the **Präteritum** of **sein**, **haben**, and modal verbs, rather than the **Perfekt**.

  Hattet ihr am Mittwoch keine Hausaufgaben?
  *Didn't you **have** any homework on Wednesday?*

  Meine alte Wohnung **war** ein Saustall.
  *My old apartment **was** a pigsty.*

  Die Kinder **wollten** das Gemüse nicht essen.
  *The kids **didn't want** to eat their vegetables.*

  Solltet ihr gestern nicht staubsaugen?
  *Weren't you **supposed** to vacuum yesterday?*

- The **Präteritum** is also preferred by most speakers after the subordinating conjunction **als**.

  Als wir Kinder **waren**, haben wir viel Hausarbeit gemacht.
  *When we **were** kids, we did a lot of housework.*

  Als ich die Garage **aufräumte**, habe ich viele alte Bücher gefunden.
  *When I **cleaned up** the garage, I found lots of old books.*

- German verbs are usually listed in dictionaries and vocabulary lists by their *principal parts* (**Stammformen**): the infinitive, the third-person singular form of the **Präteritum**, and the past participle. For verbs with stem changes in the **Präsens**, the third-person singular form is given in parentheses. For completely regular verbs, only the infinitive is listed.

  geben (gibt)
  to give (gives)

  gab
  gave

  gegeben
  given

- Knowing the principal parts of a verb allows you to produce all of its conjugations in any tense. Here are the principal parts of some of the verbs you've learned so far.

infinitive	*Präteritum*	past participle
bringen	brachte	gebracht
denken	dachte	gedacht
essen (isst)	aß	gegessen
helfen (hilft)	half	geholfen
laufen (läuft)	lief	ist gelaufen
nehmen (nimmt)	nahm	genommen
schlafen (schläft)	schlief	geschlafen
sehen (sieht)	sah	gesehen
sitzen	saß	gesessen
verstehen	verstand	verstanden
waschen (wäscht)	wusch	gewaschen
wissen (weiß)	wusste	gewusst

Sie **nahm** einen Besen und **gab** ihrem Bruder den Staubsauger.
*She **took** a broom and **gave** her brother the vacuum cleaner.*

Ich **habe** nur einen Keks **genommen** und habe Peter die anderen **gegeben**.
*I only **took** one cookie and **gave** the rest to Peter.*

Suggestion Go over the verbs in this list and make sure students remember their meanings. Then have them close their books and quiz them on the past tense forms. Give them infinitives from the list and have them call out the preterite and perfect forms.

Expansion Give students the first sentence of a story using the preterite. One at a time, have students add a sentence to the story, on a piece of paper folded so that only the previous sentence is visible. When everyone has contributed, unfold the paper and share the story with the class.

QUERVERWEIS

See **Appendix A** for a complete list of strong verbs with their principal parts.

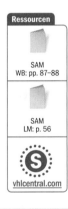

Ressourcen

SAM
WB: pp. 87–88

SAM
LM: p. 56

S
vhlcentral.com

 Jetzt sind Sie dran! Wählen Sie die richtige Zeitform (*tense*) für die folgenden Sätze.

1. Es war einmal ein Mädchen mit dem Namen Rapunzel. (Perfekt / Präteritum)

2. Der Junge saß allein in seinem Zimmer und weinte. (Perfekt / Präteritum)

3. Donnerstags wusch ich die Wäsche. (Perfekt / Präteritum)

4. Was hast du an der Universität studiert? (Perfekt / Präteritum)

5. Meine Eltern haben ein Haus in München gemietet. (Perfekt / Präteritum)

6. Sie wollten schon immer in Bayern wohnen. (Perfekt / Präteritum)

7. Hast du schon den Balkon gefegt? (Perfekt / Präteritum)

8. Heute Morgen war die Mikrowelle noch sauber. (Perfekt / Präteritum)

9. In meiner alten Wohnung hatte ich eine Spülmaschine. (Perfekt / Präteritum)

10. Die ganze Familie hat Alex bei seinem Umzug geholfen. (Perfekt / Präteritum)

11. In seiner neuen Wohnung konnte er sehr gut schlafen. (Perfekt / Präteritum)

12. Er hat wirklich Glück gehabt. (Perfekt / Präteritum)

Anwendung

1 **Perfekt oder Präteritum?** Welche Zeitform benutzt man gewöhnlich (*generally*) in diesen Situationen?

 BEISPIEL Perfekt

1. _____ Präteritum

2. _____ Perfekt   3. _____ Perfekt   4. _____ Präteritum

2 **Was fehlt?** Ergänzen Sie die Tabelle mit den fehlenden Informationen.

	Infinitiv	Präteritum	Perfekt
1.	dürfen	durfte	hat gedurft
2.	gehen	ging	ist gegangen
3.	fahren	fuhr	ist gefahren
4.	nehmen	nahm	hat genommen
5.	kommen	kam	ist gekommen
6.	sehen	sah	hat gesehen
7.	bringen	brachte	hat gebracht
8.	mögen	mochte	hat gemocht

3 **Ein kurzes Gespräch** Ergänzen Sie die Sätze mit den fehlenden Verbformen im Perfekt oder im Präteritum.

BEISPIEL **SARA** Was _hast_ du gestern Abend _gemacht_? (*machen*)

ANNA Ich (1) _sollte_ in die Bibliothek gehen, aber Michael (2) _wollte_ mit mir spazieren gehen. Es (3) _war_ langweilig. (sollen, wollen, sein)

SARA Ach ja? (4) _Musste_ er nicht mit Mira einkaufen gehen? (müssen)

ANNA Mira (5) _konnte_ nicht, denn ihre Eltern (6) _sind_ zum Abendessen (7) _gekommen_. (können, kommen)

SARA Haha! Das (8) _hat_ sie bestimmt toll (9) _gefunden_. (finden)

ANNA Das weiß ich nicht. Ich (10) _habe_ heute nicht mit ihr (11) _gesprochen_. (sprechen)

 Practice more at **vhlcentral.com**.

Kommunikation

4 **Ein bisschen Geschichte** Erraten Sie zusammen mit Ihrem Partner / Ihrer Partnerin, welches Ereignis (*event*) zu welchem historischen Datum passt.

BEISPIEL

S1: *Was ist im Jahr 2005 passiert?*
S2: *2005 ist Angela Merkel als erste Frau Bundeskanzlerin von Deutschland geworden.*

Historisches Datum	Ereignis
_b_ **1.** 1295	**a.** Die Berliner Mauer fiel.
_d_ **2.** 1492	**b.** Marco Polo brachte chinesische Nudeln nach Italien.
_c_ **3.** 1824	**c.** Ludwig van Beethoven komponierte seine 9. Sinfonie.
_e_ **4.** 1918	**d.** Christoph Kolumbus reiste nach Amerika.
_a_ **5.** 1989	**e.** Deutschland verlor den Ersten Weltkrieg (*World War*).
_f_ **6.** 2005	**f.** Angela Merkel wurde als erste Frau Bundeskanzlerin von Deutschland.

5 **Julians Kalender** Erzählen Sie zusammen mit Ihrem Partner / Ihrer Partnerin, was Julian im April alles gemacht hat. Benutzen Sie das Perfekt und/oder Präteritum. Sample answers are provided.

BEISPIEL

S1: *Am 6. April hat er einen Film gesehen.*
S2: *Und am 7. April war er beim Friseur.*

Am 2. April hat er ein Basketballspiel gehabt. / Am 4. April musste er ein Geschenk kaufen. / Am 6. April ist er ins Kino gegangen. / Am 11. April hatte seine Mutter Geburtstag. / Am 15. April ist er auf die Party bei Tom gegangen. / Am 19. April war er auf dem Coldplay-Konzert. / Am 23. April ist er mit Lara im Restaurant gewesen. / Am 27. April hatte er einen Deutschtest.

APRIL

MO	DI	MI	DO	FR	SA	SO
						1 / Basketballspiel 2
3	Geschenk kaufen 4	5	Film „Sophie Scholl" 6	Friseur 7	8	9
10	Mama Geburtstag 11	12	13	14	Party bei Tom 15	16
17	18	Coldplay-Konzert 19	20	21	22	Essen mit Lara 23
24	25	26	Deutschtest 27	28	29	30

5 **Suggestion** Verify that students remember how to read dates out loud. Ex.: **am zweiten April, am fünften April, am siebten April.**

5 **Expansion** Have students create their own calendar (real or fictional) for the last month and have them share their activities with the class, using complete sentences in the present perfect.

6 **Ein Märchen** Schreiben Sie mit Ihrem Partner / Ihrer Partnerin das Märchen zu Ende. Sie dürfen auch Ihr eigenes Märchen erfinden (*make up*). Schreiben Sie sechs bis acht Sätze im Präteritum. Answers will vary.

1. Es war einmal ein junges Mädchen. Sie hatte einen gemeinen Stiefbruder. Eines Tages...

2. Es waren einmal ein Hund, eine Katze, ein Hamster und ein Vogel. Sie wohnten alle bei einer alten Frau. Eines Tages...

3. Es war einmal ein kleiner Hund. Er wohnte allein im Wald und wollte so gern eine Familie haben. Eines Tages...

Suggestion Tell students that **Es war einmal...** is a standard fairy tale beginning in German. Provide them with a standard ending that they can use for their fairy tales, such as: **Und wenn sie nicht gestorben sind, dann leben sie noch heute.**

6B.2

Separable and inseparable prefix verbs in the *Perfekt*

 **Presentation**

Startblock In **4A.3** you learned about separable and inseparable prefix verbs in the present tense. In the **Perfekt**, the past participles of verbs with prefixes are formed slightly differently than those of other verbs.

> Du **hast** den Boden nicht gefegt und auch die Möbel nicht **abgestaubt**.

> Wir **haben** die Töpfe **weggeräumt** und eklige Dinge aus dem Kühlschrank **entfernt**.

- Verbs with prefixes can be either strong, weak, or mixed.

Ihr **habt** das Zimmer **aufgeräumt**.	Wir **haben** Kuchen **mitgebracht**.	Sie **sind** nach Berlin **umgezogen**.
*You **cleaned up** the room.*	*We **brought** cake.*	*They **moved** to Berlin.*

- To form the past participle of a separable prefix verb, add the separable prefix to the past participle of the root verb, before the **-ge-** prefix.

infinitive	participle	infinitive	participle
anrufen	**an**gerufen	rausbringen	**raus**gebracht
aufräumen	**auf**geräumt	umtauschen	**um**getauscht
ausgehen	(ist) **aus**gegangen	umziehen	(ist) **um**gezogen
einkaufen	**ein**gekauft	vorstellen	**vor**gestellt
mitbringen	**mit**gebracht	wegräumen	**weg**geräumt

> Sie **haben** mich zum Tee zu sich **eingeladen**.

> Wir **haben** Staub gesaugt und **abgestaubt**.

Wir **haben** das Geschirr **weggeräumt**.
*We **put away** the dishes.*

Ich **habe** den kaputten Staubsauger **umgetauscht**.
*I **exchanged** the broken vacuum cleaner.*

- The past participles of inseparable prefix verbs are formed like those of separable prefix verbs, but without the **-ge-** prefix.

infinitive	participle	infinitive	participle
bedeuten	**be**deutet	erklären	**er**klärt
beginnen	**be**gonnen	gehören	**ge**hört
besuchen	**be**sucht	verkaufen	**ver**kauft
bezahlen	**be**zahlt	verschmutzen	**ver**schmutzt
entdecken	**ent**deckt	verstehen	**ver**standen

Herr Koch **hat** uns einen neuen
   Gefrierschrank **verkauft**.
*Mr. Koch **sold** us a new freezer.*

Der Vermieter **hat** das Loch in der Wand
   entdeckt.
*The landlord **discovered** the hole in the wall.*

Sarahs Bruder **hat** uns einmal **besucht**.
*Sarah's brother **came to visit** us once.*

Ich **habe** die Frage nicht **verstanden**.
*I **didn't understand** the question.*

- Remember that the prefixes of inseparable prefix verbs are never stressed, while the prefixes of separable prefix verbs are always stressed.

Wie viel hast du für den
   Toaster be**zahlt**?
How much did you pay for the toaster?

Wir haben viele
   Gäste **ein**geladen.
We invited a lot of guests.

- Most separable and inseparable prefix verbs are conjugated with **haben**. However, prefixed verbs that indicate a change in condition or location and do not take a direct object are conjugated with **sein**.

Der Hund **hat** den sauberen
   Boden **verschmutzt**.
*The dog **got** the clean floor **dirty**.*

Wir **sind** mit unseren Großeltern in die
   Schweiz **mitgefahren**.
*We **went** to Switzerland with our grandparents.*

Du **hast** den dreckigen Teppich **rausgebracht**.
*You **took out** the dirty rug.*

Tobias **ist** gestern Abend **ausgegangen**.
*Tobias **went out** last night.*

- Since prefixes change the meaning of a verb, in some cases a prefixed verb is conjugated with **sein**, while its base form is conjugated with **haben**.

Sie **sind** vor einem Jahr **umgezogen**.
*They **moved** a year ago.*

Die Hunde **haben** den Schlitten **gezogen**.
*The dogs **pulled** the sled.*

Expansion Have students write a fictional journal entry using the following verbs in the present perfect tense: **aufräumen, verkaufen, einkaufen, anrufen, bekommen, bestellen, verlieren, vergessen.**

QUERVERWEIS

See **5B.1** to review the formation of the **Perfekt** with **sein**.

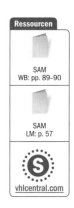

Ressourcen

SAM
WB: pp. 89–90

SAM
LM: p. 57

S
vhlcentral.com

Jetzt sind Sie dran!   **Ergänzen Sie die Sätze mit den richtigen Formen der Verben im Perfekt.**

Suggestion Before they begin this **Jetzt sind Sie dran!** activity, have students identify the verbs with inseparable prefixes.

1. Paul _____*hat*_____ den Müll nicht *rausgebracht*. (rausbringen)

2. Liebe Kinder, _____*habt*_____ ihr eure Zimmer schon _____*aufgeräumt*_____? (aufräumen)

3. Frau Schulz _____*hat*_____ den Wäschetrockner _____*verkauft*_____. (verkaufen)

4. David _____*hat*_____ seine Freundin _____*angerufen*_____. (anrufen)

5. Anna, _____*habe*_____ ich dir meinen neuen Freund _____*vorgestellt*_____? (vorstellen)

6. Mama _____*hat*_____ eine schöne Vase zu Weihnachten _____*bekommen*_____. (bekommen)

7. Du _____*hast*_____ den Ring in der Waschmaschine _____*entdeckt*_____. (entdecken)

8. Ich _____*bin*_____ mit meinem Freund _____*ausgegangen*_____. (ausgehen)

9. Wir _____*haben*_____ eine Kaffeemaschine im Internet _____*bestellt*_____. (bestellen)

10. Wie viel _____*habt*_____ ihr für den Wäschetrockner _____*bezahlt*_____? (bezahlen)

11. Maria, _____*hast*_____ du das Geschirr _____*weggeräumt*_____? (wegräumen)

12. Ich _____*habe*_____ die Hausaufgaben zu Hause _____*vergessen*_____! (vergessen)

Anwendung

1 Perfektformen Formen Sie die Sätze vom Präsens ins Perfekt um.

 BEISPIEL Er ruft seine Schwester an.
Er hat seine Schwester angerufen.

1. Mein Bruder kommt mit.
   Mein Bruder ist mitgekommen.
2. Ich stelle meine Eltern vor.
   Ich habe meine Eltern vorgestellt.
3. Georg kommt in Zürich an.
   Georg ist in Zürich angekommen.
4. Du besuchst das Museum.
   Du hast das Museum besucht.

5. Wir bringen ein Geschenk mit.
   Wir haben ein Geschenk mitgebracht.
6. Sara vergisst ihre Handtasche.
   Sara hat ihre Handtasche vergessen.
7. Der Professor wiederholt die Grammatik.
   Der Professor hat die Grammatik wiederholt.
8. Ihr schaut bei dem Fußballmatch zu.
   Ihr habt bei dem Fußballmatch zugeschaut.

2 Letzten Freitag Was haben diese Leute letzten Freitag gemacht? Bilden Sie Sätze im Perfekt.

 ▶ **BEISPIEL** Paula / ihre Schwester anrufen
Paula hat ihre Schwester angerufen.

1. Klara / nicht früh aufstehen
   Klara ist nicht früh aufgestanden.

2. Moritz / sein Fahrrad verkaufen
   Moritz hat sein Fahrrad verkauft.
3. Herr Huber / neue Schuhe anziehen
   Herr Huber hat neue Schuhe angezogen.
4. Ali / sein Zimmer aufräumen
   Ali hat sein Zimmer aufgeräumt.
5. Marie und ihre Freundin / ausgehen
   Marie und ihre Freundin sind ausgegangen.

3 Das war früher anders Sarah ist heutzutage (*nowadays*) sehr fleißig und nett, aber das war nicht immer so. Erzählen Sie, was Sarah alles gemacht hat, als sie jünger war. Answers will vary. Sample answers are provided.

BEISPIEL Heutzutage ruft sie ihre Mutter oft an.
Früher (Before) hat sie ihre Mutter selten angerufen.

1. Heutzutage steht sie immer früh auf.
   Früher ist sie immer spät aufgestanden.
2. Heutzutage geht sie oft einkaufen.
   Früher ist sie selten einkaufen gegangen.
3. Heutzutage bereitet sie täglich Essen vor.
   Früher hat sie selten Essen vorbereitet.

4. Heutzutage bringt sie immer den Müll raus.
   Früher hat sie selten den Müll rausgebracht.
5. Heutzutage geht sie nur selten aus.
   Früher ist sie oft ausgegangen.
6. Heutzutage schläft sie immer früh ein.
   Früher ist sie selten früh eingeschlafen.

4 Was ist passiert? Was hat Georg letztes Wochenende in Zürich gemacht? Schreiben Sie acht Sätze im Perfekt. Answers will vary.

BEISPIEL *Georg ist am frühen Morgen in Zürich angekommen.*

ankommen	ausgehen	bezahlen	mitkommen
anrufen	bekommen	einkaufen	vergessen
aufstehen	besuchen	mitbringen	zurückkommen

 Practice more at **vhlcentral.com.**

Kommunikation

5 Kindheitserinnerungen

5 Kindheitserinnerungen Stellen Sie Ihrem Partner / Ihrer Partnerin acht logische Fragen über seine/ihre Kindheit. Benutzen Sie das Perfekt und verwenden Sie Wörter aus jeder Spalte. Sie dürfen auch andere Elemente hinzufügen (*add*). Answers will vary.

5 Suggestion Before students begin writing, have them review the past participle of each verb and identify which ones will have **sein** as the auxiliary.

BEISPIEL

S1: Wie oft hast du dein Zimmer aufgeräumt?
S2: Ich habe es einmal in der Woche aufgeräumt.

A	B	C
Mit wem?	einmal in der Woche	aufhängen
Wen?	immer sehr spät	aufräumen
Wann?	in ein neues Haus	aufstehen
Was?	Poster von Rockstars	ausgehen
Wie oft?	deine Verwandten	bekommen
Wer?	mit Freunden	besuchen
deine Eltern	immer dein Zimmer	einschlafen
deine Geschwister	im Unterricht	umziehen
du	zum Geburtstag	vorbereiten

6 Nicht nur Hausarbeiten

6 Nicht nur Hausarbeiten Was haben diese Personen am Wochenende gemacht? Schreiben Sie mit Ihrem Partner / Ihrer Partnerin zu jedem Bild einen Satz im Perfekt. Sample answers are provided.

▶ **BEISPIEL** Greta und Jan
Greta und Jan sind ausgegangen.

1. Martin
Martin hat seine Schwester angerufen.

2. Jonas
Jonas ist spät aufgestanden.

3. Nils und Max
Nils und Max haben den Müll rausgebracht.

4. Frau Lange
Frau Lange hat das Wohnzimmer aufgeräumt.

5. Yusuf
Yusuf hat seine Freundin besucht.

7 Die neugierige Oma

7 Die neugierige Oma Ihre Oma will wissen, was Sie dieses Semester schon alles gemacht haben. Spielen Sie mit Ihrem Partner / Ihrer Partnerin einen Dialog und benutzen Sie die Perfektformen. Answers will vary.

BEISPIEL

Kaffee trinken
S1: Hast du viel Kaffee getrunken?
S2: Ja, Oma, ich habe viel Kaffee getrunken.

oft die Eltern anrufen	immer das Bett machen
früh aufstehen	die Badewanne putzen
oft ausgehen	den Müll rausbringen
oft Freunde einladen	die Hausaufgaben vorbereiten
fleißig lernen	die Kleider waschen

8 Die Haushaltsführung

8 Die Haushaltsführung Schreiben Sie zu zweit einen Dialog. Ein Hotelbesitzer / Eine Hotelbesitzerin spricht mit einem Fachmann / einer Fachfrau Hauswirtschaft über die Haushaltsführung (*housekeeping*). Answers will vary.

BEISPIEL **S1:** Haben Sie den Dachboden aufgeräumt?
S2: Ja, ich habe ihn aufgeräumt und habe auch die Wäsche gewaschen.

Wiederholung

1 Expansion Take survey of the class, based on this activity.
Ex.: **Haben wir saubere Zimmer? Wie viele von uns haben diese Woche Staub gewischt? Wer hat gestaubsaugt?**, etc.

1 Hausarbeit Fragen Sie Ihren Partner / Ihre Partnerin, was für Hausarbeit er/sie diese Woche gemacht hat.

1 Suggestion Before they begin the activity, have students review the past participles of the verbs listed.

BEISPIEL

S1: *Hast du diese Woche den Boden gewischt?*
S2: *Ja, ich habe den Boden gewischt. Du auch?*

Kleider bügeln	den Müll rausbringen
den Tisch decken	Geschirr spülen
die Küche fegen	staubsaugen
das Bett machen	Wäsche waschen
Hausarbeit machen	den Boden wischen

2 Arbeitsblatt Sie bekommen von Ihrem Professor / Ihrer Professorin eine Liste mit Aktivitäten. Fragen Sie Ihre Klassenkameraden, ob sie die Aktivitäten letzten Monat gemacht haben. Finden Sie eine Person für jede Aktivität.

BEISPIEL

S1: *Hast du letzten Monat deine Eltern angerufen?*
S2: *Ja, ich habe sie angerufen.*

Die neue Küche Machen Sie zu dritt ein Rollenspiel. Eine Person spielt einen Hausbesitzer / eine Hausbesitzerin. Die anderen zwei spielen Lieferanten (*delivery people*) von Haushaltgeräten. Die Lieferanten fragen, wohin sie die Geräte stellen sollen.

BEISPIEL

S1: *Wohin sollen wir die Waschmaschine stellen?*
S2: *Stellen Sie sie links neben die Tür.*
S3: *Und die Kaffeemaschine?*

der Gefrierschrank	die Mikrowelle
der Herd	der Ofen
die Kaffeemaschine	die Spülmaschine
der Kühlschrank	der Wäschetrockner

Diskutieren und kombinieren Sie und Ihr Partner / Ihre Partnerin bekommen zwei verschiedene Blätter mit Alexandras Aktivitäten. Ergänzen Sie Alexandras Tageslauf. Schreiben Sie dann eine Erzählung darüber.

BEISPIEL

S1: *Um halb fünf ist Alexandra im Park gelaufen.*
S2: *Danach, um fünf Uhr...*

5 Ein Luxushotel Erstellen Sie (*Create*) mit einem Partner / einer Partnerin einen Text für die Website von einem Luxushotel in der Schweiz. Beschreiben Sie das Hotel, die Zimmer und Aktivitäten im Hotel und in der Gegend (*area*).

2 Suggestion Have students compete to see who can be the first to get a positive answer for all eight questions. Circulate around the classroom, monitoring production and keeping students on task.

BEISPIEL

DAS HOTEL
Schweiz HOME | ROOMS & SUITES | RESTAURANT

Kommen Sie zu Besuch!

In unseren wunderschönen Zimmern finden Sie Kühlschrank, Mikrowelle und Kaffeemaschine.

6 Die Mitbewohner Schreiben Sie mit Ihrem Partner / Ihrer Partnerin eine Geschichte (*story*) über zwei Mitbewohner. Ein Mitbewohner ist sehr fleißig, aber der andere ist ganz anders (*completely different*). Benutzen Sie das Präteritum.

BEISPIEL

Es waren einmal zwei Mitbewohner, Daniel und Fabian. Daniel war sehr fleißig. Er lernte viel, machte jeden Abend seine Hausaufgaben, und machte jedes Wochenende die Hausarbeit. Aber Fabian...

7 Ein Festessen

Die Studenten im Studentenwohnheim wollen Gäste zum Essen einladen. Besprechen Sie mit zwei Partnern/Partnerinnen die Vorbereitungen für den Abend. Schreiben Sie auf, wer was macht.

BEISPIEL

S1: Das Wohnzimmer ist ein Saustall! Wir müssen es putzen. Wer will staubsaugen?
S2: Ich kann staubsaugen. Und du? Kannst du...

8 Was ist passiert?

Fragen Sie Ihren Partner / Ihre Partnerin, was er/sie letzte Woche gemacht hat. Schreiben Sie dann einen Bericht (*report*) über seine/ihre Aktivitäten. Benutzen Sie das Präteritum. Answers will vary.

BEISPIEL

S1: Hast du letzte Woche den Boden gefegt?
S2: Nein, aber ich habe mein Bett gemacht.
S1: (*Schreibt*) Sie fegte den Boden nicht, aber sie machte ihr Bett.

9 Eine Lebensgeschichte

Wählen Sie eine berühmte Person, und schreiben Sie mit einem Partner / einer Partnerin eine kurze Biographie über diese Person. Sie dürfen auch eine Person erfinden (*invent*).

BEISPIEL

Brad Pitt (1963–)

Mit zwei musste er mit seiner Familie nach Springfield Missouri umziehen, denn sein Vater hatte da einen Job. Im Gymnasium hat er...

Mein Wör | ter | buch

Schreiben Sie noch fünf weitere Wörter in Ihr persönliches Wörterbuch zu den Themen **zu Hause** und **Hausarbeit**.

der Staub

Übersetzung
dust

Wortart
Substantiv

Gebrauch
Ich putze mein Zimmer, denn es liegt zu viel Staub unterm Bett.

Synonyme
—

Antonyme
—

Vocabulary tools

Panorama Interactive Map

Die Schweiz und Liechtenstein

NATIONAL connections cultures STANDARDS

Die Schweiz in Zahlen

▶ **Fläche:** *41,277 km²*

▶ **Offizielle Sprachen:** *Deutsch (64,9%), Französisch (22,6%), Italienisch (8,3%), Rätoromanisch° (0,5%)*

▶ **Bevölkerung:** *8,1 Millionen*

▶ **Religion:** *römisch-katholisch 38,2%, evangelisch 26,9%*

▶ **Hauptstadt:** *Bern*

▶ **Städte:** *Zürich (390.000 Einwohner), Genf (192.000), Basel (193.000) und Bern (134.000)*

▶ **Berge:** *Hohe Dufourspitze (4.634 m), Dom (4.545 m), Matterhorn (4.478 m)*

▶ **Flüsse:** *der Rhein, die Aare, die Rhone*

▶ **Wichtige Industriezweige:** *Uhrenindustrie°, Maschinenbau, Banken und Versicherungen°*

▶ **Touristenattraktionen:** *St.-Gotthard-Pass, Burgen von Bellinzona, Schweizerischer Nationalpark, Jungfraujoch bei Grindelwald.*

QUELLE: Offizielles Informationsportal der Schweiz

Liechtenstein in Zahlen

▶ **Offizieller Name:** *Fürstentum° Liechtenstein*

▶ **Fläche:** *160 km²*

▶ **Bevölkerung:** *37.313*

▶ **Religion:** *römisch-katholisch 76%, evangelisch 8%*

▶ **Hauptstadt:** *Vaduz (5.372 Einwohner)*

▶ **Berge:** *Vorderer Grauspitz (2.599 m), Naafkopf (2.570 m)*

▶ **Niedrigster Punkt:** *Ruggeller Riet (430 m)*

▶ **Flüsse:** *der Rhein, die Samina*

▶ **Wichtige Industriezweige:** *Maschinenbau, Nahrungsmittel°*

▶ **Touristenattraktionen:** *Schloss Vaduz, Kathedrale St. Florin, Kunstmuseum Liechtenstein.*

QUELLE: Portal des Fürstentums Liechtenstein

Expansion For homework, have students find online pictures of the people and places mentioned on this page. Depending on the size of your class, each student could be responsible for one or two pictures.

Rätoromanisch Romansch **Uhrenindustrie** clock and watch industry **Versicherungen** insurance companies **Fürstentum** principality **Nahrungsmittel** food products **Kriminalitätsrate** crime rate **niedrig** low **Gefängnissen** prisons **Häftlinge** inmates **Haftstrafen** sentences

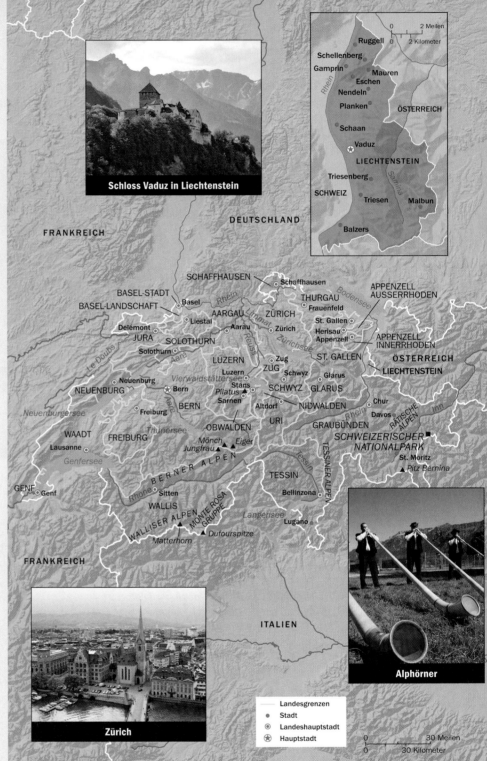

Schloss Vaduz in Liechtenstein

Zürich

Alphörner

Landesgrenzen
● Stadt
◎ Landeshauptstadt
✪ Hauptstadt

Unglaublich, aber wahr!

In Liechtenstein ist die Kriminalitätsrate° extrem niedrig°. In den Gefängnissen° sitzen nur wenige Häftlinge°. Die Kollaboration zwischen Liechtenstein, Österreich und der Schweiz ist sehr eng. Zum Beispiel kommen alle Liechtensteiner Häftlinge mit Haftstrafen° über zwei Jahren in österreichische Gefängnisse.

Politik

Fürstentum Liechtenstein

Liechtenstein ist ein Binnenland° in Mitteleuropa.
Es liegt in den Alpen zwischen Österreich und der
Schweiz. Unabhängig° ist das Land seit 1806.
Liechtenstein ist ein Fürstentum. Fürst Hans-Adam II.
von und zu Liechtenstein ist das Staatsoberhaupt°,
aber Adrian Hasler ist seit 2013 der demokratisch
gewählte Regierungschef°. Das Land hat keine Armee.
Liechtenstein ist das kleinste deutschsprachige Land.
Allerdings ist Deutsch nur in Liechtenstein die alleinige
Amts- und Landessprache°.

Industrie

Präzisionszeitmessgeräte°

In der Schweiz gibt es eine sehr
lange Tradition für die Produktion von
Präzisionszeitmessgeräten. Ein Beispiel ist
das Marinechronometer. Auf einem Schiff°
kann man mit diesem Gerät Längengrade
bestimmen° und es für astronomische
Ortsbestimmungen benutzen. Der Schweizer
Uhrmacher° Louis Berthoud (1753–1813)
stellte ein Präzisions-Taschenchronometer
her°, das Alexander von Humboldt 1799 auf
seinen Schiffsreisen testete. Heute müssen
Chronometer extrem exakt sein. Nur eine
Organisation weltweit, das unabhängige
Schweizer Observatorium *Contrôle officiel
suisse des chronomètres* (COSC) darf die
Präzision von Chronometern prüfen°
und zertifizieren.

Kultur

Vier Amtssprachen

In der Schweiz gibt es vier offizielle
Sprachen: Deutsch, Französisch, Italienisch
und Rätoromanisch. Kantone haben aber
meistens nur eine Amtssprache. Im Westen,
an der Grenze zu Frankreich, dominiert
Französisch und im Südosten, an der Grenze
zu Italien, Italienisch. Im Norden, Zentrum
und Osten dominiert Deutsch. Nur im Kanton
Graubünden gibt es drei Amtssprachen:
Deutsch, Rätoromanisch und Italienisch.
Die meisten Schweizer sprechen nur eine
Sprache als Muttersprache. Dafür lernen
viele Schweizer mindestens eine weitere°
Sprache. Einige sind auch dreisprachig.

Menschen

Roger Federer

Roger Federer ist ein Schweizer Tennisspieler.
Viele Experten halten° ihn für den besten
Tennisspieler aller Zeiten. Er gewann 17 Grand-
Slam-Turniere (Australian Open, French Open,
Wimbledon, US Open) und stand 237 Wochen
lang auf Platz 1 der Tennisweltrangliste. Er ist
einer von sieben Spielern, die in ihrer Karriere
alle Grand-Slam-Turniere gewannen. 2008
gewann er zusammen mit Stanislas Wawrinka
in Beijing eine olympische Goldmedaille im
Doppel. In den Jahren 2005–2008 war er
Weltsportler des Jahres.

 IM INTERNET

1. Suchen Sie Informationen über
   andere berühmte Schweizer Sportler.
   Welchen Sport machen sie? Was
   haben sie gewonnen?

2. Suchen Sie weitere Informationen
   über Schweizer Uhren: Was können
   Sie über die Uhrenproduktion in der
   Schweiz finden? Was sind bekannte
   Marken? Warum sind sie bekannt?

Find out more at **vhlcentral.com**.

Binnenland *land-locked country* **Unabhängig** *Independent* **Staatsoberhaupt** *head of state* **Regierungschef** *head of government*
Amts- und Landessprache *official and national language* **halten** *consider* **weitere** *more* **Präzisionszeitmessgeräte**
precision time measuring instruments **Schiff** *ship* **Längengrade bestimmen** *determine longitude* **Uhrmacher** *watchmaker*
stellte... her *produced* **prüfen** *test*

 Was haben Sie gelernt? Ergänzen Sie die Sätze.

1. In Liechtenstein ist die Kriminalitätsrate extrem ___niedrig___.

2. Ein Häftling mit über zwei Jahren Haft sitzt in ___Österreich___ im Gefängnis.

3. Liechtenstein liegt zwischen Österreich und ___der Schweiz___.

4. Liechtenstein hat ein Staatsoberhaupt sowie einen ___Regierungschef___.

5. Roger Federer stand ___237___ Wochen lang an der Spitze
   der Tennisweltrangliste.

6. In den Jahren 2005–2008 war Federer ___Weltsportler___ des Jahres.

7. Die vier Amtssprachen der Schweiz sind Deutsch, ___Französisch___, Italienisch
   und Rätoromanisch.

8. Die meisten Schweizer sprechen eine Sprache als ___Muttersprache___.

9. Alexander von Humboldt testete ___1799___ ein Schweizer Präzisions-
   Taschenchronometer auf seinen Schiffsreisen.

10. Nur eine ___Organisation___ weltweit darf Chronometer prüfen.

 Practice more at **vhlcentral.com**.

Lesen Audio: Reading

Vor dem Lesen

Strategien

Recognizing word families

Recognizing related words can help you guess the meaning of words in context. Using this strategy will improve your reading comprehension and enrich your German vocabulary.

Text untersuchen

Suchen Sie im Text ein anderes Wort aus der gleichen Wortfamilie. Answers will vary. Sample answers are provided.

BEISPIEL

Zimmer _Zweizimmerwohnung_

1. Möbel _Möblierung_
2. Küche _Einbauküche_
3. Monat _monatlich_
4. Garage _Tiefgarage_
5. Miete _Kaltmiete_
6. Wohnung _Luxuswohnung_
7. Internet _Internetanschluss_
8. Bett _Bettwäsche_

Präfixe

Suchen Sie mit einem Partner / einer Partnerin im Text ein neues Verb für jede Wortfamilie.

1. mieten _vermieten_ untermieten
2. kaufen verkaufen _einkaufen_
3. fangen _anfangen_ verfangen
4. _stehen_ aufstehen verstehen
5. lassen _verlassen_ entlassen
6. _bieten_ anbieten verbieten

Suggestion Learning to break down long compound words and identify their roots is an important reading strategy. For homework, have students find long German words online or in a dictionary. Have students write their words on the board, then break them down together into their component words.

IEN +41 56 5559990 SCHWEIZER IMMOBILIEN +41 56 5559990 SCHWEIZER

Wohnung im historischen Fribourg

SIE SUCHEN eine kuschelige° Wohnung für zwei? Sie möchten das Leben in der historischen Innenstadt Fribourgs nicht verlassen°? Dann ist diese Zweizimmerwohnung ideal!

Die Schlafzimmer sind mit Einbauschränken ausgestattet°. Die Wohnung hat eine moderne Einbauküche mit Gasherd und Backofen. Sie bietet° ein modernes Bad, ein großes Wohn- und Esszimmer mit direktem Zugang° zur Küche. Einkaufen können Sie natürlich bequem° in einem Umkreis von fünf Minuten. Sie haben ein Auto? Kein Problem! Sie können Ihr Auto für monatlich SFr 75 auf einen Parkplatz in der Tiefgarage stellen. Zu vermieten ab Juli für SFr 1.100 Kaltmiete.

SIE SUCHEN FÜR IHRE FAMILIE ein neues Zuhause im Kanton Tessin? Ihnen gefällt die Kombination von Kultur und Natur? Sie lieben traditionelle Architektur, viel Holz und warmes Wetter? Dann ist dieses Einfamilienhaus perfekt!

Das Chalet liegt direkt am Lago Maggiore in der Nähe° von Locarno. Es ist als typisches Chalet mit Holzfassaden gebaut. Für eine Familie bieten Esszimmer, Wohnzimmer, zwei Badezimmer plus drei Schlafzimmer viel Platz. Die Küche mit Einbauküche und Frühstücksecke° ist familienfreundlich. Im Keller stehen Waschmaschine und Trockner. Im Garten können Kinder spielen, Hunde herumlaufen und Eltern Grillpartys feiern. Das Haus liegt fünf Minuten entfernt von Locarnos Innenstadt und in 20 Minuten ist man in den Bergen. Zu vermieten ab August. Die Miete beträgt monatlich SFr 2.000 ohne Nebenkosten°.

Expansion Give students a fictional profile of someone looking for an apartment and have them decide which of the three dwellings would be best for that person. Ex: **Bettina: ledig, ist eine 29-jährige Rechtsberaterin, die von Fribourg nach Zürich umziehen möchte. Sie ist ambitiös und perfektionistisch. Am liebsten mag sie alles schlicht und modern. Sie arbeitet viel und hat keine Zeit zu putzen. Welche Wohnung ist am besten für sie?**

IMMOBILIEN +41 56 5559990 SCHWEIZER IMMOBILIEN +41 56 5559990 S[

Hochmoderne Luxuswohnung in Zürich

SIE LEBEN ALLEIN? Nur das Beste ist gut genug? Sie arbeiten in Zürich bei einer Bank oder einer Versicherung? Dann ist diese Luxuswohnung genau das Richtige! Top gestylte, neu renovierte Zweizimmerwohnung in der Nähe des Züricher Bankenviertels ab sofort zu vermieten. Moderne Möblierung. Nur das Beste! Küche mit Espressomaschine und Mikrowelle vorhanden. Im Wohnzimmer stehen ein Fernseher° und eine Bar. Internetanschluss in allen Zimmern. Die wöchentliche Apartmentreinigung und das Wechseln° der Bettwäsche sind im Mietpreis inklusive. Mietverträge° können sofort anfangen. Die Miete beträgt SFr 2.100 pro Monat.

Chalet im Tessin

Nach dem Lesen

Was fehlt? Ergänzen Sie die Sätze.

1. Die Wohnung in Fribourg hat eine Einbauküche mit _Gasherd und Backofen_.

2. Im _Schlafzimmer_ gibt es Einbauschränke.

3. Die Miete für die Wohnung in Fribourg kostet _SFr 1.100_ inklusive Parkplatz.

4. _Das Chalet_ liegt im Tessin.

5. Im Chalet stehen im Keller _Waschmaschine und Trockner_.

6. Beim Chalet können Kinder _im Garten_ spielen.

7. In der Wohnung in Zürich stehen _ein Fernseher und eine Bar_ im Wohnzimmer.

8. Die Miete der Züricher Wohnung beträgt _SFr 2.100_ pro Monat.

Richtig oder falsch? Sind die Sätze richtig oder falsch? Korrigieren Sie die falschen Sätze.

Sample answers are provided.

	richtig	falsch
1. Die Wohnung in Fribourg ist ideal für eine Familie. *Falsch. Die Wohnung ist ideal für zwei Personen.*	☐	☑
2. Einkaufen ist in der Nähe der Fribourger Wohnung sehr schwierig. *Falsch. Man kann hier bequem einkaufen.*	☐	☑
3. Das Chalet ist ein sehr modernes Haus. *Falsch. Das Chalet hat traditionelle Architektur.*	☐	☑
4. Die Tessiner Wohnung hat viel Platz.	☑	☐
5. Natur und Stadtleben sind dem Chalet sehr nah.	☑	☐
6. Die Züricher Zweizimmerwohnung ist nicht sehr modern. *Falsch. Sie ist top gestylt und neu renoviert.*	☐	☑
7. In allen Zimmern der Züricher Wohnung ist ein Internetanschluss.	☑	☐
8. Die Wohnung in Zürich reinigt (*cleans*) man jede Woche.	☑	☐

Die beste Wohnung Diskutieren Sie in einer kleinen Gruppe: Welche ist die beste Wohnung? Answers will vary.

BEISPIEL

S1: *Die Zweizimmerwohnung in Zürich ist klein, aber sie liegt in der Innenstadt. Man braucht kein Auto.*

S2: *Leider ist sie auch sehr teuer! Ich mag das Haus im Tessin.*

S3: *Ja, es ist ideal für eine Familie!*

kuschelig *cozy* **verlassen** *leave* **mit Einbauschränken ausgestattet** *equipped with built-in cabinets* **bietet** *offers* **Zugang** *access* **bequem** *conveniently* **in der Nähe** *in the vicinity* **Frühstücksecke** *breakfast nook* **Nebenkosten** *additional charges* **Fernseher** *television* **Wechseln** *changing* **Mietverträge** *rental agreements*

Hören

Strategien

Using background knowledge

If you know the topic being discussed, using knowledge you already have about the subject can help you to predict the kind of information you might hear.

 To help you practice this strategy, you will listen to a commercial for a cleaning product. Before you listen, jot down some key words related to the topic of cleaning that you might expect to hear in the commercial.

Vorbereitung

Sehen Sie sich das Foto an. Wer sind die Menschen auf dem Foto? Was machen sie? Könnte das eine Werbung (*advertisement*) sein?

Zuhören

Hören Sie der Sprecherin der Firma *Zauber* (*Magic*) bis *sauber* zu. Hören Sie die Werbung ein zweites Mal und wählen Sie die Dienstleistungen (*services*), die die Firma anbietet (*offers*).

1. (staubsaugen)
2. Wäsche waschen
3. bügeln
4. Geschirr spülen
5. (Kühlschränke putzen)
6. den Müll rausbringen
7. (Böden putzen)
8. (Fenster sauber machen)

Verständnis

 Was fehlt? Welche Wörter oder Ausdrücke fehlen?

arbeiten	Experten	neu
Bad	Fenster	putzen
Böden	kostenloses	sauber
bügeln	Kühlschränke	schnell

1. Die Reinigungsfirma (*cleaning company*) heißt Zauber bis ___sauber___.
2. Die Kunden der Reinigungsfirma ___arbeiten___ oft viel und haben keine Zeit zum Putzen.
3. Andere Kunden ___putzen___ einfach nicht gern.
4. Die Reinigungsfirma ist Experte für Küche, ___Bad___ und Wohnzimmer.
5. Sie staubsaugen und reinigen die ___Böden___.
6. Sie putzen auch ___Kühlschränke___ und Herde.
7. Die Leute der Reinigungsfirma sind ___Experten___ beim Saubermachen.
8. Diese Leute sind ___schnell___ und gründlich (*thorough*).
9. Die Zimmer sehen am Ende immer wie ___neu___ aus.
10. Die Reinigungsfirma gibt Kunden ein ___kostenloses___ Angebot (*offer*).

Die Reinigungsfirma Machen Sie mit zwei Mitstudenten eine Werbung für ein neues Produkt oder eine Dienstleistung.

BEISPIEL

S1: Mit *Sauberküche* können Sie Ihre Küche einfach reinigen!
S2: Sie brauchen keine anderen Produkte! Mit *Sauberküche* können Sie putzen, waschen, wischen...

Schreiben

Strategien

Reporting on an interview

When you transcribe a conversation in German, you should pay careful attention to format and punctuation. You can indicate a dialogue format by including the names of the speakers, or by using a dash (**der Gedankenstrich**) to indicate a new speaker. Compare these two formats.

> **MARIA** Nina, was hast du gestern Abend gemacht?
> **NINA** Ich war zu Hause.
> **MARIA** Oh, schade! Wolltest du nicht zu Davids Party?
> **NINA** Ja, aber ich musste noch putzen.

> —Hallo, Jonas!
> —Hallo, Sarah!
> —Wie geht's?
> —Gut. Und dir?

Whichever format you choose, your interview should begin with a brief introduction of the person you're interviewing, answering the six W-questions (**Wer?**, **Was?**, **Wann?**, **Wo?**, **Warum?**, and **Wie?**) about the topic of the interview.

Thema

Schreiben Sie ein Interview

Anton Krüger ist Architekt. Er hat ein neues Buch über energiesparendes (*energy-efficient*) Wohnen geschrieben. Diese Woche gibt er an der Universität eine Präsentation darüber. Sie arbeiten für die Studentenzeitung (*student newspaper*) und interviewen Herrn Krüger.

● Schreiben Sie zuerst 2–3 Sätze über den Autor.

● Schreiben Sie ein erfundenes Gespräch (etwa 10–12 Zeilen) zwischen Ihnen und Anton Krüger. Geben Sie mit einem Gedankenstrich oder mit dem Namen der Person an, wer spricht.

BEISPIEL

> Anton Krügers Buch kann man in Buchläden und im Internet kaufen. Er hielt diese Woche einen Vortrag…
>
> **Journalistin** Guten Tag Herr Krüger. Herzlichen Glückwunsch! Ihr neues Buch ist sehr interessant. Ich habe es wirklich toll gefunden.
>
> **Krüger** Vielen Dank!
>
> **Journalistin** Unsere Leser interessiert: Warum haben Sie dieses Buch geschrieben?

Vocabulary Tools

Zimmer

das Arbeitszimmer, -	home office
das Badezimmer, -	bathroom
der Balkon, - e	balcony
der Dachboden, ⸚	attic
das Erdgeschoss, -e	ground floor
das Esszimmer, -	dining room
der Flur, -e	hall
die Garage, -n	garage
der Keller, -	cellar
die Küche, -n	kitchen
das Schlafzimmer, -	bedroom
der erste/ zweite Stock	second/third floor
die Toilette, -n	toilet
das Wohnzimmer, -	living room

Möbel

die Badewanne, -n	bathtub
das Bett, -en	bed
das Bild, -er	picture
die Blume, -n	flower
der Boden, ⸚	floor
das Bücherregal, -e	bookshelf
die Kommode, -n	dresser
die Lampe, -n	lamp
das Möbelstück, -e	piece of furniture
der Nachttisch, -e	night table
die Pflanze, -n	plant
das Poster, -	poster
der Schrank, ⸚e	cabinet; closet
die Schublade, -n	drawer
der Sessel, -	armchair
das Sofa, -s	sofa
der Spiegel, -	mirror
der Teppich, -e	rug
die Treppe, -n	stairway
die Vase, -n	vase
der Vorhang, ⸚e	curtain
die Wand, ⸚e	wall

Orte

das Haus, ⸚er	house
das Wohnheim, -e	dorm
die Wohnung, -en	apartment
nach rechts/links	to the right/left

die Hausarbeit

den Tisch decken	to set the table
das Bett machen	to make the bed
den Müll rausbringen	to take out the trash
Geschirr (n.) spülen	to do the dishes
staubsaugen	to vacuum
Wäsche waschen	to do laundry

Haushaltsartikel

der Besen, -	broom
die Bettdecke, - n	duvet
das Bügelbrett, -er	ironing board
das Bügeleisen, -	iron
die Decke, -n	blanket
der Gefrierschrank, ⸚e	freezer
der Herd, -e	stove
die Kaffeemaschine, -n	coffeemaker
das Kissen, -	pillow
der Kühlschrank, ⸚e	refrigerator
das Laken, -	sheet
die Mikrowelle, -n	microwave
der Ofen, ⸚	oven
die Pfanne, -n	pan
die Spüle, -n	kitchen sink
die Spülmaschine, -n	dishwasher
der Staubsauger, -	vacuum cleaner
der Toaster, -	toaster
der Topf, ⸚e	pot
die Wäsche	laundry
der Wäschetrockner, -	dryer
die Waschmaschine, -n	washing machine

zum Beschreiben

dreckig	filthy
ordentlich	tidy
sauber	clean
schmutzig	dirty
Es ist ein Saustall!	It's a pigsty!

Verben

aufräumen (räumt... auf)	to clean up
bügeln	to iron
fegen	to sweep
mieten	to rent
putzen	to clean
umziehen (zieht... um)	to move
waschen	to wash
wischen	to wipe; to mop
wohnen	to live

The *Präteritum*	See pp. 240–241.
Da-, *wo-*, *hin-*, and *her-* compounds	See pp. 244–245.
Coordinating conjunctions	See p. 248.
Principal parts of verbs	See p. 261.
Perfekt of verbs with prefixes	See pp. 264–265.

Urlaub und Ferien

Suggestion Ask students where they think George and Meline are, and what they might be doing.

Communicative Goals

You will learn how to:

- discuss the weather and seasons
- talk about the months of the year

Jahreszeiten Vocabulary Tools

Suggestion Point out that all months and seasons are masculine. Remind students to use **im** to talk about what happens during specific months and seasons. Ex., **im Winter**, **im März**, etc.

Expansion Mime various weather conditions, (ex., fanning yourself to indicate **Es ist heiß.**), and ask students: **Wie ist das Wetter?**

Wortschatz

das Datum	*date*	**Suggestion** Remind students that they first learned to talk about dates and birthdays in **2A.3**. Point out that they can say either **Ich habe am 23. Mai Geburtstag** or **Mein Geburtstag ist am 23. Mai**.
das Jahr, -e	*year*	
die Jahreszeit, -en	*season*	
der Monat, -e	*month*	
der Tag, -e	*day*	
die Woche, -n	*week*	
Wann hast du Geburtstag?	*When is your birthday?*	
Am 23. Mai.	*May 23rd.*	
das Wetter	*weather*	
Wie ist das Wetter?	*What's the weather like?*	
Es ist schön draußen.	*It's nice out.*	
Das Wetter ist gut/ schlecht.	*The weather is nice/bad.*	
Das Wetter ist furchtbar.	*The weather is awful.*	
Wie warm/kalt ist es?	*How warm/cold is it?*	
Es sind 18 Grad draußen.	*It's 18 degrees out.*	
der Blitz, -e	*lightning*	
der Donner, -	*thunder*	
das Gewitter, -	*thunderstorm*	
der Hagel	*hail*	**Suggestion** Ask students to describe today's weather, using vocabulary from this section.
der Nebel, -	*fog; mist*	
der Regen	*rain*	
der Schnee	*snow*	
der Sturm, ̈-e	*storm*	
der Wetterbericht, -e	*weather report*	
die Wolke, -n	*cloud*	

ACHTUNG

You have already learned to ask **Der Wievielte ist heute?** to find out the date. You can also use the question **Was ist heute?** to ask about the date or the day of the week.

Suggestion Have students review the use of ordinal numbers, taught in **2A.3**.

Suggestion Teach students the song **Immse wimmse Spinne** (the German version of "Eensy Weensy Spider"), which includes references to rain and sun. Lyrics can be found online.

Es schneit. (schneien)

Es ist kalt.

der Winter: Dezember, Januar, Februar

Es ist sonnig.

Sommerfest

Es ist heiß.

– Welcher Tag ist heute?
– Der 15. August.

der Sommer: Juni, Juli, August

Expansion Have students create a "word chain." The first student names a word from the vocabulary list, such as **Sommer**. The next student names a related word, such as **sonnig** or **heiß**, etc. When a student can't think of a word, the chain is "broken," and he or she must start a new "chain."

Es regnet. (regnen)

der Regenschirm, -e

der Regenmantel, ¨

der Frühling: März, April, Mai

Es ist kühl.

Es ist wolkig.

Es ist windig.

der Herbst: September, Oktober, November

Anwendung

1 **Was fehlt?** Ergänzen Sie die Sätze.

1 **Suggestion** Students may not be familiar with the Celsius scale. Explain that **8° C** is 46.4° F; **17° C** is 62.6° F; and **25° C** is 77° F. Tell students that the conversion formula is: F = (C x 9/5) + 32; C = (F - 32) x 5/9.

regnet	warm
schneit	windig
Sturm	wolkig

BEISPIEL **Nürnberg: 25° C** In Nürnberg ist es sehr warm und _sonnig_

1. **Wien: 8° C** In Wien ist es kühl und _wolkig_.

2. **Genf: 17° C** In Genf ist es _windig_.

3. **Konstanz: 32° C** In Konstanz kommt am Abend ein _Sturm/Gewitter_.

4. **Innsbruck -5° C** In Innsbruck ist es kalt und es _schneit_.

5. **Basel: 12° C** In Basel ist es wolkig und es _regnet_.

6. **Hamburg: 21° C** In Hamburg ist es windig, aber _warm_.

2 **Was ist richtig?** Entscheiden Sie, welche Aussage zu welchem Bild passt.

a. Es ist heute wieder furchtbar heiß!
b. Wenn es regnet, braucht man einen Regenschirm.
c. Es kommt ein starker Sturm!
d. Auf dicke Wolken folgt schlechtes Wetter.

1. _c_

2. _a_   3. _b_   4. _d_

3 **Der Wetterbericht** 🎧 Hören Sie den Wetterbericht an und entscheiden Sie danach, ob (whether) die Aussagen richtig oder falsch sind.

3 **Suggestion** Have students correct the false statements.

	richtig	falsch
1. Der Wetterbericht ist für die ganze Woche.	☐	☑
2. Am Freitag beginnt der Winter.	☑	☐
3. Im Norden ist es sonnig.	☐	☑
4. Die Wetterfront im Norden kommt aus Skandinavien.	☑	☐
5. In Stuttgart regnet es am Freitag.	☐	☑
6. Am Wochenende schneit es in ganz Deutschland.	☑	☐

3 **Expansion** Have students work in small groups to predict the weather for the coming days, using simple sentences. Ex.: **Unsere Wettervorhersage: Am Montag schneit es. Am Dienstag gibt es Regen. Am Mittwoch ist es 18 Grad.**

Practice more at **vhlcentral.com.**

Kommunikation

4 Suggestion To get students started, find the first statement for each dialogue together as a class.

4   Vom Wetter und den Jahreszeiten
Arbeiten Sie mit einem Partner / einer Partnerin und bringen Sie die Sätze in jedem Dialog in eine logische Reihenfolge (*order*).

4 Expansion After the dialogues have been put in order, have volunteers read them out loud to the class.

Dialog 1

___2___ Schön. Die Sonne scheint und es ist ziemlich warm für die Jahreszeit.

___4___ Es regnet oft und die Sonne kommt selten durch die Wolkendecke hervor.

___1___ Paul, wie ist das Wetter heute in Köln?

___3___ Ja? Wie ist das typische Herbstwetter?

Dialog 2

___3___ April? Da ist es noch kühl und Schnee gibt es auch oft.

___2___ Der Monat, in dem ich Geburtstag habe. Der April.

___1___ Was ist dein Lieblingsmonat?

___4___ Ja, aber die Natur ist grün, die Vögel singen, alles beginnt neu.

5   Gute Ratschläge
Schreiben Sie mit einem Partner / einer Partnerin eine E-Mail an eine Studentin in Deutschland. Sie will ab Herbst an Ihrer Universität studieren und möchte etwas über das Wetter und passende (*appropriate*) Kleidung wissen. Answers will vary.

5 Suggestion Have students peer-edit each other's e-mails.

BEISPIEL

Wetter und Kleidung

Von: Anna Webber [anna.webber@students.uni.edu]
An: Jasmin Peters [peterchen@gigglepost.de]
Datum: 26. Juni
Betreff: Wetter und Kleidung

Hallo Jasmin,
wie geht es dir? Wie läuft es mit deinen Prüfungen?
In deiner letzten E-Mail hast du mich nach dem Wetter hier in Atlanta gefragt. Also, du kommst im August an und da ist es hier einfach nur heiß und sonnig! Ab Mitte September…

7 Expansion Encourage students to choose a German-speaking city and use the Internet to find an actual weather report (in German) for that city.

6   Arbeitsblatt
Fragen Sie acht Personen in der Gruppe, wann sie Geburtstag haben, und schreiben Sie das Datum auf.

BEISPIEL

S1: *Sarah, in welcher Jahreszeit hast du Geburtstag?*
S2: *Ich habe im Frühling Geburtstag. Mein Geburtstag ist am achten April.*

6 Suggestion Before they start the activity, give students a moment to write down their birthdays and to practice pronouncing the date. Provide a model by writing your own birthday on the board.

Alles Gute zum Geburtstag!!!

6 Expansion Teach your class a short and simple birthday song, such as **Hoch soll er/sie leben** or **Zum Geburtstag viel Glück**. Lyrics can be found online.

7   Ein Wetterbericht
Schreiben Sie mit einem Partner / einer Partnerin einen Wetterbericht.

- Sagen Sie, welches Datum und welche Jahreszeit es ist.
- Berichten Sie über das Wetter für die nächsten sieben Tage.
- Illustrieren Sie Ihren Wetterbericht mit Hilfe von einem Poster.
- Sagen Sie, was man an den einzelnen (*individual*) Tagen machen kann oder soll.

Der Wetterbericht für Juli: Hamburg

Mittwoch, der 14. Juli	Donnerstag, der 15. Juli	Freitag, der 16. Juli
25° C	32° C	30° C
sonnig	sehr wolkig	stürmisch

Heute ist Mittwoch, der 14. Juli. Der Sommer zeigt seine schöne Seite. Die Sonne scheint den ganzen Tag und es ist das perfekte Wetter für das Schwimmbad…

7 Expansion Have students create short videos of their own **Wetterbericht**.

Aussprache und Rechtschreibung (S) Audio

Long and short vowels

German vowels can be either long or short. Long vowels are longer in duration and typically occur before a single consonant, before the letter **h**, or when the vowel is doubled. Short vowels are shorter in duration and usually occur before two consonants.

Meter	**me**hr	**Mee**r	**Me**sser	**me**lden

The long **a** is pronounced like the *a* in the English word *calm*, but with the mouth wide open. The short **a** sounds almost like the long **a**, but it is held for a shorter period of time and pronounced with the mouth more closed.

mahnen	**Ma**nn	**la**sen	**la**ssen

The long **e** sounds like the *a* in the English word *late*. The short **e** sounds like the *e* in *pet*. The long **i** may be written as **i** or **ie**. It is pronounced like the *e* in *be*. The short **i** is pronounced like the *i* in *mitt*.

wen	**we**nn	**Vi**sum	**flie**gen	**Zi**mmer

The long **o** is pronounced like the *o* in *hope*, but with the lips firmly rounded. The short **o** is pronounced like the *o* in *moth*, but with the lips rounded. The long **u** is pronounced like the *u* in *tuna*, but with the lips firmly rounded. The short **u** is pronounced like the *u* in *put*, but with the lips rounded.

Zoo	**Zo**ll	**Flu**g	**Hu**nd

Suggestion Model the mouth position needed to produce the **o** and **u** sounds, with lips rounded and pushed forward.

 1 **Aussprechen** Wiederholen Sie die Wörter, die Sie hören.

1. Haken / hacken
2. den / denn
3. Bienen / binnen
4. Sohn / Sonne
5. buchen / Bucht

6. Nase / nass
7. fehl / Fell
8. Miete / Mitte
9. wohne / Wonne
10. Humor / Hummer

11. Wagen / Wangen
12. Zehner / Zentner
13. Linie / Linde
14. Lot / Lotto
15. Mus / muss

1 **Expansion** Conduct a dictation based on these word pairs. For each pair, read only one of the words out loud and tell students to circle the word they hear.

 2 **Nachsprechen** Wiederholen Sie die Sätze, die Sie hören.

1. Viele machen im Sommer Urlaub am Strand.
2. Wolf und Monika wollen den ganzen Tag in der Sonne liegen.
3. Sabine und Michael schwimmen lieber im Meer.
4. Alle sieben Studenten übernachten in einer Jugendherberge.
5. Hast du den Flug schon gebucht?
6. Wenn das Wetter schlecht ist, gehen wir ins Museum.

Ende gut, alles gut.[2]

Montag   Dienstag

 3 **Sprichwörter** Wiederholen Sie die Sprichwörter, die Sie hören.

Liebe geht durch den Magen.[1]

[1] The way to the heart is through the stomach.
(lit. *Love goes through the stomach.*)
[2] All's well that ends well.

Berlin von oben Video

Sabites Kunst gefällt Meline nicht, aber sie sind trotzdem Freundinnen. George und Hans sprechen über ihre Nachbarinnen und wollen hoch hinaus.

Vorbereitung Have students look closely at scenes 1, 2, 9, and 10 and describe the weather in each one.

SABITE Meline! Hallo.
MELINE Hallo.
SABITE Wie findest du es? Gut, es gefällt dir nicht.
MELINE Wie bitte?
SABITE Ich weiß, dass dir meine Kunst nicht gefällt. Ich mag VWL auch nicht, aber wir sind dennoch Freundinnen.

GEORGE Es ist schön draußen. Ich liebe diese Jahreszeit. Es ist kalt, aber nicht zu windig.
HANS Wie ist das Wetter gerade in Wisconsin?
GEORGE Milwaukee liegt am Lake Michigan. Er beeinflusst das Klima. Ich habe gestern mit meiner Mutter gesprochen. Dort liegen etwa zwei Fuß Schnee, etwa 60 cm.

HANS Wie ist das Wetter im Sommer?
GEORGE Im August ist es heiß und feucht. Es regnet, donnert und hagelt. Ich mag alle vier Jahreszeiten, aber der Frühling ist meine Lieblingsjahreszeit.
HANS Warum?
GEORGE Mein Geburtstag ist am 26. April. Und deiner?
HANS Am 17. Juli.

GEORGE Hey, was meinst du zu dieser Krawatte?
HANS Sie ist ganz okay. Warum?
GEORGE Ich habe mit Meline eingekauft. Sie hat sie ausgewählt. Ich war „zu amerikanisch" angezogen, also probiere ich neue Kleidung aus.

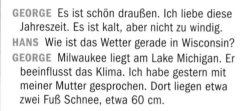

HANS Meline. Magst du sie?
GEORGE Ja. Nein, also nicht auf diese Weise. Zu Hause bin ich nicht mit Frauen befreundet. Wir haben Spaß zusammen. Ich habe gesehen, wie du mit ihr gelacht hast, also magst du sie doch.

SABITE Istanbul ist nicht weit von Berlin. Etwa 2.200 Kilometer. George ist 8.000 Kilometer von zu Hause entfernt.
MELINE George hat auch keine Freundin. Wann hast du zum ersten Mal über die Idee gesprochen?

1 **Richtig oder falsch?** Entscheiden Sie, ob die folgenden Sätze richtig oder falsch sind.

1. Meline und Sabite mögen dieselbe (*the same*) Kunst. Falsch.
2. In Milwaukee gibt es keinen Schnee. Falsch.
3. Im August ist es dort heiß und feucht. Richtig.
4. Der Frühling ist Georges Lieblingsjahreszeit. Richtig.
5. Der Geburtstag von Hans ist im Herbst. Falsch.
6. Hans findet Georges Krawatte hässlich. Falsch.
7. Istanbul ist etwa 8.000 Kilometer von Berlin entfernt. Falsch.
8. Sabite hat mit Lorenzo über Istanbul gesprochen. Richtig.
9. Der Berliner Fernsehturm ist das höchste Gebäude in Deutschland. Richtig.
10. Von dort kann man den Reichstag und das Brandenburger Tor sehen. Richtig.

PERSONEN   George   Hans   Meline   Sabite

7

SABITE An dem Abend, als wir dich und Lorenzo im Restaurant gesehen haben. Ich stand auf, ging Richtung Toilette und kam an deinem Tisch vorbei.

MELINE Torsten war also überrascht?

SABITE Ja.

MELINE Das ist das Problem! Du hast es ihm nicht zuerst gesagt.

8

SABITE Das ist doch dumm.

MELINE Sabite. Männer können manchmal dumm sein. Liebst du ihn? Sabite?

SABITE Ich weiß nicht.

9

GEORGE Der Fernsehturm ist 365 Meter hoch! Von dort kann man den Reichstag und das Brandenburger Tor sehen! Hans, ist alles in Ordnung?

HANS Ja. Mir geht's gut.

GEORGE Dies ist das höchste Gebäude in ganz Deutschland.

HANS Ich weiß.

10

HANS Mir geht's gut. Genieß den Ausblick. Ich bleibe solange hier stehen. Weit weg vom Rand.

GEORGE Hey, ist das Sabite?

HANS Wo?

GEORGE Fühlst du dich besser, Kumpel? Lass uns auf den Turm gehen und von dort oben Berlin sehen.

HANS Wow.

Nützliche Ausdrücke

- **Wie bitte?**
  Excuse me?
- **dennoch**
  nevertheless
- **beeinflussen**
  to influence
- **feucht**
  moist
- **auswählen**
  to choose
- **ausprobieren**
  to try
- **Nein, also nicht auf diese Weise.**
  No, not like that.
- **weit**
  far
- **Du hast es ihm nicht zuerst gesagt.**
  You didn't tell him first.
- **Dies ist das höchste Gebäude in ganz Deutschland.**
  This is the tallest building in all of Germany.
- **genießen**
  to enjoy
- **Fühlst du dich besser, Kumpel?**
  Are you feeling better, buddy?

7A.1
- **Ich stand auf, ging Richtung Toilette und kam an deinem Tisch vorbei.**
  I got up, went towards the restroom, and stopped by your table.

7A.2
- **Milwaukee liegt am Lake Michigan.**
  Milwaukee is on Lake Michigan.
- **Wann hast du zum ersten Mal über die Idee gesprochen?**
  When was the first time you mentioned the idea?

2 **Zum Besprechen** Sprechen Sie mit Ihren Klassenkameraden und finden Sie heraus, wer im gleichen Monat Geburtstag hat. Wie ist das Wetter in diesem Monat? Besprechen Sie es mit einem Partner.
Answers will vary.

Suggestion Tell students that in 1961, West Germany and Turkey signed a labor recruitment agreement which allowed Turkish citizens to move to Germany as guest workers (**Gastarbeiter**). Today, there are approximately 3 million people of Turkish descent living in Germany.

3 **Vertiefung** Sabite möchte ein Semester lang in Istanbul studieren. Es ist das Heimatland (*country of origin*) von Faik, Sabites Vater. Finden Sie Informationen über Türken in Deutschland. Wie viele Türken leben in Deutschland? Wann sind sie nach Deutschland gekommen? *Answers may vary.*

Expansion Tell students that Berlin is home to the largest Turkish community outside of Turkey. There are some 300,000 people with Turkish roots living in Berlin.

Ressourcen

SAM
VM: p. 13

vhlcentral.com

IM FOKUS

Windenergie Reading

> ### TIPP
> The **Deutsche Mark** (**DM** or **D-Mark**) was Germany's currency prior to the adoption of the **Euro** in 2002.

SCHLESWIG-HOLSTEIN LIEGT ZWISCHEN zwei Meeren, der Nordsee und der Ostsee. Dieses Bundesland ist relativ flach° und wegen der Nähe° zum Meer gibt es viel Wind. Schon seit 1982 investiert man hier immer mehr Geld in diese erneuerbare Energiequelle°.

Am Anfang waren es noch fünfzehn Windturbinen in einem Windpark in Braderup. Dreiunddreißig Privatbürger° finanzierten das Projekt mit einem Darlehen° von 12 Millionen DM (etwa 6 Millionen Euro).

Heute gibt es in Schleswig-Holstein über 2.400 Windturbinen. Bis zu ein Drittel des Strombedarfs° produziert man durch Windenergie in dem Bundesland. Aber Windturbinen stehen nicht nur auf dem Land. Seit 2009 kann man die Turbinen auch im Meer° finden. Hier, wo der Wind sehr stark bläst°, installiert man Turbinen in 30 Meter tiefem Wasser. Zwölf Turbinen produzieren bereits den Strom für etwa 50.000 Haushalte.

In Deutschland will man bis zum Jahr 2025 mit Windenergie 25% des Strombedarfs produzieren. 2014 gab es bereits 24.867 Windkraftanlagen in ganz Deutschland. Die Produktion von Strom mit Wind – aber auch mit Sonne, Wasser, Geothermie und Bioenergie – produziert weniger Stickstoff° im Vergleich° mit Atom-, Kohle- und Gaskraftwerken. Man braucht weniger Öl aus anderen Ländern. Und es gibt neue Arbeitsplätze° in Regionen wie Schleswig-Holstein.

Windenergie			
	Deutschland	**Österreich**	**Schweiz**
Windkraftanlagen°:	24.867	1.016	37
Stromproduktion:	4.750 MW (Megawatt)	2.095 MW	60 MW
Anteil am Strombedarf:	5,8%	7,2%	0,5%

QUELLE: Bundesverband WindEnergie, IG Windkraft, Suisse Eole

flach *flat* **wegen der Nähe** *due to its closeness* **erneuerbare Energiequelle** *renewable energy source* **Privatbürger** *private citizens* **Darlehen** *loan* **ein Drittel des Strombedarfs** *one third of electricity requirements* **im Meer** *at sea* **bläst** *blows* **Stickstoff** *nitrogen* **Vergleich** *comparison* **Arbeitsplätze** *jobs* **Windkraftanlagen** *wind power plants*

ÜBUNGEN

1 **Richtig oder falsch?** Sind die Aussagen **richtig** oder **falsch**? Korrigieren Sie die falschen Aussagen.

1. Schleswig-Holstein liegt zwischen der Nord- und Ostsee. Richtig.
2. Seit 1982 investiert man in Schleswig-Holstein in Windenergie. Richtig.
3. Der Staat baute in Braderup 15 Windturbinen. Falsch. 33 Privatbürger bauten die Windturbinen.
4. In Schleswig-Holstein gibt es 24.867 Windturbinen. Falsch. In ganz Deutschland gibt es 24.867 Windturbinen.
5. Seit 2009 gibt es auch Windturbinen im Meer. Richtig.

6. Diese Turbinen sind in 30 Meter tiefem Wasser installiert. Richtig.
7. In Deutschland will man mit Windenergie ein Viertel des Stroms produzieren. Richtig.
8. In Schleswig-Holstein gibt es wegen der Windturbinen mehr Arbeit. Richtig.
9. In Österreich ist der Windenergie-Anteil am Strombedarf weniger als 1%. Falsch. In der Schweiz ist der Windenergie-Anteil am Strombedarf weniger als 1%.
10. In der Schweiz gibt es nur 37 Windkraftanlagen. Richtig.

 Practice more at **vhlcentral.com.**

Deutsch im Alltag Ask students: **Welcher Ausdruck passt am besten zu dem heutigen Wetter?**

DEUTSCH IM ALLTAG

Wetterausdrücke

Hundewetter	*terrible weather*
Kaiserwetter	*beautiful, sunny weather*
Schmuddelwetter	*dreary, wet weather*
Es schüttet wie aus Eimern!	*It's raining cats and dogs!*
Petrus meint es gut!	*The weather's great!*

DIE DEUTSCHSPRACHIGE WELT

Planten un Blomen

Im Sommer kann man im Zentrum Hamburgs den berühmten Park Planten un Blomen besuchen. Hier gibt es einen alten Botanischen Garten. Außerdem finden Besucher den größten Japanischen Garten Europas in dem Park. Die einzelnen Gärten haben verschiedene Themen: der Rosengarten, der Apothekergarten° und die Tropengewächshäuser°. Im Musikpavillon finden im Sommer Konzerte statt° und man kann Wasserlichtkonzerte bewundern°. Kinder können auf Spielplätzen oder der Trampolinanlage spielen und auf Ponys reiten.

Suggestion Point out that the name of the park, **Planten un Blomen**, is **Plattdeutsch**. Have students translate the phrase into **Hochdeutsch**.

Apothekergarten *apothecary's garden* **Tropengewächshäuser** *tropical greenhouses* **finden... statt** *take place* **bewundern** *admire*

PORTRÄT

Klima in Deutschland

Das Wetter in Deutschland ist gemäßigt°: Im Winter ist es nicht sehr kalt und im Sommer nicht sehr warm. Im Durchschnitt° ist die Jahrestemperatur 8,1° C. Im Januar liegt die Durchschnittstemperatur bei -0,4° C und im Juli bei 16,9° C. Im Jahr fallen etwa 790 Millimeter Regen, besonders viel fällt im Juni. Die absolute Höchsttemperatur gab es 2003 in Karlsruhe und in Freiburg: 40,2° C. Freiburg liegt im Schwarzwald und gilt als° wärmste und sonnigste Stadt Deutschlands. Man kann hier jedes Jahr 1650 Sonnenstunden genießen. Die absolute Tiefsttemperatur gab es 2001 am Funtensee in den Bayrischen Alpen: -45,9° C.

Suggestion Point out that the German annual average of **8,1° C** is equivalent to 46.58° F, while the extreme temperatures of **-45,9° C** and **40,2° C** correspond to -50.62° F and 104.36° F, respectively.

gemäßigt *moderate* **Durchschnitt** *average* **gilt als** *is regarded as*

⟟ IM INTERNET

Finden Sie einen Plan von Planten un Blomen in Hamburg. Welche Gärten möchten Sie besuchen? Machen Sie eine Liste und planen Sie eine Tour.

Find out more at **vhlcentral.com**.

---

2 **Was fehlt?** Ergänzen Sie die Sätze.

1. Der Park Planten un Blomen liegt __im Zentrum__ Hamburgs.
2. Besucher finden hier den größten __Japanischen Garten__ Europas.
3. Es gibt einzelne Gärten wie zum Beispiel den Apothekergarten, __den Rosengarten__ und die Tropengewächshäuser.
4. Der Winter in Deutschland ist nicht __sehr kalt__.
5. In __Freiburg__ kann man viel Sonne genießen.

3 **Lieblingsjahreszeit** Diskutieren Sie mit einem Partner / einer Partnerin Ihre Lieblingsjahreszeit. Warum lieben Sie diese Jahreszeit? Was machen Sie in der Jahreszeit? Welche Kleidung tragen Sie?

7A.1

Separable and inseparable prefix verbs (*Präteritum*)

 **Presentation**

QUERVERWEIS

See **4A.3** to review the **Präsens** of separable and inseparable prefix verbs.

———

See **6B.2** to review the **Perfekt** of verbs with prefixes. To review the difference between **Perfekt** and **Präteritum**, see **6B.1**.

Suggestion Have students brainstorm a list of separable and inseparable prefix verbs they've already learned. Have them write sentences to demonstrate how each type of verb functions in the present and perfect tenses.

Startblock Both separable and inseparable prefix verbs can be used in the **Präteritum** to describe past events.

Ich **stand auf**, ging Richtung Toilette und **kam** an deinem Tisch **vorbei**.

Opa Otto **bereitete** die Weihnachtsgans **zu**. George **überraschte** ihn und...

- In the **Präteritum**, just like the **Präsens**, some prefixes are always attached to the verb, and others can be separated from it. When using a separable prefix verb in the **Präteritum**, move the prefix to the end of the sentence or clause.

Jan **verbrachte** den Sommer in der Schweiz.
*Jan **spent** the summer in Switzerland.*

Einmal **brachten** wir unseren Hund zur Schule **mit**.
*Once we **brought** our dog to school.*

Der Lehrer **erklärte** die Aufgabe.
*The teacher **explained** the assignment.*

Jans Schwester **rief** ihn zu seinem Geburtstag **an**.
*Jan's sister **called** him on his birthday.*

QUERVERWEIS

To review the formation of the **Präteritum**, see **6A.1**. See **Appendix A** for a complete list of strong verbs with their principal parts.

- You learned in **6B.2** that verbs with prefixes can be either strong, weak, or mixed. The **Präteritum** of a verb with a prefix is the same as the **Präteritum** of its base verb, but with the prefix added to the front of the conjugated verb, if it is inseparable, or to the end of the clause, if it is separable.

Suggestion Review the meaning of these verbs, making sure students recall which prefixes are separable and which are not.

Präteritum of separable and inseparable prefix verbs			
weak verbs			
kaufen → kaufte		verkaufen → verkaufte	
schauen (to look) → schaute		anschauen (to watch, look at) → schaute an	
strong verbs			
finden → fand		erfinden (to invent) → erfand	
sprechen → sprach		besprechen (to discuss) → besprach	
sehen → sah		fernsehen (to watch TV) → sah fern	
mixed verbs			
bringen → brachte		mitbringen → brachte mit	
		verbringen (to spend (time)) → verbrachte	
kennen → kannte		erkennen (to recognize) → erkannte	

Die Lehrerin **schaute** die Schüler **an**.
*The teacher **looked at** the students.*

Ich **erkannte** meine Tante nicht auf
dem alten Foto.
*I didn't **recognize** my aunt in
the old photo.*

Wir **sahen** als Kinder immer am
Samstagmorgen **fern**.
*When we were kids, we always **watched TV**
on Saturday mornings.*

Wer **erfand** das Internet?
*Who **invented** the Internet?*

- Remember that the prefix of a separable prefix verb is always stressed, while the prefix of an inseparable prefix verb is never stressed.

Als wir am Freitag **ausgingen**, regnete es
noch nicht.
*When we **went out** on Friday, it wasn't
raining yet.*

Wir **bestellten** zwei Pizzas zum
Abendessen.
*We **ordered** two pizzas
for dinner.*

- In a negative sentence, put **nicht** before the separable prefix.

Erik **rief** mich gestern **nicht an**.
*Erik **didn't** call me yesterday.*

Meine Mitbewohnerin **räumte** ihre Sachen **nicht auf**.
*My roommate **didn't** pick up her things.*

- When you talk about past events using a modal and a verb with a prefix, put the modal verb in the **Präteritum**. The prefixed verb goes at the end of the sentence in the infinitive form.

Frau Müller **musste** den kaputten
Regenschirm **umtauschen**.
*Mrs. Müller **had to exchange** the
broken umbrella.*

Niklas **wollte** sein altes
Fahrrad **verkaufen**.
*Niklas **wanted to sell** his
old bicycle.*

Suggestion Before they begin the **Jetzt sind Sie dran!** activity, verify that
students know the meanings of each of the verbs, and have them identify which
verbs have separable prefixes and which do not. Do the first few items as a class.

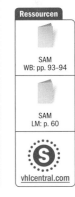

Ressourcen

SAM
WB: pp. 93–94

SAM
LM: p. 60

Ⓢ

vhlcentral.com

 Jetzt sind Sie dran! **Ergänzen Sie die Tabelle mit den Verben im Präteritum.**

Infinitiv	Präteritum		Infinitiv	Präteritum
1. bedeuten	*bedeutete*	7. wegräumen	räumte weg
2. einschlafen	schlief ein	8. wiederholen	wiederholte
3. beschreiben	beschrieb	9. besuchen	besuchte
4. zurückkommen	kam zurück	10. entdecken	entdeckte
5. umziehen	zog um	11. mitbringen	brachte mit
6. erkennen	erkannte	12. verstehen	verstand

Anwendung

1 **Was fehlt?** Ergänzen Sie die Sätze mit den richtigen Formen der Verben im Präteritum.

> **BEISPIEL** Frau Behrens ___rief___ ihre Tochter jeden Tag ___an___. (anrufen)

1. Im Sand ___entdeckten___ wir eine alte Halskette. (entdecken)

2. Wann ___fing___ der Regen ___an___? (anfangen)

3. Ich ___verkaufte___ mein Auto vor einem Monat. (verkaufen)

4. Meine Großeltern ___sahen___ immer nach dem Essen ___fern___. (fernsehen)

5. Wir ___besuchten___ unsere Cousinen oft im Sommer. (besuchen)

6. Markus ___verstand___ als Schüler nichts von Mathematik. (verstehen)

2 **Was für ein Tag** Ergänzen Sie die Sätze mit den richtigen Verben aus der Liste im Präteritum.

| aufräumen | besuchen | erklären |
| aufwachen | einkaufen | verkaufen |

▶ **BEISPIEL** Tobias ___wachte___ um acht Uhr ___auf___.

1. Michael ___kaufte___ fürs Abendessen ___ein___.

2. Am Samstag ___besuchte___ Julian seine Schwester in Heidelberg.

3. Frau Hölzel ___erklärte___ den Schülern die Aufgabe.

4. Ich ___räumte___ mein Zimmer ___auf___.

5. Wir ___verkauften___ gestern viel Currywurst.

3 **Noch einmal** Schreiben Sie die Sätze im Präteritum. Benutzen Sie dabei das Modalverb in Klammern.

> **BEISPIEL** Wir tauschten unser Geld auf der Bank um. (wollen)
> *Wir wollten unser Geld auf der Bank umtauschen.*

1. Thomas sah den ganzen Morgen fern. (wollen)
Thomas wollte den ganzen Morgen fernsehen.

2. Wir bereiteten ein schönes Essen vor. (wollen) Wir wollten ein schönes Essen vorbereiten.

3. Erik rief seine Freundin nicht an. (dürfen)
Erik durfte seine Freundin nicht anrufen.

4. Herr Roth verkaufte sein Auto nicht. (können) Herr Roth konnte sein Auto nicht verkaufen.

5. Die Lehrerin wiederholte den Satz. (müssen)
Die Lehrerin musste den Satz wiederholen.

6. Ich brachte meinen Computer in den Urlaub mit. (dürfen)
Ich durfte meinen Computer in den Urlaub mitbringen.

Practice more at vhlcentral.com.

Kommunikation

4 **Eine Überraschungsfeier** Lukas und Lena planten letzten Herbst eine Überraschungsfeier für ihre Eltern. Bilden Sie mit einem Partner / einer Partnerin zu jedem Bild einen Satz im Präteritum. Answers may vary.

▶ **BEISPIEL** Lukas und Lena
*bereiteten eine
Überraschungsfeier
für ihre Eltern vor.*

1. Lukas und Lena
kauften Sachen für die Feier ein.

2. Lena
lud viele Verwandte und Freunde ein.

3. Die Gäste
kamen am Nachmittag an.

4. Frau Braun
brachte eine Schokoladentorte mit.

5. Die Großeltern
überraschten Svens und Lenas Eltern mit einer Reise nach Amerika.

5 **Historische Personen** Bilden Sie mit einem Partner / einer Partnerin logische Fragen im Präteritum. Wechseln Sie sich bei den Fragen und Antworten ab.

BEISPIEL

S1: *Wer entdeckte die Stadt Troja?*
S2: *Heinrich Schliemann.*

Wer...

entdecken / die Allgemeine (*General*) Relativitätstheorie

erklären / die genetischen Regeln (*rules*)

erfinden / den Buchdruck (*printing press*)

bekommen / einen Nobelpreis für Literatur

> Gregor Johann Mendel
> Günter Grass
> Heinrich Schliemann
> Albert Einstein
> Johannes Gutenberg

Sample answers:
Wer entdeckte die Allgemeine Relativitätstheorie? Albert Einstein
Wer erklärte die genetischen Regeln? Gregor Johann Mendel
Wer erfand den Buchdruck? Johannes Gutenberg
Wer bekam einen Nobelpreis für Literatur? Günter Grass

6 **Eine spannende Geschichte** Schreiben Sie mit einem Partner / einer Partnerin eine Geschichte. Benutzen Sie das Präteritum und mindestens (*at least*) drei Elemente aus der Liste. Answers will vary.

BEISPIEL Es war eine dunkle und stürmische Nacht.
*Ich schlief schlecht und stand um drei Uhr nachts wieder auf.
Ich sah aus dem Fenster hinaus...*

den Regenmantel anziehen	hinausgehen
aufräumen	weggehen
aufstehen	das Handy vergessen
Angst bekommen	die Orientierung verlieren
wieder einschlafen	(nicht) verstehen

7A.2

Prepositions of location
Prepositions in set phrases

 **Presentation**

Startblock When describing locations, and in certain fixed expressions, many German prepositions are used in ways that differ from their English counterparts.

Milwaukee liegt **am Lake Michigan**.

Hat Sabite **über mich** gesprochen?

Suggestion English speakers may find phrases like **auf der Post**, **auf der Bank**, and **auf dem Markt** counter-intuitive. Encourage students to simply memorize these phrases as "sound bites."

QUERVERWEIS

See **5B.3** to review two-way prepositions.

Suggestion Remind students that the expression **zu Hause**, which they learned in **4B.2**, is an exception to the general rule of using **in** with enclosed spaces.

Suggestion Point out that most masculine and neuter country names are directly preceded by **in** with no article, but there are a few that always take a definite article, and are thus preceded by **im** in the dative, ex. **Er lebt im Libanon.**

ACHTUNG

Note that the idea of an enclosed space includes the radio, television, or Internet: **Das habe ich im Radio gehört; Das können wir im Internet finden.**

Suggestion Remind students that they have already seen the phrase **Im Internet** in the activity boxes at the end of each **Kultur** section.

QUERVERWEIS

You will learn more about using prepositions with geographical locations in **10B.1**.

Prepositions of location

- In **5B.3** you learned to use two-way prepositions with the dative to indicate location and with the accusative to show movement toward a destination.

  Neben dem Schreibtisch steht ein großes Bücherregal.
  *There's a big bookcase **next to the desk**.*

  Stell den Stuhl bitte **neben den Tisch**.
  *Please put the chair **next to the table**.*

- Use **auf** with the dative to indicate that something is located on a horizontal surface or to describe a location in a public building or open space.

  Deine Bücher liegen **auf dem Tisch**.
  *Your books are **on the table**.*

  Ich war gestern **auf der Bank**.
  *I was **at the bank** yesterday.*

  Greta hat schöne Blumen **auf dem Markt** gekauft.
  *Greta bought beautiful flowers **at the market**.*

- Use **an** with the dative to indicate a location *on* or *at* a border, wall, or body of water.

  An der Wand hängt ein schöner Kalender.
  *There's a nice calendar hanging **on the wall**.*

  Am Strand war es heute kühl und windig.
  *It was cool and windy **at the beach** today.*

- Use **in** with the dative to indicate a location *on* or *in* an enclosed space.

  Die Sonnenbrille ist **in meiner Handtasche**.
  *The sunglasses are **in my purse**.*

  Die Kinder spielen gern **im Park**.
  *The kids like to play **in the park**.*

  Ich wohne **in der Joachimstraße**.
  *I live **on Joachim Street**.*

- To indicate location in a country whose name is feminine or plural, use **in** with the dative form of the definite article, plus the country name.

  Wagner wohnte **in der Schweiz**.
  *Wagner lived **in Switzerland**.*

  Meine Mutter ist jetzt **in den USA**.
  *My mother is **in the U.S.** right now.*

- In **5B.3** you learned that **bei** is always used with the dative case. Use **bei** with a noun referring to a person or business to indicate a location at that person's home or at that place of business.

  Ich kaufe gern **bei Aldi** ein.
  *I like shopping **at Aldi's**.*

  Anna war gestern **beim Friseur**.
  *Anna was **at the hairdresser's** yesterday.*

Als Student wohnte Nils im Sommer **bei seinen Eltern**.
*When he was a student, Nils lived **with his parents** during the summer.*

Heute Abend spielen wir **bei mir** Karten.
*We're playing cards **at my place** tonight.*

Suggestion Remind students that they can also use **bei** with a person's name to refer to that person's home. Ex.: **Wir waren *bei Jonas*.**

- You can also use **bei** to mean *near* a location or *in the presence of* a condition.

Das Restaurant liegt **bei Wilhelmshaven**.
*The restaurant is **near Wilhelmshaven**.*

Bei schönem Wetter gehen wir gern spazieren.
*We like to go for walks **when the weather is nice**.*

Suggestion Point out that **bei** + dative can also be used to "set the scene" for the action in a sentence. Ex.: **Beim Abendessen haben wir über die Ferien geredet**.

Prepositions in set phrases

- Certain combinations of verbs and prepositions have specific, idiomatic meanings. The prepositions in these fixed expressions are always followed by the same case, regardless of whether the verb they are associated with indicates location or movement.

Jasmin **erzählte** uns **von ihren Problemen**.
*Jasmin **told** us **about her problems**.*

Max muss einen Brief **an seine Tante schreiben**.
*Max has to **write** a letter **to his aunt**.*

Suggestion Students may have difficulty with these German verb/ preposition combinations. Point out that English also has specific verb/ preposition combinations with specific, idiomatic meanings. Ex: "to wait for" *vs.* "to wait on".

- Use the *dative* after the following set phrases.

Verb phrases with the dative	
Angst haben vor	*to be afraid of*
arbeiten an	*to work on*
erzählen von	*to talk about; to tell a story about*
fragen nach	*to ask about*
handeln von	*to be about; to have to do with*
helfen bei	*to help with*
träumen von	*to dream of*

Meine Nichte **hat Angst vor** Hunden.
*My niece **is afraid of** dogs.*

Professor Weiss **arbeitet an** einem neuen Buch.
*Professor Weiss **is working on** a new book.*

Expansion Have students ask each other **Wovor hast du Angst?** Provide humorous model answers.

- Use the *accusative* after the following expressions.

Verb phrases with the accusative	
antworten auf	*to answer*
denken an	*to think about*
schreiben an	*to write to*
sprechen/reden über	*to talk about*
warten auf	*to wait for*

Wir haben lange **auf** den Bus **gewartet**.
*We **waited** a long time **for** the bus.*

Antworte bitte **auf** die Frage.
*Please **answer** the question.*

Ressourcen

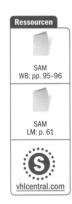

SAM
WB: pp. 95–96

SAM
LM: p. 61

S

vhlcentral.com

| **Jetzt sind Sie dran!** | **Wählen Sie die passenden Präpositionen.** |

1. Wir haben (mit / (auf)/ über) dem Markt Obst gekauft.
2. Mein Hund hat Angst (über / von / (vor)) Donner und Blitz.
3. Nach dem Sturm lag viel Hagel ((auf)/ an / in) der Straße.
4. Sara verbringt ihren Sommer (mit / aus / (in)) der Türkei.
5. Wir helfen unserer Mutter ((bei)/ vor / in) der Hausarbeit.
6. ((An)/ Mit / Unter) der Berliner Mauer gibt es viel Graffiti.
7. Du hast nicht (über / bei / (auf)) meine Frage geantwortet.
8. Wohnt dein Bruder immer noch (an / (bei)/ auf) dir?
9. Hast du schon (bei / (an)/ nach) Oma geschrieben?
10. Sophia hat mir (mit / nach / (von)) ihrem Wochenende erzählt.

Anwendung

1 **Präpositionen** Ergänzen Sie die passenden Präpositionen.

BEISPIEL ___Bei___ schlechtem Wetter werde ich oft müde.

1. Wir campen jeden Sommer ___auf___ dem Campingplatz.
2. Maria reitet oft ihr Pferd ___im___ Park.
3. Gehst du oft ___bei___ Aldi einkaufen?
4. Cuxhaven liegt ___an___ der Nordsee.
5. Unsere Katze sitzt gern ___auf___ dem Balkon und schaut den Vögeln zu.

2 **Was fehlt?** Ergänzen Sie die Lücken mit den richtigen Präpositionen.

▶ **BEISPIEL** Meine Schlüssel sind nicht _in_ meiner Tasche.

1. Meine Hunde haben immer Angst _vor_ einem Sturm.

2. Der Film handelt _von_ einer Naturkatastrophe.

3. Im Sommer mieten wir ein kleines Haus _an_ einem Strand.

4. Die Frau fragt den Verkäufer _nach_ dem Preis.

5. Elias arbeitet _an_ seiner Dissertation.

3 **Kombinieren** Ergänzen Sie die passenden Präpositionen und wählen Sie dann die beste Antwort auf jede Frage.

_a_ 1. Hast du das _im_ Internet gefunden?

_d_ 2. Warum hat deine Mutter Angst _vor_ Hunden?

_b_ 3. Oma, erzähl mir bitte _von_ deiner Kindheit.

_e_ 4. Bleibt Daniel die ganzen Semesterferien _bei_ seinen Eltern?

_c_ 5. Arbeitet Greta schon _an_ ihrem Referat?

a. Nein, ich habe es im Radio gehört.

b. Ach Kindchen, das war vor so langer Zeit.

c. Ja, sie hat schon damit angefangen.

d. Ich weiß nicht, aber sie mag Katzen.

e. Nein, er macht einen Sprachkurs in Spanien für vier Wochen.

4 **Fragen** Stellen Sie einem Partner / einer Partnerin diese Fragen. Answers will vary.

1. An wen schreibst du oft E-Mails?
2. Worüber redest du mit deinen Freunden?
3. Wo verbringst du deine Semesterferien?
4. Wo kaufst du deine Lebensmittel ein?
5. Wovon träumst du?
6. Wovor hast du Angst?

 Practice more at **vhlcentral.com.**

Kommunikation

5 **Kettenreaktion** Sagen Sie abwechselnd, wo diese Dinge in Ihrem Klassenzimmer sind. Answers will vary.

> **BEISPIEL**
>
> **S1:** *die Uhr*
> **S2:** *Die Uhr hängt an der Wand.*
> **S3:** *der Stuhl*
> **S4:** *Oliver sitzt auf dem Stuhl.*

der Boden	die Lampen	die Tafel
das Buch	das Poster	die Uhr
der Computer	der Stuhl	die Wand

6 **Was und wo ist das?** Wählen Sie ein Objekt aus dem Bild und beschreiben Sie seine Lage (*location*). Ihr Partner / Ihre Partnerin muss erraten, welchen Ort oder Objekt Sie beschreiben. Answers will vary.

> **BEISPIEL**
>
> **S1:** *Ein blaues Auto steht davor.*
> **S2:** *Ist es der Supermarkt?*
> **S1:** *Ja.*

das Café · das Hotel · die Bibliothek · das Restaurant · die Bank · das Kino · das Museum · der Supermarkt

7 **Was kann man wo machen?** Entscheiden Sie (*Decide*) mit einem Partner / einer Partnerin, wo Sie die folgenden Aktivitäten machen können. Answers will vary.

> **BEISPIEL**
>
> **S1:** *Wo kann ich ein Buch kaufen?*
> **S2:** *Das kannst du im Buchgeschäft machen.*

Wo kann ich... ?	Das kannst du... machen.
eine Tasse Kaffee bestellen	beim Bäcker
Obst und Gemüse kaufen	auf der Bank
leckere Brötchen kaufen	in der Bibliothek
in der Sonne liegen	im Café
ein Bild von Picasso sehen	im Internetcafé
ein Wörterbuch finden	im Museum
Geld bekommen	am Strand
im Internet surfen	im Supermarkt

8 **Persönliche Fragen** Machen Sie ein Interview mit einem Partner / einer Partnerin und finden Sie ein paar persönliche Informationen heraus. Answers will vary.

1. Hast du Angst vor: ___ Gewitter ___ Hunden? ___ schlechten Noten?
2. Redest du gern über: ___ Politik? ___ Musik? ___ Sport?
3. Arbeitest du heute an: ___ einem Referat? ___ deinen Hausaufgaben? ___ nichts?
4. Denkst du oft an: ___ deine Freunde? ___ deine Kurse? ___ deine Familie?
5. Handeln deine Träume von: ___ deiner Kindheit? ___ deinem Leben jetzt? ___ anderen Situationen?

Wiederholung

1 In der Stadt
Wechseln Sie sich mit einem Partner / einer Partnerin ab: Beschreiben Sie, wo Yusuf gestern in der Stadt war. Sample answers are provided.

1 Suggestion Do the first few sentences together as a class. Remind students that since they will be talking about Yusuf's *location*, they will use the dative with any two-way prepositions.

▶ **BEISPIEL** *Zuerst war Yusuf auf der Post. Dann war er...*

2 Suggestion Remind students that in sentences beginning with a time expression, the conjugated verb will appear in 2nd position, *before* the subject. Provide model answers that say what you like to do.

1.
Dann war er auf der Bank.

2.
Dann hat er im Restaurant gegessen.

3.
Im Park hat er in der Sonne gelegen.

4.
In der Metzgerei hat er Wurst gekauft.

5.
In der Bäckerei hat er frisches Brot gekauft.

2 Bei so einem Wetter
Fragen Sie Ihren Partner / Ihre Partnerin, was er/sie bei verschiedenem Wetter macht.
Answers may vary.

BEISPIEL

S1: *Was machst du bei windigem Wetter?*
S2: *Bei windigem Wetter gehe ich spazieren.*

1. windig
2. sonnig
3. schlecht
4. kalt
5. heiß
6. schön

3 Hausarbeit
Beschreiben Sie mit einem Partner / einer Partnerin, wie Sie und Ihre Mitbewohner (*roommates*) am Wochenende die Wohnung putzten. Benutzen Sie Vokabeln aus der Liste. Answers will vary.

BEISPIEL

S1: *Am Wochenende mussten wir viel Hausarbeit machen.*
S2: *Im Bad putzte Eric die Toilette und die Badewanne.*

abstauben	Müll rausbringen
aufräumen	Geschirr spülen
fegen	staubsaugen
Bett machen	Wäsche waschen
putzen	wischen

4 Arbeitsblatt
Sie bekommen ein Arbeitsblatt von Ihrem Professor / Ihrer Professorin mit verschiedenen Aktivitäten. Wer in der Gruppe hat diese Aktivitäten gemacht? Answers will vary.

BEISPIEL

S1: *Hast du deinen Freunden von einem guten Buch erzählt?*
S2: *Ja, ich habe meinen Freunden von einem guten Buch erzählt.*

5 Diskutieren und kombinieren
Tauschen Sie mit Ihrem Partner / Ihrer Partnerin Informationen aus: Was machten Paul und Sara gestern? Füllen Sie die Tabelle für Ihren Partner / Ihre Partnerin und sich selber (*yourself*) aus. Answers will vary.

BEISPIEL

S1: *Was hat Sara am Donnerstag gemacht?*
S2: *Sie hat bei A&P eingekauft.*

6 Als ich zehn war
Erzählen Sie Ihrem Partner / Ihrer Partnerin, was Sie machten, als Sie zehn Jahre alt waren. Was machten Sie im Frühling, im Sommer, im Herbst und im Winter?

BEISPIEL

S1: *Was hast du mit zehn im Herbst gemacht?*
S2: *Im Herbst bin ich Fahrrad gefahren. Im Winter...*

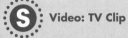

Video: TV Clip

Expansion Pause the video on the image of the map at the beginning. Ask:
• Wo liegt „das grüne Binnenland"?
• Welches Land liegt nördlich von Schleswig-Holstein?
• Schleswig-Holstein liegt zwischen zwei Meeren. Wie heißen die zwei Meere?

Urlaub im grünen Binnenland

Im Norden Schleswig-Holsteins, zwischen Nord- und Ostsee, an der Grenze zu Dänemark, liegt das grüne Binnenland. In dieser Gegend können Touristen Wiesen°, Flüsse und zwei sehr unterschiedliche° Meere° finden. Die wunderschöne Fluss- und Seenlandschaft° ist sehr flach und hat nur sanfte Hügel°. Zu den Hauptattraktionen gehören der Nationalpark Wattenmeer mit tollen Stränden, Schlössern und Wikingerdörfern. Neben der Natur gibt es viel Kultur in Städten wie Flensburg und Schleswig zu sehen.

Suggestion After showing students the scene in the tourist center, ask:
• Wie begrüßt die Frau die Touristen? Warum?
• Wie lange will das Paar hier Urlaub machen?

Reetdachdecker° bei ihrer Arbeit

Sie sind im Land der Wikinger!

Badeurlaub° genießen Sie im Seebad°, an Sandstränden oder Naturbadestellen.

Expansion Have students name activities featured in the video and organize them into things to do **in der Natur** and things to do **in der Stadt**.

Wiesen *meadows* **unterschiedliche** *different* **Meere** *seas* **Seenlandschaft** *lake landscape* **sanfte Hügel** *gentle hills*
Reetdachdecker *roof thatchers* **Badeurlaub** *beach vacation* **Seebad** *beach resort*

 Verständnis Markieren Sie alle richtigen Antworten.

1. Was kann man in der Region Grünes Binnenland Schleswig-Holstein *nicht* sehen?
   a. Meere   (b. hohe Berge)   c. Flüsse   d. Strände

2. Welche Aktivitäten kann man in dieser Region *nicht* machen?
   a. Rad fahren   b. einkaufen   (c. Ski fahren)
   d. schwimmen

 Diskussion Diskutieren Sie die folgenden Fragen mit einem Partner / einer Partnerin. Answers will vary.

1. Was möchten Sie gerne im grünen Binnenland Schleswig-Holsteins sehen und machen? Warum?

2. Sie sind die Touristen am Anfang des Videos und besuchen die Touristeninformation: Welche Fragen wollen Sie der Frau stellen?

Communicative Goals

You will learn how to:

- talk about travel
- talk about vacations and tourism

Reisen  Ⓢ **Vocabulary Tools**

Suggestion Model correct pronunciation of **Passagier**. Point out that the **g** is soft.

Wortschatz

am Flughafen	*at the airport*
der Abflug	departure
die Ankunft	arrival
die Businessklasse	business class
der Flug, ¨e	flight
das Flugticket, -s	ticket
das Gepäck	luggage
der Koffer, -	suitcase
der Passagier, -e	passenger
die Passkontrolle, -n	passport control
der Personalausweis, -e	ID card
die Reise, -n	trip
das Reisebüro, -s	travel agency
die Touristenklasse	economy class
die Verspätung, -en	delay
das Visum (*pl.* die Visa)	visa
der Zoll	customs
fliegen	*to fly*
das Ausland	abroad
pünktlich	on time
die Ferien	*vacation*
die Kreuzfahrt, -en	cruise
der Skiurlaub, -e	ski vacation
packen	*to pack*
übernachten	to spend the night
Unterkünfte	*accommodations*
der Fahrstuhl, ¨e	elevator
der Gast, ¨e	(hotel) guest
das (Fünf-Sterne-)Hotel	(five-star) hotel
die Jugendherberge, -n	youth hostel
der Schlüssel, -	key
der Zimmerservice	room service
abbrechen (bricht... ab)	to cancel
buchen	to make a (hotel) reservation
voll besetzt	*fully occupied*

Expansion Ask students: **Fliegen Sie gerne? Warum? Warum nicht?** Have them brainstorm a list of things they associate with flying.

Ressourcen

SAM
WB: pp. 97–98

SAM
LM: p. 62

Ⓢ
vhlcentral.com

Image labels:

Sonne und Meer

der Ausgang, ¨e

Er liest eine Karte.

der Strand, ¨e

das Meer, -e

die Reisenden (*pl.*) (*sing.* der Reisende)

die Bordkarte, -n

die Zeitung, -en

Sport

das Handgepäck

Es landet. (landen)

Es fliegt ab. (abfliegen)

das Flugzeug, -e

Sie machen Urlaub.

Sie stehen Schlange.

Die Welt

Anwendung

Expansion Have students write and act out short dialogues that take place at an airport, using at least six vocabulary words from this lesson.

1 **Vergleiche** Ergänzen Sie die Vergleiche mit dem richtigen Wort.

1. das Hotel : der Gast :: das Flugzeug : (der Passagier / der Familienstand)
2. heimkommen : ausgehen :: ankommen : (abfliegen / aufstehen)
3. früh : spät :: frei : (besorgt / besetzt)
4. buchen : die Reise :: packen : (der Koffer / der Keller)
5. das Zimmer : der Schlüssel :: das Ausland : (das Seminar / das Visum)
6. der Skiurlaub : die Alpen :: die Kreuzfahrt : (das Meer / der Park)

2 **Kategorien** Schreiben Sie die Wörter aus der Liste in die passenden Kategorien. Answers may vary slightly.

die Bordkarte	die Kreuzfahrt	das Reisebüro
das Hotel	die Passkontrolle	der Tourist
die Jugendherberge	der Personalausweis	der Zimmerservice

Unterkunft	Flughafen	Urlaub
die Jugendherberge	die Bordkarte	das Hotel
das Hotel	der Personalausweis	die Kreuzfahrt
der Zimmerservice	der Tourist	der Tourist
der Personalausweis	die Passkontrolle	das Reisebüro

2 **Expansion** Have students add at least one additional word to each category.

3 **Kombinationen** Kombinieren Sie die Wörter mit ihren Definitionen.

c	1. der Reisende	a. den braucht man für eine Reise ins Ausland
d	2. der Zoll	b. hier kann man billig übernachten
f	3. die Verspätung	c. eine Person macht eine Reise
e	4. die Businessklasse	d. hier kontrolliert man Importe aus dem Ausland
b	5. die Jugendherberge	e. hier sitzt man im Flugzeug mit allem Komfort
a	6. der Pass	f. nicht pünktlich ankommen

4 **Ansagen** 🎧 Hören Sie die Ansagen (*announcements*) an und entscheiden Sie, welche Ansage am besten zu welchem Satz passt.

Ansage 4 1. Die Passagiere fliegen nach Russland.

Ansage 5 2. Das Flugzeug ist gerade gelandet.

Ansage 1 3. Der Check-in für Air France ist im Terminal 1.

Ansage 3 4. Der Flug nach Hamburg fliegt bald ab.

Ansage 2 5. Die Passagiere kommen mit Verspätung in Rom an.

4 **Suggestion** Students may need to hear the recording several times in order to complete the exercise.

🚀 Practice more at **vhlcentral.com**.

Kommunikation

5   Reisen
Beantworten Sie die Fragen mit ganzen Sätzen. Vergleichen Sie dann Ihre Antworten mit den Antworten Ihres Partners / Ihrer Partnerin. Answers will vary.

1. In welcher Jahreszeit machen Sie gern Urlaub? Warum?
2. Mit wem reisen Sie nicht gern? Warum?
3. Was bringen Sie mit auf eine Kreuzfahrt nach Europa?
4. Was packen Sie normalerweise in Ihr Handgepäck?
5. Wo haben Sie schon Urlaub gemacht?
6. Wohin möchten Sie gern reisen? Warum?

5 Suggestion Have students share their answers to items 5 and 6 with the class.

6   Diskutieren und kombinieren
Ihr Lehrer / Ihre Lehrerin gibt Ihnen verschiedene Blätter mit Durchsagen. Fragen Sie Ihren Partner / Ihre Partnerin nach den fehlenden Informationen und wechseln Sie sich dabei ab. Answers will vary.

6 Suggestion Before beginning the activity, clarify the meaning of any unfamiliar vocabulary and practice pronunciation of the longer words.

BEISPIEL

S1: Wer kann zum Ausgang gehen?
S2: Nur Passagiere mit Bordkarten.

7   Beschreibungen
Schreiben Sie mit einem Partner / einer Partnerin eine Beschreibung (*description*) von jedem (*each*) Bild. Lesen Sie danach einem anderen Paar Ihre Beschreibung vor. Das andere Paar soll erraten, welches Bild zu welcher Beschreibung passt. Answers will vary.

BEISPIEL

S1: Es ist Abend. Ein Mädchen sitzt auf einem Koffer.
S1: Sie liest Zeitung.
S3: Das ist Bild 1.

7 Suggestion Point out that in the expression **Zeitung lesen** the article is not used.

1.

2.

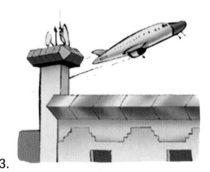

3.

4.

5.

6.

Aussprache und Rechtschreibung Audio

 Pure vowels versus diphthongs

You learned in **2B** that German has three diphthongs: **au**, **ai/ei**, and **eu/äu**. In these vowel combinations, two vowel sounds are pronounced together in the same syllable.

Haus	Mai	meine	scheu	läuft

All other German vowel sounds are pure vowels. Whether long or short, they never glide into another vowel sound.

kalt	Schnee	Spiel	Monat	Schule

Be sure to pronounce the vowels in German words as pure vowel sounds, even when they resemble English words with similar pronunciations.

kann	Stereo	Apfel	Boot	Schuh

Suggestion Have students pronounce each German word alongside its English counterpart, to help them hear the difference in the vowel sounds: "**kann**, *can*", "**Stereo**, *stereo*", etc.

1 **Aussprechen** Wiederholen Sie die Wörter, die Sie hören.

1. Hagel	5. minus	9. Januar	13. Zeit
2. wann	6. Winter	10. Geburtstag	14. heute
3. Regen	7. Oktober	11. August	15. Häuser
4. Wetter	8. Sommer	12. Mai	16. Gasthaus

2 **Nachsprechen** Wiederholen Sie die Sätze, die Sie hören.

1. Es hat fast den ganzen Tag geregnet.
2. Im Juli ist es am Nachmittag zu heiß.
3. Im Winter gehe ich gern langlaufen.
4. Trink eine Tasse Tee, damit du wieder wach wirst!
5. Im Mai wird es schön warm und sonnig.
6. Im Sommer schwimmen die Kinder im See.
7. Im Herbst muss Max sein Segelboot reparieren lassen.
8. Meine Freundin besucht mich heute.

3 **Sprichwörter** Wiederholen Sie die Sprichwörter, die Sie hören.

Nach Regen kommt Sonnenschein.[2]

Morgen, morgen, nur nicht heute, sagen alle faulen Leute.[1]

[1] Tomorrow, tomorrow, just not today, that is what all lazy people say.

[2] Things will look brighter tomorrow. (lit. *After the rain comes sunshine.*)

Ressourcen

SAM
LM: p. 63

vhlcentral.com

Ein Sommer in der Türkei? Ⓢ Video

Anke hat Pläne für den Sommer: Die ganze Familie soll den Sommer in der Türkei verbringen.

NATIONAL
communication
cultures
STANDARDS

ANKE Ich habe eine Überraschung für euch.
ZEYNEP Ich weiß schon, was es ist!
ANKE Zeynep, psst!
SABITE Was ist es denn?
ANKE Wir verbringen den Sommer in der Türkei.
SABITE Warum?
ZEYNEP Ja, warum wohl!

ANKE Es ist das Heimatland von deinem Vater. Und du und deine Schwester wart nicht mehr im Ausland seit... unseren Ferien in Frankreich vor drei Jahren. Wir wollen dort etwas über die Kunststudiengänge für dich erfahren, deshalb machen wir die Reise gemeinsam.

SABITE Ich kann es kaum erwarten, George, Hans und Meline davon zu erzählen.
ZEYNEP Und Torsten?

SABITE Mama, ich brauche deine Hilfe. Kann ich dich was fragen?
ANKE Du bittest mich doch sonst nie um Hilfe. Das muss ein großes Problem sein.

SABITE Torsten und ich haben uns gestritten. Ich habe ihm gesagt, dass ich überlege, in der Türkei Kunst zu studieren. Naja, ich habe es zuerst Meline gesagt. Ich habe mich mit Melines Freund über Kunst unterhalten und er stand daneben.

ANKE Du hast es ihm nicht zuerst gesagt. Und jetzt ist er unglücklich?
SABITE Ja. Und jetzt werden wir den Sommer nicht zusammen sein.
ANKE Wir müssen nicht in die Türkei fahren.
ZEYNEP Ähm, doch!
SABITE Oh, doch, das müssen wir. Aber ich will es ihm noch nicht sagen.

1 **Was fehlt?** Ergänzen Sie die Sätze mit den richtigen Informationen.

1. Anke möchte den (Sommer / Herbst) in der Türkei verbringen.
2. Die Türkei ist das Heimatland von (Anke / Faik).
3. Sabite und Zeynep waren schon in (Italien / Frankreich) im Urlaub.
4. Familie Yilmaz möchte etwas über (Jugendherbergen / Kunststudiengänge) in der Türkei erfahren.
5. Sabite bittet ihre Mutter um (Hilfe / Geld).

6. Sie hat Meline zuerst davon erzählt, in der Türkei (Kunst zu studieren / Urlaub zu machen).
7. Deshalb (*Therefore*) ist Torsten jetzt (unglücklich / unangenehm).
8. Anke glaubt, dass Beziehungen (einfach / kompliziert) sind.
9. Vor einem (Monat / Jahr) hat Sabite einige Arbeiten bei einer Galerie eingereicht.
10. Meline mag (Zeynep / Torsten) nicht.

PERSONEN Anke Sabite Zeynep

ANKE Was noch? Bei Problemen zwischen zwei Partnern geht es nie nur um eine Sache. Beziehungen sind kompliziert.
SABITE Er versteht meine Kunst nicht.
ZEYNEP Niemand versteht deine Kunst, ohne dass er verrückt ist.
ANKE Hör auf, deine Schwester zu ärgern.

SABITE Er möchte meine Kunst nicht verstehen. Vor einem Monat habe ich einige Arbeiten bei einer Galerie in der Torstraße eingereicht. Torsten sagte... sie werden das niemals ausstellen.

ZEYNEP Das ist gemein.
ANKE Er darf so etwas nicht zu dir sagen.
SABITE Meline mag ihn nicht.
ZEYNEP Meline ist komisch.

SABITE Aber sie versteht, dass ich Künstlerin bin, ohne meine Kunst zu verstehen. Mama, was soll ich tun?
ANKE Liebst du ihn, Sabite?

Nützliche Ausdrücke

- **Heimatland**
  homeland, country of origin

- **der Kunststudiengang**
  art course

- **gemeinsam**
  together

- **erwarten**
  to expect

- **Du bittest mich doch sonst nie um Hilfe.**
  You never ask for my help.

- **Torsten und ich haben uns gestritten.**
  Torsten and I have been fighting.

- **zuerst**
  first

- **daneben**
  aside, on the side

- **zwischen**
  between

- **ausstellen**
  to exhibit

- **komisch**
  weird

7B.1
- **Aber sie versteht, dass ich Künstlerin bin, ohne meine Kunst zu verstehen.**
  But she understands that I'm an artist, without understanding my art.

7B.2
- **Vor einem Monat habe ich einige Arbeiten bei einer Galerie in der Torstraße eingereicht.**
  A month ago, I submitted some work to a gallery on Torstraße.

7B.3
- **Niemand versteht deine Kunst, ohne dass er verrückt ist.**
  Nobody can understand your art, unless they're crazy.

2 **Zum Besprechen** Familie Yilmaz möchte zusammen Urlaub in der Türkei machen. Planen Sie mit einem Partner/einer Partnerin die Reise. Besprechen Sie das Ziel (*destination*), die Dauer der Reise, die Transportmittel, die Unterkünfte und weitere Details. Answers will vary.

3 **Vertiefung** Anke, Sabite und Zeynep sind im Bauhaus-Museum. Suchen Sie weitere Museen in Berlin und finden Sie heraus (*find out*), welche Ausstellungen zur Zeit dort zu sehen sind. Answers will vary.

2 **Expansion** Instead of having them write a paragraph, ask students to act out a conversation about vacation planning.

Suggestion Have students figure out the literal English translation of **Kofferwort**.

IM FOKUS

Flughafen Frankfurt Ⓢ Reading

> **TIPP**
>
> **The Squaire** comes from a combination of the English words *square* and *air*. This type of word combination is called a **Kofferwort** in German.

DER FRANKFURT AIRPORT (AUCH Rhein-Main-Flughafen) ist der größte Flughafen in Deutschland. Fast 60 Millionen Passagiere kamen hier 2014 an oder flogen von hier ab. In München waren es 2014 39,7 Millionen und in Düsseldorf 21,8 Millionen. In Europa fliegen Passagiere nur London-Heathrow und Paris-Charles de Gaulle öfter an.

Weltweit ist der Frankfurter Flughafen die Nummer 11. Der Flughafen ist sehr praktisch für Passagiere, weil es direkt im Flughafen einen Bahnhof° gibt. Man kann Flug und Zureise bequem miteinander kombinieren. Über dem Bahnhof findet man auch „The Squaire", ein großes Gebäude mit Büros, zwei Hotels und Geschäften.

Neben dem Passagierverkehr° ist der Frankfurt Airport auch für den Cargoverkehr wichtig. Innerhalb Europas werden nur in Paris-Charles de Gaulle mehr Güter° transportiert. Wegen der vielen Passagiere und der Güter nennt man den Frankfurt Airport auch ein wichtiges Luftfahrtdrehkreuz°. Der Flughafen ist aber nicht nur für Passagiere und Cargotransport wichtig. Hier arbeiten insgesamt über 78.000 Menschen. Innerhalb Deutschlands gilt der Flughafen als größte lokale Arbeitsstätte°. Er ist so groß, dass er seine eigene Postleitzahl° hat!

Flughafen	Passagiere (2014)	Flüge (2014)	Fluggesellschaften°
Frankfurt Airport	59,6 Millionen	469.000	109
London-Heathrow (größter in Europa)	73,4 Millionen	471.000	80
Atlanta International Airport (größter weltweit)	96,2 Millionen	868.000	58

QUELLE: Frankfurt Airport, Heathrow Airport, Atlanta International Airport

Bahnhof *train station* **Passagierverkehr** *passenger traffic* **Güter** *freight* **Luftfahrtdrehkreuz** *aviation hub* **Arbeitsstätte** *place of employment* **Postleitzahl** *zip code* **Fluggesellschaften** *airline companies*

Suggestion Before they begin the reading, have students describe the picture to you, using as many vocabulary words as possible.

1 **Richtig oder falsch?** Sind die Aussagen richtig oder falsch? Korrigieren Sie die falschen Aussagen.

1. Frankfurt Airport ist der größte Flughafen in Deutschland. Richtig.
2. Der Flughafen Nummer 2 in Deutschland ist Düsseldorf.
   Falsch. Der Flughafen Nummer 2 ist München.
3. Leider gibt es am Frankfurt Airport keinen Bahnhof.
   Falsch. Direkt im Flughafen gibt es einen Bahnhof.
4. Am Frankfurt Airport können Reisende übernachten.
   Richtig.
5. In London-Heathrow transportiert man mehr Güter als in Frankfurt.
   Falsch. Nur in Paris-Charles de Gaulle transportiert man an einem europäischen Flughafen mehr Güter.

6. Am Frankfurt Airport arbeiten 74.000 Menschen.
   Falsch. Am Frankfurt Airport arbeiten über 78.000 Menschen.
7. Der Frankfurt Airport ist die größte lokale Arbeitsstätte in Deutschland.
   Richtig.
8. Frankfurt Airport hat seine eigene Postleitzahl. Richtig.
9. Der Frankfurt Airport hat mehr Fluggesellschaften als London. Richtig.
10. Am größten Flughafen Europas flogen 2014 96,2 Millionen Passagiere ab. Falsch. In London-Heathrow flogen 2014 73,4 Millionen Passagiere ab.

 Practice more at **vhlcentral.com.**

Deutsch im Alltag You may want to teach the verb **zelten**. Ask the class: **Wer zeltet gern?**

DEUTSCH IM ALLTAG

Urlaub für Studenten

die Pension, -en	guesthouse
das Zelt, -e	tent
der Zeltplatz, ⁻e	camping area
der Zug, ⁻e	train
Sofa-surfen	to couch surf
Zimmer frei	vacancy

DIE DEUTSCHSPRACHIGE WELT

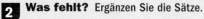

Sylt

Sylt ist die größte deutsche Insel in der Nordsee. Sie heißt auch „die Hamburger Badewanne". Jedes Jahr machen hier über 800.000 Menschen Urlaub. Berühmt ist Sylt für seine langen Strände (mehr als 40 Kilometer) und die Wanderdünen° in List. Sie sind bis zu 1.000 Meter lang und 35 Meter hoch. Sie „wandern" jedes Jahr bis zu 4 Meter. Interessant ist auch das Wattenmeer, wo viele Fische und Vögel leben. Auf Sylt findet man auch seltene° Pflanzen, Tiere und Schmetterlinge°. Die Heide° ist auch eine bekannte Landschaft° der Insel.

Wanderdünen hiking dunes **seltene** rare
Schmetterlinge butterflies **Heide** heath
Landschaft landscape

PORTRÄT

Der ICE

Der ICE, oder Intercity-Express, ist die schnellste Zugart° in Deutschland. Dieser Zug fährt in Deutschland und 6 Nachbarländern (Belgien, Dänemark, Frankreich, Niederlande, Österreich und der Schweiz) 180 ICE-Bahnhöfe an. Für Passagiere ist der ICE interessant, weil die Züge nicht nur extrem schnell fahren, sondern auch sehr bequem sind. Passagiere haben viel Platz. Alle Wagen haben Klimaanlagen°. Es gibt auch ein Bordrestaurant im Zug und oft ein Abteil° für Kinder. Mit Kopfhörern° kann man Musik- und Sprachprogramme hören und für Computer gibt es Steckdosen°.

Zugart type of train **Klimaanlagen** air conditioning **Abteil** section
Kopfhörern headphones **Steckdosen** electrical outlets

⚡S IM INTERNET

Suchen Sie Informationen über die Vogelfluglinie: Was ist die Vogelfluglinie? Wo liegt sie? Ist sie nur für Vögel?

Find out more at **vhlcentral.com**.

---

2 **Was fehlt?** Ergänzen Sie die Sätze.

⚡S
1. Die Insel Sylt liegt in der ___Nordsee___.
2. Die Insel Sylt hat lange ___Strände___ und Wanderdünen.
3. Eine Attraktion ist das ___Wattenmeer___, wo viele Fische und Vögel leben.
4. Die schnellste Zugart in Deutschland ist der ___ICE___.
5. Der ICE ist extrem schnell und auch ___(sehr) bequem___.
6. Es gibt Bordrestaurants und Abteile für ___Kinder___.

3 **Urlaub** Diskutieren Sie mit einem Partner / einer Partnerin, wo Sie in Deutschland, Österreich oder der Schweiz Urlaub machen wollen. Wählen Sie ein Urlaubziel (destination). Warum wollen Sie diese Orte besuchen? Was möchten Sie hier gerne sehen? Was möchten Sie hier gerne machen? Mit wem möchten Sie diese Orte besuchen?

Suggestion After reading the article about Sylt, have students search the text for words that describe the island. Ask comprehension questions, ex.: **Wo ist die Insel Sylt? Warum heißt sie wohl die „Hamburger Badewanne"?**

Ressourcen

vhlcentral.com

NATIONAL comparisons STANDARDS

7B.1

Infinitive expressions and clauses  Presentation

Suggestion Emphasize that **zu** is not used with modals. Write an example of an incorrect sentence on the board, such as **Ich will zu schlafen**, and have students identify the error. Have a volunteer come to the board to cross out the **zu**.

Startblock When you use a non-modal verb with an infinitive clause, add the preposition **zu** before the infinitive.

Ich habe Sabite letzte Woche geholfen, ihre Wohnung **zu putzen**.

Ich habe ihm gesagt, dass ich überlege, ein Semester in der Türkei Kunst **zu studieren**.

- In **3B.1**, you learned that when a conjugated modal verb modifies the meaning of another verb, the infinitive moves to the end of the sentence. The preposition **zu** is not needed in this case.

> Ich möchte Checkpoint Charlie **besuchen**.
> *I want **to visit** Checkpoint Charlie.*

> Es regnet. Wir müssen unsere Regenmäntel **anziehen**.
> *It's raining. We need **to put on** our raincoats.*

- After most other verbs, however, you need to put **zu** before the infinitive clause. Place **zu** plus the infinitive at the end of the sentence.

> Es macht viel Spaß **zu reisen**!
> ***Travelling** is so much fun!*

> Ich hatte keine Zeit, Postkarten **zu schreiben**.
> *I didn't have time **to write** postcards.*

- When using a double verb expression like **spazieren gehen**, put the preposition **zu** between the two verbs.

> Philip hat Angst, **schwimmen zu gehen**.
> *Philip is afraid **to go swimming**.*

> Es ist uns zu teuer, jeden Abend **essen zu gehen**.
> ***Going out to eat** every night is too expensive for us.*

- If the verb in the infinitive clause is a separable prefix verb, place **zu** between the prefix and the main part of the verb.

> Es macht keinen Spaß, die Küche **aufzuräumen**.
> ***Cleaning** the kitchen is no fun.*

> Vergiss bitte nicht, den Müll **rauszubringen**.
> *Please don't forget **to take out** the trash.*

- Infinitive constructions with **zu** often occur after the verbs **anfangen**, **beginnen**, **helfen**, **vergessen**, and **versuchen** (*to try*), the expressions **Lust haben** (*to be in the mood*), **Angst haben**, and **Spaß machen**, and the adjectives **einfach**, **wichtig** (*important*), and **schön**.

> Ich **habe vergessen**, meine Eltern **anzurufen**.
> *I **forgot to call** my parents.*

> Kannst du mir bitte **helfen**, meine Bordkarte **zu finden**?
> *Can you please **help** me **find** my boarding pass?*

> Wir **haben** keine **Lust**, heute Abend **auszugehen**.
> *We don't **feel like going out** this evening.*

> Ich finde es **wichtig**, pünktlich **zu sein**.
> *I think it's **important to be** on time.*

- Impersonal expressions beginning with **Es ist/war...** are also frequently followed by an infinitive clause.

Expansion Ask students to explain why they are learning German and answer using the expression **um... zu**. Emphasize that **um** sets off the clause, while **zu** and the infinitive appear at the very end.

> **Es war** so schön, in einem Fünf-Sterne-Hotel **zu übernachten**.
> *It was so nice **to spend the night** at a five-star hotel.*

> **Es ist** nicht gut, bei Nebel **zu fliegen**.
> *It's not good **to fly** when it's foggy.*

- The expressions **um... zu** (*in order to*), **ohne... zu** (*without*), and **anstatt... zu** (*instead of*) are frequently used in infinitive clauses. **Anstatt** is often shortened to **statt**, especially in informal conversation.

> Ich esse viel Gemüse und gehe jeden Tag schwimmen, **um** fit **zu bleiben**.
> *I eat lots of vegetables and swim every day **to stay** fit.*

> Man kann einen schönen Urlaub machen, **ohne** ins Ausland **zu fahren**.
> *You can have a nice vacation **without going** abroad.*

> Sie sind in die Schweiz gefahren, **anstatt** nach Rom **zu fliegen**.
> ***Instead of flying*** *to Rome, they drove to Switzerland.*

> Fahrt ihr nach Hamburg, **um** eure Freunde **zu besuchen**?
> *Are you driving to Hamburg **to visit** your friends?*

- In sentences with **um... zu, ohne... zu,** or **(an)statt... zu**, the infinitive clause may be the first element in a sentence. When the infinitive clause is the first element, the conjugated verb becomes the second element, and the subject comes after the conjugated verb.

> **Statt zu schlafen**, **hat Peter** die ganze Nacht gelesen.
> ***Instead of sleeping**, Peter spent all night reading.*

> **Um** ein Zimmer in diesem Hotel **zu bekommen**, **muss man** sehr früh buchen.
> ***To get** a room at that hotel, you have to book early.*

> **Ohne** vorher **zu fragen**, **haben sie** die Kekse gegessen.
> *They ate the cookies **without asking** first.*

> **Anstatt** meine Hausaufgaben **zu machen**, **bin ich** gestern Abend ausgegangen.
> ***Instead of doing** my homework, I went out last night*

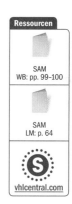

Ressourcen

SAM
WB: pp. 99–100

SAM
LM: p. 64

vhlcentral.com

 Jetzt sind Sie dran!   **Wählen Sie das passende Wort.**

1. Ich bin rausgegangen, (um / ~~ohne~~ / anstatt) den Schlüssel mitzunehmen!

2. (Um / Ohne / ~~Anstatt~~) einen Skiurlaub zu machen, fahren wir ans Meer.

3. Der Student hat eine gute Note in seiner Prüfung bekommen, (um / ~~ohne~~ / anstatt) dafür zu lernen.

4. (Um / Ohne / ~~Anstatt~~) mit dem Auto zu fahren, fliegt Jana nach Italien.

5. Willst du Deutsch lernen, (~~um~~ / ohne / anstatt) in Deutschland zu studieren?

6. Michael hat das Hotel gefunden, (um / ~~ohne~~ / anstatt) auf den Stadtplan zu schauen.

7. (Um / Ohne / ~~Anstatt~~) Zeitung zu lesen, schlafe ich gern im Flugzeug.

8. Der Geschäftsmann bestellte Zimmerservice, (um / ~~ohne~~ / anstatt) nach dem Preis zu fragen.

9. Wir fahren zwei Stunden vor unserem Flug zum Flughafen, (~~um~~ / ohne / anstatt) pünktlich zu sein.

10. Nina ist faul und fährt mit dem Fahrstuhl, (um / ohne / ~~anstatt~~) die Treppe zu nehmen.

11. Ich trage einen Mantel bei schlechtem Wetter, (~~um~~ / ohne / anstatt) warm zu bleiben.

12. Das Gute an Jugendherbergen ist, man kann dort übernachten, (um / ~~ohne~~ / anstatt) ein Bett zu reservieren.

Anwendung

1 **Was fehlt?** Ergänzen Sie die Sätze mit der richtigen Form des Verbs im Infinitiv.

1. Wir helfen unseren Eltern, die Koffer ___zu packen___. (packen)
2. Mama fängt an, die Zimmer im Hotel ___zu reservieren___. (reservieren)
3. Es macht Spaß, in Europa ___zu reisen___. (reisen)
4. Papa hat vergessen, unsere Personalausweise ___mitzubringen___. (mitbringen)
5. Der Taxifahrer hatte keine Zeit, ___zurückzufahren___. (zurückfahren)
6. Er musste sehr schnell fahren, um am Flughafen pünktlich ___anzukommen___. (ankommen)

2 **Ausdrücke** Ergänzen Sie die Sätze mit dem passenden Ausdruck **um... zu, ohne... zu** oder **(an)statt... zu.**

> **BEISPIEL** Im Flugzeug lese ich viel, _(an)statt_ zu schlafen.

1. Wir gehen mit unseren Freunden am Abend vor unserer Reise aus, ___(an)statt___ unsere Koffer zu packen.
2. Die Studenten reisen viel, ___um___ verschiedene Länder kennen zu lernen.
3. Maria hat eine gute Note in Deutsch geschrieben, ___ohne___ viel dafür zu lernen.
4. Warum habt ihr stundenlang in der Sonne gestanden, ___ohne___ einen Hut zu tragen?
5. Am Freitag gehen wir ins Theater, ___um___ das neue Theaterstück anzusehen.
6. ___Anstatt / Statt___ ein Hotelzimmer zu buchen, werden wir in der Jugendherberge übernachten.

3 Suggestion Do the first few items as a class to make sure that students understand the activity.

3 **Wozu braucht man das?** Sagen Sie, wozu man die abgebildeten Dinge braucht. Sample answers are provided.

| fit bleiben | tanzen gehen | E-Mails schreiben |
| im Regen trocken bleiben | Deutsch lernen | in den Bergen wandern |

▶ **BEISPIEL**
Man braucht einen Badeanzug, um schwimmen zu gehen.

1. Man soll viel Gemüse essen, um fit zu bleiben.

2. Man braucht einen Regenschirm, um im Regen trocken zu bleiben.

3. Man braucht ein Wörterbuch, um Deutsch zu lernen.

4. Man braucht einen Rucksack, um in den Bergen zu wandern.

5. Man braucht einen Computer, um E-Mails zu schreiben.

6. Man braucht ein schönes Kleid, um tanzen zu gehen.

Kommunikation

4 **Viel gereist** Sie waren im Sommer in Deutschland. Besprechen Sie mit einem Partner / einer Partnerin, wo Sie waren und warum Sie dort waren. Answers will vary.

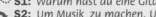 **BEISPIEL** in München
S1: Wo warst du im Sommer?
S2: Ich war in München, um meine Familie zu besuchen. Meine Schwester wohnt dort.

in den Alpen	in Hamburg
in Berlin	in Heidelberg
an der Donau	in München
in Füssen	an der Ostseeküste

4 **Expansion** Review various cultural attractions unique to the cities and landmarks on the list. Encourage students to research points of interest on their own or in groups, and share what they have discovered with the class.

5 **Ein schwerer Koffer** Sie haben viel in den Urlaub mitgebracht. Erzählen Sie einem Partner / einer Partnerin, wieso Sie so viel im Gepäck haben. Answers will vary.

BEISPIEL
S1: Warum hast du eine Gitarre mitgebracht?
S2: Um Musik zu machen. Und du? Warum hast du einen Badeanzug gepackt?
S1: Um schwimmen zu gehen.

einen gestreiften Anzug	eine kurze Hose	einen Rucksack
einen Badeanzug	ein Kleid	viele Bücher
die Brille	eine Krawatte	eine Sonnenbrille
eine Gitarre	eine Mütze	ein langärmliges T-Shirt
eine schöne Halskette	einen Regenschirm	Turnschuhe

6 **Wohin wollen wir reisen?** Denken Sie an drei mögliche Urlaubsziele. Fragen Sie Ihren Partner / Ihre Partnerin, wohin er/sie reisen möchte, und besprechen Sie dabei die Sehenswürdigkeiten in jeder Stadt. Answers will vary.

BEISPIEL
S1: Wo machen wir im Sommer Urlaub?
S2: Ich will nach Disneyland fahren, anstatt Museen zu besuchen.
S1: Warum?
S2: Um Mickey Mouse zu treffen. Ich finde ihn toll!

7 **Meiner Meinung nach** Ergänzen Sie die folgenden Aussagen mit Ihrer Meinung. Vergleichen Sie die Antworten mit anderen Studenten.

1. Ich finde es schwer...
2. Es macht mir Spaß...
3. Ich habe keine Lust...
4. Ich versuche immer...
5. Ich finde es wichtig...
6. Es ist schön...

7 **Suggestion** Make sure students know to use a **zu** + infinitive clause in each answer.

7B.2

QUERVERWEIS

See **2A.3** and **2B.2** to review times and dates in German.

To review word order with time expressions, see **4A.2**.

Expansion Write on the board: **0X, 1X, 2X, 3X, ...20X**, etc. and have students verbalize what these shorthand forms indicate: **niemals, einmal, zweimal, dreimal, ...zwanzigmal**, etc. You may also wish to introduce the colloquialism **zigmal**, "a zillion times".

Suggestion To practice the use of **seit** and **schon**, ask students how long they've been doing a particular activity and write their responses on the board. Ex.: **Carrie spielt seit einem Jahr Gitarre. Tom lernt seit Januar Deutsch.** Underline the verbs and emphasize that they are in the present tense.

Ressourcen

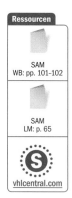

SAM
WB: pp. 101-102

SAM
LM: p. 65

vhlcentral.com

Time expressions  Presentation

Suggestion Ask travel-related questions that can be answered with these expressions, such as: **Wie oft waren Sie in Europa? Wie oft waren Sie am Strand? Wie viele Male sind Sie geflogen?**

Startblock German has two main concepts related to expressions of time. **Zeit** describes a span of time, while **Mal** refers to specific occurrences and repetitions.

Ich habe noch **50 Minuten Zeit** vor meinem Flug.
*I still have **50 minutes** before my flight.*

Ich war nur **einmal** in Hamburg.
*I've only been to Hamburg **once**.*

- Many German time expressions use **Mal** or a compound word containing **-mal**:

diesmal	*this time*	**manchmal**	*sometimes*
das erste Mal	*the first time*	**niemals**	*never*
einmal	*once*	**zum ersten/letzten Mal**	*for the first/last time*

- Use the accusative case to talk about a particular span of time or point in time. To describe how long something lasted, use **dauern** with the accusative.

Die Kreuzfahrt dauerte **einen Monat**.
*The cruise lasted **a month**.*

Nächsten Sommer fahren wir an den Strand.
Next summer we're going to the beach.

Letzten Montag haben meine Ferien angefangen.
*My break started **last Monday**.*

Die Studenten tanzten **die ganze Nacht**.
*The students danced **all night long**.*

- Use the present tense with **seit** plus a dative time expression or **schon** plus an accusative time expression to indicate how long something has been going on.

Seit einem Monat wohnt Patrick in Berlin.
*Patrick has been living in Berlin **for a month**.*

Er studiert **schon zwei Jahre** in Deutschland.
*He's been studying in Germany **for two years**.*

- The two-way prepositions **an, in,** and **vor** can all be used to answer the question **wann?** Use the dative case with these time expressions.

Vor einem Jahr studierte ich im Ausland.
A year ago I was studying abroad.

Mein Geburtstag ist **am 18. Februar**.
*My birthday is **on February 18**.*

- Use the time expressions **zuerst** (*first*), **dann** (*then*), **danach** (*after that*), and **zuletzt** (*last*) or **schließlich** (*finally*) to narrate a series of events.

Zuerst musst du die wichtigen Papiere in das Handgepäck packen.
***First** you have to pack your important papers in the carry-on bag.*

Dann kannst du die anderen Sachen in den großen Koffer packen.
***Then** you can pack the other things in the big suitcase.*

 Jetzt sind Sie dran!   **Wählen Sie die passenden Wörter.**

Expansion Have students work in small groups to write a short travel cartoon using **zuerst, dann, danach,** and **zuletzt**. Remind them of correct verb position.

1. (Im/ In den) Frühling regnet es viel.
2. In (der/ die) Nacht habe ich schlecht geträumt.
3. Laura reist für (ein / einen) Monat nach Österreich.
4. Vor (einer / eine) Woche haben wir unsere Flugtickets bekommen.
5. (Nächster / Nächsten) Sommer musst du in den Urlaub mitkommen.
6. (Am / An das) Wochenende fahre ich nach Zürich.
7. Herr Boas wartet schon (einer / eine) Stunde auf ein Taxi.
8. Wir waren (letzter / letzten) Dienstag nicht zu Hause.
9. Hugo arbeitet seit (ein / einem) Jahr an seinem neuen Buch.
10. In (einer / eine) Woche macht er eine Kreuzfahrt.

Anwendung und Kommunikation

1 **Was fehlt?** Ergänzen Sie die Sätze mit den passenden Zeitergänzungen aus der Liste.

einmal	das erste Mal	einen Monat
letztes Jahr	35 Minuten	nächste Woche

1. Saras Geburtstag ist __nächste Woche__ und dann wird sie zweiundzwanzig.
2. Mit 18 Jahren durfte ich __das erste Mal__ allein in Urlaub fahren.
3. Silvester ist __letztes Jahr__ auf einen Sonntag gefallen.
4. Der Flug von München nach Nürnberg dauert nur __35 Minuten__.
5. Wir haben noch __einen Monat__ bis zum Ende von unserem Semester.
6. Meine Großeltern planen eine Familienfeier, denn Goldene Hochzeit hat man nur __einmal__ im Leben.

2 **Ein kleines Interview** Beantworten Sie die Fragen von Ihrem Partner / Ihrer Partnerin. Answers will vary.

BEISPIEL seit wann / Deutsch lernen

S1: Seit wann lernst du Deutsch?
S2: Seit letztem Semester.

1. wann / Geburtstag haben Wann hast du Geburtstag?
2. seit wann / hier studieren Seit wann studierst du hier?
3. was / zuerst machen nach dem Semesterende / Und danach?
   Was machst du zuerst nach dem Semesterende? Und danach?
4. wann und wo / zuletzt am Strand sein
   Wann und wo bist du zuletzt am Strand gewesen?
5. vor wie vielen Jahren / zum ersten Mal im Flugzeug fliegen
   Vor wie vielen Jahren bist du zum ersten Mal im Flugzeug geflogen?
6. wen / einmal kennen lernen möchten Wen möchtest du einmal kennen lernen?

3 **Reiselust** Erfinden Sie mit Ihren Mitstudenten eine kurze Geschichte über eine Reise. Benutzen Sie Wörter aus der Liste oder Ihre eigenen.

BEISPIEL

Thomas und seine Familie wollten zum ersten Mal eine Kreuzfahrt von Marseille nach Palermo machen. Zuerst...

Zeitausdrücke	Hauptwörter	Verben
danach	die Crew	einkaufen
dann	das Gepäck	einpacken
niemals	das Meer	essen
seit	der Pass	regnen
vor	der Sandstrand	schwimmen
zuerst	das Souvenir	tanzen
zuletzt	das Wetter	vergessen

2 **Suggestion** Give students some time to write out the questions before they conduct their interviews. Point out that they will need to use the past tense to construct logical questions for items 4 and 5.

3 **Suggestion** Invite the groups to share their stories with the class.

7B.3

QUERVERWEIS

To review the use of subject, accusative, and dative pronouns, see **1.A.3**, **5A.2**, and **5A.3**.

Suggestion Provide sample sentences that demonstrate the different case endings. Ex.: **Niemand war im Zimmer. Wir sahen niemanden im Zimmer. Wir gaben niemandem die Blumen.**

Expansion Provide your class with a list of travel destinations and have students find out who has been to those places. Then have them summarize their results. Ex.: **Niemand ist nach Wyoming gereist. Maria war schon in Kuba, aber niemand aus der Klasse ist in Ecuador gewesen.**

ACHTUNG

In conversation, **etwas** may be shortened to **was**. Ex.: **Kann ich dich was fragen?**

Remember that **man** is singular. When **man** is the subject, always use a verb in the third-person singular.

Suggestion Emphasize that the declension of **alles** parallels the declension of **das**: the nominative form is **alles**, the accusative form is **alles**, and the dative form is **allem**.

Indefinite pronouns  Presentation

Startblock Pronouns that refer to an unknown or nonspecific person or thing are called indefinite pronouns.

Alles in Ordnung?

Niemand bestellt Zimmerservice.

- Two indefinite pronouns that refer to people are **jemand** (*someone*) and **niemand** (*no one*). Use the ending **-en** for the accusative case and **-em** for the dative.

  Jemand hat seinen Personalausweis an der Passkontrolle vergessen.
  Someone left his I.D. card at passport control.

  Herr Klein will mit **niemandem** sprechen.
  Mr. Klein doesn't want to speak with anyone.

- To talk about indefinite things, use **alles** (*everything*), **etwas** (*something*), or **nichts** (*nothing*). **Etwas** and **nichts** do not change in different cases; **alles** is declined like the neuter definite article **das**.

  Wir haben noch **nichts** gegessen.
  We haven't eaten anything yet.

  Möchten Sie **etwas** zu trinken bestellen?
  Would you like to order something to drink?

  Ich habe **alles** ins Handgepäck gepackt.
  I packed everything in the carry-on.

  Meine Schwester kann dir mit **allem** helfen.
  My sister can help you with everything.

- Use the pronoun **man** to talk about people in general.

  Man darf im Flugzeug nicht rauchen.
  You're not allowed to smoke on an airplane.

  In Hamburg ist **man** froh, wenn es im Winter nicht zu viel schneit.
  In Hamburg we're happy if it doesn't snow too much in winter.

  In Liechtenstein spricht **man** Deutsch.
  In Liechtenstein they speak German.

  Man soll zwei Stunden vor dem Abflug am Flughafen sein.
  One should be at the airport two hours before departure.

Ressourcen

SAM
WB: pp. 103–104

SAM
LM: p. 66

vhlcentral.com

Jetzt sind Sie dran! Wählen Sie das passende Wort.

1. Anna vergisst oft ihre Hausaufgaben, aber Emil vergisst (nichts / etwas).
2. (Etwas / Niemand) will arbeiten, wenn das Wetter draußen so schön ist.
3. Wenn (man / alles) nicht ins Ausland will, gibt es auch in Deutschland viele schöne Ferienorte (*vacation spots*).
4. (Nichts / Jemand) hat vergessen, das Fenster zu schließen.
5. Hast du (niemand / etwas) gesagt?
6. Ich möchte (alles / man) in dieser Stadt sehen!
7. Ich will im Urlaub (jemand / nichts) machen – nur schlafen und essen!
8. Sollen wir (man / jemanden) fragen, oder findest du die Antwort im Internet?
9. Jasmin ist sehr schüchtern – sie will mit (niemandem / etwas) reden.
10. (Nichts / Man) kann in diesem Geschäft viele schöne Sachen finden.

Suggestion Tell students that **man** cannot be replaced by **er**, and that in the accusative or dative it is replaced by **einen/einem**. Have students write down sample sentences; ex.: **Wenn man traurig ist, dann soll man spazieren gehen. Dann geht es einem besser.**

Anwendung und Kommunikation

1 **Fragen zur Grammatik** Ergänzen Sie die Sätze mit den passenden Wörtern aus der Liste.

alles	nichts
etwas	niemand
jemand	niemandem

1. Hat _____jemand_____ noch Fragen zur Grammatik?
2. Professor Krause, können Sie uns _____alles_____ noch einmal erklären?
3. _____Niemand_____ hat die Grammatik verstanden.
4. Sie haben wirklich _____nichts_____ verstanden?
5. Also kann ich leider _____niemandem_____ helfen.
6. Sie können _____etwas_____ lernen, liebe Studenten, aber nur wenn Sie Ihre Hausaufgaben machen!

2 **Was macht man hier?** Schreiben Sie zu jedem Foto einen Satz mit **man**. Benutzen Sie die angegebenen Wörter.

▶ **BEISPIEL**

hier / können / Medikamente kaufen
Hier kann man Medikamente kaufen.

1. bei Rot / müssen / stoppen
Bei Rot muss man stoppen.

2. hier / kommen / zum Marienplatz
Hier kommt man zum Marienplatz.

3. hier / sprechen / Deutsch
Hier spricht man Deutsch.

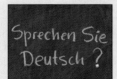

4. hier / dürfen / parken
Hier darf man parken.

5. hier / können / einkaufen
Hier kann man einkaufen.

3 **Armer Niklas** Es geht Ihrem Freund Niklas wirklich schlecht. Besprechen Sie mit Ihrem Partner / Ihrer Partnerin, was Niklas machen muss oder was man machen soll, um Niklas zu helfen. Answers will vary. Suggested answers.

 BEISPIEL

S1: *Niklas hat heute nichts gegessen.*
S2: *Er muss etwas essen!*

1. Niklas muss morgen ein Referat halten und hat noch nichts dazu vorbereitet.
Er muss etwas dazu vorbereiten!
2. Die Professorin hat ihm nichts erklärt.
Sie muss ihm alles erklären!
3. Im Unterricht hat er nichts zu sagen.
Er soll im Unterricht etwas sagen.
4. Niemand hilft ihm.
Jemand soll ihm helfen.
5. Er hat Angst vor allem.
Er muss vor nichts Angst haben!
6. Er hat mit niemandem über seine Probleme gesprochen.
Er muss mit jemandem über seine Probleme sprechen.

 Practice more at **vhlcentral.com.**

3 Suggestion Make sure students take turns describing Niklas' problems and proposing solutions.

Wiederholung

NATIONAL communication STANDARDS

1 Die vergesslichen Schröders
Sehen Sie sich die Bilder an. Sagen Sie, was die Familie Schröder vergessen hat.

Sample answers are provided.

▶ **BEISPIEL** *Jan hat vergessen, das Geschirr zu spülen.*

1 Expansion Ask students: **Und Sie? Was haben Sie diese Woche vergessen?**

Jan

1. Opa
Opa hat vergessen, den Müll rauszutragen.

2. Tobias Tobias hat vergessen, das Schlafzimmer aufzuräumen.

3. Tante Ingrid Tante Ingrid hat vergessen, das Fenster zu schließen.

4. Onkel Paul Onkel Paul hat vergessen, im Wohnzimmer zu staubsaugen.

5. Greta Greta hat vergessen, ihre Hausaufgaben zu machen.

2 Wie viel verstehst du?
Wie viel verstehen Sie und Ihr Partner / Ihre Partnerin von den Themen auf der Liste? Etwas? Nichts? Alles? Wechseln Sie sich ab.

Answers will vary.

BEISPIEL

S1: *Wie viel verstehst du von Politik?*
S2: *Ich verstehe etwas von Politik. Und du?*

Chemie	Geographie	Popmusik
Fotographie	Geschichte	Skateboard fahren
Fußball spielen	Politik	Tanzen

3 Diskutieren und kombinieren
Sie und Ihr Partner / Ihre Partnerin bekommen zwei verschiedene Arbeitsblätter von Ihrem Professor / Ihrer Professorin. Finden Sie heraus, warum die einzelnen Personen etwas tun.

Sample answers are provided.

BEISPIEL

S1: *Warum geht Kiara in die Bibliothek?*
S2: *Sie geht dahin, um ein Buch für ein Referat zu suchen.*

4 Arbeitsblatt
Fragen Sie die anderen Studenten, wann sie die Dinge auf der Liste das letzte Mal gemacht haben. Finden Sie zu jedem Wochentag eine Person.

Answers will vary.

BEISPIEL in die Bibliothek gehen

S1: *Wann bist du das letzte Mal in die Bibliothek gegangen?*
S2: *Am Mittwoch bin ich dahin gegangen.*

5 Wie lange?
Fragen Sie Ihren Partner / Ihre Partnerin, wie lange er/sie die Dinge auf der Liste schon macht. Answers will vary.

BEISPIEL Deutsch lernen

S1: *Wie lange lernst du schon Deutsch?*
S2: *Seit 6 Monaten.*

Konzerte besuchen	schwimmen
Auto fahren	ein Musikinstrument spielen
Rad fahren	Videospiele spielen
Bücher lesen	an der Uni studieren

6 Wie oft?
Arbeiten Sie mit einem Partner / einer Partnerin. Fragen Sie nach seinen/ihren Urlaubserfahrungen. Wie oft ist er/sie ins Ausland gereist oder in einem Hotel geblieben? Wie oft hat er/sie einen Nationalpark besucht? Wie oft hat er/sie Familie in einer anderen Stadt besucht? Answers will vary.

BEISPIEL

S1: *Wie oft bist du ins Ausland gereist?*
S2: *Ich bin zweimal ins Ausland gereist, einmal nach Mexiko und einmal nach Frankreich.*

3 Suggestion In this activity, students will be practicing the **um… zu** + infinitive construction. To prepare them, ask a few **warum** questions and write student responses on the board, using **um… zu**.

7 Beim Reisen Diskutieren Sie mit Ihren Mitstudenten, was man beim Reisen alles beachten (*consider*) muss. Benutzen Sie Wörter aus der Liste oder Ihre eigenen. Answers will vary.

BEISPIEL

S1: Man braucht einen Pass für eine Reise nach Europa.
S2: Und man muss das Flugticket circa drei Monate vor der Reise kaufen.
S3: Man darf nicht zu spät am Flughafen ankommen.

abfliegen	das Flugticket
ankommen	das Geld
bestellen	das Handy
buchen	die Kleidung
kaufen	die Kreditkarte
mitbringen	der Pass
packen	die Reservierung
vergessen	das Visum

8 Suggestion If students are having difficulty coming up with ideas for this role play, interrupt the activity to brainstorm ideas as a class.

8 Rollenspiel Spielen Sie mit einem Partner / einer Partnerin die Rollen von zwei älteren Menschen, die über ihr Leben nachdenken. Jede Person sagt etwas über einen anderen Abschnitt (*phase*) des Lebens. Answers will vary.

BEISPIEL

S1: Mit 5 zog meine Familie in die USA.
S2: Mit 6 ging ich zum ersten Mal in die Schule.

9 Eine Geschichte Schauen Sie sich das Bild an und schreiben Sie eine Geschichte dazu. Jede Person schreibt zwei Sätze der Geschichte und gibt sein Stück Papier an die nächste Person weiter. Der erste Satz beginnt mit „zuerst", der dritte mit „dann", der fünfte mit „danach" und so weiter. Answers will vary.

BEISPIEL Zuerst spazierten zwei Freunde auf der Straße...

Mein Wör|ter|buch

Schreiben Sie noch fünf weitere Wörter in Ihr persönliches Wörterbuch zu den Themen **Jahreszeiten** und **Reisen**.

der Altweibersommer

Übersetzung
Indian summer

Wortart
ein Substantiv

Gebrauch
Mitte September hatten wir den Altweibersommer. Das Wetter war warm und sonnig und wir haben alle Sommerkleidung getragen.

Synonyme
—

Antonyme
—

 **Vocabulary tools**

Panorama Interactive Map

Schleswig-Holstein, Hamburg und Bremen

Schleswig-Holstein in Zahlen

▶ **Fläche:** *15.800 km²*

▶ **Einwohner:** *2,8 Millionen*

▶ **Sprachen:** *Deutsch (2,7 Millionen), Plattdeutsch (1,3 Millionen), Dänisch (65.000), Friesisch (10.000)*

▶ **Städte:** *Kiel (240.000), Lübeck (212.000)*

▶ **Industrie:** *Landwirtschaft°, Seehandel°, Windenergie*

▶ **Touristenattraktionen:** *Danewerk und Haithabu (Wikingerstätten°), Karl-May-Festspiele° in Bad Segeberg*

Berühmte Schleswig-Holsteiner

▶ **Max Planck,** *Physiker (1858–1947)*

▶ **Thomas Mann,** *Literaturnobelpreisträger (1875–1955)*

Quelle: Landesportal Schleswig-Holstein

Hamburg in Zahlen

▶ **Fläche:** *755.000 km²*

▶ **Einwohner der Hansestadt Hamburg:** *1,7 Millionen*

▶ **Industrie:** *Flugzeugbau, Hafen, Schiffbau, Tourismus*

▶ **Touristenattraktionen:** *Altonaer Fischmarkt, Hamburger Michel, Museumsschiff Rickmer Rickmers*

Berühmte Hamburger

▶ **Johannes Brahms,** *Komponist (1833–1897)*

▶ **Jil Sander,** *Modedesignerin (1943–)*

Quelle: Landesportal Hamburg

Bremen in Zahlen

▶ **Fläche:** *325 km² (kleinstes deutsches Bundesland)*

▶ **Einwohner der Hansestadt Bremen:** *657.000*

▶ **Industrie:** *Außenhandel°, Automobilindustrie*

▶ **Touristenattraktionen:** *Böttcherstraße, Rathaus, Bremer Stadtmusikanten, Marktplatz, Schnoor*

Berühmte Bremer

▶ **Ernst Rowohlt,** *Verleger° (1887–1960)*

▶ **James Last,** *Komponist und Bandleader (1929–)*

Quelle: Landesportal Bremen

Landwirtschaft agriculture **Seehandel** maritime trade **Wikingerstätten** Viking sites **Festspiele** festivals **Außenhandel** foreign trade **Verleger** publisher **Brücken** bridges **überqueren** cross **Venedig** Venice

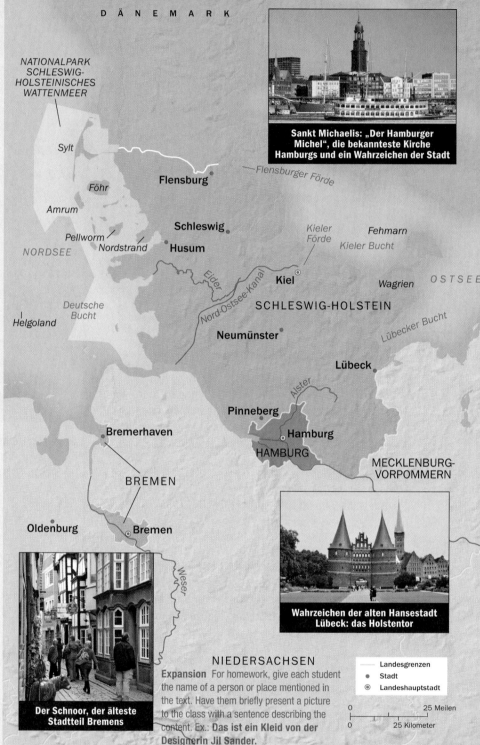

Suggestion Tell students that Hamburg is home to several German newspapers and magazines, including *Der Spiegel*, *Die Zeit*, and *Stern*.

Suggestion Ask students if they are familiar with any of Brahms' music. You may want to play them part of his **Wiegenlied**.

Sankt Michaelis: „Der Hamburger Michel", die bekannteste Kirche Hamburgs und ein Wahrzeichen der Stadt

Wahrzeichen der alten Hansestadt Lübeck: das Holstentor

Der Schnoor, der älteste Stadtteil Bremens

Expansion For homework, give each student the name of a person or place mentioned in the text. Have them briefly present a picture to the class with a sentence describing the content. Ex.: Das ist ein Kleid von der Designerin Jil Sander.

— Landesgrenzen
• Stadt
◉ Landeshauptstadt

0 — 25 Meilen
0 — 25 Kilometer

Unglaublich, aber wahr!

In Hamburg gibt es mehr als 2.400 Brücken°. Die Brücken überqueren° die Alster, Süderelbe, Norderelbe und Kanäle der Stadt. Es gibt mehr Brücken in Hamburg als in Venedig°, Amsterdam und London zusammen.

Suggestion Tell students that the Beatles spent a few years in Hamburg in the early sixties. They also recorded German versions of "**Komm gib mir deine Hand**" and "**Sie liebt dich**"; videos for both can be found online.

Expansion A series of puppet shows called **Märchen der Welt** is available online, including a production of **Bremer Stadtmusikanten**. Show students the final five minutes, in which the thieves are driven away by the animals.

Märchen
Bremer Stadtmusikanten

Auf dem Marktplatz der Stadt Bremen gibt es eine Statue: Man kann einen Hahn° auf einer Katze auf einem Hund auf einem Esel° stehen sehen. Diese Tiere spielen die Hauptrollen eines Märchens der Gebrüder Grimm mit dem Namen „Die Bremer Stadtmusikanten". Es ist interessant, dass die Tiere in dem Märchen nie in Bremen ankamen. Zwar wollten sie am Anfang der Geschichte nach Bremen, hielten dann aber in einem Haus außerhalb der Stadt an. Trotzdem sind die Stadtmusikanten ein wichtiges Symbol der Stadt.

Natur
Nationalpark Schleswig-Holsteinsches Wattenmeer

Das Wattenmeer liegt in der Nordsee. Große Teile des Wattenmeers stehen unter Naturschutz°. Der Nationalpark Schleswig-Holsteinisches Wattenmeer hat eine Fläche von 4.410 Quadratkilometern und erstreckt sich von der deutsch-dänischen Seegrenze bis zur Elbmündung°. Er ist der größte deutsche Nationalpark. 70% des Nationalparks stehen permanent unter Wasser. Tiere und Pflanzen, die in diesem Nationalpark leben, sind Schweinswale°, Brandgänse° und diverse Seegräser. Seit 2009 ist das Wattenmeer ein UNESCO-Welterbe°.

Tradition
Hafengeburtstag Hamburg

Ungefähr 13.000 Seeschiffe aus aller Welt laufen jährlich den zweitgrößten Seehafen° Europas an. Kaiser Friedrich Barbarossa hatte den Hamburgern am 7. Mai 1189 Zollfreiheit° für ihre Schiffe auf der Elbe von der Stadt bis an die Nordsee gewährt. Das Tor zur Welt war damit geöffnet, der Hamburger Hafen geboren. Seit 1977 feiert man Anfang Mai den Hafengeburtstag Hamburg. Mit vielen Attraktionen zu Wasser und in der Luft und einem ausgedehnten° Bühnenprogramm° zieht das Fest zahlreiche Touristen aus dem In- und Ausland an.

Piraten
Störtebeker

Klaus Störtebeker ist der berühmteste deutsche Pirat (wahrscheinlich 1360–1401). Viele Legenden existieren über ihn. Der Name Störtebeker (Stürz den Becher) kommt aus dem Niederdeutschen: angeblich konnte Störtebeker einen 4-Liter-Becher° in einem Schluck° austrinken. 1401 exekutierte man Störtebeker mit 30 Gefährten° in Hamburg. Laut einer Sage° durften alle Gefährten weiterleben°, an denen Störtebeker nach seiner Exekution ohne Kopf vorbeilief°. Er schaffte 11 Kameraden! Heute ist das Interesse an diesem Mann immer noch sehr groß. Einige Schiffe tragen seinen Namen und es gibt auch Filme und Festspiele über ihn.

⚙ IM INTERNET

1. Suchen Sie Informationen über die Umwelthauptstadt Hamburg: Machen Sie eine Liste mit Aktionen, die es in Hamburg gab.

2. Suchen Sie Informationen über die Stadt Lübeck: Was kann man hier machen? Warum ist diese Stadt berühmt? Was kann man hier essen?

Find out more at **vhlcentral.com**.

Hahn *rooster* **Esel** *donkey* **Naturschutz** *conservation* **Elbmündung** *Elbe delta* **Schweinswale** *porpoises* **Brandgänse** *shelducks* **Welterbe** *world heritage site* **zweitgrößten Seehafen** *second largest seaport* **Zollfreiheit** *guaranteed duty exemption* **ausgedehnten** *extensive* **Bühnenprogramm** *stage program* **Becher** *mug* **Schluck** *gulp* **Gefährten** *companions* **Sage** *tale* **weiterleben** *be spared* **ohne Kopf vorbeilief** *ran by without his head*

Was haben Sie gelernt? Ergänzen Sie die Sätze.

1. Die Brücken Hamburgs überqueren die __Alster, Norderelbe, Süderelbe__ und Kanäle der Stadt.

2. In Hamburg gibt es mehr Brücken als in __Venedig, Amsterdam und London__ zusammen.

3. Auf dem Bremer Marktplatz gibt es eine Statue mit vier __Tieren__.

4. __Die Gebrüder Grimm__ haben das Märchen der Bremer Stadtmusikanten aufgeschrieben.

5. Der Hamburger Hafen wurde im Jahr __1189__ gegründet.

6. Jedes Jahr kommen ungefähr 13.000 __Seeschiffe__ in den Hamburger Hafen.

7. Der berühmteste Pirat Deutschlands heißt __Klaus Störtebeker__.

8. Er wurde __1401__ in Hamburg exekutiert.

9. Der Nationalpark Wattenmeer ist der größte deutsche __Nationalpark__.

10. Im Nationalpark leben Tiere wie Schweinswale und __Brandgänse__.

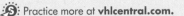 Practice more at **vhlcentral.com**.

Lesen   Audio: Reading

Vor dem Lesen

Strategien
Predicting content from the title You can often use titles and subheadings to predict the content of a text before you read it. For example, you can usually predict the content of a newspaper article from its headline. Predicting content from titles will help you increase your reading comprehension in German.

Untersuchen Sie den Text

Lesen Sie die Überschriften (*titles*) des Textes. Was für eine Textart ist das? Schreiben Sie mit einem Partner / einer Partnerin eine Liste: welche Informationen können Sie in jedem Teil des Textes finden? Answers will vary.

Überschriften

Lesen Sie die Überschriften: Was ist das Thema des Textes, der dieser Überschrift folgt (*follows*)? Wo kann man diese Überschriften finden (in einer Tageszeitung, einem Magazin, einer Broschüre, einem Reiseführer, etc.)? Sample answers are provided.

Regensburg entdecken
eine Broschüre, ein Reiseführer

Diese Woche in Berlin
eine Tageszeitung

Die Pyramiden Ägyptens in 8 Tagen!
eine Broschüre, ein Reiseführer

DFB-Team verliert Fußball-Länderspiel gegen Frankreich
eine Tageszeitung

Am Frankfurter Flughafen wird gestreikt
eine Tageszeitung

Die 15 besten Rezepte zum Grillen
ein Magazin

Gute Restaurants für Studenten in Kiel
eine Broschüre, ein Reiseführer

Suggestion Make sure students understand the difference between **Tageszeitung**, **Broschüre**, **Reiseführer**, etc. You may want to bring examples of each.

Die Nordseeküste° Schleswig-Holsteins in 6 Tagen

6 Tage Naturerlebnis° für 450 Euro!

1. Tag: Hamburg-Büsum Mit dem Bus von Hamburg nach Brunsbüttel. Hier besichtigen° wir die Schleusen° des Nord-Ostsee-Kanals. Weiter geht es mit dem Bus nach Friedrichskoog. Wir besuchen die Seehundstation° Friedrichskoog, die einzige Seehundstation in Schleswig-Holstein. Per Bus geht es weiter nach Büsum, unserer Endstation heute. Am Nachmittag besuchen wir das „Museum am Meer" mit Informationen über das Fischen an der Nordseeküste. Danach gibt es einen Besuch der 'Sturmflutenwelt° Blanker Hans' mit Demonstration der Flutkatastrophe von 1962.

2. Tag: Büsum-Tönning-St. Peter Ording-Husum Nach einer Busfahrt von Büsum nach Tönning besuchen wir das Multimar Wattforum. Hier kann man in Aquarien Wale und andere Tiere des Wattenmeers sehen. Mit dem Bus geht es weiter nach St. Peter Ording. Wir werden einen Spaziergang am Strand machen und dann den Westküstenpark mit Robbinarium° besuchen (bei schlechtem Wetter gehen wir in der Dünentherme im Freizeit- und Erlebnisbad schwimmen). Nach einer weiteren Busfahrt besuchen wir das Schloss° vor Husum und den Schlosspark mit seinen wunderschönen Blumen.

Nordseeküste *North Sea coast* **Naturerlebnis** *nature experience* **besichtigen** *tour*
Schleusen *locks* **Seehundstation** *harbor seal ward* **Sturmflutwelt** *world of the storm tide*
Robbinarium *seal zoo* **Schloss** *castle*

3. Tag: Husum-Insel Föhr

In Husum machen wir eine Stadtführung° mit dem Fahrrad: Wo hat der berühmte Autor Theodor Storm gelebt und gearbeitet? Mit dem Bus geht es dann nach Dagebüll und mit einer Fähre° auf die Insel° Föhr. Hier besuchen wir ein typisches friesisches Dorf°: Nieblum.

4. Tag: Insel Föhr-Insel Amrum

Mit der Fähre fahren wir von Föhr zu der Insel Amrum. Wir sehen uns die Stadt Wittdün an, besuchen den Amrumer Leuchtturm° (gebaut 1875) und gehen auf der Kniepsand-Sandbank spazieren.

5. Tag: Insel Amrum-Sylt

Mit der Fähre fahren wir von Amrum nach Sylt. Wir wandern zum Roten Kliff Kampen. Nachmittags besuchen wir eine Einkaufsarkade in Westerland und das Sylt Aquarium mit 2.000 verschiedenen Kreaturen aus dem Meer.

6. Tag: Sylt-Seebüll-Friedrichstadt-Hamburg

Mit der Fähre geht es zurück zur Küste nach Niebüll und dann weiter nach Seebüll. Hier besuchen wir das Emil-Nolde-Museum. Mit dem Bus weiter nach Friedrichstadt. Diese Stadt heißt auch die „Holländerstadt". Die Stadtführung ist inklusive einer Schiffsfahrt° auf den Grachten° und Kanälen der Stadt. Das Ende unserer Tour ist in Hamburg.

Stadtführung tour of the town **Fähre** ferry **Insel** island **friesisches Dorf** Frisian village
Leuchtturm lighthouse **Schiffsfahrt** boat tour **Grachten** town canals

Nach dem Lesen

Richtig oder falsch? Korrigieren Sie die falschen Sätze. Sample answers are provided.

	richtig	falsch
1. Den Nord-Ostsee-Kanal kann man in Brunsbüttel besuchen.	☑	☐
2. In Schleswig-Holstein gibt es viele Seehundstationen.	☐	☑
In Schleswig-Holstein gibt es nur in Friedrichskoog eine Seehundstation.		
3. In der Nordsee gibt es keine Wale.	☐	☑
In der Nordsee gibt es Wale.		
4. Im Schlosspark in Husum kann man wunderschöne Blumen sehen.	☑	☐
5. Dagebüll ist ein typisches friesisches Dorf.	☐	☑
Nieblum ist ein typisches friesisches Dorf.		
6. Die Insel Amrum ist für ihre lange Sandbank aus Kniepsand bekannt.	☑	☐
7. Die Insel Amrum ist berühmt für das Rote Kliff.	☐	☑
Die Insel Sylt ist berühmt für das Rote Kliff in Kampen.		
8. In Seebüll, der „Holländerstadt", gibt es viele Grachten und Kanäle.	☐	☑
In Friedrichstadt gibt es viele Grachten und Kanäle.		

Kombinieren Sie Verbinden Sie jede Aktivität mit dem passenden Ort.

_b_ 1. das Emil-Nolde-Museum besuchen

_d_ 2. auf der Kniepsand-Sandbank spazieren gehen

_a_ 3. eine Seehundstation besuchen

_c_ 4. eine Stadtführung mit dem Fahrrad machen

_e_ 5. das „Museum am Meer" besuchen

   a. Friedrichskoog

   b. Seebüll

   c. Husum

   d. Insel Amrum

   e. Büsum

Suggestion Explain that **Kniepsand** is the name of a wandering sand dune that currently juts up against the western dunes of the island **Amrum**.

Urlaub in Schleswig-Holstein
Führen Sie zu dritt eine Diskussion.

Sie werden Schleswig-Holstein drei Wochen lang besuchen. Sie wollen eine organisierte Tour machen, die in Hamburg beginnt. Sie besuchen das Reisebüro für weitere Informationen. Stellen Sie Fragen über Städte, Aktivitäten, Ausflüge, Hotels, den Transport, etc.

Suggestion Make sure students understand that the group activity is a role-play and that two people in the group will play tourists, while a third will play the travel agent.

Hören

Strategien

Using visual cues

Visual cues can provide useful context to help you make sense of information you hear.

 To practice this strategy, you will listen to an advertisement.
As you listen, jot down information you hear that relates to the image below.

Vorbereitung

Schauen Sie sich das Foto rechts an. Worüber diskutieren Lisa und Martina?

Zuhören

Hören Sie sich das Gespräch an. Welchen Ort möchte Lisa besuchen und welchen Martina? Wo werden sie Urlaub machen?

Suggestion Before students listen to the conversation, pre-teach the words **gebongt** ("agreed") and **KaDeWe** (**Kaufhaus des Westens**, a large mall in Berlin).

www.wilkommenimurlaub.de

| Hauptseite | Angebote | Preise | Anfrage und Buchung |

Teichhof Fehmarn. Direkt an der Nordsee. 2-Zimmer Wohnung mit Küche, Bad und Seeblick. 100 Euro pro Nacht.

Ferienwohnung Zugspitze. Gelegen in den Bayerischen Alpen. Wohnung für 2 Personen in traditionellem Haus mit Küche, Bad und Balkon. 50 Euro pro Nacht.

Ferienwohnung Schliemannstraße. Sehr zentral am Prenzlauer Berg in Berlin. Moderne Wohnung mit Küche und Bad. 36 Euro pro Person pro Nacht.

Verständnis

 Details Hören Sie sich den Dialog noch einmal an. Wer mag welche Aktivitäten? Wo wollen sie diese Aktivitäten machen?

	wandern	Touristen-attraktionen besuchen	Fahrrad fahren	schwimmen	Theater besuchen	einkaufen
Fehmarn	Lisa		Lisa	Lisa		
Bayerische Alpen	Martina	Martina				
Berlin		Lisa	Martina		Lisa	Martina

 Urlaubsziele Besprechen Sie mit einem Partner / einer Partnerin, wo Sie gerne Urlaub machen und was Sie dort gerne machen. Fahren Sie gerne im Winter, Frühling, Sommer oder Herbst in Urlaub? Wohin fährt Ihr Partner / Ihre Partnerin gerne? Was macht er/sie gerne im Urlaub? Welchen Urlaub wollen Sie gerne zusammen machen?

BEISPIEL

S1: Ich besuche jeden Sommer einen Nationalpark in den USA. Und du?

S2: Ich mag keine Nationalparks. Ich besuche Chicago mit meiner Familie.

Expansion After they complete the chart, ask students why Lisa doesn't want to go to the Alps. Play the audio again, if necessary. (She says: **Ich habe Angst vor hohen Bergen! Und Schlösser finde ich langweilig.**)

Schreiben

Strategien

Making an outline

Making an outline (**eine Gliederung**) before you write helps you to identify topics and subtopics, and provides a framework for presenting the information. Consider the following outline for a travel brochure.

I. Das Urlaubsziel

   A. Das Hotel

      1. Die Lage (*location*)

      2. Die Ausstattung (*facilities*)

      3. Die Bewertung (*rating*)

   B. Die Landschaft

   C. Die Sehenswürdigkeiten

II. Die Reisezeit

   A. Das Klima

   B. Der Preis

Eine Mindmap

Idea maps provide a useful way to help you visualize information before you create an outline. The larger circles in an idea map correspond to the Roman numerals in an outline. The smaller circles correspond to the outline's capital letters, numbers, and so on. Consider the idea map that led to the outline above.

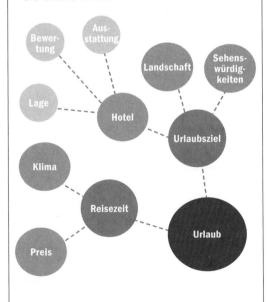

Thema

Schreiben Sie eine Broschüre

Schreiben Sie eine Tour-Broschüre für ein Reiseziel (*destination*) in einem deutschsprachigen Land.

Bevor Sie die Broschüre schreiben, schreiben Sie sich Ideen für die Broschüre auf. Hier ist eine Liste mit wichtigen Fragen:

• Welches Reiseziele wollen Sie beschreiben?

• Wie lange soll die Tour dauern?

• Wie ist das Wetter am Reiseziel?

• Welche Kleidung brauchen die Teilnehmer (*participants*)?

• Wo übernachten sie?

• Wo kann man essen gehen?

• Was soll man besuchen?

• Welche Aktivitäten gibt es (Sport, Einkaufen etc.)?

• Wie viel kostet der Urlaub pro Person?

Suggestion Tell students that they may use information from the articles in this unit, and/or do additional research online.

Organisieren Sie Ihre Ideen mit einer Mindmap. Schreiben Sie mit der fertigen Mindmap eine Gliederung. Jetzt können Sie eine Broschüre schreiben. Benutzen Sie Überschriften (*titles*), damit die Leser die Organisation der Broschüre verstehen können. In guten Broschüren sind oft Anschauungsmaterialien (*visual aids*) (Fotos, Tabellen etc.) integriert. Verwenden Sie Vokabeln und Grammatik, die Sie in diesem Kapitel gelernt haben.

Expansion Have students prepare a poster or short PowerPoint presentation in which they talk about a trip to Germany as though they have really taken it, using the past tense. Encourage them to be creative and to use real destinations featured in the unit.

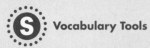 **Vocabulary Tools**

Jahreszeiten

der Winter, -	winter
der Frühling, -e	spring
der Sommer, -	summer
der Herbst, -e	fall

Monate

der Januar	January
der Februar	February
der März	March
der April	April
der Mai	May
der Juni	June
der Juli	July
der August	August
der September	September
der Oktober	October
der November	November
der Dezember	December

das Datum

Welcher Tag ist heute?	What day is it today?
Der 15. August.	The 15th of August.
Wann hast du Geburtstag?	When is your birthday?
Am 23. Mai.	May 23rd.
das Jahr, -e	year
die Jahreszeit, -en	season
der Monat, -e	month
der Tag, -e	day
die Woche, -n	week

die Ferien

die Kreuzfahrt, -en	cruise
das Meer, -e	sea; ocean
der Skiurlaub, -e	ski vacation
der Strand, ⸚e	beach
eine Karte lesen	to read a map
Urlaub machen	to go on vacation

das Wetter

Wie ist das Wetter?	What's the weather like?
Es ist schön draußen.	It's nice out.
Das Wetter ist gut/ schlecht.	The weather is nice/bad.
Wie warm/kalt ist es?	How warm/cold is it?
Es sind 18 Grad draußen.	It's 18 degrees out.
Es ist heiß.	It's hot.
Es ist kalt.	It's cold.
Es ist kühl.	It's cool.
Es ist sonnig.	It's sunny.
Es ist windig.	It's windy.
Es ist wolkig.	It's cloudy.
Es regnet.	It's raining.
Es schneit.	It's snowing.
der Blitz, -e	lightning
der Donner, -	thunder
das Gewitter, -	thunderstorm
der Hagel	hail
der Nebel, -	fog; mist
der Regen	rain
der Regenmantel, ⸚	raincoat
der Regenschirm, -e	umbrella
der Schnee	snow
der Sturm, ⸚e	storm
der Wetterbericht, -e	weather report
die Wolke, -n	cloud

Unterkünfte

der Fahrstuhl, ⸚e	elevator
der Gast, ⸚e	(hotel) guest
das (Fünf-Sterne-)Hotel	(five-star) hotel
die Jugendherberge, -n	youth hostel
der Schlüssel, -	key
der Zimmerservice	room service

zum Beschreiben

voll besetzt	fully occupied
pünktlich	on time

am Flughafen

der Abflug	departure
die Ankunft	arrival
der Ausgang ⸚e	exit
das Ausland	abroad
die Bordkarte, -n	boarding pass
die Businessklasse	business class
der Flug, ⸚e	flight
das Flugticket, -s	ticket
das Flugzeug, -e	airplane
das Gepäck	luggage
das Handgepäck	carry-on luggage
der Koffer, -	suitcase
der Passagier, -e	passenger
die Passkontrolle, -n	passport control
der Personalausweis, -e	ID card
die Reise, -n	trip
das Reisebüro, -s	travel agency
der Reisende, -n	traveler
die Touristenklasse	economy class
die Verspätung, -en	delay
das Visum (pl. die Visa)	visa
die Zeitung, -en	newspaper
der Zoll	customs

Verben

abbrechen (bricht... ab)	to cancel
abfliegen (fliegt... ab)	to take off
buchen	to make a (hotel) reservation
fliegen	to fly
landen	to land
packen	to pack
Schlange stehen	to stand in line
übernachten	to spend the night

Präteritum of verbs with prefixes	See p. 286.
Prepositions of location	See p. 290.
Infinitive expressions	See p. 304.
Time expressions	See p. 308.
Indefinite pronouns	See p. 310.

Ressourcen

vhlcentral.com

Verkehrsmittel und Technologie

Suggestion Ask students to identify who is in the picture and what type of transportation they are using.

Communicative Goals

You will learn how to:
- talk about cars and driving
- talk about public transportation

Auto und Rad fahren

S Vocabulary Tools

Suggestion Tell students that **Rad** means *wheel*. Ask them to guess the meaning of words like **Einrad**, **Dreirad**, and **Motorrad**.

Wortschatz

Auto fahren	*driving*
die Autobahn, -en	highway
der Fahrer, - /	driver
die Fahrerin, -nen	
die Straße, -n	street
geradeaus fahren	to go straight ahead
einen Unfall haben	to have an accident
parken	to park
rechts/links abbiegen	to turn right/left
(biegt... ab)	
das Verkehrsmittel	*means of transportation*
das Boot, -e	boat
der Bus, -se	bus
der LKW, -s	truck
das Schiff, -e	ship
das Taxi, -s	taxi
die U-Bahn, -en	subway
der Zug, ⁻e	train
Auto	*cars*
das Benzin	gas
die Bremse, -n	brakes
das Nummernschild, -er	license plate
reparieren	to repair
die öffentlichen	*public*
Verkehrsmittel	*transportation*
der Bahnsteig, -e	track; platform
die Bushaltestelle, -n	bus stop
das Bußgeld, -er	fine
die erste/zweite Klasse, -n	first/second class
der Fahrkartenschalter, -	ticket office
der Fahrplan, ⁻e	schedule
der Schaffner, -	ticket collector
(die Fahrkarte) entwerten	to validate (a ticket)

Suggestion Students may be unfamiliar with the process of buying a ticket in advance from an **Automat** and stamping it when entering a bus or tram. Make sure they understand the phrase **die Fahrkarte entwerten**.

Suggestion Remind students that the **-in** suffix is often added to refer to female practitioners of a profession or activity. Say: **Ein Mann, der Autos repariert, ist** *Mechaniker*. **Wie heißt eine Frau, die Autos repariert?**

Ressourcen

SAM
WB: pp. 105–106

SAM
LM: p. 67

S
vhlcentral.com

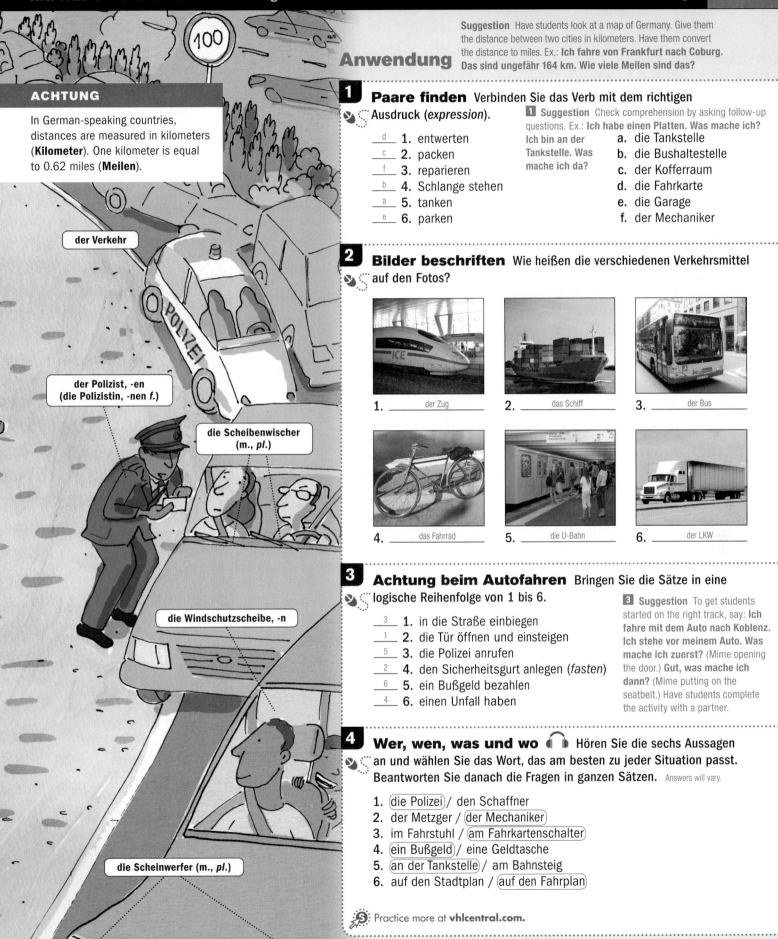

der Verkehr

der Polizist, -en
(die Polizistin, -nen *f.*)

die Scheibenwischer
(*m.*, *pl.*)

die Windschutzscheibe, -n

die Scheinwerfer (*m.*, *pl.*)

Anwendung

Suggestion Have students look at a map of Germany. Give them the distance between two cities in kilometers. Have them convert the distance to miles. Ex.: **Ich fahre von Frankfurt nach Coburg. Das sind ungefähr 164 km. Wie viele Meilen sind das?**

1 **Paare finden** Verbinden Sie das Verb mit dem richtigen Ausdruck (*expression*).

1 Suggestion Check comprehension by asking follow-up questions. Ex.: **Ich habe einen Platten. Was mache ich? Ich bin an der Tankstelle. Was mache ich da?**

_d_ 1. entwerten
_c_ 2. packen
_f_ 3. reparieren
_b_ 4. Schlange stehen
_a_ 5. tanken
_e_ 6. parken

a. die Tankstelle
b. die Bushaltestelle
c. der Kofferraum
d. die Fahrkarte
e. die Garage
f. der Mechaniker

2 **Bilder beschriften** Wie heißen die verschiedenen Verkehrsmittel auf den Fotos?

1. ___der Zug___   2. ___das Schiff___   3. ___der Bus___

4. ___das Fahrrad___   5. ___die U-Bahn___   6. ___der LKW___

3 **Achtung beim Autofahren** Bringen Sie die Sätze in eine logische Reihenfolge von 1 bis 6.

3 Suggestion To get students started on the right track, say: **Ich fahre mit dem Auto nach Koblenz. Ich stehe vor meinem Auto. Was mache ich zuerst?** (Mime opening the door.) **Gut, was mache ich dann?** (Mime putting on the seatbelt.) Have students complete the activity with a partner.

_3_ 1. in die Straße einbiegen
_1_ 2. die Tür öffnen und einsteigen
_5_ 3. die Polizei anrufen
_2_ 4. den Sicherheitsgurt anlegen (*fasten*)
_6_ 5. ein Bußgeld bezahlen
_4_ 6. einen Unfall haben

4 **Wer, wen, was und wo** Hören Sie die sechs Aussagen an und wählen Sie das Wort, das am besten zu jeder Situation passt. Beantworten Sie danach die Fragen in ganzen Sätzen. Answers will vary.

1. die Polizei / den Schaffner
2. der Metzger / der Mechaniker
3. im Fahrstuhl / am Fahrkartenschalter
4. ein Bußgeld / eine Geldtasche
5. an der Tankstelle / am Bahnsteig
6. auf den Stadtplan / auf den Fahrplan

Practice more at **vhlcentral.com**.

Kommunikation

5 **Aus dem Polizeibericht** Schauen Sie sich das Bild an und lesen Sie den kurzen Zeitungsartikel dazu. Beantworten Sie danach die Fragen. Arbeiten Sie mit einem Partner / einer Partnerin zusammen. Sample answers provided.

5 Suggestion Before they read the article, ask students if there is a **Handyverbot** in their city or state: **Darf man hier sein Handy benützen, während man fährt?**

Unfall in Frankfurter Innenstadt

Ein 23-jähriger Peugeotfahrer hat nicht aufgepasst und fuhr am Donnerstagabend bei Rot über die Kreuzung (*intersection*) Kaiserstraße und Friedensstraße. Ein LKW kam von links und die zwei Fahrzeuge sind zusammengestoßen (*collided*). Beim Unfall ist der Peugeotfahrer auch gegen ein geparktes Motorrad gestoßen. Beide Fahrer trugen Sicherheitsgurte und blieben unverletzt (*unhurt*). Der junge Mann sagte aus, er wollte nur schnell auf sein Handydisplay schauen und sah dann den LKW nicht. Der 23-Jährige bekam ein Bußgeld von 400 Euro. Seit 2001 gibt es ein Handyverbot am Steuer. Man darf nicht mit dem Auto fahren und dabei sein Handy benutzen.

1. Was ist am Donnerstagabend passiert? Ein Unfall zwischen einem Peugeot und einem LKW ist passiert.
2. Welche Fahrzeuge waren in den Unfall verwickelt (*involved*)? Ein Peugeot, ein LKW und ein Motorrad waren in den Unfall verwickelt.
3. Warum hat der Peugeotfahrer nicht bei Rot gehalten? Der Peugeotfahrer hat auf sein Handydisplay geschaut.
4. War jemand beim Unfall verletzt? Nein, niemand war verletzt.
5. Musste der Peugeotfahrer ein Bußgeld bezahlen? Ja, er musste 400 Euro Bußgeld bezahlen.
6. Was ist ein Handyverbot? Man darf nicht mit dem Auto fahren und dabei sein Handy benutzen.

7 Suggestion Before beginning the activity, ask students if public transportation is available in their hometowns. Explain that in Germany, the well-developed network of buses, trains, subways, and trams makes it easy to get around without a car.

6 **Diskutieren und kombinieren** Ihr Professor / Ihre Professorin gibt Ihnen zwei verschiedene Blätter. Finden Sie sieben Unterschiede zwischen Ihrem Bild und dem Bild Ihres Partner / Ihrer Partnerin. Answers will vary.

BEISPIEL

S1: Ich sehe vier Fahrräder.
S2: Mein Bild hat zwei Fahrräder. Und es gibt eine Bushaltestelle.
S1: Ich sehe keine Bushaltestelle...

7 **Verkehrsmittel** Diskutieren Sie in kleinen Gruppen, welche Verkehrsmittel Sie nehmen, um an die verschiedenen Orte zu kommen. Machen Sie danach eine Liste mit allen Verkehrsmitteln, die Sie normalerweise (*usually*) benutzen. Vergleichen Sie schließlich Ihre Liste mit der Liste einer anderen Gruppe. Answers will vary.

BEISPIEL

S1: Um in die Innenstadt zu kommen, nehme ich die U-Bahn.
S2: Wirklich? Ich fahre mit meinem Fahrrad.
S3: Ich gehe zu Fuß, aber...

Verkehrsmittel	Orte
das Auto	das Ausland
der Bus	das Haus von meinen Eltern
das Fahrrad	das Fußballstadion
das Flugzeug	der Supermarkt
zu Fuß	die Diskothek
das Taxi	die Innenstadt
die U-Bahn	die Unibibliothek
der Zug	?

Aussprache und Rechtschreibung Audio

🎧 Long and short vowels with an *Umlaut*

You have already learned that adding an **Umlaut** to the vowels **a**, **o**, and **u** changes their pronunciation. Vowels with an **Umlaut** have both long and short forms.

Räder **Männer** **löhnen** **löschen** **Züge** **fünf**

The long **ä** is pronounced similarly to the *a* in the English word *bay*, without the final *y* sound. The short **ä** is pronounced like the *e* in *pet*.

Faxgerät **Unterwäsche** **Fahrpläne** **Spaziergänge**

To produce the long **ö** sound, start by saying the German long **e**, but round your lips as if you were about to whistle. To produce the short **ö** sound, start by saying the short **e**, but keep your lips rounded.

Öl **öffentlich** **schön** **Töchter**

To produce the long **ü** sound, start to say the German long **i**, but round your lips tightly. To produce the short **ü** sound, make the short **i** sound, but with tightly rounded lips. In some loanwords, the German **y** is pronounced like **ü**. In other loanwords, the German **y** is pronounced like the English consonant *y*.

Schüler **zurück** **Typ** **Physik**

Suggestion To help students pronounce the long **ü** sound, have them position their tongues behind the back of the lower front teeth and round their lips, as if they were about to whistle.

1 **Aussprechen** Wiederholen Sie die Wörter, die Sie hören.

1. Rad / Räder   4. Käse / Kästchen   7. kämen / kämmen   10. typisch
2. Kopf / Köpfe   5. mögen / möchten   8. lösen / löschen   11. MP3-Player
3. Zug / Züge   6. fühlen / füllen   9. Dünen / dünn   12. Handy

2 **Nachsprechen** Wiederholen Sie die Sätze, die Sie hören.

1. In der Küche kocht die Köchin mit einem großen Kochlöffel.
2. Sie ändern morgen alle Fahrpläne für die Züge in Österreich.
3. Lösch alles auf der Festplatte, bevor du deinen PC verkaufst.
4. Jürgen fährt mit den öffentlichen Verkehrsmitteln zur Universität.
5. Grüne Fahrräder sind schöner als rote oder schwarze Fahrräder.
6. Der blonde Typ da hat sein Handy verloren.

3 **Sprichwörter** Wiederholen Sie die Sprichwörter, die Sie hören.

Der Apfel fällt nicht weit vom Stamm.[2]

Ein goldener Schlüssel öffnet alle Türen.[1]

[1] A golden key opens all doors.
[2] The apple doesn't fall far from the tree.

Ressourcen

SAM
LM: p. 68

vhlcentral.com

Ein Ende mit Schrecken Video

Sabite und Torsten gehen zusammen auf der Museumsinsel spazieren.
Es ist Sabites Lieblingsort, aber es wird ein trauriger Tag.

NATIONAL
communication
cultures
STANDARDS

Vorbereitung Have students read the episode title and try to predict what will happen in this episode. What do they think is going to end? Can they guess what **Schrecken** might mean? You may want to share with students the proverb **Besser ein Ende mit Schrecken als ein Schrecken ohne Ende.**

GEORGE Berlin hat die besten öffentlichen Verkehrsmittel! In Milwaukee haben wir nur Busse und kein S-Bahn-System.
HANS Hast du kein Auto?
GEORGE Doch, aber es ist alt und hat oft Pannen. Das Ölwarnlicht leuchtet ständig, und die Kupplung rutscht.
HANS Warum behältst du es?
GEORGE Es bringt mich zur Uni und zurück.

TORSTEN Sabite... es tut mir leid.
SABITE Wie bitte?
TORSTEN Es tut mir leid. An dem Abend im Restaurant, als ich von deinen Plänen erfahren habe...

SABITE Ich habe nicht darüber geredet, weil es nur eine Idee war. Ich hatte die Idee schon gehabt, bevor ich mit Lorenzo im Restaurant darüber gesprochen habe. Wir haben über Kunst geredet und da habe ich es zum ersten Mal laut ausgesprochen.
TORSTEN Ich habe das einfach nicht gewusst und bin wütend geworden.

SABITE Torsten, ich... ich glaube nicht...
TORSTEN Ich möchte nicht, dass du aus Berlin weggehst.
SABITE Warum?
TORSTEN Weil ich dich liebe.

SABITE Oh, Torsten, ich habe letzte Woche mit meiner Mutter zu Mittag gegessen. Wir haben etwas beschlossen. Meine ganze Familie verbringt den Sommer in der Türkei.

TORSTEN Ach so. Ich möchte nicht, dass du gehst, aber ich weiß, dass ich dich nicht davon abhalten kann. Du bist so stark, wie du schön bist. Was ich jetzt sagen muss, ist sehr schwer.
SABITE Torsten, machst du Schluss mit mir?
TORSTEN Liebst du mich?

1 **Richtig oder falsch?** Entscheiden Sie, ob die folgenden Sätze richtig oder falsch sind.

1. In Milwaukee gibt es Busse und ein S-Bahn-System.   Falsch.
2. Georges Auto ist alt und hat oft Pannen.   Richtig.
3. Sabite hat mit Lorenzo im Restaurant über Kunst gesprochen.   Richtig.
4. Dort hat sie zum ersten Mal laut über die Türkei gesprochen   Richtig.
5. Torsten war im Restaurant geduldig und ist ruhig geblieben.   Falsch.

6. Sabite hat letzte Woche mit ihrer Mutter zu Abend gegessen.   Falsch.
7. Torsten möchte, dass Sabite nach Istanbul geht.   Falsch.
8. George und Hans fahren mit dem Bus in Berlin herum.   Falsch.
9. Torsten hat mit Sabite auf der Museumsinsel Schluss gemacht.   Richtig.
10. Sabite mag die Museumsinsel nicht.   Falsch.

PERSONEN George Hans Meline Sabite Torsten

Nützliche Ausdrücke

MELINE Hallo, Sabite. Wie geht's? Okay... Süße... es ist schon okay. Wo bist du? Bleib dort, ich bin gerade an einer U-Bahn-Station vorbeigekommen. Ich bin in einer Viertelstunde da. (*Zu sich selbst.*) Torsten. Er ist so dumm, wie er gemein ist.

GEORGE Sabite, hey. Hans und ich fahren mit der Bahn in der ganzen Stadt herum. Das ist die interessanteste Weise, Berlin zu sehen. Was? Jetzt mal ganz ruhig. Du bist wo? Er hat was? Wo sind wir?
HANS Spandau. Wir sind in der U-Bahn-Station Altstadt Spandau! Wo ist sie?
GEORGE Museumsinsel. Wir kommen so schnell wie möglich.

MELINE Er hat dich bis hierher zur Museumsinsel geschleppt, nur um mit dir Schluss zu machen?
SABITE Es war meine Idee, hierher zu kommen. Ich liebe diesen Ort. Ah, da kommen sie.
HANS Hey, Sabite, es tut mir so, so, so leid.
MELINE Hans. Hans!

HANS Also... du hast mit ihm Schluss gemacht?
SABITE Ich wollte mit ihm Schluss machen. Aber er... er war schneller als ich!

- **die Panne**
  breakdown
- **Das Ölwarnlicht leuchtet ständig, und die Kupplung rutscht.**
  The oil warning light is always on, and the clutch slips.
- **erfahren (von)**
  to find out (about)
- **Wir haben über Kunst geredet und da habe ich es zum ersten Mal laut ausgesprochen.**
  We were talking about art, and that was the first time I said it out loud.
- **wütend**
  furious
- **Wir haben etwas beschlossen.**
  We decided something.
- **Ich möchte nicht, dass du gehst, aber ich weiß, dass ich dich nicht davon abhalten kann.**
  I don't want you to go, but I know I can't stop you.
- **vorbeikommen**   **herumfahren**
  to pass   *to ride around*
- **Wir kommen so schnell wie möglich.**
  We'll be there as soon as possible.
- **schleppen**
  to drag

8A.1
- **Berlin hat die besten öffentlichen Verkehrsmittel!**
  Berlin has the best public transportation!

8A.2
- **Ich hatte die Idee schon gehabt, bevor ich mit Lorenzo im Restaurant darüber gesprochen habe.**
  I'd already had the idea before Lorenzo and I discussed it at the restaurant.

---

2 **Zum Besprechen** Bilden Sie zu zweit einen Dialog zwischen Sabite und Torsten. Versuchen Sie, die Beziehung zu retten (*to save the relationship*). Answers will vary.

3 **Vertiefung** In Deutschland gibt es viele Autobahnen. Wie sind sie nummeriert? Welche haben eine, welche zwei und welche drei Ziffern (*digits*)? Welche haben gerade (*even*) und welche ungerade Nummern? Answers will vary.

3 **Expansion** Have students find out the speed limits for different types of vehicles on the German **Autobahnen**.

Ressourcen

 SAM VM: p. 15

 vhlcentral.com

IM FOKUS

Die deutsche Autobahn

TIPP

The German **Autobahn** is toll-free for cars, but Austria and Switzerland charge a toll (**eine Maut**) for use of all limited-access highways. Cars in each country must display a toll sticker (**eine Mautvignette**) in their windshields to show that they have paid an annual fee to use the country's **Autobahnnetz**.

DIE GESCHICHTE DER DEUTSCHEN Autobahn geht mehr als 80 Jahre zurück. Die AVUS (Automobil-Verkehrs- und Übungs-Straße), heute Teil der Autobahn A115, war die erste nur für Autos zugelassene° Straße Europas. Schon seit 1921 erstreckte sie sich° zwischen den Berliner Stadtteilen Charlottenburg und Nikolassee. Um einmal darüber zu fahren, musste man zehn Mark bezahlen. Damals war das ziemlich teuer!

Am 6. August 1932 eröffnete der Kölner Oberbürgermeister Konrad Adenauer die erste so genannte „Autobahn". Ihr Bau hatte drei Jahre gedauert. Sie war 20 Kilometer lang und erstreckte sich zwischen Köln und Bonn. In beide Fahrtrichtungen war sie zweispurig° und kreuzungsfrei° Damit entsprach° sie einer Autobahn, wie wir sie heute kennen, mit einem Unterschied: Es gab keinen Mittelstreifen°. Deshalb bekam der Abschnitt erst 1958, nach weiterem Ausbau°, den offiziellen Status der Autobahn.

Heute hat Deutschland eines der dichtesten Autobahnnetze° der Welt und der Bau geht immer weiter. Es gilt zwar in Deutschland eine Richtgeschwindigkeit° von 130 Kilometern pro Stunde, ein generelles Tempolimit° gibt es aber nicht. Trotzdem haben 45 Prozent aller deutschen Autobahnkilometer Tempolimits. An fast allen Autobahnen gibt es mittlerweile komfortable Raststätten°, wo es neben Tankstellen, Hotels, Restaurants und Läden sogar Kinderspielplätze gibt.

Längste Autobahnnetze der Welt	
Land	**Strecke°**
USA	97.355 km
China	75.932 km
Spanien	16.204 km
Deutschland	12.917 km

zugelassene *permitted* **erstreckte... sich** *extended*
zweispurig *two-lane* **kreuzungsfrei** *intersection-free*
entsprach *conformed to* **Mittelstreifen** *median strip*
Ausbau *extension* **Autobahnnetze** *interstate highway networks* **Richtgeschwindigkeit** *target speed*
Tempolimit *speed limit* **Raststätten** *service areas*
Strecke *distance*

ÜBUNGEN

1 Richtig oder falsch? Sind die Aussagen richtig oder falsch? Korrigieren Sie die falschen Aussagen.

1. Die Geschichte der deutschen Autobahn geht 60 Jahre zurück.
   Falsch. Die Geschichte der deutschen Autobahn geht mehr als 80 Jahre zurück.
2. Konrad Adenauer eröffnete 1921 die erste so genannte „Autobahn".
   Falsch. Er eröffnete 1932 die erste so genannte „Autobahn".
3. Die AVUS erstreckte sich zwischen Köln und Bonn.
   Falsch. Die AVUS erstreckte sich zwischen Charlottenburg und Nikolassee.
4. Man baute die erste so genannte „Autobahn" in drei Jahren. Richtig
5. Eine Autobahn muss zweispurig und kreuzungsfrei sein. Richtig

6. Deuschland hat das dichteste Autobahnnetz der Welt.
   Falsch. Deuschland hat eines der dichtesten Autobahnnetze der Welt.
7. In Deutschland gibt es eine Richtgeschwindigkeit von 130 Kilometern pro Stunde. Richtig
8. Es gibt auf deutschen Autobahnen keine Tempolimits.
   Falsch. Etwa 45 Prozent aller deutschen Autobahnkilometer haben permanente Tempolimits
9. Heute umfasst das Autobahnnetz in Deutschland mehr als 75.000 Kilometer.
   Falsch. Heute umfasst das Autobahnnetz in Deutschland mehr als 12.000 Kilometer.
10. Nach Spanien hat Deutschland das längste Autobahnnetz Europas. Richtig

 Practice more at **vhlcentral.com**.

Verkehrsschilder

die Kreuzung	intersection
das Stoppschild	stop sign
(die) Ausfahrt	exit
(die) Baustelle	construction zone
(die) Einbahnstraße	one-way street
(die) Umleitung	detour

Fahrrad fahren

In Deutschland besitzen mehr Haushalte° Fahrräder als ein Auto. Bei Familien haben sogar 96% der Haushalte Fahrräder. Deshalb gibt es in vielen Städten separate Fahrradwege°. Für das Fahrradfahren gibt es besondere Regeln°: Wenn es keinen Fahrradweg gibt, müssen Fahrradfahrer, die über 11 Jahre alt sind, auf der rechten Seite der Straße fahren. Besondere Schilder zeigen, wann Fahrradfahrer in Einbahnstraßen entgegen der Fahrtrichtung° fahren dürfen. In Fußgängerzonen° dürfen Radfahrer nur im Schritttempo° fahren. Außerdem muss jedes Fahrrad ein festes Fahrradlicht haben.

Haushalte *households* **Fahrradwege** *bike lanes* **Regeln** *rules* **entgegen der Fahrtrichtung** *against the flow of traffic* **Fußgängerzonen** *pedestrian zones* **Schritttempo** *walking speed*

Fräulein Stinnes' Weltreise°

Clärenore Stinnes kommt am 21. Januar 1901 als Tochter eines Großindustriellen zur Welt. Mit 24 Jahren nimmt sie zum ersten Mal an einem Autorennen° teil. Bis 1927 gewinnt sie 17 Rennen, darunter auch eine internationale Rallye in Russland. Sie ist die einzige Frau unter 53 Teilnehmern! Im Mai 1927 bricht Clärenore zu einer Weltreise auf. Sie finanziert die Reise mit Sponsoren wie Bosch und Aral. Auch das Außenministerium° und deutsche Auslandsvertretungen° unterstützen sie. Sie legt 47.000 Kilometer zurück und ist zwei Jahre und einen Monat unterwegs. Das Auto, ein Adler Standard 6, steht heute im Deutschen Museum in München.

Weltreise *world tour* **Autorennen** *car race* **Außenministerium** *Ministry of Foreign Affairs* **Auslandsvertretungen** *embassies*

IM INTERNET

Suchen Sie Informationen zu der Internationalen Automobil-Ausstellung (IAA). Wo und wann war die letzte Ausstellung?

Find out more at **vhlcentral.com**.

---

2 **Was fehlt?** Ergänzen Sie die Sätze.

1. In deutschen Haushalten gibt es öfter <u>Fahrräder</u> als ein Auto.
2. In vielen Städten gibt es seperate <u>Fahrradwege</u> für Fahrräder.
3. Jedes Fahrrad in Deutschland muss <u>ein Fahrradlicht</u> haben.
4. Ihre Weltumrundung hat <u>zwei Jahre</u> und einen Monat gedauert.
5. Das Auto, das Clärenore Stinnes bei ihrer Weltreise gefahren hat, kann man heute im <u>Deutschen Museum</u> in München finden.

3 **Lieblingstransportmittel** Diskutieren Sie mit einem Partner / einer Partnerin Ihr Lieblingstransportmittel.

Wie bewegen Sie sich am liebsten fort? Sind Sie ein Fan von Fahrrad, Auto oder Bus? Gehen Sie am liebsten zu Fuß? Warum bewegen Sie sich gerne so fort? Was sind die Vorteile und Nachteile?

8A.1 ### Das Plusquamperfekt Presentation

Startblock Use the **Plusquamperfekt** tense to refer to a past event that occurred before another event in the past.

> Ich **hatte** die Idee schon **gehabt**, bevor ich mit Lorenzo im Restaurant darüber gesprochen habe.

> Wir **hatten** über Kunst **geredet** und da habe ich es zum ersten Mal laut ausgesprochen.

Das Plusquamperfekt

- To form the **Plusquamperfekt**, use the **Präteritum** form of **haben** or **sein** with the past participle of the verb that expresses the action.

  Ich **hatte vergessen**, die Tür zu schließen.
  *I **had forgotten** to close the door.*

  Jasmin **war** noch nie nach Zürich **gefahren**.
  *Jasmin **had** never **been** to Zurich.*

- Since the **Plusquamperfekt** refers to a past event that was completed prior to another past event, both events are often described in the same sentence.

Der Zug fährt ab.   Ich komme am Bahnsteig an.

14.45 Uhr   **Plusquamperfekt**   14.47 Uhr   **Perfekt/Präteritum**

PRÄTERITUM
Als ich am Bahnsteig **ankam**,
*When I **arrived** at the platform,*

PLUSQUAMPERFEKT
war der Zug schon **abgefahren**.
*the train **had** already **left**.*

Bevor Stefan in die Stadt gezogen ist, **hatte** er nie öffentliche Verkehrsmittel **benutzt**.
*Before Stefan moved to the city, he **had** never **used** public transportation.*

Nachdem der Mechaniker das Auto **repariert hatte**, **fuhr** er damit zur Tankstelle.
*After the mechanic **had fixed** the car, he **drove** it to the gas station.*

Bevor ich nach England **reiste, hatte** ich meinen Neffen noch nie **gesehen**.
***Before** I **went** to England, I **had** never **met** my nephew.*

Als wir im Kino **ankamen, hatte** der Film schon **angefangen**.
***When** we **got** to the movie theater, the film **had** already **started**.*

Conjunctions *als, bevor, nachdem*

Suggestion Tell students that subordinating conjunctions like **bevor**, **nachdem**, and **als** "send" or "kick" the verb to the end of the clause.

- Use the subordinating conjunctions **als** (*when*), **bevor** (*before*), and **nachdem** (*after*) to indicate the sequence in which two past events occurred.

> **Als** Jan ins Restaurant **kam, hatte** seine Freundin schon **bestellt**.
> *By the time Jan **got** to the restaurant, his girlfriend **had** already **ordered**.*

> Unsere Eltern sind erst nach Hause gekommen, **nachdem** wir schon ins Bett **gegangen waren**.
> *By the time our parents came home, we **had** already **gone** to bed.*

- When a clause begins with **als**, **bevor**, or **nachdem**, move the conjugated verb to the end of the clause.

> **Bevor** ich in Deutschland **wohnte**...
> *Before I **lived** in Germany...*

> **Als** Hanna **anrief**...
> *When Hanna **called**...*

- After **bevor** and **als**, use the **Perfekt** or **Präteritum** and put the main clause in the **Plusquamperfekt**.

> **Als** Tom zur Bushaltestelle **kam, war** der Bus schon **abgefahren**.
> *By the time Tom **got** to the bus stop, the bus **had** already **left**.*

> **Bevor** ich Kalifornien **besucht habe, hatte** ich noch nie Artischocken **gegessen**.
> *Before I **visited** California, I **had** never **eaten** artichokes.*

- After **nachdem**, use the **Plusquamperfekt** and put the main clause in the **Perfekt** or **Präteritum**.

> Der Bus **ist** endlich **gekommen, nachdem** wir schon 30 Minuten **gewartet hatten**.
> *The bus finally **came**, after we **had been waiting** for 30 minutes.*

> **Nachdem** Sara ins Bett **gegangen war, hat** ihre Mutter **angerufen**.
> *After Sara **had gone** to bed, her mother **called**.*

- If the clause with **bevor**, **nachdem**, or **als** is first in the sentence, the main clause after the comma begins with the verb. If that verb is in the **Plusquamperfekt** or **Perfekt**, put the helping verb first and the past participle at the end.

> Als wir am Flughafen **ankamen, war** das **Flugzeug** schon **abgeflogen**.
> *By the time we **got** to the airport, the plane **had** already **taken off**.*

> Das Flugzeug **war** schon **abgeflogen**, als wir am Flughafen **ankamen**.
> *The plane **had** already **taken off** by the time we **got** to the airport.*

Suggestion Point out to students that this word order is consistent with the "verb-in-second-position" rule. The dependent clause, set off by the comma, functions as the first sentence element, and the verb comes as the second element.

QUERVERWEIS

You will learn more about subordinating conjunctions in **10A.3**. To review coordinating conjunctions, see **6A.3**.

ACHTUNG

If the main clause comes first in the sentence, use the normal subject-verb word order.

Suggestion You may want to mention that in conversation, people often use the **Perfekt** tense instead of the **Plusquamperfekt** along with time expressions to help clarify the sequence of events: **Nachdem Ulrich einen Unfall gehabt hat, hat er sein Auto zum Mechaniker gebracht.**

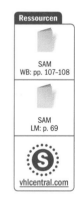

Ressourcen

SAM
WB: pp. 107–108

SAM
LM: p. 69

(S)
vhlcentral.com

Jetzt sind Sie dran!   Schreiben Sie die Sätze ins Plusquamperfekt um.

1. Haben Sie Ihre Freundin angerufen?
   Hatten Sie Ihre Freundin angerufen?

2. Ich habe das Auto zum Mechaniker gebracht.
   Ich hatte das Auto zum Mechaniker gebracht.

3. Bist du zu spät aufgestanden?
   Warst du zu spät aufgestanden?

4. Benjamin ist noch nie in Berlin gewesen.
   Benjamin war noch nie in Berlin gewesen.

5. Ihr habt die Fahrkarte schon entwertet, nicht?
   Ihr hattet die Fahrkarte schon entwertet, nicht?

6. Die Mechanikerin hat den LKW schon repariert.
   Die Mechanikerin hatte den LKW schon repariert.

7. Oma und Opa sind gerade zurückgekommen.
   Oma und Opa waren gerade zurückgekommen.

8. Wir haben falsch geparkt.
   Wir hatten falsch geparkt.

9. Papa hat das Auto letzte Woche verkauft.
   Papa hatte das Auto letzte Woche verkauft.

10. Wir haben das Buch noch nicht gelesen.
    Wir hatten das Buch noch nicht gelesen.

11. Seid ihr in die Stadt gefahren?
    Wart ihr in die Stadt gefahren?

12. Hast du das gewusst?
    Hattest du das gewusst?

Anwendung

1 **Was passt zusammen?** Welche Sätze in der rechten Spalte
ergänzen die Sätze in der linken Spalte?

<u>d</u> 1. Nachdem Paul seine Sachen
gepackt hatte,

<u>b</u> 2. Als Amila nach Hause kam,

<u>a</u> 3. Wir haben noch lange geredet,

<u>f</u> 4. Bevor du zurückkamst,

<u>c</u> 5. Hattest du meinen Geburtstag
vergessen,

<u>e</u> 6. Ich war sehr traurig,

a. nachdem wir gegessen hatten.

b. hatte ihre Familie schon mit dem Essen
angefangen.

c. oder wolltest du mich überraschen?

d. hat er eine Karte an Greta geschrieben.

e. nachdem du weggegangen warst.

f. hatte ich dich überall gesucht.

2 **Was fehlt?** Ergänzen Sie die Sätze mit den richtigen Plusquamperfektformen.

1. Vor meiner Reise nach Paris __hatte__ ich viel darüber __gelesen__. (lesen)

2. Nachdem wir __gelandet__ __waren__, sind wir zuerst ins Hotel gefahren. (landen)

3. Wir __hatten__ kein Auto __gemietet__, sondern sind immer mit der U-Bahn gefahren. (mieten)

4. Jasmin __hatte__ ihr Geld in den Hotelsafe __gelegt__, bevor sie ausgegangen ist. (legen)

5. Sie sind ins Museum gegangen, nachdem sie __getankt__ __hatten__. (tanken)

6. Als sie dort ankamen, __hatten__ ihre Freunde schon lange auf sie __gewartet__. (warten)

3 **Dornröschen** Im Jahr 2015 wacht Dornröschen auf (*Sleeping Beauty
wakes up*). Erzählen Sie, was für sie alles neu ist. Bilden Sie Sätze im
Plusquamperfekt.

> **BEISPIEL** in einem Auto fahren
> *Sie war noch nie in einem Auto gefahren.*

1. in einem Flugzeug sein
Sie war (noch) nie in einem Flugzeug gewesen.
2. einen Film sehen
Sie hatte (noch) nie einen Film gesehen.
3. mit dem Zug reisen
Sie war (noch) nie mit dem Zug gereist.

4. ein Taxi nehmen
Sie hatte (noch) nie ein Taxi genommen.
5. eine Fahrkarte entwerten
Sie hatte (noch) nie eine Fahrkarte entwertet.
6. einen Sicherheitsgurt tragen
Sie hatte (noch) nie einen Sicherheitsgurt getragen.

4 **Was hatten sie gemacht?** Schreiben Sie zu jedem Bild einen Satz im
Plusquamperfekt und erzählen Sie, was diese Personen gemacht hatten, bevor
sie jemand fotografiert hat. Benutzen Sie Wörter aus der Liste oder Ihre
eigenen. Seien Sie kreativ. Sample answers are provided.

> **BEISPIEL**
> **Manfred**
> *war zur Tankstelle gefahren.*

besuchen	kaufen
fahren	parken
gehen	warten (auf)

1. Herr Maier
hatte sein Auto geparkt.

2. Karl
hatte schon 15 Minuten auf
Klara gewartet.

3. Birgit und Lara
hatten Fahrkarten gekauft.

4. Sebastian
war zur U-Bahn gegangen.

 Practice more at **vhlcentral.com**.

communication NATIONAL STANDARDS

Kommunikation

5 **Faul oder fleißig** Besprechen Sie mit Ihrem Partner / Ihrer Partnerin, was Jan und Maria gestern gemacht haben. Wechseln Sie sich ab. Answers will vary.

BEISPIEL

S1: *Maria hat um 8 Uhr gefrühstückt.*
S2: *Um 8 Uhr war Jan noch nicht aufgestanden.*

	Jan	Maria
8.00	--	frühstücken
9.00	aufstehen	mit dem Bus zur Uni fahren
10.00	Kaffee trinken	Chemieprüfung schreiben
11.00	mit Freunden chatten	mit der Professorin sprechen
12.00	Musik hören	ins Fitnessstudio gehen
13.00	mit Martin Videospiele spielen	--

6 **Warum wohl?** Stellen Sie Ihrem Partner / Ihrer Partnerin zu jedem Bild eine Frage und erfinden Sie eine Antwort. Answers will vary.

die Küche nicht aufräumen	im Regen dreckig werden	keine Brille tragen
eine gute Note bekommen	kein Hotelzimmer buchen	zu spät nach Hause kommen

Philip / einen Unfall haben

BEISPIEL

S1: *Warum hat Philip einen Unfall gehabt?*
S2: *Er war vielleicht zu schnell gefahren.*

1. Hasan und Greta / diskutieren

2. Sophia / Kopfschmerzen (*headache*) haben

3. Günther / laut singen

4. Paula und Rolf / Hund waschen

5. Ben und Hans / im Wald campen

6. Tom / einen Platten haben

7 **Wichtige Ereignisse** Sagen Sie Ihren Mitstudenten, in welchem Jahr Sie geboren sind. Ein anderer Student / eine andere Studentin nennt dann ein Ereignis (*event*), das schon vorher (*before that*) passiert war. Answers will vary.

BEISPIEL

S1: *Ich bin 1994 geboren.*
S2: *25 Jahre vorher waren Astronauten schon auf dem Mond gelandet.*

1946: man baut das erste Mobiltelefon	1984: Steve Jobs stellt den ersten Mac vor
1959: die Barbiepuppe kommt auf den Markt	1989: die Berliner Mauer fällt
1973: in Deutschland gibt es eine Ölkrise	

7 **Suggestion** To prepare students for this activity, have them convert the information provided into complete **Plusquamperfekt** sentences. Ex.: **Man hatte das erste Mobiltelefon gebaut.**

QUERVERWEIS

8A.2

Comparatives and superlatives  Presentation

See **3A.2** to review the use of adjectives. See **4A.2** to review the use of adverbs.

Startblock Use the comparative and superlative forms of adjectives and adverbs to compare two or more people or things.

Mein Vater fährt gern **schneller als** 150.

Es ist einer der **schönsten** Orte in Berlin.

Der Komparativ

- There are three forms of adjectives and adverbs: **die Grundform** (**schnell**), **der Komparativ** (**schneller**), and **der Superlativ** (**am schnellsten**). When describing similarities between two people or things, use the expression **so... wie** (*as... as*) or **genauso... wie** (*just as... as*) with the **Grundform** of an adjective or adverb.

Suggestion Model correct pronunciation of the **Grundformen** and comparative forms and have students repeat after you.

> Dieser LKW ist **so groß wie** ein Bus.
> *That truck is **as big as** a bus.*

> Der Zug fährt **genauso schnell wie** ein Auto.
> *The train goes **just as fast as** a car.*

- To describe differences between two people or things, you can use the expression **nicht so... wie** (*not as... as*), or you can use the **Komparativ**. Form the **Komparativ** by adding the ending **-er** to the **Grundform** of an adjective or adverb, followed by the word **als**.

> Lina fährt **nicht so langsam wie** Sara.
> *Lina **doesn't** drive **as slowly as** Sara.*

> Sara fährt **langsamer als** Lina.
> *Sara drives **more slowly than** Lina.*

- Common one-syllable words with the stem vowel **a**, **o**, or **u** often have an umlaut on the vowel in the comparative.

ACHTUNG

The two-syllable word **gesund** (*healthy*) also has an umlaut on the **u** in the comparative form:

gesund ⟶ gesünder

For adjectives ending in **-el** or **-er**, German speakers usually drop the **-e-** before adding the comparative **-er** ending.

teuer ⟶ teurer
dunkel ⟶ dunkler

a ⟶ ä		o ⟶ ö		u ⟶ ü	
alt	älter	groß	größer	dumm (*dumb*)	dümmer
lang	länger	oft	öfter	jung	jünger
stark	stärker	rot	röter	kurz	kürzer

> Meine Geschwister sind alle **älter** als ich.
> *My siblings are all **older** than I am.*

> Die Fahrt nach Frankfurt dauert mit dem Auto **länger** als mit dem Zug.
> *The trip to Frankfurt takes **longer** by car than by train.*

- A small number of adjectives and adverbs have irregular comparative forms.

Expansion Provide additional examples for each adjective or adverb. Ex.: **Sarahs Haare sind länger als Bens. Lady Gaga ist jünger als Donald Trump.**

GRUNDFORM		KOMPARATIV
gern	⟶	lieber
gut	⟶	besser

> Ich fahre **lieber** mit der U-Bahn als mit dem Bus.
> *I'd **rather** take the subway than the bus.*

GRUNDFORM		KOMPARATIV
hoch	⟶	höher
viel	⟶	mehr

> Benzin kostet in Deutschland **mehr** als in den USA.
> *Gasoline is **more expensive** in Germany than in the USA.*

- When a comparative adjective precedes a noun, add the appropriate case ending after the **-er** ending.

  Leider kostet der **schnellere** Zug mehr.
  *Unfortunately the **faster** train costs more.*

  Ich brauche einen **größeren** Koffer.
  *I need a **bigger** suitcase.*

Der Superlativ

- Use the **Superlativ** form of an adjective or adverb to indicate that a person or thing has more of a particular quality than anyone or anything else.

  Welches ist **das größte** Tier der Welt?
  *What's **the biggest** animal in the world?*

  Wie komme ich **am besten** zur Tankstelle?
  *What's **the best** way to get to the gas station?*

- To form the superlative of an adjective, add **-st** to the **Grundform**. If the **Grundform** ends in **-d**, **-t**, or an **s** sound, add **-est**. When an adjective in the superlative precedes a noun, use a definite article before the superlative and add the appropriate case ending.

  Warum habt ihr **die teuersten**
    Fahrkarten gekauft?
  *Why did you buy **the most expensive** tickets?*

  Wir wollten mit **dem schnellsten**
    Zug fahren.
  *We wanted to take **the fastest** train.*

- To form the superlative of adverbs and of adjectives that come after **sein**, **werden**, or **bleiben**, use the word **am** before the adverb or adjective and add **-(e)sten** as the superlative ending.

  Wer fährt **am langsamsten**?
  *Who drives **the slowest**?*

  Welches Auto ist **am schnellsten**?
  *Which car is **the fastest**?*

- If an adjective or adverb has an added umlaut in the comparative, it will also have an umlaut in the superlative.

a ⟶ ä			o ⟶ ö			u ⟶ ü		
alt	älter	ältest-	rot	röter	rötest-	jung	jünger	jüngst-

- If an adjective or adverb is irregular in the comparative form, the superlative form is also irregular.

GRUNDFORM	KOMPARATIV	SUPERLATIV
gern	lieber	liebst-
groß	größer	größt-
gut	besser	best-
hoch	höher	höchst-
viel	mehr	meist-

QUERVERWEIS

See **3A.2** to review adjective agreement.

Expansion Bring in a few items or pictures that lend themselves to comparison, and ask questions that model comparative and superlative forms. Ex.: **Was ist größer, dieser Roman oder das Deutschbuch? Welcher Hut ist lustiger, der oder der? Welcher steht mir besser?**

ACHTUNG

The adjective **nah** (*near*) has a stem vowel change, as well as an additional spelling change in the superlative:
nah / näher / nächst-

Most German speakers do not use the superlative form **öftest-**; instead, they use **(am) häufigst-** (*most often*).

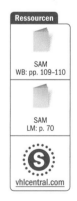

Ressourcen

SAM
WB: pp. 109–110

SAM
LM: p. 70

vhlcentral.com

 Jetzt sind Sie dran! Ergänzen Sie die Lücken mit den richtigen Formen der Adjektive.

	Base form	Komparativ	Superlativ		Base form	Komparativ	Superlativ
1.	groß	größer	am größten	7.	jung	jünger	am jüngsten
2.	gut	besser	am besten	8.	kurz	kürzer	am kürzesten
3.	lang	länger	am längsten	9.	gesund	gesünder	am gesündesten
4.	klein	kleiner	am kleinsten	10.	einfach	einfacher	am einfachsten
5.	hoch	höher	am höchsten	11.	viel	mehr	am meisten
6.	spät	später	am spätesten	12.	gern	lieber	am liebsten

Anwendung

1 **Meinungen** Ergänzen Sie die Sätze mit dem Adjektiv oder dem Adverb im Superlativ.

> **BEISPIEL** Von allen Verkehrsmitteln benutzen wir die U-Bahn
> _am häufigsten_. (häufig)

1. Von allen Automodellen findet Ingrid einen Mercedes ___am schönsten___. (schön)
2. Von allen meinen Kursen finde ich Chemie ___am schwierigsten___. (schwierig)
3. Von allen Getränken trinkt Emil Tee ___am seltensten___. (selten)
4. Von allen Obstsorten schmecken dir Bananen ___am besten___? (gut)
5. Von allen meinen Kursen interessiert mich Mathematik ___am meisten___. (viel)
6. Von allen meinen Freunden habe ich Peter ___am liebsten___. (gern)

2 **Komparative** Bilden Sie Sätze im Komparativ. **+** bedeutet **-er als**, **=** bedeutet **(genau)so... wie** und **≠** bedeutet **nicht so... wie**.

> **BEISPIEL** ein Auto / ist / ≠ groß / ein LKW
> _Ein Auto ist nicht so groß wie ein LKW._

1. die Mozartstraße / ist / + lang / die Beethovenstraße   Die Mozartstraße ist länger als die Beethovenstraße.
2. Kiara / fährt / + gut / Dana   Kiara fährt besser als Dana.
3. der Verkehr am Freitagabend / ist / = schlecht / der Verkehr am Montagmorgen
   Der Verkehr am Freitagabend ist (genau)so schlecht wie der Verkehr am Montagmorgen.
4. ich / reise / + gern / mit dem Zug / mit dem Flugzeug   Ich reise lieber mit dem Zug als mit dem Flugzeug.
5. Die erste Klasse / ist / + teuer / die zweite Klasse   Die erste Klasse ist teurer als die zweite Klasse.
6. heute / ist / es / ≠ warm / gestern   Heute ist es nicht so warm wie gestern.

3 **Vergleichen Sie** Bilden Sie Sätze und benutzen Sie dabei die Komparativformen der angegebenen Adjektive. Sample answers are provided.

> ▶ **BEISPIEL** ein Bus / ein Auto (klein)
> _Ein Auto ist kleiner als ein Bus._

1. eine U-Bahn / ein Flugzeug (schnell)
   Ein Flugzeug ist schneller als eine U-Bahn.

2. Niklas / Lisa (alt)
   Niklas ist nicht so alt wie Lisa.

3. Ben bezahlt 350 € Miete. / Jana bezahlt 320 € Miete. (viel)
   Ben bezahlt mehr Miete als Jana.

4. Ihr esst Fisch einmal pro Monat. / Ihr esst Hähnchen einmal pro Woche. (gern)
   Ihr esst lieber Hähnchen als Fisch.

 Practice more at **vhlcentral.com.**

Kommunikation

4 **Komparative** Ergänzen Sie die Fragen mit den Komparativformen der angegebenen Adjektive und beantworten Sie die Fragen Ihres Partners. Answers will vary.

> **BEISPIEL** Wer ist _schüchterner_, du oder dein bester Freund? (schüchtern)
>
> **S1:** *Wer ist schüchterner, du oder dein bester Freund?*
> **S2:** *Ich bin viel schüchterner!*

1. Was isst du _____lieber_____, Joghurt oder Schokolade? (gern)
2. Womit fährst du _____seltener_____, mit dem Fahrrad oder mit dem Auto? (selten)
3. Welche Sängerin findest du _____besser_____, Rihanna oder Beyoncé? (gut)
4. Welches Fach findest du _____interessanter_____, Marketing oder Anthropologie? (interessant)
5. Wovon verstehst du _____mehr_____, von Mode oder von Sport? (viel)
6. Was machst du am Wochenende _____häufiger_____, Hausaufgaben oder schlafen? (häufig)

5 **Wie gut ist Ihr Allgemeinwissen?** Finden Sie mit Ihrem Partner / Ihrer Partnerin zu jedem Begriff (*concept*) zwei Sachen, die man vergleichen kann, und stellen Sie einem anderen Paar Ihre Fragen. Answers will vary.

> **BEISPIEL** welcher Kontinent / groß
>
> **S1:** *Welcher Kontinent ist größer, Europa oder Asien*
> **S2:** *Natürlich ist Asien größer!*

1. welches Land / klein
2. welche Stadt / alt
3. welcher Fluss / lang
4. welcher Flughafen / groß
5. welches Auto / schnell
6. welches Hotel / teuer
7. welche Person / reich
8. welche Universität / gut

6 **Beschreiben Sie** Besprechen Sie mit einem Partner / einer Partnerin die Leute im Bild. Machen Sie so viele Vergleiche wie möglich.

> **BEISPIEL**
>
> **S1:** *Sarah ist so groß wie Sabrina.*
> **S2:** *Ja, aber David ist am größten.*

Sabrina David Lukas Sarah Emma

7 **Ein kleines Interview** Interviewen Sie zwei Mitstudenten und schreiben Sie ihre Antworten auf. Stellen Sie dann Ihre Informationen vor. Benutzen Sie dabei Komparativ- und Superlativformen. Answers will vary.

> **BEISPIEL**
>
> **S1:** *Wie alt bist du, Emily?*
> **S2:** *Ich bin 18. Und du, Michael?*
> **S3:** *Ich bin 21.*
> **S1:** *Ich bin älter als Emily und jünger als Michael. Michael ist am ältesten.*

> Name:
> Wie alt bist du?
> Wie groß bist du?
> Wie viele Geschwister hast du?
> Wie oft machst du Sport?

4 Expansion After students have done this activity with comparatives, have them ask each other similar questions using superlatives.

6 Expansion Have pairs of students choose two very different celebrities and write sentences comparing the two. You may want to have them bring in photographs and present their comparisons to the class.

Wiederholung

4 Suggestion Remind students to "kick" the verb to the end of the clause when using conjunctions like **bevor** or **nachdem**.

1 Vergleiche
Schreiben Sie mit einem Partner / einer Partnerin auf, was Sie auf den Fotos sehen. Benutzen Sie so viele Vergleiche wie möglich. Arbeiten Sie dann mit einem anderen Paar zusammen: Diskutieren Sie, was sie über die Bilder geschrieben haben. Answers will vary.

BEISPIEL

S1: Taxis sind teurer als Busse.
S2: Aber Busse fahren nicht so schnell wie Taxis.

1.

2.

2 Diskutieren und kombinieren
Sie und Ihr Partner / Ihre Partnerin bekommen von Ihrem Professor / Ihrer Professorin verschiedene Autostatistiken. Sehen Sie sich die Statistiken der vier Autos an und vergleichen Sie dann, wie schnell, wie stark und wie teuer die Autos sind. Entscheiden Sie auch, welches Auto den größten Kofferraum hat. Answers will vary.

2 Suggestion Pre-teach the vocabulary **Marke**, **Geschwindigkeit**, and **Kraft**, and explain that **PS** is short for **Pferdestärken** (horsepower). Make sure students know how to pronounce **VW**. Explain that all car brands are masculine.

BEISPIEL

S1: Wie schnell ist der Audi?
S2: Der Audi ist 247 Stundenkilometer schnell.
S1: Also ist der Audi am schnellsten.

3 Werbung
Entwerfen Sie (Design) in einer Dreiergruppe ein Zukunftsfahrzeug (vehicle of the future). Wie heißt das Fahrzeug? Machen Sie auch eine Liste mit der Ausstattung (features). Schreiben Sie dann eine Werbung, in der Sie das Zukunftsfahrzeug mit einem Auto von heute vergleichen. Answers will vary.

BEISPIEL

S1: „Futura" – das Auto des 21. Jahrhunderts. Es kann CO_2 tanken.
S2: Unser Auto verbraucht viel weniger als die Autos von gestern.

3 Suggestion You may wish to provide markers and paper so that students can make their ads more colorful. Set a time limit and make sure everyone stays on task.

4 Arbeitsblatt
Fragen Sie andere im Unterricht, was sie gestern gemacht haben. Berichten Sie dann, wer was wann gemacht hat. Benutzen Sie das Plusquamperfekt. Answers will vary.

BEISPIEL

S1: Bist du gestern zum Englischunterricht gegangen?
S2: Ja.
S1: Wann?
S2: Um 8.15 Uhr.
S1 (schreibt): Peter war schon zum Englischunterricht gegangen, bevor Julia Kaffee getrunken hat.

5 Die Party
Sie geben eine Party mit Ihren Freunden. Besprechen Sie, was Sie alle gemacht haben, um die Party vorzubereiten. Answers will vary.

BEISPIEL

S1: Seid ihr einkaufen gegangen?
S2: Ja, aber bevor wir einkaufen gegangen sind, hatten wir die Küche geputzt.

6 Eine Reise nach Erfurt
Sie planen eine Zugfahrt von Marburg nach Erfurt. Spielen Sie mit Ihrem Partner / Ihrer Partnerin ein Gespräch im Reisebüro der Deutschen Bahn. Der Reiseberater (travel agent) hilft dem Reisenden, sich für eine Zugverbindung zu entscheiden. Answers will vary.

BEISPIEL

S1: Wie kann ich Ihnen helfen?
S2: Ich möchte von Marburg nach Erfurt fahren und brauche eine Fahrkarte.
S1: Wann möchten Sie abfahren...?

TIPP

Here are some abbreviations used in train schedules.

Umst. = Umsteigen (transfer)
RE = Regional-Express
IC = Intercity
ICE = Intercity-Express

ZUG		Ihre Hinfahrtmöglichkeiten			
Bahnhof	**Zeit**	**Dauer**	**Umst.**	**Produkte**	**Preis**
MARBURG ERFURT	ab 8.21 an 12.40	4.19	2	RE, IC	51€
MARBURG ERFURT	ab 10.04 an 13.33	3.29	1	IC, ICE	65€
MARBURG ERFURT	ab 10.56 an 14.40	3.44	2	IC	51€
MARBURG ERFURT	ab 13.50 an 16.28	2.38	1	IC	51€

Video

Mercedes Benz

Im Jahr 1886 bekam der deutsche Ingenieur Carl Benz das Patent für das erste Automobil der Welt. 40 Jahren später fusionierte seine Firma mit der Daimler-Motoren-Gesellschaft und legte den Grundstein für eine schnelle Entwicklung der Autoindustrie in ganz Deutschland. Neben Volkswagen, Audi und BMW gilt Mercedes Benz als die bekannteste Automarke. Vor allem auf den Gebieten° Sicherheit und Komfort ist Mercedes Benz unschlagbar°. Laut einer Statistik, gesammelt über 30 Jahre vom Pannendienst° des ADAC (Allgemeiner Deutscher Automobilclub), hat Mercedes die wenigsten Pannen aller deutschen Automarken.

Suggestion Tell students that the ADAC is the German equivalent
of the AAA service in the United States.

Entschuldigung. Welche deutschen Automarken kennen Sie?

Volkswagen, Opel, BMW, Audi, Porsche...

Klar, Mercedes Benz gibt's natürlich auch.

auf den Gebieten *in the area of* **unschlagbar** *unbeatable* **Pannendienst** *breakdown service*

 Verständnis Beantworten Sie die Fragen mit den Informationen aus dem Video.

1. Wer ist der befragte Mann?
   a. ein Polizist
   b. ein Pannendienst-Mitarbeiter
   c. ein Autoverkäufer

2. Warum denkt der Mann nicht sofort an Mercedes Benz?
   a. Weil es eine unbekannte Automarke ist.
   b. Weil er nichts über Autos weiß.
   c. Weil Mercedes Benz selten Pannen hat.

 Diskussion Diskutieren Sie die folgenden Fragen mit einem Partner / einer Partnerin. Answers will vary.

1. Gibt es Automarken mit einer langen Tradition in Ihrem Land? Vergleichen Sie (*Compare*) diese Automarken mit Mercedes Benz.

2. Sind Sie oder Ihre Familie Mitglied in einem Automobilclub? Haben Sie den Pannendienst schon einmal zu Hilfe gerufen? Warum?

Communicative Goals

You will learn how to:

- talk about electronic communication
- talk about computer technology

Technik und Medien 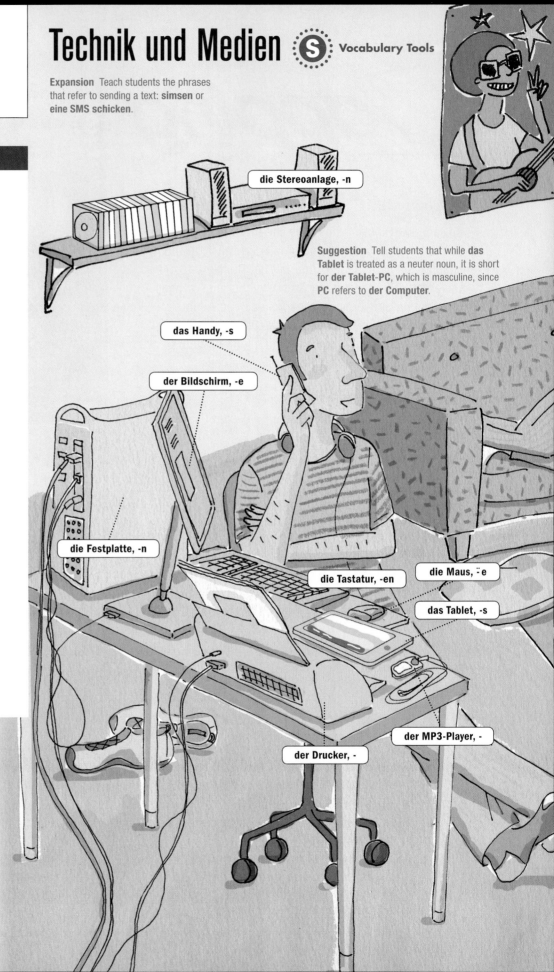 Vocabulary Tools

Expansion Teach students the phrases that refer to sending a text: **simsen** or **eine SMS schicken**.

Wortschatz

Technik bedienen	*using technology*
anmachen (macht... an)	*to turn on*
aufnehmen (nimmt... auf)	*to record*
ausmachen (macht... aus)	*to turn off*
drucken	*to print*
fernsehen (sieht... fern)	*to watch television*
funktionieren	*to work, to function*
herunterladen (lädt... herunter)	*to download*
laden (lädt)	*to charge; to load*
löschen	*to delete*
online sein	*to be online*
schicken	*to send*
speichern	*to save*
starten	*to start*
im Internet surfen	*to surf the Web*
die Technik	*technology*
der Benutzername, -n	*screen name*
die CD, -s	*compact disc, CD*
die Datei, -en	*file*
die Digitalkamera, -s	*digital camera*
das Dokument, -e	*document*
die E-Mail, -s	*e-mail*
der Kopfhörer, -	*headphones*
das Ladegerät, -e	*battery charger*
der Laptop, -s	*laptop (computer)*
das Mikrofon, -e	*microphone*
das Passwort, ¨er	*password*
das Programm, -e	*program*
der Sender, -	*channel*
das Smartphone, -s	*smartphone*
die SMS, -	*text message*
die Website, -s	*Web site*

Suggestion Tell students that while **das Tablet** is treated as a neuter noun, it is short for **der Tablet**-PC, which is masculine, since **PC** refers to **der Computer**.

Labels in illustration:
die Stereoanlage, -n
das Handy, -s
der Bildschirm, -e
die Festplatte, -n
die Tastatur, -en
die Maus, ¨e
das Tablet, -s
der MP3-Player, -
der Drucker, -

ACHTUNG

The word **Gerät**, found in the compound noun **Ladegerät**, is used by itself to refer to any kind of device or appliance.

Das Telefon klingelt.
(klingeln)

die Fernbedienung, -en

der Fernseher, -

der DVD-Player, -

die DVD, -s

die Spielkonsole, -n

Anwendung

1 Bilder beschriften Wie heißen die Geräte auf den Fotos?

a. der Drucker c. der Fernseher e. der Laptop
b. die Fernbedienung d. die Kamera f. das Mikrofon

1. _c_

2. _d_

3. _f_

4. _a_

5. _b_

6. _e_

2 Was fehlt? Ergänzen Sie die Sätze mit einem passenden Wort aus der Vokabelliste.

1. Vergessen Sie nicht, Ihr Dokument zu ____speichern____, bevor Sie den Computer ausmachen.
2. Um das Handy zu laden, braucht man ein ____Ladegerät____.
3. Man soll nicht für jede Website dasselbe ____Passwort____ benutzen.
4. Recyceln Sie Ihren Computer nicht, ohne alle Dokumente zu ____löschen____.
5. Der Klingelton auf meinem ____Handy____ ist ein Lied von Lady Gaga.
6. X-Box und Playstation sind ____Spielkonsolen____.

3 Kategorien Finden Sie für jede Kategorie passende Wörter aus Ihrer Vokabelliste. Answers may vary slightly.

Computer	Telefon	Fernseher
die Maus	das Handy	fernsehen
die E-Mail	das Smartphone	die Fernbedienung
die Tastatur	klingeln	der Sender
speichern	die SMS	das Programm

4 Hören Sie zu 🎧 Hören Sie sich die Dialoge 1-4 an und entscheiden Sie dann, welche Geräte die Personen brauchen. Schreiben Sie zu jedem Gerät die Nummer des passenden Dialogs. Answers will vary.

1. _4_ das Telefon 3. _2_ die Stereoanlage
2. _1_ die Kamera 4. _3_ die Fernbedienung

3 Suggestion Instead of filling in the answers in the book, have students write the words for each category on the board.

 Practice more at **vhlcentral.com.**

Kommunikation

5 Im Elektronikladen
Was kann man hier im Elektronikladen (*electronics store*) alles kaufen? Fragen Sie Ihren Partner / Ihre Partnerin, wie er/sie die verschiedenen elektronischen Geräte findet. Answers will vary.

BEISPIEL

S1: *Wie findest du den Laptop?*
S2: *Er ist in Ordnung. Die Festplatte ist ziemlich groß.*

| der Bildschirm | die Festplatte | die Tastatur |
| der Fernseher | der Drucker | die Videokamera |

5 Suggestion Before beginning the activity, have the class look at the picture together. Ask students to tell you what they see, using as many vocabulary words as possible.

6 Diskutieren und kombinieren
Sie und Ihr Partner / Ihre Partnerin bekommen zwei verschiedene Versionen desselben Kreuzworträtsels (*crossword puzzle*). Lesen Sie sich gegenseitig die fehlenden Definitionen vor. Answers will vary.

6 Suggestion Before they begin this activity, have students prepare written definitions (in German) for the words in their **Kreuzworträtsel**, either in class or as homework.

BEISPIEL

S1: *Eins senkrecht: Man macht das mit einem neuen Programm.*
S2: *Das ist LADEN.*

7 Technische Geräte
Erzählen Sie in Dreiergruppen, welche technischen Geräte Sie und die Mitglieder Ihrer Familie haben und auch oft benutzen. Answers will vary.

BEISPIEL

S1: *Meine Schwester kann ohne ihr Handy nicht leben. Sie schreibt bestimmt zweihundert SMS jeden Tag!*
S2: *Meine Eltern haben eine super Stereoanlage. Sie hören gern klassische Musik.*

8 Wie macht man das?
Beschreiben Sie mit einem Partner / einer Partnerin zusammen möglichst genau, was Sie tun müssen, um die folgenden Tätigkeiten auszuführen (*carry out*). Answers will vary.

BEISPIEL

S1: *Zuerst muss man die Fernbedienung finden.*
S2: *Dann macht man den Fernseher an und...*

- DVD ansehen
- Fotos drucken
- ein Buch herunterladen
- Informationen für ein Referat finden
- eine SMS schicken

8 Suggestion Tell students to describe each process in at least five steps. Give them time to prepare, and provide vocabulary as needed.

Aussprache und Rechtschreibung Audio

🎧 The German *l*

To pronounce the German **l**, place your tongue firmly against the ridge behind your top front teeth and open your mouth wider than you would for the English *l*.

| lang | Laptop | Telefon | normal | stellen |

> **Suggestion** Pronounce German and English cognates side by side, and ask students if they can hear the difference in the articulation of the l sound. Ex.: **Ball** and *ball*; **Spiel** and *spiel*.

Unlike the English *l*, the German **l** is always produced with the tongue in the same position, no matter what sound comes before or after it. Practice saying **l** after the following consonants and consonant clusters.

| Platten | schlafen | Kleid | pflegen | fleißig |

Practice saying **l** at the end of words and before the consonants **d**, **m**, and **n**. Be sure to use the German **l**, even in words that are spelled the same in English and German.

| Ball | Spiel | Wald | Film | Zwiebeln |

Practice saying the German **l** in front of the consonant clusters **sch** and **ch**.

| solch | falsch | Milch | Kölsch | Elch |

1 **Aussprechen** Wiederholen Sie die Wörter, die Sie hören.

1. Lenkrad
2. Fahrplan
3. Öl
4. Klasse
5. schlank
6. Geld
7. Köln
8. welch

2 **Nachsprechen** Wiederholen Sie die Sätze, die Sie hören.

1. Viele warten an der Bushaltestelle auf den letzten Bus nach Ludwigsfelde.
2. Luise, kannst du das Nummernschild von dem LKW lesen?
3. Lothar hatte leider einen Platten auf einer verlassenen Landstraße.
4. Man soll den Ölstand im Auto regelmäßig kontrollieren.
5. Natürlich hat der Laptop einen DVD-Player und eine Digitalkamera.
6. Klicken Sie auf das Bild, um den Film herunterzuladen.

3 **Sprichwörter** Wiederholen Sie die Sprichwörter, die Sie hören.

Wer im Glashaus sitzt, sollte nicht mit Steinen werfen.[1]

Ein Unglück kommt selten allein.[2]

[1] People in glass houses shouldn't throw stones.

[2] It never rains, but it pours. (lit. *Misfortune seldom comes alone.*)

Ressourcen

SAM
LM: p. 72

vhlcentral.com

Fotoroman

Ein Spaziergang durch Spandau  Video

George und Sabite haben Spaß zusammen, doch ein älteres Paar sieht mehr in ihnen. Hans und Meline haben leider nicht so viel Spaß.

Vorbereitung Tell students to look at scene 2 and scene 4. Have them write a brief description of the relationship between George and Sabite, and between Meline and Hans. After they have watched the video episode, have them reconsider their descriptions.

1

GEORGE Unter uns sind zwei Flüsse. Dieser Fluss ist die Havel, und das da ist die Spree. Die Spandauer Zitadelle wurde im 16. Jahrhundert anstelle einer alten Burg erbaut. Endlich besuche ich sie mal. Viel besser, als nur darüber im Internet zu lesen. Die Architektur Deutschlands ist sagenhaft!

2

SABITE Er hat nicht angerufen, keine E-Mail und keine SMS geschickt. Ich habe seine Nummer von meinem Handy gelöscht. Doch trotz meiner Gefühle habe ich seinen Schal behalten.
GEORGE Die Farbe steht dir gut.
SABITE Danke. Sie steht dir besser.

3

HANS Ich habe mich aus meiner Wohnung ausgeschlossen. Darf ich hier warten, bis George zurückkommt?
MELINE Wieso gehst du nicht in ein Café oder in die Bibliothek? Oder... oder... machst einen Spaziergang im Viertel.
HANS Mein Mantel, mein Handy und mein Geldbeutel sind in meiner Wohnung.

4

MELINE Hier ist etwas Geld und Lorenzos Pullover. Geh solange ins Café um die Ecke. Ich schicke George dann zu dir.
HANS Warum hast du den Pullover deines Ex-Freundes noch?
MELINE Tschüss, Hans.

5

GEORGE Wie nennst du es?
SABITE „Spandau... Spandau Ballet." Dein Handy klingelt.
GEORGE Es ist eine SMS von Meline. „Dein Mitbewohner, der Idiot, hat sich ausgeschlossen. Ich habe ihn ins Café geschickt. Bitte hol ihn dort ab. Lass dir Zeit."

6

MANN Berlin ist ein herrlicher Ort, um verliebt zu sein.
GEORGE Wie bitte?
FRAU Sie haben eine Verbindung. Wenn sie lacht, leuchten Ihre Augen.
MANN Katharinas Lächeln wärmt mein Herz noch immer.
FRAU Haben Sie noch viel Spaß.

---

1 **Wer ist das?** Welche Personen beschreiben die folgenden Sätze: George, Hans, Meline oder Sabite?

1. Er/Sie hat über die Spandauer Zitadelle im Internet gelesen. George
2. Er/Sie hat Torstens Nummer von seinem/ihrem Handy gelöscht. Sabite
3. Er/Sie hat sich aus seiner/ihrer Wohnung ausgeschlossen. Hans
4. Er/Sie hat Lorenzos Pullover behalten. Meline
5. Sein/Ihr Handy klingelt. George

6. Sein/Ihr Mitbewohner hat sich aus der Wohnung ausgeschlossen. George
7. Das ältere Paar glaubt, dass sie verliebt sind. George und Sabite
8. Er/Sie entschuldigt sich (apologizes) bei Hans. Meline
9. Er/Sie isst ein Stück Kuchen. Hans
10. Er/Sie hat ein Problem mit dem Computer. Meline

PERSONEN

George   Hans   Meline   Sabite   Frau   Mann

> **GEORGE** Das ist verrückt. Wir sind Freunde. Gute Freunde.
> **SABITE** Genau.

> **GEORGE** Es tut mir leid, Sabite.
> **SABITE** Es tut mir leid. Das war schrecklich.
> **GEORGE** Ja, schrecklich. Die beiden waren trotz ihres Alters nicht wirklich weise.

> **MELINE** Hans, es tut mir leid.
> **HANS** Was willst du, Meline?
> **MELINE** Ich? Nichts. Ich... ich bin unhöflich zu dir gewesen und bin hierher gekommen, um mich zu entschuldigen.
> **HANS** Danke, ich nehme an. Setz dich doch. Kuchen?

> **MELINE** Danke. Also, du kennst dich gut mit Computern aus?
> **HANS** Ja...
> **MELINE** Ich habe während eines Chats eine Datei runtergeladen, dann wurde mein Bildschirm plötzlich dunkel und die Festplatte hat angefangen, ein komisches Geräusch zu machen.
> **HANS** Speichere deine Dateien ab und schalte den Computer aus.

Nützliche Ausdrücke

- **Die Spandauer Zitadelle wurde im 16. Jahrhundert anstelle einer alten Burg erbaut.**
  The Spandau Citadel was built during the 16th century, on the site of an old castle.

- **sagenhaft**
  legendary

- **das Gefühl**
  feeling

- **Die Farbe steht dir gut.**
  The color looks good on you.

- **Ich habe mich aus meiner Wohnung ausgeschlossen.**
  I'm locked out of my apartment.

- **das Viertel**
  neighborhood

- **der Geldbeutel**
  wallet

- **Berlin ist ein herrlicher Ort, um verliebt zu sein.**
  Berlin is a beautiful place to be in love.

- **Katharinas Lächeln wärmt mein Herz noch immer.**
  Katharina's smile still warms my heart.

- **schrecklich**
  terrible

- **unhöflich**
  rude

8B.1

- **Die beiden waren trotz ihres Alters nicht wirklich weise.**
  In spite of their age, those two weren't really wise.

8B.2

- **Dieser Fluss ist die Havel, und das da ist die Spree.**
  This river is the Havel and that one is the Spree.

---

2 **Zum Besprechen** Beschreiben Sie zu zweit, wie Sie Technologie täglich nutzen. Haben Sie einen Computer? Wofür benutzen Sie ihn? Schreiben Sie einen Blog? Was machen Sie, wenn Sie Probleme mit dem Computer haben? Answers will vary.

2 Expansion Have students write a blog entry about their reaction to George and Sabite's relationship.

3 **Vertiefung** Viele technische Erfindungen (*inventions*) kommen aus Deutschland, Österreich, Liechtenstein oder der Schweiz. Suchen Sie im Internet nach einer Erfindung und informieren Sie Ihre Klasse über den Erfinder, Ort und Zeit der Erfindung sowie den Zweck (*purpose*).

Answers may include: automobile, combustion engine, movable type, aspirin, MP3s, Swiss Army knife.

Ressourcen

SAM
VM: p. 16

vhlcentral.com

IM FOKUS

Max-Planck-Gesellschaft°

(S) Reading

MAX PLANCK (1858–1947) WAR EIN deutscher Physiker. Er entwickelte° die Quantentheorie und bekam dafür 1918 den Nobelpreis für Physik. Nach ihm ist die deutsche Max-Planck-Gesellschaft (MPG) benannt.

Diese Gesellschaft existiert seit 1948. Sie ist Nachfolgerin° der Kaiser-Wilhelm-Gesellschaft, die Kaiser Wilhelm II. 1911 in Berlin gegründet hatte. In beiden Gesellschaften bekamen und

bekommen Spitzenforscher° weltweit beste Arbeitsbedingungen°, um sich voll auf ihre Forschungsinteressen konzentrieren zu können. Niemand sagt ihnen, was sie machen müssen, und die Forscher dürfen sich ihre Mitarbeiter selber aussuchen.

Heute besteht die MPG aus 80 Instituten in den Bereichen° Natur-, Sozial- und Geisteswissenschaften°. Immer wieder entstehen° neue Institute in neuen Forschungsbereichen und alte Institute schließen wieder. Zwischen 1948 und 2014 waren 18 Nobelpreisträger Mitglieder° der MPG, ein weiteres Zeichen für die herausragende° Arbeit dieser Gesellschaft. Bisher war Christiane Nüsslein-Volhard die einzige Frau unter ihnen, aber das könnte sich ändern°. Im Jahre 2015 waren immerhin 28% der Wissenschaftler an den Instituten Frauen.

Nobelpreisträger der Max-Planck-Gesellschaft		
Chemie	**Medizin**	**Physik**
Stefan W. Hell (2014)	Christiane Nüsslein-Volhard (1995)	Theodor Hänsch (2005)
Gerhard Ertl (2007)	Erwin Neher (1991)	Ernst Ruska (1986)
Paul Crutzen (1995)	Bert Sakmann (1991)	Klaus von Klitzing (1985)
Robert Huber (1988)	Georges Köhler (1984)	Walter Bothe (1954)
Hartmut Michel (1988)	Konrad Lorenz (1973)	
Johann Deisenhofer (1988)	Feodor Lynen (1964)	
Manfred Eigen (1967)		
Karl Zigler (1963)		

Gesellschaft *society* **entwickelte** *developed*
Nachfolgerin *successor* **Spitzenforscher** *top researchers*
Arbeitsbedingungen *work conditions* **Bereichen** *areas*
Geisteswissenschaften *humanities* **entstehen** *form*
Mitglieder *members* **herausragende** *outstanding*
sich ändern *to change*

1 **Richtig oder falsch?** Sind die Aussagen richtig oder falsch? Korrigieren Sie die falschen Aussagen.

1. Max Planck war Chemiker. Falsch. Max Planck war Physiker.

2. Planck entwickelte die Quantentheorie. Richtig.

3. Die MPG entstand nach dem Zweiten Weltkrieg. Richtig.

4. Vor der MPG gab es in Deutschland die Kaiser-Wilhelm-Gesellschaft. Richtig.

5. In der MPG dürfen sich die Forscher ihre Mitarbeiter selber aussuchen. Richtig.

6. Die 80 Institute der MPG arbeiten im Bereich Naturwissenschaft. Falsch. Die Insitute arbeiten in den Bereichen Natur-, Sozial- und Geisteswissenschaften.

7. Siebzehn Forscher der MPG erhielten einen Nobelpreis. Richtig.

8. Nur ein Prozent aller Wissenschaftler der MPG sind Frauen. Falsch. Immerhin 28% der Wissenschaftler der MPG sind Frauen.

9. Der erste Nobelpreisträger der MPG war Feodor Lynen. Falsch. Der erste Nobelpreisträger der Gesellschaft war Walter Bothe.

10. Die meisten Nobelpreisträger der MPG waren Chemiker. Richtig.

 Practice more at **vhlcentral.com**.

Suggestion Before they read the **Deutschsprachige Welt** article, ask students: **Welche Zeitungen, Zeitschriften oder Blogs lesen Sie? Kennen Sie auch deutsche Zeitungen?** If possible, bring a copy of *Bild* to show the class.

DEUTSCH IM ALLTAG

Wortfeld: machen

aufmachen	*to open*
durchmachen	*to experience*
mitmachen	*to participate*
nachmachen	*to imitate*
vormachen	*to fool somebody*
wettmachen	*to make up for something*
zumachen	*to close*

DIE DEUTSCHSPRACHIGE WELT

Deutsche Mediengiganten°

Die zwei deutschen Mediengiganten sind die Bertelsmann AG und die Axel Springer AG. Die Bertelsmann AG, ein 1835 in Gütersloh gegründetes deutsches Familienunternehmen°, ist das größte Medienhaus Europas. Weltweit arbeiten 104.000 Mitarbeiter für dieses Unternehmen. Neben Buchclubs sind auch Software-Entwicklung° und Fernsehsender Teil des Unternehmens. Die 1946 gegründete Axel Springer AG ist der zweite deutsche Mediengigant. Sie verlegt° mehr als 230 Zeitungen und Zeitschriften°. Die bekannteste ist die *Bild*, eine Zeitung mit täglich mehr als 12 Millionen Lesern.

Mediengiganten *media giants* **Familienunternehmen** *family-owned company* **Entwicklung** *development* **verlegt** *publishes* **Zeitschriften** *magazines*

PORTRÄT

Darmstadt

Darmstadt, eine Stadt in Hessen, gilt als Wissenschaftsstadt°. Hier wohnen zwar nur 144.000 Einwohner, aber es gibt drei Universitäten mit insgesamt mehr als 35.000 Studenten. Neben den Universitäten gibt es auch Forschungseinrichtungen° wie zum Beispiel das Europäische Raumflugkontrollzentrum° (ESOC), die Europäische Organisation für die Nutzung° meteorologischer Satelliten (EUMETSAT) und drei Institute der Fraunhofer-Gesellschaft. Im GSI Helmholtzzentrum für Schwerionenforschung° entdeckten Forscher 1994 das chemische Element Darmstadtium, das man unter der Ordnungsnummer 110 im Periodensystem finden kann.

Wissenschaftsstadt *city of science* **Forschungseinrichtungen** *research institutions* **Raumflugkontrollzentrum** *space flight control center* **Nutzung** *use* **Schwerionenforschung** *heavy ion research*

◈ IM INTERNET

Suchen Sie Informationen über digitale Medien in der deutschsprachigen Welt. Was sind die neuesten Trends?

Find out more at **vhlcentral.com**.

Expansion After reading about **Darmstadt**, have students suggest other examples of **Wissenschaftsstädte** or **-orte** like Silicon Valley. Ask them to list advantages and disadvantages of living in research and manufacturing centers such as these.

2 **Was fehlt?** Ergänzen Sie die Sätze.

1. Die Bertelsmann AG ist ein deutsches <u>Familienunternehmen</u> in Gütersloh.
2. Bertelsmann ist das <u>größte</u> Medienhaus Europas.
3. Die <u>Bild</u> ist die bekannteste Zeitung der Axel Springer AG.
4. Darmstadt gilt auch als <u>Wissenschaftsstadt</u>.
5. In Darmstadt studieren mehr als <u>35.000</u> Studenten.
6. Forscher entdeckten 1994 das chemische Element <u>Darmstadtium</u>.

3 **Technologie und digitale Medien** Diskutieren Sie mit einem Partner / einer Partnerin digitale Medien und Technologien, die Sie gerne benutzen. Warum mögen Sie sie? Gibt es ältere Technologien, die Sie bevorzugen? Warum?

BEISPIEL

S1: *Welche digitalen Medien und Technologien benutzt du gerne?*

S2: *Ich schreibe gerne E-Mails. Und du?*

Ressourcen

vhlcentral.com

8B.1 The genitive case  **Presentation**

Startblock German speakers often use constructions with **von** to indicate a relationship of ownership or close connection between two nouns. To talk about these relationships in more formal speech or writing, use the genitive case (**der Genitiv**).

- In conversation, the preposition **von** is used with a noun in the dative case to indicate ownership or a close relationship.

Hast du den neuen Klingelton **von meinem Handy** schon gehört?
*Have you heard **my cell phone's** new ringtone?*

Um die Website **von Professor Giese** zu sehen, braucht man ein Passwort.
*You need a password to access **Professor Giese's** website.*

- Another way to indicate ownership or a close relationship, especially in more formal speech and writing, is to use the genitive case.

Tim hat die Rede **des Bundespräsidenten** heruntergeladen.
*Tim downloaded **the president's** speech.*

Das Mikrofon **der Professorin** hat nicht funktioniert.
***The professor's** microphone didn't work.*

- The forms of definite articles, indefinite articles, and possessive adjectives used with genitive nouns differ from the nominative, accusative, and dative forms. Masculine and neuter nouns also change in the genitive case: those with more than one syllable add **-s**, and those with only one syllable add **-es**.

QUERVERWEIS

See **1A.3** to review the nominative case, **1B.1** and **3B.2** for the accusative case, and **4B.1** and **4B.2** for the dative case.

ACHTUNG

Possessive adjectives have the same genitive endings as the indefinite articles: **meines Druckers, meiner Festplatte, meines Handys, meiner E-Mails.**

definite articles				
	masculine	**feminine**	**neuter**	**plural**
nominative	**der** Drucker	**die** Festplatte	**das** Handy	**die** E-Mails
accusative	**den** Drucker	**die** Festplatte	**das** Handy	**die** E-Mails
dative	**dem** Drucker	**der** Festplatte	**dem** Handy	**den** E-Mails
genitive	**des** Druckers	**der** Festplatte	**des** Handys	**der** E-Mails

indefinite articles				
	masculine	**feminine**	**neuter**	**plural**
nominative	**ein** Drucker	**eine** Festplatte	**ein** Handy	**keine** E-Mails
accusative	**einen** Drucker	**eine** Festplatte	**ein** Handy	**keine** E-Mails
dative	**einem** Drucker	**einer** Festplatte	**einem** Handy	**keinen** E-Mails
genitive	**eines** Druckers	**einer** Festplatte	**eines** Handys	**keiner** E-Mails

Was ist der Preis **der Spielkonsole**?
*What is the price **of the game console**?*

Der Bildschirm **dieses Computers** ist sehr schmutzig.
***This computer's** screen is very dirty.*

Ich habe diese Fotos mit der Kamera **meines Vaters** gemacht.
*I took these photos with **my father's** camera.*

Ich kann die Telefonnummer **meiner Schwester** nicht finden.
*I can't find **my sister's** phone number.*

- You learned in **4B.1** that some masculine nouns add **-n** or **-en** in the accusative and dative cases: **der Herr, den Herrn, dem Herrn**. This is also true for the genitive case: **des Herrn**.

  Ich habe **dem Polizisten** meinen Personalausweis gezeigt.
  *I showed **the police officer** my ID card.*

  Die Kamera **des Touristen** funktioniert nicht.
  ***The tourist's** camera isn't working.*

- In the genitive case, an adjective *preceded by* an **ein**-word or a **der**-word always ends in **-en**. *Unpreceded* adjectives in the genitive case have the endings: **-en, -er, -en,** and **-er**.

  Ich mag das Aroma **schwarzen Kaffees.**
  *I like the smell **of black coffee.***

  Mögen Sie den Geschmack **grüner Paprikas**?
  *Do you like the taste **of green peppers**?*

- When using the name of a person or place in the genitive, add **-s** to the end of the name. If the name already ends with an **s** sound, add an apostrophe instead.

  Magst du **Laras** Website?
  *Do you like **Lara's** website?*

  Benjamin hat **Hans'** Ladegerät verloren.
  *Benjamin lost **Hans's** charger.*

- Most nouns in the genitive case follow the noun they modify. However, the name of a person or place comes before the noun it modifies.

  Die Eltern **meines Freundes** sind sehr nett.
  ***My boyfriend's** parents are really nice.*

  Jans Digitalkamera ist sehr klein.
  ***Jan's** digital camera is really small.*

- Use the genitive question word **wessen** to ask *whose*?

nominative	accusative	dative	genitive
wer?	wen?	wem?	wessen?

  Wessen Telefon klingelt?
  ***Whose** phone is ringing?*

  Ich glaube, es ist **Josefs** Handy.
  *I think it's **Josef's** cell phone.*

- The genitive case is also used after certain prepositions.

prepositions with the genitive			
(an)statt	*instead of*	trotz	*despite, in spite of*
außerhalb	*outside of*	während	*during*
innerhalb	*inside of, within*	wegen	*because of*

  Anstatt einer Stereoanlage bekam mein Bruder ein Handy zum Geburtstag.
  ***Instead of a stereo**, my brother got a cell phone for his birthday.*

  Trotz des Regens wollten unsere Freunde wandern gehen.
  ***Despite the rain**, our friends wanted to go hiking.*

QUERVERWEIS

See **2B.3, 3A.1, 3A.2,** and **4B.1** to review **ein**-words. See **3A.2** and **4B.1** to review **der**-words. You will learn more about **der**-words in **8B.2**.

See **3B.2** to review accusative prepositions. See **4B.2** to review dative prepositions. See **5B.3** to review two-way prepositions.

ACHTUNG

Be careful not to confuse the genitive **-s** ending with the **'s** ending used in English. In German, the apostrophe is added instead of an **s**, never before it.

Ressourcen

SAM
WB: pp. 113-114

SAM
LM: p. 73

vhlcentral.com

Suggestion
Tell students that in colloquial German, people tend to use the dative instead of the genitive, especially with the prepositions **trotz** and **wegen**.

Jetzt sind Sie dran!   **Wählen Sie die richtigen Genitivformen.**

1. Das ist der Computer (meines Bruders / meinen Bruder).
2. Wo ist der Kopfhörer (die Studenten / des Studenten)?
3. Der Fernseher (eures Vaters / euren Vater) steht im Wohnzimmer.
4. Die Website (der neuen Professorin / die neue Professorin) ist sehr interessant.
5. Ich darf den DVD-Player (meine ältere Schwester / meiner älteren Schwester) benutzen.
6. Der Bildschirm (unserem neuen Laptop / unseres neuen Laptops) ist kaputt.

Anwendung

1 **Wessen?** Beantworten Sie die Fragen mit einem ganzen Satz und benutzen Sie dabei den Genitiv der angegebenen Substantive.

▶ **BEISPIEL** Wessen Bücher sind das? (die Professorin)
Das sind die Bücher der Professorin.

1. Wessen Laptop ist das?
(die Ingenieurin) Das ist der Laptop der Ingenieurin.
2. Wessen Fahrrad ist das? (das Kind)
Das ist das Fahrrad des Kindes.
3. Wessen Auto war das? (Tobias)
Das war Tobias' Auto.
4. Wessen Mikrofon ist das?
(der Journalist) Das ist das Mikrofon des Journalisten.

5. Wessen Kamera ist das? (Johanna)
Das ist Johannas Kamera.
6. Wessen Personalausweis ist das? (Julian)
Das ist Julians Personalausweis.
7. Wessen Fahrplan ist das? (der Schaffner)
Das ist der Fahrplan des Schaffners.
8. Wessen Abschlussparty war das?
(die Deutschstudenten)
Das war die Abschlussparty der Deutschstudenten.

2 **Was fehlt?** Ergänzen Sie die Sätze mit der Genitivform der Wörter in Klammern.

BEISPIEL

Das Auto _meiner kleinen Schwester_ ist ein Mercedes. (meine kleine Schwester)

1. Gefällt dir die Farbe __meines tollen Kleides__? (mein tolles Kleid)
2. Der Blog __der neuen Dozentin__ ist sehr interessant. (die neue Dozentin)
3. Wir müssen immer über die Eskapaden __unserer jungen Hunde__ lachen.
(unsere jungen Hunde)
4. Die Digitalkamera __des amerikanischen Touristen__ ist kaputt. (der amerikanische Tourist)
5. Der Klingelton __ihres billigen Handys__ ist sehr laut. (ihr billiges Handy)
6. Der Bildschirm __des teuren Fernsehers__ ist größer als ein Fenster. (der teure Fernseher)
7. Der DVD-Player __meines alten Computers__ funktioniert nicht mehr. (mein alter Computer)

3 Suggestion Remind students that **Neffe** (item 7) is an **n**-noun and does not take an **-s** in the genitive.

3 **Dativ oder Genitiv?** Schreiben Sie die Sätze so um, dass Sie statt des Dativs den Genitiv benutzen.

BEISPIEL Der Benutzername von meinem Partner ist wirklich sehr lustig.
Der Benutzername meines Partners ist wirklich sehr lustig.

1. Die Vorlesungen von unserem Professor sind interessant.
Die Vorlesungen unseres Professors sind interessant.
2. Die Website von der Universität ist nicht sehr schön.
Die Website der Universität ist nicht sehr schön.
3. Die Stereoanlage von Alexander ist alt.
Alexanders Stereoanlage ist alt.
4. Die Festplatte von deinem Computer ist nicht groß.
Die Festplatte deines Computers ist nicht groß.
5. Meine Eltern verkaufen das Auto von meinen Großeltern.
Meine Eltern verkaufen das Auto meiner Großeltern.
6. Der Fußball von dem Jungen ist zwischen die geparkten Autos gefallen.
Der Fußball des Jungen ist zwischen die geparkten Autos gefallen.
7. Die Katze von meinem Neffen ist sehr aggressiv.
Die Katze meines Neffen ist sehr aggressiv.
8. Die neue CD von Herbert Grönemeyer ist gerade (*just now*) auf den Markt gekommen.
Herbert Grönemeyers neue CD ist gerade auf den Markt gekommen.

 Practice more at **vhlcentral.com.**

Kommunikation

4 **Bilder beschreiben** Beschreiben Sie mit einem Partner / einer Partnerin zusammen, was man auf den Bilder sehen kann. Benutzen Sie den Genitiv und verwenden Sie dabei die Wörter aus der Liste. Answers will vary.

▶ **BEISPIEL**
S1: *Was sieht man auf diesem Bild?*
S2: *Man sieht den Bildschirm eines Fernsehers.*

der Ausgang	der Motor	die Tastatur
der Bildschirm	der Seminarraum	

1. Man sieht die Tastatur eines Computers.
2. Man sieht den Seminarraum einer Universität.
3. Man sieht den Motor eines Autos.
4. Man sieht den Ausgang eines Flughafens.

5 **Bedeutende Erfinder** Finden Sie zusammen mit einem Partner / einer Partnerin heraus, was diese Personen erfunden (*invented*) haben. Verwenden Sie in Ihren Antworten den Genitiv und wechseln Sie sich ab. Answers will vary.

 BEISPIEL
S1: *Wer war Melitta Bentz?*
S2: *Sie war die Erfinderin des Kaffeefilters.*

der Bunsenbrenner	das Luftschiff
der Dieselmotor	die Röntgenstrahlen (*X-rays*)
die Jeans	der Rorschachtest
der Kaffeefilter	der Sportschuh

1. Rudolf Diesel
2. Levi Strauss
3. Wilhelm Röntgen
4. Ferdinand von Zeppelin

5. Hermann Rorschach
6. Robert Bunsen
7. Adi Dassler
8. Melitta Bentz

6 **Wann machst du das?** Fragen Sie Ihren Partner / Ihre Partnerin, wann er/sie diese Aktivitäten macht. Verwenden Sie bei Ihren Antworten einen Zeitausdruck aus jeder (*each*) Spalte. Answers will vary.

  BEISPIEL
S1: *Wann schreibst du die meisten Prüfungen?*
S2: *Am Ende des Semesters.*

Am Ende	das Semester
Am Anfang	die Woche
Während	der Tag
	das Jahr
	der Sommer
	die Ferien
	das Abendessen

1. Wann lernst du neue Mitstudenten kennen?
2. Wann surfst du im Internet?
3. Wann fährst du mal für ein paar Tage weg?
4. Wann rufst du deine Familie an?
5. Wann bekommst du deine Noten?
6. Wann suchst du einen Ferienjob?

5 **Suggestion** Tell students that Adi Dassler's name provides a clue about his invention. Dassler is the founder of the sportswear company **Adidas**.

5 **Suggested answers:**
1. Wer war Rudolf Diesel? Er war der Erfinder des Dieselmotors.

2. Wer war Levi Strauss? Er war der Erfinder der Jeans.

3. Wer war Wilhelm Röntgen? Er war der Erfinder der Röntgenstrahlen.

4. Wer war Ferdinand von Zeppelin? Er war der Erfinder des Luftschiffes.

5. Wer war Hermann Rorschach? Er war der Erfinder des Rorschachtests.

6. Wer war Robert Bunsen? Er war der Erfinder des Bunsenbrenners.

7. Wer war Adi Dassler? Er war der Erfinder des Sportschuhs.

8. Wer war Melitta Bentz? Sie war die Erfinderin des Kaffeefilters.

8B.2

Demonstratives  Presentation

Startblock Use demonstrative pronouns and adjectives to refer to something that has already been mentioned, or to point out a specific person or thing.

> **Dieser** Fluss ist die Havel, und **das** da ist die Spree.

> Es war meine Idee, hierher zu kommen. Ich liebe **diesen** Ort.

Demonstrative pronouns

Suggestion The humorous '90s song **Die Da!?!** by **Die Fantastischen Vier** can be found online and provides a good illustration of the use of demonstratives.

- Use demonstrative pronouns to refer to a person or thing that has already been mentioned or whose identity is clear, instead of repeating the noun.

Ist Greta online?
—Ja, **die** schreibt eine E-Mail.
Is Greta online?
*—Yes, **she**'s writing an e-mail.*

Gefällt dir dein neuer Drucker?
—Ja, **der** funktioniert sehr gut!
Do you like your new printer?
*—Yes, **it** works really well!*

- The forms of the demonstrative pronoun are identical to the definite article, except for the genitive and dative plural forms. Use the demonstrative pronoun that agrees in gender and number with the noun it is replacing.

ACHTUNG

When referring to people, the demonstrative pronoun is equivalent to *she, he, it,* or *they.* When referring to things, it is equivalent to *it, that,* or *those.*

A demonstrative pronoun usually appears at or near the beginning of a clause, even when it is an object.

Dem kann man nicht helfen.

Das will ich schnell löschen.

demonstrative pronouns				
	masculine	**feminine**	**neuter**	**plural**
nominative	der	die	das	die
accusative	den	die	das	die
dative	dem	der	dem	denen
genitive	dessen	deren	dessen	deren

Dieser Laptop ist wirklich alt. **Den** habe ich schon seit Jahren.
*This laptop is really old. I've had **it** for years.*

Lara ist sehr zuverlässig. **Die** wird nicht zu spät kommen.
*Lara is very reliable. **She** won't come too late.*

Was sagen deine Eltern? Hast du **denen** schon dein Zeugnis gezeigt?
*What do your parents say? Have you shown **them** your report card yet?*

Ich habe nur eine Fernbedienung, aber mit **der** kann man alles an- und ausmachen.
*I only have one remote, but you can turn everything on and off with **it**.*

- Use the genitive demonstrative pronouns **dessen** or **deren** in cases where the possessive adjectives **sein** or **ihr** might cause confusion.

Erik hat Daniel auf **seinem** neuen Boot gesehen.
*Erik saw Daniel on **his** (Erik's? Daniel's?) new boat.*

Erik hat Daniel auf **dessen** neuen Boot gesehen.
*Erik saw Daniel on **his** (Daniel's) new boat.*

- Use **hier** or **da** with a demonstrative to distinguish between *this one* or *that one*.

Der da gefällt Klara besser.
*Klara likes **that one** better.*

Vergiss nicht, **das hier** zu drucken!
*Don't forget to print **this one**!*

Der-words

- **Der**-words include **dieser** (*this; that*), **jeder** (*each, every*) and its plural counterpart **alle** (*all*), **mancher** (*some*), and **solcher** (*such*), as well as the question word **welcher** (*which*).

Nina, **welcher** Laptop gefällt dir am besten?
*Nina, **which** laptop do you like best?*

Ich finde **diesen** Laptop am schönsten.
*I think **this** laptop is the nicest.*

- **Der**-words are so called because they have the same endings as the definite articles. The chart below shows only **dieser**, but all the other **der**-words have the same endings.

der-words			
	masculine	**feminine**	**neuter**	**plural**
nominative	dies**er** Mann	dies**e** Frau	dies**es** Kind	dies**e** Kinder
accusative	dies**en** Mann	dies**e** Frau	dies**es** Kind	dies**e** Kinder
dative	dies**em** Mann	dies**er** Frau	dies**em** Kind	dies**en** Kindern
genitive	dies**es** Mannes	dies**er** Frau	dies**es** Kindes	dies**er** Kinder

Mit **dieser** Tastatur können Sie viel schneller tippen.
*With **this** keyboard, you can type much faster.*

Speichert dein neues Handy **jede** SMS?
*Does your new cellphone save **every** text message?*

Manche Sender haben keine guten Programme.
Some stations don't have any good programs.

Solche Websites gefallen mir nicht.
*I don't like **those kinds of** websites.*

- Adjectives after **der**-words have the same endings as adjectives after definite articles.

Diese kleine Digitalkamera macht sehr schöne Fotos.
***That little** digital camera takes great photos.*

Welchen neuen Film wollt ihr heute Abend sehen?
***Which new** film do you want to see tonight?*

Suggestion Provide students with a few memorable **so ein** phrases to help them understand its idiomatic use. Ex.: **So ein Tag! So ein Zufall! So ein tolles Auto!**

ACHTUNG

Jeder is only used with singular nouns while **alle** is only used in the plural. The accusative forms of **jeder** appear in time expressions such as **jeden Tag/Monat**, **jede Woche**, and **jedes Jahr**.

Solcher is used mainly in the plural. Instead of using **solcher** in the singular, German speakers typically use **so ein** to mean *that kind of* or *such a*:
So einen Mann möchte ich heiraten.

QUERVERWEIS

To review adjective endings after **der**-words, see **3A.2**, **4B.1**, and **8B.1**.

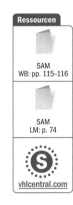

Ressourcen

SAM
WB: pp. 115–116

SAM
LM: p. 74

vhlcentral.com

Jetzt sind Sie dran!   Wählen Sie die passende Form.

1. (**Welches** / Welcher) Mikrofon funktioniert am besten?
2. Simon speichert (jede / **jedes**) Dokument auf der Festplatte.
3. Frau Kaufmann hat einen neuen Laptop gekauft. (Die / **Der**) hat 700 € gekostet.
4. Von (**welcher** / welchem) Schwester hast du die Stereoanlage zum Geburtstag bekommen?
5. Danke für den guten Saft! (**Den** / Dem) trinken wir heute Abend.
6. Bringst du bitte das Ladegerät mit? (**Das** / Dem) brauche ich sofort (*right away*).
7. Mira speichert (manchen / **manche**) E-Mails und löscht den Rest.
8. Ich schreibe (jeder / **jeden**) Benutzernamen auf, um ihn nicht zu vergessen.
9. Mit (solche / **solchen**) Handys kann man E-Mails schreiben, SMS schicken und telefonieren.
10. Ihr wolltet den Fernseher mit der Fernbedienung anmachen, aber (**die** / das) war nirgendwo (*nowhere*) zu finden.
11. (Welches / **Welcher**) Freund hat dir mit deiner Website geholfen?
12. Antonia hat Nils und (**dessen** / deren) Frau das Dokument gezeigt.

Anwendung

1 **Was fehlt?** Ergänzen Sie die Sätze mit den richtigen Demonstrativpronomen.

1. Kennst du die Deutschdozentin? Nein, __die__ kenne ich nicht.
2. Welcher Computer ist der bessere? __Der__ da für 1.200 €.
3. Welches Kleid ziehst du auf die Party an? __Das__ da auf meinem Bett.
4. Welchem Kind gehört der Fußball? __Dem__ dort auf dem Spielfeld.
5. Haben Schmidts dich schon angerufen? __Deren__ Tochter hat letzte Woche ihren Abschluss gemacht.
6. Was machen deine Großeltern? Ach, __denen__ geht's leider nicht sehr gut.
7. Bringt ihr euren Hund ins Hundehotel während eurer Reise? Nein, __den__ nehmen wir natürlich mit.
8. Welcher Zug geht nach Kassel? __Der__ fährt dort drüben auf Bahnsteig 7A.

2 **Was ist richtig?** Wählen Sie die passenden **der**-Wörter.

1. (Solches / Welches) Auto hast du denn jetzt gekauft?
2. (Jede / Manche) Modelle haben nur einen kleinen Kofferraum.
3. Heute kann man mit (jedem / welchem) Handy im Internet surfen.
4. Hast du (diese / jede) Website schon gesehen? Die ist wirklich interessant!
5. (Manche / Solche) Probleme möchte ich haben!
6. Mit (solchen / welchen) Leuten kann man leider nicht reden.

3 Sample answers: 1. Ja, mit allen günstigen Smartphones kann man auch SMS schreiben. 2. Nein, so ein kleiner Laptop hat keinen DVD-Player. 3. Nein, diese amerikanische Tastatur kann man nicht in Deutschland benutzen. 4. Nein, ich möchte diese alte Videokamera nicht kaufen. 5. Nein, ich kann mit diesem nutzlosen Kopfhörer nichts hören.

3 **Suggestion** Do the first few items aloud and have students complete the rest in writing. Circulate around the classroom and check their answers.

3 **Elektronische Geräte** Beantworten Sie die Fragen mit **ja** oder **nein**. Verwenden Sie die **der**-Wörter in Klammern und ein passendes Adjektiv aus der Liste. Achten Sie auf die Adjektivendungen. Sample answers are provided.

| alt | amerikanisch | günstig | flach (*flat*) | kaputt | klein | nutzlos |

> **BEISPIEL**
>
> Hat der Bildschirm des Fernsehers eine bessere Bildqualität? (so ein)
> *Ja, der Bildschirm so eines flachen Fernsehers hat wirklich eine bessere Bildqualität.*

1. Kann man mit dem Smartphone auch SMS schreiben? (all-)

2. Hat der Laptop auch einen DVD-Player? (so ein)

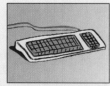

3. Kann man diese Tastatur auch in Deutschland benutzen? (dies-)

4. Möchtest du die Videokamera meiner Mutter kaufen? (dies-)

5. Kannst du mit deinem Kopfhörer alles hören? (dies-)

 Practice more at **vhlcentral.com.**

Kommunikation

4 **Wie findest du das?** Fragen Sie Ihren Partner / Ihre Partnerin nach seiner/ihrer Meinung (*opinion*). Benutzen Sie Demonstrativpronomen und wechseln Sie sich ab. Answers will vary.

> **BEISPIEL**
>
> **S1:** *Wie findest du die Band* Train?
> **S2:** *Die ist einfach fantastisch!*

egoistisch	langweilig
eingebildet	lustig
fade	romantisch
fantastisch	schlecht
hübsch	süß
intelligent	toll
interessant	

Wie findest du...

1. die Musik von...?

2. die Kunst von...?

3. den Fernsehsender...?

4. den Film...?

5. die Kurse von Professor/Professorin...?

6. die Bücher von...?

5 **Immer das Gleiche** Schreiben Sie, was Sie jeden Tag, jede Woche, jeden Monat und jedes Jahr machen, und dann interviewen Sie Ihre Mitstudenten. Answers will vary.

> **BEISPIEL**
>
> **S1:** *Was machst du jeden Tag?*
> **S2:** *Ich esse jeden Tag in der Mensa.*
> *Und du, was machst du jeden Tag?*

jeden Tag:	
jede Woche:	
jeden Monat:	
jedes Jahr:	

6 **Rollenspiel: Im Modehaus** Sie sind Verkäufer / Verkäuferin in einem Modehaus. Leider hat der Kunde / die Kundin immer etwas auszusetzen (*criticize*). Erfinden Sie mit einem Partner / einer Partnerin einen Dialog. Answers will vary.

6 **Suggestion** Have students write their dialogues and perform them for the class.

> **BEISPIEL**
>
> **S1:** *Wie finden Sie diesen Pullover?*
> **S2:** *Der ist viel zu klein!*
> **S1:** *Und wie gefällt Ihnen dieses rote Kleid?*
> **S2:** *So ein hässliches Kleid habe ich noch nie gesehen!*

der Anzug	die Krawatte	billig	gestreift
die Baseballmütze	die Lederjacke	dunkel	hässlich
das Baumwollkleid	der Minirock	einfach	lang
die Halskette	die Sandalen	elegant	langweilig
die Handtasche	der Schal	eng	schmutzig
die Hose	das Trägerhemd	furchtbar	teuer

Wiederholung

1 Logische Verbindungen

Sehen Sie sich mit einem Partner / einer Partnerin die Wortliste und die Bilder an. Welche Wörter passen zu welchen Bildern?

Sample answers are provided.

▶ **BEISPIEL**

Das ist die Schwimmerin des Jahres.

> **1** Suggestion Make sure students understand that each of their answers must contain a genitive construction.

das Jahr	die Schülerin
der Monat	der Tag
das Restaurant	

1.

Das ist das Restaurant des Monats.

2.

Das sind die Bleistifte der Schülerin.

3.

Das ist das Auto des Jahres.

4.

Das ist der Koch des Restaurants.

2 Diskutieren und kombinieren

Sehen Sie sich die Tabelle mit statistischen Informationen über Deutschland, Liechtenstein und die Schweiz an. Fragen Sie Ihren Partner / Ihre Partnerin nach den fehlenden Informationen.

> **2** Suggestion If you notice that students are having difficulty forming the questions, interrupt the activity to write the questions as a class.

BEISPIEL

S1: Wie lang ist der längste Fluss der Schweiz?
S2: Das ist der Rhein. Er ist 375 Kilometer lang.

3 Manche Leute

Viele Menschen machen komische Sachen (*strange things*). Was denken Sie und Ihr Partner / Ihre Partnerin darüber? Was sollen diese Menschen anders machen?

> **3** Suggestion Encourage students to be creative, and provide vocabulary help as needed. If your class is fairly small, invite students to share their answers on the board.

BEISPIEL

S1: Manche Menschen tanzen im Regen.
S2: Solche Menschen sind dynamisch, aber sie sollen sich einen Regenschirm kaufen.

im Haus Rad fahren	draußen schlafen
unter dem Bett lesen	im Regen tanzen
auf dem Dach lesen	im Winter kurze Kleider tragen

4 Wem gehört's?

Sehen Sie sich die Bilder an. Fragen Sie einen Partner / eine Partnerin, wem die Dinge gehören. Wechseln Sie sich ab. Sample answers are provided.

▶ **BEISPIEL**

S1: Wessen Stereoanlage ist das?
S2: Das ist die Stereoanlage des Studenten.

meine Eltern	mein Opa
David	der Journalist
das Mädchen	der Student

1.

Das ist der Drucker meines Opas.

2.

Das ist die Videokamera des Journalisten.

3.

Das ist das Fotoalbum des Mädchens.

4.

Das ist der Fernseher meiner Eltern.

5 Arbeitsblatt

Fragen Sie andere im Unterricht, was ihnen gefällt. Schreiben Sie sich die Antworten auf.

BEISPIEL Autor: Stephen King / Jane Austen

S1: Wen liest du lieber, Stephen King oder Jane Austen?
S2: Mir ist Stephen King lieber.

6 Technologie

Unterhalten Sie sich mit Ihrem Partner / Ihrer Partnerin, über die Geräte, die sie besitzen. Was halten Sie von solchen Geräten? Benutzen sie viele Menschen? Sind sie für jeden geeignet (*suitable*)?

▶ **BEISPIEL**

S1: Ich habe eine Spielkonsole.
S2: Ich habe auch eine Spielkonsole. Viele Studenten mögen sie.
S1: Was spielst du am liebsten?
S2: Am liebsten spiele ich...

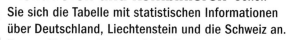

7 Im Kleidergeschäft
Sehen Sie sich die Kleidung an und fragen Sie Ihren Partner / Ihre Partnerin nach seiner/ihrer Meinung.

BEISPIEL

S1: Gefällt dir der blaue Rock?
S2: Der gefällt mir, aber diese grüne Hose gefällt mir nicht.

> **7 Suggestion** You may wish to briefly review adjective endings before having students begin this activity.

8 Genitivpräpositionen
Schreiben Sie mit einem Partner / einer Partnerin ein Gedicht (*poem*) aus fünf Sätzen. Außer der letzten Zeile (*line*) muss jede Zeile mit einer Genitivpräposition beginnen.

BEISPIEL

> Außerhalb der Stadt stürmt es.
> Trotz des schlechten Wetters spielen wir Tennis.
> Während des Spiels rollt der Ball in den Fluss.
> Wegen des verlorenen Balls können wir nicht mehr spielen.
> Das nächste Mal bleiben wir lieber mit der
> Spielkonsole zu Hause.

9 Wahrheiten und Lügen
Schreiben Sie zwei Sätze darüber, was Sie schon vor Ihrem 14. Geburtstag gemacht haben. Eine der Aussagen ist wahr (*true*), eine Aussage ist eine Lüge (*lie*). Ihre Mitstudenten müssen erraten, welcher Satz die Lüge ist. Answers will vary.

BEISPIEL

Ich war schon zweimal nach Europa geflogen.
Ich hatte schon zwei Fremdsprachen gelernt.

> **9 Suggestion** Provide a model with two truths and a lie about what you had already done before you turned 14. Have students guess which one is the lie.

Mein Wör | ter | buch

Schreiben Sie noch fünf weitere Wörter in Ihr persönliches Wörterbuch zu den Themen **Verkehrsmittel** und **Technologie**.

der Führerschein

Übersetzung
driver's license

Wortart
ein Substantiv

Gebrauch
In Amerika darf man den Führerschein mit 16 Jahren machen. In Deutschland muss man 18 Jahre alt sein und der Führerschein ist viel teurer.

Synonyme
die Fahrerlaubnis

Antonyme
—

 **Vocabulary tools**

Panorama 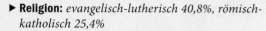 Interactive Map

Hessen und Thüringen

Hessen in Zahlen

▶ **Fläche:** *21.114 km²*

▶ **Bevölkerung:** *6 Millionen Menschen*

▶ **Religion:** *evangelisch-lutherisch 40,8%, römisch-katholisch 25,4%*

▶ **Städte:** *Frankfurt (701.000 Einwohner), Wiesbaden (274.000), Kassel (194.000)*

▶ **Flüsse:** *der Main, der Neckar, die Fulda*

▶ **Wichtige Industriezweige:** *chemische Industrie, Pharmaindustrie, Fahrzeugbau, Banken*

▶ **Touristenattraktionen:** *Römischer Grenzwall° Limes, Fossilienlagerstätte° Grube Messel, Benediktiner-Abtei° und Kloster° Lorsch*
Touristen können in Marburg die Märchen der Gebrüder Grimm entdecken. Wirtschaftlich ist Hessen für die Banken in Frankfurt und die chemische und Pharmaindustrie bekannt.

QUELLE: Landesportal Hessen

Thüringen in Zahlen

▶ **Fläche:** *16.172 km²*

▶ **Bevölkerung:** *2,2 Millionen Menschen*

▶ **Religion:** *keine Religion 66%, evangelisch-lutherisch 26%*

▶ **Städte:** *Erfurt (205.000 Einwohner), Jena (108.000), Gera (95.000)*

▶ **Wichtige Industriezweige:** *Automobil, Metallverarbeitung, Lebensmittelindustrie, Tourismus*

▶ **Touristenattraktionen:** *Weimar, Wartburg (Eisenach), Schloss Friedenstein (Gotha)*
Touristen können in Eisenach die Spuren berühmter Deutscher wie Luther und Bach entdecken. Wirtschaftlich ist Thüringen eines der erfolgreichsten° ostdeutschen Bundesländer.

QUELLE: Thüringen Tourismus

Berühmte Hessen und Thüringer

▶ **Johann Sebastian Bach,** *Komponist (1685–1750)*

▶ **Johann Wolfgang von Goethe,** *Autor (1749–1832)*

▶ **Anne Frank,** *Autorin und Opfer° des Nationalsozialismus (1929–1945)*

römischer Grenzwall *Roman boundary wall* **Fossilienlagerstätte** *natural fossil deposit* **Abtei** *abbey* **Kloster** *monastery* **erfolgreichsten** *most successful* **Opfer** *victim* **Karfreitag** *Good Friday* **Tanzverbot** *ban on dancing* **drohen** *threaten* **Geldstrafen** *fines*

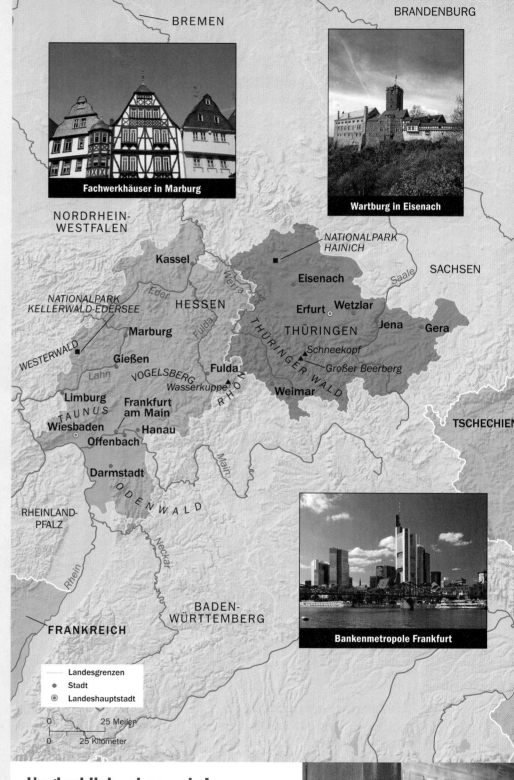

Fachwerkhäuser in Marburg

Wartburg in Eisenach

Bankenmetropole Frankfurt

Landesgrenzen
• Stadt
◉ Landeshauptstadt

0 — 25 Meilen
0 — 25 Kilometer

Unglaublich, aber wahr!

Am Karfreitag° und an anderen religiösen Feiertagen darf man in vielen Bundesländern nicht tanzen. Hessen und Thüringen sind zwei von dreizehn Bundesländern, in denen das Tanzverbot° am Karfreitag 24 Stunden dauert. Seit 1952 dürfen Diskotheken an diesem Tag keine Tanzveranstaltungen organisieren oder es drohen° hohe Geldstrafen°.

Suggestion Point out that the term **Bußgeld** typically refers to fines incurred for parking violations, speeding, or fare evasion, while **Geldstrafe** is a more general term for a fine or legal penalty.

Städte

Suggestion Have students read a short poem by Goethe, such as *Wanderers Nachtlied II* or *Heidenröslein*.

Weimar

Weimar ist die viertgrößte Stadt in Thüringen. Im Jahre 1919 beschloss die Nationalversammlung° hier die deutsche Verfassung°. Deshalb nennt man die erste deutsche Demokratie auch „Weimarer Republik". Für die Literatur ist Weimar wichtig, weil Autoren wie Goethe, Schiller und Nietzsche hier lebten. Berühmte Musiker, die in Weimar komponierten, waren Johann Sebastian Bach und Franz Liszt. Im Bereich der Architektur entwickelte° der Architekt Walter Gropius die Bauhaus-Schule in Weimar.

Kultur

Skat

Skat ist eines der beliebtesten Kartenspiele in Deutschland. Manche Menschen nennen es auch „das Spiel der Deutschen". Etwa 20 Millionen Deutsche spielen Skat. Das Spiel wurde circa 1810 in der thüringischen Stadt Altenburg erfunden°. Seit 1938 gibt es deutsche Meisterschaften°. Altenburg ist immer noch die Skathauptstadt der Welt, in welcher der Deutsche Skatverband seine Geschäftsstelle° hat. Hier gibt es auch die berühmte Kartenfabrik Altenburger Spielkarten. 2007 feierte die Firma ihr 175-jähriges Jubiläum.

Geographie

Wald und Jagd° in Deutschland

In Hessen und Thüringen bestehen große Landesflächen aus Wäldern. In Hessen gibt es 8.472 Quadratkilometer Wald, etwa 40% der Landesfläche, mehr als in jedem anderen deutschen Bundesland. Der Nationalpark Thüringer Wald bietet ein sehr beliebtes Urlaubsziel für Wanderer, Fahrradfahrer und Skifahrer an. Seit dem 19. Jahrhundert nennt man Thüringen „das grüne Herz Deutschlands". Auch Jäger° besuchen diese Region gerne zur Jagd von Rehen und Hirschen°.

Menschen

Heilige Elisabeth

Die heilige° Elisabeth, auch bekannt als Landgräfin Elisabeth von Thüringen, lebte zwischen 1207 und 1231. Sie war die Tochter des ungarischen° Königs Andreas II. und lebte die meiste Zeit ihres Lebens im hessischen Marburg. Sie starb im Alter von 24 Jahren, aber die Menschen liebten sie, weil sie sehr vielen Menschen während ihres Lebens geholfen hatte. Nur vier Jahre nach ihrem Tod sprach Papst Gregor IX. Elisabeth heilig°. In Marburg kann man heute ihr Grab° in der Elisabethkirche besuchen.

IM INTERNET

1. Suchen Sie im Internet Informationen über Weimar: Was sind die berühmtesten Gebäude Weimars? Machen Sie eine Liste. Wie viele Touristen besuchen Weimar jedes Jahr?

2. Suchen Sie im Internet andere Spiele, die man in Deutschland spielt. Wo spielt man diese Spiele?

Find out more at **vhlcentral.com**.

Nationalversammlung *national assembly* **Verfassung** *constitution* **entwickelte** *developed* **erfunden** *invented*
Meisterschaften *championships* **Geschäftsstelle** *office* **Wald und Jagd** *forest and hunting* **Jäger** *hunters*
Rehen und Hirschen *deer and stags* **heilige** *saint* **ungarischen** *Hungarian* **sprach... heilig** *canonized* **Grab** *grave*

Was haben Sie gelernt? Ergänzen Sie die Sätze.

1. In vielen deutschen Bundesländern darf man an religiösen Feiertagen nicht __tanzen__.

2. Seit __1952__ gibt es Karfreitag ein Tanzverbot.

3. Die erste deutsche __Demokratie__ nennt man auch die „Weimarer Republik".

4. Autoren, die in Weimar gelebt haben, sind __Goethe__, Schiller und Nietzsche.

5. Skat wurde circa __1810__ in Altenburg in Thüringen erfunden.

6. Etwa __20 Millionen__ Deutsche spielen heute Skat.

7. In Hessen sind __40%__ der Landesfläche Wald.

8. Der Nationalpark __Thüringer Wald__ ist ein beliebtes Urlaubsziel in Thüringen.

9. Die heilige Elisabeth starb schon mit __24__ Jahren.

10. In der Elisabethkirche in __Marburg__ ist das Grab von Elisabeth.

 Practice more at **vhlcentral.com**.

Lesen Audio: Reading

Vor dem Lesen

Strategien

Guessing meaning from context

As you read in German, you will often see words you have not learned. You can guess their meaning by looking at surrounding words. Read this e-mail and guess what **erleichtert** means.

> Hallo Sylvia! Ich habe heute meinen Führerschein gemacht. Zuerst musste ich durch die Stadt fahren. Das war ziemlich schwer, denn alle Ampeln waren rot. Danach ging es auf die Autobahn. Ich war sehr nervös und wollte keinen Fehler machen. Am Ende war ich sehr erleichtert, als ich die Prüfung bestanden hatte, weil es sehr stressig war. Jetzt darf ich endlich Auto fahren.
> Liebe Grüße,
> Lina

If you guessed *relieved*, you are correct. You can conclude that Lina is feeling happy about the outcome of the test.

Untersuchen Sie den Text 👥 Sehen Sie sich mit einem Partner / einer Partnerin den Text an und beschreiben Sie das Format. Um was geht es in dem Text Ihrer Meinung nach (*in your opinion*)? Suchen Sie die folgenden Wörter und Ausdrücke im Text. Benutzten Sie den Kontext, um die Bedeutung zu erraten.

- Zubehör
  components
- Luftfeuchtigkeit
  humidity
- Tintenpatrone
  ink cartridge
- Steckdose
  electric outlet
- Papiergröße
  paper size
- Laufwerk
  drive

Inhalt erraten Sie wissen schon etwas über das Format des Texts und einige Wörter: sagen Sie, was Sie wahrscheinlich in dem Text lernen werden.

- wie man eine Internetverbindung einrichtet
- wie man eine CD brennt
- wie man einen Drucker anschließt
- wie man ein Dokument druckt
- wie man Tintenpatronen recycelt

Drucker MI6-0070
Vierfarbdrucker Installationsanleitung

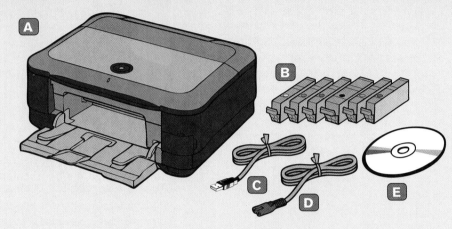

A. Drucker **B.** Tintenpatronen **C.** USB-Kabel **D.** Netzkabel **E.** CD

Schritt ① Auspacken

Heben Sie den Drucker und das Zubehör vorsichtig aus dem Karton. Prüfen Sie°, ob Sie alle Komponenten haben. Entfernen Sie° das Klebeband° vom Drucker. Entfernen Sie auch das Klebeband an der Rückseite des Druckers.

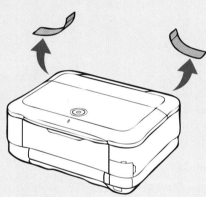

Schritt ② Aufstellen des Druckers

Der Drucker darf nicht zu nahe an anderen Geräten stehen. Es muss genügend Platz um den Drucker herum sein, damit er nicht zu heiß wird. Die ideale Zimmertemperatur für den Drucker ist 23°C. Die Zimmertemperatur darf aber zwischen 10°C und 32°C variieren. Die Luftfeuchtigkeit darf zwischen 20% und 80% variieren. Die ideale Luftfeuchtigkeit beträgt 60%.

23°C | 60%

Schritt ③ Tintenpatrone einsetzen

Vor der ersten Verwendung° des Druckers müssen Sie die Tintenpatrone einsetzen. Öffnen Sie zuerst die obere Abdeckung° des Druckers. Nehmen Sie die Tintenpatronen aus der Verpackung°. Ziehen Sie den Schutzstreifen vorsichtig ab. Setzen Sie die Tintenpatrone in den Drucker ein. Drücken Sie fest auf die mit *PUSH HERE* gekennzeichneten° Stellen. Schließen Sie jetzt den Drucker.

PUSH HERE

Schritt ④ Drucker an den Computer anschließen

Schließen Sie ein Ende des USB-Kabels an der Rückseite des Druckers an. Schließen Sie das andere Ende des USB-Kabels an den USB-Anschluss des Computers an.

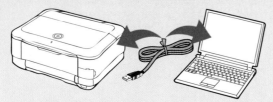

Schritt ⑤ Netzkabel anschließen

Verwenden Sie nur das Kabel, das mit dem Drucker geliefert wurde. Wenn der Drucker ausgeschaltet ist, schließen Sie das Netzkabel an den Anschluss° auf der Rückseite des Druckers an. Schließen Sie dann das andere Ende des Netzkabels an eine Steckdose an.

Schritt ⑥ Papier in Kassette einlegen

Sie können 250 Blatt Papier in die Papierkassette einlegen. Ziehen Sie zuerst die Papierkassette aus dem Drucker heraus. Legen Sie jetzt das Papier in die Kassette ein und schließen Sie den Drucker wieder.

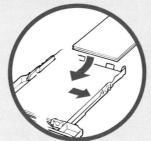

Schritt ⑦ Installation der Treiber

Schalten Sie den Drucker ein und schieben Sie die CD in das CD-Laufwerk. Installieren Sie das Programm „Drucker.exe" auf Ihrem Computer. Wenn Sie mit der Installation fertig sind, öffnet sich automatisch ein neues Fenster. Jetzt ist Ihr Drucker fertig installiert.

Schritt ⑧ Statusseite drucken

Testen Sie den Drucker, indem Sie eine Statusseite drucken. Schalten Sie den Drucker ein. Drücken Sie mindestens 3 Sekunden auf den EIN/AUS Knopf. Der Drucker sollte jetzt eine Statusseite drucken.

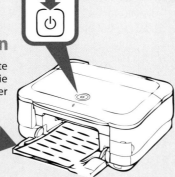

Prüfen Sie *Check* **Entfernen Sie** *Remove* **Klebeband** *adhesive tape* **Verwendung** *use*
Abdeckung *cover* **Verpackung** *packaging* **gekennzeichneten** *marked* **Anschluss** *connection*

Nach dem Lesen

Richtig oder falsch Sind die Sätze **richtig** oder **falsch**? Korrigieren Sie die falschen Sätze. Sample answers are provided.

	richtig	falsch
1. In dem Karton ist nur der Drucker. Im Karton sind der Drucker und die Komponenten.	☐	☑
2. Die Zimmertemperatur muss immer 23°C sein. Die ideale Zimmertemperatur ist 23°C.	☐	☑
3. Man muss erst die Tintenpatrone einsetzen, bevor man das erste Mal drucken kann.	☑	☐
4. Den Drucker muss man mit einem USB-Kabel an den Computer anschließen.	☑	☐
5. Das Netzkabel schließt man auf der Vorderseite des Druckers an. Das Netzkabel schließt man auf der Rückseite des Druckers an.	☐	☑
6. Man kann nur 150 Blatt Papier in die Kassette einlegen. Man kann 250 Blatt Papier in die Kassette einlegen.	☐	☑
7. Den Treiber für den Drucker installiert man mit einer CD auf dem Computer.	☑	☐
8. Am Ende kann man eine Statusseite drucken.	☑	☐

Druckerprobleme Arbeiten Sie mit einem Partner / einer Partnerin. Einer von Ihnen hat ein Problem mit dem Drucker. Beschreiben Sie das Problem. Versuchen Sie dann mit Ihrem Partner / Ihrer Partnerin, das Problem zu lösen.

BEISPIEL

S1: *Ich habe meinen Drucker gerade installiert. Aber ich kann die Statusseite nicht drucken.*
S2: *Hast du den Drucker eingeschaltet?*

Suggestion Make sure students understand that they should refer back to the text to solve their **Druckerprobleme**.

Hören

Strategien

Recognizing the genre of spoken discourse

You will encounter many different types of speech in German. For example, you may hear a political speech, a radio interview, a commercial, a voicemail message, or a news broadcast. Try to identify the context of the speech you hear, so that you can activate your background knowledge about that type of discourse and identify the speakers' motives and intentions.

 To practice this strategy, you will listen to two short selections. Identify the genre of each one.

Vorbereitung

Über was sollte man nachdenken, bevor man ein neues Handy kauft? Machen Sie eine Liste. Welche Funktionen sind Ihnen bei einem neuen Handy wichtig?

Zuhören

Hören Sie Rolf und Karin zu, wie sie den Kauf eines neuen Handys diskutieren. Welche Funktionen von Ihrer Liste diskutieren Rolf und Karin? Kreisen Sie die richtigen Antworten ein. Hören Sie sich dann das Gespräch nochmal an. Schreiben Sie jetzt die anderen Antworten in die Tabelle. Answers may vary slightly.

Name + Kosten	Anbieter	Beschreibung	andere Merkmale
1. Samsung Galaxy (235 Euro)	T-Mobile	silber	unbegrenztes Datenvolumen
2. Apple iPhone (450 Euro)	Vodafone	einfach zu benutzen	bis zu 8 Stunden Gesprächszeit
3. Doro PhoneEasy (129 Euro)	o2	rot	extra große Tasten
4. LG P700 (259 Euro)	E-Plus	dünn	Surf-Flatrate

Verständnis

Suggestion Point out to students that cell phone brand names are neuter: **das iPhone, das Samsung,** etc.

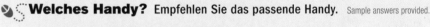Welches Handy? Empfehlen Sie das passende Handy. Sample answers provided.

1. Ich will lange telefonieren.
   Kauf dir das iPhone.

2. Ich brauche nur ein einfaches Telefon.
   Kauf dir das Doro.

3. Ich will ein dünnes Telefon.
   Kauf dir das LG.

4. Ich habe nicht viel Geld für ein Handy.
   Kauf dir das Doro.

5. Ich will ein Telefon, damit ich viel im Internet surfen kann.
   Kauf dir das LG.

6. Ich will ein Telefon, das nicht sehr kompliziert ist.
   Kauf dir das iPhone.

7. Ich will viele Videos sehen und viel Musik hören.
   Kauf dir das Samsung.

Das beste Telefon
Sie haben gehört, wie Rolf und Karin den Kauf eines neuen Handys diskutieren. Sprechen Sie mit einem Partner / einer Partnerin über die Vorteile der Handys. Entscheiden Sie, welches Handy das beste für Sie und Ihren Partner / Ihre Partnerin ist.

Suggestion Have students present their partner's preferences using **denn: Das LG ist am besten für meinen Partner, denn er surft viel im Internet mit seinem Handy.**

Expansion Use this listening activity as a lead-in to a discussion of the pros and cons of cell phones. Ask students how often they use their cell phones. Could they imagine giving up their phones? Do they ever see people use cell phones in a rude manner?

Schreiben

Strategien

Expressing and supporting opinions

Written reviews are one of the many kinds of writing that require you to state your opinions. In order to convince your reader to take your opinions seriously, it is important to support them as thoroughly as possible, using details, facts, examples, and other forms of evidence. In a car review, for example, readers will want details about size, speed, fuel consumption, comfort, extra features, etc.

It is easier to include details that support your opinions if you plan ahead. Before trying out a product or going to an event that you are planning to review, write a list of questions that your readers might ask. Decide which aspects of the experience you are going to rate, and list the details that will help you decide upon a rating. You can then organize these lists into a questionnaire and a rating sheet. Bring these with you to remind you of the kind of information you need to gather in order to support your opinions. Later, the information you wrote down will help you organize your review into logical categories. It can also provide the details and evidence you need to convince your readers of your opinions.

Suggestion Assign this writing task as homework. Give students clear guidelines for word count, typing expectations, deadline, etc., and remind them to include a brief introduction and conclusion. Mark up the first version they submit and have them rewrite the paper to turn in as a final draft.

Thema

Schreiben Sie einen Bericht

Schreiben Sie einen Bericht (*review*) über ein Auto. Nennen Sie zuerst den Namen des Autos und sprechen Sie dann die folgenden Kategorien an. Bilden Sie sich zum Schluss eine eigene Meinung. Ist das ein gutes Auto?

- **Beschreibung**
  Wie groß ist das Auto? Wie viel wiegt (*weighs*) das Auto? Was für einen Motor hat es? Wie viele Liter verbraucht es je 100 Kilometer? Wie viele Gänge (*gears*) hat es? Was ist die Höchstgeschwindigkeit (*top speed*)? Wie viel Platz (*room*) haben die Passagiere? Wie groß ist der Kofferraum?

- **Ausstattung**
  Welche Farbe hat das Auto? Wie sieht es im Innenraum aus? Hat es hinten ein Kamerasystem zum Ein- und Ausparken? Kann es automatisch parken? Wie viele Türen hat das Auto? Hat es ein Sonnenfenster? Ist es ein Kombi (*station wagon*)?

- **Fahrzeugtyp**
  Ist es ein Familienauto? Ist es ein Sportauto? Ist es ein Geländewagen (*SUV*)?

- **Andere Funktionen**
  Welche Art von Elektronik hat das Auto? Wie bequem ist das Auto? Hat das Auto ein gutes Image? Wie viel kostet das Auto? Ist das Auto umweltfreundlich (*environmentally friendly*)? Wie ist der Wiederverkaufswert (*resale value*) des Autos?

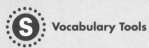 **Vocabulary Tools**

Auto fahren

die Autobahn, -en	highway
der Fahrer, - / die Fahrerin, -nen	driver
der Polizist, -en / die Polizistin, -nen	police officer
die Straße, -n	street
die Tankstelle, -n	gas station
der Verkehr	traffic
geradeaus fahren	to go straight ahead
einen Platten haben	to have a flat tire
einen Unfall haben	to have an accident
parken	to park
rechts/links abbiegen (biegt... ab)	to turn right/left

Auto

das Benzin	gas
die Bremse, -n	brakes
der Kofferraum, ¨e	trunk
das Lenkrad, ¨er	steering wheel
der Mechaniker, - / die Mechanikerin, -nen	mechanic
der Motor, -en	engine
die Motorhaube, -n	hood
das Nummernschild, -er	license plate
das Öl, -e	oil
der Scheibenwischer, -	windshield wiper
der Scheinwerfer, -	headlight
der Sicherheitsgurt, -e	seatbelt
die Windschutzscheibe, -n	windshield
reparieren	to repair
tanken	to fill up

die öffentlichen Verkehrsmittel

der Bahnsteig, -e	track; platform
die Bushaltestelle, -n	bus stop
der Fahrkartenschalter, -	ticket office
der Fahrplan, ¨e	schedule
das Bußgeld, -er	fine
die erste/zweite Klasse, -n	first/second class
der Schaffner, -	ticket collector
(die Fahrkarte) entwerten	to validate (a ticket)

Technik bedienen

anmachen (macht... an)	to turn on
aufnehmen (nimmt... auf)	to record
ausmachen (macht... aus)	to turn off
drucken	to print
fernsehen (sieht... fern)	to watch television
funktionieren	to work, to function
herunterladen (lädt... herunter)	to download
klingeln	to ring
laden (lädt)	to charge; to load
löschen	to delete
online sein	to be online
schicken	to send
speichern	to save
starten	to start
im Internet surfen	to surf the Web

das Verkehrsmittel

das Auto, -s	car
das Boot, -e	boat
der Bus, -se	bus
das Fahrrad, ¨er	bicycle
der LKW, -s	truck
das Schiff, -e	ship
das Taxi, -s	taxi
die U-Bahn, -en	subway
der Zug, ¨e	train

die Technik

der Benutzername, -n	screen name
der Bildschirm, -e	screen
die CD, -s	compact disc, CD
die Datei, -en	file
die Digitalkamera, -s	digital camera
das Dokument, -e	document
der Drucker, -	printer
die DVD, -s	DVD
der DVD-Player, -	DVD-player
die E-Mail, -s	e-mail
die Fernbedienung, -en	remote control
der Fernseher, -	television
die Festplatte, -n	hard drive
das Handy, -s	cell phone
der Kopfhörer, -	headphones
das Ladegerät, -e	battery charger
der Laptop, -s	laptop (computer)
die Maus, ¨e	mouse
das Mikrofon, -e	microphone
der MP3-Player, -	mp3 player
das Passwort, ¨er	password
das Programm, -e	program
der Sender, -	channel
das Smartphone, -s	smartphone
die SMS, -	text message
die Spielkonsole, -n	game console
die Stereoanlage, -n	stereo system
das Tablet, -s	tablet
die Tastatur, -en	keyboard
das Telefon, -e	telephone
die Website, -s	Web site

Das Plusquamperfekt	*See pp. 330–331.*
Comparatives and superlatives	*See pp. 334–335.*
The genitive case	*See pp. 348–349.*
Demonstratives	*See pp. 352–353.*

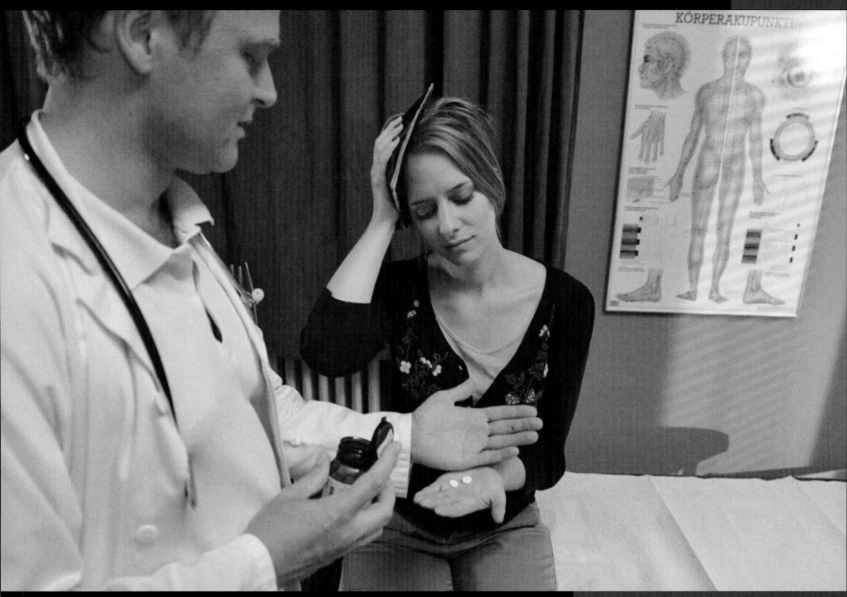

Gesundheit

Suggestion Ask students: **Wo ist Meline? Warum ist sie da? Wer ist der Mann neben ihr? Was macht er?**

Communicative Goals

You will learn how to:

- talk about morning routines
- discuss personal hygiene

Die Alltagsroutine

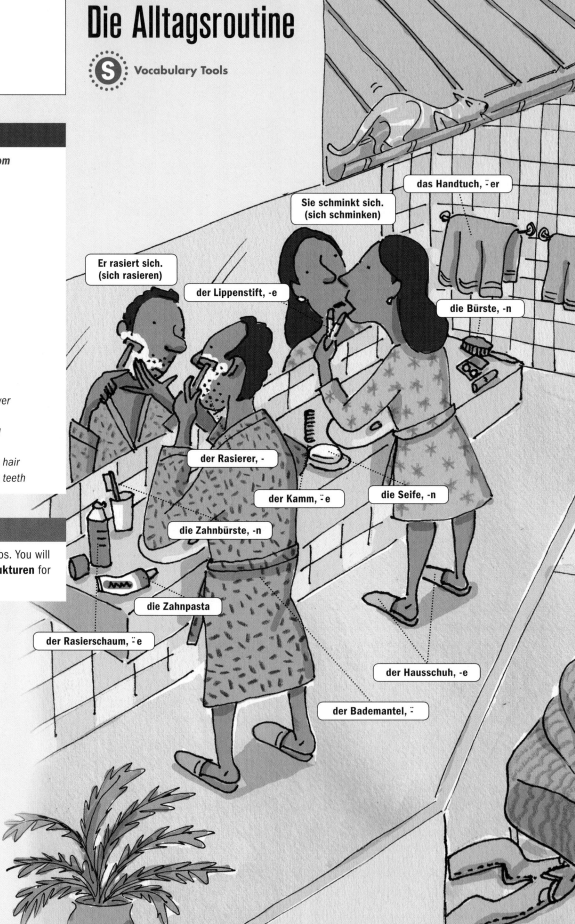

(S) Vocabulary Tools

Wortschatz

im Badezimmer	*in the bathroom*
der Haartrockner, -	hair dryer
das Shampoo, -s	shampoo
der Körper, -	*body*
die Augenbraue, -n	eyebrow
der Bart, ⁻e	beard
das Gesicht, -er	face
das Haar, -e	hair
die Hand, ⁻e	hand
die Lippe, -n	lip
der Rücken, -	back
die Schulter, -n	shoulder
Verben	*verbs*
aufwachen (wacht...auf)	to wake up
(sich) duschen	to take a shower
ins Bett gehen	to go to bed
sich anziehen (zieht sich...an)	to get dressed
sich die Haare bürsten	to brush one's hair
sich die Zähne putzen	to brush one's teeth

ACHTUNG

The pronoun **sich** is used with reflexive verbs. You will learn more about reflexive verbs in the **Strukturen** for this lesson.

Suggestion Remind students that they learned to use the verb **anziehen** without a reflexive pronoun in 5B. Ex.: **Ich ziehe das Hemd an. Er zieht die Jacke an.**

Picture labels:

das Handtuch, ⁻er

Sie schminkt sich. (sich schminken)

Er rasiert sich. (sich rasieren)

der Lippenstift, -e

die Bürste, -n

der Rasierer, -

der Kamm, ⁻e

die Seife, -n

die Zahnbürste, -n

die Zahnpasta

der Rasierschaum, ⁻e

der Hausschuh, -e

der Bademantel, ⁻

der Kopf, ⸚e
die Nase, -n
das Auge, -n
der Mund, ⸚er
das Ohr, -en
der Hals, ⸚e
der Arm, -e
der Finger, -
der Ell(en)bogen, -
der Bauch, ⸚e
der Schlafanzug, ⸚e
das Bein, -e
der Fuß, ⸚e
das Knie, -
der Zeh, -en

Anwendung

1 Was passt nicht? Welches Wort passt nicht zu den anderen?

BEISPIEL Bart, Mund, Lippe, (Rücken)

1 Expansion Ask students to explain why each word doesn't belong.

1. Ohr, (Bauch), Auge, Nase
2. Zahnbürste, Mundwasser, (Mineralwasser), Zahnpasta
3. (Handtuch), Schlafanzug, Nachthemd, Bademantel
4. duschen, schminken, rasieren, (anziehen)
5. Shampoo, Seife, (Haar), Duschgel
6. (Gesicht), Lippenstift, Mascara, Make-up
7. Haartrockner, (Rasierer), Bürste, Kamm
8. Bein, Fuß, Zeh, (Schulter)

2 Bild beschriften Wie heißen die verschiedenen Körperteile (*parts of the body*)?

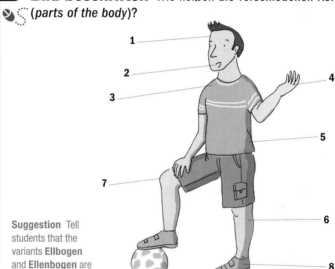

Suggestion Tell students that the variants **Ellbogen** and **Ellenbogen** are used interchangeably to refer to the elbow.

1.	der Kopf	5.	der Rücken
2.	der Mund	6.	das Bein
3.	die Schulter	7.	das Knie
4.	die Hand	8.	der Fuß

3 Paulas Morgenroutine 🎧 Hören Sie sich an, was Paula über ihre Morgenroutine erzählt. Bringen Sie danach ihre morgendlichen Aktivitäten in die richtige Reihenfolge.

1. _2_ Ich dusche mich.
2. _5_ Ich ziehe mich an.
3. _4_ Ich schminke mich.
4. _1_ Ich frühstücke.
5. _3_ Ich putze mir die Zähne.

3 Expansion Have students put the items in order according to their own morning routines.

Suggestion Call out the names of various body parts and have students point to each body part. Then move to "active recall" by pointing to a body part and asking: **Was ist das?**

 Practice more at **vhlcentral.com**.

Kommunikation

4 Was haben wir? Fragen Sie Ihren Partner / Ihre Partnerin, welche Badezimmer- und Kosmetikartikel er/sie besitzt und wie viele davon er/sie hat. Answers will vary.

▶ **BEISPIEL**

S1: Hast du einen Spiegel?
S2: Ja, ich habe einen. Wie viele Spiegel hast du?

4 Suggestion Quickly review the plural form of each noun by asking: **Was ist das? Und wenn ich zwei davon habe, wie heißt das denn?**

1.

2.

3.

4.

5.

6.

7.

8.

5 Diskutieren und kombinieren Sie und Ihr Partner / Ihre Partnerin bekommen zwei verschiedene Bilder der Außerirdischen (*extraterrestrials*) von Ihrem Professor / Ihrer Professorin. Finden Sie die sieben Unterschiede auf den Bildern.

BEISPIEL

S1: Wie viele Augen hat dein Außerirdischer?
S2: Mein Außerirdischer hat drei Augen.
S1: Aha. Mein Außerirdischer hat nur ein Auge.

6 So ein Saustall! Sie und Ihr Partner / Ihre Partnerin wollen mal wieder das Badezimmer sauber machen. Aber leider sind diverse Kosmetikartikel in der ganzen Wohnung verstreut (*scattered*). Fragen Sie Ihren Partner / Ihre Partnerin, wo Ihre Sachen sind. Answers will vary.

BEISPIEL

6 Suggestion Remind students to use the dative with two-way prepositions when describing location.

S1: Wo ist mein Rasierer?
S2: Den habe ich in der Küche neben der Spüle gesehen. Aber wo ist mein...

5 Expansion Model the pronunciation of **Außerirdischer**. Have students come up with a fictional profile for their aliens. Have them ask one another: **Wie heißt dein Außerirdischer? Woher kommt er? Was sind seine Hobbys?** etc.

7 Berühmte Leute Wählen Sie eine berühmte Person und schreiben Sie sechs Dinge über das Aussehen dieser Person. Lesen Sie Ihre Aussagen zwei Mitstudenten vor, die erraten müssen, von welcher Person Sie sprechen. Answers will vary.

BEISPIEL

S1: Er ist Spanier, 1,85 Meter groß, hat dunkle Augen und dunkelbraune Haare. Er ist Linkshänder und hat die schnellsten Beine auf dem Tennisplatz.
S2: Ist es Rafael Nadal?
S1: Ja, genau!

7 Suggestion Circulate around the class to make sure students stay on task and to offer vocabulary support.

Aussprache und Rechtschreibung Audio

🎧 Vocalic *r*

After a vowel, the German **r** often sounds more like a vowel than a consonant. When the syllable **er** occurs at the end of a word, it is pronounced with the *vocalic* **r** sound, similar to the letter *a* in the English word *sofa*.

Schulter	Pfleger	Schwester	guter	Badezimmer

....

The vocalic **r** also appears in unstressed prefixes, such as **er-**, **ver-** or **zer-**. In these prefixes, the sound of the **e** and the vocalic **r** are pronounced as separate sounds, blended together in a single syllable.

Verletzung	Erkältung	zerbrechen	verstauchen	erklären

....

The vocalic **r** also appears at the end of words after a long vowel sound. After a long **a** sound, the vowel and the vocalic **r** blend together. Otherwise, the long vowel and the vocalic **r** are pronounced as two separate sounds in a single syllable.

Ohr	vier	sehr	Haar	Bart

---

1 Aussprechen Wiederholen Sie die Wörter, die Sie hören.

1. Mutter	4. schwanger	7. zerstechen	10. schwer
2. Vater	5. verstopft	8. verstehen	11. hier
3. Rasierer	6. erkälten	9. Paar	12. Fahrt

2 Nachsprechen Wiederholen Sie die Sätze, die Sie hören.

1. Mir tut das rechte Ohr weh.
2. Die Krankenschwester und der Krankenpfleger suchen den Rasierer.
3. Mein kleiner Bruder hatte eine verstopfte Nase und Fieber.
4. Ohne Haar und ohne Bart friert man im Winter sehr.
5. Wie konnte Oliver mit dem verstauchten Fuß den 400-Meter-Lauf gewinnen?
6. Der erkältete Busfahrer hat eine lange Fahrt vor sich.

3 Sprichwörter Wiederholen Sie die Sprichwörter, die Sie hören.

> *Verbotene Früchte schmecken am besten.*[2]

> *Es ist alles in Butter.*[1]

[1] Everything is just great. (lit. *Everything is in butter.*)
[2] Forbidden fruit tastes the sweetest.

Ressourcen

SAM
LM: p. 76

vhlcentral.com

Fotoroman

Guten Morgen, Herr Professor!  Video

Meline schläft beim Lernen ein und hat einen interessanten Traum.
Er spielt in der Zukunft und wir begegnen einem guten Bekannten.

Vorbereitung Before showing students this
episode, draw their attention to the reflexive
verbs and other expressions used to talk about
daily routines. Explain that reflexive pronouns
always correspond to their subject pronouns.
Ex.: **ich - mich/mir, du - dich/dir**, etc.

MELINE Schatz... es ist Zeit, dass du
aufwachst und dich anziehst. Hase, ich habe
um halb zehn eine Besprechung. Du musst
dich für deinen ersten Unterrichtstag noch
duschen und rasieren. Du darfst nicht
zu spät kommen.

MELINE Da ist ja mein schöner Ehemann.
Guten Morgen, Herr Professor.
HANS Wie haben wir uns nur so
ineinander verliebt?
MELINE Tja, wahrscheinlich einfach
Glück gehabt.

SABITE Meline? Meline, ist alles in Ordnung?
MELINE Hans?
SABITE Meline? Meline, beweg dich nicht.
George? George!

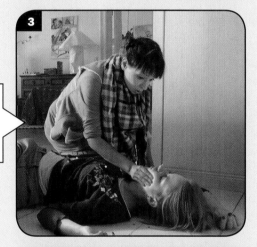

MELINE Ich erinnere mich, du warst noch
ein Junge. Dein Vater und ich – ist er
schon aufgewacht? – dein Vater und ich
haben uns diesen Tag immer vorgestellt.
Wir haben nur nicht gedacht, dass er
so schnell kommt. Heute machst du
deinen Universitätsabschluss.

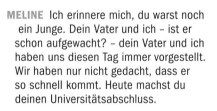

HANS Guten Morgen, mein Sohn.
WOLFGANG Paps.
HANS Mein Liebling.
WOLFGANG Mama, Paps, mir dreht sich der
Magen um. Hört bitte auf, euch zu küssen.

MELINE Eines Tages, Wolfgang, wirst du
erstaunt sein, wie es sich anfühlt, sich in
jemanden zu verlieben. Ach Hans, putz
dir die Zähne!
HANS Für dich tu ich doch alles, mein
Liebling. Dann dusche ich mich, rasiere
mich und wasche mir die Haare.

---

1 **Was fehlt?** Ergänzen Sie die Sätze mit den richtigen Informationen.

1. (Meline/ Hans) hat um halb zehn eine Besprechung.
2. Hans muss sich noch duschen und (schminken / rasieren).
3. Er darf nicht zu (früh / spät) kommen.
4. Meline begrüßt ihren schönen (Schwiegervater / Ehemann).
5. In Melines Traum ist Hans (Professor/ Ingenieur).
6. Wolfgang macht heute seinen (Universitätsabschluss/ Urlaub).

7. Nach dem Frühstück geht Hans sich duschen, rasieren und die
(Haare/ Füße) waschen.
8. Als Meline aufwacht, liegt sie auf dem (Sofa / Boden).
9. Im Traum hat Meline gesagt, dass sie Hans (liebt/ heiratet).
10. Sabite und George wollen Meline zum (Friseur/ Arzt) bringen.

PERSONEN

 George

 Hans

 Meline

 Sabite

 Wolfgang

HANS Heute ist ein besonderer Tag. Genießen wir ihn.

MELINE Besonderer Tag. Hans, ich liebe dich. Hans?
GEORGE Meline! Wach auf, Meline.
MELINE Hans?
GEORGE Ich bin's, George.

MELINE Oh, mein Kopf. Was ist passiert? Warum bin ich am Boden?
GEORGE Okay, Meline. Jetzt ganz langsam. Versuche, aufzustehen.

SABITE Sollen wir Hans holen?
MELINE Was? Nein. Warum wollt ihr ihn holen?
GEORGE Ähm, du hast gesagt, du liebst ihn.
MELINE Das ist nicht lustig. Jetzt wird mir erst recht schlecht.
SABITE Komm, wir bringen dich zum Arzt.

Nützliche Ausdrücke

- **Besprechung**
  meeting
- **Du darfst nicht zu spät kommen.**
  You don't want to be late.
- **Meline, beweg dich nicht.**
  Meline, don't move.
- **sich erinnern**
  to remember
- **sich vorstellen**
  to imagine
- **Mama, Paps, mir dreht sich der Magen um.**
  Mom, Dad, my stomach is churning.
- **Hört bitte auf, euch zu küssen.**
  Please stop kissing each other.
- **Eines Tages, Wolfgang, wirst du erstaunt sein, wie es sich anfühlt, sich in jemanden zu verlieben.**
  One day, Wolfgang, you will be amazed at what it feels like to fall in love with someone.
- **Heute ist ein besonderer Tag.**
  Today is a special day.
- **der Arzt**
  doctor

9A.1
- **Du musst dich für deinen ersten Unterrichtstag noch duschen und rasieren.**
  You need to shower and shave for your first day of classes.

9A.2
- **Ach Hans, putz dir die Zähne!**
  Oh, Hans, brush your teeth!

9A.3
- **Wie haben wir uns nur so ineinander verliebt?**
  How did we get to be so in love with each other?

---

2 Zum Besprechen Wählen Sie zu zweit eine Person aus dem Fotoroman und beschreiben Sie seinen/ihren Morgen im Badezimmer. Benutzen Sie Informationen dieser Episode und Ihre Fantasie. Answers will vary.

2 Suggestion Before students begin this activity, ask them to brainstorm words and expressions used to talk about daily routines. Write these suggestions on the board for reference.

3 Vertiefung Im Deutschen gibt es viele Sprichwörter, die sich auf den Körper beziehen (*refer to*), zum Beispiel „Das geht mir nicht aus dem Kopf" (*It's always on my mind*). Finden Sie drei Sprichwörter mit Wörtern aus dieser Lektion. Answers will vary.

3 Suggestion Encourage students to share their selected proverbs. As a class, discuss the meaning of each proverb.

Ressourcen

 SAM VM: p. 17

 vhlcentral.com

IM FOKUS

Die Kur°  Reading

Suggestion Read the first sentence out loud as a class and have students guess what a **Kurort** might be. Explain that in Germany, health spas are very common, and prescribing a long **Kur** is a fairly standard medical practice.

Suggestion Tell students that the designation **Bad** typically indicates that a location has natural hotsprings and was the site of ancient Roman baths.

IN DEUTSCHLAND GIBT ES UNGEFÄHR 300 Kurorte. An diesen Orten können Patienten sich erholen°. Nach einem schweren Unfall, bei psychischer Erschöpfung° oder wegen schwerer gesundheitlicher Probleme brauchen Patienten oft längere Pflege°: Kuraufenthalte° dauern normalerweise zwischen drei und sechs Wochen. Deutsche Krankenkassen° bezahlen einen großen Teil dieser Kurbesuche.

Kurorte in Deutschland bieten saubere Luft° und viel Ruhe°, damit Patienten sich auf ihre Gesundheit konzentrieren können. Patienten sollen in einer Kur physisch fit werden, indem sie wandern, schwimmen oder Rad fahren. Patienten sollen auch lernen, ihr Leben gesünder zu gestalten: Was kann man anders machen, damit man nicht wieder krank wird?

Einige der berühmtesten Kurorte in Deutschland sind Oberstdorf (Bayern), Bad Wörishofen (Bayern), Baden-Baden (Baden-Württemberg) und Westerland (Schleswig-Holstein). Oberstdorf liegt im Allgäu und ist die südlichste Gemeinde Deutschlands. Die Luft ist so klar, dass Patienten mit Allergien hier wenige Probleme haben. Hier hat man auch fantastische Wintersportmöglichkeiten. Das bayerische Bad Wörishofen im Allgäu ist berühmt wegen Sebastian Kneipp (1821–1897), einem katholischen Priester, der hier die Kneipp-Kur erfand. Teil der Kur ist Wassertreten° in einem kalten Wasserbad.

Baden-Baden liegt im Schwarzwald in der Nähe von Karlsruhe. Es ist bekannt für seine Thermalquellen°. Die Römer° haben die Stadt bereits im Jahr 80 nach Christus gegründet. Westerland liegt auf der Insel Sylt. Es ist ein sehr bekanntes Seeheilbad. Für Patienten ist die Nähe zur Nordsee und die Faszination des Wattenmeers interessant.

Anzahl an Kurorten pro Bundesland	
Baden-Württemberg – 56	Nordrhein-Westfalen – 34
Bayern – 53	Rheinland-Pfalz – 21
Brandenburg – 8	Saarland – 4
Hessen – 31	Sachsen – 11
Mecklenburg-Vorpommern – 30	Sachsen-Anhalt – 5
	Schleswig-Holstein – 45
Niedersachsen – 46	Thüringen – 16

QUELLE: Portal Bäderland Deutschland

Kur *health spa treatment* **sich erholen** *recover* **Erschöpfung** *exhaustion* **Pflege** *care* **Kuraufenthalte** *spa visits* **Krankenkassen** *health insurance* **Luft** *air* **Ruhe** *quiet* **Wassertreten** *treading water* **Thermalquellen** *hot springs* **Römer** *Romans*

1 **Richtig oder falsch?** Sagen Sie, ob die Sätze richtig oder falsch sind. Korrigieren Sie die falschen Sätze.

1. An etwa 300 Orten kann man in Deutschland eine Kur machen. Richtig.
2. Eine Kur dauert zwischen drei und sechs Wochen. Richtig.
3. Patienten müssen selber für eine Kur bezahlen.
   Falsch. Deutsche Krankenkassen bezahlen einen Teil einer Kur.
4. Kurorte bieten Patienten Ruhe und saubere Luft. Richtig.
5. In Bad Wörishofen wurde die Kneipp-Kur erfunden. Richtig.

6. In Oberstdorf ist das Klima so gut, dass Patienten wenige Probleme mit Allergien haben. Richtig.
7. Baden-Baden liegt in Baden-Württemberg. Richtig.
8. Westerland ist ein Seeheilbad in der Ostsee.
   Falsch. Westerland liegt auf Sylt in der Nordsee.
9. Die meisten Kurorte gibt es in Bayern.
   Falsch. Die meisten Kurorte gibt es in Baden-Württemberg.
10. Viele Kurorte gibt es im Saarland.
    Falsch. Die wenigsten Kurorte gibt es im Saarland.

 Practice more at **vhlcentral.com**.

Ausdrücke mit Körperteilen

Hand und Fuß haben	to make sense
jemandem ins Auge springen	to catch somebody's eye
sich die Augen aus dem Kopf weinen	to cry one's eyes out
Hals- und Beinbruch!	Break a leg!
Hand aufs Herz!	Cross my heart!

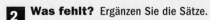

Öffentliche Schwimmbäder

Das erste öffentliche Schwimmbad° in Deutschland wurde 1860 in Marburg eröffnet. Heute gibt es viele verschiede Arten von Schwimmbädern. Fast jede deutsche Stadt besitzt ein Freibad, das an warmen Sommertagen normalerweise voll ist. Dann gibt es auch noch Hallenbäder°, wo man das ganze Jahr über baden kann. Schwimmbäder mit moderneren Anlagen° wie Wellenbad°, Rutschen° und Saunen heißen entweder Spaßbad oder Erlebnisbad. Entlang der Meeresküsten gibt es Strandbäder, wo man in Meerwasser schwimmt, aber auch Flüsse und Seen, besonders Baggerseen°, sind sehr beliebt.

Schwimmbad *swimming pool* **Hallenbäder** *indoor swimming pools* **Anlagen** *facilities* **Wellenbad** *wave pool* **Rutschen** *slides* **Baggerseen** *quarry ponds*

Nivea

Suggestion Ask students if they use any Nivea products. Tell them that Germany's cosmetics industry is the third largest in the world, after the U.S. and Japan.

Die Marke Nivea gibt es schon seit 1911. Sie ist Teil der deutschen Firma Beiersdorf. Ihr bekanntestes Produkt ist die Nivea Hautcreme°. Seit 1925 verkauft Nivea diese Hautcreme in der bekannten, blauen Dose°. Neben der traditionellen weißen Hautcreme gibt es heute auch viele andere Produkte, zum Beispiel Cremes für Babys, Rasiercremes, Aftershaves und verschiedene Sonnenschutzmittel°. Wichtig ist auch, dass bei der Entwicklung und Produktion von Nivea Produkten keine Tierversuche° gemacht werden. Heute kann man Nivea auf allen Kontinenten und in fast allen Ländern kaufen.

Hautcreme *skin cream* **Dose** *jar* **Sonnenschutzmittel** *sunscreen* **Tierversuche** *animal testing*

⛛⒮ IM INTERNET

Suchen Sie im Internet den Katalog eines öffentlichen Schwimmbads. Was kann man hier alles machen? Wie viel kostet der Eintritt?

Find out more at **vhlcentral.com**.

---

2 **Was fehlt?** Ergänzen Sie die Sätze.

1. In Magdeburg wurde das erste deutsche Schwimmbad ___1860___ eröffnet.
2. Ein ___Freibad/ Schwimmbad___ hat fast jede deutsche Stadt.
3. ___Strandbäder___ gibt es entlang der Meeresküsten.
4. Die Marke Nivea gibt es seit ___1911___.
5. Die Nivea Hautcreme kommt in einer blauen ___Dose___.
6. Für Nivea-Produkte finden keine ___Tierversuche___ statt.

3 **Ein Kurbesuch** Planen Sie mit einem Partner / einer Partnerin einen Besuch bei einer Kur. Was machen Sie jeden Tag? Was essen und trinken Sie? Was machen Sie in Ihrer Freizeit?

9A.1

Reflexive verbs with accusative reflexive pronouns

 **Presentation**

Startblock A reflexive verb indicates an action you do to yourself or for yourself. The subject of a reflexive verb is also its object.

Du musst **dich** zum ersten Unterrichtstag **duschen** und **rasieren**.

Ich **erinnere mich**, du warst noch ein Junge.

- Reflexive verbs always use reflexive pronouns. When the subject of a reflexive verb is also its direct object, it takes an accusative reflexive pronoun.

personal pronouns						
nominative	ich	du	er/sie/es	wir	ihr	Sie/sie
accusative reflexive	mich	dich	sich	uns	euch	sich

ACHTUNG

The accusative reflexive pronouns are the same as the accusative personal pronouns, except that all of the third person pronouns and **Sie** are replaced by **sich**. Note that **sich** is never capitalized, even when it refers to **Sie**.

Suggestion Ask students: "If my subject is **ich**, what reflexive pronoun will I use?" etc.

- When a reflexive verb is conjugated, the verb and the reflexive pronoun must both agree with the subject. In the infinitive, reflexive verbs are always listed with the third person reflexive pronoun.

sich rasieren	
ich rasiere mich	wir rasieren uns
du rasierst dich	ihr rasiert euch
er/sie/es rasiert sich	Sie/sie rasieren sich

- Some verbs can be used both non-reflexively and reflexively. Note that certain verbs have a change in meaning when they are used reflexively.

ACHTUNG

Verbs that are reflexive in German do not always have reflexive equivalents in English: **Ich frage mich, wo meine Schlüssel sind.** *I wonder where my keys are.*

Suggestion Note that students will learn to use **sich (etwas) vorstellen** to mean *to imagine (something)* in **9A.2**.

non-reflexive verbs		reflexive verbs	
anziehen	*to put on*	sich anziehen	*to get dressed*
legen	*to put; to lay*	sich (hin)legen	*to lie down*
setzen	*to put; to set*	sich (hin)setzen	*to sit down*
fragen	*to ask*	sich fragen	*to wonder, ask oneself*
vorstellen	*to introduce*	sich vorstellen	*to introduce oneself*
umziehen	*to move*	sich umziehen	*to change clothes*
waschen	*to wash (something)*	sich waschen	*to wash (oneself)*

Ich **ziehe** den Mantel **an**.
I'm putting on my coat.

Ich **ziehe mich an**.
I'm getting dressed.

- A number of verbs related to daily routines, personal hygiene, and health take an accusative reflexive pronoun.

common reflexive verbs			
sich abtrocknen	*to dry oneself off*	sich entspannen	*to relax*
sich ausruhen	*to rest*	sich erkälten	*to catch a cold*
sich ausziehen	*to get undressed*	sich (wohl) fühlen	*to feel (well)*
(sich) baden	*to bathe, take a bath*	sich rasieren	*to shave*
sich beeilen	*to hurry*	sich schminken	*to put on makeup*
(sich) duschen	*to take a shower*	sich verspäten	*to be late*

Ich **fühle mich** nicht **wohl**.
I don't feel well.

Wir **haben uns** am Wochenende **entspannt**.
We relaxed this weekend.

- When the subject is the first word in a sentence, put the reflexive pronoun after the conjugated verb. When the verb and subject are inverted, put the reflexive pronoun after the subject.

Klara schminkt **sich** jeden Morgen.
Klara puts on makeup every morning.

Heute Morgen schminkt sie **sich** nicht.
She's not putting on makeup this morning.

Ziehst du **dich** an?
Are you getting dressed?

Setzen Sie **sich**, bitte!
Please be seated.

- In informal imperatives, since the pronoun **du** or **ihr** is dropped, the reflexive pronoun comes immediately after the verb.

Zieh **dich** bitte an!
Get dressed, please.

Setzt **euch**, bitte!
Please sit down.

- When the conjugated verb is a modal, the reflexive pronoun comes immediately after the modal, or immediately after the subject, if the word order is inverted.

Wir müssen **uns** beeilen.
We need to hurry up.

Möchtet ihr **euch** hier setzen?
Would you like to sit here?

- Use the auxiliary verb **haben** with reflexive verbs in the **Perfekt** and **Plusquamperfekt**.

Ich **habe mich** heute Morgen **rasiert**.
I shaved this morning.

Wir **hatten uns** schon **geduscht**.
We had already showered.

Suggestion Emphasize the point that *any* verb used reflexively takes **haben** in the perfect and the past perfect.

ACHTUNG

The verbs **baden** and **duschen** can also be used non-reflexively, with no difference in meaning: **Ich dusche jeden Morgen**.

Expansion Have students work in pairs to write a short text about getting ready for an evening out, using common reflexive verbs.

QUERVERWEIS

See **3B.3** to review the formation of imperatives.

See **3B.1** to review the use of modals.

See **5A.1** to review the **Perfekt** with **haben**.

See **8A.1** to review the **Plusquamperfekt**.

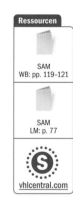

Ressourcen

SAM
WB: pp. 119–121

SAM
LM: p. 77

vhlcentral.com

Jetzt sind Sie dran! Ergänzen Sie die Tabelle mit den fehlenden Formen.

		sich fragen	sich beeilen	sich ausziehen
1.	ich	ich frage mich	*ich beeile mich*	*ich ziehe mich aus*
2.	du	du fragst dich	du beeilst dich	du ziehst dich aus
3.	er/sie	er fragt sich	er beeilt sich	er zieht sich aus
4.	wir	wir fragen uns	wir beeilen uns	wir ziehen uns aus
5.	ihr	ihr fragt euch	ihr beeilt euch	ihr zieht euch aus
6.	sie	sie fragen sich	sie beeilen sich	sie ziehen sich aus
7.	Sie	Sie fragen sich	Sie beeilen sich	Sie ziehen sich aus

Anwendung

1 Suggestion You may wish to provide a context for this activity. Ex.: **Es ist Montag um 6 Uhr 30, und die Familie Bauer ist gerade aufgestanden. Wie bereiten sich alle auf den Tag vor?**

1 **Reflexive Verben** Ergänzen Sie die Sätze mit den richtigen Reflexivformen der Verben in Klammern.

1. Birgit ist müde und __legt sich__ (sich legen) aufs Sofa.

2. Wie __fühlen__ Sie __sich__ (sich fühlen) heute, Frau Neumann?

3. Bei dem schlechten Wetter __erkälten sich__ (sich erkälten) manche Leute.

4. __Beeil dich__ (sich beeilen)! Du musst vor 17 Uhr noch einkaufen.

5. Torsten __duscht sich__ (sich duschen) schnell.

6. Ich __schminke mich__ (sich schminken) nur, wenn ich ausgehe.

7. Jana! Erik! __Setzt euch__ (sich setzen) hier zu uns an den Tisch!

8. Wir __fragen uns__ (sich fragen), wie das passieren konnte.

2 **Sätze bilden** Bilden Sie Sätze und achten Sie dabei auf die Wortstellung. Answers may vary. Sample answers provided.

BEISPIEL Zuerst / Herr Bauer / sich duschen
Zuerst duscht sich Herr Bauer.

1. Danach / er / sich rasieren / langsam
Danach rasiert er sich langsam.

2. Seine Frau / sich schminken / vor dem Spiegel
Seine Frau schminkt sich vor dem Spiegel.

3. Dann / sie / sich umziehen / schnell
Dann zieht sie sich schnell um.

4. Die Kinder / sich anziehen / für die Schule
Die Kinder ziehen sich für die Schule an.

5. Heute / alle in der Familie / sich verspäten
Heute verspäten sich alle in der Familie.

6. Später / der Hund / sich legen / auf das Bett
Später legt sich der Hund auf das Bett.

3 Suggestion To verify comprehension, ask students: **Hat Claudia den Job bekommen? Warum nicht?**

3 **Ein schlechter Tag** Gestern hat Claudia einen sehr schlechten Tag gehabt. Schreiben Sie ihre Geschichte ins Perfekt um.

BEISPIEL Claudia steht erst um halb zehn auf.
Sie fühlt sich nicht wohl.
Claudia ist erst um halb zehn aufgestanden.
Sie hat sich nicht wohl gefühlt.

1. Sie duscht sich, und dann schminkt sie sich. Sie hat sich geduscht, und dann hat sie sich geschminkt.

2. Sie zieht sich schön an. Sie hat sich schön angezogen.

3. Sie beeilt sich, zur U-Bahn zu kommen. Sie hat sich beeilt, zur U-Bahn zu kommen.

4. Um 10.15 Uhr stellt sie sich bei der Firma *Werner Elektronik* vor.
Um 10.15 Uhr hat sie sich bei der Firma *Werner Elektronik* vorgestellt.

5. Sie verspätet sich, und deshalb (*for that reason*) bekommt sie den Job nicht.
Sie hat/hatte sich verspätet, und deshalb hat sie den Job nicht bekommen.

6. Sie geht traurig nach Hause, und dann legt sie sich aufs Sofa.
Sie ist traurig nach Hause gegangen, und dann hat sie sich aufs Sofa gelegt.

 Practice more at **vhlcentral.com.**

Kommunikation

4 **Bilder beschreiben** Beschreiben Sie mit einem Partner / einer Partnerin, was die Personen auf den Bildern gerade machen. Benutzen Sie reflexive Verben. Sample answers are provided.

▶ **BEISPIEL**
Er zieht sich an.

1.
Er duscht sich.

2.
Das Kind wäscht sich.

3.
Sie schminkt sich.

4.
Er rasiert sich.

5.
Sie legt sich hin.

6.
Er beeilt sich.

5 **Pantomimen** Sie spielen eine Tätigkeit (*activity*) aus der Liste vor und Ihre zwei Mitstudenten erraten, was Sie vorgespielt haben (*mimed*). Wechseln Sie sich ab. Answers will vary.

BEISPIEL
S1: (spielt „sich rasieren" vor)
S2: Du hast dich rasiert!

sich abtrocknen	sich umziehen
sich erkälten	sich vorstellen
sich hinsetzen	sich (nicht) wohl fühlen
sich rasieren	

6 **Machst du das?** Fragen Sie Ihre Mitstudenten, ob (*whether*) sie diese Sachen machen. Finden Sie für jede Frage eine Person, die das macht. Answers will vary.

BEISPIEL
S1: Verspätest du dich oft?
S2: Nein, ich verspäte mich nie!
S3: Ja, ich verspäte mich immer am Montagmorgen.

Tätigkeiten	Name
sich oft verspäten	
sich vor einer Prüfung entspannen	
sich zweimal am Tag duschen	
sich nachmittags hinlegen	
sich am Abend duschen	
sich im Winter immer erkälten	

7 **Was soll ich machen?** Geben Sie Ihrem Partner / Ihrer Partnerin Ratschläge (*advice*) für seine/ihre Probleme. Wechseln Sie sich ab. Answers will vary.

BEISPIEL
S1: Ich fühle mich so schmutzig!
S2: Du musst dich duschen.

Die Probleme:

1. Ich bin sehr müde.
2. Ich kenne meinen Kommilitonen nicht und möchte mit ihm sprechen.
3. Ich habe in fünf Minuten ein Seminar und muss mich noch anziehen.
4. Ich habe beim Essen mein neues T-Shirt verschmutzt.

4 **Suggestion** You may want to do this activity as a class. Ask: **Was macht der Mann? Was macht das Kind?** etc.

5 **Suggestion** Act out a few reflexive verbs yourself, such as **sich kämmen** or **sich anziehen.** Ask: **Was habe ich gerade gemacht?**

6 **Suggestion** Formulate the questions together before students begin circulating.

9A.2

Reflexive verbs with dative reflexive pronouns

 **Presentation**

Startblock In **9A.1**, you learned that when the subject of a reflexive verb is also its direct object, it takes an accusative reflexive pronoun. When the subject of a reflexive verb is not its direct object, it takes a dative reflexive pronoun.

Dann dusche ich mich, rasiere ich mich und **wasche mir** die Haare.

Ach Hans, **putz dir** die Zähne!

- The dative reflexive pronouns are the same as the dative personal pronouns, except that all of the third person pronouns and the formal **Sie** are replaced by **sich**. Remember that the pronoun **sich** is never capitalized, even when it refers to the formal **Sie**.

personal pronouns						
nominative	ich	du	er/sie/es	wir	ihr	Sie/sie
accusative reflexive	mich	dich	sich	uns	euch	sich
dative reflexive	mir	dir	sich	uns	euch	sich

- Many verbs take an accusative reflexive pronoun when used on their own but a dative reflexive pronoun when used with a different direct object.

reflexive verbs used with direct objects	
sich (die Hände) abtrocknen	*to dry (one's hands)*
sich (eine Jacke) anziehen	*to put on (a jacket)*
sich (einen Mantel) ausziehen	*to take off (a coat)*
sich die Haare bürsten	*to brush one's hair*
sich die Haare färben	*to dye one's hair*
sich die Haare kämmen	*to comb one's hair*
sich die Zähne putzen	*to brush one's teeth*
sich (die Beine) rasieren	*to shave (one's legs)*
sich (die Augen) schminken	*to put on (eye) makeup*
sich (das Gesicht) waschen	*to wash (one's face)*
sich etwas vorstellen	*to imagine something (for oneself)*
sich etwas wünschen	*to wish for something (for oneself)*

Ich wasche **mich**.
I'm washing (myself).

Ich wasche **mir** das Gesicht.
I'm washing my face.

- Note that the meaning of the verb **sich vorstellen** changes when it is used with a direct object and a dative reflexive pronoun.

Hast du **dich** vorgestellt?
Did you introduce yourself?

Kannst du **dir** das vorstellen?
Can you imagine that?

- To refer to a part of the body or a particular piece of clothing after a reflexive verb in German, use a definite article where you would use a possessive adjective in English.

Ela putzt sich **die** Zähne.
*Ela is brushing **her** teeth.*

Habt ihr euch **die** Haare gebürstet?
*Did you brush **your** hair?*

Ich ziehe mir **den** Mantel aus.
*I'm taking off **my** coat.*

Zieh dir **die** Schuhe schnell an!
*Put **your** shoes on quickly!*

- Some verbs can be used reflexively to emphasize that the subject of the verb is also its indirect object.

Ich **bestelle (mir)** einen Kaffee.
I'm ordering (myself) a coffee.

Hast du **(dir)** eine Jacke **gekauft**?
Did you buy (yourself) a jacket?

- If the direct object is a *noun*, put the dative reflexive pronoun before it. If the direct object is a *pronoun*, put the dative reflexive pronoun after it.

Machst du **dir** eine Tasse Tee?
*Are you making (**yourself**) a cup of tea?*

Ja, ich habe sie **mir** schon gemacht.
*Yes, I've already made it (**for myself**).*

- In a sentence with more than one object, the dative object comes before the accusative object. However, when one object is a pronoun, the pronoun comes first. If there are two pronouns, the accusative pronoun comes before the dative.

Ich kaufe **meiner Schwester einen Hund**.
*I'm buying **my sister a dog**.*

Ich kaufe **ihn meiner Schwester**.
*I'm buying **it for my sister**.*

Ich kaufe **ihr** einen Hund.
*I'm buying **her** a dog.*

Ich kaufe **ihn ihr**.
*I'm buying **it for her**.*

Suggestion You may want to translate these phrases literally into English, to humorously emphasize the pattern. Ex: *She brushes herself the teeth. Did you brush yourself the hair?*

ACHTUNG

When the verbs **anziehen** and **ausziehen** are used with a direct object, the reflexive pronoun is optional: **Zieh (dir) die Schuhe aus!**

QUERVERWEIS

See **4B.1** for a note on word order with dative and accusative objects.

Suggestion You may want to translate these phrases literally into English, to humorously emphasize the pattern. Ex: *She brushes herself the teeth. Did you brush yourself the hair?*

Ressourcen

SAM
WB: 121-122

SAM
LM: p. 78

S
vhlcentral.com

Jetzt sind Sie dran!   **Ergänzen Sie die Sätze mit den richtigen Reflexivpronomen.**

1. Niklas kauft (sich / ihm) ein Sandwich.
2. Hast du (dich / dir) einen Salat gemacht?
3. Wir haben (euch / uns) ein kleines Auto gemietet.
4. Max und Lara haben (sich / ihnen) eine Pizza bestellt.
5. Nina wünscht (sich / ihm) eine Spielkonsole zum Geburtstag.
6. Ich backe (mich / mir) einen Schokoladenkuchen.

Anwendung

1 Suggestion Do the first few items as a class to verify that students understand the pattern.

1 **Körperteile und Kleidung** Bilden Sie Sätze mit den reflexiven Verben in Klammern. Achten Sie (*Pay attention*) auf die Artikel!

> **BEISPIEL** ihre Beine (sich rasieren)
> Jasmin *rasiert sich die Beine* .

1. meine Nase (sich putzen)
Ich ___putze mir die Nase___ .

2. deine Hände (sich abtrocknen)
Du ___trocknest dir die Hände ab___ .

3. seine Uniform (sich anziehen)
Julius ___zieht sich die Uniform an___ .

4. eure Füße (sich waschen)
Ihr ___wascht euch die Füße___ .

5. deine Jacke (sich ausziehen)
Du ___ziehst dir die Jacke aus___ .

6. meine Handschuhe (sich anziehen)
Ich ___ziehe mir die Handschuhe an___ .

2 **Was machen sie?** Schreiben Sie die Sätze um.

> **BEISPIEL** Putzt du dir die Zähne? (ihr)
> *Putzt ihr euch die Zähne?*

1. Kauft David sich neue Hausschuhe? (du)
Kaufst du dir neue Hausschuhe?

2. Sie machen sich eine Tasse Tee. (ich)
Ich mache mir eine Tasse Tee.

3. Hat Anna sich die Haare gefärbt? (du)
Hast du dir die Haare gefärbt?

4. Ich bestelle mir etwas zu trinken. (Ben und Lisa)
Ben und Lisa bestellen sich etwas zu trinken.

5. Stell dir das vor! (Sie)
Stellen Sie sich das vor!

3 **Sätze mit Dativ** Schreiben Sie zu jedem Bild einen Satz. Benutzen sie ein reflexives Verb mit einem Reflexivpronomen im Dativ. Sample answers are provided.

> **BEISPIEL**
> Lina
> *Lina schminkt sich den Mund.*

1. Fabian
Fabian rasiert sich das Gesicht.

2. du
Du wäschst dir die Haare.

3. wir
Wir waschen uns das Gesicht.

4. Nils
Nils bürstet sich die Haare.

5. ich
Ich putze mir die Zähne.

Kommunikation

4 **Was macht man damit?** Ihr kleiner Bruder möchte wissen, was man mit den Sachen unten macht. Schreiben Sie gemeinsam einen Dialog. Answers will vary.

BEISPIEL Haartrockner
S1: Was ist das?
S2: Das ist ein Haartrockner.
S1: Und was machst du damit?
S2: Damit trockne ich mir die Haare.

1. ein Lippenstift
2. ein Rasierer
3. ein Kamm
4. eine Zahnbürste
5. Shampoo
6. eine Kaffeemaschine

4 **Suggestion** Have students act out their dialogues for the class.

5 **Und nun?** Ihr Partner / Ihre Partnerin hat Probleme. Helfen Sie ihm/ihr mit guten Ratschlägen (*advice*). Benutzen Sie den Imperativ und wechseln Sie sich ab. Answers will vary.

BEISPIEL

S1: Ich habe kalte Hände.
S2: Zieh dir doch Handschuhe an!

1. Meine Füße sind sehr schmutzig.
2. Meine Haare hängen mir ins Gesicht.
3. Ich habe so einen Hunger!
4. Mir ist kalt.

> sich die Füße waschen
> sich die Haare kämmen
> sich einen Pullover anziehen
> sich etwas zu essen machen

6 **Wann machst du das?** Fragen Sie Ihren Partner / Ihre Partnerin, wann oder wie oft er/sie diese Dinge macht. Answers will vary.

BEISPIEL
S1: Wann wäschst du dir die Haare?
S2: Ich wasche mir jeden zweiten Tag die Haare.

> jeden Tag/Morgen/Abend | wenn ich Lust habe
> ein/zwei Mal am Tag | jeden zweiten Tag
> vor/nach dem Essen | wenn ich kalte Füße habe
> nie | bevor ich ins Bett gehe

1. sich die Haare waschen
2. sich die Zähne putzen
3. sich etwas zu essen machen
4. sich die Hände waschen
5. sich die Haare föhnen
6. sich Hausschuhe anziehen

7 **Gewonnen** Sie haben 500.000 Dollar gewonnen! Sagen Sie, was Sie sich zuerst kaufen, und dann fragen Sie Ihre Mitstudenten, was sie sich kaufen wollen. Answers will vary.

BEISPIEL
S1: Ich kaufe mir ein großes Boot. Und was kaufst du dir, Tim?
S2: Ich kaufe mir ein Flugticket nach Sydney. Was kaufst du dir, Sophie?
S3: Ich gehe ins Restaurant und bestelle mir...

7 **Suggestion** Circulate and provide vocabulary help, if needed. Set a time limit for this activity. As a follow-up, have students share answers, using the 3rd person. Ex.: **Sophie kauft sich einen Roboter.**

9A.3 **Reciprocal verbs and reflexives used with prepositions**

 **Presentation**

Startblock Reciprocal verbs express an action done by two or more people or things to or for one another.

> Hört bitte auf, **euch** zu **küssen**.

> Torsten und ich **haben uns gestritten**.

Reciprocal verbs

- Because reciprocal verbs refer to more than one person, they are only used with the plural reflexive pronouns **uns**, **euch**, and **sich**.

Wir rufen **uns** jeden Tag an.
*We call **each other** every day.*

Meine Großeltern lieben **sich** sehr.
*My grandparents love **each other** very much.*

Woher kennt **ihr euch**?
*How do **you** know **each other**?*

Sie schrieben **sich** zweimal im Monat.
*They wrote to **one another** twice a month.*

- Here are some common verbs with reciprocal meanings.

common reciprocal verbs	
sich anrufen	*to call each other*
sich kennen	*to know each other*
sich kennen lernen	*to meet (each other) for the first time*
sich küssen	*to kiss (each other)*
sich lieben	*to love each other*
sich schreiben	*to write to one another*
sich streiten	*to argue (with one another)*
sich trennen	*to separate, split up*
sich treffen	*to meet up*
sich unterhalten	*to chat, have a conversation*
sich verlieben	*to fall in love (with one another)*

Wir **kennen uns** schon seit Jahren.
*We've **known each other** for years.*

Habt ihr **euch** gestern **gestritten**?
*Did you **argue (with each other)** yesterday?*

Unsere Eltern **haben sich** vor fünfundzwanzig Jahren **verliebt**.
*Our parents **fell in love** twenty-five years ago.*

Die Studenten **treffen sich** gern im Restaurant, um **sich zu unterhalten**.
*Students like to **meet (each other)** at the restaurant **to talk (with one another)**.*

- In some cases, it may be unclear whether a verb is being used reflexively or reciprocally. To clarify or emphasize a verb's reciprocal meaning, use the expression **einander** (*each other, one another*) instead of, or in addition to, a reflexive pronoun.

Sie haben **sich** vorgestellt.
They introduced themselves (to one another, or to someone else).

Sie haben sich **einander** vorgestellt.
They introduced themselves
to one another.

Reflexive verbs with prepositions

- Some reflexive verbs are typically used in set phrases with a preposition. Use accusative reflexive pronouns with these verbs. The prepositions in the following fixed expressions also take the accusative case.

common reflexive verbs with prepositions	
sich ärgern über	*to get angry about*
sich erinnern an	*to remember*
sich freuen auf	*to look forward to*
sich freuen über	*to be happy about*
sich gewöhnen an	*to get used to*
sich informieren über	*to find out about*
sich interessieren für	*to be interested in*
sich verlieben in	*to fall in love with*
sich vorbereiten auf	*to prepare oneself for*

Suggestion Tell students that in some cases, reflexive pronouns can be used after prepositions to mean myself, herself, etc. Ex.: **Mein Freund denkt nur an** *sich*.

Mama **hat sich über** mein unordentliches Zimmer **geärgert**.
*Mom **got mad about** my messy room.*

Nach der Reise **freuten** wir **uns auf** ein warmes Bad.
*After our trip, we **were looking forward to** a warm bath.*

Meine kleine Schwester **interessiert sich für** Computer.
*My little sister **is interested in** computers.*

Ich **habe mich an** das kalte Wetter **gewöhnt**.
*I've **gotten used to** the cold weather.*

ACHTUNG

When using **einander** with a preposition, attach it to the end of the preposition to form a single word: **Die Kinder spielen immer so schön <u>miteinander</u>.**

Klara und Paul haben sich <u>ineinander</u> verliebt.

QUERVERWEIS

In **6B.2**, you learned to form the past participles of verbs with separable and inseparable prefixes. Note that **erinnern**, **gewöhnen**, and **verlieben** all have inseparable prefixes. The verb **vorbereiten** has a separable prefix, but because its root verb, **bereiten**, has an inseparable prefix, there is no **-ge-** added to its past participle: **Ich bereite mich auf einen Marathon vor. Wie hast du dich auf die Prüfung vorbereitet?**

See **7A.2** to review other verbs that are used in set phrases with prepositions.

Ressourcen

SAM
WB: 123–124

SAM
LM: p. 79

Ⓢ
vhlcentral.com

Jetzt sind Sie dran! Geben Sie an, ob die Verben in den Sätzen eine reflexive oder reziproke Bedeutung (*meaning*) haben.

	reflexiv	reziprok		reflexiv	reziprok
1. Wir treffen uns um 16 Uhr im Café.	☐	☑	5. Seht ihr euch heute Abend?	☐	☑
2. Max und ich kennen uns seit drei Jahren.	☐	☑	6. Tom verliebte sich in Lena.	☑	☐
3. Die Schüler freuten sich auf die Ferien.	☑	☐	7. Lena freute sich sehr darüber.	☑	☐
4. Sara und Felix schreiben einander über 100 SMS am Tag.	☐	☑	8. Dana und ihr Freund streiten sich nur selten.	☐	☑

Anwendung

1 **Was fehlt?** Ergänzen Sie die Sätze mit den passenden Reflexivpronomen.

> **BEISPIEL** Mira und Hasan rufen __*sich*__ dreimal pro Tag an.

1. Heute küssten sie __sich__ zum ersten Mal.
2. Unsere Großeltern kennen __sich__ seit 60 Jahren.
3. Es ist klar, dass ihr __euch__ liebt.
4. Philip und Daniel unterhalten __sich__ gern.
5. Wo sollen wir __uns__ treffen?
6. Ich kann __mich__ nicht an seinen Namen erinnern.
7. Hast du __dich__ über den neuen Film informiert?
8. Ihr sollt __euch__ vorstellen.

2 **Bilder beschreiben** Beschreiben Sie die Bilder mit reziproken reflexiven Verben. Benutzen Sie das Perfekt.

▶ **BEISPIEL** die Geschäftsleute
Die Geschäftsleute haben sich getroffen.

sich jeden Tag anrufen	sich streiten
sich küssen	sich treffen
sich oft schreiben	sich unterhalten

Tobias und ich
1. haben uns geküsst.

Klara und Mia
2. haben sich jeden Tag angerufen.

Ihr
3. habt euch gestritten.

Wir
4. haben uns oft geschrieben.

Sie
5. haben sich unterhalten.

3 **Sätze schreiben** Schreiben Sie mindestens (*at least*) sechs logische Sätze mit Wörtern aus jeder Spalte.

> **BEISPIEL** *Die Studenten bereiten sich auf das Abschlussexamen vor.*

Julia	sich ärgern über	das Abschlussexamen
der Hotelgast	sich aufregen über	sein ehemaliger (*former*) Lehrer
die Enkelkinder	sich erinnern an	die Geburt ihres Enkelkindes
Simon	sich freuen auf	die Laptopangebote im Internet
Oma und Opa	sich freuen über	der schlechte Zimmerservice
die Passagierin	sich informieren über	ihr verlorenes (*lost*) Handgepäck
die Studenten	sich vorbereiten auf	die vielen Geschenke

 Practice more at **vhlcentral.com**.

Kommunikation

4 **Suggestion** As a class project, compile the stories into a "class book" of **Liebesgeschichten**.

4 **Beste Freunde** Stellen Sie Ihrem Partner / Ihrer Partnerin Fragen über seinen besten Freund / ihre beste Freundin. Antworten Sie in ganzen Sätzen und wechseln Sie sich ab. Answers will vary.

BEISPIEL

S1: Seit wann kennt ihr euch schon?
S2: Wir kennen uns schon seit 10 Jahren.

1. Seit wann kennt ihr euch schon?
2. Wo und wie habt ihr euch kennen gelernt?
3. Wie oft seht ihr euch?
4. Wo trefft ihr euch meistens?

5. Schreibt ihr euch viele SMS?
6. Ruft ihr euch an? Wie oft?
7. Worüber unterhaltet ihr euch?
8. Streitet ihr euch manchmal? Worüber?

5 **Eine Liebesgeschichte** Schreiben Sie mit Ihrem Partner / Ihrer Partnerin eine Liebesgeschichte über Lisa und David. Verwenden Sie die reflexiven Verben aus der Liste und benutzen Sie das Perfekt. Answers will vary.

▶ **BEISPIEL** Lisa und David haben sich auf einer Party kennen gelernt.

sich anrufen	sich treffen
sich kennen lernen	sich trennen
sich küssen	sich unterhalten
sich schreiben	sich verlieben
sich streiten	sich vorstellen

6 **Interessen** Wofür interessieren sich Ihre Mitstudenten? Machen Sie eine kurze Umfrage in Ihrem Kurs. Answers will vary.

BEISPIEL

S1: Ich interessiere mich für Technologie. Und du, Max, wofür interessierst du dich?
S2: Ich interessiere mich für Musik. Und du, Hanna, wofür interessierst du dich?
S3: Ich interessiere mich für...

7 **Suggestion** Formulate the questions as a class before students begin the group activity.

7 **Fragen über Fragen** Stellen Sie Fragen an Ihre Mitstudenten. Finden Sie für jede Frage mindestens eine Person, die sie mit ja beantwortet. Answers will vary.

BEISPIEL

S1: Freust du dich auf das Semesterende?
S2: Ja, ich freue mich total auf das Semesterende. Und du, freust du dich auf das Semesterende?
S1: Nein, gar nicht! Ich muss in den Ferien arbeiten.

	Name
sich auf das Semesterende freuen	
sich gern an den letzten Sommer erinnern	
sich für Politik interessieren	
sich über das Essen in der Mensa aufregen	
sich über schlechte Noten ärgern	

Wiederholung

1 Welches Bild? Beschreiben Sie sich gegenseitig die Bilder und erraten Sie, welches Bild Ihr Partner / Ihre Partnerin beschreibt. Answers will vary.

BEISPIEL

S1: Es ist im Badezimmer…
S2: Auf Bild eins?
S1: Nein, es ist im Badezimmer vor dem Spiegel …

1.

2.

3.

4.

5.

6.

2 Lebensregeln Schreiben Sie eine Regelliste (*list of rules*) für Ihre Mitbewohner. Benutzen Sie reflexive Verben und Reflexivpronomen. Answers will vary.

2 Expansion Have the groups compare their lists and decide which rules are most important.

BEISPIEL

Mitbewohner müssen einander jeden Tag helfen…

3 Arbeitsblatt Schreiben Sie drei Aktivitäten auf, die Sie diese Woche gemacht haben. Dann fragen Sie vier Personen im Unterricht, was sie gemacht haben. Answers will vary.

BEISPIEL

S1: Hast du dich diese Woche über etwas geärgert?
S2: Ja.
S1: Worüber hast du dich geärgert?
S2: Über das schlechte Essen in der Mensa.

4 Körperteile Arbeiten Sie mit einem Partner / einer Partnerin und beschreiben Sie Tätigkeiten, die mit den verschiedenen Körperteilen zu tun haben. Benutzen Sie die reflexiven und reziproken Verben aus der Liste. Answers will vary.

4 Expansion Have students come up with additional statements involving parts of the body and reflexive verbs.

BEISPIEL

S1: Wir schreiben einander mit den Händen.
S2: Wir kämmen uns die Haare.

A	B
Gesicht	sich anrufen
Haare	sich kämmen
Hände	sich küssen
Lippen	sich rasieren
Mund	sich schminken
Ohren	sich schreiben
	sich sprechen

5 Diskutieren und kombinieren Sie und Ihr Partner / Ihre Partnerin bekommen zwei verschiedene Blätter mit Jasmins Alltagsroutine. Wechseln Sie sich ab und fragen Sie, was Jasmin jeden Abend und jeden Morgen macht. Answers will vary.

BEISPIEL

S1: Um 23 Uhr zieht sich Jasmin aus und zieht ihren Schlafanzug an. Was macht sie danach?
S2: Danach…

6 In der Stadt Schreiben Sie mit einem Partner / einer Partnerin einen kurzen Text über eine Shoppingtour, die Sie zusammen am Wochenende machen wollen. Beantworten Sie die Fragen. Answers will vary.

BEISPIEL

S1: Wir treffen uns am Samstagmorgen um 9 Uhr auf dem Markt vor der Bank.
S2: Wir haben uns einen Monat lang nicht gesehen. Wir freuen uns auf den Tag zusammen.

- Wo und wann treffen Sie sich?
- Worauf freuen Sie sich?
- Was kaufen Sie sich?
- Worüber ärgern Sie sich?
- Gehen Sie in ein Restaurant oder in ein Café?
- Was bestellen Sie sich?
- Worüber unterhalten Sie sich?
- Was machen Sie noch?

Gesundheit bewegt uns

Deutschland hat ein duales Krankenversicherungssystem°.
Zum einen gibt es die gesetzliche° Krankenversicherung.
Sie ist eine verpflichtende° Versicherung für alle Personen
in Deutschland. Zum anderen gibt es private Unternehmen,
die Krankenversicherungen anbieten.
Die Central Krankenversicherung ist so eine private
Krankenversicherung. Sie wurde 1913 als Aktiengesellschaft°
in Köln gegründet und ist die älteste private Krankenversicherung
Deutschlands. Die Central hat mehr als 1,75 Millionen
Versicherte und bietet, neben der vollen Krankenversicherung,
auch verschiedene Zusatzmodelle° an. Sie zählt mit
mehr als 1.000 Mitarbeitern zu den führenden° privaten
Krankenversicherungen in Deutschland.

central

Gesundheit bewegt uns.

Es gibt Spezialisten für die Gesundheit Ihrer Knochen°, ...   **Ihres Herz-Kreislaufsystems°...**   **und Ihren Spezialisten für die private Krankenversicherung.**

Krankenversicherungssystem *health insurance system* **gesetzliche** *compulsory* **verpflichtende** *obligatory* **Aktiengesellschaft** *corporation* **Zusatzmodelle** *additional plans*
führenden *leading* **Knochen** *bones* **Herz-Kreislaufsystem** *cardiovascular system*

 Verständnis Beantworten Sie die Fragen mit den Informationen aus dem Video.

1. Wofür wirbt (*advertises*) der Mann?
   a. eine Arztpraxis   b. ein Krankenhaus
   c. eine Krankenversicherung

2. Wofür ist Central Spezialist?
   a. für Knochen   b. für die private Krankenversicherung
   c. für das Herz-Kreislaufsystem

 Diskussion Diskutieren Sie die folgenden Fragen mit einem Partner / einer Partnerin. Answers will vary.

1. Welche Unterschiede gibt es zwischen den Krankenversicherungen in Deutschland und denen in Ihrem Land?

2. Was macht Ihrer Meinung nach eine gute Krankenversicherung aus? Erarbeiten Sie ein Modell.

Communicative Goals

You will learn how to:
- talk about health
- talk about remedies and well-being

Wortschatz

die Gesundheit	*health*
die Allergie, -n	*allergy*
die Apotheke, -n	*pharmacy*
allergisch sein (gegen)	*to be allergic (to)*
krank/gesund werden	*to get sick/better*
in guter/schlechter Form sein	*to be in/out of shape*
sich verletzen	*to hurt oneself*
zum Arzt gehen	*to go to the doctor*
Symptome	*symptoms*
der Schmerz, -en	*pain*
die verstopfte Nase	*stuffy nose*
Zahnschmerzen (*pl.*)	*toothache*
leicht	*mild*
schwer	*serious*
schwindlig	*dizzy*
übel	*nauseous*
im Krankenhaus	*at the hospital*
der Arzt, ⸚e / die Ärztin, -nen	*doctor*
das Medikament, -e	*medicine*
die Grippe, -n	*flu*
der Krankenwagen, -	*ambulance*
die Notaufnahme, -n	*emergency room*
das Pflaster, -	*adhesive bandage*
das Rezept, -e	*prescription*
das Thermometer, -	*thermometer*
der Zahnarzt, ⸚e / die Zahnärztin, -nen	*dentist*
sich (das Handgelenk / den Fuß) verstauchen	*to sprain (one's wrist/ankle)*
sich (den Arm / das Bein) brechen	*to break (an arm / a leg)*
weh tun (tut...weh)	*to hurt*
weinen	*to cry*
krank	*sick*

Expansion Ask students: **Wer hier studiert Medizin? Möchte jemand Arzt oder Krankenpfleger werden? Hat jemand hier sich schon mal was gebrochen, einen Arm oder ein Bein?** etc.

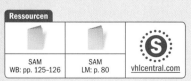
Beim Arzt (S) Vocabulary Tools

Suggestion Point out that when reporting symptoms, it's common to say: **Ich *habe* Husten und Schnupfen**, rather than using the conjugated verbs.

Suggestion Model pronunciation of **Patient** and **Patientin**.

ACHTUNG

To describe how you feel, use an adjective with a dative noun or pronoun:

Mir ist schwindlig. Ihr ist übel.

Also use a dative noun or pronoun with the phrase **weh tun**:

Tut dir das Bein weh? *Does your leg hurt?*

RAUCHEN VERBOTEN

der Krankenpfleger, -

Sie treibt Sport. (Sport treiben)

die Krankenschwester, -n

Sie hat Kopfschmerzen.

Er hat Bauchschmerzen.

Anwendung

1 **Assoziationen** Wählen Sie ein Wort aus der Liste, das Sie mit einem der Ausdrücke assoziieren.

die Allergie	die Notaufnahme
die Apotheke	das Thermometer
das Ibuprofen	die Zahnschmerzen

1 **Expansion** Have students create four additional associations for a partner to complete.

1. sich den Arm brechen ___die Notaufnahme___
2. eine verstopfte Nase haben ___die Allergie___
3. zum Zahnarzt gehen ___die Zahnschmerzen___
4. 39 Grad Celsius Fieber haben ___das Thermometer___
5. Kopfschmerzen haben ___das Ibuprofen___
6. Medikamente kaufen ___die Apotheke___

2 **Bilder beschriften** Finden Sie ein passendes Wort oder einen passenden Ausdruck für jedes Bild. Sample answers are provided.

1. ___weinen___

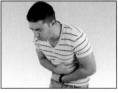

2. ___Bauchschmerzen haben___

3. ___Fieber haben___

4. ___die Ärztin___

5. ___schwanger sein___

6. ___in schlechter Form sein___

3 **Beim Arzt** Hören Sie sich das Gespräch zwischen Elias und seinem Arzt an und markieren Sie dabei die Ausdrücke, die Sie hören.

1. Ich habe Halsschmerzen. ☑
2. Mir ist übel. ☐
3. Ich habe Fieber. ☑
4. Mein Bauch tut weh. ☐
5. Ich schlafe schlecht. ☑
6. Mir tut alles weh. ☑
7. Ich habe eine Erkältung. ☐
8. Meine Nase ist verstopft. ☑
9. Ich treibe Sport. ☐
10. Ich huste. ☑

3 **Suggestion** To prepare for the listening activity, ask students to be your "doctor." Provide a list of symptoms and have them diagnose the problem.

 Practice more at **vhlcentral.com**.

Kommunikation

4 Ratschläge geben
Sehen Sie sich mit einem Partner / einer Partnerin die Bilder an. Was ist passiert und welche Ratschläge (*advice*) geben Sie den Personen auf den Bildern, so dass es ihnen dann besser geht? Answers will vary.

▶ **BEISPIEL** Hanna

S1: *Hanna hat Zahnschmerzen*
S2: *Sie soll den Zahnarzt anrufen.*

1. Emma

2. Frau Schmidt

3. Jasmin

4. Moritz

5. Herr Meyer

6. Michaela

7. Klara

8. Jonas

5 Fragen und Antworten
Beantworten Sie mit einem Partner / einer Partnerin die Fragen. Answers will vary.

BEISPIEL

S1: *Was machst du bei Kopfschmerzen?*
S2: *Ich lege mich ins Bett.*

1. Bist du gegen etwas allergisch?
2. Bekommst du jedes Jahr eine Spritze gegen die Grippe?
3. Hast du dir schon mal etwas gebrochen?
4. Wie oft gehst du zum Arzt?
5. Was machst du, um fit zu bleiben?

6 Diskutieren und kombinieren
Sie und Ihr Partner / Ihre Partnerin bekommen zwei verschiedene Blätter von Ihrem Professor / Ihrer Professorin. Fragen Sie Ihren Partner / Ihre Partnerin nach den Patienten, die in der Notaufnahme sind. Answers will vary.

BEISPIEL

S1: *Wer hat sich den Arm gebrochen?*
S2: *Frau Zimmermann hat sich den Arm gebrochen. Welches Problem hat Herr Arslan?*
S1: *Er hat...*

7 Wörter erraten
Erraten Sie mit zwei Mitstudenten zusammen Wörter aus Ihrer neuen Vokabelliste. Eine Person beschreibt ein Wort und die anderen zwei müssen es erraten. Wechseln Sie sich ab. Answers will vary.

BEISPIEL

S1: *Man putzt sie sich, wenn sie verstopft ist.*
S2: *Die Nase!*

7 Suggestion Give students a few minutes beforehand to prepare their definitions.

Aussprache und Rechtschreibung **S** Audio

🎧 Syllabic Stress

When a syllable in a word is stressed, it is pronounced with more emphasis than the other syllables. In German, the main stress is usually on the first syllable of a word.

| Sei**fe** | **Na**se | **Au**ge | **Tech**niker | **fern**sehen |

You have already learned that separable prefixes are always stressed, while inseparable prefixes are never stressed.

| **auf**wachen | **an**kommen | be**sprechen** | Ver**kehr** | **wie**dersehen |

In compound words, the first part of the compound is usually stressed.

| **Schlaf**anzug | **Spei**sekarte | **Ba**demantel | **Zahn**pasta | **Haus**schuh |

In words borrowed from other languages, the placement of stress varies. In nouns ending with **–ei** or **-ie**, the final syllable is stressed. In verbs ending in **–ieren**, the stress is on the **ie** sound.

| Com**pu**ter | Stu**dent** | Bäcke**rei** | Aller**gie** | ra**sie**ren |

Expansion Give students examples of words that change meaning if stress is placed on the prefix: **wieder**holen *to repeat*, wieder**holen** *to fetch*; **über**fahren *to run over*, über**fahren** *to ferry*; **durch**schlagen *to smash*; durch**schlagen** *to split in two*.

 1 **Aussprechen** Wiederholen Sie die Wörter, die Sie hören.

1. Rücken
2. duschen
3. anziehen
4. Einkauf
5. Gesicht
6. verlieren
7. überraschen
8. Handtuch
9. Bauchschmerzen
10. Hotel
11. Metzgerei
12. Psychologie

 2 **Nachsprechen** Wiederholen Sie die Sätze, die Sie hören.

1. Ich nehme immer eine Zahnbürste, Zahnpasta und saubere Unterwäsche mit.
2. Mein Arzt verschreibt mir solche Medikamente nicht.
3. Robert rasiert sich nur mit Rasierschaum.
4. Die Studenten lernen am liebsten in der Bäckerei.
5. In den Ländern war die Demokratie nicht nur Theorie.
6. Wenn ich zu früh aufstehe, bekomme ich Kopfschmerzen.

 3 **Sprichwörter** Wiederholen Sie die Sprichwörter, die Sie hören.

Was du heute kannst besorgen, das verschiebe nicht auf morgen.[1]

Aller Anfang ist schwer.[2]

[1] Never put off till tomorrow what you can do today.
[2] The first step is always the hardest. (lit. Every beginning is hard.)

Ressourcen

SAM
LM: p. 81

S vhlcentral.com

Im Krankenhaus Video

George und Sabite haben Meline ins Krankenhaus gebracht. Der Arzt möchte sie eine Nacht dabehalten und Meline beginnt wieder, von Hans zu träumen. Oder ist es gar kein Traum?

Vorbereitung Have students look at the video stills and guess what the episode will be about.

1

GEORGE Sie wird wieder gesund, Sabite. Sie ist auf den Kopf gefallen. Der Arzt untersucht sie gleich und dann gehen wir wieder nach Hause. Mein Bruder ist einmal aus einem Baum gefallen, ohne schwere Verletzungen zu haben.

2

SABITE Was ist passiert?
GEORGE Er hat sich den Knöchel verstaucht. Und den Arm gebrochen. Und ihm war mehrere Stunden lang schlecht und schwindlig. Tage. Aber jetzt ist er gesund, in toller Form und schmerzfrei. Aber er meidet Bäume.

ARZT Das ist eine schöne Beule auf Ihrem Kopf. Erinnern Sie sich, was passiert ist?
MELINE Ich habe gelernt und bin eingeschlafen. Und dann bin ich aufgewacht und vom Stuhl gefallen.
ARZT Und nachdem Sie das Bewusstsein wiedererlangt hatten?
MELINE Ich bin am Boden gelegen und meine Freunde haben mich gefunden.

3

MELINE Es geht mir gut, Dr. Klompenhouwer. Ist das holländisch?

4

5

ARZT Haben Sie ein Schwindelgefühl?
MELINE Ein bisschen.
ARZT Übelkeit?
MELINE Ahhh. Ja.
ARZT Ohrgeräusche?
MELINE Haben vor einer Stunde aufgehört.
ARZT Gut. Haben wir noch andere Symptome?
MELINE Außer Kopfschmerzen? Nein.

6

ARZT Okay. Hier ist ein Schmerzmittel. Lassen Sie mich die Schwester holen, damit wir eine Computertomographie machen können. Sie bleiben heute Nacht bei uns.
MELINE Och, Herr Doktor. Ich...
ARZT Frau... Meline. Es sieht so aus, als hätten Sie eine leichte Gehirnerschütterung.

1 **Richtig oder falsch?** Entscheiden Sie, ob die folgenden Sätze richtig oder falsch sind.

1. Meline ist auf ihren Arm gefallen. Falsch.
2. Georges Bruder ist einmal von der Garage gefallen. Falsch.
3. Georges Bruder hat sich einmal den Arm gebrochen. Richtig.
4. Meline hat eine Beule am Kopf. Richtig.
5. Sie ist aufgewacht und aus dem Bett gefallen. Falsch.

6. Jetzt hat sie ein Schwindelgefühl, Ohrgeräusche und Fieber. Falsch.
7. Dr. Klompenhouwer gibt Meline eine Spritze. Falsch.
8. Er will die Krankenschwester rufen, um eine CT zu machen. Richtig.
9. Meline hat wahrscheinlich eine leichte Gehirnerschütterung. Richtig.
10. Hans trägt einen Mundschutz (face mask), weil er Schnupfen und Husten hat. Richtig.

Expansion Point out that Meline says **bin am Boden gelegen** instead of **habe am Boden gelegen**. Explain that in Southern Germany and Austria, **sein** is used with **liegen** instead of **haben**. Explain also that the use of **am Boden** implies that she fell to the floor, whereas **auf dem Boden** would imply that she lay down intentionally.

PERSONEN

Dr. Klompenhouwer Hans George Meline Sabite

7

ARZT George Bachman, Sabite Yilmaz?

ARZT Wir würden Meline heute Nacht gern im Krankenhaus behalten. Es geht ihr gut. Wir möchten auf Nummer sicher gehen.

SABITE Können wir sie sehen?

ARZT Sie würde heute lieber keine Besucher mehr haben.

8

MELINE Dr. Klompenhouwer? Sind Sie Chirurg? Ich verstehe das nicht.

HANS Ich musste mit meinen eigenen Augen sehen, dass es dir gut geht.

MELINE Hans, ich liebe dich!

9

ARZT Ihre Freunde sind hier, um Sie abzuholen.

MELINE Oh, Dr. Klompenhouwer, ganz herzlichen Dank. Sie haben mein Leben gerettet. Sie sind ein ausgezeichneter Arzt.

ARZT Danke, Meline. Wenn Sie Symptome haben, dann rufen Sie uns bitte auf jeden Fall an.

10

MELINE Wo ist George?

SABITE Er wäre hier, wenn er keine Uni hätte. Hans ist mit mir gekommen.

HANS Na, wie geht es unserer Patientin heute morgen? Das hier hat mir die Schwester gegeben, weil ich Schnupfen und Husten habe. Ich soll ja niemanden anstecken.

Nützliche Ausdrücke

- **untersuchen**
  to examine
- **der Baum**
  tree
- **der Knöchel**
  ankle
- **meiden**
  to avoid
- **die Beule**
  bump
- **Und nachdem Sie das Bewusstsein wiedererlangt hatten?**
  And after you regained consciousness?
- **das Schmerzmittel**
  painkiller
- **die Gehirnerschütterung**
  concussion
- **der Chirurg**
  surgeon
- **abholen**
  to pick (someone) up
- **ausgezeichnet**
  excellent

9B.1
- **Er wäre hier, wenn er keine Uni hätte.**
  He would have come if he weren't in class.

9B.2
- **Wir würden Meline heute Nacht gern im Krankenhaus behalten.**
  We would like to keep Meline in the hospital tonight.

2 **Zum Besprechen** Stellen Sie sich vor, Meline hat andere Symptome, als sie ins Krankenhaus kommt. Spielen Sie einen Dialog zwischen Meline und Dr. Klompenhouwer. Answers will vary.

2 **Expansion** Have students act out their dialogues for the class.

3 **Vertiefung** Wilhelm Conrad Röntgen hat etwas erfunden, das heute in jedem Krankenhaus täglich benutzt wird. Finden Sie heraus, was es ist und wie er es erfunden hat. Answers may include X-rays or electromagnetic radiation.

Apotheken  Reading

Suggestion Tell students that in Germany, supermarkets are not allowed to sell over-the-counter drugs. Before they read the article, have students skim for familiar words and cognates.

TIPP

Die Medizin refers to the practice of medicine, while **das Medikament** refers to medication.

In jeder Stadt ist immer mindestens eine Apotheke geöffnet. Das bedeutet, dass die Menschen 24 Stunden am Tag wichtige Medikamente bekommen können.

Apotheken sind Geschäfte, in denen man nicht nur Medikamente, sondern auch andere gesundheitsfördernde° Produkte kaufen kann. Neben Medikamenten findet man normalerweise auch Nahrungsergänzungsmittel° wie zum Beispiel Vitamine, Kosmetikprodukte, sowie Produkte für Diäten, Haut- und Fußpflege° und für die Kontaktlinsenpflege.

In Deutschland gibt es neben der traditionellen Medizin auch viele Menschen, die homöopathische Mittel° benutzen. Beide Medikamentensorten kann man in Apotheken kaufen, aber manche Ärzte und Apotheken spezialisieren sich auf die traditionelle Medizin oder auf die homöopathische Medizin.

DEUTSCHLAND IST DER GRÖSSTE Apothekenmarkt in Europa. Hier gibt es etwa 21.500 Apotheken. Jede Apotheke muss von einem staatlich geprüften° Apotheker geleitet werden°. Apotheken sind keine Ketten°, daher darf ein Apotheker höchstens vier davon besitzen. Die Medikamentenpreise werden von der Regierung° reglementiert. Relativ neu sind Versandapotheken°, bei denen man im Internet Medikamente bestellen kann.

Typische homöopathische Mittel	
Belladonna	Fieber und Kopfschmerzen
Kamille	Ohren- und Zahnschmerzen
Echinacea	Erkältung und Fieber
Hopfen	Schlafstörung°

staatlich geprüften *state certified* **geleitet werden** *headed* **Ketten** *chains* **Regierung** *government* **Versandapotheken** *mail-order pharmacies* **gesundheitsfördernde** *health promoting* **Nahrungsergänzungsmittel** *dietary supplements* **Fußpflege** *foot care* **Mittel** *remedy* **Schlafstörung** *insomnia*

Expansion Have students compare and contrast German pharmacies with their local drugstores.

ÜBUNGEN

1 Richtig oder falsch? Sagen Sie, ob die Sätze richtig oder falsch sind. Korrigieren Sie die falschen Sätze.

1. Die Schweiz ist der größte Apothekenmarkt in Europa.
   Falsch. Deutschland ist der größte Apothekenmarkt in Europa.
2. In Deutschland gibt es etwa 23.400 Apotheken.
   Falsch. In Deutschland gibt es etwa 21.500 Apotheken.
3. Es dürfen nicht mehr als vier Apotheken zusammengehören. Richtig.
4. Die deutsche Regierung reglementiert den Apothekerberuf. Richtig.
5. Bei Versandapotheken kann man online Medikamente bestellen. Richtig.

6. In deutschen Städten ist immer mindestens eine Apotheke geöffnet. Richtig.
7. In Apotheken kann man keine Vitamine kaufen.
   Falsch. In Apotheken kann man Vitamine kaufen.
8. Deutsche Apotheken verkaufen traditionelle und homöopathische Medikamente. Richtig.
9. Echinacea ist ein homöopatisches Mittel gegen Erkältung und Fieber. Richtig.
10. Ein homöopatisches Mittel gegen Schlafstörung ist Kamille.
    Falsch. Ein homöopatisches Mittel gegen Schlafstörung ist Hopfen.

 Practice more at **vhlcentral.com**.

Expansion Have students create short skits using the **Deutsch im Alltag** expressions.

DEUTSCH IM ALLTAG

Ausdrücke zur Gesundheit

der Blutdruck	blood pressure
der blaue Fleck	bruise
der Hitzschlag	heat stroke
der Muskelkater	sore muscles
der Sonnenbrand	sunburn
der steife Hals	stiff neck

DIE DEUTSCHSPRACHIGE WELT

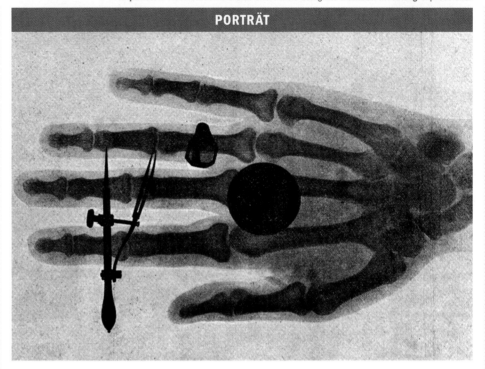

10°C   20°C

Föhn

Föhn heißt ein Windsystem in den Alpen. Dieser Wind, auch Fallwind genannt, ist sehr trocken°, weil er beim Aufsteigen° auf der Südseite der Alpen Wasser in der Form von Regen verliert. Wenn er von den Gipfeln° der Alpen nach Norden ins Voralpengebiet° weht°, ist die Luftmasse° trocken und warm. Das Wetter in Bayern ist bei Föhn sonnig und trocken. Aber viele Menschen haben bei Föhn Kopfschmerzen.

trocken dry **Aufsteigen** rising **Gipfeln** peaks **Voralpengebiet** foothills of the Alps **weht** blows **Luftmasse** air mass

PORTRÄT

Röntgen
Suggestion Tell students that **der Föhn, -e** is also used as a synonym for **Haartrockner**.

Wilhelm Conrad Röntgen (1845–1923) war ein deutscher Physiker. Er arbeitete als Professor an der Universität Würzburg, als er 1895 zufällig° eine besondere Art von Strahlen° entdeckte: die X-Strahlen. Mit diesen Strahlen konnte man durch viele Materialien hindurchsehen. Für diese Entdeckung° bekam Röntgen 1901 als erster Wissenschaftler den Nobelpreis für Physik. Vor allem für die Medizin war diese Entdeckung sehr wichtig: Ärzte konnten mit den X-Strahlen zum Beispiel Knochenbrüche° diagnostizieren. In seinem Testament° schrieb Röntgen, dass die Strahlen nicht seinen Namen tragen dürfen. Trotzdem nennt man die X-Strahlen heute in Deutschland und in Polen Röntgenstrahlen.

zufällig accidentally **Strahlen** rays **Entdeckung** discovery **Knochenbrüche** bone fractures **Testament** will

⟡ IM INTERNET

Suchen Sie im Internet eine deutsche Versandapotheke. Was kann man bei der Versandapotheke bestellen? Kann man hier homöopathische Mittel kaufen?

Find out more at **vhlcentral.com**.

---

2 **Was fehlt?** Ergänzen Sie die Sätze.

1. Föhn ist ein Windsystem in den ___Alpen___.
2. Bei Föhn ist das Wetter sonnig, warm und ___trocken___.
3. Viele Menschen haben bei Föhn ___Kopfschmerzen___.
4. Wilhelm Conrad Röntgen war ein deutscher ___Physiker___.
5. Er entdeckte die ___X-Strahlen___.
6. In Deutschland und Polen heißen die X-Strahlen ___Röntgenstrahlen___.

3 **Leben Sie gesund?** Diskutieren Sie mit einem Partner / einer Partnerin: Was machen Sie, damit Sie gesund bleiben? Sollten Sie mehr machen?

3 Suggestion Have students prepare a list of their healthy and unhealthy habits before they speak with their partners.

Ressourcen

vhlcentral.com

9B.1

Der Konjunktiv II (S) Presentation

Startblock Use the subjunctive, also called the **Konjunktiv II**, to talk about hypothetical or unreal conditions, to express wishes, and to make polite requests.

Könnte es auch schlimmer sein?

Er **wäre** hier, wenn er keinen Unterricht **hätte**.

- To form the subjunctive of weak verbs and the modal verbs **sollen** and **wollen**, add the subjunctive endings -e, -est, -e; -en, -et, -en to the **Präteritum** stem. The subjunctive forms of these verbs are identical to their **Präteritum** forms.

wünschen (*to wish*)	
Präteritum	**Konjunktiv II**
ich wünschte	ich wünschte
du wünschtest	du wünschtest
er/sie/es wünschte	er/sie/es wünschte
wir wünschten	wir wünschten
ihr wünschtet	ihr wünschtet
Sie/sie wünschten	Sie/sie wünschten

Wir **sollten** vier Mal pro Woche Sport treiben.
*We **should** exercise four times a week.*

Ich **wünschte**, ich **spielte** besser Fußball.
*I **wish** I **played** soccer better.*

- To form the subjunctive of strong verbs, add the subjunctive endings to the **Präteritum** stem. If the stem vowel is a, o, or u, add an **Umlaut**. The verbs **sein** and **haben** and the modals **dürfen**, **können**, **mögen**, and **müssen** also follow this pattern.

Infinitiv	Präteritum	Konjunktiv II		Infinitiv	Präteritum	Konjunktiv II
bleiben	ich blieb	ich bliebe		dürfen	ich durfte	ich dürfte
geben	du gabst	du gäbest		können	du konntest	du könntest
gehen	er/sie/es ging	er/sie/es ginge		mögen	er/sie/es mochte	er/sie/es möchte
kommen	wir kamen	wir kämen		müssen	wir mussten	wir müssten
lassen	ihr ließt	ihr ließet		haben	ihr hattet	ihr hättet
tun	Sie/sie taten	Sie/sie täten		sein	Sie/sie waren	Sie/sie wären

- The only mixed verb commonly used in the subjunctive is **wissen**. Its subjunctive forms are the same as its **Präteritum** forms, but with an added **Umlaut** on the stem vowel.

Wüssten Sie, wo die Apotheke ist?
***Would** you **happen to know** where the pharmacy is?*

Wenn ich das nur **wüsste**!
*If only I **knew** that!*

- Modals and the verbs **haben** and **sein** are often used in the subjunctive to make polite requests or ask questions.

  Hätten Sie Lust, diesen Film mit mir zu sehen?
  ***Do** you feel like seeing this movie with me?*

  Könntest du mir bitte ein Taschentuch reichen?
  ***Could** you hand me a tissue, please?*

- To express a wish that is contrary to reality, use the subjunctive form of **wünschen** with another clause in the subjunctive.

  Ich wünschte, wir hätten mehr Zeit!
  ***I wish we had** more time!*

  Ich wünschte, ich könnte heute schwimmen gehen.
  ***I wish I could** go swimming today!*

- The conjunction **wenn** (*if*) is often used with **nur** to mean *if only*. Move the conjugated verb to the end of a clause beginning with **wenn**.

  Wenn wir **nur** mehr Zeit **hätten**!
  ***If only** we **had** more time!*

  Wenn ich heute **nur** schwimmen gehen **könnte**!
  ***If only** I **could** go swimming today!*

- To express a condition that is hypothetical or contrary to fact, use a **wenn**-clause with a second clause that indicates what would happen if the **wenn**-clause were true.

  Wenn du Zeit **hättest, könnten** wir heute Abend ins Konzert gehen.
  ***If** you **had** time, we **could** go to a concert this evening.*

  Wenn mir die Füße nicht so **weh täten, käme** ich **gern** mit euch wandern.
  ***If** my feet didn't **hurt** so much, I'**d be happy to come** hiking with you.*

- You can use the conjunction **dann** to introduce the second clause in a hypothetical statement.

  Wenn du nicht so spät ins Bett **gingest**...
  ***If** you **didn't go** to bed so late,...*

  dann wärest du nicht so müde.
  ***then** you **wouldn't be** so tired.*

- Use **als ob** with the subjunctive, instead of **wenn**, to mean *as if*.

  Er tut, **als ob** er krank **wäre**.
  *He's acting **as if** he **were** sick.*

  Du siehst aus, **als ob** du eine Grippe hättest.
  *You look **as if** you **had** the flu.*

  Es hört sich an, **als ob** Paul Husten und Schnupfen **hätte**.
  *It sounds **like** Paul **has** a cough and the sniffles.*

  Sara tut so, **als ob** sie am besten Tennis **spielte**.
  *Sara's acting **like** she's the best tennis player.*

QUERVERWEIS

In **4A.1**, you learned to use the subjunctive forms of **mögen** to make polite requests.

———

Wenn and **als ob** are subordinating conjunctions. You learned about the subordinating conjunctions **bevor**, **nachdem**, and **als** in **8A.1**. You will learn more about subordinating conjunctions in **10A.3**.

ACHTUNG

Ich möchte is typically used instead of **ich wollte** as the polite equivalent of **ich will**. **Ich hätte gern** is also frequently used for ordering in a restaurant.

Ressourcen

SAM
WB: pp. 127–128

SAM
LM: p. 82

vhlcentral.com

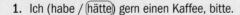

Jetzt sind Sie dran!   **Wählen Sie die passenden Verbformen.**

1. Ich (habe / hätte) gern einen Kaffee, bitte.

2. (Soll / Sollte) man immer wegen Rückenschmerzen zum Arzt gehen?

3. Ihr tut immer, als ob ihr keine Zeit zum Rad fahren (hättet / habt).

4. Wenn ich dagegen nicht allergisch (bin / wäre), (könnte / kann) ich Erdbeeren essen.

5. Ich (will / wollte), mein Computer (funktionierte / funktioniert) besser!

6. Wenn ich nur (wüsste / weiß), wo das Rezept für die Tabletten ist!

7. Die Zahnärztin (wünscht / wünschte), dass nicht so viele Patienten vor ihr Angst (haben / hätten).

8. Wenn Sie mehr Sport (treiben / trieben), dann (sind / wären) Sie in besserer Form.

9. (Könnten / Können) Sie die Krankenschwester rufen, bitte?

10. Wenn Roland kein Fieber (hätte / hat), (kommen / käme) er mit uns ins Restaurant.

11. (Dürfte / Darf) ich bitte die Tabletten und ein Glas Wasser haben?

12. Wenn es Lina nur nicht so schlecht (geht / ginge)!

Anwendung

1 Expansion Have students work in pairs to write about a hypothetical situation using the verbs from this activity.

1 **Konjunktivformen** Ergänzen Sie die Tabelle mit den fehlenden Verbformen im Präteritum und im Konjunktiv II.

Präsens	Präteritum	Konjunktiv II
wir kommen	wir kamen	wir kämen
ich gebe	ich gab	ich gäbe
sie will	sie wollte	sie wollte
ihr arbeitet	ihr arbeitetet	ihr arbeitetet
du hast	du hattest	du hättest
er geht	er ging	er ginge

2 **Hypothesen** Ergänzen Sie die Sätze mit den richtigen Konjunktivformen der Verben in Klammern.

> **BEISPIEL** Wenn ich das ___wüsste___ (wissen), könnte ich dir helfen.

1. Wenn Jan nicht krank wäre, ___könnte___ (können) er ins Konzert gehen.
2. Wenn das Baby nicht so laut ___weinte___ (weinen), könnte die Ärztin ihm eine Spritze geben.
3. Wenn Julian Zeit hätte, ___ginge___ (gehen) er mit uns zum Fußballspiel.
4. Es sieht aus, als ob Sophia sehr unglücklich ___wäre___ (sein).
5. Ali sieht aus, als ob er Fieber ___hätte___ (haben).

3 Suggestion Remind students of how the conjunction **wenn** impacts word order. Do the first few sentences together as a class.

3 **Wünsche** Was würden (*would*) die Personen sagen? Schreiben Sie zu jedem Bild einen Satz im Konjunktiv II und benutzen Sie die angegebenen Verben.

> ▶ **BEISPIEL**

Kopfschmerztabletten haben
Wenn ich nur Kopfschmerztabletten hätte!

1. nicht so früh aufwachen müssen ___Wenn ich nur nicht so früh aufwachen müsste!___

2. ihre Handynummer wissen ___Wenn ich nur ihre Handynummer wüsste!___

3. Tennis spielen können ___Wenn ich nur Tennis spielen könnte!___

4. nicht so viele Patienten haben ___Wenn ich nur nicht so viele Patienten hätte!___

 Practice more at **vhlcentral.com**.

Kommunikation

4 **Drei Wünsche** Fragen Sie einander, was Sie sich wünschen. Benutzen Sie dabei den Konjunktiv II. Answers will vary.

BEISPIEL

S1: *Was hättest du am liebsten?*
S2: *Ich hätte am liebsten ein Motorrad.*

1. Was hättest du am liebsten?
2. Wo wärest du am liebsten?
3. Was wüsstest du am liebsten?
4. Was möchtest du am liebsten?

5 **Stell dir mal vor...** Fragen Sie Ihren Partner / Ihre Partnerin, was er/sie wäre, wenn er/sie eine andere Person, ein Tier oder ein Ding sein könnte. Answers will vary.

BEISPIEL

S1: *Wenn du ein Tier wärest, welches Tier wärest du und warum?*
S2: *Ich wäre ein Vogel, denn dann könnte ich fliegen. Und welches Tier wärest du?*

1. ein Tier
2. eine berühmte Person
3. ein Möbelstück
4. eine Person aus einem Film/Buch

6 **Wenn es nur anders wäre!** Erzählen Sie einander, was Sie stört (*bothers*) und was Sie sich wünschen. Benutzen Sie den Konjunktiv II. Answers will vary.

BEISPIEL

S1: *Ich habe nicht viel Zeit für meine Hobbys. Ich wünschte, ich hätte mehr Zeit!*
S2: *Mein Computer ist so langsam. Ich wünschte, mein Computer wäre schneller!*

7 **Rollenspiel: Im Restaurant** Sie sind im Restaurant. Fragen Sie den Kellner / die Kellnerin, was er/sie Ihnen empfehlen kann. Answers will vary.

BEISPIEL

S1: *Guten Tag, was möchten Sie trinken?*
S2: *Ich hätte gern ein Mineralwasser.*
S3: *Und könnte ich bitte Apfelsaft bekommen?*

Kellner(in)	Gäste
Möchten Sie etwas trinken/essen? Was hätten Sie gern?	Dürfte/Könnte ich bitte... Hätten Sie vielleicht...? Ich hätte gern... Könnten Sie etwas empfehlen? Könnten Sie mir/uns bitte sagen...? Wir möchten bitte... Was / Wie viel macht das?

Speisekarte

Vorspeisen
Tomatensuppe	€4,80
Großer Salatteller	€9,50
Kleiner Salatteller	€3,60
Brotteller (Wurst oder Käse)	€6,80

Nachspeisen
Schokoladentorte	€6,45
Apfelkuchen	€5,80
Gemischtes Eis	€5,30
Obstsalat mit Pfirsich, Melone, Erdbeeren und Birne	€4,10

Hauptspeisen
Currywurst mit Pommes frites	€8,20
Hähnchen mit Reis, Pilzen und Gemüse	€18,80
Wiener Schnitzel mit Kartoffeln und kleinem Salat	€15,60
Thunfisch mit Bratkartoffeln und grünen Bohnen	€21,30
Scampi: Garnelen mit Reis und Knoblauch	€20,50

Getränke
Mineralwasser 0,2 l	€1,50
Limonade (Cola, Orange, Zitrone) 0,2 l	€1,80
Saft (Apfel, Ananas, Orange) 0,2 l	€2,20
Tasse Kaffee, Tee	€1,50

5 **Expansion** Have students report what they learned about their partners to the class.

7 **Suggestion** Have students repeat the items in the word bank after you to practice pronunciation. Remind them to use the accusative with **Ich hätte gern...** and **Ich möchte...**,

9B.2

Würden with the infinitive  Presentation

Startblock The subjunctive of **werden** is **würden**. It is the subjunctive form used most commonly in conversation.

Wir **würden** Meline heute Nacht gern im Krankenhaus behalten.

Sie **würde** heute lieber keine Besucher mehr haben.

- The subjunctive forms of **werden** are the same as its **Präteritum** forms, but with an added **Umlaut** on the stem vowel.

QUERVERWEIS

You will learn about other uses of **werden** in **12B.2**.

werden		
Indikativ	**Präteritum**	**Konjunktiv II**
ich werde	ich wurde	ich würde
du wirst	du wurdest	du würdest
er/sie/es wird	er/sie/es wurde	er/sie/es würde
wir werden	wir wurden	wir würden
ihr werdet	ihr wurdet	ihr würdet
Sie/sie werden	Sie/sie wurden	Sie/sie würden

- **Würden** functions like a modal verb. When you use it with an infinitive, place **würden** in the position of the conjugated verb and place the infinitive at the end of the clause.

Würden Sie mir bitte **helfen?**
*Would you **help** me, please?*

An deiner Stelle **würde** ich zum Arzt **gehen.**
*If I were you, I **would go** to the doctor.*

Ich glaube, ich **würde** mit ihr **gehen.**
*I think I **would go** with her.*

Wenn er nur **mitkommen würde!**
*If only he **would come** with us!*

- Since all weak verbs, and some strong and mixed verbs, have identical subjunctive and **Präteritum** forms, German speakers typically use **würden** with the infinitive to express a subjunctive meaning for those verbs.

Sie **rannte** nach Hause.
*She **ran** home. / She **would** run home.*

Sie **würde** nach Hause rennen.
*She **would** run home.*

Ich **fragte** die Krankenschwester nach einem Pflaster.
*I **asked** the nurse for a bandage. / I **would ask** the nurse for a bandage.*

Ich **würde** die Krankenschwester nach einem Pflaster **fragen.**
*I **would ask** the nurse for a bandage.*

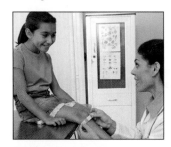

- Use **würden** + *infinitive* with a **wenn**-clause in the subjunctive to describe a hypothetical situation.

Wenn du vorsichtiger **wärest, würdest** du dich nicht so oft **verletzen.**
*If you were more careful, you **wouldn't hurt** yourself so much.*

Wenn ich Zahnschmerzen **hätte, würde** ich zum Zahnarzt **gehen.**
*If I **had** a toothache, I **would go** to the dentist.*

Wenn du mehr **Sport treiben würdest, wärst** du in besserer Form.
*If you **exercised more**, you'd be in better shape.*

Wenn Jan und Susanna **sich** nicht so oft **streiten würden, dann würden** sie sich **nicht trennen.**
*If Jan and Susanna **didn't fight** with each other so much, they **wouldn't be splitting up**.*

- Use **würden** + *infinitive* to express wishes, give advice, make polite requests, or ask questions.

Ich **würde** gern in die Türkei **reisen.**

An Ihrer Stelle **würde** ich die Wahrheit **sagen.**

Sie **würden gern** nach Bern **fahren.**
*They'**d love** to go to Bern.*

An deiner Stelle **würde** ich das nicht **tun.**
*I **wouldn't do** that if I were you.*

Würdest du bitte das Fenster **schließen?**
***Would** you **close** the window, please?*

Wir **würden** das nie **tun.**
*We **would** never **do** that.*

Expansion Have students pick a famous person and give them a few words of advice: **An Ihrer Stelle würde ich…**

ACHTUNG

The subjunctive forms of **haben, sein, wissen,** and the modal verbs are commonly used in conversation. These verbs are rarely used as infinitives with **würden.**

ACHTUNG

To give advice, use the expression **An deiner/Ihrer Stelle,** meaning *In your place…* or *If I were you…*

Ressourcen

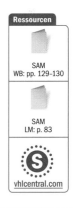

SAM
WB: pp. 129–130

SAM
LM: p. 83

S

vhlcentral.com

Jetzt sind Sie dran! Geben Sie an, wie der Konjunktiv mit **würden** in jedem Satz verwendet wird (*is used*):
a. Frage b. Wunsch c. Ratschlag (*advice*) d. hypothetische Situation

1. _a_ Würden Sie die Tür bitte schließen?
2. _a_ Würdest du dich auf einen Besuch freuen?
3. _c_ An Ihrer Stelle würde ich mehr Gemüse essen.
4. _b_ Sie würden gern Musik hören.
5. _a_ Würden Sie bitte den Arzt rufen?
6. _c_ An seiner Stelle würde ich keinen Kaffee trinken.

7. _d_ Er würde sich nicht verletzen.
8. _d_ Wenn ich Rückenschmerzen hätte, würde ich mich hinlegen.
9. _b_ Ich würde gern nach Hause gehen.
10. _c_ An deiner Stelle würde ich zum Zahnarzt gehen.
11. _a_ Würdest du mir bitte das Thermometer geben?
12. _a_ Würden Sie lieber mit der Ärztin oder dem Arzt sprechen?

Anwendung

1 **Konjunktivformen** Schreiben Sie die Verben in die Konjunktivform mit **würden** + *Infinitiv* um.

> **BEISPIEL** ich käme *ich würde kommen*

1. sie sagte _____ sie würde sagen _____
2. du nähmest _____ du würdest nehmen _____
3. ich gäbe _____ ich würde geben _____
4. wir zögen um _____ wir würden umziehen _____

5. er lernte _____ er würde lernen _____
6. ihr schriebet _____ ihr würdet schreiben _____
7. sie arbeitete _____ sie würde arbeiten _____
8. sie informierten sich _____ sie würden sich informieren _____

2 **Was tun?** Was würden Sie an Stelle dieser Personen machen? Schreiben Sie zu jedem Bild einen Satz mit **würden** + *Infinitiv*. Benutzen Sie die Wörter im Wortschatz.

> den Automechaniker anrufen | an Land schwimmen
> Brille tragen | sehr still bleiben
> ein Boot bauen

▶ **BEISPIEL**

An seiner Stelle
würde ich ein Boot bauen.

1. An seiner Stelle
würde ich eine Brille tragen.

2. An ihrer Stelle
würde ich sehr still bleiben.

3. An seiner Stelle
würde ich den Automechaniker anrufen.

4. An ihrer Stelle
würde ich an Land schwimmen.

3 **Sätze umschreiben** Schreiben Sie die Sätze mit **würden** + *Infinitiv* um. Sample answers are provided.

> **BEISPIEL** Öffnen Sie bitte die Tür!
> *Würden Sie bitte die Tür öffnen?*

1. Räumt bitte eure Zimmer auf! Würdet ihr bitte eure Zimmer aufräumen?
2. Mach bitte den Fernseher aus! Würdest du bitte den Fernseher ausmachen?
3. Fahr bitte langsamer! Würdest du bitte langsamer fahren?
4. Zeigen Sie mir Ihre Bordkarte, bitte! Würden Sie mir Ihre Bordkarte zeigen, bitte?
5. Ladet dieses Dokument für mich herunter! Würdet ihr dieses Dokument für mich herunterladen?

Kommunikation

4 **An deiner Stelle würde ich...** Erzählen Sie Ihrem Partner / Ihrer Partnerin von Ihren Gesundheitsproblemen. Er/Sie sagt dann, was er/sie an Ihrer Stelle machen würde. Answers will vary.

▶ **BEISPIEL**

S1: Mir tun die Füße weh.
S2: An deiner Stelle würde ich mich öfter hinsetzen.

Probleme	Ratschläge (Advice)
Ich bin immer müde.	früher ins Bett gehen
Ich habe Rückenschmerzen.	mehr Sport treiben
Ich bin in schlechter Form.	sich öfter hinsetzen
Mir ist schwindlig.	sich hinlegen
Mir tun die Füße weh.	Tabletten nehmen
Ich bin allergisch gegen...	zum Arzt gehen

5 **Wenn es so wäre, ...** Erzählen Sie einander, was Sie machen würden, wenn diese Situationen echt wären. Answers will vary.

BEISPIEL

S1: Wenn ich mehr Zeit hätte, würde ich öfter ausgehen. Und du?
S2: Ich würde mehr Sport treiben.

1. Wenn es jetzt Sommer wäre, ...
2. Wenn ich wieder ein Kind wäre, ...
3. Wenn ich den ganzen Tag frei hätte, ...
4. Wenn ich eine Zeitmaschine hätte, ...
5. Wenn ich fliegen könnte, ...
6. Wenn ich viel Geld hätte, ...

6 **Austauschstudenten** Zwei Austauschstudenten (*exchange students*) aus Deutschland sind für ein paar Tage bei Ihnen. Diskutieren Sie, was Sie in der Zeit alles zusammen machen könnten. Benutzen Sie den Konjunktiv II. Answers will vary.

BEISPIEL

S1: Sollten wir vielleicht ins Kino gehen?
S2: Das wäre okay, aber ich würde lieber ein Museum besuchen.
S3: Wir könnten auch...

Wir könnten vielleicht...	Das wäre toll/langweilig/schön/okay...
Möchtet ihr...	Ich hätte nicht so viel Lust auf...
Sollten wir vielleicht...	Es würde bestimmt viel/keinen Spaß machen, zu...
Ich würde gern / lieber / am liebsten...	

7 **Ein neues Konzept** Was würden Sie an Ihrer Schule oder Ihrer Universität anders machen? Machen Sie einen Plan und überzeugen (*convince*) Sie dann Ihre Mitstudenten von den Vorteilen (*advantages*) Ihres Konzepts. Answers will vary.

BEISPIEL

S1: Wir würden zuerst allen Studenten einen Tag frei geben.
S2: Und Kurse würden niemals vor 10 Uhr beginnen.

4 **Suggestion** Tell students they don't have to stick to the **Ratschläge** in the word bank, as long as they use the **würde** + infinitive construction.

4 **Expansion** Have students repeat the activity, this time coming up with **schlechte Ratschläge**.

6 **Suggestion** Give students a few minutes to brainstorm ideas before they begin working in groups.

7 **Expansion** Have pairs share some of their suggestions with the class, and have students vote on whether or not the suggestions should be implemented.

Wiederholung

1 Suggestion Point out that although some speakers still treat **backen** (item 2) as a strong verb, it is more frequently conjugated as a weak verb in current usage.

Als ob! Diese Leute tun, als ob sie alles machen könnten. Beschreiben Sie mit einem Partner / einer Partnerin, was sie machen und wie sie sich benehmen (*act*). Sample answers are provided.

> **BEISPIEL** Florian / vom Tennisspielen sprechen
>
> **S1:** Florian spricht immer vom Tennisspielen.
> **S2:** Als ob er am besten spielte!

1. Tim / vom
   Singen sprechen
   Als ob er am besten sänge!
2. Antonia und Jan / vom
   Backen sprechen
   Als ob sie am besten backten!
3. Simon / von seinen
   Reisen sprechen
   Als ob er am meisten reiste!
4. Mia / vom
   Laufen sprechen
   Als ob sie am schnellsten liefe!
5. Herr und Frau Schulz / vom
   Tanzen sprechen
   Als ob sie am schönsten tanzten!
6. Sara / vom
   Schreiben sprechen
   Als ob sie am schönsten schriebe!

Diskutieren und kombinieren Sie und Ihr Partner / Ihre Partnerin bekommen zwei Blätter mit verschiedenen Informationen über Familie Weber. Was hat jedes Familienmitglied gemacht und was ist danach passiert? Finden Sie für jede Wirkung (*effect*) eine Ursache (*cause*). Answers will vary.

> **BEISPIEL**
>
> **S1:** Wie hat David sich den Arm gebrochen?
> **S2:** Er ist beim Baseballspiel gefallen.

3 Wenn nur... Schauen Sie sich mit einem Partner / einer Partnerin die Bilder an. Sagen Sie, was die Personen alles machen würden, wenn sie gesund wären. Answers will vary.

> **BEISPIEL**
>
> **S1:** Wenn Emma kein gebrochenes Bein hätte, könnte sie Fußball spielen.
> **S2:** Auch könnte sie...

1. Emma

2. Herr Yildirim

3. Frau Krüger

4. Michael

4 Sätze bilden Bilden Sie mit einem Partner / einer Partnerin logische Sätze. Verwenden Sie den Konjunktiv II für den Satzanfang und **würden** + *Infinitiv* für das Satzende. Sample answers are provided.

> **BEISPIEL** ich / Zahnschmerzen haben / den Zahnarzt anrufen
>
> *Wenn ich Zahnschmerzen hätte, würde ich den Zahnarzt anrufen.*

1. ich / mehr Geld haben / dir ein Geschenk mitbringen
   Wenn ich mehr Geld hätte, würde ich dir ein Geschenk mitbringen.

2. ihr / nicht so erkältet sein / campen gehen
   Wenn ihr nicht so erkältet wärt, würdet ihr campen gehen.

3. er / nicht arbeiten müssen / Zeit mit seiner Familie verbringen
   Wenn er nicht arbeiten müsste, würde er Zeit mit seiner Familie verbringen.

4. wir / spät ausgehen / morgen lange schlafen
   Wenn wir spät ausgingen, würden wir morgen lange schlafen.

5. du / nicht so viele Hausaufgaben haben / mehr Sport treiben
   Wenn du nicht so viele Hausaufgaben hättest, würdest du mehr Sport treiben.

5 Kritische Meinungen Schauen Sie sich mit einem Partner / einer Partnerin die Bilder an. Fragen Sie ihn/sie, wie er/sie die Geräte findet. Answers will vary.

> **BEISPIEL**
>
> **S1:** Wie findest du das Handy?
> **S2:** Ich fände es besser, wenn es nicht so alt wäre. Wie findest du es?

6 Arbeitsblatt Wählen Sie eine schwierige Situation aus der Liste. Fragen Sie vier Personen, was sie in der Situation machen würden. Answers will vary.

> **BEISPIEL**
>
> **S1:** Was würdest du machen, wenn du einen Unfall sähest?
> **S2:** Wenn ich einen Unfall sähe, würde ich den Krankenwagen rufen.

7 Im Kleidergeschäft

Sie sind Verkäufer/Verkäuferin in einem Kleidergeschäft und versuchen Ihrem Partner / Ihrer Partnerin etwas zu verkaufen, aber ihm/ihr gefällt das Kleidungsstück nicht. Answers will vary.

BEISPIEL

S1: Hätten Sie gern das rote Kleid?
S2: Vielleicht... wenn es nur nicht so rot wäre.

7 Suggestion Bring in photos from fashion magazines and have students use them for this activity.

8 Ich wünschte, ...

Sprechen Sie im Kurs über Ihre Wünsche. Verwenden Sie den Konjunktiv II mit **sein**, **haben**, **können**, **müssen** oder **dürfen**. Answers will vary.

BEISPIEL

S1: Ich wünschte, ich müsste nicht so früh aufwachen. Was wünschst du dir?
S2: Ich wünschte, ich wäre in wirklich guter Form.

9 Mir geht's nicht gut

Sagen Sie Ihrem Partner / Ihrer Partnerin, warum Sie sich nicht wohl fühlen. Beschreiben Sie alle Symptome. Der Partner / Die Partnerin sagt Ihnen, was Sie machen sollen, um sich besser zu fühlen. Answers will vary.

BEISPIEL

S1: Ich fühle mich nicht gut. Ich habe eine verstopfte Nase, und ich huste. Ich glaube, ich habe auch Fieber.
S2: Es hört sich an, als ob du eine schwere Erkältung hättest. Du solltest...

8 Expansion As a final project on the subjunctive, have students work in groups to prepare a poster with 10 statements about a hypothetical topic of their choice, such as their ideal world, what it would be like to be a cat, etc. Encourage them to use **würde** + infinitive constructions, except with the modals and **haben**, **sein**, **wissen**, **wünschen**.

Mein Wör | ter | buch

Schreiben Sie noch fünf weitere Wörter in Ihr persönliches Wörterbuch zu den Themen **Tagesroutine** und **Gesundheit**.

sich ankleiden

Übersetzung
to get dressed

Wortart
Verb

Gebrauch
Ich kleide mich nach der Dusche an.
Im Winter sollen die Kinder sich warm ankleiden.

Synonyme
sich anziehen, sich Kleidung anlegen

Antonyme
sich ausziehen, sich auskleiden

 **S** Vocabulary tools

Panorama ⓢ Interactive Map

Mecklenburg-Vorpommern und Brandenburg

Mecklenburg-Vorpommern in Zahlen

▶ **Fläche:** *23.193 km²*

▶ **Bevölkerung:** *1,6 Millionen Menschen*

▶ **Städte:** *Rostock (204.000 Einwohner), Schwerin (96.000), Neubrandenburg (63.000)*

▶ **Wichtige Industriezweige:** *Schiffbau°, Reedereien°, Energiesektor, Tourismus*

▶ **Touristenattraktionen:** *Usedom, Rügen, Hiddensee, Greifswald, Stralsund*

Mecklenburg-Vorpommern zieht jedes Jahr viele Touristen an, die die Ostseeinseln° Usedom, Rügen und Hiddensee oder die historischen Hafenstädte° Rostock und Schwerin besuchen wollen.

QUELLE: Landesportal Mecklenburg-Vorpommern

Suggestion Tell students that **Buchenwald** was a concentration camp during the Nazi regime.

Brandenburg in Zahlen

▶ **Fläche:** *29.654 km²*

▶ **Bevölkerung:** *2,5 Millionen Menschen*

▶ **Städte:** *Potsdam (163.000 Einwohner), Cottbus (99.000), Brandenburg (71.000)*

▶ **Wichtige Industriezweige:** *Holzgewerbe°, Ernährungsindustrie°, Landwirtschaft°, Tourismus*

▶ **Touristenattraktionen:** *Potsdam, Schloss Sanssouci, Buchenwald im Grumsiner Forst*

Viele Touristen besuchen Potsdam mit seinen kaiserlichen Schlössern und Parkanlagen°.

QUELLE: Landesportal Brandenburg

Berühmte Menschen aus Mecklenburg-Vorpommern und Brandenburg

▶ **Heinrich von Kleist,** *Autor (1777–1811)*

▶ **Marie Christine Eleonora Prochaska,** *Soldatin (1785–1813)*

▶ **Heinrich Schliemann,** *Archäologe und Entdecker der Ruinen von Troja (1822–1890)*

▶ **Otto Lilienthal,** *Flugpionier (1848–1898)*

▶ **Gerhart Hauptmann,** *Autor und Literaturnobelpreisträger (1862–1946)*

Schiffbau shipbuilding **Reedereien** shipping companies **Ostseeinseln** Baltic Sea islands **Hafenstädte** port cities **Holzgewerbe** wood industry **Ernährungsindustrie** food industry **Landwirtschaft** agriculture **Parkanlagen** parks **Innere** inside

DÄNEMARK

OSTSEE

NATIONALPARK VORPOMMERSCHE BODDENLANDSCHAFT

RÜGEN

MECKLENBURGER BUCHT

Stralsund

SCHLESWIG-HOLSTEIN

Greifswald

POMMERSCHE BUCHT

Rostock

USEDOM

Wismar

MECKLENBURG-VORPOMMERN

Schwerin

Neubrandenburg

NATIONALPARK MÜRITZ

Müritz

Elbe

Havel

Oder

NIEDERSACHSEN

BRANDENBURG

POLEN

Oranienburg

BERLIN

Havel

Berlin

Frankfurt an der Oder

Brandenburg

Potsdam

Oder

Spree

SACHSEN-ANHALT

Cottbus

Neiße

SACHSEN

Landesgrenzen
● Stadt
◉ Landeshauptstadt
✪ Hauptstadt

0 — 25 Meilen
0 — 25 Kilometer

TSCHECHIEN

Schloss Güstrow

Hafen von Rostock

Segeln in Brandenburg

Suggestion You may want to mention the comedian Loriot as another example of a **berühmte Brandenburger**. Many of his classic sketches, such as **Die Nudel** or **Die Jodelschule**, can be found online.

Unglaublich, aber wahr!

Auf Rügen gibt es seit 2010 eine neue Touristenattraktion: Das „Haus-Kopf-über". Hier kann man ein Haus besuchen, das auf dem Dach steht. Besucher stehen auf der Unterseite des Hauses und können sich das Innere° des Hauses ansehen.

Architektur
Schloss Sanssouci

Suggestion Before they read about the Potsdam Conference, have students briefly share what they know about the situation in Germany in 1945.

Schloss Sanssouci war der Lieblingsort von Friedrich dem Großen, König von Preußen. Das Schloss war seine Sommerresidenz, in der er sein Privatleben genießen wollte. Der Name Sanssouci bedeutet „ohne Sorge°". Es wurde von 1745 bis 1747 von Georg Wenzeslaus von Knobelsdorff nach den Ideen des Königs auf einem terrassierten Weinberg° gebaut°. Es gilt als Hauptwerk deutscher Rokokoarchitektur. Die prächtigen° und eleganten Räume sind noch original ausgestattet°. Das Schloss und die Parks sind eine der größten Touristenattraktionen Brandenburgs.

Geschichte
Die Potsdamer Konferenz

Zwischen dem 17. Juli und dem 2. August 1945 trafen sich in Potsdam die Alliierten Großbritannien, USA und UdSSR. Sie berieten°, was mit dem ehemaligen Kriegsgegner° Deutschland passieren sollte. An der Konferenz nahmen der sowjetische Diktator Josef Stalin, der US-Präsident Harry S. Truman und die britischen Premierminister Winston Churchill und Clement Attlee teil. Sie entschieden°, dass Deutschland eine Demokratie werden sollte, alle Naziparteien verboten werden und Deutschland eine wirtschaftliche Einheit° werden sollte. Konflikte zwischen Stalin und den anderen Alliierten führten aber später zur Teilung° Deutschlands.

Archäologie
Megalithgräber°

In Mecklenburg-Vorpommern bauten Menschen während der Jungsteinzeit° fast 5.000 große Grabmonumente. Diese Gräber heißen auch Megalithgräber. Die ersten Gräber stammen aus der Zeit um 3.500 vor Christus. Anfangs waren diese Gräber nur für Familienoberhäupter°, später wurden sie immer größer, und ganze Familien wurden in den Gräbern beerdigt°. Etwa 1.000 dieser Grabanlagen° gibt es noch, und wenn man durch die flache Landschaft Mecklenburg-Vorpommerns fährt, kann man sie heute noch gut erkennen.

Geographie
Rügen

Die Ostseeinsel Rügen ist mit 926 km² die größte deutsche Insel und gehört zum Bundesland Mecklenburg-Vorpommern. 70.000 Menschen leben hier ständig. Dazu kommen rund 800.000 Urlauber, die die Insel jedes Jahr besuchen.

Zu den meistbesuchten Touristenattraktionen zählen die Kreidefelsen° im Nationalpark Jasmund und die rund 80 km langen Sand- und Naturstrände.

IM INTERNET

1. Suchen Sie Informationen über die Potsdamer Konferenz: Warum traf man sich in Potsdam? Was wollten die Alliierten mit Deutschland machen?

2. Suchen Sie Informationen über Schloss Sanssouci: Welche Gärten sind Teil der Parkanlage?

Find out more at **vhlcentral.com**.

Sorge *worry* **Weinberg** *vineyard* **wurde... gebaut** *was built* **prächtigen** *grand* **ausgestattet** *furnished* **berieten** *deliberated* **Kriegsgegner** *wartime enemy* **entschieden** *decided* **Einheit** *unity* **Teilung** *division* **Kreidefelsen** *chalk rocks* **Megalithgräber** *megalith graves* **Jungsteinzeit** *New Stone Age* **Familienoberhäupter** *patriarchs* **wurden... beerdigt** *were buried* **Grabanlagen** *burial sites*

 Was haben Sie gelernt? Ergänzen Sie die Sätze.

1. Auf Rügen gibt es ein Haus, das auf dem ___Kopf___ steht.

2. Wenn man das ___Innere___ des Hauses sehen will, muss man auf der Unterseite des Hauses stehen.

3. Schloss Sanssouci war das Schloss von ___Friedrich dem Großen___.

4. Die Architektur von Sanssouci ist ein Beispiel der ___Rokokoarchitektur___.

5. Die Potsdamer Konferenz fand im Jahre ___1945___ statt.

6. An der Konferenz nahmen Churchill, Truman und ___(Josef) Stalin___ teil.

7. Rügen ist die ___größte___ deutsche Insel.

8. Sie liegt an der ___Ostsee___.

9. Die großen Grabmonumente in Mecklenburg-Vorpommern heißen auch ___Megalithgräber___.

10. Die größeren Gräber sind nicht nur für ___Familienoberhäupter___, sondern auch für die ganze Familie.

 Practice more at **vhlcentral.com**.

Lesen Audio: Reading

Vor dem Lesen

Strategien

Reading for the main idea

You have already learned to make predictions about the content of a reading by looking at its format, titles, and subtitles, looking for cognates, skimming to get the gist, and scanning for specific information. Reading for the main idea involves locating the topic sentences of each paragraph to determine the author's purpose. Topic sentences can provide clues about the content of each paragraph, as well as the general organization of the reading. Your choice of which reading strategies to use will depend on the style and format of the reading selections you encounter.

Untersuchen Sie den Text

Sehen Sie sich beide Texte kurz an. Welche Ähnlichkeiten (*similarities*) und Unterschiede (*differences*) können Sie erkennen? Welche Strategien können Sie benutzen, um die Art (*type*) der Texte zu identifizieren? Vergleichen Sie Ihre Ideen mit denen eines Partners / einer Partnerin.

Vergleichen Sie die Texte

- Analysieren Sie das Format des ersten Texts. Gibt es eine Überschrift (*heading*)? Gibt es viele Abschnitte (*sections*)? Wie ist der Text gegliedert (*structured*)? Sehen Sie sich jetzt den Inhalt an. Was für Vokabeln benutzt man? Was ist die Hauptidee von jedem Abschnitt?

- Ist der zweite Text genauso gegliedert wie der erste? Gibt es Überschriften und verschiedene Abschnitte? Ist die Information ähnlich der im ersten Text? Welche Vokabeln werden benutzt? Was für eine Art Text ist es? Was ist die Hauptidee von jedem Abschnitt? Haben beide Texte das gleiche Thema?

Andis Blog

Kommentare

Vorheriger Eintrag

Nächster Eintrag

Archiv

3. Juni 2012

Meine Gesundheitspläne

Heute war ich beim Arzt für eine allgemeine Untersuchung°. Er hat mir gesagt, dass ich in keiner guten Form bin! Meine Blutdruckwerte sind zu hoch. Ich muss gesünder leben! Besser essen und mehr Sport treiben. Das soll ich machen:

Als Erstes muss ich mehr schlafen. Jeden Tag mindestens sieben Stunden. Vielleicht kann ich ja weniger Videospiele spielen!

Vor allem muss ich mich mehr bewegen°. Auf der Arbeit werde ich jeden Tag zum Büro Treppen steigen und nicht mit dem Aufzug° fahren! Ich bin früher immer gerne gelaufen. Also werde ich wieder anfangen zu joggen. Drei Mal die Woche möchte ich eine halbe Stunde joggen. Das wäre super! Ich habe einen tollen Artikel gefunden, der zeigt, wie man drei kurze Übungen machen kann, um fit zu werden. Ich möchte diese Übungen auch drei Mal die Woche machen.

Im Allgemeinen darf ich nicht so viel Stress in meinem Leben haben. Schlafen, Bewegung und besser essen sind ein guter Start. So hoffe ich, bald wieder gesünder zu sein.

Andi

Untersuchung *check-up* **mich... bewegen** *move around* **Aufzug** *elevator*

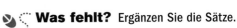

Fit in 10 Minuten!

Sie wollen fit werden? Hier sind 3 kurze Übungen für Bauch und Po°.
Machen Sie dreimal die Woche 5 bis 10 Wiederholungen jeder Übung.

Aufwärmen

Stehen sie aufrecht°, die Füße hüftweit° auseinander.
Gehen Sie 2 Minuten lang auf der Stelle. Die Arme schwingen mit.

Obere Bauchmuskeln

Übung 1

Legen Sie sich mit dem Rücken auf ein Handtuch.
Ziehen Sie jetzt die Knie an. Fassen Sie das
Handtuch mit den Händen an den Enden hinter
dem Kopf. Rollen Sie nun den Oberkörper°
langsam auf. Halten Sie kurz die Position und
rollen Sie langsam wieder in die erste Position.

Schräge° Bauchmuskeln

Legen Sie sich auf den Rücken und ziehen Sie die
Knie an. Heben Sie die Unterschenkel°, bis diese
parallel zum Boden sind. Verschränken° Sie nun die
Hände hinter dem Kopf. Jetzt heben Sie den linken
Ellenbogen zum rechten Knie und zurück, ohne dass
die rechte Schulter den Boden berührt°. Der Rücken
bleibt auf dem Boden. Wiederholen Sie die Übung
mit der anderen Seite.

Übung 2

Po

Übung 3

Hände und Knie berühren den Boden. Heben
Sie nun das linke Knie, bis Oberschenkel
und Boden etwa parallel sind. Halten Sie
kurz diese Position und senken Sie das Knie
langsam wieder zum Boden. Wiederholen
Sie die Übung auch mit der anderen Seite.

Suggestion If you have a lively class and a suitable
space, have students try out the exercises described.

Po *glutes* **aufrecht** *upright* **hüftweit** *hip-wide* **Oberkörper** *upper body* **Schräge** *Oblique*
Unterschenkel *lower leg* **Verschränken** *Cross* **berührt** *touches*

Nach dem Lesen

 Was fehlt? Ergänzen Sie die Sätze.

1. Andi war heute beim _____Arzt_____.

2. Andi muss besser essen und mehr
   _____Sport_____ treiben.

3. Andi darf nicht so viel _____Stress_____ in seinem
   Leben haben.

4. Die Übungen, die Andi gefunden hat, sind für
   _____Bauch_____ und Po.

5. In der zweiten Übung verschränkt man die
   _____Hände_____ hinter dem Kopf.

6. In der dritten Übung berühren Hände und
   _____Knie_____ den Boden.

 Richtig oder falsch? Sind die Sätze richtig
oder falsch? Korrigieren Sie die falschen Sätze.

Sample answers are provided.

	richtig	falsch
1. Andis Arzt sagt, dass alles in Ordnung ist. *Der Arzt sagt, dass Andi gesünder leben muss.*	☐	☑
2. Andi muss sich mehr bewegen.	☑	☐
3. Andi will jeden Tag joggen gehen. *Andi will 3 Mal die Woche joggen gehen.*	☐	☑
4. Andi will jeden Tag mindestens 7 Stunden schlafen.	☑	☐
5. Vor der ersten Übung soll man die Muskeln aufwärmen.	☑	☐
6. In der ersten Übung liegt man mit dem Gesicht nach unten. *In der ersten Übung liegt man auf dem Rücken.*	☐	☑
7. In der zweiten Übung trainiert man die Rückenmuskeln. *In der zweiten Übung trainiert man die Bauchmuskeln.*	☐	☑
8. Alle Übungen kann man in 5 Minuten machen. *Alle Übungen kann man in 10 Minuten machen.*	☐	☑

Bessere Gesundheit Diskutieren Sie
mit einem Partner / einer Partnerin: Sie wollen
gesünder leben. Was müssen Sie machen? Welche
Ziele (*goals*) haben Sie? Wie können Sie diese Ziele
erreichen (*achieve*)?

BEISPIEL

S1: *Ich muss endlich gesünder leben.*
S2: *Was willst du machen?*
S1: *Ich will...*

Hören

NATIONAL communication cultures STANDARDS

Strategien

Using background information

Once you figure out the topic of a conversation, take a minute to consider what you already know about the subject. Using this background information will help you guess the meaning of unknown words or linguistic structures.

 To help you practice this strategy, you will listen to a short commercial. Once you figure out the topic, use your knowledge of the subject to listen for and jot down the main points mentioned.

Vorbereitung

Wie ist es, mit anderen Menschen zusammenzuwohnen? Schreiben Sie vier Dinge auf, die man mit Mitbewohnern planen oder diskutieren muss, damit das Zusammenwohnen ohne Probleme funktioniert. Answers will vary.

Zuhören

Hören Sie sich den Dialog zwischen Marco, Annette und Simone an. Worüber diskutieren sie? Schreiben Sie mindestens sechs Sachen auf. Sample answers are provided.

Frühstück machen
Küche sauber machen
Badezimmer benutzen
Abfall raustragen
Zeitung lesen
Geschirr spülen

Verständnis

Richtig oder falsch Sind die Sätze richtig oder falsch? Korrigieren Sie die falschen Sätze. Sample answers are provided.

1. Marco, Simone und Annette wohnen in einer Wohnung zusammen.
   Richtig.

2. Marco möchte um 7 Uhr ins Badezimmer.
   Falsch. Simone möchte um 7 Uhr ins Badezimmer.

3. Alle Personen bleiben 20 Minuten im Badezimmer.
   Falsch. Marco bleibt nur 15 Minuten im Badezimmer.

4. Simone wird sich nicht im Badezimmer schminken.
   Richtig.

5. Annette muss das Frühstück um 7 Uhr machen.
   Falsch. Annette muss das Frühstück vor 7 Uhr machen.

6. Um 7.20 Uhr darf Annette ins Badezimmer.
   Richtig.

7. Simone muss den Abfall runterbringen.
   Falsch. Annette muss den Abfall runterbringen.

8. Marco liest jeden Morgen Zeitung.
   Richtig.

Morgenroutine Sie und Ihre Partner / Partnerinnen wohnen in einer Wohngemeinschaft (WG) zusammen. Wie funktioniert das Zusammenleben? Wer benutzt wann das Bad? Wie lange? Wie organisieren Sie das Frühstück? Wer räumt auf? Planen Sie die WG-Regeln.

BEISPIEL

S1: Zuerst müssen wir über das Badezimmer sprechen.
S2: Ich möchte als Erster ins Badezimmer.
S3: Und wann?
S1: Kann ich es um 7 Uhr benutzen?

Schreiben

Strategien

Using linking words

You can make your writing more sophisticated by using linking words (**Verbindungswörter**) to connect simple sentences or clauses, creating more complex sentences.

Consider these two passages.

> Heute Morgen war ich beim Arzt. Ich hatte starke Kopfschmerzen. Ich hatte einen schlimmen Schnupfen. Es waren viele Leute im Wartezimmer. Ich musste über eine Stunde warten. Der Arzt hat mich behandelt. Er hat gesagt, dass ich eine Grippe habe.

> Heute Morgen war ich beim Arzt, **denn** ich hatte starke Kopfschmerzen und einen schlimmen Schnupfen. Es waren viele Leute im Wartezimmer. **Deshalb** musste ich über eine Stunde warten. **Endlich** hat der Arzt mich behandelt. Er hat gesagt, dass ich eine Grippe habe.

Expansion Have students work in groups to create a plan and then pitch it to the rest of the class in a Q & A session.

Bio-Produkte haben's drauf.

Thema

Unsere neue Firma

Sie wollen eine Firma im Bereich Gesundheit gründen und brauchen einen Businessplan. Die neue Firma kann ein Fitness-Center, ein Wellness-Center, ein Bioladen (*health-food store*) oder etwas Ähnliches sein.

Schreiben Sie einen Businessplan für potentielle Investoren. Bevor Sie anfangen, überlegen Sie sich Antworten auf die folgenden Fragen:

- Warum gibt es Ihre Firma?
- Welche Art von Service oder welche Produkte bieten Sie an (*offer*)?
- Warum braucht man diesen Service oder diese Produkte?
- Wer sind die Kunden Ihrer Firma?
- Wie erfüllt Ihre Firma die Bedürfnisse (*needs*) Ihrer Kunden?
- Wie ist Ihre Firma anders als ähnliche Firmen?
- Wie heißt Ihre Firma?

Benutzen Sie Verbindungswörter, damit die Präsentation Ihrer Geschäftsidee überzeugend (*persuasive*) wird.

Verbindungswörter

aber	*but*	deswegen	*that's why*
als erstes	*first*	endlich	*finally*
also	*so*	manchmal	*sometimes*
außerdem	*moreover*	normalerweise	*usually*
danach	*then, after that*	oder	*or*
dann	*then*	oft	*often*
denn	*because*	sondern	*however*
deshalb	*so*	sowie	*as well as*

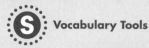 **Vocabulary Tools**

im Badezimmer

der Bademantel, ⸚	bathrobe
die Bürste, -n	brush
der Haartrockner, -	hair dryer
das Handtuch, ⸚er	towel
der Hausschuh, -e	slipper
der Kamm, ⸚e	comb
der Lippenstift, -e	lipstick
der Rasierer, -	razor
der Rasierschaum	shaving cream
der Schlafanzug, ⸚e	pajamas
die Seife, -n	soap
das Shampoo, -s	shampoo
die Zahnbürste, -n	toothbrush
die Zahnpasta (*pl.* Zahnpasten)	toothpaste

der Körper

der Arm, -e	arm
das Auge, -n	eye
die Augenbraue, -n	eyebrow
der Bart, ⸚e	beard
der Bauch, ⸚e	belly
das Bein, -e	leg
der Ell(en)bogen, -	elbow
der Finger, -	finger
der Fuß, ⸚e	foot
das Gesicht, -er	face
das Haar, -e	hair
der Hals, ⸚e	neck
die Hand, ⸚e	hand
das Knie, -	knee
der Kopf, ⸚e	head
die Lippe, -n	lip
der Mund, ⸚er	mouth
die Nase, -n	nose
das Ohr, -en	ear
der Rücken, -	back
die Schulter, -n	shoulder
der Zeh, -en	toe

Verben

aufwachen (wacht...auf)	to wake up
(sich) duschen	to take a shower
ins Bett gehen	to go to bed
sich anziehen (zieht sich...an)	to get dressed
sich die Haare bürsten	to brush one's hair
sich die Zähne putzen	to brush one's teeth
sich rasieren	to shave
sich schminken	to put on makeup

die Gesundheit

die Allergie, -n	allergy
die Apotheke, -n	pharmacy
die Erkältung, -en	cold
allergisch sein (gegen)	to be allergic (to)
krank/gesund werden	to get sick/better
in guter/schlechter Form sein	to be in/out of shape
sich verletzen	to hurt oneself
Sport treiben	to exercise
zum Arzt gehen	to go to the doctor

Symptome

die Bauchschmerzen (*pl.*)	stomachache
die Kopfschmerzen (*pl.*)	headache
die Rückenschmerzen (*pl.*)	backache
der Schmerz, -en	pain
die verstopfte Nase	stuffy nose
die Zahnschmerzen (*pl.*)	toothache
Fieber haben	to have a fever
husten	to cough
niesen	to sneeze
leicht	mild
schwer	serious
schwindlig	dizzy
übel	nauseous

im Krankenhaus

der Arzt, ⸚e / die Ärztin, -nen	doctor
das Medikament, -e	medicine
die Grippe, -n	flu
der Krankenpfleger, -	nurse (m.)
die Krankenschwester, -n	nurse (f.)
der Krankenwagen, -	ambulance
die Notaufnahme, -n	emergency room
der Patient, -en / die Patientin, -nen	patient
das Pflaster, -	adhesive bandage
das Rezept, -e	prescription
die Tablette, -n	pill
das Taschentuch, ⸚er	tissue
das Thermometer, -	thermometer
die Verletzung, -en	injury
der Zahnarzt, ⸚e / die Zahnärztin, -nen	dentist
sich (das Handgelenk / den Fuß) verstauchen	to sprain (one's wrist/ankle)
sich (den Arm / das Bein) brechen	to break (an arm / a leg)
eine Spritze geben	to give a shot
weh tun (tut...weh)	to hurt
weinen	to cry
gesund	healthy
krank	sick
schwanger	pregnant

Accusative reflexive pronouns	See pp. 374–375.
Dative reflexive pronouns	See pp. 378–379.
Reflexives used with prepositions	See pp. 382–383.
Der Konjunktiv II	See pp. 396–397.
würden	See pp. 400–401.

Stadtleben

Suggestion Have students brainstorm a list of things they associate with city life. Ask them which of those things they can identify in the picture.

Communicative Goals

You will learn how to:

- talk about errands and banking
- talk about places and businesses in town

Wortschatz

Orte	*places*
das Blumengeschäft, -e	*flower shop*
die Drogerie, -n	*drugstore*
das Kino, -s	*movie theater*
die Polizeiwache, -n	*police station*
das Rathaus, ¨er	*town hall*
der Waschsalon, -s	*laundromat*
geöffnet	*open*
geschlossen	*closed*
die Post	*mail*
die Adresse, -n	*address*
die Briefmarke, -n	*stamp*
der Briefumschlag, ¨e	*envelope*
die Postkarte, -n	*postcard*
auf der Bank	*at the bank*
das Geld	*money*
das Konto (*pl.* die Konten)	*bank account*
die Münze, -n	*coin*
das Kleingeld	*change*
Geld abheben	*to withdraw money*
Geld einzahlen	*to deposit money*
Ausdrücke	*expressions*
das Bargeld	*cash*
bar bezahlen	*to pay in cash*
Besorgungen machen	*to run errands*
ein Formular ausfüllen	*to fill out a form*
mit der Karte bezahlen	*to pay by (credit) card*
unterschreiben	*to sign*

Suggestion Model the pronunciation of Waschsalon.

ACHTUNG

Post is short for **das Postamt, ¨er** or **die Postfiliale, -n**. It is also used to refer to the mail in general: **Wann kommt die Post?** *When does the mail arrive?*

Suggestion Ask students if they ever send or receive letters. Tell them that a pen pal is a **Brieffreund** or **Brieffreundin**.

Besorgungen (S) Vocabulary Tools

Suggestion Point out the separable-prefix verbs on this page: **abschicken, abheben, einzahlen, ausfüllen.** Remind students that these are listed in the end-of-unit **Wortschatz** with their 3rd-person forms in parentheses. Tell students that **unterschreiben** is an inseparable-prefix verb, and ask them to guess its past-tense forms.

das Schreibwarengeschäft, -e

das Juweliergeschäft, -e

das Internetcafé, -s

die Post

das Paket, -e

der Briefkasten, ¨

Sie schickt einen Brief ab. (abschicken)

der Kiosk, -e

die Zeitschrift, -en

die Zeitung, -en

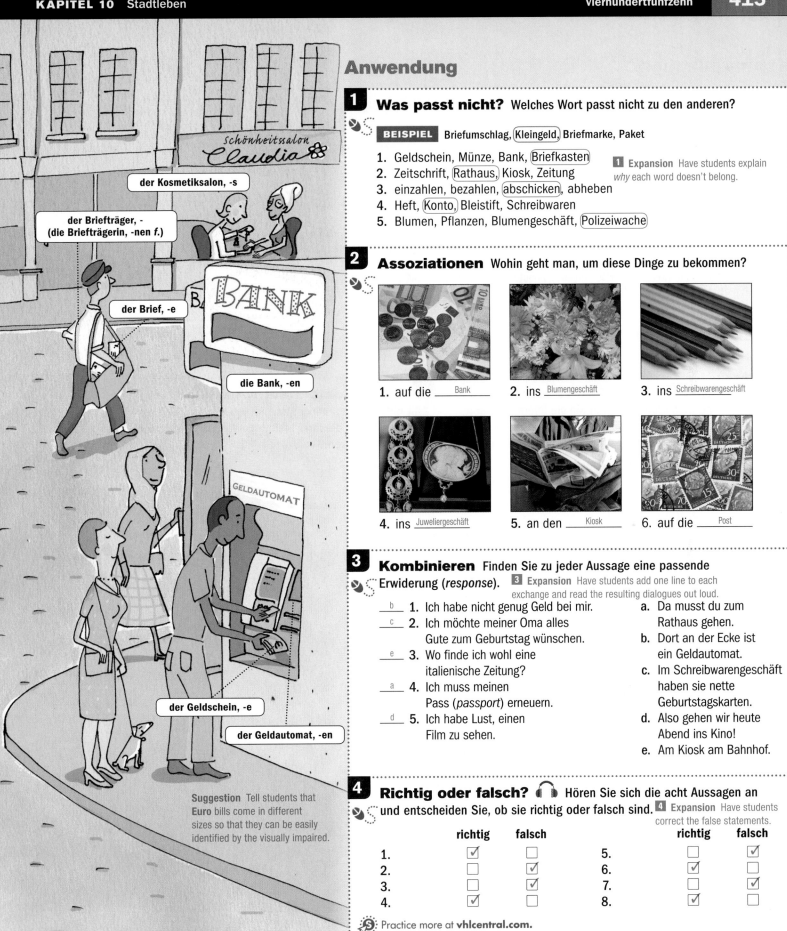

der Kosmetiksalon, -s

der Briefträger, -
(die Briefträgerin, -nen f.)

der Brief, -e

die Bank, -en

GELDAUTOMAT

der Geldschein, -e

der Geldautomat, -en

Schönheitssalon Claudia

BANK

Suggestion Tell students that **Euro** bills come in different sizes so that they can be easily identified by the visually impaired.

Anwendung

1 Was passt nicht? Welches Wort passt nicht zu den anderen?

BEISPIEL Briefumschlag, (Kleingeld,) Briefmarke, Paket

1. Geldschein, Münze, Bank, (Briefkasten)
2. Zeitschrift, (Rathaus,) Kiosk, Zeitung
3. einzahlen, bezahlen, (abschicken), abheben
4. Heft, (Konto,) Bleistift, Schreibwaren
5. Blumen, Pflanzen, Blumengeschäft, (Polizeiwache)

1 Expansion Have students explain *why* each word doesn't belong.

2 Assoziationen Wohin geht man, um diese Dinge zu bekommen?

1. auf die ___Bank___   2. ins ___Blumengeschäft___   3. ins ___Schreibwarengeschäft___

4. ins ___Juweliergeschäft___   5. an den ___Kiosk___   6. auf die ___Post___

3 Kombinieren Finden Sie zu jeder Aussage eine passende Erwiderung (*response*).

3 Expansion Have students add one line to each exchange and read the resulting dialogues out loud.

__b__ 1. Ich habe nicht genug Geld bei mir.
__c__ 2. Ich möchte meiner Oma alles Gute zum Geburtstag wünschen.
__e__ 3. Wo finde ich wohl eine italienische Zeitung?
__a__ 4. Ich muss meinen Pass (*passport*) erneuern.
__d__ 5. Ich habe Lust, einen Film zu sehen.

a. Da musst du zum Rathaus gehen.
b. Dort an der Ecke ist ein Geldautomat.
c. Im Schreibwarengeschäft haben sie nette Geburtstagskarten.
d. Also gehen wir heute Abend ins Kino!
e. Am Kiosk am Bahnhof.

4 Richtig oder falsch? 🎧 Hören Sie sich die acht Aussagen an und entscheiden Sie, ob sie richtig oder falsch sind.

4 Expansion Have students correct the false statements.

	richtig	falsch		richtig	falsch
1.	☑	☐	5.	☐	☑
2.	☐	☑	6.	☑	☐
3.	☐	☑	7.	☐	☑
4.	☑	☐	8.	☑	☐

Practice more at **vhlcentral.com**.

Kommunikation

4 Expansion Have two volunteers act out the dialogue.

4 Besorgungen Bringen Sie mit Ihrem Partner / Ihrer Partnerin die folgenden Sätze in eine logische Reihenfolge.

_7_ **MICHAELA** Ja, ich muss dir nämlich unbedingt erzählen, wen ich im Juweliergeschäft gesehen habe.

_3_ **MICHAELA** Weißt du was? Ich gehe mit dir auf die Post. Ich brauche sowieso Briefmarken. Und danach gehe ich dann auf die Bank, Geld abheben.

_6_ **JULIA** Klar, für einen Kaffee immer. Dann können wir uns dabei auch noch ein bisschen unterhalten.

_2_ **JULIA** Ich muss ein paar Besorgungen machen. Ich muss auf die Post, ein Paket an meine Freundin abschicken, und dann wollte ich noch nach einem Geburtstagsgeschenk für meinen Bruder suchen.

_1_ **MICHAELA** Hallo Julia! Was machst du heute Schönes in der Stadt?

_4_ **JULIA** Du, dort auf der anderen Straßenseite ist ein Geldautomat. Ich will auch noch Bargeld holen.

_8_ **JULIA** Ach ja?! Da bin ich jetzt aber neugierig. Also komm.

_5_ **MICHAELA** Okay, dann lass uns das schnell machen und dann können wir ja noch im Wiener Café einen Kaffee trinken. Hast du Zeit und Lust?

5 Definitionen Schreiben Sie zuerst zu jedem Begriff eine Definition und lesen Sie sie Ihrem Partner / Ihrer Partnerin vor. Er/sie muss dann den passenden Begriff aus der unten stehenden Liste identifizieren.
Suggested answers provided.

S1: Es ist ein Automat, wo man Geld abheben kann.
S2: Ein Geldautomat!

1. Internetcafé Es ist kein Café, wo man nur Kaffee trinkt, sondern wo man im Internet surft.
2. Briefmarken Man macht sie auf einen Umschlag, um einen Brief abzuschicken.
3. Kiosk Hier kauft man Zeitungen und Magazine.
4. Kreditkarte Mit ihr kann man ohne Bargeld bezahlen.
5. Briefträger Diese Person bringt die Post ans Haus.
6. Waschsalon Hier stehen viele Waschmaschinen und Wäschetrockner.

6 Diskutieren und kombinieren Sie und Ihr Partner / Ihre Partnerin bekommen zwei verschiedene Blätter von Ihrem Professor / Ihrer Professorin. Erzählen Sie abwechselnd wohin Anna geht und was sie macht.
Suggested answers provided.

S1: Um zehn Uhr geht Anna auf die Post, um Briefmarken zu kaufen.
S2: Danach...

6 Expansion Ask students to compare their day with Anna's. Ex.: **Haben Sie etwas gemacht, was Anna gemacht hat? Sind Sie auf die Post gegangen?**

7 Die perfekte Stadt Wählen Sie mit zwei Mitstudenten mindestens (*at least*) sechs Orte und Geschäfte, die Ihrer Meinung nach zu einer perfekten Stadt gehören. Answers will vary.

S1: Für mich muss es in einer perfekten Stadt ein Internetcafé geben.
S2: Gute Idee. Ich hätte auch gern eine leckere Konditorei.
S3: Ach, das ist doch nicht so wichtig! Was ich brauche, ist ...

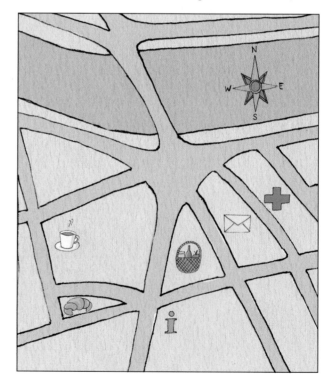

Aussprache und Rechtschreibung Audio

🎧 The Glottal Stop

The glottal stop is the sound you hear in the middle of the English phrase *uh oh*. In German, there is a glottal stop before all words that begin with a vowel.

obwohl	Ampel	Innenstadt	abbiegen	einkaufen

Glottal stops occur within words, when one syllable ends with a vowel and the next syllable begins with a vowel. They also occur in compound words, when the second part of the compound begins with a vowel.

geradeaus	beeilen	Geldautomat	Zahnarzt	Wochenende

A glottal stop also occurs when one syllable of a word ends with a consonant and the next syllable begins with a vowel.

nachahmen	überall	nebenan	überaus	bergab

Suggestion Point out that the glottal stop is also used in English before words beginning with vowel sounds. Write the sentence *I eat an egg at eight*. Have students try saying it without using glottal stops between the words.

1 Aussprechen Wiederholen Sie die Wörter, die Sie hören.

1. abheben
2. Orte
3. einzahlen
4. Ecke
5. bearbeiten
6. Schlafanzug
7. Hausaufgaben
8. Freizeitaktivität
9. Mittagessen
10. hinab
11. fortan
12. bergauf

2 Nachsprechen Wiederholen Sie die Sätze, die Sie hören.

1. Auch am Abend kann man Geld vom Geldautomaten abheben.
2. Am Wochenende arbeitet Amanda in der Apotheke.
3. Im Internetcafé essen acht Engländer Erdbeereis.
4. Auf dem Briefumschlag steht die Adresse allerdings nicht.
5. Fortan bearbeitet ihr alles vor Ort.
6. Das Nadelöhr am Autobahndreieck wird ab morgen ausgebaut.

3 Sprichwörter Wiederholen Sie die Sprichwörter, die Sie hören.

Erst die Arbeit, dann das Vergnügen.[1]

Unkraut vergeht nicht.[2]

[1] Business before pleasure.
[2] Bad weeds grow tall. (*lit.*, Weeds don't die.)

Ressourcen

SAM
LM: p. 85

vhlcentral.com

Gute Neuigkeiten S Video

Sabite bekommt einen Anruf vom Manager der Galerie. Die Freunde wollen die guten
Neuigkeiten feiern. Dann erzählt George von seinem Kuss mit Sabite...

NATIONAL
communication
cultures
STANDARDS

Vorbereitung Have students read the title
of the episode and discuss in pairs what they
think will happen in the episode.

HANS Sind wir an einer Bank vorbeigekommen?
Ich muss Geld vom Bankautomaten abheben.
GEORGE Ich zahle nie bar. Ich zahle mit
meiner Bankkarte.
HANS Immer wenn ich eine Zeitung oder einen
Kaffee kaufe, zahle ich bar. Ich vergesse
immer, die kleinen Artikel aufzuschreiben, und
dann geht mir das Geld auf dem Bankkonto
aus. Ich gebe jede Woche gleich viel aus.
GEORGE Ich habe auf der anderen
Straßenseite eine Bank gesehen, dort.

MELINE Hallo? Oh, hallo Sabite. Was
gibt's Neues? Gutes oder Schlechtes?
Okay, okay. Ich komme gerade aus dem
Salon und treffe dich in einer Stunde im
Biergarten. Bis dann. „Ich sage es dir,
wenn ich dich sehe." Künstler sind
so dramatisch.

HANS Was musst du heute Nachmittag sonst
noch erledigen?
GEORGE Ich muss zur Post gehen und diese
Karten abschicken. Als ich die USA verlassen
habe, habe ich meiner kleinen Schwester Olivia
versprochen, ihr Postkarten zu schicken. Ich
habe sie schon geschrieben, habe sie aber noch
nicht in den Briefkasten geworfen.

GEORGE Hallo Sabite. Hat er angerufen?
Okay... okay. Wir sehen uns dann im
Biergarten. Das brauchst du nicht, er
steht direkt hier. Alles klar. Tschüss.
Sabite hat Neuigkeiten von der Galerie in
der Torstraße bekommen. Sie wollte sie
nicht am Telefon sagen. Wir werden beim
Blumengeschäft Halt machen müssen.

HANS Das müssen um die 20 Karten
sein. ... Potsdamer Platz, Alexanderplatz,
Brandenburger Tor, Jüdisches Museum,
Checkpoint Charlie...
GEORGE Ich werde sie in ein Päckchen legen
mit etwas Schokolade und diesem hier.

SABITE Es geht ihr jetzt wieder gut. Ja, was
komisch ist, ist, dass sie nach Hans gefragt
hat, als sie aufgewacht ist. Ich weiß. Ich
weiß. Oh, Mama, ich muss auflegen. Ich habe
auf diesen Anruf gewartet. Ok, ich gebe dir
Bescheid. Tschüss. Hallo, hier ist Sabite.
Guten Tag, Herr Kleinedler, wie geht es Ihnen?

1 **Wer ist das?** Welche Person(en) beschreiben die folgenden Sätze:
George, Hans, Meline oder Sabite?

1. __Hans__ muss Geld vom Bankautomaten abheben.
2. __George__ zahlt nie bar, sondern immer mit der Karte.
3. __Hans__ gibt jede Woche gleich viel Geld aus.
4. __George__ muss zur Post gehen und Karten abschicken.
5. __George__ will ein Päckchen mit Schokolade abschicken.

6. __Sabite__ bekommt einen Anruf von Herrn Kleinedler.
7. __Meline__ kommt gerade aus dem Salon.
8. __George__ möchte beim Blumengeschäft Halt machen.
9. __George__ erzählt Hans von dem Kuss.
10. __Sabite__ hat gute Neuigkeiten von der Galerie.

PERSONEN

 George   Hans   Meline   Sabite

HANS Immer wenn etwas passiert, ruft sie dich an.
GEORGE Wir sind Freunde.
HANS Mehr nicht?
GEORGE Nein. Als wir uns geküsst haben, da wussten wir beide...
HANS Als ihr was?

GEORGE Wenn ich richtig rate, hast du gute Neuigkeiten. Komisch, ich habe es in deiner Stimme gehört, als du angerufen hast.
MELINE Herzlichen Glückwunsch, Sabite!

SABITE Danke. Wow. Wo ist Hans?
GEORGE Er, ähm...
MELINE Er hat ein Problem mit der Beziehung zwischen... dir und George.
SABITE Welche Beziehung? Wir sind Freunde.
GEORGE Ich habe ihm aus Versehen von unserem Kuss erzählt.

MELINE Von was?
SABITE Oh, George, wie konntest du nur?
GEORGE Frauen bringen mich ganz durcheinander.
MELINE So soll es ja auch sein. Hast du Hunger? Lass uns bestellen.

Nützliche Ausdrücke

- **vorbeikommen**
  to pass
- **aufschreiben**
  to write down
- **erledigen**
  to run an errand
- **verlassen**
  to leave
- **versprechen**
  to promise
- **einen Brief einwerfen**
  to mail a letter
- **das Päckchen**
  little package
- **auflegen**
  to hang up
- **Halt machen**
  to stop by
- **raten**
  to guess
- **die Beziehung**
  relationship
- **aus Versehen**
  by mistake
- **durcheinanderbringen**
  to confuse

10A.1
- **Ich werde sie in ein Päckchen legen mit etwas Schokolade und diesem hier.**
  I'm going to put them all in a little package with some chocolate and this.

10A.2
- **Was gibt's Neues? Gutes oder Schlechtes?**
  What's the news? Is it good or bad?

10A.3
- **Wenn ich richtig rate, hast du gute Neuigkeiten.**
  If I'm right, you have good news.

2 **Zum Besprechen** Machen Sie zu zweit Pläne für einen Tag in der Stadt. Entscheiden Sie, wohin Sie gehen und was Sie machen wollen. Erklären Sie Ihre Entscheidungen. Answers will vary.

2 **Expansion** Have students act out their dialogue in front of the class.

3 **Vertiefung** In den deutschsprachigen Ländern wird der Begriff ‚Kreditkarte' anders verwendet als in den USA. Benutzen Sie das Internet, um herauszufinden, wo genau die Unterschiede (*differences*) liegen.
Suggested answer: In German-speaking countries, the term refers to real credit cards as well as debit, prepaid, or charge cards.

Ressourcen

SAM
VM: p. 19

vhlcentral.com

IM FOKUS

Fußgängerzonen°

 **Reading**

IN VIELEN EUROPÄISCHEN STÄDTEN findet man im Stadtzentrum oder in der historischen Altstadt eine Fußgängerzone, in der man nur zu Fuß gehen darf. Radfahrer müssen langsam fahren oder das Fahrrad schieben°, und Autos dürfen hier nur fahren, wenn sie Geschäfte in der Fußgängerzone beliefern° oder zur Polizei, Feuerwehr oder anderen Notdiensten° gehören. Aber auch sie müssen hier Schritttempo° fahren und sehr vorsichtig sein.

Viele Leute kommen in die Fußgängerzone, weil man in den vielen Geschäften gut einkaufen und in schönen Cafés oder Restaurants im Freien sitzen kann.

Die erste Fußgängerzone Europas gibt es seit 1953 in der Lijnbaan im holländischen Rotterdam. Im selben Jahr eröffnete man in der Kasseler Treppenstraße, die erste Fußgängerzone Deutschlands. Nachdem große Teile Kassels während des Zweiten Weltkriegs zerstört wurden°, gab es einen Wiederaufbauwettbewerb°, um die Innenstadt Kassels neu zu gestalten°. 1961 folgte in Klagenfurt die erste Fußgängerzone in Österreich: die Kramergasse.

Historische Innenstädte° in Deutschland	
Dresden	Im 2. Weltkrieg wurde Dresden fast komplett zerstört. Heute kann man in der Altstadt wieder die Semperoper, den Zwinger und die Frauenkirche besuchen.
Heidelberg	Heidelberg, die Stadt mit der ältesten Universität im heutigen Deutschland, hat die längste Fußgängerzone Deutschlands.
Köln	Die Schildergasse in Köln ist die meistbesuchte Einkaufsmeile Europas.
Regensburg	Die Regensburger Altstadt geht auf die Römer° zurück. Das Schloss der Familie von Thurn und Taxis, die die erste Post in Deutschland gründete, ist Teil dieser Altstadt.

Fußgängerzonen *traffic-free zones* **schieben** *push*
beliefern *supply* **Notdiensten** *emergency services*
Schritttempo *walking pace* **zerstört wurden** *were destroyed*
Wiederaufbauwettbewerb *reconstruction competition*
gestalten *design* **Innenstädte** *city centers* **Römer** *Romans*

1 **Richtig oder falsch?** Sagen Sie, ob die Sätze richtig oder falsch sind. Korrigieren Sie die falschen Sätze.

1. Fußgängerzonen findet man meistens in der Innenstadt. Richtig.

2. Viele Menschen besuchen die Fußgängerzonen einer Stadt. Richtig.

3. In Fußgängerzonen gibt es nur Straßen mit vielen Geschäften.
Falsch. In Fußgängerzonen gibt es auch viele Cafés, Restaurants, Bänke, Brunnen und Bäume.

4. In einer Fußgängerzone dürfen keine Autos fahren.
Falsch. Nur wenige Autos dürfen in einer Fußgängerzone fahren.

5. In Cafés und Restaurants kann man draußen sitzen. Richtig.

6. In Kassel baute man eine Fußgängerzone nach dem Zweiten Weltkrieg, weil große Teile der Innenstadt zerstört waren. Richtig.

7. Die Fußgängerzone in Kassel heißt Kramergasse.
Falsch. Die Fußgängerzone in Kassel heißt Treppenstraße.

8. Die erste Fußgängerzone in Europa gab es in Klagenfurt.
Falsch. Die erste Fußgängerzone in Europa gab es in Rotterdam.

9. Die längste Fußgängerzone in Deutschland ist in Dresden.
Falsch. Die längste Fußgängerzone in Deutschland ist in Heidelberg.

10. Die meistbesuchte Fußgängerzone ist in Köln. Richtig.

 Practice more at **vhlcentral.com**.

DEUTSCH IM ALLTAG

Geschäfte

der Antiquitätenladen	*antiques shop*
der Buchladen	*bookshop*
der Makler	*real estate agent*
der Schneider	*tailor*
der Schuster	*shoemaker*
das Spielwarengeschäft	*toy store*

DIE DEUTSCHSPRACHIGE WELT

Heimat

Für Deutsche, Österreicher und Schweizer ist Heimat ein sehr wichtiger Begriff°. Es ist der Ort, wo man geboren und aufgewachsen ist. Oft haben an diesem Ort schon mehrere Generationen einer Familie gelebt. Heimat bedeutet aber auch die Sprache, die man spricht, und zwar nicht nur Deutsch, sondern auch den Dialekt der Region. Heimat sind auch die Traditionen der Region. Im Allgemeinen ist Heimat ein sehr emotionales Konzept. Man kann dieses Wort nicht direkt ins Englische übersetzen. Oft sagt man *home* oder *homeland*.

Suggestion Ask students what
Begriff *term*   place they consider home and why.

PORTRÄT

Die Deutsche Post

Die Post hat in Deutschland eine lange Tradition. Seit 1615 organisierte die Familie Thurn und Taxis in Deutschland den Postverkehr. Aus dieser Zeit stammt° auch das Symbol der Post: das Posthorn. Reiter benutzten es, wenn sie in Städte oder über Grenzen ritten. Ab 1660 führte die Familie Thurn und Taxis eine Fahrpost ein°, mit der sie Briefe und Personen beförderte°. Die erste Strecke führte von Halle über Magdeburg nach Hamburg. Ab 1710 gab es die ersten Briefträger in Deutschland und ab 1874 gab es dann in ganz Deutschland auch Briefkästen an Häusern. Heute ist die Deutsche Post kein staatliches Unternehmen° mehr, sondern eine private Aktiengesellschaft°.

Suggestion Point out that the **Deutsche Post** has become one of the world's largest courier companies.

stammt *stems* **führte ... ein** *instituted* **beförderten** *transported* **Unternehmen** *organization*
Aktiengesellschaft *corporation*

⟆ IM INTERNET

Suchen Sie im Internet Informationen über eine bekannte Innenstadt in Deutschland. Was können Touristen und Besucher hier alles machen? Welche Geschäfte gibt es? Welche anderen Attraktionen?

Find out more at **vhlcentral.com**.

---

2 **Was fehlt?** Ergänzen Sie die Sätze.

1. Den Begriff Heimat gibt es vor allem in <u>deutschsprachigen</u> Ländern.

2. Heimat ist der Ort, wo man _____<u>geboren</u>_____ und aufgewachsen ist.

3. Für viele Menschen ist Heimat ein sehr _____<u>emotionales</u>_____ Konzept.

4. Die Familie _<u>Thurn und Taxis</u>_ hat in Deutschland die erste Post organisiert.

5. Briefträger gibt es in Deutschland seit _____<u>1710</u>_____.

6. Die erste Poststrecke war von Halle über Magdeburg nach _____<u>Hamburg</u>_____.

3 **Traumstadt** Diskutieren Sie mit einem Partner / einer Partnerin: Wo möchten Sie gerne leben? In einer großen Stadt? In einer kleinen Stadt? Was muss eine Stadt für Sie bieten (*offer*)?

3 **Expansion** Ask students whether they would prefer to live in a big city or a small town.

Ressourcen

vhlcentral.com

10A.1 Subordinating conjunctions (S) Presentation

Startblock In **6A.3**, you learned to use coordinating conjunctions to combine two independent clauses in a single sentence. Use subordinating conjunctions to combine a subordinate clause with a main clause.

Suggestion Have students find the conjugated verbs in each example on this page. Ask if they notice a pattern.

„Ich sage es dir, **wenn** ich dich sehe."

Wenn ich richtig rate, hast du gute Neuigkeiten.

QUERVERWEIS

See **6A.3** to review coordinating conjunctions. See **8A.1** to review the use of the subordinating conjunctions **bevor**, **nachdem**, and **als** with the **Plusquamperfekt**. See **9B.1** to review the use of the subordinating conjunction **wenn** in hypothetical statements.

- A subordinate clause explains, how, when, why, or under what circumstances the action in the main clause occurs. Subordinate clauses always begin with a subordinating conjunction and normally end with the conjugated verb. Always use a comma to separate the subordinate clause from the main clause.

MAIN CLAUSE	SUBORDINATE CLAUSE
Ich lese die Zeitung,	**wenn** ich Zeit **habe**.
I read the newspaper	***when** I **have** the time.*

Suggestion Tell students that **obwohl** is the "conjunction of contradictions." Give examples, ex: **Obwohl ich krank war, musste ich zu Arbeit gehen**.

- Here is a list of commonly used subordinating conjunctions:

subordinating conjunctions

als	*as, when*	ob	*whether, if*
bevor	*before*	obwohl	*although*
bis	*until*	seit	*since*
damit	*so that*	während	*while; whereas*
dass	*that*	weil	*because*
nachdem	*after*	wenn	*when; whenever; if*

ACHTUNG

The conjunctions **denn** and **weil** both mean *because*. Since **denn** is a coordinating conjunction, it does not affect word order: **Ich komme nicht, denn ich bin krank.** Since **weil** is a subordinating conjunction, the verb moves to the end of the clause: **Ich komme nicht, weil ich krank bin**.

___

The conjunction **dass** is often used to report what somebody else said.

Jonas sagt, dass er seine Familie im Herbst besucht.

Vergiss nicht, **dass** wir nächste Woche ins Konzert **gehen**.
*Don't forget **that** we're going to a concert next week.*

Ich bezahle immer bar, **weil** ich keine Kreditkarte **habe**.
*I always pay cash, **because** I don't have a credit card.*

- When you begin a sentence with a subordinate clause, the entire clause is treated as the first element of the sentence. The verb in the main clause moves to second position, after the comma, and is followed by its subject.

SUBORDINATE CLAUSE	MAIN CLAUSE
Wenn ich nach Deutschland fahre,	**spreche** ich immer Deutsch.
Weil meine Familie deutsch ist,	**habe** ich als Kind Deutsch gelernt.
Obwohl ich Deutsch spreche,	**möchte** ich lieber in Italien wohnen.

Suggestion Remind students that the coordinating conjunctions *don't* cause subject-verb inversion and are simply inserted between two clauses.

- When using a separable prefix verb in a subordinate clause, attach the prefix to the beginning of the conjugated verb.

Ich **rufe dich** heute Abend **an**.
*I'll **call** you tonight.*

Ich warte, **bis** du mich **anrufst**.
*I'll wait **until** you **call** me.*

- When using a modal verb in a subordinate clause, put the conjugated form of the modal at the end of the clause, after the infinitive of the verb it modifies.

> Wir **müssen** heute Nachmittag Briefmarken **kaufen**.
> *We **need to buy** stamps this afternoon.*

> Wir gehen zur Post, **weil** wir Briefmarken **kaufen müssen**.
> *We're going to the post office **because** we **need to buy** stamps.*

- For a subordinate clause in the **Perfekt** or **Plusquamperfekt**, move the conjugated form of **sein** or **haben** to the end of the clause, after the past participle.

> Ich **bin** heute früher nach Hause **gegangen**.
> *I **went** home early today.*

> Ich habe Besorgungen gemacht, **bevor** ich nach Hause **gegangen bin**.
> *I ran some errands **before** I **went** home.*

- Use **als** to refer to a one-time event or continuing situation in the past. Use **wenn** to refer to a one-time event in the present or future. Use **(immer) wenn** to refer to a recurring event in the past, present, or future.

> **Als** wir Kinder waren, gab uns Papa Münzen aus anderen Ländern.
> ***When** we were kids, Dad used to give us coins from other countries.*

> **Wenn** du nächsten Sommer nach Hannover fährst, musst du mir eine Postkarte schicken.
> ***When** you go to Hannover next summer, you'll have to send me a postcard.*

Indirect questions

- Indirect questions are a type of subordinate clause. They are introduced by a main clause beginning with a phrase such as **Weißt du**, **Ich möchte wissen**, **Kannst du mir sagen**, **Ich weiß nicht**, or **Ich frage mich**.

> Ich möchte wissen, **ob** ich ein Formular ausfüllen muss.
> *I'd like to know **whether** I need to fill out a form.*

> Ich frage mich, **warum** es so viele Internetcafés in Berlin gibt.
> *I wonder **why** there are so many Internet cafés in Berlin.*

> Erzähl uns bitte, **was** passiert ist.
> *Please tell us **what** happened.*

> Sag mir, **wie viele** Briefmarken du brauchst.
> *Tell me **how many** stamps you need.*

- Use the subordinating conjunction **ob** to ask indirect yes-or-no questions.

> Wissen Sie, **ob** man hier mit der Karte bezahlen kann?
> *Do you know **if** I can pay by card here?*

> Weißt du, **ob** die Post schon da ist?
> *Do you know **if** the mail has come yet?*

- For all other indirect questions, use the question words you learned in **2A.2** as subordinating conjunctions.

> Sie wissen, **wohin** man gehen soll.
> *They know **where** to go.*

> Ich weiß, **wie** du dich fühlst.
> *I know **how** you feel.*

QUERVERWEIS

See **1B.2** to review basic word order.

———

See **5B.2** to review the conjugations of the verb **wissen**.

———

See **2A.2** to review question words.

ACHTUNG

Both **ob** and **wenn** are sometimes translated as *if*, but only **ob** is used in indirect yes-or-no questions. Use **wann**, rather than **als** or **wenn**, to mean *when* in an indirect question.

Expansion Write on the board: **ob** = *whether*. Then, have students complete the sentence, **Ich möchte wissen, ob...** and share their sentences.

Expansion Write two simple sentences, putting each word on a separate card. In class, distribute the cards and have students stand in the correct order to form the sentences. Then, add a card with a subordinating conjunction. Have students place the card between the sentences and rearrange themselves accordingly.

Ressourcen

SAM
WP: pp. 133–134

SAM
LM: p. 86

vhlcentral.com

Jetzt sind Sie dran! Wählen Sie die richtigen Konjunktionen.

1. Lara geht zur Post, (weil / ob) sie Briefmarken braucht.

2. Der Kunde erklärte der Verkäuferin, (dass / ob) er kein Kleingeld hat.

3. Ich habe ein Paket bekommen, (obwohl / ob) ich nichts bestellt habe.

4. (Damit / Nachdem) die Touristen im Internetcafé ihre E-Mails gelesen hatten, sind sie zum Hotel gegangen.

5. (Als / Bevor) man einen Brief abschickt, muss man die Adresse auf den Briefumschlag schreiben.

6. Weißt du, (ob / damit) es beim Kiosk noch Zeitungen gibt?

Anwendung

1 **Ausflug nach München** Ergänzen Sie die Sätze mit **als** oder **wenn**.

BEISPIEL _Wenn_ wir nach München fahren, besuchen wir die Frauenkirche.

1. _Wenn_ es 12 Uhr mittags ist, sollte man am Münchner Rathaus das Glockenspiel anschauen.

2. _Als_ wir das letzte Mal in München waren, hat es nur geregnet.

3. _Wenn_ wir Ende September hier wären, könnten wir auch aufs Oktoberfest gehen.

4. Das erste Oktoberfest hat man 1810 gefeiert, _als_ Kronprinz Ludwig Prinzessin Therese heiratete.

5. Vielleicht fahren wir morgen zum Schloss Neuschwanstein, _wenn_ wir Zeit haben.

6. Ludwig II baute Schloss Neuschwanstein, _als_ er 1864 König (_king_) von Bayern wurde.

2 **Suggestion** Tell students that **Klatsch** means gossip.

2 **Klatsch** Schreiben Sie, was Petra sagt und verbinden Sie die Sätze mit der Konjunktion **dass**.

BEISPIEL Mein kleiner Bruder will immer etwas kaputt machen.
Anna sagt, _dass ihr kleiner Bruder immer etwas kaputt machen will._

1. Max hat noch nie Sushi gegessen.
Anna sagt, dass Max noch nie Sushi gegessen hat.

2. Simon und Greta freuen sich nicht auf ihre Reise.
Anna sagt, dass Simon und Greta sich nicht auf ihre Reise freuen.

3. Die Katze hat eine Ratte im Garten gefangen.
Anna sagt, dass die Katze eine Ratte im Garten gefangen hat.

4. Die Eltern von Antonia haben sich getrennt.
Anna sagt, dass die Eltern von Antonia sich getrennt haben.

5. Mia kommt wegen Nina nicht auf die Feier mit.
Anna sagt, dass Mia wegen Nina nicht auf die Feier mitkommt.

3 **Ein kurzes Interview** Ändern Sie die direkten Fragen in indirekte Fragen um und verwenden Sie dabei die Ausdrücke aus der Liste. Sample answers provided.

BEISPIEL Warum lernst du Deutsch und nicht Spanisch?
Darf ich dich fragen, warum du Deutsch und nicht Spanisch lernst?

Darf ich dich fragen	Ich weiß nicht
Erzähl mir bitte	Kannst du mir sagen
Ich frage mich	Sag mir
Ich möchte gern wissen	Weißt du

1. Kommen deine Großeltern aus Deutschland?
Weißt du, ob deine Großeltern aus Deutschland kommen?
2. Hast du Geschwister?
Ich frage mich, ob du Geschwister hast.
3. Wie oft bist du schon nach Europa geflogen?
Sag mir, wie oft du schon nach Europa geflogen bist.
4. Welches Land möchtest du gern mal besuchen?
Erzähl mir bitte, welches Land du gern mal besuchen möchtest.

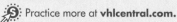 Practice more at **vhlcentral.com.**

Kommunikation

4 Besorgungen

4 **Besorgungen** Fragen Sie Ihren Partner / Ihre Partnerin, wohin er/sie geht, um die folgenden Besorgungen zu machen. Answers will vary.

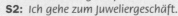
▶ **BEISPIEL**
S1: Wohin gehst du, wenn du einen schönen Ring kaufen willst?
S2: Ich gehe zum Juweliergeschäft.

einen schönen
Ring kaufen

1. Geld abheben

2. schöne Rosen
kaufen

3. ein Paket
abschicken

4. eine Zeitung
kaufen

5. schmutzige
Wäsche waschen

5 **Was und wenn** Fragen Sie Ihren Partner / Ihre Partnerin, was er/sie normalerweise in den folgenden Situationen macht. Achten Sie auf die Wortstellung. Answers will vary.

BEISPIEL
S1: Was machst du normalerweise, wenn du richtig Hunger hast?
S2: Wenn ich richtig Hunger habe, esse ich einen Hamburger.

1. Hunger haben
2. sich schlecht fühlen
3. müde sein

4. sich verspäten
5. ein Paket abschicken wollen
6. traurig sein

6 **Was weißt du?**
A. Schreiben Sie vier Dinge auf, die Sie schon über die deutschsprachigen Länder gelernt haben. Beginnen Sie jede Aussage mit „**Ich weiß, dass...**". Answers will vary.

BEISPIEL
Ich weiß, dass Berlin die Hauptstadt Deutschlands ist.

B. Machen Sie jetzt ein kleines Quiz, um herauszufinden, ob Ihr Partner / Ihre Partnerin dasselbe Wissen hat. Beginnen Sie jede Frage mit **Weißt du, ...** und einem passenden Fragewort – **wer, was, wann, wo, wie**. Answers will vary.

BEISPIEL
S1: Weißt du, was die Hauptstadt Deutschlands ist?
S2: Natürlich! Berlin ist die Hauptstadt Deutschlands!

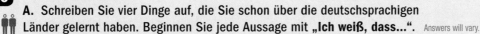

5 Suggestion Tell students that they can be creative with their answers.

6 Expansion After students complete part B, have everyone switch partners and repeat the quiz.

10A.2

Adjectives used as nouns  Presentation

Suggestion Explain that adjectival nouns referring to men are masculine, those referring to women are feminine, and those referring to more than one person are plural.

Startblock Many adjectives in German can also be used as nouns.

Herr Miller ist ein sehr **alter** Mann.
*Mr. Miller is a very **old** man.*

Was sollen wir machen, um **den Alten** zu helfen?
*What should we do to help **the elderly**?*

- The endings for adjectival nouns change depending on the gender, number, or case of the noun, and whether it is preceded by a **der**-word or an **ein**-word. When you use an adjective as a noun, add the same ending that you would add to the adjective form.

adjective	noun after a *der*-word	noun after an *ein*-word
arbeitslos *unemployed*	**der/die Arbeitslose** *unemployed person*	**ein Arbeitsloser / eine Arbeitslose**
bekannt *(well-)known*	**der/die Bekannte** *acquaintance*	**ein Bekannter / eine Bekannte**
erwachsen *grown(-up)*	**der/die Erwachsene** *adult*	**ein Erwachsener / eine Erwachsene**
jugendlich *young, youthful*	**der/die Jugendliche** *young person*	**ein Jugendlicher / eine Jugendliche**
verlobt *engaged*	**der/die Verlobte** *fiancé(e)*	**ein Verlobter / eine Verlobte**
verwandt *related*	**der/die Verwandte** *relative*	**ein Verwandter / eine Verwandte**

QUERVERWEIS

See **3A.2** to review adjective endings in the nominative and accusative cases, **4B.1** to review dative endings, and **8B.1** to review genitive endings.

See **7B.3** to review indefinite words.

ACHTUNG

Common expressions with neuter adjectival nouns are **nichts Besonderes** (*nothing special*) and **etwas anderes** (*something else*). Notice that there is no capitalization in the expression **etwas anderes**.

- When adjectival nouns refer to people, the gender of the noun matches the gender of the person. When they refer to previously mentioned objects, the gender of the noun matches the gender of the object.

Marias **Verlobter** ist sehr nett.
*Maria's **fiancé** is very nice.*

Seine **Verwandten** habe ich nicht so gern.
*I'm not so crazy about his **relatives**.*

Welche **Krawatte** hast du gekauft?
*Which **tie** did you buy?*

Ich habe die **Blaue** gekauft.
*I bought the **blue one**.*

- Adjectival nouns that refer to concepts are always neuter and are only used in the singular. They often follow indefinite words such as **alles**, **etwas** and **nichts**, or the quantity words **viel** and **wenig** (*little, not much*). For adjectival nouns after **etwas**, **nichts**, **viel**, or **wenig**, use the endings for unpreceded neuter adjectives. After **alles**, use the endings you would use after a **der**-word. **Suggestion** Have students memorize the phrase **Alles Gute!** as a reminder that adjectival nouns after **alles** take the -e ending.

Wir wünschen dir **alles Gute**!
*We wish you **all the best**!*

Möchtest du **etwas Kaltes** trinken?
*Do you want **something cold** to drink?*

Ressourcen

SAM
WP: pp. 135-136

SAM
LM: p. 87

vhlcentral.com

Suggestion Emphasize that **etwas anderes** is an exception to the rule that adjectival nouns are always capitalized.

Suggestion Demonstrate the pattern by writing on the board **etwas Altes** and **etwas Neues**. Underline the capital letters and the -es endings. Have students guess how to say "*something blue*," etc. Repeat with **wenig, viel**, and **nichts**.

Jetzt sind Sie dran! Wählen Sie das Wort, das in jedem Satz am besten passt.

1. Meine __c__ sind alle sportlich, vor allem mein Onkel.
2. Ich will dir etwas __a__ erzählen.
3. Du __e__! Hast du dich schwer verletzt?
4. Dein __b__ hat dir einen wunderschönen Ring geschenkt.
5. Amila bestellt alles __d__, das sie auf der Speisekarte sieht.

a. Lustiges
b. Verlobter
c. Verwandten
d. Leckere
e. Arme

Anwendung und Kommunikation

1 **Was fehlt?** Ergänzen Sie die Sätze mit den richtigen Endungen der substantivierten Adjektive.

1. Wer ist die hübsche Rothaarig<u>e</u> dort drüben?

2. Ich finde, dass Tom nichts Interessant<u>es</u> zu sagen hat.

3. Er ist ein Bekannt<u>er</u>, aber kein Freund.

4. In dem Gestreift<u>en</u> siehst du wirklich gut aus.

5. Macht ihr heute noch etwas Besonder<u>es</u>?

1 **Suggestion** Do the first few items as a class. After students have completed the activity, have them explain how they chose the correct endings.

2 **Interview** Stellen Sie Fragen mit einem passenden Paar aus der Liste. Answers will vary.

BEISPIEL

S1: Was isst du lieber, etwas Süßes oder etwas Scharfes?
S2: Ich esse lieber etwas Scharfes.

einfach / kompliziert	kalt / warm
fantastisch / realistisch	lecker / gesund
hell / dunkel	modern / klassisch
italienisch / mexikanisch	süß / scharf

1. Was isst du lieber, ... ?

2. Was trinkst du am häufigsten, ... ?

3. Was schaust du dir im Fernsehen lieber an, ... ?

4. Welche Musik hörst du dir meistens an, ... ?

5. Welche Kleidung steht dir besser, ... ?

3 **Bilder beschreiben** Beschreiben Sie mit einem Partner / einer Partnerin die Bilder und verwenden Sie dabei substantivierte Adjektive aus der Liste. Answers will vary.

3 **Suggestion** Have students work through this activity twice: first orally, with an emphasis on communication and content; then in writing, with an emphasis on accuracy.

dick	klein	verlobt
jugendlich	krank	verwandt

▶ **BEISPIEL**

Die Kleine hat einen Brief an den Weihnachtsmann geschrieben.

1.

2.

3.

4.

 Practice more at **vhlcentral.com**.

10A.3

QUERVERWEIS

See **2B.2** to review the use of the present tense with future meaning. See **2B.1** or **9B.2** to review the present tense forms of **werden**.

In **11B.1**, you will learn about the future perfect tense, **das Futur II**

ACHTUNG

Do not confuse the modal **wollen** with the future auxiliary **werden**: **Ich will gehen.** *I want to go.* BUT: **Ich werde** gehen. *I will go. / I'm going to* go.

In a subordinate clause, the infinitive of the modal comes at the end of the clause, preceded by the infinitive of the verb it modifies. The conjugated form of **werden** comes *before* both infinitives.: **Er weiß nicht, wie lange er wird arbeiten müssen.**

Suggestion Since this is a common mistake among students, you may want to have your class highlight the first note in the **Achtung** box. Write on board: **Ich will** is NOT *I will*!

Das Futur I  Presentation

Startblock You have already learned to make statements about the future using the present tense with future meaning. You can also use the future tense (**das Futur I**) to talk about the future, especially when the future meaning might not otherwise be clear from context.

Er **wird** bald hier **sein**.

Wir **werden** beim Blumengeschäft Halt machen **müssen**.

- To form the **Futur I**, use a present tense form of the verb **werden** with the infinitive of the verb that expresses the action.

  Wir **werden** uns in einer Woche wieder **treffen**.
  *We'll **meet** again in one week.*

  Werdet ihr am Wochenende Zeit **haben?**
  ***Will** you **have** time on the weekend?*

- In subordinate clauses, move the conjugated form of **werden** to the end of the clause, unless the clause contains a modal verb. When using a modal verb in the **Futur**, place the infinitive of the modal verb at the end of the clause, *after* the infinitive of the verb it modifies.

  Suggestion Tell students that a trick for remembering verb order with modals in future subordinate clauses is the acronym **AIM**: Auxiliary Infinitive Modal.

  Wir **werden** unsere Hausaufgaben **machen**, nachdem wir etwas essen.
  *We'll **do** our homework after we eat something.*

  Ich verspreche dir, dass ich dich immer **lieben werde**.
  *I promise you that I **will** always **love** you.*

  Bald **wird** man überall mit der Karte **bezahlen können**.
  *Soon, you'll **be able to pay** by credit card everywhere.*

  Sie **werden** ein Formular bei der Post **ausfüllen müssen**.
  *You **will have to fill out** a form at the post office.*

- The **Futur I** is commonly used to talk about assumptions or expectations concerning the present *or* future. Such sentences often include the words **wohl**, **wahrscheinlich**, **sicher**, or **schon**, all of which mean *probably* when used with the **Futur**.

  Daniel **wird wohl** noch bei der Ärztin **sein**.
  *Daniel **is probably** still at the doctor's office.*

  In 100 Jahren **wird** die Welt **sicher** sehr anders **aussehen**.
  *In 100 years, the world **will probably look** very different.*

Jetzt sind Sie dran! Bilden Sie Sätze im Futur.

1. ich / bar bezahlen *Ich werde bar bezahlen.*
2. wir / machen keine Besorgungen
   Wir werden keine Besorgungen machen.
3. du / jetzt ins Bett gehen / ?
   Wirst du jetzt ins Bett gehen?
4. ihr / wahrscheinlich Hunger haben
   Ihr werdet wahrscheinlich Hunger haben.
5. ich / müssen / sich schnell anziehen
   Ich werde mich schnell anziehen müssen.

6. Nina / wohl / auf der Post / sein
   Nina wird wohl auf der Post sein.
7. das Kind / schon / schlafen
   Das Kind wird schon schlafen.
8. es / heute noch / regnen
   Es wird heute noch regnen.
9. wir / müssen / früh aufstehen
   Wir werden früh aufstehen müssen.
10. Onkel Gerhard / Diät machen
    Onkel Gerhard wird Diät machen.

Anwendung und Kommunikation

1 **Sätze schreiben** Schreiben Sie die Sätze um. Benutzen Sie das Futur.

BEISPIEL Wir kommen um 10 Uhr an.

Wir werden um 10 Uhr ankommen.

1. Ich koche morgen Abend. Ich werde morgen Abend kochen.
2. Müsst ihr am Abend noch lernen? Werdet ihr am Abend noch lernen müssen?
3. Andreas ärgert sich wohl darüber. Andreas wird sich wohl darüber ärgern.
4. Das Wetter wird bald besser. Das Wetter wird bald besser werden.
5. Das Flugzeug hat vier Stunden Verspätung. Das Flugzeug wird vier Stunden Verspätung haben.
6. Bist du nächstes Jahr schon 21? Wirst du nächstes Jahr schon 21 sein?
7. Will Michaela ein Zimmer buchen? Wird Michaela ein Zimmer buchen wollen?
8. Sie ziehen im Herbst in eine größere Wohnung um. Sie werden im Herbst in eine größere Wohnung umziehen.

2 **Meine Zukunftspläne** Fragen Sie einander nach Ihren
Zukunftsplänen (*plans for the future*). Benutzen Sie die Futurformen. Answers will vary.

BEISPIEL

S1: *Was wirst du heute Abend machen?*
S2: *Heute Abend werde ich Deutsch lernen.*

1. heute Abend
2. am Wochenende
3. im Sommer
4. im Winter
5. nach dem Studium

2 Expansion Ask pairs to prepare a list of predictions about what they and their classmates will be doing in 10 years.

3 **Und dann** Schauen Sie sich mit Ihrem Partner / Ihrer Partnerin
zusammen die Fotos an und entscheiden Sie, was wohl in den nächsten
Minuten passieren wird. Benutzen Sie das Futur. Answers will vary.

BEISPIEL

S1: *Ich glaube, der Mann wird einen Käsekuchen kaufen.*
S2: *Ich glaube, er wird Brötchen fürs Frühstück kaufen.*

1.

2.

3.

4.

Wiederholung

1 Wer ist's?

Wer ist's? Wählen Sie drei Adjektive aus der Liste und beschreiben Sie Ihrem Partner / Ihrer Partnerin zu jedem Adjektiv eine Person. Ihr Partner / Ihre Partnerin sagt, was für eine Person Sie beschreiben. Answers will vary.

BEISPIEL

S1: Dieser Mann hat seine Katze verloren. Er weint den ganzen Tag.
S2: Ist das der Traurige?
S1: Ja.

1 Expansion Have students act out the characteristics described by the adjectival nouns.

dreckig	langweilig
intelligent	lustig
sportlich	nervös

2 Diskutieren und kombinieren

Diskutieren und kombinieren Sie und Ihr Partner / Ihre Partnerin bekommen verschiedene Arbeitsblätter. Fragen Sie Ihren Partner / Ihre Partnerin, welche Gegenstände die einzelnen Personen in dem Kaufhaus möchten.

BEISPIEL

S1: Was für einen Pulli möchte Paul?
S2: Er möchte einen Roten.

3 Unglaublich!

Unglaublich! Wechseln Sie sich mit einem Partner / einer Partnerin ab: Was ist den Personen in den Bildern passiert? Beginnen Sie jede Beschreibung mit „Hast du gehört, dass ..." oder „Weißt du, dass ...". Ihr Partner / Ihre Partnerin wird auf die Neuigkeiten (news) reagieren. Answers will vary.

3 Expansion Bring in additional pictures for students to work with.

BEISPIEL

S1: Hast du gehört, dass Maria einen Autounfall hatte?
S2: Nein! Unglaublich! Sie fährt aber doch immer so langsam.

1. Maria

2. Anna und Jonas

3. Emma und Felix

4. Max

5. Jan

6. Lisa und Erik

4 Versprechungen

Versprechungen Wählen Sie eine Person aus der linken Spalte und einen Zeitraum aus der rechten. Erzählen Sie Ihrem Partner / Ihrer Partnerin, was Sie jeder Person für diese Zeiträume versprochen haben. Answers will vary.

BEISPIEL

4 Suggestion Remind students that **versprechen** takes a dative object.

S1: Ich habe meinen Eltern versprochen, dass ich nach dem Abschluss einen Job finden werde.
S2: Gute Idee. Meinen Eltern habe ich versprochen, dass ...

die Eltern	in drei Wochen
der Freund	im Sommer
der Professor	nach dem Studium
du	in fünf Jahren
die Schwester	vor dem 65. Lebensjahr
die Freundin	in 15 Jahren

5 Arbeitsblatt

Arbeitsblatt Formulieren Sie in Dreiergruppen drei Fragen für eine Umfrage (poll): Wohin gehen andere Personen im Unterricht, wenn sie in die Stadt gehen? Was machen sie dort? Seien Sie höflich (polite), wenn Sie fragen! Answers will vary.

5 Suggestion Remind students to use the subjunctive for polite requests.

BEISPIEL

S1: Entschuldigung, ich möchte gern wissen, wie oft du im Monat auf die Bank gehst.
S2: Vielleicht ein- oder zweimal im Monat.
S1: Aha, und könntest du mir sagen, ob ...

6 Die Zukunft

Die Zukunft Diskutieren Sie mit einem Partner / einer Partnerin, wie die Stadt der Zukunft aussehen wird. Answers will vary.

S1: In der Zukunft wird wohl kein Mensch mehr Auto fahren.
S2: Das stimmt. Wahrscheinlich werden Computer bald Auto fahren können.

Ein Film von Andreas Schmid-Thomae

Fanny

mit Johannes Spengler, Georgia Stahl
und Sebastian Münster

Nützliche Ausdrücke

- **leben**
  to live
- **die Probe**
  rehearsal
- **sich (etwas) merken**
  to remember (something)
- **Halt die Klappe!**
  Shut your mouth!
- **fassen**
  to understand
- **Das soll nicht dein Ernst sein!**
  You can't be serious!
- **Rate mal!**
  Guess!
- **verrückt**
  crazy
- **eigentlich**
  actually

Über den Film sprechen

- **der Regenschauer**
  rain shower
- **malen**
  to paint
- **sich trennen (von)**
  to break up (with)
- **sich verabreden (mit)**
  to make a date (with)

S Video: Short Film

Fanny

Fanny erkennt Al im Park wieder und sie verabreden sich. Aber Al verliert ihre Telefonnummer. Fannys Mitbewohnerin Nora und Als Freund Max lernen einander kennen, als sie Fanny und Al helfen zueinander zu finden.

Vorbereitung

1 **Fragen und Antworten** Verbinden Sie jede Frage mit der logischsten Antwort.

__c__ 1. Hast du dich mit Sophie zum Abendessen verabredet?

__e__ 2. Soll man jeden Tag leben, als ob es der letzte wäre?

__d__ 3. Rate mal, wen ich heute im Supermarkt getroffen habe!

__a__ 4. Könnt ihr uns helfen, die Wohnung anzumalen?

__b__ 5. Soll ich dir meine Telefonnummer aufschreiben?

a. Heute können wir leider nicht, weil wir Probe haben.

b. Nein, danke. Ich kann sie mir merken.

c. Nein. Eigentlich habe ich mich gestern von ihr getrennt.

d. Das weiß ich nicht. Du musst es mir sagen.

e. Das ist verrückt! Wenn man so lebte, könnte man niemals seine Zukunft planen.

2 **Besprechen Sie** Diskutieren Sie die folgenden Sprichwörter mit einem Partner / einer Partnerin. Glauben Sie an diese Sprichwörter? Warum oder warum nicht?

Liebe macht blind.

Die Zeit vergeht - die Liebe bleibt.

Szenen: Fanny

FANNY: Al!
AL: Fanny! Hallo!
FANNY: Hallo.
AL: Was machst du hier?
FANNY: Ich lebe hier.
AL: Das kann nicht sein.

MAX: Und? Was wirst du jetzt tun?
AL: Hier hab' ich sie wiedergetroffen.
MAX: Ja, und?
AL: Hier werd' ich auf sie warten.

NORA: Ich wohn' mit ihr zusammen.
MAX: Mit Fanny?
NORA: Ja.
MAX: Zeig mir, wo ihr wohnt!

FANNY: Jean... Ich liebe dich nicht mehr.
JEAN: Ich hab' wohl einige Dinge° falsch gemacht. Gelächelt hast du, aber. Dann werde ich wohl den Rest meiner Tage im Kloster° verbringen.

AL: Sie ist nicht allein!
MAX: Ja und?
AL: Und sie hat dieses lebende° Paket geküsst.
MAX: Ja, aber das heißt doch gar nichts°.

AL: Hab' ich für dich gepflückt°.

einige Dinge *some things* **Kloster** *monastery* **lebende** *living* **gar nichts** *nothing* **gepflückt** *picked*

Analyse

3 **Wer ist das?** Welche Personen beschreiben die folgenden Sätze?

a. Al

b. Max

c. Fanny

d. Nora

e. Jean

f. der Hausmeister

___b___ **1.** Er ist ein guter Freund von Al.

___e___ **2.** Er hat sich als lebendes Paket verkleidet.

___d___ **3.** Max hat sie im Park erkannt.

___c___ **4.** Sie ist Noras Mitbewohnerin.

___a___ **5.** Er hat für Fanny Blumen angemalt.

___f___ **6.** Er will nicht, dass Jean bei ihm klingelt.

4 **Und wie geht's weiter?** Entscheiden Sie mit einem Partner / einer Partnerin, was die Personen aus diesem Film in Zukunft machen werden. Werden sowohl Fanny und Al als auch Nora und Max für immer zusammen bleiben? Wird Jean endlich seine große Liebe finden? Schreiben Sie zusammen mindestens fünf Sätze darüber.

5 **Beziehungsgespräch** In diesem Film erfährt (*learns*) man, dass Fanny und Jean sich vor einem Jahr getrennt haben. Erfinden Sie ein Gespräch zwischen Fanny und Jean, das vor der Trennung stattfindet.

6 **Diskutieren Sie** Wenn Sie verliebt wären, hätten Sie auch wie Al im Film gehandelt? Wenn Sie Max oder Nora wären, hätten Sie auch Fanny und Nora geholfen? Besprechen Sie diese Fragen mit Ihren Partnern.

Communicative Goals

You will learn how to:

- ask for and give directions
- talk about parts of a city

In der Stadt

S Vocabulary Tools

Wortschatz

die Innenstadt	*downtown*
das Einkaufszentrum, (*pl.* Einkaufszentren)	*mall; shopping center*
das Gebäude, -	*building*
das Kaufhaus, ⸚er	*department store*
die Kirche, -n	*church*
die Stadt, ⸚e	*town*
das Viertel, -	*neighborhood*
Verkehr	*traffic*
die Allee, -n	*avenue; boulevard*
der Bürgersteig, -e	*sidewalk*
die Ecke, -n	*corner*
die Hauptstraße, -n	*main road*
der Zebrastreifen, -	*crosswalk*
Menschen	*people*
der Bürgermeister, - / die Bürgermeisterin, -nen	*mayor*
der Fußgänger, - / die Fußgängerin, -nen	*pedestrian*
Wo ist ...?	*Where is ...?*
abbiegen (biegt... ab)	*to turn*
folgen	*to follow*
bis zu	*until; up to*
gegenüber von	*across from*
geradeaus	*straight*
in der Nähe von	*close to*
in Richtung	*toward*
nah(e)	*near; nearby*
weit von	*far from*
Ausdrücke	*expressions*
(jemanden) mitnehmen	*to give (someone) a ride*
(die Straße) überqueren	*to cross (the street)*

Suggestion Remind students that they encountered the numerical meaning of **Viertel** when they learned to tell time in **2A.3**. Ex: **Es ist Viertel nach vier**. Point out that the English word quarter can also refer to a neighborhood or section of a city, as in the French Quarter of New Orleans.

die Brücke, -n

Sie geht die Treppe hoch. (hochgehen)

die Statue, -n

Er geht die Treppe herunter. (heruntergehen)

der Brunnen, -

Osten · Süden · Norden · Westen

Er hat sich verlaufen. (sich verlaufen)

Sie findet sich zurecht. (sich zurechtfinden)

ACHTUNG

Folgen is used with an object in the dative case: **Folge mir! Folgen Sie dem Bus!** To tell someone to follow a road, use **entlanggehen** if the person is on foot or **entlangfahren** for someone in a vehicle: **Gehen Sie die Hauptstraße entlang, bis Sie zur ersten Kreuzung kommen.**

die Ampel, -n

die Kreuzung, -en

die Straße, -n

Suggestion Explain that telephone booths are used mainly with phone cards for international calls.

die Telefonzelle, -n

Suggestion Point out that when **die Bank** refers to a *bank* the plural form is **Banken**, and when it refers to a *bench*, the plural is **Bänke**.

die Bank, ¨e

Anwendung

1 Paare finden Welche Tätigkeit verbinden Sie mit welcher Person oder mit welchem Ort?

b	1. nach rechts abbiegen	a. die Bank
e	2. mit der Bürgermeisterin sprechen	b. die Kreuzung
d	3. auf dem Bürgersteig gehen	c. die Telefonzelle
a	4. sich kurz hinsetzen	d. der Fußgänger
c	5. telefonieren	e. das Rathaus
g	6. hochgehen	f. das Kaufhaus
f	7. einkaufen gehen	g. die Treppe

2 Bilder beschriften Finden Sie ein passendes Wort für jedes Bild.

Sample answers provided.

1. ____die Ecke____   2. ____die Kirche____   3. ____der Brunnen____

4. ____die Ampel____   5. ____die Statue____   6. ____die Brücke____

3 Definitionen Lesen Sie die Definitionen und wählen Sie das dazu gehörige Wort aus Ihrer Vokabelliste.

1. Hier darf man die Straße überqueren. ___der Zebrastreifen___
2. Manchmal ist sie rot, gelb oder grün. ___die Ampel___
3. Man muss über sie gehen, um den Fluss zu überqueren. ___die Brücke___
4. Hier kreuzen sich zwei Straßen. ___die Kreuzung/die Ecke___
5. Man geht sie hoch oder herunter. ___die Treppe___
6. Normalerweise ist es eine Skulptur aus Stein in Gestalt einer Person. ___die Statue___

4 Gespräche 🎧 Hören Sie sich die Kurzdialoge an und entscheiden Sie dann, wo diese Gespräche stattfinden (*take place*).

1. Brücke / (Einkaufszentrum)
2. (Bänke) / Kirchen
3. Kaufhaus / (Brunnen)
4. (Ampel) / Zebrastreifen
5. Kiosk / (Statue)

4 Expansion Have students close their books before you play the dialogues. Have them guess the locations without looking at the options.

Practice more at **vhlcentral.com.**

Kommunikation

5 Wegbeschreibungen
Sehen Sie sich den Stadtplan an und fragen Sie Ihren Partner / Ihre Partnerin, wie Sie zu den angegebenen Orten kommen. Ihre Ausgangsposition (*starting point*) ist mit einem "X" gekennzeichnet. Wechseln Sie sich ab. Answers will vary.

BEISPIEL

S1: *Entschuldigen Sie bitte, können Sie mir sagen, wie man zur Peterskirche kommt?*
S2: *Gehen Sie auf der Karolinenstraße geradeaus bis zum Bismarckplatz. Dann…*

1. die Peterskirche
2. der Tiergarten
3. die Universitätsbibliothek
4. der Herkulesbrunnen
5. das Einkaufszentrum "Königsarkaden"
6. die Post

Suggestion Review the phrases listed on p. 434 under the headings **Wo ist…?** and **Ausdrücke**. To help students use these phrases correctly, begin with a listening task: Have students start at the "X" and move along the map as you give directions to different locations. Repeat a few times before having them work in pairs.

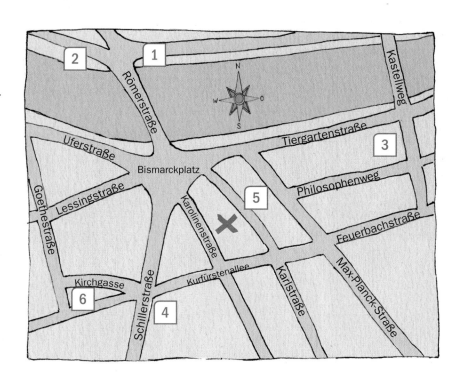

6 Nach der Ankunft
Schreiben Sie zusammen mit Ihrem Partner / Ihrer Partnerin eine E-Mail an Toni, eine Freundin aus Österreich, die Sie nächste Woche besuchen kommt. Erklären Sie ihr, wie man am besten zu Ihnen nach Hause findet. Answers will vary.

Von:	Vogel.Scheuche@online.de
An:	toni.meltzer@epost.au
Betreff:	Dein Besuch

Hallo Toni!

Wir freuen uns schon sehr auf deinen Besuch. Wenn du am Flughafen ankommst, solltest du erst mit dem Bus 51 in die Stadtmitte fahren. Dann…

7 Diskutieren und kombinieren
Sie und Ihr Partner / Ihre Partnerin bekommen zwei verschiedene Versionen des- selben Kreuzworträtsels (*crossword puzzle*). Geben Sie einander die Definitionen der fehlenden Wörter, um die beiden Versionen des Kreuzworträtsels auszufüllen.

BEISPIEL

S1: *Eins waagerecht: hier treffen sich vier Straßen.*
S2: *Das ist eine Kreuzung.*

8 Mein Viertel
Zeichnen Sie zuerst eine Karte Ihres Viertels und beschreiben Sie es danach Ihrem Partner / Ihrer Partnerin. Er/Sie versucht eine eigene Karte zu zeichnen. Answers will vary.

BEISPIEL

S1: *Ich wohne um die Ecke, zwischen der Hauptstraße und dem Park. Wenn du bei mir aus der Haustür rausgehst und dann gleich nach rechts, dann…*

Aussprache und Rechtschreibung  Audio

🎧 Loan Words (Part 1)

Some German words borrowed from other languages retain elements of their original pronunciation. For example, the German consonant **v** is normally pronounced like the *f* in the English word *fan*. But in certain loan words, the **v** is pronounced like the *v* in *van*.

| In**v**estor | Uni**v**ersität | **V**entilator | Ad**v**okat | **V**egetarier |

The **ch** letter combination has a variety of pronunciations in loan words. Depending on the word, it may be pronounced like the *k* in *kitten*, like the *sh* in *shop*, or with a sound similar to the *j* in *jungle*. In some loan words, it is pronounced like the **ch** in the word **ich**.

| **Ch**arakter | **Ch**ef | che**ck**en | **Ch**emie | **Ch**ina |

The **sk** in the German word **Ski** and related compound words is pronounced like the *sh* in *shirt*.

| **Sk**ilift | **Sk**ier | **Sk**iläufer | **Sk**ipiste | **Sk**iurlaub |

Suggestion Point out to students that many borrowed words are pronounced with standard German pronunciation, ex.: **informativ**, **aktiv**.

Suggestion Tell students about regional variations in pronunciation of **ch** at the beginning of loanwords. For example, an Austrian would typically pronounce **China**, "keen ah," while someone from Wuppertal might say "sheen ah."

◆Ⓢ **1** Aussprechen Wiederholen Sie die Wörter, die Sie hören.

1. Interview
2. Vase
3. Video
4. investieren
5. Chaos
6. Champignon
7. Charter
8. Chance
9. chinesisch
10. Skifahrer
11. Skihütte
12. Skispringen

Suggestion Have students refer to the **Ausprache** and **Rechtschreibung** sections of **5B** and **6A** to review the pronunciation of **ch** in German words.

◆Ⓢ **2** Nachsprechen Wiederholen Sie die Sätze, die Sie hören.

1. Der kreative und aktive Vegetarier war in Wirklichkeit ein Vampir.
2. Mit den chaotischen Zuständen in China kommt der Chef nicht zurecht.
3. Die Skiläufer fahren mit dem Skilift zu den Skipisten.
4. Das Interview mit dem Investor von der Bank war sehr informativ.
5. Auch im Winter essen wir oft Vanilleeis in unserer Villa in Venedig.
6. Der charmante Chemiker war ein Mann von Charakter.

◆Ⓢ **3** Sprichwörter Wiederholen Sie die Sprichwörter, die Sie hören.

Auf dem Vulkan tanzen.[1]

„*Wer nichts als Chemie versteht, versteht auch die nicht recht.*"[2]
–Georg Christoph Lichtenberg

[1] To laugh in the face of danger. (*lit.*, To dance on the volcano.)
[2] Whoever understands nothing other than chemistry, does not truly understand even that.

Fotoroman

Sabites Nacht Video

Die Freunde wollen ausgehen, um Sabites Erfolg zu feiern. Leider ist Berlin ziemlich groß. Wo war nochmal dieses spanische Restaurant?

Vorbereitung Have students look at scenes 5 and 6 and try to predict what the characters are reacting to. After they have watched the video, have them review their predictions.

GEORGE Hans? Hans! Du verlierst noch das Gehör, wenn du diese Dinger die ganze Zeit auf den Ohren trägst. Es sind jetzt schon drei Tage, Hans. Könntest du bitte mit mir darüber reden?
HANS Ich kann dich nicht hören.
GEORGE Geh heute Abend mit uns aus. Idiot.

GEORGE Sabite, ich bin's, George!
SABITE Ich komme! Kein Hans?
MELINE Hallo! Lass mal sehen. Sehr europäisch. Spricht Hans immer noch nicht mit dir? Idiot. Gib mir deine Schlüssel.

MELINE Hans, ich sage es nur einmal – hör also gut zu. Die Galerie in der Torstraße stellt Sabites Kunst in ein paar Wochen aus. Heute Abend feiern wir diese Neuigkeiten. Wir laufen nach Charlottenburg, um in einem spanischen Restaurant zu Abend zu essen. Und danach gehen wir in einen Club tanzen. George und Sabite sind nur Freunde. Das musst du einfach kapieren.

GEORGE Kommst du mit?
HANS Ich muss mich noch umziehen. Wir sehen uns dann in Kreuzberg.
SABITE Ich habe Melines Handtasche. Beeil dich. Wir treffen dich dann dort.

MELINE Du bist Berlinerin, Sabite! Wie kann man sich denn hier verlaufen?
SABITE Ich bin noch nie in diesem Stadtteil gewesen.
GEORGE Ich habe zwei Häuserblocks weiter unten an der Kreuzung mit der Straßenampel ein koreanisches Restaurant gesehen. Wir sollten umkehren.
SABITE Ich will kein koreanisches Essen essen, ich wollte doch spanisches Essen. Es ist mein Abend.

MELINE Mir ist es egal, wo wir essen gehen.
SABITE Hallo Hans. Wo bist du? Beweg dich nicht. Wir treffen dich dort in ein paar Minuten.

ÜBUNGEN

1 Was fehlt? Ergänzen Sie die Sätze mit den richtigen Informationen.

1. (George / Hans) spricht seit drei Tagen mit niemandem.
2. Die Galerie in der Torstraße will Sabites Kunst (kaufen / ausstellen).
3. Alle möchten diese Neuigkeiten in Charlottenburg (erzählen / feiern).
4. Sie wollen in einem (italienischen / spanischen) Restaurant essen gehen.
5. Anschließend wollen sie in einem Club (tanzen / singen).
6. George hat an der (Kreuzung / Brücke) ein koreanisches Restaurant gesehen.

7. Sabite möchte kein (koreanisches / spanisches) Essen.
8. Hans hat eine (Notiz / Karte) ausgedruckt, bevor er die Wohnung verlassen hat.
9. Sie müssen an der Kreuzung abbiegen und Richtung (Brücke / Tankstelle) gehen.
10. Das Restaurant ist gegenüber von einer (Telefonzelle / Statue).

PERSONEN

 George   Hans   Meline   Sabite

7

SABITE Er ist an der U-Bahn-Station Görlitzer Bahnhof. Wir sind nicht weit weg davon. Ich kann mich erinnern, sie gesehen zu haben. Sie ist einen Häuserblock von der Falckensteinstraße entfernt. Wir sollten über diese Straße gehen und dann in diese Richtung weitergehen.

8

HANS Ich hatte es online nachgesehen, bevor ich die Wohnung verlassen habe. Ich habe uns eine Karte ausgedruckt. So, wir sind nicht weit vom Restaurant entfernt. Wir gehen einen Häuserblock weiter, biegen an der Kreuzung ab und gehen in Richtung Brücke. Es ist gegenüber von einer Statue.

9

GEORGE Es tut mir leid, Sabite.
SABITE Mir auch.
HANS Ich... Ich muss gehen.

10

SABITE Hans, warte! Hans! Geh ihm hinterher!
MELINE Ich laufe Jungen nicht hinterher, Sabite, Jungen laufen mir hinterher. Lass nicht zu, dass er uns den Spaß verdirbt. Essen und Tanzen warten auf dich. Es ist Sabites Nacht!

Nützliche Ausdrücke

- **das Gehör verlieren**
  to lose one's hearing
- **kapieren**
  to understand
- **umkehren**
  to turn around
- **sich bewegen**
  to move
- **Ich laufe Jungen nicht hinterher, Sabite, Jungen laufen mir hinterher.**
  I don't chase boys, Sabite; they chase me.
- **Lass nicht zu, dass er uns den Spaß verdirbt.**
  Don't let him ruin our fun.

10B.1
- **Wir sollten über diese Straße gehen und dann in diese Richtung weitergehen.**
  We should cross this street, and continue in this direction.

10B.2
- **Ich will kein koreanisches Essen essen, ich wollte doch spanisches Essen.**
  I don't want Korean food, I wanted Spanish food.

---

2 **Zum Besprechen** Stellen Sie sich vor, Hans kommt als Tourist in Ihre Stadt. Spielen Sie einen Dialog, in dem Sie ihm drei Orte empfehlen, die er sehen sollte. Erklären Sie ihm den Weg von Ihrer Schule oder Uni aus. Answers will vary.

2 Expansion Ask each pair of students what their three favorite places in town are and have them describe how you can get there.

3 **Vertiefung** Hans, George, Meline und Sabite wollen im Berliner Stadtteil (*district*) Charlottenburg spanisch essen gehen. Finden Sie weitere Stadtteile von Berlin.
Possible answers: Mitte, Tiergarten, Wedding, Prenzlauer Berg, Friedrichshain, Wilmersdorf, Kreuzberg, Spandau, Zehlendorf, Schöneberg, Steglitz, Tempelhof, Neukölln, Treptow, Köpenick, Lichtenberg, Weißensee, Pankow, Reinickendorf.

3 Expansion Have students identify which districts were formerly part of East Berlin.

Kabarett  Reading

Suggestion As a pre-reading activity, have students ask each other about their favorite comedians, late-night TV shows, and theater acts. Do any of these engage in social criticism or political satire?

TIPP

Many of the terms used to describe theatrical forms in German, like **Pantomime**, **Satire**, and **Komödie**, are similar to their English counterparts.

KABARETT IST EINE FORM DES THEATERS. Es wird auch Kleinkunst genannt. Beim Kabarett kombinieren und verbinden° Künstler Monologe, Dialoge, Pantomime und schauspielerische Szenen. Auch Aspekte der Lyrik (Gedichte° und Balladen) und Musik sind Teil° des Kabaretts. Im Kabarett kritisieren Künstler oft Aspekte der Gesellschaft°, indem sie Satire, Parodie, Sarkasmus und Ironie für diese Kritik benutzen. Dabei wollen sie auch das Publikum unterhalten° und zum Lachen bringen. Man kann Kabarett vor allem auf kleinen Bühnen° sehen. Die deutsche Kultshow „Mitternachtsspitzen", moderiert vom Kabarettisten Jürgen Becker, ist ein Beispiel dafür, dass es Kabarett auch im Fernsehen gibt.

Kabarett begann ursprünglich in Frankreich. 1901, etwa 20 Jahre später, gründete° Ernst von Wolzogen in Berlin das Kabarett „Überbrettl". Während des Kaiserreichs am Anfang des 20. Jahrhunderts und während des Dritten Reichs hatten Kabarettisten große politische Probleme. Erst nach dem 2. Weltkrieg durften Künstler im Kabarett wieder sagen, was sie wollten, und freie Kritik an Politik und Gesellschaft üben. In Mainz kann man heute das Deutsche Kabarettarchiv finden, wo es für die herausragenden° deutschen Kaberettisten ähnlich dem° *Hollywood Walk of Fame* einen Weg „Sterne der Satire" gibt.

Berühmte Kabarettisten	
Dieter Hallervorden (1935–)	Gründete 1960 das Kabarett Die Wühlmäuse und ist berühmt für die Figur Didi. In dem Film „Didi und die Rache der Enterbten" spielt Hallervorden sieben Rollen!
Dieter Hildebrandt (1927–)	Einer der wichtigsten Kaberettisten Deutschlands und Mitbegründer° der Münchner Lach- und Schießgesellschaft.
Urban Priol (1961–)	Berühmt für seine Arbeit im Kabarett und im Fernsehen. 2015 wurde ein Asteroid nach ihm benannt: (233880) Urbanpriol.

QUELLE: Das deutsche Kaberett Portal

Expansion One of the more accessible **Kabarett** artists for first-year students is the American Gayle Tufts, who performs in a language of her own invention: "Denglisch."
verbinden *combine* **Gedichte** *poems* **Teil** *part* **Gesellschaft** *society* **unterhalten** *entertain* **Bühnen** *stages* **gründete** *founded* **herausragenden** *outstanding* **ähnlich dem** *similar to the* **Mitbegründer** *co-founder*

1 **Richtig oder falsch?** Sind die Aussagen richtig oder falsch? Korrigieren Sie die falschen Aussagen mit einem Partner / einer Partnerin.

1. Ein anderer Name für Kabarett ist Kleinkunst. Richtig.
2. Kabarett ist eine Kombination von vielen Kunstformen. Richtig.
3. Kabarett kann man nur im Fernsehen sehen. Falsch. Kabarett kann man vor allem auf kleinen Bühnen sehen.
4. Das erste Kabarett in Deutschland hieß Überbrettl. Richtig.
5. Eine berühmte Kabarettshow im deutschen Radio heißt „Mitternachtsspitzen". Falsch. Die Show spielt im deutschen Fernsehen.
6. Das Deutsche Kabarettarchiv ist in Mainz. Richtig.
7. In Berlin gibt es einen Weg „Sterne der Satire". Falsch. Er ist in Mainz.
8. Urban Priol spielt auf der Bühne und im Fernsehen. Richtig.

 Practice more at **vhlcentral.com**.

Orte der Kunst

die Freilichtbühne, -n	open air theater
die Galerie, -n	gallery
das Kabarett, -s	cabaret
das Museum, Museen	museum
die Oper, -n	opera
das Theater, -	theater

Religion

Die beiden größten Religionsgruppen in Deutschland sind der Katholizismus (die Römisch-Katholische Kirche) und der Protestantismus (Evangelische Landeskirchen). Etwa 30% der Deutschen sind römisch-katholisch und 35% evangelisch. Im Süden und Westen sind mehr Menschen katholisch. Im Norden sind mehr Menschen evangelisch. Diese Aufteilung° geht auf den Dreißigjährigen Krieg° zurück, als Länder im Norden die protestantische Seite unterstützten° und Länder im Süden die römisch-katholische Kirche. Neben den beiden Hauptreligionen ist der Islam mit 3% die drittgrößte Religionsgruppe, aber etwa ein Drittel der Bevölkerung (29%), vor allem in Ostdeutschland, ist konfessionslos.

Aufteilung *division* **Krieg** *war* **unterstützten** *supported*

Pina Bausch

Suggestion You may want to show students excerpts from the 3-D documentary by Wim Wenders, *Pina*, 2012. Other clips that showcase Bausch's choreography are available online.

Pina Bausch (1940–2009) war neben Mary Wigman die bedeutendste° deutsche Choreographin der Gegenwart°. Sie begann ihre Ausbildung° als Tänzerin an der Folkwangschule in Essen. Sie studierte auch an der Juilliard School in New York. 1973 wurde sie choreographische Leiterin° bei den Wuppertaler Bühnen und das Tanzensemble wird schon bald in Tanztheater Wuppertal umbenannt.

Bausch entwickelte° eine neue Tanzform, das Tanztheater, eine Kombination von Tanz, Gesang, Pantomime und Akrobatik. Es war sehr radikal und die Aufführungen° waren am Anfang oft kontrovers. Bausch war international anerkannt° und sie bekam Preise in Deutschland, England, Frankreich, Italien, Japan, Russland, der Türkei und den USA.

bedeutendste *most significant* **Gegenwart** *present times* **Ausbildung** *training* **Leiterin** *director* **entwickelte** *developed* **Aufführungen** *performances* **anerkannt** *recognized*

◉S IM INTERNET

Suchen Sie mehr Informationen zum Thema Religion in Deutschland: Welche Religionen gibt es in Deutschland? Welche religiösen Feste feiern die Deutschen? Welche offiziellen Feiertage gibt es?

Find out more at **vhlcentral.com**.

Suggestion Point out that the religious landscape of Germany is changing rapidly as immigrants bring their own beliefs with them.

---

2 **Was fehlt?** Ergänzen Sie die Sätze.

1. Etwa 35% der Deutschen sind ___evangelisch___.
2. Mehr katholische Deutsche wohnen im ___Süden___ und Westen.
3. Das Tanztheater Pina Bausch ist in ___Wuppertal___.
4. Tanztheater ist eine neue ___Tanzform___.
5. Pina Bauschs Tanztheater ist eine Kombination von Tanz, Gesang, Pantomime und ___Akrobatik___.

3 **Kabarett!** Schreiben Sie mit einem Partner / einer Partnerin ein kurzes Kabarettstück, um es vor der Klasse zu spielen. Wählen Sie zuerst ein Thema. Überlegen Sie sich dann, was Sie darüber sagen oder zeigen wollen. Wollen Sie soziale oder politische Kommentare in Ihr Stück integrieren? Wollen Sie Satire oder Sarkasmus integrieren? Wie können Sie Ihre Ideen am besten zeigen: durch ein Gedicht (*poem*), mit Pantomime oder in der Form von Musik?

3 **Suggestion** Help students with planning a few days before the actual performance, and encourage them to rehearse. Clarify your expectations in terms of length of performance, props, etc. Ideally, students should memorize their lines instead of reading them.

Ressourcen

vhlcentral.com

10B.1

QUERVERWEIS

See **3B.3**, **4B.2** and **5B.3**, to review the use of prepositions with the accusative and dative cases. See **7A.2**, to review the use of prepositions to indicate location.

You will learn more about country names in **10B.2**.

ACHTUNG

Remember that **nach Hause** means *(to) home*, while **zu Hause** means *(at) home*. Note that you cannot use **zu Hause** to express going to someone else's home.

Remember that certain prepositions are typically combined with the definite article to form a contraction. You have already learned the accusative contractions **ans**, **aufs**, **durchs**, **fürs**, **ins**, **ums** and the dative contractions **am**, **beim**, **im**, **vom**, **zum**, **zur**.

Suggestion Tell students that the patterns described here are helpful as guidelines, but that the use of prepositions is not always clear cut. Point out, for example, that the phrases **zum Kunstmuseum** and **ins Kunstmuseum** are both acceptable, but that **ins** emphasizes going *inside* to look at exhibits. Point out that **in**, **auf**, and **an** are also sometimes used interchangeably.

Prepositions of direction  Presentation

Startblock In **7A.2**, you learned to use prepositions to talk about where things are located. You can also use prepositions to talk about movement toward or away from a location.

Wir müssen **nach** Kreuzberg zurück.

Wir sollten **über** die Straße gehen und dann **in** diese Richtung weitergehen.

- Use **nach** with geographical place names to talk about traveling to a destination. Use **in** with the accusative if a place name includes a definite article.

Fliegt ihr morgen **nach** Istanbul?
*Are you flying **to** Istanbul tomorrow?*

Wir wollten schon immer **in** die Türkei fahren.
*We've always wanted to go **to** Turkey.*

- Use **zu** with the dative to talk about going to a destination within a town or city, such as a store or building. You can also use **zu** with a dative personal pronoun or a person's name or title to say that you are going to their home or business.

Dieser Bus fährt **zum** Einkaufszentrum.
*This bus goes **to** the shopping center.*

Ich muss noch schnell **zu** Aldi, um Milch zu kaufen.
*I still have to go **to** Aldi to buy milk.*

Die Fahrt **zu** meinen Großeltern dauert zwei Stunden.
*The drive **to** my grandparents' house takes two hours.*

Vergiss nicht, dass du morgen **zur** Zahnärztin gehen musst!
*Don't forget that you have to go **to** the dentist tomorrow!*

- Use **in** with the accusative to talk about going to a location inside a building, into a geographical area, or to a certain street.

Heute Abend gehe ich **in** die Bibliothek.
*I'm going **to** the library tonight.*

Mia geht **in** den Waschsalon.
*Mia's going **into** the laundromat.*

Am Wochenende fahren wir gern **in** die Berge.
*On weekends, we like to drive up **into** the mountains.*

Biegen Sie links ab **in** die Waldstraße!
*Take a left **onto** Wald Street!*

- Use **auf** with the accusative to talk about movement toward a horizontal surface, an open space, or a public building, and also in idiomatic expressions such as **auf eine Party gehen**.

Legen Sie die Papiere bitte **auf** meinen Schreibtisch.
*Please put the papers **on** my desk.*

Am Sonntag gehen wir **auf** den Markt.
*On Sunday, we're going **to** the market.*

Könntest du bitte **auf** die Post gehen und Briefmarken kaufen?
*Could you please go **to** the post office and buy some stamps?*

Morgen fahren Herr und Frau Maier **aufs** Land.
*Tomorrow, Mr. and Mrs. Maier are driving **out to** the country.*

- Use **an** with the accusative to talk about movement toward a vertical surface or a body of water.

Emma hängt ihre Poster **an** die Wand.
*Emma is putting her posters up **on** the wall.*

Fahren wir zusammen **ans** Meer!
*Let's go **to** the seaside together!*

Im Sommer gehen wir immer **an** den Strand.
*We always go **to** the beach in the summer.*

Sie fahren im Urlaub **an** die Nordsee.
*They're going **to** the North Sea on vacation.*

- Use **über** with the accusative to talk about movement over, across, or by way of something, such as a street, a bridge, or a mountain.

Radfahrer sollen ihre Fahrräder **über** die
Straße schieben.
*Bicyclists are supposed to push their bikes
across the street.*

Sie fahren **über** München nach Salzburg.
*They're driving to Salzburg **by way of** Munich.*

Nur bei Grün darf man **über** die
Kreuzung fahren.
*You can only drive **through** the intersection
when the light is green.*

Wir sind **über** die Berge nach Österreich gereist.
*We traveled **over** the mountains to Austria.*

- Use **aus** with place names to express where someone is from. If the place name includes a definite article, use the dative case.

Unsere Eltern kommen **aus** Österreich.
*Our parents are **from** Austria.*

Die beste Schokolade kommt **aus** der Schweiz.
*The best chocolate comes **from** Switzerland.*

- When using modals with prepositions of location, German speakers often omit the infinitive after the modal.

Wir müssen **nach Hause**.
*We have to **go home**.*

Ich will **ins Bett**.
*I want to **go to bed**.*

Ressourcen

SAM
WB: pp. 141–142

SAM
LM: p. 91

S

vhlcentral.com

 Jetzt sind Sie dran!   **Wählen Sie die passenden Präpositionen.**

1. Ich fliege morgen früh (nach)/ in / auf) Spanien.
2. Tim und Greta fahren (in / auf / (an)) den Strand.
3. In zwei Wochen fliegen wir alle (über / (nach)/ zu) Hause.
4. Wie kommt man am schnellsten (an den / (zum)) / in den) Deutschen Museum?
5. Ich fahre gern (in)/ über / auf) die Schweiz.
6. Geht ihr am Wochenende (an / nach / (auf)) Annikas Party?
7. Schaut in beide Richtungen, bevor ihr (nach / (über)/ in) den Zebrastreifen lauft.
8. Der Lehrer hat seinen Namen (an)/ in / nach) die Tafel geschrieben.
9. Warst du schon (in / zu / (auf)) der Post?
10. Fahren Sie (an / (in)/ auf) die Albstraße hinein und suchen Sie dort einen Parkplatz.
11. Mama, ich gehe (nach / über / (zu)) einer Freundin.
12. Der Mann ist bei Rot (zu / (über)/ aus) die Kreuzung gefahren.
13. Ich fliege morgen (zu / (nach)/ auf) München.
14. Wir gehen (zu / (auf)/ an) den Markt.

Anwendung

1 **Was fehlt?** Ergänzen Sie die Sätze mit **nach** oder **in**.

 ▶ **BEISPIEL** Italien
Nächsten Freitag fahre ich
nach Italien.

die Fußgängerzone
1. Zum Einkaufen
geht man
in die Fußgängerzone.

Paris
2. Macht ihr
eine Reise
nach Paris ?

die Schweiz
3. Jan und
Maria fahren
in die Schweiz.

Mexiko
4. Kiara würde gern
nach Mexiko
fliegen.

die Staatsbibliothek
5. Am Freitag
gehen wir
in die Staatsbibliothek.

2 **Kombinieren Sie** Ergänzen Sie die Sätze mit den passenden
Präpositionen: **an, auf, in, über, zu**.

BEISPIEL Kommst du nach dem Konzert noch mit uns _zu_ Paul?

1. Mein Opa legt sich nach dem Mittagessen immer _auf_ das Sofa.
2. Um zu Sarah zu kommen, musst du _über_ die Brücke fahren und dann links abbiegen.
3. Wisst ihr, ob Annika und Lena _in_ die Bibliothek gegangen sind?
4. Ich muss noch schnell _auf_ die Bank gehen und Geld abheben.
5. Warum fährst du im Winter nie in die Berge, sondern immer nur _an_ den Strand?

3 **Persönliche Fragen** Beantworten Sie die Fragen in ganzen Sätzen.
Achten Sie darauf, dass Sie die passenden Präpositionen bei Ihren
Antworten benutzen. Sample answers provided.

BEISPIEL Wohin werden Sie am Ende des Semesters fahren?
Ich werde zu meinen Eltern fahren.

1. Wohin gehen Sie, wenn Sie richtig Spaß haben wollen? Ich gehe zu meinem besten Freund.
2. Wohin gehen Sie, wenn Sie mal ganz allein sein wollen? Ich gehe in den Wald.
3. Wohin gehen Sie, wenn Sie ein schönes Geschenk für Ihre Mutter suchen?
Ich gehe in ein Juweliergeschäft.
4. Wohin gehen Sie, wenn Sie Briefmarken brauchen? Ich gehe auf die Post.
5. Wohin fahren Sie lieber: in die Berge oder an den Strand? Ich fahre lieber an den Strand.
6. Wohin möchten Sie in Urlaub fahren? Ich möchte gern in die Schweiz in Urlaub fahren.

Practice more at **vhlcentral.com**.

Kommunikation

4 **Wohin?** Wohin sind die Leute in den Bildern gegangen, gefahren oder geflogen? Schreiben Sie Sätze mit einem Partner / einer Partnerin und benutzen Sie dabei das Perfekt und die passenden Präpositionen. Answers will vary.

> | Italien | der See | der Supermarkt |
> | das Konzert | der Strand | |

▶ **BEISPIEL** Simone und Emil

Simone und Emil sind an den See gefahren.

1. Herr und Frau Kaymaz

2. Julian

3. Mira

4. Familie Lehmann

5 **Wie oft…?** Fragen Sie Ihren Partner / Ihre Partnerin, wie oft er/sie zu den angegebenen Orten geht. Answers will vary.

BEISPIEL

S1: *Wie oft gehst du ins Theater?*
S2: *Vielleicht einmal im Jahr. Und wie oft gehst du auf eine Party?*
S1: *Jedes Wochenende.*

1. das Kino
2. das Einkaufszentrum
3. der Arzt
4. die Großeltern
5. die Bank

6 **Spielen im Unterricht** Zwei Studenten verlassen (*leave*) das Klassenzimmer. Der Rest der Klasse ändert die Position von ein paar Sachen im Klassenzimmer. Die zwei Studenten kommen wieder herein und müssen herausfinden, was die anderen Studenten gemacht haben. Answers will vary.

BEISPIEL

S1: *Ihr habt Bücher unter den Tisch gelegt.*
S2: *Und ihr habt einen Rucksack an die Wand gehängt.*

5 **Suggestion** Write the questions as a class, to verify that students are forming the prepositional phrases correctly.

10B.2

Talking about nationality  Presentation

Startblock In German, both nouns and adjectives are used to talk about nationality.

ACHTUNG

The United States may be refered to as **Amerika**, **die USA** (*pl.*), or **die Vereinigten Staaten** (*pl.*). To talk about travelling to a country, use the preposition **in** with country names that begin with an article and **nach** with those that do not. **Ich fliege morgen <u>nach</u> Deutschland. Ich fahre dann <u>in</u> die Schweiz.**

Schweizer is used as an adjective in certain fixed expressions, such as **Schweizer Käse** and **Schweizer Schokolade**. It ends in **-er** regardless of the gender or number of the noun that follows it.

- Unlike in English, German adjectives of nationality are never capitalized and are rarely used to refer to people. To describe a person's nationality, use **sein** with a noun of nationality, dropping the article before the noun.

Magst du **deutsches** Essen?
*Do you like **German** food?*

Sarah ist **Deutsche**.
*Sarah is **German**.*

Suggestion Point out that one can also form nouns and adjectives from city names. Ex: **Er ist Münchner. Ich esse gern Wiener Würstchen.**

countries and nationalities		
Amerika	der Amerikaner,- / die Amerikanerin,-nen	amerikanisch
China	der Chinese,-n / die Chinesin,-nen	chinesisch
Deutschland	der Deutsche,-n / die Deutsche,-n	deutsch
England	der Engländer,- / die Engländerin,-nen	englisch
Frankreich	der Franzose,-n / die Französin,-nen	französisch
Indien	der Inder,- / die Inderin,-nen	indisch
Italien	der Italiener,- / die Italienerin,-nen	italienisch
Japan	der Japaner, - / die Japanerin, -nen	japanisch
Kanada	der Kanadier,- / die Kanadierin,-nen	kanadisch
Korea	der Koreaner,- / die Koreanerin,-nen	koreanisch
Mexiko	der Mexikaner,- / die Mexikanerin,-nen	mexikanisch
Österreich	der Österreicher,- / die Österreicherin,-nen	österreichisch
Russland	der Russe,-n / die Russin,-nen	russisch
die Schweiz	der Schweizer,- / die Schweizerin,-nen	schweizerisch, Schweizer
Spanien	der Spanier,- / die Spanierin,-nen	spanisch
die Türkei	der Türke,-n / die Türkin,-nen	türkisch

QUERVERWEIS

Note that **der/die Deutsche** is an adjectival noun. Its endings follow the patterns you learned about in **10A.2**. The endings shown in the chart are for the nominative case after a definite article.

Chinese, **Franzose**, and **Russe** are **n**-nouns. See **8B.1** to review **n**-nouns.

See **3A.2** to review adjective endings.

- You can use either **nicht** or **kein** before a noun of nationality.

Marie **ist Französin**.
*Marie **is French**.*

Yasmin **ist keine Türkin**.
*Yasmin **isn't Turkish**.*

Max **ist nicht Kanadier**.
*Max **isn't Canadian**.*

- Most nouns referring to languages are identical to the corresponding adjective of nationality, but are capitalized and have no added endings. Nouns referring to a language are always neuter. They do not take definite articles.

Ben spricht fließend **Deutsch**.
*Ben speaks **German** fluently.*

Wir sprechen **kein Italienisch**.
*We don't speak **Italian**.*

Ihr **Französisch** ist sehr gut.
*Your **French** is very good.*

Ich spreche nicht so gut **Russisch**.
*I don't speak **Russian** very well.*

Ressourcen

SAM
WB: pp. 143–144

SAM
LM: p. 92

S

vhlcentral.com

S

Jetzt sind Sie dran! Wählen Sie das passende Wort.

1. Niklas spricht (deutsch / Ⓓeutsch).
2. Ich finde (Chinesisches / chinesisches) Essen sehr lecker.
3. Arnold Schwarzenegger ist (Österreich / Ⓞsterreicher).
4. Karl studiert seit zwei Jahren in Rom und spricht fließend (Ⓘtalienisch / italienisch).
5. Die (Deutsche / Ⓓeutsche) Flagge ist schwarz, rot und gold.
6. Lara kommt aus der Türkei und ist (eine Türkin / Ⓣürkin).
7. Daniela wohnt in Madrid und ist (spanisch / Ⓢpanierin).
8. In Kanada spricht man (englisch / Ⓔnglisch) und Französisch.

Anwendung und Kommunikation

1 **Nationalitäten** Geben Sie die Nationalitäten und die Muttersprachen dieser Personen an.

> **BEISPIEL** Marie / Frankreich
> *Marie ist Französin. Sie spricht wohl Französisch.*

1. Manfred / Deutschland Manfred ist Deutscher. Er spricht (wohl) Deutsch.
2. Francesca / Italien Francesca ist Italienerin. Sie spricht (wohl) Italienisch.
3. Jasmin / Türkei Jasmin ist Türkin. Sie spricht (wohl) Türkisch.
4. Sergio / Spanien Sergio ist Spanier. Er spricht (wohl) Spanisch.
5. Emily / die USA Emily ist Amerikanerin. Sie spricht (wohl) Englisch.

2 **Was fehlt?** Ergänzen Sie die Sätze mit den Adjektiven, die zu den Orten in Klammern gehören. Benutzen Sie die richtigen Adjektivendungen.

> **BEISPIEL** (Türkei) Im Pergamonmuseum kann man etwas über die ___türkische___ Geschichte lernen.

1. (Österreich) Das Wiener Schnitzel ist eine ___österreichische___ Spezialität.
2. (Spanien) Das Guggenheim-Museum in der ___spanischen___ Stadt Bilbao ist sehr modern.
3. (die Schweiz) Emmentaler und Münster sind ___Schweizer___ Käse.
4. (Korea) Ich esse sehr gern ___koreanisches___ Essen.
5. (Deutschland) Der ___deutsche___ Journalist ist sehr neugierig.

3 **Aus aller Welt** Fragen Sie Ihren Partner / Ihre Partnerin, welche Sachen aus verschiedenen Ländern er/sie (nicht) gern mag. Benutzen Sie die Wörter aus der Liste oder Ihre eigenen. Answers will vary.

> **BEISPIEL**
> **S1:** *Isst du gern Käse aus Holland?*
> **S2:** *Ja, ich esse gern holländischen Käse.*
> *Am liebsten esse ich aber französischen Käse.*

Architektur (*f.*)	Musik (*f.*)
Essen (*n.*)	Olivenöl (*n.*)
Filme (*pl.*)	Schokolade (*f.*)
Käse (*m.*)	Tee (*m.*)
Kaffee (*m.*)	Würstchen (*n.*)
Literatur (*f.*)	Zeitungen (*pl.*)

Wiederholung

1 Diskutieren und kombinieren
Sie und Ihr Partner / Ihre Partnerin bekommen Blätter mit ähnlichen Bildern einer Straße. Suchen Sie die Unterschiede und notieren Sie sie. Answers will vary.

BEISPIEL

S1: Auf meinem Bild gibt es zwei Zeitungskioske. Wie viele hast du?
S2: Ich habe nur einen.

2 Geografie
Fragen Sie Ihren Partner / Ihre Partnerin, in welches Land man fahren muss, um die abgebildeten Sehenswürdigkeiten zu besichtigen. Sample answers are provided.

BEISPIEL

S1: Wohin reist man, wenn man den Eiffelturm sehen will?
S2: Wenn man den Eiffelturm sehen will, muss man nach Frankreich reisen.

der Eiffelturm in Paris
Nach Frankreich.

die Brooklyn-Brücke in New York In die USA.

der Westminster-Palast in London Nach England.

die Sultan-Ahmed-Moschee in Istanbul In die Türkei.

das Matterhorn in den Alpen In die Schweiz.

das Brandenburger Tor in Berlin Nach Deutschland.

3 In der Stadt
Wählen Sie eine Aktivität aus der Liste. Sagen Sie Ihrem Partner / Ihrer Partnerin, was Sie in der Stadt machen wollen. Er/Sie sagt Ihnen, wohin Sie gehen müssen, um das zu machen. Answers will vary.

BEISPIEL

S1: Ich möchte mit dem Bürgermeister sprechen.
S2: Hmmm, da musst du ins Rathaus.

> mit dem Bürgermeister sprechen
> schwimmen gehen
> eine Sportzeitschrift kaufen
> frisches Obst und Gemüse kaufen
> Blumen kaufen
> Wäsche waschen
> im Grünen spazieren gehen
> im Internet surfen

4 Wer isst das?
Erzählen Sie Ihrem Partner / Ihrer Partnerin, was Sie gerne essen würden. Ihr Partner / Ihre Partnerin sagt, in welches Restaurant Sie gehen sollen. Answers will vary.

BEISPIEL

S1: Ich würde gern Pasta oder Pizza essen.
S2: Gehen wir doch in ein italienisches Restaurant!

5 Arbeitsblatt
Wählen Sie drei Orte in Ihrer Stadt aus. Fragen Sie zwei Personen, wie man von der Bibliothek zu jedem Ort kommt. Schreiben Sie die Antwort auf, und entscheiden Sie, welche Antwort besser ist. Answers will vary.

BEISPIEL

S1: Wie kommt man am besten von der Bibliothek zu Martins Waschsalon?
S2: Wenn du vor der Bibliothek stehst, geh erst nach links und dann geradeaus bis zum Broadway, dann...

2 Expansion Have students name additional landmarks from other countries for their partners to guess.

6 Ein Festessen

 Sie und Ihr Partner / Ihre Partnerin haben Ihre Eltern zu einem schönen Abendessen eingeladen. Planen Sie erst das Menü und was Sie alles dazu brauchen. Dann schauen Sie auf das Bild und sagen Sie, was Sie in jedem Geschäft kaufen. Answers will vary.

BEISPIEL

S1: Mein Vater will immer Brot zum Abendessen. Ich kaufe es in der Bäckerei.
S2: Und wie wär's mit Garnelen? Ich kann dafür ins Fischgeschäft gehen.

6 Suggestion Verify that students remember the genders of the shops shown in the drawing.

7 Stadtführer

Wählen Sie mit einem Partner / einer Partnerin fünf Orte in Ihrer Stadt, die Besucher unbedingt sehen sollen. Beschreiben Sie jeden Ort. Besprechen Sie dann, wie man von einem Ort zum nächsten kommt. Answers will vary.

BEISPIEL

S1: Ich finde, Besucher sollten das Kunstmuseum sehen.
S2: Du hast recht! Da kann man...

8 Wer und woher?

Beschreiben Sie Ihrem Partner / Ihrer Partnerin eine berühmte Person. Er/Sie rät, wer das ist, und sagt, woher er/sie kommt. Answers will vary.

BEISPIEL

S1: Man kennt diesen Mann durch seine Opern und Symphonien. Er war Österreicher und lebte im 18. Jahrhundert und ist jung gestorben.
S2: Das ist Mozart, der österreichische Musiker.

Mein Wör|ter|buch

Schreiben Sie fünf weitere Wörter in Ihr persönliches Wörterbuch zu den Themen **Besorgungen** und **In der Stadt**.

Schmuckgeschäft

Übersetzung
jewelry store

Wortart
Substantiv

Gebrauch
Im Schmuckgeschäft will ich mir eine neue Halskette aussuchen.

Synonyme
Juweliergeschäft, Juwelier

Antonyme
—

 **Vocabulary tools**

Panorama (S) Interactive Map

Niedersachsen und Nordrhein-Westfalen

NATIONAL
connections
cultures
STANDARDS

Niedersachsen in Zahlen

▶ **Fläche:** *47,634 km²*

▶ **Bevölkerung:** *7,9 Millionen Menschen*

▶ **Städte:** *Hannover (514.000 Einwohner), Braunschweig (249.000), Osnabrück (160.000)*

▶ **Wichtige Industriezweige:** *Automobil, Stahl°, Windenergie, Messen°*

▶ **Touristenattraktionen:** *Cuxhaven, Ostfriesische Inseln, Hannover, Otterndorf, Lüneburger Heide*

Touristen können in Niedersachsen Urlaub an der Nordseeküste machen oder die Natur in der Lüneburger Heide oder im Harz genießen. Die Industrie wird vor allem durch den Autohersteller VW mit seinem Sitz in Wolfsburg dominiert.

QUELLE: Landesportal Niedersachsen

Nordrhein-Westfalen in Zahlen

▶ **Fläche:** *34,088 km²*

▶ **Bevölkerung:** *17,6 Millionen Menschen*

▶ **Städte:** *Köln (1.039.500 Einwohner), Düsseldorf (601.000), Dortmund (578.000)*

▶ **Wichtige Industriezweige:** *Maschinenbau, Elektroindustrie, Banken, Tourismus*

▶ **Touristenattraktionen:** *Teutoburger Wald, Siegerland, Wittgensteiner Land*

Viele Touristen besuchen Nordrhein-Westfalen wegen der schönen Natur und der vielen Bäder im Teutoburger Wald. Nordrhein-Westfalen ist nicht nur das Bundesland mit der größten Bevölkerung, sondern auch mit der stärksten Wirtschaft°.

QUELLE: Landesportal Nordrhein-Westfalen

Berühmte Menschen aus Niedersachsen und Nordrhein-Westfalen

▶ **Wilhelm Busch,** *Autor (1832–1908)*

▶ **Lena Meyer-Landrut,** *Sängerin (1991–)*

▶ **Baron Münchhausen,** *Aristokrat (1720–1797)*

▶ **Michael Schumacher,** *Formel-1-Rennfahrer (1969–)*

▶ **Werner von Siemens,** *Erfinder° (1816–1892)*

Stahl *steel* **Messen** *trade shows* **Wirtschaft** *economy* **Erfinder** *inventor* **Würfen** *throws* **eine bestimmte Strecke schaffen** *complete a predetermined route* **freien Feldern** *open fields*

Karnevalskostüm in Köln

VW-Werk in Wolfsburg

Der Harz liegt in Niedersachsen, Sachsen-Anhalt und Thüringen

HAMBURG

■ NATIONALPARK NIEDERSÄCHSISCHES WATTENMEER

Bremerhaven

BREMEN   Lüneburg

Oldenburg   *Elbe*

LÜNEBURGER

HEIDE

NIEDERSACHSEN

Ems   *Weser*

Wolfsburg

NIEDERLANDE   Osnabrück   ⊙ Hannover

Braunschweig

WESERBERGLAND

Münster   Bielefeld   NATIONALPARK HARZ   SACHSEN-ANHALT

Lippe   Paderborn   *H A R Z*

Wurmberg ▲

NORDRHEIN-WESTFALEN   Göttingen

Langenberg ▲

○ Düsseldorf   *SAUERLAND*

Rhein   *Ruhr*

Köln   *BERGISCHES LAND*

Aachen   *ROTHAARGEBIRGE*   HESSEN

Bonn

E I F E L

BELGIEN

RHEINLAND-PFALZ

RUHRGEBIET

Gelsenkirchen   Dortmund

Duisburg   Essen   Bochum

Ruhr

Rhein

— Landesgrenzen
● Stadt
⊙ Landeshauptstadt

0 ────── 50 Meilen
0 ────── 50 Kilometer

0 ──── 25 Meilen
0 ──── 25 Kilometer

Unglaublich, aber wahr!

Boßeln ist ein Ballsport in Norddeutschland. Ein Spieler muss mit einem Ball in so wenig Würfen° wie möglich eine bestimmte Strecke schaffen°. Man kann auf freien Feldern° oder auf Straßen spielen. Normalerweise ist Boßeln ein Mannschaftssport.

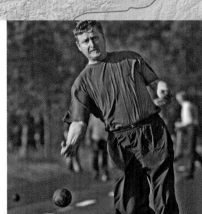

Landschaftsarchitektur
Landschaftspark Duisburg-Nord

Suggestion Point out that the combination **ui** in **Duisburg** is pronounced **ü**.

Als die Stahlproduktion unrentabel° wurde, veränderte sich die gesamte Region. Aus dem Stahlwerk° in Duisburg-Meiderich ist so der Landschaftspark Duisburg-Nord geworden. Viele Industrieelemente sind im Park noch erhalten, aber sie wurden mit Bäumen, Blumen und Freizeitgeländen° kombiniert. Das Resultat ist eine bemerkenswerte Integration von Industriestrukturen und Landschaft. Der Landschaftspark gilt als eins der wichtigsten Projekte der Landschaftsarchitektur der Jahrtausendwende°.

Öffentlicher Verkehr
Schwebebahn° Wuppertal

In Wuppertal gibt es nicht nur Busse für den öffentlichen Verkehr, sondern auch eine Schwebebahn, die seit 1901 Menschen zwischen Vohwinkel und Oberbarmen transportiert. Sie ist das Wahrzeichen° der Stadt Wuppertal und steht seit 1997 unter Denkmalschutz. Im Jahr 1950 sollte der Elefant Tuffi zwischen zwei Stationen mit der Schwebebahn fahren. Als der Elefant erschrak°, sprang er aus der Schwebebahn und landete in der Wupper. Dem Tier passierte dabei nichts, aber die Stadt ist seither dafür berühmt.

Natur
Lüneburger Heide

Suggestion Have students scan for the following information: **Wo ist die Lüneberger Heide? Wie viele Touristen kommen jedes Jahr? Welche Tiere findet man dort?**

Die Lüneburger Heide° ist eine Naturlandschaft in Niedersachsen. Sie liegt zwischen Hamburg, Bremen und Hannover. Die Heide ist eine der wichtigsten Touristenattraktion in Niedersachsen: mehr als vier Millionen Touristen besuchen die Heide jedes Jahr. In dieser flachen Region kann man Wald- und Heidelandschaften finden. Im Naturschutzgebiet° darf man nicht mit dem Auto fahren. Selbst die Polizisten reiten auf Pferden°. Besonders interessant für Touristen sind die vielen Heidschnuckenherden°, die es auf der Heide gibt.

Berühmte Personen
Karl der Große°

Suggestion Tell students that **schweben** means *to float* or *to hover*, and that **die Wupper** is the river that runs through Wuppertal.

Karl der Große (circa 747–814) gilt als einer der bedeutendsten Herrscher° Europas. Er war ab dem Jahr 768 König des fränkischen Reiches° und ab dem Jahr 800 Römischer Kaiser. Er regierte das heutige Deutschland, Frankreich, die Niederlande, Belgien, Italien und Polen. Er gilt als der erste Europäer, weil er in dieser Region eine Art europäische Kultur geprägt° hat. Zum Beispiel war Latein die wichtigste Sprache in dem gesamten Reich. Nach seinem Tod wurde er in der Pfalzkapelle in seiner Residenzstadt Aachen, die heute in Nordrhein-Westfalen liegt, begraben°.

---

unrentabel *unprofitable* **Stahlwerk** *steel mill* **Freizeitgeländen** *recreational facilities* **Jahrtausendwende** *turn of the millennium*
Heide *heath* **Naturschutzgebiet** *protected landscape* **Pferden** *horses* **Heidschnuckenherden** *flocks of moorland sheep*
Schwebebahn *suspended monorail* **Wahrzeichen** *landmark* **erschrak** *became scared* **Karl der Große** *Charlemagne*
Herrscher *rulers* **des fränkischen Reiches** *of the Frankish Empire* **geprägt** *shaped* **begraben** *buried*

IM INTERNET

1. Suchen Sie Touristeninformationen über die Lüneburger Heide: Was kann man hier machen? Wo kann man wohnen?

2. Suchen Sie mehr Informationen zu Karl dem Großen: Was weiß man über seine Familie? Warum war sein Reich so wichtig für Europa?

Find out more at **vhlcentral.com**.

Was haben Sie gelernt? Ergänzen Sie die Sätze.

1. Boßeln ist ein ___Ballsport___ in Norddeutschland.

2. Normalerweise spielt man Boßeln als ___Mannschaft___.

3. Aus einem Stahlwerk hat man im Ruhrgebiet einen ___Park___ gemacht.

4. Der Landespark Duisburg-Nord ist eine Kombination aus ___Industrieelementen___ und Landschaft.

5. Die Lüneburger Heide liegt zwischen ___Hamburg___, Bremen und Hannover.

6. Mehr als ___vier Millionen___ Touristen besuchen die Heide jedes Jahr.

7. Die Wuppertaler Schwebebahn gibt es seit ___1901___.

8. 1950 sprang ein ___Elefant___ aus der Schwebebahn.

9. Karl der Große hat in seinem Reich eine europäische ___Kultur___ geprägt.

10. Karl der Große ist in ___Aachen___ begraben.

 Practice more at **vhlcentral.com**.

Lesen

 Audio: Reading

Vor dem Lesen

Strategien

Repetition

Poets often use repetition of sounds, syllables, words, rhymes, or rhythms to emphasize certain images or themes, to establish a particular mood or tone, or to create a musical effect. A poet may also repeat a particular verse or phrase with slight variations, using these subtle differences to create a shift in tone or change of focus. Paying attention to the effects of recurring words, phrases, and sounds will help you gain insight into the meaning of a poem.

Untersuchen Sie den Text

Sehen Sie sich diese beiden Gedichte (*poems*) an. Beachten Sie die Wiederholung von Wörtern und Zeilen. Gibt es auch Wiederholungen mit kleinen Unterschieden (*differences*)?

Autoren
Hermann Hesse

Der deutsche Schriftsteller (*writer*) Hermann Hesse (1877–1962) war weit gereist. In einigen Werken (z.B. seinem Roman *Siddhartha*) merkt man den Einfluss der indischen Kultur. Während beider Weltkriege wohnte Hesse in der Schweiz, wo er viel über Pazifismus schrieb.

Paul Celan

Paul Celan (1920–1970) wurde in Rumänien geboren. Seine Familie waren deutschsprachige Juden (*Jews*). 1941 deportierten die Nazis Celans Familie in ein Konzentrationslager. Beide Eltern sind dort gestorben. Celan überstand (*survived*) das Konzentrationslager. Nach dem Krieg ging er nach Paris, wo er sich niederließ (*settled*). In vielen Gedichten schrieb er über die Vernichtung der Juden im Zweiten Weltkrieg.

Allein

Hermann Hesse

Es führen° über die Erde°
Strassen und Wege° viel,
Aber alle haben
Dasselbe Ziel°

Du kannst reiten und fahren
Zu zwein und zu drein°,
Den letzten Schritt°
Mußt du gehen allein.
Drum° ist kein Wissen
Noch Können so gut,
Als daß man alles Schwere
Alleine tut.

führen *lead* Erde *earth* Wege *paths*
Ziel *goal* Zu zwein...zu drein *in twos and threes*
Schritt *step* Drum *Because of that* Todesfuge *death fugue*
schaufeln *shovel* Grab *grave* Lüften *air* Schlangen *snakes*
tritt *steps* blitzen *flash* Sterne *stars* pfeift *whistles*
Rüden *hounds* Erde *earth* befiehlt *commands*
aschenes *ash-colored* stecht *stab* tiefer *deeper*
Eisen *iron* Gurt *belt* Spaten *shovels* Meister *master*
streicht *play* Geigen *violins* Rauch *smoke* Wolken *clouds*
bleierner Kugel *lead bullet* genau *exactly* hetzt...auf *stirs up*

Todesfuge°

Paul Celan

Schwarze Milch der Frühe wir trinken sie abends
wir trinken sie mittags und morgens wir trinken sie nachts
wir trinken und trinken
wir schaufeln° ein Grab° in den Lüften° da liegt man nicht eng
Ein Mann wohnt im Haus der spielt mit den Schlangen° der schreibt
der schreibt wenn es dunkelt nach Deutschland dein goldenes Haar Margarete
er schreibt es und tritt° vor das Haus und es blitzen° die Sterne° er pfeift°
    seine Rüden° herbei
er pfeift seine Juden hervor läßt schaufeln ein Grab in der Erde°
er befiehlt° uns spielt auf nun zum Tanz

Schwarze Milch der Frühe wir trinken dich nachts
wir trinken dich morgens und mittags wir trinken dich abends
wir trinken und trinken
Ein Mann wohnt im Haus der spielt mit den Schlangen der schreibt
der schreibt wenn es dunkelt nach Deutschland dein goldenes Haar Margarete
Dein aschenes° Haar Sulamith wir schaufeln ein Grab in den Lüften da liegt
    man nicht eng

Er ruft stecht° tiefer° ins Erdreich ihr einen ihr andern singet und spielt
er greift nach dem Eisen° im Gurt° er schwingts seine Augen sind blau
stecht tiefer die Spaten° ihr einen ihr andern spielt weiter zum Tanz auf

Schwarze Milch der Frühe wir trinken dich nachts
wir trinken dich mittags und morgens wir trinken dich abends
wir trinken und trinken
ein Mann wohnt im Haus dein goldenes Haar Margarete
dein aschenes Haar Sulamith er spielt mit den Schlangen

Er ruft spielt süßer den Tod der Tod ist ein Meister° aus Deutschland
er ruft streicht° dunkler die Geigen° dann steigt ihr als Rauch° in die Luft
dann habt ihr ein Grab in den Wolken° da liegt man nicht eng

Schwarze Milch der Frühe wir trinken dich nachts
wir trinken dich mittags der Tod ist ein Meister aus Deutschland
wir trinken dich abends und morgens wir trinken und trinken
der Tod ist ein Meister aus Deutschland sein Auge ist blau
er trifft dich mit bleierner Kugel° er trifft dich genau°
ein Mann wohnt im Haus dein goldenes Haar Margarete
er hetzt seine Rüden auf° uns er schenkt uns ein Grab in der Luft
er spielt mit den Schlangen und träumet der Tod ist ein Meister aus Deutschland

dein goldenes Haar Margarete
dein aschenes Haar Sulamith

Nach dem Lesen

 Verständnis Antworten Sie auf die folgenden Fragen. Sample answers are provided.

1. Worüber führen laut Hesse die Straßen und die Wege? Sie führen über die Erde.

2. Wie geht man den letzen Schritt?
Den letzten Schritt geht man allein.

3. Was machen die Juden in dem Gedicht von Celan?
Sie schaufeln ein Grab (in den Lüften/in der Erde).

4. Welche Farbe haben die Augen des Mannes?
Seine Augen sind blau.

5. Womit spielt der Mann? Er spielt mit Schlangen.

6. Wann schreibt der Mann nach Deutschland?
Er schreibt nach Deutschland, wenn es dunkelt.

 Diskutieren Sie Suchen Sie mit einem Partner/einer Partnerin alle Wörter in dem Gedicht „Allein", die ähnliche Geräusche (*similar sounds*) oder Bedeutungen haben. Suchen Sie auch alle Zeilen (*lines*) in „Todesfuge", die sich wiederholen. Wie benutzt jeder Dichter (*poet*) diese Wiederholungen (*repetitions*)?

 Fragen Sie einander Was sind laut Hermann Hesse sowohl dasselbe Ziel als auch der letzte Schritt? Hat Hesse Recht? Ist man immer allein, wenn man stirbt?
Sind die Juden in Celans Gedicht allein vor ihrem Tod, wie Hesse glaubt? Warum oder warum nicht?

 Schreiben Sie Sie haben hier zwei Arten von Gedichten: Ein Gedicht hat Verse und Strophen (*stanzas*) und hält sich an die Regeln (*rules*) der Interpunktion (*punctuation*) und der Rechtschreibung. Das zweite Gedicht hat zwar Verse und Strophen, hält sich aber nicht an die Regeln. Welche Wirkung (*effect*) haben diese verschiedenen Stile? Welches Gedicht gefällt Ihnen besser? Warum?

Expansion Hand out photocopies of **Todesfuge** and have students fill in punctuation, adding quotation marks, periods, and capitalization at the beginning of sentences. Ask them how the addition of punctuation changes the effect of the poem.

Suggestion Explain to students that **Margarete** is a common German women's name, while **Sulamith** (or Shulamite) is a Jewish woman's name meaning "peace." In the biblical Song of Solomon, it is the name of Solomon's beloved.

Hören

NATIONAL communication cultures STANDARDS

Strategien

Guessing the meaning of words from context

When you hear an unfamiliar word, you can often guess its meaning based on the context in which it is used...

 To practice this strategy, you will listen to a tour guide talking about Bonn. Jot down some of the familiar words or place names that you hear. Then, listen again and try to guess the meaning of two unfamiliar words based on context. Suggested answers.

Hilfreiche Wörter	Unbekannte Wörter
Haupstadt, Berlin	Regierungssitz
Politiker, gearbeitet	Abgeordnetenhaus

Vorbereitung

Sehen Sie sich das Bild an. Was meinen Sie; welchen Beruf hat die Frau in der weißen Bluse?

Zuhören

Hören Sie sich den Dialog an. Benutzen Sie den Kontext, um die Wörter in Spalte A zu verstehen. Welche Wörter in Spalte B passen zu den Wörtern in Spalte A?

Spalte A	Spalte B
1. __c__ Büro	a. Viertel
2. __d__ Umbau	b. Geschäfte
3. __b__ Läden	c. Arbeitszimmer für Geschäftsleute
4. __a__ Nachbarschaft	d. Renovierung eines Hauses
5. __e__ Tiefgarage	e. Parkplätze unter einem Haus

Suggestion Have students match the concepts in columns A and B *before* listening to the audio. Play the dialogue 2-3 times, and have students complete the true/false questions in **Verständnis**. Then, have them reevaluate their answers in **Zuhören**.

 Practice more at **vhlcentral.com.**

Verständnis

Richtig oder falsch Sind die Sätze richtig oder falsch? Korrigieren Sie die falschen Sätze. Sample answers are provided.

1. Das renovierte Gebäude soll nur für Büros sein.
   Falsch. Das Gebäude soll für Läden, Büros und Wohnungen sein.

2. Das Gebäude soll 100 Büros haben.
   Falsch. Das Gebäude soll 200 Büros haben.

3. Der Umbau soll ein Jahr dauern.
   Richtig.

4. Es wird definitiv einen Supermarkt und ein Fitnessstudio in dem Gebäude geben.
   Falsch. Es könnten ein Supermarkt und ein Fitnessstudio in dem Gebäude sein.

5. Es wird Drei- und Vier-Zimmer-Wohnungen geben.
   Falsch. Es wird Zwei-, Drei- und Vier-Zimmer-Wohnungen geben.

6. Die Architektur ist eine Kombination aus alt und neu.
   Richtig.

7. Es werden neue Parkplätze neben dem Gebäude gebaut.
   Falsch. Man baut eine Tiefgarage.

8. Die Renovierung soll den Charakter der Nachbarschaft nicht verändern.
   Richtig.

Neue Architektur Identifizieren Sie in einer Gruppe ein Gebäude auf Ihrem Campus oder in Ihrer Stadt, das man renovieren oder neu bauen sollte. Was sind die Vor- und Nachteile (*advantages and disadvantages*) einer Renovierung oder eines Neubaus? Was ist für die Bewohner und Nutzer des Gebäudes besser? Was ist effizienter? Was ist für die Nachbarschaft am besten?

Suggestion Play the **Strategien** recording once and ask comprehension questions: **Wie lange war Bonn die Hauptstadt Westdeutschlands? Wer hat früher in dem Alten Abgeordnetenhaus gearbeitet?** Then, play it again, and have students compile their word lists.

Schreiben

Strategien

Using note cards

When you write, note cards can help you organize and sequence the information you wish to present.

For example, if you were going to write an article about a new apartment complex being built in your town, you would jot down notes about each feature of the development on a different note card. Then you could easily organize the cards once you decide how you want to present the information. For example, you could include the best and worst features of the apartment complex, the different uses incorporated into the design, the size of the various facilities, etc.

Here are some helpful techniques:

- Label the top of each card with a general subject, such as **Geschäfte** or **Wohnungen**.

- Use only the front side of each note card so that you can easily flip through them to find information.

- On each card, jot down only those specifics that correspond to the topic of the card.

- As a last step, number the cards in each subject category in the upper right corner to help you organize them.

Wohnungskriterien 6

- *2–3 Schlafzimmer*
- *2 Badezimmer*
- *Einbauküche*
- *große Fenster*
- *Fitnesscenter im Haus*
- *Einkaufsmöglichkeiten im Haus*

Thema

Eine virtuelle Stadttour

Wählen Sie eine Stadt, die Sie kennen und mögen. Schreiben Sie einen Text für eine virtuelle Stadttour für deutschsprechende Besucher. Schreiben Sie für jede Besonderheit (*feature*) der Stadt eine Notizkarte mit einigen Details, die Sie diskutieren wollen.

- Jede Notizkarte soll ein allgemeines Thema und eine spezifische Sehenswürdigkeit (*point of interest*) haben. Ein allgemeines (*general*) Thema kann auf verschiedene Karten verteilt sein, jede mit einer anderen Sehenswürdigkeit. Wenn die Stadt zum Beispiel mehrere Viertel hätte, wäre „Viertel" das allgemeine Thema und jedes Viertel hätte seine eigene Karte mit einer Beschreibung.

- Benutzen Sie die Notizkarten, um die Tour zu organisieren. Sie können sie nach Nähe (*proximity*), Zweck (Wohnen, Geschäfte, Industrie, Unterhaltung), historischer Entwicklung (ältester Teil bis neuester Teil), saisonalen Interessen oder Art der Bewohner (Studenten, Geschäftsleute, Künstler (*artists*), Rentner (*retirees*)) organisieren.

- Wenn Sie die Tour beginnen, heißen Sie die Besucher willkommen und geben Sie eine allgemeine Übersicht (*orientation*) über die Stadt. Wenn Sie die Tour beenden, sagen Sie den Besuchern, dass Sie hoffen, dass ihnen die Tour gefallen hat und dass sie bald wiederkommen.

 **Vocabulary Tools**

Orte

das Blumengeschäft, -e	flower shop
das Internetcafé, -s	internet café
das Juweliergeschäft, -e	jewelry store
das Kino, -s	movie theater
der Kiosk, -e	newspaper kiosk
die Drogerie, -n	drugstore
die Polizeiwache, -n	police station
das Rathaus, ¨er	town hall
der Kosmetiksalon, -s	beauty salon
das Schreibwarengeschäft, -e	paper-goods store
der Waschsalon, -s	laundromat
geöffnet	open
geschlossen	closed

die Post

die Adresse, -n	address
der Brief, -e	letter
der Briefkasten, ¨	mailbox
die Briefmarke, -n	stamp
der Briefträger, - / die Briefträgerin, -nen	mail carrier
der Briefumschlag, ¨e	envelope
das Paket, -e	package
die Post	post office
die Postkarte, -n	postcard
abschicken (schickt... ab)	to mail

in der Bank

die Bank, -en	bank
das Geld	money
der Geldautomat, -en	ATM
der Geldschein, -e	bill
das Konto (pl. die Konten)	bank account
die Münze, -n	coin
das Kleingeld	change
abheben (hebt... ab)	to withdraw
einzahlen (zahlt... ein)	to deposit

Ausdrücke

das Bargeld	cash
das Formular, -e	form
die Zeitschrift, -en	magazine
die Zeitung, -en	newspaper
bar bezahlen	to pay in cash
Besorgungen machen	to run errands
ausfüllen (füllt... aus)	to fill out
mit der Karte bezahlen	to pay by (credit) card
unterschreiben	to sign

die Innenstadt

das Einkaufszentrum, (pl. Einkaufszentren)	mall; shopping center
das Gebäude, -	building
das Kaufhaus, ¨er	department store
die Kirche, -n	church
die Stadt, ¨e	town
die Telefonzelle, -n	phone booth
das Viertel, -	neighborhood

Verkehr

die Allee, -n	avenue; boulevard
die Ampel, -n	traffic light
die Bank, ¨e	bench
die Brücke, -n	bridge
der Brunnen, -	fountain
der Bürgersteig, -e	sidewalk
die Ecke, -n	corner
die Hauptstraße, -n	main road
die Kreuzung, -en	intersection
die Statue, -n	statue
die Straße, -n	street
die Treppe, -n	stairs
der Zebrastreifen, -	crosswalk

Menschen

der Bürgermeister, - / die Bürgermeisterin, -nen	mayor
der Fußgänger, - / die Fußgängerin, -nen	pedestrian

Wo ist...?

abbiegen (biegt... ab)	to turn
folgen	to follow
bis zu	until; up to
gegenüber von	across from
geradeaus	straight
in der Nähe von	close to
in Richtung	toward
nah(e)	near; nearby
weit von	far from

Ausdrücke

mitnehmen (nimmt... mit)	to give a ride
überqueren	to cross
hochgehen (geht... hoch)	to go up/climb
heruntergehen (geht... herunter)	to go down
sich verlaufen	to be/get lost
sich zurechtfinden (findet sich... zurecht)	to find one's way

Subordinating conjunctions	See p. 422.
Adjectives as nouns	See p. 426.
Das Futur I	See p. 428.
Prepositions of direction	See pp. 442–443.
Talking about nationality	See p. 446.

Beruf und Karriere

Suggestion Have students look at the photo. Ask: Wo ist Meline? Was macht sie?

Communicative Goals

You will learn how to:
- talk about jobs and qualifications
- talk about job applications and interviews

Im Büro

(S) Vocabulary Tools

Wortschatz

eine Stelle suchen	*looking for a job*
die Ausbildung, -en	education
der Beruf, -e	profession
die Berufsausbildung, -en	professional training
die Besprechung, -en	meeting
der Bewerber, - / die Bewerberin, -nen	applicant
das Empfehlungsschreiben, -	letter of recommendation
die Erfahrung, -en	experience
das Geschäft, -e	business
das (hohe/niedrige) Gehalt (*pl.* die (hohen/niedrigen) Gehälter)	(high/low) salary
das Praktikum (*pl.* die Praktika)	internship
die Referenz, -en	reference
die Stelle, -n	position; job
der Termin, -e	appointment
der Vertrag, -e	contract
Arbeit finden	to find a job
einen Termin vereinbaren	to make an appointment
sich bewerben um (bewirbt sich)	to apply for
Büromaterial	*office supplies*
die Büroklammer, -n	paperclip
das Büromaterial, -ien	office supplies
die Pinnwand, ¨e	bulletin board
der Hefter, -	stapler
am Telefon	*on the phone*
Wer spricht?	Who's calling?
Bleiben Sie bitte am Apparat.	Please hold.
eine Nachricht hinterlassen	to leave a message

Suggestion Tell students that **sich bewerben** is typically used with the preposition **um** (+ *acc.*). Ex.: **Julius bewirbt sich um eine Stelle bei einer Bank in Frankfurt**. However, some speakers also use it with **auf** or **für**. You may want to provide past tense forms: **bewarb sich, hat sich beworben**. Also remind students that complete conjugations for all verb types are listed in **Appendix A**.

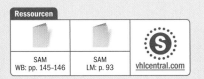
ACHTUNG

In the singular, **Stellenangebot** typically refers to a specific job offer: **Die Firma macht dem Bewerber ein Stellenangebot.** In the plural, it usually refers to job listings: **Der Arbeitslose liest jeden Tag die Stellenangebote in der Zeitung.**

die Personalchefin, -nen
(der Personalchef, -s *m.*)

der Lebenslauf, ⸚e

Personalbüro

das Vorstellungsgespräch, -e

die Assistentin, -nen
(der Assistent, -en *m.*)

der Hörer, -

das Stellenangebot, -e

Lotmeyer GmbH

die Firma (*pl.* die Firmen)

Suggestion Explain that **GmbH** stands for **Gesellschaft mit beschränkter Haftung**, a type of limited partnership, similar to "*Ltd.*" in English.

Anwendung

1 Bilder beschriften Wählen Sie das richtige Wort für jedes Foto.

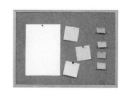

1. (die Büroklammer)/ die Stellen
2. der Bewerber / (die Pinnwand)
3. (die Besprechung)/ der Vertrag

4. die Referenz / (der Hefter)
5. das Praktikum / (der Hörer)
6. (der Lebenslauf)/ das Gehalt

2 Definitionen Finden Sie die passende Definition.

1. _c_ die Personalchefin
2. _e_ der Beruf
3. _b_ das Praktikum
4. _f_ die Warteschleife
5. _a_ die Stellenangebote
6. _d_ das Empfehlungsschreiben

2 Expansion Have students write additional definitions and have classmates guess the words they refer to. Ex.: **In diesem Dokument steht meine Berufserfahrung. Was ist das? (der Lebenslauf)**

a. Die liest man, wenn man eine neue Stelle sucht.
b. Studenten machen das, um praktische Erfahrungen in einem Beruf zu bekommen.
c. Mit dieser Person führt man ein Vorstellungsgespräch.
d. Das schickt man zusammen mit einer Bewerbung ab.
e. Das ist die Arbeit, die man jeden Tag macht.
f. Hier bleibt man oft lange, wenn zu viele Telefonanrufe zur selben Zeit ankommen.

3 Das Vorstellungsgespräch 🎧 Hören Sie sich den Dialog an und zeigen Sie die Worte an, die die Bewerberin spricht.

1. Empfehlungsschreiben ☐
2. Gehaltshöhe ☑
3. Praktikum ☑
4. Chefassistentin ☐
5. Bewerbung ☐
6. Ausbildung ☑
7. Berufserfahrungen ☐
8. Vorstellungsgespräch ☑

3 Expansion After they complete the listening activity, ask students if they think Frau Mellert will get the job and why. Have them come up with additional interview questions to ask her.

🔧 Practice more at **vhlcentral.com.**

Kommunikation

4 Bewerber Verwenden Sie die angegebenen Vorschläge (*suggestions*)
und berichten Sie in ganzen Sätzen, welche Qualifikationen die Bewerber
für die aufgelisteten Stellen brauchen. Sample answers are provided.

BEISPIEL

*Für die Stelle als Fußballtrainer braucht der Bewerber mindestens
fünf Jahre Erfahrung als Fußballspieler in der Bundesliga.*

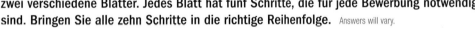

1. __f__ Fußballtrainer
2. __b__ Journalistin
3. __a__ Koch
4. __e__ Kosmetikerin
5. __d__ Mechaniker
6. __c__ Polizistin

a. fünf Jahre Berufserfahrung in einem Restaurant
b. ein abgeschlossenes (*completed*) Studium und ein Praktikum
   bei einer Zeitung, einer Zeitschrift oder einem Fernsehsender
c. eine zweijährige juristische (*legal*) Ausbildung in Praxis und Theorie
d. eine abgeschlossene technische Lehre (*apprenticeship*)
e. mindestens eine dreijährige Ausbildung in einer Drogerie oder einem Kosmetiksalon
f. mindestens fünf Jahre Erfahrung als Fußballspieler in der Bundesliga

5 Diskutieren und kombinieren Sie und Ihr Partner / Ihre Partnerin bekommen
zwei verschiedene Blätter. Jedes Blatt hat fünf Schritte, die für jede Bewerbung notwendig
sind. Bringen Sie alle zehn Schritte in die richtige Reihenfolge. Answers will vary.

5 Suggestion Make sure
students understand all
vocabulary before beginning
the activity.

BEISPIEL

S1: *Als Erstes würde ich eine Liste mit Namen und Adressen
einiger Firmen aufstellen. Was meinst du?*
S2: *Ich würde mich zuerst mal über mögliche Stellenangebote
informieren, bevor ich eine Liste der Firmen aufstelle.*

5 Expansion Ask students
questions about their personal
experience with job searches.
Ex.: **Haben** *Sie* **jemals eine
Stelle gesucht? Haben Sie
die Stelle bekommen? Was
für eine Stelle war sie?**

6 Stellenangebote Wählen Sie in Dreiergruppen zwei der abgebildeten
Fotos aus und schreiben Sie zu jedem Foto ein Stellenangebot. Es sollte
Informationen über gewünschte Qualifikationen enthalten (*contain*), sowie
über das Gehalt und die Anzahl der bezahlten Urlaubstage. Machen Sie Ihr
Stellenangebot so attraktiv wie möglich. Answers will vary.

BEISPIEL

S1: *Wir suchen einen Piloten/eine Pilotin.*
S2: *Der/die ideale Bewerber (-in) sollte...*
S3: *Unsere Firma ist...*

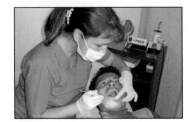

Aussprache und Rechtschreibung Audio

🎧 Loan words (Part 2)

You have already learned that the main stress in German words usually falls on the first syllable. However, in words borrowed from other languages, the first syllable may not be stressed.

Kandidat **Immobilien** **Karriere** **Politiker** **Fabrik**

....

Some loan words in German are pronounced similarly to their English equivalents.

Computer **Sektor** **Komma** **Semester**

....

In other loan words, the stress falls on a different syllable in German than it does in English.

Referenz **Assistent** **Psychologe** **Material**

....

The stress in a loan word may shift to a different syllable in the plural form of a word, or in the feminine form of a noun.

Doktor **Doktorin** **Doktoren** **Sektor** **Sektoren**

Suggestion Tell students that since the stress patterns for loan words are so variable, they should learn the pronunciation on a case-by-case basis. Emphasize the important words for this unit: **Karriere, Computer, Personal, Assistent, Referenz.**

1 **Aussprechen** Wiederholen Sie die Wörter, die Sie hören.

1. Jurist
2. Kosmetik
3. Identität
4. Hotel
5. Laptop
6. Thermometer
7. Sekretär
8. Temperatur
9. Akrobat
10. Student
11. Faktor
12. Faktoren

2 **Nachsprechen** Wiederholen Sie die Sätze, die Sie hören.

1. Am Computer sitzt der Student im ersten Semester.
2. Die Kandidaten werden vor der Wahl sehr nervös.
3. Der Atlas, den du suchst, liegt unter den anderen Atlanten.
4. In dem Sektor findet man weniger Arbeitslosigkeit als in den anderen Sektoren.
5. Die Assistentin kocht sich oft eine Tomatensuppe im Labor.
6. Aus diesem Katalog kann man sehr günstig Büromaterial bestellen.

3 **Sprichwörter** Wiederholen Sie die Sprichwörter, die Sie hören.

Je ärgrer Student, je frömmerer Pastor.[1]

Schlaf ist die beste Medizin.[2]

[1] The worse the student, the more devout the pastor.
[2] Sleep is the best medicine.

Ressourcen

SAM
LM: p. 94

vhlcentral.com

Sag niemals nie Video

Hans hat Meline seit Tagen nicht mehr gesehen. Er besucht sie, um sich für den Kuss zu entschuldigen. Aber dann kommt alles ganz anders.

Vorbereitung Have students preview the images and write down 3 questions they want to have answered in the video.

1

SABITE Ich habe euch nicht mehr gesehen seit... Was macht ihr hier?
HANS Der Reichstag verkörpert deutsche Geschichte.

2

HANS Der Reichstag war bis 1918 Sitz des Parlamentes im Deutschen Kaiserreich. Hier verabschiedeten die Abgeordneten Gesetze, erließen Beschlüsse und wählten ihren Präsidenten. Nach dem Ersten Weltkrieg rief Philipp Scheidemann hier die Weimarer Republik aus. Ich habe vor, mich für ein Praktikum zu bewerben. Was genau machst du denn hier?

3

SABITE Der Reichstag bietet eine große Sammlung zeitgenössischer deutscher Kunst, die ich mir gern anschaue. Als ich ein Kind war, hat der Künstler Christo das gesamte Gebäude in Stoff verpackt. Ich schreibe darüber eine Hausarbeit.

4

HANS Hast du Meline gesehen?
SABITE Ich weiß, dass sie viel zu tun hat und in Wien nach Arbeit sucht und Lebensläufe und Bewerbungsschreiben abgeschickt hat. Ich glaube, sie hat nächste Woche ein Vorstellungsgespräch. Ich habe sie nicht mehr gesehen seit...

5

GEORGE Hans, mein Freund, Vergiss es. Sie flirtet mit Männern, bekommt ihre Nummern und schmeißt sie danach in den Abfall.
SABITE Oh, George, du hast doch keine Ahnung von der Liebe. Hans, wenn Meline mit dir nicht geredet hat, ist es deshalb, weil sie Angst hat, dass ihr Herz gebrochen wird.

MELINE Hallo?
HANS Hallo, Meline. Ich bin's, Hans. Leg bitte nicht auf. Ich bin draußen. Ich wollte mit dir reden über...

6

ÜBUNGEN

1 **Richtig oder falsch?** Entscheiden Sie, ob die folgenden Sätze **richtig** oder **falsch** sind.

1. Der Reichstag war bis 1918 Sitz des Parlamentes im Deutschen Kaiserreich. Richtig.
2. Philipp Scheidemann rief im Reichstag die Weimarer Republik aus. Richtig.
3. Hans möchte sich als Geschäftsführer bewerben. Falsch.
4. Als Sabite ein Kind war, hat der Künstler Christo das Reichstagsgebäude in Stoff verpackt. Richtig.

5. Sie schreibt darüber ihr Examen. Falsch.
6. Meline sucht in Berlin nach Arbeit. Falsch.
7. Sie flirtet mit Männern, bekommt ihre Nummern und ruft sie an. Falsch.
8. Hans schreibt Meline eine SMS. Falsch.
9. Hans möchte sich für sein Verhalten entschuldigen. Richtig.
10. George glaubt, dass Meline und Hans zu unterschiedlich sind. Richtig.

PERSONEN George Hans Meline Sabite

HANS Also, ich bin hierhergekommen, um dir zu sagen, dass das, was neulich Abend passiert ist, nie wieder passieren wird. Ich möchte mich für mein Verhalten entschuldigen.
MELINE Ich bin froh, dass du das so siehst. Wir hätten das nicht tun sollen.

HANS Dann haben wir also eine Abmachung?
MELINE Ja.
HANS Du siehst hübsch aus, wenn du nicht total... fabelhaft aussiehst.
MELINE Danke, Hans. Das ist sehr nett von dir.

GEORGE Du liegst falsch, Sabite. Es würde zwischen den beiden niemals klappen. Sie sind zu unterschiedlich.
SABITE Glaubst du nicht, dass sich Gegensätze anziehen?
GEORGE Ich glaube nicht, dass Hans und Meline... Was ich gemeint habe, ist...

MELINE Genug. Alle raus. Ich muss arbeiten. Ja. Du auch, Sabite.

Nützliche Ausdrücke

- **verkörpern**
  to embody
- **ein Gesetz verabschieden**
  to pass a law
- **einen Beschluss erlassen**
  to adopt a resolution
- **ausrufen**
  to proclaim
- **das Gebäude**
  building
- **schmeißen**
  to throw
- **Oh, George, du hast doch keine Ahnung von der Liebe.**
  Oh, George, you don't know anything about love.
- **jemandem das Herz brechen**
  to break someone's heart
- **eine Abmachung haben**
  to have a deal
- **fabelhaft**
  fabulous
- **der Gegensatz**
  opposite

11A.1
- **Der Reichstag bietet eine große Sammlung zeitgenössischer deutscher Kunst, die ich mir gern anschaue.**
  The Reichstag holds a large collection of contemporary German art, which I like looking at.

11A.2
- **Der Reichstag war bis 1918 Sitz des Parlamentes im Deutschen Kaiserreich.**
  Until 1918, the Reichstag housed the parliament of the German Reich.

2 **Zum Besprechen** Was passiert zwischen Hans und Meline? Schreiben Sie in kleinen Gruppen einen kurzen Absatz darüber, wie es mit den beiden weitergehen wird. Bereiten Sie sich darauf vor, Ihre Prognose der Klasse zu präsentieren. Answers will vary.

2 **Suggestion** Have all the groups read their predictions to the class. Ask them to keep their paragraphs until they watch the last episode, so that they can find out which predictions were correct.

3 **Vertiefung** Hans sagt, dass der Reichstag deutsche Geschichte verkörpert. Finden Sie mehr über das Reichstagsgebäude heraus. Wann wurde es gebaut? Welche historischen Ereignisse fanden hier statt? Possible answers: The Reichstag was built between 1884 and 1894. Philipp Scheidemann proclaimed the Weimarer Republik from the balcony in 1918. In 1990, the official German reunification ceremony took place in the Reichstag.

3 **Suggestion** Have students present their findings to the class.

Ressourcen

SAM
VM: p. 21

vhlcentral.com

Familienunternehmen  Reading

TIPP

Die Firma is a general term for a business or company. **Das Geschäft** is a shop or small business. **Der Betrieb** refers to a factory or other business operation, and **die Wirtschaft** can refer to a specific business or to the economy in general.

LAUT EINER STUDIE DES INSTITUTS für Mittelstandsforschung sind etwa

Bekannte deutsche Familienunternehmen	
Meggle	(Butter) Gründer°: Josef Anton Meggle (1877)
Oetker	(Pudding) Gründer: August Oetker (1891)
Porsche	(Autos) Gründer: Ferdinand Porsche (1931)
Ritter Sport	(Schokolade) Gründer: Clara und Alfred E. Ritter (1912)
Steiff	(Plüschtiere°) Gründerin: Margarete Steiff (1880)

3 Millionen deutsche Firmen in Familienbesitz. Diese Familienunternehmen sind ungefähr 95% aller Firmen und Betriebe. Über 41% des Umsatzes° aller Firmen wird von Familienunternehmen erwirtschaftet°. Bei diesen Zahlen ist es kein Wunder, dass Experten Familienunternehmen den wichtigsten Aspekt der deutschen Wirtschaft nennen.

Die Liste bekannter deutscher Familienunternehmen ist lang. Die Familie Quandt besitzt zum Beispiel fast 50% des Automobilbauers BMW. Auch

die Familie Bertelsmann ist mit dem größten deutschen Medienkonzern sehr erfolgreich. Die Familie Heraeus besitzt Heraeus Holding GmbH, die im Bereich Edelmetall° jährlich über 22 Milliarden Euro erwirtschaftet. Andere berühmte Familienunternehmen sind Henkel (Reinigungsmittel), Marquard und Bahls (Mineralöl) und Fresenius (Arzneimittel).

Neben diesen großen Unternehmen findet sich in ganz Deutschland eine große Anzahl kleinerer Familieunternehmen, die oft auf eine lange Tradition zurückschauen° können. Das Familienunternehmen Hipp produziert Babynahrung. Die Gebrüder Mehler produzieren Stoffe° im Bayerischen Wald. Und das Familieunternehmen Rombach & Haas stellt in vierter Generation im Schwarzwald Kuckucksuhren° her.

Umsatzes *sales* **erwirtschaftet** *generated*
Edelmetall *precious metal* **zurückschauen** *look back*
Stoffe *fabrics* **Kuckucksuhren** *cuckoo clocks*
Gründer *founder* **Plüschtiere** *stuffed animals*

ÜBUNGEN

1 Richtig oder falsch Sagen Sie, ob die Sätze richtig oder falsch sind. Korrigieren Sie die falschen Sätze.

1. Etwa 5 Millionen deutsche Firmen sind in Familienbesitz.
   Falsch. Etwa 3 Millionen Firmen sind in Familienbesitz.
2. Familienunternehmen sind etwa 95% aller deutschen Firmen. Richtig.
3. Mehr als 50% des Umsatzes aller Firmen wird von Familienunternehmen erwirtschaftet.
   Falsch. Etwa 41% des Umsatzes aller Firmen wird von Familienunternehmen erwirtschaftet.
4. Familienunternehmen sind der wichtigste Teil der deutschen Wirtschaft.
   Richtig.
5. Die Firma BMW ist zu über 50% im Besitz der Familie Quandt. Richtig.

6. Die Familie Heraeus verdient viel Geld durch den Handel mit Edelmetallen.
   Richtig.
7. In allen Teilen Deutschlands gibt es Familienunternehmen mit einer langen Tradition. Richtig.
8. Eine bekannte Firma für Babynahrung ist Hipp. Richtig.
9. Die Firma Rombach & Haas produziert Kuckucksuhren. Richtig.
10. Die Firma Mehler produziert Stoffe Im Schwarzwald.
    Falsch. Die Firma Mehler ist im Bayerischen Wald.

 Practice more at **vhlcentral.com**.

Expansion Have students repeat each phrase from the **Deutsch im Alltag** aloud after you. Have pairs write short dialogues using at least four of the words.

DEUTSCH IM ALLTAG

Im Büro

der Arbeitgeber	employer
der Arbeitnehmer	employee
die Abteilung	department
das Bewerbungsschreiben	cover letter
die Stellenanzeige	job advertisement
die Visitenkarte	business card

DIE DEUTSCHSPRACHIGE WELT

Kuckucksuhren

Kuckucksuhren haben in Deutschland und vor allem im Schwarzwald große Tradition. Die meisten Kuckucksuhren sind Wanduhren aus Holz. Jede volle Stunde° kommt ein Kuckuck mechanisch aus der Uhr und man kann einen Kuckucksruf° hören. Traditionelle Kuckucksuhren müssen alle 24 Stunden bis 8 Tage aufgezogen° werden, damit sie funktionieren. Im Schwarzwald werden heute noch viele dieser Uhren von Hand gemacht. Die ältesten Kuckucksuhren stammen aus dem 18. Jahrhundert.

volle Stunde *top of the hour* **Kuckucksruf** *call of a cuckoo* **aufgezogen** *wound up*

PORTRÄT

Robert Bosch

Robert Bosch, 1861 in Albeck geboren und 1942 in Stuttgart gestorben, war ein deutscher Erfinder°, Unternehmer°, Sozialreformer und Philanthrop. Seine bedeutendste Erfindung war die Zündkerze°, mit der man Autos leichter starten konnte. Diese Zündkerzen und andere Erfindungen machten sein Unternehmen bald zu einem multinationalen Unternehmen. Bosch war aber auch ein deutscher Philanthrop und Sozialreformer. In seinen Firmen mussten Arbeiter zum Beispiel nur acht Stunden am Tag arbeiten. Außerdem war ihm wichtig, dass es viel Licht und frische Luft in den Fabriken° gab. Bosch war auch ein spendabler Stifter°. Im Jahr 1910 schenkte er der Technischen Hochschule Stuttgart 1.000.000 Mark, um die Forschung zu unterstützen°. **Suggestion** Ask students whether they think Robert Bosch was a good boss, and why.

Erfinder *inventor* **Unternehmer** *entrepreneur* **Zündkerze** *spark-plug* **Fabriken** *factories* **spendabler Stifter** *generous donor* **Forschung zu unterstützen** *to support research*

⟍S IM INTERNET

Suchen Sie im Internet mehr Informationen über ein deutsches Familienunternehmen: Welche Informationen können Sie über die Familie finden?

Find out more at **vhlcentral.com**.

---

2 **Was fehlt?** Ergänzen Sie die Sätze.

1. Kuckucksuhren haben vor allem im ___Schwarzwald___ große Tradition.
2. Die meisten Kuckucksuhren sind aus ___Holz___.
3. Die ältesten Kuckucksuhren stammen aus dem ___18. Jahrhundert___.
4. Die bedeutendste Erfindung von Robert Bosch war die ___Zündkerze___.
5. Eine soziale Reform für Arbeiter von Robert Bosch war, dass sie nur acht ___Stunden___ am Tag arbeiten mussten.

3 **Vorbereitung auf ein Vorstellungsgespräch** Diskutieren Sie mit einem Partner / einer Partnerin, wie man sich am besten auf ein Vorstellungsgespräch vorbereitet. Was muss man vor dem Gespräch alles wissen? Welche Fragen sind typisch für ein Bewerbungsgespräch?

BEISPIEL

3 Expansion Have pairs compile a list of tips for a successful interview and share them with the class.

S1: *Wenn ich mich auf ein Vorstellungsgespräch vorbereite, will ich alles Mögliche über die Firma wissen.*
S2: *Wo findest du die Informationen?*

Ressourcen

vhlcentral.com

11A.1

QUERVERWEIS

See **10A.1** to review subordinate clauses.

ACHTUNG

Relative pronouns are not optional in German, even though they are sometimes omitted in English.

Relative pronouns  Presentation

Startblock In 8B.2, you learned to use demonstrative pronouns to refer to someone or something mentioned in a previous sentence. Demonstratives can also be used as relative pronouns, to introduce a subordinate clause that refers to someone or something mentioned in the main clause.

Er ist der Künstler, **der** im Central Park in New York das Kunstwerk „The Gates" errichtet hat.

Sie ist eine Frau, **die** mit Typen flirtet, ihre Telefonnummern bekommt und sie dann in den Abfall wirft.

Suggestion Point out that the relative pronouns are identical to the definite articles except in the dative plural (**denen**) and the genitive forms (**dessen** and **deren**).

- Use relative pronouns to combine two statements about the same subject into a single sentence. German relative pronouns correspond to the English relative pronouns *who, whom, whose, that,* and *which.*

relative pronouns				
	masculine	**feminine**	**neuter**	**plural**
nominative	der	die	das	die
accusative	den	die	das	die
dative	dem	der	dem	denen
genitive	dessen	deren	dessen	deren

Ich arbeite bei **einer** kleinen **Firma**.
*I work for a small **company.***

Die Firma verkauft Möbel.
***The company** sells furniture.*

Ich arbeite bei einer kleinen Firma, **die** Möbel verkauft.
*I work for a small company **that** sells furniture.*

- Separate a relative clause from the main clause with a comma, and put the conjugated verb at the end. As in English, a relative clause may come in the middle of a main clause. In this case, put commas both before and after the relative clause.

Wer hat den Hefter genommen, **der** auf meinem Schreibtisch stand?
*Who took the stapler **that** was on my desk?*

Die Personalchefin, **die** meinen Anruf entgegengenommen hat, war sehr nett.
*The HR manager **who** took my call was very nice.*

- The gender and number of a relative pronoun matches the gender and number of the noun it refers to. The case depends on whether the relative pronoun is functioning as a subject, direct object, indirect object, or possessive in the relative clause.

Ich habe eine gute Freundin, **die** eine
  Stelle sucht.
*I have a good friend **who** is looking
  for a job.*

Die Bewerberin, **der** wir die Stelle anbieten,
  hat sehr gute Referenzen.
*The applicant **to whom** we're offering the job
  has very good references.*

Der Lebenslauf, **den** wir gestern bekommen
  haben, hatte viele Schreibfehler.
*The résumé **(that)** we received yesterday had
  a lot of spelling mistakes.*

Das ist der Geschäftsführer, **dessen** Tochter ein
  Praktikum bei unserer Firma macht.
*That's the manager **whose** daughter is doing
  an internship at our company.*

Suggestion You may want to explain the concept of an antecedent to students. Tell them that the antecedent is the word in the main clause that the relative clause refers to. Have students identify the antecedent in each of the example sentences.

- Use **was** as the relative pronoun if the noun in the main clause is an indefinite pronoun such as **alles**, **etwas**, **nichts**, **viel**, or **wenig**.

Ist das alles, **was** du mir
  sagen wolltest?
*Is that all **(that)** you wanted to
  say to me?*

Das ist etwas, **was** nur die Geschäftsführerin
  entscheiden darf.
*That's something **(that)** only the manager
  can decide.*

Expansion Teach students the saying **Nicht alles, was glänzt, ist Gold**. Have them make up their own sayings by completing the following sentences: **Nichts, was... Etwas, was... Viel, was... Wenig, was...**

- If a relative pronoun is the object of a preposition, put the preposition at the beginning of the clause, *before* the relative pronoun. Remember to use a relative pronoun in the appropriate case for the preposition that precedes it.

Der Kalender, **auf den** ich meine Termine
  schreibe, ist hinter den Schreibtisch gefallen.
*The calendar **on which** I write my
  appointments fell behind the desk.*

Wie heißt die Firma, **für die** Sie gerne
  arbeiten würden?
*What's the name of the company **(that)**
  you'd like to work **for**?*

- You may also use **wo** instead of a prepositional phrase to indicate location in a relative clause.

In dem Gebäude, **wo** ich arbeite, gibt es
  ein gutes Restaurant.
*There's a good restaurant in the building
  where I work.*

Ich kenne ein Geschäft, **wo** man Schweizer
  Schokolade kaufen kann.
*I know a shop **where** you can buy
  Swiss chocolate.*

Ressourcen

SAM
WB pp. 147–148

SAM
LM: p. 95

S
vhlcentral.com

Jetzt sind Sie dran! **Wählen Sie die passenden Relativpronomen.**

1. Hast du das Paket bekommen, (das/ dem) ich dir letzte Woche geschickt habe?

2. Die Telefonnummer, (der / die) er mir gegeben hat, funktioniert nicht.

3. Die Firma, bei (die / der) Franz sich beworben hat, hat viele Angestellte.

4. Ich kenne den Geschäftsführer, mit (dem/ der) du sprichst, schon seit Jahren.

5. Ich muss den Lebenslauf, an (dem/ das) ich jetzt arbeite, bis morgen abschicken.

6. Ist das die Assistentin, (der / die) dir bei der Arbeit hilft?

7. Kennen Sie die Angestellten, (der / die) ihre Ausbildung in Wien gemacht haben?

8. Herr Vögele, (dessen/ der) Frau Geschäftsführerin ist, arbeitet als Personalchef.

9. Wie heißt die Bewerberin, mit (die / der) Sie gesprochen haben?

10. Das ist die nette Frau, (der / die) im Schreibwarengeschäft arbeitet.

11. Das Paket, auf (das/ dem) ich seit Wochen warte, ist heute angekommen.

12. Die Assistenten, (den / denen) der Personalchef gute Referenzen gegeben hat, freuten sich sehr.

1 Suggestion Have students write their answers on the board. Correct any mistakes and explain the correct answers.

Anwendung

1 Falschbestellungen
Sie haben einige neue Artikel im Internet bestellt, aber bei der Bestellung gab es ein Durcheinander (*mix-up*). Sagen Sie, dass Sie diese Artikel nicht bestellt haben.

▶ **BEISPIEL** Computer

Das ist nicht der Computer, den ich bestellt habe.

Stuhl

1. Das ist nicht der Stuhl, den ich bestellt habe.

Uhr

2. Das ist nicht die Uhr, die ich bestellt habe.

Fahrrad

3. Das ist nicht das Fahrrad, das ich bestellt habe.

Schuhe

4. Das sind nicht die Schuhe, die ich bestellt habe.

Haartrockner

5. Das ist nicht der Haartrockner, den ich bestellt habe.

2 Suggestion Remind students that **was** is used as the relative pronoun when the antecedent is **alles**, **etwas**, **nichts**, **viel**, or **wenig**.

2 Relativpronomen
Ergänzen Sie die Sätze mit den Relativpronomen aus der Liste.

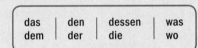

| das | den | dessen | was |
| dem | der | die | wo |

BEISPIEL Dort ist der Student, *dessen* Eltern Immobilienmakler sind.

1. Meine Schwester hat einen neuen Freund, __den__ ich nicht mag.
2. Das Geschichteprojekt, an __dem__ die Studenten arbeiten, ist sehr interessant.
3. Die alte Frau, __der__ Martin immer beim Einkaufen hilft, ist heute krank.
4. An der Ecke ist eine Eisdiele, __wo__ es leckeres italienisches Eis gibt.
5. Die Brücke, über __die__ man gehen muss, um in die Altstadt zu kommen, ist für den Fahrverkehr geschlossen.
6. Es gibt nicht viel, __was__ mein Mann nicht isst.
7. Das ist das neue Handy, __dessen__ Display die Größe von einem Tablet-Computer hat.
8. Wo ist das Silberbesteck, __das__ wir zur Hochzeit bekommen haben?

3 Die Tierarztpraxis
Ergänzen Sie den Dialog mit der richtigen Form der passenden Relativpronomen.

BEISPIEL JASMIN: Hanna, kennst du den Tierarzt, bei _dem_ Nina ihr Praktikum macht?

HANNA: Ja, ist das nicht der, (1) __dessen__ Büro gegenüber vom Juweliergeschäft Wagner ist?

JASMIN: Meinst du das Geschäft, (2) __wo__ es die tollen Halsketten gibt?

HANNA: Ja, genau. Und was sagt Nina so über die Arbeit, (3) __die__ sie da machen muss?

JASMIN: Sie sagt, sie lernt viele Dinge, von (4) __denen__ sie vorher nichts wusste.

 Practice more at **vhlcentral.com.**

Kommunikation

4 **Was passt zusammen?** Finden Sie mit einer Partnerin / einem Partner die richtige Definition für jeden Begriff und ergänzen Sie dann das passende Relativpronomen.

> **BEISPIEL**
>
> *Ein Geschäftsführer ist eine Person,*
> *die die Angestellten leitet.*

1. Ein Geschäftsführer ist eine Person, _f_.
2. Ein Praktikum ist eine Arbeit, _c_.
3. Ein Gehalt ist Geld, _e_.
4. Ein Personalchef ist ein Mann, _b_.
5. Ein Bewerber ist eine Person, _a_.
6. Ein Lebenslauf ist ein Dokument, _d_.

a. _die_ sich um eine Stelle bewirbt.
b. _der_ Vorstellungsgespräche vereinbart.
c. _die_ oft unbezahlt ist.
d. _das_ zu einer Bewerbung gehört.
e. _das_ man für seine Arbeit bekommt.
f. _die_ die Angestellten leitet.

5 **Definitionen** Erfinden Sie mit einem Partner / einer Partnerin Ihre eigenen Definitionen und benutzen Sie Relativpronomen.   Sample answers provided.

> **BEISPIEL** Büromaterialien sind Sachen, ____*die man bei der Arbeit benutzt*____.

1. Ein Terminkalender ist ein Kalender, _in den man wichtige Termine und Besprechungen schreibt._
2. Ein Vorstellungsgespräch ist ein Interview, _das ein Bewerber mit einem Personalchef oder einem Geschäftsführer hat_.
3. Arzt ist ein Beruf, ____*für den man lange studieren muss*____.
4. Ein Kosmetiksalon ist ein Geschäft, _wo man einen neuen Haarschnitt bekommen kann_
5. Ein Briefträger ist ein Mann, ____*der die Post bringt*____.

6 **Stadt, Land, Fluss** Denken Sie sich mit Ihrem Partner / Ihrer Partnerin fünf Fragen zu den Themen Geografie, Sprachen, bekannte Leute und Architektur aus. Machen Sie dann ein Quiz mit zwei Mitstudenten. Benutzen Sie Relativsätze.   Answers will vary.

> **BEISPIEL**
>
> **S1:** *Wie heißt der Fluss, der in Deutschland beginnt*
> *und ins Schwarze Meer fließt?*
> **S2:** *Das ist die Donau. Wie heißt der berühmteste*
> *Tennisspieler, der aus der Schweiz kommt?*
> **S3:** *Das ist Roger Federer.*

7 **Im Konferenzzimmer** Beschreiben Sie mit einem Partner / einer Partnerin, was in dieser Szene passiert. Verwenden Sie auch Ihre Fantasie dabei. Benutzen Sie Relativsätze.   Answers will vary.

> **BEISPIEL**
>
> *Die Angestellten sind in einer Besprechung,*
> *in der sie über die Bewerberin für die Stelle*
> *als Chefsektretärin reden. Frau Weber, die*
> *eine der Bewerbungen liest, arbeitet schon*
> *lange in der Firma und hat ein Gehalt, das…*

11A.2 ## The past tenses (review)  **Presentation**

Startblock You have learned to use weak, strong, and mixed verbs, including verbs with separable and inseparable prefixes, in both the **Perfekt** and the **Präteritum**.

QUERVERWEIS

See **5A.1** and **6B.2** to review the formation of past participles. See **5B.1** to review verbs that use **sein** as the auxiliary in the **Perfekt**.

See **6A.1** and **7A.1** to review the formation of the **Präteritum**. See **Appendix A** for a complete list of strong verbs and their **Perfekt** and **Präteritum** forms.

Remember that the **Plusquamperfekt** is often used with the subordinating conjunctions **als**, **bevor**, and **nachdem**. See **8A.1** to review the formation of the **Plusquamperfekt** and its use with these conjunctions.

- The **Perfekt** tense is used in conversation and informal writing to talk about the past. It is formed with a conjugated form of **haben** or **sein** and a past participle. Suggestion Make sure students remember the meanings of the verbs reviewed in this section.

  Hat Herr Schwartz eine Nachricht **hinterlassen**?
  *Did Mr. Schwartz **leave** a message?*

  Wir **sind** gestern erst sehr spät **angekommen**.
  *We **got here** very late yesterday.*

- To form the **Perfekt** of a reflexive verb, place the reflexive pronoun between the conjugated form of **haben** or **sein** and the past participle.

  Ich **habe mich** um fünfzehn Stellen **beworben**.
  *I **applied** for fifteen jobs.*

  Hast du **dir** die Zähne **geputzt**?
  *Did you **brush** your teeth?*

- The **Präteritum** is used to talk about the past in writing or in formal spoken contexts. **Präteritum** forms of **sein**, **haben**, **werden**, and the modal verbs are used more commonly than **Perfekt** forms, even in informal speech.

  Sie **suchten** Arbeit.
  *They **were looking for** work.*

  Lena **blieb** am Apparat.
  *Lena **stayed** on the line.*

- The **Plusquamperfekt** is used to talk about an action that happened before another event in the past. It is formed with the **Präteritum** of **haben** or **sein** and a past participle.

  Jasmin **hatte vergessen**, das Telefon aufzulegen.
  *Jasmin **had forgotten** to hang up the phone.*

  Sie **war** eine halbe Stunde in der Warteschleife **gewesen**.
  *She **had been** on hold for half an hour.*

ACHTUNG

Remember that the prefixes of separable prefix verbs are always stressed, while the prefixes of inseparable prefix verbs are never stressed: **Die Assistentin ist ein**geschlafen. Der Chef hat viel ver**dient**.

verb type	*Infinitiv*	*Präteritum*	*Perfekt*	*Plusquamperfekt*
weak	suchen besuchen	suchte besuchte	hat gesucht hat besucht	hatte gesucht hatte besucht
modal	dürfen wollen	durfte wollte	hat gedurft hat gewollt	hatte gedurft hatte gewollt
mixed	bringen mitbringen	brachte brachte mit	hat gebracht hat mitgebracht	hatte gebracht hatte mitgebracht
strong	kommen ankommen	kam kam an	ist gekommen ist angekommen	war gekommen war angekommen

Ressourcen

SAM
WB: pp. 149–150

SAM
LM: p. 96

vhlcentral.com

Jetzt sind Sie dran! Ergänzen Sie die Tabelle mit den fehlenden Verbformen.

	Präteritum (er/sie/es)	Perfekt (er/sie/es)	Plusquamperfekt (er/sie/es)
abheben	hob ab	hat abgehoben	hatte abgehoben
sich anziehen	zog sich an	hat sich angezogen	hatte sich angezogen
haben	hatte	hat gehabt	hatte gehabt
nehmen	nahm	hat genommen	hatte genommen
sein	war	ist gewesen	war gewesen
mitbringen	brachte mit	hat mitgebracht	hatte mitgebracht
gehen	ging	ist gegangen	war gegangen

Anwendung und Kommunikation

1 **Was fehlt?** Ergänzen Sie die Sätze mit den Verben in Klammern.
Benutzen Sie die richtigen Präteritumsformen.

1. Ben __bewarb sich__ (sich bewerben) für eine Stelle bei einer Bank.

2. Er __stand auf__ (aufstehen) und zog seinen besten Anzug an.

3. Nach dem Frühstück __wurde__ (werden) es Zeit, dass er sich auf den Weg machte.

4. Er __hatte__ (haben) nur noch fünfzehn Minuten, um zu seinem Termin zu kommen.

5. Er __wollte__ (wollen) einen guten Eindruck (*impression*) machen.

6. Aber als er die Kreuzung __überquerte__ (überqueren), hatte er einen Unfall!

7. Als er Stunden später bei seinem Vorstellungsgespräch __ankam__ (ankommen),
   sagte man ihm, dass er wieder gehen konnte.

8. Er __war__ (sein) sehr traurig.

2 **Sätze umschreiben** Schreiben Sie die Sätze um. Benutzen Sie das
Perfekt anstelle des Präsens und das Plusquamperfekt anstelle des Perfekt.

1. Ich habe vier Karten für ein Konzert bekommen, also lade ich drei Freunde dazu ein.
   Ich hatte vier Karten für ein Konzert bekommen, also habe ich drei Freunde dazu eingeladen.
2. Nachdem wir im Restaurant gegessen haben, fahren wir zusammen zum Konzert.
   Nachdem wir im Restaurant gegessen hatten, sind wir zusammen zum Konzert gefahren.
3. Obwohl Jan die Wegbeschreibung (*directions*) im Internet heruntergeladen hat,
   biegen wir zweimal falsch ab.
   Obwohl Jan die Wegbeschreibung im Internet heruntergeladen hatte, sind wir zweimal falsch abgebogen.
4. Als wir endlich in der Konzerthalle ankommen, hat das Konzert schon begonnen.
   Als wir endlich in der Konzerthalle angekommen sind, hatte das Konzert schon begonnen.

3 **Im Märchenland** Wählen Sie mit Ihrem Partner / Ihrer Partnerin eine
Märchenfigur (*fairy-tale character*). Auf was für eine Stelle würde diese
Figur sich bewerben und wie würde ihr Lebenslauf aussehen? Schreiben Sie
aus der Ich-Perspektive und benutzen Sie das Präteritum. Answers will vary.

3 **Expansion** Have students role-play a job interview with their fairy-tale character.

> **BEISPIEL**
>
> **Aschenputtels Lebenslauf:**
>
> Meine Mutter starb, als ich sehr jung war. Ich musste
> also viele Jahre lang die ganze Hausarbeit für meine
> Stiefmutter und zwei Stiefschwestern machen. Ich putzte
> täglich das ganze Haus, kochte das Essen und hatte nie
> einen freien Tag …

4 **Wer hat das gemacht?** Benutzen Sie die Verben aus der Liste
und erfinden Sie mit einem Partner / einer Partnerin sechs Quizfragen
zu dem Thema, was berühmte Leute gemacht haben. Stellen Sie Ihre
Fragen dann zwei anderen Mitstudenten. Verwenden Sie das Perfekt
und das Plusquamperfekt. Wechseln Sie sich ab. Answers will vary.

> **BEISPIEL**
>
> **S1:** Wer hat *Der Steppenwolf* geschrieben?
> **S2:** Hermann Hesse.

bauen	gewinnen	singen
bekommen	heiraten	(mit)spielen
entdecken	landen	sterben
erfinden	schreiben	verlieren

Wiederholung

1 Die Familie

Wählen Sie eine Person von der Liste aus. Beschreiben Sie die Person mit einem Relativsatz. Ihr Partner / Ihre Partnerin muss die Person erraten, die Sie beschreiben. Answers will vary.

BEISPIEL

S1: Das ist der junge Mann, dessen Vater mein Onkel ist.
S2: Ist es dein Cousin?

die Mutter	die Schwester
der Onkel	die Cousine
die Schwiegertochter	die Nichte
der Urgroßvater	die Tante

2 Diskutieren und kombinieren

Sie und Ihr Partner / Ihre Partnerin bekommen unterschiedliche Blätter. Fragen Sie Ihren Partner / Ihre Partnerin, was jede Person gemacht hat. Answers will vary.

BEISPIEL

S1: Was wollte die Geschäftsführerin?
S2: Sie wollte, dass die Assistentin Anrufe entgegennimmt.

3 Was trägst du?

Beschreiben Sie abwechselnd die Kleidung der Personen in Ihrer Gruppe. Die anderen erraten, wen Sie beschreiben. Verwenden Sie möglichst viele Relativsätze. Answers will vary.

BEISPIEL

S1: Ich denke an eine Frau, die eine schwarze Hose und eine weiße Bluse trägt.
S2: Denkst du an Sarah?

3 Expansion Have students describe the attributes of a famous person and have group members guess who is being described.

4 Arbeitsblatt

Fragen Sie drei Personen in der Gruppe, über welches Thema sie viel, alles, ein bisschen oder nichts wissen. Schreiben Sie die Antworten auf. Answers will vary.

BEISPIEL

S1: Worüber weißt du viel?
S2: Ich weiß viel über alles, was mit Mathematik zu tun hat.

5 Arbeitsuchender

Felix sucht eine neue Stelle. Sehen Sie mit einem Partner / einer Partnerin seinen Terminkalender an und besprechen Sie, was er gestern morgen gemacht hat, um eine Stelle zu finden. Benutzen Sie das Präteritum und das Plusquamperfekt. Answers will vary.

BEISPIEL

Felix hatte die Stellenangebote schon gelesen, bevor er gefrühstückt hat...

8.00	Stellenangebote lesen
9.00	Frühstück
10.00	dem Personalchef der Computerfirma meinen Lebenslauf schicken
11.00	mich aufs Vorstellungspräch vorbereiten
12.00	Vorstellungsgespräch bei „Maxifirma"
13.00	Mittagessen

6 Generationen

Diskutieren Sie mit einem Partner / einer Partnerin, wie das Leben der älteren Generationen war. Answers will vary.

BEISPIEL

S1: Meine Eltern sind beide 1960 geboren. Als sie Kinder waren, gab es kein Internet. Sie haben meistens Musik im Radio gehört.
S2: Das war bei meinen Eltern genauso. Aber meine Großeltern...

Arbeit	Kochen
Familie	Schule
Freizeit	Technologie
Gesundheit	Urlaub
Hausarbeit	

6 Suggestion Have students prepare notes individually, before they begin working with a partner.

Die Berliner Mauer

Gewinner: Short Film Jury Prize Hong Kong International Film Festival

Ein Film von Paul Cotter

mit Joost Siedhoff, Fritz Roth und Dominik Bender

S Video: Short Film

Die Berliner Mauer

Nach dem Tod seiner Ehefrau baut ein alter Mann eine Mauer (*wall*), wo die Berliner Mauer früher in seinem Dorf stand. Niemand weiß warum. Die Kinder in der Nachbarschaft (*neighborhood*) helfen ihm, während die Erwachsenen über die Bedeutung der neuen Mauer für Westdeutsche, Ostdeutsche und Ausländer diskutieren.

Vorbereitung

1 **Was fehlt?** Schreiben Sie die Wörter aus den zwei Listen, die die Sätze unten ergänzen.

1. Die Witwe war sehr __einsam__ nach dem Tod ihres Ehemannes.
2. Wir wollen keinen __Ärger__ mit der Polizei.
3. Viele Menschen glauben, dass sie zu hohe __Steuern__ zahlen.
4. Sich nicht sicher zu sein ist kein __Grund__, etwas nicht zu tun.
5. Ich weiß nicht, ob sie freundlich oder __feindlich__ sind.
6. In diesem Land gibt es manchmal __Diskriminierung__ von Ausländern.
7. Ist das Rauchen (*smoking*) __erlaubt__ in diesem Gebäude?
8. Sie waren __anscheinend__ glücklich, obwohl sie viele Probleme gehabt hatten.

2 **Diskutieren** Sprechen Sie über die folgenden Themen.

1. Was wissen Sie schon über die Berliner Mauer und die Wiedervereinigung (*reunification*) Deutschlands? Welche Probleme kann es geben, wenn Menschen, die sehr unterschiedliche Lebenserfahrungen gehabt haben, zusammenleben müssen?

2. Erzählen Sie einander über etwas, was Ihnen nicht erlaubt war, das Sie aber trotzdem getan haben. Glauben Sie, dass Sie das Richtige getan haben, obwohl es verboten war?

Nützliche Ausdrücke

- **anscheinend**
  apparently
- **Das reicht!**
  That's enough!
- **das Grundstück, -e**
  piece of land
- **erlaubt**
  allowed
- **die Steuer, -n**
  tax
- **der Ärger, -**
  trouble
- **der Grund, ⸚e**
  reason
- **eingreifen**
  to intervene
- **ermutigen**
  to encourage
- **zustimmen**
  to approve; to agree

Über den Film sprechen

- **der Ausländer, - / Ausländerin, -nen**
  foreigner
- **die Diskriminierung, -en**
  discrimination
- **einsam**
  lonely
- **feindlich (zu)**
  hostile (to)
- **der Nachbar, -n / Nachbarin, -nen**
  neighbor
- **hassen**
  to hate

Suggestion Point out that **Nachbar** is an **n**-noun.

Szenen: Die Berliner Mauer

MANN: Sie wird in Frieden ruhen°.

KATJA: Was macht er da?
KATJAS MANN: Ich hab' keine Ahnung°. Da macht er schon seit über einer Stunde 'rum.
KATJAS MANN: Werden wir auch so, wenn wir alt sind? Drehst du auch durch°, wenn ich sterbe?
KATJA: Der arme alte Mann. Sieht aus, als hätte er nicht mehr alle Tassen im Schrank.

MÄDCHEN: Aber wir sind schon fast fertig°!
POLIZIST: Das ist egal! Das ist ein öffentliches Grundstück. Hier können Sie nicht ohne Genehmigung° bauen. Da müssen Sie erst die Zustimmung° der Stadtplanung einholen. Und die haben Sie nicht, oder? Ja, dann muss es alles hier weg!

HELMUT: Herr Schlömerkemper, was machen Sie denn da? Sie können doch hier nicht einfach die Mauer wieder aufbauen. Die ist ja aus gutem Grund abgerissen worden°, nicht wahr? Sicher, es gibt schon Momente... da hätte ich sie auch schon gerne wieder, schon allein wegen des Gesindels° da, nicht wahr? Aber... Herr Schlömerkemper, das kann man nicht machen... Das ist nicht erlaubt!

HELMUT: Tut mir leid, Werner. Wir haben es versucht°.

POLIZIST: Okay! Stoppt, stoppt! Das reicht! Genug° jetzt! Die Mauer wird abgerissen! Räumen sie alle Ihre Gerätschaften° hier weg! Sie auch! Das muss hier alles weg!

in Frieden ruhen *rest in peace* **keine Ahnung** *no idea* **Drehst du...durch** *Will you go crazy*
ist... abgerissen worden *was torn down* **Gesindels** *scum* **Genug** *Enough* **Gerätschaften** *equipment*
fertig *finished* **Genehmigung** *permit* **Zustimmung** *approval* **haben...versucht** *tried*

Analyse

3 **Verständnis** Lesen Sie die folgenden Sätze aus dem Film und bringen Sie sie in die richtige Reihenfolge (1-8).

<u>3</u> „Werden wir auch so, wenn wir alt sind?"

<u>6</u> „Aber wir sind fast fertig!"

<u>2</u> „Ihr sollt nicht mal mit diesen Kindern spielen!"

<u>4</u> „Herr Schlömerkemper, das kann man nicht machen."

<u>5</u> „Die Mauer wird abgerissen!"

<u>8</u> „Tut mir leid, Werner."

<u>7</u> „Können wir das kleine Stückchen Mauer nicht einfach stehen lassen?"

<u>1</u> „Sie wird in Frieden ruhen."

4 **Dialoge** Erfinden Sie mit einem Partner / einer Partnerin einen Dialog zu einer der folgenden Situationen.

- Stellen Sie sich vor, dass Sie Katja und ihr Ehemann sind. Was besprechen Sie zusammen, nachdem die Polizei die Mauer zerstört (*destroyed*) hat? Wollen Sie Herrn Schlömerkemper und die anderen Nachbarn besser kennen lernen?

- Spielen Sie die Szene von dem Tag im Jahre 1962, als Werner Schlömerkemper und Theresa ihre Namen in den Stein eingeritzt (*carved*) haben. Welche Gedanken über die Zukunft hatten Sie? Was waren Ihre Träume für Ihr Leben zusammen?

5 **Zum Besprechen** Diskutieren Sie die folgenden Sprichwörter. Glauben Sie an diese Sprichwörter? Welche Verbindung haben sie zu dem Film?

Stille Wasser sind tief.

Liebe deinen Nachbarn, reiß aber den Zaun (*fence*) nicht ein (*tear down*).

Suggestion Ask students if they can think of contemporary examples where the building of a wall or fence has been a source of controversy.

Communicative Goals

You will learn how to:

- talk about professions
- talk about work

 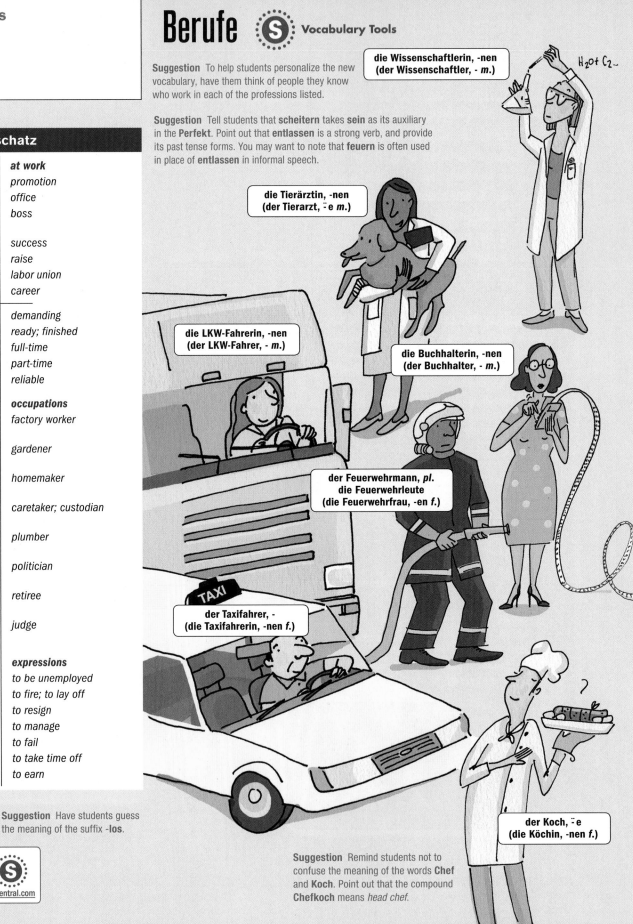
Suggestion To help students personalize the new vocabulary, have them think of people they know who work in each of the professions listed.

Suggestion Tell students that **scheitern** takes **sein** as its auxiliary in the **Perfekt**. Point out that **entlassen** is a strong verb, and provide its past tense forms. You may want to note that **feuern** is often used in place of **entlassen** in informal speech.

Wortschatz

auf der Arbeit	*at work*
die Beförderung, -en	*promotion*
das Büro, -s	*office*
der Chef, -s / die Chefin, -nen	*boss*
der Erfolg, -e	*success*
die Gehaltserhöhung, -en	*raise*
die Gewerkschaft, -en	*labor union*
die Karriere, -n	*career*
anspruchsvoll	*demanding*
fertig	*ready; finished*
ganztags	*full-time*
halbtags	*part-time*
zuverlässig	*reliable*
Berufe	*occupations*
der Fabrikarbeiter, - / die Fabrikarbeiterin, -nen	*factory worker*
der Gärtner, - / die Gärtnerin, -nen	*gardener*
der Hausmann, ̈er / die Hausfrau, -en	*homemaker*
der Hausmeister, - / die Hausmeisterin, -nen	*caretaker; custodian*
der Klempner, - / die Klempnerin, -nen	*plumber*
der Politiker, - / die Politikerin, -nen	*politician*
der Rentner, - / die Rentnerin, -nen	*retiree*
der Richter, - / die Richterin, -nen	*judge*
Ausdrücke	*expressions*
arbeitslos sein	*to be unemployed*
entlassen	*to fire; to lay off*
kündigen	*to resign*
leiten	*to manage*
scheitern	*to fail*
Urlaub nehmen	*to take time off*
verdienen	*to earn*

die Wissenschaftlerin, -nen (der Wissenschaftler, - m.)

die Tierärztin, -nen (der Tierarzt, ̈e m.)

die LKW-Fahrerin, -nen (der LKW-Fahrer, - m.)

die Buchhalterin, -nen (der Buchhalter, - m.)

der Feuerwehrmann, pl. die Feuerwehrleute (die Feuerwehrfrau, -en f.)

der Taxifahrer, - (die Taxifahrerin, -nen f.)

der Koch, ̈e (die Köchin, -nen f.)

Suggestion Have students guess the meaning of the suffix **-los**.

Suggestion Remind students not to confuse the meaning of the words **Chef** and **Koch**. Point out that the compound **Chefkoch** means *head chef*.

der Bankangestellte, -n
(die Bankangestellte, -n *f.*)

die Immobilienmaklerin, -nen
(der Immobilienmakler, - *m.*)

der Bauer, -n
(die Bäuerin, -nen *f.*)

die Elektrikerin, -nen
(der Elektriker, - *m.*)

der Psychologe, -n
(die Psychologin, -nen *f.*)

ACHTUNG

The adverbs **gut** and **schlecht** can be used with **verdienen** to indicate how well a person is paid: **Ich will gut verdienen.**

Suggestion Explain that **Bankangestellte(r)** is a compound adjectival noun, derived from the adjective **angestellt** (*employed*). Remind students that the ending of an adjectival noun changes depending on the article that precedes it.

Anwendung

1 **Assoziationen** Wählen Sie die Berufsbezeichnung, die Sie mit jedem Foto assoziieren.

<u>c</u> 1. Feuerwehrmann <u>e</u> 3. LKW-Fahrer <u>d</u> 5. Bankangestellter
<u>f</u> 2. Richterin   <u>a</u> 4. Gärtnerin <u>b</u> 6. Tierärztin

a.

b.

c.

d.

e.

f.

2 **Vergleiche** Ergänzen Sie die Vergleiche mit einem passenden Wort.

Suggested answers provided.

1. Garten : Gärtner :: Fabrik : _____Fabrikarbeiter_____
2. Küche : Koch :: Labor (*lab*) : _____Wissenschaftler_____
3. LKW : LKW-Fahrer :: Taxi : _____Taxifahrer_____
4. Auto : Mechaniker :: Toilette : _____Klempner_____
5. Musik : Musiker :: Politik : _____Politiker_____
6. Friseurin : Friseur :: Hausfrau : _____Hausmann_____

2 **Expansion** Have students explain which of these jobs they would or would not like to have, and why.

3 **Die Beförderung** 🎧 Hören Sie sich das Gespräch zwischen Lukas und seinem Chef an, und entscheiden Sie dann, ob die folgenden Aussagen richtig oder falsch sind.

	richtig	falsch
1. Der Chef hatte eine Besprechung mit dem Geschäftsführer.	☑	☐
2. Er bietet Lukas eine Halbtagsstelle an.	☐	☑
3. Lukas hat ein abgeschlossenes Studium.	☑	☐
4. Lukas nimmt das Angebot nicht an.	☐	☑
5. Der Buchhalter schickt Lukas einen neuen Vertrag.	☐	☑
6. Lukas bekommt eine Stelle als Assistent.	☑	☐
7. Die neue Stelle ist nicht sehr anspruchsvoll.	☐	☑
8. Der Chef denkt, dass Lukas eine große Karriere machen wird.	☑	☐

3 **Expansion** Have groups of students write a conversation between a manager and an employee and then act it out.

🖋️ Practice more at **vhlcentral.com.**

Kommunikation

4 Definitionen Schreiben Sie mit einem Partner / einer Partnerin zu jedem Begriff eine Definition. Sample answers are provided.

1. die Gehaltserhöhung ___Man bekommt ein höheres Gehalt.___
2. halbtags arbeiten ___Man arbeitet nur zwanzig Stunden die Woche.___
3. arbeitslos sein ___Man hat keine Arbeitsstelle und muss eine suchen.___
4. die Gewerkschaft ___Das ist eine Organisation, die sich für die Interessen der Arbeiter oder Angestellten stark macht.___
5. Urlaub nehmen ___Man nimmt sich ein paar Tage frei.___
6. die Beförderung ___Man bekommt eine bessere Stelle.___

4 Expansion Have partners play a guessing game. One student says the definition, and the other guesses the correct word.

---

5 Berufe raten Wählen Sie aus der Vokabelliste einen Beruf und beschreiben Sie, was man in diesem Beruf macht. Ihr Partner / Ihre Partnerin muss erraten, um welchen Beruf es geht. Answers will vary.

BEISPIEL

S1: Diese Frau arbeitet an biologischen, chemischen oder physikalischen Experimenten.
S2: Ist sie Wissenschaftlerin?

---

6 Diskutieren und kombinieren Sie und Ihr Partner / Ihre Partnerin bekommen zwei unterschiedliche Bilder. Finden Sie die sieben Unterschiede auf den Bildern. Wechseln Sie sich bei Ihren Fragen und Antworten ab.

BEISPIEL

S1: Sind auf deinem Bild Taxifahrer zu sehen?
S2: Ja, drei. Und auf deinem?
S1: Auf meinem sind zwei.

7 Heute im Büro Wählen Sie zwei der Zeichnungen und erfinden Sie eine Geschichte, in der Sie erzählen, was diesen Personen heute alles passiert ist. Sie können über die zwei Zeichnungen getrennt erzählen oder sie zu einer Geschichte verbinden. Answers will vary.

BEISPIEL

S1: Heute Morgen hat Lisa zu lange geschlafen.
S2: Sie kam eine halbe Stunde zu spät zur Arbeit.
S3: Im Büro hat sie dann ...

Aussprache und Rechtschreibung $\textcircled{S}$ Audio

🎧 Recognizing near-cognates

Because English and German belong to the same language family, the two languages share some related sounds. Knowing these relationships makes it easier to recognize English and German cognates. For example, for many English words that contain a *d* sound, the German equivalent has a **t** in the same position.

Ta**g**	un**t**er	Bro**t**	ro**t**	Tür

For many English words that contain a *p* sound, the German equivalent has an **f** or **pf** in the same position, while a *t* sound in an English word may correspond to a German **z** or **s** sound.

Pfanne	Schi**ff**	**z**wei	au**s**	e**ss**en

In some German words, the **ch** corresponds to an English *k* or *gh*.

ma**ch**en	Bu**ch**	la**ch**en	Na**ch**t	ho**ch**

In many German words, the **d** corresponds to the English *th* sound, and in a few words, the **g** corresponds to an English *y*.

Bru**d**er	**D**onner	Le**d**er	**g**estern	**g**elb

Suggestion Tell students that these relationships are the result of the **Hochdeutsche Lautverschiebung** (High German consonant shift), which occurred between the 5th and 9th centuries A.D. Since English branched off from German prior to this shift, many of its consonant sounds correspond to the German spoken around 400 A.D. You may want to point out that the **Plattdeutsch** dialect likewise skipped the shift. For example, in **Plattdeutsch** *water* is **Water** and *ship* is **Schip**.

1 **Aussprechen** Wiederholen Sie die Wörter, die Sie hören.

1. trinken
2. Wort
3. sitzen
4. zu
5. Pfeffer
6. Apfel
7. helfen
8. brechen
9. denken
10. Bad
11. recht
12. Garn

2 **Nachsprechen** Wiederholen Sie die Sätze, die Sie hören.

1. Der alte Koch arbeitet nur noch halbtags.
2. Die Gärtnerin findest du unter einem großen Baum im Hinterhof.
3. Ich suche gerade seine Telefonnummer in meinem Adressbuch.
4. Wir wollen nicht den ganzen Tag vor einem Computer sitzen.
5. Es ist besser länger zu schlafen, als soviel Kaffee zu trinken.
6. Seit einer Woche leitet sie das Büro.

2 **Expansion** Have students underline the cognates and provide English equivalents.

3 **Sprichwörter** Wiederholen Sie die Sprichwörter, die Sie hören.

Wo sich Fuchs und Hase gute Nacht sagen.[1]

Die Nacht zum Tage machen.[2]

[1] In the middle of nowhere. (lit. Where the fox and hare say "good night" to each other.)

[2] To party all night. (lit. To turn the night into day.)

Ressourcen

SAM
LM: p. 98

$\textcircled{S}$
vhlcentral.com

Schlechte Nachrichten

(S) Video

Sabite bekommt schlechte Nachrichten aus der Galerie. Zum Glück ist Hans gut in Wirtschaft und kann Sabite trösten.

Vorbereitung Have students look at scene 1, and discuss with a partner why they think Sabite is sad. After they have watched the episode, have students get together with their partners again and check their predictions.

HERR KLEINEDLER Danke, dass Sie zu dieser Besprechung in die Galerie gekommen sind, Sabite. Ich hoffe, Sie mussten dafür nicht Ihre Uni ausfallen lassen.
SABITE Ich hatte heute nur einen Kurs. Dies ist die erste Ausstellung meiner Karriere, drum möchte ich... Herr Kleinedler, es gibt doch noch eine Ausstellung, oder?

HERR KLEINEDLER Sabite, sie sind eine junge und talentierte Künstlerin, aber es gibt noch so viele ausgezeichnete Künstler mit vielen neuen aufregenden Werken. Wir werden den Schwerpunkt unserer Ausstellung ändern auf Berlins Nachwuchskünstler. Wir werden nur zwei Ihrer Werke anstatt zehn brauchen.

HANS Mein Vater ist Forscher und Wissenschaftler. Meine Mutter arbeitet in einer Versicherungsagentur. Sie ist Buchhalterin. Und Max plant eine Karriere als Psychologe.

SABITE Aber nur zwei Werke? Das ist nicht fair.
HERR KLEINEDLER Diese beiden Werke werden fünf Wochen in der Ausstellung sein, zusammen mit den Werken aller anderen Künstler. Dadurch werden viel mehr Leute Ihre Kunst sehen. Es ist die bessere Lösung.

MELINE Ich möchte, dass bereits etwas organisiert ist, wenn ich nach Wien komme.
HANS Ich war noch nie in Wien.
MELINE Wien ist eine wunderschöne Kulturstadt. Du solltest Wien besuchen kommen...

MELINE Also, Hans, jetzt wohne ich schon seit fast einem Jahr neben dir, und ich weiß immer noch nicht einmal, was du studierst.
HANS Geschichte und Politik.
MELINE Willst du Politiker werden?
HANS Ich glaube nicht, dass ich ein guter Politiker wäre.

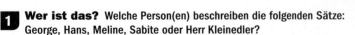

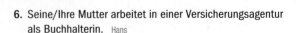

ÜBUNGEN

1 **Wer ist das?** Welche Person(en) beschreiben die folgenden Sätze: George, Hans, Meline, Sabite oder Herr Kleinedler?

1. Er/Sie hat die erste Ausstellung seiner/ihrer Karriere. Sabite

2. Er/Sie muss den Schwerpunkt der Ausstellung ändern. Herr Kleinedler

3. Er/Sie wird nur zwei seiner/ihrer Werke ausstellen können. Sabite

4. Er/Sie weiß nicht, was Hans studiert. Meline

5. Er/Sie glaubt nicht, dass er/sie ein guter Politiker/eine gute Politikerin wäre. Hans

6. Seine/Ihre Mutter arbeitet in einer Versicherungsagentur als Buchhalterin. Hans

7. Sein/Ihr Bruder möchte Psychologe werden. Hans

8. Er/Sie möchte eine Stelle in Wien finden. Meline

9. Er/Sie hatte in den letzten Monaten sehr viele Notfälle. Sabite

10. Es tut ihm/ihr leid, dass er/sie so anstrengend ist. Sabite

PERSONEN

 Herr Kleinedler   Hans   Meline   Sabite   George

MELINE Hallo Sabite. Gut. Wir treffen dich dann in einer halben Stunde da. Mann. Sabite hatte in den letzten drei Monaten mehr Notfälle als ich in meinem ganzen Leben.

SABITE Und das alles, nachdem ich allen, die ich kenne, davon erzählt habe. Könnt ihr das glauben?

HANS Sabite, wir sind deine Freunde, die dich immer unterstützen. Aber Kleinedlers Idee ist wirklich nicht schlecht. Die Nachfrage nach deiner Kunst wird sich erhöhen, wenn weniger Werke über einen längeren Zeitraum ausgestellt werden.

MELINE VWL, Einführungskurs. Hans hat recht.

HANS Es werden auch Leute wegen der anderen Künstler kommen. Und die werden dann wieder deine Kunst gesehen haben, wenn sie wieder gehen.

SABITE Danke, Hans. Du überraschst mich immer wieder aufs Neue. Es tut mir leid, dass ich so anstrengend bin.

HANS Ist schon okay, Sabite.

MELINE Wenn ich es mir so recht überlege, Hans, könntest du doch auch ein guter Politiker sein.

Nützliche Ausdrücke

- **die Ausstellung**
  exhibition
- **der Künstler / die Künstlerin**
  artist
- **der Schwerpunkt**
  focus
- **der Nachwuchskünstler**
  emerging artist
- **die Lösung**
  solution
- **die Versicherungsagentur**
  insurance agency
- **Wien ist eine wunderschöne Kulturstadt.**
  Vienna is a beautiful cultural city.
- **der Notfall**
  emergency
- **die Nachfrage**
  demand
- **unterstützen**
  support
- **der Zeitraum**
  period of time
- **VWL, Einführungskurs.**
  Economics 101.

11B.1
- **Und die werden dann wieder deine Kunst gesehen haben, wenn sie wieder gehen.**
  Plus, they will have seen your art, too, by the time they leave.

11B.2
- **Sabite, sie sind eine junge und talentierte Künstlerin, aber es gibt noch so viele ausgezeichnete Künstler mit vielen neuen aufregenden Werken.**
  Sabite, you are a talented young artist, but there are so many new exciting works by other fine artists as well.

2 **Zum Besprechen** Zuerst ist Sabite sehr enttäuscht (*disappointed*), dass Herr Kleinedler nur zwei ihrer Werke ausstellen kann. Schreiben Sie zu zweit einen Absatz, in dem Sie Sabite erklären, dass es besser ist, weniger Werke länger auszustellen. Answers will vary.

2 **Suggestion** Students can also write a conversation between Sabite and her friends.

3 **Vertiefung** Meline sagt, dass Wien eine wunderschöne Kulturstadt ist. Finden Sie heraus, warum. Was gibt es in Wien zu sehen? Für welche Art von Kultur ist Wien besonders berühmt? Answers will vary.

3 **Suggestion** On the board, make a list of the cultural highlights that students identified.

Ressourcen

SAM
VM: p. 22

vhlcentral.com

Suggestion Point out that **Sozialversicherung** has a broader meaning in German than its English translation *social security*.

IM FOKUS

Sozialversicherungen Ⓢ Reading

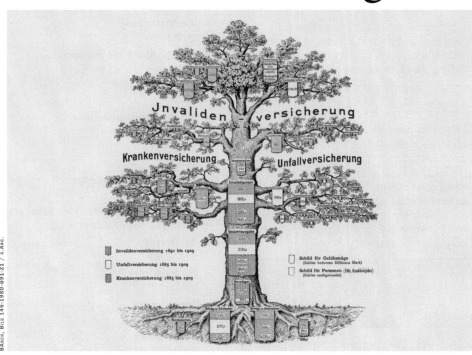

GESETZLICHE SOZIALVERSICHERUNGEN° gibt es in Deutschland schon seit Ende des 19. Jahrhunderts. Im Jahr 1883 führte° der deutsche Reichskanzler Otto von Bismarck die gesetzliche Krankenversicherung ein. Er wollte soziale Unruhen verhindern° und den Sozialismus bekämpfen°. Später kamen die Rentenversicherung und die Arbeitslosenversicherung. Diese drei Versicherungen bilden heute die gesetzliche Sozialversicherung. Dieses System wird nicht durch Steuern°, sondern durch geteilte Beiträge° von Arbeitgebern und Arbeitnehmern° finanziert.

In Österreich und in der Schweiz ist dieses System sehr ähnlich. In Österreich sind Unfall- Kranken-, Pensions- und Arbeitslosenversicherung Teil der gesetzlichen Sozialversicherungen. In der Schweiz gibt es eine Kranken- und eine Arbeitslosenversicherung so wie auch die Altersversicherung und die Invalidenversicherung. Anders als in Österreich und in Deutschland gibt es eine separate Versicherung für Erwerbsersatz° für den Fall, dass man Militär- oder Zivildienst leisten muss oder Erziehungsurlaub° machen muss.

Neben diesen Sozialversicherungen gibt es noch andere Ähnlichkeiten: festgelegte Wochenarbeitsstunden, ein gesetzliches Rentenalter° eine bestimmte Anzahl an Urlaubstagen und Feiertage, an denen nicht gearbeitet wird.

Zusatzleistungen° in deutschsprachigen Ländern			
	Deutschland	**Österreich**	**Schweiz**
Wochenarbeitszeit (Stunden pro Woche)	35–42	40	42
gesetzliches Rentenalter	Männer: 67 Frauen: 67	Männer: 65 Frauen: 60	Männer: 65 Frauen: 64
Urlaubstage pro Jahr	30	28	20
gesetzliche Feiertage	9–13	17–18	8–14

Sozialversicherungen *social security* **führte... ein** *established* **soziale Unruhen verhindern** *avoid social unrest* **bekämpfen** *combat* **Steuern** *taxes* **geteilte Beiträge** *shared contributions* **Arbeitgebern und Arbeitnehmern** *employers and employees* **Erwerbsersatz** *compensation for loss of income* **Erziehungsurlaub** *maternity leave* **gesetzliches Rentenalter** *legal retirement age* **Zusatzleistungen** *job benefits*

BArch, Bild 146-1980-091-21 / o.Ang.

Expansion Have students compare these statistics to the corresponding data for their home country.

ÜBUNGEN

1 **Richtig oder falsch?** Sagen Sie, ob die Sätze richtig oder falsch sind. Korrigieren Sie die falschen Sätze.

1. Die gesetzliche Sozialversicherung hat in Deutschland keine lange Tradition. Falsch. Sie hat eine lange Tradition.

2. Otto von Bismarck führte die gesetzliche Krankenversicherung in Deutschland ein. Richtig.

3. Das Sozialversicherungssystem wird durch Steuern finanziert. Falsch. Es wird durch Beiträge finanziert.

4. Österreicher haben auch die Unfallversicherung. Richtig.

5. In der Schweiz gibt es eine Erwerbsersatzversicherung, wenn man Militärdienst leisten muss. Richtig.

6. Das Sozialversicherungssystem in Deutschland, Österreich und der Schweiz ist sehr ähnlich. Richtig.

7. In Deutschland können Männer vor Frauen in Rente gehen. Falsch. In Deutschland können beide mit 67 Jahren in Rente gehen.

8. In der Schweiz gibt es die meisten gesetzlichen Feiertage. Falsch. In Österreich gibt es die meisten gesetzlichen Feiertage.

 Practice more at **vhlcentral.com.**

Berufe

der Fotograf, -en / die Fotografin, -nen	photographer
der Künstler, - / die Künstlerin, -nen	artist
der Optiker, - / die Optikerin, -nen	optician
der Schauspieler, - / die Schauspielerin, -nen	actor
der Schreiner, - / die Schreinerin, -nen	carpenter

Angestellte, Arbeiter, Beamte

Angestellte, Arbeiter und Beamte: Diese drei Wörter bezeichnen° Personen, die arbeiten. Was sind aber die Unterschiede zwischen diesen Bezeichnungen? Angestellte sind Personen, die vor allem in Büros arbeiten. In Firmen haben sie oft auch eine leitende° Funktion. Sie bekommen ein festes monatliches Gehalt. Arbeiter sind Personen, die Lohn° bekommen. Es kann zum Beispiel ein Stück- oder Stundenlohn sein. Arbeiter verrichten typischerweise manuelle Tätigkeiten°. Beamte sind Personen, die für die Regierung arbeiten, wie zum Beispiel Polizisten und Lehrer.

bezeichnen *designate* **leitende** *managerial*
Lohn *wage* **Tätigkeiten** *tasks*

Der Marshallplan

Suggestion Tell students that in today's dollars, the Marshall Plan would cost around $137.5 billion.

Nach dem Zweiten Weltkrieg war Europa zu großen Teilen zerstört°. Am 3. April 1948 verabschiedete° der amerikanische Kongress einen Plan, den Marshallplan oder auch *European Recovery Program*, um Westeuropa wieder aufzubauen°. Teil des Plans war es, Kredite, Rohstoffe°, Lebensmittel und Waren nach Westeuropa zu schicken. Die drei Gründe für den Marshallplan waren Hilfe für Westeuropa, Eindämmung° der Sowjetunion und des Kommunismus, und Erschaffung° eines Marktes für amerikanische Waren. Das Volumen des Plans betrug 1948 13,1 Milliarden Dollar. Der Plan war nach dem US-Außenminister George C. Marshall benannt, der 1953 den Friedensnobelpreis bekam.

zerstört *destroyed* **verabschiedete** *passed* **aufzubauen** *rebuild* **Rohstoffe** *raw materials*
Eindämmung *containment* **Erschaffung** *creation*

◦S IM INTERNET

Suchen Sie im Internet weitere Informationen zum Marshallplan. Wie war die wirtschaftliche Situation 1948 in Deutschland? Was war die Reaktion auf den Marshallplan in Europa?

Find out more at **vhlcentral.com**.

Suggestion Point out that the differences between **Angestellte**, **Arbeiter**, and **Beamter** are similar to the distinction in English between "blue-collar" and "white-collar" workers.

---

2 **Was fehlt?** Ergänzen Sie die Sätze.

1. Angestellte kann man vor allem in ___Büros___ finden.
2. Für den Staat arbeiten ___Beamte___.
3. Beispiele von Beamten sind ___Polizisten___ und Lehrer.
4. Der amerikanische Kongress verabschiedete 1948 den ___Marshallplan___.
5. Europa war nach dem Zweiten ___Weltkrieg___ zu großen Teilen zerstört.
6. 1953 bekam George C. Marshall den ___Friedensnobelpreis___.

3 **Arbeitsbedingungen** Diskutieren Sie mit einem Partner / einer Partnerin: Was wäre Ihnen am Arbeitsplatz wichtig? Wo möchten Sie arbeiten? Mit wie vielen Mitarbeitern möchten Sie arbeiten? Wie sollte die Hierarchie an Ihrem Arbeitsplatz sein? Welche Sozialleistungen (*benefits*) wären Ihnen wichtig?

3 **Expansion** Have students describe their dream boss. Ask them what a good boss does or doesn't do.

NATIONAL comparisons STANDARDS

11B.1

Suggestion Tell students that the **Futur II** is the "will-have-happened" tense.

Das Futur II  Presentation

Startblock In **10A.3** you learned about the future tense (**das Futur I**). Although it is rarely used, German also has a future perfect tense (**das Futur II**).

Bis zum Ende des Tages **werde** ich mit vier weiteren Künstlern **gesprochen haben**.

Die **werden** dann auch deine Kunst **gesehen haben**, wenn sie wieder gehen.

Suggestion Summarize the pattern on the board:
werden (conjugated) +
Partizip + **haben/sein**.

ACHTUNG

The combination of the past participle and the infinitive of **haben** or **sein** is called a *past infinitive*.

QUERVERWEIS

See **10A.3** to review the **Futur I**. See **5A.1** and **5B.1** to review past participles and the use of **haben** and **sein** with verbs in the perfect tense.

- Use the **Futur II** to indicate that an event is expected to have happened by or before a particular point in the future.

Ich arbeite an einem Brief, den meine Chefin heute Nachmittag abschicken will.
I'm working on a letter that my boss wants to send this afternoon.

Bis heute Nachmittag **werde** ich den Brief **geschrieben haben**.
*By this afternoon, I **will have written** the letter.*

- To form the **Futur II**, use the present tense of **werden** with the past participle of the verb that expresses the action plus the infinitive of **haben** or **sein**.

Wir **werden** Urlaub **genommen haben**.
*We **will have taken** time off.*

Nils **wird** im Büro **geblieben sein**.
*Nils **will have stayed** at the office.*

- Standard word order rules apply in the **Futur II**. Use **bis** to indicate the time by which a future action will have happened.

Herr Mauer **wird bis** morgen die Arbeit **beendet haben**.
*Herr Mauer **will have completed** the work **by** tomorrow.*

Ich denke, dass er die ganze Nacht **gearbeitet haben wird**.
*I think that he **will have worked** the whole night.*

- Use the **Futur II** with **wohl**, **wahrscheinlich**, **schon**, or **sicher**, to express the likelihood that something has happened or will have happened by or before a particular time.

Peter wird **wahrscheinlich** heute gekündigt haben.
*Peter **probably** (will have) quit today.*

Bis nächste Woche wird er **wohl** eine neue Stelle gefunden haben.
*By next week he will **likely** have found a new job.*

Ressourcen

SAM
WB: pp. 153–154

SAM
LM: p. 99

S
vhlcentral.com

 Jetzt sind Sie dran! **Formulieren Sie die folgenden Sätze ins Futur II um.**

1. Wir werden früh ins Bett gehen.
   Wir werden früh ins Bett gegangen sein.
2. Ich werde Arbeit finden.
   Ich werde Arbeit gefunden haben.
3. Die Assistentin wird kündigen.
   Die Assistentin wird gekündigt haben.
4. Ihr werdet einen wichtigen Termin haben.
   Ihr werdet einen wichtigen Termin gehabt haben.
5. Wie viele Fabrikarbeiter werden sie wohl entlassen?
   Wie viele Fabrikarbeiter werden sie wohl entlassen haben?
6. Dieses Projekt wird wohl scheitern.
   Dieses Projekt wird wohl gescheitert sein.

Anwendung und Kommunikation

1 **Was fehlt?** Ergänzen Sie die Sätze mit den Verben in Klammern.
Benutzen Sie das **Futur II**.

> **BEISPIEL** Bis morgen Abend ___werden___ wir den Film
> schon ___gesehen haben___. (sehen)

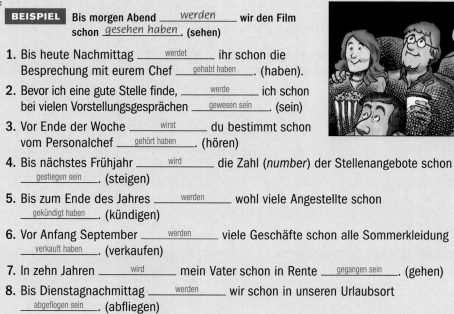

1. Bis heute Nachmittag ___werdet___ ihr schon die
   Besprechung mit eurem Chef ___gehabt haben___. (haben).
2. Bevor ich eine gute Stelle finde, ___werde___ ich schon
   bei vielen Vorstellungsgesprächen ___gewesen sein___. (sein)
3. Vor Ende der Woche ___wirst___ du bestimmt schon
   vom Personalchef ___gehört haben___. (hören)
4. Bis nächstes Frühjahr ___wird___ die Zahl (*number*) der Stellenangebote schon
   ___gestiegen sein___. (steigen)
5. Bis zum Ende des Jahres ___werden___ wohl viele Angestellte schon
   ___gekündigt haben___. (kündigen)
6. Vor Anfang September ___werden___ viele Geschäfte schon alle Sommerkleidung
   ___verkauft haben___. (verkaufen)
7. In zehn Jahren ___wird___ mein Vater schon in Rente ___gegangen sein___. (gehen)
8. Bis Dienstagnachmittag ___werden___ wir schon in unseren Urlaubsort
   ___abgeflogen sein___. (abfliegen)

2 **Bis zum 30. Geburtstag** Fragen Sie Ihren Partner / Ihre Partnerin,
was er/sie wohl bis zum 30. Geburtstag alles gemacht haben wird.
Benutzen Sie das **Futur II**. Answers will vary.

> **BEISPIEL**
>
> **S1:** *Wirst du bis zu deinem 30. Geburtstag geheiratet haben?*
> **S2:** *Nein, ich werde nicht bis zu meinem 30. Geburtstag geheiratet haben.*
> *Und du, wirst du geheiratet haben?*

> den Uni-Abschluss machen
> heiraten
> Kinder bekommen
> in ein anderes Land umziehen
> deinen Traumberuf (*dream job*) finden
> viel Geld verdienen
> nach Europa reisen

3 **Vor nächster Woche** Sagen Sie Ihrem Partner / Ihrer Partnerin
vier Sachen, die Sie diese Woche machen müssen oder wollen. Benutzen
Sie dabei das **Futur I**. Danach sagen Sie dem Rest der Klasse, was Sie
voneinander gelernt haben. Benutzen Sie dabei das **Futur II**. Answers will vary.

> **BEISPIEL**
>
> **S1:** *Ich werde diese Woche zwei Referate schreiben.*
> *Ich werde auch ein neues Handy kaufen.*
> **S2:** *Paul wird bis nächste Woche zwei Referate geschrieben haben.*
> *Er wird auch ein neues Handy gekauft haben...*

 Practice more at **vhlcentral.com**.

2 **Suggestion** Before
students begin the activity,
ask them which verbs in the
word bank take **sein**, and
verify that they know all of the
past participles.

3 **Expansion** Ask students
to make realistic predictions
about what you will have done
by the end of the week. Tell
them whether or not their
predictions are correct.

QUERVERWEIS

See **8B.2** to review **der**-words and **2B.3** to review **ein**-words.

Suggestion Point out that since **der**-words already carry information about case and gender, the adjective ending doesn't have to.

11B.2 Adjective endings (review)  Presentation

Startblock Adjectives that precede a noun take different endings depending on the case, gender, and number of the noun and whether they are preceded by a **der**-word, an **ein**-word, or neither.

- Adjectives that are preceded by **der**-words have the following endings.

	masculine	feminine	neuter	plural
	adjective endings after *der*-words			
nom.	der gut**e** Chef	die gut**e** Chefin	das gut**e** Geschäft	die gut**en** Stellen
acc.	den gut**en** Chef	die gut**e** Chefin	das gut**e** Geschäft	die gut**en** Stellen
dat.	dem gut**en** Chef	der gut**en** Chefin	dem gut**en** Geschäft	den gut**en** Stellen
gen.	des gut**en** Chefs	der gut**en** Chefin	des gut**en** Geschäfts	der gut**en** Stellen

- Adjectives that are preceded by **ein**-words have the following endings.

	masculine	feminine	neuter	plural
	adjective endings after *ein*-words			
nom.	ein gut**er** Chef	eine gut**e** Chefin	ein gut**es** Geschäft	keine gut**en** Stellen
acc.	einen gut**en** Chef	eine gut**e** Chefin	ein gut**es** Geschäft	keine gut**en** Stellen
dat.	einem gut**en** Chef	einer gut**en** Chefin	einem gut**en** Geschäft	keinen gut**en** Stellen
gen.	eines gut**en** Chefs	einer gut**en** Chefin	eines gut**en** Geschäfts	keiner gut**en** Stellen

ACHTUNG

Remember that these endings are used with comparatives and superlatives, as well as with adjectival nouns.

Remember that adjectives that come directly after **sein**, **bleiben**, or **werden** do not have added endings.

Remember that adjectives ending in **-el** and **-er** drop the **-e-** when they take a case ending:
teue**r** → teur**e**, teur**en**, teur**er**, teur**es**

Suggestion Remind students that unpreceded adjectives and those after **ein**-words have "strong" endings because they must carry the case information that is not shown by the article.

Thomas hat eine sehr **gute** Stelle gefunden.
*Thomas found a really **good** job.*

Hast du mein **kleines** Adressbuch gesehen?
*Have you seen my **little** address book?*

- Unpreceded adjectives have the following endings.

	masculine	feminine	neuter	plural
	unpreceded adjective endings			
nom.	warm**er** Regen	hell**e** Sonne	schön**es** Wetter	farbig**e** Blumen
acc.	warm**en** Regen	hell**e** Sonne	schön**es** Wetter	farbig**e** Blumen
dat.	warm**em** Regen	hell**er** Sonne	schön**em** Wetter	farbig**en** Blumen
gen.	warm**en** Regens	hell**er** Sonne	schön**en** Wetters	farbig**er** Blumen

Ressourcen

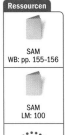
SAM
WB: pp. 155–156

SAM
LM: 100

vhlcentral.com

Jetzt sind Sie dran! **Wählen Sie die passenden Adjektivformen.** **Suggestion** Before students select the adjective endings, have them determine whether the article is a **der**-word or an **ein**-word, or if there is no article.

1. Ein Gärtner muss auch bei (schlechtes / schlechte / (schlechtem)) Wetter oft draußen arbeiten.

2. Wissenschaftler machen (wichtig / (wichtige) / wichtigen) Entdeckungen.

3. Ein ((kaputter) / kaputten / kaputte) Wäschetrockner ist für einen Elektriker kein Problem.

4. Die Immobilienmaklerin hat das Haus trotz des (hohes / hoch / (hohen)) Preises verkaufen können.

5. Unser Hausmeister geht nicht gern in den (dunkle / (dunklen) / dunkler) Keller.

6. Ingrid arbeitet seit (kurze / kurzen / (kurzer)) Zeit als Buchhalterin.

Anwendung und Kommunikation

1 **Beim Vorstellungsgespräch** Ergänzen Sie die Sätze mit den richtigen Formen der Adjektive in Klammern.

1. Wer träumt nicht von einer ___erfolgreichen___ Karriere? (erfolgreich)

2. Auf ein ___persönliches___ Vorstellungsgespräch sollte man sich gut vorbereiten. (persönlich).

3. Suchen Sie sich ___nützliche___ Informationen über die Firma aus dem Internet. (nützlich)

4. Machen Sie dem Personalchef klar, dass Sie ein ___zuverlässiger___ Mitarbeiter sind. (zuverlässig)

5. Sagen Sie, dass Sie an einer ___längeren___ Zusammenarbeit interessiert sind. (länger)

6. Bleiben Sie immer freundlich und locker trotz ___stressiger___ Fragen. (stressig)

7. Ziehen Sie sich lieber konservativ an und kommen Sie in ___sauberer___ Kleidung zu Ihrem Termin. (sauber)

8. Zeigen Sie sich von Ihrer ___besten___ Seite. (best-)

2 **Lebensläufe** Beschreiben Sie mit einem Partner / einer Partnerin die drei Personen auf dem Bild und erfinden Sie zu jeder Person einen kurzen Lebenslauf: Wer sind sie, woher kommen sie, was haben sie gemacht, und so weiter. Verwenden Sie attributive Adjektive. Answers will vary.

> **BEISPIEL**
>
> **S1:** Die Frau in dem roten Kleid ist eine berühmte Musikerin.
> **S2:** Sie kommt aus einer kleinen Stadt in der Schweiz...

3 **Mein Traumjob** Fragen Sie einander, was Sie sich von Ihrem Traumberuf (nicht) erhoffen. Answers will vary.

> **BEISPIEL**
>
> **S1:** Was für eine Stelle möchtest du?
> **S2:** Ich möchte eine interessante, anspruchsvolle Stelle.

anspruchsvoll	großzügig	modern
dynamisch	intelligent	ordentlich
ernst	interessant	schön
freundlich	kreativ	zuverlässig

1. Was für eine Arbeitsstelle möchtest du (nicht)?

2. Was für ein Gehalt möchtest du (nicht)?

3. Was für einen Chef oder eine Chefin möchtest du (nicht)?

4. In was für einem Büro möchtest du (nicht) arbeiten?

5. Mit was für Mitarbeitern möchtest du (nicht) arbeiten?

 Practice more at **vhlcentral.com.**

1 Expansion For more practice, bring in assorted postcards and have students work in pairs to describe what they see on each card, using complete sentences and as many adjectives as possible. Collect the descriptions and correct any mistakes in adjective endings.

3 Expansion Allow students to focus on communication and content during the activity, but follow up by having them write down a few of their answers with a focus on accuracy. Have them trade with a partner and check each other's adjective endings.

Wiederholung

1 Diskutieren und kombinieren Sie und Ihr

Partner / Ihre Partnerin haben einige Personen, die Arbeit suchen, und einige Stellenangebote. Sprechen Sie über die Arbeitssuchenden und die Stellenagebote und entscheiden Sie, wer zu welcher Stelle passt. Answers will vary.

BEISPIEL

S1: Martin Richter hat sieben Jahre lang als Feuerwehrmann in Hamburg gearbeitet.

S2: Ich habe die perfekte Stelle für ihn. In Dresden gibt es einige Stellen für Feuerwehrleute.

1 Expansion Have students write a "want ad" together using the texts as models.

2 Semesterende Was werden Sie vor Ende des

Semesters gemacht haben? Vergleichen Sie Ihre Antworten mit denen Ihres Partners / Ihrer Partnerin. Answers will vary.

BEISPIEL

S1: Bis Ende des Semesters werde ich noch zwei Stücke auf dem Saxophon gelernt haben. Und du?

S2: Ich werde ... **2 Suggestion** Remind students to use the **Futur II.**

> Projekte fertig machen
> für die Abschlussprüfungen lernen
> ein Referat halten
> einen Ferienjob finden
> Aufsätze schreiben
> eine Sportveranstaltung besuchen
> Prüfungen machen
> aus meinem Zimmer ausziehen

3 Weltpolitik Sagen Sie, was mit jedem der Länder auf

der Liste in der Zukunft passieren wird. Sagen Sie auch, wann das passieren wird. Vergleichen Sie Ihre Antworten mit denen Ihres Partners / Ihrer Partnerin. Answers will vary.

BEISPIEL

S1: Bis 2035 wird China sicher eine Demokratie geworden sein.

S2: Ich glaube, dass es wohl ein kommunistisches Land geblieben sein wird.

> | Kanada | Russland |
> |---|---|
> | Österreich | Deutschland |
> | die USA | die Schweiz |

4 Der schönste Geburtstag Beschreiben Sie

Ihrem Partner / Ihrer Partnerin den schönsten Geburtstag Ihres Lebens. Benutzen Sie Adjektive, um den Tag zu beschreiben. Answers will vary.

BEISPIEL

Als ich neun wurde, habe ich den schönsten Geburtstag meines Lebens gehabt. Der Tag begann mit einem leckeren Frühstück. Wir aßen...

5 Kleine Geschichte Schreiben Sie mit Ihrem

Partner / Ihrer Partnerin die Geschichte von Frank, der in seinem Beruf nicht immer erfolgreich war. Gebrauchen Sie die angegebenen Worte. Beachten Sie den Gebrauch des Präteritums. Answers will vary.

> eine Gehaltserhöhung bekommen
> eine große Überraschung sein
> die Firma verlassen
> ins Büro kommen
> eine Beförderung anbieten
> entlassen
> an der Qualität der Arbeit scheitern
> sich um eine neue Stelle bewerben

6 Arbeitsblatt Fragen Sie drei Kommilitonen nach

ihrer Lieblingsfarbe. Bitten Sie sie, zwei Dinge, die sie in dieser Farbe besitzen, detailliert zu beschreiben. Answers will vary.

BEISPIEL

S1: Was ist deine Lieblingsfarbe?

S2: Meine Lieblingsfarbe ist Grün.

S1: Was hast du alles in Grün?

S2: Ich habe eine warme, grüne Bettdecke, die mir meine Großmutter geschenkt hat...

6 Expansion Conduct a poll to find out students' favorite colors and the most common items they have in those colors.

7 Berufsberatung

Berufsberatung Arbeiten Sie mit einem Partner / einer Partnerin. Beschreiben Sie was für eine Person Sie sind, Ihre Erfahrungen und die Art Arbeit, die Sie gerne machen wollen. Ihr Partner / Ihre Partnerin wird die Rolle des Berufsberaters / der Berufsberaterin (*career counselor*) spielen, Ihnen Fragen stellen und Sie beraten, welche Berufe für Sie in Frage kommen. Wechseln Sie dann die Rollen. Answers will vary.

BEISPIEL

S1: Ich bin ein kreativer Mensch und ich bin auch sehr logisch.
S2: Arbeiten Sie lieber allein oder mit anderen?
S1: Lieber allein, aber nicht immer...

7 Suggestion Before they begin the role-play, give students time to jot down relevant information and potential questions.

8 Beim Immobilienmakler

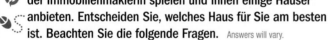

Beim Immobilienmakler Beschreiben Sie Ihrem Partner / Ihrer Partnerin das Haus, das Sie suchen. Er/Sie wird die Rolle des Immobilienmaklers / der Immobilienmaklerin spielen und Ihnen einige Häuser anbieten. Entscheiden Sie, welches Haus für Sie am besten ist. Beachten Sie die folgende Fragen. Answers will vary.

BEISPIEL

S1: Ich suche ein kleines Haus auf dem Land nicht weit vom Meer. Ich brauche ein ziemlich großes Grundstück für meine drei Hunde.
S2: Hmmm... Ich habe hier drei Häuser, die Ihnen gefallen könnten.

- Wo möchten Sie gerne wohnen?
- Wie groß soll das Haus sein?
- Was für einen Stil soll das Haus haben?
- Wer wird in dem Haus wohnen?
- Wie viele Zimmer brauchen Sie?
- Brauchen Sie besondere Zimmer oder Einrichtungen (*features*)?
- Wie muss das Haus ausgestattet (*equipped*) sein?
- Würden Sie sich für ein Haus interessieren, das renoviert werden muss?
- Wie viel wollen Sie maximal bezahlen?

Mein Wör | ter | buch

Schreiben Sie noch fünf weitere Wörter in Ihr persönliches Wörterbuch zu den Themen **Im Büro** und **Berufe**.

der Ferienjob

Übersetzung
vacation job

Wortart
Substantiv

Gebrauch
Fast alle Studenten suchen für den Sommer einen Ferienjob, damit sie etwas Geld verdienen können.

Synonyme
die Ferienarbeit

Antonyme
fester Arbeitsplatz

 **Vocabulary tools**

Weiter geht's

Panorama (S) Interactive Map

Baden-Württemberg, das Saarland und Rheinland-Pfalz

Baden-Württemberg in Zahlen

- ▶ **Fläche:** *35.751 km²*
- ▶ **Bevölkerung:** *10,7 Millionen Menschen*
- ▶ **Städte:** *Stuttgart (603.000 Einwohner), Mannheim (314.000), Karlsruhe (300.000)*
- ▶ **Wichtige Industriezweige:** *Maschinenbau, Automobilindustrie, Metallerzeugnisse°*
- ▶ **Touristenattraktionen:** *Schwarzwald, Bodensee, Baden-Baden*

QUELLE: Tourismusportal Baden-Württemberg

Expansion Divide the class into small groups and assign each student one of these famous people to research and present to their group. You may want to provide additional names, ex.: **Hildegard von Bingen, Gottlieb Daimler, Oskar Lafontaine**.

Das Saarland in Zahlen

- ▶ **Fläche:** *2.569 km²*
- ▶ **Bevölkerung:** *1 Million Menschen*
- ▶ **Städte:** *Saarbrücken (177.000 Einwohner), Neunkirchen (46.000)*
- ▶ **Wichtige Industriezweige:** *Automobilbau, Keramikindustrie, Informatik*
- ▶ **Touristenattraktionen:** *Ludwigskirche in Saarbrücken, Völklinger Hütte, römische Villa in Borg*

QUELLE: Tourismus Zentrale Saarland GmbH

Suggestion Tell students that the **Limes** was a protective wall built by the ancient Romans to secure their territory and hold back Germanic invaders.

Rheinland-Pfalz in Zahlen

- ▶ **Fläche:** *19.853 km²*
- ▶ **Bevölkerung:** *4 Millionen Menschen*
- ▶ **Städte:** *Mainz (203.000 Einwohner), Ludwigshafen (167.000), Koblenz (110.000)*
- ▶ **Wichtige Industriezweige:** *Weinanbau°, chemische Industrie, pharmazeutische Industrie, Tourismus*
- ▶ **Touristenattraktionen:** *Speyerer Dom, Kulturlandschaft Oberes Mittelrheintal, Limes*

QUELLE: Rheinland-Pfalz Tourismus GmbH

Berühmte Baden-Württemberger, Saarländer und Rheinland-Pfälzer

- ▶ **Friedrich Schiller,** *Dichter° (1759–1805)*
- ▶ **Nicole (Seibert),** *Sängerin (1964–)*
- ▶ **Helmut Kohl,** *Politiker (1930–)*

Metallerzeugnisse *metal products* **Weinanbau** *vineyards* **Dichter** *poet* **Dom** *cathedral* **Kelten** *Celts* **Grab** *grave* **Fürstin** *princess* **starb** *died* **ausweichen** *yield*

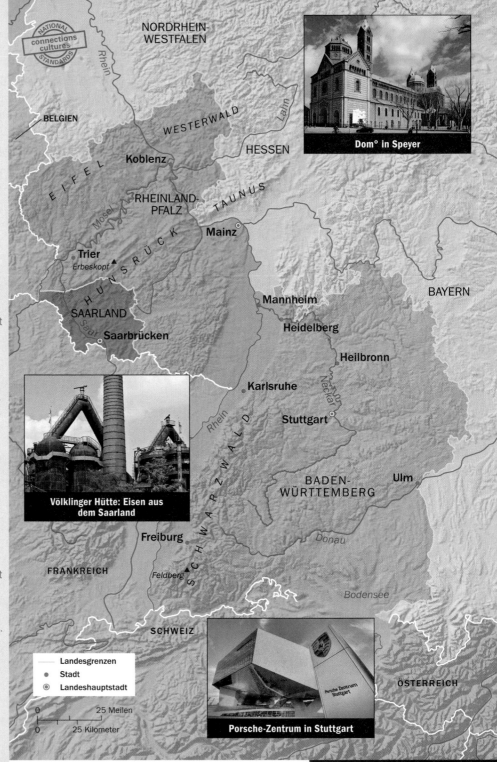

NORDRHEIN-WESTFALEN

BELGIEN

WESTERWALD

EIFEL

Koblenz

HESSEN

RHEINLAND-PFALZ

TAUNUS

Mainz

MOSEL

HUNSRÜCK

Trier
Erbeskopf

SAARLAND

Saarbrücken

Saar

BAYERN

Mannheim

Heidelberg

Heilbronn

Karlsruhe

Neckar

Stuttgart

Rhein

SCHWARZWALD

BADEN-WÜRTTEMBERG

Ulm

Freiburg

Donau

FRANKREICH

Feldberg

Bodensee

SCHWEIZ

ÖSTERREICH

Dom° in Speyer

Völklinger Hütte: Eisen aus dem Saarland

Porsche-Zentrum in Stuttgart

— Landesgrenzen
• Stadt
◎ Landeshauptstadt

0 — 25 Meilen
0 — 25 Kilometer

Unglaublich aber wahr!

Die Kelten° lebten früher in der Nähe der Donau im heutigen Baden-Württemberg, dem östlichen Frankreich und der Schweiz. Das älteste Grab° einer keltischen Fürstin° fand man 2010 in Ludwigsburg. Die Fürstin starb° etwa im Jahr 600 vor Christus. Erst später mussten die Kelten ins westliche Europa der britischen Inseln ausweichen°.

Geographie
Rhein

Der Rhein ist der längste Fluss Deutschlands. Er ist 1.233 Kilometer lang, 865 Kilometer davon fließen° durch Deutschland zwischen dem Bodensee im Süden und Holland im Norden. Er ist eine der verkehrsreichsten Wasserstraßen der Welt. Er ist auch eine wichtige Grenze° zwischen Deutschland und Frankreich. Die vielen Schlösser°, die man bei einer Bootsfahrt durch das Obere Mittelrheintal zwischen Bingen und Koblenz sehen kann, sind historische Beispiele der Grenzfunktion des Flusses.

Technologie
Gutenberg

Johannes Gutenberg (1400–1468) gilt als Erfinder des Buchdrucks mit beweglichen Metalllettern° in Europa. Diese Erfindung startete eine Medienrevolution. Bücher und andere Publikationen wie zum Beispiel Pamphlete konnten mit der neuen Erfindung wesentlich schneller und billiger produziert werden. Mit Hilfe von Pamphleten konnte Martin Luther (1483–1546), der 1517 mit seinen 95 Thesen in direkte Konfrontation zur römisch-katholischen Kirche getreten war, seine neuen Ideen schnell und billig den Menschen mitteilen°. Ohne diese technische Neuerung wäre er isoliert und ohne Publikum gewesen.

Sport
Das Saarland bei Olympischen Spielen

An der Grenze zwischen Deutschland, Luxemburg und Frankreich liegt das Saarland, wegen seiner Bodenschätze ein oft umstrittenes° Land. 1952 war das Saarland politisch unabhängig°, gehörte wirtschaftlich aber zu Frankreich. Bei den ersten Olympischen Sommerspielen nach dem Zweiten Weltkrieg im finnischen Helsinki trat zum einzigen Mal eine saarländische Mannschaft bei der Olympiade an°. Sechsunddreißig saarländische Sportler fuhren nach Finnland, gewannen dort aber keine Medaille. Ab 1956 waren die Saarländer dann Teil der deutschen Mannschaft.

Kultur
Trier

Trier ist eine Stadt in Rheinland-Pfalz. Sie gilt als älteste Stadt Deutschlands. Vor mehr als 2000 Jahren gründeten die Römer die Stadt unter dem Namen Augusta Treverorum. Aus der Zeit der Römer kann man noch das Amphitheater, die Thermen°, die Konstantinbasilika und die Igeler Säule° besuchen. Die Römerbrücke ist die älteste Brücke Deutschlands. Das bekannteste Bauwerk° ist aber die Porta Nigra, ein römisches Stadttor° und Wahrzeichen° der Stadt. Alle diese Bauwerke sind Teil des UNESCO-Weltkulturerbes.

fließen *flow* **Grenze** *border* **Schlösser** *castles* **umstrittenes** *disputed* **unabhängig** *independent* **trat...an** *took part*
beweglichen Metalllettern *movable metal type* **mitteilen** *communicate* **Thermen** *thermal baths* **Säule** *column*
Bauwerk *building* **Stadttor** *city gate* **Wahrzeichen** *landmark*

⚙ IM INTERNET

1. Suchen Sie weitere Informationen über die Kelten in Deutschland: Wo genau haben sie gelebt? Was weiß man über sie?

2. Suchen Sie mehr Informationen über Johannes Gutenberg: Wer war er? Was hat er noch gemacht?

Find out more at **vhlcentral.com**.

 Was haben Sie gelernt? Ergänzen Sie die Sätze.

1. Das älteste Grab einer keltischen Fürstin fand man in __Ludwigsburg__.

2. Die Kelten lebten in __Baden-Württemberg__ und Teilen Frankreichs, bevor sie auf die britischen Inseln ausweichen mussten.

3. Im Süden Deutschlands beginnt der Rhein am __Bodensee__.

4. Der Rhein war schon immer eine __Grenze__ zwischen Deutschland und Frankreich.

5. Die saarländische Mannschaft gewann keine __Medaille__.

6. Nach 1952 waren die Saarländer Teil der __deutschen__ Mannschaft.

7. Johannes Gutenberg erfand den __Buchdruck__ mit beweglichen Metalllettern.

8. Luthers __Pamphlete__ konnte man schneller und billiger produzieren.

9. Trier hieß früher __Augusta Treverorum__.

10. Das bekannteste Bauwerk Triers ist die __Porta Nigra__.

 Practice more at **vhlcentral.com**.

Lesen

 Audio: Reading

Vor dem Lesen

Untersuchen Sie den Text

Sehen Sie den Titel und die Bilder an. Was wissen Sie sofort über diese Geschichte? Lesen Sie die ersten Sätze der Geschichte. Glauben Sie, dass der Erzähler dieser Geschichte allwissend (*omniscient*) ist?

Autor

Peter Bichsel

Peter Bichsel ist Schweizer. Er wurde 1935 in Luzern geboren. Er hat als Lehrer in einer Grundschule, als freier Journalist, und als Berater in der Politik gearbeitet. Jetzt ist er freier Schriftsteller. Er schreibt Kurzgeschichten und Essays. Oft schreibt er humorvolle Erzählungen aus der Perspektive junger Kinder. Bichsel hat einige Literaturpreise gewonnen. Er hat viele Einladungen an amerikanische Universitäten bekommen, wo er weitere Texte verfasst und seine Werke vorgelesen hat. Peter Bichsel wohnt heute im schweizerischen Solothurn.

Suggestion Point out to students that Bichsel uses pre-reform spelling on some words, ex.: **Mikrophon**, instead of **Mikrofon**.

Der Erfinder

(Ausschnitt°)

Erfinder ist ein Beruf, den man nicht lernen kann; deshalb ist er selten; heute gibt es ihn überhaupt nicht mehr.

Früher aber gab es noch Erfinder. Einer von ihnen hieß Edison. Er erfand das Mikrophon und baute einen Apparat, mit dem man die Filme abspielen konnte.

1931 starb er.

1890 wurde zwar noch einer geboren, und der lebt noch. Niemand kennt ihn, weil er jetzt in einer Zeit lebt, in der es keine Erfinder mehr gibt. Seit dem Jahre 1931 ist er allein. Das weiß er nicht, weil er schon damals nicht mehr hier in der Stadt wohnte und nie unter die Leute ging; denn Erfinder brauchen Ruhe°.

Er berechnete° und zeichnete° den ganzen Tag. Er saß stundenlang da, legte seine Stirn° in Falten°, fuhr sich mit der Hand immer wieder übers Gesicht und dachte nach.

Dann nahm er seine Berechnungen, zerriss° sie und warf sie weg und begann wieder von neuem, und abends war er mürrisch° und schlecht gelaunt°, weil die Sache wieder nicht gelang.

Er ging früh zu Bett, stand früh auf und arbeitete den ganzen Tag. Er bekam keine Post, las keine Zeitungen und wusste nichts davon, dass es Radios gibt.

Und nach all den Jahren kam der Abend, an dem er nicht schlecht gelaunt war, denn er hatte seine Erfindung erfunden, und er legte sich jetzt überhaupt nicht mehr schlafen. Tag und Nacht saß er über seinen Plänen und prüfte sie nach, und sie stimmten°.

Dann rollte er sie zusammen und ging nach Jahren zum ersten Mal in die Stadt. Sie hatte sich völlig verändert°. Wo es früher Pferde gab, da gab es jetzt Automobile, und im Warenhaus° gab es eine Rolltreppe°, und die Eisenbahnen° fuhren nicht mehr mit Dampf°. Der Erfinder staunte°. Aber weil er ein Erfinder war, begriff er alles sehr schnell. Er sah einen Kühlschrank und sagte: „Aha." Er sah ein Telefon und sagte: „Aha." Und als er rote und grüne Lichter sah, begriff er, dass man bei Rot warten muss und bei Grün gehen darf.

Ausschnitt *excerpt* **Ruhe** *quiet* **berechnete** *calculated* **zeichnete** *sketched* **Stirn** *forehead* **Falten** *wrinkles* **zerriss** *tore* **mürrisch** *grumpy* **schlecht gelaunt** *in a bad mood* **stimmten** *were correct*

Und er begriff alles, aber er staunte, und fast hätte er dabei seine eigene Erfindung vergessen.

Als sie ihm wieder einfiel, ging er auf einen Mann zu, der eben bei Rot wartete und sagte: „Entschuldigen Sie, mein Herr, ich habe eine Erfindung gemacht." Und der Herr war freundlich und sagte: „Und jetzt, was wollen Sie?" Und der Erfinder wusste es nicht. „Es ist nämlich eine wichtige Erfindung", sagte der Erfinder, aber da schaltete die Ampel auf Grün, und sie mussten gehen.

Was hätten die Leute sagen sollen, zu denen der Erfinder sagte: „Ich habe eine Erfindung gemacht."

Er sprang auf in der Straßenbahn, breitete seine Pläne zwischen den Beinen der Leute auf den Boden aus und rief: „Hier schaut mal, ich habe einen Apparat erfunden, in dem man sehen kann, was weit weg geschieht°." „Der hat das Fernsehen erfunden", rief jemand, und alle lachten. „Warum lachen Sie?" fragte der Mann, aber niemand antwortete, und er stieg aus, ging durch die Straßen, blieb bei Rot stehen und ging bei Grün weiter, setzte sich in ein Restaurant und bestellte einen Kaffee, und als sein Nachbar° zu ihm sagte: „Schönes Wetter heute", da sagte der Erfinder: „Helfen Sie mir doch, ich habe das Fernsehen erfunden, und niemand will es glauben – alle lachen mich aus." „Sie lachen", sagte der Mann, „weil es das Fernsehen schon lange gibt und weil man das nicht mehr erfinden muss", und er zeigte in die Ecke des Restaurants, wo ein Fernsehapparat stand, und fragte: „Soll ich ihn einstellen°?"

Aber der Erfinder sagte: „Nein, ich möchte das nicht sehen."Er stand auf und ging.

Er ging durch die Stadt, achtete nicht mehr auf Grün und Rot, und die Autofahrer schimpften° und tippten mit dem Finger an die Stirn.

Seither kam der Erfinder nie mehr in die Stadt.

Er ging nach Hause und erfand jetzt nur noch für sich selbst.

Er nahm einen Bogen Papier, schrieb darauf „Das Automobil", rechnete und zeichnete wochenlang und monatelang und erfand das Auto noch einmal, dann erfand er die Rolltreppe, er erfand das Telefon, und er erfand den Kühlschrank. Alles, was er in der Stadt gesehen hatte, erfand er noch einmal. Und jedes Mal, wenn er eine Erfindung gemacht hatte, zerriss er die Zeichnungen, warf sie weg und sagte: „Das gibt es schon."

Doch er blieb sein Leben lang ein richtiger Erfinder, denn auch Sachen, die es gibt, zu erfinden, ist schwer und nur Erfinder können es.

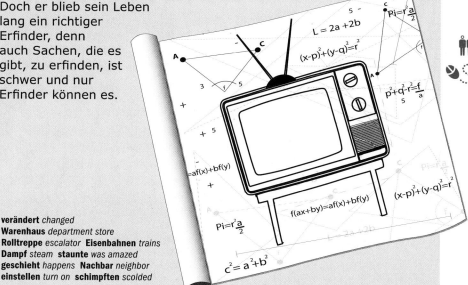

verändert changed
Warenhaus department store
Rolltreppe escalator **Eisenbahnen** trains
Dampf steam **staunte** was amazed
geschieht happens **Nachbar** neighbor
einstellen turn on **schimpften** scolded

Nach dem Lesen

Richtig oder falsch? Laut dieser Geschichte sind die Sätze richtig oder falsch?

	Richtig	Falsch
1. Man kann den Beruf Erfinder lernen.	☐	☑
2. Thomas Edison erfand das Mikrofon.	☑	☐
3. Der Erfinder wurde 1931 geboren.	☐	☑
4. Der Erfinder war selten gut gelaunt.	☑	☐
5. Eisenbahnen in der Stadt fuhren noch mit Dampf.	☐	☑
6. Der Erfinder wollte, dass der Nachbar im Restaurant den Fernsehapparat einstellt.	☐	☑
7. Der Erfinder wartete immer bei Rot und ging immer bei Grün.	☐	☑
8. Der Erfinder zeichnete ein Automobil auf das Papier.	☑	☐

Fragen Antworten Sie auf die folgenden Fragen.
Sample answers provided.

1. Was erfand Edison?   Er erfand das Mikrophon und einen Apparat, mit dem man die Filme abspielen konnte.
2. Was erfand der Erfinder?   Er erfand das Fernsehen.
3. Was gibt es nicht mehr in der Stadt?   Pferde gibt es nicht mehr in der Stadt.
4. Was sind die neuen Erfindungen in der Stadt?   Automobile, Rolltreppe und Eisenbahnen sind die neuen Erfindungen in der Stadt.
5. Was will der Erfinder den Leuten in der Straßenbahn zeigen?   Er will den Leuten seine Pläne zeigen.

Schreiben Wie finden Sie diese Geschichte? Beschreiben Sie, was Sie davon denken. Ist die Geschichte traurig oder lustig? Warum?

Zum Besprechen Sprechen Sie mit einem Partner / einer Partnerin über vier Erfindungen, die Sie für wichtig halten (*consider important*). Wozu benutzen Sie diese vier Geräte? Warum sind diese Dinge wichtig in Ihrem Leben?

Hören

Strategien

Listening for linguistic clues

You can enhance your listening comprehension by listening for specific cues. For example, if you listen for the endings of conjugated verbs or for familiar constructions, such as the **Perfekt**, **Futur**, or **Konjunktiv**, you can find out whether a person did something in the past, is going to do something in the future, or would do something under certain conditions.

 To practice this strategy, you will listen to questions and statements from an interview. As you listen, note whether each question or statement refers to a past, present, or future action.

Vorbereitung

Sehen Sie sich das Bild an. Welche Art von Arbeit sucht wohl der Bewerber? Läuft das Bewerbungsgespräch gut oder schlecht? Glauben Sie, dass der Mann die Stelle bekommen wird?

Zuhören

Hören Sie sich das Gespräch zweimal an. Machen Sie sich Notizen über den Bewerber, nachdem Sie das Gespräch ein zweites Mal gehört haben.

Name des Bewerbers: _Herr Huber_

Stelle: _Programmierer_

Studienabschluss: _Informatik_

Arbeitserfahrung: _keine_

Praktika: _zwei: Softwarefirmen in Karlsruhe und Mannheim_

Forschung (*research*): _Computerspiele_

Teilzeitarbeit: _Studentenjobs_

Suggestion Have students listen to the conversation again, before they complete the **richtig oder falsch** activity.

Verständnis

Richtig oder falsch Sind die Sätze richtig oder falsch?

1. Herr Huber ist gerade erst mit dem Studium fertig geworden.
   Richtig.

2. Herr Huber hat sein Studium mit der Note 1,5 beendet.
   Richtig.

3. Das erste Praktikum von Herrn Huber dauerte zwei Monate.
   Falsch.

4. Das erste Praktikum war bei einer Firma in Stuttgart.
   Falsch.

5. Das zweite Praktikum hat Herr Huber bei einer Softwarefirma gemacht.
   Richtig.

6. Das zweite Praktikum dauerte drei Monate lang.
   Richtig.

7. In seiner Forschung konzentrierte sich Herr Huber auf Softwareprogramme für die Buchhaltung.
   Falsch.

8. Herr Huber wird erst in zwei Wochen wieder von der Firma hören.
   Falsch.

Brief an den Interviewer Stellen Sie sich vor, dass Sie sich für ein Praktikum bei einer deutschen Firma beworben haben. Es war ein gutes Bewerbungsgespräch und Sie wollen sich bei der Firma bedanken. Schreiben Sie mit einem Partner / einer Partnerin einen Brief an den Interviewer: Bedanken Sie sich für das Interview und das Interesse der Firma. Wiederholen Sie nochmal Ihre Qualifikationen für die Stelle. Verwenden Sie die Sie-Form.

Suggestion Teach students formal letter openers and closers such as **Sehr geehrte Frau/geehrter Herr...** and **Mit freundlichen Grüßen**.

Schreiben

Strategien

Writing strong introductions and conclusions

Introductions and conclusions serve a similar purpose: both are intended to focus the reader's attention on the topic being discussed. The introduction presents a brief preview of the topic and informs the reader of the important points that will be covered in the body of the text. The conclusion reaffirms those points and concisely sums up the information that has been provided.

If you were writing a cover letter for a job application, you might start by identifying the job posting to which you are responding. The rest of your introductory paragraph could outline the areas you will cover in the body of your letter, such as your work experience and your reasons for wanting the job. In your conclusion, you might sum up the most important and convincing points of your letter and tie them together in a way that would leave your reader impressed and curious to learn more. You could, for example, use your conclusion to state why your qualifications make you the ideal candidate for the job and convince your reader of your enthusiasm for the position.

Suggestion You may want to share a few sample **Bewerbungsschreiben** with the class. Examples can be found online by searching with the keywords **Beispiele Bewerbungsschreiben** or **Muster Bewerbungsschreiben**.

Thema

Bewerbungsschreiben

Schreiben Sie eine Bewerbung, um sich auf Ihren Traumjob zu bewerben. Der Brief sollte drei Teile haben: Einleitung (*introduction*), Hauptteil (*body*) und Schluss (*conclusion*). Nennen Sie in der Einleitung kurz den Grund (*reason*) für den Brief. Beschreiben Sie dann im Detail Ihre Qualifikationen und Interessen. Fassen Sie am Ende die diversen Aspekte zusammen und erklären Sie, warum Sie ein guter Bewerber / eine gute Bewerberin für die Stelle sind.

Einleitung

- Nennen Sie den Titel der Stelle, auf die Sie sich bewerben.
- Erklären Sie, warum Sie sich auf die Stelle bewerben.

Hauptteil

- Fassen Sie Ihre (Schul-)Ausbildung und Erfahrungen zusammen.
- Beschreiben Sie, was Sie dadurch gelernt haben.
- Erklären Sie, warum Sie wegen dieser Erfahrungen für die Stelle qualifiziert sind.
- Beschreiben Sie, welche von Ihren Eigenschaften (*characteristics*) für die Firma wichtig sein könnten.

Schluss

- Bestätigen Sie (*Confirm*) Ihren Enthusiasmus für diese Stelle und Ihr Interesse daran.
- Erklären Sie, warum diese Stelle Ihrer Karriere helfen kann und auch, wie Sie dem Arbeitgeber nützen (*be of use*) können.

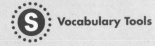 **Vocabulary Tools**

eine Stelle suchen

der/die Angestellte, -n	employee
der Assistent, -en / die Assistentin, -nen	assistant
die Ausbildung, -en	education
der Beruf, -e	profession
die Berufsausbildung, -en	professional training
die Besprechung, -en	meeting
der Bewerber, - / die Bewerberin, -nen	applicant
das Empfehlungsschreiben, -	letter of recommendation
die Erfahrung, -en	experience
die Firma (pl. die Firmen)	firm; company
das Geschäft, -e	business
der Geschäftsführer, - / die Geschäftsführerin, -nen	manager
das (hohe/niedrige) Gehalt (pl. die (hohen/niedrigen) Gehälter	(high/low) salary
der Lebenslauf, ¨e	résumé; CV
der Personalchef, -s / die Personalchefin, -nen	human resources manager
das Praktikum (pl. die Praktika)	internship
die Referenz, -en	reference
die Stelle, -n	position; job
das Stellenangebot, -e	job opening
der Termin, -e	appointment
der Vertrag, -e	contract
das Vorstellungsgespräch, -e	job interview
Arbeit finden	to find a job
einen Termin vereinbaren	to make an appointment
sich bewerben um (bewirbt sich)	to apply for

Büromaterial

die Büroklammer, -n	paperclip
das Büromaterial, -ien	office supplies
die Pinnwand, ¨e	bulletin board
der Hefter, -	stapler

am Telefon

der Hörer, -	receiver
die Telefonnummer, -n	telephone number
Wer spricht?	Who's calling?
Bleiben Sie bitte am Apparat.	Please hold.
auflegen	to hang up
einen Anruf entgegennehmen	to answer the phone
eine Nachricht hinterlassen	to leave a message
in der Warteschleife sein	to be on hold

auf der Arbeit

die Beförderung, -en	promotion
das Büro, -s	office
der Chef, -s / die Chefin, -nen	boss
der Erfolg, -e	success
die Gehaltserhöhung, -en	raise
die Gewerkschaft, -en	labor union
die Karriere, -n	career
anspruchsvoll	demanding
fertig	ready; finished
ganztags	full-time
halbtags	part-time
zuverlässig	reliable

Ausdrücke

arbeitslos sein	to be unemployed
entlassen	to fire; to lay off
kündigen	to resign
leiten	to manage
scheitern	to fail
Urlaub nehmen	to take time off
verdienen	to earn

Berufe

der/die Bankangestellte, -n	bank employee
der Bauer, -n / die Bäuerin, -nen	farmer
der Buchhalter, - / die Buchhalterin, -nen	accountant
der Elektriker, - / die Elektrikerin, -nen	electrician
der Fabrikarbeiter, - / die Fabrikarbeiterin, -nen	factory worker
der Feuerwehrmann (pl. die Feuerwehrleute) / die Feuerwehrfrau, -en	firefighter
der Gärtner, - / die Gärtnerin, -nen	gardener
der Hausmann, ¨er / die Hausfrau, -en	homemaker
der Hausmeister, - / die Hausmeisterin, -nen	caretaker; custodian
der Immobilienmakler, - / die Immobilienmaklerin-nen	real estate agent
der Klempner, - / die Klempnerin, -nen	plumber
der Koch, ¨e / die Köchin, -nen	cook, chef
der LKW-Fahrer, - / die LKW-Fahrerin, -nen	truck driver
der Politiker, - / die Politikerin, -nen	politician
der Psychologe, -n / die Psychologin, -nen	psychologist
der Rentner, - / die Rentnerin, -nen	retiree
der Richter, - / die Richterin, -nen	judge
der Taxifahrer, - / die Taxifahrerin, -nen	taxi driver
der Tierarzt, ¨e / die Tierärztin, -nen	veterinarian
der Wissenschaftler, - / die Wissenschaftlerin, -nen	scientist

Relative pronouns	See pp. 466–467.
Perfekt versus Präteritum (review)	See p. 470.
Das Futur II	See p. 484.
Adjective endings (review)	See p. 486.

Ressourcen

vhlcentral.com

Natur

Suggestion Ask students: **Wo sind George und Sabite?** Ask them how this image relates to the unit theme (**Natur**).

Communicative Goals

You will learn how to:

- talk about nature
- talk about outdoor activities

In der Natur  Vocabulary Tools

Suggestion Have students brainstorm nature-related vocabulary they have already learned: **Blume**, **Pflanze**, **Park**, **Vogel**, **klettern**, **spazieren**, etc.

Wortschatz	
die Natur	*nature*
der Bauernhof, ⸚e	*farm*
der Berg -e	*mountain*
das Blatt, ⸚er	*leaf*
das Feld, -er	*field*
der Fluss, ⸚e	*river*
die Küste, -n	*coast*
die Landschaft, -en	*countryside*
die Luft	*air*
das Meer, -e	*sea*
die Sonne, -n	*sun*
der Sonnenaufgang, ⸚e	*sunrise*
der Sonnenuntergang, ⸚e	*sunset*
der Wasserfall, ⸚e	*waterfall*
der Weg, -e	*path*
nass	*wet*
trocken	*dry*
Tiere	*animals*
der Fisch, -e	*fish*
das Huhn, ⸚er	*chicken*
die Maus, ⸚e	*mouse*
das Pferd, -e	*horse*
das Schaf, -e	*sheep*
Verben	*verbs*
aufgehen (geht...auf)	*to rise (sun)*
erforschen	*to explore*
untergehen (geht...unter)	*to set (sun)*
wandern	*to hike*

Suggestion Provide students with the past tense forms of the new verbs.

ACHTUNG

Kaninchen (*rabbits*) in the German-speaking world are almost exclusively domesticated. Their cousins **Hasen** (*hares*) are found in the wild.

Suggestion Point out that **aufgehen** and **untergehen** are used with other celestial bodies besides the sun.

der Himmel

der Baum, ⸚e

der Busch, ⸚e

das Tal, ⸚er

der Wald, ⸚er

Sie machen ein Picknick (*n.*).

das Eichhörnchen, -

die Kuh, ⸚e

das Gras

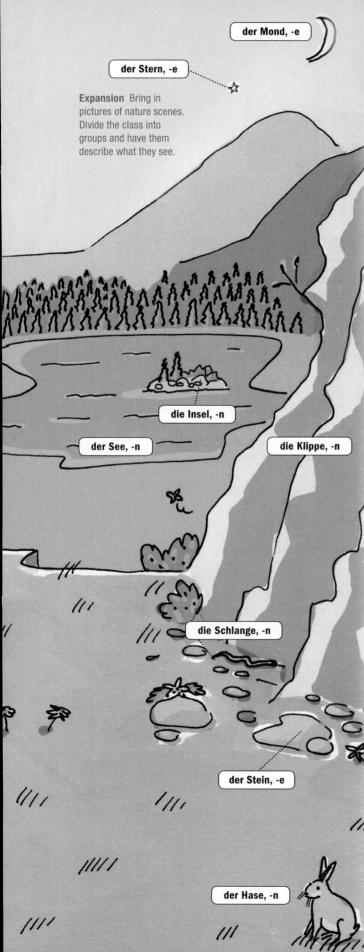

der Mond, -e

der Stern, -e

Expansion Bring in pictures of nature scenes. Divide the class into groups and have them describe what they see.

die Insel, -n

der See, -n

die Klippe, -n

die Schlange, -n

der Stein, -e

der Hase, -n

Anwendung

1 Was passt zusammen? Wählen Sie das richtige Wort zu jedem Foto.

1. __b__ der Baum

2. __f__ der Wasserfall

3. __e__ das Feld

4. __a__ der Sonnenaufgang

5. __d__ die Klippe

6. __c__ der Berg

a.

b.

c.

d.

e.

f.

2 Kategorien Geben Sie zu jeder Kategorie drei passende Begriffe an.

Sample answers are provided.

BEISPIEL Waldtiere _der Hase, die Maus, das Eichhörnchen_

1. Pflanzen _der Baum, das Gras, der Busch_

2. Landschaftliche Formationen _die Klippen, die Insel, das Tal_

3. Lebensräume (*habitats*) von wilden Tieren _der Wald, der Fluss, das Feld_

4. Gewässer (*bodies of water*) _das Meer, der See, der Wasserfall_

5. Tiere auf dem Bauernhof _die Kuh, das Schaf, das Pferd_

6. Himmelskörper (*celestial bodies*) _der Mond, die Sterne, die Sonne_

2 Expansion Have students come up with additional words for each category.

3 Momentaufnahmen 🎧 Hören Sie sich die Dialoge an und entscheiden Sie, welches Bild am besten zu jeder Situation passt. Schreiben Sie außerdem zu allen Bildern einen kurzen Satz darüber, was jedes Paar in diesem Moment gerade macht oder gemacht hat.

Sample answers are provided.

BEISPIEL Sie hören:

— *Wie rosa der Himmel ist!*
— *Ja, da hinten am Horizont geht die Sonne unter.*

Gespräch __1__
Sie schauen sich einen Sonnenuntergang an.

1. Gespräch __4__
Sie machen ein Picknick.

2. Gespräch __3__
Sie schwimmen im See.

3. Gespräch __2__
Sie sehen sich die Sterne an.

Suggestion Point out to students that **Hase** is an **n**-noun.

🔄 Practice more at **vhlcentral.com**.

Kommunikation

4 Ein schöner Urlaub Bringen Sie zusammen mit Ihrem Partner / Ihrer Partnerin die Sätze in eine logische Reihenfolge.

__5__ **FABIAN** Ja, nur gut, dass wir den Stall gefunden haben, wo wir uns unterstellen konnten. Wir wären sonst bis auf die Knochen *(to the bone)* nass geworden.

__1__ **FABIAN** Ich habe gerade nochmal die Fotos von unserem letzten Urlaub angeschaut. Ich glaube, das war der schönste Urlaub, den wir bis jetzt gemacht haben.

__4__ **LINA** Nicht nur an den. Auch an den Bergsee. Das Blau des Wassers—einfach unbeschreiblich! Und die vielen Tiere: die Kühe, die Schafe, die Hasen und die süßen Eichhörnchen! Leider zog dann am Nachmittag plötzlich ein Gewitter auf.

__3__ **FABIAN** Was waren wir kaputt am nächsten Tag! Denk mal an die vielen Kilometer, die wir gelaufen sind! Durch die Täler, über die Felder und dann auf den Berg hoch. Erinnerst du dich noch an den Wasserfall, der da senkrecht nach unten ging?

__2__ **LINA** Ich erinnere mich auch gern daran. Wir hatten so viel Spaß und haben so viel unternommen und gesehen. Die Wanderung, die wir gleich am zweiten Tag gemacht haben, war beeindruckend.

5 Richtig oder falsch? Entscheiden Sie mit einem Partner / einer Partnerin, ob die folgenden Aussagen richtig oder falsch sind. Korrigieren Sie die falschen Aussagen. Answers to false items may vary.

	richtig	falsch
1. Der Mond ist ein braves Haustier.	☐	☑
2. Die Sonne geht im Osten unter.	☐	☑
3. Aus Schafsmilch macht man Käse.	☑	☐
4. Der Rhein ist ein europäischer Fluss.	☑	☐
5. Hasen sind Pflanzenfresser.	☑	☐
6. Schafe sind kleiner als Mäuse.	☐	☑
7. Eichhörnchen wohnen auf Bäumen.	☑	☐
8. Steine verlieren im Herbst ihre Blätter.	☐	☑

5 Expansion Have pairs of students write four more true-false statements to exchange with another pair.

6 Diskutieren und kombinieren Sie und Ihr Partner / Ihre Partnerin bekommen zwei verschiedene Bilder. Finden Sie die sieben Unterschiede auf den Bildern. Wechseln Sie sich bei Ihren Fragen und Antworten ab. Sample answers are provided.

BEISPIEL

S1: *Wie viele Flüsse sind auf deinem Bild zu sehen?*
S2: *Ein Fluss. Und auf deinem?*
S1: *Auf meinem Bild ist auch nur ein Fluss.*

7 Der perfekte Tag Beschreiben Sie mit einem Partner / einer Partnerin, wie ein perfekter Tag in der freien Natur aussehen würde. Wie ist die Landschaft? Was würden Sie um sich herum sehen? Mit wem würden Sie den Tag verbringen? Was würden Sie machen? Und warum mögen Sie gerade diese Landschaft? Answers may vary.

BEISPIEL

S1: *Mein perfekter Tag beginnt in den Bergen. Ich würde bei Sonnenaufgang aufstehen und ein großes Bauernfrühstück mit meiner Familie essen.*
S2: *Und was macht ihr nach dem Frühstück?*
S1: *Danach...*

7 Expansion Have students take notes and describe their partner's perfect day to the class. Have the class identify similarities and differences.

Aussprache und Rechtschreibung (S) Audio

 **Intonation**

Intonation refers to the rise and fall of the voice in speaking. In German, different intonation is used for different types of questions and statements.

Es regnet.   **Es regnet?**   **Wenn es regnet...**

....

In general, statements and commands end with a drop in pitch. A speaker may use rising intonation at the end of a command or statement to communicate a friendly or encouraging tone.

Werfen Sie das nicht weg!   **Bring doch deine Schwester mit.**

....

Yes-or-no questions typically end with a rising intonation. Questions that begin with a question word end with falling intonation. In questions where multiple options are presented, the pitch rises before each pause and falls at the end of the last option.

Schwimmst du gern?   **Wo liegt diese Insel?**   **Ist das gut oder schlecht?**

....

The pitch neither rises nor falls at the end of incomplete sentences. It remains flat or neutral. This is also the case before a comma in a complex sentence. The final clause in a complex sentence usually ends with a drop in pitch.

Und wenn die Blätter bunt werden...   **Wenn die Sonne scheint, fahren wir.**

Suggestion Write an English sentence on the board to demonstrate how pitch functions in English. Have students say the sentence with different stress patterns to express questioning intonation, insistence, hesitation, friendliness, etc.

 1 Aussprechen Wiederholen Sie die Sätze die Sie hören.

1. Der Müllwagen kommt zweimal in der Woche.
2. Wie retten wir uns vor der Erderwärmung?
3. Schlagen Sie eine bessere Lösung vor!
4. Warst du schon mal auf einem Bauernhof?
5. Willst du die Schafe, Kühe oder die Pferde sehen?
6. Wenn du nicht gleich ins Bett gehst, geht bald die Sonne auf.

 2 Nachsprechen Wiederholen Sie die Sätze, die Sie hören.

1. Machen wir heute ein Picknick im Wald?
2. Ich weiß nicht, ob ich kommen kann.
3. Bleib stehen! Siehst du die Schlange nicht?
4. Wohnst du lieber in den Bergen oder an der Küste?

 3 Sprichwörter Wiederholen Sie die Sprichwörter, die Sie hören.

Es ist noch kein Meister vom Himmel gefallen.[2]

Wo ein Wille ist, ist auch ein Weg.[1]

Ressourcen

SAM
LM: p. 102

(S) vhlcentral.com

Fotoroman

In der Kunstgalerie Video

Endlich ist der Tag für Sabites Ausstellung gekommen. Sabite und Karl, ein anderer
Künstler, kommen sich näher, aber Meline und Hans haben Probleme.

Vorbereitung Have students scan the script to
find words and expressions related to nature.

NATIONAL
communication
cultures
STANDARDS

1

KARL Ich finde deine Werke toll.
SABITE Danke, aber deine Kunst ist auch nicht
schlecht. Und Herr Kleinedler hat mir gesagt,
dass du noch nicht einmal eine formelle
Ausbildung hast.

2

KARL Danke. Du bist sehr liebenswürdig.
Erschaffen ist das, worin ich am besten
bin. Durch die Arbeit mit meinen Händen
erforsche ich meine Gefühle. Sag mir,
liebst du die Natur? Ich gehe oft bei
Sonnenaufgang in den Tiergarten, um unter
den Eichen zu spazieren. Möchtest du mich
morgen begleiten?

3

HANS Ciao, meine Damen! Na, wie geht's uns
heute Abend?
SABITE Hans? Was trägst du da? Und deine
Haare... sind sie... kürzer?
HANS Ich probiere einen eleganteren Look aus.
Also, was meint ihr?
SABITE Ich glaube, du solltest du selbst sein.
Wer immer das auch sein mag.

4

GEORGE Meline, was meinst du?
MELINE Fast so schön wie Lederhosen.
HANS Was ist an Lederhosen auszusetzen?
Das Tragen von Lederhosen ist eine stolze
urbayrische Tradition. Die Österreicher... ja,
dein Großvater trug sicher auch Lederhosen!
Diese Intoleranz macht mich rasend.

5

MELINE Hans, du verstehst nicht, worum
es geht. Schon wieder nicht. Du bist
manchmal so schwierig.
HANS Ich? Du bist die schwierigste Person,
die ich jemals kennen gelernt habe!
MELINE Das stimmt nicht!

HANS Du hast recht. Es gibt schon etwas,
das dir gefällt: du selbst!
MELINE Entschuldigt mich bitte.

6

1 **Was fehlt?** Ergänzen Sie die Sätze mit den richtigen Informationen.

1. Karl hat keine (Erfahrung / (Ausbildung)) als Künstler.

2. Durch die Arbeit mit seinen Händen erforscht er seine (Probleme / (Gefühle)).

3. Er geht oft in den Tiergarten, um unter den (Sternen zu schlafen /
(Eichen zu spazieren)).

4. Hans probiert einen neuen ((eleganteren) / sportlicheren) Look aus.

5. Das Tragen von Lederhosen ist eine ((bayrische) / norddeutsche) Tradition.

6. Für Hans ist Meline die ((schwierigste) / schönste) Person, die er jemals
kennen gelernt hat.

7. George findet, dass Hans sich (rasieren / (entschuldigen)) sollte.

8. Er denkt, Hans sollte Meline Zeit geben, sich zu (schminken / (beruhigen)).

9. Meline möchte nicht über ((Hans) / Kunst) reden.

10. Karl hat früher die Wälder erkundet und ist im ((See) / Fluss) geschwommen.

PERSONEN

 George

 Hans

 Meline

 Sabite

 Faik

 Karl

 Herr Kleinedler

7

HANS Ich hätte das nicht sagen sollen? Ich muss mich entschuldigen?
SABITE Noch nicht. Du würdest es nur schlimmer machen.
GEORGE Lass sie sich erst einmal beruhigen.
HANS Ich gehe nach Hause.

8

GEORGE Wer war das?
MELINE Mikhail Zagoruychenko.
GEORGE Russe?
MELINE Ja.
GEORGE Langweilig? Und Hans?
MELINE Ich möchte nicht darüber reden.

SABITE Hallo.
KARL Hallo. Schön, dass wir uns treffen.
SABITE Ich liebe diesen Ort.

10

SABITE Woher kommst du?
KARL Wir kommen aus einem Tal in der Nähe von Zürich. Wir haben die Wälder erkundet und sind im See geschwommen. Es war eine herrliche Landschaft mit singenden Vögeln und blühenden Blumen.

Nützliche Ausdrücke

- **liebenswürdig**
  amiable

- **erschaffen**
  to create

- **erforschen**
  to explore

- **die Eiche**
  oak tree

- **begleiten**
  to accompany

- **Wer immer das auch sein mag.**
  Whoever that may be.

- **Was ist an Lederhosen auszusetzen?**
  What's wrong with lederhosen?

- **rasend**
  furious

- **sich beruhigen**
  to calm down

12A.1
- **Ich hätte das nicht sagen sollen?**
  I shouldn't have said that?

12A.2
- **Es war eine herrliche Landschaft mit singenden Vögeln und blühenden Blumen.**
  It was a beautiful countryside with singing birds and blooming flowers.

2 **Zum Besprechen** Organisieren Sie ein Picknick für das nächste Wochenende. Wohin soll es gehen? Wann geht es los? Wie kommen Sie dorthin? Was gibt es zu essen? Wen laden Sie ein? Besprechen Sie die Pläne Ihrer Gruppe mit dem Rest der Klasse. Answers will vary.

2 **Expansion** Ask students which group's picnic they would most like to attend and why.

3 **Vertiefung** Karl kommt aus einem Tal in der Nähe von Zürich. Finden Sie heraus, welche Freizeitaktivitäten unter freiem Himmel (*outdoors*) dieser Teil der Schweiz bietet. Was würden Sie dort am liebsten tun? Answers will vary.

Landschaften Deutschlands  Reading

Vom Wattenmeer° im hohen Norden bis zu den bayerischen Alpen: Deutschland ist ein Land mit vielen verschiedenen Landschaften und einer Vielzahl an heimischen Tieren. Besonders in den Nationalparks findet man seltene Tiere, Vögel und Pflanzen.

Nationalpark Bayerischer Wald

Der Nationalpark Bayerischer Wald ist der älteste Nationalpark Deutschlands. Nirgendwo zwischen Atlantik und Ural gibt es einen so großen Wald, der sich ganz natürlich entwickeln° darf. Es ist ein wilder Wald, in dem es 17 Fledermausarten° gibt. Außerdem kann man Luchse° in freier Natur sehen und acht verschiedene Spechtarten° entdecken.

Biosphärenreservat Spreewald

Dieses Reservat in Brandenburg ist mit 500 Quadratkilometern eine der größten Fluss- und Auenlandschaften° Mitteleuropas. Die Flüsse und Kanäle sind hier etwa 1.500 Kilometer lang: ein Traum für Kanu- und Kajakfreunde. Wer Tiere mag, kann hier Otter, Biber°, Eisvogel° und Prachtlibelle° bewundern. Auch zu sehen sind etwa 1.600 Pflanzenarten wie zum Beispiel diverse Orchideen, Schwertlilien° und die Kuckuckslichtnelke°.

Nationalpark Sächsische Schweiz

Der Nationalpark Sächsische Schweiz, der in Sachsen liegt und an die Tschechische Republik angrenzt°, ist erst 20 Jahre alt. Er ist ein Paradies für Kletterfans und Wanderer. Seltene Pflanzen gibt es hier; das Gelbe Veilchen° ist noch ein Relikt aus der Eiszeit°. Vogelfans können hier Schwarzstörche, Uhus° und Wanderfalken° sehen. Außerdem gibt es Feuersalamander und Fischotter.

Gefährdete° Arten Deutschlands			
Säugetiere°:	6	Fische:	21
Vögel:	6	Weichtiere°:	9
Reptilien:	0	Pflanzen:	12

QUELLE: Rote Liste gefährdeter Arten (2009)

Suggestion Remind students that they read about another bio-diverse landscape, **National Park Niedersächsisches Wattenmeer**, in Unit 7.

Wattenmeer *intertidal zone* **entwickeln** *develop* **Fledermausarten** *bat species* **Luchse** *lynxes* **Spechtarten** *woodpecker species* **Auenlandschaften** *meadow landscapes* **Biber** *beaver* **Eisvogel** *kingfisher* **Prachtlibelle** *banded damselfly* **Schwertlilien** *irises* **Kuckuckslichtnelke** *ragged robin* **angrenzt** *borders* **Gelbe Veilchen** *twoflower violet* **Eiszeit** *Ice Age* **Uhus** *eagle owls* **Wanderfalken** *peregrine falcons* **Gefährdete** *Endangered* **Säugetiere** *mammals* **Weichtiere** *molluscs*

Expansion Ask students: **Welche Nationalparks haben Sie besucht? Was hat Ihnen da gefallen? Was haben Sie alles gesehen? Gibt es da irgendwelche besonderen Tiere, Pflanzen usw?**

1 **Richtig oder falsch?** Sagen Sie, ob die Sätze richtig oder falsch sind. Korrigieren Sie die falschen Sätze.

1. Der älteste deutsche Nationalpark ist der Nationalpark Bayerischer Wald. Richtig.
2. Der Nationalpark Bayerischer Wald ist der größte wilde Wald in Europa. Richtig.
3. Das Biosphärenreservat Spreewald liegt in Sachsen. Falsch. Es liegt in Brandenburg.
4. Kanu- und Kajakfreunde finden Flüsse und Kanäle im Bayerischen Wald. Falsch. Man findet sie im Biosphärenreservat Spreewald.
5. Schwertlilien findet man in der Sächsischen Schweiz. Falsch. Man findet sie im Biosphärenreservat Spreewald.
6. Der Nationalpark Sächsische Schweiz liegt in der Nähe der Tschechischen Republik. Richtig.
7. Der Nationalpark Sächsische Schweiz ist noch sehr jung. Richtig.
8. Eine der ältesten Blumenarten im Nationalpark Sächsische Schweiz ist das Gelbe Veilchen. Richtig.
9. Es gibt in Deutschland keine gefärdeten Fischarten. Falsch. Es gibt in Deutschland 21 gefährdete Fischarten.
10. Es gibt in Deutschland sechs gefährdete Vogelarten. Richtig.

Practice more at **vhlcentral.com**.

Naturkatastrophen

das Erdbeben, -	*earthquake*
die Lawine, -en	*avalanche*
der Tornado, -s	*tornado*
der Treibsand	*quicksand*
der Vulkan, -e	*volcano*

Der Weißstorch

Der Weißstorch ist ein mitteleuropäischer Vogel, den man vor allem in Deutschland, Österreich, Polen und der Schweiz finden kann. Er ist weiß mit schwarzen Flügeln°. Beine und Schnabel° sind rot. Er überwintert in Afrika. Der Storch kehrt jedes Jahr zum gleichen Nest zurück, und so kann es nach vielen Jahren über eine Tonne wiegen. In Deutschland gelten Störche als Glücksbringer°. Der Sage° nach bringen sie auch die neugeborenen Kinder.

Flügeln *wings* **Schnabel** *beak* **Glücksbringer** *good luck charms* **Sage** *legend*

Alexander von Humboldt

Suggestion You may want to read students an excerpt from Daniel Kehlmann's popular book *Die Vermessung der Welt*, which offers a fictionalized account of Humboldt's travels through South America.

Friedrich Wilhelm Heinrich Alexander von Humboldt wurde am 14. September 1769 in Berlin geboren und starb dort am 6. Mai 1859. Er war Naturforscher und Begründer° der heutigen Geographie. Vor allem durch seine Reise nach Amerika, auf der er zwischen 1799 und 1804 das heutige Venezuela, Peru, Mexiko und die USA besuchte, wurde er weltweit berühmt. Seine Entdeckungen in den Bereichen der Botanik, Zoologie, Klimatologie und Ozeanographie dokumentierte er in seinem Werk *Kosmos*. Wegen seines großen Einflusses auf Botanik und Zoologie tragen heute eine Orchideen-, eine Lilien-, eine Kaktus°-, eine Pinguin-, eine Fledermaus- und mehrere Affenarten° seinen Namen. Allein in den USA heißen acht Städte Humboldt und der wichtige Humboldtstrom fließt entlang der Küste Südamerikas.

Begründer *founder* **Kakteen** *cactus* **Affenarten** *monkey species*

 IM INTERNET

Suchen Sie im Internet eine europäische Pflanze oder ein europäisches Tier, über das Sie gerne mehr wissen möchten: Wie sieht es aus? Wo kann man es finden? Was frisst es?

Find out more at **vhlcentral.com**.

---

2 **Was fehlt?** Ergänzen Sie die Sätze.

1. Der Weißstorch hat schwarze ___Flügel___.
2. Der Weißstorch fliegt im Winter nach ___Afrika___.
3. Weißstörche benutzen jedes ___Jahr___ dasselbe Nest.
4. Alexander von Humboldt hat die heutige ___Geographie___ begründet.
5. Die Erlebnisse seiner Reise dokumentierte er in seinem Werk ___Kosmos___.
6. Viele Pflanzen und Tiere tragen seinen ___Namen___.

3 **Die Natur** Diskutieren Sie mit einem Partner / einer Partnerin Ihre Einstellung (*attitude*) zur Natur. Sind Sie gerne in der Natur oder nicht? Warum? Was sind einige positive und negative Aspekte der Natur?

12A.1

Suggestion Point out that the **Konjunktiv der Vergangenheit** is often used to express regrets.

Expansion Have students convert other **Perfekt** or **Plusquamperfekt** sentences into the **Konjunktiv der Vergangenheit** by changing the auxiliary to the appropriate **Konjunktiv II** form. Make sure they understand the difference in meaning between the two sentences.

Der Konjunktiv der Vergangenheit  Presentation

Startblock In 9B.1, you learned to use the **Konjunktiv II** to talk about hypothetical events or to express wishes about the present or the future. You can use a past form, **der Konjunktiv der Vergangenheit**, to speculate about events that could have happened, or to express wishes about the past.

Ich **hätte** nie **gedacht**, dass du solche Gefühle hast.

Das **hätte** ich nie **sagen sollen**.

- The formation of the **Konjunktiv der Vergangenheit** is similar to that of the **Plusquamperfekt**.

PLUSQUAMPERFEKT	KONJUNKTIV DER VERGANGENHEIT
Ich **hatte** ihm das **gesagt**.	Ich wünschte, ich **hätte** ihm das **gesagt**.
*I **had said** that to him.*	*I wish I **had said** that to him.*

QUERVERWEIS

See **9B.1** to review the formation and use of present forms of the **Konjunktiv II**.

- To form the **Konjunktiv der Vergangenheit**, use the **Konjunktiv II** of **sein** or **haben** with a past participle.

Konjunktiv der Vergangenheit			
	wissen	**gehen**	**sich informieren**
ich	hätte gewusst	wäre gegangen	hätte mich informiert
du	hättest gewusst	wärest gegangen	hättest dich informiert
er/sie/es	hätte gewusst	wäre gegangen	hätte sich informiert
wir	hätten gewusst	wären gegangen	hätten uns informiert
ihr	hättet gewusst	wäret gegangen	hättet euch informiert
Sie/sie	hätten gewusst	wären gegangen	hätten sich informiert

ACHTUNG

Remember to use the subjunctive form of **wünschen** with a subjunctive clause to express a wish that is contrary to reality.

Ich wünschte, ich **hätte** den Sonnenaufgang **gesehen**.
*I wish I **had seen** the sunrise.*

Wenn wir früher **angekommen wären**, **hätten** wir mehr Zeit **gehabt**.
*If we **had arrived** earlier, we **would have had** more time.*

Wenn du nur früher **aufgewacht wärest**!
*If only you **had woken up** earlier!*

Wenn ich mehr Zeit gehabt **hätte**, **hätte** ich **mich** besser darüber **informiert**.
*If I **had had** more time, I **would have found out** more about it.*

Suggestion Remind students that the auxiliary used with modals is always **haben**, and never **sein**.

- To use a modal in the **Konjunktiv der Vergangenheit**, replace the past participle with a double infinitive (verb infinitive + modal infinitive). This construction is most common with the modals **können**, **müssen**, and **sollen**.

Ich **hätte** es **wissen sollen**.
*I **should have known**.*

Sie **hätte** uns **helfen können**.
*She **could have helped** us.*

Sie **hätten sich** nicht **streiten sollen**.
*They **shouldn't have argued**.*

Du **hättest** den Wasserfall **fotografieren sollen**.
*You **should have taken a picture** of the waterfall.*

- In a subordinate clause with a modal, place the conjugated form of **haben** *before* the double infinitive at the end of the clause.

Suggestion Help students remember this word order with the acronym **AIM**: **A**uxiliary, then **I**nfinitive, then **M**odal.

Die Lehrerin hat Paul gesagt, dass er seine
   Hausaufgabe **hätte machen sollen**.
*The teacher told Paul that he **should
   have done** his homework.*

Wir wussten nicht, dass wir hier ein
   Picknick **hätten machen können**.
*We didn't know that we **could have
   had** a picnic here.*

- When a modal is used without an accompanying infinitive, the **Konjunktiv der Vergangenheit** is formed as with other verbs.

Er **hätte** das nicht **gekonnt**.
*He **wouldn't have been able to do** that.*

Wir **hätten** das nicht **gewollt**.
*We **wouldn't have wanted** that.*

- Use the **Konjunktiv der Vergangenheit** to express wishes about events that are already past.

Ich wünschte, ich **hätte** mehr Zeit **gehabt**,
   um den Wald zu erforschen.
*I wish I **had had** more time to explore
   the forest.*

Wenn wir nur länger auf der Insel
   hätten bleiben können!
*If only we **could have stayed** on
   the island longer!*

- Use the **Konjunktiv der Vergangenheit** to make statements or ask questions about hypothetical situations in the past.

Was **wäre passiert**, wenn ich dort nicht
   pünktlich **angekommen wäre**?
*What **would have happened** if I **hadn't
   gotten** there in time?*

Was **hättet** ihr an seiner
   Stelle **gemacht**?
*What **would** you **have done**
   in his place?*

Wenn das Wetter schön **gewesen wäre**,
   hätten wir ein Picknick **gemacht**.
*If the weather **had been nice**, we **would
   have had** a picnic.*

Wenn sie sehr krank **gewesen wäre**, **hätten** wir
   sie ins Krankenhaus **bringen müssen**.
*If she **had been** really sick, we **would have had
   to take** her to the hospital.*

Ressourcen

SAM
WB: pp. 159–160

SAM
LM: p. 103

S
vhlcentral.com

 Jetzt sind Sie dran! **Wählen Sie die passenden Wörter.**

1. Wenn ich nur nichts gesagt (hätte/ wäre)!

2. Wir wünschten, wir (wären/ hätten) am Wochenende wandern gegangen.

3. Wenn er keinen Unfall (gehabt/ haben) hätte, hätte er sein Fahrrad nicht reparieren müssen.

4. Wenn die Klippe nicht so hoch (gewesen/ sein) wäre, wären wir hinaufgeklettert.

5. Ich wünschte, ich (haben/ hätte) als Kind ein Kaninchen gehabt.

6. Er wusste nicht, dass er den Hausmeister hätte (anrufen sollen/ sollen anrufen).

7. Wenn wir den Bauernhof (wären/ hätten) finden können, hätten wir frische Milch gekauft.

8. Welchen Weg (hättest/ wärest) du durch den Wald genommen?

9. Was für ein Wasserfall! Wenn ihr ihn nur hättet (sehen/ gesehen) können!

10. Ich (wäre/ hätte) gern mit euch aufs Land gefahren.

Anwendung

1 Sätze umschreiben Schreiben Sie die Sätze in den Konjunktiv der Vergangenheit um.

BEISPIEL

Wir kämen mit.
Wir wären mitgekommen.

Wir würden sie anrufen.
Wir hätten sie angerufen.

1. Ich schliefe länger. Ich hätte länger geschlafen.
2. Gingest du mit ihnen aus?
   Wärest du mit ihnen ausgegangen?
3. Er würde viel wandern. Er wäre viel gewandert.
4. Ihr solltet kündigen. Ihr hättet kündigen sollen.
5. Sie gäben eine Party. Sie hätten eine Party gegeben.
6. Ich könnte das nicht. Ich hätte das nicht gekonnt.
7. Wir müssten trainieren. Wir hätten trainieren müssen.
8. Sie würde nach Hause fahren.
   Sie wäre nach Hause gefahren.

2 Hypothesen Bilden Sie Sätze im Konjunktiv der Vergangenheit. Suggested answers provided.

2 Suggestion Quickly review the **Partizipien** of the verbs provided and have students identify which verbs take **hätte** and which take **wäre**.

2 Expansion Have students choose one sentence, build a scenario around it, and turn it into a short dialogue to share with the class.

BEISPIEL wenn der Personalchef / mich / nur / früher anrufen
Wenn der Personalchef mich nur früher angerufen hätte!

1. wenn die Assistentin / nur nicht / kündigen
   Wenn die Assistentin nur nicht gekündigt hätte!
2. wenn seine Empfehlungsschreiben / nur / besser sein
   Wenn seine Empfehlungsschreiben nur besser gewesen wären!
3. wenn ich / nur / mehr Geld haben Wenn ich nur mehr Geld gehabt hätte!
4. wenn die Katze / nur nicht / die Maus fangen Wenn die Katze nur nicht die Maus gefangen hätte!
5. wenn Jonas / nur nicht / seinen Schlüssel verlieren
   Wenn Jonas nur nicht seinen Schlüssel verloren hätte!
6. wenn die Blätter / nur nicht / vom Baum fallen
   Wenn die Blätter nur nicht vom Baum gefallen wären!
7. wenn das Gras / nur nicht / so nass werden Wenn das Gras nur nicht so nass geworden wäre!
8. wenn ich / nur / länger bleiben können Wenn ich nur länger hätte bleiben können!

3 Wenn es anders gewesen wäre Schreiben Sie die Sätze um. Sagen Sie, was passiert wäre, wenn die Situation anders gewesen wäre. Verwenden Sie dabei den Konjunktiv der Vergangenheit. Suggested answers provided.

BEISPIEL Ich bin spät nach Hause gekommen
und ich war am nächsten Tag müde.
Wenn ich nicht spät nach Hause gekommen wäre, wäre ich am nächsten Tag nicht müde gewesen.

1. Der Boden war so nass, dass die Frau hingefallen ist.
   Wenn der Boden nicht so nass gewesen wäre, wäre die Frau nicht hingefallen.
2. Es hat einen Sturm gegeben und die Wanderer konnten ihre Bergtour nicht machen.
   Wenn es keinen Sturm gegeben hätte, hätten die Wanderer ihre Bergtour machen können.
3. Die Kinder haben Angst gehabt und sind ins Haus gelaufen.
   Wenn die Kinder keine Angst gehabt hätten, wären sie nicht ins Haus gelaufen.
4. Wir hatten Vollmond (*full moon*) und ich habe nicht schlafen können.
   Wenn wir keinen Vollmond gehabt hätten, hätte ich schlafen können.
5. Weil der Weg an einer Klippe endete, mussten sie zurückgehen.
   Wenn der Weg nicht an einer Klippe geendet hätte, hätten sie nicht zurückgehen müssen.
6. Mein Hund hat nicht auf mich gehört und ist auf die Straße gerannt.
   Wenn mein Hund auf mich gehört hätte, wäre er nicht auf die Straße gerannt.

 Practice more at **vhlcentral.com.**

Kommunikation

4 **Ich nicht** Schauen Sie sich die Bilder an und erzählen Sie sich, was Sie anders gemacht hätten. Benutzen Sie den Konjunktiv der Vergangenheit. Answers will vary.

4 **Suggestion** If students have difficulty spontaneously producing the past subjunctive in this activity, have them prepare their answers as written homework, and then share them with a partner during the next class.

▶ **BEISPIEL**

S1: Ich wäre nicht so schnell gefahren!
S2: Ich hätte länger an der Kreuzung gewartet!

5 **Wenn nur!** Was hätte im letzten Jahr anders sein sollen? Arbeiten Sie mit einem Partner / einer Partnerin und verwenden Sie den Konjunktiv der Vergangenheit. Answers will vary.

BEISPIEL

S1: Wenn ich nur fleißiger gelernt hätte!
S2: Wenn der Winter nur nicht so kalt gewesen wäre!

6 **Was hättest du lieber gemacht?** Berichten Sie Ihrem Partner / Ihrer Partnerin von zwei Aktivitäten, die Sie letztes Wochenende gemacht haben. Erzählen Sie sich, was Sie lieber gemacht hätten, und verwenden Sie dabei den Konjunktiv der Vergangenheit. Answers will vary.

BEISPIEL

S1: Was hast du am Wochenende gemacht?
S2: Am Samstag habe ich ein Referat für Geschichte geschrieben und am Sonntag bin ich zum Waschsalon gefahren.
S1: Und was hättest du lieber gemacht?
S2: Ich hätte lieber länger geschlafen. Ich wäre auch lieber ins Kino gegangen.

7 **Vor 100 Jahren** Was hätten Sie (nicht) machen können, müssen oder dürfen, wenn Sie vor hundert Jahren gelebt hätten? Answers will vary.

BEISPIEL

S1: Ich hätte nicht im Internet surfen können.
S2: Ich hätte keinen Minirock tragen dürfen.

12A.2 **Das Partizip Präsens**  Presentation

Startblock The present participle (**das Partizip Präsens**) can be used as an adjective or an adverb. It is used more often in writing than in spoken German.

> ... es gibt auch von anderen ausgezeichneten Künstlern so viele neue **aufregende** Werke.

> Es war eine herrliche Landschaft mit **singenden** Vögeln und **blühenden** Blumen.

- To form the present participle in German, add **-d** to the infinitive.

Suggestion Emphasize to students that *any* infinitive can be turned into an adjective or adverb by adding **-d**, followed by an adjective ending where necessary.

present participle	
klingelnd	*ringing*
lachend	*laughing*
wachsend	*growing*

Suggestion Point out that the second example sentence is a **Sprichwort**, similar to the English proverb, "Let sleeping dogs lie."

- When you use present participles as adjectives, follow the normal rules for adjective endings.

Der **aufgehende** Mond war sehr schön.
*The **rising** moon was beautiful.*

Schlafende Hunde soll man nicht wecken.
*You shouldn't wake a **sleeping** dog.*

Michael Hanekes Filme sind **bedeutend**.
*Michael Haneke's films are **important**.*

- Present participles can also be used as adverbs. When used as adverbs, they do not have added endings.

Nachdem der Junge vom Baum gefallen war, lief er **weinend** nach Hause.
*After the boy fell out of the tree, he ran home **crying**.*

Er sah ihr **suchend** in die Augen.
*He looked **searchingly** into her eyes.*

Suggestion Point out that a present participle and a past participle can be used together as attributive adjectives. Ex.: **die folgenden vergessenen historischen Orte.**

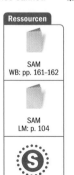

Jetzt sind Sie dran! **Wählen Sie die passenden Wörter.**

1. Peter ist ein gut (aussehend / aussehender / aussehenden) Bauer.

2. Die (spielend / spielenden / spielende) Eichhörnchen sind niedlich (*cute*).

3. Wir fahren am (kommend / kommenden / kommendes) Wochenende an den See.

4. Hast du auch die (passend / passende / passenden) Schuhe zu diesem Kleid?

5. Das Mädchen lief (singend / singende / singender) durch den Wald.

6. Wo ist hier ein (funktionierend / funktionierender / funktionierenden) Drucker?

7. Die Kinder laufen (lachend / lachende / lachendes) durch das Feld.

8. Das war ein (überraschend / überraschenden / überraschender) Besuch!

9. (Anschließend / Anschließende / Anschließenden) gingen wir alle ins Kino.

10. Bitte beantworten Sie die (folgend / folgenden / folgende) Fragen.

Anwendung und Kommunikation

1 **Partizipien** Ergänzen Sie die richtigen Partizipendungen. Wenn Sie keine Endung brauchen, machen Sie einen Strich (*slash*).

> **BEISPIEL** Der Zirkus hatte einen tanzend*en* Bären (*bear*).
> Sein Tanzen war überraschend——— gut.

1. Die laufend*en* Kosten sind circa 120 Euro monatlich.
2. Sie hat das weinend*e* Baby nicht beruhigen (*calm down*) können.
3. Wir fahren in der kommend*en* Woche an den Strand.
4. Der Film war aufregend———.
5. Wegen stark steigend*er* Ölpreise wird alles teurer.
6. Ein schlafend*er* Hund liegt vor der Tür.
7. Die Prüfung war überraschend——— einfach.
8. Sein klingelnd*es* Handy ist allen auf die Nerven gegangen.

2 **Bilder beschreiben** Beschreiben Sie bei jedem Bild, was gerade passiert. Benutzen Sie dabei die Verben aus der Liste. Danach wiederholt Ihr Partner / Ihre Partnerin den Satz, aber er/sie muss das Verb in ein Partizip umändern (*change*). Answers will vary.

klingeln	spielen
scheinen	weinen
schlafen	

► **BEISPIEL**
> **S1:** *Der Mond scheint hell diese Nacht.*
> **S2:** *Ja, das ist ein hell scheinender Mond.*

Der Mond...

Die Katze...

Das Kind...

Der Wecker...

Die Mädchen...

3 **Umweltprobleme** Schlagen Sie sich gegenseitig mögliche Lösungen (*solutions*) für die folgenden Probleme vor. Answers will vary.

> **S1:** *Die Temperaturen steigen.*
> **S2:** *Was können wir gegen die steigenden Temperaturen tun?*
> **S1:** *Wir könnten weniger Auto fahren.*

1. Die Temperaturen steigen.
2. Der Müll stinkt.
3. Die Regenwälder (*rainforests*) sterben.
4. Die Wasserqualität sinkt.

 Practice more at **vhlcentral.com**.

1 **Suggestion** Make sure students understand that the participle ending **-d** has already been added, and they just need to decide what, if any, adjective ending is needed. Also, remind students that **wegen** (in item 5) is a genitive preposition. In item 7, point out that **überraschend** is being used as an adverb, not as an adjective.

3 **Suggestion** Remind students that since **gegen** is an accusative preposition, their participles will need accusative endings.

Wiederholung

1 Wie wäre es gewesen? Wählen Sie eine Angabe (*condition*) aus der Liste und bilden Sie mit einem Partner / einer Partnerin eine logische Folgerung (*conclusion*) daraus. Benutzen Sie den Konjunktiv der Vergangenheit.
Answers will vary.

BEISPIEL

Wenn wir früh aufgestanden wären, hätten wir den Sonnenaufgang gesehen.

früh aufstehen	mehr regnen
das Feld nicht so klein sein	auf den Berg steigen
wandern gehen	ein Boot haben

2 Diskutieren und kombinieren Auf Ihrem Blatt finden Sie Informationen über vier Personen und vier Urlaubsorte. Berichten Sie Ihrem Partner / Ihrer Partnerin, was Ihre Personen gerne im Urlaub machen.
Answers will vary.

BEISPIEL

S1: *Julian Koch liebt das Leben in der Stadt. Aber er segelt auch gerne und geht gerne klettern.*
S2: *Er sollte Salzburg besuchen. Da gibt es viele Theater und Konzerte. Die Berge sind sehr nah und es gibt auch Seen in der Nähe.*

3 Was hätten Sie gemacht? Sehen Sie sich mit einem Partner / einer Partnerin die Fotos an. Sagen Sie, was jede Person gemacht hat, und fragen Sie einander, was Sie in der gleichen Situation gemacht hätten. Benutzen Sie den Konjunktiv der Vergangenheit. Answers will vary.

BEISPIEL

S1: *Sarah ist auf diesem Weg gelaufen. Wärest du darauf gelaufen?*
S2: *Nein. Obwohl dieser Weg sehr schön aussieht, wäre ich dort nicht gelaufen, weil es zu viele Insekten im hohen Gras gibt.*

Sarah / laufen

David / spielen

Lara / schwimmen

Nina / nahekommen

Jonas / klettern gehen

Max / angeln gehen

Hanna / springen

4 Arbeitsblatt Zeichnen Sie (*draw*) ein Bild mit Tieren, die etwas Unerwartetes (*unexpected*) machen. Bitten Sie drei Personen im Unterricht, das Bild mit Partizipien der Gegenwart zu beschreiben. Schreiben Sie die Antworten auf.
Answers will vary.

BEISPIEL

S1: *Was siehst du auf meinem Bild?*
S2: *Die sprechende Kuh fragt das stehende Pferd, was das singende Huhn sagt.*
S3: *Das singende Huhn erzählt dem denkenden Pferd ...*

5 Regeln Schreiben Sie mit einem Partner / einer Partnerin Sicherheitsregeln für die folgenden Situationen.
Answers will vary.

BEISPIEL in den Bergen wandern

S1: *Wenn man in den Bergen wandert, soll man auf das Wetter achten.*
S2: *Wenn man in den Bergen wandert, muss man Trinkwasser mitbringen.*

im Wald Fahrrad fahren	auf eine Klippe klettern
in einem See baden	unter einem Wasserfall baden
auf dem Meer segeln	ein Pferd reiten

6 Die Traumlandschaft Beschreiben Sie einem Partner / einer Partnerin Ihre Traumlandschaft. Benutzen Sie so viele Details wie möglich für Ihre Beschreibung. Ihr Partner / Ihre Partnerin macht sich Notizen, um später allen diese Traumlandschaft beschreiben zu können.
Answers will vary.

BEISPIEL

Neulich habe ich einen komischen Traum gehabt. Ich wanderte in den Bergen und kam auf ein Feld. Beim aufgehenden Mond sah ich einen laufenden Hasen aus dem Wald kommen. Der Hase...

GEWINNER
16. Gütersloher
Kurzfilmfestival

Bienenstich
ist aus

Thilo Berndt, Renate Fuhrmann, Lotte Becker,
Eva Pliego und Lucius Woytt
Buch und Regie: Sarah Winkenstette

Eine Produktion der Kunsthochschule
für Medien Köln

© 2009 KHM/Winkenstette

Nützliche Ausdrücke

- **das Apfelmus, -e**
  apple sauce
- **erschrecken**
  to frighten
- **Ich muss dann mal los.**
  I have to go now.
- **der Kirschkuchen, -**
  cherry cake
- **das Lied, -er**
  song
- **das Mittagsschläfchen, -**
  mid-day nap
- **der Seemann, ¨er**
  sailor
- **verrückt**
  crazy
- **wasserscheu**
  afraid of water

Über den Film sprechen

- **der Schlaganfall**
  stroke
- **der Schrebergarten**
  community garden
- **stottern**
  to stutter
- **vermissen**
  to miss

Kurzfilm

(S) **Video: Short Film**

Bienenstich ist aus

Paul stottert und weigert sich (*refuses*) zu sprechen. Seine Eltern reisen viel und Paul ist oft alleine. Er hat keine Freunde. Aber er hat seine Oma, die er sehr lieb hat. In ihrem Garten essen sie oft zusammen Kuchen, am liebsten Bienenstich (*cream-filled cake*). Dort lernt er auch Emma und ihren Hund Anton kennen, die seine Freunde werden.

Vorbereitung

Suggestion Tell students that **Bienenstich** (literally "bee sting" cake) is filled with vanilla cream and topped with caramelized almonds. You may want to bring in a recipe to share with the class.

1 **Was fehlt?** Ergänzen Sie die Sätze mit einem passenden Wort oder Ausdruck aus den Listen.

1. Der ____Kirschkuchen____ kommt frisch aus dem Ofen.
2. Lina geht nicht gern schwimmen, weil sie ____wasserscheu____ ist.
3. Frau Müller ist im Krankenhaus, weil sie letzte Woche einen ____Schlaganfall____ hatte.
4. Diese laute Musik macht mich ganz ____verrückt____.
5. Mit Äpfeln, die vom Baum gefallen sind, könnten wir ____Apfelmus____ machen.
6. Nach einem ____Mittagsschläfchen____ würdest du dich nicht so müde fühlen.
7. Wir haben heute einen Baum im ____Schrebergarten____ gepflanzt.
8. Paul spricht nicht gern, weil er ____stottert____.
9. Die Schlangen ____erschrecken____ mich sehr.
10. Ich habe gestern ein schönes ____Lied____ im Radio gehört.

2 **Partnerarbeit** Besprechen Sie mit einem Partner / einer Partnerin die folgenden Themen.

1. In vielen deutschen Städten gibt es Schrebergärten. Gibt es solche Gärten auch in ihrer Stadt? Wie unterscheiden sie sich von anderen Gärten?
2. In Deutschland kauft man Brot und Kuchen oft bei einem Bäcker und nicht im Supermarkt. Ist dies in ihrem Land auch so? Diskutieren Sie die Vor- und Nachteile der beiden Läden.

Szenen: Bienenstich ist aus

TIM: Ey... Hast du seit Neuestem auch was auf den Augen, oder was?
STEFAN: Lass ihn doch.
TIM: Was, lass ihn doch? Der hätte doch wohl mal eben den Ball aufheben können.
STEFAN: Du weißt doch, wie er ist ...

VERKÄUFERIN: Der Bienenstich ist leider schon aus, tut mir leid. Darf ich dir denn irgendwas anderes geben? Wie wär's denn mit Kirschkuchen? Der ist ganz frisch aus dem Ofen. Ja? Zwei Stück, wie immer?

NACHBARIN: Ach, vielleicht hat sie sich ja auch was gebrochen.
NACHBAR: Gebrochen?
NACHBARIN: Ich weiß nicht, was das ist...
HERR SCHULTE: Das muss ganz plötzlich°, offensichtlich°... Eben hat sie noch gestanden. Ich verstehe das nicht.

HERR SCHULTE: Jetzt reicht's!° Stellen Sie die Musik leiser, Frau Hoffmann!
OMA: (singend) ... deine Freunde sind die Sterne, über Rio und Shanghai, über Bali und Hawaii...
HERR SCHULTE: Ja, ein Seemann müsste man sein. Dann hätte man wenigstens seine Ruhe!

EMMA: Meinst du nicht, dass es deiner Oma stinklangweilig° ist, so alleine im Krankenhaus? Sie vermisst dich bestimmt.
PAUL: Kommst du mit?

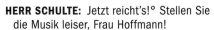

OMA: Och, der sieht doch noch ganz gut aus.
PAUL: Bienenstich gab's nicht mehr.
OMA: Mmm, boah°, ist der lecker!

Jetzt reicht's! *That does it!* **boah** *wow* **plötzlich** *suddenly* **offensichtlich** *obviously* **stinklangweilig** *really boring*

Analyse

3 **Richtig oder falsch?** Entscheiden Sie, ob die folgenden Sätze richtig oder falsch sind.

	richtig	falsch
1. Paul hat etwas auf den Augen und sieht nicht gut.	☐	☑
2. Seine Eltern sind nicht oft zu Hause.	☑	☐
3. Pauls Oma singt nicht gern.	☐	☑
4. Paul kann nicht sprechen und auch nicht singen.	☐	☑
5. Emmas Hund heißt Anton.	☑	☐
6. Anton hat alle vier Würstchen aufgegessen.	☑	☐
7. Im Schrebergarten wird Pauls Oma von einer Biene (*bee*) gestochen.	☐	☑
8. Die Nachbarn haben den Krankenwagen gerufen.	☑	☐

4 **Fortsetzung** Überlegen Sie sich mit einem Partner / einer Partnerin, wie der Kurzfilm weitergehen könnte. Wird Pauls Oma wieder gesund? Wie können Paul und seine Eltern ihr dabei helfen? Wird Paul wieder sprechen und sein Stottern überwinden (*overcome*)? Schreiben Sie einen Dialog zwischen Paul und seinen Eltern sowie zwischen Paul und Emma.

5 **Diskutieren** Besprechen Sie die folgenden Themen im Kurs.

- Für Paul ist der Schrebergarten seiner Oma ein Ort, wo er sich gut und sicher fühlt. Haben Sie auch einen Ort, an dem Sie sich besonders gut fühlen? Ist es irgendwo in der freien Natur oder woanders?

- Großeltern spielen eine wichtige Rolle im Leben von vielen Kindern. Besprechen Sie, warum Pauls Oma so wichtig für ihn ist. Versteht er sich gut mit seinen Eltern?

- Werden Menschen diskriminiert, die stottern oder andere Sprachfehler haben? Was kann man tun, um einem Freund, der stottert, zu helfen?

6 **Nachgedacht** Lesen Sie die folgenden Zitate (*quotations*) des römischen Politikers Cicero und des schweizerischen Schriftstellers Curt Goetz. Welchen Bezug (*connection*) haben sie zum Film? Finden Sie, dass die beiden Zitate richtig sind? Begründen Sie Ihre Meinung. Besprechen Sie diese Fragen mit einem Partner / einer Partnerin.

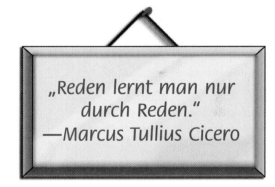

„Reden lernt man nur durch Reden." —Marcus Tullius Cicero

„Eine Gelegenheit (*opportunity*), den Mund zu halten, sollte man nie vorübergehen lassen." — Curt Goetz

6 Suggestion Make sure students understand the meaning of the quotations before discussing them in pairs. Alternatively, you may wish to discuss them as a class.

 Practice more at **vhlcentral.com.**

Communicative Goals

You will learn how to:

- talk about pollution
- talk about environmentalism

Die Umwelt  Vocabulary Tools

Wortschatz

die Umwelt	*environment*
die Art, -en	*species*
die Erde, -n	*earth*
die Gefahr, -en	*danger*
das Hochwasser, -	*flood*
das Licht, -er	*light*
die Ökologie	*ecology*
der Umweltschutz	*environmentalism*
die Welt, -en	*world*
biologisch	*organic*
gefährdet	*endangered*
ökologisch	*ecological*
umweltfreundlich	*environmentally friendly*
Energie	*energy*
die Windenergie	*wind energy*
Probleme	*problems*
das Aussterben	*extinction*
die Erderwärmung	*global warming*
der Giftmüll	*toxic waste*
die Überbevölkerung	*overpopulation*
Lösungen	*solutions*
das Gesetz, -e	*law*
die erneuerbare Energie (*pl.* die erneuerbaren Energien)	*renewable energy*
das Hybridauto, -s	*hybrid car*
die Regierung, -en	*government*
Verben	*verbs*
ausschalten (schaltet... aus)	*to turn off*
(den Planeten) retten	*to save (the planet)*
einschalten (schaltet... ein)	*to turn on*
entwickeln	*to develop*
erhalten	*to preserve*
schützen	*to protect*
verbessern	*to improve*
verschmutzen	*to pollute*
vorschlagen (schlägt... vor)	*to propose*
wegwerfen (wirft... weg)	*to throw away*

der saure Regen

die Kernenergie

die Sonnenenergie

das Kernkraftwerk, -e

Fabrik

die Fabrik, -en

die Verschmutzung

Sie bilden eine Fahrgemeinschaft.

Ressourcen

SAM
WB: pp. 163-164

SAM
LM: p. 105

vhlcentral.com

ACHTUNG

The terms **Wiederverwertung** and **wiederverwerten**
are sometimes used instead of the English loan words
Recycling and **recyceln**: Durch Wiederverwertung
von Glas und Papier können wir alle unseren
täglichen Haushaltsmüll stark reduzieren.

der Müllwagen, -

Sie recycelt.
(recyceln)

das Recycling

der Müll

Anwendung

Suggestion Ask students: **Ist Umweltschutz ein Thema, das Sie interessiert? Welche Umweltprobleme sind am dringendsten? Machen Sie sich Sorgen um die Umwelt?** etc. Students may have conflicting views about environmental issues, so remind them to approach each other's opinions with respect.

1 **Was passt nicht?** Geben Sie an, welches Wort nicht zu den anderen passt.

1 Expansion Have students write one more group of words on a piece of paper. Have volunteers read their lists aloud and have their classmates find the word that doesn't belong.

1. Glas, Papier, (Gras), Plastik
2. erforschen, erfinden, entdecken, (einladen)
3. Smog, (Lösung), Wasserverschmutzung, Giftmüll
4. (Körperenergie), Windenergie, Sonnenenergie, Kernenergie
5. Regierung, Gesetz, Minister, (Gefahr)
6. biologisch, ökologisch, (gefährdet), umweltfreundlich

2 **Bilder beschriften** Beschriften Sie jedes Bild mit einem passenden Wort aus der Vokabelliste.

1. ___die Sonnenenergie___

2. ___der Müllwagen___

3. ___das Hochwasser___

4. ___das Kernkraftwerk___

5. ___der Müll___

6. ___die Windenergie___

3 **Was ist richtig?** Ergänzen Sie die Sätze mit einem passenden Ausdruck.

1. Um unsere Umwelt zu schützen, müssen wir alle mehr (recyceln) / wegwerfen).
2. Der saure Regen (verbessert / (verschmutzt)) die Wälder.
3. Viele Tierarten sind (gefährdet) / erneuerbar).
4. Wenn es plötzlich zu viel regnet, haben die Flüsse (Giftmüll / (Hochwasser)).
5. Es ist wichtig, dass die Regierungen umweltfreundliche (Gesetze) / Gefahren) vorschlägt.

4 **Jeder muss seinen Teil tun** 🎧 Sie hören im Radio einen öffentlichen Aufruf (*public service announcement*) zum Thema Umweltschutz. Hören Sie zu und ergänzen Sie dann jeden Satz mit dem richtigen Wort.

1. Jeder muss seinen Teil (*part*) tun, um unsere ___Umwelt___ zu schützen.
2. Wir sollen Papier und ___Glas___ recyceln.
3. Wir können Strom (*electricity*) sparen, wenn wir nicht in allen Zimmern das ___Licht___ anlassen.
4. Man sollte weniger Produkte konsumieren, die ___Giftmüll___ produzieren.
5. Bio-Lebensmittel sind nicht nur gesünder, sondern auch ___umweltfreundlicher___.

🖎 Practice more at **vhlcentral.com**.

4 Suggestion Prepare students for the listening activity by having them work in pairs to make a list of **Dinge in unserem täglichen Leben, die wir machen können, um die Erde zu retten.**

Kommunikation

5 **Ein Umweltproblem** Lesen Sie den folgenden Artikel und ergänzen Sie mit
einem Partner / einer Partnerin die Sätze. Sample answers are provided.

1. Wir haben eine Krise, weil zu viel ___Energie___
   verbraucht wird.
2. Alte Fabriken ___verschmutzen___ den Planeten.
3. Es gibt viele ___Lösungen___ für die Energiekrise.
4. Solar-, Wind- und Kernenergie sind
   ___erneuerbare___ Energiequellen.
5. Öffentliche Verkehrsmittel und ___Hybridautos___ verbrauchen
   weniger Energie pro Person.
6. Zusammen können wir den Planeten ___retten___.

5 Expansion Ask students: **Was kann man
sonst noch machen um den Planeten zu retten?**

Fokus Umwelt

ENERGIEVERBRAUCH

Die Energiekrise wird zu einem immer ernsteren Problem, das wir so schnell wie möglich angehen (*address*) müssen. Unsere Fabriken sind alt, verbrauchen (*use*) zu viel Energie und tragen (*contribute*) zur Verschmutzung des Planeten bei. Unsere Autos verbrauchen zu viel Benzin und verursachen (*cause*) Smog. Man kann die Energiekrise auf verschiedene Art und Weise lösen (*solve*). Erstens müssen wir weitere erneuerbare Energiequellen wie Solar-, Wind- oder Kernenergie verwenden. In der Stadt könnten wir alle öffentliche Verkehrsmittel oder Hybridautos benutzen. In den Häusern sollten wir versuchen, weniger Energie zu verbrauchen und unseren Stromverbrauch zu kontrollieren. Wir müssen zusammenarbeiten, um den Planeten zu retten!

6 **Diskutieren und kombinieren** Sie und Ihr
Partner / Ihre Partnerin bekommen zwei verschiedene
Arbeitsblätter. Jeder von Ihnen hat nur die Hälfte der
Informationen über die verschiedenen Umweltprobleme
auf der Welt. Finden Sie heraus, welche Information
Ihnen fehlt. Sample answers are provided.

6 Expansion Have pairs create a public-service
announcement about an environmental problem.

BEISPIEL

S1: *Welches Land auf deiner Karte hat Probleme mit Smog?*
S2: *Mexiko hat Probleme mit Smog. Und auf deiner Karte?*
S1: *Großbritannien hat auch Probleme damit.*

7 **Sätze bilden** Bringen Sie die Sätze zu einem
logischen Schluss. Vergleichen Sie danach Ihre Antworten
mit denen Ihres Partners / Ihrer Partnerin. Answers will vary.

BEISPIEL Das Gute an Hybridautos ist,...

dass sie die Luftverschmutzung in den Städten reduzieren.

1. Die größten Umweltprobleme sind...
2. Die Überbevölkerung ist ein weltweites Problem,...
3. Viele Tierarten sind vom Aussterben bedroht,...
4. Recyceln ist wichtig,...
5. Erneuerbare Energien sind solche,...
6. Um unseren Planeten zu retten,...

8 **Karrieren mit Zukunftschancen** Beschreiben
Sie in Gruppen drei Berufe, die Ihrer Meinung nach große
Zukunftschancen haben. Beschreiben Sie für jeden Beruf
die Tätigkeit (*type of work*), den Nutzen in der heutigen
Zeit, und warum Ihrer Meinung nach dieser Beruf in der
Zukunft noch wichtiger sein wird.
Answers will vary.

BEISPIEL

S1: *In der Zukunft wird die Erderwärmung weiter zunehmen.*
S2: *Ein nützlicher Beruf wäre deshalb einer, der...*

Aussprache und Rechtschreibung  Audio

🎧 Tongue Twisters

> **Zungenbrecher** (*Tongue twisters*) are a part of German culture. Mastering a tongue twister means being able to say it quickly several times in a row. One popular type of tongue twister reverses sounds, syllables or words.
>
> **Rauchlachs mit Lauchreis.**   **Allergischer Algerier, algerischer Allergiker.**
>
> ⋯⋯⋯⋯⋯⋯⋯⋯⋯⋯⋯⋯⋯⋯⋯⋯⋯⋯⋯⋯⋯⋯⋯⋯⋯⋯⋯⋯⋯⋯⋯⋯⋯⋯⋯⋯
>
> Other tongue twisters repeat syllables, words, or phrases that contain similar sounds.
>
> **In Ulm, um Ulm und um Ulm herum.**   **Der dicke Dachdecker deckte das dicke Dach.**
>
> ⋯⋯⋯⋯⋯⋯⋯⋯⋯⋯⋯⋯⋯⋯⋯⋯⋯⋯⋯⋯⋯⋯⋯⋯⋯⋯⋯⋯⋯⋯⋯⋯⋯⋯⋯⋯
>
> German allows for the construction of very long compound words. Many such compounds appear in tongue twisters, sometimes as nonsense words.
>
> **Postkutschkasten**   **Fichtendickicht**   **Kirschenmirschen**

1   **Aussprechen** Wiederholen Sie die Zungenbrecher, die Sie hören.

1. zwischen zwei Zwetschgenzweigen
2. ein krummer Krebs kroch
3. der Cottbuser Postkutscher
4. allergischer Algerier

Expansion Have students take turns trying to read these **Zungenbrecher** out loud. Have them search online for additional examples and variations.

2   **Nachsprechen** Wiederholen Sie die Sätze, die Sie hören.

1. Hinter Hermann Hansens Haus hängen hundert Hemden raus.
2. Esel essen Nesseln nicht, Nesseln essen Esel nicht.
3. Der Cottbuser Postkutscher putzt den Cottbuser Postkutschkasten blank.
4. Fischers Fritz fischt frische Fische, frische Fische fischt Fischers Fritz.
5. Zehn Ziegen zogen zehn Zentner Zucker zum Zoo.
6. Es klapperten die Klapperschlangen, bis ihre Klappern schlapper klangen.

3   **Sprichwörter** Wiederholen Sie die Sprichwörter, die Sie hören.

> *Blaukraut bleibt Blaukraut und Brautkleid bleibt Brautkleid.*[1]

> *Zwischen zwei Zwetschgenzweigen zwitschern zwei Schwalben.*[2]

[1] You can't make a silk purse out of a sow's ear. (lit. Red cabbage remains red cabbage and a wedding dress remains a wedding dress.)

[2] Between two plum branches twitter two swallows.

Auf Wiedersehen, Berlin! Video

Zum letzten Mal treffen sich unsere Freunde im Biergarten, um den Abschied von George zu feiern.

Vorbereitung Have students read the title and discuss what they expect to happen in the episode.

communication cultures
NATIONAL STANDARDS

HANS Hey, an was arbeitest du?
GEORGE Ich schreibe meine Hausarbeit über ökologische Architektur fertig. Damit der Planet gerettet werden kann, sollten erneuerbare Energien wie Solar- und Windenergie in neuen Gebäuden verwendet werden. Regierungen müssen Gesetze verabschieden, die die Umwelt erhalten. Die Bedrohung durch Abforstung und Verschmutzung darf nicht ignoriert werden. Außerdem...

HANS Ich habe meine Abschlussarbeit für das Semester gestern abgegeben.
GEORGE Ich schlage eine Lösung vor, die Fabriken helfen wird, weniger zu verschmutzen und mehr zu recyceln. Mein Professor sagt, es sei eine gute Sache.

HANS Meline, ich bin's. Bist du da? Es tut mir leid wegen neulich Abend in der Galerie. Können wir darüber reden? Meline?
SABITE Hans! Was machst du denn hier draußen? Oh, Mann.
HANS Meline?
SABITE Sie ist wohl nicht zu Hause.

HANS Sie ist mir immer noch böse, oder? Sie gibt mir gar keine Chance, mich zu entschuldigen. Manchmal verstehe ich sie überhaupt gar nicht. Ich glaube, George hatte recht, wir sind einfach zu unterschiedlich.
SABITE Vielleicht.

SABITE Bist du Hans immer noch böse? Es tut ihm wirklich leid.
MELINE Er hat sehr liebe Nachrichten hinterlassen. Ich bin ihm nicht böse. Ich glaube, dass er ein guter Mensch ist, aber ich... ja...
SABITE Du mochtest ihn mehr, als du ihn nicht mochtest.
MELINE Genau!

MELINE Hallo! George! Das ist für dich. Von uns.
HANS Öffne es, öffne es!
SABITE Vorsichtig!
GEORGE Das ist wunderbar. Habt vielen herzlichen Dank.
GEORGE Ich hätte keine besseren Freunde finden können. Wegen euch war das Jahr in Berlin so großartig.

1 **Richtig oder falsch?** Entscheiden Sie, ob die folgenden Sätze **richtig** oder **falsch** sind.

1. George schreibt eine Hausarbeit über Ökotourismus. Falsch.
2. Er schlägt vor, dass in neuen Gebäuden Solar- und Windenergie verwendet wird. Richtig.
3. Hans hat seine Abschlussarbeit für das Semester schon abgegeben. Richtig.
4. Georges Professor gefällt die Lösung nicht, die George vorschlägt. Falsch.

5. Meline versteckt sich in ihrem Zimmer, weil sie Hans nicht sehen möchte. Richtig.
6. Hans hat Meline einen Kuchen mitgebracht. Falsch.
7. Meline ist immer noch böse auf Hans. Falsch.
8. Seine Freunde schenken George einen Stadtplan von Milwaukee. Falsch.
9. Hans möchte mit George die nächsten paar Wochen verreisen. Falsch.
10. Meline und Hans möchten weiterhin Freunde sein. Richtig.

PERSONEN

 George   Hans   Meline   Sabite

7

MELINE Ich hoffe, wir bleiben in Verbindung?
GEORGE Das werden wir. Ich möchte Wien besuchen.
HANS Ich habe gehört, es soll eine wunderschöne Kulturstadt sein.
SABITE Ähh, George, lass uns...
GEORGE Ja, definitiv.

8

HANS Das war nicht nett von mir, tut mir leid. Und wegen neulich Abend, ich... ich war wütend und ich hätte diese Dinge nicht zu dir sagen sollen.
MELINE Es ist schon okay, Hans. Du hast vielleicht gar nicht so falsch gelegen. Es tut mir leid, dass ich dich nicht angerufen habe.

9

HANS Max und ich, wir werden die nächsten paar Wochen verreisen, bevor ich wieder nach Hause zurückkehre, und ich... ich möchte dir nicht weh tun, aber ich kann mich im Moment nicht binden. Ich hoffe, du hast Verständnis dafür.
MELINE Ja, das habe ich. Können wir weiterhin Freunde sein?

10

HANS Auf ein tolles Jahr in Berlin, und neue Freunde.
GEORGE Richtig! Bravo!

Nützliche Ausdrücke

- **ein Gesetz verabschieden**
  to pass a law
- **neulich**
  the other day
- **unterschiedlich**
  different
- **eine Nachricht hinterlassen**
  to leave a message
- **in Verbindung bleiben**
  to stay in touch
- **falsch liegen**
  to be wrong

12B.1
- **Mein Professor sagt, es sei eine gute Sache.**
  My professor says it's a worthy cause.

12B.2
- **Die Bedrohung durch Abforstung und Verschmutzung darf nicht ignoriert werden.**
  The threat of deforestation and pollution shouldn't be ignored.

---

2   **Zum Besprechen** Am Ende dieser Episode trennen sich Hans und Meline. Denken Sie sich zu zweit ein alternatives Ende der Episode aus. Wie könnte es mit Hans und Meline weitergehen? Entwickeln Sie einen Dialog zwischen Hans und Meline und präsentieren Sie ihn Ihrer Klasse. Answers will vary.

   2 **Expansion** Have students write a dialogue in which Hans and Meline meet again after Hans comes back from his vacation.

3   **Vertiefung** Suchen Sie im Internet nach dem „Grünen Punkt". Welches System steckt dahinter? Wann wurde es eingeführt (*introduced*)? In welchen Ländern gibt es den Grünen Punkt?
Answers may include: recycling of packaging materials, Duales System Deutschland, introduced 1990 in Germany, most European countries participate.

Ressourcen

 SAM VM: pp. 24   vhlcentral.com

IM FOKUS

Grüne Berufe in Sachsen  Reading

Bauernhöfe und landwirtschaftliche Betriebe haben heute viele verschiedene Funktionen. Sie produzieren nicht nur landwirtschaftliche Produkte wie Fleisch, Obst, Gemüse, Milch und Eier; sie sind auch für den Umweltschutz verantwortlich. Außerdem sind sie sowohl Kunden als auch Arbeitgeber im ländlichen Raum° und deshalb sehr wichtig für die wirtschaftliche Entwicklung einer Region.

Grüne Berufe geben jungen Menschen die Möglichkeit°, viele verschiedene berufliche Tätigkeiten zu lernen. Eine Ausbildung dauert normalerweise drei Jahre. In dieser Zeit sammeln Auszubildende° praktische Kenntnisse bei der Arbeit. Regelmäßig besuchen sie auch die Berufsschule, wo sie die theoretischen Aspekte ihres neuen Berufes lernen. Durch Fort- und Weiterbildungsmöglichkeiten° haben Berufstätige auch die Chance, später in ihrer Karriere eine bessere Perspektive als verantwortliche° Mitarbeiter oder selbstständige Unternehmer° zu bekommen.

GRÜNE BERUFE IN SACHSEN IST EINE Initiative der Regierung, um Jugendliche, die sich für Natur und Umwelt interessieren, in sogenannte „grüne Berufe" zu bringen. Warum sind grüne Berufe so wichtig? Moderne

Grüne Berufe	Stellenbeschreibungen
Fischwirt/ Fischwirtin	Fischwirte arbeiten an den vielen Seen und Flüssen in Deutschland: sie fangen Fische und ziehen sie in Seen auf°.
Milchtechnologe/ Milchtechnologin	Milchtechnologen bedienen° die modernen Produktions- und Abfüllanlagen° und überwachen° die Produktionsprozesse von Milch und Milchprodukten wie Käse oder Jogurt.
Pferdewirt/ Pferdewirtin	Pferdewirte lernen, wie man Pferde richtig hält°, wie man sie reitet und wie man sie züchtet°.

ländlichen Raum rural area **Möglichkeit** opportunity **Auszubildende** apprentices **Fort- und Weiterbildungsmöglichkeiten** continuing education **verantwortliche** responsible **selbstständige Unternehmer** independent entrepreneur **ziehen... auf** breed **bedienen** operate **Abfüllanlagen** bottling systems **überwachen** monitor **hält** keeps **züchtet** breeds

ÜBUNGEN

1 **Richtig oder falsch?** Sagen Sie, ob die Sätze richtig oder falsch sind. Korrigieren Sie die falschen Sätze.

1. In Sachsen gibt es viele grüne Berufe. Richtig.

2. Menschen in grünen Berufen tragen grüne Kleider. Falsch. Sie arbeiten in Berufen, die mit Natur oder Umwelt zu tun haben.

3. Die Arbeit auf Bauernhöfen ist wichtig für den Umweltschutz. Richtig.

4. Auf Bauernhöfen werden Produkte wie Eier, Fleisch, Milch, Obst und Gemüse produziert. Richtig.

5. Eine Ausbildung dauert normalerweise zwei Jahre. Falsch. Sie dauert normalerweise drei Jahre.

6. Bauernhöfe sind nicht mehr so wichtig für die Wirtschaft im ländlichen Raum. Falsch. Sie sind sehr wichtig für die Wirtschaft im ländlichen Raum.

7. In der Ausbildung arbeitet man und geht in die Berufsschule. Richtig.

8. Ein Milchtechnologe holt die Milch von den Kühen. Falsch. Ein Milchtechnologe produziert Milchprodukte.

9. Fischwirte fangen Fische und kochen sie. Falsch. Sie fangen Fische und ziehen sie in Seen auf.

10. Pferdewirte lernen, wie man Pferde reitet. Richtig.

 Practice more at **vhlcentral.com**.

Suggestion Read the **Deutsch im Alltag** words together and ask students which of these things they recycle.

DEUTSCH IM ALLTAG

Abfall und Recycling

der Abfall, ⸚e	waste
die Altkleider	second-hand clothing
das Altpapier	used paper
der Gartenabfall, ⸚e	yard waste
der Schrott	scrap metal
der Verpackungsmüll	packaging waste

DIE DEUTSCHSPRACHIGE WELT

Umweltschutzorganisationen°

Deutschland

Seit 1975 gibt es in Deutschland den Bund für Umwelt und Naturschutz. Diese Organisation engagiert° sich für ökologische Landwirtschaft, gesunde Lebensmittel, den Klimaschutz und den Ausbau° regenerativer Energien.

Österreich In Österreich gibt es seit 1913 den Naturschutzbund Österreich. Diese Organisation war bei der Gründung° der österreichischen Nationalparks sehr aktiv und hilft auch bei der Erhaltung des Wiener Waldes, der Krimmler Wasserfälle und der Hainburger Au.

Die Schweiz In der Schweiz setzt sich die Organisation Pro Natura seit 1909 für den Naturschutz ein°. Zu den Erfolgen dieser Organisation zählt ein Netz° von 600 Naturschutzgebieten°.

Umweltschutzorganisationen *ecology groups* **engagiert** *gets involved in* **Ausbau** *development* **Gründung** *founding* **setzt sich... ein** *advocates* **Netz** *network* **Naturschutzgebieten** *nature reserves*

PORTRÄT

Michael Braungart

Suggestion Ask students: **Gibt es hier irgendwelche Organisationen, die sich für den Umweltschutz einsetzen? Wie heißen sie? Was tun sie alles?**

Michael Braungart, ein Chemiker aus Schwäbisch-Gmünd, arbeitet heute als Professor an der Erasmus-Universität Rotterdam. In den 80er Jahren war er aktives Mitglied° von Greenpeace Deutschland. Seither sucht er Antworten auf die folgenden Fragen: Wie kann der Mensch sich in das Leben auf der Erde integrieren? Wie kann er nicht nur wenig Schaden anrichten°, sondern wie kann er selbst einen Beitrag für die Umwelt leisten? Braungart ist bekannt für die Entwicklung von Umweltschutz-Konzepten und die Konzeption umweltverträglicher Produktionsverfahren°.

Mitglied *member* **Schaden anrichten** *do damage* **umweltverträglicher Produktionsverfahren** *environmentally friendly production*

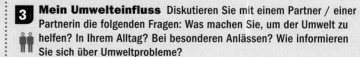

⚙ IM INTERNET

Wählen Sie einen Umweltaspekt aus, der Sie besonders interessiert. Suchen Sie Informationen darüber. Machen Sie eine Liste mit Initiativen, die es auf diesem Gebiet gibt.

Find out more at **vhlcentral.com**.

---

2   **Was fehlt?** Ergänzen Sie die Sätze.

1. Der Bund für Umwelt und Naturschutz engagiert sich für den Ausbau regenerativer __Energien__.

2. Der Naturschutzbund Österreich war bei der Gründung der österreichischen __Nationalparks__ aktiv.

3. Michael Braungart war in den 80er Jahren ein aktives __Mitglied__ von Greenpeace Deutschland.

4. Braungart will vor allem Antworten auf zwei __Fragen__ finden.

3   **Mein Umwelteinfluss** Diskutieren Sie mit einem Partner / einer Partnerin die folgenden Fragen: Was machen Sie, um der Umwelt zu helfen? In Ihrem Alltag? Bei besonderen Anlässen? Wie informieren Sie sich über Umweltprobleme?

12B.1

Der Konjunktiv I and indirect speech Presentation

Startblock You learned in **9B.1** and **12A.1** about the **Konjunktiv II** and its present and past tense forms. There is another subjunctive, **der Konjunktiv I**, which is used to report what someone else has said.

Mein Professor sagt, es **sei** eine gute Sache.

Sie hat gesagt, sie **werde** sein Geschenk **mitnehmen**.

Der Konjunktiv I

- To form the present tense of the **Konjunktiv I**, add the endings **-e, -est, -e, -en, -et, -en** to the infinitive stem. Only the verb **sein** is irregular: its stem is **sei-** and the first and third person singular have no added endings.

Konjunktiv I Präsens				
	geben	**können**	**haben**	**sein**
ich	geb**e**	könn**e**	hab**e**	sei
du	geb**est**	könn**est**	hab**est**	sei(e)st
er/sie/es	geb**e**	könn**e**	hab**e**	sei
wir	geb**en**	könn**en**	hab**en**	seien
ihr	geb**et**	könn**et**	hab**et**	seiet
Sie/sie	geb**en**	könn**en**	hab**en**	seien

Herr Braun sagt, die Erde **sei** wegen Erderwärmung gefährdet.
*Herr Braun says the earth **is** in danger because of global warming.*

Er meint, dass er die Lösung dafür **habe**.
*He believes that he **has** the solution for it.*

- To form the past tense of the **Konjunktiv I**, use the **Konjunktiv I** of **haben** or **sein** with the past participle.

Der *Spiegel* berichtete, dass es gestern sauren Regen **gegeben habe**.
Der Spiegel *reported that acid rain **fell** yesterday.*

Papa sagte, das Paket **sei** heute Morgen **gekommen**.
*Dad said the package **came** this morning.*

- Use the **Konjunktiv I** of **werden** with an infinitive to report a statement someone else has made about the future.

Frau Müller sagte, sie **werde** ein Hybridauto **kaufen**.
*Ms. Müller said she **would buy** a hybrid car.*

Wissenschaftler sagen, sie **werden** eine Lösung für die Erderwärmung **finden**.
*Scientists say they **will find** a solution for global warming.*

Indirect Speech

Expansion Bring in German-language newspapers, or printouts from online newspapers, and have students find statements containing the **Konjunktiv I**.

- In conversation, you can report what someone else said using the **Indikativ**, especially when you want to show that you agree with what was said or that you believe it to be true. If you wish to express skepticism or doubt, however, use the **Konjunktiv I**.

QUERVERWEIS

See **10A.1** to review indirect questions.

Die Nachbarn sagten, sie **haben** eine Maus **gesehen**.	Murat sagte, er **werde** später **wiederkommen**.
*The neighbors said they **saw** a mouse.*	*Murat said he **would come back** later.*

- In more formal contexts, such as news reports, political speeches, and scientific writing, the **Konjunktiv I** is used to report what people have said without implying that the information is necessarily true or accurate. It is typically introduced with a verb that denotes speech or belief, such as **sagen, berichten** (*to report*), **behaupten** (*to claim*), **meinen** (*to mean, to opine*), or **glauben**.

ACHTUNG

When you are reporting what someone else said, personal pronouns, possessive adjectives, and adverbs of time and place may need to be changed accordingly:

Paul: „*Ich* freue *mich* auf *meinen* Urlaub."

Paul sagte, dass *er sich* auf *seinen* Urlaub freue.

Die *Zeit* berichtet, dass es einen Atomkraftwerkunfall **gegeben habe**.	Wissenschaftler glauben, dass viele Menschen und Tiere in Gefahr **seien**.
Die Zeit *reports that there **was** a nuclear power plant accident.*	*Scientists believe that many people and animals **are** in danger.*

- The **Konjunktiv I** is used mainly with modals, **wissen, sein,** and third-person singular verbs. In cases where the **Konjunktiv I** conjugation is identical to the present-tense indicative, it is more common to use the **Konjunktiv II** or **würden** + infinitive.

QUERVERWEIS

See **9B.1** and **9B.2** to review **Konjunktiv II** and the **würden** + infinitive construction.

Thomas behaupte, er **habe** das nicht **gewusst**.	Sarah sagte, dass sie uns vielleicht morgen **besuchen werde**.
*Thomas claimed he **didn't know** that.*	*Sarah said that she **might visit** us tomorrow.*

Suggestion Show students an ambiguous sentence in which the indicative and **Konjunktiv II** forms are identical. Ex.: **Natasha sagt, ich gebe Ihnen all mein Geld**. Then, restate it using the **Konjunktiv II** to avoid the ambiguity: **Natasha sagt, ich gäbe Ihnen all mein Geld**.

- To express imperatives in indirect speech, use the **Konjunktiv I** or **II** of the modals **sollen** or **müssen**.

Suggestion Mention that the modal mögen can be used in indirect speech describing polite requests. Ex.: **Die Chefin sagte, der Bewerber möge jetzt eintreten**.

Die Studenten meinen, die Uni **solle/sollte** nicht so viel Papier **verschwenden**.	Die Geschäftsführerin sagte, wir **müssten** mehr **recyceln**.
*The students feel that the university **should**n't **waste** so much paper.*	*Our manager said we **should recycle** more.*

- The tense of the verb in indirect speech is the same as the tense in the original direct speech.

Ressourcen

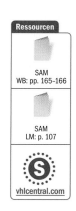

SAM
WB: pp. 165–166

SAM
LM: p. 107

vhlcentral.com

Der Bundespräsident: „Unser Land **braucht** mehr Windenergie."	Der Bundespräsident meint, unser Land **brauche** mehr Windenergie.
*The President: "Our country **needs** more wind energy."*	*The President believes that our country **needs** more wind energy.*

Jetzt sind Sie dran! **Entscheiden Sie, ob die folgenden Sätze im Indikativ oder im Konjunktiv I stehen.**

Expansion Write two sentences on the board, one in the **Indikativ** and one in the **Konjunktiv I**. Ex.: **Er hat keine Schuhe. Er habe keine Schuhe**. Ask students to explain the difference in English.

	Indikativ	Konjunktiv I		Indikativ	Konjunktiv I
1. Maria sagte, sie sei krank.	☐	☑	7. Ihr sagt, ihr benutzt wenig Energie.	☑	☐
2. Du sagst, du fährst nur Hybridautos.	☑	☐	8. Er sagte, er werde Lösungen entwickeln.	☐	☑
3. Er meinte, die Umwelt bleibe in Gefahr.	☐	☑	9. Sie meinte, sie habe ihren Müll getrennt.	☐	☑
4. Sie sagte, sie habe eine Lösung vorgeschlagen.	☐	☑	10. Erika sagte, sie kaufe nur biologische Lebensmittel.	☐	☑
5. Max sagt, er wird Windenergie benutzen.	☑	☐	11. Alex sagt, er wird die Umwelt schützen.	☑	☐
6. Er glaubt, er werde den Planeten retten.	☐	☑	12. Ihr sagt, ihr habt keinen Giftmüll produziert.	☑	☐

Anwendung

1 Was ist richtig? Ihr Freund hat keine Lust mit Ihnen ins Konzert zu gehen. Berichten Sie Ihren anderen Freunden, was er gesagt hat. Wählen Sie die passenden Verbformen des Konjunktiv I.

> **BEISPIEL** Er sagte, er (war /sei) zu müde, um ins Konzert zu gehen.

Er sagte, ...

1. er (müsse / muss) noch für eine schwere Prüfung am nächsten Tag lernen.
2. er (hatte / habe) nicht genug Geld, eine Konzertkarte zu kaufen.
3. er (wollte / wolle) heute Abend früh ins Bett gehen.
4. das Konzert (werde / wird) schon ausverkauft (*sold out*) sein.
5. ich (solle / soll) jemand anders einladen.

2 Welche Zeitform? Markieren Sie die richtigen Zeitformen.

	Indikativ	Konjunktiv I Präsens	Konjunktiv I Vergangenheit	Konjunktiv I Zukunft
1. er habe nichts gemacht	☐	☐	☑	☐
2. sie werde ihn heiraten	☐	☐	☐	☑
3. ich dürfe das nicht	☐	☑	☐	☐
4. sie sind angekommen	☑	☐	☐	☐
5. du werdest kündigen	☐	☐	☐	☑
6. sie seien abgefahren	☐	☐	☑	☐
7. sie wollte umziehen	☑	☐	☐	☐
8. ihr habet eine Idee	☐	☑	☐	☐

3 Suggestion Do the first few items together as a class.

3 Unsere Gegenwart Formen Sie die Sätze in indirekte Rede um. Suggested answers provided.

> **BEISPIEL** „Der Wasserspiegel (*water level*) der Weltmeere steigt."Der Wissenschaftler erklärte, dass *der Wasserspiegel der Weltmeere steige*.

1. „Die Regenwald (*rainforest*) muss gerettet werden."
   Die Wissenschaftlerin sagte, dass ___der Regenwald gerettet werden müsse___.
2. „Die Solarzellen werden Ihre Energiekosten reduzieren."
   Der Elektriker sagte dem Mann, dass ___die Solarzellen seine Energiekosten reduzieren würden___.
3. „Wollen Sie in dieser Firma ein Praktikum machen?"
   Der Personalchef fragte mich, ob ___ich in dieser Firma ein Praktikum machen wolle___.
4. „Warum recycelst du nicht deinen alten Computer?"
   Jan fragte seine Freundin, warum ___sie nicht ihren alten Computer recycle___.
5. „Die Papierfabrik hat seit Jahren die Luft verschmutzt."
   Der Bürgermeister klagte (*complained*), dass ___die Papierfabrik seit Jahren die Luft verschmutzt habe___.
6. „Ich weiß nicht, ob man diesen Nationalpark erhalten kann."
   Die Innenministerin sagte, ___sie wisse nicht, ob man diesen Nationalpark erhalten könne___.

 Practice more at **vhlcentral.com**.

Kommunikation

4 **Ein Streitgespräch** Schreiben Sie mit einem Partner / einer Partnerin einen kurzen Dialog zu dem Bild. Dann berichten Sie zwei anderen Studenten, was die Leute auf dem Bild gesagt haben. Verwenden Sie den Konjunktiv I. Answers will vary.

BEISPIEL

Dialog:
Mann: *Warum bist du so böse (angry) auf mich?*
Frau: *Weil du niemals bei der Hausarbeit hilfst.*
Mann: *Das ist nicht wahr! ...*

Bericht:
Der Mann hat die Frau gefragt, warum sie so böse auf ihn sei. Die Frau hat geantwortet, er helfe niemals bei der Hausarbeit. Der Mann hat dann gesagt, das sei nicht wahr. ...

5 **Glaubst du das?** Erzählen Sie zwei Partnern/Partnerinnen zwei Dinge über sich, die wahr oder eine Lüge (*lie*) sein könnten. Ein Partner / Eine Partnerin berichtet davon. Der andere Partner / Die andere Partnerin sagt, ob er/sie das glaubt oder nicht. Wechseln Sie sich ab. Answers will vary.

BEISPIEL

S1: *Ich bin 18 Jahre alt.*
S2: *Melanie hat gesagt, sie sei 18 Jahre alt. Glaubst du das?*
S3: *Nein, das glaube ich nicht. Ich glaube, sie ist 19.*

6 **Klatschkolumnen** Schreiben Sie mit Ihrem Partner / Ihrer Partnerin eine Klatschkolumne (*gossip column*) über einen Prominenten. Benutzen Sie Indikativformen. Tauschen Sie (*exchange*) Ihre Kolumne mit zwei Mitstudenten aus. Berichten Sie dem Rest der Klasse, was in der Kolumne Ihrer Mitstudenten steht. Verwenden Sie dabei den Konjunktiv I. Answers will vary.

BEISPIEL

S1/S2: *In der Klatschkolumne steht, dass die große Schauspielerin Tanja ihr ganzes Geld der Tierschutzorganisation „Ein Herz für Tiere" gegeben habe. Sie sei gestern in die Schweiz geflogen, habe das Geld abgehoben und dann ihre Konten gekündigt. Sie sei noch nie so glücklich gewesen, sagte Tanja.*

Die große Schauspielerin (*actress*) Tanja hat ihr ganzes Vermögen (*fortune*) der Tierschutzorganisation „Ein Herz für Tiere" gegeben. Sie ist gestern in die Schweiz geflogen, hat das Geld abgehoben und dann ihre Konten gekündigt. „Ich bin noch nie so glücklich gewesen", sagte Tanja.

5 **Suggestion** Tell students to use statements with **Ich bin...**, **Ich habe..., Ich will...,** or **Ich kann...** Provide model subjunctive forms on the board: **Sie sagt, sie sei... Er sagt, er habe... Sie sagt, sie wolle... Er sagt, er könne...** Circulate and provide help as needed.

6 **Suggestion** After they swap columns, give students time to convert the verbs into indirect speech. It may be helpful to have them underline all of the verbs first. Point out that since they'll be using the 3rd person throughout their reports, the pattern will be: *verb stem* + -e.

12B.2

The passive voice  Presentation

Startblock Most sentences in German are in the *active* voice. Use the *passive* voice to put the focus on the action itself, or on the receiver of the action.

ACHTUNG

When you convert an active sentence to the passive voice, pay attention to changes in case. The direct object of the verb in an active sentence becomes the subject of the sentence in the passive voice.
Die Regierung entwickelt einen neuen Plan. ⟶ **Ein neuer Plan wird entwickelt.**

Suggestion Make sure students do not confuse passive voice constructions with the **Futur I**.

- To form a sentence using the passive voice, use a conjugated form of **werden** with the past participle of the verb that describes the action of the sentence. Sentences using the passive voice are usually in the present tense or the **Präteritum**.

In diesem Land **wird** zu viel Müll **produziert**. *Too much trash **is being produced** in this country.*	Im Jahr 2009 **wurden** 455 kg Müll pro Kopf **weggeworfen**. *In 2009, 455 kilos of trash per person **were thrown out**.*

- The subject of a passive sentence is the receiver of the action.

Wir **schalten** immer die Lichter **aus**. *We always **turn out** the lights.*	Die Lichter **werden ausgeschaltet**. *The lights **are being turned out**.*

- In a passive voice sentence, the doer of the action is often unidentified. To indicate who or what performed or is performing the action, use the preposition **von** after the conjugated form of **werden**, followed by a noun in the dative case.

Neue Hybridautos werden (**von Wissenschaftlern**) entwickelt. *New hybrid cars are being developed **(by scientists)**.*	Das Wasser wurde (**von der Fabrik**) verschmutzt. *The water was polluted **(by the factory)**.*

- In passive sentences with a modal verb, use the conjugated form of the modal and move the infinitive **werden** to the end of the sentence, after the past participle.

Ein neues Gesetz **soll vorgeschlagen werden**. *A new law **needs to be proposed**.*	Die Technologie **musste** erst **verbessert werden**. *The technology **had to be improved** first.*

- In an impersonal statement, where there is no specific subject, the sentence may begin with **es**, or with an adverb of time or place.

Es wird hier nur Deutsch gesprochen. *Only German is spoken here.*	**Gestern** wurde viel gearbeitet. *A lot of work was done **yesterday**.*

- You can often replace a statement in the passive voice with an active sentence using the indefinite pronoun **man** as the subject.

In den USA **benutzt man** zu viel Benzin. ***People*** *in the U.S.* ***use*** *too much gasoline.*	**Man soll** Energie sparen. *We **should save** energy.*

Ressourcen

SAM
WB: pp. 167–168

SAM
LM: p. 108

vhlcentral.com

Jetzt sind Sie dran! Markieren Sie, ob die folgenden Sätze aktiv oder passiv sind.

	aktiv	passiv		aktiv	passiv
1. Es muss mehr getan werden.	☐	☑	4. Heute wird mehr wiederverwertet.	☐	☑
2. Viele Tierarten sind jetzt gefährdet.	☑	☐	5. Man muss mehr Wasser sparen.	☑	☐
3. Fahrgemeinschaften sollen oft benutzt werden.	☐	☑	6. Der Müll wurde von dem Müllfahrer abgeholt (*picked up*).	☐	☑

Anwendung und Kommunikation

1 **Was fehlt?** Ergänzen Sie die Sätze mit den Passivformen der Verben in Klammern.

> **BEISPIEL** In meiner Familie ___werden___ keine Batterien in den Müll ___geworfen___. (werfen)

1. Innovative Ideen, unseren Planeten zu retten, ___werden___ dringend (*urgently*) ___gesucht___. (suchen)

2. Die Luft ___wird___ immer mehr ___verschmutzt___. (verschmutzen)

3. Stofftaschen (*Cloth bags*) statt Plastiktaschen sollen beim Einkaufen ___benutzt___ ___werden___. (benutzen)

4. Wasserreservoirs, um Trinkwasser zu speichern, müssen ___gebaut___ ___werden___. (bauen)

5. In welchem Land ___wird___ das meiste Altpapier ___recycelt___? (recyceln)

6. Die Tier- und Pflanzenwelt darf nicht ___vergessen___ ___werden___. (vergessen)

2 **Was wird hier gemacht?** Beschreiben Sie mit einem Partner / einer Partnerin, was auf den Bildern gerade passiert. Benutzen Sie die Präsensformen des Passivs. Answers will vary.

> **BEISPIEL**
> **S1:** *Hier wird Mathematik gelernt.*

1.

 2.

 3.

 4.

 5.

Bücher / verkaufen	Müll / recyceln
ein Hund / baden	Pizza / essen
Mathematik / lernen	die Umwelt / verschmutzen

3 **Lösungsvorschläge** Diskutieren Sie mit einem Partner / einer Partnerin, was (nicht) gemacht werden kann/muss/soll/darf, um unsere Umweltprobleme zu lösen. Gebrauchen Sie Modalverben im Passiv. Answers will vary.

> **BEISPIEL**
> **S1:** *Die Windenergie muss ausgebaut werden.*

ausbauen	das Kernkraftwerk / der Reaktor...
entwickeln	die Landschaft
erfinden	die Luft / das Wasser /...
finden	die Natur / die Flora / die Fauna...
recyceln	das Papier / das Glas / das Plastik / das Aluminium...
reduzieren	die Windenergie / die Solarenergie / die Kernenergie...
retten	die Wissenschaft
verbessern	

 Practice more at **vhlcentral.com.**

3 Expansion Ask students if they think people will start living in a more environmentally aware manner in the near future. Are they optimistic or pessimistic about the environment?

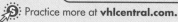

Wiederholung

1 Ein Zeitungsartikel

Identifizieren Sie mit einem Partner / einer Partnerin Beispiele indirekter Rede in dem Artikel über eine Umweltinitiative. Wechseln Sie sich dann ab und sagen Sie in indirekter Rede, was gesagt wurde. Answers will vary.

BEISPIEL

S1: Die Polizei erklärte: „Am Wochenende haben mehr als 250.000 Menschen in ganz Deutschland für den Atomausstieg demonstriert."

Zehntausende demonstrieren für raschen Atomausstieg

Das Wochenende stand im Zeichen des Atomausstiegs (*nuclear phase-out*). Die Polizei erklärte, am Wochenende hätten mehr als 250.000 Menschen in ganz Deutschland für den Atomausstieg demonstriert. Sie berichtete außerdem, Demonstrationen hätten in 20 Städten stattgefunden. Atomgegner erzählten, es habe Demonstrationen in mehr als 20 Städten gegeben. Organisatoren meinten auch, diese Demonstrationen seien größer gewesen als die vorherigen Demonstrationen. Zu dem Protest aufgerufen hatten Umweltschutzinitiativen, Gewerkschaften und Parteien. Diese Organisationen sagten, sie wollten Druck (*pressure*) auf die Politiker in Berlin machen. Sie meinten auch, es sei Zeit für eine neue Umweltpolitik. Ohne Atomkraft hätten die Kinder eine Chance auf eine sicherere Welt.

2 Arbeitsblatt

Stellen Sie den anderen im Unterricht die Fragen auf dem Arbeitsblatt, das Sie bekommen. Schreiben Sie die Antworten auf. Diskutieren Sie dann mit der Gruppe, um zu sehen, was die typischsten Antworten waren. Answers will vary.

BEISPIEL

S1: Was wäre, wenn weniger Leute Kinder bekämen?
S2: Wenn weniger Leute Kinder bekämen, hätten wir kein Problem mit Überbevölkerung.

2 Suggestion Make sure that students understand they will be practicing **Konjunktiv II** in this activity, not **Konjunktiv I**.

3 Wer hat's gesagt?

Entscheiden Sie, wer wahrscheinlich die folgenden Sätze gesagt hat. Berichten Sie, was die Personen gesagt haben. Wechseln Sie sich mit einem Partner / einer Partnerin ab. Sample answers are provided.

BEISPIEL Man hat viele Tiere aus dem Tierheim adoptiert.

S1: Die Tierärztin war froh, dass man viele Tiere aus dem Tierheim adoptiert habe.
S2: Der Biologe berichtete, dass ...

die Bankangestellte	die Psychologin
der Biologe	der Rentner
der Elektriker	die Richterin
der Koch	die Tierärztin
der LKW-Fahrer	

1. Man muss jeden Tag arbeiten, bis das Restaurant schließt.
   Der Koch sagte, man müsse jeden Tag arbeiten, bis das Restaurant schließe.
2. Viele Menschen haben Depressionen.
   Die Psychologin berichtete, viele Menschen hätten Depressionen.
3. Niemand interessiert sich für alte Menschen.
   Der Rentner meinte, niemand interessiere sich für alte Menschen.
4. Es ist ein Problem, dass Benzin immer teurer wird.
   Der LKW-Fahrer sagte, es sei ein Problem, dass Benzin immer teurer werde.
5. Es gibt immer mehr Jugendliche, die Probleme mit dem Gesetz haben.
   Die Richterin sagte, es gebe immer mehr Jugendliche, die Probleme mit dem Gesetz hätten.
6. Online-Banking wird immer beliebter.
   Die Bankangestellte berichtete, Online-Banking werde immer beliebter.

4 Gut oder schlecht?

Bitten Sie Ihren Partner / Ihre Partnerin, auf die folgenden Fotos zu reagieren. Wie erklärt Ihr Partner / Ihre Partnerin diese Reaktion? Answers will vary.

BEISPIEL

S1: Wie findest du die Insel im See?
S2: Ich finde sie schön, weil man da die frische Luft genießen kann.

1.　　　　2.　　　　3.

4.　　　　5.　　　　6.

4 Expansion Have students describe each picture in detail before giving their reactions.

5 **Wenn nur...** Machen Sie anhand der Bilder eine Liste mit fünf Dingen, die Sie während Ihrer Unikarriere gerne gemacht hätten. Lesen Sie dann in Vierergruppen Ihre Sätze vor. Answers will vary.

▶ **BEISPIEL**

S1: *Wenn ich gelernt hätte, anstatt zu spielen, hätte ich bessere Noten gehabt.*

2.

3.

4.

5.

6.

6 **In der Zukunft** Was muss man in der Zukunft machen, um der Umwelt zu helfen? Schreiben Sie in Dreiergruppen mindestens sechs Antworten auf diese Frage. Benutzen Sie das Futur I. Answers will vary.

BEISPIEL

6 Suggestion Remind students to use **werden** with an infinitive to form the **Futur I**.

S1: *In der Zukunft wird unsere Mensa das gesamte Papier und den gesamten Kunststoff recyceln.*
S2: *Ja, und es wird...*

7 **Diskutieren und kombinieren** Auf Ihrem Arbeitsblatt finden Sie Informationen über Jasmin und ihre Mutter. Überlegen Sie sich, wie Jasmins Mutter reagieren würde, wenn Jasmin das machen würde, was Sie auf den Bildern sehen können. Answers will vary.

BEISPIEL

7 Suggestion Remind students that **werden** can be used in its subjunctive form for hypotheses and contrary-to-fact situations.

S1: *Was würde passieren, wenn Jasmin mit dem Flugzeug flöge?*
S2: *Wenn Jasmin mit dem Flugzeug flöge, würde ihre Mutter sie am Flughafen anrufen.*

8 **Eine bessere Stadt** Schreiben Sie mit einem Partner / einer Partnerin eine Liste mit sechs Umwelt-problemen, die in Städten existieren. Schlagen Sie für jedes Problem eine Lösung vor. Benutzen Sie das Passiv. Answers will vary.

BEISPIEL

S1: *Zu viele Batterien werden in den Müll geworfen.*
S2: *Batterien sollen recycelt werden.*

Mein Wör | ter | buch

Schreiben Sie fünf weitere Wörter in Ihr persönliches Wörterbuch zu den Themen **In der Natur** und **Die Umwelt**.

unbehandelt

Übersetzung
untreated

Wortart
Adjektiv

Gebrauch
Bei unbehandeltem Gemüse benutzen Bauern keine Pestizide, wenn es auf dem Feld wächst.

Synonyme
biologisch, ungespritzt

Antonyme
behandelt, gespritzt

S Vocabulary tools

Panorama Interactive Map

Sachsen-Anhalt und Sachsen

Sachsen-Anhalt in Zahlen

▶ **Fläche:** *20.446 km²*

▶ **Bevölkerung:** *2,3 Millionen Menschen*

▶ **Städte:** *Halle (233.000 Einwohner), Magdeburg (231.000)*

▶ **Wichtige Industriezweige:** *Chemieindustrie, Maschinenbau, Landwirtschaft*

▶ **Touristenattraktionen:** *Lutherstadt Wittenberg; das Bauhaus, Dessau; Burg Falkenstein Für Touristen ist in Sachsen-Anhalt neben Wittenberg, wo Martin Luther seine 95 Thesen an die Tür der Schlosskirche nagelte°, auch das Bauhaus in Dessau interessant. Das Grüne Band Deutschland, wo einmal die Mauer stand, liegt zum größten Teil in Sachsen-Anhalt. Es ist jetzt Naturschutzgebiet.*

Quelle: Investitions- und Marketinggesellschaft Sachsen-Anhalt mbH

Sachsen in Zahlen

▶ **Fläche:** *18.415 km²*

▶ **Bevölkerung:** *4,1 Millionen Menschen*

▶ **Städte:** *Leipzig (532.000 Einwohner), Dresden (530.000), Chemnitz (243.000)*

▶ **Wichtige Industriezweige:** *Automobilindustrie, Mikroelektronik, Maschinenbau*

▶ **Touristenattraktionen:** *Weihnachtsmärkte im Erzgebirge, Dresden, Meißener Porzellan Dresden, das Elbflorenz, ist eine der größten Touristenattraktionen Sachsens. Touristen sollten den Zwinger, die Frauenkirche und die Semperoper besuchen.*

Quelle: Tourismus Marketing Gesellschaft Sachsen mbH

Berühmte Menschen aus Sachsen-Anhalt und Sachsen

▶ **Otto Fürst von Bismarck,** *Politiker (1815–1898)*

▶ **Erich Kästner,** *Autor (1839–1974)*

▶ **Gottfried Wilhelm Leibniz,** *Mathematiker und Wissenschaftler (1646–1716)*

▶ **Christiane Nüsslein-Volhard,** *Wissenschaftlerin (1942–)*

▶ **Katharina Witt,** *Sportlerin (1965–)*

Expansion For homework, have students research one of these famous individuals and find one piece of information about them to share with the class.

nagelte *nailed* **Kurfürst** *prince-elector* **Manufaktur** *factory* **gekreuzten Schwerter** *crossed swords*

Das Bauhaus in Dessau

Die Silhouette der Dresdener Innenstadt

Suggestion Tell students that the former no-man's land between East and West Germany remained relatively untouched for nearly 40 years and is now a protected area of rich biodiversity.

Das Grüne Band Deutschland

Landesgrenzen
● Stadt
◎ Landeshauptstadt

0 — 25 Meilen
0 — 25 Kilometer

Unglaublich, aber wahr!

Im Jahr 1708 erfanden Johann Friedrich Böttger und Walther von Tschirnhaus das europäische Porzellan. 1710 gründete der sächsische Kurfürst° August der Starke dann die Porzellan-Manufaktur° Meißen. Dieses auch heute noch weltberühmte Porzellan trägt das Symbol der gekreuzten Schwerter°.

Technologie

Solar Valley

Das Solar Valley, auch Sonnenallee bezeichnet, liegt in Sachsen-Anhalt in der Nähe der Stadt Bitterfeld-Wolfen. Es gilt als eines der Zentren der Photovoltaikindustrie. Zu den Firmen, die hier vertreten° sind, gehören Q-Cells SE, Calyxo GmbH und Sontor GmbH.

Das Solar Valley gilt als einer der größten Solarstandorte Europas und ist Symbol für das deutsche Engagement im Bereich erneuerbarer Energiequellen. Bis zu 3.000 Menschen arbeiten in diesem Industriebereich in Sachsen-Anhalt.

Völker

Die Sorben

Die Sorben, ein westslawisches Volk, leben heute in der Ober- und Niederlausitz in den Bundesländern Brandenburg und Sachsen, wo Sorbisch eine offizielle Sprache ist. Es gibt heute noch etwa 60.000 Sorben in Deutschland, wo sie als offizielle Minderheit° anerkannt° sind. Die meisten Sorben sind deutsche Staatsangehörige°. Einer der bekanntesten sorbischen Bräuche° ist das alljährliche Osterreiten. Jährlich sehen mehr als 30.000 Besucher zu, wenn rund 1.700 Reiter in Frack und Zylinder° die Botschaft von der Auferstehung Jesu Christi verkünden°.

Musik

Barockmusiker aus Sachsen-Anhalt

Johann Sebastian Bach, Georg Philipp Telemann und Georg Friedrich Händel sind weltberühmte Barockmusiker aus Sachsen-Anhalt, deren Werke man heute noch hört. Telemann, der Musik im Selbststudium lernte, komponierte mehr als 3.600 Stücke. Bach ist vor allem für seine Chorwerke und Musik für Tasteninstrumente° berühmt. Händel hatte in England mit seinen dramatischen Opern und Oratorien großen Erfolg. Trotz der Entfernung waren Telemann und Händel gut befreundet, und alle drei studierten und führten die Musik der anderen auf°.

Politik

Leipziger Montagsdemonstrationen

Im Herbst 1989 kam es in der DDR zu der Friedlichen Revolution. Die gewaltfreien° Montagsdemonstrationen in Leipzig und einigen anderen ostdeutschen Städten galten als Katalysator für die Wende° und das Ende der DDR. Nachdem sich am 4. September 1.200 Demonstranten vor der Leipziger Nikolaikirche getroffen hatten, waren es am 6. November, drei Tage vor dem Fall der Berliner Mauer, 500.000 Menschen, die Slogans wie "Wir sind das Volk" oder "Für ein offenes Land mit freien Menschen" riefen°.

🔵 IM INTERNET

1. Suchen Sie weitere Informationen über die Leipziger Montagsdemonstrationen und die Friedliche Revolution: Wann fingen diese Demonstrationen an? Wer organisierte sie?

2. Suchen Sie mehr Informationen über Bach, Telemann und Händel. Warum kommen so viele Barockmusiker aus Sachsen-Anhalt? Was für Musik haben diese drei Komponisten geschrieben?

Find out more at **vhlcentral.com**.

vertreten *represented* **gewaltfreien** *nonviolent* **Wende** *reunification* **riefen** *called* **Minderheit** *minority* **anerkannt** *recognized* **Staatsangehörige** *citizens* **Bräuche** *customs* **Frack und Zylinder** *tails and top hat* **verkünden** *announce* **Musik für Tasteninstrumente** *keyboard music* **führten... auf** *performed*

🔵 Was haben Sie gelernt? Ergänzen Sie die Sätze.

1. Im Jahr 1708 erfanden Böttger und von Tschirnhaus __europäisches__ Porzellan.

2. Gekreuzte Schwerter sind das __Symbol__ der Porzellan-Manufaktur Meißen.

3. Das Solar Valley heißt auch __Sonnenallee__.

4. Bis zu 3.000 Menschen arbeiten hier in der __Photovoltaikindustrie__.

5. Die Leipziger Montagsdemonstrationen waren Teil der Friedlichen __Revolution__ in der ehemaligen DDR.

6. 500.000 Menschen nahmen an der Demonstration am 6. November 1989 in __Leipzig__ teil.

7. Die __Sorben__ sind eine anerkannte Minderheit in Deutschland.

8. Rund 1.700 sorbische Reiter nehmen am __Osterreiten__ teil.

9. Bach komponierte Werke für Chor und für __Tasteninstrumente__.

10. Händels __Opern__ und Oratorien hatten in England großen Erfolg.

Lesen Ⓢ Audio: Reading

Vor dem Lesen

Strategien

Imagery

Poets often use vivid imagery to convey a particular sensory experience to the reader. A poet may also use specific images as symbols, to represent certain abstract themes or ideas, or as metaphors, to draw a comparison between apparently dissimilar objects or concepts. Paying close attention to the words of a poem and the images those words convey can help you to gain a deeper understanding of the poem.

Untersuchen Sie den Text

Lesen Sie einmal die beiden Gedichte. Welche Wörter und Bilder kommen in beiden Gedichten immer wieder vor?

Autoren
Rose Ausländer

Rose Ausländer (1901–1988) wurde in Czernowitz, Bukowina (damals Österreich-Ungarn) als Kind jüdischer Eltern geboren. 1921 wanderte sie nach Amerika aus, aber 1931 kam sie in ihre Heimatstadt zurück, um ihre Mutter zu pflegen (*care for*). Die Jahre von 1941 bis 1944 verbrachte sie mit ihrer Mutter und ihrem Bruder in einem Kellerversteck (*cellar hiding-place*). Nach dem Krieg wanderte sie wieder nach Amerika aus. Dort fing sie an, Gedichte auf Englisch zu schreiben. Erst im Jahre 1956 begann sie ihre Gedichte wieder auf Deutsch zu schreiben.

Rainer Maria Rilke

Rainer Maria Rilke (1875–1926) ist einer der bekanntesten Dichter (*poets*) der deutschen Sprache. Er stammte aus Prag, das damals zu Österreich-Ungarn gehörte. Neben Gedichten schrieb er Erzählungen, einen Roman und Aufsätze über Kunst und Kultur. Der Panther gilt als eines der berühmtesten Gedichte Rilkes.

Meine Nachtigall°

Rose Ausländer

—— ❧ ——

Meine Mutter war einmal ein Reh°
Die goldbraunen Augen
die Anmut°
blieben ihr aus der Rehzeit

Hier war sie
halb Engel° halb Mensch-
die Mitte° war Mutter
Als ich sie fragte was sie gern geworden wäre
sagte sie: eine Nachtigall

Jetzt ist sie eine Nachtigall
Nacht um Nacht höre ich sie
im Garten meines schlaflosen Traumes°
Sie singt das Zion der Ahnen°
sie singt das alte Österreich
sie singt die Berge und Buchenwälder°
der Bukowina
Wiegenlieder°
singt mir Nacht um Nacht
meine Nachtigall
im Garten meines schlaflosen Traumes

—— ——

Nachtigall *nightingale* **Reh** *deer* **Anmut** *grace* **Engel** *angel*
Mitte *middle* **schlaflosen Traumes** *sleepless dream* **Ahnen** *ancestors*
Buchenwälder *beech tree forests* **Wiegenlieder** *lullabies*

Suggestion Point out that Rilke omits the letter 'e' in certain words (**Vorübergehen**, **müde**) to fit the meter of the poem.

～ Der Panther ～

Rainer Maria Rilke

Im Jardin des Plantes, Paris

Sein Blick° ist vom Vorübergehn° der Stäbe°
so müd geworden, daß er nichts mehr hält°.
Ihm ist, als ob es tausend Stäbe gäbe
und hinter tausend Stäben keine Welt.

Der weiche° Gang geschmeidig° starker Schritte,
der sich im allerkleinsten Kreise° dreht,
ist wie ein Tanz von Kraft um eine Mitte,
in der betäubt° ein großer Wille steht.

Nur manchmal schiebt der Vorhang der Pupille
sich lautlos° auf. – Dann geht ein Bild hinein,
geht durch der Glieder° angespannte Stille –
und hört im Herzen auf zu sein.

Blick *gaze* **Vorübergehn** *passing by* **Stäbe** *bars*
hält *holds* **weiche** *smooth* **geschmeidig** *sleek*
allerkleinsten Kreise *smallest circles*
betäubt *numbed* **lautlos** *silently* **Glieder** *limbs*

Nach dem Lesen

 Die Nachtigall Wählen Sie die richtige Antwort auf jede Frage.

1. Was wollte die Mutter laut Ausländers Gedicht werden?
   a. Sie wollte ein Reh werden.
   b. Sie wollte eine Nachtigall werden.

2. Was hatte die Mutter noch aus der Zeit, als sie ein Reh war?
   a. Sie hatte noch goldbraune Augen und Anmut.
   b. Sie hatte noch schlaflose Träume.

3. Was für Lieder singt die Nachtigall?
   a. Sie singt Wiegenlieder.
   b. Sie singt Volkslieder.

 Der Panther Wählen Sie die richtige Antwort auf jede Frage.

1. Wo lebt der Panther?
   a. Er lebt in der freien Natur.
   b. Er lebt in Gefangenschaft.

2. Warum sieht er die Welt nicht mehr?
   a. Weil er alt und blind geworden ist.
   b. Weil sein Blick müde geworden ist.

3. Wer hat laut Rilkes Gedicht einen großen Willen?
   a. Der Panther hat einen großen Willen.
   b. Die Welt hat einen großen Willen.

 Zum Besprechen Sprechen Sie mit einem Partner / einer Partnerin über die zwei Gedichte. Was finden beide Dichter so gut an den Tieren? Was unterscheidet die Situation der Nachtigall von der des Panthers?

 Aufsatz Schreiben Sie einen Aufsatz über eins der folgenden Themen.

1. Wofür stehen die Tiere in den Gedichten? Was wollen die Autoren mit Hilfe der Tiere ausdrücken?

2. Gibt es Menschen, die wie der Panther in Rilkes Gedicht sind? Begründen Sie Ihre Meinung.

3. Welche Wörter und Verse kommen in beiden Gedichten immer wieder vor? Welche Wirkung (*effect*) hat die Wiederholung der Wörter und Verse?

4. Schreiben Sie ein Gedicht über ein Tier, das Sie besonders interessant finden.

Suggestion Reassure students that Rilke's poetry can be challenging even for native speakers, and they should not worry if they don't understand all of it.

Hören

Strategien

Taking notes

Jotting down notes while you listen can help you keep track of the important points of a speech or oral presentation. It will help you to focus actively on comprehension rather than on remembering what you heard.

 To practice this strategy, listen as Katrin Schneider describes her recent vacation. Jot down notes about the main points you hear. Suggested answers are provided.

Urlaub auf einem Bauernhof; biologisches Obst und Gemüse; in Wäldern gewandert; Picknicks an romantischen Bergseen

Vorbereitung

Sehen Sie sich das Foto an: Wer sind diese Leute? Was machen sie? Warum protestieren sie? Was sagen sie vielleicht?

Zuhören

Hören Sie dem Organisator zu, der mit den Demonstranten spricht, und nennen Sie die Themen, über die er spricht.

1. ____ Recycling
2. _X_ Abfall
3. _X_ Sonnenenergie
4. ____ Überbevölkerung
5. ____ Gesetz
6. _X_ Windenergie
7. _X_ Umwelt
8. ____ Waldsterben
9. _X_ Kernenergie
10. _X_ erneuerbare Energie
11. ____ Erderwärmung
12. _X_ Giftmüll

Suggestion For the first round of listening, have students keep their books closed and jot down as many words as they can catch. Ask them to share their lists and make a projection about the purpose of the speech.

 Practice more at **vhlcentral.com.**

Verständnis

 Ergänzen Sie die Sätze mit der richtigen Antwort.

1. Die Demonstration ist gegen __die Kernkraft__.
   a. die Sonnenenergie
   b. die Kernkraft
   c. die Windenergie

2. Die Demonstration findet in __Berlin__ statt.
   a. Sachsen
   b. Berlin
   c. Schleswig-Holstein

3. Es sind __30.000__ Menschen bei der Demonstration.
   a. 13.000
   b. 30.000
   c. 3.000

4. Windenergie wird vor allem in __Schleswig-Holstein__ produziert.
   a. Sachsen
   b. Berlin
   c. Schleswig-Holstein

5. Die Technologie für Sonnenenergie wird in __Sachsen__ entwickelt.
   a. Sachsen
   b. Berlin
   c. Schleswig-Holstein

Expansion Ask students to identify the rhetorical devices that they hear such as repetition of words, phrases, and structures, rhetorical questions, etc.

Suggestion Tell students that **Atomenergie** and **Solarenergie** are frequently used as synonyms for **Kernenergie** and **Sonnenenergie**, respectively.

Neue Gesetze Ein Repräsentant einer internationalen Umweltorganisation besucht Ihre Universität, um Umweltprobleme und Umweltschutz zu diskutieren. Wählen Sie in kleinen Gruppen ein Umweltproblem aus, das heute sehr wichtig ist. Versuchen Sie den Repräsentanten zu überzeugen, dass Regierungen und Politiker mehr auf diesem Gebiet machen sollten. Sie müssen das Problem erklären können. Was muss sich ändern, damit es besser wird? Überlegen Sie sich auch neue Gesetze, die Sie dem Repräsentanten vorschlagen wollen.

Schreiben

Strategien

Considering audience and purpose

Before you begin a piece of writing, you must determine to whom you are addressing the piece and what you want to express to your reader. Once you have defined both your audience and your purpose, you will be able to decide which genre, vocabulary, and grammatical structures will best serve your composition.

Suppose you want to share your thoughts on local traffic problems. Your audience might be either the local government or the community. You could choose to write a newspaper article, a letter to the editor, or a letter to the city's governing board. You should first decide the focus of your piece:

1. Are there specific problems you want to highlight?

2. Is your goal to register a complaint or to increase public awareness?

3. Are you trying to persuade others to adopt your point of view?

4. Are you hoping to inspire others to take concrete actions?

The answers to these questions will help you establish the purpose of your writing and determine your audience. Of course, your writing may have more than one purpose. For example, you may intend both to inform others of a problem and to inspire them to take action.

Whatever the topic you choose, defining your purpose and your audience before you begin will help to make your writing more focused and effective.

Thema

Schreiben Sie einen Brief oder einen Bericht

Schreiben Sie über ein Umweltproblem, das Ihrer Meinung nach (*in your opinion*) sehr wichtig ist. Beantworten Sie die folgenden Fragen.

1. Wählen Sie zuerst ein Problem, über das Sie schreiben wollen. Ist es ein Problem vor Ort (z. B., Recycling auf dem Campus) oder ein Problem auf globaler Ebene (z. B. die Überbevölkerung)?

2. Wer sind die Leser Ihres Briefs/Berichts: Schreiben Sie einen Brief an einen Freund? Schreiben Sie einen Brief an einen Politiker? An eine Studentengruppe der Universität? Schreiben Sie einen Bericht oder einen Artikel für eine Zeitung oder eine Zeitschrift?

3. Nennen Sie den Grund für den Brief oder den Bericht: Informieren Sie die Leser oder wollen Sie auch Ihre Meinung sagen?

4. Schreiben Sie eine kurze Einleitung (*introduction*). Stellen Sie das Problem, das Sie ausgewählt haben, hier vor.

5. Wenn Sie Ihre Meinung sagen wollen, müssen Sie gute Gründe für ihre Position angeben, damit man Ihnen glaubt.

6. Schreiben Sie eine Schlussfolgerung (*conclusion*) für den Brief oder Bericht.

Expansion Before leaving the topic of the environment, ask students for their closing thoughts: **Wie sieht die Zukunft unseres Planeten aus? Möchten Sie versuchen, umweltfreundlicher zu leben? Warum, warum nicht? Wie? Kann der Einzelne was bewirken?**

Suggestion Remind students of the techniques introduced in earlier chapters for organizing their ideas, such as idea-maps and note cards, as well as linking words such as adverbs and conjunctions for creating logical connections and emphasis.

 **Vocabulary Tools**

die Natur

der Bauernhof, ⸚e	farm
der Baum, ⸚e	tree
der Berg -e	mountain
das Blatt, ⸚er	leaf
der Busch, ⸚e	bush
das Feld, -er	field
der Fluss, ⸚e	river
das Gras , ⸚er	grass
der Himmel	sky
die Insel, -n	island
die Klippe, -n	cliff
die Küste, -n	coast
die Landschaft, -en	countryside
die Luft	air
das Meer, -e	sea
der Mond, -e	moon
der See, -n	lake
die Sonne, -n	sun
der Sonnenaufgang, ⸚e	sunrise
der Sonnenuntergang, ⸚e	sunset
der Stein, -e	rock
der Stern -e	star
das Tal, ⸚er	valley
der Wald, ⸚er	forest
der Wasserfall, ⸚e	waterfall
der Weg, -e	path
aufregend	exciting
bedeutend	important
nass	wet
trocken	dry

Tiere

das Eichhörnchen, -	squirrel
der Fisch, -e	fish
der Hase, -n	hare
das Huhn, ⸚er	chicken
die Kuh, ⸚e	cow
die Maus, ⸚e	mouse
das Pferd, -e	horse
das Schaf, -e	sheep
die Schlange, -n	snake

Verben

aufgehen (geht... auf)	to rise
erforschen	to explore
untergehen (geht... unter)	to set
wandern	to hike
ein Picknick (*n.*) machen	to have a picnic

die Umwelt

die Art, -en	species
die Erde, -n	earth
die Fabrik, -en	factory
die Gefahr, -en	danger
das Hochwasser, -	flood
das Licht, -er	light
der Müll	waste
der Müllwagen, -	garbage truck
die Ökologie	ecology
der Umweltschutz	environmentalism
die Welt, -en	world
biologisch	organic
gefährdet	endangered
ökologisch	ecological
umweltfreundlich	environmentally friendly

Energie

die Kernenergie	nuclear energy
das Kernkraftwerk, -e	nuclear power plant
die Sonnenenergie	solar energy
die Windenergie	wind energy

Probleme

das Aussterben	extinction
die Erderwärmung	global warming
der Giftmüll	toxic waste
der saure Regen	acid rain
die Überbevölkerung	overpopulation
die Verschmutzung	pollution

Lösungen

das Gesetz, -e	law
die erneuerbare Energie (*pl.* die erneuerbaren Energien)	renewable energy
die Fahrgemeinschaft, -en	carpool
das Hybridauto, -s	hybrid car
das Recycling	recycling
die Regierung, -en	government

Verben

ausschalten (schaltet... aus)	to turn off
(den Planeten) retten	to save (the planet)
einschalten (schaltet... ein)	to turn on
entwickeln	to develop
erhalten (erhält)	to preserve
recyceln	to recycle
schützen	to protect
verbessern	to improve
verschmutzen	to pollute
vorschlagen (schlägt... vor)	to propose
wegwerfen (wirft... weg)	to throw away

Der Konjunktiv der Vergangenheit	See pp. 506–507.
Das Partizip Präsens	See p. 510.
Der Konjunktiv I	See pp. 524–525.
The passive voice	See p. 528.

Ressourcen

vhlcentral.com

Appendix A

Appendix B

Appendix C

Glossary of Grammatical Terms

ADJECTIVE Words that describe people, places, or things. An attributive adjective comes before the noun it modifies and takes an ending that matches the gender and case of the noun. A predicate adjective comes after the verb **sein**, **werden**, or **bleiben** and describes the noun that is the subject of the sentence. Predicate adjectives take no additional endings.

Thomas hat eine sehr **gute** Stelle gefunden.
*Thomas found a really **good** job.*

Hast du mein **kleines** Adressbuch gesehen?
*Have you seen my **little** address book?*

Mein Bruder ist **klein**.
*My brother is **short**.*

Deine Schwester wird **groß**.
*Your sister is getting **tall**.*

Possessive adjectives Words that are placed before a noun to indicate ownership or belonging. Each personal pronoun has a corresponding possessive adjective. Possessive adjectives take the same endings as the indefinite article **ein**.

Meine Schwester ist hier.
***My** sister is here.*

Wo ist **dein** Vater?
*Where is **your** father?*

ADVERB Words or phrases that modify a verb, an adjective, or another adverb. Adverbs and adverbial phrases describe *when*, *how*, or *where* an action takes place.

Der Kuchen ist **fast** fertig.
*The cake is **almost** ready.*

Du isst **viel zu** schnell.
*You eat **much too** quickly.*

ARTICLE A word that precedes a noun and indicates its gender, number, and case.

Definite article Equivalent to *the* in English. Its form indicates the gender and case of the noun, and whether it is singular or plural.

der Tisch (*m. s.*)
the table
die Tische (*m. pl.*)
the tables
die Tür (*f. s.*)
the door

die Türen (*f. pl.*)
the doors
das Fenster (*n. s.*)
the window
die Fenster (*n. pl.*)
the windows

Indefinite article Corresponds to *a* or *an* in English. It precedes the noun and matches its gender and case. There is no plural indefinite article in German.

ein Tisch (*m.*)
a table
eine Tür (*f.*)
a door

ein Fenster (*n.*)
a window

CASE There are four cases in German. The case indicates the function of each noun in a sentence. The case of a noun determines the form of the definite or indefinite article that precedes the noun, the form of any adjectives that modify the noun, and the form of the pronoun that can replace the noun.

Nominativ (*nominative*): **Der Professor** ist alt.
***The professor** is old.*

Akkusativ (*accusative*): Ich verstehe **den Professor**.
*I understand **the professor**.*

Dativ (*dative*): Der Assistent zeigt **dem Professor** den neuen Computer.
*The assistant is showing **the professor** the new computer.*

Genitiv (*genitive*): Das ist der Assistent **des Professors**.
*This is **the professor's** assistant.*

The nominative case The grammatical subject of a sentence is always in the nominative case. The nominative case is also used for nouns that follow a form of **sein**, **werden**, or **bleiben**. In German dictionaries, nouns, pronouns, and numbers are always listed in their nominative form.

Das ist **eine gute Idee**.
*That's **a good idea**.*

Die Kinder schlafen.
***The kids** are sleeping.*

The accusative case A noun that functions as a direct object is in the accusative case.

Der Lehrer hat **den Stift**.
*The teacher has **the pen**.*

Sie öffnet **die Tür**.
*She's opening **the door**.*

Ich kaufe **einen Tisch**.
*I'm going to buy **a table**.*

Ich habe **ein Problem**.
*I have **a problem**.*

The dative case An object in the dative case indicates to whom or for whom an action is performed.

Ich bringe **dem Lehrer** einen Apfel.
*I'm bringing **the teacher** an apple.*

Zeig **der Professorin** deine Arbeit.
*Show your work **to the professor**.*

The genitive case A noun in the genitive case modifies another noun. The genitive case indicates ownership or a close relationship between the genitive noun and the noun it modifies, which may be a subject or an object.

Thorsten hat die Rede **des Bundespräsidenten** heruntergeladen.
*Thorsten downloaded **the president's** speech.*

Das Mikrofon **der Professorin** funktioniert nicht.
***The professor's** microphone doesn't work.*

CLAUSE A group of words that contains both a conjugated verb and a subject, either expressed or implied.

Main (or independent) clause A clause that can stand alone as a complete sentence.

Ich bezahle immer bar, weil ich keine Kreditkarte habe.
I always pay cash, because I don't have a credit card.

Subordinate clause A subordinate clause explains how, when, why, or under what circumstances the action in the main clause occurs. The conjugated verb of a subordinate clause is placed at the end of that clause.

Ich lese die Zeitung, **wenn** ich Zeit **habe.**
*I read the newspaper **when** I **have** the time.*

COMPARATIVE The form of an adjective or adverb that compares two or more people or things.

Meine Geschwister sind alle **älter** als ich.
*My siblings are all **older** than I am.*

Die Fahrt dauert mit dem Auto **länger** als mit dem Zug.
*The trip takes **longer** by car than by train.*

CONJUNCTION A word used to connect words, clauses, or phrases.

Coordinating conjunctions Words that combine two related sentences, words, or phrases into a single sentence. There are five coordinating conjunctions in German: **aber** (*but*), **denn** (*because; since*), **oder** (*or*), **sondern** (*but, rather*), **und** (*and*). All other conjunctions are subordinating.

Ich möchte eine große Küche, **denn** ich koche gern.
*I want a big kitchen, **because** I like to cook.*

Lola braucht einen Schrank **oder** eine Kommode.
*Lola needs a closet **or** a dresser.*

Subordinating conjunctions Words used to combine a subordinate clause with a main clause.

Ich lese die Zeitung, **wenn** ich Zeit **habe.**
*I read the newspaper **when** I **have** the time.*

DEMONSTRATIVE Pronouns or adjectives that refer to something or someone that has already been mentioned, or that point out a specific person or thing.

Ist Greta online? –Ja, **die** schreibt eine E-Mail.
*Is Greta online? –Yes, **she's** writing an e-mail.*

Gefällt dir dieser Sessel? –Ja, **der** ist sehr bequem!
*Do you like that chair? –Yes, **it's** very comfortable!*

DER-WORDS Words that take the same endings as the forms of the definite article **der**. These include the demonstrative pronouns **dieser** (*this; that*), **jeder** (*each, every*), **jener** (*that*), **mancher** (*some*), and **solcher** (*such*), and the question word **welcher** (*which*).

Welcher Laptop gefällt dir am besten?
***Which** laptop do you like best?*

Ich finde **diesen** Laptop am schönsten.
*I think **this** laptop is the nicest.*

DIRECT OBJECT A noun or pronoun that directly receives the action of the verb. Direct objects are in the accusative.

Kennst du **diesen Mann**?   Ich mache **eine Torte.**
*Do you know **that man**?   I'm making **a cake**.*

EIN-WORDS Words that take the same endings as the forms of the indefinite article **ein**. These include the negation **kein** and all of the possessive adjectives.

Hast du **einen** Hund?   Ich habe **keinen** Fußball.
*Do you have **a** dog?   I don't have **a** soccer ball.*

GENDER The grammatical categorization of nouns, pronouns, and adjectives as masculine, feminine, or neuter.

Masculine
articles: **der, ein**
pronouns: **er, der**
adjectives: **guter, schöner**

Feminine
articles: **die, eine**
pronouns: **sie, die**
adjectives: **gute, schöne**

Neuter
articles: **das, ein**
pronouns: **es, das**
adjectives: **gutes, schönes**

HELPING VERB *See VERB, Auxiliary verb.*

IMPERATIVE Imperatives are verb forms used to express commands, requests, suggestions, directions, or instructions.

Mach deine Hausaufgaben!   **Backen wir** einen Kuchen!
***Do** your homework!   **Let's bake** a cake!*

INDIRECT OBJECT A noun or pronoun that receives the action of the verb indirectly. The indirect object is often a person to whom or for whom the action of the sentence is performed. Indirect objects are in the dative case.

Manfred hat **seinem Bruder** ein Buch geschenkt.
*Manfred gave **his brother** a book.*

INFINITIVE The basic, unconjugated form of a verb. Most German infinitives end in **-en**. A few end in **-ern** or **-eln**.

sehen, essen, lesen, wandern, sammeln
to see, to eat, to read, to hike, to collect

NOUN A word that refers to one or more people, animals, places, things, or ideas. Nouns in German may be masculine, feminine, or neuter, and are either singular or plural.

der **Junge**, die **Katze**, das **Café**
the boy, the cat, the café

Compound noun Two or more simple nouns can be combined to form a compound noun. The gender of a compound noun matches the gender of the last noun in the compound.

die Nacht + das Hemd = **das Nachthemd**
night + shirt = nightshirt

NUMBER A grammatical term that refers to the quantity of a noun. Nouns in German are either singular or plural. The plural form of a noun may have an added umlaut and/or an added ending. Adjectives, articles, and verbs also have different endings, depending on whether they are singular or plural.

Singular:
der **Mann**, die **Frau**, das **Kind**
the man, the woman, the child

Plural:
die **Männer**, die **Frauen**, die **Kinder**
the men, the women, the children

NUMBERS Words that represent quantities.

Cardinal numbers Numbers that indicate specific quantities. Cardinal numbers typically modify nouns, but do not add gender or case endings.

zwei Männer, **fünfzehn** Frauen, **sechzig** Kinder
two men, fifteen women, sixty children

Ordinal numbers Words that indicate the order of a noun in a series. Ordinal numbers add the same gender and case endings as adjectives.

der **erste** Mann, die **zweite** Frau, das **dritte** Kind
the first man, the second woman, the third child

PARTICIPLE A participle is formed from a verb but may be used as an adjective or adverb. Present participles are used primarily in written German. Past participles are used in compound tenses, including the **Perfekt** and the **Plusquamperfekt**.

Der **aufgehende** Mond war sehr schön.
The rising moon was beautiful.

Habt ihr schon **gegessen**?
Have you already eaten?

PREPOSITION A preposition links a noun or pronoun to other words in a sentence. Combined with a noun or pronoun, it forms a prepositional phrase, which can be used like an adverb to answer the question *when, how,* or *where*. In German, certain prepositions are always followed by a noun in the accusative case, while others are always followed by a noun in the dative case. A small number of prepositions are used with the genitive case.

ohne das Buch   **mit** dem Auto
without the book   *by car*

trotz des Regens
in spite of the rain

Two-way prepositions can be followed by either the dative or the accusative, depending on the situation. They are followed by the accusative when used with a verb that indicates movement toward a destination. With all other verbs, they are followed by the dative.

Stell deine Schuhe nicht **auf den Tisch**!
Don't put your shoes on the table!

Dein Schal liegt **auf dem Tisch**.
Your scarf is lying on the table.

PRONOUN A word that takes the place of a noun.

Subject pronouns Words used to replace a noun in the nominative case.

Maria ist nett.   **Der Junge** ist groß.
Maria is nice.   *The boy is tall.*

Sie ist nett.   **Er** ist groß.
She is nice.   *He is tall.*

Accusative pronouns Words used to replace a noun that functions as the direct object.

Wer hat **die Torte** gebacken?   Ich habe **sie** gebacken.
Who baked the cake?   *I baked it.*

Dative pronouns Words used to replace a noun that functions as the indirect object.

Musst du **deiner Oma** eine E-Mail schicken?
Do you need to send an e-mail to your grandma?

Nein, ich habe **ihr** schon geschrieben.
No, I already wrote to her.

Indefinite pronouns Words that refer to an unknown or nonspecific person or thing.

Jemand hat seinen Personalausweis vergessen.
Someone forgot his I.D. card.

Herr Klein will mit **niemandem** sprechen.
Mr. Klein doesn't want to speak with anyone.

Reflexive pronouns The pronouns used with reflexive verbs. When the subject of a reflexive verb is also its direct object, it takes an accusative reflexive pronoun. When the subject of a reflexive verb is not its direct object, it takes a dative reflexive pronoun.

Ich wasche **mich**.	Ich wasche **mir** das Gesicht.
I'm washing (myself).	*I'm washing my face.*

SUBJUNCTIVE A verb form (**der Konjunktiv II**) used to talk about hypothetical, unlikely or impossible conditions, to express wishes, and to make polite requests. German also has an additional subjunctive tense, der **Konjunktiv I**, used to report what someone else has said without indicating whether the information is true or false.

Ich **hätte** gern viel Geld.
I'd like to have a lot of money.

Wenn er sportlicher **wäre**, **würde** er häufiger trainieren.
If he were more athletic, he would exercise more.

SUPERLATIVE The form of an adjective or adverb used to indicate that a person or thing has more of a particular quality than anyone or anything else.

Welches ist **das größte** Tier der Welt?
What's the biggest animal in the world?

Wie komme ich **am besten** zur Tankstelle?
What's the best way to get to the gas station?

TENSE A set of verb forms that indicates if an action or state occurs in the past, present, or future.

Compound tense A tense made up of an auxiliary verb and a participle or infinitive.

Wir **haben** ihren Geburtstag **gefeiert**.
We celebrated her birthday.

VERB A word that expresses actions or states of being. German verbs are classified as *weak, mixed,* or *strong,* based on the way their past participles are formed.

weak: Ich **habe** eine Torte **gemacht**.	strong: Wir **haben** Kekse **gegessen**.
I made a cake.	*We ate cookies.*

mixed: Er **hat** eine CD **gebrannt**.
He burned a CD.

Auxiliary verb A conjugated verb used with the participle or infinitive of another verb. The auxiliary verbs **haben** and **sein** are used with past participles to form compound tenses including the **Perfekt** and **Plusquamperfekt**. **Werden** is used with an infinitive to form the future tense, and with a past participle to form a passive construction. Modals are also frequently used as auxiliary verbs.

Habt ihr den Tisch **gedeckt**?
Did you set the table?

Jasmin **war** noch nie nach Zürich **gefahren**.
Jasmin had never been to Zurich.

Wir **werden** uns in einer Woche wieder **treffen**.
We'll meet again in one week.

Es **wird** hier nur Deutsch **gesprochen**.
Only German is spoken here.

Modal verbs Verbs that modify the meaning of another verb. Modals express an attitude toward an action, such as permission, obligation, ability, desire, or necessity.

Ich **muss** Französisch **lernen**.	Ich **will** Französisch **lernen**.
I have to study French.	*I want to learn French.*

Principal parts German verbs are usually listed in dictionaries by their *principal parts* (**Stammformen**): the infinitive, the third-person singular present tense form (if the verb is irregular in the present), the third-person singular **Präteritum** form, and the past participle. Knowing the principal parts of a verb allows you to produce all of its conjugations in any tense.

geben (gibt)	**gab**	**gegeben**
to give (gives)	*gave*	*given*

Reflexive verbs Verbs that indicate an action you do to yourself or for yourself. The subject of a reflexive verb is also its object.

Ich **fühle mich** nicht **wohl**.	Wir **haben uns entspannt**.
I don't feel well.	*We've been relaxing.*

Reciprocal reflexive verbs Verbs that express an action done by two or more people or things to or for one another.

Wir rufen **uns** jeden Tag an.	**Meine Großeltern** lieben **sich** sehr.
We call each other every day.	*My grandparents love each other very much.*

Declension of articles

definite articles				
	masculine	**feminine**	**neuter**	**plural**
nominative	der	die	das	die
accusative	den	die	das	die
dative	dem	der	dem	den
genitive	des	der	des	der

der-words				
	masculine	**feminine**	**neuter**	**plural**
nominative	dieser	diese	dieses	diese
accusative	diesen	diese	dieses	diese
dative	diesem	dieser	diesem	diesen
genitive	dieses	dieser	dieses	dieser

indefinite articles				
	masculine	**feminine**	**neuter**	**plural**
nominative	ein	eine	ein	-
accusative	einen	eine	ein	-
dative	einem	einer	einem	-
genitive	eines	einer	eines	-

ein-words				
	masculine	**feminine**	**neuter**	**plural**
nominative	mein	meine	mein	meine
accusative	meinen	meine	mein	meine
dative	meinem	meiner	meinem	meinen
genitive	meines	meiner	meines	meiner

Declension of nouns and adjectives

nouns and adjectives with *der*-words			
	masculine	**feminine**	**neuter**	**plural**
nominative	der gute Rat	die gute Landschaft	das gute Brot	die guten Freunde
accusative	den guten Rat	die gute Landschaft	das gute Brot	die guten Freunde
dative	dem guten Rat	der guten Landschaft	dem guten Brot	den guten Freunden
genitive	des guten Rates	der guten Landschaft	des guten Brotes	der guten Freunde

nouns and adjectives with *ein*-words			
	masculine	**feminine**	**neuter**	**plural**
nominative	ein guter Rat	eine gute Landschaft	ein gutes Brot	meine guten Freunde
accusative	einen guten Rat	eine gute Landschaft	ein gutes Brot	meine guten Freunde
dative	einem guten Rat	einer guten Landschaft	einem guten Brot	meinen guten Freunden
genitive	eines guten Rates	einer guten Landschaft	eines guten Brotes	meiner guten Freunde

unpreceded adjectives			
	masculine	**feminine**	**neuter**	**plural**
nominative	guter Rat	gute Landschaft	gutes Brot	gute Freunde
accusative	guten Rat	gute Landschaft	gutes Brot	gute Freunde
dative	gutem Rat	guter Landschaft	gutem Brot	guten Freunden
genitive	guten Rates	guter Landschaft	guten Brotes	guter Freunde

Declension of pronouns

personal pronouns									
nominative	ich	du	Sie	er	sie	es	wir	ihr	Sie	sie
accusative	mich	dich	Sie	ihn	sie	es	uns	euch	Sie	sie
accusative reflexive	mich	dich	sich	sich	sich	sich	uns	euch	sich	sich
dative	mir	dir	Ihnen	ihm	ihr	ihm	uns	euch	Ihnen	ihnen
dative reflexive	mir	dir	sich	sich	sich	sich	uns	euch	sich	sich

Verb conjugation tables

Here are the infinitives of all verbs introduced as active vocabulary in **SAG MAL**. Each verb is followed by a model verb that follows the same conjugation pattern. The number in parentheses indicates where in the verb tables, pages **A10–19**, you can find the conjugated forms of the model verb. The word (*sein*) after a verb means that it is conjugated with **sein** in the **Perfekt** and **Plusquamperfekt**. For irregular reflexive verbs, the list may point to a non-reflexive model verb. A full conjugation of the simple forms of a reflexive verb is presented in Verb table 6 on page **A11**. Verbs followed by an asterisk (*) have a separable prefix.

abbiegen* (*sein*) like schieben (42)	**beschreiben** like bleiben (20)	**(sich) erkälten** like arbeiten (1)	**joggen** (*sein*) like machen (3)
abbrechen* like sprechen (47)	**besprechen** like sprechen (47)	**erkennen** like rennen (17)	**(sich) kämmen** like machen (3)
abfahren* (*sein*) like tragen (51)	**bestehen** like stehen (48)	**erklären** like machen (3)	**kaufen** like machen (3)
abfliegen* (*sein*) like schieben (42)	**bestellen** like machen (3)	**erzählen** like machen (3)	**kennen** like rennen (17)
abheben* like heben (29)	**besuchen** like machen (3)	**essen** (21)	**klettern** (*sein*) like fordern (26)
abschicken* like machen (3)	**(sich) bewegen** like heben (29)	**fahren** (*sein*) like tragen (51)	**klingeln** like sammeln (5)
abstauben* like machen (3)	**(sich) bewerben** like helfen (31)	**fallen** (*sein*) (22)	**kochen** like machen (3)
(sich) abtrocknen* like arbeiten (1)	**bezahlen** like machen (3)	**fangen** (23)	**kommen** (*sein*) (32)
adoptieren like probieren (4)	**bieten** like schieben (42)	**(sich) färben** like machen (3)	**können** (11)
anbieten* like schieben (42)	**bleiben** (*sein*) (20)	**faulenzen** like machen (3)	**korrigieren** like probieren (4)
anfangen* like fangen (23)	**braten** like schlafen (43)	**fegen** like machen (3)	**kosten** like arbeiten (1)
angeln like sammeln (5)	**brauchen** like machen (3)	**feiern** (2)	**küssen** like machen (3)
ankommen* (*sein*) like kommen (32)	**brechen** like sprechen (47)	**fernsehen*** like geben (27)	**lächeln** like sammeln (5)
anmachen* like machen (3)	**brennen** like rennen (17)	**finden** like trinken (52)	**lachen** like machen (3)
anrufen* like rufen (40)	**bringen** like denken (16)	**fliegen** (*sein*) like schieben (42)	**laden** like tragen (51)
anschauen* like machen (3)	**buchen** like machen (3)	**folgen** (*sein*) like machen (3)	**landen** (*sein*) like arbeiten (1)
anstoßen* like stoßen (50)	**büffeln** like sammeln (5)	**(sich) fragen** like machen (3)	**lassen** like fallen (22)
antworten like arbeiten (1)	**bügeln** like sammeln (5)	**(sich) freuen** (6)	**laufen** (*sein*) (33)
(sich) anziehen* like schieben (42)	**bürsten** like arbeiten (1)	**(sich) fühlen** like sich freuen (6)	**leben** like machen (3)
arbeiten (1)	**danken** like machen (3)	**füllen** like machen (3)	**legen** like machen (3)
(sich) ärgern like fordern (26)	**decken** like machen (3)	**funktionieren** like probieren (4)	**leiten** like arbeiten (1)
aufgehen* (*sein*) like gehen (28)	**denken** like denken (16)	**geben** (27)	**lernen** like machen (3)
auflegen* like machen (3)	**drücken** like machen (3)	**gefallen** like fallen (22)	**lesen** (34)
aufmachen* like machen (3)	**drucken** like machen (3)	**gehen** (*sein*) (28)	**lieben** like machen (3)
aufnehmen* like nehmen (38)	**durchfallen*** (*sein*) like fallen (22)	**gehören** like machen (3)	**liegen** (35)
aufräumen* like machen (3)	**durchmachen*** like machen (3)	**genießen** like fließen (25)	**löschen** like tragen (51)
aufstehen* (*sein*) like stehen (48)	**dürfen** (10)	**gewinnen** like schwimmen (44)	**lügen** (36)
aufwachen* (*sein*) like machen (3)	**(sich) duschen** like sich freuen (6)	**(sich) gewöhnen** like sich freuen (6)	**machen** (3)
ausfüllen like machen (3)	**einkaufen*** like machen (3)	**glauben** like machen (3)	**meinen** like machen (3)
ausgehen like gehen (28)	**einladen*** like tragen (51)	**gratulieren** like probieren (4)	**mieten** like arbeiten (1)
ausmachen like machen (3)	**einschlafen*** (*sein*) like schlafen (43)	**grüßen** like machen (3)	**mitbringen*** like denken (16)
(sich) ausruhen like sich freuen (6)	**einzahlen*** like machen (3)	**haben** like haben (7)	**mitkommen*** (*sein*) like kommen (32)
ausschalten* like arbeiten (1)	**empfehlen** like stehlen (49)	**handeln** like sammeln (5)	**mitmachen*** like machen (3)
(sich) ausziehen* like schieben (42)	**entdecken** like machen (3)	**hängen** like machen (3)	**mitnehmen*** like nehmen (38)
backen like mahlen (37)	**entfernen** like machen (3)	**heiraten** like arbeiten (1)	**mögen** (12)
(sich) baden like arbeiten (1)	**entgegennehmen*** like nehmen (38)	**heißen** (30)	**müssen** (13)
bauen like machen (3)	**entlassen** like fallen (22)	**helfen** (31)	**nachmachen*** like machen (3)
beantworten like arbeiten (1)	**(sich) entschließen** like fließen (25)	**heruntergehen*** (*sein*) like gehen (28)	**nehmen** (38)
bedeuten like arbeiten (1)	**(sich) entschuldigen** like machen (3)	**herunterladen*** like tragen (51)	**(sich) nennen** like rennen (17)
bedienen like machen (3)	**(sich) entspannen** like sich freuen (6)	**(sich) hinlegen*** like machen (3)	**niesen** like machen (3)
(sich) beeilen like sich freuen (6)	**entwerten** like arbeiten (1)	**(sich) hinsetzen*** like machen (3)	**öffnen** like arbeiten (1)
beginnen like schwimmen (44)	**entwickeln** like sammeln (5)	**hinterlassen** like fallen (22)	**packen** like machen (3)
behaupten like arbeiten (1)	**erfinden** like trinken (52)	**hochgehen*** (*sein*) like gehen (28)	**parken** like machen (3)
bekommen like kommen (32)	**erforschen** like machen (3)	**hören** like machen (3)	**passen** like machen (3)
belegen like machen (3)	**ergänzen** like machen (3)	**husten** like arbeiten (1)	**passieren** (*sein*) like probieren (4)
benutzen like machen (3)	**erhalten** like fallen (22)	**(sich) informieren** like probieren (4)	**probieren** (4)
berichten like arbeiten (1)	**(sich) erinnern** like fordern (26)	**(sich) interessieren** like probieren (4)	**putzen** like machen (3)

(sich) rasieren like probieren (4)
rauchen like machen (3)
recyceln like sammeln (5)
reden like arbeiten (1)
regnen like arbeiten (1)
reisen (*sein*) like machen (3)
reiten (*sein*) like pfeifen (39)
rennen (*sein*) (17)
reparieren like probieren (4)
retten like arbeiten (1)
sagen like machen (3)
schauen like machen (3)
scheitern (*sein*) like fordern (26)
schenken like machen (3)
schicken like machen (3)
schlafen (43)
schmecken like machen (3)
(sich) schminken like machen (3)
schneien like machen (3)
schreiben like bleiben (20)
schützen like machen (3)
schwänzen like machen (3)
schwimmen (*sein*) (44)
sehen like lesen (34)
sein (*sein*) (8)
(sich) setzen like machen (3)
singen like trinken (52)
sitzen (46)

sollen (14)
sortieren like probieren (4)
spazieren (*sein*) like probieren (4)
speichern like fordern (26)
spielen like machen (3)
sprechen (47)
springen (*sein*) like trinken (52)
spülen like machen (3)
starten (*sein*) like arbeiten (1)
staubsaugen like saugen (41)
stehen (48)
stehlen (49)
steigen (*sein*) like bleiben (20)
stellen like machen (3)
sterben (*sein*) like helfen (31)
(sich) streiten like pfeifen (39)
studieren like probieren (4)
suchen like machen (3)
surfen (*sein*) like machen (3)
tanken like machen (3)
tanzen like machen (3)
tragen (51)
träumen like machen (3)
(sich) treffen (*sein*) like sprechen (47)
treiben (*sein*) like bleiben (20)
(sich) trennen like sich freuen (6)
trinken (52)
tun (53)

üben like machen (3)
(sich) überlegen like machen (3)
übernachten like arbeiten (1)
überqueren like machen (3)
überraschen like machen (3)
umtauschen* like machen (3)
(sich) umziehen* (*sein*) like schieben (42)
untergehen* (*sein*) like gehen (28)
(sich) unterhalten* like fallen (22)
unterschreiben like bleiben (20)
(sich) verbessern like fordern (26)
verbringen like denken (16)
verdienen like machen (3)
vereinbaren like machen (3)
vergessen like essen (21)
verkaufen like machen (3)
verkünden like arbeiten (1)
(sich) verlaufen like laufen (33)
(sich) verletzen like machen (3)
(sich) verlieben like machen (3)
verlieren like schieben (42)
verschmutzen (*sein*) like machen (3)
(sich) verspäten like sich freuen (6)
(sich) verstauchen like machen (3)
verstehen like stehen (48)
versuchen like machen (3)
(sich) vorbereiten* like arbeiten (1)

vormachen* like machen (3)
vorschlagen* like tragen (51)
(sich) vorstellen* like machen (3)
wachsen (*sein*) like waschen (54)
wandern (*sein*) like fordern (26)
warten like arbeiten (1)
(sich) waschen (54)
wegräumen* like machen (3)
wegwerfen* like helfen (31)
weinen like machen (3)
werden (*sein*) (9)
wettmachen* like machen (3)
wiederholen like machen (3)
wiegen like schieben (42)
wischen like machen (3)
wissen (55)
wohnen like machen (3)
wollen (15)
(sich) wünschen like machen (3)
zeigen like machen (3)
ziehen (*sein*) like schieben (42)
zubereiten* like arbeiten (1)
zumachen* like machen (3)
(sich) zurechtfinden* like trinken (52)
zurückkommen* (*sein*) like kommen (32)
zuschauen* like machen (3)

Regular verbs: simple tenses

Infinitiv	INDIKATIV			KONJUNKTIV I	KONJUNKTIV II		IMPERATIV
Partizip I / Partizip II / Perfekt	Präsens	Präteritum	Plusquamperfekt	Präsens	Präsens	Perfekt	
1 **arbeiten** (to work) arbeitend gearbeitet gearbeitet haben	arbeite arbeitest arbeitet arbeiten arbeitet arbeiten	arbeitete arbeitetest arbeitete arbeiteten arbeitetet arbeiteten	hatte gearbeitet hattest gearbeitet hatte gearbeitet hatten gearbeitet hattet gearbeitet hatten gearbeitet	arbeite arbeitest arbeite arbeiten arbeitet arbeiten	arbeitete arbeitetest arbeitete arbeiteten arbeitetet arbeiteten	hätte gearbeitet hättest gearbeitet hätte gearbeitet hätten gearbeitet hättet gearbeitet hätten gearbeitet	arbeite — arbeiten wir arbeitet arbeiten Sie
2 **feiern** (to celebrate) feiernd gefeiert gefeiert haben	feiere feierst feiert feiern feiert feiern	feierte feiertest feierte feierten feiertet feierten	hatte gefeiert hattest gefeiert hatte gefeiert hatten gefeiert hattet gefeiert hatten gefeiert	feiere feierest feiere feiern feiert feiern	feierte feiertest feierte feierten feiertet feierten	hätte gefeiert hättest gefeiert hätte gefeiert hätten gefeiert hättet gefeiert hätten gefeiert	feiere — feiern wir feiert feiern Sie
3 **machen** (to make; to do) machend gemacht gemacht haben	mache machst macht machen macht machen	machte machtest machte machten machtet machten	hatte gemacht hattest gemacht hatte gemacht hatten gemacht hattet gemacht hatten gemacht	mache machest mache machen machet machen	machte machtest machte machten machtet machten	hätte gemacht hättest gemacht hätte gemacht hätten gemacht hättet gemacht hätten gemacht	mache/mach — machen wir macht machen Sie
4 **probieren** (to try) probierend probiert probiert haben	probiere probierst probiert probieren probiert probieren	probierte probiertest probierte probierten probiertet probierten	hatte probiert hattest probiert hatte probiert hatten probiert hattet probiert hatten probiert	probiere probierest probiere probieren probieret probieren	probierte probiertest probierte probierten probiertet probierten	hätte probiert hättest probiert hätte probiert hätten probiert hättet probiert hätten probiert	probiere/probier — probieren wir probiert probieren Sie
5 **sammeln** (to collect) sammelnd gesammelt gesammelt haben	sammle sammelst sammelt sammeln sammelt sammeln	sammelte sammeltest sammelte sammelten sammeltet sammelten	hatte gesammelt hattest gesammelt hatte gesammelt hatten gesammelt hattet gesammelt hatten gesammelt	sammle sammelst sammle sammeln sammelt sammeln	sammelte sammeltest sammelte sammelten sammeltet sammelten	hätte gesammelt hättest gesammelt hätte gesammelt hätten gesammelt hättet gesammelt hätten gesammelt	sammle — sammeln wir sammelt sammeln Sie

Reflexive verbs

6

Infinitiv: sich freuen (*to be happy*)
Partizip I: sich freuend
Partizip II: sich gefreut
Perfekt: sich gefreut haben

	INDIKATIV Präsens	INDIKATIV Präteritum	INDIKATIV Plusquamperfekt	KONJUNKTIV I Präsens	KONJUNKTIV II Präsens	KONJUNKTIV II Perfekt	IMPERATIV
	freue mich	freute mich	hatte mich gefreut	freue mich	freute mich	hätte mich gefreut	
	freust dich	freutest dich	hattest dich gefreut	freuest dich	freutest dich	hättest dich gefreut	freue/freu dich
	freut sich	freute sich	hatte sich gefreut	freue sich	freute sich	hätte sich gefreut	
	freuen uns	freuten uns	hatten uns gefreut	freuen uns	freuten uns	hätten uns gefreut	freuen wir uns
	freut euch	freutet euch	hattet euch gefreut	freuet euch	freutet euch	hättet euch gefreut	freut euch
	freuen sich	freuten sich	hatten sich gefreut	freuen sich	freuten sich	hätten sich gefreut	freuen Sie sich

Auxiliary verbs

7

Infinitiv: haben (*to have*)
Partizip I: habend
Partizip II: gehabt
Perfekt: gehabt haben

	INDIKATIV Präsens	INDIKATIV Präteritum	INDIKATIV Plusquamperfekt	KONJUNKTIV I Präsens	KONJUNKTIV II Präsens	KONJUNKTIV II Perfekt	IMPERATIV
	habe	hatte	hatte gehabt	habe	hätte	hätte gehabt	habe/hab
	hast	hattest	hattest gehabt	habest	hättest	hättest gehabt	
	hat	hatte	hatte gehabt	habe	hätte	hätte gehabt	
	haben	hatten	hatten gehabt	haben	hätten	hätten gehabt	haben wir
	habt	hattet	hattet gehabt	habet	hättet	hättet gehabt	habt
	haben	hatten	hatten gehabt	haben	hätten	hätten gehabt	haben Sie

8

Infinitiv: sein (*to be*)
Partizip I: seiend
Partizip II: gewesen
Perfekt: gewesen sein

	INDIKATIV Präsens	INDIKATIV Präteritum	INDIKATIV Plusquamperfekt	KONJUNKTIV I Präsens	KONJUNKTIV II Präsens	KONJUNKTIV II Perfekt	IMPERATIV
	bin	war	war gewesen	sei	wäre	wäre gewesen	sei
	bist	warst	warst gewesen	seiest/seist	wärst/wärest	wärst/wärest gewesen	
	ist	war	war gewesen	sei	wäre	wäre gewesen	
	sind	waren	waren gewesen	seien	wären	wären gewesen	seien wir
	seid	wart	wart gewesen	seiet	wärt/wäret	wärt/wäret gewesen	seid
	sind	waren	waren gewesen	seien	wären	wären gewesen	seien Sie

9

Infinitiv: werden (*to become*)
Partizip I: werdend
Partizip II: geworden
Perfekt: geworden sein

	INDIKATIV Präsens	INDIKATIV Präteritum	INDIKATIV Plusquamperfekt	KONJUNKTIV I Präsens	KONJUNKTIV II Präsens	KONJUNKTIV II Perfekt	IMPERATIV
	werde	wurde	war geworden	werde	würde	wäre geworden	werde
	wirst	wurdest	warst geworden	werdest	würdest	wärst geworden	
	wird	wurde	war geworden	werde	würde	wäre geworden	
	werden	wurden	waren geworden	werden	würden	wären geworden	werden wir
	werdet	wurdet	wart geworden	werdet	würdet	wärt geworden	werdet
	werden	wurden	waren geworden	werden	würden	wären geworden	werden Sie

Compound tenses

Hilfsverb	INDIKATIV		KONJUNKTIV I		KONJUNKTIV II	
	Perfekt	**Plusquamperfekt**	**Präsens**	**Perfekt**	**Präsens**	**Perfekt**
haben	habe	hatte	habe		hätte	
	hast	hattest	habest		hättest	
	hat	hatte	habe		hätte	
	haben	hatten	haben		hätten	
	habt	hattet	habet		hättet	
	haben	hatten	haben		hätten	
	gemacht / gearbeitet / studiert / gefeiert / gesammelt	gemacht / gearbeitet / studiert / gefeiert / gesammelt	gemacht / gearbeitet / studiert / gefeiert / gesammelt		gemacht / gearbeitet / studiert / gefeiert / gesammelt	
sein	bin gegangen	war gegangen	sei gegangen		wäre gegangen	
	bist gegangen	warst gegangen	seiest/seist gegangen		wärst/wärest gegangen	
	ist gegangen	war gegangen	sei gegangen		wäre gegangen	
	sind gegangen	waren gegangen	seien gegangen		wären gegangen	
	seid gegangen	wart gegangen	seiet gegangen		wärt/wäret gegangen	
	sind gegangen	waren gegangen	seien gegangen		wären gegangen	

	Futur I/II	**Futur I/II**	**Futur I/II**
werden	werde machen / gemacht haben	werde machen / gemacht haben	würde machen / gemacht haben
	wirst machen / gemacht haben	werdest machen / gemacht haben	würdest machen / gemacht haben
	wird machen / gemacht haben	werde machen / gemacht haben	würde machen / gemacht haben
	werden machen / gemacht haben	werden machen / gemacht haben	würden machen / gemacht haben
	werdet machen / gemacht haben	werdet machen / gemacht haben	würdet machen / gemacht haben
	werden machen / gemacht haben	werden machen / gemacht haben	würden machen / gemacht haben

Modal verbs

10 dürfen

Infinitiv: dürfen *(to be permitted to)*; **Partizip I:** dürfend; **Partizip II:** gedurft/dürfen; **Perfekt:** gedurft haben

	INDIKATIV			KONJUNKTIV I	KONJUNKTIV II		IMPERATIV
	Präsens	Präteritum	Plusquamperfekt	Präsens	Präsens	Perfekt	
	darf	durfte	hatte gedurft	dürfe	dürfte	hätte gedurft	*Modal verbs are not used in the imperative.*
	darfst	durftest	hattest gedurft	dürfest	dürftest	hättest gedurft	
	darf	durfte	hatte gedurft	dürfe	dürfte	hätte gedurft	
	dürfen	durften	hatten gedurft	dürfen	dürften	hätten gedurft	
	dürft	durftet	hattet gedurft	dürfet	dürftet	hättet gedurft	
	dürfen	durften	hatten gedurft	dürfen	dürften	hätten gedurft	

11 können

Infinitiv: können *(to be able to)*; **Partizip I:** könnend; **Partizip II:** gekonnt/können; **Perfekt:** gekonnt haben

	INDIKATIV			KONJUNKTIV I	KONJUNKTIV II		IMPERATIV
	Präsens	Präteritum	Plusquamperfekt	Präsens	Präsens	Perfekt	
	kann	konnte	hatte gekonnt	könne	könnte	hätte gekonnt	*Modal verbs are not used in the imperative.*
	kannst	konntest	hattest gekonnt	könnest	könntest	hättest gekonnt	
	kann	konnte	hatte gekonnt	könne	könnte	hätte gekonnt	
	können	konnten	hatten gekonnt	können	könnten	hätten gekonnt	
	könnt	konntet	hattet gekonnt	könnet	könntet	hättet gekonnt	
	können	konnten	hatten gekonnt	können	könnten	hätten gekonnt	

12 mögen

Infinitiv: mögen *(to like)*; **Partizip I:** mögend; **Partizip II:** gemocht/mögen; **Perfekt:** gemocht haben

	INDIKATIV			KONJUNKTIV I	KONJUNKTIV II		IMPERATIV
	Präsens	Präteritum	Plusquamperfekt	Präsens	Präsens	Perfekt	
	mag	mochte	hatte gemocht	möge	möchte	hätte gemocht	*Modal verbs are not used in the imperative.*
	magst	mochtest	hattest gemocht	mögest	möchtest	hättest gemocht	
	mag	mochte	hatte gemocht	möge	möchte	hätte gemocht	
	mögen	mochten	hatten gemocht	mögen	möchten	hätten gemocht	
	mögt	mochtet	hattet gemocht	möget	möchtet	hättet gemocht	
	mögen	mochten	hatten gemocht	mögen	möchten	hätten gemocht	

13 müssen

Infinitiv: müssen *(to have to)*; **Partizip I:** müssend; **Partizip II:** gemusst/müssen; **Perfekt:** gemusst haben

	INDIKATIV			KONJUNKTIV I	KONJUNKTIV II		IMPERATIV
	Präsens	Präteritum	Plusquamperfekt	Präsens	Präsens	Perfekt	
	muss	musste	hatte gemusst	müsse	müsste	hätte gemusst	*Modal verbs are not used in the imperative.*
	musst	musstest	hattest gemusst	müssest	müsstest	hättest gemusst	
	muss	musste	hatte gemusst	müsse	müsste	hätte gemusst	
	müssen	mussten	hatten gemusst	müssen	müssten	hätten gemusst	
	müsst	musstet	hattet gemusst	müsset	müsstet	hättet gemusst	
	müssen	mussten	hatten gemusst	müssen	müssten	hätten gemusst	

14 sollen

Infinitiv: sollen *(to be supposed to)*; **Partizip I:** sollend; **Partizip II:** gesollt/sollen; **Perfekt:** gesollt haben

	INDIKATIV			KONJUNKTIV I	KONJUNKTIV II		IMPERATIV
	Präsens	Präteritum	Plusquamperfekt	Präsens	Präsens	Perfekt	
	soll	sollte	hatte gesollt	solle	sollte	hätte gesollt	*Modal verbs are not used in the imperative.*
	sollst	solltest	hattest gesollt	sollest	solltest	hättest gesollt	
	soll	sollte	hatte gesollt	solle	sollte	hätte gesollt	
	sollen	sollten	hatten gesollt	sollen	sollten	hätten gesollt	
	sollt	solltet	hattet gesollt	sollet	solltet	hättet gesollt	
	sollen	sollten	hatten gesollt	sollen	sollten	hätten gesollt	

15 wollen

Infinitiv: wollen *(to want to)*; **Partizip I:** wollend; **Partizip II:** gewollt/wollen; **Perfekt:** gewollt haben

	INDIKATIV			KONJUNKTIV I	KONJUNKTIV II		IMPERATIV
	Präsens	Präteritum	Plusquamperfekt	Präsens	Präsens	Perfekt	
	will	wollte	hatte gewollt	wolle	wollte	hätte gewollt	*Modal verbs are not used in the imperative.*
	willst	wolltest	hattest gewollt	wollest	wolltest	hättest gewollt	
	will	wollte	hatte gewollt	wolle	wollte	hätte gewollt	
	wollen	wollten	hatten gewollt	wollen	wollten	hätten gewollt	
	wollt	wolltet	hattet gewollt	wollet	wolltet	hättet gewollt	
	wollen	wollten	hatten gewollt	wollen	wollten	hätten gewollt	

Mixed verbs

16. denken *(to think)* — Partizip I: denkend — Partizip II: gedacht — Perfekt: gedacht haben

	INDIKATIV			KONJUNKTIV I	KONJUNKTIV II		IMPERATIV
	Präsens	Präteritum	Plusquamperfekt	Präsens	Präsens	Perfekt	
	denke	dachte	hatte gedacht	denke	dächte	hätte gedacht	
	denkst	dachtest	hattest gedacht	denkest	dächtest	hättest gedacht	denke/denk
	denkt	dachte	hatte gedacht	denke	dächte	hätte gedacht	
	denken	dachten	hatten gedacht	denken	dächten	hätten gedacht	denken wir
	denkt	dachtet	hattet gedacht	denket	dächtet	hättet gedacht	denkt
	denken	dachten	hatten gedacht	denken	dächten	hätten gedacht	denken Sie

17. rennen *(to run)* — Partizip I: rennend — Partizip II: gerannt — Perfekt: gerannt sein

	INDIKATIV			KONJUNKTIV I	KONJUNKTIV II		IMPERATIV
	Präsens	Präteritum	Plusquamperfekt	Präsens	Präsens	Perfekt	
	renne	rannte	war gerannt	renne	rennte	wäre gerannt	
	rennst	ranntest	warst gerannt	rennest	renntest	wärest gerannt	renne/renn
	rennt	rannte	war gerannt	renne	rennte	wäre gerannt	
	rennen	rannten	waren gerannt	rennen	rennten	wären gerannt	rennen wir
	rennt	ranntet	wart gerannt	rennet	renntet	wärt gerannt	rennt
	rennen	rannten	waren gerannt	rennen	rennten	wären gerannt	rennen Sie

18. senden *(to send)* — Partizip I: sendend — Partizip II: gesendet — Perfekt: gesendet haben

	INDIKATIV			KONJUNKTIV I	KONJUNKTIV II		IMPERATIV
	Präsens	Präteritum	Plusquamperfekt	Präsens	Präsens	Perfekt	
	sende	sandte	hatte gesandt	sende	sendete	hätte gesandt	
	sendest	sandtest	hattest gesandt	sendest	sendetest	hättest gesandt	sende
	sendet	sandte	hatte gesandt	sende	sendete	hätte gesandt	
	senden	sandten	hatten gesandt	senden	sendeten	hätten gesandt	senden wir
	sendet	sandtet	hattet gesandt	sendet	sendetet	hättet gesandt	sendet
	senden	sandten	hatten gesandt	senden	sendeten	hätten gesandt	senden Sie

Irregular verbs

19. bitten *(to ask)* — Partizip I: bittend — Partizip II: gebeten — Perfekt: gebeten haben

	INDIKATIV			KONJUNKTIV I	KONJUNKTIV II		IMPERATIV
	Präsens	Präteritum	Plusquamperfekt	Präsens	Präsens	Perfekt	
	bitte	bat	hatte gebeten	bitte	bäte	hätte gebeten	
	bittest	batest	hattest gebeten	bittest	bätest	hättest gebeten	bitte
	bittet	bat	hatte gebeten	bitte	bäte	hätte gebeten	
	bitten	baten	hatten gebeten	bitten	bäten	hätten gebeten	bitten wir
	bittet	batet	hattet gebeten	bittet	bätet	hättet gebeten	bittet
	bitten	baten	hatten gebeten	bitten	bäten	hätten gebeten	bitten Sie

20. bleiben *(to stay)* — Partizip I: bleibend — Partizip II: geblieben — Perfekt: geblieben sein

	INDIKATIV			KONJUNKTIV I	KONJUNKTIV II		IMPERATIV
	Präsens	Präteritum	Plusquamperfekt	Präsens	Präsens	Perfekt	
	bleibe	bliebe	war geblieben	bleibe	bliebe	wäre geblieben	
	bleibst	bliebst	warst geblieben	bleibest	bliebest	wärest geblieben	bleibe/bleib
	bleibt	blieb	war geblieben	bleibe	bliebe	wäre geblieben	
	bleiben	blieben	waren geblieben	bleiben	blieben	wären geblieben	bleiben wir
	bleibt	bliebt	wart geblieben	bleibet	bliebet	wärt geblieben	bleibt
	bleiben	blieben	waren geblieben	bleiben	blieben	wären geblieben	bleiben Sie

21 essen (to eat) — essend / gegessen / gegessen haben

	INDIKATIV Präsens	Präteritum	Plusquamperfekt	KONJUNKTIV I Präsens	KONJUNKTIV II Präsens	KONJUNKTIV II Perfekt	IMPERATIV
	esse	aß	hatte gegessen	esse	äße	hätte gegessen	
	isst	aßest	hattest gegessen	essest	äßest	hättest gegessen	iss
	isst	aß	hatte gegessen	esse	äße	hätte gegessen	
	essen	aßen	hatten gegessen	essen	äßen	hätten gegessen	essen wir
	esst	aßt	hattet gegessen	esset	äßet	hättet gegessen	esst
	essen	aßen	hatten gegessen	essen	äßen	hätten gegessen	essen Sie

22 fallen (to fall) — fallend / gefallen / gefallen sein

	INDIKATIV Präsens	Präteritum	Plusquamperfekt	KONJUNKTIV I Präsens	KONJUNKTIV II Präsens	KONJUNKTIV II Perfekt	IMPERATIV
	falle	fiel	war gefallen	falle	fiele	wäre gefallen	
	fällst	fielst	warst gefallen	fallest	fielest	wärest gefallen	falle/fall
	fällt	fiel	war gefallen	falle	fiele	wäre gefallen	
	fallen	fielen	waren gefallen	fallen	fielen	wären gefallen	fallen wir
	fallt	fielt	wart gefallen	fallet	fielet	wäret gefallen	fallt
	fallen	fielen	waren gefallen	fallen	fielen	wären gefallen	fallen Sie

23 fangen (to catch) — fangend / gefangen / gefangen haben

	INDIKATIV Präsens	Präteritum	Plusquamperfekt	KONJUNKTIV I Präsens	KONJUNKTIV II Präsens	KONJUNKTIV II Perfekt	IMPERATIV
	fange	fing	hatte gefangen	fange	finge	hätte gefangen	
	fängst	fingst	hattest gefangen	fangest	fingest	hättest gefangen	fange/fang
	fängt	fing	hatte gefangen	fange	finge	hätte gefangen	
	fangen	fingen	hatten gefangen	fangen	fingen	hätten gefangen	fangen wir
	fangt	fingt	hattet gefangen	fanget	finget	hättet gefangen	fangt
	fangen	fingen	hatten gefangen	fangen	fingen	hätten gefangen	fangen Sie

24 flechten (to braid) — flechtend / geflochten / geflochten haben

	INDIKATIV Präsens	Präteritum	Plusquamperfekt	KONJUNKTIV I Präsens	KONJUNKTIV II Präsens	KONJUNKTIV II Perfekt	IMPERATIV
	flechte	flocht	hatte geflochten	flechte	flöchte	hätte geflochten	
	flichtst	flochtest	hattest geflochten	flechtest	flöchtest	hättest geflochten	flicht
	flicht	flocht	hatte geflochten	flechte	flöchte	hätte geflochten	
	flechten	flochten	hatten geflochten	flechten	flöchten	hätten geflochten	flechten wir
	flechtet	flochtet	hattet geflochten	flechtet	flöchtet	hättet geflochten	flechtet
	flechten	flochten	hatten geflochten	flechten	flöchten	hätten geflochten	flechten Sie

25 fließen (to flow) — fließend / geflossen / geflossen sein

	INDIKATIV Präsens	Präteritum	Plusquamperfekt	KONJUNKTIV I Präsens	KONJUNKTIV II Präsens	KONJUNKTIV II Perfekt	IMPERATIV
	fließe	floss	war geflossen	fließe	flösse	wäre geflossen	
	fließt	flossest/flosst	warst geflossen	fließest	flössest	wärest geflossen	fließe/fließ
	fließt	floss	war geflossen	fließe	flösse	wäre geflossen	
	fließen	flossen	waren geflossen	fließen	flössen	wären geflossen	fließen wir
	fließt	flosst	wart geflossen	fließet	flösset	wärt geflossen	fließt
	fließen	flossen	waren geflossen	fließen	flössen	wären geflossen	fließen Sie

26 fordern (to demand) — fordernd / gefordert / gefordert haben

	INDIKATIV Präsens	Präteritum	Plusquamperfekt	KONJUNKTIV I Präsens	KONJUNKTIV II Präsens	KONJUNKTIV II Perfekt	IMPERATIV
	ford(e)re	forderte	hatte gefordert	fordere	forderte	hätte gefordert	
	forderst	fordertest	hattest gefordert	forderest	fordertest	hättest gefordert	fordere/fordre
	fordert	forderte	hatte gefordert	fordere	forderte	hätte gefordert	
	fordern	forderten	hatten gefordert	forderen	forderten	hätten gefordert	fordern wir
	fordert	fordertet	hattet gefordert	forderet	forderet	hättet gefordert	fordert
	fordern	forderten	hatten gefordert	forderen	forderten	hätten gefordert	fordern Sie

27 geben (to give) — gebend / gegeben / gegeben haben

	INDIKATIV Präsens	Präteritum	Plusquamperfekt	KONJUNKTIV I Präsens	KONJUNKTIV II Präsens	KONJUNKTIV II Perfekt	IMPERATIV
	gebe	gab	hatte gegeben	gebe	gäbe	hätte gegeben	
	gibst	gabst	hattest gegeben	gebest	gäbest	hättest gegeben	gib
	gibt	gab	hatte gegeben	gebe	gäbe	hätte gegeben	
	geben	gaben	hatten gegeben	geben	gäben	hätten gegeben	geben wir
	gebt	gabt	hattet gegeben	gebet	gäbet	hättet gegeben	gebt
	geben	gaben	hatten gegeben	geben	gäben	hätten gegeben	geben Sie

28 gehen (to go)

Partizip I: gehend · Partizip II: gegangen · Perfekt: gegangen sein

	INDIKATIV			KONJUNKTIV I	KONJUNKTIV II		IMPERATIV
	Präsens	Präteritum	Plusquamperfekt	Präsens	Präsens	Perfekt	
	gehe	ging	war gegangen	gehe	ginge	wäre gegangen	gehe/geh
	gehst	gingst	warst gegangen	gehest	gingest	wärest gegangen	
	geht	ging	war gegangen	gehe	ginge	wäre gegangen	
	gehen	gingen	waren gegangen	gehen	gingen	wären gegangen	gehen wir
	geht	gingt	wart gegangen	gehet	ginget	wäret gegangen	geht
	gehen	gingen	waren gegangen	gehen	gingen	wären gegangen	gehen Sie

29 heben (to lift)

Partizip I: hebend · Partizip II: gehoben · Perfekt: gehoben haben

	INDIKATIV			KONJUNKTIV I	KONJUNKTIV II		IMPERATIV
	Präsens	Präteritum	Plusquamperfekt	Präsens	Präsens	Perfekt	
	hebe	hob	hatte gehoben	hebe	höbe	hätte gehoben	hebe/heb
	hebst	hobst	hattest gehoben	hebest	höbest/höbst	hättest gehoben	
	hebt	hob	hatte gehoben	hebe	höbe	hätte gehoben	
	heben	hoben	hatten gehoben	heben	höben	hätten gehoben	heben wir
	hebt	hobt	hattet gehoben	hebet	höbet/höbt	hättet gehoben	hebt
	heben	hoben	hatten gehoben	heben	höben	hätten gehoben	heben Sie

30 heißen (to be called)

Partizip I: heißend · Partizip II: geheißen · Perfekt: geheißen haben

	INDIKATIV			KONJUNKTIV I	KONJUNKTIV II		IMPERATIV
	Präsens	Präteritum	Plusquamperfekt	Präsens	Präsens	Perfekt	
	heiße	hieß	hatte geheißen	heiße	hieße	hätte geheißen	heiß/heiße
	heißt	hießest	hattest geheißen	heißest	hießest	hättest geheißen	
	heißt	hieß	hatte geheißen	heiße	hieße	hätte geheißen	
	heißen	hießen	hatten geheißen	heißen	hießen	hätten geheißen	heißen wir
	heißt	hießt	hattet geheißen	heißet	hießet	hättet geheißen	heißt
	heißen	hießen	hatten geheißen	heißen	hießen	hätten geheißen	heißen Sie

31 helfen (to help)

Partizip I: helfend · Partizip II: geholfen · Perfekt: geholfen haben

	INDIKATIV			KONJUNKTIV I	KONJUNKTIV II		IMPERATIV
	Präsens	Präteritum	Plusquamperfekt	Präsens	Präsens	Perfekt	
	helfe	half	hatte geholfen	helfe	hälfe	hätte geholfen	hilf
	hilfst	halfst	hattest geholfen	helfest	hälfest/hälfst	hättest geholfen	
	hilft	half	hatte geholfen	helfe	hälfe	hätte geholfen	
	helfen	halfen	hatten geholfen	helfen	hälfen	hätten geholfen	helfen wir
	helft	halft	hattet geholfen	helfet	hälfet/hälft	hättet geholfen	helft
	helfen	halfen	hatten geholfen	helfen	hälfen	hätten geholfen	helfen Sie

32 kommen (to come)

Partizip I: kommend · Partizip II: gekommen · Perfekt: gekommen sein

	INDIKATIV			KONJUNKTIV I	KONJUNKTIV II		IMPERATIV
	Präsens	Präteritum	Plusquamperfekt	Präsens	Präsens	Perfekt	
	komme	kam	war gekommen	komme	käme	wäre gekommen	komme/komm
	kommst	kamst	warst gekommen	kommest	kämest	wärest gekommen	
	kommt	kam	war gekommen	komme	käme	wäre gekommen	
	kommen	kamen	waren gekommen	kommen	kämen	wären gekommen	kommen wir
	kommt	kamt	wart gekommen	kommet	kämet	wäret gekommen	kommt
	kommen	kamen	waren gekommen	kommen	kämen	wären gekommen	kommen Sie

33 laufen (to run)

Partizip I: laufend · Partizip II: gelaufen · Perfekt: gelaufen sein

	INDIKATIV			KONJUNKTIV I	KONJUNKTIV II		IMPERATIV
	Präsens	Präteritum	Plusquamperfekt	Präsens	Präsens	Perfekt	
	laufe	lief	war gelaufen	laufe	liefe	wäre gelaufen	laufe/lauf
	läufst	liefst	warst gelaufen	laufest	liefest	wärest gelaufen	
	läuft	lief	war gelaufen	laufe	liefe	wäre gelaufen	
	laufen	liefen	waren gelaufen	laufen	liefen	wären gelaufen	laufen wir
	lauft	lieft	wart gelaufen	laufet	liefet	wäret gelaufen	lauft
	laufen	liefen	waren gelaufen	laufen	liefen	wären gelaufen	laufen Sie

34 lesen (to read)

Partizip I: lesend · Partizip II: gelesen · Perfekt: gelesen haben

	INDIKATIV			KONJUNKTIV I	KONJUNKTIV II		IMPERATIV
	Präsens	Präteritum	Plusquamperfekt	Präsens	Präsens	Perfekt	
	lese	las	hatte gelesen	lese	läse	hätte gelesen	lies
	liest	la(se)st	hattest gelesen	lesest	läsest	hättest gelesen	
	liest	las	hatte gelesen	lese	läse	hätte gelesen	
	lesen	lasen	hatten gelesen	lesen	läsen	hätten gelesen	les en wir
	lest	last	hattet gelesen	leset	läset	hättet gelesen	lest
	lesen	lasen	hatten gelesen	lesen	läsen	hätten gelesen	lesen Sie

35 liegen *(to lie; to be lying)* — Partizip I: liegend · Partizip II: gelegen · Perfekt: gelegen haben

	INDIKATIV			KONJUNKTIV I	KONJUNKTIV II		IMPERATIV
	Präsens	Präteritum	Plusquamperfekt	Präsens	Präsens	Perfekt	
	liege	lag	hatte gelegen	liege	läge	hätte gelegen	liege/lieg
	liegst	lagst	hattest gelegen	liegest	lägest	hättest gelegen	
	liegt	lag	hatte gelegen	liege	läge	hätte gelegen	
	liegen	lagen	hatten gelegen	liegen	lägen	hätten gelegen	liegen wir
	liegt	lagt	hattet gelegen	lieget	läget	hättet gelegen	liegt
	liegen	lagen	hatten gelegen	liegen	lägen	hätten gelegen	liegen Sie

36 lügen *(to lie)* — Partizip I: lügend · Partizip II: gelogen · Perfekt: gelogen haben

	Präsens	Präteritum	Plusquamperfekt	Präsens	Präsens	Perfekt	IMPERATIV
	lüge	log	hatte gelogen	lüge	löge	hätte gelogen	lüge/lüg
	lügst	logst	hattest gelogen	lügest	lögest	hättest gelogen	
	lügt	log	hatte gelogen	lüge	löge	hätte gelogen	
	lügen	logen	hatten gelogen	lügen	lögen	hätten gelogen	lügen wir
	lügt	logt	hattet gelogen	lüget	löget	hättet gelogen	lügt
	lügen	logen	hatten gelogen	lügen	lögen	hätten gelogen	lügen Sie

37 mahlen *(to grind)* — Partizip I: mahlend · Partizip II: gemahlt/gemahlen · Perfekt: gemahlt/gemahlen haben

	Präsens	Präteritum	Plusquamperfekt	Präsens	Präsens	Perfekt	IMPERATIV
	mahle	mahlte	hatte gemahlt/gemahlen	mahle	mahlte	hätte gemahlt/gemahlen	mahle/mahl
	mahlst	mahltest	hattest gemahlt/gemahlen	mahlest	mahltest	hättest gemahlt/gemahlen	
	mahlt	mahlte	hatte gemahlt/gemahlen	mahle	mahlte	hätte gemahlt/gemahlen	
	mahlen	mahlten	hatten gemahlt/gemahlen	mahlen	mahlten	hätten gemahlt/gemahlen	mahlen wir
	mahlt	mahltet	hattet gemahlt/gemahlen	mahlet	mahltet	hättet gemahlt/gemahlen	mahlt
	mahlen	mahlten	hatten gemahlt/gemahlen	mahlen	mahlten	hätten gemahlt/gemahlen	mahlen Sie

38 nehmen *(to take)* — Partizip I: nehmend · Partizip II: genommen · Perfekt: genommen haben

	Präsens	Präteritum	Plusquamperfekt	Präsens	Präsens	Perfekt	IMPERATIV
	nehme	nahm	hatte genommen	nehme	nähme	hätte genommen	nimm
	nimmst	nahmst	hattest genommen	nehmest	nähmest	hättest genommen	
	nimmt	nahm	hatte genommen	nehme	nähme	hätte genommen	
	nehmen	nahmen	hatten genommen	nehmen	nähmen	hätten genommen	nehmen wir
	nehmt	nahmt	hattet genommen	nehmet	nähmet	hättet genommen	nehmt
	nehmen	nahmen	hatten genommen	nehmen	nähmen	hätten genommen	nehmen Sie

39 pfeifen *(to whistle)* — Partizip I: pfeifend · Partizip II: gepfiffen · Perfekt: gepfiffen haben

	Präsens	Präteritum	Plusquamperfekt	Präsens	Präsens	Perfekt	IMPERATIV
	pfeife	pfiff	hatte gepfiffen	pfeife	pfiffe	hätte gepfiffen	pfeife/pfeif
	pfeifst	pfiffst	hattest gepfiffen	pfeifest	pfiffest	hättest gepfiffen	
	pfeift	pfiff	hatte gepfiffen	pfeife	pfiffe	hätte gepfiffen	
	pfeifen	pfiffen	hatten gepfiffen	pfeifen	pfiffen	hätten gepfiffen	pfeifen wir
	pfeift	pfifft	hattet gepfiffen	pfeifet	pfiffet	hättet gepfiffen	pfeift
	pfeifen	pfiffen	hatten gepfiffen	pfeifen	pfiffen	hätten gepfiffen	pfeifen Sie

40 rufen *(to call)* — Partizip I: rufend · Partizip II: gerufen · Perfekt: gerufen haben

	Präsens	Präteritum	Plusquamperfekt	Präsens	Präsens	Perfekt	IMPERATIV
	rufe	rief	hatte gerufen	rufe	riefe	hätte gerufen	rufe/ruf
	rufst	riefst	hattest gerufen	rufest	riefest	hättest gerufen	
	ruft	rief	hatte gerufen	rufe	riefe	hätte gerufen	
	rufen	riefen	hatten gerufen	rufen	riefen	hätten gerufen	rufen wir
	ruft	rieft	hattet gerufen	rufet	riefet	hättet gerufen	ruft
	rufen	riefen	hatten gerufen	rufen	riefen	hätten gerufen	rufen Sie

41 saugen *(to suck)* — Partizip I: saugend · Partizip II: gesaugt/gesogen · Perfekt: gesaugt/gesogen haben

	Präsens	Präteritum	Plusquamperfekt	Präsens	Präsens	Perfekt	IMPERATIV
	sauge	saugte/sog	hatte gesaugt/gesogen	sauge	saugte/söge	hätte gesaugt/gesogen	sauge/saug
	saugst	saugtest/sogst	hattest gesaugt/gesogen	saugest	saugtest/sögest	hättest gesaugt/gesogen	
	saugt	saugte/sog	hatte gesaugt/gesogen	sauge	saugte/söge	hätte gesaugt/gesogen	
	saugen	saugten/sogen	hatten gesaugt/gesogen	saugen	saugten/sögen	hätten gesaugt/gesogen	saugen wir
	saugt	saugtet/sogt	hattet gesaugt/gesogen	sauget	saugtet/söget	hättet gesaugt/gesogen	saugt
	saugen	saugten/sogen	hatten gesaugt/gesogen	saugen	saugten/sögen	hätten gesaugt/gesogen	saugen Sie

Infinitiv / Partizip I / Partizip II / Perfekt	INDIKATIV Präsens	INDIKATIV Präteritum	INDIKATIV Plusquamperfekt	KONJUNKTIV I Präsens	KONJUNKTIV II Präsens	KONJUNKTIV II Perfekt	IMPERATIV
42 schieben (to push) schiebend geschoben geschoben haben	schiebe schiebst schiebt schieben schiebt schieben	schob schobst schob schoben schobt schoben	hatte geschoben hattest geschoben hatte geschoben hatten geschoben hattet geschoben hatten geschoben	schiebe schiebest schiebe schieben schiebet schieben	schöbe schöbest schöbe schöben schöbet schöben	hätte geschoben hättest geschoben hätte geschoben hätten geschoben hättet geschoben hätten geschoben	schiebe/schieb schieben wir schiebt schieben Sie
43 schlafen (to sleep) schlafend geschlafen geschlafen haben	schlafe schläfst schläft schlafen schlaft schlafen	schlief schliefst schlief schliefen schlieft schliefen	hatte geschlafen hattest geschlafen hatte geschlafen hatten geschlafen hattet geschlafen hatten geschlafen	schlafe schlafest schlafe schlafen schlafet schlafen	schliefe schliefest schliefe schliefen schliefet schliefen	hätte geschlafen hättest geschlafen hätte geschlafen hätten geschlafen hättet geschlafen hätten geschlafen	schlafe/schlaf schlafen wir schlaft schlafen Sie
44 schwimmen (to swim) schwimmend geschwommen geschwommen sein	schwimme schwimmst schwimmt schwimmen schwimmt schwimmen	schwamm schwammst schwamm schwammen schwammt schwammen	war geschwommen warst geschwommen war geschwommen waren geschwommen wart geschwommen waren geschwommen	schwimme schwimmest schwimme schwimmen schwimmet schwimmen	schwömme schwömmest schwömme schwömmen schwömmet schwömmen	wäre geschwommen wärest geschwommen wäre geschwommen wären geschwommen wäret geschwommen wären geschwommen	schwimme/schwimm schwimmen wir schwimmt schwimmen Sie
45 schwören (to swear) schwörend geschworen geschworen haben	schwöre schwörst schwört schwören schwört schwören	schwor schworst schwor schworen schwort schworen	hatte geschworen hattest geschworen hatte geschworen hatten geschworen hattet geschworen hatten geschworen	schwöre schwörest schwöre schwören schwöret schwören	schwüre schwürest/schwürst schwüre schwüren schwüret schwüren	hätte geschworen hättest geschworen hätte geschworen hätten geschworen hättet geschworen hätten geschworen	schwöre/schwör schwören wir schwört schwören Sie
46 sitzen (to sit) sitzend gesessen gesessen haben	sitze sitzt sitzt sitzen sitzt sitzen	saß saßest saß saßen saßet saßen	hatte gesessen hattest gesessen hatte gesessen hatten gesessen hattet gesessen hatten gesessen	sitze sitzest sitze sitzen sitzet sitzen	säße säßest säße säßen säßet säßen	hätte gesessen hättest gesessen hätte gesessen hätten gesessen hättet gesessen hätten gesessen	sitze/sitz sitzen wir sitzt sitzen Sie
47 sprechen (to speak) sprechend gesprochen gesprochen haben	spreche sprichst spricht sprechen sprecht sprechen	sprach sprachst sprach sprachen spracht sprachen	hatte gesprochen hattest gesprochen hatte gesprochen hatten gesprochen hattet gesprochen hatten gesprochen	spreche sprechest spreche sprechen sprechet sprechen	spräche sprächest spräche sprächen sprächet sprächen	hätte gesprochen hättest gesprochen hätte gesprochen hätten gesprochen hättet gesprochen hätten gesprochen	sprich sprechen wir sprecht sprechen Sie
48 stehen (to stand) stehend gestanden gestanden haben	stehe stehst steht stehen steht stehen	stand standest/standst stand standen standet standen	hatte gestanden hattest gestanden hatte gestanden hatten gestanden hattet gestanden hatten gestanden	stehe stehest stehe stehen stehet stehen	stünde/stände stündest/ständest stünde/stände stünden/ständen stündet/ständet stünden/ständen	hätte gestanden hättest gestanden hätte gestanden hätten gestanden hättet gestanden hätten gestanden	stehe/steh stehen wir steht stehen Sie

49 — stehlen (to steal) / stehlend / gestohlen / gestohlen haben

Indikativ Präsens	Präteritum	Plusquamperfekt	Konjunktiv I Präsens	Konjunktiv II Präsens	Konjunktiv II Perfekt	Imperativ
stehle	stahl	hatte gestohlen	stehle	stähle/stöhle	hätte gestohlen	
stiehlst	stahlst	hattest gestohlen	stehlest	stählest/stöhlest	hättest gestohlen	stiehl
stiehlt	stahl	hatte gestohlen	stehle	stähle/stöhle	hätte gestohlen	
stehlen	stahlen	hatten gestohlen	stehlen	stählen/stöhlen	hätten gestohlen	stehlen wir
stehlt	stahlt	hattet gestohlen	stehlet	stählet/stöhlet	hättet gestohlen	stehlt
stehlen	stahlen	hatten gestohlen	stehlen	stählen/stöhlen	hätten gestohlen	stehlen Sie

50 — stoßen (to bump) / stoßend / gestoßen / gestoßen haben

Indikativ Präsens	Präteritum	Plusquamperfekt	Konjunktiv I Präsens	Konjunktiv II Präsens	Konjunktiv II Perfekt	Imperativ
stoße	stieß	hatte gestoßen	stoße	stieße	hätte gestoßen	
stößt	stießest/stießt	hattest gestoßen	stoßest	stießest	hättest gestoßen	stoße/stoß
stößt	stieß	hatte gestoßen	stoße	stieße	hätte gestoßen	
stoßen	stießen	hatten gestoßen	stoßen	stießen	hätten gestoßen	stoßen wir
stoßt	stießt	hattet gestoßen	stoßet	stießet	hättet gestoßen	stoßt
stoßen	stießen	hatten gestoßen	stoßen	stießen	hätten gestoßen	stoßen Sie

51 — tragen (to carry) / tragend / getragen / getragen haben

Indikativ Präsens	Präteritum	Plusquamperfekt	Konjunktiv I Präsens	Konjunktiv II Präsens	Konjunktiv II Perfekt	Imperativ
trage	trug	hatte getragen	trage	trüge	hätte getragen	
trägst	trugst	hattest getragen	tragest	trügest	hättest getragen	trage/trag
trägt	trug	hatte getragen	trage	trüge	hätte getragen	
tragen	trugen	hatten getragen	tragen	trügen	hätten getragen	tragen wir
tragt	trugt	hattet getragen	traget	trüget	hättet getragen	tragt
tragen	trugen	hatten getragen	tragen	trügen	hätten getragen	tragen Sie

52 — trinken (to drink) / trinkend / getrunken / getrunken haben

Indikativ Präsens	Präteritum	Plusquamperfekt	Konjunktiv I Präsens	Konjunktiv II Präsens	Konjunktiv II Perfekt	Imperativ
trinke	trank	hatte getrunken	trinke	tränke	hätte getrunken	
trinkst	trankst	hattest getrunken	trinkest	tränkest	hättest getrunken	trinke/trink
trinkt	trank	hatte getrunken	trinke	tränke	hätte getrunken	
trinken	tranken	hatten getrunken	trinken	tränken	hätten getrunken	trinken wir
trinkt	trankt	hattet getrunken	trinket	tränket	hättet getrunken	trinkt
trinken	tranken	hatten getrunken	trinken	tränken	hätten getrunken	trinken Sie

53 — tun (to do) / tuend / getan / getan haben

Indikativ Präsens	Präteritum	Plusquamperfekt	Konjunktiv I Präsens	Konjunktiv II Präsens	Konjunktiv II Perfekt	Imperativ
tue	tat	hatte getan	tue	täte	hätte getan	
tust	tatest	hattest getan	tuest	tätest	hättest getan	tue/tu
tut	tat	hatte getan	tue	täte	hätte getan	
tun	taten	hatten getan	tuen	täten	hätten getan	tun wir
tut	tatet	hattet getan	tuet	tätet	hättet getan	tut
tun	taten	hatten getan	tuen	täten	hätten getan	tun Sie

54 — waschen (to wash) / waschend / gewaschen / gewaschen haben

Indikativ Präsens	Präteritum	Plusquamperfekt	Konjunktiv I Präsens	Konjunktiv II Präsens	Konjunktiv II Perfekt	Imperativ
wasche	wusch	hatte gewaschen	wasche	wüsche	hätte gewaschen	
wäschst	wuschest/wuschst	hattest gewaschen	waschest	wüschest/wüschst	hättest gewaschen	wasche/wasch
wäscht	wusch	hatte gewaschen	wasche	wüsche	hätte gewaschen	
waschen	wuschen	hatten gewaschen	waschen	wüschen	hätten gewaschen	waschen wir
wascht	wuscht	hattet gewaschen	waschet	wüschet/wüscht	hättet gewaschen	wascht
waschen	wuschen	hatten gewaschen	waschen	wüschen	hätten gewaschen	waschen Sie

55 — wissen (to know) / wissend / gewusst / gewusst haben

Indikativ Präsens	Präteritum	Plusquamperfekt	Konjunktiv I Präsens	Konjunktiv II Präsens	Konjunktiv II Perfekt	Imperativ
weiß	wusste	hatte gewusst	wisse	wüsste	hätte gewusst	
weißt	wusstest	hattest gewusst	wissest	wüsstest	hättest gewusst	wisse
weiß	wusste	hatte gewusst	wisse	wüsste	hätte gewusst	
wissen	wussten	hatten gewusst	wissen	wüssten	hätten gewusst	wissen wir
wisst	wusstet	hattet gewusst	wisset	wüsstet	hättet gewusst	wisst
wissen	wussten	hatten gewusst	wissen	wüssten	hätten gewusst	wissen Sie

Irregular verbs

The following is a list of the principal parts of all strong and mixed verbs that are introduced as active vocabulary in **SAG MAL**, as well as other sample verbs. For the complete conjugations of these verbs, consult the verb list on pages **A8–A9** and the verb charts on pages **A10–A19**. The verbs listed here are base forms. See **Strukturen 6B.2** and **7A.1** to review **Perfekt** and **Präteritum** forms of separable and inseparable prefix verbs.

Infinitiv		Präteritum	Partizip II
backen	*to bake*	backte	gebacken
beginnen	*to begin*	begann	begonnen
bieten	*to bid, to offer*	bot	geboten
binden	*to tie, to bind*	band	gebunden
bitten	*to request*	bat	gebeten
bleiben	*to stay*	blieb	(ist) geblieben
braten (brät)	*to fry, to roast*	briet	gebraten
brechen (bricht)	*to break*	brach	gebrochen
brennen	*to burn*	brannte	gebrannt
bringen	*to bring*	brachte	gebracht
denken	*to think*	dachte	gedacht
dürfen (darf)	*to be allowed to*	durfte	gedurft
empfehlen (empfiehlt)	*to recommend*	empfahl	empfohlen
essen (isst)	*to eat*	aß	gegessen
fahren (fährt)	*to go, to drive*	fuhr	(ist) gefahren
fallen (fällt)	*to fall*	fiel	(ist) gefallen
fangen (fängt)	*to catch*	fing	gefangen
finden	*to find*	fand	gefunden
fliegen	*to fly*	flog	(ist) geflogen
fließen	*to flow, to pour*	floss	(ist) geflossen
frieren	*to freeze*	fror	gefroren
geben (gibt)	*to give*	gab	gegeben
gehen	*to go, to walk*	ging	(ist) gegangen
gelten (gilt)	*to be valid*	galt	gegolten
genießen	*to enjoy*	genoss	genossen
geschehen (geschieht)	*to happen*	geschah	(ist) geschehen
gewinnen	*to win*	gewann	gewonnen
gleichen	*to resemble*	glich	geglichen
graben (gräbt)	*to dig*	grub	gegraben
haben (hat)	*to have*	hatte	gehabt
halten (hält)	*to hold, to keep*	hielt	gehalten
hängen	*to hang*	hing	gehangen
heben	*to raise, to lift*	hob	gehoben
heißen	*to be called, to mean*	hieß	geheißen
helfen (hilft)	*to help*	half	geholfen
kennen	*to know*	kannte	gekannt
klingen	*to sound, to ring*	klang	geklungen
kommen	*to come*	kam	(ist) gekommen
können (kann)	*to be able to, can*	konnte	gekonnt
laden (lädt)	*to load, to charge*	lud	geladen
lassen (lässt)	*to let, to allow*	ließ	gelassen
laufen (läuft)	*to run, to walk*	lief	(ist) gelaufen

Infinitiv		Präteritum	Partizip II
leiden	*to suffer*	litt	gelitten
leihen	*to lend*	lieh	geliehen
lesen (liest)	*to read*	las	gelesen
liegen	*to lie, to rest*	lag	gelegen
lügen	*to lie, to tell lies*	log	gelogen
meiden	*to avoid*	mied	gemieden
messen (misst)	*to measure*	maß	gemessen
mögen (mag)	*to like*	mochte	gemocht
müssen (muss)	*to have, to must*	musste	gemusst
nehmen (nimmt)	*to take*	nahm	genommen
nennen	*to name, to call*	nannte	genannt
preisen	*to praise*	pries	gepriesen
raten (rät)	*to guess*	riet	geraten
reiben	*to rub, to grate*	rieb	gerieben
riechen	*to smell*	roch	gerochen
rufen	*to call, to shout*	rief	gerufen
schaffen	*to accomplish*	schuf	geschaffen
scheiden	*to divorce, to depart*	schied	(ist) geschieden
scheinen	*to shine, to appear*	schien	geschienen
schieben	*to push, to shove*	schob	geschoben
schießen	*to shoot*	schoss	geschossen
schlafen (schläft)	*to sleep*	schlief	geschlafen
schlagen (schlägt)	*to beat, to hit*	schlug	geschlagen
schließen	*to close*	schloss	geschlossen
schlingen	*to loop, to gulp*	schlang	geschlungen
schneiden	*to cut*	schnitt	geschnitten
schreiben	*to write*	schrieb	geschrieben
schwimmen	*to swim*	schwamm	(ist) geschwommen
sehen (sieht)	*to see*	sah	gesehen
sein (ist)	*to be*	war	(ist) gewesen
senden	*to send*	sandte/sendete	gesandt/gesendet
singen	*to sing*	sang	gesungen
sinken	*to sink*	sank	(ist) gesunken
sitzen	*to sit*	saß	gesessen
sollen (soll)	*to be supposed to*	sollte	gesollt
sprechen (spricht)	*to speak*	sprach	gesprochen
stehen	*to stand*	stand	gestanden
stehlen (stiehlt)	*to steal*	stahl	gestohlen
steigen	*to climb, to rise*	stieg	(ist) gestiegen
sterben (stirbt)	*to die*	starb	(ist) gestorben
stoßen	*to push, to thrust*	stieß	gestoßen
streichen	*to paint, to cancel*	strich	gestrichen
streiten	*to argue*	stritt	gestritten
tragen (trägt)	*to carry*	trug	getragen
treffen (trifft)	*to hit, to meet*	traf	getroffen
treten (tritt)	*to kick*	trat	getreten
trinken	*to drink*	trank	getrunken
tun	*to do*	tat	getan
vergessen (vergisst)	*to forget*	vergaß	vergessen

Infinitiv		Präteritum	Partizip II
verlieren	to lose	verlor	verloren
wachsen (wächst)	to grow	wuchs	(ist) gewachsen
waschen (wäscht)	to wash	wusch	gewaschen
weisen	to indicate, to show	wies	gewiesen
wenden	to turn, to flip	wandte/wendete	gewandt/gewendet
werben (wirbt)	to advertise	warb	geworben
werden (wird)	to become	wurde	(ist) geworden
werfen (wirft)	to throw	warf	geworfen
winden	to wind	wand	gewunden
wissen (weiß)	to know	wusste	gewusst
wollen (will)	to want	wollte	gewollt
ziehen	to pull, to draw	zog	gezogen

Glossary

This glossary includes all active vocabulary introduced in **SAG MAL**, as well as some additional words and expressions. The singular and plural endings listed for adjectival nouns are those that occur after a definite article. See **10A.2** to review the complete set of endings.

Abbreviations used in this glossary

acc.	accusative	*gen.*	genitive	*poss.*	possessive
adj.	adjective	*inf.*	informal	*prep.*	preposition
adv.	adverb	*interr.*	interrogative	*pron.*	pronoun
conj.	conjunction	*m.*	masculine noun	*sing.*	singular
dat.	dative	*n.*	neuter noun	*v.*	verb
f.	feminine noun	*nom.*	nominative		
form.	formal	*pl.*	plural		

Deutsch-Englisch

A

abbiegen *v.* to turn **8A**
  rechts/links abbiegen *v.* to turn right/left **8A**
abbrechen *v.* to cancel **7B**
Abend, -e *m.* evening **2B**
  abends *adv.* in the evening **2A**
Abendessen, - *n.* dinner **4B**
aber *conj.* but **1B**
abfahren *v.* to leave **8A**
Abfall, ⸚e *m.* waste **12B**
abfliegen *v.* to take off **7B**
Abflug, ⸚e *m.* departure **7B**
abheben *v.* to withdraw (money) **10A**
Absatz, ⸚e *m.* paragraph **5B**
abschicken *v.* to send **11B**
Abschied, -e *m.* leave-taking; farewell **1A**
Abschluss, ⸚e *m.* degree **2A**
  einen Abschluss machen *v.* to graduate **5A**
Abschlusszeugnis, -se *n.* diploma (transcript) **2A**
abstauben *v.* to dust **6B**
sich abtrocknen *v.* to dry oneself off **9A**
acht eight **2A**
Achtung! Attention!
adoptieren *v.* to adopt **3A**
Adresse, -n *f.* address **10A**
Allee, -n *f.* avenue **10B**
allein *adv.* alone; by oneself **4A**
Allergie, -n *f.* allergy **9B**
allergisch (gegen) *adj.* allergic (to) **9B**
alles *pron.* everything **7B**
  Alles klar? Everything OK? **1A**
  alles Gute all the best **10A**
  Alles Gute zum Geburtstag! Happy birthday! **5A**
Alltagsroutine, -n *f.* daily routine **9A**
  im Alltag in everyday life
als *conj.* as; when **8A**
  als ob as if **10A**
also *conj.* therefore; so **9B**
alt *adj.* old **3A**
Altkleider *pl.* second-hand clothing **12B**
Altpapier *n.* used paper **12B**
Amerika *n.* America **10B**
amerikanisch *adj.* American **10B**
Amerikaner, - / Amerikanerin, -nen *m./f.* American **10B**
Ampel, -n *f.* traffic light **10B**
an *prep.* at; on; by; in; to **5B**, **10B**
Ananas, - *f.* pineapple **4A**
anbieten *v.* to offer **12B**

anfangen *v.* to begin **4A**
Angebot, -e *n.* offer
  im Angebot on sale **5B**
angeln gehen *v.* to go fishing **2B**
angenehm *adj.* pleasant **3B**
  Angenehm. Nice to meet you. **1A**
angesagt *adj.* trendy **5B**
Angestellte, -n *m./f.* employee **11A**
Angst, ⸚e fear *f.* **7A**
  Angst haben (vor) *v.* to be afraid (of) **7A**
ankommen *v.* to arrive **4A**
Ankunft, ⸚e *f.* arrival **7B**
Anlass, ⸚e *m.* occasion **5A**
  besondere Anlässe *m. pl.* special occasions **5A**
anmachen *v.* to turn on **8B**
Anruf, -e *m.* phone call **11A**
  einen Anruf entgegennehmen *v.* to answer the phone **11A**
anrufen *v.* to call **4A**
  sich anrufen *v.* to call each other **9A**
anschauen *v.* to watch, look at **7A**
anspruchsvoll *adj.* demanding **11B**
anstatt *prep.* instead of **8B**
anstoßen *v.* to toast **5A**
Antwort, -en *f.*
antworten (auf) *v.* to answer **2A**
Anwendung *f.* application; usage
anziehen *v.* to put on **5B**
  sich anziehen *v.* to get dressed **9A**
Anzug, ⸚e *m.* suit **5B**
Apfel, ⸚ *m.* apple **1A**
Apotheke, -n *f.* pharmacy **9B**
April *m.* April **2A**, **7A**
Arbeit, -en *f.* work **11B**
  Arbeit finden *v.* to find a job **11A**
arbeiten (an) *v.* to work (on) **2A**, **7A**
arbeitslos *adj.* unemployed **10A**
Arbeitszimmer, - *n.* home office **6A**
Architekt, -en / Architektin, -nen *m./f.* architect **3B**
Architektur, -en *f.* architecture **2A**
sich ärgern (über) *v.* to get angry (about) **9A**
arm *adj.* poor; unfortunate **3B**
Arm, -e *m.* arm **9A**
Art, -en *f.* species; type **12B**
Artischocke, -n *f.* artichoke **4A**
Arzt, ⸚e / Ärztin, -nen *m./f.* doctor **9B**
  zum Arzt gehen *v.* to go to the doctor **9B**
Assistent, -en / Assistentin, -nen *m./f.* assistant **11A**
Aubergine, -n *f.* eggplant **4A**
auch *adv.* also **1A**

auf *prep.* on, onto, to **5B**
  Auf Wiedersehen. Good-bye. **1A**
aufgehen *v.* to rise (sun) **12A**
auflegen *v.* to hang up **11A**
aufmachen *v.* to open **8B**
aufnehmen *v.* to record **8B**
aufräumen *v.* to clean up **6B**
aufregend *adj.* exciting **12A**
aufrichtig *adj.* sincere **3B**
aufstehen *v.* to get up **4A**
aufwachen *v.* to wake up **9A**
Auge, -n *n.* eye **3A**; **9A**
Augenbraue, -n *f.* eyebrow **9A**
August *m.* August **2A**, **7A**
aus *prep.* from **4A**
Ausbildung, -en *f.* education **11A**
Ausdruck, ⸚e *m.* expression
Ausfahrt, -en *f.* exit **8A**
ausfüllen *v.* to fill out **10A**
  ein Formular ausfüllen *v.* to fill out a form **10A**
Ausgang ⸚e *m.* exit **7B**
ausgefallen *adj.* offbeat **5B**
ausgehen *v.* to go out **4A**
Ausland *n.* abroad **7B**
ausmachen *v.* to turn off **8B**
sich ausruhen *v.* to rest **9A**
ausschalten *v.* turn out, to turn off **12B**
Aussehen *n.* look (style) **5B**
außer *prep.* except (for) **4B**
außerhalb *prep.* outside of **8B**
Aussprache *f.* pronunciation
Aussterben *n.* extinction **12B**
sich ausziehen *v.* to get undressed **9A**
Auto, -s *n.* car **1A**, **8A**
Autobahn, -en *f.* highway **8A**

B

Baby, -s *n.* baby **3A**
Bäckerei, -en *f.* bakery **4A**
Badeanzug, ⸚e *m.* bathing suit **5B**
Bademantel, ⸚ *m.* bathrobe **9A**
sich baden *v.* to bathe, take a bath **9A**
Badewanne, -n *f.* bathtub **6A**
Badezimmer, - bathroom *n.* **6A**, **9A**
Bahnsteig, -e *m.* track; platform **8A**
bald *adv.* soon
  Bis bald. See you soon. **1A**
Balkon, -e/-s *m.* balcony **6A**
Ball, ⸚e *m.* ball **2B**
Ballon, -e/-s *m.* balloon **5A**
Banane, -n *f.* banana **4A**

Bank, ⸚e *f.* bench **10B**
Bank, -en *f.* bank **10A**
  auf der Bank *f.* at the bank **10B**
Bankangestellte, -n *m./f.* bank employee **11B**
bar *adj.* cash **10A**
  bar bezahlen *v.* to pay in cash **10A**
Bargeld *n.* cash **10A**
Bart, ⸚e *m.* beard **9A**
Baseball *m.* baseball **2B**
Basketball *m.* basketball **2B**
Bauch, ⸚e *m.* belly **9A**
Bauchschmerzen *m. pl.* stomachache **9B**
bauen *v.* to build **2A**
Bauer, -n / Bäuerin, -nen *m./f.* farmer **11B**
Bauernhof, ⸚e *m.* farm **12A**
Baum, ⸚e *m.* tree **12A**
Baumwolle *f.* cotton **5B**
Baustelle, -n *f.* construction zone **8A**
beantworten *v.* to answer **4B**
bedeuten *v.* to mean **2A**
bedeutend *adj.* important **12A**
bedienen *v.* to operate, use **8B**
sich beeilen *v.* to hurry **9A**
Beförderung, -en *f.* promotion **11B**
beginnen *v.* to begin **6A**
Begrüßung, -en *f.* greeting **1A**
behaupten *v.* to claim **12B**
bei *prep.* at; near; with **4A**
Beilage, -n *f.* side dish **4B**
Bein, -e *n.* leg **9A**
Beitrag ⸚e *m.* contribution **12B**
bekannt *adj.* well-known **10A**
bekommen *v.* to get, to receive **5A**
belegen *v.* to take (a class) **2A**
benutzen *v.* to use **8A**
Benutzername, -n *m.* screen name **8B**
Benzin, -e *n.* gasoline **8A**
Berg -e *m.* mountain **2B, 12A**
berichten *v.* to report **12B**
Beruf, -e *m.* profession; job **3B, 11A**
Berufsausbildung, -en *f.* professional training **11A**
bescheiden *adj.* modest **3B**
beschreiben *v.* to describe **2A**
Beschreibung, -en *f.* description **3B**
Besen, - *m.* broom **6B**
Besitzer, - / Besitzerin, -nen *m./f.* owner **3B**
besonderes special *adj.* **10A**
  nichts Besonderes *adj.* nothing special **10A**
besorgt worried *adj.* **3B**
Besorgung, -en *f.* errand **10A**
  Besorgungen machen *v.* to run errands **10A**
besprechen *v.* to discuss **7A**
Besprechung, -en *f.* meeting **11A**
besser *adj.* better **8A**
Besserwisser, - / Besserwisserin, -nen *m./f.* know-it-all **2A**
beste *adj.* best **8A**
Besteck *n.* silverware **4B**
bestehen *v.* to pass (a test) **1B**
bestellen *v.* to order **4A**
bestimmt *adv.* definitely. **4A**

besuchen *v.* to visit **4A**
Bett, -en *n.* bed **6A**
  das Bett machen *v.* to make the bed **6B**
  ins Bett gehen *v.* to go bed **9A**
Bettdecke, - n *f.* duvet **6B**
bevor *conj.* before **8A**
sich bewegen *v.* to move (around)
sich bewerben *v.* to apply **11A**
Bewerber, - / die Bewerberin, -nen *m./f.* applicant **11A**
Bewertung, -en *f.* rating **7B**
bezahlen *v.* to pay (for) **4A**
Bibliothek, -en *f.* library **1B**
Bier, -e *n.* beer **4B**
bieten *v.* to offer **9B**
Bild, -er *n.* picture **6A**
Bildschirm, -e *m.* screen **8B**
Bioladen, ⸚ *m.* health-food store **9B**
Biologie *f.* biology **2A**
biologisch *adj.* organic **12B**
Birne, -n *f.* pear **4A**
bis *prep.* until **3B**
  Bis bald. See you soon. **1A**
  Bis dann. See you later. **1A**
  Bis gleich. See you soon. **1A**
  Bis morgen. See you tomorrow. **1A**
  Bis später. See you later. **1A**
  bis zu *prep.* up to; until **10B**
Bitte. Please.; You're welcome. **1A**
Blatt, ⸚er *n.* leaf **12A**
blau *adj.* blue. **3A**
  blaue Fleck, -e *m.* bruise **9B**
bleiben *v.* to stay **5B**
  Bleiben Sie bitte am Apparat. *v.* Please hold. **11A**
Bleistift, -e *m.* pencil **1B**
Blitz, -e *m.* lightning **7A**
blond *adj.* blond **3A**
  blonde Haare *n. pl.* blond hair **3A**
Blume, -n *f.* flower **1A**
Blumengeschäft, -e *n.* flower shop **10A**
Bluse, -n *f.* blouse **5B**
Blutdruck *m.* blood pressure **9B**
Boden, ⸚ *m.* floor; ground **6A**
Bohne, -n *f.* bean **4A**
  grüne Bohne *f.* green bean **4A**
Boot, -e *n.* boat **8A**
Bordkarte, -n *f.* boarding pass **7B**
braten *v.* to fry **2B**
brauchen *v.* to need **2A**
braun *adj.* brown **5B**
braunhaarig *adj.* brown-haired, brunette **3A**
brechen *v.* to break **2B**
  sich (den Arm / das Bein) brechen *v.* to break (an arm / a leg) **9B**
Bremse, -n *f.* brake **8A**
brennen *v.* to burn **5A**
Brief, -e *m.* letter **10A**
  einen Brief abschicken *v.* to mail a letter **10A**
Briefkasten, ⸚ *m.* mailbox **10A**
Briefmarke, -n *f.* stamp **10A**
Briefträger, - / Briefträgerin, -nen *m./f.* mail carrier **10A**

Briefumschlag, ⸚e *m.* envelope **10A**
Brille, -n *f.* glasses **5B**
bringen *v.* to bring **2A**
Brot, -e *n.* bread **4A**
Brötchen, - *n.* roll **4A**
Brücke, -n *f.* bridge **10B**
Bruder, ⸚ *m.* brother **1A**
Brunnen, - *m.* fountain **10B**
Buch, ⸚er *n.* book **1A**
buchen *v.* to make a (hotel) reservation **7B**
Bücherregal, -e *n.* bookshelf **6A**
Buchhalter, - / Buchhalterin, -nen *m./f.* accountant **11B**
büffeln *v.* to cram (for a test) **2A**
Bügelbrett, -er *n.* ironing board **6B**
Bügeleisen, - *n.* iron **6B**
bügeln *v.* to iron **6B**
Bundespräsident, -en / Bundespräsidentin, -nen *m./f.* (federal) president **8B**
bunt *adj.* colorful **10A**
Bürgermeister, - / Bürgermeisterin, -nen *m./f.* mayor **10B**
Bürgersteig, -e *m.* sidewalk **10B**
Büro, -s *n.* office **11B**
Büroklammer, -n *f.* paperclip **11A**
Büromaterial *n.* office supplies **11A**
Bürste, -n *f.* brush **9A**
bürsten *v.* to brush
  sich die Haare bürsten *v.* to brush one's hair **9A**
Bus, -se *m.* bus **8A**
Busch, ⸚e *m.* bush **12A**
Bushaltestelle, -n *f.* bus stop **8A**
Businessklasse *f.* business class **7B**
Bußgeld, -er *n.* fine (monetary) **8A**
Butter *f.* butter **4A**

C

Café, -s *n.* café **2A**
Camping *n.* camping **2B**
CD, -s *f.* compact disc, CD **8B**
Chef, -s / Chefin, -nen *m./f.* boss **11B**
Chemie *f.* chemistry **2A**
China *n.* China **10B**
Chinese, -n / Chinesin, -nen *m./f.* Chinese (person) **10B**
Chinesisch *n.* Chinese (language) **10B**
Computer, - *m.* computer **1B**
Cousin, -s / Cousine, -n *m./f.* cousin **3A**

D

da there **1A**
  Da ist/sind… There is/are… **1A**
Dachboden, ⸚ *m.* attic **6A**
dafür *adv.* for it **6A**
daher *adv.* from there **6A**
dahin *adv.* there **6A**
damit *conj.* so that **10A**
danach *conj.* then, after that **9B**
danken *v.* to thank **2A**
  Danke. Thank you. **1A**
dann *adv.* then **7B**
daran *adv.* on it **6A**

darauf *adv.* on it **6A**
darin *adv.* in it **6A**
das *n.* the; this/that **1A**
dass *conj.* that **10A**
Datei, - en *f.* file **8B**
Datum (*pl.* Daten) *n.* date **7A**
davon *adv.* of it **6A**
davor *adv.* before it **6A**
Decke, -n *f.* blanket **6B**
decken *v.* to cover **6B**
  den Tisch decken *v.* to set the table **6B**
denken *v.* to think **5A**
  denken an *v.* to think about **7A**
denn *conj.* for; because **6A**
der *m.* the **1A**
deshalb *conj.* therefore; so **9B**
deswegen *conj.* that's why; therefore **9B**
deutsch German *adj.* **10B**
Deutsch German (language) *n.* **10B**
Deutsche *m./f.* German (man/woman) **10B**
Deutschland *n.* Germany **4A**
deutschsprachig *adj.* German-speaking
Dezember *m.* December **2A, 7A**
Diät, -en *f.* diet **4B**
  auf Diät sein *v.* to be on a diet **4B**
dick *adj.* fat **3A**
die *f./pl.* the **1A**
Dienstag, -e *m.* Tuesday **2A**
  dienstags *adv.* on Tuesdays **2A**
dieser/diese/dieses *m./f./n.* this; these **8B**
diesmal *adv.* this time **7B**
Digitalkamera, -s *f.* digital camera **8B**
Ding, -e *n.* thing **2A**
Diplom, -e *n.* diploma (degree) **2A**
diskret *adj.* discreet **3B**
doch *adv.* yes (contradicting a negative statement or question) **2B**
Dokument, -e *n.* document **8B**
Donner, - *m.* thunder **7A**
Donnerstag, -e *n.* Thursday **2A**
  donnerstags *adv.* on Thursdays **2A**
dort *adv.* there **1A**
Dozent, -en / Dozentin, -nen *m./f.* college instructor **2A**
draußen *prep.* outside; *adv.* out **7A**
  Es ist schön draußen. It's nice out. **7A**
dreckig *adj.* filthy **6B**
drei three **2A**
dritte third *adj.* **2A**
Drogerie, -n *f.* drugstore **10A**
drüben *adv.* over there **4A**
drücken *v.* to push **3B**; to print **8B**
Drucker, - *m.* printer **8B**
du *pron.* (*sing. inf.*) you **1A**
dumm *adj.* dumb **8A**
dunkel *adj.* dark **3A**
dunkelhaarig *adj.* dark-haired **3A**
dünn *adj.* thin **3A**
durch *prep.* through **3B**
durchfallen *v.* to flunk; to fail **1B**
durchmachen *v.* to experience **8B**
dürfen *v.* to be allowed to; may **3B**
(sich) duschen *v.* to take a shower **9A**

Dutzend, -e *n.* dozen **4A**
DVD, -s *f.* DVD **8B**
DVD-Player, - *m.* DVD-player **8B**

E

Ecke, -n *f.* corner **10B**
egoistisch *adj.* selfish **3B**
Ehe, -n *f.* marriage **5A**
Ehefrau, -en *f.* wife **3A**
Ehemann, -̈er *m.* husband **3A**
Ei, -er *n.* egg **4A**
Eichhörnchen, - *n.* squirrel **12A**
eifersüchtig *adj.* jealous **3B**
ein/eine *m./f./n.* a **1A**
Einbahnstraße, -n *f.* one-way street **8A**
einfach *adj.* easy **2A**
einfarbig *adj.* solid colored **5B**
eingebildet *adj.* arrogant **3B**
einkaufen *v.* to shop **4A**
  einkaufen gehen *v.* to go shopping **4A**
Einkaufen *n.* shopping **5B**
Einkaufszentrum, (*pl.* Einkaufszentren) *n.* mall; shopping center **10B**
Einkommensgruppe, -n *f.* income bracket **6B**
einladen *v.* to invite **5A**
einmal *adv.* once **7B**
eins one **2A**
einschlafen *v.* to go to sleep **4A**
einzahlen *v.* to deposit (money) **10A**
Einzelkind, -er *n.* only child **3A**
Eis *n.* ice cream **5A**
Eisdiele, -n *f.* ice cream shop **4A**
Eishockey *n.* ice hockey **2B**
Eiswürfel, - *m.* ice cube **5A**
elegant *adj.* elegant **5B**
Elektriker, - / Elektrikerin, -nen *m./f.* electrician **11B**
elf eleven **2A**
Ell(en)bogen, - *m.* elbow **9A**
Eltern *pl.* parents **3A**
E-Mail, -s *f.* e-mail **8B**
empfehlen *v.* to recommend **2B**
Empfehlungsschreiben, - *n.* letter of recommendation **11A**
endlich *adv.* finally **9B**
Energie, -n *f.* energy **12A**
energiesparend *adj.* energy-efficient **6B**
eng *adj.* tight **5B**
England *n.* England **10B**
Engländer, - / Engländerin, -nen *m./f.* English (person) **10B**
Englisch *n.* English (language) **10B**
Enkelkind, -er *n.* grandchild. **3A**
Enkelsohn, -̈e *m.* grandson **3A**
Enkeltochter, -̈ *f.* granddaughter **3A**
entdecken *v.* to discover **6B**
entfernen *v.* to remove **6B**
entlang *prep.* along, down **3B**
entlassen *v.* to fire; to lay off **11B**
sich entschließen *v.* to decide **4B**
(sich) entschuldigen *v.* to apologize; to excuse
  Entschuldigen Sie. Excuse me. (*form.*) **1A**

Entschuldigung. Excuse me. **1A**
sich entspannen *v.* to relax **9A**
entwerten *v.* to validate **8A**
  eine Fahrkarte entwerten *v.* to validate a ticket **8A**
entwickeln *v.* to develop **12B**
er *pron.* he **1A**
Erdbeben, - *n.* earthquake **12A**
Erdbeere, -n *f.* strawberry **4A**
Erde, -n *f.* earth **12B**
Erderwärmung *f.* global warming **12B**
Erdgeschoss, -e *n.* ground floor **6A**
Erfahrung, -en *f.* experience **11A**
erfinden *v.* to invent **7A**
Erfolg, -e *m.* success **11B**
erforschen *v.* to explore **12A**
ergänzen *v.* complete
Ergebnis, -se *n.* result; score **1B**
erhalten *v.* to preserve **12B**
sich erinnern (an) *v.* to remember **9A**
sich erkälten *v.* to catch a cold **9A**
Erkältung, -en *f.* cold **9B**
erkennen *v.* to recognize **7A**
erklären *v.* to explain **4A**
erneuerbare Energie, -n *f.* renewable energy **12B**
ernst *adj.* serious **3B**
erster/erste/erstes *adj.* first **2A**
erwachsen grown-up *adj.* **10A**
erzählen *v.* to tell **7A**
  erzählen von *v.* to talk about **7A**
es *pron.* it **1A**
  Es geht. (I'm) so-so. **1A**
  Es gibt... There is/are... **2B**
Essen, - *n.* food **4A**
essen *v.* to eat **2B**
  essen gehen *v.* to eat out **2B**
Esslöffel, - *m.* soup spoon **4B**
Esszimmer, - *n.* dining room **6A**
etwas *pron.* something **7B**
  etwas anderes something else **10A**
euer (*pl. inf.*) *poss. adj.* your **3A**

F

Fabrik, -en *f.* factory **12B**
Fabrikarbeiter, - / Fabrikarbeiterin, -nen *m./f.* factory worker **11B**
Fach, -̈er *n.* subject **2A**
fade *adj.* bland **4B**
fahren to drive; to go *v.* **2B**
  Auto fahren *v.* to drive a car **8A**
  Fahrrad fahren *v.* to ride a bicycle **2B**
  geradeaus fahren *v.* to go straight ahead **8A**
Fahrer, - / Fahrerin, -nen *m./f.* driver **8A**
Fahrgemeinschaft, -en *f.* carpool **12B**
Fahrkarte, -n *f.* ticket **8A**
  eine Fahrkarte entwerten *v.* to validate a ticket **8A**
Fahrkartenschalter, - *m.* ticket office **8A**
Fahrplan, -̈e *m.* schedule **8A**
Fahrrad, -̈er *n.* bicycle **2B, 8A**
Fahrstuhl, -̈e *m.* elevator **7B**
fallen *v.* to fall **2B**

Familie, -n *f.* family **3A**
Familienstand, -̈e *m.* marital status **3A**
Fan, -s *m.* fan **2B**
fangen *v.* to catch **2B**
fantastisch *adj.* fantastic **10A**
Farbe, -n *f.* color **5B**
färben *v.* to dye
 sich die Haare färben *v.* to dye one's hair **9A**
fast *adv.* almost **4A**
faul *adj.* lazy **3B**
Februar *m.* February **2A, 7A**
fegen *v.* to sweep **6B**
feiern *v.* to celebrate **5A**
Feiertag, -e *m.* holiday **5A**
Feinkostgeschäft, -e *n.* delicatessen **4A**
Feld, -er *n.* field **12A**
Fenster, - *n.* window **1A**
Ferien *pl.* vacation **7A**
Fernbedienung, -en *f.* remote control **8B**
fernsehen *v.* to watch television **8B**
Fernsehen *n.* television (programming)
Fernseher, - *m.* television set **8B**
fertig *adj.* ready; finished **11B**
Fest, -e *n.* festival; celebration **5A**
Festplatte, -n *f.* hard drive **8B**
**Feuerwehrmann, -̈er / Feuerwehrfrau, -en
 (pl. Feuerwehrleute)** *m./f.* firefighter **11B**
Fieber, - *n.* fever **9B**
 Fieber haben *v.* to have a fever **9B**
finden *v.* to find **2A**
Finger, - *m.* finger **9A**
Firma (pl. die Firmen) *f.* firm; company **11A**
Fisch, -e *m.* fish **4A, 12A**
Fischgeschäft, -e *n.* fish store **4A**
fit *adj.* in good shape **2B**
Flasche, -n *f.* bottle **4B**
Fleisch *n.* meat **4A**
fleißig *adj.* hard-working **3B**
fliegen *v.* to fly **7B**
Flug, -̈e *m.* flight **7B**
Flughafen, -̈ *m.* airport **7B**
Flugticket, -s *n.* (plane) ticket **7B**
Flugzeug, -e *n.* airplane **7B**
Flur, -e *m.* hall **6A**
Fluss, -̈e *m.* river **3B, 12A**
folgen *v.* to follow **5A, 10B**
Form, -en *f.* shape, form
 in guter/schlechter Form sein *v.* to be in/out of shape **9B**
Formular, -e *n.* form **10A**
 ein Formular ausfüllen *v.* to fill out a form **10A**
Foto, -s *n.* photo, picture **1B**
Frage, -n *f.* question **1B**
fragen *v.* to ask **2A**
 fragen nach *v.* to ask about **7A**
 sich fragen *v.* to wonder, ask oneself **9A**
Frankreich *n.* France **10B**
Franzose, -n / Französin, -nen *m./f.* French (person) **10B**
Französisch *n.* French (language) **10B**
Frau, -en *f.* woman **1A**; wife **3A**
 Frau... Mrs./Ms.... **1A**
Freitag, -e *m.* Friday **2A**

freitags *adv.* on Fridays **2A**
Freizeit, -en *f.* free time, leisure **2B**
Freizeitaktivität, - en *f.* leisure activity **2B**
Fremdsprache, -n *f.* foreign language **2A**
sich freuen (über) *v.* to be happy (about) **9A**
 Freut mich. Pleased to meet you. **1A**
 sich freuen auf *v.* to look forward to **9A**
Freund, -e / Freundin, -nen *m./f.* friend **1A**
freundlich *adj.* friendly **3B**
 Mit freundlichen Grüßen Yours sincerely **3B**
Freundschaft, -en *f.* friendship **5A**
Frischvermählte, -n *m./f.* newlywed **5A**
Friseur, -e / Friseurin, -nen *m./f.* hairdresser **3B**
froh *adj.* happy **3B**
 Frohe Ostern! Happy Easter! **5A**
 Frohe Weihnachten! Merry Christmas! **5A**
früh *adj.* early; in the morning **2B**
 morgen früh tomorrow morning **2B**
Frühling, -e *m.* spring **2B, 7A**
Frühstück, -e *n.* breakfast **4B**
fühlen *v.* to feel **2A**
 sich (wohl) fühlen *v.* to feel (well) **9A**
füllen *v.* to fill
fünf five **2A**
funktionieren *v.* to work, function **8B**
für *prep.* for **3B**
furchtbar *adj.* awful **7A**
Fuß, -̈e *m.* foot **9A**
Fußball *m.* soccer **2B**
Fußgänger, - / Fußgängerin, -nen *m./f.* pedestrian **10B**

G

Gabel, -n *f.* fork **4B**
Gang, -̈e *m.* course **4B**
 erster/zweiter Gang *m.* first/second course **4B**
ganz *adj.* all, total **7B**
ganztags *adj.* full-time **11B**
Garage, -n *f.* garage **5B**
Garnele, -n *f.* shrimp **4A**
Gartenabfall, -̈e *m.* yard waste **12B**
Gärtner, - /Gärtnerin, -nen *m./f.* gardener **11B**
Gast, -̈e *m.* guest **5A**
Gastfamilie, -n *f.* host family **4B**
Gastgeber, - / Gastgeberin, -nen *m./f.* host/ hostess **5A**
Gebäck, -e *n.* pastries; baked goods **5A**
Gebäude, - *n.* building **10A**
geben *v.* to give **2B**
 Es gibt... There is/are... **2B**
Geburt, -en *f.* birth **5A**
Geburtstag, -e *m.* birthday **5A**
 Wann hast du Geburtstag? When is your birthday? **7A**
geduldig *adj.* patient **3B**
Gefahr, -en *f.* danger **12B**
gefährdet *adj.* endangered; threatened **12B**
gefallen *v.* to please **5A**
Gefrierschrank, -̈e *m.* freezer **6B**
gegen *prep.* against **3B**
gegenüber (von) *prep.* across (from) **10B**
Gehalt, -̈er *n.* salary **11A**

hohes/niedriges Gehalt, -̈er high/low salary *n.* **11A**
Gehaltserhöhung, -en *f.* raise **11B**
gehen to go *v.* **2A**
 Es geht. (I'm) so-so. **1A**
 Geht es dir/Ihnen gut? *v.* Are you all right? (*inf./form.*) **1A**
 Wie geht es Ihnen? (*form.*) How are you? **1A**
 Wie geht's (dir)? (*inf.*) How are you? **1A**
gehören *v.* to belong to **4B**
Geländewagen, - *m.* SUV **8B**
gelb *adj.* yellow **5B**
Geld, -er *n.* money **10A**
 Geld abheben/einzahlen *v.* to withdraw/deposit money **10A**
Geldautomat, -en *m.* ATM **10A**
Geldschein, -e *m.* bill (money) **10A**
gemein *adj.* mean **3B**
Gemüse, - ** *n.* vegetables **4A
genau *adv.* exactly
 genauso wie just as **8A**
genießen *v.* to enjoy
geöffnet *adj.* open **10A**
Gepäck *n.* luggage **7B**
geradeaus straight ahead *adv.* **8A**
gern *adv.* with pleasure **2B**
 gern (+verb) to like to (+verb) **2B**
 ich hätte gern... I would like... **4A**
 Gern geschehen. My pleasure.; You're welcome. **1A**
Geschäft, -e *n.* business **11A**; store **4A**
Geschäftsführer, - / Geschäftsführerin, -nen *m./f.* manager **11A**
Geschäftsmann, -̈er / Geschäftsfrau, -en (pl. Geschäftsleute) *m./f.* businessman/ businesswoman **3B**
Geschenk, -e *n.* gift **5A**
Geschichte, -n *f.* history **2A**; story
geschieden *adj.* divorced **3A**
Geschirr *n.* dishes **6B**
 Geschirr spülen *v.* to do the dishes **6B**
geschlossen *adj.* closed **10A**
Geschmack, -̈e *m.* flavor; taste **4B**
Geschwister, - *n.* sibling **3A**
Gesetz, -e *n.* law **12B**
Gesicht, -er *n.* face **9A**
gestern *adv.* yesterday **5B**
gestreift *adj.* striped **5B**
gesund *adj.* healthy **8A; 9B**
 gesund werden *v.* to get better **9B**
Gesundheit *f.* health **9B**
geteilt durch divided by **1B**
Getränk, -e *n.* beverage **4B**
getrennt *adj.* separated **3A**
gewaltfrei *adj.* nonviolent **12B**
Gewerkschaft, -en *f.* labor union **11B**
gewinnen *v.* to win **2B**
Gewitter, - *n.* thunderstorm **7A**
sich gewöhnen an *v.* to get used to **9A**
gierig *adj.* greedy **3B**
Giftmüll *m.* toxic waste **12B**
Glas, -̈er *n.* glass **4B**
glatt *adj.* straight **3A**
 glatte Haare *n. pl.* straight hair **3A**

glauben *v.* to believe **5A**
gleich *adj.* same
  ist gleich *v.* equals, is **1B**
Glück *n.* happiness **5A**
glücklich *adj.* happy **3B**
Golf *n.* golf **2B**
Grad *n.* degree **7A**
  Es sind 18 Grad draußen. It's 18 degrees out. **7A**
Gramm, -e *n.* gram **4A**
Granit, -e *m.* granite **6B**
Gras, ̈er *n.* grass **12A**
gratulieren *v.* to congratulate **5A**
grau *adj.* grey **5B**
grausam *adj.* cruel
Grippe, -n *f.* flu **9B**
groß *adj.* big; tall **3A**
großartig *adj.* terrific **3A**
Großeltern *pl.* grandparents **1A**
Großmutter, ̈ *f.* grandmother **3A**
Großvater, ̈ *m.* grandfather **3A**
großzügig *adj.* generous **3B**
grün *adj.* green **5B**
  grüne Bohne (*pl.* die grünen Bohnen) *f.* green bean **4A**
Gruß, ̈e *m.* greeting
  Mit freundlichen Grüßen Yours sincerely **3B**
grüßen *v.* to greet **2A**
günstig *adj.* cheap **5B**
Gürtel, - *m.* belt **5B**
gut *adj.* good; *adv.* well **1A**
  gut aussehend *adj.* handsome **3A**
  gut gekleidet *adj.* well-dressed **5B**
  Gute Besserung! Get well! **5A**
  Guten Appetit! Enjoy your meal! **4B**
  Guten Abend! Good evening. **1A**
  Guten Morgen! Good morning. **1A**
  Gute Nacht! Good night. **1A**
  Guten Tag! Hello. **1A**

H

Haar, -e hair *n.* **3A, 9A**
Haartrockner, - *m.* hair dryer **9A**
haben to have *v.* **1B**
Hagel *m.* hail **7A**
Hähnchen, - *n.* chicken **4A**
halb half; half an hour before **2A**
Halbbruder, ̈ *m.* half brother **3A**
Halbschwester, -n *f.* half sister **3A**
halbtags *adj.* part-time **11B**
Hallo! Hello. **1A**
Hals, ̈e *m.* neck **9A**
  Hals- und Beinbruch! Break a leg! **5A**
Halskette, -n *f.* necklace **5B**
Hand, ̈e *f.* hand **9A**
handeln *v.* to act
  handeln von *v.* to be about; have to do with **7A**
Handgelenk, -e *n.* wrist **9B**
Handgepäck *n.* carry-on luggage **7B**
Handschuh, -e *m.* glove **5B**
Handtasche, -n *f.* purse **5B**
Handtuch, ̈er *n.* towel **9A**
Handy, -s *n.* cell phone **8B**

hängen *v.* to hang **5B**
Hase, -n *m.* hare **12A**
hässlich *adj.* ugly **3A**
Hauptspeise, -n *f.* main course **4B**
Hauptstraße, -n *f.* main road **10B**
Haus, ̈er *n.* house **6A**
  nach Hause *adv.* home **5B**
  zu Hause *adv.* at home **4A**
Hausarbeit *f.* housework **6B**
  Hausarbeit machen *v.* to do housework **6B**
Hausaufgabe, -n *f.* homework **1B**
Hausfrau, -en / Hausmann, ̈er *f./m.* homemaker **11B**
hausgemacht *adj.* homemade **4B**
Hausmeister, - / Hausmeisterin, -nen *m./f.* caretaker; custodian **11B**
Hausschuh, -e *m.* slipper **9A**
Haustier, -e *n.* pet **3A**
Heft, -e *n.* notebook **1B**
Hefter, - *m.* stapler **11A**
heiraten *v.* to marry **3A**
heiß *adj.* hot **7A**
heißen *v.* to be named **2A**
  Ich heiße... My name is... **1A**
helfen *v.* to help **2B**
  helfen bei *v.* to help with **7A**
hell *adj.* light **3A**; bright **5B**
Hemd, -en *n.* shirt **5B**
herauf *adv.* up; upwards **6A**
heraus *adv.* out **6A**
Herbst, -e *m.* fall, autumn **2B, 7A**
Herd, -e *m.* stove **6B**
Herr Mr. **1A**
herunter *adv.* down; downwards **6A**
heruntergehen *v.* to go down **10B**
  die Treppe heruntergehen *v.* to go downstairs **10B**
herunterladen *v.* to download **8B**
Herz, -en *n.* heart
  Herzlichen Glückwunsch! Congratulations! **5A**
heute *adv.* today **2B**
  Heute ist der... Today is the... **2A**
  Welcher Tag ist heute? What day is it today? **7A**
  Der Wievielte ist heute? What is the date today? **2A**
hier *adv.* here **1A**
  Hier ist/sind... Here is/are... **1B**
Himmel *m.* sky **12A**
hin und zurück there and back **7B**
sich hinlegen *v.* to lie down **9A**
sich hinsetzen *v.* to sit down **9A**
hinter *prep.* behind **5B**
hinterlassen *v.* to leave (behind)
eine Nachricht hinterlassen *v.* to leave a message **11A**
Hobby, -s *n.* hobby **2B**
hoch *adj.* high **8A**
hochgehen *v.* to go up, climb up **10B**
  die Treppe hochgehen *v.* to go upstairs **10B**
Hochwasser, - *n.* flood **12B**
Hochzeit, -en *f.* wedding **5A**
Hockey *n.* hockey **2B**
Höflichkeit, -en *f.* courtesy; polite expression **1A**
Holz, ̈er *n.* wood **6B**

hören *v.* to hear; listen to **2A**
Hörer, - *m.* receiver **11A**
Hörsaal (*pl.* Hörsäle) *m.* lecture hall **2A**
Hose, -n *f.* pants **5B**
  kurze Hose *f.* shorts **5B**
Hotel, -s *n.* hotel **7B**
  Fünf-Sterne-Hotel *n* five-star hotel. **7B**
Hotelgast, ̈e *m.* hotel guest **7B**
hübsch *adj.* pretty **3A**
Hund, -e *m.* dog **3A**
Hundewetter *n.* terrible weather **7A**
husten *v.* to cough **9B**
Hut, ̈e *m.* hat **5B**
Hybridauto, -s *n.* hybrid car **12B**

I

ich *pron.* I **1A**
Idee, -n *f.* idea **1A**
Ihr (*form., sing/pl.*) *poss. adj.* your **3A**
ihr (*inf., pl.*) *pron.* you **1A**; *poss. adj.* her, their **3A**
immer *adv.* always **4A**
Immobilienmakler, - / Immobilienmaklerin, -nen *m./f.* real estate agent **11B**
in *prep.* in **5B**
Inder, - / Inderin, -nen *m./f.* Indian (person) **10B**
Indien *n.* India **10B**
indisch *adj.* Indian **10B**
Informatik *f.* computer science **2A**
sich informieren (über) *v.* to find out (about) **9A**
Ingenieur, -e / Ingenieurin, -nen *m./f.* engineer **3B**
Innenstadt, ̈e *f.* city center; downtown **10B**
innerhalb *prep.* inside of, within **8B**
Insel, -n *f.* island **12A**
intellektuell *adj.* intellectual **3B**
intelligent *adj.* intelligent **3B**
interessant *adj.* interesting **2A**
sich interessieren (für) *v.* to be interested (in) **9A**
Internet *n.* Web **8B**
  im Internet surfen *v.* to surf the Web **8B**
Internetcafé, -s *n.* internet café **10A**
Italien *n.* Italy **10B**
Italiener, - / Italienerin, -nen *m./f.* Italian (person) **10B**
Italienisch *n.* Italian (language) **10B**

J

ja yes **1A**
Jacke, -n *f.* jacket **5B**
Jahr, -e *n.* year **7A**
  Ein gutes neues Jahr! Happy New Year! **5A**
  Ich bin... Jahre alt. I am... years old **1B**
Jahrestag, -e *m.* anniversary **5A**
Jahreszeit, -en *f.* season **7A**
Januar *m.* January **2A, 7A**
Japan *n.* Japan **10B**
Japaner, - / Japanerin, -nen *m./f.* Japanese (person) **10B**
Japanisch *n.* Japanese (language) **10B**
Jeans *f.* jeans **5B**
jeder/jede/jedes *adj.* any, every, each **8B**

jemand *pron.* someone **7B**
jetzt *adv.* now **4A**
joggen *v.* to jog **2B**
Joghurt, -s *m.* yogurt **4A**
Journalist, -en / Journalistin, -nen *m./f.*
  journalist **3B**
Jugendherberge, -n *f.* youth hostel **7B**
jugendlich *adj.* young; youthful **10A**
Juli *m.* July **2A, 7A**
jung *adj.* young **3A**
Junge, -n *m.* boy **1A**
Juni *m.* June **2A, 7A**
Juweliergeschäft, -e *n.* jewelry store **10A**

K

Kaffee, -s *m.* coffee **4B**
Kaffeemaschine, -n *f.* coffeemaker **6B**
Kalender, - *m.* calendar **1B**
kalt *adj.* cold **7A**
sich (die Haare) kämmen *v.* to comb (one's hair)
  9A
Kanada *n.* Canada **10B**
Kanadier, - / Kanadierin, -nen *m./f.*
  Canadian **10B**
Kandidat, -en *m.* candidate **11A**
Kaninchen, - *n.* rabbit **12A**
Karotte, -n *f.* carrot **4A**
Karriere, -n *f.* career **11B**
Karte, -n *f.* map **1B**, *f.* card **2B; 5A**
  eine Karte lesen *v.* to read a map **7B**
  mit der Karte bezahlen *v.* to pay by (credit)
    card **10A**
Kartoffel, -n *f.* potato **4A**
Käse, - *m.* cheese **4A**
Katze, -n *f.* cat **3A**
kaufen *v.* to buy **2A**
Kaufhaus, -er *n.* department store **10B**
Kaution, -en *f.* security deposit **6A**
kein *adj.* no **2B**
  Keine Zufahrt. Do not enter. **3B**
Keks, -e *m.* cookie **5A**
Keller, - *m.* cellar **6A**
Kellner, - / Kellnerin, -nen *m./f.* waiter/
  waitress **3B, 4B**
kennen *v.* to know, be familiar with **5B**
  sich kennen *v.* to know each other **9A**
  (sich) kennen lernen *v.* to meet (one another) **1A**
Keramik, -en *f.* ceramic **6B**
Kernenergie *f.* nuclear energy **12B**
Kernkraftwerk, -e *n.* nuclear power plant **12B**
Kind, -er *n.* child **1A**
Kino, -s *n.* movie theater **10A**
Kiosk, -e *m.* newspaper kiosk **10A**
Kirche, -n *f.* church **10B**
Kissen, - *n.* pillow **6B**
Klasse, -n *f.* class **1B**
  erste/zweite Klasse, -n first/second class **8A**
Klassenkamerad, -en / Klassenkameradin,
  -nen *m./f.* (K-12) classmate **1B**
Klassenzimmer, - *n.* classroom **1B**
klassisch *adj.* classical **10A**
Kleid, -er *n.* dress **5B**
Kleidergröße, -n *f.* clothing size **5B**

Kleidung *f. pl.* clothes **5B**
klein *adj.* small; short (stature) **3A**
Kleingeld *n.* change (money) **10A**
Klempner, - / Klempnerin, -nen *m./f.* plumber **11B**
klettern *v.* to climb (mountain) **2B**
klingeln *v.* to ring **8B**
Klippe, -n *f.* cliff **12A**
Knie, - *n.* knee **9A**
Knoblauch, -e *m.* garlic **4A**
Koch, -e / Köchin, -nen *m./f.* cook, chef **4B**
kochen *v.* to cook **2B**
Koffer, - *m.* suitcase **7B**
Kofferraum, -e *m.* trunk **8A**
Kombi, -s *m.* station wagon **8B**
Komma, -s *n.* comma **1B**
kommen *v.* to come **2A**
Kommilitone, -n / Kommilitonin, -nen *m./f.*
  (university) classmate **1B**
Kommode, -n *f.* dresser **6A**
kompliziert *adj.* complicated **10A**
Konditorei, -en *f.* pastry shop **4A**
können *v.* to be able, can **3B**
Konto (pl. Konten) *n.* bank account **10A**
Konzert, -e *n.* concert **5B**
Kopf, -e *m.* head **9A**
Kopfhörer, - *m.* headphones **8B**
Kopfschmerzen *m. pl.* headache **9B**
Korea *n.* Korea **10B**
der Koreaner, - / die Koreanerin, -nen *m./f.*
  Korean (person) **10B**
Koreanisch *n.* Korean (language) **10B**
Körper, - *m.* body **9A**
korrigieren *v.* to correct **2A**
Kosmetiksalon, -s *m.* beauty salon **10A**
kosten *v.* to cost **2A**
  Wie viel kostet das? *v.* How much is that? **4A**
krank *adj.* sick **9B**
  krank werden *v.* to get sick **9B**
Krankenhaus, -er *n.* hospital **9B**
Krankenpfleger, - / Krankenschwester, -n *m./f.*
  nurse **9B**
Krankenwagen, - *m.* ambulance **9B**
Krawatte, -n *f.* tie **5B**
Kreuzfahrt, -en *f.* cruise **7B**
Kreuzung, -en *f.* intersection **10B**
Küche, -n *f.* kitchen **6A**
Kuchen, - *m.* cake; pie **4A**
Kuh, -e *f.* cow **12A**
kühl *adj.* cool **7A**
Kühlschrank, -e *m.* refrigerator **6B**
Kuli, -s *m.* (ball-point) pen **1B**
Kunde, -n / Kundin, -nen *m./f.* customer **5B**
kündigen *v.* to resign **11B**
Kunst, -e *f.* art **2A**
Kunststoff, -e *m.* plastic **6B**
kurz *adj.* short **3A**
  kurze Haare *n. pl.* short hair **3A**
  kurze Hose *f.* shorts **5B**
kurzärmlig *adj.* short-sleeved **5B**
Kurzfilm, -e *m.* short film
Kuss, -e *m.* kiss **5A**
küssen *v.* to kiss **5A**
  sich küssen *v.* to kiss (each other) **9A**
Küste, -n *f.* coast **12A**

L

lächeln *v.* to smile **3B**
lachen *v.* to laugh **3B**
Ladegerät, -e *n.* battery charger **8B**
laden *v.* to charge; load **8B**
Lage, -n *f.* location **7B**
Laken, - *n.* sheet **6B**
Lampe, -n *f.* lamp **6A**
Land, -er *n.* country **7B**
landen *v.* to land **7B**
Landkarte, -n *f.* map **7B**
Landschaft, -en *f.* landscape;
  countryside **12A**
lang *adj.* long **3A**
  lange Haare *n. pl.* long hair **3A**
langärmlig *adj.* long-sleeved **5B**
langsam *adj* slow. **3B**
  Langsam fahren. Slow down. **3B**
langweilig *adj.* boring **2A**
Laptop, -s *m./n.* laptop (computer) **8B**
lassen *v.* to let, allow **2B**
laufen *v.* to run **2B**
leben *v.* to live **2A**
Lebenslauf, -e *m.* résumé; CV **11A**
Lebensmittelgeschäft, -e *n.* grocery store **4A**
lecker *adj.* delicious **4B**
Leder, - *n.* leather **5B**
ledig *adj.* single **3A**
legen *v.* to lay **5B**; *v.* to put; lay **9A**
Lehrbuch, -er *n.* textbook (university) **1B**
Lehrer, - / Lehrerin, -nen *m./f.* teacher **1B**
leicht *adj.* light **4B**; mild **9B**
Leichtathletik *f.* track and field **2B**
leider *adv.* unfortunately **4A**
leiten *v.* to manage **11B**
Lenkrad, -er *n.* steering wheel **8A**
lernen *v.* to study; to learn **2A**
lesen *v.* to read **2B**
letzter/letzte/letztes *adj.* last **2B**
Leute *pl.* people **3B**
Licht, -er *n.* light **12B**
Liebe, -n *f.* love **5A**
  Lieber/Liebe *m./f.* Dear **3B**
lieben *v.* to love **2A**
  sich lieben *v.* to love each other **9A**
lieber *adj.* rather **8A**
liebevoll *adj.* loving **3B**
Liebling, -e *m.* darling
  Lieblings- favorite **4B**
liegen *v.* to lie; to be located **5B**
lila *adj.* purple **5B**
Linie, -n *f.* line
Lippe, -n *f.* lip **9A**
Lippenstift, -e *m.* lipstick **9A**
Literatur, -en *f.* literature **2A**
LKW, -s *m.* truck **8A**
LKW-Fahrer, - / LKW-Fahrerin, -nen *m./f.* truck
  driver **11B**
lockig *adj.* curly **3A**
  lockige Haare *n. pl.* curly hair **3A**
Los! Start!; Go! **2B**
löschen *v.* to delete **8B**
Lösung, -en *f.* solution **12B**

eine Lösung vorschlagen *v.* to propose a solution **12B**
Luft, ⁼e *f.* air **12A**
lügen *v.* to lie, tell a lie
Lust, ⁼e *f.* desire
   Lust haben *v.* to feel like **7B**
lustig *adj.* funny **3B**

M

machen *v.* to do; make **2A**
   Mach's gut! *v.* All the best! **3B**
Mädchen, - *n.* girl **1A**
Mahlzeit, -en *f.* meal **4B**
Mai *m.* May **2A, 7A**
Mal, -e *n.* time
   das erste/letzte Mal the first/last time **7B**
   zum ersten/letzten Mal for the first/last time **7B**
mal times **1B**
Mama, -s *f.* mom **3A**
man *pron.* one **7B**
mancher/manche/manches *adj.* some. **8B**
manchmal *adv.* sometimes **7B**
Mann, ⁼er *m.* man **1A**; *m.* husband **3A**
Mannschaft, -en *f.* team **2B**
Mantel, ⁼ *m.* coat **5B**
Markt, ⁼e *m.* market **4A**
Marmelade, -n *f.* jam **4A**
Marmor *m.* marble **6B**
März *m.* March **2A, 7A**
Material, -ien *n.* material **5B**
Mathematik *f.* mathematics **2A**
Maus, ⁼e *f.* mouse **8B**
Mechaniker, - / Mechanikerin, -nen *m./f.* mechanic **8A**
Medikament, -e *n.* medicine **9B**
Medizin *f.* medicine **2A**
Meer, -e *n.* sea; ocean **12A**
Meeresfrüchte *f. pl.* seafood **4A**
mehr *adj.* more **8A**
mein *poss. adj.* my **3A**
meinen *v.* to mean; to believe; to maintain **12B**
Meisterschaft, -en *f.* championship **2B**
Melone, -n *f.* melon **4A**
Mensa (*pl.* Mensen) *f.* cafeteria (college/university) **1B**
Mensch, -en *m.* person
Messer, - *n.* knife **4B**
Metzgerei, -en *f.* butcher shop **4A**
Mexikaner, - / Mexikanerin, -nen *m./f.* Mexican (person) **10B**
mexikanisch *adj.* Mexican **10B**
Mexiko *n.* Mexico **10B**
Miete, -n *f.* rent **6A**
mieten *v.* to rent **6A**
Mikrofon, -e *n.* microphone **8B**
Mikrowelle, -n *f.* microwave **6B**
Milch *f.* milk **4B**
Minderheit, -en *f.* minority **12B**
Mineralwasser *n.* sparkling water **4B**
minus minus **1B**
mir *pron.* myself, me **7A**

Mir geht's (sehr) gut. *v.* I am (very) well. **1A**
Mir geht's nicht (so) gut. *v.* I am not (so) well. **1A**
mit with **4B**
Mitbewohner, - / Mitbewohnerin, -nen *m./f.* roommate **2A**
mitbringen *v.* to bring along **4A**
mitkommen *v.* to come along **4A**
mitmachen *v.* to participate **8B**
mitnehmen *v.* to bring with **10B**
   jemanden mitnehmen *v.* to give someone a ride **10B**
Mittag, -e *m.* noon **2A**
Mittagessen *n.* lunch **4B**
Mitternacht *f.* midnight **2A**
Mittwoch, -e *m.* Wednesday **2A**
   mittwochs *adv.* on Wednesdays **2A**
Möbel, - *n.* furniture **6A**
Möbelstück, -e *n.* piece of furniture **6A**
möbliert *adj.* furnished **6A**
modern *adj.* modern **10A**
modisch *adj.* fashionable **5B**
mögen *v.* to like **4B**
   Ich möchte... I would like… **4B**
Monat, -e *m.* month **2A, 7A**
Mond, -e *m.* moon **12A**
Montag, -e *m.* Monday **2A**
   montags *adv.* on Mondays **2A**
Morgen, - *m.* morning **2B**
   morgens *adv.* in the morning **2A**
morgen *adv.* tomorrow **2B**
   morgen früh tomorrow morning **2B**
Motor, -en *m.* engine **8A**
Motorhaube, -n *f.* hood (of car) **8A**
MP3-Player, - *m.* mp3 player **8B**
müde *adj.* tired **3B**
Müll *m.* trash **6B**; *m.* waste **12B**
   den Müll rausbringen *v.* to take out the trash **6B**
Müllwagen, - *m.* garbage truck **12B**
Mund, ⁼er *m.* mouth **9A**
Münze, -n *f.* coin **10A**
Musiker, - / Musikerin, -nen *m./f.* musician **3B**
müssen *v.* to have to; must **3B**
mutig *adj.* brave **3B**
Mutter, ⁼ *f.* mother **1A**
Mütze, -n *f.* cap **5B**

N

nach *prep.* after; to; according to **4B**; *prep.* past (time) **2A**
   nach rechts/links to the right/left **6A**
nachdem *conj.* after **10A**
nachmachen *v.* to imitate **8B**
Nachmittag, -e *m.* afternoon **2B**
   nachmittags *adv.* in the afternoon **2A**
Nachname, -n *m.* last name **3A**
Nachricht, -en *f.* message **11A**
   eine Nachricht hinterlassen *v.* to leave a message **11A**
nächster/nächste/nächstes *adj.* next **2B**
Nacht, ⁼e *f.* night **2B**
Nachtisch, -e *m.* dessert **4B**
Nachttisch, -e *m.* night table **6A**

nah(e) *adj.* near; nearby **10B**
Nähe *f.* vicinity **10B**
   in der Nähe von *f.* close to **10B**
naiv *adj.* naïve **3B**
Nase, -n *f.* nose **9A**
   verstopfte Nase *f.* stuffy nose **9A**
nass *adj.* wet **12A**
Natur, *f.* nature **12A**
Naturkatastrophe, -n *f.* natural disaster **12A**
Naturwissenschaft, -en *f.* science **2A**
Nebel, - *m.* fog; mist **7A**
neben *prep.* next to **5B**
Nebenkosten *pl.* additional charges **6A**
Neffe, -n *m.* nephew **8B**
nehmen *v.* to take **2B**
nein no **1A**
nennen *v.* to call **5A**
nervös *adj.* nervous **3B**
nett *adj.* nice **3B**
neugierig *adj.* curious **3B**
neun nine **2A**
nicht *adv.* not **2B**
   nicht schlecht not bad **1A**
nichts *pron.* nothing **7B**
nie *adv.* never **4A**
niedrig *adj.* low **11A**
niemals *adv.* never **7B**
niemand *pron.* no one **7B**
niesen *v.* to sneeze **9B**
noch *adv.* yet; still; in addition **4A**
normalerweise *adv.* usually **9B**
Notaufnahme, -n *f.* emergency room **9B**
Note, -n *f.* grade (on an assignment) **1B**
Notfall, ⁼e *m.* emergency **11B**
Notiz, -en *f.* note **1B**
November *m.* November **2A, 7A**
Nummernschild, -er *n.* license plate **8A**
nur *adv.* only **4A**
nützlich *adj.* useful **2A**
nutzlos *adj.* useless **2A**

O

ob *conj.* whether; if **10A**
Obst *n.* fruit **4A**
obwohl *conj.* even though **6A**; *conj.* although **10A**
oder *conj.* or **1B**
Ofen, ⁼ *m.* oven **6B**
öffentlich *adj.* public **8A**
   öffentliche Verkehrsmittel *n.* public transportation **8A**
öffnen *v.* to open **2A**
oft *adv.* often **4A**
ohne *prep.* without **3B**
Ohr, -en *n.* ear **9A**
Ökologie *f.* ecology **12B**
ökologisch *adj.* ecological **12B**
Oktober *m.* October **2A, 7A**
Öl, -e *n.* oil **4A**
Olivenöl, -e *n.* olive oil **4A**
Oma, -s *f.* grandma **3A**
online sein *v.* to be online **8B**
Opa, -s *m.* grandpa **3A**

orange *adj.* orange **5B**
Orange, -n *f.* orange **4A**
ordentlich *adj.* neat, tidy **6B**
Ort, -e *m.* place **1B**
Österreich *n.* Austria **10B**
Österreicher, - / Österreicherin, -nen *m./f.*
  Austrian (person) **10B**

P

Paar, -e *n.* couple **3A**
packen *v.* to pack **7B**
Paket, -e *n.* package **10A**
Papa, -s *m.* dad **3A**
Papier, -e *n.* paper
  Blatt Papier (*pl.* Blätter Papier) *n.* sheet of paper
  1B
Papierkorb, ⁻e *m.* wastebasket **1B**
Paprika, - *f.* pepper **4A**
  grüne/rote Paprika *f.* green/red pepper **4A**
Park, -s *m.* park **1A**
parken *v.* to park **8A**
  Parkverbot. No parking. **3B**
Party, -s *f.* party **5A**
  eine Party geben *v.* to throw a party **5A**
Passagier, -e / Passagierin, -nen *m./f.*
  passenger **7B**
passen *v.* to fit; to match **5A**
passieren *v.* to happen **5B**
Passkontrolle, -n *f.* passport control **7B**
Passwort, ⁻er *n.* password **8B**
Pasta *f.* pasta **4A**
Patient, -en / Patientin, -nen *m./f.* patient **9B**
Pause, -n *f.* break, recess **1B**
Pension, -en *f.* guesthouse **7B**
Person, -en *f.* person **1A**
Personalausweis, -e *m.* ID card **7B**
Personalchef, -s / die Personalchefin, -nen *m./f.*
  human resources manager **11A**
persönlich *adj.* personal **3B**
Pfanne, -n *f.* pan **6B**
Pfeffer, - *m.* pepper **4B**
Pferd, -e *n.* horse **2B**
Pfirsich, -e *m.* peach **4A**
Pflanze, -n *f.* plant **6A**
Pfund, -e *n.* pound **4A**
Physik *f.* physics **2A**
Picknick, -s, *n.* picnic **12A**
  ein Picknick machen *v.* to have a picnic **12A**
Pilz, -e *m.* mushroom **4A**
Pinnwand, ⁻e *f.* bulletin board **11A**
Planet, -en *m.* planet **12B**
  den Planeten retten *v.* to save the planet **12B**
Platten, - *m.* flat tire **8A**
  einen Platten haben *v.* to have a flat tire **8A**
Platz, ⁻e *m.* court **1A**
plus plus **1B**
Politiker, - / Politikerin, -nen *m./f.* politician **11B**
Polizeiwache, -n *f.* police station **10A**
Polizist, -en / Polizistin, -nen *m./f.* police
  officer **8A**
Post *f.* post office; mail **10A**
  zur Post gehen *v.* to go to the post office **10A**

Poster, - *n.* poster **6A**
Postkarte, -n *f.* postcard **10A**
Praktikum (*pl.* die Praktika) *n.* internship **11A**
prima *adj.* great **1A**
probieren *v.* to try **3B**
  Probieren Sie mal! Give it a try!
Problem, -e *n.* problem **1A**
Professor, -en / Professorin, -nen *m./f.*
  professor **1B**
Programm, -e *n.* program **8B**
Prost! Cheers! **4B**
Prozent, -e *n.* percent **1B**
Prüfung, -en *f.* exam, test **1B**
Psychologe, -n / Psychologin, -nen *m./f.*
  psychologist **11B**
Psychologie *f.* psychology **2A**
Pullover, - *m.* sweater **5B**
Punkt, -e *m.* period **1B**
pünktlich *adj.* on time **7B**
putzen *v.* to clean **6B**
  sich die Zähne putzen *v.* to brush one's teeth **9A**

Q

Querverweis, -e *m.* cross-reference

R

Radiergummi, -s *m.* eraser **1B**
Rasen, - *m.* lawn, grass **3B**
  Betreten des Rasens verboten. Keep off the
  grass. **3B**
sich rasieren *v.* to shave **9A**
Rasierer, - *m.* razor **9A**
Rasierschaum, ⁻e *m.* shaving cream **9A**
Rathaus, ⁻er *n.* town hall **10A**
rauchen *v.* to smoke
  Rauchen verboten. No smoking. **3B**
rausbringen *v.* to bring out **6B**
  den Müll rausbringen *v.* to take out the trash **6B**
realistisch *adj.* realistic **10A**
Rechnung, -en *f.* check **4B**
Rechtsanwalt, ⁻e / Rechtsanwältin, -nen *m./f.*
  lawyer **3B**
Rechtschreibung *f.* spelling
recyceln *v.* to recycle **12B**
reden *v.* to talk **5A**
  reden über *v.* to talk about **7A**
Referat, -e *n.* presentation **2A**
Referenz, -en *f.* reference **11A**
Regen *m.* rain **7A**
Regenmantel, ⁻ *m.* raincoat **7A**
Regenschirm, -e *m.* umbrella **7A**
Regierung, -en *f.* government **12B**
regnen *v.* to rain **2A, 7A**
reich *adj.* rich **3B**
Reis *m.* rice **4A**
Reise, -n *f.* trip **7B**
Reisebüro, -s *n.* travel agency **7B**
reisen *v.* to travel **2A**
Reisende, -n *m./f.* traveler **7B**
Reiseziel, -e *n.* destination **7B**
reiten *v.* to ride **2B**

rennen *v.* to run **5A**
Rente, -n *f.* pension
  in Rente gehen *v.* to retire **5A**
Rentner, - / Rentnerin, -nen *m./f.* retiree **11B**
reparieren *v.* to repair **8A**
Restaurant, -s *n.* restaurant **4B**
retten *v.* to save **12B**
Rezept, -e *n.* recipe **4A**; prescription **9B**
Richter, - / Richterin, -nen *m./f.* judge **11B**
Richtung, -en *f.* direction **10B**
  in Richtung *f.* toward **10B**
Rindfleisch *n.* beef **4A**
Rock, ⁻e *m.* skirt **5B**
rosa *adj.* pink **5B**
rot *adj.* red **3A**
rothaarig *adj.* red-haired **3A**
Rücken, - *m.* back **9A**
Rückenschmerzen *m. pl.* backache **9B**
Rucksack, ⁻e *m.* backpack **1B**
ruhig *adj.* calm **3B**
Russe, -n / Russin, -nen *m./f.* Russian
  (person) **10B**
Russisch *n.* Russian (language) **10B**
Russland *n.* Russia **10B**

S

Sache, -n *f.* thing **1B**
Saft, ⁻e *m.* juice **4B**
sagen *v.* to say **2A**
Salat, -e *m.* lettuce; salad **4A**
Salz, -e *n.* salt **4B**
salzig *adj.* salty **4B**
Samstag, -e *m.* Saturday **2A**
  samstags *adv.* on Saturdays **2A**
sauber *adj.* clean **6B**
saurer Regen *m.* acid rain **12B**
Saustall *n.* pigsty **6B**
  Es ist ein Saustall! It's a pigsty! **6B**
Schach *n.* chess **2B**
Schaf, -e *n.* sheep **12A**
Schaffner, - / Schaffnerin, -nen *m./f.* ticket
  collector **8A**
Schal, -s *m.* scarf **5B**
scharf *adj.* spicy **4B**
schauen *v.* to look **7A**
Scheibenwischer, - *m.* windshield wiper **8A**
Scheinwerfer, - *m.* headlight **8A**
scheitern *v.* to fail **11B**
schenken *v.* to give (a gift) **5A**
schicken *v.* to send **8B**
Schiff, -e *n.* ship **8A**
Schinken, - *m.* ham **4A**
Schlafanzug, ⁻e *m.* pajamas **9A**
schlafen *v.* to sleep **2B**
Schlafzimmer, - *n.* bedroom **6A**
Schlange, -n *f.* line **7B**; *f.* snake **12A**
  Schlange stehen *v.* to stand in line **7B**
schlank *adj.* slim **3A**
schlecht *adj.* bad **3B**
  schlecht gekleidet *adj.* badly dressed **5B**
schließlich *adv.* finally **7B**
Schlüssel, - *m.* key **7B**

schmecken *v.* to taste **4B**
Schmerz, -en *m.* pain **9B**
sich schminken *v.* to put on makeup **9A**
schmutzig *adj.* dirty **6B**
Schnee *m.* snow **7A**
schneien *v.* to snow **7A**
schnell *adj.* fast **3B**
schon *adv.* already, yet **4A**
schön *adj.* pretty; beautiful **3A**
  Schön dich/Sie kennen zu lernen. Nice to meet you. **1A**
  Schönen Tag noch! Have a nice day! **1A**
  Es ist schön draußen. It's nice out. **7A**
Schrank, ⁻e *m.* cabinet; closet **6A**
schreiben *v.* to write **2A**
  schreiben an *v.* to write to **7A**
  sich schreiben *v.* to write one another **9A**
Schreibtisch, -e *m.* desk **1B**
Schreibwarengeschäft, -e *n.* paper-goods store **10A**
Schublade, -n *f.* drawer **6A**
schüchtern *adj.* shy **3B**
Schuh, -e *m.* shoe **5B**
Schulbuch, ⁻er *n.* textbook (K–12) **1B**
Schule, -n *f.* school **1B**
Schüler, - / Schülerin, -nen (K–12) *m./f.* student **1B**
Schulleiter, - / Schulleiterin, -nen *m./f.* principal **1B**
Schulter, -n *f.* shoulder **9A**
Schüssel, -n *f.* bowl **4B**
schützen *v.* to protect **12B**
schwach *adj.* weak **3B**
Schwager, ⁻ *m.* brother-in-law **3A**
Schwägerin, -nen *f.* sister-in-law **3A**
schwanger *adj.* pregnant **9B**
schwänzen *v.* to cut class **1B**
schwarz *adj.* black **5B**
schwarzhaarig *adj.* black-haired **3A**
Schweinefleisch *n.* pork **4A**
Schweiz (die) *f.* Switzerland **7A**
Schweizer, - / Schweizerin, -nen *m./f.* Swiss (person) **10B**
schwer *adj.* rich, heavy **4B**; *adj.* serious, difficult **9B**
Schwester, -n *f.* sister **1A**
Schwiegermutter, ⁻ *f.* mother-in-law **3A**
Schwiegervater, ⁻ *m.* father-in-law **3A**
schwierig *adj.* difficult **2A**
Schwimmbad, ⁻er *n.* swimming pool **2B**
schwimmen *v.* to swim **2B**
schwindlig *adj.* dizzy **9B**
sechs six **2A**
See, -n *m.* lake **12A**
sehen *v.* to see **2B**
sehr *adv.* very **3A**
Seide, -n *f.* silk **5B**
Seife, -n *f.* soap **9A**
sein *v.* to be **1A**
  (gleich) sein *v.* to equal **1B**
sein *poss. adj.* his, its **3A**
seit since; for **4B**
Sekt, -e *m.* champagne **5A**
selten *adv.* rarely **4A**

Seminar, -e *n.* seminar **2A**
Seminarraum, -räume *m.* seminar room **2A**
Sender, - *m.* channel **8B**
September *m.* September **2A, 7A**
Serviette, -n *f.* napkin **4B**
Sessel, - *m.* armchair **6A**
setzen *v.* to put, place **5B**; *v.* to put, set **9A**
Shampoo, -s *n.* shampoo **9A**
sicher *adv.* probably **10A**
Sicherheitsgurt, -e *m.* seatbelt **8A**
sie *pron.* she/they **1A**
Sie *pron.* (*form., sing./pl.*) you **1A**
sieben seven **2A**
Silvester *n.* New Year's Eve **5A**
singen *v.* to sing **2B**
sitzen *v.* to sit **5B**
Ski fahren *v.* to ski **2B**
Smartphone, -s *n.* smartphone **8B**
SMS, - *f.* text message **8B**
Snack, -s *m.* snack **4B**
so *adv.* so **4A**
Socke, -n *f.* sock **5B**
Sofa, -s *n.* sofa; couch **6A**
  Sofa surfen *v.* to couch surf **7B**
Sohn, ⁻e *m.* son **3A**
solcher/solche/solches *pron.* such **8B**
sollen *v.* to be supposed to **3B**
Sommer, - *m.* summer **2B, 7A**
sondern *conj.* but rather; instead **6A**
Sonne, -n *f.* sun **12A**
Sonnenaufgang, ⁻e *m.* sunrise **12A**
Sonnenbrand, ⁻e *m.* sunburn **9B**
Sonnenbrille, -n *f.* sunglasses **5B**
Sonnenenergie *f.* solar energy **12B**
Sonnenuntergang, ⁻e *m.* sunset **12A**
sonnig *adj.* sunny **7A**
Sonntag, -e *m.* Sunday **2A**
  sonntags *adv.* on Sundays **2A**
Spanien *n.* Spain **10B**
Spanier, - / Spanierin, -nen *m./f.* Spanish (person) **10B**
Spanisch *n.* Spanish (language) **10B**
spannend *adj.* exciting **10A**
Spaß fun *m.* **2B**
  Spaß haben/machen *v.* to have fun/to be fun **2B**
  (keinen) Spaß haben *v.* to (not) have fun **5A**
spät *adj.* late
  Wie spät ist es? What time is it? **2A**
spazieren gehen *v.* to go for a walk **2B**
Spaziergang, ⁻e *m.* walk
speichern *v.* to save **8B**
Speisekarte, -n *f.* menu **4B**
Spiegel, - *m.* mirror **6A**
Spiel, -e *n.* match, game **2B**
spielen *v.* to play **2A**
Spieler, - / Spielerin, -nen *m./f.* player **2B**
Spielfeld, -er *n.* field **2B**
Spielkonsole, -n *f.* game console **8B**
Spitze! *adj.* great! **1A**
Sport *m.* sports **2B**
  Sport treiben *v.* to exercise **9B**
Sportart, -en *f.* sport; type of sport **2B**
Sporthalle, - n *f.* gym **2A**

sportlich *adj.* athletic **3A**
sprechen *v.* to speak **2B**
  sprechen über *v.* to speak about **7A**
Spritze, -n *f.* shot **9B**
  eine Spritze geben *v.* to give a shot **9B**
Spüle, -n *f.* (kitchen) sink **6B**
spülen *v.* to rinse **6B**
  Geschirr spülen *v.* to do the dishes **6B**
  Spülmaschine, -n *f.* dishwasher **6B**
Stadion (pl. Stadien) *n.* stadium **2B**
Stadt, ⁻e *f.* city **5B**; *f.* town **10B**
Stadtplan, ⁻e *m.* city map **7B**
Stahl *m.* steel **6B**
stark *adj.* strong **3B**
starten *v.* to start **8B**
statt *conj.* instead of
Statue, -n *f.* statue **10B**
staubsaugen *v.* to vacuum **6B**
Staubsauger, - *m.* vacuum cleaner **6B**
stehen *v.* to stand **5B**
  Schlange stehen *v.* to stand in line **7B**
stehlen *v.* to steal **2B**
steif *adj.* stiff **9B**
steigen *v.* to climb **5B**
Stein, -e *m.* rock **12A**
Stelle, -n *f.* place, position **10A**; job **11A**
  an deiner/Ihrer Stelle *f.* if I were you **10A**
  eine Stelle suchen *v.* to look for a job **11A**
stellen *v.* to put, place **5B**
Stellenangebot, -e *n.* job opening **11A**
sterben *v.* to die **5B**
Stereoanlage, -n *f.* stereo system **8B**
Stern -e *m.* star **12A**
Stiefel, - *m.* boot **5B**
Stiefmutter, ⁻ *f.* stepmother **3A**
Stiefsohn, ⁻e *m.* stepson **3A**
Stieftochter, ⁻ *f.* stepdaughter **3A**
Stiefvater, ⁻ *m.* stepfather **3A**
Stift, -e *m.* pen **1B**
Stil, -e *m.* style **5B**
still *adj.* still **4B**
  stilles Wasser *n.* still water **4B**
Stipendium, (pl. Stipendien) *n.* scholarship, grant **2A**
Stock, ⁻e *m.* floor **6A**
  erster/zweiter Stock first/second floor **6A**
stolz *adj.* proud **3B**
Stoppschild, -er *n.* stop sign **8A**
Strand, ⁻e *m.* beach **2B**
Straße, -n *f.* street **8A**
sich streiten *v.* to argue **9A**
Strom, ⁻e *m.* stream **12A**
Student, -en / Studentin, -nen *m./f.* (college/university) student **1A**
Studentenwohnheim, -e *n.* dormitory **2A**
studieren *v.* to study; major in **2A**
Studium (pl. Studien) *n.* studies **2A**
Stuhl, ⁻e *m.* chair **1A**
Stunde, -n *f.* lesson **1B**; hour **2A**
Stundenplan, ⁻e *m.* schedule **2A**
Sturm, ⁻e *m.* storm **7A**
suchen *v.* to look for **2A**
  eine Stelle suchen *v.* to look for a job **11A**

Supermarkt, ⁝e *m.* supermarket **4A**
Suppe, -n *f.* soup **4B**
surfen *v.* to surf **8B**
　im Internet surfen *v.* to surf the Web **8B**
süß *adj.* sweet, cute **3B, 4B**
Süßigkeit, -en *f.* candy **5A**
Sweatshirt, -s *n.* sweatshirt **5B**
Symptom, -e *n.* symptom **9B**

T

Tablet, -s *n.* tablet **8B**
Tablette, -n *f.* pill **9B**
Tafel, -n *f.* board, black board **1B**
Tag, -e *m.* day **1A, 7A**
　Welcher Tag ist heute? What day is it today? **7A**
täglich *adv.* every day; daily **4A**
Tal, ⁝er *n.* valley **12A**
tanken *v.* to fill up **8A**
Tankstelle, -n *f.* gas station **8A**
Tante, -n *f.* aunt **3A**
tanzen *v.* to dance **2B**
Taschenrechner, - *m.* calculator **1B**
Taschentuch, ⁝er *n.* tissue **9B**
Tasse, -n *f.* cup **4B**
Tastatur, -en *f.* keyboard **8B**
Taxi, -s *n.* taxi **8A**
Taxifahrer, - / Taxifahrerin, -nen *m./f.* taxi driver **11B**
Technik *f.* technology **8B**
　Technik bedienen *v.* to use technology **8B**
Tee, -s *m.* tea **4B**
Teelöffel, - *m.* teaspoon **4B**
Telefon, -e *n.* telephone **8B**
　am Telefon on the telephone **11A**
Telefonnummer, -n *f.* telephone number **11A**
Telefonzelle, -n *f.* phone booth **10B**
Teller, - *m.* plate **4B**
Tennis *n.* tennis **2B**
Teppich, -e *m.* rug **6A**
Termin, -e *m.* appointment **11A**
　einen Termin vereinbaren *v.* to make an appointment **11A**
teuer *adj.* expensive **5B**
Thermometer, - *n.* thermometer **9B**
Thunfisch, -e *m.* tuna **4A**
Tier, -e *n.* animal **12A**
Tierarzt, ⁝e / Tierärztin, -nen *m./f.* veterinarian **11B**
Tisch, -e *m.* table, desk **1B**
　den Tisch decken *v.* to set the table **6B**
Tischdecke, -n *f.* tablecloth **4B**
Toaster, - *m.* toaster **6B**
Tochter, ⁝ *f.* daughter **3A**
Toilette, -n *f.* toilet **6A**
Tomate, -n *f.* tomato **4A**
Topf, ⁝e *m.* pot **6B**
Tor, -e *n.* goal (in soccer, etc.) **2B**
Tornado, -s *m.* tornado **12A**
Torte, -n *f.* cake **5A**
Touristenklasse *f.* economy class **7B**
tragen *v.* to carry; wear **2B**
Trägerhemd, -en *n.* tank top **5B**

trainieren *v.* to practice (sports) **2B**
Traube, -n *f.* grape **4A**
träumen *v.* to dream **7A**
traurig *adj.* sad **3B**
treffen *v.* to meet; to hit **2B**
　sich treffen *v.* to meet (each other) **9A**
treiben *v.* to float; to push
　Sport treiben *v.* to exercise **9B**
Treibsand *m.* quicksand **12A**
sich trennen *v.* to separate, split up **9A**
Treppe, -n *f.* stairway **6A**
trinken *v.* to drink **3B**
Trinkgeld, -er *n.* tip **4B**
trocken *adj.* dry **12A**
trotz *prep.* despite, in spite of **8B**
Tschüss. Bye. **1A**
T-Shirt, -s *n.* T-shirt **5B**
　tun *v.* to do **9B**
　Es tut mir leid. I'm sorry. **1A**
　weh tun *v.* to hurt **9B**
Tür, -en *f.* door **1B**
　Türen schließen. Keep doors closed. **3B**
Türkei (die) *f.* Turkey **10B**
Türke, -n / die Türkin, -nen *m./f.* Turkish (person) **10B**
Türkisch *n.* Turkish (language) **10B**
Turnschuhe *m. pl.* sneakers **5B**

U

U-Bahn, -en *f.* subway **8A**
übel *adj.* nauseous **9B**
über *prep.* over, above **5B**
übernachten *v.* to spend the night **7B**
überall *adv.* everywhere **4A**
Überbevölkerung *f.* overpopulation **12B**
überlegen *v.* to think over **4A**
übermorgen *adv.* the day after tomorrow **2B**
überqueren *v.* to cross **10B**
überraschen *v.* to surprise **5A**
Überraschung, -en *f.* surprise **5A**
überzeugend *adj.* persuasive **9B**
Übung, -en *f.* practice, exercise
Uhr, -en *f.* clock **1B**
　um... Uhr at... o'clock **2A**
　Wie viel Uhr ist es? *v.* What time is it? **2A**
um *prep.* around; at (time) **3B**
　um... zu in order to **7B**
Umleitung, -en *f.* detour **8A**
umtauschen *v.* to exchange **6B**
Umwelt, -en *f.* environment **12B**
umweltfreundlich *adj.* environmentally friendly **12B**
Umweltschutz *m.* environmentalism **12B**
umziehen *v.* to move **6A, 9A**
　sich umziehen *v.* to change clothes **9A**
unangenehm *adj.* unpleasant **3B**
und *conj.* and **1B**
Unfall, ⁝e *m.* accident **8A**
　einen Unfall haben *v.* to have an accident **8A**
Universität, -en *f.* university; college **1B**
unmöbliert *adj.* unfurnished **6A**
unser *poss. adj.* our **3A**

unter *prep.* under, below **5B**
untergehen *v.* to set (sun) **12A**
sich unterhalten *v.* to chat, have a conversation **9A**
Unterkunft, ⁝e *f.* accommodations **7B**
Unterricht, -e *m.* class **1B**
unterschreiben *v.* to sign **10A**
Unterwäsche *f.* underwear **5B**
Urgroßmutter, ⁝ *f.* great grandmother **3A**
Urgroßvater, ⁝ *m.* great grandfather **3A**
Urlaub, -e *m.* vacation **7B**
　Urlaub machen *v.* to go on vacation **7B**
　Urlaub nehmen *v.* to take time off **11B**
USA (die) *pl.* USA **10B**

V

Vase, -n *f.* vase **6A**
Vater, ⁝ *m.* father **3A**
Veranstaltung, -en *f.* class; course **2A**
Verb, -en *n.* verb **9A**
verbessern *v.* to improve **12B**
verbringen *v.* to spend **4A**
verdienen *v.* to earn **11B**
Vereinigten Staaten (die) *pl.* United States **10B**
Vergangenheit, -en *f.* past **12A**
vergessen *v.* to forget **2B**
verheiratet *adj.* married **3A**
verkaufen *v.* to sell **4A**
Verkäufer, - / Verkäuferin, -nen *m./f.* salesperson **5B**
Verkehr *m.* traffic **8A**
Verkehrsmittel *n.* transportation **8A**
　öffentliche Verkehrsmittel *n. pl.* public transportation **8A**
verkünden *v.* to announce **12B**
sich verlaufen *v.* to get lost **10B**
sich verletzen *v.* to hurt oneself **9B**
Verletzung, -en *f.* injury **9B**
sich verlieben (in) *v.* to fall in love (with) **9A**
verlieren *v.* to lose **2B**
verlobt *adj.* engaged **3A**
Verlobte, -n *m./f.* fiancé(e) **3A**
verschmutzen *v.* to pollute **12B**
Verschmutzung *f.* pollution **12B**
sich verspäten *v.* to be late **9A**
Verspätung, -en *f.* delay **7B**
Verständnis, -se *n.* comprehension
sich (das Handgelenk / den Fuß) verstauchen *v.* to sprain (one's wrist/ankle) **9B**
verstehen *v.* to understand **2A**
verstopfte Nase *f.* stuffy nose **9B**
versuchen *v.* to try **7B**
Vertrag, ⁝e *m.* contract **11A**
verwandt *adj.* related **10A**
Verwandte, -n *m.* relative **3A**
viel *adv.* much, a lot (of) **4A**
　Viel Glück! Good luck! **5A**
　Vielen Dank. Thank you very much. **1A**
vielleicht *adv.* maybe **4A**
vier four **2A**
Viertel, - *n.* quarter **2A**; neighborhood **10B**
　Viertel nach/vor quarter past/to **2A**

Visum(pl. Visa) n. visa **7B**
Vogel, ⸚ m. bird **3A**
voll adj. full **7B**
  voll besetzt adj. fully occupied **7B**
Volleyball m. volleyball **2B**
von prep. from **4B**
vor prep. in front of, before **5B**; prep. to **2A**
vorbei adv. over, past **7A**
vorbereiten v. to prepare **4A**
  sich vorbereiten (auf) v. to prepare oneself
    (for) **9A**
  Vorbereitung, -en f. preparation
Vorhang, ⸚e m. curtain **6A**
Vorlesung, -en f. lecture **2A**
vormachen v. to fool **8B**
Vormittag, -e m. midmorning **2B**
vormittags adv. before noon **2A**
Vorspeise, -n f. appetizer **4B**
vorstellen v. to introduce **9A**
  sich vorstellen v. to introduce oneself **9A**
  sich (etwas) vorstellen v. to imagine
    (something) **9A**
Vorstellungsgespräch, -e n. job interview **11A**
Vortrag, ⸚e m. lecture **6B**
Vulkan, -e m. volcano **12A**

W

wachsen v. to grow **5B**
während prep. during **8B**
wahrscheinlich adv. probably **10A**
Wald, ⸚er m. forest **2B, 12A**
Wand, ⸚e f. wall **5B**
wandern v. to hike **2A**
wann interr. when **2A**
  Wann hast du Geburtstag? When is your
    birthday? **2B**
warm adj. warm **10A**
warten v. to wait (for) **2A**
  warten auf v. to wait for **7A**
  in der Warteschleife sein v. to be on hold **11B**
warum interr. why **2A**
was interr. what **2A**
  Was geht ab? What's up? **1A**
  Was ist das? What is that? **1B**
Wäsche f. laundry **6B**
waschen v. to wash **2B**
  sich waschen v. to wash (oneself) **9A**
  Wäsche waschen v. to do laundry **6B**
Wäschetrockner, - m. dryer **6B**
Waschmaschine, -n f. washing machine **6B**
Waschsalon, -s m. laundromat **10A**
Wasser n. water **4B**
Wasserfall, ⸚e m. waterfall **12A**
Wasserkrug, ⸚e m. water pitcher **4B**
Website, -s f. web site **8B**
Weg, -e m. path **12A**
wegen prep. because of **8B**
wegräumen v. to put away **6B**
wegwerfen v. to throw away **12B**
weh tun v. to hurt **9B**
Weihnachten, - n. Christmas **5A**
weil conj. because **10A**

Wein, -e m. wine **4B**
weinen v. to cry **3B**
weise adj. wise **3B**
weiß adj. white **5B**
weit adj. loose; big **5B**; adj. far **10B**
  weit von adj. far from **10B**
  weiter geht's moving forward
welcher/welche/welches interr. which **2A**
  Welcher Tag ist heute? What day is it today? **7A**
Welt, -en f. world **12B**
wem interr. whom (dat.) **4B**
wen interr. whom (acc.) **2A**
Wende, -n f. turning point **12B**
wenig adj. little; not much **10A**
wenn conj. when; whenever; if **10A**
  wenn... dann if… then **10A**
  wenn... nur if… only **10A**
wer interr. who **2A**
  Wer ist das? Who is it? **1B**
  Wer spricht? Who's calling? **11A**
werden v. to become **2B**
werfen v. to throw **2B**
Werkzeug, -e n. tool kit
wessen interr. whose **8B**
Wetter n. weather **7A**
  Wie ist das Wetter? What's the weather like? **7A**
Wetterbericht, -e m. weather report **7A**
wichtig adj. important **7B**
wie interr. how **2A**
  wie viel? interr. how much? **1B**
  wie viele? interr. how many? **1B**
  Wie alt bist du? How old are you? **1B**
  Wie heißt du? (inf.) What's your name? **1A**
wiederholen v. to repeat **2A**
Wiederholung, -en f. repetition; revision
wiegen v. to weigh **8B**
willkommen welcome **1A**
  Herzlich willkommen! Welcome! **1A**
Windenergie f. wind energy **12B**
windig adj. windy **7A**
Windschutzscheibe, -n f. windshield **8A**
Winter, - m. winter **2B, 7A**
wir pron. we **1A**
wirklich adv. really **4A**
Wirtschaft, -en f. business; economy **2A**
wischen v. to wipe, mop **6B**
wissen v. to know (information) **5B**
Wissenschaftler, - / Wissenschaftlerin, -nen m./f.
  scientist **11B**
Witwe, -n f. widow **3A**
Witwer, - m. widower **3A**
wo interr. where **2A**
woanders adv. somewhere else **4A**
Woche, -n f. week **2A**
Wochenende, -n n. weekend **2A**
woher interr. from where **2A; 6A**
wohin interr. where to **2A**
wohl adv. probably **10A**
wohnen v. to live (somewhere) **2A**
Wohnheim, -e n. dorm **6A**
Wohnung, -en f. apartment **6A**
Wohnzimmer, - n. living room **6A**
Wolke, -n f. cloud **7A**

wolkig adj. cloudy **7A**
Wolle f. wool **5B**
wollen v. to want **3B**
Wörterbuch, ⸚er n. dictionary **1B**
Wortschatz, ⸚e m. vocabulary
wünschen v. to wish **9A**
  sich (etwas) wünschen v. to wish (for
    something) **9A**
Würstchen, - n. sausage **4A**

Z

Zahn, ⸚e m. tooth **9A**
  sich die Zähne putzen m. to brush one's teeth **9A**
Zahnarzt, ⸚e / Zahnärztin, -nen m./f. dentist **9B**
Zahnbürste, -n f. toothbrush **9A**
Zahnpasta (pl. Zahnpasten) f. toothpaste **9A**
Zahnschmerzen m. pl. toothache **9B**
Zapping n. channel surfing
Zebrastreifen, - m. crosswalk **10B**
Zeh, -en m. toe **9A**
zehn ten **2A**
zeigen v. to show **4B**
Zeit, -en f. time **2A**
Zeitschrift, -en f. magazine **10A**
Zeitung, -en f. newspaper **7B, 10A**
Zelt, -e n. tent **7B**
Zeltplatz, ⸚e m. camping area **7B**
Zeugnis, -se n. report card, grade report **1B**
ziehen v. to pull **3B**
ziemlich adv. quite **4A**
  ziemlich gut pretty well **1A**
Zimmer, - n. room **5A**
  Zimmer frei vacancy **6A**
Zimmerservice m. room service **7B**
Zoll, ⸚e m. customs **7B**
zu adv. too **4A**; prep. to; for; at **4B**
  bis zu prep. until **10B**
  um... zu (in order) to **7B**
  Zum Wohl! Cheers! **4B**
zubereiten v. to prepare **7A**
zuerst adv. first **7B**
Zug, ⸚e m. train **8A**
zumachen v. to close **8B**
sich zurechtfinden v. to find one's way **10B**
zurückkommen v. to come back **4A**
zusammen adv. together **3A**
zuschauen v. to watch **4A**
Zutat, -en m. ingredient **4A**
zuverlässig adj. reliable **11B**
zwanzig twenty **2A**
zwei two **2A**
zweite adj. second **2A**
Zwiebel, -n f. onion **4A**
Zwilling, -e m. twin **3A**
zwischen prep. between **5B**
zwölf twelve **2A**

Englisch-Deutsch

A

a ein/eine **1A**
able: to be able to können *v.* **3B**
about über *prep.* **5B**
  to be about handeln von *v.* **7A**
above über *prep.* **5B**
abroad Ausland *n.* **7B**
accident Unfall, -e *m.* **8A**
  to have an accident einen Unfall haben *v.* **8A**
accommodation Unterkunft, -e *f.* **7B**
according to nach *prep.* **4B**
accountant Buchhalter, - / Buchhalterin, -nen *m./f.* **11B**
acid rain saurer Regen *m.* **12B**
across (from) gegenüber (von) *prep.* **10B**
address Adresse, -n *f.* **10A**
adopt adoptieren *v.* **3A**
afraid: to be afraid of Angst haben vor *v.* **7A**
after nach *prep.* **4B**; nachdem *conj.* **10A**
afternoon Nachmittag, -e *m.* **2B**
  in the afternoon nachmittags *adv.* **2A**
against gegen *prep.* **3B**
air Luft, -e *f.* **12A**
airplane Flugzeug, -e *n.* **7B**
airport Flughafen, - *m.* **7B**
all ganz *adj.* **7B**; alle *pron.* **7B**
allergic (to) allergisch (gegen) *adj.* **9B**
allergy Allergie, -n *f.* **9B**
allow lassen *v.* **2B**
  to be allowed to dürfen *v.* **3B**
almost fast *adv.* **4A**
alone allein *adv.* **4A**
along entlang *prep.* **3B**
already schon **4A**
alright: Are you alright? Alles klar? **1A**
also auch *adv.* **4A**
although obwohl *conj.* **10A**
always immer *adv.* **4A**
ambulance Krankenwagen, - *m.* **9B**
America Amerika *n.* **10B**
American amerikanisch *adj.* **10B**; **(person)** Amerikaner, - / Amerikanerin, -nen *m./f.* **10B**
  American football American Football *m.* **2B**
and und *conj.* **1B**
animal Tier, -e *n.* **12A**
angry böse *adj.*
  to get angry (about) sich ärgern (über) *v.* **9A**
anniversary Jahrestag, -e *m.* **5A**
announce verkünden *v.* **12B**
answer antworten *v.* **2A**; beantworten *v.* **4A**; Antwort, -en *f.*
  to answer the phone einen Anruf entgegennehmen *v.* **11A**
anything: Anything else? Noch einen Wunsch? **4B**; Sonst noch etwas? **4A**
apartment Wohnung, -en *f.* **6A**
appetizer Vorspeise, -n *f.* **4B**
apple Apfel, - *m.* **1A**
applicant Bewerber, - / Bewerberin, -nen *m./f.* **11A**
apply sich bewerben *v.* **11A**

appointment Termin, -e *m.* **11A**
April April *m.* **2A**
architect Architekt, -en / Architektin, -nen *m./f.* **3B**
architecture Architektur, -en *f.* **2A**
argue sich streiten *v.* **9A**
arm Arm, -e *m.* **9A**
armchair Sessel, - *m.* **6A**
around um *prep.* **3B**
arrival Ankunft, -e *f.* **7B**
arrive ankommen *v.* **4A**
arrogant eingebildet *adj.* **3B**
art Kunst, -e *f.* **2A**
artichoke Artischocke, -n *f.* **4A**
as als *conj.* **8A**
  as if als ob **10A**
ask fragen *v.* **2A**
  to ask about fragen nach *v.* **7A**
assistant Assistent, -en / Assistentin, -nen *m./f.* **11A**
at um *prep.* **3B**; bei *prep.* **4A**; an *prep.* **5B**
  at...o'clock um...Uhr **2A**
athletic sportlich *adj.* **2B**
ATM Geldautomat, -en *m.* **10A**
Attention! Achtung!
attic Dachboden, - *m.* **6A**
August August *m.* **2A**
aunt Tante, -n *f.* **3A**
Austria Österreich *n.* **10B**
Austrian österreichisch *adj.* **10B**; **(person)** Österreicher, - / Österreicherin, -nen *m./f.* **10B**
autumn Herbst, -e *m.* **2B**
avenue Allee, -n *f.* **10B**
awful furchtbar *adj.* **7A**

B

baby Baby, -s *n.* **3A**
back Rücken, - *m.* **9A**
backache Rückenschmerzen *m. pl.* **9B**
backpack Rucksack, -e *m.* **1B**
bad schlecht *adj.* **3B**
  badly dressed schlecht gekleidet *adj.* **5B**
baked goods Gebäck *n.* **5A**
bakery Bäckerei, -en *f.* **4A**
balcony Balkon, - e *m.* **6A**
ball Ball, -e *m.* **2B**
balloon Ballon, -e *m.* **5A**
ball-point pen Kuli, -s *m.* **1B**
banana Banane, -n *f.* **4A**
bank Bank, -en *f.* **10A**
  at the bank auf der Bank *f.* **10B**
bank account Konto (*pl.* Konten) *n.* **10A**
bank employee Bankangestellte, -n *m./f.* **11B**
baseball Baseball *m.* **2B**
basketball Basketball *m.* **2B**
bath: to take a bath sich baden *v.* **9A**
bathing suit Badeanzug, -e *m.* **5B**
bathrobe Bademantel, - *m.* **9A**
bathroom Badezimmer, - *n.* **9A**
bathtub Badewanne, -n *f.* **6A**
battery charger Ladegerät, -e *n.* **8B**
be sein *v.* **1A**

Is/Are there... Ist/Sind hier...? *v.* **1B**; Gibt es...? **2B**
  There is/are... Da ist/sind... *v.* **1A**; Es gibt... **2B**
beach Strand, -e *m.* **2B**
bean Bohne, -n *f.* **4A**
beard Bart, -e *m.* **9A**
beautiful schön *adj.* **3A**
beauty salon Kosmetiksalon, -s *m.* **10A**
because denn *conj.* **6A**; weil *conj.* **10A**
  because of wegen *prep.* **8B**
become werden *v.* **2B**
bed Bett, -en *n.* **6A**
  to go to bed ins Bett gehen *v.* **9A**
  to make the bed das Bett machen *v.* **6B**
bedroom Schlafzimmer, - *n.* **6A**
beef Rindfleisch *n.* **4A**
beer Bier, -e *n.* **4B**
before vor *prep.* **5B**; bevor *conj.* **8A**
  before noon vormittags *adv.* **2A**
begin anfangen *v.* **4A**; beginnen *v.* **6A**
behind hinter *prep.* **5B**
believe glauben *v.* **5A**; meinen *v.* **12B**
belly Bauch, -e *m.* **9A**
belong gehören *v.* **4B**
below unter *prep.* **5B**
belt Gürtel, - *m.* **5B**
bench Bank, -e *f.* **10B**
best beste/bester/bestes *adj.* **8A**
  All the best! Mach's gut! *v.* **3B**; alles Gute **10A**
better besser *adj.* **8A**
  to get better gesund werden *v.* **9B**
between zwischen *prep.* **5B**
beverage Getränk, -e *n.* **4B**
bicycle Fahrrad, -er *n.* **2B**
big groß, weit *adj.* **3A**
bill (money) Geldschein, -e *m.* **10A**
biology Biologie *f.* **2A**
bird Vogel, - *m.* **3A**
birth Geburt, -en *f.* **5A**
birthday Geburtstag, -e *m.* **5A**
  When is your birthday? Wann hast du Geburtstag? **2B**
black schwarz *adj.* **5B**
  black board Tafel, -n *f.* **1B**
  black-haired schwarzhaarig *adj.* **3A**
bland fade *adj.* **4B**
blanket Decke, -n *f.* **6B**
blond blond *adj.* **3A**
  blond hair blonde Haare *n. pl.* **3A**
blood pressure Blutdruck *m.* **9B**
blouse Bluse, -n *f.* **5B**
blue blau *adj.* **3A**
board Tafel, -n *f.* **1B**
boarding pass Bordkarte, -n *f.* **7B**
boat Boot, -e *n.* **8A**
body Körper, - *m.* **9A**
book Buch, -er *n.* **1A**
bookshelf Bücherregal, -e *n.* **6A**
boot Stiefel, - *m.* **5B**
boring langweilig *adj.* **2A**
boss Chef, -s / Chefin, -nen *m./f.* **11B**
bottle Flasche, -n *f.* **4B**
bowl Schüssel, -n *f.* **4B**

boy Junge, -n *m.* **1A**
brakes Bremse, -n *f.* **8A**
brave mutig *adj.* **3B**
bread Brot, -e *n.* **4A**
break brechen *v.* **2B**
  to break (an arm / a leg) sich (den Arm/Bein) brechen *v.* **9B**
  Break a leg! Hals- und Beinbruch! **5A**
breakfast Frühstück, -e *n.* **4B**
bridge Brücke, -n *f.* **10B**
bright hell *adj.* **5B**
bring bringen *v.* **2A**
  to bring along mitbringen *v.* **4A**
  to bring out rausbringen **6B**
  to bring with mitnehmen *v.* **10B**
broom Besen, - *m.* **6B**
brother Bruder, ⸚ *m.* **1A**
brother-in-law Schwager, ⸚ *m.* **3A**
brown braun *adj.* **5B**
  brown-haired braunhaarig *adj.* **3A**
bruise blauer Fleck, -e *m.* **9B**
brush Bürste, -n *f.* **9A**
  to brush one's hair sich die Haare bürsten *v.* **9A**
  to brush one's teeth sich die Zähne putzen *v.* **9A**
build bauen *v.* **2A**
building Gebäude, - *n.* **10A**
bulletin board Pinnwand, ⸚e *f.* **11A**
burn brennen *v.* **5A**
bus Bus, -se *m.* **8A**
bus stop Bushaltestelle, -n *f.* **8A**
bush Busch, ⸚e *m.* **12A**
business Wirtschaft, -en *f.* **2A**; Geschäft, -e *n.* **11A**
  business class Businessklasse *f.* **7B**
  businessman / businesswoman Geschäftsmann, ⸚er / Geschäftsfrau, -en *m./f.* (*pl.* Geschäftsleute) **3B**
but aber *conj.* **1B**
  but rather sondern *conj.* **6A**
butcher shop Metzgerei, -en *f.* **4A**
butter Butter *f.* **4A**
buy kaufen *v.* **2A**
by an *prep.* **5B**; bei; von **4B**
Bye! Tschüss! **1A**

C

cabinet Schrank, ⸚e *m.* **6A**
café Café, -s *n.* **2A**
cafeteria Cafeteria, (*pl.* Cafeterien) *f.*; **(college/university)** Mensa, Mensen *f.* **1B**
cake Kuchen, - *m.* **4A**; Torte, -n *f.* **5A**
calculator Taschenrechner, - *m.* **1B**
calendar Kalender, - *m.* **1B**
call anrufen *v.* **4A**; sich anrufen **9A**; nennen *v.* **5A**
  Who's calling? Wer spricht? **11A**
calm ruhig *adj.* **3B**
(to go) camping campen gehen *n.* **2B**
camping area Zeltplatz, ⸚e *m.* **7B**
can können *v.* **3B**
Canada Kanada *n.* **10B**
Canadian kanadisch *adj.* **10B**; **(person)** Kanadier, - / Kanadierin, -nen *m./f.* **10B**
cancel abbrechen *v.* **7B**

candidate Kandidat, -en *m.* **11A**
candy Süßigkeit, -en *f.* **5A**
cap Mütze, -n *f.* **5B**
car Auto, -s *n.* **1A**
to drive a car Auto fahren *v.* **8A**
card Karte, -n *f.* **2B**
career Karriere, -n *f.* **11B**
caretaker Hausmeister, - / Hausmeisterin, -nen *m./f.* **11B**
carpool Fahrgemeinschaft, -en *f.* **12B**
carrot Karotte, -n *f.* **4A**
carry tragen *v.* **2B**
carry-on luggage Handgepäck *n.* **7B**
cash bar *adj.* **10A**; Bargeld *n.* **10A**
  to pay in cash bar bezahlen *v.* **10A**
cat Katze, -n *f.* **3A**
catch fangen *v.* **2B**
  to catch a cold sich erkälten *v.* **9A**
celebrate feiern *v.* **5A**
celebration Fest, -e *n.* **5A**
cell phone Handy, -s *n.* **8B**
cellar Keller, - *m.* **6A**
ceramic Keramik, -en *f.* **6B**
chair Stuhl, ⸚e *m.* **1A**
champagne Sekt, -e *m.* **5A**
championship Meisterschaft, -en *f.* **2B**
change Kleingeld *n.* **10A**
  to change clothes sich umziehen *v.* **9A**
channel Sender, - *m.* **8B**
  channel surfing Zapping *n.*
charge laden *v.* **8B**
chat sich unterhalten *v.* **9A**
cheap günstig *adj.* **5B**
check Rechnung, -en *f.* **4B**
Cheers! Prost! **4B**; Zum Wohl! **4B**
cheese Käse, - *m.* **4A**
chemistry Chemie *f.* **2A**
chess Schach *n.* **2B**
chicken Huhn, ⸚er *n.* **12A**; **(food)** Hähnchen, - *n.* **4A**
child Kind, -er *n.* **1A**
China China *n.* **10B**
Chinese (person) Chinese, -n / Chinesin, -nen *m./f.* **10B**; **(language)** Chinesisch *n.* **10B**
Christmas Weihnachten, - *n.* **5A**
church Kirche, -n *f.* **10B**
city Stadt, ⸚e *f.* **5B**
  city center Innenstadt, ⸚e *f.* **10B**
claim behaupten *v.* **12B**
class Klasse, -n *f.* **1B**; Unterricht *m.* **1B**; Veranstaltung, -en *f.* **2A**
  first/second class erste/zweite Klasse **8A**
classical klassisch *adj.* **10A**
classmate Kommilitone, -n / Kommilitonin, -nen; Klassenkamerad, -en / Klassenkameradin, -nen *m./f.* **1B**
classroom Klassenzimmer, - *n.* **1B**
clean sauber *adj.* **6B**; putzen *v.* **6B**
  to clean up aufräumen *v.* **6B**
cliff Klippe, -n *f.* **12A**
climb steigen *v.* **5B**
  to climb (mountain) klettern *v.* **2B**
  to climb (stairs) (die Treppe) hochgehen *v.* **10B**
clock Uhr, -en *f.* **1B**

at... o'clock um... Uhr **2A**
close zumachen *v.* **8B**; nah *adj.* **10B**
  close to in der Nähe von *prep.* **10B**
closed geschlossen *adj.* **10A**
closet Schrank, ⸚e *m.* **6A**
clothes Kleidung *f.* **5B**
cloud Wolke, -n *f.* **7A**
cloudy wolkig *adj.* **7A**
coast Küste, -n *f.* **12A**
coat Mantel, ⸚ *m.* **5B**
coffee Kaffee, -s *m.* **4B**
coffeemaker Kaffeemaschine, -n *f.* **6B**
coin Münze, -n *f.* **10A**
cold kalt *adj.* **7A**; Erkältung, -en *f.* **9B**
  to catch a cold sich erkälten *v.* **9A**
college Universität, -en *f.* **1B**
college instructor Dozent, -en / Dozentin, -nen *m./f.* **2A**
color Farbe, -n *f.* **5B**
  solid colored einfarbig *adj.* **5B**
colorful bunt *adj.* **10A**
comb Kamm, ⸚e *m.* **9A**
  to comb (one's hair) sich (die Haare) kämmen *v.* **9A**
come kommen *v.* **2A**
  to come along mitkommen *v.* **4A**
  to come back zurückkommen *v.* **4A**
comma Komma, -s *f.* **1B**
compact disc CD, -s *f.* **8B**
company Firma (*pl.* die Firmen) *f.* **11A**
complicated kompliziert *adj.* **10A**
computer Computer, - *m.* **1B**
computer science Informatik *f.* **2A**
concert Konzert, -e *n.* **5B**
congratulate gratulieren *v.* **5A**
  Congratulations! Herzlichen Glückwunsch! **5A**
construction zone Baustelle, -n *f.* **8A**
contract Vertrag, ⸚e *m.* **11A**
conversation: to have a conversation sich unterhalten *v.* **9A**
cook kochen *v.* **2B**; Koch, ⸚e / Köchin, -nen *m./f.* **4B**
cookie Keks, -e *m.* **5A**
cool kühl *adj.* **7A**
corner Ecke, -n *f.* **10B**
correct korrigieren *v.* **2A**
cost kosten *v.* **2A**
cotton Baumwolle *f.* **5B**
couch Sofa, -s *n.* **7B**
  to couch surf Sofa surfen *v.* **7B**
cough husten *v.* **9B**
country Land, ⸚er *n.* **7B**
countryside Landschaft, -en *f.* **12A**
couple Paar, -e *n.* **3A**
courageous mutig *adj.*
course Veranstaltung, -en *f.* **2B**; Gang, ⸚e *m.* **4B**
  first/second course erster/zweiter Gang *m.* **4B**
  main course Hauptspeise, -en *f.* **4B**
court Platz, ⸚e *m.* **1A**
cousin Cousin, -s / Cousine, -n *m./f.* **3A**
cover decken *v.* **6B**
cow Kuh, ⸚e *f.* **12A**
cram (for a test) büffeln *v.* **2A**

cross überqueren *v.* **10B**
  to cross the street die Straße überqueren *v.* **10B**
cross-reference Querverweis, -e *m.*
crosswalk Zebrastreifen, - *pl.* **10B**
cruel grausam *adj.*; gemein *adj.* **3B**
cruise Kreuzfahrt, -en *f.* **7B**
cry weinen *v.* **3B**
cup Tasse, -n *f.* **4B**
curious neugierig *adj.* **3B**
curly lockig *adj.* **3A**
curtain Vorhang, ¨-e *m.* **6A**
custodian Hausmeister, - / Hausmeisterin, -nen *m./f.* **11B**
customer Kunde, -n /Kundin, -nen *m./f.* **5B**
customs Zoll *m.* **7B**
cut Schnitt, -e *m.* **5B**
  to cut class schwänzen *v.* **1B**
cute süß *adj.* **3B**
CV Lebenslauf, ¨-e *m.* **11A**

D

dad Papa, -s *m.* **3A**
daily täglich *adv.* **4A**
  daily routine Alltagsroutine *f.* **9A**
dance tanzen *v.* **2B**
danger Gefahr, -en *f.* **12B**
dark dunkel *adj.* **3A**
  dark-haired dunkelhaarig *adj.* **3A**
darling Liebling, -e *m.*
date Datum (*pl.* Daten) *n.* **7A**
  What is the date today? Der wievielte ist heute? **2A**
daughter Tochter, ¨ *f.* **3A**
day Tag, -e *m.* **1A**
  every day täglich *adv.* **4A**
Dear Lieber/Liebe *m./f.* **3B**
December Dezember *m.* **2A**
decide sich entschließen *v.* **4B**
definitely bestimmt *adv.* **4A**
degree Abschluss, ¨-e *m.* **2A**; Grad *n.* **7A**
  It's 18 degrees out. Es sind 18 Grad draußen. **7A**
delay Verspätung, -en *f.* **7B**
delete löschen *v.* **8B**
delicatessen Feinkostgeschäft, -e *n.* **4A**
delicious lecker *adj.* **4B**
demanding anspruchsvoll *adj.* **11B**
dentist Zahnarzt, ¨-e / Zahnärztin, -nen *m./f.* **9B**
department store Kaufhaus, ¨-er *n.* **10B**
departure Abflug, ¨-e *m.* **7B**
deposit (money) (Geld) einzahlen *v.* **10A**
describe beschreiben *v.* **2A**
description Beschreibung, -en *f.* **3B**
desk Schreibtisch, -e *m.* **1B**
despite trotz *prep.* **8B**
dessert Nachtisch, -e, *m.* **4B**
destination Reiseziel, -e *n.* **7B**
detour Umleitung, -en *f.* **8A**
develop entwickeln *v.* **12B**
dictionary Wörterbuch, ¨-er *n.* **1B**
die sterben *v.* **5B**
diet Diät, -en *f.* **4B**

to be on a diet auf Diät sein *v.* **4B**
difficult schwierig *adj.* **2A**
digital camera Digitalkamera, -s *f.* **8B**
dining room Esszimmer, - *n.* **6A**
dinner Abendessen, - *n.* **4B**
diploma Abschlusszeugnis, -se *n.* **2A**; Diplom, -e *n.* **2A**
direction Richtung, -en *f.* **10B**
dirty schmutzig *adj.* **6B**
discover entdecken *v.* **6B**
discreet diskret *adj.* **3B**
discuss besprechen *v.* **4A**
dish Gericht, -e *n.* **4B**
dishes Geschirr *n.* **6B**
  to do the dishes Geschirr spülen **6B**
dishwasher Spülmaschine, -n *f.* **6B**
dislike nicht gern (+*verb*) **3A**
divided by geteilt durch **1B**
divorced geschieden *adj.* **3A**
dizzy schwindlig *adj.* **9B**
do machen *v.* **2A**; tun *v.* **9B**
  to do laundry Wäsche waschen *v.* **6B**
  to do the dishes Geschirr spülen *v.* **6B**
  to have to do with handeln von **7A**
doctor Arzt, ¨-e / Ärztin, -nen *m./f.* **9B**
  to go to the doctor zum Arzt gehen *v.* **9B**
document Dokument, -e *n.* **8B**
dog Hund, -e *m.* **3A**
door Tür, -en *f.* **1B**
dormitory (Studenten)wohnheim, -e *n.* **6A**
down entlang *prep.* **3B**; herunter *adv.* **6A**
  to go down heruntergehen *v.* **10B**
download herunterladen *v.* **8B**
downtown Innenstadt, ¨-e *f.* **10B**
dozen Dutzend, -e *n.* **4A**
  a dozen eggs ein Dutzend Eier **4A**
drawer Schublade, -n *f.* **6A**
dream träumen *v.* **7A**
dress Kleid, -er *n.* **5B**
  to get dressed sich anziehen *v.* **9A**
  to get undressed sich ausziehen *v.* **9A**
dresser Kommode, -n *f.* **6A**
drink trinken *v.* **3B**
drive fahren *v.* **8A**
  to drive a car Auto fahren *v.* **8A**
driver Fahrer, - / Fahrerin, -nen *m./f.* **8A**
drugstore Drogerie, -n *f.* **10A**
dry trocken *adj.* **12A**
  to dry oneself off sich abtrocknen *v.* **9A**
dryer Wäschetrockner, - *m.* **6B**
dumb dumm *adj.* **8A**
during während *prep.* **8B**
dust abstauben *v.* **6B**
duvet Bettdecke, - n *f.* **6B**
DVD DVD, -s *f.* **8B**
DVD-player DVD-Player, - *m.* **8B**
dye (one's hair) sich (die Haare) färben *v.* **9A**

E

ear Ohr, -en *n.* **9A**
early früh *adj.* **2B**
earn verdienen *v.* **11B**

earth Erde, -n *f.* **12B**
earthquake Erdbeben, - *n.* **12A**
easy einfach *adj.* **2A**
eat essen *v.* **2B**
  to eat out essen gehen *v.* **2B**
ecological ökologisch *adj.* **12B**
ecology Ökologie *f.* **12B**
economy Wirtschaft, -en *f.* **2A**
  economy class Touristenklasse *f.* **7B**
education Ausbildung, -en *f.* **11A**
egg Ei, -er *n.* **4A**
eggplant Aubergine, -n *f.* **4A**
eight acht **2A**
elbow Ell(en)bogen, - *m.* **9A**
electrician Elektriker, - / Elektrikerin, -nen *m./f.* **11B**
elegant elegant *adj.* **5B**
elevator Fahrstuhl, ¨-e *m.* **7B**
eleven elf **2A**
e-mail E-Mail, -s *f.* **8B**
emergency Notfall, ¨-e *m.* **11B**
emergency room Notaufnahme, -n *f.* **9B**
employee Angestellte, -n *m./f.* **11A**
endangered gefährdet *adj.* **12B**
energy Energie, -n *f.* **12B**
energy-efficient energiesparend *adj.* **6B**
engaged verlobt *adj.* **3A**
engine Motor, -en *m.* **8A**
engineer Ingenieur, -e / Ingenieurin, -nen *m./f.* **3B**
England England *n.* **10B**
English (person) Engländer, - / Engländerin, -nen *m./f.* **10B**; **(language)** Englisch *n.* **10B**
enjoy genießen *v.*
  Enjoy your meal! Guten Appetit! **4B**
envelope Briefumschlag, ¨-e *m.* **10A**
environment Umwelt, -en *f.* **12B**
  environmentally friendly umweltfreundlich *adj.* **8B**
environmentalism Umweltschutz *m.* **12B**
equal (gleich) sein *v.* **1B**
eraser Radiergummi, -s *m.* **1B**
errand Besorgung, -en *f.* **10A**
  to run errands Besorgungen machen *v.* **10A**
even though obwohl *conj.* **6A**
evening Abend, -e *m.* **2A**
  in the evening abends *adv.* **2A**
every jeder/jede/jedes *adv.* **8B**
everything alles *pron.* **7B**
  Everything OK? Alles klar? **1A**
everywhere überall *adv.* **4A**
exam Prüfung, -en *f.* **1B**
except (for) außer *prep.* **4B**
exchange umtauschen *v.* **6B**
exciting spannend *adj.* **10A**; aufregend *adj.* **12A**
Excuse me. Entschuldigung. **1A**
exercise Sport treiben *v.* **9B**
exit Ausgang, ¨-e *m.* **7B**; Ausfahrt, -en *f.* **8A**
expensive teuer *adj.* **5B**
experience durchmachen *v.* **8B**; Erfahrung, -en *f.* **11A**
explain erklären *v.* **4A**
explore erforschen *v.* **12A**

expression Ausdruck, ⸚e *m.*
extinction Aussterben *n.* 12B
eye Auge, -n *n.* 3A
eyebrow Augenbraue, -n *f.* 9A

F

face Gesicht, -er *n.* 9A
factory Fabrik, -en *f.* 12B
factory worker Fabrikarbeiter, - / Fabrikarbeiterin, -nen *m./f.* 11B
fail durchfallen *v.* 1B; scheitern *v.* 11B
fall fallen *v.* 2B; (season) Herbst, -e *m.* 2B
  to fall in love (with) sich verlieben (in) *v.* 9A
familiar bekannt *adj.*
  to be familiar with kennen *v.* 5B
family Familie, -n *f.* 3A
fan Fan, -s *m.* 2B
fantastic fantastisch *adj.* 10A
far weit *adj.* 10B
  far from weit von *adj.* 10B
farm Bauernhof, ⸚e *m.* 12A
farmer Bauer, -n / Bäuerin, -nen *m./f.* 11B
fashionable modisch *adj.* 5B
fast schnell *adj.* 3B
fat dick *adj.* 3A
father Vater, ⸚ *m.* 3A
father-in-law Schwiegervater, ⸚ *m.* 3A
favorite Lieblings- 4B
fear Angst, ⸚e *f.* 7A
February Februar *m.* 2A
feel fühlen *v.* 2A; sich fühlen *v.* 9A
  to feel like Lust haben *v.* 7B
  to feel well sich wohl fühlen *v.* 9A
fever Fieber, - *n.* 9B
  to have a fever Fieber haben *v.* 9B
fiancé(e) Verlobte, -n *m./f.* 3A
field Spielfeld, -er *n.* 2B; Feld, -er *n.* 12A
file Datei, -en *f.* 8B
fill füllen *v.*
  to fill out ausfüllen *v.* 10A
  to fill up tanken *v.* 8A
filthy dreckig *adj.* 6B
finally schließlich *adv.* 7B
find finden *v.* 2A
  to find one's way sich zurechtfinden *v.* 10B
  to find out (about) sich informieren (über) *v.* 9A
fine (monetary) Bußgeld, -er *n.* 8A
  I'm fine. Mir geht's gut. 1A
finger Finger, - *m.* 9A
fire entlassen *v.* 11B; Feuer, - *n.*
firefighter Feuerwehrmann, ⸚er / Feuerwehrfrau, -en (*pl.* Feuerwehrleute) *m./f.* 11B
firm Firma (*pl.* die Firmen) *f.* 11A
first erster/erste/erstes *adj.* 2A; zuerst *adv.* 7B
  first course erster Gang *m.* 4B
  first class erste Klasse *f.* 8A
fish Fisch, -e *m.* 4A
  to go fishing angeln gehen *v.* 2B
fish store Fischgeschäft, -e *n.* 4A
fit passen *v.* 5A; fit *adj.* 2B
five fünf 2A

flat tire Platten, - *m.* 8A
  to have a flat tire einen Platten haben *v.* 8A
flavor Geschmack, ⸚e *m.* 4B
flight Flug, ⸚e *m.* 7B
flood Hochwasser, - *n.* 12B
floor Stock, ⸚e *m.*; Boden, ⸚ *m.* 6A
  first/second floor erster/zweiter Stock 6A
flower Blume, -n *f.* 1A
  flower shop Blumengeschäft, -e *n.* 10A
flu Grippe, -n *f.* 9B
flunk durchfallen *v.* 1B
fly fliegen *v.* 7B
fog Nebel, - *m.* 7A
follow folgen *v.* 5A
food Essen, - *n.* 4A
foot Fuß, ⸚e *m.* 9A
football American Football *m.* 2B
for für *prep.* 3B; seit; zu *prep.* 4B
foreign language Fremdsprache, -n *f.* 2A
forest Wald, ⸚er *m.* 2B
forget vergessen *v.* 2B
fork Gabel, -n *f.* 4B
form Formular, -e *n.* 10A
  to fill out a form ein Formular ausfüllen *v.* 10A
fountain Brunnen, - *m.* 10B
four vier 2A
France Frankreich *n.* 10B
French (person) Franzose, -n / Französin, -nen *m./f.* 10B; (language) Französisch *n.* 10B
free time Freizeit, -en *f.* 2B
freezer Gefrierschrank, ⸚e *m.* 6B
Friday Freitag, -e *m.* 2A
  on Fridays freitags *adv.* 2A
friend Freund, -e / Freundin, -nen *m./f.* 1A
friendly freundlich *adj.* 3B
friendship Freundschaft, -en *f.* 5A
from aus *prep.* 4A; von *prep.* 4B
  where from woher *interr.* 2A
front: in front of vor *prep.* 5B
fruit Obst *n.* 4A
fry braten *v.* 2B
full voll *adj.* 7B
full-time ganztags *adj.* 11B
fully occupied voll besetzt *adj.* 7B
fun Spaß *m.* 2B
  to be fun Spaß machen *v.* 2B
  to (not) have fun (keinen) Spaß haben *v.* 5A
function funktionieren *v.* 8B
funny lustig *adj.* 3B
furnished möbliert *adj.* 6A
furniture Möbel, - *n.* 6A
  piece of furniture Möbelstück, ⸚e *n.* 6A

G

game Spiel, -e *n.* 2B
game console Spielkonsole, -en *f.* 8B
garage Garage, -n *f.* 5B
garbage truck Müllwagen, - *m.* 12B
gardener Gärtner, - / Gärtnerin, -nen *m./f.* 11B
garlic Knoblauch *m.* 4A
gas Benzin, -e *n.* 8A

gas station Tankstelle, -n *f.* 8A
generous großzügig *adj.* 3B
German (person) Deutsche *m./f.* 10B; (language) Deutsch *n.* 10B
Germany Deutschland *n.* 4A
get bekommen *v.* 5A
  to get up aufstehen *v.* 4A
  to get sick/better krank/gesund werden *v.* 9B
gift Geschenk, -e *n.* 5A
girl Mädchen, - *n.* 1A
give geben *v.* 2B
  to give (a gift) schenken *v.* 5A
glass Glas, ⸚er *n.* 4B
glasses Brille, -n *f.* 5B
global warming Erderwärmung *f.* 12B
glove Handschuh, -e *m.* 5B
go gehen *v.* 2A; fahren *v.* 2B
  to go out ausgehen *v.* 4A
  Go! Los! 2B
goal (in soccer) Tor, -e *n.* 2B
golf Golf *n.* 2B
good gut *adj.*; nett *adj.* 1A
  Good evening. Guten Abend! 1A
  Good morning. Guten Morgen! 1A
  Good night. Gute Nacht! 1A
  Good-bye. Auf Wiedersehen! 1A
  Good luck! Viel Glück! 5A
government Regierung, -en *f.* 12B
grade Note, -n *f.* 1B
grade report Zeugnis, -se *n.* 1B
graduate Abschluss machen, ⸚e *v.* 5A
graduation Abschluss, ⸚e *m.* 1B
gram Gramm, -e *n.* 4A
  100 grams of cheese 100 Gramm Käse 4A
granddaughter Enkeltochter, ⸚ *f.* 3A
grandson Enkelsohn, ⸚e *m.* 3A
grandchild Enkel, - *m.* 3A; Enkelkind, -er *n.* 3A
grandfather Großvater, ⸚ *m.* 3A
grandma Oma, -s *f.* 3A
grandmother Großmutter, ⸚ *f.* 3A
grandpa Opa, -s *m.* 3A
grandparents Großeltern *pl.* 1A
grape Traube, -n *f.* 4A
grass Gras, ⸚er *n.* 12A
gray grau *adj.* 5B
great toll *adj.* 3B; prima *adj.*; spitze *adj.* 1A
great grandfather Urgroßvater, ⸚ *m.* 3A
great grandmother Urgroßmutter, ⸚ *f.* 3A
greedy gierig *adj.* 3B
green grün *adj.* 5B
green bean grüne Bohne (*pl.* die grünen Bohnen) *f.* 4A
greet grüßen *v.* 2A
greeting Begrüßung, -en *f.* 1A; Gruß, ⸚e *m.* 1A
grocery store Lebensmittelgeschäft, -e *n.* 4A
ground floor Erdgeschoss, -e *n.* 6A
grow wachsen *v.* 5B
grown-up erwachsen *adj.* 10A
guest Gast, ⸚e *m.* 5A
  hotel guest Hotelgast, ⸚e *m.* 7B
guesthouse Pension, -en *f.* 7B
gym Sporthalle, -n *f.* 2A

H

hail Hagel *m.* **7A**
hair Haar, -e *n.* **3A**
hair dryer Haartrockner, - *m.* **9A**
hairdresser Friseur, -e / Friseurin, -nen *m./f.* **3B**
half halb *adj.* **2A**
half brother Halbbruder, ¨ *m.* **3A**
half sister Halbschwester, -n *f.* **3A**
hall Flur, -e *m.* **6A**
ham Schinken, - *m.* **4A**
hand Hand, ¨e *f.* **9A**
handsome gut aussehend *adj.* **3A**
hang hängen *v.* **5B**
  to hang up auflegen *v.* **11A**
happen passieren *v.* **5B**
happiness Glück *n.* **5A**
happy glücklich *adj.* **3B** froh *adj.* **3B**
  Happy birthday! Alles Gute zum Geburtstag! **5A**
  Happy Easter! Frohe Ostern! **5A**
  Happy New Year! Ein gutes neues Jahr! **5A**
  to be happy (about) sich freuen (über) *v.* **9A**
hard schwer *adj.* **9B**
hard drive Festplatte, -en *f.* **8B**
hard-working fleißig *adj.* **3B**
hare Hase, -n *m.* **12A**
hat Hut, ¨e *m.* **5B**
have haben *v.* **1B**
  Have a nice day! Schönen Tag noch! **1A**
  to have to müssen *v.* **3B**
he er *pron.* **1A**
head Kopf, ¨e *m.* **9A**
headache Kopfschmerzen *m. pl.* **9B**
headlight Scheinwerfer, -e *m.* **8A**
headphones Kopfhörer, - *m.* **8B**
health Gesundheit *f.* **9B**
health-food store Bioladen, ¨ *m.* **9B**
healthy gesund *adj.* **8A**
hear hören *v.* **2A**
heat stroke Hitzschlag, ¨e *m.* **9B**
heavy schwer *adj.* **4B**
hello Guten Tag!; Hallo! **1A**
help helfen *v.* **2B**
  to help with helfen bei *v.* **7A**
her ihr *poss. adj.* **3A**
here hier *adv.* **1A**
  Here is/are... Hier ist/sind... **1B**
high hoch *adj.* **8A**
highway Autobahn, -en *f.* **8A**
hike wandern *v.* **2A**
his sein *poss. adj.* **3A**
history Geschichte, -en *f.* **2A**
hit treffen *v.* **2B**
hobby Hobby, -s *n.* **2B**
hockey Hockey *n.* **2B**
hold: to be on hold in der Warteschleife sein *v.* **11B**
  Please hold. Bleiben Sie bitte am Apparat! **11A**
holiday Feiertag, -e *m.* **5A**
home Haus, ¨er *adv.* **5B**
  at home zu Hause *adv.* **4A**
home office Arbeitszimmer, - *n.* **6A**
homemade hausgemacht *adj.* **4B**
homemaker Hausfrau, -en / Hausmann,
  ¨er *f./m.* **11B**

homework Hausaufgabe, -n *f.* **1B**
hood Motorhaube, -en *f.* **8A**
horse Pferd, -e *n.* **2B**
hospital Krankenhaus, ¨er *n.* **9B**
host / hostess Gastgeber, - / Gastgeberin,
  -nen *m./f.* **5A**
host family Gastfamilie, -n *f.* **4B**
hot heiß *adj.* **7A**
hotel Hotel, -s *n.* **7B**
  five-star hotel Fünf-Sterne-Hotel *n.* **7B**
hour Stunde,-n *f.* **2A**
house Haus, ¨er *n.* **6A**
housework Hausarbeit *f.* **6B**
  to do housework Hausarbeit machen *v.* **6B**
how wie *interr.* **2A**
  How are you? (form.) Wie geht es Ihnen? **1A**
  How are you? (inf.) Wie geht's (dir)? **1A**
  how many wie viele *interr.* **1B**
  how much wie viel *interr.* **1B**
human resources manager Personalchef, -s / die
  Personalchefin, -nen *m./f.* **11A**
humble bescheiden *adj.*
hurry sich beeilen *v.* **9A**
hurt weh tun *v.* **9B**
  to hurt oneself sich verletzen *v.* **9B**
husband Ehemann, ¨er *m.* **3A**
hybrid car Hybridauto, -s *n.* **12B**

I

I ich *pron.* **1A**
ice cream Eis *n.* **5A**
ice cream shop Eisdiele, -n *f.* **4A**
ice cube Eiswürfel, - *m.* **5A**
ice hockey Eishockey *n.* **2B**
ID card Personalausweis, -e *m.* **7B**
idea Idee, -n *f.* **1A**
if wenn *conj.;* ob *conj.* **10A**
  as if als ob **10A**
  if I were you an deiner/Ihrer Stelle *f.* **10A**
  if... only wenn... nur **10A**
  if... then wenn... dann **10A**
imagine sich (etwas) vorstellen *v.* **9A**
imitate nachmachen *v.* **8B**
important wichtig *adj.* **7B**; bedeutend *adj.* **12A**
improve verbessern *v.* **12B**
in in *prep.* **5B**
  in the afternoon nachmittags *adv.* **2A**
  in the evening abends *adv.* **2A**
  in the morning morgens *adv.* **2A**
  in spite of trotz *prep.* **8B**
India Indien *n.* **10B**
Indian indisch *adj.* **10B**; **(person)** Inder, - /
  Inderin, -nen *m./f.* **10B**
ingredient Zutat, -en *f.* **4A**
injury Verletzung, -en *f.* **9B**
inside (of) innerhalb *prep.* **8B**
instead sondern *conj.* **6A**
  instead of statt *prep.;* anstatt *prep.* **8B**
intellectual intellektuell *adj.* **3B**
intelligent intelligent *adj.* **3B**
interested: to be interested (in) sich interessieren
  (für) *v.* **9A**
interesting interessant *adj.* **2A**

internet café Internetcafé, -s *n.* **10A**
internship Praktikum (*pl.* die Praktika) *n.* **11A**
intersection Kreuzung, -en *f.* **10B**
introduce: to introduce (oneself) (sich)
  vorstellen *v.* **9A**
invent erfinden *v.* **7A**
invite einladen *v.* **5A**
iron Bügeleisen, - *n.* **6B**; bügeln *v.* **6B**
ironing board Bügelbrett, -er *n.* **6B**
island Insel, -n *f.* **12A**
it es *pron.* **1A**
Italian (person) Italiener, - / Italienerin,
  -nen *m./f.* **10B**; **(language)** Italienisch *n.* **10B**
Italy Italien *n.* **10B**
its sein *poss. adj.* **3A**

J

jacket Jacke, -n *f.* **5B**
jam Marmelade, -n *f.* **4A**
January Januar *m.* **2A**
Japan Japan *n.* **10B**
Japanese (person) Japaner, - / Japanerin,
  -nen *m./f.* **10B**; **(language)** Japanisch *n.* **10B**
jealous eifersüchtig *adj.* **3B**
jeans Jeans, - *f.* **5B**
jewelry store Juweliergeschäft, -e *n.* **10A**
job Beruf, -e *m.* **11B**; Stelle, -n *f.* **11A**
  to find a job Arbeit finden *v.* **11A**
job interview Vorstellungsgespräch, -e *n.* **11A**
job opening Stellenangebot, -e *n.* **11A**
jog joggen *v.* **2B**
journalist Journalist, -en / Journalistin,
  -nen *m./f.* **3B**
judge Richter, - / Richterin, -nen *m./f.* **11B**
juice Saft, ¨e *m.* **4B**
July Juli *m.* **2A**
June Juni *m.* **2A**
just as genauso wie **8A**

K

key Schlüssel, - *m.* **7B**
keyboard Tastatur, -en *f.* **8B**
kind nett *adj.*
kiosk Kiosk, -e *m.* **10A**
kiss Kuss, ¨e *m.* **5A**; küssen *v.* **5A**
  to kiss (each other) sich küssen *v.* **9A**
kitchen Küche, -n *f.* **6A**
knee Knie, - *n.* **9A**
knife Messer, - *n.* **4B**
know kennen *v.* **5B**; wissen *v.* **5B**
  to know each other sich kennen *v.* **9A**
know-it-all Besserwisser, - / Besserwisserin
  -nen *m./f.* **2A**
Korea Korea *n.* **10B**
Korean (person) Koreaner, - / Koreanerin,
  -nen *m./f.* **10B**; **(language)** Koreanisch *n.* **10B**

L

labor union Gewerkschaft, -en *f.* **11B**
lake See, -n *m.* **12A**
lamp Lampe, -n *f.* **6A**

land landen *v.* **7B**; Land, ¨er *n.* **7B**
landscape Landschaft, -en *f.* **12A**
laptop (computer) Laptop, -s *m./n.* **8B**
last letzter/letzte/letztes *adj.* **2B**
last name Nachname, -n *m.* **3A**
late spät *adj.* **2A**
  to be late sich verspäten *v.* **9A**
laugh lachen *v.* **2A**
laundromat Waschsalon, -s *m.* **10A**
laundry Wäsche *f.* **6B**
  to do laundry Wäsche waschen *v.* **6B**
law Gesetz, -e *n.* **12B**
lawyer Rechtsanwalt, ¨e / Rechtsanwältin,
  -nen *m./f.* **3B**
lay legen *v.* **5B**
lazy faul *adj.* **3B**
leaf Blatt, ¨er *n.* **12A**
learn lernen *v.* **2A**
leather Leder, - *n.* **5B**
leave abfahren *v.* **8A**
lecture Vorlesung, -en *f.* **2A**; Vortrag, ¨e *m.* **6B**
lecture hall Hörsaal (*pl.* Hörsäle) *m.* **2A**
leg Bein, -e *n.* **9A**
leisure Freizeit *f.* **2B**
lesson Stunde, -n *f.* **1B**
let lassen *v.* **2B**
letter Brief, -e *m.* **10A**
  to mail a letter einen Brief abschicken *v.* **10A**
  letter of recommendation
    Empfehlungsschreiben, - *n.* **11A**
lettuce Salat, -e *m.* **4A**
library Bibliothek, -en *f.* **1B**
license plate Nummernschild, -er *n.* **8A**
lie liegen *v.* **5B**
  to lie down sich (hin)legen *v.* **9A**
  to tell a lie lügen *v.*
light hell *adj.* **3A**; leicht *adj.* **4B**; Licht, -er *n.* **12B**
lightning Blitz, -e *m.* **7A**
like mögen *v.* **4B**; gern (+*verb*) *v.* **2B**; gefallen *v.* **5A**
  I would like... ich hätte gern… **4A**; Ich möchte…
    4B
line Schlange, -n *f.* **7B**; Linie, -n *f.*
  to stand in line Schlange stehen *v.* **7B**
lip Lippe, -n *f.* **9A**
lipstick Lippenstift, -e *m.* **9A**
listen (to) hören *v.* **2A**
literature Literatur, -en *f.* **2A**
little klein *adj.* **3A**; wenig *adj.* **10A**
live wohnen *v.* **2A**; leben *v.* **2A**
living room Wohnzimmer, - *n.* **6A**
load laden *v.* **8B**
location Lage, -n *f.* **7B**
long lang *adj.* **3A**
  long-sleeved langärmlig *adj.* **5B**
look schauen *v.* **7A**
  to look at anschauen *v.* **7A**
  to look for suchen *v.* **2A**
  to look forward to sich freuen auf *v.* **9A**
loose weit *adj.* **5B**
lose verlieren *v.* **2B**
  to get lost sich verlaufen *v.* **10B**
love lieben *v.* **2A**; Liebe *f.* **5A**
  to fall in love (with) sich verlieben (in) *v.* **9A**
  to love each other sich lieben *v.* **9A**

loving liebevoll *adj.* **3B**
low niedrig *adj.* **11A**
luggage Gepäck *n.* **7B**
lunch Mittagessen, - *n.* **4B**

M

magazine Zeitschrift, -en *f.* **10A**
mail Post *f.* **10A**
  to mail a letter einen Brief abschicken *v.* **10A**
mail carrier Briefträger, - / Briefträgerin,
  -nen *m.* **10A**
mailbox Briefkasten, ¨ *m.* **10A**
main course Hauptspeise, -n *f.* **4B**
main road Hauptstraße, -n *f.* **10B**
major: to major in studieren *v.* **2A**
make machen *v.* **2A**
makeup: to put on makeup sich schminken *v.* **9A**
mall Einkaufszentrum (*pl.* Einkaufszentren) *n.* **10B**
man Mann, ¨er *m.* **1A**
manage leiten *v.* **11B**
manager Geschäftsführer, - / die
  Geschäftsführerin, -nen *m./f.* **11A**
map Karte, -n *f.* **1B**; Landkarte, -n *f.* **7B**
  city map Stadtplan, ¨e *m.* **7B**
  to read a map eine Karte lesen *v.* **7B**
marble Marmor *m.* **6B**
March März *m.* **2A**
marital status Familienstand, ¨e *m.* **3A**
market Markt, ¨e *m.* **4A**
marriage Ehe, -n *f.* **5A**
married verheiratet *adj.* **3A**
marry heiraten *v.* **3A**
match Spiel, -e *n.* **2B**; passen *v.* **5A**
material Material, -ien *n.* **5B**
mathematics Mathematik *f.* **2A**
May Mai *m.* **2A**
may dürfen *v.* **3B**
maybe vielleicht *adv.* **4A**
mayor Bürgermeister, - / Bürgermeisterin,
  -nen *m./f.* **10B**
meal Mahlzeit, -en *f.* **4B**
mean bedeuten *v.* **2A**; meinen *v.* **12B**; gemein *adj.*
  3B
meat Fleisch *n.* **4A**
mechanic Mechaniker, - / Mechanikerin,
  -nen *m./f.* **8A**
medicine Medizin *f.* **2A**; Medikament, -e *n.* **9B**
meet (sich) treffen *v.* **2B**; **(for the first time)** (sich)
  kennen lernen *v.* **9A**
  Pleased to meet you. Schön dich/Sie kennen zu
    lernen! **1A**
meeting Besprechung, -en *f.* **11A**
melon Melone, -n *f.* **4A**
menu Speisekarte, -n *f.* **4B**
Merry Christmas! Frohe Weihnachten! **5A**
message Nachricht, -en *f.* **11A**
Mexico Mexiko *n.* **10B**
Mexican mexikanisch *adj.* **10B**; **(person)**
  Mexikaner, - / Mexikanerin, -nen *m./f.* **10B**
microphone Mikrofon, -e *n.* **8B**
microwave Mikrowelle, -n *f.* **6B**
midmorning Vormittag, -e *m.* **2B**
midnight Mitternacht *f.* **2A**

mild leicht *adj.* **9B**
milk Milch *f.* **4B**
minority Minderheit, -en *f.* **12B**
minus minus **1B**
mirror Spiegel, - *m.* **6A**
mist Nebel, - *m.* **7A**
modern modern *adj.* **10A**
modest bescheiden *adj.* **3B**
mom Mama, -s *f.* **3A**
Monday Montag, -e *m.* **2A**
  on Mondays montags *adv.* **2A**
money Geld, -er *n.* **10A**
month Monat, -e *m.* **2A**
moon Mond, -e *m.* **12A**
mop wischen *v.* **6B**
more mehr *adj.* **8A**
morning Morgen, - *m.* **2B**
  in the morning vormittags **2A**
  tomorrow morning morgen früh **2B**
mother Mutter, ¨ *f.* **1A**
mother-in-law Schwiegermutter, ¨ *f.* **3A**
mountain Berg, -e *m.* **2B**; **12A**
mouse Maus, ¨e *f.* **8B**
mouth Mund, ¨er *m.* **9A**
move umziehen *v.* **6A**; sich bewegen *v.*
movie Film, -e *m.*
movie theater Kino, -s *n.* **10A**
mp3 player MP3-Player, - *m.* **8B**
Mr. Herr **1A**
Mrs. Frau **1A**
Ms. Frau **1A**
much viel *adv.* **4A**
mushroom Pilz, -e *m.* **4A**
musician Musiker, - / Musikerin, -nen *m./f.* **3B**
must müssen *v.* **3B**
my mein *poss. adj.* **3A**
myself mich *pron.*; mir *pron.* **9A**

N

naïve naiv *adj.* **3B**
name Name, -n *m.* **1A**
  to be named heißen *v.* **2A**
  What's your name? Wie heißen Sie? (form.) /
    Wie heißt du? (inf.) *v.* **1A**
napkin Serviette, -n *f.* **4B**
natural disaster Naturkatastrophe, -n *f.* **12A**
nature Natur, -en *f.* **12A**
nauseous übel *adj.* **9B**
near bei *prep.* **4B**; nah *adj.* **10B**
neat ordentlich *adj.* **6B**
neck Hals, ¨e *m.* **9A**
necklace Halskette, -n *f.* **5B**
need brauchen *v.* **2A**
  to need to müssen *v.* **3B**
neighborhood Viertel, - *n.* **10B**
nephew Neffe, -n *m.* **8B**
nervous nervös *adj.* **3B**
never nie *adv.* **4A**; niemals *adv.* **7B**
New Year's Eve Silvester *n.* **5A**
newlywed Frischvermählte, -n *m./f.* **5A**
newspaper Zeitung, -en *f.* **7B**
next nächster/nächste/nächstes *adj.* **2B**

next to neben *prep.* **5B**
nice nett *adj.* **3B**
  It's nice out. Es ist schön draußen. **7A**
  Nice to meet you. Schön dich/Sie kennen zu lernen! **1A**
  The weather is nice. Das Wetter ist gut. **7A**
night Nacht, ¨e *f.* **2B**
  to spend the night übernachten *f.* **7B**
night table Nachttisch, -e *m.* **6A**
nine neun **2A**
no nein **1A**; kein *adj.* **2B**
no one niemand *pron.* **7B**
nonviolent gewaltfrei *adj.* **12B**
noon Mittag, -e *m.* **2A**
nose Nase, -n *f.* **9A**
not nicht *adv.* **2B**
  Do not enter. Keine Zufahrt. **3B**
  not bad nicht schlecht **1A**
  not much wenig *adj.* **10A**
note Notiz, -en *f.* **1B**
notebook Heft, -e *n.* **1B**
nothing nichts *pron.* **7B**
November November *m.* **2A**
now jetzt *adv.* **4A**
nuclear energy Kernenergie *f.* **12B**
nuclear power plant Kernkraftwerk, -e *n.* **12B**
nurse Krankenpfleger, - / Krankenschwester, -n *m./f.* **9B**

O

ocean Meer, -e *n.* **12A**
occasion Anlass, ¨e *m.* **5A**
  special occasions besondere Anlässe *m. pl.* **5A**
October Oktober *m.* **2A**
offer Angebot, -e *n.* **5B**; bieten *v.* **9B**; anbieten *v.* **12B**
office Büro, -s *n.* **11B**
office supplies Büromaterial, -ien *n.* **11A**
often oft *adv.* **4A**
oil Öl, -e *n.* **4A**
old alt *adj.* **3A**
  How old are you? Wie alt bist du? **1B**
  I am... years old. Ich bin… Jahre alt. **1B**
olive oil Olivenöl, -e *n.* **4A**
on an *prep.*; auf *prep.* **5B**
once einmal *adv.* **7B**
one eins **2A**; man *pron.* **7B**
  by oneself allein *adv.* **4A**
one-way street Einbahnstraße, -n *f.* **8A**
onion Zwiebel, -n *f.* **4A**
online: to be online online sein *v.* **8B**
only nur *adv.* **4A**
  only child Einzelkind, -er *n.* **3A**
on-time pünktlich *adj.* **7B**
onto auf *prep.* **5B**
open öffnen *v.* **2A**; aufmachen *v.* **8B**; geöffnet *adj.* **10A**
or oder *conj.* **1B**
orange Orange, -n *f.* **4A**; orange *adj.* **5B**
order bestellen *v.* **4A**
organic biologisch *adj.* **12B**
our unser *poss. adj.* **3A**

out draußen *adv.* **7A**; heraus *adv.* **6A**
  It's nice out. Es ist schön draußen. **7A**
  to go out ausgehen *v.* **4A**
  to bring out rausbringen **6B**
outside draußen *prep.* **7A**
  outside of außerhalb *prep.* **8B**
oven Ofen, ¨ *m.* **6B**
over über *prep.* **5B**; vorbei *adv.* **7A**
  over there drüben *adv.* **4A**
overpopulation Überbevölkerung *f.* **12B**
owner Besitzer, - / Besitzerin, -nen *m./f.* **3B**

P

pack packen *v.* **7B**
package Paket, -e *n.* **10A**
pain Schmerz, -en *m.* **9B**
pajamas Schlafanzug, ¨e *m.* **9A**
pan Pfanne, -n *f.* **6B**
pants Hose, -n *f.* **5B**
paper Papier, -e *n.* **1B**
  sheet of paper Blatt Papier (*pl.* Blätter) Papier *n.* **1B**
paperclip Büroklammer, -n *f.* **11A**
paper-goods store Schreibwarengeschäft, -e *n.* **10A**
paragraph Absatz, ¨e *m.* **5B**
parents Eltern *pl.* **3A**
park Park, -s *m.* **1A**; parken *v.* **8A**
  No parking. Parkverbot. **3B**
participate mitmachen *v.* **8B**
part-time halbtags *adj.* **11B**
party Party, -s *f.* **5A**
  to go to a party auf eine Party gehen *prep.* **10B**
  to throw a party eine Party geben *v.* **5A**
pass (a test) bestehen *v.* **1B**
passenger Passagier, -e *m.* **7B**
passport control Passkontrolle, -n *f.* **7B**
password Passwort, ¨er *n.* **8B**
past Vergangenheit, -en *f.* **12A**; nach *prep.* **2A**
pasta Pasta *f.* **4A**
pastries Gebäck *n.* **5A**
pastry shop Konditorei, -en *f.* **4A**
path Weg, -e *m.* **12A**
patient geduldig *adj.* **3B**; Patient, -en / Patientin, -nen *m./f.* **9B**
pay (for) bezahlen *v.* **4A**
  to pay by (credit) card mit der Karte bezahlen *v.* **10A**
  to pay in cash bar bezahlen *v.* **10A**
peach Pfirsich, -e *m.* **4A**
pear Birne, -n *f.* **4A**
pedestrian Fußgänger, - / Fußgängerin, -nen *m./f.* **10B**
pen Kuli, -s *m.* **1B**
pencil Bleistift, -e *m.* **1B**
people Leute *pl.* **3B**; Menschen *pl.*
pepper Paprika, - *f.* **4A**; Pfeffer, - *m.* **4B**
percent Prozent, -e *n.* **1B**
period Punkt, -e *m.* **1B**
person Person, -en *f.* **1A**; Mensch, -en *m.*
personal persönlich *adj.* **3B**
pet Haustier, -e *n.* **3A**
pharmacy Apotheke, -n *f.* **9B**

phone booth Telefonzelle, -n *f.* **10B**
photo Foto, -s *n.* **1B**
physics Physik *f.* **2A**
picnic Picknick, -s *n.* **12A**
  to have a picnic ein Picknick machen *v.* **12A**
picture Foto, -s *n.* **1B**; Bild, -er *n.* **6A**
pie Kuchen, - *m.* **4A**
pigsty Saustall, ¨e *n.* **6B**
  It's a pigsty! Es ist ein Saustall! **6B**
pill Tablette, -n *f.* **9B**
pillow Kissen, - *n.* **6B**
pineapple Ananas, - *f.* **4A**
pink rosa *adj.* **5B**
place Ort, -e *m.* **1B**; Lage, -n *f.* **7B**; setzen *v.* **5B**
  in your place an deiner/Ihrer Stelle *f.* **10A**
plant Pflanze, -n *f.* **6A**
plastic Kunststoff, -e *m.* **6B**
plate Teller, - *m.* **4B**
platform Bahnsteig, -e **8A**
play spielen *v.* **2A**
player Spieler, - / Spielerin, -nen *m./f.* **2B**
pleasant angenehm *adj.* **3B**
please bitte **1A**; gefallen *v.* **5A**
  Pleased to meet you. Freut mich! **1A**
plumber Klempner, - / Klempnerin, -nen *m./f.* **11B**
plus plus **1B**
police officer Polizist, -en / Polizistin, -nen *m./f.* **8A**
police station Polizeiwache, -n *f.* **10A**
politician Politiker, - / Politikerin, -nen *m./f.* **11B**
pollute verschmutzen *v.* **12B**
pollution Verschmutzung *f.* **12B**
poor arm *adj.* **3B**
pork Schweinefleisch *n.* **4A**
position Stelle, -n *f.* **11A**
post office Post, - *f.* **10A**
  to go to the post office zur Post gehen *v.* **10A**
postcard Postkarte, -n *f.* **10A**
poster Poster, - *n.* **6A**
pot Topf, ¨e *m.* **6B**
potato Kartoffel, -n *f.* **4A**
pound Pfund, -e *n.* **4A**
  a pound of potatoes ein Pfund Kartoffeln **4A**
practice (sports) trainieren *v.* **2B**; Übung, -en *f.*
pregnant schwanger *adj.* **9B**
preparation Vorbereitung, -en *f.*
prepare vorbereiten *v.* **4A**; zubereiten *v.* **7A**
  to prepare oneself (for) sich vorbereiten (auf) *v.* **9A**
prescription Rezept, -e *n.* **9B**
presentation Referat, -e *n.* **2A**
preserve erhalten *v.* **12B**
president Präsident, - / Präsidentin, -nen *m./f.* **8B**
  federal president Bundespräsident, - / Bundespräsidentin, -nen *m./f.* **8B**
pretty hübsch *adj.* **3A**
  pretty well ziemlich gut *adv.* **1A**
principal Schulleiter, - *m.* / Schulleiterin, -nen *f.* **1B**
print drucken *v.* **8B**
printer Drucker, - *m.* **8B**
probably wohl ; wahrscheinlich *adv.* **10A**; sicher *adv.* **10A**

problem Problem, -e *n.* **1A**
profession Beruf, -e *m.* **3B**
professional training Berufsausbildung, -en *f.* **11A**
professor Professor, -en / Professorin,
  -nen *m./f.* **1B**
program Programm, -e *n.* **8B**
promotion Beförderung, -en *f.* **11B**
pronunciation Aussprache *f.*
propose vorschlagen *v.* **12B**
protect schützen *v.* **12B**
proud stolz *adj.* **3B**
psychologist Psychologe, -n / Psychologin,
  -nen *m./f.* **11B**
psychology Psychologie *f.* **2A**
public öffentlich *adj.* **8A**
  public transportation öffentliche
    Verkehrsmittel *n. pl.* **8A**
pull ziehen *v.* **3B**
purple lila *adj.* **5B**
purse Handtasche, -n *f.* **5B**
push drücken *v.* **3B**
put stellen *v.* **5B**; legen *v.* **9A**; setzen *v.* **9A**
  to put away wegräumen *v.* **6B**
  to put on anziehen *v.* **5B**

Q

quarter Viertel, - *n.* **2A**
  quarter past/to Viertel nach/vor **2A**
question Frage, -n *f.* **1B**
quicksand Treibsand *m.* **12A**
quite ziemlich *adv.* **4A**

R

rabbit Kaninchen, - *n.* **12A**
rain Regen *m.* **7A**; regnen *v.* **2A**
raincoat Regenmantel, ¨ *m.* **7A**
raise Gehaltserhöhung, -en *f.* **11B**
rarely selten *adv.* **4A**
rather lieber *adj.* **8A**
rating Bewertung, -en *f.* **7B**
razor Rasierer, - *m.* **9A**
read lesen *v.* **2B**
ready fertig *adj.* **11B**
real estate agent Immobilienmakler, - /
  Immobilienmaklerin, -nen *m./f.* **11B**
realistic realistisch *adj.* **10A**
really wirklich *adv.* **4A**
receive bekommen *v.* **5A**
receiver Hörer, - *m.* **11A**
recess Pause, -n *f.* **1B**
recipe Rezept, -e *n.* **4A**
recognize erkennen *v.* **7A**
recommend empfehlen *v.* **2B**
record aufnehmen *v.* **8B**
recycle recyceln *v.* **12B**
red rot *adj.* **3A**
  red-haired rothaarig *adj.* **3A**
reference Referenz, -en *f.* **11A**
refrigerator Kühlschrank, ¨e *m.* **6B**
related verwandt *adj.* **10A**
relative Verwandte, -n *m.* **3A**

relax sich entspannen *v.* **9A**
reliable zuverlässig *adj.* **3B**
remember sich erinnern (an) *v.* **9A**
remote control Fernbedienung, -en *f.* **8B**
remove entfernen *v.* **6B**
renewable energy erneuerbare Energie, -en *f.* **12B**
rent Miete, -n *f.* **6A**; mieten *v.* **6A**
repair reparieren *v.* **8A**
repeat wiederholen *v.* **2A**
repetition Wiederholung, -en *f.*
report berichten *v.* **12B**
report card Zeugnis, -se *n.* **1B**
reservation: to make a (hotel) reservation
  buchen *v.* **7B**
resign kündigen *v.* **11B**
rest sich ausruhen *v.* **9A**
restaurant Restaurant, -s *n.* **4B**
result Ergebnis, -se *n.* **1B**
résumé Lebenslauf, ¨e *m.* **11A**
retire in Rente gehen *v.* **5A**
retiree Rentner, - / Rentnerin, -nen *m./f.* **11B**
review Besprechung, -en *f.* **8B**
rice Reis *m.* **4A**
rich reich *adj.* **3B**
ride fahren *v.* **2B**; reiten *v.* **2B**
  to give (someone) a ride (jemanden)
    mitnehmen *v.* **10B**
  to ride a bicycle Fahrrad fahren *v.* **2B**
ring klingeln *v.* **8B**
rinse spülen *v.* **6B**
rise (sun) aufgehen *v.* **12A**
river Fluss, ¨e *m.* **3B**
rock Stein, -e *m.* **12A**
roll Brötchen, - *n.* **4A**
room Zimmer, - *n.* **5A**
room service Zimmerservice *m.* **7B**
roommate Mitbewohner, - / Mitbewohnerin,
  -nen *m./f.* **2A**
rug Teppich, -e *m.* **6A**
run laufen *v.* **2B**; rennen *v.* **5A**
Russia Russland *n.* **10B**
Russian (person) Russe, -n / Russin,
  -nen *m./f.* **10B**; (**language**) Russisch *n.* **10B**

S

sad traurig *adj.* **3B**
salad Salat, -e *m.* **4A**
salary Gehalt, ¨er *n.* **11A**
  high/low salary hohes/niedriges Gehalt,
    ¨er *n.* **11A**
sale Verkauf, ¨e *m.*
  on sale im Angebot **5B**
salesperson Verkäufer, - / Verkäuferin,
  -nen *m./f.* **5B**
salt Salz, -e *n.* **4B**
salty salzig *adj.* **4B**
same gleich *adj.*
Saturday Samstag, -e *m.* **2A**
  on Saturdays samstags *adv.* **2A**
sausage Würstchen, - *n.* **4A**
save speichern *v.* **8B**; retten *v.* **12B**
  to save the planet den Planeten retten *v.* **12B**
say sagen *v.* **2A**

scarf Schal, -s *m.* **5B**
schedule Stundenplan, ¨e *m.* **2A**; Fahrplan,
  ¨e *m.* **8A**
scholarship Stipendium (*pl.* Stipendien) *n.* **2A**
school Schule, -n *f.* **1B**
science Naturwissenschaft, -en *f.* **2A**
scientist Wissenschaftler, - / Wissenschaftlerin,
  -nen *m./f.* **11B**
score Ergebnis, -se *n.* **1B**
screen Bildschirm, -e *m.* **8B**
screen name Benutzername, -n *m.* **8B**
sea Meer, -e *n.* **12A**
seafood Meeresfrüchte *f. pl.* **4A**
season Jahreszeit, -en *f.* **7A**
seatbelt Sicherheitsgurt, -e *m.* **8A**
second zweite *adj.* **2A**
  second-hand clothing Altkleider *pl.* **12B**
see sehen *v.* **2B**
  See you later. Bis später! **1A**
  See you soon. Bis gleich! / Bis bald. **1A**
  See you tomorrow. Bis morgen! **1A**
selfish egoistisch *adj.* **3B**
sell verkaufen *v.* **4A**
seminar Seminar, -e *n.* **2A**
seminar room Seminarraum (*pl.* Seminarräume)
  m. **2A**
send schicken *v.* **8B**; abschicken *v.* **11B**
separate (sich) trennen *v.* **9A**
separated getrennt *adj.* **3A**
September September *m.* **2A**
serious ernst *adj.* **3B**; schwer *adj.* **9B**
set setzen *v.* **9A**; (**sun**) untergehen *v.* **12A**
  to set the table den Tisch decken *v.* **6B**
seven sieben **2A**
shampoo Shampoo, -s *n.* **9A**
shape Form, -en *f.* **9B**
  in good shape fit *adj.* **2B**
  to be in/out of shape in guter/schlechter Form
    sein *v.* **9B**
shave sich rasieren *v.* **9A**
shaving cream Rasierschaum, ¨e *m.* **9A**
she sie *pron.* **1A**
sheep Schaf, -e *n.* **12A**
sheet Laken, - *n.* **6B**
  sheet of paper Blatt Papier (*pl.* Blätter)
    Papier *n.* **1B**
ship Schiff, -e *n.* **8A**
shirt Hemd, -en *n.* **5B**
shoe Schuh, -e *m.* **5B**
shop einkaufen *v.* **4A**; Geschäft, -e *n.* **4A**
  to go shopping einkaufen gehen *v.* **4A**
shopping Einkaufen *n.* **5B**
shopping center Einkaufszentrum,
  -(*pl.* Einkaufszentren) *n.* **10B**
short kurz *adj.* **3A**; (**stature**) klein *adj.* **3A**
  short film Kurzfilm, -e *m.* **10A**
  short-sleeved kurzärmlig *adj.* **5B**
shorts kurze Hose, -n *f.* **5B**
shot Spritze, -n *f.* **9B**
  to give a shot eine Spritze geben *v.* **9B**
shoulder Schulter, -n *f.* **9A**
show zeigen *v.* **4B**
shower: to take a shower (sich) duschen *v.* **9A**
shrimp Garnele, -n *f.* **4A**

shy schüchtern *adj.* **3B**
sibling Geschwister, - *n.* **3A**
sick krank *adj.* **9B**
  to get sick krank werden *v.* **9B**
side dish Beilage, -n *f.* **4B**
sidewalk Bürgersteig, -e *m.* **10B**
sign unterschreiben *v.* **10A**; Schild, -er *n.*
silk Seide, -n *f.* **5B**
silverware Besteck *n.* **4B**
since seit **4B**
sincere aufrichtig *adj.* **3B**
  Yours sincerely Gruß, ¨e **3B**
sing singen *v.* **2B**
single ledig *adj.* **3A**
sink Spüle, -n *f.* **6B**
sister Schwester, -n *f.* **1A**
sister-in-law Schwägerin, -nen *f.* **3A**
sit sitzen *v.* **5B**
  to sit down sich (hin)setzen *v.* **9A**
six sechs **2A**
size Kleidergröße, -n *f.* **5B**
ski Ski fahren *v.* **2B**
skirt Rock, ¨e *m.* **5B**
sky Himmel *m.* **12A**
sleep schlafen *v.* **2B**
  to go to sleep einschlafen *v.* **4A**
slim schlank *adj.* **3A**
slipper Hausschuh, -e *m.* **9A**
slow langsam *adj.* **3B**
  Please speak more slowly. Sprechen Sie bitte
    langsamer! **3B**
  Slow down. Langsam fahren. **3B**
small klein *adj.* **3A**
smartphone Smartphone, -s *n.* **8B**
smile lächeln *v.* **5A**
smoke rauchen *v.*
  No smoking. Rauchen verboten. **3B**
snack Snack, -s *m.* **4B**
snake Schlange, -n *f.* **12A**
sneakers Turnschuhe *m. pl.* **5B**
sneeze niesen *v.* **9B**
snow Schnee *m.* **7A**; schneien *v.* **7A**
so so *adv.* **4A**
  so far, so good so weit, so gut **1A**
  so that damit *conj.* **10A**
soap Seife, -n *f.* **9A**
soccer Fußball *m.* **2B**
sock Socke, -n *f.* **5B**
sofa Sofa, -s *n.* **6A**
soil verschmutzen *v.* **6B**
solar energy Sonnenenergie *f.* **12B**
solid colored einfarbig *adj.* **5B**
solution Lösung, -en *f.* **12B**
some mancher/manche/manches *pron.* **8B**
someone jemand *pron.* **7B**
something etwas *pron.* **7B**
  something else etwas anderes *n.* **10A**
sometimes manchmal *adv.* **7B**
somewhere else woanders *adv.* **4A**
son Sohn, ¨e *m.* **3A**
soon bald **1A**
  See you soon. Bis bald.; Bis gleich. **1A**
sorry: I'm sorry. Es tut mir leid. **1A**

so-so (I'm so-so) Es geht. **1A**
soup Suppe, -n *f.* **4B**
soup spoon Esslöffel, - *m.* **4B**
Spain Spanien *n.* **10B**
Spanish (person) Spanier, - / Spanierin,
  -nen *m./f.* **10B**; **(language)** Spanisch *n.* **10B**
sparkling water Mineralwasser *n.* **4B**
speak sprechen *v.* **2B**
  to speak about sprechen über; reden über *v.* **7A**
special besonderes *adj.* **10A**
  nothing special nichts Besonderes *adj.* **10A**
species Art, -en *f.* **12B**
spelling Rechtschreibung *f.*
spend verbringen *v.* **4A**
spicy scharf *adj.* **4B**
split up sich trennen *v.* **9A**
spoon Löffel, - *m.* **4B**
sport Sport *m.* **2B**; Sportart, -en *f.* **2B**
sprain (one's wrist/ankle) sich (das Handgelenk /
  den Fuß) verstauchen *v.* **9B**
spring Frühling, -e *m.* **2B**
squirrel Eichhörnchen, - *n.* **12A**
stadium Stadion (*pl.* Stadien) *n.* **2B**
stairs Treppe, -n *f.* **6A**
  to go up/down stairs die Treppe hochgehen/
    heruntergehen *v.* **10B**
stamp Briefmarke, -n *f.* **10A**
stand stehen *v.* **5B**
  to stand in line Schlange stehen *v.* **7B**
stapler Hefter, - *m.* **11A**
star Stern, -e *m.* **12A**
start starten *v.* **8B**; anfangen *v.* **4A**; beginnen *v.* **6A**
station wagon Kombi, -s *m.* **8B**
statue Statue, -n *f.* **10B**
stay bleiben *v.* **5B**
steal stehlen *v.* **2B**
steering wheel Lenkrad, ¨er *n.* **8A**
stepbrother Halbbruder, ¨ *m.* **3A**
stepdaughter Stieftochter, ¨ *f.* **3A**
stepfather Stiefvater, -s¨ *m.* **3A**
stepmother Stiefmutter, ¨ *f.* **3A**
stepsister Halbschwester, -n *f.* **3A**
stepson Stiefsohn, ¨ *m.* **3A**
stereo system Stereoanlage, -n *f.* **8B**
still noch *adv.* **4A**; still *adj.* **4B**
  still water stilles Wasser *n.* **4B**
stomachache Bauchschmerzen *m. pl.* **9B**
stop sign Stoppschild, -er *n.* **8A**
store Geschäft, -e *n.* **4A**
storm Sturm, ¨e *m.* **7A**
stove Herd, -e *m.* **6B**
straight glatt *adj.* **3A**
  straight hair glatte Haare *n. pl.* **3A**
  straight ahead geradeaus *adv.* **8A**
strawberry Erdbeere, -n *f.* **4A**
stream Strom, ¨e *m.* **12A**
street Straße, -n *f.* **8A**
  to cross the street die Straße überqueren *v.* **10B**
striped gestreift *adj.* **5B**
strong stark *adj.* **3B**
student Schüler, - / Schülerin, -nen *m./f.* **1B**;
  (college/university) Student, -en / Studentin,
  -nen *m./f.* **1A**

studies Studium (*pl.* Studien) *n.* **2A**
study lernen *v.* **2A**
stuffy nose verstopfte Nase *f.* **9B**
style Stil, -e *m.* **5B**
subject Fach, ¨er *n.* **2A**
subway U-Bahn, -en *f.* **8A**
success Erfolg, -e *m.* **11B**
such solcher/solche/solches *pron.* **8B**
suit Anzug, ¨e *m.* **5B**
suitcase Koffer, - *m.* **7B**
summer Sommer, - *m.* **2B**
sun Sonne, -n *f.* **12A**
sunburn Sonnenbrand, ¨e *m.* **9B**
Sunday Sonntag, -e *m.* **2A**
  on Sundays sonntags *adv.* **2A**
sunglasses Sonnenbrille, -n *f.* **5B**
sunny sonnig *adj.* **7A**
sunrise Sonnenaufgang, ¨e *m.* **12A**
sunset Sonnenuntergang, ¨e *m.* **12A**
supermarket Supermarkt, ¨e *m.* **4A**
supposed: to be supposed to sollen *v.* **3B**
surf surfen *v.* **8B**
  to surf the Web im Internet surfen *v.* **8B**
surprise überraschen *v.* **5A**; Überraschung,
  -en *f.* **5A**
sweater Pullover, - *m.* **5B**
sweatshirt Sweatshirt, -s *n.* **5B**
sweep fegen *v.* **6B**
sweet süß *adj.* **3B**
swim schwimmen *v.* **2B**
swimming pool Schwimmbad, ¨er *n.* **2B**
Switzerland die Schweiz *f.* **7A**
Swiss schweizerisch, Schweizer *adj.* **10B**; **(person)**
  Schweizer, - / Schweizerin, -nen *m./f.* **10B**
symptom Symptom, -e *n.* **9B**

T

table Tisch, -e *m.* **1B**
  to set the table den Tisch decken **6B**
tablecloth Tischdecke, -n *f.* **4B**
tablet Tablet, -s *n.* **8B**
take nehmen *v.* **2B**
  to take (a class) belegen *v.* **2A**
  to take out the trash den Müll rausbringen **6B**
  to take a shower (sich) duschen *v.* **9A**
  to take off abfliegen *v.* **7B**
talk reden *v.* **5A**
  to talk about erzählen von; sprechen/reden
    über *v.* **7A**
tall groß *adj.* **3A**
tank top Trägerhemd, -en *n.* **5B**
taste schmecken *v.* **4B**; Geschmack, ¨e *m.* **4B**
taxi Taxi, -s *n.* **8A**
taxi driver Taxifahrer, - / Taxifahrerin,
  -nen *m./f.* **11B**
tea Tee, -s *m.* **4B**
teacher Lehrer, - / Lehrerin, -nen *m./f.* **1B**
team Mannschaft, -en *f.* **2B**
teaspoon Teelöffel, - *m.* **4B**
technology Technik *f.* **8B**
  to use technology Technik bedienen *v.* **8B**
telephone Telefon, -e *n.* **8B**

on the telephone am Telefon **11A**
telephone number Telefonnummer, -n *f.* **11A**
television Fernsehen *n.*
   television (set) Fernseher -*m.* **8B**
tell erzählen *v.* **7A**
   to tell a story about erzählen von *v.* **7A**
temperature Temperatur, -en *f.*
   What's the temperature? Wie warm/kalt ist
   es? **7A**
tennis Tennis *n.* **2B**
tent Zelt, -e *n.* **7B**
ten zehn **2A**
terrific großartig *adj.* **3A**
test Prüfung, -en *f.* **1B**
text message SMS, - *f.* **8B**
textbook Lehrbuch, ¨er *n.*; Schulbuch, ¨er *n.* **1B**
thank danken *v.* **2A**
   Thank you. Danke! **1A**
   Thank you very much. Vielen Dank! **1A**
that das **1A**; dass *conj.* **10A**
the das/der/die **1A**
their ihr *poss. adj.* **3A**
then dann *adv.* **7B**
there da **1A**
   Is/Are there...? Ist/Sind hier...? **1B**;
   Gibt es...? **2B**
   There is/are... Da ist/sind... **1A**; Es gibt... **2B**
   there and back hin und zurück **7B**
   over there drüben *adv.* **4A**
therefore also; deshalb *conj.* **9B**
thermometer Thermometer, - *n.* **9B**
these diese *pron.* **8B**
   These are... Das sind... **1A**
they sie *pron.* **1A**
thick dick *adj.* **3A**
thin dünn *adj.* **3A**
thing Sache, -n *f.* **1B**; Ding, -e *n.*
think denken *v.* **5A**
   to think about denken an *v.* **7A**
   to think over überlegen *v.* **4A**
third dritter/dritte/drittes *adj.* **2A**
this das **1A**; dieser/diese/dieses *pron.* **8B**
   This is... Das ist... **1A**
three drei **2A**
through durch *prep.* **3B**
throw werfen *v.* **2B**
   to throw away wegwerfen *v.* **12B**
thunder Donner, - *m.* **7A**
thunderstorm Gewitter, - *n.* **7A**
Thursday Donnerstag, -e *m.* **2A**
   on Thursdays donnerstags *adv.* **2A**
ticket Flugticket, -s *n.* **7B**; Fahrkarte, -n *f.* **8A**
ticket collector Schaffner, - / Schaffnerin,
   -nen *m./f.* **8A**
ticket office Fahrkartenschalter, - *m.* **8A**
tidy ordentlich *adj.* **6B**
tie Krawatte, -n *f.* **5B**
tight eng *adj.* **5B**
time Zeit, -en *f.* **2A**; Mal, -e *n.* **7B**
   for the first/last time zum ersten/letzten
   Mal **7B**
   the first/last time das erste/letzte Mal **7B**
   this time diesmal *adv.* **7B**

What time is it? Wie spät ist es?; Wie viel Uhr
   ist es? **2A**
times mal **1B**
tip Trinkgeld, -er *n.* **4B**
tired müde *adj.* **3B**
tissue Taschentuch, ¨er *n.* **9B**
to vor *prep.* **2A**; nach; zu *prep.* **4B**; auf, an *prep.* **5B**
   (in order) to um...zu **7B**
   to the right/left nach rechts/links **6A**
toast anstoßen *v.* **5A**
toaster Toaster, - *m.* **6B**
today heute *adv.* **2B**
   Today is... Heute ist der... **2A**
   What day is it today? Welcher Tag ist heute? **7A**
toe Zeh, -en *m.* **9A**
together zusammen *adv.* **3A**
toilet Toilette, -n *f.* **6A**
tomato Tomate, -n *f.* **4A**
tomorrow morgen *adv.* **2B**
   the day after tomorrow übermorgen *adv.* **2B**
   tomorrow morning morgen früh **2B**
too zu *adv.* **4A**; auch *adv.* **1A**
tool kit Werkzeug, -e *n.*
tooth Zahn, ¨e *m.* **9A**
toothache Zahnschmerzen *m. pl.* **9B**
toothbrush Zahnbürste, -n *f.* **9A**
toothpaste Zahnpasta (*pl.* Zahnpasten) *f.* **9A**
tornado Tornado, -s *m.* **12A**
toward in Richtung *f.* **10B**
towel Handtuch, ¨er *n.* **9A**
town Stadt, ¨e *f.* **10B**
town hall Rathaus, ¨er *n.* **10A**
toxic waste Giftmüll *m.* **12B**
track Bahnsteig, -e *m.* **8A**
track and field Leichtathletik *f.* **2B**
traffic Verkehr *m.* **8A**
traffic light Ampel, -n *f.* **10B**
train Zug, ¨e *m.* **8A**
transportation Verkehrsmittel, - *n.* **8A**
   public transportation öffentliche
   Verkehrsmittel *n. pl.* **8A**
trash Müll *m.* **6B**
   to take out the trash den Müll rausbringen **6B**
travel reisen *v.* **2A**
travel agency Reisebüro, -s *n.* **7B**
traveler Reisende, -n *m./f.* **7B**
tree Baum, ¨e *m.* **12A**
trendy angesagt *adj.* **5B**
trip Reise, -n *f.* **7B**
truck LKW, -s *m.* **8A**
truck driver LKW-Fahrer, - / LKW-Fahrerin,
   -nen *m./f.* **11B**
trunk Kofferraum, ¨e *m.* **8A**
try probieren *v.* **3B**; versuchen *v.* **7B**
   Give it a try! Probieren Sie mal!
T-shirt T-Shirt, -s *n.* **5B**
Tuesday Dienstag, -e *m.* **2A**
   on Tuesdays dienstags *adv.* **2A**
tuition fee Studiengebühr, -en *f.* **2A**
tuna Thunfisch, -e *m.* **4A**
Turkey die Türkei *f.* **10B**
Turkish (person) Türke, -n / Türkin, -nen *m./f.* **10B**;
   Turkish (language) Türkisch *n.* **10B**

turn abbiegen *v.* **10B**
   to turn right/left rechts/links abbiegen *v.* **8A**
   to turn off ausmachen *v.* **8B**; einschalten *v.* **12B**
   to turn on anmachen *v.* **8B**; auschalten *v.* **12B**
turning point Wende, -n *f.* **12B**
twelve zwölf **2A**
twenty zwanzig **2A**
twin Zwilling, -e *m.* **3A**
two zwei **2A**

U

ugly hässlich *adj.* **3A**
umbrella Regenschirm, -e *m.* **7A**
under unter *prep.* **5B**
understand verstehen *v.* **2A**
underwear Unterwäsche *f.* **5B**
undressed: to get undressed sich ausziehen *v.* **9A**
unemployed arbeitslos *adj.* **10A**
unfortunate arm *adj.* **3B**
unfortunately leider *adv.* **4A**
unfurnished unmöbliert *adj.* **6A**
university Universität, -en *f.* **1B**
unpleasant unangenehm *adj.* **3B**
until bis *prep.* **3B**; bis zu *prep.* **10B**
up herauf *adv.* **6A**
   to get up aufstehen *v.* **4A**
   to go up hochgehen *v.* **10B**
USA die USA *pl.*; die Vereinigten Staaten *pl.* **10B**
use benutzen *v.* **8A**; bedienen *v.* **8B**
   to get used to sich gewöhnen an *v.* **9A**
useful nützlich *adj.* **2A**
useless nutzlos *adj.* **2A**

V

vacancy Zimmer frei *f.* **6A**
vacation Ferien *pl.*; Urlaub, -e *m.* **7B**
   to go on vacation Urlaub machen *v.* **7B**
vacuum staubsaugen *v.* **6B**
vacuum cleaner Staubsauger, - *m.* **6B**
validate entwerten *v.* **8A**
   to validate a ticket eine Fahrkarte
   entwerten *v.* **8A**
valley Tal, ¨er *n.* **12A**
vase Vase, -n *f.* **6A**
vegetables Gemüse *n.* **4A**
verb Verb, -en *n.* **9A**
very sehr *adv.* **3A**
   very well sehr gut **1A**
veterinarian Tierarzt, ¨e / Tierärztin,
   -nen *m./f.* **11B**
visa Visum (*pl.* Visa) *n.* **7B**
visit besuchen *v.* **4A**
vocabulary Wortschatz, ¨e *m.*
volcano Vulkan, -e *m.* **12A**
volleyball Volleyball *m.* **2B**

W

wait warten *v.* **2A**
   to wait for warten auf *v.* **7A**
waiter / waitress Kellner, - / Kellnerin,

-nen *m./f.* **3B**

Waiter! Herr Ober! **4B**

wake up aufwachen *v.* **9A**

walk Spaziergang, ⸚e *m.*

to go for a walk spazieren gehen *v.* **2B**

wall Wand, ⸚e *f.* **5B**

want wollen *v.* **3B**

warm warm *adj.* **10A**

wash waschen *v.* **2B**

to wash (oneself) sich waschen *v.* **9A**

washing machine Waschmaschine, -n *f.* **6B**

waste Müll *m.* **12B**; Abfall, ⸚e *m.* **12B**

wastebasket Papierkorb, ⸚e *m.* **1B**

watch zuschauen *v.* **4A**; anschauen *v.* **7A**

to watch television fernsehen *v.* **8B**

water Wasser *n.*

sparkling water Mineralwasser *n.* **4B**

still water stilles Wasser *n.* **4B**

water pitcher Wasserkrug, ⸚e *m.* **4B**

waterfall Wasserfall, ⸚e *m.* **12A**

we wir *pron.* **1A**

weak schwach *adj.* **3B**

wear tragen *v.* **2B**

weather Wetter *n.* **7A**

What's the weather like? Wie ist das Wetter? **7A**

weather report Wetterbericht, -e *m.* **7A**

Web Internet *n.* **8B**

to surf the Web im Internet surfen *v.* **8B**

Web site Website, -s *f.* **8B**

wedding Hochzeit, -en *f.* **5A**

Wednesday Mittwoch, -e *m.* **2A**

on Wednesdays mittwochs *adv.* **2A**

week Woche, -n *f.* **2A**

weekend Wochenende, -n *n.* **2A**

weigh wiegen *v.* **8B**

welcome (herzlich) willkommen **1A**

You're welcome. Gern geschehen! **1A**

well gut *adv.*

I am (very) well. Mir geht's (sehr) gut. **1A**

I am not (so) well. Mir geht's nicht (so) gut. **1A**

Get well! Gute Besserung! **5A**

well-dressed gut gekleidet *adj.* **5B**

well-known bekannt *adj.* **10A**

wet nass *adj.* **12A**

what was *interr.* **2A**

What is that? Was ist das? **1B**

What's up? Was geht ab? **1A**

when wann *interr.* **2A**

whenever wenn *conj.* **10A**

where wo *interr.* **2A**

where from woher *interr.* **2A**

where to wohin *interr.* **2A**

whether ob *conj.* **10A**

which welcher/welche/welches *interr.* **2A**

white weiß *adj.* **5B**

who wer *interr.* **2A**

Who is it? Wer ist das? **1B**

whom wen *acc. interr.* **2A**; wem *dat. interr.* **4B**

whose wessen *interr.* **8B**

why warum *interr.* **2A**

widow Witwe, -n *f.* **3A**

widower Witwer, - *m.* **3A**

wife Ehefrau, -en *f.* **3A**

win gewinnen *v.* **2B**

wind energy Windenergie *f.* **12B**

window Fenster, - *n.* **1A**

windshield Windschutzscheibe, -n *f.* **8A**

windshield wiper Scheibenwischer, - *m.* **8A**

windy windig *adj.* **7A**

wine Wein, -e *m.* **4B**

winter Winter, - *m.* **2B**

wipe wischen *v.* **6B**

wise weise *adj.* **3B**

wish wünschen *v.* **9A**

to wish (for something) sich (etwas) wünschen *v.* **9A**

with mit **4B**

withdraw (money) (Geld) abheben *v.* **10A**

within innerhalb *prep.* **8B**

without ohne *prep.* **3B**

woman Frau, -en *f.* **1A**

wonder sich fragen *v.* **9A**

wood Holz *n.* **6B**

wool Wolle *f.* **5B**

work Arbeit, -en *f.* **11B**; arbeiten *v.* **2A**; funktionieren *v.* **8B**

at work auf der Arbeit **11B**

to work on arbeiten an *v.* **7A**

world Welt, -en *f.* **12B**

worried besorgt *adj.* **3B**

write schreiben *v.* **2A**

to write to schreiben an *v.* **7A**

to write to one another sich schreiben *v.* **9A**

Y

year Jahr, -e *n.* **7A**

yellow gelb *adj.* **5B**

yes ja **1A**; (**contradicting**) doch *adv.* **2B**

yesterday gestern *adv.* **5B**

yet noch *adv.* **4A**

yogurt Joghurt, -s *m.* **4A**

you du/ihr/Sie *pron.* **1A**

young jung *adj.* **3A**; jugendlich *adj.* **10A**

your euer/Ihr *poss. adj.* **3A**

youth hostel Jugendherberge, -n *f.* **7B**

Index

Europa

die Welt

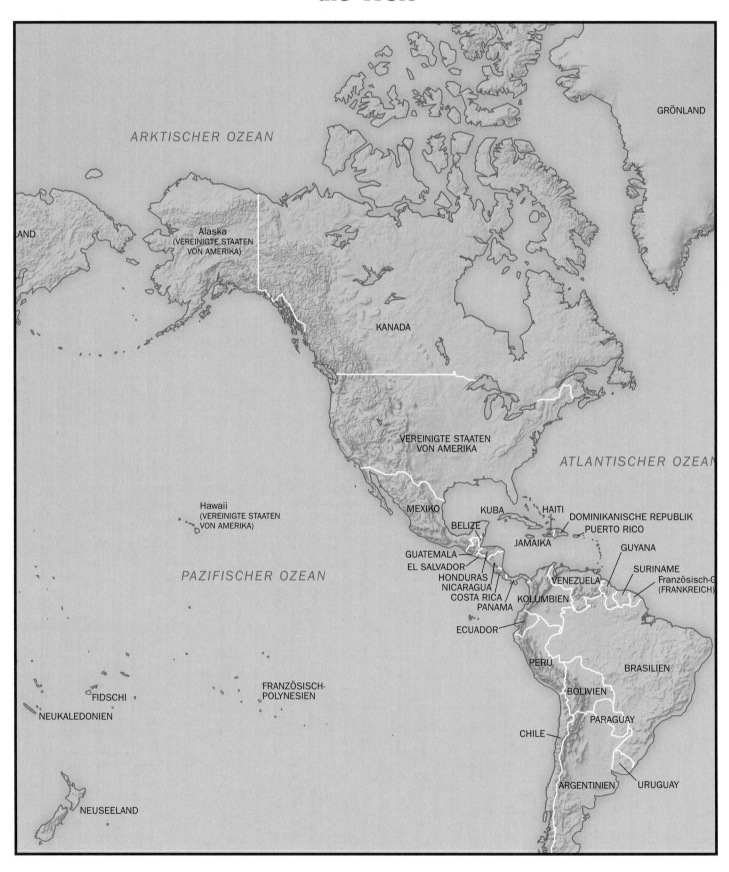

GRÖNLAND

ARKTISCHER OZEAN

Alaska
(VEREINIGTE STAATEN
VON AMERIKA)

KANADA

VEREINIGTE STAATEN
VON AMERIKA

ATLANTISCHER OZEAN

Hawaii
(VEREINIGTE STAATEN
VON AMERIKA)

MEXIKO

KUBA

HAITI

DOMINIKANISCHE REPUBLIK

PUERTO RICO

BELIZE

JAMAIKA

GUATEMALA

EL SALVADOR

HONDURAS

NICARAGUA

COSTA RICA

PANAMA

GUYANA

SURINAME

Französisch-G
(FRANKREICH)

VENEZUELA

KOLUMBIEN

ECUADOR

PAZIFISCHER OZEAN

PERU

BRASILIEN

BOLIVIEN

FRANZÖSISCH-
POLYNESIEN

FIDSCHI

NEUKALEDONIEN

PARAGUAY

CHILE

ARGENTINIEN

URUGUAY

NEUSEELAND

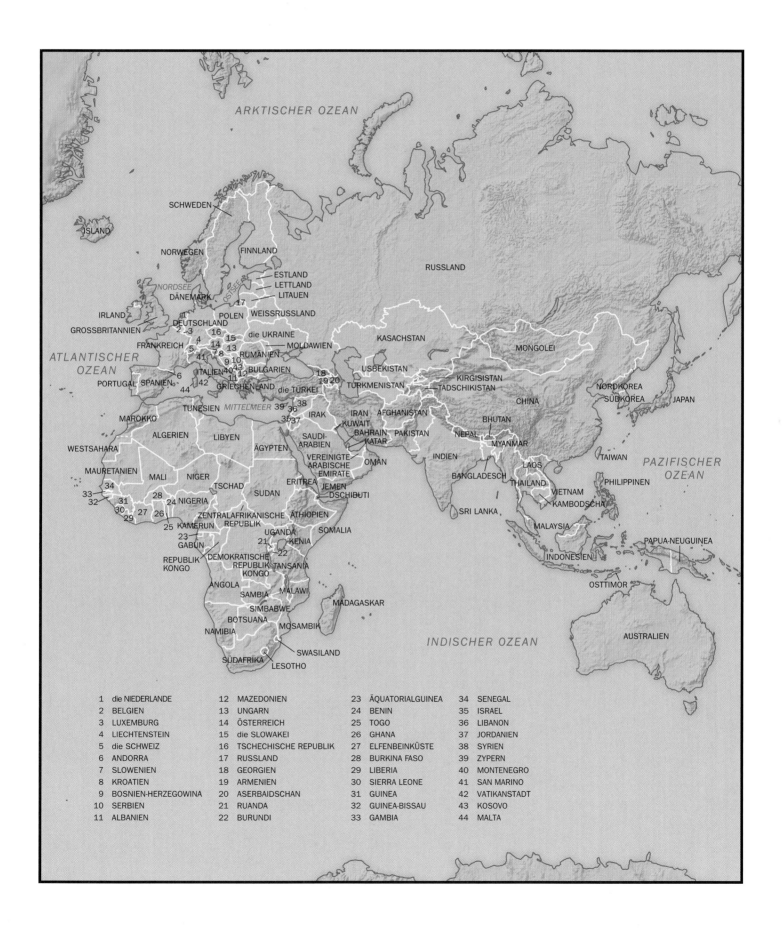

1 die NIEDERLANDE	12 MAZEDONIEN	23 ÄQUATORIALGUINEA	34 SENEGAL
2 BELGIEN	13 UNGARN	24 BENIN	35 ISRAEL
3 LUXEMBURG	14 ÖSTERREICH	25 TOGO	36 LIBANON
4 LIECHTENSTEIN	15 die SLOWAKEI	26 GHANA	37 JORDANIEN
5 die SCHWEIZ	16 TSCHECHISCHE REPUBLIK	27 ELFENBEINKÜSTE	38 SYRIEN
6 ANDORRA	17 RUSSLAND	28 BURKINA FASO	39 ZYPERN
7 SLOWENIEN	18 GEORGIEN	29 LIBERIA	40 MONTENEGRO
8 KROATIEN	19 ARMENIEN	30 SIERRA LEONE	41 SAN MARINO
9 BOSNIEN-HERZEGOWINA	20 ASERBAIDSCHAN	31 GUINEA	42 VATIKANSTADT
10 SERBIEN	21 RUANDA	32 GUINEA-BISSAU	43 KOSOVO
11 ALBANIEN	22 BURUNDI	33 GAMBIA	44 MALTA

Deutschland

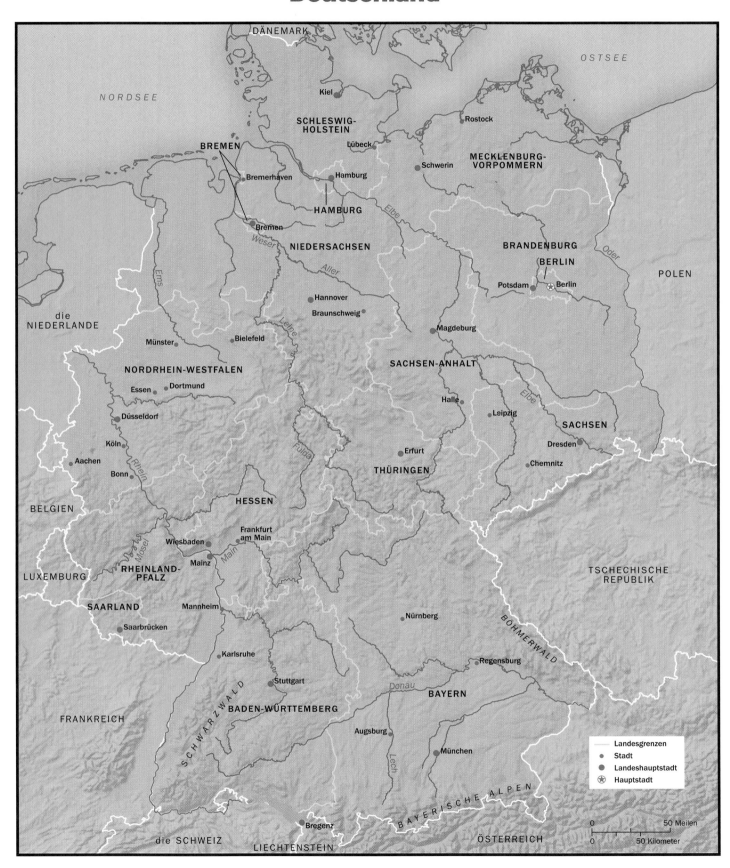

DÄNEMARK

NORDSEE

OSTSEE

Kiel

SCHLESWIG-HOLSTEIN

Rostock

Lübeck

BREMEN

Schwerin

MECKLENBURG-VORPOMMERN

Bremerhaven

Hamburg

HAMBURG

Bremen

Weser

NIEDERSACHSEN

Elbe

BRANDENBURG

Oder

BERLIN

POLEN

Aller

Potsdam

Berlin

die NIEDERLANDE

Ems

Hannover

Braunschweig

Leine

Magdeburg

Münster

Bielefeld

SACHSEN-ANHALT

NORDRHEIN-WESTFALEN

Essen

Dortmund

Halle

Elbe

Leipzig

Düsseldorf

SACHSEN

Köln

Rhein

Fulda

Erfurt

Dresden

Aachen

Chemnitz

Bonn

THÜRINGEN

HESSEN

BELGIEN

Frankfurt am Main

Mosel

Wiesbaden

Main

RHEINLAND-PFALZ

Mainz

TSCHECHISCHE REPUBLIK

LUXEMBURG

SAARLAND

Mannheim

Nürnberg

BÖHMERWALD

Saarbrücken

Karlsruhe

Regensburg

Donau

Stuttgart

BAYERN

SCHWARZWALD

BADEN-WÜRTTEMBERG

FRANKREICH

Augsburg

Lech

München

Landesgrenzen

Stadt

Landeshauptstadt

Hauptstadt

BAYERISCHE ALPEN

Bregenz

die SCHWEIZ

LIECHTENSTEIN

ÖSTERREICH

0   50 Meilen

0   50 Kilometer

Österreich

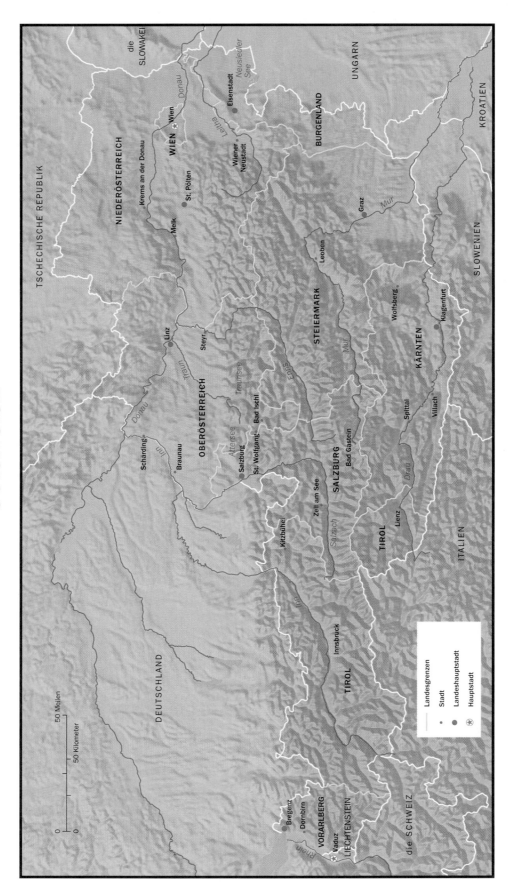

Liechtenstein

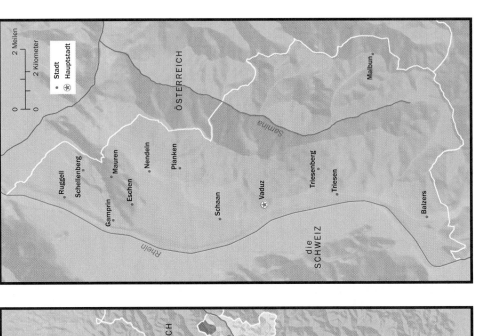

die Schweiz

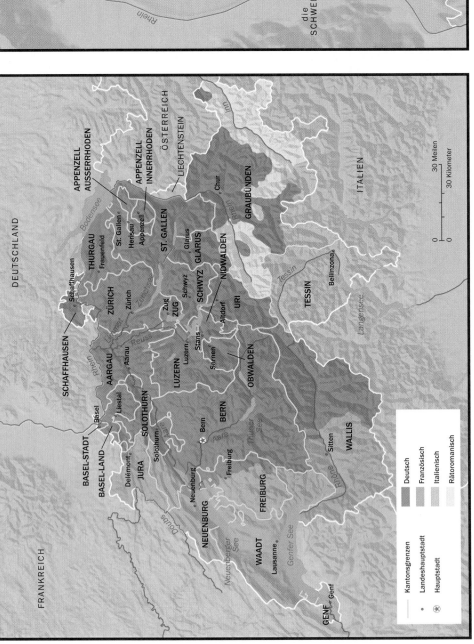

About the Authors

Christine Anton, a native of Germany, is Associate Professor of German and Director of the Language Resource Center at Berry College. She received her B.A. in English and German from the Universität Erlangen and her graduate degrees in Germanic Languages and Literatures from the University of North Carolina at Chapel Hill. She has published two books on German realism and German cultural memory of National Socialism, and a number of articles on 19th and 20th century German and Austrian literature, as well as on second language acquisition. Dr. Anton has received several awards for excellence in teaching and was honored by the American Association of Teachers of German with the Duden Award for her "outstanding efforts and achievement in the teaching of German." Dr. Anton previously taught at the State University of New York and the University of North Carolina, Chapel Hill.

Tobias Barske, a native of Bavaria, is an Associate Professor of German and Applied Linguistics at the University of Wisconsin-Stevens Point. He has a Ph.D. in German Applied Linguistics from the University of Illinois at Urbana-Champaign with emphases on language and social interaction as well as language pedagogy. He has also studied at the Universität Regensburg in Germany. Tobias has over 10 years of experience teaching undergraduate and graduate courses at the university level and has earned numerous awards for excellence in teaching.

Megan McKinstry has an M.A. in Germanics from the University of Washington. She is an Assistant Teaching Professor of German Studies and Co-Coordinator for Elementary German at the University of Missouri, where she received the University's "Purple Chalk" teaching award and an award for "Best Online Course." Ms. McKinstry has been teaching for over fifteen years.

Credits

Every effort has been made to trace the copyright holders of the works published herein. If proper copyright acknowledgment has not been made, please contact the publisher and we will correct the information in future printings.

Text Credits

page 452 Reproduced from: "Allein" by Hermann Hesse, Sämtliche Werke in 20 Bänden. Herausgegeben von Volker Michels. Band 10: Die Gedichte. © Suhrkamp Verlag Frankfurt am Main 2002. All rights with and controlled by Suhrkamp Verlag Berlin.

page 453 Reproduced from: "Todesfuge" by Paul Celan, Mohn und Gedächtnis © 1952, Deutsche Verlags-Anstalt, München, in der Verlagsgruppe Randome House GmbH.

page 492 "Der Erfinder", from: Peter Bichsel, Kindergeschichten. © Suhrkamp Verlag Frankfurt am Main 1997. All rights with and controlled by Suhrkamp Verlag Berlin.

page 534 Reproduced from: "Meine Nachtigall" by Rose Ausländer. Aus: Rose Ausländer. Gesammelte Werke in sieben Bänden. Band II, Die Sichel mäht die Zeit zu Heu. Gedichte 1957-1965. ©1985 S. Fischer Verlag GmbH, Frankfurt am Main.

Film Credits

page 431 Courtesy of Kurzfilm Agentur Hamburg.

page 473 Courtesy of Kurzfilm Agentur Hamburg.

page 513 Courtesy of Sarah Winkenstette, Director.

Television Credits

page 21 Courtesy of Deutsche Bahn AG.

page 67 Courtesy of Technische Universität Berlin. First broadcast 2008. Technische Universität Berlin disclaims all liability for any information appearing herein that may be outdated or incorrect. Please view Technische Universität Berlin's website for the most current information.

page 113 Courtesy of Privatmolkerei Bauer GmbH & Co. KG.

page 161 Courtesy of Jung von Matt Agency.

page 203 Courtesy of Real,-.

page 251 Courtesy of Schweizer Radio und Fernsehen and TELEPOOL GmbH.

page 295 Courtesy of the Grünes Binnenland Tourist Information Office.

page 339 Courtesy of Daimler AG.

page 387 Courtesy of Central Krankenversicherung AG and Philipp und Keuntje GmbH.

Photography and Art Credits

All images © Vista Higher Learning unless otherwise noted.

Cover: Pidjoe/Getty Images.

Front Matter (SE): xiii: Petr Z/Shutterstock.

Front Matter (IAE): IAE-14: Mike Flippo/Shutterstock; **IAE-17:** Petr Z/Shutterstock.

Unit 1: 1: Xavier Roy; **3:** 36clicks/iStockphoto; **4:** Paula Díez; **8:** Laurence Mouton/Media Bakery; **9:** (l) Michaeljung/iStockphoto; (tr) Sashagala/Shutterstock; (br) Imac/Alamy; **13:** (tl) Anne Loubet; (tm) Igor Tarasov/Fotolia; (tr) Jack Hollingsworth/Corbis; (ml) Gualtiero Boffi/Shutterstock; (mml) Tupungato/Shutterstock; (mmr) Nicole Winchell; (mr) Tabitha Patrick/iStockphoto; (b) Eugenio Marongiu/Shutterstock; **15:** (tl) Lazar Mihai-Bogdan/Shutterstock; (tr) Vanessa Bertozzi; (ml, mr, bm) Nicole Winchell; (mm) Anne Loubet; (bl) Gudrun Hommel; (br) Paula Díez; **16:** Auremar/Fotolia; **20:** Richard Foreman/iStockphoto; **28:** Woodapple/Fotolia; **29:** (l) ChristArt/Fotolia; (tr) Arnd Wiegmann/RTR/Newscom; (br) Kyle Monk/Blend Images/Getty Images; **36:** (all) Nicole Winchell; **38:** Sarah2/Shutterstock; **39:** Monkey Business Images/Shutterstock; **40:** (t) Shishic/iStockphoto; (m) PeterSVETphoto/Shutterstock; (b) Hollandse Hoogte/Redux; **41:** (tl) Vaclav Volrab/Shutterstock; (tr) Steve Raymer/Corbis; (bl) CrazyD/iStockphoto; (br) Horst Galuschka/DPA/Corbis; **44:** Chris Schmidt/iStockphoto; **45:** StockLite/Shutterstock.

Unit 2: 47: Xavier Roy; **50:** Chris Schmidt/iStockphoto; **54:** Sabine Lubenow/AGE Fotostock; **55:** (l) Heinz-Peter Bader/Reuters/Newscom; (tr) Ingolf Pompe/AGE Fotostock; (br) Laviana/Shutterstock; **56:** (l) Nicole Winchell; (r) Martín Bernetti; **58:** Nicole Winchell; **66:** (left col: t) IDP Manchester Airport Collection/Alamy; (left col: ml) Javier Larrea/AGE Fotostock; (left col: mm) Noam/Fotolia; (left col: mr) Martín Bernetti; (left col: bl) Ana Cabezas Martín; (left col: bm) Tetra Images/Alamy; (left col: br) Jacob Wackerhausen/iStockphoto; (right col) Martinap/Shutterstock; **74:** Roland Syba/Shutterstock; **75:** (tl) Imagebroker /SuperStock; (tm) Daniel Karmann/Picture-Alliance/DPA/AP Images; (tr) Imago Sportfotodienst/Imago/Moritz Müller/Newscom; (b) Allan Grosskrueger/Shutterstock; **78:** (t) Nicole Winchell; (ml) Polka Dot Images/JupiterImages; (mm) Martín Bernetti; (mr) Michael Chamberlin/Fotolia; (bl) Losevsky Photo and Video/Shutterstock; (bm) Gudrun Hommel; (br) Nicole Winchell; **83:** Janne Hämäläinen/Shutterstock; **84:** Auremar/Shutterstock; **85:** (tl) Ilyashenko Oleksiy/Shutterstock; (tm) Martín Bernetti; (tr) Carlos Gaudier; (bl) Karens4/Big Stock Photo; (bml) Val Thoermer/Big Stock Photo; (bmr) Ben Blankenburg/Corbis; (br) Danny Warren/iStockphoto; **86:** (l) Neustockimages/iStockphoto; (r) JupiterImages; **87:** (tl) Martín Bernetti; (tm) Monkey Business/Fotolia; (tr) Katie Wade; (bl) Brand X Pictures/Fotosearch; (bml) Ana Cabezas Martín; (bmr) Anne Loubet; (br) Harry Neave/Fotolia; **88:** (tl) Gudrun Hommel; (tr) Steffen/Shutterstock; (ml) Nicole Winchell; (mr) VVO/Shutterstock; (b) Bettmann/Corbis; **89:** (tl) Riccardo Sala/Alamy; (tr) Adam Berry/Getty Images; (bl) Fox Photos/Getty Images; (br) Philip Lange/Shutterstock; **90-91:** Jorg Greuel/Getty Images; **92:** Jack Hollingsworth/Cardinal/Corbis; **93:** (t) Kzenon/Fotolia; (b) Nadezda Verbenko/Shutterstock.

Unit 3: 95: Xavier Roy; **102:** Westend61/Getty Images; **103:** (l) John Dowland/Getty Images; (tr) Michael Gottschalk/AFP/Getty Images; (br) Wrangler/Shutterstock; **105:** George Olsson/iStockphoto; **106:** (tl, tr, bl, bmr) Martín Bernetti; (tm) Ray Levesque; (bml) David N. Madden/Shutterstock; (br) Prism68/Shutterstock; **112:** (t) Aspen Stock/AGE Fotostock; (ml) Martín Bernetti; (mm) Carlos Gaudier; (mr) Alexander Rochau/Fotolia; (bl) Imag'In Pyrénées/Fotolia; (bm) Pixtal/AGE Fotostock; (br) Raberry/Big Stock Photo; **116:** (top row: tl) José Blanco; (top row: tm, br) Martín Bernetti; (top row: tr) Anne Loubet; (top row: bl) Rasmus Rasmussen/iStockphoto; (top row: bml) Ana Cabezas Martín; (top row: bmr) Javier Larrea/AGE Fotostock; (bottom row: l) Vanessa Nel/Shutterstock; (bottom row: r) Photoinjection/Shutterstock; **120:** Michelangelo Gratton/Getty Images; **121:** (tl) Tatiana Lebedeva/Shutterstock; (tr) David Fernandez/EPA/Newscom; (b) Sonya Etchison/Shutterstock; **123:** Anne Loubet; **125:** Minerva Studio /Shutterstock; **131:** Nicole Winchell; **132:** (left col: tl) Lichtmeister/Shutterstock; (left col: tr, left col: br) Gudrun Hommel; (left col: bl) Martín Bernetti; (right col) Anne Loubet; **134:** (tl) Andre Jenny/Alamy; (tr) ShyMan/iStockphoto; (m) RosaIreneBetancourt 3/Alamy; (b) Frymire Archive/Alamy; **135:** (tl) Aspen Rock/Shutterstock; (tr) Ruggles Susan/AGE Fotostock; (bl) MWaits/Shutterstock; (br) Sergey Peterman/Shutterstock; **136:** Aleksandar Mijatovic/Shutterstock; **137:** Serg64/Shutterstock; **138:** Gudrun Hommel; **139:** Gudrun Hommel.

Unit 4: 141: Xavier Roy; **143:** (tl) VHL; (tr) Smit/Shutterstock; (bl) Susan Schmitz/Shutterstock; (bml) Smileus/Shutterstock; (bmr, br) Vanessa Bertozzi; **144:** (tl) Nancy Camley; (tr, bl) Vanessa Bertozzi; (bml) Nicole Winchell; (bmr) Monkey Business Images/Shutterstock; (br) Martín Bernetti; **148:** Xyno/iStockphoto; **149:** (l) Karandaev/Fotolia; (tr) Ted Soqui/Corbis; (br) StockPixstore/Fotolia; **151:** Tyler Olson/Shutterstock; **153:** (tl) Rafael Rios; (tr) Steve Debenport/iStockphoto; (bl) Nicole Winchell; (bml) Oscar Artavia Solano; (bmr) Anne Loubet; (br) José Blanco; **155:** (tl) Moori/Big Stock Photo; (tr) Alexey Tkachenko/iStockphoto; (bl, bmr) Martín Bernetti; (bml) Pixtal/AGE Fotostock; (br) Gudrun Hommel; **157:** Javier Larrea/AGE Fotostock; **158:** (tl) Pixart/Big Stock Photo; (tm) Pictrough/Big Stock Photo; (tr) Monkey Business Images/Shutterstock; (bl) PhotoAlto/Alamy; (bml) Nicole Winchell; (bmr) Janet Dracksdorf; (br) Sonyae/Big Stock Photo; **159:** Haveseen/Shutterstock; **163:** (hot dog) Sapik/Shutterstock; (bread) Kheng Guan Toh/Shutterstock; (pie) Notkoo/Shutterstock; **164:** (tl, tm) Katie Wade; (tr) Stocksnapp/Big Stock Photo; (bl) Barry Gregg/Corbis; (bml) Carlos Hernandez/Media Bakery; (bmr) Jack Puccio/iStockphoto; (br) Ruth Black/Shutterstock; **168:** Jean-Pierre Lescourret/Corbis; **169:** (l) Mimmo Lobefaro/Alamy; (tr) Stefan Liewehr; (br) Norbert Enker/laif/Redux; **175:** (t) Alistair Scott/Alamy; (bl) Paula Díez; (bml) Photo courtesy of www.Tahiti-Tourisme.com; (bmr) Gudrun Hommel; (br) Andersen Ross/Blend Images/Corbis; **176:** (t) Gudrun Hommel; (ml) Subbotina Anna/Big Stock Photo; (mm) Willmetts/Big Stock Photo; (mr) LepasR/Big Stock Photo; (bl) Jacek Chabraszewski/Fotolia; (bm) Karandaev/Fotolia; (br) Nicole Winchell; **177:** YinYang/iStockphoto; **178:** (t) Tupungato/123RF; (ml) Michal Durinik/Shutterstock; (mr) Phil Emmerson/Shutterstock; (b) Catherine Lane/iStockphoto; **179:** (tl) Mac99/iStockphoto; (tr) Nikonaft/Crestock/Masterfile; (m) Bettmann/Corbis; (b) Brian Kersey/UPI/Newscom; **180:** OPIS Zagreb/Shutterstock; **181:** PavleMarjanovic/Shutterstock; **182:** Webphotographeer/iStockphoto; **183:** Wavebreakmedia/Shutterstock.

Unit 5: 185: Xavier Roy; **188:** Darío Eusse Tobón; **192:** Nagelestock.com/Alamy; **193:** (l) H. Brauer/Shutterstock; (tr) Vario Images GmbH & Co.KG/Alamy; (br) JTB Media Creation, Inc/Alamy; **196:** (tl) Palladium/AGE Fotostock; (tm) Ana Cabezas Martín; (tr) Pascal Pernixl; (bl, bmr) Martín Bernetti; (bml) Dmitriy Shironosov/Shutterstock; (br) Paula Díez; **199:** (tl) Nicole Winchell; (tr) Andrew Park/Shutterstock; (bl) Aspen Stock/AGE Fotostock; (bml) Moodboard/Fotolia; (bmr) Katie Wade; (br) Martín Bernetti; **205:** (tl) Vanessa Bertozzi; (tm) José Blanco; (tr) Danilo Calilung/Corbis; (bl, bm) Katie Wade; (br) Peter Scholz/Scholz Press/Corbis; **206:** (tl) Rolfbodmer/iStockphoto; (tm, tr, bl, bmr, br) Martín Bernetti; (bml) Darío Eusse Tobón; **210:** A-way!/Splash News/Newscom; **211:** (l) Free Agents Limited/Corbis; (tr) Thomas Rabsch/laif/Redux; (br) Splash News/Newscom; **212:** (l) Diego Cervo/123RF; (r) Artur Bogacki/123RF; **220:** (tl, bmr) Martín Bernetti; (tr) Marc Pinter/Alamy; (bl) Nicole Winchell; (bml) Celso Diniz/Shutterstock; (br) Silky/Shutterstock; **222:** (all) Arbit/Shutterstock; **223:** Javier Larrea/AGE Fotostock; **224:** (tl) Hirotaka Ihara/123RF; (tr) Vaclav Volrab/Shutterstock; (m) Paha_L/Big Stock Photo; (b) Fabián Montoya; **225:** (tl) Enrico Nawrath/DPA/Corbis; (tr) Maugli/Shutterstock; (m) Tibor Bognár/AGE Fotostock; (b) Bloomberg/Getty Images; **226:** Gordon Welters/laif/Redux; 226-227: Petr Z/Shutterstock; **227:** (t) Arnold Morascher/laif/Redux; (b) Georg Knoll/laif/Redux; **228:** Masterfile; **229:** SE Media/Shutterstock.

Unit 6: 231: Xavier Roy; **234:** David Hughes/123RF; **238:** F1 Online/SuperStock; **239:** (l) Canebisca/Shutterstock; (tr) Bettmann/Corbis; (br) Zoonar GmbH/Alamy; **242:** Anopa/Shutterstock; **243:** (t) Mark Bowden/iStockphoto; (b) Zoe Michelle/Big Stock Photo; **245:** Pushkin/Shutterstock; **246:** (tl) Martín Bernetti; (tr) Clayton Hansen/iStockphoto; (bl) José Blanco; (bm) Vanessa Bertozzi; (br) Rolf Fischer/iStockphoto; **254:** Ricardo Miguel/123RF; **258:** BERNINA International AG; **259:** (l) DreamPictures/VStock/Media Bakery; (tr) Interfoto/Alamy; (br) Martín Bernetti; **262:** (tl) Pixtal/AGE Fotostock; (tr) Martín Bernetti; (bl) Katie Wade; (bm) Radius Images/Corbis; (br) Adam Kazmierski/iStockphoto; **263:** Sean Locke Photography/Shutterstock; **268:** (tablet) Petr Z/Shutterstock; (hotel) Phillip Minnis/123RF; **269:** Anne Loubet; **270:** (t) Sergey Telegin/Shutterstock; (ml) Hongjiong Shi/AGE Fotostock; (mr) Christian Kober/Robert Harding World Imagery/Corbis; (b) Photo courtesy of National Police of the Principality of Liechtenstein; **271:** (tl) Richard Wareham Fotografie/Alamy; (tr) Yvan Reitserof/Fotolia; (m) Robyn Beck/AFP/Getty Images; (b) GAPS/iStockphoto; **272:** Fotosearch; **273:** (t) Ant Clausen/Shutterstock; (b) Clu/iStockphoto; **274:** Brian McEntire/iStockphoto; **275:** Purestock/Alamy.

Unit 7: 277: Xavier Roy; **280:** Notkoo/Shutterstock; **284:** Frank Krahmer/Corbis; **285:** (l) David Ball/Alamy; (tr) LOOK Die Bildagentur der Fotografen GmbH/Alamy; (br) Christian Ohde/Chromorange/Picture Alliance/Newscom; **287:** (l) Martín Bernetti; (r) BananaStock/JupiterImages; **288:** (tl, bml) Martín Bernetti; (tr, br) Nicole Winchell; (bl) IT Stock Free/JupiterImages; (bmr) Oredia/Alamy; **294:** (tl, tr) Nicole Winchell; (bl) Darío Eusse Tobón; (bml) Georgios Alexandris/Shutterstock; (bmr) MyasNick/Big Stock Photo; (br) Gudrun Hommel; **297:** Ana Cabezas Martín; **302:** Mlenny Photography/iStockphoto; **303:** (l) DeVIce/Fotolia; (tr) Tupungato/Shutterstock; (br) ImageBroker/SuperStock; **307:** (t) Gudrun Hommel; (m) Elisabeth Holm/Shutterstock; (b) Karel Gallas/Shutterstock; **311:** (tl, bmr, br) Nicole Winchell; (tr) Raimund Linke/Media Bakery; (bl) Lance Bellers/Fotolia; (bml) Marekuliasz/Shutterstock; **313:** Design Pics Inc/Alamy; **314:** (t) ImageBroker/SuperStock; (ml) Tibor Bognár/AGE Fotostock; (mr) Clearlens/Fotolia; (b) Imagebroker/Alamy; **315:** (tl) David Harding/Shutterstock; (tr) Daniel Bockwoldt/DPA/Picture-Alliance/Newscom; (m) Bronswerk/iStockphoto; (b) ImageBroker/SuperStock; 316–317: Manuel Gutjahr/Getty Images; **317:** (l) Imagebroker/Alamy; (m) Sabine Lubenow/Media Bakery; (r) INSADCO Photography/Alamy; **318:** (left col) Rob Schoenbaum/ZUMA Press; (right col: background) Bloomua/Shutterstock; (right col: t/window) Bronswerk/iStockphoto; (right col: t/chairs) Kuttig-RF-Travel/Alamy; (right col: m) Captblack76/Fotolia; (right col: b) Artono9/123RF; **319:** Pascal Pernix.

Unit 8: 321: Xavier Roy; **323:** (tl, bm) Gudrun Hommel; (tm) Sascha Burkard/Shutterstock; (tr) Nicole Winchell; (bl) Martín Bernetti; (br) Herb Greene/Big Stock Photo; **324:** Nicole Winchell; **328:** Manfred Steinbach/Shutterstock; **329:** (l) Nicole Winchell; (tr) Taglichtmedia/Ullstein Bild/Getty Images; (br) Imaginechina/Corbis; **330:** (l) Emese/Shutterstock; (r) Naphtalina/iStockphoto; **332:** (t, br) Nicole Winchell; (bl) Ale Ventura/Media Bakery; (bml) Camilo Torres/Shutterstock; (bmr) Gudrun Hommel; **336:** (tl, ml, bl, bml) Gudrun Hommel; (tr) Vanessa Bertozzi; (mml) IDP Manchester Airport Collection/Alamy; (mmr) Aspen Stock/AGE Fotostock; (mr) Aspen Photo/Shutterstock; (bmr) Olgany/Big Stock Photo; (br) Jack Puccio/iStockphoto; **338:** (tl, tr, bl) Nicole Winchell; (br) Gudrun Hommel; **339:** Courtesy of Daimler AG; **341:** (tl) Dmitry Kutlayev/iStockphoto; (tm) Aleksandr Kurganov/Shutterstock; (tr, bm) Ray Levesque; (bl) Greg Nicholas/iStockphoto; (br) LdF/iStockphoto; **346:** Library of Congress/Digital VE/Science Faction/Corbis; **347:** (l, br) Nicole Winchell; (tr) Khabar/Big Stock Photo; **351:** (t) Ronen/iStockphoto; (bl) Annie Pickert Fuller; (bml) Mauricio Osorio; (bmr) CandyBox Images/Fotolia; (br) Gudrun Hommel; **356:** Aspen Stock/AGE Fotostock; **357:** (tl, tr) Arbit/Shutterstock; (b) Robert Kneschke/Shutterstock; **358:** (tl) P.lange/Big Stock Photo; (tr) Pecold/Shutterstock; (m) Zsolt Biczo/Shutterstock; (b) Frieder Blickle/laif/Redux; **359:** (t) AKG-Images/Newscom; (ml) Ina Van Hateren/123RF; (mr) Media Bakery; (b) *St. Elizabeth* (c. 1529/30), Nikolaus Glockendon. AKG-Images; **362:** Wavebreak Media Ltd/Big Stock Photo; **363:** Lexan/123RF.